The Politics of Agriculture in Japan

Aurelia George Mulgan's truly magisterial work on Japanese agriculture is simultaneously a masterful analysis of the Japanese political system and the role of powerful interest groups in it. Her new book is the best treatment in English of how the Japanese policy process actually works.

Chalmers Johnson
Japan Policy Research Institute

Agriculture is one of the most politically powerful sectors in Japanese national politics. This book provides the first, comprehensive account of the political power of Japanese farmers. This definitive text analyses the organisational and electoral basis of farmers' political power, including the role of agricultural interest groups, the mobilisation of the farm vote and links between farmers and politicians in the Diet. Agrarian power has helped to produce the distinctly pro-rural, anti-urban bias of post-war Japanese governments, resulting in a general neglect of urban consumer interests and sustained opposition to market opening for farm products.

The book represents a major study of Japanese agricultural organisations in their multifarious roles as interest groups, agents of agricultural administration, electoral resource providers and mammoth business groups. It describes the policy issues that engage farmers' concerns and identifies the agricultural commodities that carry the greatest political significance.

Using extensive primary sources including interviews and questionnaires conducted in Japan, the book taps the vast literature in the Japanese language on the political economy of Japanese agriculture, including studies of agricultural organisations, agricultural policies and farmers' politics, and investigates the standard stereotype of farmers' political power, providing much of the empirical data missing from long-standing generalisations about agrarian power in Japan. In so doing, it reveals a more complex picture of pluralist organisation, diversity of political connection and long-term decline. *The Politics of Agriculture in Japan* is written for specialists in Asian studies, Japanese politics and comparative politics, as well as for agricultural policy specialists and economists.

Aurelia George Mulgan lectures in the School of Politics at the University of New South Wales, Australian Defence Force Academy, and is an internationally renowned authority in this field of Japanese politics and the Japanese political system. She is co-author of *Dynamic and Immobilist Politics in Japan* and co-editor of *Australian Agriculture* and *Newly Industrialising Asia*.

Biotechnology in Japan
Malcolm Brock

Britain's Educational Reform: a Comparison with Japan
Michael Howarth

Language and the Modern State: the Reform of Written Japanese
Nanette Twine

Industrial Harmony in Modern Japan: the Intervention of a Tradition
W. Dean Kinzley

Japanese Science Fiction: a View of a Changing Society
Robert Matthew

The Japanese Numbers Game: the Use and Understanding of Numbers in Modern Japan
Thomas Crump

Ideology and Practice in Modern Japan
Roger Goodman and Kirsten Refsing

Technology and Industrial Development in pre-War Japan
Yukiko Fukasaku

Japan's Early Parliaments 1890–1905
Andrew Fraser, R. H. P. Mason and Philip Mitchell

Japan's Foreign Aid Challenge
Alan Rix

Emperor Hirohito and Shōwa Japan
Stephen S. Large

Japan: Beyond the End of History
David Williams

Ceremony and Ritual in Japan: Religious Practices in an Industrialized Society
Jan van Bremen and D. P. Martinez

Understanding Japanese Society: Second Edition
Joy Hendry

The Fantastic in Modern Japanese Literature: The Subversion of Modernity
Susan J. Napier

Militarization and Demilitarization in Contemporary Japan
Glenn D. Hook

The Politics of Agriculture in Japan

Aurelia George Mulgan

London and New York

First published 2000 by Routledge
2 Park Square, Milton Park, Abingdon, Oxon, OX14 4RN

Simultaneously published in the USA and Canada
by Routledge
270 Madison Ave, New York NY 10016

Routledge is an imprint of the Taylor & Francis Group

Transferred to Digital Printing 2005

© 2000 Aurelia George Mulgan

Typeset in Times by Steven Gardiner Ltd, Cambridge

British Library Cataloguing in Publication Data
A catalogue record for this book is available from the British Library

Library of Congress Cataloging in Publication Data

ISBN 0-415-22346-6
Printed and bound by Antony Rowe Ltd, Eastbourne

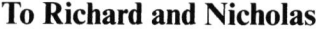

To Richard and Nicholas

Contents

Figures

Tables

Series editor's preface

By the time this book is published, the new millennium will have begun. At the very end of the old one, Japan, widely seen as a 'miracle country' in view of the spectacular achievements of its economy between the late 1950s and early 1990s, was struggling out of its 1990s recession, which became particularly acute between 1997 and 1999. The 1990s have been a time of turbulence in Japanese politics as in the economy, and pressure for restructuring has been strong. Grave weaknesses in the banking system were revealed in the form of a massive overhang of bad debt inherited from the boom period of the late 1980s and subsequent collapse. An ambitious programme of reform of the political system was announced by the Hosokawa coalition Government that replaced single-party rule by the Liberal Democratic Party (LDP) in 1993, but the path towards implementing reform proved far from smooth. Indeed, after a brief period out of office, the LDP was soon back in power as part of a succession of coalition arrangements, during which it gradually clawed back its dominant political position. Even at the end of the decade, however, the LDP was still unable to run the country without help from other parties, and curiously enough this help was beginning to bring about results in the form of the implementation of a reformist agenda. In particular the dominant role of the government bureaucracy over policy-making was now being challenged through parliamentary legislation. Even the 1946 Constitution, which had inhibited Japan from acting as a 'normal nation' in defence matters, was now to be the subject of scrutiny by parliamentary commissions. Although it was too early (as of November 1999) to say that Japan was into a recovery phase, the outlook was certainly rather more optimistic than it had been for several years.

The Nissan Institute/Routledge Japanese Studies Series seeks to foster an informed and balanced, but not uncritical, understanding of Japan. One aim of the series is to show the depth and variety of Japanese institutions, practices and ideas. Another is, by using comparisons, to see what lessons, positive or negative, can be drawn for other countries. The tendency in commentary on Japan to resort to out-dated, ill-informed or sensational stereotypes still remains, and needs to be combated.

The politics of Japanese agriculture have always intrigued observers.

Even though some other countries (notably in Europe) have protected their farmers to an extent hardly justified by contemporary notions of economic rationality, in Japan this process went to extremes after the Second World War. While protection of Japan's rice producers was the most notorious, producers of many other agricultural products (beef, for instance) have enjoyed levels of protection almost beyond the imagination of farming communities elsewhere. Even though protection levels have declined in recent years, the Japanese agricultural world still retains extraordinary degrees of regulation and organisation, in which the state is heavily involved.

In this magisterial work, Dr Aurelia George Mulgan penetrates deep into the structures of agricultural organisation, and unravels their complexities. An astonishing picture emerges of bureaucratic intricacy, enlivened by surprising elements of entrepreneurial spirit. The Agricultural Cooperative Association, which since soon after the war has been the principal interest group representing farmers, is shown to be a mixture of interest group, conglomerate enterprise and branch of government bureaucracy. It exhibits considerable flexibility in the face of pressures caused by the declining agricultural population and predominance of farmers who tend their mini-plots at weekends only.

The book is not only about agriculture. The author provides important new insights into the structure of the Japanese political system as a whole. She shows why it is that despite the pressures of 'globalisation', Japanese politics has proved so slow to change during the recessions of the 1990s. The entrenched position of vested interests at many levels of the political system serve to protect producers in declining industries such as agriculture, but at the expense of the vast mass of people now resident in cities. Perhaps the future of Japanese politics may encompass a revolt of the urban masses against the exploitation to which they have long been subjected by vested interests in conjunction with the political-bureaucratic Establishment. For more reasons than can be enumerated here, this book may well turn out to be the most significant single work on how Japan's politics actually functions in practice to appear for the past decade or more.

J.A.A. Stockwin

Preface

The larger study, of which this book is the first volume, was conceived almost two and a half decades ago and has been that long in the research and writing. Two further volumes are at the penultimate stage of production. Their provisional titles are *Politicians and Bureaucrats: Agricultural Policies and Policymaking in Japan*, and *The Challenge to Vested Interests: Contesting Agricultural Power in Japan*. It is to this larger project that many of following remarks serve as a preface.

The study of agricultural politics in Japan has been a journey of personal discovery. The subject was initially selected not because agriculture was a politically dominant sectoral interest or because political factors appeared to be so central to explaining why foreign agricultural exporters had such a hard time trying to crack open the Japanese market, but because my desired focus of analysis was powerholders and the organised interests that seek to influence them. As a political science graduate newly arrived in Japan from New Zealand in the early 1970s, my selected topic of research was Japanese interest groups. I was advised by my initial supervisor, Professor Hayashi Shigeru of Tokyo University, to examine the Rice Price Advisory Council because it was such a conspicuous locale for the activities of agricultural interest groups. Some months after beginning this work, I learned quite by chance that a doctoral student from Canada, Michael Donnelly, had just completed his PhD fieldwork on the Rice Price Advisory Council. He wisely suggested that I reorientate my focus to Japan's agricultural cooperatives (Nokyo).

It was serendipitous that Professor Ishida Takeshi replaced Professor Hayashi as my supervisor on the former's retirement. Professor Ishida introduced me to his voluminous writings on Nokyo and to the sociological significance of the agricultural cooperatives and their organisational predecessors in the countryside, as well as to their political role as interest groups. In retrospect, I benefitted greatly from his enlightened comparativism, his welcoming attitude towards foreign scholars, and his well-earned reputation as one of Japan's leading political scientists, a meticulous empiricist who could nevertheless explain Japanese politics (and particularly interest groups) in terms and concepts used by Western political scientists. Looking back, I also greatly enjoyed his sceptical and radical views of the Japanese political establishment, something of which, by the late 1970s, Nokyo had become very much a part. With Professor Ishida's help, I managed to find enough grist for my mill to produce a doctoral thesis at the Australian National University, under the wise and temperate guidance of Arthur Stockwin.

The project began as an endeavour to turn my doctoral thesis into a major publication, but it expanded far beyond that into a broad-brush attempt to locate agricultural politics in all its multidimensional aspects in the system of Japanese politics as a whole. As the project progressed, the need to satisfy academic convention was soon replaced by a wish to respond positively to those friends and colleagues who, over the years, greeted me with the refrain: 'When are you going to finish that book on Nokyo?', and 'Are you *still* studying Japanese agriculture?'

The initial writing began while I was working as a Research Fellow at the Australia–Japan Research Centre, Australian National University. This was a time when Japan's farm trade barriers, and the agricultural interests standing resolutely behind them, began to create a lot of problems for Japan's major agricultural suppliers – countries like the United States, Australia and New Zealand – which gave my research a relevance to policymakers in all three countries. It was also a time when I was introduced to the writings and views of economists, agricultural economists and trade economists, to whom agricultural protection was a cross-national phenomenon dogged by many of the same economic and political problems, and producing many of the same 'pernicious' agricultural trade consequences.

This first volume is an attempt to measure and account for the political power of Japanese farmers and agricultural organisations. The approach of the book is thematic: each chapter is discrete and can be read as a complete whole. At the same time, the chapters are broadly sequenced in a historical way – both in terms of their content and in terms of their order in the book. Moreover, given that the perspective is basically postwar – from 1945 until 2000 – one cannot help but be alert to the advance and retreat of the rice-roots power of Japanese farmers over this period. Why and how this occurred is an integral part of the story. The book is also a story of the preeminent farmers' organisation in Japan – Nokyo – and its rise and decline in the postwar period.

The further I proceeded with empirical research, the more sceptical I became of the futility of two popular academic enterprises in the field of Japanese politics. The first is transposing, without careful analytical modification – as Professor Ishida sought to do – the concepts of Western political science into studies of Japan. For example, even basic concepts like 'interest group' can be called into question by the kinds of organisations one comes up against in conducting a study such as this. If there is a predominant characteristic of Japanese 'interest groups', it is that they are frequently not organised for interest representational purposes at all, but for something else. Their primary rationale can be economic, or even quasi-bureaucratic. They are often formally apolitical – as Nokyo itself claims to be. Thus, one finds oneself dealing with entities that sometimes behave like interest groups but which do not necessarily conform to the standard Western definition of such bodies in terms of their fundamental rationale, organisational attributes, or relations with government and rice-roots interests.

Likewise, the term 'lobby' requires careful transposition in a Japanese political context. To some extent it presupposes clear boundaries between the groups doing the lobbying and those in the legislature or in the government being lobbied. Sometimes clear boundaries can be discerned in the Japanese case; sometimes they cannot. If researchers confine their focus to examples of lobbying in the commonly accepted Western sense, they can miss more important and productive types of interest representation being undertaken by intermediaries from within the political process.

This observation touches on another analytical problem that has to be confronted in the study of Japanese politics: the ill-defined boundary between the public and private sectors. The dividing line is often simply indistinguishable. Countless agricultural organisations operate at the interface between the public and private sectors and incorporate the facets of both. Indeed, some operate in three different institutional settings simultaneously: within the administration as auxiliary agencies of government; in the political marketplace as interest groups combining voluntary membership, internal democracy and interest representational functions; and in the Diet and political parties through the medium of their executive leaders.

Standard Western notions of 'interest group', 'lobby' and the public/private dichotomy thus have difficulty in accommodating the kind of organisations one encounters in a study of agricultural politics in Japan. Moreover, just as public and private structures are hard to discern, so are public and private interests. Interests can become fused in the same way as organisations and institutions can. This 'fusion of public and private interests' – a phrase coined by former US ambassador to Japan, Michael Armacost – is one of the reasons why the agricultural sector represents such a solid bulwark to deregulatory reform and market liberalisation in Japan.

The second popular enterprise in the field of Japanese politics which I have tried to avoid is pursuing the standard methodological approach of a literature survey, followed by an explication and then illustration of a single theoretical framework. As I got deeper and deeper into the subject of agricultural politics, I became increasingly convinced of the ultimate futility of trying to characterise the Japanese political system as exemplifying one type of interest-group politics or another. A dizzying array of concepts greets the student in the literature: the proliferation of hyphenated pluralisms and corporatisms as well as the various power elite and statist paradigms. Applied and adapted to a Japanese setting, these all turn out to be over-generalised constructs based on the observable characteristics of certain key groups and their relations with government. In all cases, they fail to capture the whole convincingly.

This is not to deny the analytical utility of these concepts, merely to point out that their value is primarily heuristic rather than explanatory. They may or may not be a consistently reliable description of the real world; their explanatory value needs to be carefully determined in each case. One can try to establish which terms offer an appropriate description in one's own field of investigation. Hence the exercise in Chapter 2, where the pattern of interest groups in the agricultural sector is tested against traditional notions of pluralism, corporatism and the tripartite power elite model. Even in the agricultural sector, it is difficult to find concepts that sufficiently encapsulate the degree of variation that is present in the organisational form and inter-connections between groups and different parts of the political system. The agricultural sector embraces groups of multiple organisational type which complicates the picture considerably.

Thus, for reasons of both content and preferred methodology, this book does not attempt to generate systemic-level descriptions of Japanese politics or Japanese interest-group politics. In fact it tries to redress the balance of emphasis for students and scholars away from literature-driven studies. Increasingly, students of Japanese politics do not learn about Japanese politics, they learn about the artificial constructs that politicial scientists have devised to describe and explain Japanese politics – in short, the latest theories, models, frameworks in the discipline. In the end, students get further and further away from the documented realities of Japanese politics; they some-times reside in an artificial world of spurious scientism, grand theories that exhibit selective blindness to contradictory facts, and studies of Japanese politics that quote from general theoretical texts in order to substantiate specific observations about the Japanese case. Too many students feel obliged to make a literary trek through these writings in order to set their empirical work in a theoretical context. Thesis examiners, and journal article and book referees continually entrench this requirement. The result can be a perpetuation of vacuous theories that are founded on logical deduction and not on empirical research, and which retain their academic currency long after their use-by date because graduate students feel obliged to genuflect to them in order to place their own work in a disciplinary context.

The overarching objective of this book and the larger project of which it is a part, is to uncover the complexities of the real world, rather than simplifying these complexities to fit theoretical assumptions or ignoring them in order to make the real world conform to some deductive theory. The study seeks to impose no 'theoretical order' on the data, or to provide a simple, single-factor explanation for the political phenomena it describes and explains. The methodological approach is inductive and the theoretical aspirations modest.

Towards the end of its writing, the project was motivated by a desire to move beyond Western economic analyses of Japan's agricultural policies, in particular, the works of economists, agricultural economists and trade economists who, meritorious as they are, proceed from the confining assumptions of neo-classical economic theory. Too often they 'explain' Japan's agricultural 'protection' as just a cross-national phenomenon, or are circumscribed in their scholarly understanding of the Japanese case by their need to define aggregate welfare by the single, measurable phenomenon of price differentials. Their concession to the role of politics in explaining agricultural protection is to resort to the economic theory of politics, the over-simplified, ahistorical, culture-bound, institutionally reductionist premises of rational choice theory. Furthermore, much of their work has a negative, carping quality about it. Western economic analysts of Japanese agricultural policies, in keeping with their presumptions of universal validity, have not delved sufficiently into the voluminous works of their Japanese counterparts writing in their own language – economists and non-economists alike – and the radically different values on which much of their work is premised. More disturbing is the fact that the agenda of Western economists, both inside and outside government, is not always made clear to readers. Many of them have been motivated by the desire to further the trading interests of their own countries, and/or by a belief in the ideological principles of global free trade institutions such as the GATT and now the WTO. Others, particularly Japanese writers, have understandably been concerned about the so-called 'welfare losses' wrought by agricultural protection and the intrinsically unfair distribution of the nation's resources mandated by the government's pro-rural bias. Their policy aim has been to rectify these distortions in Japan's political economy, improve what they saw was an inefficient system of agricultural production, and secure Japan's global trading interests.

The recent bursting of the Japanese economic bubble and some of its associated fallout in the agricultural sector, including the shady deals and investments of the agricultural cooperatives and the extraordinary exposure of Nokyo's financial institutions to the bankrupt housing finance companies (*jusen*), suggest that there is another, more sensationalist story to be told. Clearly Japanese farmers and consumers have both suffered from the fact that one giant cartel – Nokyo – has been running the agricultural economy for most of the postwar period. If Nokyo had been a private corporation, it might have been outlawed long ago, but because it was a cooperative, it got away with practices not permitted to Japanese business. Nokyo's special status has been preserved with the connivance of the agricultural bureaucracy in maintaining a highly regulated and subsidised agricultural sector, and with the benefit of protection from political allies in the ruling Liberal Democratic Party. Because this book is not a journalistic account, however, explicit moral judgements have been eschewed. For the most part, the author has allowed Japanese critics to speak for themselves.

Two notes for readers: the politically incorrect terminology of 'he', 'his' 'man' and 'men' is used throughout because the fact of the matter is that in 99.9 per cent of cases, it is a male that is being referred to. The term 'Socialist' is used to describe the Japan Socialist Party and its predecessor organisations. When the Democratic Socialist Party is lumped together with the Japan Socialist Party, the term 'socialist' is used. Japanese names are in the order in which they are used by the writer/individuals themselves.

Acknowledgements

Many people have directly and indirectly contributed to the information and analytical interpretations offered in this book and the larger project of which it is a part. Not the least are a host of Japanese writers on agriculture-related subjects who have been working energetically for decades with little acknowledgement from Western scholars, but whose writings I have tried to bring to a wider audience in the English language.

The project would have been so much the poorer had the author not been able to draw on the intelligence, knowledge, time and indulgence of friends and academic colleagues. I am especially grateful to those scholars who have taken the time to read and comment on individual chapters and pieces of work that later became book chapters or part chapters. They are Peter Drysdale, Chalmers Johnson, Kawagoe Toshihiko, Hayden Lesbirel, Ozawa Kenji, David Rapkin, Arthur Stockwin and Ezra Vogel.

To all those individuals whom I interviewed in Japan amongst Diet politicians, party officials, Ministry of Agriculture, Forestry and Fisheries' bureaucrats, agricultural journalists, academic researchers, executive and staff members of Nokyo and other agricultural organisations, and to many Japanese farmers, I am indebted for revealing some of the rich detail of the subject matter of this volume and the others to follow. The material has continued to fascinate the writer through many years of research and writing. I am especially indebted to the farm and other dwellers of *Koromokawa-mura* and *Maesawa-machi* in *Iwate-ken* who opened their homes, lives, and views on politics and agricultural policy to the author so long ago.

Several individuals deserve specific mention. Kobori Iwao, formerly of the Department of Geography, University of Tokyo, quite outside his formal obligations, provided much-needed arrangements for my fieldwork in one of Japan's frontier agricultural prefectures. The Food and Agricultural Policy Research Centre in Tokyo provided extensive intellectual, financial and research support over the years, particularly its former President, the scion of Japanese agricultural policy, Ogura Takekazu, as well as his staff member, Hayashi Toshimune. A special thanks to Takahashi Teiji and Takahashi Yoshitada formerly of the Ministry of Agriculture, Forestry and Fisheries, and to the many other members of the ministry and its Food Agency who assisted me over the years, including Tsujiyama Yayoi. I am also grateful to Matsumoto Tokuo, formerly of the National Central Union of Agricultural Cooperatives (Zenchu) who provided many insightful comments about Nokyo and its associated organisations. I remain forever indebted to the late Hosoe Yoshihisa, Secretary of the Agricultural Policy Research Association and his encouragement to the pregnant woman who, ignoring time-honored traditions of Japanese etiquette, boldly knocked on his door and introduced herself and her research so many years ago. Hosoe-san provided critical input into the printing and dissemination of my first questionnaire survey of Japanese farm politicians in 1977. I am also greatly obliged to those members of the Japanese Diet who answered my questionnaires honestly and sincerely. Since 1995, I have received the publications of the National Council of Farmers' Agricultural Policy Campaign Organisations through the kind offices of Odagiri Kiku. My thanks also to journalists Tanaka Toyotoshi, Tomioka Yoshiyuki, Yamaji Susumu and Sugawara Hiroshi.

Friends and colleagues who have gone beyond the obligations of friendship include Urasaki Miyuki, who provided invaluable assistance in the distribution of questionnaires to Japanese Diet members in 1990, and Kobayashi Shinichi of Nihon University, who managed to circumvent bureaucratic rigidities and stonewalling to provide information that was sensitive, but not confidential. The author is particularly pleased to learn of an Information Disclosure Bill recently passed in the Japanese Diet, which will enable researchers such as myself, some form of legal redress against officials too long accustomed to the arbitrary exercise of informational power.

The project has been supported by the funding of several organisations and institutions, including the Japan Foundation, the Japan Foundation Center for Global Partnership, Nanzan University, and the Program on U.S.-Japan Relations at Harvard University. At various times these organisations released me from teaching to do fruitful research and writing during the course of the project's completion. I owe an enormous debt of gratitude to the Japanese taxpayer who has funded the bulk of my research over the years, and also to the Australian taxpayer, who through my own institution, the University of New South Wales, and the generosity of numerous Special Research Grants, has enabled me to travel to Tokyo and beyond on a regular basis, and to receive research assistance. In addition I express my thanks to the Australia–Japan Research Centre at the Australian National University which provided support in the form of research assistance and data-based searches. I am also deeply indebted to the Japan Foundation for contributing to the publication costs of the volume.

Towards the end of the project, I benefited immeasurably from the dedication, hard work and intelligence of research assistants such as Koko Clark, Akemi Inoue, Hidetaka Yoshimatsu and Shunichi Ishihara. They provided invaluable insights, particularly with respect to the vagaries and complexities of the written and spoken Japanese language.

Finally, I owe an irredeemable debt of gratitude to my husband, Richard Mulgan, who not only bravely read the entire manscript, but who also provided unstinting practical contributions in the household enabling me to squeeze in extra hours of research and writing. I have benefited immeasurably from his wise counsel, strategic advice, illuminating intelligence, and great knowledge and understanding of political phenomena.

Finally, it is fitting that this book will appear just as Japan's New Food, Agriculture and Rural Areas Basic Law, which will serve as a guideline for the nation's agricultural policies into the 21st century, takes effect. Although politics has been a significant shaper of the content of the new law, it has also been guided by values that redress the overemphasis on 'rational' efficiency considerations held in such high regard by Western economists and treasuries.

This book is dedicated to my sons, Richard born in Tokyo in 1973, and Nicholas born in Canberra in 1977, whose lives have spanned the writing of the three-volume work.

Canberra,
October 1999

1   Introduction

Japanese agriculture reflects Japanese politics. To understand Japanese agriculture one must know the mechanisms of Japanese politics . . . which in turn leads to an understanding of Japan.[1]

An abiding assumption amongst scholars of Japanese politics is that agriculture has been one of the most powerful sectoral interests in the national polity and that, as a result, farmers have sheltered under a broad umbrella of political largesse and administrative regulation throughout most of the postwar period. Certainly the farm sector has been far more politically important than the contribution of agriculture to the national economy warrants. Amongst a number of uncompetitive and low-productivity sectors in the Japanese economy, agriculture has stood out at once as the most highly protected and the most politically powerful.

Although a complete explanation for relatively high levels of agricultural support and protection in Japan requires a complex multifactoral account of the diverse political, historical, economic, bureaucratic, ideological and other elements involved, political factors are often regarded as paramount. Agricultural producers and their organisations have successfully extracted preferential treatment from government almost without regard to the impact of relentlessly high food prices on consumers and the ire of Japan's trading partners.

Why do farmers wield such great political power? The answer lies in a mix of organisational, electoral and party-political factors encapsulating some of the best-known facts of Japanese political life. Firstly, the organisational basis of farmers' political power is formidable. Farmers have been well mobilised across a spectrum of groups at the same time as unifying in a single, universal system of agricultural cooperatives, which has played a comprehensive role in shaping farm politics, the rural economy and society. Secondly, farmers have been a potent political constituency because they form a coherent voting bloc in an electoral system that has overweighted the value of their votes throughout most of the postwar period. Thirdly, farmers have secured the loyalties of large numbers of Diet politicians because the predominant ruling party has been electorally indebted to farm voters and farm organisations. All these factors have combined to produce a highly organised, politically powerful sectoral interest that is well represented in national politics.

This book aims to clarify all these important elements in the rural political equation. On the organisational level, the analysis focuses on how farmers form a cohesive, collective interest, what policy issues engage their concerns, how agricultural organisations interact with political parties and the bureaucracy, what resources and connections they mobilise to make their demands effective, what strategies they deploy to pursue their political goals and what challenges they face in an era of liberalisation and deregulation. On the electoral and party-political levels, the book evaluates the size and composition of the agricultural electorate, the strength of electoral ties between ruling Liberal Democratic Party (LDP) politicians and farmers, how agricultural groups function as electoral organisations, how the farm sector is represented in the Diet, and the various policymaking settings in which politicians act on behalf of agricultural interests.

Importantly, the book unravels the stereotype of farmers' political power, underscoring its elemental truths and revealing its hidden complexities. The accompanying analysis provides much of the empirical data missing from long-standing generalisations about agrarian power in Japan. It also raises the question whether the traditional stereotype of Japanese agrarian power still holds, or whether manifest social, economic and political changes are working to undermine it.

Agriculture in the domestic economy

Farming in Japan represents the classic case of an inefficient, protected industry, which contrasts markedly with Japan's much more competitive manufacturing export sector.[2] A densely populated mountainous country, Japan has only 13 per cent of land under cultivation.[3] The dominant unit of agricultural production is the family farm whose members work mostly in non-agricultural occupations.[4] All too often the 'farm' consists of scattered plots amounting to little more than one hectare (ha) in total size.[5]

The role of government in the agricultural sector has been markedly interventionist, with most aspects of farm production and the operations of the agricultural market subject to various kinds of assistance and control. The extensive and complex structure of agricultural support and protection encompasses agricultural laws, farm policies, fiscal and other financial measures as well as diverse institutions and organisations designed to assist farm production, to regulate agricultural marketing and commodity distribution, and to promote the farmers' welfare. The effect has been to insulate farmers and the farm economy from the full impact of domestic and international market forces and from the consequences of economic and social change.

The effects of government intervention on Japanese agriculture have been palliative and insufficient to prevent its slow and inexorable decline. Although farm output and productivity have been elevated by technological improvements, the economic and social significance of farming as an occupation,[6] way of life, form of land utilisation[7] and industrial sector contributing to national income and national output[8] has continued to contract since the mid-1950s.[9] Japanese agriculture is losing key factors of production such as capital[10] and skilled labour.[11] The number of farm households has decreased continuously from 6.2 million in 1950 to 5.4 million in 1970 and 3.3 million in 1998.[12] Farm household population has diminished commensurately, from 37.7 million in 1950 to 26.3 million in 1970,[13] and 14.8 million in 1998.[14] The very government policies designed to preserve and protect agriculture have also contributed to its wane, chiefly by encouraging small-scale, inefficient farmers to stay on the land.[15]

Japanese agricultural policies in comparative perspective

Japan has not been the only country to shield its farmers with an elaborate framework of agricultural support and protection.[16] Assisting weak agricultural sectors has been a global phenomenon, particularly amongst industrialised countries lacking comparative advantage in agriculture.[17] The regime in Japan shares many common features with interventionist systems found elsewhere,[18] including similarities in the instruments used (such as price supports, import restrictions and subsidies on agricultural production inputs), associated domestic effects (such as commodity surpluses, budget deficits and economic 'losses'[19]) and consequent impact on international trade in agricultural commodities.[20]

Furthermore, Japan has not been the only country in the grip of agricultural interests and subject to the lobbying power of farmers and their representative organisations. In spite of the Uruguay Round (UR) agreement to liberalise world agricultural trade negotiated in December 1993, demonstrations of the power of farm lobbies continue to reverberate around the globe. The ingredients in this story are all too familiar: routinised exchanges of farm votes for agricultural subsidies;[21] electoral promises by politicians to maintain protective tariffs on agricultural imports,[22] to preserve farm subsidies and price support,[23] to cut taxes paid by farmers[24] and to compensate farmers for loss of income arising from agricultural trade access agreements;[25] blatant trading of votes by farm organisations for rural benefits;[26] and large political donations by farm organisations to ensure that politicians sympathetic to agricultural interests will be elected.[27] Almost no country is blameless when it comes to buying farmers' votes in this fashion.[28]

Nonetheless, amongst the major trading nations protecting agriculture, Japan has occupied 'a uniquely protectionist niche' in the world market for rice and other agricultural commodities.[29] As early as 1965, steady annual increases in the price paid by the government to rice farmers (the so-called 'producer rice price', or *seisansha beika*) made Japan the leading industrialised country in level of support for agriculture.[30] Assessed by a range of measures devised by economists, Japan's agricultural sector has revealed itself to be more highly protected than any other in the major world economies.[31]

As in many industrialised countries, agricultural support and protection in Japan is now on the wane, with political action by farmers focused more on retaining benefits rather than on increasing them. In Japan's case, the turning point can be traced back to the early 1980s when the government imposed a zero-growth framework on budget spending for agriculture and froze farm support and stabilisation prices as a forerunner to actual reductions. The government subsequently made both major and minor retreats over import barriers and, in the 1990s, all remaining quantitative restrictions on farm imports have been abolished. Several events stand out in their symbolic importance: the decision to lower the producer rice price for the first time in 31 years in 1987; the agreement with the United States and other suppliers in 1988 to abolish prospectively import quotas on beef and orange imports in 1991, and on citrus juice imports in 1992; and the commitment to allow foreign exporters 'minimum access' to the Japanese rice market along with tariffication of other agricultural import barriers as part of the 1993 UR Agreement on Agriculture. These reforms signalled a regression in the two main Japanese agricultural support and protection policies – measures to support agricultural prices and measures to restrict imports.[32]

Further changes have been predicated on the UR agreement. The Food Control (FC) system (*shokuryo kanri seido*, or *shokkan seido*) which governed the collection, distribution and sale of rice and which was administered by the Food Agency (Shokuryocho) of the Ministry of Agriculture, Forestry and Fisheries, or MAFF (Norinsuisansho) underwent an overhaul in 1994. In July 1999, the government passed a new Food, Agriculture and Rural Areas Basic Law (*Shokuryo, Nogyo, Noson Kihonho*) in the Diet which embodies a fundamental shift away from conventional methods of supporting agricultural prices to a market-orientated system in which supply-demand conditions and product quality will determine prices and farmers will receive direct income compensation from the government. The legislation represents the first full-scale revision of agricultural policies since the passage of the original Agricultural Basic Law (*Nogyo Kihonho*) in 1961. The new law was preceded by the release of an 'Agricultural Policy Reform Outline' and 'Agricultural Policy Reform Program' which are being touted as a 'New Agricultural Policy Constitution'.[33] Other policy changes have been less dramatic; nevertheless the cumulative impact of these policy shifts, both incremental and more radical, and their consistent direction, has been to pare back the agricultural support system and reduce expectations of what the government is willing to deliver.

While the changes taking place in the agricultural sector and in agricultural policy give the appearance of an avalanche slowly gathering speed, the forces of resistance remain entrenched and active. In defiance of expectations, the steadily increasing exposure of Japanese agricultural producers to domestic and international market forces has not signalled the permanent retreat of the Japanese farm lobby or marked the demise of the agricultural support and protection regime. Indeed, many important battles remain to be fought – on a whole panoply of agricultural subsidies, on regulated distribution systems and not the least on questions of market access. Agricultural trade remains a contentious issue in negotiations conducted at a regional level under the umbrella of the Asia Pacific Economic Cooperation (APEC) forum as well as those due to be held under the auspices of the World Trade Organisation (WTO) beginning in November 1999. Although Japan accepted the option of converting quantitative controls over rice imports to tariffs in December 1998, implementing early tariffication enabled the government to reduce levels of obligatory rice imports, ensuring that rice would be one of the key items on the agenda of the WTO farm trade liberalisation talks.

The fact that Japanese agricultural support and protection policies are still generating controversy both domestically and internationally suggests that the power of the farm lobby remains far from negligible. On every occasion, reports of its political demise have proved to be premature. The basis of agrarian power in Japan and the processes of adjustment that it is undergoing are, therefore, worthy of detailed investigation.

The remainder of this chapter identifies the major policy benefits that shape farmers' interests as well as the interests of their agricultural organisations. It sets out the main factors that serve to politicise price and marketing issues relating to particular commodities and isolates the key institutions through which agrarian interests achieve political representation. It also briefly out-lines the principal legal and administrative structures through which the agricultural support and protection regime is maintained.

The structure of agrarian interests

Farmers

Policies to assist and protect agriculture have provided farmers with major benefits. From a producer's perspective, the most important programmes are: government-engineered income support through commodity price subsidy and stabilisation schemes operated in concert with controls on imports; crop-related incentive payments such as subsidies to convert farmland from rice to other crops; mutual aid benefits paid in the event of crop damage and other natural calamities; subsidies and subsidised loans for production inputs such as agricultural facilities and land infrastructure development; preferential tax treatment for agricultural income compared to the incomes of wage and salary earners;[34] lower fixed property taxes on agricultural land[35] compared with residential land; electricity charges that are less than those for urban consumers; and supplementary old age pensions.[36] The range of benefits helps to perpetuate a vested interest amongst farm households in some form of agricultural production, even if their level of participation is minimal and their production efficiency is low. The majority of Japan's farmers are accustomed to living their lives as part-timers with the aid of subsidies from government.[37] For a variety of reasons, they want to retain their farmland and the benefits that go with it. Thus, although farmers' agriculture-related interests are not necessarily homogenous (given a measure of specialisation in terms of commodity production and the differing needs of full- and part-time farmers), the dominant interest amongst Japanese farmers is that of part-time agricultural producers earning the bulk of their income off the land.[38] Furthermore, the fact that this group is the largest (and growing) category of agricultural producers is in part testimony to the extent to which they have been cosseted by the government.

Farmers as well as non-farming residents of farm households also benefit from public works subsidies for the provision of social and economic infrastructure in rural areas (and from the construction jobs associated with this industry), an interest that is shared with rural dwellers generally. Thus, in addition to the benefits that are specific to farm households such as farm income support, government loan assistance to farmers, and the quality of amenities and employment prospects in rural areas, those that advantage both farmers and rural dwellers must therefore be considered as politically significant, such as rural public works.

Of all the policy benefits directed to the agricultural sector, producer prices have the most direct and immediate impact on farm household income from agriculture. Nearly 80 per cent of agricultural commodities in Japan have been subject to administered pricing systems of one kind or another.[39] The incorporation of a majority of farm products into price support and stabilisation arrangements has subjected producer prices to regular annual review procedures and to political negotiations between government and farmers' representatives. Although in the official rhetoric the neutral term 'administrative prices' is used and price calculations are subject to the application of certain pseudo-objective mathematical formulae, the final decision is ultimately the responsibility of the Minister of Agriculture, Forestry and Fisheries (Norinsuisan Daijin). Administrative prices are also subject to certain mandatory deliberation procedures by advisory councils and to decisionmaking by LDP agricultural committees. They are, therefore, ultimately political rather than purely administrative decisions.

Japan's agricultural commodity pricing systems involve different types of subsidy and stabilisation schemes and different price calculation methods. They have also been linked to variable systems of import control. Indeed, price support and stabilisation have gone hand in hand with quantitative restrictions on imports, given that in the absence of import controls, foreign agricultural products would enter the Japanese market and undermine domestic price support and stabilisation systems.[40] As farm trade liberalisation inevitably impacts on domestic agricultural prices, market access issues have thus loomed large politically because of their likely impact on farm incomes. The principal price and import schemes operating over the postwar period are outlined in Table 1.1.

Not all commodity prices have been of equal political importance however.[41] The demand from farmers for price intervention and other forms of support and protection has been higher in relation to some products than others. Major factors affecting the scale and intensity of their demand include the size of the commodity constituency in question (for example, gross production weightings and values, numbers of producers etc.), the extent of farm income dependence on the sale of a particular product, the scale of production by area or livestock numbers which affects production efficiencies, and the overall level of support and protection afforded to particular products.

The higher the demand for support and protection, the more intense the focus of political action by farmers. In short, some agricultural products have been much more politicised than others. The following section constructs a series of commodity profiles which indicates, using a series of common statistical measures, which products in Japan are likely to have the greatest political significance from this perspective. The results are presented in Table 1.2.

The analysis begins with general indices such as total volume of production, the value of a particular commodity in gross output value and the extent of land utilisation given over to particular products. These provide a general background to the discussion of politically more significant indices of commodity production.

General indices

1. Gross output (tonnage)

The total output of a particular commodity can be sufficiently prominent to give it national importance. As Table 1.2 reveals, rice is clearly the dominant single crop in gross output terms (10.0 million tonnes), although greater tonnages are recorded by the composite categories of livestock products (15.3 million tonnes) and vegetables (13.2 million tonnes). Industrial crops (5.2 million tonnes), fruit (4.4 million tonnes), potatoes and sweet potatoes (4.5 million tonnes) as well as single products such as raw milk (8.6 million tonnes) also register substantial levels of output. Minor products according to this measure are wheat and barley (766,000 tonnes), miscellaneous beans and pulses (307,000 tonnes) and sericulture (3,000 tonnes of silk cocoons).

2. Gross output (by value)

As shown in Table 1.2, the rank ordering of Japanese agricultural commodities begins with the 'big three': rice, which produces a little under one-third of gross output value, or 29.8 per cent; livestock products, which generate more

Table 1.1 Main agricultural product price support and import control systems

Product	Administering agency	Relevant law(s)	Price support system	Import control measures pre-1995	Date of quota liberalisation
Rice for government sale	Food Agency	Food Control Law (1942); Staple Food Law (1994)[a]	Price control system: government controls all aspects of market distribution. Buying and selling prices under government management are officially decided by the MAFF Minister. Government purchases rice from farmers at a guaranteed price.	State trade (Food Agency) monopoly (effectively import prohibition)	1995 – minimum access IQ system; April 1999 tariffication (¥351.17 per kg) – Food Agency buys minimum access amount; private firms may import freely provided tariff is paid
Independently distributed rice (1969–)	Independently Distributed Rice Price Formation Organisation/Centre		Government-administered market distribution system: buying price of rice negotiated between agricultural cooperatives and rice wholesalers; purchase price for government rice acts as floor price; from 1990, auction price for commercial rice became standard price for independently distributed rice.		
Commercial Rice (20% of independently distributed rice) (1990–)	None, apart from the requirement to declare volumes to the Food Agency		Government-monitored market distribution system: buying price of rice determined at auction where wholesalers may bid.		
Free Market Rice (1995–)			Direct sales from farmers to consumers and wholesalers at 'market' prices.		

Commodity	Agency	Law	Price support mechanism	Border measures	1995 reforms
Wheat, barley and naked barley[b]	Food Agency		Government purchase of wheat, barley and naked barley from farmers at a guaranteed price.	State trade (Food Agency) monopoly and IQ system	1995 (abolition of state trade monopoly; Food Agency remained only buyer of imported wheat and barley within the tariff quota)
Raw milk for processing (into butter, skim milk powder, sweetened condensed whole milk and skim milk, whole milk powder, sweetened milk powder, unsweetened condensed whole milk, skim milk for calf feed and natural cheese)	Livestock Industry Promotion Corporation[c] (LIPC)	Provisional Measures Law for Subsidies to Producers of Raw Milk for Processing (1965)	Subsidy (deficiency payment) system: LIPC pays subsidies to producers to compensate for the difference between the guaranteed price and the standard transaction price (processors' buying price).[d]	IQ system for milk and cream (fresh)	1995 (a degree of natural protection)
Designated dairy products (butter, skim milk powder, sweetened condensed whole milk and sweetened condensed skim milk)		Livestock Products Price Stabilisation Law (1961)	Price stabilisation system: LIPC purchases designated dairy products if prices drop, or are likely to drop, below 90% of the stabilisation indicative prices and sells stock if prices rise, or are likely to rise, above 104% of the stabilisation indicative prices.[e]	IQ system and state trade (LIPC) monopoly of designated dairy product imports, except skim milk powder for school lunches and for feed; 25–35 per cent customs duty	1995 (abolition of state trade monopoly of designated dairy products; ALIC buys minimum access amount; balance bought by private companies who pay tariff equivalent to ALIC; tariff quotas for skimmed milk powder for school lunches and for other purposes)

Table 1.1 (continued)

Product	Administering agency	Relevant law(s)	Price support system	Import control measures pre-1995	Date of quota liberalisation
Non-designated dairy products (butter milk powder, whole milk powder and whey powder); cheese	No administering agency			Natural cheese – tariff quota system – primary tariff rates applied to imports up to certain quantities and elevated rates levied on quantities exceeding quantity quotas (dairy processors permitted to import 2 kg of foreign cheese free of duty for every 1 kg of domestic cheese purchased for producing processed cheese). Imports above this limit subject to an *ad valorem* duty of 35 per cent	1995 (tariff quotas for whey, butter, cheese for processed cheese)
Pork			Price stabilisation system: LIPC maintains market price within a certain predetermined price range (i.e. floor and ceiling prices in a price stabilisation band) through buying	Variable levies (a 5% basic tariff which can be raised when prices in the	1971 (Specific duties, differential duties or 4.9% duty applied to import price)

Commodity	Institution	Law	Domestic policy	Border measures	Year
			...and selling operations of domestically produced pork.	...domestic market fall below designated levels)	
Beef			Price stabilisation system: LIPC maintains market price within a certain predetermined price range (i.e. floor and ceiling prices in a price stabilisation band) through buying and selling operations of imported beef 1966–91 and domestic beef 1975–.	State trade; IQ system; 25% *ad valorem* tariff and import surcharges	1991
Beef calves		Special Measures Law for Beef Calf Production Stabilisation etc. (1988); original law passed in 1983	Subsidy (deficiency payment) system cum stabilisation fund system: when the average selling price has dropped below the guaranteed standard price, a part of the difference exceeding the rationalisation target price (an import parity price adjusted for quality differences) is covered with a subsidy paid by the LIPC through prefectural beef calf price stabilisation fund associations, and another part of the difference below the target price is covered with funds accumulated by the government, producers, etc.	Duty (initially 60–100 per cent *ad valorem* paid per head, later ¥45,000 per head under 300 kg); also a tariff-exempt quota. Because subject to strict quarantine requirements, numbers limited by the availability of quarantine facilities	1971
Sugar beet and cane	Silk and Sugar Price Stabilisation Corporation (SSPSC)[c]	Sugar Price Stabilisation Law (1965)	Minimum price guarantee system: when market price has dropped below a certain predetermined level, the government guarantees minimum price through buying operations by the SSPSC.	Import levy imposed to protect domestic market price	1972 (refined beet and cane sugar)

Table 1.1 (continued)

Product	Administering agency	Relevant law(s)	Price support system	Import control measures pre-1995	Date of quota liberalisation
Soybeans, rapeseed	MAFF	Provisional Measures Law for Soybean and Rapeseed Subsidies (1961)	Subsidy (deficiency payment) system: subsidies are paid to compensate for deficit between standard price and producers' selling price.	Initially 13% tariff; in 1973 tariff abolished	1961
Potatoes and sweet potatoes for processing	MAFF	Agricultural Products Price Stabilisation Law (1953)	Minimum price guarantee system.	IQ system (starch)	1995 (starch)
Designated vegetable[f]	Vegetable Price Stabilisation Fund		Stabilisation fund system: when market price has dropped below a certain given level, part of the difference is covered by funds accumulated by the government, producers etc.	Some degree of natural protection (freshness); 5–10 per cent tariff; IQ system for tomato juice, tomato ketchup and tomato paste	1963
Raw fruit for processing, feeder hogs, calves, pulses, hen eggs, broilers			Stabilisation fund system: when market price has dropped below a certain given level, part of the difference is covered by funds accumulated by the government, producers etc.	Oranges (IQ system and seasonal tariff of 40 per cent from December to May); processed pineapple products, fruit	Apples 1971; fruit puree and fruit pastes 1988; apple juice 1990; oranges 1991; citrus juice 1992

Commodity	Agency	Law	Policy	Trade/tariff measures	Date
				juices, fruit puree and fruit pastes (IQ system; pineapple products 55% tariff); poultry meat *ad valorem* tariff of 10–14 % depending on the cut	
Feed grains (corn, sorghum, mixed feed)				Purchased by bonded feed mills duty free; otherwise subject to a specific duty of ¥15 per kg (corn); and *ad valorem* 5% duty (sorghum); 15% duty on mixed feed	1995 (tariff quota on corn)
Raw silk	SSPSC	Cocoon and Silk Price Stabilisation Law (1951)	Price stabilisation band operates for silk cocoons; from 1985 a standard grade cocoon price.	State trade (monopoly) in raw silk and dried cocoons since 1974; Prior Approval (AA – Automatic Approval system); import levy imposed to protect domestic market price	1995 (tariff quota on silk-worm cocoons suitable for reeling)

Table 1.1 (continued)

Notes:

a The table encompasses the changes to the domestic rice marketing arrangements which came into effect in November 1995 under the new Staple Food Law. It also includes the 1998 rice tariffication decision, but it does not cover the new income compensation system for rice farmers introduced in the government's 'new rice policy' of November 1997, nor the changes to the operating system of the Independently Distributed Rice Price Formation Centre in June 1998.

b The table does not encompass the proposed alteration to the domestic wheat marketing system, in which the Food Agency will shift to a free market, combined with compensation to wheat growers for a possible decline in their income.

c The Livestock Industry Promotion Corporation was renamed the Agriculture & Livestock Industries Corporation (ALIC) in October 1996, when it amalgamated with the Silk and Sugar Price Stabilisation Corporation.

d The table does not include the anticipated changes to the deficiency payment system for milk for dairy products in 2001 under the reform programme for the dairy and milk sector decided in December 1998, involving a transition to a dairy farmers' farm management stabilisation scheme.

e The table does not encompass the anticipated changes to the marketing of dairy products with the establishment of a new trading centre for dairy products in 1999, under the reform programme for the dairy and milk sector decided in December 1998.

f Designated vegetables include cabbage, cucumber, taro, Japanese radish, tomato, eggplant, carrot, Welsh onion, Chinese cabbage, pimento, spinach, lettuce, onion and potato.

Sources: OECD, *Agricultural Policies, Markets and Trade in OECD Countries*, Paris, OECD 1996, pp. 50, 53; Junko Yamamiya, 'Japan's Declining Food Self-Sufficiency Rate', *Mitsui Research Institute Business Report*, March 1991, p. 4 (quoting MAFF sources); *Norinsuisansho Tokeihyo*, 1996–97, pp. 590–591; Tachibana Takashi, *Nokyo: Kyodai na Chosen* [Nokyo: The Enormous Challenge], Tokyo, Asahi Shinbunsha, 1980, p. 335; Foreign Agricultural Service, United States Department of Agriculture, *Agricultural Trade Policy*, June 1972, pp. 5–7; *Livestock Industry Promotion Corporation: Corporate Profile*, 1996; John W. Longworth, *Beef in Japan: Politics, Production, Marketing and Trade*, St Lucia, University of Queensland Press, 1983, pp. 171–238; Loek Boonekamp, *Agriculture in Japan: Current Issues and Possible Implications of the Uruguay Round Agreement*, Tokyo, National Research Institute of Agricultural Economics, Ministry of Agriculture, Forestry and Fisheries, March 1995; Kobayashi, Morison and Riethmuller, 'A Review of Recent Developments', p. 224; *Jiji Press Newswire*, 26 May 1998; *Kyodo News Service*, 18 December 1998.

Table 1.2 Main commodity production profiles[a]

Product[b]	Gross output ('000 tonnes)	Agricultural income produced (¥ billion)	% of gross output value	Planted area ('000 hectares)	% of land utilisation	Regions/ prefectures with the highest numbers of marketing households	No's of farm households marketing product ('000 households)	% of gross agricultural income from commodity (average per commercial farm household)	% of commercial farms one hectare or less	% PSE
Rice	10,004[c]	3,053.4	29.8	1,944[c]	41.2[c]	Kanto-Tosan, Tohoku, Hokuriku (Niigata), Kyushu	2,044[d]	29.7	75.6[d]	88
Wheat and Barley	766[c]	92.1	0.9	216	4.3	Hokkaido, Kanto-Tosan, Kyushu	149[d]	1.2	70.4[d]	99 (wheat) 94 (barley)[n]
Miscellaneous beans and pulses	289	82.1	0.8	199	4.0		n/a	0.7	n/a	n/a
of which soybeans	148			82	1.6	Hokkaido, Iwate	67[d]			
of which peanuts	30			13	0.3	Chiba	n/a			

Table 1.2 (continued)

Product[b]	Gross output ('000 tonnes)	Agricultural income produced (¥ billion)	% of gross output value	Planted area ('000 hectares)	% of land utilisation	Regions/prefectures with the highest numbers of marketing households	No's of farm households marketing product ('000 households)	% of gross agricultural income from commodity (average per commercial farm household)	% of commercial farms one hectare or less	% PSE
Fruit	3,727	887.1	8.7	288	5.8		489[d]	9.6	87.1[d]	n/a
of which apples	899			50	1.0	Aomori, Nagano	78[d]		84.6[d]	
of which mikan	1,153			68	1.4	Ehime, Wakayama, Shizuoka, Kyushu	115[d]		87.0[d]	
Potatoes and sweet potatoes	4,546	243.7	2.4	151	3.0	Hokkaido (potatoes); Kagoshima (sweet potatoes)	107[d] 68[d]	1.7	n/a	n/a
Vegetables	13,541	2,284.6	22.3	475	9.5	Kanto-Tosan, Kyushu, Tohoku	881[d]	22.6	97.0[d]	n/a
Industrial crops	5,200	396.6	3.9	187	3.7			5.0	n/a	n/a
of which tobacco	66			26		Kyushu, Tohoku	27[d]			
of which tea	402			53		Shizuoka, Kyushu	59[d]			
of which rape seed	1			.6		Aomori	n/a			

Item	Output (¥100 million)	Volume ('000 t)	Share (%)	Self-sufficiency (%)	Main producing regions	Commercial farm households raising livestock ('000 households)	Average head per household
of which sugar cane	1,284		24	70	Okinawa	17[d]	
of which sugar beet	3,295		70		Hokkaido	13[d]	
of which konnyaku	90		—		Gumma	n/a	
Sericulture	3[e]	4.9	0.05	49	Gumma, Fukushima	0.1 / 8[f]	
Livestock and livestock products	14,649[dg]	2,584.4	25.2	—		19.7	
of which raw milk	8,657	708.2	6.9	83		9.1	
of which beef	601[dh]			43		n/a	
of which *wagyu* beef	250	430.9 (beef cattle)	4.2 (beef cattle)		Tohoku, Miyazaki, Kagoshima	143[c] (beef cattle)	20.0[c] (beef cattle)
of which dairy beef	340	801.6 (dairy cattle)[i]	7.8 (dairy cattle)[i]		Hokkaido, Kanto-Tosan, Iwate	39[c] (dairy cattle)	48.2[c] (dairy cattle)
of which pork	1,322[d]	541.5 (pigs)	5.3	61	Miyagi, Ibaraki, Miyazaki, Kagoshima	3.1[l] / 14[c]	618.8
of which chicken	1,793[d]	753.9 (chickens)[j]	7.4[j]	12	Miyazaki, Kagoshima	3.1[m] / 7[c]/4[k]	28,141[c]/32,800[k]
of which eggs	2,567	466.7 (hen eggs)	4.6	18	Aichi, Chiba, Kagoshima		
Total	10,248.9	—	—	4,718[c]	—	2,522[o]	71

Table 1.2 (continued)

Notes:

a These figures are for 1996, unless otherwise indicated.

b Commodities omitted include flowers, seed and seedlings and processed agricultural products. Accordingly there is no figure for total gross output ('000 tonnes) in the table.

c These figures are for 1997. In the case of rice production, the 1998 crop year is estimated at about 8.95 million tonnes, down 1.05 million tonnes from the 1997 crop year. In the case of rice acreage, the total planted area in 1998 was 1.79 million ha, down 151,000 ha on the 1997 figure.

d These figures are for 1995.

e This is the total for cocoon production.

f This is the number of households raising silkworms.

g This total is only for the livestock commodities designated below in 1995.

h This includes beef and veal.

i This is inclusive of the figure above for raw milk.

j This is inclusive of the figure below for hen eggs

k The first figure is for the number of farm households raising layers; the second is for the number of farm households shipping broilers. The extent to which these overlap is unclear.

l This is the figure for pig raising.

m This is the figure for hen and chicken raising.

n Strictly speaking, this is the percentage PSE for 'other grains'.

o This figure is for 1998.

Sources: Ministry of Agriculture, Forestry and Fisheries, *The Long-Term Prospects for Demand and Production of Agricultural Products*, Japan's Agricultural Review, Vol. 25, March 1996, p. 9; *Norinsuisansho Tokeihyo*, 1996–97, pp. 59–405; *Poketto*, 1998, pp. 100–301; OECD, *Agricultural Policies in OECD Countries*, p. 99; MAFF *Update*, No. 270, 31 July 1998, http://www.maff.go.jp; *Japan Agrinfo Newsletter*, Vol. 16, No. 4, December 1998, p. 2.

than one-quarter, or 25.2 per cent; and vegetables, which yield somewhat less than one-quarter, or 22.3 per cent.[42] As vegetables can be broken down into a large number of sub-sectors,[43] the national significance of any single product is diminished. Livestock products, on the other hand, divide into a few large sub-sectors. The main ones are dairy cattle (producing 7.8 per cent of gross output value, including raw milk 6.9 per cent),[44] beef cattle 4.2 per cent, pigs 5.3 per cent, and chickens 7.4 per cent (including hen eggs at 4.6 per cent).

The gross output value of fruit farming (at 8.7 per cent of the total) is greater than any single livestock product but again, it consists of multiple sub-sectors, the main ones being apples and Japanese mandarins (*mikan*). In gross value terms, the minor products are non-rice grains, such as wheat and barley (0.9 per cent), miscellaneous beans and pulses (0.8 per cent), sericulture (0.05 per cent), while potatoes and sweet potatoes at 2.4 per cent are marginally more important.

Overall, rice and the broad categories of livestock products, vegetables and fruit are relatively more significant than the other agricultural commodities in terms of production value. As a single crop, however, rice once again dominates by a large margin.

3. Planted area

Rice is also predominant in land area terms, with the largest number of ha devoted to its production (almost 2 million ha, or just over 40 of the total area of cultivated land in 1997). In contrast to rice, other 'land-intensive' products such as wheat and barley occupy only 215,000 ha (a little over one-tenth of the area planted in rice). For all other crops or categories of products, production area is relatively small. Fruit cropping is somewhat larger than the category of wheat and barley (274,000 ha), but vegetables are intensively farmed: a greater tonnage than rice is produced from just over one-quarter of the area.

Politically significant variables

Variables that are more important in political terms are total numbers of farm households involved in the sale of particular commodities, production geography (that is the location of producers both nationally and regionally), the extent of farm household reliance on income generated by different products (the nationwide average), and lastly, factors relating to the scale of production.

Numbers of farm households are significant because they point to the quantity of votes linked to particular products (bearing in mind that some households engage in mixed farming). Production geography can be politically relevant if a commodity is dominant nationally, and/or is dominant regionally, because this affects the distribution of commodity-relevant votes. An agricultural product may be relatively minor in national terms, but quite major in regional terms, with a potentially important effect on electoral outcomes in particular constituencies. National averages for farm household income dependence on particular products are also useful for indicating the size of the stake that the average producer household has in the market for a particular product, and therefore, their interest in the policies that influence that market, such as price intervention, import protection and supply controls. Scale of production management, on the other hand, is an indirect indicator of farming efficiency, and consequently of farmers' need for support and protection.

The percentage producer subsidy equivalent (PSE) is indicative as a composite figure that reveals the level of support received by the producers of particular commodities.[45] It shows the degree to which producers are assisted by means of market price support programmes, direct payments, reduced input costs and/or indirect support. The higher the percentage PSE, the greater the likelihood of political resistance from farmers to any declines in support.

1. Numbers of farm households

Farm household numbers for all major commodities are shown in Table 1.2. Clearly, as a marketed commodity, rice is by far the most important production item for farmers. More than three-quarters of all Japanese commercial farm households[46] in 1995 sold rice (2.04 million out of 2.65 million), while just over two-thirds, or 2.3 million of Japan's 3.4 million Japanese farm households harvested rice in that year.[47] These figures exceed those for any other single product by a large margin. Rice farmers therefore constitute the largest single voting group in the total farming population.

The next largest category of commercial producers is the composite group of vegetable growers who number more than 800,000 households, but they divide into much smaller numbers producing particular commodities or groups of commodities. In comparison with rice and vegetables, all other categories of farm producers are much smaller in total size. Somewhat under half a million farm households market fruit (although the individual totals for *mikan* and apple growers are much smaller), with about one-quarter or less that number marketing wheat, potatoes and sweet potatoes. For other agricultural production sectors such as industrial crops and sericulture, the numbers of farmers involved are too small to be politically significant on a national scale. In the livestock category, farm households raising beef cattle are the most numerous – 143,000 – which is more than three times the number raising dairy cattle (39,000). The pig and poultry sectors have lower numbers of producer households: 14,000 pig farms and 11,000 or so poultry farms nationwide.[48]

2. Production geography

In terms of production geography, the most outstanding characteristic of rice growing in Japan is that it is a nationwide industry. Certain areas of Northern and Central Honshu such as Tohoku, Kanto-Tosan and Hokuriku (particularly Niigata Prefecture) do, however, have substantial concentrations of rice producers. In these regions, the rice produced constitutes 27.0 per cent (Tohoku), 17.2 per cent (Kanto-Tosan) and 12.4 per cent (Hokuriku) of total rice output.[49]

Most other commodities (apart from vegetables which are grown everywhere) share these general production characteristics: nationwide spread combined with marked regional intensities, although on a smaller scale than rice. They include wheat (more than half of which is grown in Hokkaido, with significant percentages also produced in Kanto-Tosan and Kyushu); two-row barley (Tochigi and Saga produce more than half the total); soybeans (almost half are produced in Hokkaido and Tohoku); sweet potatoes (approximately one-third are grown in Kyushu); grapes (well over a third are produced in the two prefectures of Yamanashi and Nagano); and livestock farming. The regions in which dairy cattle and milk production are prominent are Hokkaido and Kanto-Tosan, and to a lesser extent Tohoku and Kyushu. Hokkaido in particular is the biggest dairy farming region in Japan. Of gross agricultural output in Hokkaido, the dairy cattle sector comprises 28.3 per cent, including raw milk production at 24.0 per cent.[50] Furthermore, Hokkaido accounts for around 40 per cent of Japan's total milk output and, as far as milk for butter and other processed dairy products are concerned, Hokkaido supplies nearly 80 per cent of the country's total demand.[51] Almost one-third of all farms specialising in dairy production are located in Hokkaido (just under 10,500 farms), followed by Chiba (over 1,800) and Iwate (almost 1,700).[52]

Beef cattle farms are prominent in Kyushu, particularly Miyazaki, Kagoshima, Nagasaki and Kumamoto as well as in the Tohoku prefecture of Iwate. Altogether, these prefectures account for over 60 per cent of all specialist beef-cattle farms in Japan.[53] Keeping 1–2 head, however, is a common sideline for farmers growing crops throughout Japan (only around 32,000 farm households out of 142,000 are specialist beef producers).[54]

Lastly, there are other products that are limited in geographic dispersion, usually for climatic or other physical reasons. For example, major concentrations of *mikan* producers can be found in Ehime, Wakayama, Shizuoka and Kyushu (particularly Kumamoto, Nagasaki and Saga), while Aomori is the premier apple-growing prefecture, producing more than double any other prefecture (Nagano comes in second).[55] Other farm commodities with a high degree of regional specialisation are peanuts (well over two-thirds are produced in Chiba); *azuki* beans (almost all are produced in Hokkaido); naked barley (Shikoku grows over two-thirds of all of this grain); *konnyaku* (elephant foot, or yam jelly, more than 80 per cent of which is produced in Gumma); sugar cane (nearly 60 per cent is grown in Okinawa, the rest in Southwest Kagoshima); green tea (more than 40 per cent of total output comes from Shizuoka, with a good proportion of the remainder produced in Kyushu); sugar beets (all are grown in Hokkaido).[56] In addition, over one-third of all farm households raising silk worms are found in Gumma, and three-quarters of the entire potato crop (some of which is used for starch) is grown in Hokkaido.[57] Indeed, almost all potato-based starch is produced in Hokkaido. On the other hand, sweet potatoes grow well in the volcanic ash soil area of Southern Kyushu and so this is a concentrated production region for this crop. For those commodities that are relatively minor on a national scale, regional concentrations help to counterbalance their lower national importance because of the potential for cohesive mobilisation of producer-votes in particular constituencies.[58] The exception is silkworm-raising farm households which have diminished in number so dramatically in recent years that their political influence has been severely attenuated.[59]

3. Income dependence

Average agricultural gross income figures indicate the extent of farmers' reliance on particular farm commodities as an income source. As Table 1.2 reveals, rice once again dominates as the single most important crop. Under the government's farm incomes policy instituted with the passage of the 1961 Agricultural Basic Law (ABL), maintaining high producer rice prices became the most convenient and effective means of raising farm incomes to the level of urban workers because rice producers constituted the majority of farm households.[60] Rice still provides 29.7 per cent of average agricultural gross farm household income, followed by vegetables (22.6 per cent), livestock products (19.7 per cent) – raw milk generates the most at 9.1 per cent – and fruit farming (9.6 per cent). Wheat and barley (1.2 per cent) are minor products, as are industrial crops (5.0 per cent) and sericulture (0.1 per cent).

Rice is also overwhelmingly predominant amongst those farm households that depend on a single crop. In 1997, more than half of all farm households marketing agricultural products grew only rice,[61] which means that the agricultural income of one-half of Japanese farm households is solely dependent on the price they receive for their rice. This factor, more than any other, helps to account for the central place that the producer rice price issue has occupied in Japan's agricultural policymaking and the electoral sensitivity of rice price, production, marketing and import issues for Japanese politicians. It also helps to explain why policies to curb production through rice acreage reductions (*gentan*) have been so unpopular amongst farmers.

In the beef industry, the two halves of the dairy beef industry are closely linked. Dairy producers earn 10–20 per cent of their income from the sale of steers and culled cows for beef production. This magnifies the significance of any policy issue affecting either side of the industry.

Regional variations in farm income dependence can also be politically important. The most vulnerable regions are those where income from particular commodity sales represent a substantial proportion of the total agricultural income of farm households. For example, in fiscal year (FY) 1996, rice constituted 71.7 per cent of the average farm household gross agricultural income in Hokuriku, 48.0 per cent in Tohoku, with Chugoku

(40.5 per cent) and Kinki (35.9 per cent) also relatively high.[62] On a prefecture-wide basis, rice was most significant in the Hokuriku prefectures of Toyama (87.3 per cent) and Niigata (72.6 per cent), and the Tohoku prefectures of Akita (69.6 per cent) and Yamagata (50.5 per cent).[63] Because farmers in these regions derive the bulk of their agricultural income from rice sales, and only rice sales, they will have a keen interest in rice issues such as producer rice prices, rice acreage set-aside subsidies and rice import policies.

Other notable commodity income dependencies on a regional basis are livestock and livestock products (32.8 per cent of gross agricultural receipts per farm household in Hokkaido and 27.5 per cent in Kyushu); fruit farming (production of fruit, particularly grapes and peaches generates 71.3 per cent of gross receipts in Yamanashi, in Wakayama, fruit – mainly *mikan* – produces 59.5 per cent of gross farm receipts and in Ehime, 45.4 per cent, in Aomori, fruit – mainly apples – accounts for 29.1 per cent); industrial crops (in Gumma, 9.7 per cent of agricultural income comes from industrial crops, with almost all of this generated by *konnyaku* production); and potatoes for potato starch (which generate 7.8 per cent of gross agricultural receipts in Hokkaido).[64] While most of these products lack significance in gross production terms, they represent important commodity sectors because they support regional economies.[65]

Regional income dependencies can be compounded by farm household specialisation factors. For example, almost all farm households that specialise in the production of *konnyaku* are situated in Gumma, nearly one-third of all specialist dairy farmers are located in Hokkaido, around one-half of specialist sericulture farms can be found in Gumma, and about the same proportion of all specialist beef cattle producers are located in Miyazaki and Kagoshima.[66]

Commodity specialisation usually signifies reduced production alternatives, which makes these farms economically vulnerable to price changes and more competitive market environments. For small-scale beef producers in the mountainous regions of Kagoshima and Miyazaki, the alternatives are limited which increases their vulnerability to enterprise failure in the face of competitive pressures. Similarly, sugar beets, sweet potatoes, potatoes and soybeans are agricultural products that form a crop rotation system in the dry field farming areas of Hokkaido.[67] This means that policies affecting one of these products ultimately impacts on the whole crop system in such areas.

4. Production efficiency

Generally speaking, most farms in Japan are reliant in varying degrees on assistance and protection from government. Farm viability is extremely low. In 1960 only 8.6 per cent of farm operations were estimated to be viable farm units.[68] By 1990, this proportion had diminished even further, to just 6.3 per cent of the total number of farm households.[69] The less viable the farm, the more dependent the farm household is on government support for agricultural income and on wages and salaries earned in non-agricultural occupations.

Rice farming, for example, continues to be prevalent among the smallest land holders. In 1990, just on 80 per cent of all commercial farms cultivating rice paddy were 1 ha or less; by 1995, the percentage had dipped slightly to 75.6 per cent, as Table 1.2 indicates. Furthermore, even in 1995 the number of commercial farms cultivating rice paddy in the smallest category (less than 0.5 ha) still constituted 45.9 per cent of all rice-producing households.[70] This proportion is declining only slowly (it was 51.6 per cent in 1990[71]). Somewhat less than a half of all farms that market rice in Japan, therefore, cultivate 0.5 ha or less; only 7.8 per cent of the total are larger than 2 ha,[72] while viable units account for only 10 per cent of gross output in the rice growing sector.[73]

For a sizeable proportion of Japanese farmers cultivating rice on their minuscule rice paddies, their basic concern is to retain all the direct and indirect benefits of growing rice, even if only on a small scale. These benefits are realised not only through price supports, but also through associated benefits such as mutual aid insurance payouts for crop damage and the whole panoply of general concessions available to farmers such as lower tax rates on agricultural land amongst others. For many farm households, growing rice is a way of profitably maintaining farmland as an asset inherited down through the generations.[74]

The political significance of rice is not, therefore, simply a reflection of its overwhelming predominance in Japan's total agricultural output and the large number of rice cultivators. It is also a question of the scale of agricultural enterprise involved, and the fact that rice farms are, on average, very small and therefore usually inefficient. Most rice farmers are dependent on price supports to yield higher returns than an unfettered market would produce. Rice income is important as supplementary income for the household. The other concessions and handouts from government also generate the necessary economic incentives to keep rice growers in the business of farming. If these concessions were withdrawn, farming would become a distinctly less attractive option. Many of this group are not serious agricultural producers; rice growing suits them for a host of other reasons. They are basically concession seekers and they constitute the vast majority of Japanese farmers.

Most farm households marketing other crops are not much larger than rice farms in terms of their overall scale of enterprise, as the figures in Table 1.2 indicate. Except for wheat and barley producers, they are all on average smaller in scale than rice farms which suggests that the endeavours of the government to expand the scale of enterprise in the rice sector has had some small success. Vegetable farms are particularly minuscule (97 per cent are less than 1.0 ha), while orchards are not much larger on average. Amongst *mikan* growers, for example, the area of land cultivated per unit is still very small. The vast majority have less than 1.0 ha, and only 3,000 have 2.0 ha or more.[75]

Japanese beef farming has also been a small-scale, high-cost sector, although there are now marked variations between the dairy and beef sectors. Dairy cattle farming is now characterised by larger-scale, more efficient farms compared with the beef cattle sector, rationalisation and restructuring steadily taking place from the 1970s onwards. This has meant a substantial increase in dairy beef head per household. In 1996, as Table 1.2 indicates, there was an average of 48.2 head per household, an increase from an average of only 3.4 in 1965.[76] Nevertheless, by world standards, the number of head per household is still relatively low. Somewhat under half of all dairy beef households have less than 30 head (16,620), while only 950 households have more than 100 head.[77] Beef cattle-raising households are much smaller again. The average farm has 20.0 head as Table 1.2 indicates. A large number (31,700) have only 1–2 head of cattle (in 1991 the comparable figure was 76,900 indicating some progress in expanding the scale of production), while only 2,540 have more than 200.[78]

The figures for cattle farming in Table 1.2 contrast with those for the pig and chicken sectors which are characterised by a smaller number of farms running much larger and more cost-efficient operations (there are thousands of pigs and sometimes hundreds of thousands of layers and broilers per farm). Despite the fact that most are viable units in terms of production scale, their international competitiveness remains in doubt. According to one study, few or none of the individual farm commodity sectors in Japan, including all sub-sectors of the livestock industry, have a size that would enable them to compete with international market prices: 'Under the assumption that the critical size of farms to be internationally competitive is somewhere in the neighborhood of 50 ha. of rice, 100 dairy cows, 200 head of beef cattle, 2000 fattening pigs or 300,000 head of poultry, then only a dozen or so rice producers, less than 1 per cent of beef and dairy producers, 2 to 3 per cent of pig and egg producers and about 6 per cent of broiler producers would currently fall into this category.'[79] This suggests a continuing need for government assistance and protection, although products such as *wagyu* beef caters to a speciality demand, and raw milk enjoys a degree of natural protection.

5. Producer subsidy equivalents

The PSE is a measure of current levels of assistance and support to Japan's farmers (including by commodity) and, therefore, the vulnerability of farmers who produce these commodities to a reduction in government support, and indirectly, to market opening. The percentage PSE for rice in 1995 was 97,[80] sliding to 88 in 1996 (see Table 1.2). This is the highest of any agricultural product in Japan except for wheat and other non-rice grains such as barley. The figures indicate that rice farmers would need to be paid the equivalent of 97 per cent (88 per cent in 1996) of the producer rice price to compensate them for loss of income if all producer subsidies to rice growers were withdrawn.

Rice also accounted for 65.3 per cent of the total PSE value for Japanese agricultural commodities in 1995,[81] rising to 65.7 per cent in 1996.[82] Table 1.2 discloses that certain sectors of the livestock industry also register relatively high percentage PSEs, for instance 83 for milk, 61 for pigmeat and 43 for beef and veal. The only livestock products that are relatively low on this scale are chicken and eggs. Sugar also enjoyed a high percentage PSE (70).

The range of variables used in the above analysis, economic and geographic, provide a general indication of the extent to which farmers, their organisations and political representatives are motivated to rally around particular commodity issues and the political cost factors for the LDP relating to farmers' votes nationwide and in particular regions. Rice scores highest on almost all the statistical indices used. Not surprisingly, rice is considered synonymous with Japanese agriculture and the producer rice price the most prominent symbol of Japan's protection of agriculture.[83] For most Japanese farmers, an increase in the producer rice price has been the equivalent of a wage hike. The annual producer price decision has dominated the agricultural policymaking agenda, a 'political price'[84] marked by large-scale mobilisation of farmers in public assemblies, gatherings and demonstrations. Rice has also featured as the most contentious agricultural trade liberalisation issue in the postwar period. For all these reasons, rice excites greater political sensitivities than any other single agricultural product. As Donnelly puts it, rice is 'the political commodity par excellence'.[85]

On a nationwide basis as well as amongst specialist regional producers, livestock products likewise loom large in political terms, particularly the beef and dairy sectors. Livestock price decisionmaking for beef and raw milk for processing has been politicised, as have associated market liberalisation issues.

In contrast, support and stabilisation prices for crops such as soybeans, sugar beets, potatoes and sweet potatoes rank fairly low on the politicisation scale according to most of the above criteria. Because of the relatively small number of producers involved, price policymaking for these commodities passes with little or no public campaigning by farmers. Nevertheless, the farmers' main representative body, the agricultural cooperative organisation, submits formal requests to government in relation to all products subject to price intervention. Furthermore, discussions or negotiations involving MAFF officials, the MAFF Minister and LDP representatives are held on all these agricultural prices. In other cases, because of greater efficiencies of production scale (such as *mikan* and chicken meat) price intervention from government is minimal or non-existent.

Commodities for which price decisionmaking is not contentious have, however, in some cases become politicised in relation to agricultural market access issues. These include citrus, potatoes for starch, sugar beets, apples, *konnyaku*, peanuts, miscellaneous beans and so on. In particular, agricultural items that loom large in regional economies have tended to figure politically when assailed by external demands for market opening.

Farmers' organisations

Farmers in Japan, like farmers in many other developed economies that protect agriculture, benefit from strong organisations with an established voice in government representing a clearly defined sector of the economy. In the Japanese case, one farmers' organisation has been overwhelmingly important – Nokyo – which in April 1992 retitled itself the JA Group (JA Guruupu). 'JA' is short for 'Japan Agricultural Cooperatives'. Nokyo changed its name in order to establish a new corporate identity.[86] The aim was to revamp the image or impression of Nokyo to the wider public. For the purposes of this study, however, the traditional term 'Nokyo' will be used.

'Nokyo' is an acronym for the nationwide organisation of agricultural cooperative unions (*nogyo kyodo kumiai*, or *nokyo*), terminology that is still used in relevant legislation. Used with the lower case, '*nogyo kyodo kumiai*', or '*nokyo*' is the generic term. It refers to a type of organisation, that is, an 'agricultural cooperative union', or 'agricultural cooperative'.[87] The term '*nokyo*' used by itself also denotes a single municipal (city, town or village) agricultural cooperative.

On the other hand, Nokyo with a capital 'N' is the name given to the collection of agricultural cooperative organisations operating at municipal, prefectural and national levels, whose core functions consist of a comprehensive range of economic businesses (either as a specialisation or in combination) and which come together as a nationwide grouping.[88] Nokyo therefore stands for a group of interrelated organisations, all of which are agricultural cooperatives in the generic sense, but which are also components of Nokyo, the nationwide organisation. All prefectural and national agricultural cooperative organisations, whatever their functional specialisation, have Nokyo in their title (and may now be additionally prefixed by the letters 'JA'). At the municipal level, the title 'Nokyo' is combined with the locality in which they operate.

Nokyo's presence in the Japanese countryside is ubiquitous. Almost all farm households, no matter what they produce or the level of their engagement in agriculture, belong to their local agricultural cooperative. In addition to Nokyo's primary functions which involve the provision of a multitude of economic and other kinds of services to farmers and local communities, the wider Nokyo system also encompasses diverse social and political activities. Its coverage of the farm sector, in both membership and functional terms, is comprehensive, projecting an image of a multifaceted organisational giant. Chapter 2 on 'Interest Group Politics' outlines Nokyo's hierarchical structure and details its diverse economic and policy-related functions, while chapter 4 on 'Organisational Politics' analyses its membership, organisational resources and other distinctive features of its organisational setup.

Nokyo has no equivalent amongst rural producer groups in the Western world. Comparison with cooperatives in other industrialised democracies provides only a limited guide to the diversity, scope and state-guided nature of its operations. Nokyo's character is not simply economic as are most farm cooperatives elsewhere. It is not like the agricultural cooperatives in the United States, for example, which are purely business ventures. Nokyo is a social institution, an entity that encapsulates, expresses and reinforces social and cultural mores in the countryside. It is also a vast bureaucracy with a multitude of officials extending the organisation's reach into the remotest areas of Japan, and an arm of government in the implementation of agricultural policy. In popular and scholarly literature it is called both an interest group (*rieki dantai*) and a pressure group (*atsuryoku dantai*), with policy interests that range over the entire agricultural economy. It has also been likened to a corporate enterprise network (*keiretsu*) that competes with other giant Japanese financial and trading corporations on equal terms. Last, but not least, Nokyo has been identified as an institutional obstacle to structural adjustment and deregulatory reform in the agricultural sector, and a powerful non-tariff barrier to an expansion in farm imports. The fact that Japan's farmers have been a well mobilised and vocal political force is in no small part due to Nokyo. It is an enduring element in the rural political equation and one of the nation's most politically powerful interest groups.

Nokyo's primary policy concerns relating to farmers centre on matters that impact directly on producer incomes. Its agricultural policy activities (*nosei katsudo*) focus on producer prices, market liberalisation, budget subsidies for farm assistance programmes, levels of crop incentive payments and associated questions. The panoply of agricultural policy issues targeted by Nokyo are a measure of the level of government intervention in the agricultural economy. Because agricultural prices have been subject to government intervention, for example, decisions made by the government on agricultural pricing issues have become the direct focus of pressure from Nokyo seeking the highest returns for farmers. Nokyo has submitted 'demand' prices for agricultural commodities and backed these up with public and behind-the-scenes lobbying as well as direct negotiations with government. The scale of organisational mobilisation behind a price demand has been greatest in the case of the producer rice price which has occasioned annual rituals of Nokyo-led public demonstrations and marches by farmers and co-op leaders. During the Nokyo-led rice price campaign (*beika undo*), Nokyo has taken on the characteristics of a pressure group most visibly.[89] Chapter 8 on 'Policy Campaigning' describes Nokyo's strategies and activities as a farm pressure group on a range of issues and explains how the changing nature of agricultural policy is affecting the conduct of Nokyo's policy campaigns.

The agricultural cooperatives are deeply and intimately involved through their leaders, members and organisational offshoots in a great deal of electoral activity (*senkyo katsudo*), both official and unofficial, at all levels of government. In terms of Nokyo's organisational genre, however, perhaps one of the few things it is not, is a mass *political* movement of farmers. Its formal definition is economic: it is a self-help cooperative that conducts a range of businesses for its members. Nevertheless, a particular combination of factors support the extension of Nokyo's activity into politics in general and electoral politics in particular.

Firstly, the agricultural cooperatives have incorporated the electorally over-represented farm bloc within their membership. The electoral power of the agricultural cooperatives has been enhanced by the over-representation of more sparsely populated rural districts, which has magnified the political significance of the farm vote. Chapter 5 on 'The Political Demography of Agriculture' provides changing figures for the number of farm voters and discusses their overall weighting in the national voting population. Secondly, the agricultural cooperatives and their associated political groupings have provided a rice-roots electoral infrastructure for the LDP in the countryside, acting as some of the main organisational intermediaries linking conservative party Diet members to their supporters in rural areas.[90] Indeed, Nokyo's powers as a pressure group are directly related to the role of agricultural cooperative groups as the primary link between farm voters and the LDP.[91] Chapter 6 describes the diverse electoral activities of individuals and groups connected to the Nokyo system, including an assessment of Nokyo's much vaunted vote-mobilisation power.

Nokyo is also an economic group with vested interests in its own right, not simply a farmers' organisation. Its business functions include not only basic farm cooperative activities like marketing farmers' produce and providing farm inputs such as agricultural machinery, equipment and agro-chemicals, they also extend to the manufacture of these inputs such as stockfeed and fertilisers through subsidiary companies. Moreover, agricultural cooperatives and their associated companies are also engaged in agricultural product processing, such as drinking milk, fruit juice and livestock products of all kinds.

Nokyo's financial activities extend beyond providing basic banking services to members to stock and bond purchases as well as channelling large quantities of loans to other financial institutions and investments in agriculture-related industries. Another key area of economic activity has centred around admin-istratively sanctioned monopolies, such as rice collection and distribution, for which Nokyo has been paid commissions and various other service fees and subsidies by the government. Nokyo also receives government financial assistance for rationalising agricultural cooperative management and for carrying out agriculture-related projects, programmes and functions on behalf of the government. Chapter 2 delineates Nokyo's role as an adjunct to agricultural administration, evaluating the costs and benefits of corporatised connections with the bureaucracy.

Profits and other benefits generated by Nokyo's concessionary-related businesses, by its economic and financial enterprises and by agricultural budget subsidies have assumed greater prominence in its policy agenda over the years. These concerns directly affect its own performance and prospects as an organisation as well as the rewards flowing back to its executive and staff personnel. Such interests can be distinguished from farmers' policy interests. Nokyo's position on many issues is shaped by its long-term organisational maintenance strategies. In particular, Nokyo is concerned with the management viability of individual agricultural cooperative organisations and levels of profit generated by its different businesses. Its political priorities on its own account reflect the size of its economic stake in particular economic or financial enterprises or farm-related industries. Its stake in the domestic production of particular agricultural commodities is also related to the economic benefits it derives from the marketing, supply and distribution businesses associated with these products. These can determine how prominently certain products and issues figure in its *nosei katsudo*. Nokyo's involvement in subsidiary industries has generated considerable resistance to deregulation of agricultural input markets as well as to liberalisation of agricultural product markets where Nokyo processors have long enjoyed near-monopolies. Nokyo's massive investments in domestic livestock processing and feed supply manufacture and distribution, for example, have generated a considerable stake in the survival of the domestic livestock industry and its protection from international competition. Chapter 4 identifies Nokyo's organisational interests in commodity distribution systems and associated businesses as well as the current challenges it faces in an evolving economic, financial and policy environment.

Nokyo is a particular class of Japanese farmers' organisation: a government-sponsored body created to perform designed functions under law. Other farmers' groups also fall into this category, although they do not have the broad functional scope or universal membership characteristics of the agricultural cooperatives. These groups are the land improvement groups (*tochi kairyo dantai*), the agricultural mutual aid associations (*nogyo kyosai kumiai*) and the agricultural committee (*nogyo iinkai*) system, each of which performs a narrower range of functions than Nokyo and has a more restricted farmer membership, although all are involved in policy-related and electoral activities to some degree. Chapter 2 details these organisations as well as other categories of farmers' groups, including associations of commodity producers and the farmers' unions (*nomin kumiai*).

The institutional interface of agrarian interests

The Diet

A dominant feature of the exercise of agrarian power in Japan has been the extent to which farming interests have penetrated Diet and party policy processes. The bias of the electoral system in favour of voters in more sparsely populated rural areas and the active connections between farmers, agricultural organisations and politicians work to facilitate the articulation of agricultural interests from within Parliamentary and party circles.

Nokyo's electoral activities, for example, have resulted in direct representation in the Diet by its own leaders and indirect representation by politicians on whom it bestows various forms of electoral and organisational backing in exchange for sponsorship of Nokyo's and the farmers' interests in national politics. Chapter 7 on 'Representative Politics' identifies the different types of politicians who receive electoral support from agricultural cooperative organisations, the party alignment of these politicians and the linkages between types of electoral support and quality of representation. This analysis is part of a wider examination of direct and indirect agricultural representation in the Diet and of how this representation has changed over time, both quantitatively and in terms of the party affiliations of politicians with connections to the farm sector. The study evaluates the proximity of different political parties to the range of agricultural interest groups, the extent of policy specialisation amongst agricultural representatives and the locus of their Diet and party activity.

Farmers' parties

The LDP, in power continuously between 1955 and 1993, and back in government since June 1994,[92] has been overwhelmingly dominant as the party representing agricultural interests in Japan. Although elements of the pre-1993 Opposition – the Japan Socialist Party, or JSP (Nihon Shakaito),[93] the Democratic Socialist Party, or DSP (Minshato) and the Japan Communist Party, or JCP (Nihon Kyosanto), particularly the JSP – sought and obtained varying levels of electoral support from rural areas with the help of their farmers' union organisations, these parties were never really serious electoral alternatives for farmers, particularly from the late 1970s onwards. Attempts to organise more distinctively farmers' parties failed in the first decade after the war, as chapter 3 on 'Farmers' Politics' explains.

The LDP's long-standing pro-farmer bias and electoral dominance in rural areas are basic features of the Japanese political landscape. Like all parties in power, the LDP pays close heed to electoral imperatives, which have induced a high level of responsiveness to a strategically important agricultural electorate. The party has rewarded its rural clients with an unwavering predisposition towards transferring financial resources from the cities to the countryside.

The electoral foundation of the LDP's rural bias is documented in chapters 5 and 6. Japan's farmers have provided the electoral bedrock for successive conservative governments since 1955. The LDP forged a broadly based (but not exclusive) alliance with farm voters and Nokyo from the very earliest period of its rule. Lacking party-based, rice-roots organisations in the countryside, LDP candidates turned to the organised power of the agricultural cooperatives and their associated organisations to help them secure electoral victories in rural and semi-rural constituencies.[94] In this way, Nokyo provided the organisational means whereby LDP politicians could penetrate rural society and mobilise support.[95] Electoral malapportionment,

999

meanwhile, guaranteed that farmers' votes continued to be more politically important than their absolute numbers.

Although the LDP diversified the range of its supporting groups over time, farmers have remained a traditional constituency for the party and the core of its electoral support base. The question for the future is whether, in the face of inexorable demographic and economic change, rural support will remain critical to the maintenance of the LDP's Diet majorities and hence to its political dominance as the ruling party.[96] Chapters 5 and 6 assess the likely impact of socio-economic change on the voting power of farmers and their contribution to continuing LDP victories.

MAFF and the legislative framework

The chief instrument of state intervention in the farm sector has been the bureaucracy, and in particular the MAFF[97] and its associated agencies. The MAFF administers agriculture through all the legal, institutional, financial and administrative means at its disposal, drafts agricultural legislation and the agricultural budget, and negotiates agricultural policies with the ruling party(ies).

As in the case of the Ministry of International Trade and Industry (MITI), MAFF's basic rights of intervention in the agricultural economy are embedded in its founding legislation, the 1949 Law Establishing the Ministry of Agriculture, Forestry and Fisheries (*Norinsuisansho Setchiho*). The purpose of this law was to establish an organisation to implement the administrative duties and projects within MAFF's jurisdiction[98] as well as to set out clearly the scope and competence of this administration. MAFF is additionally charged with administering around 121 other laws[99] as well as ministerial ordinances governing various aspects of the operations of the agricultural economy.

The 'big five' laws have formed the core of agricultural legislation in the postwar period. They are the Food Control (FC) Law (*Shokuryo Kanriho*, or *Shokkanho*) of 1942, the Agricultural Cooperative Union Law, or Nokyo Law (*Nogyo Kyodo Kumiaiho*) of 1947, the Land Improvement Law (*Tochi Kairyoho*) of 1949, the Agricultural Land Law (*Nochiho*) of 1952, and the Agricultural Basic Law of 1961.[100]

From 1942 onwards, and throughout most of the postwar period, the FC Law regulated the domestic rice market through price control, distribution control and trade control.[101] Although some aspects of Food Control relating to consumer rationing were completely liberalised in the early postwar period, government regulation of rice collection and distribution remained an entrenched feature of the system. So did ministerial intervention in the price-setting process. Imports of rice (and wheat, barley and naked barley) except as state-traded items were also banned under Article 11 of the FC Law. The FC system continued in operation until November 1995, when the Law for Stabilisation of Supply-Demand and Price of Staple Food (*Shuyo Shokuryo no Jukyu oyobi Kakaku no Anteiho*), commonly referred to as the new Staple Food Law (*Shokuryoho*) came into effect and the FC Law was abolished.

The 1947 Agricultural Cooperative Union Law provided for the establishment of a nationwide system of farm cooperatives in order to promote the livelihood and agricultural production activities of farmers through a system self-help and mutual cooperation. The legislation (Article 1) states that the fundamental aim of the law is 'to encourage the development of farmers' cooperative organisations, and thereby to promote agricultural productivity and elevate farmers' economic and social position, as well as to promote the development of the national economy.'[102]

The purpose of the 1949 Land Improvement Law was 'to lay down the necessary means to implement properly and smoothly projects relating to the improvement, development, conservation and collectivisation of agricultural land with the aim of developing and consolidating the agricultural production base, thereby contributing to rises in agricultural productivity, increases in gross agricultural output, a selective expansion of agricultural production and improvement in agricultural structure. In carrying out land improvement projects, works will be compatible with the advancement of the national economy and will contribute to the comprehensive development and conservation of national land resources.'[103] In general terms, the law provided a postwar legal foundation for large-scale, government-subsidised land improvement works designed to expand the scale of agricultural production and consolidate land holdings.

The 1952 Agricultural Land Law laid down regulations relating to farmland ownership, use, and transfers through sales and leasing arrangements.[104] In so doing it established the fundamental principle that those who cultivate the land should own the land, thus providing a firm basis for the family farm tradition. Article 1 of the law describes its purpose as 'promoting the acquisition of agricultural land by cultivators and protecting their rights, as well as coordinating land use relationships in order to encourage the effective agricultural use of land and thereby stabilise the position of farmers and improve agricultural productivity.'[105] Following the land reform of the late 1940s and the passage of the Agricultural Land Law, the three primary components of farming – land ownership, farm management, and farm labour – all came under the control of the family farm.[106]

The 1961 ABL embodied the government's most fundamental set of aims with respect to the farm sector. Objectives included preservation of agriculture as an industry vital to the nation, improving farm structure, raising agricultural productivity and efficiency, promoting greater responsiveness of farm producers to consumer demand for particular commodities,[107] and last but not least, 'narrowing the gap between agriculture and other industries through . . . higher incomes for those engaged in agriculture so that they may expect to achieve parity in living standards with those engaged in other industries.'[108] This precept inscribed a farm incomes policy into law and formed the basis on which a much more extensive postwar system of support and assistance to agriculture was built.

MAFF-sponsored administrative groups

The MAFF has established multiple organisational and institutional linkages to bridge the policy implementation gap between administrators and agricultural producers. These auxiliary organs are called government-affiliated agencies (*gaikaku dantai*). They number in the hundreds. Their primary role is to assist the process of administering the agricultural sector. They operate under varying degrees of MAFF supervision and control with funding derived in varying proportions from government sources. They have a dual function: to perform public-policy functions as well as to provide private services to group members (principally other agricultural organisations). In many cases, they form an important channel for the distribution of agricultural subsidies and, in some instances, of funding generated by state trades in farm products. Some are directly represented in the policy process by influential politicians recruited to serve in executive positions in the groups.

Over time these intermediary organisations have developed a vested interest in the maintenance of government support to agriculture, both as a basis for group functioning and as a source of financial benefits. Collectively, they form a substantial organisational and institutional bulwark against the abolition of regulatory controls on the agricultural economy and the largesse flowing from high levels of government intervention.

Advisory councils

Advisory councils or government inquiry organs (*shimon kikan*) are an important vehicle for the expression of special interests in the Japanese policymaking process. Most advisory councils are official standing organs created by a minister and composed of members selected by him to inquire into and discuss policies and legislation proposed by the ministries and agencies to which the councils are attached. One of their basic functions is to provide non-ministry input into the process of bureaucratic policy formulation. In 1996, a total of 213 advisory councils of this type were operating.[109]

The ministry-attached advisory councils are theoretically constituted so as to reflect the diversity of opinion and interests of groups most affected by the policies in question. Representation from stakeholders is cross-sectional. It includes leaders of interest groups that come within the ambit of ministerial jurisdiction (including ministry *gaikaku dantai*) who have differing and potentially conflicting interests in the policy in question. For the sake of balance, representatives from groups formally outside the ministry constituency are also included. Partisan representation is tempered by the informed expertise and professional input of 'persons of learning and experience' (*gakushiki keikensha*) such as academics and other kinds of technical experts, as well as other 'neutral' parties such as journalists. Council deliberations and the compilation of reports on ministry submissions are a means of dealing with 'interest arbitration' amongst the parties to an issue.[110]

In practice, advisory councils generally support ministry policies and legitimise new policy directions drafted by ministry officials. As consultative bodies, their formal role is limited to suggestion and advice. Nevertheless, the largest and most prestigious of the advisory councils set or endorse basic goals for different sectors of the economy, such as industry, agriculture and the financial system, in the light of which more detailed matters of policy are decided.

In 1996, the MAFF main ministry had 14 advisory councils, the most important being the Agricultural Policy Advisory Council, or APAC (Nosei Shingikai, or Noseishin),[111] the Livestock Industry Promotion Advisory Council, or LIPAC (Chikusan Shinko Shingikai), the Silk Manufacturing Industry Promotion Council (Sanshigyo Shinko Shingikai), the Fruit Tree Agriculture Promotion Advisory Council (Kaju Nogyo Shinko Shingikai), the Food Distribution Advisory Council (Shokuhin Ryutsu Shingikai), the Central Raw Milk Trading Arbitration Advisory Council (Chuo Seinyu Torihiki Chotei Shingikai) and the Sweet Resources Advisory Council (Kanmi Shigen Shingikai).[112] One of the largest is the Agriculture, Forestry and Fisheries Statistics Observation Advisory Council with around 80 members. The Food Agency had one advisory council, the Rice Price Advisory Council, or RPAC (Beika Shingikai, or Beishin), the Forestry Agency two, and the Fisheries Agency five (to make a total of 22) (MITI for example had 20).[113]

Of all the MAFF advisory councils, the RPAC has been the best known because of the publicity and Nokyo-sponsored action surrounding its deliberations on the producer rice price. In spite of the focus on the 'political price' of rice, the RPAC has endorsed the government's recommendation in the majority of cases.[114] APAC on the other hand is the most prestigious: it proposes basic goals for agriculture in addition to outlining more specific objectives for the development of the farm sector. Its reports are jointly issued with the MAFF, and are used as a policy guide by administrators, the agricultural cooperatives and the farming industry in general.

MAFF advisory councils have representation from Nokyo, other agricultural groups including MAFF *gaikaku dantai*, consumer organisations, academia, business associations including those operating in the food manufacturing sector, private companies, the media, and other interested parties and experts. The RPAC, when first established in 1949, was composed of 32 members: 11 representatives from the producer side (including one from Nokyo), five from the consumer side (consumer and labour union groups), two from business organisations, eight Diet members from the conservative and socialist parties,[115] and a miscellaneous category of 'other' members including 'persons of learning and experience' such as university professors.[116] Four decades later in 1987, the RPAC was composed of five academics, two representatives from Nokyo, five representatives from various agricultural

organisations including MAFF *gaikaku dantai*[117] and the national organisation of agricultural committees, three representatives from consumer groups
and cooperatives, one from the rice wholesaling industry (the National
Federation of Staple Food Collection Cooperatives (Zenkoku Shushoku
Shuka Kyodo Kumiai Rengokai, or Zenshuren)) two mass media representatives (NHK and the *Nikkei* newspaper), one farmers' union representative,
one prefectural agricultural guidance expert, two local government representatives (including the Governor of Shiga Prefecture and the vice-chairman of
a local government association), one company representative, and two
representatives from economic research groups affiliated with the government
(one public and one private) for a total of 25 members.[118] No radical changes
in this membership structure were evident even 10 years later in 1996, except
that the actual membership had fallen to 16 and a Managing Director of
the Federation of Economic Organisations (Keidanren) was present as a
representative of business.[119]

While most ministry advisory councils have a more or less permanent
existence,[120] others appear from time to time to deal with specific policy
issues. In 1990, for example, the Director-General of the Food Agency set up
a special inquiry organ entitled the Independently Distributed Rice Price
Formation Arena Investigation Committee (Jishu Ryutsumai Kakaku Keisei
no Ba Kentokai) to examine the agency's proposal to introduce the market
mechanism into the distribution and sale of rice marketed directly to wholesalers rather than to the government, which by 1990, comprised around 70 per
cent of the total amount of edible rice marketed in Japan.

In addition, specific-purpose advisory councils are set up from time to time
by the Prime Minister. These are often charged with making recommendations in relation to national policy issues that cut across ministerial
jurisdictions, or issues that may engage ministries in defence of their own
interests. Such councils have often made recommendations relevant to agricultural policy. Because they are not attached to specific ministries, these
councils do not function to legitimise ministerial policy initiatives and hence
their recommendations often call for more radical innovation than individual
ministries are prepared to contemplate in their own spheres. In April 1997,
for example, an advisory committee to the Prime Minister called the Food,
Agriculture and Rural Areas Basic Problems Investigation Committee
(Shokuryo, Nogyo, Noson Kihon Mondai Chosakai) was established to
propose new medium- and long-range plans for agriculture, and in particular
to review the ABL and to formulate a New Agricultural Basic Law (*Arata na
Nogyo Kihonho*).

Basic approach and methodology

As this introductory discussion indicates, the subject matter of this book is
predominantly interests: farmers' interests; the interests of agricultural
organisations; politicians' interests; how the interests of farmers and farm

organisations are articulated and represented in national politics; how and why these interests influence the decisions of policymakers and so on. Such a subject focus appears tailormade for the rational choice approach, which applies the assumptions and methods of micro-economics to politics, arguing that individuals in a range of political contexts (as voters, as members of interest groups, as politicians, as organisational leaders etc.) are motivated by rational calculations of their personal utility (self-interest) defined in terms of a single, uniform variable.

The rational choice approach would thus proceed from the fundamental assumption that farmers will invariably vote for the candidate who is most likely to maximise their benefits; that LDP politicians will invariably be motivated to deliver policy benefits to the agricultural sector in order to maximise farmers' voting support; that Nokyo leaders will automatically pursue policies that yield the greatest returns for their organisation and thus increased personal status, job security, monetary rewards and so on. Rational choice theorists, for example, have tried to sheet home all the obstacles to Japan's market liberalisation to the peculiar construction of Japan's electoral system, the incentives this generates for candidates to pursue the particularistic interests of constituents and the LDP's electoral dependencies.[121]

The objections to the rational choice approach are both methodological and evidential. Firstly, because the rational choice approach proceeds by means of *a priori* deduction rather than through empirical-inductive analysis, what it gains in analytical clarity and simplification, it loses in accuracy of detail and comprehensiveness of explanation. This work prefers to derive general conclusions from observed evidence rather than pursue evidence to support single-factor universal explanations.

Secondly, while rational choice assumptions about, for example, the motivations that drive the electoral choices of farmers and the policy choices of politicians may be useful as loose working assumptions, they should not be treated as universally valid propositions. There is a considerable 'leap of faith' from one to the other, which no doubt accounts for rational choice theorists' air of doctrinal conviction. Not *all* agricultural policy choices of LDP politicians will be solely attributable to a vote-maximising calculus; not *all* farmers will *always* vote purely on the basis of self-interest (defined in terms of expected economic benefit). The assumptions of rational choice theory are simply too confining and too easily challenged by contradictory evidence.

This work prefers a simpler, basic standpoint: societal groupings (defined in terms of their membership of particular political, institutional, social or economic organisations or categories) are broadly conceived as pursuing their interests in politics; and the extent to which the interests of any particular societal grouping are realised will depend on the relative power of these groups. This approach encapsulates a traditional, political science perspective that defines the focus of analysis in terms of interests and power which are assumed to be multifaceted and multidimensional.

In analysing Japanese agricultural politics from this standpoint, several analytical objectives are appropriate. The first is to explain in historical-empirical terms the evolution of agricultural interest groups and farmers' parties, the formation and continuation of the LDP-farmer electoral alliance, the expansion and contraction of agrarian electoral power, the penetration of Diet and party systems by agricultural interests, the waxing and waning of Nokyo's economic and political influence, the record of agricultural cooperative policy campaigns, and the conflation of representative and administrative roles by interest groups and semi-governmental institutions in the agricultural sector. The book's historical timeframe extends over the entire postwar period, although the analysis proceeds thematically rather than by means of historical narrative.

Secondly, because the politics of agriculture incorporates some of the best known features of Japanese political life, the analysis of agricultural politics and political economy can be used as a case study to illustrate salient features of Japan's political system, in particular the way in which vested interests wield power through Japan's electoral, party, Diet and institutional structures. At this level of inquiry, the purpose is to explain more clearly the nature of Japanese politics by using agricultural politics to generate some key propositions which are related to existing generalisations, understandings, models and 'theories' in the field.

Thirdly, and less directly, the study is designed to have relevance for a number of broader theoretical questions in comparative politics and comparative political economy relating to interest group behaviour, corporatism, electoral systems, political participation, organisational maintenance, the preservation of protectionist regimes and so on. The analysis of the agricultural cooperative organisation, for example, may be valuable to comparativists studying interest groups in general and farm interest groups in particular. This study provides a good deal of information that is relevant to the common headings under which interest groups are analysed, such as organisational capabilities, resources, goals and constraints as well as group lobbying tactics and strategies of political representation. Likewise, the analysis of how agricultural interests are represented in the Diet, the role of agricultural organisations in elections and the relationship between these organisations and political parties provides rich material for those wishing to adopt a more comparative approach. It is hoped that scholars working in these and other areas covered by the book will find material useful to their theoretical and comparative concerns.

2   Interest group politics

The representation of farm interests in Japan takes diverse organisational forms. The all-encompassing nature of Nokyo's activities ensures its dominance at the rice roots, yet the agricultural cooperatives by no means exercise a monopoly on the organised representation of farm interests. This role is shared by a range of groups with various organisational characteristics, capabilities and functional attributes. The differences are explicable primarily in terms of historical background and legal status, factors that also determine the way in which these organisations operate as interest groups, their proximity to government, their predominant policy concerns and their overall political orientation and strategies.

Agricultural interest groups fall into three main sub-types: statutory interest groups, rice-roots farmers' organisations and institutional interest groups. At the same time, they relate in similar ways to the political world, particularly in their electoral activities and connections to Diet and local assembly members. Many agricultural organisations are led by politicians, a subject that is explored in greater detail in later chapters.

The following discussion traces the evolution of farmers' groups from the earliest postwar years culminating in the establishment of Nokyo in 1947 and its assumption of a dominant role as farmers' representative by the mid-1950s. The structure and functions of diverse agricultural cooperative organisations are outlined and pertinent aspects of their historical, organisational and legal heritage examined. Nokyo belongs in the category of statutory interest group along with three other farmers' organisations representing more narrowly defined interests. These bodies are contrasted with the rice-roots farmers' groups operating without government sponsorship. The latter include Nokyo's organisational offshoots (the farmers' political leagues), various commodity associations and farmers' unions. The overall picture is one of organisational heterogeneity and interest group pluralism, although without the more competitive aspects of the pluralist model.

The third category of agricultural organisation, the institutional interest groups, encompasses the profusion of quasi-governmental entities that assume promotional and protective roles in the course of their administrative duties for the MAFF. Various sub-categories of these organisations are delineated, along with specific examples illustrating the defining character-istics of each type. That many of them, as well as the statutory interest groups, are so close to government inevitably raises the question of corporatisation in the agricultural sector. This prompts further questions about the complexities of public–private functioning by agricultural interest groups, organisational independence and dependence, and the balance between compliance with government directives and the unfettered representation of agricultural interests, particularly in the case of Nokyo, the 'peak' organisation of farmers.

Farmers' organisations in the early postwar period

The early postwar period was a time of organisational flux, formation, dissolution and reformation. The most visible manifestation of democracy in the countryside was the creation of a number of mass organisations of farmers (*nomin no taishuteki soshiki*). Most were reincarnations of prewar groups, although wartime agricultural organisations initially carried over into the postwar years.

It took at least a decade for the final shape of the agricultural interest group system to emerge and for the full range of organisations to develop. The following analysis discusses the rise of farmers' groups during this period, tracing their historical roots, extent of government sponsorship, varying political concerns and emerging rivalry for representation of the farm sector during the 1950s and 1960s.

The agricultural societies (nogyokai)

The *nogyokai* comprised a nationwide network of agricultural organisations established in 1943 to serve the wartime economy.[1] Designated by law as state policy organs (*kokusaku kikan*), they provided a medium for state control of farmers.[2] They were allocated various tasks in accordance with state policies, such as the collection of agricultural commodities and the distribution of pro-duction materials and farming techniques. The main focus of their economic business lay in the collection and distribution of commodities under the FC Law, especially rice.[3] The *nogyokai* were permitted to impose production quotas on farmers; membership of all farmers, both landowners and tenants, was compulsory; and *nogyokai* executives were effectively appointed by government. As Mitsukawa observes, the *nogyokai* were one of the eminently powerful wartime institutions.[4] Immediately after the war, they were democ-ratised by the Occupation authorities[5] and continued to operate as a transitional type of group until their abolition in 1948. During this period, they retained their primary functions in the area of rice collection and distribution on behalf of the government.

At the time of their formation the *nogyokai* brought under a single organ-isational umbrella the two principal farmers' organisations that had been operating in prewar Japan: the industrial or producer cooperatives (*sangyo kumiai*)[6] and the agricultural associations (*nokai*). In this respect, the *nogyokai* were an amalgam of prewar farmers' organisations that had been dominated by the large landholders and owner-cultivators and which had incorporated a strong tradition of supervision by agricultural administrators and association with conservative parties.

The *sangyo kumiai* were established by the Industrial Cooperatives Law (*Sangyo Kumiaiho*) of 1900. The government's original purpose was to provide a source of credit at non-usurious rates for petty or smaller land-holders, the large group of hard-pressed owner-cultivators (*jisakuno*) who came to dominate the *sangyo kumiai*.[7] The industrial cooperatives also helped to rationalise the distribution process for agricultural and other products,[8] with a 1906 amendment to the law empowering them to expand their operations to include marketing of agricultural commodities, purchasing of farm inputs and processing of agricultural products through joint-use facilities.[9] In this respect, the industrial cooperatives became the prototype of the postwar multi-purpose agricultural cooperatives.[10]

The *sangyo kumiai* were organised into a tri-level pyramid of municipal (city, town and village) cooperatives, prefectural federations and national federations, with the National Central Union of Industrial Cooperatives (Zenkoku Sangyo Kumiai Chuokai) at the top. The central union was established in 1909 by an amendment to the *Sangyo Kumiaiho*. Its tasks were guidance and inspection of the cooperatives as well as education, information and publication activities.

From these beginnings, the number of *sangyo kumiai* multiplied rapidly until by 1912, 10,455 cooperatives were operating and 57 per cent of farm households were members.[11] By 1915, 93 per cent of cities, towns and villages had a local chapter of the *sangyo kumiai*.[12] Apart from the provision of credit, active business areas were fertiliser sales, and rice and silk marketing. In some areas specialist producer cooperatives were established to handle the needs of specialist farmers such as cocoon producers and orange growers.

Further expansion of the producer cooperatives took place in the 1920s when a number of national federations were set up for handling economic functions such as marketing, and a Central Bank for Industrial Cooperatives (Sangyo Kumiai Chuo Kinko) was established under its own organising legislation.[13] During the depression years of the 1930s, the government provided considerable stimulus for a further strengthening of the *sangyo kumiai* system, including support for federations of producer cooperatives and the marketing and purchasing divisions of the local *sangyo kumiai*. Proactive government efforts to revise laws, assist with the necessary subsidies and allow the cooperatives to diversify their activities into new and different areas provided much of the impetus behind the growth and consolidation of the producer cooperatives during this period.[14] The *sangyo kumiai* were also singled out by the government to coordinate cooperation amongst farmers with regard to alleviating rural debt which reached crisis proportions during the 1930s. The critical role of the *sangyo kumiai* in the government's Rural Rehabilitation Programme of 1932–35 enabled them to achieve greater control over village economies and encourage all farmers to join.[15]

As offshoots of the *sangyo kumiai*, youth divisions were established from 1927 onwards, and a Federation of Industrial Cooperative Youth Leagues, the Sangyo Kumiai Seinen Renmei, or Sanseiren was formed in 1933.[16] This became the most politically active and progressive sector of the producer cooperative organisation. As Ishida describes it, the movement 'embraced some young socialists and, supported by the presence of widespread grievances in villages, strove to safeguard the interests of middle-class farmers against the expansion of the interests of the landowning class and business man. The government feared that the activities of this movement might become extreme and go beyond their control, so they tried to suppress it, while at the same time attempting to use it as a means to strengthen the integration of the nation under government control.'[17]

The impetus behind the establishment of the *nokai*, on the other hand, came from a government anxious to hasten the technological advancement of agriculture in order to improve agricultural productivity. The 1899 Agricultural Association Law (*Nokaiho*) required every municipal and prefectural political unit to have an agricultural association 'to serve as agricultural extension associations for the state.'[18] The state dictated the conditions of membership: it was made compulsory for landlords and optional for other farmers giving 'large landholders de facto domination'.[19] The *nokai* were basically semi-official organisations supported by public funds[20] and were, therefore, subject to a high degree of bureaucratic control. They not only functioned as state-sponsored guidance organisations to disseminate new farm technology and improvements in agricultural management, they also acted in a broader sense as organs for implementing government agricultural policy.

In 1910, the Imperial Agricultural Association (Teikoku Nokai) was set up under legislation as the national-level organisation of the prefectural and municipal *nokai*. The government appointed its leadership. The Teikoku Nokai was permitted by law to conduct *nosei katsudo* which involved it in making recommendations on the producer rice price almost every year as well as undertaking activities for maintaining cocoon prices, promoting the agricultural insurance system and advancing various other policies for agriculture and forestry.[21] It was particularly active during periods of agricultural crisis after WWI and in the late 1920s. In addition, it issued reports on the state of the *nokai* and agriculture in response to government requests.[22]

Nevertheless, as organisations articulating farmers' interests, the *nokai* were quite circumscribed. In essence, they were 'sounding boards for the interests of landlords',[23] and were 'under the control of landlords and bureaucrats'.[24] Over time, their state-sponsored functions grew even stronger.[25] Compared to the *sangyo kumiai*, however, the *nokai* were very active in *nosei katsudo*.[26] Whilst the *sangyo kumiai* were economic organisations of farmers, the *nokai* specialised in lobbying as well as technical training in the agricultural villages. Close personal ties were forged with farmers in the course of these technical activities. *Nokai* advisers came to act as advisers of farmers on a day-to-day basis. Because of the utility of this technical training and the power of landowners as executives of the *nokai*, the latter became a powerful political force in the agricultural villages.[27]

On the other hand, as part of the government's pro-active policy for the *sangyo kumiai* during the 1930s, it put a lot of effort into expanding the membership of the producer cooperatives to include the poorer class of farmers. The aim was 'to bring all classes of the village community [into the cooperatives in order to] . . . make even tighter the social-collectivity aspect of the bonds between members'.[28] By 1936, all towns and villages had cooperatives and all farmers were affiliated with them. While the government's drive to expand the producer cooperative movement was successful, it also entailed a commensurate entrenchment of government control over the organisation.[29]

In the late 1930s and early 1940s, the *sangyo kumiai* came under even greater state direction and the role of the *nokai* in policy implementation was strengthened and expanded. After the outbreak of war, rice control regulations were instituted and progressively applied to all agricultural products. Under this regime, agricultural organisations took on the function of collection and distribution groups. The *nokai* controlled the production of agricultural products and the *sangyo kumiai* worked as collection organisations. In 1943 the passage of the Agricultural Groups Law (*Nogyo Dantaiho*) created the *nogyokai* organisation which unified these two groups (as well as other lesser farmers' groups).[30] With the establishment of the *nogyokai*, the government-control features of the cooperatives and the *nokai* became absolute. In the same year, the Central Bank for Industrial Cooperatives became the Central Bank for Agriculture and Forestry (Norin Chuo Kinko, or Norinchukin).[31]

The farmers' unions (nomin kumiai)

The lead in representing the interests of non-landowning farmers immediately after the war was taken by the farmers' unions around the issue of land reform. Abolition of the landlord class and the distribution of their land to tenants had been the primary plank in the activities of the prewar farmers' unions, first organised in the 1920s. Land reform and the democratisation policies of the Occupation provided the impetus for the spectacular early development of the farmers' unions.[32] Initial development and consolidation of the movement took place with the formation of a national organisation, the Japan Farmers' Union (Nihon Nomin Kumiai, or Nichino), in February 1946.[33] Its speedy foundation was assisted by a veteran Socialist agrarian leadership poised to resume the struggle for land reform immediately the war was over.

The membership of Nichino underwent rapid expansion. By April 1946, more than 2,000 branches had been organised with over 282,609 members.[34] Land reform began in December 1946 but there was rising rural frustration at the slow pace of the reform effort in its initial stages. This prompted further membership growth with 1.25 million members organised into 6,000 affiliated farmers' unions by the time of the second national convention in February 1947,[35] reaching a peak of 1.7 million when the third national convention was held in early 1949.[36] The farmers' unions attracted the support of farmers by promoting agricultural land reform and organising protest campaigns against heavy taxes and compulsory deliveries of rice.[37] Official endorsement of the farmers' unions was granted in the form of encouragement to participate in the administration of land reform as representatives of tenants on the land committees (*nochi iinkai*).[38]

The climax of land reform in 1947 is generally regarded as coinciding with the peak in the political influence of the farmers' union movement. The completion of both stages of land reform deprived the farmers' unions of their principal *raison d'être* and undermined the basis of their popular appeal.[39] When the business of land reform came to an end, the farmers' unions faced 'a virtual impasse . . . At this point their organizational weaknesses came to the surface and they could not find a way to realize their interest demands through legitimate organizational activities.'[40] These were more readily expressed through the newly established and legally authorised agricultural cooperatives which were all-inclusive of farmers and which gradually assumed the role of the farmers' unions as a representative organisation of farmers.[41] The *nomin kumiai* could not find either a clear function to perform (the farmers' economic interest group function, for example, was taken over by Nokyo), nor any major national issue around which to organise a vigorous national movement.[42]

Another potent factor weakening the farmers' unions was the refocussing of their leaders on other causes. Many of those active in these groups in the immediate postwar period were later elected to positions of responsibility in other agricultural organisations, such as the agricultural cooperatives[43] and agricultural committees,[44] as well as in local, prefectural and national politics, and lost interest in protest movements.[45] Furthermore, some of the other issues that had driven the early protests and activism had been resolved or lost their urgency, such as food requisitions and democratisation of the agricultural societies. The last was achieved in the form of the newly established agricultural cooperatives.[46]

The party-political connections of the farmers' unions were another complicating factor. Although the movement was non-partisan in theory, in practice it was highly political and led by politicians.[47] The main parent party of Nichino was the JSP, although activists engaged in the farmers' union movement were members of both the JSP and JCP. The politicisation of the farmers' unions by these parties increasingly identified them as no more than farmers' departments of left-wing political parties or as sources of votes for

JSP or JCP candidates. As a result, the farmers' unions lost their independence and became more distant from farmers.[48]

The politicisation of Nichino made it vulnerable to political and ideological disputes taking place within the JSP in particular. Intensification of conflict within the party along ideological and factional lines produced serious divisions in the farmers' union movement from 1947 onwards (see Figure 2.1). The extreme right wing of the farmers' union movement was expelled from Nichino in February 1947, forming the League for Revivifying the Japan Farmers' Union (Nichino Sasshin Domei) under the leadership of Hirano Rikizo,[49] finally establishing a separate organisation, the National Farmers' Union (Zenkoku Nomin Kumiai, or Zenno) in July 1947. At the time of its formation this group claimed 705 affiliated local farmers' unions and a total membership of 163,092.[50]

A subsequent division separated Nichino along Socialist–Communist lines in April 1949. The JCP and JSP had often confronted each other over the direction in which the movement should go and had competed to take control of Nichino.[51] The mainstream Nichino organisation fractured internally into two practically separate groupings, the Independence Group (Shutaiseiha) of Socialist supporters and the pro-Communist Unity Group (Toitsuha). These two organisations tended to be stronger in certain prefectures and not in others. The Shutaiseiha, for example, was strong in Yamagata, Akita and Tottori.

The organisational decline of the farmers' unions was most evident at the local level where membership numbers fell dramatically after the 1949 split. In many agricultural prefectures, farmers' union organisations became moribund. From a peak membership of 1.7 million just prior to the split in April 1949, in December 1949 the membership of the Independence Group stood at 209,614, while the Unity Group had a membership of 121,387.[52] A year later membership figures had halved – to 133,372 and 68,792 respectively.[53] Membership of the right-wing farmers' union group, Zenno, meanwhile declined commensurately from 219,355 in December 1949 to 144,203 in December 1950.[54]

The JSP's split into the Right and Left Socialists in 1951 contributed to a further splintering of the farmers' union movement, with the formation in November 1952 of a New Village Construction Group of the Japan Farmers' Union (Nichino Shinnoson Kensetsuha) led by agrarian leaders of the Right Socialist Party. At that time, members in affiliated farmers' unions numbered 85,398.[55] This group later merged in January 1953 with a breakaway group from Zenno (with 101,608 members) to become a loose federation called the General Federation of Farmers' Unions (Nomin Kumiai Sodomei). This meant that by early 1953, four national federations of farmers' union were operating: Zenno, Nomin Kumiai Sodomei, Nichino Shutaiseiha and Nichino Toitsuha (plus a breakaway group from the latter) – as shown in Figure 2.1. Nevertheless, despite the divisions amongst the farmers' unions, the movement as a whole started to show signs of recovery

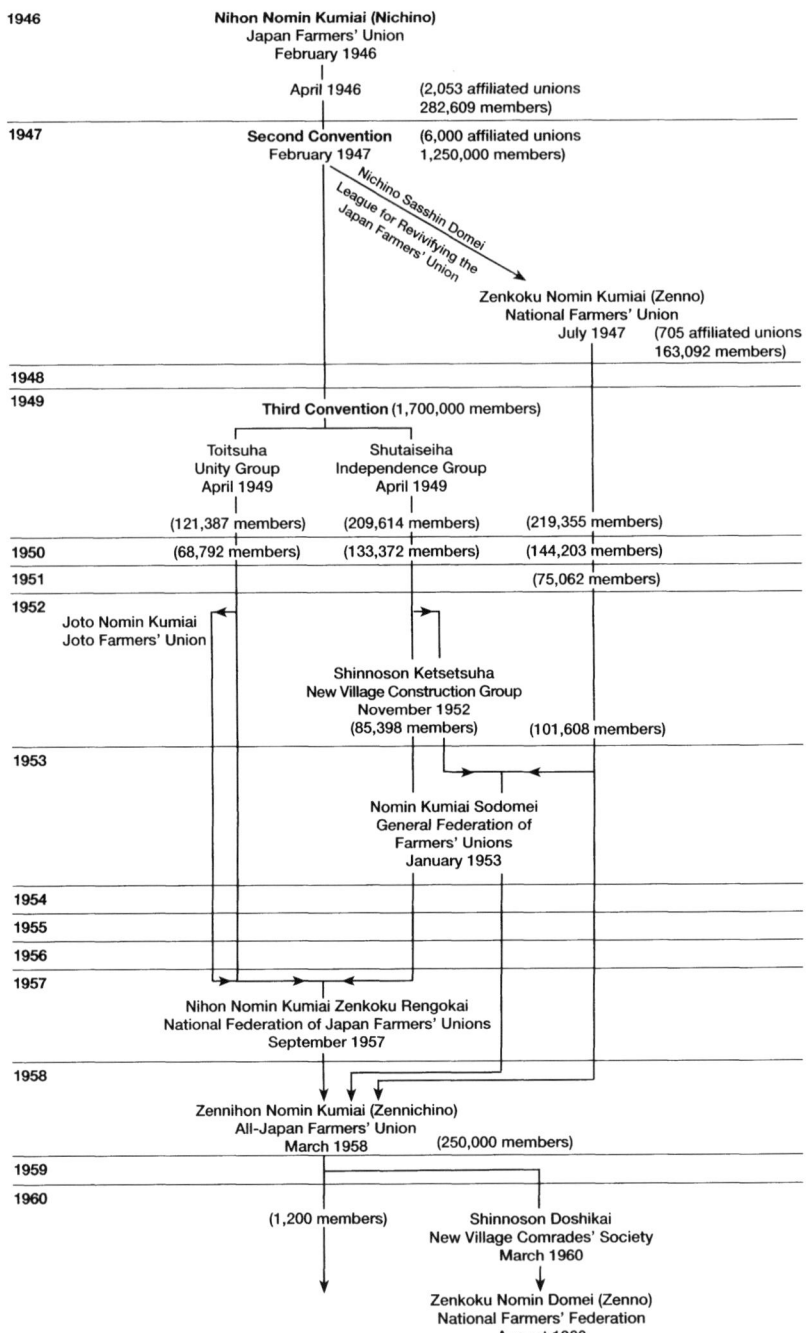

Figure 2.1 Genealogy of main farmers' union organisations, 1946–58
  Source: *Nihon Kindaishi Jiten*, Furoku No. 36; Dore, 'The Socialist Party',
  pp. 372–373, 401.

in 1953. Several factors were responsible: a poor harvest, natural disasters, US military base issues, the establishment of landowners' groups and so on. The farmers' union movement also gained strong support from labour, including the General Council of Japanese Trade Unions (Sohyo).[56]

The rural youth leagues

Local agricultural leaders, many of whom had previous histories in the government-sponsored *nokai* and *sangyo kumiai*, and who rejected any connection with left-wing farmers' unions, helped to establish a number of voluntary farmers' groups in the initial years after the war. The most important of these were the rural youth leagues (*nomin seinen renmei*, or *noseiren*). Prefectural rural youth leagues comprising town and village associations combined to form a nationwide body, the National Rural Youth League (Zenkoku Noson Seinen Renmei, or Zennoseiren) in June 1946. It claimed a founding membership of 363,886, which grew to 432,499 by 1949.[57]

Although described by some writers as a farmers' union (*nomin kumiai*), the Zennoseiren had a separate and distinct organisational genealogy.[58] The term 'farmers' organisation' (*nomin no soshiki*) was considered by others to be a more appropriate label for these groups.[59] The rural youth league organisation shared with the farmers' unions their goals of land reform, abolition of the landlord system and the modernisation of agriculture, but differed from the Socialists on key points of political ideology. It acknowledged a social class standpoint but rejected the notion of farmers as workers for wages, preferring to equate emancipated tenants with members of the managerial class.[60] It also included non-farmers as members, although core members were relatively larger-scale, full-time owner-farmers and group activities were orientated around the demands of these farmers.[61] Zennoseiren had strong links with the newly democratised but conservatively-orientated *nogyokai* and received considerable organisational support from them.[62] Historical ties between the *nogyokai* and the *noseiren* were strong. The rural youth leagues traced their origins back to the youth leagues of the industrial cooperatives, which later became incorporated into the wartime *nogyokai*.

Zennoseiren's associations with the prewar industrial cooperatives also influenced its objectives.[63] The establishment of a postwar equivalent of the producer cooperative organisation was its primary aim, and it invested this with an ideology of political independence, democratisation and freedom from bureaucratic control. Its basic objective was to ensure that the newly established agricultural cooperatives would be free from the coercive organisational aspects of the *nogyokai* (such as compulsory membership) and the bureaucratic authoritarianism of the prewar period at the hands of the Ministry of Agriculture and Forestry (MAF). Zennoseiren conducted the first producer rice price campaign after the war in 1946.[64]

The Agriculture Reconstruction Council

Around 40 groups, including Nichino and the national body of the *nogyokai* (the National Agricultural Society, or Zenkoku Nogyokai),[65] Norinchukin and the National Rural Youth League participated in an Agriculture Reconstruction Council (Nogyo Fukko Kaigi) organised in June 1947. Such a conference had been advocated by Nichino at its second convention in 1947.[66] The task of the conference was to act as an official channel for the presentation of agricultural policy demands to the government.

In the new climate of democracy that flourished under the Occupation, the producer rice price quickly became subject to pressure from farm organisations on all sides. In 1947, council members cooperated in a rice price campaign, and in 1948 the council coordinated the first general meeting of farmers after the war – the National Farmers' Convention (Zenkoku Nomin Taikai). The focus of the convention was the producer rice price and more particularly farmers' objections to the government's method of calculating it (the so-called 'Parity Method').[67] In 1948, the council coordinated another rice price campaign, requesting that the state-guaranteed rice price be decided in the Diet. This was followed up by a national farmers' representatives' meeting, where participants decided to raise the demand price to a level higher than the council's.[68]

The high rate of participation by farmers' groups in the council was due to a number of factors. Firstly, it reflected the encouragement given by the Occupation authorities to the establishment of consultative and participatory groupings in which the opinions of reorganised, democratic farmers' associations could be canvassed on matters vital to their membership. Secondly, it reflected the desire for mutual cooperation and joint action which leaders of the entire spectrum of farmers' organisations shared at that time.

Thirdly, one of the main subjects of debate in the council was the establishment of an agricultural cooperative organisation in which it was duly recognised that all farmers had a stake. With the publicised intention of the Occupation authorities to recreate a system of agricultural cooperatives and the democratisation of the *nogyokai*, heightened interest in the issue of organisational reform was evident amongst all groups in the agricultural sector. The role of the *nogyokai* was limited to filling the organisational vacuum until the re-establishment of the agricultural cooperatives, given the order of the Supreme Commander of the Allied Powers (SCAP) that the agricultural associations be dissolved and agricultural cooperatives be set up.[69] The question of what legal form the proposed cooperatives should take became the subject of continuous consultation between the government led by the Occupation's General Headquarters (GHQ) and the MAF, and various organisational representatives of the farmers under the aegis of the council, which became the main instrumentality in the creation of the cooperatives.[70]

In summary, the radical initiatives emanating from the Occupation authorities contributed to the rapid growth and distinctive shape of postwar Japanese farm groups. The issue of land reform provided a political focus for the early revival of the farmers' unions while its implementation sustained their organisational rationale until the late 1940s. Meanwhile the urgent priority of policies to increase agricultural production and to supply food to the national population raised the additional question of the official powers of the agricultural cooperatives and their assistance in areas such as rice production and distribution. This encouraged the formation of local farmers' groups linked to the notional idea of an agricultural cooperative system and their participation in the national debate on this issue. The postwar atmosphere of political freedom and democratisation was also conducive to demands for a voluntary agricultural cooperative organisation independent of government supervision and control. Indeed, this concept of a revived agricultural cooperative organisation accorded with the basic vision of the Occupation authorities.

During this early postwar period, farm organisations thus participated in a common struggle for official recognition of farmers' demands of all kinds, rather than for concessions to particular organisational interests.[71] A platform shared by almost all groups was the need for land reform and the redevelopment of the agricultural cooperatives.[72] These shared goals were underscored by an awareness amongst agrarian leaders of all political colourings that unprecedented changes in the nature of farm organisation were inevitable under the Occupation. Farm leaders were keenly aware of the historic nature of the decisions in which they were involved, and that unprecedented times called for unprecedented action. Cooperation amongst farmers' groups was institutionalised in the Agriculture Reconstruction Council which oversaw concerted lobbying on issues such as the producer rice price.

The agricultural cooperatives

On 19 November 1947, the coalition government led by the Socialists passed the Agricultural Cooperative Union Law, or Nokyo Law.[73] The aim of the law as set out in the legislation was to support the production and economic activities of the newly established owner-farmers and elevate their social and economic status through agricultural improvement based on the agricultural cooperatives.'[74] In the same month, the Cabinet decided that the role of food collection should be undertaken by the Nokyo organisation.

Following the passage of the legislation, numbers of local *nokyo* proliferated rapidly – from 4,256 in April 1948 to 14,120 in August[75] and 27,819 by December.[76] As the farmers' unions retreated, the agricultural cooperatives became the dominant force in the villages.[77] Norinchukin was reorganised with an increase in its capital on 1 April 1948. Prefectural federations of agricultural cooperatives were launched in July 1948 with 330 federations established by October 1948 and 350 by December; national federations first appeared in September 1948, with 13 operational by November 1948.[78] In March 1949, the first national Nokyo representatives' convention was held.

The structure and functions of the Nokyo organisation[79]

Nokyo Law describes the purposes for which the agricultural cooperatives were established, outlines the structure of the agricultural cooperative organisation and makes its democratic operation mandatory. Article 10 of the law itemises the 'businesses' (*jigyo*) that agricultural cooperatives or federations of agricultural cooperatives may undertake, all or in part.[80] These are comprehensive and include: supplying the necessary funds for members' business or livelihood (credit business, or *shinyo jigyo*); receiving members' savings or fixed deposits (also credit business); supplying the necessary goods for members' business or livelihood (purchasing business, or *kobai jigyo*); installing necessary joint-use facilities for members' business or livelihood (*riyo jigyo*)[81] excluding medical facilities; providing facilities for increasing farm labour efficiency or for promoting cooperation amongst farmers (*nogyo rodo no koritsu no zoshin ni kansuru jigyo*); developing, improving or managing lands supplied for agricultural purposes, selling, leasing or exchanging agricultural lands, and installing or managing agricultural irrigation facilities (*noyochi kyokyuto no jigyo*); transporting, processing, storing, or marketing of goods produced by members (*hanbai jigyo*); providing facilities for rural industries (*noson kogyo jigyo*), for mutual aid (insurance business, or *kyosai jigyo*), for medical use, or *iryo jigyo* (hospitals, clinics etc.) and for the welfare of the aged (*rojin fukushi jigyo*); providing educational facilities for achieving improvement in the management and techniques of members' farming and facilities for improving rural life and culture (*shido jigyo*); concluding collective agreements for improving the economic status of members (*dantai kyoyaku no teiketsu*); and undertaking any other business incidental to the foregoing items.

   Under Article 10, Paragraph 2 of Nokyo Law, the agricultural cooperatives may also undertake the business of farm management on trust from members (*nogyo no keiei no jigyo*), i.e. contract farming or agricultural production business;[82] under Paragraph 3, it may sell or lease agricultural lands or grasslands on trust from members (*nochi shintaku jigyo*), i.e. farm real estate; under Paragraph 5, it may sell converted-use agricultural lands and construct residences or other facilities on these lands (*takuchito kyokyu jigyo*), i.e. commercial real estate; under Paragraph 7, it may supply credit to local public organisations, banks, or other banking institutions; and under Paragraph 10, it may engage in the discounting of bills for the benefit of members and undertake domestic exchange transactions (restricted to federations of agricultural cooperatives only).[83]

The above items were not all contained in the original Nokyo Law passed in 1947. They represent the sum total of agricultural cooperative activities listed when the law was originally passed, plus a number of amendments made in subsequent years permitting the co-ops to conduct additional businesses.[84] In one of the more recent amendments, for example, agricultural cooperatives were permitted to conduct agricultural management business involving the utilisation of agricultural land which had been leased or purchased through agricultural land sales business.[85]

In their entirety agricultural cooperative activities cover a wide range of financial, management, service, technical, social, educational, advisory, welfare, social and cultural activities relating to agriculture and the farmers' lives as well as those of non-farmers.[86] Businesses divide roughly into two groups: those that produce income for the cooperatives – such as marketing, purchasing, financial and mutual aid – and those that do not. The latter fall into the broad category of guidance activities, such as education, farm management and life guidance activities.[87] In terms of businesses, unlike farm cooperatives in Western countries which are organised by function or type of business, Nokyo's businesses are highly diversified, with individual co-ops carrying on a number of different enterprises.[88]

Compared to the original four functions of the *sangyo kumiai* in relation to credit, marketing, purchasing and managing joint-utilisation facilities, the activities of the modern-day agricultural cooperatives are all-encompassing. One of the reasons for this is the integrated nature of the farm household economy, with no discrimination between household accounts and farm management accounts owing largely to the part-time and small-scale nature of much of Japanese farming. This structure calls for comprehensive agricultural cooperative services that accommodate both the daily living and farming needs of farmers and non-farmers in the household.[89]

In terms of its organisational set-up, Nokyo, in its totality, comprises a massive and highly complex grouping with a multitude of organisational offshoots. It brings together a collection of several thousand separately-constituted agricultural cooperative organisations that are independent in organisational set-up and internal decision-making structures, but highly interdependent in the flow of goods, services and finance.

The core structure of Nokyo is referred to as the 'federated Nokyo organisation' (*keito Nokyo soshiki*)[90] which is constructed along hierarchical lines in a federated three-tiered system (*keito sandankaisei*) corresponding to the three-stage pattern of national politico-administrative divisions (i.e. municipal (city, town and village), prefectural and national government). Nokyo thus forms a pyramid-shaped structure with a base line made up of primary agricultural cooperatives (*nokyo*), also called 'unit cooperatives' (*tani nokyo*, or *tankyo*, now called *tani* JA, or JA) to distinguish them from upper-level groups. Primary co-ops operate at local level as city, town and village agricultural cooperatives (*shichoson nokyo*). They group into secondary organisations at prefectural level, known as prefectural federations (*fuken rengokai*, or *kenren*), which in turn come together to form national federations (*zenkoku rengokai*, or *zenkokuren*). The Nokyo federations are now also referred to as JA *rengokai* and JA *zenkokuren*.

Within this horizontal structure a vertical division separates general-purpose or multi-purpose agricultural cooperatives (*sogo nokyo*), which conduct the full range of economic and other services, from special-purpose or specialist agricultural cooperatives (*senmon nokyo*), which perform a more limited range of functions in relation to particular farm products or which are specialised according to business function.

The unit co-ops

According to Nokyo Law, the members of unit cooperatives can be farmers (either as individuals or farm households); farmers group corporations or juridical persons (*noji kumiai hojin*) undertaking farm management,[91] and other types of juridical persons (*hojin*)[92] undertaking farm management; persons living in areas serviced by the cooperatives but not necessarily involved in agricultural activities; other agricultural cooperatives; other organisations composed chiefly of farmers which aim to promote the common interests of the farmers through the cooperative system; or organisations that have farmers as their main members or capital stock contributors. All categories except for the first (i.e. individual farmers or farm households) are classed as 'group members' of Nokyo. The first two categories are 'regular' members (*seikumiaiin*), while the latter categories are 'associate' members (*junkumiaiin*).

Depending on their place of residence, farmers join city, town or village agricultural cooperatives. They join the multi-purpose cooperatives, and depending on their production or other specialised interests, they may also become members of one or more special-purpose cooperatives. In 1975, there were 11,489 agricultural cooperatives (4,942 *sogo nokyo* and 6,547 *senmon nokyo*); in 1980, 4,546 *sogo nokyo* and 5,314 *senmon nokyo*; in 1990, 3,688 *sogo nokyo* and 4,097 *senmon nokyo*; and in 1996, 2,472 *sogo nokyo* and 3,513 *senmon nokyo* – making a total of 5,985 local co-ops nationwide.[93] By 1998, their numbers had dipped further to 5,369: 2,006 *sogo nokyo* and 3,363 *senmon nokyo* (see Figure 2.2).[94]

Within the Nokyo organisation, the difference between the general- and special-purpose cooperatives is striking. Firstly, the *sogo nokyo* have blanket coverage of all agricultural areas in Japan while there are many areas where *senmon nokyo* are not established.[95] Secondly, the *sogo nokyo* are geographically-based cooperatives, with organisational boundaries matching those of municipal (i.e. city, town and village) entities. This means that each Nokyo recruits its members from only one particular area, which puts a geographic limit on its business activities.[96] The *senmon nokyo*, however, are organised to conduct a specific functional or commodity-related purpose, with members drawn from areas that cut across fixed politico-administrative

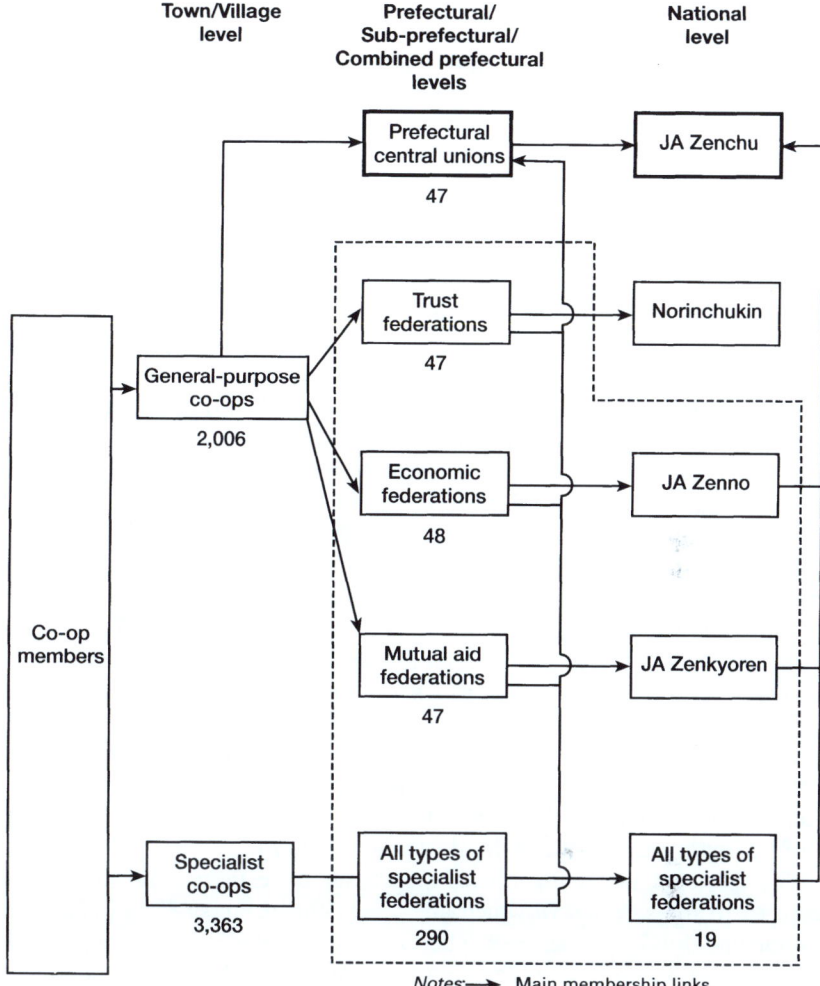

| Town/Village level | Prefectural/ Sub-prefectural/ Combined prefectural levels | National level |

Figure 2.2 Organisational chart of the Federated Nokyo Organisation, 1998
Source: *Norinsuisansho Tokeihyo*, 1996–97, pp. 578–581.

boundaries and the *sogo nokyo*, although most members of the *senmon nokyo* are simultaneously members of the *sogo nokyo*.

Secondly, a multi-purpose cooperative is exactly what its name indicates. It simultaneously conducts a range of businesses and services permitted to the cooperatives including trust (i.e. deposits and loans), purchasing, marketing, mutual aid, utilisation, farm guidance as well as welfare, cultural, informational and other activities related to the daily living of farmers. In short the *sogo nokyo* are all-round organisations that cater not only to members' agricultural production activities but also their daily lives. Moreover, the *sogo nokyo* are virtually the only co-ops that undertake general financial business in addition to their other commodity-related activities and services, effectively keeping the purse strings of Nokyo within the *sogo nokyo* side of the organisation.[97]

The *senmon nokyo*, with their more specialised functions and interests, fall into six main categories: sericulture (*yosan*), livestock (*chikusan*), horticultural and speciality production (*engei tokusan*), reclamation (*kaitaku*), rural industry (*noson kogyo*) and 'other'. In relation to specific commodities, *senmon nokyo* functions are limited to activities like farm guidance, processing, marketing and processing. The largest single category by numbers of co-ops is livestock, followed by horticulture.[98] The specialist livestock cooperatives engage in marketing, purchasing, technical guidance and production activities but only in relation to livestock farming. They do not handle the whole range of farm products as do the multi-purpose co-ops, which may be involved in all aspects of business in connection with rice, vegetable, fruit and milk production in one area.

Another contrast is to be found in the differing membership composition and characteristics of these groups. The membership of the *sogo nokyo* is all inclusive given its territorial basis of organisation. On the other hand, although the *senmon nokyo* operate for the producers of particular agricultural products, not all producers of these commodities are necessarily members.[99] Furthermore, the *senmon nokyo* are predominantly organisations of full-time specialist farmers,[100] whereas *sogo nokyo* membership covers all the farm households within a given district irrespective of management type, management scale, full- or part-time operations or whatever.[101] In practice, because they make up the large majority of the membership, part-time farmers (mainly rice farmers) dominate the *sogo nokyo*.

The specialist unit cooperatives also tend to be more self-sufficient in contrast to the *sogo nokyo* which are dependent on upper level organs for channelling goods and services. The upper level federations of the *senmon nokyo* undertake processing, facility utilisation, guidance and liaison adjustment activities.[102] Little duplication of function exists between the unit and upper-level federations unlike the multi-purpose cooperatives and their federations. In some cases, business functions (e.g. marketing) are undertaken by the unit specialist co-ops, whilst non-business functions are undertaken by their federations.[103] The *senmon nokyo* sometimes maintain close connections to private companies depending on their speciality (this is particularly true of the livestock and sericultural cooperatives).

The *sogo nokyo* and their upper-level federations, although outnumbered by the *senmon nokyo*, administer the most wide-ranging programmes and form the core of the Nokyo federated organisation.[104] They comprise the *keito Nokyo soshiki*. When compared with farm cooperatives in other countries, it is the *sogo nokyo* that give Nokyo its distinctive, multi-functional character as an agricultural cooperative organisation.[105]

The Nokyo federations

Nokyo federations exist at sub-prefectural level (primarily county, or *gun* level), as well as at prefectural, combined prefectural and national level, with prefectural and national federations predominating. Organisationally speaking, the base-level *tankyo* and the upper-level *rengokai* are characterised by two striking differences. Firstly, the federations are essentially bureaucratic entities with an organisational rather than an individual membership. Their regular membership is made up of other agricultural cooperative organisations (*tankyo* and other federations).[106] In terms of the Nokyo organisational hierarchy, each level of cooperative tends to form the membership of the federations above it, although *tankyo* can also be direct members of national federations.[107]

Secondly, the federations of the *sogo nokyo* are functionally specialised. While individual Nokyo branches are permitted to conduct various businesses from finance to the sale of producer goods, their prefectural and national federations have to be organised separately by type of business.[108] The upper level federations are, therefore, specialised according to the three core functions of the *sogo nokyo*: trust, economic (marketing and purchasing), and mutual aid (see Figure 2.2). The trust function of the multi-purpose cooperatives is represented at prefectural level by the prefectural credit Nokyo federations (*shinren*), the mutual aid function by the prefectural mutual aid Nokyo federations (*kyosairen*) and the marketing and purchasing functions by the prefectural Nokyo economic federations (*keizairen*). By law, these federations are not permitted to conduct activities relating to more than one type of business. Their regular membership is predominantly made up of multi-purpose co-ops, and to a lesser extent the *senmon nokyo* (the latter are more likely to join the trust and economic federations for obvious reasons), as well as other Nokyo federations (once again the trust and economic federations have relatively large numbers of members from the specialist side of the organisation).

Above the specialist *tankyo* sit the specialist federations (see Figure 2.2). They more frequently operate at sub-prefectural and combined prefectural levels than the mainstream federations, depending on the predominance of particular types of specialist agricultural production within and across prefectures.[109] Many *senmon nokyo* also effectively operate in a two-stage system as far as basic business functions are concerned.[110]

The members of the specialist federations are drawn from essentially the same categories as the mainstream prefectural federations: from *sogo nokyo*, from *senmon nokyo* and from other federations, including prefectural *keizairen*. In 1995 there were two sub-prefectural marketing federations, 30 prefectural welfare federations and 8 sub-prefectural federations, one sub-prefectural transport federation, five prefectural and 33 sub-prefectural sericultural federations, 11 prefectural and 47 sub-prefectural livestock federations, 24 prefectural and 29 sub-prefectural dairy federations, one prefectural poultry federation and one sub-prefectural poultry federation, eight prefectural and 35 sub-prefectural horticultural federations, and 29 'other' prefectural and 80 sub-prefectural federations, including rural industry federations, reclamation federations, guidance federations, settlers' federations[111] and agricultural broadcasting federations.[112] This made a total of 344 such federations, a figure which fell in 1998 to 290 (see Figure 2.2) as part of Nokyo's internal rationalisation and restructuring process. This resulted in the demise of the two sub-prefectural marketing federations, one sub-prefectural welfare federation, 16 sub-prefectural sericultural federations, 15 sub-prefectural livestock federations, six sub-prefectural dairy federations, eight sub-prefectural horticultural federations, 20 'other' prefectural federations and 57 'other' sub-prefectural federations.[113]

The prefectural federations of the *sogo nokyo* are organised in turn into national Nokyo federations: the National Federation of Agricultural Cooperatives (Zenno,[114] also spelled Zen-noh, or JA-Zenno), which is the national body for the prefectural Nokyo economic federations; the National Mutual Aid Nokyo Federation (Zenkyoren,[115] or JA-Zenkyoren); and Norinchukin, the national banking institution for the agricultural cooperatives (see Figure 2.2).[116] Of these main national Nokyo federations, Zenno is the most recently established. It was formed in 1972 when the National Purchasing Nokyo Federation (Zenkoren)[117] and the National Marketing Nokyo Federation (Zenhanren)[118] amalgamated.

One of Norinchukin's most important tasks is to act as a channel for public funds into agriculture via the cooperatives. Its own source of funding is limited to the agricultural, forestry and fisheries cooperatives and their federations, but the use of the capital that is collected is diverted widely into stocks and bonds, loans to related and non-related industries and other financial ventures.[119] In the opinion of the JCP, it performs a capital supply role for large enterprise.[120]

The organisational chart of the federated Nokyo organisation in Figure 2.2 shows that although the various components are formally independent, their membership structure is linked through a vertical hierarchy. Business systems are also linked in the same way. Most enterprise (particularly in the case of the multi-purpose cooperatives and their federations) is done internally amongst the different parts of the three-stage system of national federations, prefectural federations and local co-ops. For example, in marketing business, the *tankyo* utilisation rate of the *keizairen* is 93 per cent[121] and the *keizairen* utilisation rate of Zenno is 56 per cent.[122] These figures indicate that the vast bulk of agricultural commodities produced by members is delivered to the market through at least the two-stage *tankyo-keizairen* system, while some moves through all three stages. With respect to purchasing, the *tankyo* utilisation rate of the economic federations is 74 per cent,[123] while the *keizairen* utilisation rate of Zenno is 62 per cent,[124] and thus most purchasing is conducted through the three-stage federated system. As far as trust business is concerned, excluding 'system capital', a large proportion of loans are debts of the federated upper organs, and in the case of surplus capital, the *tankyo* trust federation utilisation rate is 85 per cent (1997), and the *shinren* utilisation rate of Norinchukin is 53 per cent (1997).[125] In other words, when it comes to the *sogo nokyo*, the three layers of business operations overlap to a great extent. This suggests that the unit cooperatives are not self-sufficient in their management. Rather they are dependent on upper-level organisations.[126]

Horizontal cross-linkages also characterise Nokyo's various business activities. All Nokyo's enterprises are systematically connected to one another. Take economic activities (*keizai jigyo*)[127] with respect to rice, for example. The National Central Union of Agricultural Cooperatives (Zenkoku Nogyo Kyodo Kumiai Chuokai, or Zenchu) discusses the state-guaranteed producer rice price with the government,[128] while Zenno negotiates with suppliers about the prices of producer goods such as fertiliser, pesticides and machinery.[129] The *sogo nokyo* are in charge of the collection of rice from farmers which is sold to the government as well as to private wholesalers through the federated three-stage system involving the *keizairen* and Zenno.[130] The *sogo nokyo* have some facilities for rice processing as well as outlets for selling rice to consumers, including members. In addition, the *sogo nokyo* organise the storage of rice and seeds, and the shipping to buyers at the request of producers. If members are in need of funds, they are eligible for loans from the *sogo nokyo* credit business. Thus although the activities of agricultural cooperative organisations are formally categorised as different businesses, the various enterprises are actually inseparably connected with each other,[131] both vertically and horizontally. The horizontal linkages also extend to the specialist side of the organisation through cross-cutting membership and because specialist cooperatives rely on the *sogo nokyo* and their federations for some services such as credit, although their main connections are vertical with their own upper-level federations.[132]

The national specialist Nokyo federations outnumber the mainstream multi-purpose federations by a considerable margin (see Figure 2.2). The top-level national specialist cooperative federations for the livestock and dairying industries are the National Livestock Nokyo Federation (Zenkoku Chikusan Nogyo Kyodo Kumiai Rengokai, or Zenchikuren), the National Dairy Nokyo Federation (Zenkoku Rakuno Nogyo Kyodo Kumiai Rengokai, or Zenrakuren)[133] and the National Raw Milk Demand and Supply Adjustment Nokyo Federation (Zenkoku Seinyu Jukyu Chosei Nogyo Kyodo Kumiai Rengokai).

The Japanese sericultural cooperatives are led by the National Sericultural Nokyo Federation (Zenkoku Yosan Nogyo Kyodo Kumiai Rengokai, or Zenyoren) and the Japan Raw Silk Thread Marketing Nokyo Federation (Nihon Kiito Hanbai Nogyo Kyodo Kumiai Rengokai, or Niseiren);[134] the poultry and egg industries by the Japan Poultry Nokyo Federation (Nihon Yokei Nogyo Kyodo Kumiai Rengokai, or Niyoren) and the National Egg

Marketing Nokyo Federation (Zenkoku Keiran Hanbai Nogyo Kyodo Kumiai Rengokai, or Zenkeiren); the fruit and vegetable industries by the Japan Horticultural Nokyo Federation (Nihon Engei Nogyo Kyodo Kumiai Rengokai, or Nichienren), the Japan Fruit Juice Nokyo Federation (Nihon Kaju Nogyo Kyodo Kumiai Rengokai, or Kajuren), the Japan Carrot Marketing Nokyo Federation (Nihon Ninjin Hanbai Nogyo Kyodo Kumiai Rengokai, or Ninhanren) and the Japan Shiitake Nokyo Federation (Nihon Shiitake Nogyo Kyodo Kumiai Rengokai, or Nishiiren); the hop (tobacco) industry by the National Hop Nokyo Federation (Zenkoku Hoppu Nogyo Kyodo Kumiai Rengokai, or Zenhoppuren); the reclamation and settlers' industries by the National Reclamation Nokyo Federation (Zenkoku Kaitaku Nogyo Kyodo Kumiai Rengokai, or Kaitakuren), and the National Settlers' Nokyo Federation (Zenkoku Takushoku Nogyo Kyodo Kumiai Rengokai, or Zentakuren).

Nokyo's cultural and welfare activities are represented nationally by the National Welfare Nokyo Federation (Zenkoku Kosei Nogyo Kyodo Kumiai Rengokai, or Zenkoku Koseiren) and the National Culture and Welfare Nokyo Federation (Zenkoku Bunka Kosei Nogyo Kyodo Kumiai Rengokai) and its information and PR industry by the National Newspaper and Information Nokyo Federation (Zenkoku Shinbun Joho Nogyo Kyodo Kumiai Rengokai, or Shinbunren). In addition there is a general marketing specialist federation called the Japan Marketing Nokyo Federation (Nihon Hanbai Nogyo Kyodo Kumiai Rengokai) and a National Transportation Nokyo Federation (Zenkoku Unyu Nogyo Kyodo Kumiai Rengokai, or Zenunren).[135]

Nokyo's policy leadership groups

With the establishment of the agricultural cooperatives and with the land reform completed, government rice policies provided a pivotal focus around which farmers' organisations attempted to mobilise politically and the star item in a lobbying process that Nokyo shared and increasingly came to dominate.

In November 1948 a National Guidance Nokyo Federation (Zenkoku Shido Nogyo Kyodo Kumiai Rengokai, or Zenshiren) was established as the central guiding body for the agricultural cooperatives. It was replicated at the prefectural level by prefectural guidance federations (*shidoren*). Zenshiren provided guidance to the agricultural cooperatives in three main fields: production, organisation and agricultural policy.[136] It launched *nosei katsudo* as an interest representative organ (*rieki daihyo kikan*) of the farmers and of the agricultural cooperatives on issues relating to compulsory rice deliveries, producer prices, agricultural taxes and other policy problems.[137] As a decision governed by ministerial responsibility, the producer rice price was a political as well as an administrative and economic issue affecting the vast majority of farmers and co-op members. In order to increase farmers' returns, the agricultural cooperatives turned their attention to increases in the price of rice they delivered to the government. For example, during the 1948 rice price campaign under the aegis of the Agriculture Reconstruction Council, the newly formed agricultural cooperatives led by Zenshiren decided to increase the demand price to a level higher than that requested by the council. This action proved to be successful with a government settlement at the midpoint between the two demands.[138]

Possibilities for the presentation of producer rice price demands to government by farmers' groups were considerably enhanced with the establishment of the RPAC as an inquiry organ (*shimon kikan*) of the MAF in August 1949. The call to 'democratise' the process of deciding the prices of commodities distributed through the FC system (namely rice, wheat and barley) had been made by both Nichino and the *noseiren* in 1947. They wanted farmers' representatives to be involved in the process through an agricultural commodity price council and a pricing committee respectively. In 1948, the National Farmers' Convention called for the establishment of a central advisory organ that would include both farmers and consumers' representatives in order to democratise what they considered a one-sided, bureaucratically-dominated decisionmaking process, although formally speaking the producer rice price was decided by the MAF Minister.

These various calls from the rice roots were taken up by the Lower House (LH) Agriculture, Forestry and Fisheries Committee which issued a proposal for the creation of an advisory council consisting of farmers, consumers and learned persons (*gakushikisha*) to be involved in rice price decisionmaking. This was subsequently realised with the formation of the RPAC with members appointed by the MAF Minister.[139] Eleven producer representatives were selected to the first council, including officials of Zennoseiren, Zenkoku Nomin Kumiai, Nichino, Zenshiren and Zenhanren. The main task of the RPAC was to receive and discuss a government-proposed producer rice price presented to it by the MAF Minister and to compile a final report containing the council's views on the government's recommendation. The RPAC was, therefore, established very early on as a formal consultative channel for the presentation of producer opinions to government.[140]

The early 1950s were a period when agricultural cooperative leaders were primarily concerned with internal matters of organisational establishment, financial viability and functional scope,[141] but Nokyo also consolidated its position as the political voice of farmers in relation to rival agricultural organisations at this time.[142] As a group commissioned almost exclusively by government with the task of collecting rice and selling it to the Food Agency under the FC Law,[143] Nokyo was able to voice the interests of all rice producers.[144] In many respects, Nokyo's pressure group activities evolved as an extension of its principal economic functions in relation to Food Control.[145] After the abolition of direct government control over wheat and barley distribution in 1950–51 (which Nokyo opposed), issues such as rice delivery quotas and the producer rice price became paramount. The pressing need to increase rice output assisted Nokyo's assumption of a representational role on rice-related issues. It naturally acceded to the position of policy leader in relation to requests for government subsidies to enable farmers to acquire key inputs such as fertiliser, agricultural chemicals and tools to expand rice production. Nokyo's position as spokesperson for farmers was bolstered as it inevitably found itself channelling all demands on rice production as well as price supports.[146] The assumption of the Zenshiren chairmanship by a pro-active Nokyo leader in 1951 also assisted Nokyo to assert its national leadership of the producer rice price campaign.[147] Nokyo's representatives became the most influential farmers' advocates on the RPAC.

The strength that the agricultural cooperatives were able to muster contrasted with the growing disunity of the farmers' unions and the decay of the National Rural Youth League – both dispossessed of their primary raison d'être. In 1950–51, a distinct turning point in the farmers' movement could be detected. As Tanaka puts it, the movement changed its character from one that took the farmers' unions as its core to one centring on Nokyo's agricultural policy activities. Nokyo started to take the lead in farmers' campaigns, replacing the farmers' unions.[148]

The producer rice price issue also spawned new divisions amongst farmers' groups as the era of organisational cooperation around such issues as the formation of new agricultural cooperative unions and organisational democratisation came to an end. Policy differences emerged between groups over levels of price demands. One indicator of this was the appearance of major differences between Nokyo and Nichino's attitudes to the producer rice price. The farmers' unions began to demand much higher prices compared to those being requested by Nokyo. Their different perspective largely stemmed from their divergent ideological worldviews. The membership of the farmers' unions largely derived from a select group of ideologically committed supporters of the Socialist and Communist parties. They sought to equalise 'wages' in the agricultural sector with those of modern factory workers.[149] Their appeal to some farmers at the time was their call for higher rice prices, with the enemy identified as 'monopoly capital' and the conservative government depicted as its main instrument out to plunder and sacrifice the workers and the farmers.[150] The agricultural cooperatives, on the other hand, were government-sponsored organisations acting as agents of the MAF in relation to rice collection and distribution. Their proximity to government inevitably moderated their stance compared with those of the farmers' unions.[151]

The early 1950s were also significant for the passage of an amendment to the Nokyo Law setting up a new system of agricultural cooperative leadership groups called central unions (*chuokai*) to replace the old system of guidance federations. Zenshiren lacked the status of a peak organisation of agricultural cooperatives. Nor was its role in representing the interests of the agricultural cooperatives to government clearly spelled out in the legislation. As a result, it operated on equal terms with the national Nokyo economic federations which also assumed agricultural policy functions.[152] This made it difficult for Zenshiren to unify the common will of Nokyo as a whole.[153]

At the first national Nokyo convention in 1952, a resolution to establish a National Central Union of Agricultural Cooperatives (Zenchu) as a comprehensive guidance organisation that would also oversee the conduct of agricultural policy activities was seen as urgently required.[154] In June 1954 the amendment to the Nokyo Law was duly passed. For the first time Nokyo's agricultural policy activities came under the supervision of a peak, national body.[155] At the same time, prefectural central unions (*ken chuokai*, or *kenchu*) were established in each prefecture. Like the *shidoren*, the central unions were a special type of non-economic agricultural cooperative.

The 'business' (*jigyo*) of the central unions as listed under Article 73(9) of Nokyo Law are as follows: 'providing guidance on matters of organisation, business operations and management of agricultural cooperatives; auditing of the accounts of member cooperatives; furnishing information and providing educational services for agricultural cooperatives; liaison with and mediation of disputes amongst member cooperatives; research and investigation on matters relevant to the agricultural cooperatives; and, in addition to the activities under the foregoing items, any other activities required for attaining the objectives of the central union.'[156] The central unions are different from the other agricultural cooperative organisations whose main purpose is to provide services to agricultural cooperative members. The principal function of the *chuokai* is to supervise the other agricultural cooperative groups and adjust their interests. In this respect the central unions occupy a more elevated position on the organisational ladder. They are the powerful central institutions of Nokyo which direct the lower-level organisations.[157]

The *kenchu* serve as coordinating and guiding bodies for the agricultural cooperatives within each prefecture. Because they do not conduct economic business, they are funded by levies on their organisational members, principally the *sogo nokyo*. They also receive subsidies from the government to conduct their activities. The membership of Zenchu primarily consists of the *kenchu* and the other Nokyo national federations, including the specialist federations.[158] Zenchu performs functions for its members that are the same as the prefectural central unions and derives its funding in the same way from levies on its organisational members and from government subsidies. Under the internal division of labour, the prefectural central unions serve as leadership organs for the agricultural cooperatives within individual prefectures, while Zenchu's task is to act as the overall leader of the Nokyo organisation in the nationwide sphere. Taken together, the *chuokai* have the function of concentrating the will of the agricultural cooperatives and representing it to the outside.[159]

Legal provisions establishing the central unions were not, therefore, part of the original 1947 Nokyo Law. They were added later in order to correct what were thought to be the organisational and financial deficiencies of the existing system of national and prefectural guidance federations and to

---

■ General Affairs Department (Somubu)

■ Public Relations Department (Kohobu)

■ Agricultural Policy Department (Noseibu)
  - Agricultural Policy Section (Noseika)
  - International Planning Section (Kokusai Kikakuka)
  - International Cooperation Office (Kokusai Kyoryoku Shitsu)*

■ Agricultural Countermeasures Department (Nogyo Taisakubu)*
  - Agricultural Management Countermeasures Office* (Eino Taisaku Shitsu)
  - Rice and Wheat Section (Beibakuka)
  - Livestock and Horticulture Section (Chikusan Engeika)
  - Rice Consumption Expansion Policy Department (Beishohi Kakudai Taisakubu)*

■ Regional Policy Department (Chiiki Taisakubu)*
  - Youth and Women's Section (Seinen Joseika)
  - Livelihood Section (Seikatsuka)
  - Regional Promotion Section (Chiiki Shinkoka)*

■ Management and Auditing Department (Keiei Kansabu)*

■ Organisational Countermeasures Department (Soshiki Taisakubu)*
  - Organisational Adjustment Promotion Section (Soshiki Seibi Suishinka)*

■ Education Department (Kyoikubu)

■ College Department (Gakuenbu)*

Notes: New and renamed departments are signified by an *.

Figure 2.3 Zenchu's internal structural divisions (1997)
   Source: Nokyo Pamphlet, *JA Zenchu Soshiki Kozu* [*JA Zenchu Organisational Composition*], 1998.

strengthen the agricultural cooperative movement generally. The formation of Nokyo's bureaucratic system was considerably accelerated by the creation of the *chuokai*.

The most politically significant aspect of the creation of the central unions, however, was the formal ascription under the law of what might be broadly called an 'agricultural policy function'. Central unions were allocated the task of representing the interests of the agricultural cooperative movement to government. Article 73(9)-2 of the Nokyo Law lays down that: 'A central union may make proposals to administrative authorities on matters concerning the cooperatives'.[160] Although the legislation does not include the terms *nosei katsudo* or phrases directly relevant to it, the interpretation of this

Article provides legal authority allowing *nosei katsudo*.[161] Nokyo's conduct of *nosei katsudo* was thus laid on a firm legal foundation. The *chuokai* were formally charged with coordinating Nokyo's agricultural policy activities, with Zenchu acting as the peak representative body for the agricultural cooperatives on policy-related matters.

By 1955 the stage had been set for the development of a distinctive system of Nokyo-led agricultural policy campaigns, and from this time onwards, these activities were bolstered and expanded. Located in Tokyo, the seat of government, the 'administrative authorities' in Zenchu's case were clearly the MAFF and its agencies, although in practice this provision has included all branches of the government, including the ruling party.

Zenchu's policy concerns encompass issues concerning the cooperatives as well as larger questions of state-wide farm policy. Although the legislation appears to limit its policy concerns to 'matters concerning the cooperatives', in practice these naturally extend to issues concerning its membership as a whole, and thus agriculture and farmers in general.[162] In addition, the articles of incorporation and bylaws of Zenchu greatly expand its range of activities in the policy representation sphere. According to these provisions, Zenchu is the 'sole and supreme national body that unifies the intentions, represents the interests and determines the directions of the whole movement'.[163]

Zenchu is also the supreme 'staff' body of the cooperatives and combines with the *kenchu* to form the administrative branch of the federated Nokyo organisation. Central union 'business' is mainly concerned with internal organisational matters involving the operations, management and finances of the cooperatives. Only one paragraph of the Nokyo Law concerns the relationship between the central unions and outside groups (administrative authorities).

The Zenchu secretariat constitutes its internal bureaucracy (each *kenchu* also has a secretariat). It is divided into nine departments (*bu*), seven offices (*shitsu*) and 17 sections (*ka*) in which Zenchu's salaried staff manage its affairs. Departments and their respective subdivisions (offices and sections) have been renamed and reorganised over the years as new foci of organisational interest have emerged. The 1997 setup is outlined in Figure 2.3. The department charged with formulating agricultural policy proposals for Zenchu is the Agricultural Policy Department (Noseibu). It has an Agricultural Policy Section, International Planning Section and International Cooperation Office. The latter is a new acquisition. Previously there used to be a separate International Department (Kokusaibu) in the secretariat. The structural reorganisation reflected the growing link between agricultural policy and international affairs consequent upon successive rounds of agricultural trade liberalisation, with the Noseibu now handling all questions relating to agricultural market access. Some restructuring has also gone on between the Noseibu and the Agricultural Countermeasures Department. The former lost its Livestock and Horticulture Section to the latter when it strengthened its international sections. The Agricultural Countermeasures

Department is now subdivided along the main agricultural product lines (these are concerned mainly with price and domestic production issues relating to these commodities), although it also has what amounts to a 'structural improvement' section (the Agricultural Management Countermeasures Office) in addition to a Rice Consumption Expansion Countermeasures Office, which underlines the importance of this issue to Nokyo. Zenchu's Merger Promotion Department, which operated in the early 1990s, has been taken over by the new Management Guidance Office when organisational management issues were subsumed by an expanded Management and Auditing Department (the latter used to operate as a single department). In fact, the particular subdivisions within the Zenchu secretariat are indicative of the organisation's main priorities at any particular time.

By and large the main structural divisions within the *kenchu* correspond to those of Zenchu, although not all departments are replicated exactly. The prefectural central unions have general affairs departments, public relations departments, education departments and management and auditing departments. Some also have merger promotion departments, livelihood departments and agricultural countermeasures departments. Almost all have agricultural policy departments, although these are sometimes amalgamated with agricultural management or public relations sections.

The agricultural policy departments of the central unions, particularly Zenchu, do the basic leg work of drafting various demands, requests, resolutions etc. that become the building blocks of Nokyo's *nosei katsudo*. These departments are staffed by salaried employees who are urban white collar workers and who have only indirect links to the farming world. The task of directing and monitoring their activities falls to Zenchu's full-time managing directors and its elected executives, who hold the reins of agricultural policy leadership within Nokyo.[164]

Taking the organisation as a whole, one of its most salient operational features is that the agricultural cooperatives conduct their activities in each prefecture as a block. Prefectural directors of the various Nokyo federations supervise the administration of agricultural cooperatives in each city, town and village and coordinate the differences between them. Similarly, it is up to the leadership of the prefectural central unions to adjust confrontations between different agricultural cooperative groups and to mitigate regional antagonisms of blocks of groups, or the regional antagonisms of city, town and village unit agricultural cooperatives on the policy level.[165] These conflicting interests arise because each of the cooperatives is a fundamentally separate group, and acts on the basis of its own ideas. On occasions the cooperatives may even compete with each other for business.[166]

Nokyo's historical, organisational and legal heritage

The analysis of Nokyo's historical antecedents, organisational establishment and functional attributes underlines the fact that the agricultural cooperative organisation originated as 'a creature of the government'.[167] In fact, the overall historical process of the birth and development of the agricultural cooperatives in Japan was in reverse order to the traditional pattern of the formation of agricultural organisations in industrialised nations of the West.[168] Unlike farmers' cooperatives in Europe which were established on the spontaneous initiative of their members, Nokyo's predecessors were government-sponsored groups set up under organising legislation drafted by the Japanese bureaucracy.[169] Like the *sangyo kumiai* and *nokai* that were creations of the Meiji state and which set out to organise and control farmers for purposes of agricultural development as well as for farmers' own better-ment, the modern Japanese agricultural cooperatives were founded on the initiative of governing authorities rather than agricultural producers them-selves.[170] The state passed the necessary law governing their set-up, cooperatives were then established, and only then was cooperative membership organised.

Nokyo's heritage as a state-sponsored institution was reinforced by its *de facto* inheritance of the nationwide structure of the *nogyokai* in 1947–48, including buildings, members, employees and facilities.[171] Although GHQ expected the agricultural cooperatives to play an important role in the democ-ratisation of agricultural villages, in fact, little difference existed between Nokyo and the *nogyokai*.[172] In the poverty and confusion that followed Japan's defeat, and in the controlled economy of the early postwar years, it was inevitable that the newly formed agricultural cooperatives would simply take over where the *nogyokai*, which were in the process of being dismantled, left off.[173] As one Nokyo 'old hand' commented, 'the old senior officials of the *nogyokai* and the meddling bureaucrats of the government offices got together and soon nationwide *tankyo*, prefectural federations and national federations were established.'[174]

The lack of any tradition of free and independent action by villagers, who remained bound by the communal traditions of village society,[175] also facili-tated the direct transition from the *nogyokai* to the *nokyo*. A comment that is ubiquitous in the analysis of the times notes that *nogyokai* signboards were simply taken down and replaced with *nokyo* signs.[176] As Kawagoe explains,

> the previous agricultural associations were disbanded in August 1948. Their assets, business and staff were passed on, just as they were, to the new Nokyo. This was done to avoid unnecessary social upheaval, but in addition, the government needed an implementing agency working at the local level to handle the many agricultural products and raw materials, which were still under control at that time. So the newly launched Nokyo inherited a lot from the wartime agricultural associations . . . Though the agricultural associations were disbanded, the new Nokyo inherited many of the functions as control agency in the former.[177]

The one-union-for-each-village formula was adopted 'in order to facilitate the maintenance of continuity and similarity between the old agricultural associations and the new unions.'[178] In addition, the familiar tri-level structure of local, prefectural and national organisations, including the customary division of labour into guidance, economic and financial arms was adopted as the basic framework of the newly established Nokyo organisation.[179] Moreover, as many of the new executives of Nokyo local and prefectural organisations had little experience in managing cooperatives, they had no choice but to depend on former senior staff of the *nogyokai*, which contributed to the retention of the bureaucratic nature of the *nogyokai* in the *nokyo*.[180]

In recreating agricultural cooperatives by law and putting the MAF in charge as the overall administering organ, the Japanese government also reasserted some of its regulatory and supervisory powers over the main organisation of farmers. Under its organising legislation, Nokyo was only permitted to conduct the functions ascribed to it by statute and, therefore, it could be held accountable for any activities that breached legal limits. In administering this legislation, the MAF was able to keep a close eye on the activities of the agricultural cooperatives. Within one month of the passage of the law establishing Nokyo, the MAF established a Nokyo Department (Nokyobu), which in later years became the current Agricultural Cooperative Division (Nogyo Kyodo Kumiaika) of the Economic Affairs Bureau (Keizai Kyoku). As soon as the Nokyo Department was launched, it quickly began to monitor and supervise the management and functions of the agricultural cooperatives.

An amendment to Nokyo Law in 1950 weakened early liberal policies towards Nokyo and encouraged its dependence on the administration. As a result of the law change, it became possible for the MAF to restrict Nokyo's financial dealings by ordinances and to reinforce the inspection of *sogo nokyo* and prefectural and national federations. Both of these moves signalled increased intervention by the administration in the Nokyo organisation, despite the intentions of GHQ which were to minimise the administration's influence on the newly established agricultural cooperatives.[181]

In incorporating such organisational features, legal restraints and administrative restrictions into its postwar design, Nokyo retained many of the basic characteristics of the prewar style of Japanese interest groups. As Ishida noted in his discussion of the emergence of interest groups in Japan: '(a)lmost all of the important interest groups were approved . . . or established . . . by law.'[182] As a result, the 'conduct of their activities was very often governed by the need to help spread and develop the policies of the government, while the original function of interest articulation was more or less suppressed'.[183] Understanding the peculiarities of the Nokyo system, therefore, requires an analysis of how history and the state helped to shape some of its distinctive characteristics and thus why it is a far cry from the typical farm cooperative in Western countries. At no stage of its development has Nokyo ever been a popular farmers' movement, the product of rice-roots rural initiative.[184]

Duties in relation to rice collection and distribution were critical to the timing and characteristic features of Nokyo's postwar reconstruction and to its assumption of a role in relation to government administration.[185] As Mitsukawa points out, 'Nokyo, the most powerful agricultural organisation in postwar Japan, made its start as an agent to collect rice and wheat.'[186] The need for farm organisations to accomplish tasks relating to Food Control was one of the primary objectives behind the push for the speedy rehabilitation of the agricultural cooperative system in the early postwar period. The Occupation authorities were keen to ensure the fair distribution of scarce food supplies. As noted earlier, the *nokyo* were soon allocated the role of the wartime *nogyokai* as proxy agents of government in rice collection and storage. It was mainly in this context that the newly inaugurated agricultural cooperatives 'continued to assist and support the functions of govern-ment.'[187] As Yamaguchi reiterates, 'as soon as Nokyo was established, it was used as an organisation to collect food and distribute controlled goods because of the food shortage and starvation after WWII. As a result, Nokyo became a subcontractor (*shitauke*) of the government.'[188] Organisational features of the *nogyokai* well suited to the performance of administratively-determined tasks under FC were retained by the agricultural cooperatives, including a convenient nationwide network of facilities for rice collection and handling, as well as one cooperative for each village.

Nokyo's integration into agricultural administration was facilitated by the fact that its three-tiered organisational structure matched national politico-administrative divisions. The arrangement reflected the administrative rationality of government officials anxious to ensure the complementarity of state-wide organisational structures. Since the country's agricultural policy was instituted from the top down (that is, in the form of directives emanating from the national government to prefectural governments and thence to city, town and village administrations), it was considered desirable for Nokyo to have a parallel organisational architecture in order for it to become part of the administration process.[189] As Saeki points out, the arrangement of one cooperative per city, town or village,[190] and no competition amongst the agricultural cooperatives was convenient for rice collection as well as for government administration generally.[191] Nokyo had national coverage of all administrative districts and its membership had coverage of practically all farmers.[192] This was a very effective method of infiltrating agricultural policies into the farming community.[193] Organisational complementarity between state and outside groups also meant ease of communication between administrative authorities and the cooperatives.[194] As Saeki concludes, even though the agricultural cooperatives were reborn as voluntary organisations with greater independence from government, the MAF still looked to Nokyo as an agent of its own administration and so the same policy requests penetrated from the top down as before.[195]

In the first postwar decade, Nokyo was progressively assimilated into agricultural administration under several other laws besides the FC Law. These included the 1945 Sericultural Industry Law, the Agricultural Movables Credit Law (originally passed in 1937, but amended in 1947), the 1949 Land

Improvement Law and the 1952 Agricultural Land Law. Under the Land Improvement Law, for example, agricultural cooperatives and federations of agricultural cooperatives were able to implement land improvement projects and undertake agricultural land exchange, division and merger projects.[196]

The strengthening and expansion of agricultural support systems from the early 1960s onwards integrated Nokyo even more comprehensively into the functioning of agricultural administration. The principle of price support was firmly established by the ABL, and the passage of this law was followed by others that established price support systems across a range of products. Nokyo became a proxy agent for the authorities in channelling price support payments to farmers.[197]

Nokyo also took on more diversified functions as a policy administrator under various other laws passed during the 1960s and subsequently. These included the Agricultural Modernisation Fund Assistance Law (1961), the Agricultural Credit Guarantee Insurance Law (1961), the Livestock Products Price Stabilisation Law (1961), the Provisional Measures Law for Subsidies to Producers of Raw Milk for Processing (1965), the Law Concerning the Development of Agricultural Promotion Regions (1969), the Farmers' Pension Fund Law (1970), the Law for Special Exceptions to the Agricultural Land Law etc. Concerning the Leasing of Specific Agricultural Land (1989), and others.

Under the Agricultural Modernisation Fund Assistance Law, for example, agricultural cooperatives and federations of agricultural cooperatives provide government-subsidised finance in the form of long-term, low-interest facility funds;[198] under the Farmers' Pension Fund Law, the fund can entrust agricultural cooperatives with a part of its business;[199] under the Livestock Price Stabilisation Law, agricultural cooperatives and federations of agricultural cooperatives, whose direct or indirect members are milk producers, can draw up a production plan for designated dairy products made from raw milk produced by their members in the event that prices of raw milk drop or are likely to slide substantially;[200] under the Law for Special Exceptions to the Agricultural Land Law etc. Concerning the Leasing of Specific Agricultural Land, agricultural cooperatives can lease specific farm land;[201] and under the Law Concerning the Development of Agricultural Promotion Regions, agricultural cooperatives can propose negotiations about establishing utilisation rights to owners of farm land not used for cultivation.[202]

In this way, the agricultural cooperatives became 'peripheral agencies of government economic policies'.[203] Most agricultural policies came to be implemented through Nokyo,[204] which became the 'de facto local office of MAFF',[205] and 'an extension of the MAFF bureaucracy in administering the programmes under its jurisdiction'.[206] The shared goals and parallel functioning of the MAFF and Nokyo were clearly exemplified in the campaigns both conducted to prevent further declines in the domestic consumption of rice in Japan during the 1980s and early 1990s.[207] Zenchu set up its Rice Consumption Expansion Countermeasures Office,[208] as did the Food Agency.

Other statutory agricultural interest groups

Besides Nokyo, several other agricultural interest groups operating under their own organising legislation serve to represent the interests of farmers in particular areas of policy. Nokyo shares the status of statutory interest group with the agricultural committee organisation, the agricultural mutual aid organisations and the agricultural land improvement groups.

The agricultural committee organisation

One of Nokyo's early rivals for policy leadership of the farm sector was the agricultural committee organisation. Groups called 'agricultural committees' (*nogyo iinkai*) were established at local and prefectural levels with the passage of the Agricultural Committee Law (*Nogyo Iinkaiho*) of 1951. Initially the agricultural committees acted merely as administrative bodies, amalgamating the functions of the former land committees, food adjustment committees and agricultural improvement committees.[209] In the early 1950s, however, pressure built to convert these groups into 'active leadership organizations, responsive to the needs of farmers and with the ability to represent their interests.'[210] As Mitsukawa explains, MAFF bureaucrats and former *nokai* leaders were keen to recreate the agricultural committee organisation as a body to represent the interests of farmers. Both believed that there should be two types of agricultural organisation: economic organisations of farmers (i.e. the co-ops) and agricultural organisations to conduct guidance (*shido*) and agricultural policy activities (*nosei katsudo*), i.e. the agricultural committees. The coexistence of these two organisations, which could confront and criticise each other, would improve the functioning of both.[211]

The jurisdictional competition between Nokyo and the agricultural committees over which group should represent the farmers thus began almost as soon as the latter were established in 1951. As well as being rivals for the agricultural budget in the early 1950s, 'both sides . . . agitated for legal changes to widen the sphere of their own competence.'[212] In 1952, the agricultural committees proposed that Nokyo should be restructured purely as an economic institution, and a new organisation, based on the agricultural committees, which would represent the interests of farmers, should be established. This idea naturally incited a fiercely negative response from Nokyo.[213]

In June 1954, the Agricultural Committee Law was amended to become the Law Concerning Agricultural Committees and Related Organisations (*Nogyo Iinkai to ni kansuru Horitsu*). New groups called prefectural chambers of agriculture (*ken nogyo kaigi*) replaced the agricultural committees at prefectural level, while a National Chamber of Agriculture, or NCA (*Zenkoku Nogyo Kaigisho*) was created at the national level. An interest articulation function was legally ascribed to each of these bodies which gave them the right to make 'known to the public, as well as to administrative agencies, through recommendations and submission of reports at their inquiries, the views and opinions of the farmers on themselves and agriculture in general'.[214]

Certain provisions of the law allowed other agricultural organisations including agricultural cooperatives to join the prefectural chambers of agriculture, which weakened the relationship between local agricultural committees and the prefectural chambers. In addition, the NCA permitted Nokyo national organisations as members, along with academics and prefectural chambers of agriculture. The fact that external elements were allowed to join the prefectural and national organisations undermined their unity and made it difficult for the *nogyo iinkai* to dominate NCA decision-making processes.[215] The municipal agricultural committees were also obliged by law to extend membership to local agricultural cooperatives.[216]

In the mid-1950s, another attempt was made at comprehensive reform of agricultural organisations. It was basically led by the agricultural committee system and supported by the MAF Minister, Kono Ichiro. The proposal was for the formation of a new farmers' group which, at the municipal level, which would incorporate the municipal agricultural committees and agricultural mutual aid unions.[217] The new group would also combine the functions of agricultural policy activities and technical guidance.[218] This plan pitted the MAF and the agricultural committee system against Nokyo, which directly confronted the agricultural committee system over the issue.

In January 1956, an LDP Diet member presented a plan for the reorganisation of agricultural groups which became known as the 'Hirano Private Plan', although in reality it was drafted by the head of the Economic Bureau of the MAF, who was a trusted friend of Kono Ichiro.[219] The plan proposed the establishment of federated farmers' associations (*nominkai*) based on the 'natural participation' of farmers, which would combine the agricultural committees and agricultural mutual aid associations. The Nokyo system would be reformed with its functions of conducting agricultural policy activities and technical guidance eliminated. The *kenchu* would be made into branch offices of Zenchu and the *shinren* would likewise become branch offices of Norinchukin. Credit business would be taken away from the *sogo nokyo*.[220]

The real aim of the plan was for the *nominkai* to make farmers' membership compulsory and thus abolish farmers' freedom to join or to leave, to reinstitute a system of bureaucratically controlled groups and thus to revive the prewar *nokai* and the wartime *nogyokai*.[221] The new groups would have dual functions as representatives of farmers' interests and as agencies of the administration in assisting it in communicating agricultural policy to the farmers.[222] To many in the agricultural cooperatives, the plan represented a retreat to the period of wartime control. It provoked fierce protest campaigns from Zenchu and other Nokyo organisations. Hirano became the target of strong public criticism, and what was even worse for the MAF Minister, some members of the LDP, who were surprised by the sensation caused by the plan, began to put forward their own objections. As a result, Kono who had masterminded the Hirano Private Plan, was forced to abandon it.[223]

In 1957, a further amendment to the law enlarged the scope of the municipal agricultural committees, conferring on them the role of farmers' interest groups in addition to their function as administrative councils.[224] As well as the tasks that were exclusively within their administrative competence, they were given more general duties involving the representation of farmers.[225] These involved 'publicising views and making proposals to government agencies, and advising the agencies at their inquiries regarding agriculture and farmers'.[226] As a result of the changes, the three-tiered agricultural committee organisation was fully established as a democratic body to represent farmers.

Even after the structural and functional extensions to the agricultural committee organisation in 1954 and 1957, however, the question of policy leadership of the farm sector was basically resolved in Nokyo's favour. Although reform of agricultural organisations was intended to wrest the interest group function from Nokyo, the latter fought and won the right to retain its position as a body articulating the interests of farmers. Not only were the central unions successfully established as peak representative organs of the agricultural cooperatives in 1954, but they consolidated their hold on *nosei katsudo* involving the farmers from that time onwards. In fact, Nokyo united its members and reinforced the basis of its organisation through the experience of confronting the agricultural committee system over the issue of organisational reform and defending its standing as the primary farm interest group.[227]

Moreover, the agricultural committee organisation proved a subordinate body to Nokyo in their overlapping function of 'making proposals to the relevant authorities'. This arose from the failed division of labour on agricultural policy matters as prescribed in their respective organising laws. The *nosei katsudo* of the *chuokai* were supposed to be confined to affairs directly relevant to the agricultural cooperatives (see Article 73(9)-2 of the Nokyo Law), while the agricultural committees and their higher bodies were expected to handle affairs concerning the farmers and agriculture in general. This created a problem insofar as the range of affairs directly relevant to the agricultural cooperatives naturally expanded to include matters concerning the farmers and agriculture as a whole, which coincided with the functions of the agricultural committee organisation. Thus, although a different focus of interest group activity was formally ascribed to Nokyo, in practice it shared and came to dominate the agricultural committee organisation's sphere of competence in articulating farmers' interests on agricultural policy matters.

Another early victory for Nokyo in the period of inter-organisational conflict was, as already noted, its penetration of the membership structure of the agricultural committee organisation. It successfully lobbied for membership of the local, prefectural and national groups to include representatives of the agricultural cooperatives at each level. In terms of overall membership structure, the municipal agricultural committees, prefectural chambers of agriculture and the National Chamber of Agriculture divide their membership between group and individual members, with only indirect representation of the rice roots through limited elections by farmers.[228]

The present membership composition of the agricultural committee system is as follows. Over 3,100 local agricultural committees operate with between 10 and 30 elected farmer members each (with an average of 15 per agricultural committee), and an average of six appointed members: one director each from local agricultural cooperatives and agricultural mutual aid associations, and five or less persons of learning and experience recommended by the local assembly. The chairman of the agricultural committee is elected from amongst the members. The agricultural committees send representatives to the 47 prefectural chambers of agriculture (one per prefecture) which have an average of 70 members each (except for Hokkaido with 216 members). The chambers consist of one nominated member from each local agricultural committee and an average of 16 other members: one representative each from the prefectural central union of agricultural cooperatives and the prefectural federation of agricultural mutual aid associations; a few representatives of prefectural agricultural cooperative federations and organisations carrying out agricultural improvement and development; and persons of learning and experience. The most powerful members of the prefectural chambers of agriculture have traditionally been the prefectural Nokyo federations.[229]

Membership of the National Chamber of Agriculture comprises an affiliated organisational membership of 47 prefectural chambers of agriculture; one representative from Zenchu and seven representatives from national agricultural cooperative federations; 11 members from organisations carrying out agricultural improvement and development; and 10 persons of learning and experience. The executive structure of the National Chamber of Agriculture is made up of 14 directors from the prefectural chambers of agriculture, national agricultural cooperative organisations and persons of learning and experience, plus two auditors.[230]

The administrative duties of the agricultural committee organisation are mainly taken up with managing various schemes and programmes on behalf of the government. Besides representing the interests of farmers and agriculture in general, the fundamental objectives of the National Chamber of Agriculture are 'to strive for the development of farming productivity and rationalisation of agricultural management and to enhance the status of farmers.'[231] Many of the same goals underlie the work of the prefectural chambers of agriculture, which also act in an advisory capacity to prefectural governors and thus 'play a supportive role in local government'.[232] Municipal agricultural committees are, in turn, 'held responsible for administrative work as prescribed by the relevant Laws',[233] including the Agricultural Land Law, the Land Improvement Law, the Agricultural Land Utilisation Promotion Law, the Law Concerning the Infrastructural Reorganisation for Agricultural

Development in Designated Areas and the City Residents' Farm Consolidation Development Promotion Law.[234]

One of the most important activities of the local agricultural committees is agricultural land administration, particularly relating to land transfers, whether by leasing, exchange, mergers or otherwise.[235] Under the Agricultural Land Law of 1951, these bodies are authorised to execute its provisions with the approval of prefectural governors and the MAFF. The owners of agricultural land, for example, must obtain permission from the agricultural committees for establishing or transferring legal rights of possession, leasehold and other uses of agricultural land.[236] In fact, three items out of eight on the official list of substantive functions of the local agricultural committees spelled out in the legislation relate to land administration.[237] Other functions include the determination and implementation of development plans concerning agriculture and rural areas; activities relating to improvements in agricultural technology, the prevention and alleviation of insect damage, increases in agricultural production, rationalisation of agricultural enterprises and improvements in farmers' livelihood, survey and research on agricultural production, agricultural enterprises and farmers' livelihood; and education and publicity of matters concerning agriculture and farmers.[238]

The agricultural committee organisation receives full subsidies from government for such functions as are mandated by law and partial funding for other activities. Article 2 of the Agricultural Committee Law of 1951 outlines the subsidy arrangements for the NCA, prefectural chambers of agriculture and agricultural committees. The monies are drawn from the national, prefectural and municipal budgets. The national budget provides funding for the National Chamber of Agriculture, while the prefectural chambers of agriculture are subsidised by both the national and prefectural governments. Part of the funding for the prefectural chambers also goes towards assisting the local agricultural committees. In addition, the national and municipal governments subsidise the activities of the local agricultural committees.

Since the agricultural committee organisation is not permitted to create independent sources of finance, it has no choice but to try and increase the amount of funding allocated by central and local governments, which makes it a petitioner for subsidies at budget time.[239] Each year, the NCA makes proposals to the government expressing the wishes of agricultural committee organisation members with respect to the agricultural budget and agricultural policies. The chairmen of all the agricultural committees nationwide assemble in Tokyo for the annual national convention and deliberate on their requests in relation to agricultural policies and the agricultural budget. They adopt resolutions and submit them to the government.[240]

The historical record shows that the agricultural committee system has lobbied successfully in relation to a number of laws over the years, including the Agricultural Land Law, Nokyo Law and the Agricultural Promotion Regional Consolidation Law, and for the establishment in law of the farmers' pension system.[241] Numerous other examples also illustrate the interest representational role of the NCA. In 1968, it issued a document entitled 'Concerning Policies for the Food Control System', in which it proposed the introduction of a new channel for distributing rice through Nokyo. In reply, the government decided to draw up a plan for an independently distributed rice (IDR) system (*jishu ryutsumai seido*),[242] which bypassed the normal sales route to the government and allowed Nokyo to sell rice directly to wholesalers.[243]

In the late 1960s and early 1970s, the NCA became involved in an anti-agricultural trade liberalisation campaign. In response to US demands for market opening, it requested that the government improve agriculture as an industry that could supply sufficient foodstuffs to the Japanese people and establish the principles of food self-sufficiency for major commodities as a means of ensuring the safety of the state. It also demanded that the government reject the option of liberalising agricultural trade.[244]

Constructive policy proposals emanating from the agricultural committee organisation often take the form of reports compiled in response to government requests. In 1977, the MAFF requested the NCA make input in the form of proposals into its Third Agricultural Structural Adjustment Project scheduled to begin in 1978, particularly around the issues of agricultural land policy and farm successors policy. The chamber's report was subsequently submitted to MAFF Minister Suzuki Zenko.[245] The NCA was also instrumental in the evolution of the 'new farm policy' (*shinnosei*)[246] in the early 1990s. They requested the government develop the *shinnosei* and many of their demands, particularly in relation to the development of farm management corporations (*hojinka*) are in the *shinnosei*.[247]

At a general level, the problem whether or not the agricultural committee organisation is a suitable vehicle for representing the interests of farmers has never really been resolved, and could resurface in the future.[248] In practice, the agricultural committee system, given its organisational and financial setup, has been a conservative semi-public grouping with powers limited to those of suggestion and advice. Although at the rice roots, the agricultural committees have an election system in which farmers' representatives are chosen, and although the committees are expected to reflect farmers' interests to some extent, the agricultural committee organisation as a whole has functioned largely as an instrumentality of the state in propagating and disseminating the government's agricultural policies,[249] rather than as an agent for articulating the interests of farmers.[250]

The victory for Nokyo in the jurisdictional dispute with the agricultural committee organisation over which grouping should represent the interests of the farmers reflected its greater organisational and financial autonomy, its stronger representative characteristics as a mass organisation of farmers and its importance as an electoral actor in the countryside.[251] These organisational features bestowed more independent political clout compared to the agricultural committee system.[252]

Agricultural mutual aid associations

A mixture of funding from public subsidies and levies from members has supported the operations of the agricultural mutual aid associations (*nogyo kyosai kumiai*) and their federations (*nogyo kyosai kumiai rengokai*) set up under the Agricultural Disaster Compensation Law (*Nogyo Saigai Hoshoho*) of 1947. Under the law, these organisations undertake the business of agricultural disaster compensation. They make available mutual aid funds to their members (i.e. farmers) to compensate them for losses arising from damage to crops, livestock and other farm goods and facilities caused by natural disasters.[253]

At the local level, the agricultural mutual aid associations have an individual farmer membership. Farmers pay levies to these organisations partially to insure themselves against natural disasters that impact on their farming operations. The government reinsures the insurance burden of disaster compensation funding which the federations undertake for their member associations.[254] The funds derive from the Agricultural Mutual Aid Reinsurance Special Account in the national budget.

The Agricultural Disaster Compensation Law states that agricultural disaster compensation is a mutual aid business operated by the agricultural mutual aid associations or municipalities, an insurance business of the federations of agricultural mutual aid associations, and a reinsurance business by the government. Article 14 of the law says that the state will assume the burden of office expenses of the agricultural mutual aid federations and associations from within the budget.[255] The same article also states that the treasury can subsidise the agricultural mutual aid associations for part of the costs of insect damage prevention which the main minister designates.[256]

The prefectural agricultural mutual aid federations are federated into a national body called the Agricultural Mutual Aid Fund (Nogyo Kyosai Kikin), set up under the Agricultural Mutual Aid Fund Law (*Nogyo Kyosai Kikinho*) of 1952. The fund received half its funding from the government and the other half from the agricultural mutual aid federations. Under the Agricultural Mutual Aid Fund Law, the fund loaned the money needed by its members (federations of agricultural mutual aid associations) as well as local agricultural mutual aid associations and municipalities (i.e. city, town and village governments) for mutual aid. The money was used to make payouts in the event of damage claims.[257] In 1997, however, the decision was taken to abolish the Agricultural Mutual Aid Fund under the rubric of 'administrative reform' (*gyosei kaikaku*, or *gyokaku*).[258] This leaves the conduct of agricultural mutual aid to the local associations and federations, although the Agricultural Mutual Aid Fund was still listed as receiving subsidies from the MAFF in FY 1998 (see Table 2.1).

Table 2.1 Fiscal 1998–99 national budget subsidies[a] allocated by the MAFF to statutory agricultural interest groups[b] as either primary or secondary works agents[c]

Unit: '000

Name of group[d]	Amount received and year of first subsidy[e]	Main administrative purpose for which subsidy was received[f]
*National Chamber of Agriculture	¥128,105 (1954)	Research relating to agriculture and farmers, and guidance on structural policy duties promotion system consolidation works undertaken by the prefectural agricultural councils and the agricultural committees.
	(1954)	Publishing opinions relating to agriculture and farmers, and the holding of conferences in order to make recommendation reports or proposals to administrative authorities.
	¥287,148 (1968)	Promoting structural policies for implementation of Uruguay Round Agriculture Agreement-related policies, including the advancement of increased land mobility, the rationalisation of land ownership and the cultivation of 'bearers' of agriculture.
	¥3,020 (1998)	Research relating to agricultural land utilisation in order to promote improvements in the employment of farmers.
	¥67,212 (1967)	Disseminating various policy measures in response to recent changes in the diverse conditions relating to the agricultural, forestry and fisheries industries.
*Prefectural Chambers of Agriculture	¥539,418 (1954)	Cultivating farm households with independent management intention, and the advancement of structural policy duties promotion system consolidation works.
	(1975)	Local investigations in order to fix the appropriateness of agricultural land duties.
	(1954)	Publishing opinions relating to agriculture and farmers, and the holding of conferences in order to make recommendation reports or proposals to administrative authorities.
	¥345,139 (1970)	Agricultural groups promotion works.

*Municipal Agricultural Committees	¥694,925 (1954/1987) ¥1,042,292 (1968)	Costs of councillors and staff members relating to matters laid down in ministerial ordinances. Expenses necessary for guidance relating to agricultural management which the agricultural committees undertake in order to assist the promotion of structural and other policies.

Total subsidies received by agricultural committee system ¥3,040,047

Agricultural Mutual Aid Fund	¥29,240 (1951)	Costs of agricultural mutual aid groups middle management lecture programmes.
	¥3,802 (1995)	Research into drawing up guidance for management analysis.
	¥6,449 (1997)	Research into financial management of large mutual aid associations.
*Agricultural mutual aid federations, agricultural mutual aid associations	¥744,789 (1958)	Evaluating damage to crops etc. (from natural disasters).
	(1968)	Countermeasures management works for strengthening the regional response (to natural disasters).
	¥54,141,250 (1947)	Agricultural mutual aid works office expenses.
	¥8,623,256 (1948)	Subsidy to cover part of the burden of the instalment payments which farmers have to make to the agricultural mutual aid associations to insure their crops etc., and a part or all of the insurance charge which the agricultural mutual aid unions have to pay to the federations.
	¥6,915,270 (1968)	Subsidy for agricultural mutual aid purposes.
	¥909,645 (1973)	Subsidy for agricultural mutual aid purposes.
*Agricultural mutual aid federations	¥819,021 (1967)	Subsidy to cover part of the costs of the costs of compensation which the agricultural mutual aid federations have to outlay for cattle disease.
	¥2,839,317 (1979)	Subsidy for agricultural mutual aid purposes.
Agricultural mutual aid associations	¥482,054 (1964)	Wetland rice insect damage prevention.

Total subsidies received by agricultural mutual aid organisations ¥75,514,093

Table 2.1 (continued)

Unit: '000

Name of group[e]	Amount received and year of first subsidy[e]	Main administrative purpose for which subsidy was received[f]
*National Federation of Land Improvement Industry Groups and land improvement districts	¥4,116,735 (1977)	Appropriate works for the management and upkeep of land improvement facilities.
*Federations of land improvement groups, land improvement districts	¥983,992 (1958) ¥2,051,629 (1979)	Guidance supervision for land improvement finance. Techniques management works for the management and upkeep of land improvement facilities.
*Federations of land improvement groups	¥438,234 (1979) ¥3,064,423 (1972) ¥67,985 (1958)	Land improvement facilities maintenance control. Land improvement comprehensive consolidation works. Guidance auditing for land improvement financing.
*Land improvement districts	¥4,804,290 (1997) ¥22,000,000 (1998) ¥4,293,785 (1995) ¥20,092,735 (1972) ¥6,720,346 (1972) ¥3,913,645 (1991/1992) ¥20,551,854 (1969) ¥10,864,644 (1953) ¥6,435,246 (1953) ¥2,962,619 (1970) ¥14,902,265 (1965) ¥3,658,500 (1950) ¥814,000 (1950) ¥73,000 (1949) ¥121,500 (1989) ¥30,500 (1990)	Agricultural village regions consolidation development works. Agricultural village regions consolidation development works. Works to promote the fluidity of agricultural land. Comprehensive rural consolidation works. Rural regions reorganisation consolidation works. Rural environment consolidation works to improve and maintain the beautiful natural environment of rural areas. Mountainous areas comprehensive consolidation works. Reservoir consolidation works. Agricultural land preservation works. Rural environment preservation works. Agricultural road consolidation works. Agricultural facilities disaster restoration works. Agricultural land disaster restoration works. Agricultural facilities disaster-related works. Agricultural land disaster-related block consolidation works. Disaster-related rural livelihood environment facilities restoration works.
Total subsidies received by land improvement industry groups	**¥132,961,927**	

* Those groups with an * have current or former Diet politicians in leadership positions.

Notes:

a Sources are the General Account and Special Account budgets. Only those allocations from the General Account budget by the MAFF main ministry are included. Subsidy contributions from prefectural and municipal governments and from other sources for the above administrative purposes are not included, although these may be substantial.

b Nokyo organisations are considered on a separate table.

c A group normally becomes a secondary works agent when a central government budget subsidy is channelled through prefectural or local governments. Where a group is a secondary agent, the subsidy has been treated as if the total amount was allocated to the group.

d In all cases the actual subsidy was used to cover or assist with the costs incurred by the groups in carrying out the specified function.

e In the budget documents, unspecified farmers' groups (*nogyosha dantai*), agricultural groups (*nogyo dantai*) and agricultural, forestry and fisheries groups (*noringyogyo dantai*) are often listed as primary and secondary works agents. These subsidies have been omitted from this table.

f The subsidies are given in the order in which they are listed in the record of national budget subsidies for 1998–99. Where more than one type of organisation was allocated a subsidy as a works agent, amounts have been divided equally amongst them. Hence, the actual amounts listed above are only approximate.

Source: Zaisei Chosakai (ed.), *Heisei 10 Nendo Hojokin Soran* [*A Compendium of Subsidies*, 1998], Tokyo, Nihon Densan Kikaku Kabushiki Kaisha 1998 (hereafter known as *Hojokin Soran*), pp. 192–615.

Land improvement industry groups

The 1949 Land Improvement Law created a three-tiered organisation of land improvement districts (*tochi kairyoku*),[259] prefectural federations of land improvement industry groups (*ken tochi kairyo jigyo dantai rengokai*), and a National Federation of Land Improvement Industry Groups (Zenkoku Tochi Kairyo Jigyo Dantai Rengokai, or Zendoren). Farmers join local land improvement districts if they wish to participate in government-subsidised land improvement projects. A few *nokyo* also join.[260] The land improvement districts are, in turn, members of the prefectural federations, as are municipal governments and *nokyo*. The prefectural federations as well as some land improvement districts form the membership of the national federation.

The districts are charged with the specialist tasks of land reclamation, land holding consolidation (*shudanka*), controlling irrigation water and undertaking irrigation projects, land conservation, disaster prevention and other types of land development activities. These come under the general umbrella of land improvement, but the main focus is to improve water and drainage systems for rice farming. A total of 7,000 land improvement districts are distributed throughout Japan, although their numbers are greater in Northern Japan than in Western Japan, because of the predominance of rice farming in the former.[261] The districts can only be set up on the initiative of farmers, who meet to discuss what kind of facilities are required and the specific projects involved, such as their common need for an irrigation canal.[262] After these discussions are completed, farmers have to register as a land improvement district under the law.

The expenses of the land improvement districts are raised in several different ways: through cash levies amongst their members; through payments made by those who will benefit from the land improvement activities undertaken by the local districts; and through government subsidies (from the national and prefectural governments). Article 126 of the Land Improvement Law states that the state will subsidise a part of the expenses of these groups from within the budget.[263] 'Once farmers have registered as a *tochi kairyoku*, they can then petition the prefectural and national government for subsidies. Their leaders often come to Tokyo to request the MAFF to supply funding for specific projects. They visit the Structural Improvement Bureau and the Ministry Secretariat.'[264] The MAFF budget includes very large amounts for land improvement works.[265] Construction companies that win the public works contracts actually construct the necessary facilities, although their beneficiaries are, of course, the farmers. Some of the projects are on a nation-wide or prefecture-wide scale.[266] When they are completed, the *tochi kairyoku* take over their maintenance, such as dams or ponds.

The land improvement district office in rural towns and villages is one of the three prominent local administrative organisations, the others being the town office (*yakuba*) and the agricultural cooperative. Farmers elect their own leaders to land improvement districts, just as they do to the *nokyo*. 'Small land improvement projects have no staff overseeing them (for example, projects under 300 hectares), but if the projects are bigger than that, they generally have some staff.'[267]

According to Moore, the 'land improvement district is more autonomous than either the town office or Nokyo and independently solicits project grants.'[268] In the town he researched, the district worked closely with the town office in relation to land improvement projects.[269] The districts also coordinate activity between agricultural cooperative organisations and national, prefectural and municipal governments.[270] Although *nokyo* are sometimes partially involved in land improvement projects, most are carried out by individual land improvement districts. Nokyo does, however, receive some funding in relation to these kinds of projects.

The role of the prefectural and national federations of land improvement districts is to liaise with the prefectural and national administrations and to oversee the functioning of the local groups. 'The prefectural land improvement federations, for example, have engineering technicians on their staff, because the districts do not possess human resources of this kind. The federations supply technicians to each district to supervise local projects.'[271] The national organisation has six separate departments concerned with various aspects of administering land improvement projects. Also attached is a Land Improvement Research Institute, similarly consisting of various administrative departments.[272]

Table 2.1 lists the subsidies outlaid from the MAFF main ministry budget to the land improvement industry groups in the FY 1998–99 national budget (¥133.0 billion), as well as those for the agricultural committee organisation (¥3.1 billion) and the agricultural mutual aid organisations (¥75.5 billion). The figures disclose that the land improvement industry groups receive by far the highest total subsidy allocation of these statutory agricultural interest groups.

In the case of the agricultural committee organisation, the subsidies are for its various research, educational and publicity activities, as well as for tasks relating to the promotion of structural policies and agricultural land administration, plus outlays for the costs of staff and elected personnel undertaking various designated functions. The relatively small total subsidy allocation for the agricultural committee organisation suggests that it mounts a fairly small-scale, modest operation in financial terms, which at the local level is conducted mainly by its elected or nominated members, without substantial staff back-up.

The agricultural mutual aid associations and federations benefit from very large subsidy allocations to cover part of the burden of the instalment payments that farmers have to make to the agricultural mutual aid associations (to insure their crops etc.) and a part or all of the insurance charge that the agricultural mutual aid unions have to pay to the federations (as laid down in Article 13 of the Agricultural Disaster Compensation Law of 1947).[273] The latter charge covers part of the costs of compensation which the agricultural mutual aid federations are required to outlay for cattle disease as well as the costs of their permanent operations in relation to evaluating the damage to crops and farms from natural disasters, engaging in damage prevention measures, managing disaster compensation funds (from government and farmers) and indemnifying farmers for the costs of disaster restoration works. As already noted, central government subsidies allocated for these purposes amounted to more than ¥75 billion in FY 1998.

The land improvement industry groups, particularly the local land improvement districts, obtain even greater amounts of budgetary funds for implementing all aspects of agricultural and rural public works projects relating to the reconstruction and consolidation of paddy fields and dry fields, drainage and irrigation, the development of agricultural roads, water storage, the rural environment, disaster restoration and so on. As Table 2.1 indicates, the land improvement groups received just on ¥133 billion via the MAFF for these purposes in FY 1998. In addition to the MAFF, three agencies of the Prime Minister's Office: the Hokkaido Development Agency, the Okinawa Development Agency and the Land Agency also allocate subsidies to the land improvement industry groups. In FY 1998, these amounted to an additional ¥7.5 billion.[274]

As the dates on all these various subsidy allocations reveal, the statutory agricultural interest groups have, in some cases, been routinely receiving subsidies for nominated tasks over many years and even decades, in some instances since the passage of their organising law. In other cases, subsidies for specific purposes are quite new, beginning in the late 1980s or early 1990s, with some starting in FY 1998.

Rice-roots farmers' organisations

Farmers' political leagues

A considerable number of prefectural, rice-roots farmers' political groups were launched by the regional Nokyo leadership in the late 1950s and early 1960s. These organisations went under a bewildering variety of titles, but generically speaking, they were farmers' political leagues (*nomin seiji renmei*, or *noseiren*).[275] The primary objective behind their formation was to have specialised organisations working on behalf of the agricultural cooperatives to 'organise their political power to elect Diet members and members in local government who could make real efforts to raise farmers' economic and social status.'[276] Officially, the Nokyo leadership viewed it as inappropriate for local co-ops or federations qua Nokyo organisations to become directly involved in electoral activities for a number of reasons. As laid down in an internal Nokyo report: 'Agricultural cooperative unions are economic organisations and should not be involved in election campaigns. Farmers need to form political organisations to promote their election campaigns.'[277] Other potential difficulties were created by the provisions of Nokyo's organising legislation which set fairly tight boundaries on the scope of Nokyo's political activities and also its status as a mass organisation of farmers, which meant that its members inevitably had differing ideas about politics. This necessitated the separate establishment of groups to spearhead Nokyo's activities relating to elections which members were free to join or not.

The farmers' political leagues thus became political 'front' organisations for the agricultural cooperatives. They operated under the slogan of 'groups for mobilising farmers' political power' (*nomin seiji ryoku kesshu dantai*), which was the catchcry of the National Rural Youth League in the late 1940s, and which could trace its origins back even further to the political activities of the Rural Diet Members' League (Noson Giin Domei) founded in 1937 to fight the anti-industrial cooperative movement in the Imperial Diet.[278] 'Mobilising farmers' political power' was a code-phrase for organising farmers' votes in elections behind favoured candidates.

Many farmers' political leagues had a brief and unnoteworthy history, often linked to a particular issue, election, or regional problem. As noted earlier, a more permanent and substantial set of organisations was established beginning in the late 1950s. Local Nokyo leaders recognised the need for prefecturally-based electoral support groups to operate on a continuous basis and to handle a range of elections, local, prefectural and national. These groups could offer a variety of support and commitment to one or a number of candidates in any constituency.

Although the primary purpose of the *noseiren* was electoral, in reality it was difficult to separate electoral activity from agricultural policy activity because the two were inextricably linked. The *noseiren* often used policy issues to mobilise farmers in rice-roots election campaigns. Tactically speaking, the electoral and agricultural policy functions of the leagues were highly complementary: electing supportive candidates to all levels of political office was viewed as an effective way of getting policies realised in addition to purely pressure group-type activity. The leagues that recommended and supported candidates in local and national elections also lobbied these politicians on agricultural policy and related issues.

The more predominant function of the leagues, however, was electoral rather than policy-related activity because of Zenchu's dominance of *nosei katsudo*. Nevertheless, the *noseiren* encroached on, or at least supplemented the agricultural policy activities of the mainstream agricultural cooperative organisation led by Zenchu. Indeed, when they were first set up, the central and prefectural Nokyo leadership wanted to harness the leagues as part of a more effective strategy of waging successful agricultural policy campaigns. Nokyo executives saw the leagues as providing an organised context for the political mobilisation of rank and file members at the rice roots. In particular the *noseiren* served to present to government the appearance of widespread local farmers' support for Zenchu's demands.

The leagues remained very much regional entities in rural localities, however. While they shared with their parent organisation many common aims in terms of a general recognition of farmers' basic policy demands, agreement on fundamentals was often overlaid with a strong locality consciousness. The spur to action for many of the leagues was the desire to present insights into the needs of farmers in regional areas to government and to their own national leadership. Although the leagues were prepared to participate in agricultural policy movements organised by Zenchu in recognition of the need for unified national action on issues such as the rice price, the MAFF budget, agricultural taxes and opposition to the liberalisation of agricultural trade, they also called for an emphasis in *nosei katsudo* on what they termed 'daily activities' (*nichijo katsudo*), which involved eliciting the feeling and demands of the farmers in the villages about matters impinging on policy.[279] With their political orientation often centring on local issues and grievances, the leagues were in an ideal position to realign the balance in Nokyo's *nosei katsudo* from national to local interests. The strength of localism was often behind the electoral successes of the farmers' leagues in the late 1950s and 1960s.[280]

Indeed, in some respects these groups were anti-centrist (i.e. anti-Zenchu), exemplifying the old local-activist (farmers' youth leagues) versus central-bureaucratic (*nogyokai*) theme of the early Nokyo-associated groups. The same division also endured to some extent in the centre-periphery cleavage within the mainstream agricultural cooperative organisation. Zenchu's policies tended to predominate over the demands of the agricultural cooperatives at the rice roots. It was hoped that the prefectural farmers' political leagues would reorientate the focus of Nokyo's policy activities more towards regional issues and organisations that were more in touch with the farmers and local conditions. Provincial Nokyo leaders were particularly concerned about what they saw as deleterious developments in the central echelons of Nokyo, such as lack of concern about local problems and issues and the idea that Nokyo should operate purely as an economic group. The dissatisfaction of the prefectural executive class with these developments and their desire to ensure the interests of rice-roots farmers within the agricultural cooperative organisation were manifested in league activities in each prefecture.[281] Most of the groups originated in conferences of prefecture-wide agricultural cooperative chairmen who contributed the initial impetus for their establishment and the energy for their continued functioning.

The political attachments of the agricultural cooperatives were also increasingly circumscribed by the growing emphasis amongst central Nokyo leaders on acquiring subsidies from government, which demanded closer ties to the LDP. Another consideration for more radical, Socialist-leaning local leaders was the fact that Nokyo's smallest organisational unit centred on agricultural villages in their entirety, thereby encompassing all farmers, rich and poor, full- and part-time. The comprehensive membership base of Nokyo was construed by the farmers' political league in Ibaraki Prefecture,[282] for example, as a factor undermining the agricultural cooperatives' capacity to formulate constructive political demands particularly on behalf of the poorer class of farmers.[283] As an interest group, Nokyo could at best provide only a weak common measure of the political and economic goals of all farmers.

The inherent shortcomings of the agricultural cooperatives as political and electoral organisations were, therefore, employed as the main rationale for the establishment of the farmers' political leagues in many areas. Their aim was to act as the spearhead of an agrarian political movement (*nomin undo*) that could express farmers' dissatisfaction with government agricultural policy, consolidate and unify the political activities of the agricultural cooperatives at the local level, and act as agencies for the election of Nokyo leaders.

By December 1958, 13 prefectural farmers' leagues were either up and running or in the process of being formed (their names, membership composition, dates of establishment and main objectives are shown in Table 2.2).[284] As Mitsukawa describes it, 1958 was a turning point, the year in which prefectural Nokyo central union leaders shared a sense of crisis about agricultural policy and started to consider establishing political organisations in order to promote agricultural villages and establish more 'positive' agricultural policies. In July 1958 the National Nokyo Executive and Staff Members' League (Zenkoku Nokyo Yakushokuin Renmei) adopted a resolution relating to the mobilisation of farmers' political power and in November, the sixth National Nokyo Convention passed a similar resolution relating to strengthening farmers' political power.[285] In the same month, the Agricultural Policy Promotion Council, a joint grouping of LDP agricultural and forestry Diet members (*norin giin*) and central organisations of agriculture, forestry and fisheries was established.[286] In Mitsukawa's view, these developments suggest that the sense of crisis about agricultural policy was shared by both national- and local-level Nokyo leaders at the time.[287] Moreover, it was considered crucial for both the ruling LDP and agricultural organisations to keep farmers' political activities within the framework of an agricultural policy movement dominated by Nokyo and associated groups, rather than allow them to become radicalised under the umbrella of a farmers' union-sponsored 'farmers' movement' and class struggle.[288] This threat was underlined by the formation of a newly amalgamated national farmers' union organisation, Zennichino in 1958 (see Figure 2.1).[289]

An additional 26 farmers' political leagues were established in other prefectures across the country in 1959. Their avowed objective was the realisation of 'politics for the farmers' (*nomin no tame no seiji*)[290] under the general slogan of 'mobilising farmers' political power'. In 1960, a national umbrella organisation was formed – the National Farmers' Political League (Zenkoku Nomin Seiji Renmei, or Zennoseiren[291]) – and 22 prefectural farmers' political leagues joined it.[292] The platform of the Zennoseiren was as follows: 'guaranteeing freedom of choice of political party and exclusion of domination by a political party; engaging in activities leading to the establishment of policies relating to the farmers and Nokyo such as agricultural policies and rural social policies; undertaking agricultural policy activities in harmony and

Table 2.2 Farmers' political leagues in 1958–59

Title of group[a]	Date of establishment	Main objective	Membership composition
Yamagata Prefecture Nokyo Agricultural Policy Research Association	April 1958	An agricultural policy to establish rural advancement	Private individuals who endorse this aim
Miyagi Prefecture Agricultural Policy Establishment League	September 1958	Establishment of an agricultural policy	Farmers and persons connected to agricultural groups
Iwate Prefecture Rural Youth League	October 1958	Improving the position of farmers and rural democratisation	Private individuals who endorse these aims
Fukushima Prefecture Agricultural Policy Reform League	July 1957	Political activities associated with the establishment of an agricultural policy	Farmers
Fukui Prefecture Rural Construction Political League	October 1958	Political activities in order to improve the position of farmers	Farmers
Ibaraki Prefecture Political League for Promoting Agriculture	December 1958	Improving the political and social position of farmers	Farmers and persons of learning and experience
Gumma Prefecture Agricultural Policy Research Association	April 1955	Establishment of an agricultural policy	Farmers and persons connected to agricultural groups
Shiga Prefecture Political League for the Promotion of Agricultural Policy	October 1958	Improving the position of farmers	Those employed in agriculture
Hyogo Prefecture Agricultural Policy Promotion League	November 1958	Rural advancement	Private individuals who endorse this aim
Shimane Prefecture Agricultural Policy Council	May 1958[b]	Raising farmers' political consciousness	Agricultural groups and private individuals who endorse this aim

Oita Prefecture Agriculture and Forestry Promotion League	February 1959 (scheduled)	Establishment of an agricultural policy	Private individuals
Saga Prefecture Farmers' Political League	1959 (scheduled)	Improving the position of farmers and establishment of an agricultural policy	Private individuals
Kumamoto Prefecture Agriculture, Forestry and Fisheries Political League	November 1958	Establishment of an agricultural policy	Private individuals

Notes:

a The titles of these groups were subsequently to change in some cases (cf. Table 6.5).

b According to another source, this group was formed in April 1958. See Nagase, 'Nosei Kyogikai', p. 53.

Source: Nosei Jyaanarisuto no Kai, 'Teimei Suru Nosei Undo – Nomin Seiji Ryoku Kesshu' ['Lukewarm Agricultural Policy Campaigns – The Whereabouts of the Mobilisation of Farmers' Political Power'], in *Teimei Suru Nosei Undo* [*Lukewarm Agricultural Policy Campaigns*], Kikan Nosei no Ugoki, No. 5, Tokyo, Kyodo Kumiai Kyokai, 20 December 1958, p. 7.

close contact with Nokyo's campaigns; accomplishing the mobilisation of farmers' political power with farmers as the core; and assisting in the creation of a democratic form of politics.'[293]

A dominant concern amongst the leagues at the time was the issue of urbanisation. In one sense the leagues represented the organised expression of a rural populist movement emerging from the 'deep sense of resentment towards urbanization in the villages'.[294] A number of prefectural governors were elected with the backing of the *noseiren* in the expectation that they would slow the pace of urbanisation and ameliorate its pernicious effects on rural communities.[295] It was over this issue and the attempts of the leagues to ensure that rural interests were represented in the new cities, towns and villages created by the local government amalgamations of the 1950s that importance came to be attached to Nokyo's organisational power.[296]

In 1963 the Zennoseiren moved to consolidate its position and increase its organisational strength by amalgamating with the National Farmers' Federation (Zennoren), the organisational remnant of the National Rural Youth League.[297] The new organisation amended its title to National Farmers' General Federation (Zenkoku Nomin Sorenmei, or Zennosoren) in recognition of its broader popular base.[298] It continued to operate thereafter as Nokyo's national political organisation (*Nokyo no seiji soshiki*),[299] headquartered in the Nokyo building in Tokyo and uniting a host of prefectural farmers' leagues under a single organisational umbrella.

In addition to its electoral activities,[300] Zennosoren's objective was to function as the 'lynch pin' (*kaname*) of joint Nokyo agricultural policy struggles with the farmers' unions. One of its central policy concerns was agricultural prices. According to one source, it 'took the initiative in the price war for each agricultural commodity'.[301] It also played an important role in other farmers' campaigns, such as the 'movement to protect land' (*tochi o mamoru undo*), which sought to retain the farmers' use of common lands with demands for compensation when this was disallowed.[302] Another campaign opposed the purchase of agricultural land by developers who turned it into housing estates and factory land.[303] Zennosoren also became involved in opposition to agricultural trade liberalisation and the application of residential taxes to urban agricultural land.[304]

After setting the initial electoral pace in the late 1950s and early 1960s, the organisational impetus of the *noseiren* began to wane somewhat in the 1970s and 1980s. Much of the force evaporated from the concept of 'mobilising the farmers' political power', which had inspired the activities of the farmers' political leagues in the late 1950s and 1960s. It became more of a traditional catch-phrase tying together a rather loosely knit bunch of groups than a meaningful call to action. By 1972, only 15 prefectural farmers' political leagues constituted the formal members of the Zennosoren: those from Hokkaido, Aomori, Miyagi, Fukushima, Ibaraki, Kanagawa, Nagano, Fukui, Mie, Shiga, Shimane, Fukuoka, Kumamoto, Miyazaki and Kagoshima. Farmers' political leagues in Akita, Gumma, Chiba, Yamanashi,

Tottori, Saga and Oita cooperated with Zennosoren in its activities as 'friendly' groups.[305]

The structural forms of the prefecturally based groups from which Zennosoren was composed, were fairly diverse. The more highly activist continued to be manned by core groups of politically motivated prefectural Nokyo leaders with a farmer membership that usually formally incorporated local co-op members throughout the prefecture. Often their membership was only nominal, however. Not all farmer members of the co-ops were necessarily actively involved in the leagues even though they might have been on the membership books.[306] The majority of Zennosoren-affiliated farmers' political leagues were composed of representatives of local cooperatives. Amongst the latter, conference- or council-type bodies (*kyogikai*) were common.[307]

Although Zennosoren continued to function as the only nationally organised political grouping attached to the agricultural cooperatives, at no stage did it assume the role of a centralised national coordinator or director of the electoral activities of the agricultural cooperatives or the prefectural *noseiren*.[308] Zennosoren was essentially a formal umbrella structure with a small national staff, embracing most but not necessarily all the prefectural farmers' political leagues whose electoral activities were concentrated at local, prefectural and constituency level and directed by co-op leaders at those levels. The *noseiren* remained very much locality-oriented bodies and rather more radical and politically independent than the mainstream Nokyo organisation, particularly its central executive leadership. These rice-roots farmers' groups could afford to be more politically independent than Nokyo because they were less concerned with striking a *modus vivendi* with the MAFF and the ruling party. Their central concern was to advance farmers' interests via supportive candidates irrespective of party. The central leadership of Nokyo, on the other hand, was constrained by having to cultivate and preserve cooperative relationships with agricultural administrators in the implementation of policy. They adjusted their demands more to what was 'reasonable' in the light of existing government measures, rather than simply giving free expression to the political demands of their membership. The central leadership was also acutely conscious of the need to forge close links with the government party as the influential arbiter of agricultural policy and the agricultural budget. This pragmatic approach of the centre was often at the bottom of differences between the mainstream Nokyo organisation and the farmers' political leagues over which candidates to support in elections.

In 1989 the Zennosoren underwent a metamorphosis to become the National Council of Farmers' Agricultural Policy Campaign Organisations, or National Council[309] (Zenkoku Nogyosha Nosei Undo Soshiki Kyogikai, or Zenkoku Noseikyo). This organisation was recreated from the ashes of Zennosoren as a Zenchu-sponsored initiative to revamp and revitalise farmers' policy campaigns, particularly in the light of intensifying external pressures for rice market access during the UR. The change of title signified a desire on the part of national Nokyo leaders to breathe new life into the farmers' political leagues nationwide. Impetus for the formation of the National Council came from the top – the Zenchu Board of Directors – as early as 1986. It recognised the need to revamp farmers' agricultural policy campaign organisations.

With an initial membership of 23 prefectural farmers' leagues,[310] the Zenkoku Noseikyo was officially established for the purpose of 'mobilising the political power of farmers' and for improving the rural and farm household economy.[311] It pledged to cooperate with Nokyo campaigns. As the document outlining its organisational rationale stated:

> in order to strive for the improvement in the social and economic position of farmers and the advancement of agriculture in a severe situation, it has become necessary to cultivate and consolidate nationally an agricultural policy campaign organisation of farmers which has neither too close nor too distant relations with Nokyo, which can function in parallel to Nokyo and which can complement the agricultural policy movement of the federated Nokyo organisation. There are already agricultural policy campaign organisations in many prefectures which are based on this aim, but they have not led to a mobilisation of power nationwide. Taking the Nokyo campaigns as a base, farmers will mobilise nationally, and, taking the opportunity of policy decisions such as the elections and the Diet, the National Council will exercise regular political influence in order to resolve agricultural policy issues.[312]

Zenkoku Noseikyo is a more activist, coordinating body than its predecessor. Its main objective is to sustain the momentum of Nokyo's electoral support activities and to spearhead invigorated agricultural policy activities. After its establishment on 15 June 1989, the National Council joined in the climax of the 1989 producer rice price campaign, holding a number of consultations and discussions amongst prefectural league executives as well as a national assembly of representatives (approximately 250 people from member organisations). At the same time, it made contact with Zenchu's Central Headquarters for Paddy Field Agriculture Establishment (concerned with rice acreage reduction)[313] and issued a request demanding five items: support for the existing producer rice price; opposition to the new method of calculating it; an appraisal of the role that paddy fields played in national land management; establishment of a future outlook for rice farming; and prevention of rice market opening. About 30 people from the national assembly of prefectural representatives as well as national executives undertook 'demand activities' to members of the RPAC including the Zenchu Chairman who sat on the advisory council. In each of the prefectures, the prefectural leagues engaged in request activities to Diet members from their local areas.[314] The National Council and its prefectural *noseiren* also immediately organised a list of recommended candidates in the 1989 Upper House (UH) elections.

The National Council continues to function as Nokyo's official national political arm, mobilising at election time and negotiating with government on key policy issues of primary interest to the Nokyo membership.[315] It is housed in the Nokyo Building in Tokyo and has very close links with Zenchu. Its Secretary-General is a Zenchu Managing Director and its Vice-Chairman is a Managing Director of Norinchukin. Prefectural branches, or farmers' political leagues (*noseiren*) now operate in most Japanese prefectures.[316] The decade since the creation of the National Council has seen more and more prefectural farmers' leagues affiliate with the group, plus the creation of new farmers' agricultural policy campaign organisations in some prefectures.[317] In May 1995, for example, the Gifu Prefecture Nokyo organisation launched a prefectural Farmers' Agricultural Policy Campaign Organisational Council for the stated purpose of 'mobilising the political power of farmers by unifying farmers' consciousness', and, liaising with Nokyo campaigns, achieving improvement in the rural and farm household economy and establishing an agricultural policy with a future outlook.[318]

The organisational structure of the *noseiren* forms a hierarchy of groups either in three or four layers with the prefectural body at the top. Each has a sub-set of federated branches (*rengo shibu*) consisting of sub-branches and local chapters in cities, towns and villages, which generally parallel the main-stream Nokyo organisation.[319] The prefectural groups collect the requests of lower-level units in order to reflect the demands of farmers in politics. Membership of the *noseiren* differs from prefecture to prefecture. In some cases, all the Nokyo members join; in others, only executives of Nokyo branches join.[320] Most groups fall somewhere between these two extremes. The new Gifu Agricultural Policy Council, for example, takes 'as its core, a system of private members centring on Nokyo executive and staff members'.[321] All these *noseiren* are primarily vehicles for the political and electoral mobilisation of farmers by Nokyo leaders and thus form integral elements of Nokyo's power structure as both an interest group and as an electoral support organisation.

The major activities of the prefectural *noseiren* are transmitting agricultural policy demands to Diet members, particularly those politicians who have received *noseiren* recommendation in elections, as well as to other legitimate policy targets;[322] publicity and informational activities relating to agriculture and rural development (including the publication of bulletins and news-papers) for distribution to members; activities that promote understanding of agriculture and rural areas amongst the public in general; and electoral activities of various kinds. As far as the first three are concerned, they overlap with those of the prefectural central unions and are, therefore, conducted on a cooperative basis. In short, the *noseiren* coordinate with the mainstream Nokyo organisation on policy-related matters, but retain some degree of independence when it comes to electoral backup.[323]

Zenkoku Noseikyo and the prefectural *noseiren* also maintain close liaison with each other. The National Council sponsors frequent meetings of prefectural *noseiren* leaders and provides overall organisational direction, not only on internal matters relating to the running of the groups, but also on agricultural policy matters targeted in Nokyo campaigns. In this way, the National Council provides active leadership for the prefectural leagues that are affiliated with it. In the electoral sphere, Zenkoku Noseikyo conducts public relations activities and coordinates prefectural branches which are responsible for collecting votes. The latter organise meetings and seminars to introduce candidates recommended by Nokyo to agricultural voters.[324] Guidance and coordination by the National Council does not extend to a system of centralised control, however. In contrast to the mainstream agricultural cooperative organisation, power is very much decentralised to the prefectural farmers' political leagues and their sub-units.

Farmers' commodity groups

It is often said that agricultural groups in Japan are generally devoted to rice and are not very enthusiastic about other products.[325] This is a consequence of several factors including the dominance of rice farming and rice producers within Japan's overall agricultural production profile and partly associated with this, Nokyo's overwhelming concern with rice-related interests.[326] Nevertheless, farmers who specialise in the production of particular commodities have formed organisations independently of the agricultural cooperatives around more specialised, non-rice interests. Some of these are nationwide organisations; many are simply local groups in specific areas where certain types of commodities are produced.

Dairy farmers have been a particularly well mobilised group politically and are known to have 'very strong unity of spirit'.[327] The largest and most prominent of the commodity groups is the Dairy Farmers' Political Federation of Japan (Nihon Rakuno Seiji Renmei, or Rakuseiren), a specialist political organisation representing the interests of dairy farmers. It was established in February 1955, but it became better known in the early 1960s when local farmers organised themselves around their specialist dairy cooperatives to press for higher prices for raw milk for processing. The dairy cooperatives held general meetings of farmers and decided to organise demonstrations. The milk price campaign by dairy farmers spread across a number of prefectures, and thence to the whole of Japan.[328] The federation coordinated this movement, particularly as the national specialist organisation of dairy cooperatives (Zenrakuren) was mainly a commercial, dairy processing organisation. The federation embodied a recognition of the need to consolidate the diversified demands of different types of dairy farmers and to establish a permanent organisation to coordinate the dairy farmers' movement. The federation assumed the role of political organisation for the specialist dairy cooperatives (*rakuno nokyo*).

In 1995, 32,300 dairy farmers, or 73 per cent of the total, were members of Rakuseiren.[329] According to official documents of the organisation, its avowed purpose is 'to support and bolster dairy farmers by resolving political problems to raise their living standards and social status along with sound development of the dairy industry'.[330] Membership is voluntary but has slumped dramatically in recent years because of the precipitous fall in the number of dairy farmers – from 253,850 when the organisation was founded in 1955, to the current level.[331] The organisation does not support any specific political party. Local branches (dairy farmers' political leagues, or *rakuno seiji renmei*) are located all over Japan, although in areas where rice growing is the dominant farming industry, membership rates tend to be lower.

According to Rakuseiren executives, farmers join the organisation because it works to reflect their voice in government policies. Another important consideration is the view amongst dairy farmers that their interests run the risk of being neglected by the *sogo nokyo* and therefore by the mainstream Nokyo organisation as a whole, because of its overwhelming emphasis on the interests of rice farmers. As explained by federation officials, Zenchu has always been biased in favour of rice producers, and so the federation found it necessary to submit proposals and demands to the government separately from Zenchu. As the number of dairy farmers was small, it was necessary to have an organisation that protected and represented their interests exclusively. For the same reason the federation conducted its political activities independently of the mainstream agricultural cooperative organisation.[332]

Dairy farmers in practice can belong to the *rakuno seiji renmei*, the *senmon rakuno nokyo* and the *sogo nokyo*, without any real conflict of interest.[333] Federation executives do not consider their grouping as a rival to Nokyo in any way, although when Nokyo mainstream economic federations are strong in some prefectures (such as the Hokkaido Prefecture Economic Federation, or Hokuren), they tend to overshadow the federation as the voice of dairy farmers in those districts. As far as federation executives are concerned, however, their organisation shares with Nokyo the task of looking after dairy farmers' interests at the policy level despite the independent operations of the two groupings.

The federation is funded by membership levies on dairy farmers, currently set at ¥500 per head of dairy cattle and ¥1.60 per 100 kg sold.[334] Representatives are dispatched from the central organisation to the prefectural branches to listen to local dairy farmers' demands. These are subsequently reflected in the policy resolutions and activities of the federation, which centre around public campaigns of various sorts (including marches, demonstrations and conventions), negotiation with MAFF officials, the MAFF Minister and LDP Diet members, attendance at LDP agricultural committees, and providing electoral backup for politicians. According to federation documents, several laws and amendments have passed the Diet backed up by its campaigns in cooperation with the National Dairy Farmers' Association (Zenkoku Rakuno Kyokai, or Zenraku),[335] Zenrakuren, the Central Dairy Council,[336] the Japan Holstein Registration Association (Nihon Horustain Toroku Kyokai)[337] and other farm organisations. The legislation has included the introduction of the deficiency payment scheme for producers of raw milk for processing. An important policy focus each year has been the MAFF Minister's decisions on the guaranteed price for manufacturing milk and the quota amount on which this guaranteed price would be applied, both settled in March each year. The federation is also concerned with lowering feed costs as well as increasing the price for drinking milk.[338] Other policy interests include budgetary matters relating to dairy farming and agricultural trade issues. The federation sent two delegations to Geneva during the UR negotiations to oppose tariffication of dairy products.[339]

An important issue in discussions with MAFF officials since the mid-1990s has been the subject of lowering the production costs of dairy farming in order that support prices could be reduced.[340] This has involved the MAFF's setting targets for the cost of production for dairy products in 2005, and providing guidance for dairy farmers to meet these targets. The most important issue for the federation in this process has been the issue of maintaining dairy farmers' incomes at a level equivalent to farmers in other agricultural sectors. The federation also engages in electoral support activities for candidates from dairy farming districts. It claims that 85 per cent of its candidates are successful, thus increasing the political power of the federation.[341]

The other major producers' associations at national level include the National Central Union of Tobacco Cultivation Associations (Zenkoku Tabako Kosaku Kumiai Chuokai),[342] the National Tobacco Cultivators' Political League (Zenkoku Tabako Kosakusha Seiji Renmei), the Leaf Tobacco Cooperative Struggle Council (Hatabako Kyodo Toso Kyogikai) and the National Federation of Tea Production Groups (Zenkoku Chaseisan Dantai Rengokai). The National Central Union of Tobacco Cultivation Associations, like Nokyo, was founded on the basis of a law, the Tobacco Cultivation Association Law (*Tabako Kosaku Kumiaiho*). It is not classed as a statutory agricultural interest group for purposes of this analysis, however, because its supervisory body is the Ministry of Finance (MOF), not the MAFF. Its members include 29 prefectural cultivation central unions and prefectural agricultural cooperative organisations including *kenchu*. Its task is to negotiate the farmers' selling price of tobacco leaves to Japan Tobacco, or Nihon Tabako (now a privatised corporation). Its main income source is from undertaking entrusted enterprises for Nihon Tabako; it receives no funding from the MOF.

Most commodity-based farmers' groups engage in policy-related activities as well as furnishing backup for their chosen candidates in elections. The extent of their political engagement varies, however. The tobacco cultivation associations, for example, conduct national campaigns from time to time around specific issues or elections. Their political arm is the National Tobacco Cultivators' Political League. Other organisations like the fruit associations (*kaju kumiai*) barely organise for political or electoral purposes.[343] On the other hand, other fruit growers' associations such as the Ehime Prefecture Fruit Tree Political League (Ehime-ken Kaju Seiji Renmei) and local fruit growers' associations in Ehime, such as the Nanyo Fruit Tree Comrades' Association (Nanyo Kaju Doshikai) are particularly active in elections.

Other farmers' political leagues

An important specialist interest exists around the land improvement industry. The land improvement political leagues consisting of the National Land Improvement Political League (Zenkoku Tochi Kairyo Seiji Renmei)[344] and the prefectural land improvement political leagues (*ken tochi kairyo seiji renmei*) represent the political arm of the land improvement groups. Although they are formally separate from the land improvement districts and their prefectural and national federations, they are in fact the same organisations reconstituted under a separate title. They have the advantage in that they are not restricted by the laws that define the activities of their parent organisations. The land improvement political leagues involve themselves in all kinds of electoral activity, including vote-gathering and the supply of campaign workers and political funds for their chosen LDP candidates.

The recipients of farmers' pensions are a special kind of agricultural interest group, with a selective interest in this issue. A large national interest group looks after this cause: the National Agricultural Pension Recipients' League, with branches in every prefecture, including Tokyo and Osaka.

Other sundry farmers' groupings include the National Mountain Village Promotion League (Zenkoku Sanson Shinko Renmei), the All-Japan Settlers' League (Zennihon Kaitakusha Renmei, or Kaitakuren), the national and prefectural farm migrant workers' (*dekasegisha*) federations (the national body is called the National Federation of Migrant Farm Workers' Associations, or Zenkoku Dekasegi Kumiai Rengokai) and the Agricultural Land League (Nochi Domei), which incorporates farmers involved in the land improvement districts. These groups unite farmers around specific issues at a policy and electoral level.

The All-Japan Settlers' League, for example, is the political organisation of the specialist settlers' agricultural cooperatives. Its membership consists of regional settlers' leagues (*kaitakusha renmei*) which are concerned with settlers' issues. New settlers were encouraged to start agricultural production by a series of policies aimed at increasing food production in the early post-war period.[345] At the time of their establishment, membership of the settlers' leagues stood at 200,000. The main function of the leagues is to collect the demands of agricultural settlers and relay them to government.[346] These demands have concerned issues such as the rice price, farmers' debt problems, and the establishment of policies for full-time, larger-scale farm households farming reclaimed land, and policies to promote dry-field farming.[347] As farming on reclaimed land often involves livestock – especially beef cattle – Kaitakuren has been described as the 'smallest but in some ways the most vigorous and innovative specialist group interested in beef.'[348] The settlers' leagues have also been classed as farmers' unions.[349]

The National Federation of Migrant Farm Workers' Associations is also close to the farmers' unions and to the JSP in particular. It has been particularly strong in those parts of Japan which supplied migrant farm workers as city labourers, such as Akita. In fact, the history of the organisation of *dekasegi* farmers began with the rally of 10,000 farmers 'To Maintain Food Control and Smash the Kono Plan'[350] in Tokyo in 1962. Kuribayashi Saburo, a JSP member in the Lower House for Akita (2)[351] and former chairman of Nichino's prefectural federation who was charged with mobilising 500 farmers to attend the rally from Akita noticed that many farmers were employed in Tokyo on construction works for the Olympic site. He successfully organised these *dekasegi* workers in Tokyo to attend the rally. Looking back Kuribayashi was recorded as saying: 'I was surprised at the miserable conditions at the construction site. There were farmers who were not getting paid, who were not insured for accidents in the workplace, and if they died at work, no one would be responsible. The conditions in which *dekasegi* farmers were working were totally unregulated. In order to change these conditions, I approached the JSP, Sohyo and the Labour-Farmer Council[352] and tried to organise *dekasegi* farmers'.[353]

In order to improve the conditions for temporary migrant workers, *dekasegisha kumiai* were formed with the help of progressive political elements under JSP auspices in a number of areas where the number of these workers had increased sharply, such as Akita and Yamagata.[354] The objective was to organise a farmers' movement by focusing on their situation as labourers as well as farmers. Activities were mainly concentrated in Akita (2) and Yamagata (2) electoral districts of the Lower House. Of the 35,000 *dekasegi* farmers in Akita, 25,000 of them were concentrated in Akita (2).[355] In 1965, a national meeting of migrant farm workers was held under the auspices of the JSP-attached farmers' union federation (Zennichino).[356] In 1971 the Zenkoku Dekasegi Kumiai Rengokai was established as a national organisation of these workers. It had over 100 local associations and 15,000 members.[357] Akita (2) constituency supported a number of JSP politicians who were executives of the *dekasegi* farmers' organisation over the years. Kuribayashi served as Chairman of the National Federation of Migrant Farm Workers Associations as did his successor.[358]

The farmers' unions revisited: Zennichino

The intense factional disputes amongst the various arms of the farmers' union movement in the early 1950s were largely resolved with firstly, the amalgamation of left-wing farmers' unions into the National Federation of Japan Farmers' Unions (Nihon Nomin Kumiai Zenkoku Rengokai) in September 1957, followed by the formation of a new nationwide grouping of farmers' unions, the All-Japan Farmers' Union (Zennihon Nomin Kumiai, or Zennichino) in 1958.[359] This group amalgamated the newly formed left-wing Nihon Nomin Kumiai Zenkoku Rengokai with the right-wing Nomin Kumiai

Sodomei and Zenno (see Figure 2.1).[360] The formation of Zennichino thus brought the right-wing unions back into the fold and unified the disparate farmers' union groups that had formed in the early 1950s associated with the JSP split and the Socialists' ideological feuds with the Communists. The successful amalgamation of the disparate national farmers' union groupings was attributed to a number of factors including the JCP's self-criticism in 1955 over its policies for farmers, the unification of the JSP in the same year,[361] and the agreement between the JCP and JSP that 'monopoly capital' should be the target of the farmers' union movement.[362] The major impulse for reunification, however, came from the continuing organisational weakness of the farmers' union movement as a whole. At the time of its formation, Zennichino's membership was only 250,000.

At its establishment convention, the new organisation underscored its new-found unity by insisting on the elimination of control by political parties and freedom of party choice at every juncture.[363] In the 1958 elections, Zennichino stuck to this principle by recommending candidates who had previously been affiliated to both the Right and Left Socialists as well as to the JCP. Despite these auspicious beginnings, Zennichino subsequently became almost exclusively aligned with the JSP. Farmers' union groups affiliated to the national organisation functioned mainly as electoral support groups for JSP-affiliated politician-leaders. This was despite Zennichino's retention of a more rigidly ideological Marxist stance on agricultural policy, which held that 'farming villages would never be liberated without overthrowing the power of monopoly capital'. Such a stance conflicted with the JSP's more pragmatic inclination 'to let farmers realise they can obtain benefits under monopoly capital'. The party's agricultural leadership grasped that perpetual antagonism towards the government would not bring about fundamental improvement in the farmers' standard of living, a position that implicitly criticised Zennichino's stance and political methods.[364]

The JCP, however, remained exceedingly critical of Zennichino's conversion into a political appendage of the JSP. It had assumed that Zennichino's formation in 1958 was based on the understanding that members would cooperate on common demands regardless of political views, thus protecting the freedom of members to support the party of their choice. In the JCP's view, Zennichino Central (Chuo) was immediately appropriated as a quasi-party organisation by the JSP. Executives from the JSP constituted a majority in the organisation and they managed it in an anti-democratic, partisan fashion.[365] The JCP accused them of transforming the union's policies in accordance with the JSP's more right-wing line, because they deleted the call for the abolition of the US–Japan Security Treaty (which underlay the government's support for agricultural trade liberalisation and its 'destruction of agriculture' according to the JCP) and instead, just used it as a campaign slogan. Furthermore, because Zennichino had been 'appropriated' by the JSP and local affiliated unions were just support groups for JSP election candidates, Zennichino lost its core as a farmers' organisation and renounced completely its duties and functions as the national centre of farmers' campaigns and the farmers' union movement.[366]

On the agricultural policy front, Zennichino, with the farmers' unions newly united into one body, pursued agricultural policy 'struggles' (*toso*) centring on support prices for rice, silk cocoons, milk and other livestock products, improvement in the agricultural mutual aid system and government assistance for dams and land improvement.[367] Rice price 'struggles' provided a major focus of action especially in the dominant rice-producing areas of Hokuriku and Northern Japan. Zennichino was also active in the 'struggle' to maintain the FC system. As a result, the farmers' unions were galvanised into a more cohesive force for the first time since the days of land reform.

During the 1960s, however, membership of Zennichino continued to diminish to the point where even the strongest prefectural organisations had less than 500 members, while in the weaker prefectures, membership was less than one-third this number.[368] Membership weakness may have been behind the combined activities of farmers' unions across several prefectures. Sponsored by Zennichino these were called 'cooperative struggle councils' (*kyoso kaigi*), and their specific focus was the producer rice price issue. One of these organised farmers' unions across 10 prefectures.[369]

In addition to finding common cause with each other, the farmers' unions sometimes combined their activities with other farmers' organisations of a more progressive orientation. In the late 1970s, four farmers' organisations (Zennichino, Zenno, Zennosoren and Zenkoku Dekasegiren) began cooperating with each other on the producer rice price issue by forming a Farmers' Combined Struggle Council (Nomin no Kyoso Kaigi).[370] Once again, such cooperation was symptomatic of organisational weakness rather than strength.

Initially cooperation also extended to the agricultural cooperatives, with Zennichino and Nokyo conducting joint producer rice price campaigns. In general, however, the farmers' unions were prepared to countenance much more disruptive mass action on producer rice price issues than the agricultural cooperatives. In the 1950s, Nokyo tended to confine its rice price campaigns to lobbying administrators and politicians, and presenting petitions.

It was over the issue of campaign tactics, price demand levels and other differences that the relationship between Nokyo and the farmers' unions underwent marked deterioration from the late 1950s onwards.[371] In 1958, Zennichino pursued radical campaign measures and, in 1959, it adopted a different method of calculating the producer rice price from Nokyo.[372] The result was that Nokyo decided to conduct its producer rice price campaign independently of Zennichino for the first time in 1959.[373] Likewise, Zennichino organised general assemblies of farmers separately from the agricultural cooperatives. This development heralded the parting of the ways between Zennichino-led farmers' movements and Nokyo-led agricultural policy campaigns.[374] From then on, Nokyo organised its own producer rice price campaign, pursuing its own mass-based strategies such as rallies and demonstrations in Tokyo,[375] which had the effect of channelling the demands and energies of farmers through the agricultural cooperative system. In this way, Nokyo's agricultural policy campaigns stifled the development of the more radical farmers' unions campaigns,[376] although in some local areas the farmers' unions were strong enough to dominate farmers' and agricultural cooperatives' producer rice price campaigns.[377]

The division between the two forces was also promoted by the integration of the conservative parties. Nokyo became increasingly dependent on the LDP after the integration of the two major conservative parties in 1955, because it was harder to use conflicts between the two parties to extract the necessary political leverage to achieve producer rice price increases. Nokyo started to approach LDP headquarters' officials and Diet members directly during its campaigns. On the other hand, Zennichino sent its members and representatives directly to MAF offices and to the RPAC venue, eschewing manoeuvres behind the scenes.[378]

In another development, Zennichino, in association with the General Council of Japanese Trade Unions, successfully launched more than 20 so-called Labour-Farmer Councils (Rono Kaigi) in various prefectures by 1961, although at the time, less than 1 per cent of farmers were actually members of the farmers' unions.[379] These bodies were designed to enlist the support of the labour union movement in election campaigns to win farmers' votes and to provide organisational and funding backup for the farmers' unions. The formation of the labour-farmer councils was in keeping with the Marxist worldview that saw small-landholders as exploited by capital and as essentially workers rather than landowners.

On the labour side, the core of the Labour-Farmer Councils was the labour union of MAFF employees (Zennorin Rodo Kumiai, or Zennorin), which shared a common interest with farmers in support of agriculture and which was affiliated to Sohyo. Zennorin's backing for the Rono Kaigi lay in its opposition to the draft Agricultural Basic Law of 1960–61, which it saw as a threat to farmers and therefore to agricultural bureaucrats. It interpreted the ABL as premised on the notion of a cheap agricultural policy (i.e. less support and subsidies to agriculture) and as accepting the principle of farm trade liberalisation. This would mean protecting and developing only those farmers who were able to compete internationally. The end result would be a mass exodus of farmers from the land which would threaten the basis of employment in the MAFF. Thus, the ABL was an issue not only for farmers but also for the labour force in the agricultural bureaucracy.[380]

On a more general level, the JSP and Zennichino called for farmers and workers to forge alliances in opposing government agricultural policy, but these alliances never materialised as a real political force.[381] Labour-farmer cooperation in elections and in relation to various agricultural policy issues occurred from time to time but never became regularised.[382] In some cases labour unions provided organised support for struggles to increase the rate of subsidies for land improvement or to achieve higher support prices.[383] In

1961, a Central Labour-Farmer Council was formed and it held a 'General Uprising Convention' which made various requests to the MAF Minister as well as to Zenchu.[384] In the early 1970s a Cooperative Struggle Council to Protect the Food Control System (Shokkan Seido o Mamoru Kyoso Kaigi) sponsored by Zennichino and embracing consumer groups and labour unions (Sohyo, Zennorin and the National Nokyo Labour Union Federation[385]) mounted a 'combined struggle' to maintain the FC system.[386]

The JSP–DSP split in 1960 saw another schism form in the briefly united Zennichino with the formation of the DSP-affiliated farmers' union organisation, the National Farmers' League (Zenkoku Nomin Domei, or Zenno).[387] From the time the DSP was established, Zenno set about creating prefectural federations of farmers' unions. Membership of these groups amongst farmers was based essentially on party support factors and on ideological motivation. Although membership in the early 1970s was officially 100,000 (in 18 prefectures), only a few branches such as those in Akita, Tochigi and Fukuoka, were really active.[388] They mobilised around rice price issues and other agricultural policy issues such as agricultural taxes and land problems in 'cooperative struggles' with Zennosoren, the *kaitakusha renmei* and other agricultural policy groups.[389]

On the whole, however, Zenno's role as a farmers' interest group remained largely underdeveloped. It put its energies into electoral activities, nominating its own candidates for seats in the Diet as well as prefectural assemblies and Upper and Lower House elections. Prefectural and local farmers' union branches doubled as party branches and personal support groups for politicians in rural areas. It ended up a top-heavy organisation: leadership of Zenno was dominated by DSP Diet politicians, while its prefectural leagues were little more than groups of local assembly politicians. Although it put some effort into taking up issues of concern to farmers, it had difficulty in expanding its membership and thus remained weak at the rice-roots level.[390] Zenno functioned in much the same fashion as the JSP-attached Zennichino – as a parliamentary appendage of the DSP in the countryside. Furthermore, by the 1980s, both Zenno and the DSP's electoral prospects had dwindled in rural areas.

Zennichino's prospects were not markedly different. Membership of the farmers' unions affiliated to Zennichino fell to extremely low levels by the late 1980s, while levels of organisational mobilisation also diminished dramatically. For example, in Fukushima Prefecture there were only 2,800 members in farmers' unions federated to the national body. According to the JCP, even JSP-affiliated executives of Zennichino expressed the view that 'Zennichino is no good . . . . If we continue to keep company with it, we ourselves could be finished.'[391] It was described as 'utterly weak' (*mattaku yowai*) by the secretary to a Nokyo-sponsored Diet members' organisation.[392] Zennichino also suffered from the dissolution of Sohyo in the late 1980s because it substantially relied on Sohyo's Labour-Farmer Council in terms of money and campaign backup.[393]

The JCP's farmers' union organisations

In the 1980s, the JCP decided to sponsor its own farmers' union organisation because of what it saw as the fundamental shortcomings of Zennichino: the fact that Zennichino Central (the national headquarters in Tokyo) had become the 'private property' (*shibutsuka*) of the JSP,[394] had abandoned its role as the national centre of the farmers' movement and was an organisation that ran counter to farmers' interests. The JCP saw a need to establish another rice-roots group of farmers which would be 'independent' of party. In 1984, it organised a 'Roundtable Conference to Consider a National Centre of a Farmers' Movement' (Nomin Undo no Zenkoku Sentaa o Kangaeru Kondankai, or Nomin Undo Zenkokukon). This body aimed to establish itself as a national centre of farmers with five basic objectives: voluntary development of Japanese agriculture and stability of farm management; farmers' solidarity based on demands and national unified action to pursue these demands; independence from political parties; respect for the voluntary nature of member organisations; and solidarity with all classes of people.

The JCP had ambitions for this organisation to become a nationwide body of farmers, characterising it as 'the only national centre in reality'.[395] What the JCP had in mind was, firstly, to use the organisation to align the interests of farmers with workers and consumers in opposing agricultural trade liberalisation and, secondly, to capitalise on farmers' disaffection with the LDP and Nokyo to organise a rice-roots organisation that could engage in 'joint struggles' with trade union and consumer organisations. This strategy was described as mobilising 'force in depth', by which the JCP meant organising a mass movement of farmers in the villages. The party's basic objective was to carve out a separate niche for the group, encroaching on JSP ground and trying to gain a foothold in the countryside. It hoped to establish federations in all prefectures with farmer members of at least 1000 each,[396] pointing out that there had never been a national centre with strong subsidiary organisations in all prefectures in the history of Japan's *nomin undo*. The party was aiming for a total membership of around 50,000,[397] and in the late 1980s, intensified efforts to strengthen and expand the organisation.[398] By 1988, the group had reportedly brought together more than 30,000 farmers in 45 prefectures.[399]

The public activities of the Nomin Undo Zenkokukon, however, were remarkably under-patronised by farmers. The 'National General Rally to Protect the Nation's Food and Health', attracted about 100 farmers from 30 prefectures. To some extent, lack of farmers' support was made up for by representation from 65 other groups such as labour unions, consumer groups and mothers' unions.[400] Following the rally, the Zenkokukon called a National Exchange Assembly of groups, with 43 representatives from 31 non-farmers' groups (including those just listed) attending. The JCP tried to exaggerate the significance of this move by pointing out that the total number of people who were members of these 'cooperative struggle organisations' amounted to more than 2 million people.[401] The meeting was followed up by another 'National General Rally Assembly to Protect the People's Food and Health', in which farmers and workers marched through the streets of Tokyo.[402] A farmers' assembly was also held to protest prospective liberalisation of 12 miscellaneous agricultural products that were under negotiation between Japan and the United States at the time. The JCP criticised Zennichino for doing nothing 'at this important time',[403] and pointed out that Zennichino's links with workers were weakened by the fact that Sohyo and the prefectural labour councils had been dissolved.[404]

In January 1989, the JCP held an establishment convention for a national organisation of farmers, the People's Farming Union (Nominren), the realisation of the Zenkokukon's primary objective. The party was endeavouring to seize the moment by exploiting farmers' discontent with the series of decisions to liberalise farm imports in 1988. The agenda of the Nominren was heavily influenced by workers' unions affiliated to the JCP. A list of joint objectives was drawn up, which included 'smashing' the Japan–US military alliance, protecting the lives and livelihood of the nation from LDP politics which served the interests of large enterprise, preserving democracy and so on.[405] The Nominren remained a peripheral and largely ignored presence in Japanese politics, however, isolated as a JCP-sponsored fringe group and studiously avoided by the vast majority of farmers.

Speaking with one voice?

As the preceding discussion has demonstrated, farmers' organisations in Japan are both numerous and diverse in organisational form and the interests they claim to represent. On the face of it, they display a rather fragmented picture, although this fragmentation does not necessarily mean that pronounced divisions and rivalries characterise their relationships. The representation of agricultural interests is not divided territorially (such as in a federal system like Australia or the United States); nor is it divided by crops or commodities in the sense that different farmers' groups compete with each other for the representation of certain commodity interests. Farmers' organisations representing more specialised interests generally complement the activities of generalist organisations like Nokyo. The agricultural mutual aid groups and land improvement organisations, for example, dominate representations on matters relating to their own separate spheres of activity.

Characteristically, farmers' groups in Japan do not compete for the allegiance of members. Membership of these groups is not mutually exclusive; farmers may easily belong to a range of organisations without any conflict of interest because each entity performs different functions and has a different organisational focus and rationale. Generally speaking, farmers belong to Nokyo first; when they join other groups, it is in addition to their membership of the agricultural cooperatives. This is because Nokyo is fundamentally a business and service organisation for farmers. Farmers need the agricultural cooperatives to go about their daily living and agricultural production activities. Other groups are joined to advance farmers' particular interests in more specialised fields of activity, not to switch organisational allegiance.

Furthermore, all groups share a fundamental underlying purpose: to enhance and defend benefits flowing to farmers. In this sense, a transcendental consensus exists amongst the various organisations in favour of the basic objective of government assistance to farmers. Although their foci of policy interest might vary and there may be differences of view or approach on particular issues at particular times, all farmers' groups work towards this overarching goal at the same time as seeking their particular slice of the agricultural support pie. For this reason, Japanese farmers' organisations have a remarkable record of unity.[406] They speak the same general message, even if they do not speak with the same voice or on the same matters. When different groups engage in action alongside others, it is generally to form a chorus, rather than to compete for benefits or to advance counterclaims. Certainly they do not engage in zero sum competition for benefits, where a win for one group equals a loss for another. The standard image of competitive pluralism simply does not apply to the Japanese farming sector.[407] Many farmers' organisations press their claims to government without any sense of competition and often without even encountering each other when they engage in political action.[408]

Some issues like the producer rice price, deregulation of the FC system and agricultural trade liberalisation have united a phalanx of farmers' organisations in concerted action.[409] In 1971, for example, six agricultural groups – Zennichino, Zennosoren, Zenkoku Nomin Domei, Zennihon Kaitakusha Renmei, the National Liaison Council to Protect the Food Control System (Shokkan Seido o Mamoru Zenkoku Renraku Kaigi)[410] and the Central Labour–Farmer Council (Chuo Rono Kaigi) – adopted a combined stance in the fight for the producer rice price. At the RPAC, the four organisations representing rice producers – Zenchu, Zenhanren, Zenkoku Nogyo Kaigisho and Zennichino – boycotted the deliberations, criticising the tentative price presented by the government. As a result, the council could not draft its report.[411]

This particular campaign, although evoking more extreme action from farmers' groups, highlighted the concerted action in which farmers' organisations sometimes engaged on major issues of agricultural policy. Reinforcement of farmers' demands by Zennichino was particularly useful for Nokyo in administrative councils such as the RPAC. The actions of Zennichino underscored Nokyo's own demands. In fact, the extreme nature of Zennichino's demands consistently served to make Nokyo's requests look reasonable.[412] The political objective behind Zennichino's inflated demands was to make the actual increases granted by the government appear hopelessly inadequate and thus raise the general level of dissatisfaction amongst the LDP's farm supporters. Zennichino's more exaggerated claims and strategies were reflected in the emotive and extreme nature of the terminology and tactics it used in presenting its demands. As noted earlier, it described the rice price campaign as a 'rice price battle' (*beika toso*), and the campaign to achieve its demands as a 'national uprising'. Its mass activities tended to be more unruly and undisciplined than those hosted by Nokyo, which advanced more realistic and achievable goals in its producer rice price campaigns. From time to time, Zennichino criticised Nokyo for agreeing to inadequate rice price rises and for 'capitulating' to government-proposed rice production adjustment plans and reforms of the FC system, in an effort to strengthen its reputation as an advocate of the farmers at Nokyo's expense. In this limited sense, it represented a rival group, although in a way that tended to under-line Nokyo's demands rather than conflicting with them. Furthermore, Zennichino's organisational weakness precluded any serious threat to Nokyo's dominance on rice issues.

The National Chamber of Agriculture also regularly weighed in on the producer rice price issue as well as a range of other policy questions connected to its various quasi-governmental duties, the agricultural budget and agri-cultural trade liberalisation. It was represented on the RPAC and liaised with Zenchu in the formulation of producer rice price demands. In some years, the Nokyo 'demand' price for rice was presented jointly with the NCA demand. The alignment of these two organisations generally had a mutually reinforcing effect, although Nokyo was clearly the superior entity as a farmers' interest group.

On only a limited range of issues did their differing organisational basis produce divergent perspectives. As already noted, the designated interest group functions of Zenchu and the NCA overlap, but Nokyo has the added dimension of being an economic organisation with profit-making interests relating to agricultural business.[413] The NCA conducts no economic activities at all and is, therefore, quite neutral on business matters relating to the farm economy. The result is a major difference in their structural policies. Because Nokyo undertakes economic activities, officially both full- and part-time farm households are equally important customers, and since practically all house-holds are customers of Nokyo, it cannot be openly biased against full-time farmers.[414] The NCA, on the other hand, is neutral on this issue, so it can push for structural policies aiming for the development of farm households that can be self-supporting with income only from agricultural production. The NCA thus discriminates against part-time farm households in its advocacy of a policy emphasising the need to create competitive farmers and encourage the development of full-time, economically efficient agricultural producers. So while Zenchu and the NCA have a similar view when it comes to the importance of maintaining agriculture, in terms of structural policies they do not necessarily see eye to eye.[415]

This fundamentally divergent perspective was apparent in the different responses of Nokyo and the NCA towards the prospective passage of the 1961 ABL. The NCA had a very positive attitude towards the legislation, while Nokyo was rather negative.[416] Indeed, the enactment of the law was demanded primarily by the NCA, which was pressing for legislation that would underwrite the income parity principle between farmers and workers in other industries. Zenchu's position, on the other hand, was more ambivalent. It doubted whether the parity objective could be achieved with one law, and it was concerned that some sections of the law could lead to further government restrictions and intervention. Moreover, it was anxious that it would lose its main customers if agricultural structural adjustment policies based on the law encouraged small farmers to abandon agriculture and created a number of commercial and professional farm households. Nokyo's businesses were designed to serve small-scale owner-farmers, who could not possibly manage their production without support from the agricultural cooperatives. Nokyo reasoned that larger-scale commercial and professional farmers could establish themselves as production corporations (*hojin*) and might distance themselves from Nokyo in order to deal directly with suppliers of agricultural producer goods.[417] The reduction in loyal members would undermine not only Nokyo's business power but also its political power.[418]

Despite these differing perspectives, Nokyo and the other statutory agricultural interest groups including the NCA (and also, of course, the groups that are organisational off-shoots of Nokyo) maintain many kinds of formal and informal ties with each other. In practice, they form a cross-cutting network of groupings, characterised by overlapping functions, membership, finance and leadership roles. This amounts to a legally-imposed interlocking nexus of membership, organisational and consultative links with each other and with government. The Land Improvement Law, for example, provides for consultation between the *tochi kairyoku* and the *nogyo iinkai* on agricultural land matters. Nokyo is a group member of all the other agricultural statutory interest groups, while the agricultural mutual aid associations and their federations and the land improvement districts and their federations can be associate members of the Nokyo federations. Within this enlarged set of organisations, Nokyo predominates. As Saeki puts it, the *sogo nokyo* system is in the centre of all these groups and effectively coordinates these other agricultural organisations.[419] At the same time, it is almost impossible for Nokyo alone to pursue the promotion of local agriculture. It has to coordinate its agriculture-related activities with other semi-administrative groups.[420]

Nokyo thus stands head and shoulders above all other farmers' organisations as the dominant organisation representing agricultural interests, although clearly, it does not enjoy a monopoly of the right to speak on the farmers' behalf.[421] Nokyo's leading role as the dominant interest group in the agricultural sector crystallises around the policy leadership of Zenchu. A survey of agricultural pressure groups in the 1980s revealed that only Zenchu operated as an active summit group in the agricultural sector. Zenchu seemed to hold the position of political headquarters for agricultural interests such as budgets, subsidies, price stabilisation, import control as well as agricultural problems in general and production promotion. At the same time, half of the agricultural organisations surveyed did not refer to Zenchu as the peak agricultural interest group, indicating that some farmers' groups operated in the political market without relying on Zenchu as a summit group.[422] So while Zenchu could claim the status of a peak interest group of farmers, this did not mean that all the other farmers' organisations would necessarily be under its sway or coordinate their activities with the agricultural cooperatives.[423]

On matters of policy, organisational priorities and development, co-ordination within groups may also be a problem. Nokyo suffers from a number of internal cleavages, which sometimes make it difficult for a consensus to be reached within the organisation.[424] In terms of their interest group roles, differences also exist amongst farmers' groups on the quality of access they enjoy to government circles. This varies primarily according to their organisational setup. Not all groups have been created equally in the sense that not all have been sponsored by government. Groups established by government under their own organising legislation, whose activities are sanctioned and supervised and to varying degrees subsidised by government (this category includes all the statutory agricultural interest groups), enjoy automatic access to the bureaucracy; those not formally established by government and which remain formally independent of the bureaucracy do not have the same sort of close relationship with the administration. The latter category includes organisations such as the farmers' unions, the individual commodity organisations and the farmers' political leagues.

An ideological divide also separates the farmers' unions from the rest. Zennichino, for example, has been described as the only 'class-based farmers' organisation'[425] (*kaikyuteki nomin soshiki*).[426] Moreover, the farmers' unions, given their status as organisational offshoots of parliamentary socialist parties, are the only groups with an unabashed party allegiance. With one or two exceptions such as the *dekasegi* organisations, other farmers' groups have not been ideology- or party-centred. Most farmers' organisations do not compete for the political loyalty of farmers through membership and are thus spared the fragmenting influence of ideological competition. Except for the farmers' unions, membership does not automatically carry with it a vote for a particular political party. The *noseiren* and Nokyo go out of their way to assert an official position of political neutrality, while the other statutory agricultural interest groups, without asserting any particular ideological position, simply take it for granted that the politicians with whom they form alliances will be members of the ruling party for obvious reasons. This brand of policy pragmatism is quite different from the ideological linkages tying farmers' unions leaders and members to the socialist (and, in some cases, Communist) parties. The absence of fixed party ties in the case of most farmers' organisations is characteristic of many 'functional groups' (*kino dantai*)[427] in Japan, which become politicised when they forge links with candidates and political parties but which avoid becoming partisan (*tohaka*). This is especially the case with respect to groups that are loosely associated with the LDP, like agricultural sector organisations, which are not support groups of the LDP as such, but support groups of individual LDP Diet members.[428]

The partisan divide between the farmers' unions and other farmers' groups has not been equally balanced because of the organisational weakness of the former, in terms of both membership strength and policy influence. Although the revival of the farmers' union movement in 1946 pre-dated the reorganisation of the agricultural cooperative system, its early demise after the completion of land reform considerably reduced its chances of taking the leadership position amongst agricultural groups. Basically the farmers' unions never developed as a national mass organisation of farmers except in the early postwar period, enabling Nokyo (and specifically the central unions) to consolidate their position as the farmers' interest representative organ.[429] Furthermore, the farmers' unions' intimate connections with left-wing parties condemned them to the status of minority players in the countryside.[430] Given the conservative predilections of farmers,[431] the party-attachment and ideological slant of the farmers' unions undermined their potential either to build or sustain a substantial membership in rural areas which, in turn, undermined their credibility as groups representing farmers' interests. Nevertheless, they were not excluded from the political centre altogether, given Parliamentary representation through the farmers' union leadership and their presence on some agricultural advisory councils, such as the RPAC.

When it comes to electoral activity, the agricultural cooperatives, farmers' political leagues, other statutory agricultural interest groups (and their associated political groups, such as the land improvement political leagues), farmers' commodity groups and other sundry farmers' associations also provide varying amounts of organisational and electoral backup for individual farm politicians, including mobilising votes amongst their membership and supplying political funds.[432] The dominant rationale for such electoral activity is that sympathetic politicians will support the cause of farmers and their organisations in the Diet, and if a member of the LDP, in government.[433] Amongst these politicians, current and former group leaders ensure 'direct representation' of organisational interests in national politics.[434]

The issue of which candidate to support in a given constituency, however, is very much an independent decision of the group in question. These organisations do not operate as one on questions of electoral support because, as already noted, the vast majority are formally independent of party and because their electoral support activities have been predominantly geared to individual candidates. The question of party in some cases is an open one; in others it is a foregone conclusion. In practice, most of these farmers' organisations have supported conservative candidates, although from time to time, some have thrown their weight behind progressive candidates (the farmers' political leagues for instance).[435] The result can, on occasions, be electoral rivalry amongst different groups in the same constituencies (even those in the same organisational orbit such as Nokyo).[436] Partisan differences have generally been muted, however.

Institutional interest groups in the agricultural sector

In addition to the statutory agricultural interest groups which can be called farmers' organisations because they have a rice-roots farmer membership, the MAFF has spawned large numbers of so-called 'related groups' (*kankei dantai*) to assist in the multifarious aspects of agricultural administration. These groups are all officially listed in the MAFF Personnel Directory.[437] They consist of several broad sub-categories: public corporations or special legal entities (*tokushu hojin*) – literally special juridical persons; approved corporations – literally government-approved juridical persons (*ninka hojin*); and public interest corporations (*koeki hojin*) – literally juridical persons for public benefit. These organisations can also be grouped collectively under the label of *gaikaku dantai* which translates variously as 'auxiliary organs of government', 'government-affiliated agencies', 'extra-departmental bodies' or 'affiliated associations'. Other Japanese terms such as *gaikaku kikan*[438] and *seifu kankei kikan* which both mean 'government-affiliated organs' are also in common use. From the MAFF's point of view, the existence of these groups is formally justified by their implementation of various agricultural promotion and support programmes.[439]

The MAFF is not unique in its creation and use of *gaikaku dantai* in administrative assistance roles. The Japanese bureaucracy has created an extensive network of literally thousands of semi-public institutions to supplement the administrative functions of the main ministries and agencies.[440] They form a 'vague miasma of so-called semi-governmental organizations which surrounds the great mass of central government'.[441] Their founding impetus is bureaucratic and each has an intimate client relationship with the part of the bureaucracy to which it is attached. This relationship is built around financial, functional and personnel links. Around 5,000 such groups exist in Japan. The top executives of these are predominantly retired government officials ('OBs'), although their subordinate staff ranks are usually filled by career officials.

The extra-ministerial organs form important elements in the network of organisations through which the Japanese government administers various economic and social sectors. Taken in their entirety, the auxiliary organs of government assist in the various processes of regulation, supervision and management of activities within particular sectors and provide various services, assistance and support to different categories of recipients with the help of subsidies and other forms of financial support. They represent the institutionalised expression of the protectionist, regulatory and promotional goals of the Japanese bureaucracy. Sometimes their activities are specified in law.

In essence, the *gaikaku dantai* are non-profit, 'public-purpose institutions', undertaking designated tasks that are formally commissioned by government, operating under varying degrees of control and supervision by their sponsoring ministries and agencies, and subsidised in varying degrees by these administrative organs. The *gaikaku dantai* perform various service functions for their members and other clientele, whilst at the same time implementing government policy.[442] Membership is normally group or corporate, not individual, and categories of membership are specified by the group's bureaucratic sponsors. It often includes an interest group clientele made up of those organisations who are the recipients of the administrative services undertaken by the *gaikaku dantai* and who may also participate in their execution. The *gaikaku dantai* thus incorporate a dual public-private functioning, and, in this respect, they represent the institutional interface between the public and private sectors in Japan.

From an interest group perspective, the *gaikaku dantai* could be said to represent a specialised form of administrative or institutional interest group. A by-product of the administering function of these groups is, in some cases, involvement in representations to government relating to their respective spheres of activity. In so doing, they may come to represent the interests of the client industries, activities, associated organisations and members they help to administer. In performing their various designated tasks, the *gaikaku dantai* also develop vested interests in their own jurisdictional spheres of operation.[443]

The *gaikaku dantai* thus share and complement the interest articulation function of the more orthodox interest groups. Their policy concerns focus on the acquisition of various benefits including specific policies or administrative measures, the maintenance of regulatory controls on activities they administer, and increased funding from government. Subsidies are often the main source of finance for these organisations, which also act as channels for subsidies to their members. Funding is supplied by government through the budget and from other official and semi-official sources for the various functions and projects these groups undertake as well as for the various recipients to whom these groups distribute subsidies on the government's behalf.

The extent to which *gaikaku dantai* operate as institutional interest groups depends on the policy content of their activities and the degree to which they function as subsidy distribution agents and therefore as part of the ruling LDP's patronage networks.[444] Amongst the many functions of the extensive network of semi-public institutions created by the Japanese bureaucracy is the consumption and distribution of government patronage. Patronage delivers benefits to specific sectors or groups of voters, most often in the form of subsidies, grants and other types of financial assistance which can be used as an inducement to support LDP candidates.

A large number of *gaikaku dantai* (almost 700 in 1995) are attached to the MAFF and its various bureaus and agencies. They go by a myriad of labels including corporations, associations, federations, centres, research institutes and so on.[445] The connections they maintain with the ministry are legal, financial, functional and personnel-based. Some organisations are extremely close to government with duties fixed in law, with a high public content in their activities and with funding almost entirely derived from government sources. Others are less so on all counts. Some merely submit an annual report to the ministry and are much more autonomous in their designated field. Most receive some level of funding from government. Another major source of finance is their own membership, which is usually dominated by other agricultural organisations. In some cases membership may extend to individual farmers and cooperative associations of agricultural and food companies, including processors and distributors. Finance may also be generated by the various activities that these organisations undertake.

The MAFF's *gaikaku dantai* undertake extremely diverse semi-official technical, planning, guidance, state-trading, consultancy, informational, research, inspection, promotional and public relations functions in policy areas affecting agriculture. They also administer the payment of various kinds of subsidies to their members and carry out government-assisted insurance, development, price support and price stabilisation schemes. Their active executive personnel are either seconded ministry officials or retired bureaucrats, predominantly from the MAFF.[446] Staff members are recruited as career officials. They belong to the National Agricultural Groups' Labour Union (Zenkoku Nogyo Dantai Rodo Kumiai).

The *gaikaku dantai* attached to the MAFF (as in the case of all ministries) are constituted as different types of legal entities. There is a hierarchy of groups dictated by the balance between their public and private functions, the degree of control the MAFF exerts over their activities and the amount of public funding they receive for their operations. The closer the groups are to government according to these criteria, the more powerful and prestigious they are.

Public corporations, special juridical persons, or special corporations (tokushu hojin)

The highest-ranking *kankei dantai* are the *tokushu hojin*, or special corporations. In practice, the definition of these special corporations is complex, variable and unclear. One 'broad but common definition is a "corporate body, founded by a special act of law, and entrusted with a specific administrative and public role"'.[447] Special corporations are thus statutory organisations set up under their own organising legislation. So many special corporations satisfy this definition, however, that no official tally exists.[448]

A narrower definition specifies 'corporations which are subject to investigation by the Management and Coordination Agency in the event of major structural changes'.[449] A total of 92 organisations satisfy this definition, employing over half a million people and boasting a combined investment capital of no less than ¥200 trillion, 'most, though not quite all, of that money coming from the government'.[450] Their main source of funding is the central government budget (all three accounts).[451] In addition, some receive investment loans from the government's Fiscal Investment Loan Programme (FILP)[452] and some also generate financial resources of their own as a by-product of their operations. In terms of status, financing and functional roles, the special corporations are the closest to the mainstream bureaucracy amongst the *gaikaku dantai*. The *tokushu hojin* are staffed mainly by officials on secondment from the ministries although some also have *amakudari*[453] bureaucrats. They employ whatever superannuated officials are sent to them by the ministries and agencies to which they are attached. The members of their boards of directors are also chosen by the ministries at their annual personnel reshuffles.[454] The special corporations, as public entities, are not permitted in principle to pursue profits, as similar corporatised bodies in Western countries are. When corporations run at a loss, the deficit is picked up by government subsidies.[455]

In 1995, 12 *tokushu hojin* operated in the agricultural sector under MAFF jurisdiction and control. By 1997 this number had been reduced to 10 because of an amalgamation of two public corporations in 1996 and the disestablishment of another in 1997.[456] The following discussion examines in more detail the most prominent and politicised corporations within this group.

The Livestock Industry Promotion Corporation, or LIPC (Chikusan Shinko Jigyodan) was established in December 1961 under the Livestock Products Price Stabilisation Law. It was renamed the Agriculture and Livestock Industries Corporation, or ALIC (Nochikusangyo Shinko Jigyodan) in October 1996 when it amalgamated with the Silk Thread and Sugar Price Stabilisation Corporation (SSPSC), which is discussed below. The new body now has its own organising law, the Agriculture and Livestock Industries Corporation Law (*Nochikusangyo Shinko Jigyodanho*), passed in May 1996, which stipulates details regarding the establishment, objectives and functions of the organisation.

The LIPC was designed to assist in the implementation of the two basic objectives of the Livestock Products Price Stabilisation Law: to achieve price stabilisation for the main livestock products and to raise the necessary funds for the management of dairy farms and others.[457] The LIPC's initial price stabilisation operations involving the purchase and sale of 'designated' products targeted dairy products (butter and skim milk powder) and meat (in this case, pork).[458] After 1961, the LIPC's functions were expanded (its price stabilisation and import operations are summarised in Table 1.1). In May 1962 it took on the task of allocating subsidies for milk supply under the School Lunch Programme. In April 1966 it was charged with the function of paying subsidies to producers of raw milk for processing[459] and conducting the sole importation (state trade) of designated dairy products. In July 1966 it began to import beef and sell it on the domestic market, and in May 1975 it adopted a similar role in relation to domestically-produced beef. In April 1990 it was charged with paying subsidies to producers of beef calves while in April 1995 it began the importation of designated dairy products.[460]

The LIPC's most notorious role concerned its state trade in imported beef. Once it entered the beef import trade, it quickly assumed control over the vast bulk of beef imports.[461] Furthermore, it was required to monitor movements in domestic wholesale prices for livestock products as part of its price stabil-isation operations, thus providing critical input into the decision-making process on beef import quotas. It was consulted by the MAFF in its decisions on quota allocations (announced formally by the MITI, but decided in fact by the MAFF) and it was able to make its own recommendations as to the size of the quotas required to stabilise domestic wholesale prices.

Under the Livestock Products Price Stabilisation Law, another important function of the LIPC was to 'give assistance to projects which would contribute to the promotion of the livestock industry'.[462] This task was taken up in May 1962 and involved subsidising or investing in 'designated assistance projects' designed to enhance the domestic livestock industry.[463] According to the official description:

> Using grants from the Government[464] and profits accruing from trans-actions in imported dairy products and beef, the LIPC gives assistance either through subsidizing or investing in different projects as provided for by the Law Concerning the Price Stabilization of Livestock Products. Designated assistance projects, as specified in an ordinance of the Minister of Agriculture, Forestry and Fisheries, may cover those with such objects as 1) improving livestock farm operations, 2) rationalizing livestock production and distribution, and 3) adjusting the supply-demand balance of livestock products and stabilizing their prices, and other projects aimed at contributing to the promotion of the livestock industry.[465] The basic purpose of each project is carefully reviewed from the standpoint of its importance, urgency and effectiveness, and determined by the Ministry of Agriculture, Forestry and Fisheries. In accordance with the decision, the LIPC provides subsidies or makes investments to help implement the projects. As in the case of Government assistance, these projects are subject to inspection by the Board of Audit after their completion.[466]

LIPC funding thus derived from a mixture of government budgetary allocations and profits accruing from its transactions in imported dairy products (from 1966), from the tariff revenue on the import of designated dairy products (from 1995) and from its beef import operations (between 1966–91 and after April 1991 from the beef tariff).[467] LIPC profits from the trade in imported dairy products, for example, generated some of the funding for the operation of the deficiency payment scheme for raw milk for processing.

In terms of government grants, the LIPC (now ALIC) received over ¥35 billion from the FY 1998 budget for its deficiency payment to producers of raw milk for processing, for its school milk programme, and for emergency policy works for strengthening and promoting dairy farming management as part of the government's UR agricultural agreement countermeasures policy.[468] In the same year, it received over ¥104 billion for managing the government's feeder calf price stabilisation scheme. This money was sourced from revenue generated by the beef import tariff.[469] Apart from these two programmes, however, the bulk of its funding (particularly for subsidies and investment in livestock-related projects) came from the operation of its beef and dairy product import trades.[470]

The Sugar Price Stabilisation Corporation (Toka Antei Jigyodan) was set up in 1965 to support the price of sugar and related products. In 1981 under the Silk and Sugar Price Stabilisation Corporation Law, the Sugar Price Stabilisation Corporation amalgamated with the Japan Silk and Cocoon Corporation (Nihon Sanken Jigyodan). The latter had been established in 1959 to support the price of raw silk and related products and had been reorganised as the Japan Silk Thread Corporation (Nihon Sanshi Jigyodan) in 1966. The amalgamation of the sugar and silk corporations produced the Silk Thread and Sugar Price Stabilisation Corporation (Sanshi Satorui Kakaku Antei Jigyodan), or Santo Kakaku Antei Jigyodan (SSPSC) for short.

The SSPSC operated an import monopoly on raw silk, negotiating annually with foreign countries on raw silk import quotas. As a state trading agency, it bought and stored the commodity and released it onto the domestic market according to demand. Basically it bought low and sold high to domestic textile companies, using the profits to fund its own operating costs. In 1990, the SSPSC gave up the purchase and sale of domestic silk, confining itself to buying imported silk and reselling it at inflated prices because, it maintained, stable prices were important to textile companies and silkworm breeders.[471] The corporation also received 'exceptional subsidies' from the government in order to promote a policy of establishing a stable supply system for young silk worms and promoting high-productivity zones.[472] These amounted to over ¥1 billion in FY 1995[473] dropping to ¥448 million in FY 1998 (received by ALIC).[474]

The other main task of the SSPSC was to protect Japanese sugar producers (sugar beet growers in Hokkaido and sugar cane growers in Okinawa) by purchasing their output at a high price and selling it at a lower price, with the loss made up by buying and selling cheap imported sugar at a considerable profit. In practice, profits on imports did not cover losses on the domestic trade. In FY 1995, the SSPSC received over ¥17 billion for the purchase and resale of domestically produced sugar under Article 39 of the 1981 law.[475] This subsidy fell to just under ¥16 billion in 1998 (paid to ALIC).[476] One report in the early 1990s noted that the cumulative deficit of the SSPSC's sugar price stabilisation operations had reached ¥25.7 billion by the end of FY 1992.[477] ALIC (and previously the SSPSC) also receives government subsidies for the necessary management costs of mounting the sugar price stabilisation operation (just under ¥1.6 billion in FY 1998).[478]

The basic objective of both the LIPC and the SSPSC was to support specific prices through buying and selling (including import operations) and to assist their associated domestic industries, including the provision of subsidies. In this way they acted as agents for the MAFF in promoting and protecting the interests of particular producers – livestock, sugar and silkworm farmers. At the same time, they embodied the interests of other beneficiaries of their services, for example, groups – including other *gaikaku dantai* – eligible to receive subsidies under their 'designated assistance projects' scheme, as well as their own institutional interests in maintaining the scope and scale of their operations.

The tasks of most other public corporations attached to the MAFF are not related to price support for specific commodities. Nevertheless their basic character and functioning are similar to the LIPC and SSPSC (and the new ALIC). They perform designated tasks for which they receive budget subsidies. They may also distribute subsidies to selected beneficiaries and organisations who qualify to receive them. For example, the Farmers' Pension Fund (Nogyosha Nenkin Kikin) was established in 1970 to undertake the purchase and sale of agricultural land from farmers who left farming as well as paying farmers' pensions and making payments to farmers who had abandoned agriculture.[479] In FY 1995, the Fund received just over ¥4 billion to manage the farmers' pension fund, falling to just under ¥3.5 billion in FY 1998.[480] The government subsidises farmers' pensions (some portions at a one-third rate; others at one-half) under Article 64 of the Farmers' Pension Fund Law of 1970. The cost amounted to well over ¥110 billion in FY 1995, and more than ¥82 billion in FY 1998.[481] In addition, the Fund received almost ¥1 billion in FY 1995 and around ¥700 million in FY 1998 for its activities in providing the finance for and buying and selling agricultural land.[482]

Another organisation in this category is the Agriculture, Forestry and Fisheries Finance Corporation (Noringyogyo Kinyu Koko), established in 1953.[483] Its establishment legislation specifies that its main task is to provide long-term, low-interest funds to those engaged in farming, forestry and fishing for the purpose of maintaining and promoting productivity in their industries. This funding is not provided directly to farmers but to other agricultural financial institutions. For example, the Agriculture, Forestry and Fisheries Finance Corporation Law states that the corporation provides funds for projects that Norinchukin and other general financial organisations have difficulty in financing.[484]

The corporation is officially classed as a 'government affiliated agency' for budgetary purposes, with most of its funding allocated through the Government Affiliated Agencies budget, along with 10 other public corporations.[485] Nevertheless, the corporation also receives 'supplementary compensation' subsidies from the main MAFF budget. In FY 1995, this amounted to almost ¥101 billion, while in FY 1998 it was just over ¥96 billion.[486] In addition, it benefits from loan funds provided through the FILP.[487]

The remaining public corporations attached to the MAFF are not so well known, but nevertheless perform a diverse range of functions. The Agricultural Land Development Corporation (Noyochi Seibi Kodan) undertakes 'agricultural land adjustment works'. It was initially set up in 1965 (under a different title) to engage in agricultural land development activities in order to expand food production. By degrees it acquired other functions such as servicing agricultural facilities, farm mechanisation, purchase of livestock, land reclamation, drainage projects and so on.[488] Although the original rationale of the corporation – to expand farm acreage – no longer applies, it reinvented itself by switching from new land development to areas such as 'land readjustment', soil improvement, the construction of roads and sewage networks in rural areas – in other words the maintenance of existing land plus social infrastructure construction.[489] It received well over ¥15 billion in subsidies for this purpose from the MAFF in the FY 1995 budget.[490] Like the Agriculture, Forestry and Fisheries Finance Corporation, it also receives loan funds from the FILP.[491] In 1997, it became an easy target for 'administrative reform' (downsizing the bureaucracy by getting rid of relatively useless government entities) and the decision was taken to abolish it.[492] Nevertheless, it was still listed as a recipient of just under ¥17 billion in subsidies from the MAFF in the FY 1998 budget.[493]

The Agriculture, Forestry and Fishery Groups Staff Members' Mutual Aid Association (Noringyogyo Dantai Shokuin Kyosai Kumiai) is effectively the pension fund of staff members of agriculture, forestry and fishery groups (all the *kankei dantai*). According to Article 62 of the 1958 Agriculture, Forestry and Fishery Groups Staff Members' Mutual Aid Law, every year the government will subsidise one-third of the basic pension payments made by this organisation.[494] The cost to the central government in FY 1998 was just under ¥53 billion, for a total outlay of just over ¥190 billion.[495]

The remaining special corporations attached to the MAFF are the International Cooperation Corporation (Kokusai Kyoryoku Jigyodan), the People's Livelihood Centre (Kokumin Seikatsu Sentaa), the National Association of Regional Horse Racing (Chiho Keiba Zenkoku Kyokai) and three others in the fisheries, forestry and horse racing fields. These are the Forestry Development Corporation (Shinrin Kaihatsu Kodan), the Japan Central Horse Racing Association (Nihon Chuo Keibakai) and the Fisheries' Resources Development Corporation (Suishigen Kaihatsu Kodan).

Only one MAFF privatised special juridical person (*mineika sareta tokushu hojin*) exists – Norinchukin. Its change of legal status from a public corporation to a privatised public corporation occurred in 1986 by means of an amendment to the bank's organising legislation (*Norin Chuo Kinkoho*), although the changes were largely cosmetic.[496] The executive and staff members of Norinchukin continue to be predominantly retired or seconded MAFF and MOF bureaucrats, the bank's president is still chosen from the MAFF, and Norinchukin still operates under strict legal provisions and administrative regulations. Even as a privatised *tokushu hojin*, the extent of government supervision of its operations remains strong and its largely public character has been retained. This makes the legal status of Norinchukin somewhat different from all other agricultural cooperative organisations. It belongs strictly in the category of a public corporation. Nokyo, at the highest level of its finance organisation, is thus an auxiliary organ of government.

Approved corporations, or government-approved juridical persons
(ninka hojin)

The 'approved corporations' are another category of *gaikaku dantai*, not as closely controlled and legally regulated by the bureaucracy, but nevertheless still very much under its administrative supervision. As they have been authorised by government, they can claim quasi-governmental status. The approved corporations are set up according to specified procedures in legislation in order to perform specific administrative functions.

The MAFF has nine such corporations. Most receive full or partial subsidies from government sources to conduct their operations. The most important in the agricultural sector are the Vegetable Supply Stabilisation Fund (Yasai Kyokyu Antei Kikin)[497] and the Agriculture and Fisheries' Industries Cooperative Union Savings Insurance Organisation (Nosuisangyo Kyodo Kumiai Chokin Hoken Kiko). The three national-level organisations of the agricultural cooperatives (Zenchu), the agricultural committee organisation (Zenkoku Nogyo Kaigisho) and the agricultural mutual aid organisation (Nogyo Kyosai Kikin) are also classified as *ninka hojin*.[498] These three statutory agricultural interest groups thus incorporate leadership groups of different legal status, with their national peak organisations operating as quasi-public groups.[499]

The public-private interface at which these statutory organisations function makes their interest group character more difficult to comprehend. At one level, they function as arms of the government with strictly supervised functions; on another, they represent their organisational interests and those of their membership to the government. This may be a mass membership (in the case of Nokyo), or it may be more limited (as in the case of the agricultural committee organisation and land improvement groups). The dual character of these organisations defies the usual differentiation between public and private groups.

Public interest corporations, or juridical persons for public benefit
(koeki hojin)

The third category of *gaikaku dantai* are public service or public interest corporations. In terms of organisational form, they may be incorporated associations (*shadan hojin*),[500] incorporated foundations (*zaidan hojin*)[501] or unions (*kumiai*, or, at the national level, federations of unions, *rengokai*). All are established under the Japanese Civil Code, and thus belong in the generic category of Civil Code Juridical Persons (*Minpo Hojin*). In essence, they are formally private, non-profit and non-commercial enterprises created by government.

In the case of the MAFF, they are established in all cases with the approval of the minister to undertake various semi-administrative roles in the agricultural sector. They serve both private and public policy interests, combining public functions for government with private functions for their members. The majority are 'associations' (*kyokai*, or *kai*) of various sorts. Their executive leaders are usually retired ex-bureaucrats from the MAFF who have 'descended from heaven' (*amakudari*). Their proximity to government tends to depend on the level of position in the ministry previously held by the officials. If prominent retired MAFF officials (such as the former Vice-Minister) descend into executive posts in the group, then the group can be considered as officially close and important to the MAFF.[502] Others choose to place LDP Diet politicians in their top leadership positions (see Table 7.9) in order to help them secure subsidies from the MAFF (see Table 2.3) and other government organs such as the LIPC/ALIC, and to act as brokers on their behalf in the political world. A fundamental exchange relationship underlies this political connection: the ultimate beneficiaries of group services and subsidies (farmers, agricultural cooperatives, other agricultural organisations, food traders and processors, and agricultural construction companies etc.) provide an organised basis for electoral support and the provision of funds.[503]

The *koeki hojin* are structured around ministry bureaus and agencies. Each bureau has its associated *koeki hojin*, viz., the MAFF Minister's Secretariat (Daijin Kanbo) has 11; the Economic Bureau (Keizai Kyoku) has 33; the Statistics and Information Bureau (Tokei Johobu) has three; the Structural Improvement Bureau (Kozo Kaizen Kyoku) has 34; the Agriculture, Sericulture and Horticulture Bureau (Nosan Engei Kyoku) has 96; the Livestock Bureau (Chikusan Kyoku) has 111; the Food Distribution Bureau has 102; the Technical Council (Gijutsu Kaigi) has three; the Food Agency has 52; the Forestry Agency has 83; and the Fisheries Agency has 77; to make a grand total of 605.[504]

These organisations have other agricultural *gaikaku dantai* and statutory agricultural interest groups as members (including agricultural cooperative organisations), and may also have supporting members that include private sector enterprises operating in the relevant field, such as beef processing or agricultural infrastructure construction companies. Interlocking membership is a feature of almost all these organisations. In this way, they support each other's activities. Some of these organisations operate at the national level only. Others may also have prefectural branches which form part of their membership structure, although only the national organisations are officially classed as *gaikaku dantai*.

The public interest corporations fall into a number of different categories which are not necessarily mutually exclusive. The first category is made up of national Nokyo federations. Many of these national federations are *gaikaku dantai* of various bureaus of the MAFF: Zenno, Zenkyoren, Zenkoku Koseiren and Shinbunren of the Economic Bureau; Kaitakuren and Zentakuren of the Structural Improvement Bureau; Zenyoren, Nichienren, Kajuren, Niseiren of the Agriculture, Sericulture and Horticulture Bureau; and Zenchikuren, Zenrakuren and Niyoren of the Livestock Bureau.[505] Nokyo at the national level is thus a semi-administrative arm of government,

Table 2.3 Fiscal 1998–99 national budget subsidies[a] allocated by the MAFF to MAFF public interest corporations as either primary or secondary works agents[b]

Unit: '000

Name of group	Amount received[c]	Main administrative purpose for which subsidy was received[d]
Agricultural Policy Research Committee	¥88,470	Research and investigation into agricultural basic policy
*Japan Agriculture, Forestry and Fisheries Promotion Association	¥53,623	Improvement of techniques and development of management in the agriculture, forestry and fisheries industries
Food and Agricultural Policy Research Centre	¥75,186	Research into food demand structure problems
International Food and Agriculture Association	¥68,293	FAO cooperation
*Japan–China Agriculture, Forestry and Fisheries Exchange Association	¥34,005	Fostering young Chinese farm guidance officers
Asia Agricultural Cooperatives Promotion Body	¥39,264	Agricultural and agricultural cooperative exchange activities with other countries in Asia
International Agriculture and Forestry Industries Cooperation Association	¥742,111	Reporting on foreign countries' food and agriculture
International Farmers' Exchange Association	¥194,959	Reporting on foreign countries' food and agriculture
Overseas Agricultural Development Association	¥151,371	Reporting on foreign countries' food and agriculture
*Overseas Agricultural Development Consultants' Association	¥232,664	Research on pre-agricultural development activities
Agriculture, Forestry and Fisheries Long-Term Finance Association	¥7,800,000	Interest subsidy on agricultural management improvement promotion fund
Japan Soil Association	¥74,214	Soil preservation policy control activities
Agriculture, Forestry and Fisheries Aviation Association	¥81,595	Insect damage prevention
Residual Agricultural Chemicals Research Institute	¥207,327	Insect damage prevention; agricultural chemical experiments
Japan Fumigation Techniques Association	¥81,595	Insect damage prevention
Agriculture, Forestry and Fishery Groups Staff Members' Mutual Aid Association	¥52,793,847	Mutual aid subsidy
Hometown Reporting Centre	¥586,410	Furnishing reports; food industry policy guidance promotion
*National Land Improvement Fund Association	¥17,000,000	Indemnifying land improvement financing

Organisation	Amount	Description
National Agricultural Structural Improvement Association	¥482,551	Guidance for promoting agricultural structural improvement
Agricultural Industry Promotion Encouragement Association	¥180,125	Agricultural commodities production improvement policy promotion; promoting the appropriate utilisation of fertiliser production materials; promoting the practical use of techniques in response to agricultural production reorganisation
Japan Flower Propagation Centre	¥215,402	Agricultural commodities production improvement policy promotion
Agriculture, Forestry and Fisheries Vanguard Techniques Industry Centre	¥46,953	Agricultural commodities production improvement policy promotion
Japan Speciality Agricultural Products Association	¥46,953	Agricultural commodities production improvement policy promotion
*Central Fruit Production and Delivery Stabilisation Fund Association	¥1,368,157	Promoting planned production and delivery of fruit
Japan Soba Association	¥52,918	Introduction of a quality evaluation policy
Japan Facilities Horticulture Association	¥122,758	Guidance activities for promoting agricultural production system strengthening policy; food distribution policy guidance promotion; horticultural facilities mutual aid system research
Japan Agricultural Policy Research Institute	¥123,120	Experimentation in the production of high quality agricultural products
*National Agricultural Improvement Dissemination Association	¥231,269	Supplying reports relating to new techniques to farmers on line
Rural Livelihood Comprehensive Research Centre	¥151,117	Survey research relating to all issues of farmers' and rural livelihood
Agricultural, Mountainous and Fishing Village Women's and Livelihood Activities Support Association	¥33,116	Agricultural, mountainous and fishing village livelihood development promotion
Farmers' Educational Association	¥189,341	Research and education promotion
Rural Welfare Association	¥108,307	Research and education promotion
National Rural Youth Education Promotion Association	¥124,622	Research and education promotion
*Cattle and Livestock Products Hygiene Guidance Association	¥697,110	Livestock industry reorganisation comprehensive policy promotion
Cattle Improvement Corporation	¥247,496	Livestock industry reorganisation comprehensive policy promotion
*Central Livestock Association	¥604,380	Livestock industry reorganisation comprehensive policy promotion

Table 2.3 (continued)

Name of group	Amount received[e]	Main administrative purpose for which subsidy was received[d]
Livestock Techniques Association	¥194,744	Guidance for the promotion of a feed production policy
Compound Feed Supply Stabilisation Organisation	¥3,800,000	Compound feed price stabilisation; feed products stockpiling
National Hen Egg Price Stabilisation Fund	¥763,284	Egg price stabilisation
All-Japan Egg Price Stabilisation Fund	¥763,284	Egg price stabilisation
Wheat for Feed Use Production Encouragement Association	¥868,528	Distribution promotion encouragement
Food Industry Centre	¥1,344,377	Food industry policy guidance promotion; food industry technical basis improvement
Nokyo Distribution Research Institute	¥6,407	Food distribution improvement policy
Sweet Resources Promotion Association	¥1,164,659	Potato flour factory reorganisation
Food Industry Environment Preservation Techniques Research Union	¥463,929	Leading techniques promotion
Food Distribution System Association	¥487,790	Promoting greater efficiency in the food industry
Food Distribution Structure Improvement Promotion Body	¥919,789	Promoting greater efficiency in the food industry
Food Livelihood Improvement Association	¥94,258	Exchange reports concerning agriculture and food livelihood between consumers and producers
Japan Agriculture and Forestry Standards Association	¥541,603	Improving the dissemination of Japanese agricultural and forestry standards
Food Demand and Supply Research Centre	¥281,568	Guidance promotion activities
National Vegetable Demand and Supply Adjustment Organisation	¥64,800	Vegetable demand and supply stabilisation promotion reporting
Agricultural and Forestry Statistics Association	¥270,600	Development of agricultural, forestry and fisheries statistical reporting techniques
Soybean Supply Stabilisation Association	¥588,418	Buying and selling of soybeans as part of a soybean stockpile policy
*Agriculture and Forestry Broadcasting Corporation	¥245,597	Agricultural problems research

International Agricultural Exchange and Food Support Fund ¥200,977 Research into China's agricultural directions

*Japan Agriculturral Mechanisation Association ¥53,164 Promotion of stable agricultural production

Total subsidies received by groups **¥98,448,405**

Notes:

* Those groups with an * had current or former Diet politicians in leadership positions in 1995.

a Sources are the General Account and Special Account budgets. Only those allocations from the General Account budget by the MAFF main ministry are included. Subsidy contributions from prefectural and municipal governments and from other sources for the above administrative purposes are not included, although these may be substantial.

b A group becomes a secondary recipient when a central government budget subsidy is channelled through prefectural or local governments. Where a group is a secondary agent, the subsidy has been treated as if the total amount was allocated to the group.

c Where various organisations as well as others (including local governments) shared in the subsidy, amounts have been divided equally amongst them. Figures, therefore, should be considered as approximate only.

d In almost all cases the actual subsidy was used to assist with the costs incurred by these groups in carrying out the specified function. The subsidies are given in the order in which they are listed in the record of national budget subsidies for 1998–99.

Source: Hojokin Soran, 1995, pp. 190–438.

with the most governmentalised group being Norinchukin, followed by Zenchu (a *ninka hojin*) and the rest (mainly national Nokyo economic federations) officially classified as *koeki hojin*.

This illustrates an important and frequently overlooked fact about the legal status of Nokyo. It contains groups with differing legal characteristics, depending on the level at which the group operates. At the local level the agricultural cooperatives function at arm's length from the government as largely self-governing entities. They are constrained only by the legal provisions of the *Nokyoho* and the broad administrative oversight of the MAFF. As *gaikaku dantai*, however, the main national Nokyo organisations operate at close quarters to the government and are much more tightly integrated into the administrative process. The result is a blurring of Nokyo's organisational attributes: it incorporates the structural characteristics of both interest group and auxiliary organ of government.

The second category of *koeki hojin* are organisations that Nokyo has established itself, sometimes in collaboration with other agricultural organisations such as *gaikaku dantai* and the statutory interest groups as well as interest groups operating in related fields. Various Nokyo organisations belong to these organisations as group members and they are often led by Nokyo executives. They are: Ie no Hikari Kyokai (Light in the Home Association), the national commercial publishing arm of Nokyo, the National Nokyo Tourist Association, the National Nokyo Amalgamation Promotion Support Fund, the National Nokyo Guarantee Centre, the National Agriculture, Forestry and Fishing Industry Groups Promotion Association, the National Agricultural Structural Improvement Association, the National Settlers' Promotion Association, the Regional Society Planning Centre, the National Nokyo Executive and Staff Members' Mutual Aid Association, the Nokyo Association (Nokyo Kyokai), the Nokyo Mutual Aid General Research Institute, the Nokyo Labour Problems Research Institute, the National Nokyo Milk Industry Plant Association, the Central Dairy Council (Chuo Rakuno Kaigi, or Churaku) and the Nokyo Distribution Research Institute.

These organisations operate like joint *gaikaku dantai* of Nokyo and the MAFF, with funding that comes from the organisations that form its membership in addition to government subsidies. Churaku, for example, is the specialist organisation created by Nokyo to handle the representation of its milk marketing interests. Its members are predominantly federations that engage in milk marketing on both the multi-purpose and specialist side of the organisation. Its national level members are Zenno, Zenrakuren, Zenchu, Zenkyoren, Norinchukin and Kaitakuren, which are either interested in milk policy determination or can assist in financing Churaku's activities. These extend to a range of functions: market adjustment (formulating policies to balance milk supply and demand); public relations and promotional activities with the aim of expanding milk consumption; and producer representation on milk prices (the raw milk-for-drinking price) negotiated with the major dairy companies.[506]

Another example in this category is the National Agricultural Structural Improvement Association (Zenkoku Nogyo Kozo Kaizen Kyokai). It was established by Zenchu, the National Chamber of Agriculture and the National Town and Village Association in 1963, following the passage of the ABL, in order to undertake agricultural structural improvement enterprises 'smoothly in cooperation with relevant associations'.[507] The association consists of members (22) and supporting members (27). Amongst the former are its three founding members in addition to other national Nokyo organisations such as Zenno, Zenkyoren, Kaitakuren and Zenrakuren, plus another statutory agricultural interest group (Zendoren), other agricultural *gaikaku dantai* and local government associations. Its supporting members are made up of agricultural public corporations such as the ALIC and the Agriculture, Forestry and Fisheries Finance Corporation and a long list of agricultural and general construction companies working in the 'structural improvement' field. Amongst the diverse activities of the group are supplying information and conducting public relations, training, consultancy and regional liaison support activities. The organisation also draws up regional agricultural plans, conducts special investigations for drawing up agricultural structural improvement agreements, investigates business for revitalising villages and restoring mountain villages, and undertakes agricultural land consolidation plans. Moreover, it also presents proposals and opinions to administrative authorities, in short, a recognised interest representational function. The association has offices in all Japan's main regions: Hokkaido, Tohoku, Tokai, Kinki Shikoku and Chukoku and Kyushu.[508] It receives partial financial support from the MAFF.[509] Other income is generated by consulting activities.[510]

A smaller organisation is the National Settlers' Promotion Association, originally established in 1945 to assist farmers as pioneers in various parts of the country, chiefly by providing guidance to their agricultural management. Its central members are Kaitakuren, the political association representing pioneering farmers. Its prefectural members are mainly Nokyo economic federations, settlers' promotion associations, settlers' leagues and federations of settlers' agricultural cooperatives.[511]

The third major category of public interest corporation comprises the national-level body of the remaining statutory agricultural interest group, the National Federation of Land Improvement Industry Groups (Zendoren), and associations representing the interests of the statutory agricultural interest groups: the National Agricultural Mutual Aid Association (Zenkoku Nogyo Kyosai Kyokai), the National Land Improvement Fund Association (Zenkoku Tochi Kairyo Kikin Kyokai), the Land Improvement Construction Association (Tochi Kairyo Kensetsu Kyokai) and the National Agricultural Public Works Techniques League (Zenkoku Nogyo Doboku Gijutsu Renmei).

The National Agricultural Mutual Aid Association, for example, defines its main purpose as mutual aid. Its members are the prefectural agricultural mutual aid federations and prefectural agricultural mutual aid associations. It

Table 2.4 Main public interest corporations representing specific commodity interests

Rice and Wheat:
National Rice Association (Zenkoku Beikoku Kyokai)
National Rice and Wheat Improvement Association (Zenkoku Beibaku Kairyo Kyokai)

Silk:
Raw Silk Association (Kiito Kyokai)
Central Silk Thread Association (Chuo Sanshi Kyokai)
National Silkworm Egg Card Association (Zenkoku Sanshu Kyokai)
Greater Japan Silk Thread Association (Dainihon Sanshikai)

Livestock Industry (general):
Central Livestock Association (Chuo Chikusankai)
Japan Livestock Facilities and Machinery Association (Nihon Chikusan Shisetsu Kikai Kyokai)
Horse and Livestock Hall (Baji Chikusan Kaikan)
National Livestock Compound Feed Price Stabilisation Fund (Zenkoku Chikusan Haigo Shiryo Kakaku Antei Kikin)
All Japan Compound Feed Price Stabilisation Fund (Zennihon Haigo Shiryo Kakaku Antei Kikin)
All Japan Livestock Management Stabilisation Fund Association (Zennihon Chikusan Keiei Antei Kikin Kyokai)
Compound Feed Supply Stabilisation Organisation (Haigo Shiryo Kyokyu Antei Kiko)

Beef Industry:
National Beef Association (Zenkoku Nikuyogyu Kyokai)
National Japanese Cattle Registration Association (Zenkoku Wagyu Toroku Kyokai)
Japan Cattle Business Association (Nihon Kachikusho Kyokai)
Cattle Trading Fund Association (Kachiku Torihiki Kikin Kyokai)
Japan Holstein Registration Association (Nihon Horustain Toroku Kyokai)
National Beef Calf Price Stabilisation Fund Association (Zenkoku Nikuyo Koushi Kakaku Antei Kikin Kyokai)

Dairy Farming:
National Milk Association (Zenkoku Gyunyu Kyokai)
National Dairy Farmers' Association of Japan (Zenkoku Rakuno Kyokai)
Japan International Dairy Farming Federation (Nihon Kokusai Rakuno Renmei)
National Association of Dairy Farming Helpers (Rakuno Herupaa Zenkoku Kyokai)

claims to have no direct funding relationship to the MAFF.[512] Office expenses are subsidised by the prefectural agricultural mutual aid federations.[513]

The fourth major category of public interest corporations serves specific sets of producers' commodity or special farming interests. Some of these are involved in price support and stabilisation schemes of one sort or another. They can be divided into 12 sub-categories as outlined in Table 2.4. First on the list is the National Rice Association (Zenkoku Beikoku Kyokai) in the rice

Table 2.4 (continued)

Hog Raising:
National Hog Raising Association (Zenkoku Yoton Kyokai)
Japan Hog Registration Association (Nihon Shuton Toroku Kyokai)

Poultry Farming:
Japan Poultry Association (Nihon Yokei Kyokai)
Japan Egg Industry Association (Nihon Rangyo Kyokai)
All Japan Egg Price Stabilisation Fund (Zennihon Ranka Antei Kikin)

Tea Growers:
Japan Tea Industry Central Association (Nihon Chagyo Chuokai)

Fruit Farming:
Japan Fruit Juice Association (Nihon Kaju Kyokai),
Japan Fruit Tree Seeds and Seedlings Association (Nihon Kaju Shubyo Kyokai)
Central Fruit Production and Delivery Stabilisation Fund Association (Chuo Kajitsu Seisan Shukka Antei Kikin Kyokai)

Flower Farming:
Japan Flower Association (Nihon Hana no Kai)
Japan Rose Association (Nihon Barakai)
Japan Flowering Plant Production Association (Nihon Kaki Seisan Kyokai)

Other Products:
Japan Speciality Agricultural Products Association (Nihon Tokushu Nosanbutsu Kyokai)
National Peanut Association (Zenkoku Rakkasei Kyokai)
Japan Konjak Association (Nihon Konnyaku Kyokai)
Japan Beekeeping and Honey Association (Nihon Shokuho Hachimitsu Kyokai)
Miscellaneous Beans Import Fund Association
Japan Miscellaneous Beans Fund Association (Nihon Mamerui Kikin Kyokai)

Specialised Farming:
Farmland Agriculture Promotion Association (Hatachi Nogyo Shinkokai)
Japan Grassland Association (Nihon Kusachi Kyokai)
Agricultural Settlers Association (Nogyo Takushoku Kyokai)

Source: *Norinsuisansho Meibo*, 1995, pp. 613–711.

and wheat category. Its members are prefectural rice associations, and it undertakes PR activities relating to the budget for rice as well as mediation between *gaikaku dantai* of the Food Agency and wholesale dealers of rice. It receives no funding or subsidies from the MAFF. Money is raised from membership fees. It has dealings with Nokyo insofar as both organisations are involved in the wholesaling of rice.[514]

The other organisation in this category is the National Rice and Wheat

Improvement Association (Zenkoku Beibaku Kairyo Kyokai). It is structured in a similar fashion to the National Rice Association with prefectural organisations as members. Zenno is also a member. The main task of this association is improving rice and wheat production by providing guidance for production improvement and the organisation of training programmes. It receives no funding or subsidies from the MAFF. It is financed by fees collected from its members.[515]

In the livestock category, two of the most prominent groups are the Central Livestock Association, or CLA (Chuo Chikusankai) and the National Beef Association, or NBA (Zenkoku Nikuyogyu Kyokai). These organisations function as technical, informational, guidance, advisory, research, publicity, promotional and funding bodies for the livestock industry. The NBA is particularly concerned with providing services to and advancing the interests of Japanese cattle (i.e. *wagyu*) producers. It is closely related to a sister association, the National Japanese Cattle Registration Association (Zenkoku Wagyu Toroku Kyokai) which has similar purposes.[516]

One of the most important functions of these livestock organisations is to channel various public subsidies into livestock-related projects. The primary focus of their policy interest is maintaining organisational funding and the level of subsidies being disbursed into their general field of operations and thus indirectly the interests of livestock producers, cooperatives and companies that benefit from their services. The CLA, for example, conducts livestock policy activities (*chikusei katsudo*), that involve providing suggestions and proposals on government livestock policies. The latter includes making requests relating to livestock policy and budgetary measures.[517] In FY 1998, the CLA received more than ¥600 million in subsidies from the MAFF for various livestock policy-related functions (see Table 2.3).[518]

The Compound Feed Supply Stabilisation Organisation (Haigo Shiryo Kyokyu Antei Kiko) is another regulatory and support organisation operating in the livestock sector. It was set up in 1976 to disburse government subsidies to stabilise the supply of compound feed and to stockpile materials for compound feed-making. The organisation is involved in creating preparatory assets for special subsidies, allocating special subsidies and grants, paying the interest on construction costs of storage silos, buying, selling and storing of feed grains, collecting information regarding supply and demand and price trends for feed grains, and assisting with funds to cover the costs of constructing the necessary facilities for improving the distribution of foreign wheat for fodder use.[519] In FY 1998, it received ¥3.8 billion in subsidies for compound feed price stabilisation and the stockpiling of feed products (see Table 2.3).

The National Dairy Farmers' Association, or Zenraku, is an important group in the dairy farming category. It was established in 1946 with the aim of protecting the interests of dairy farmers and improving their economic and social status. Zenraku provides extensive advisory, research, mutual aid, information and publication extension services as well as maintaining continuous political contacts with the Diet and government.[520] One of its main roles is to conduct agricultural policy activities (*nosei katsudo*). In fact, Rakuseiren is an affiliated organisation of Zenraku. The federation was set up by the association to engage exclusively in political activity for the dairy farmers, thus concentrating their political power. The directors of Zenraku are currently executives of the federation.

The key price stabilisation organisation in the fruit farming sector is the Central Fruit Production and Delivery Stabilisation Fund Association (Chuo Kajitsu Seisan Shukka Antei Kikin Kyokai). Its members are prefectural fruit production and delivery stabilisation fund associations, members of which include local agricultural cooperatives. Its main task is stabilising the price of fruit through compensation to farmers in cases where fruit prices drop. The fruit covered by the association includes oranges, Chinese citrons, nashi pears, grapes and apples (in other words, all of the main fruit in Japan). The association also conducts public relations activities with respect to fruit and investigations of the fruit market and production. It is financially supported by the MAFF. Funds flow from the MAFF to each local agricultural cooperative through the prefectural organisations of the national fund association.[521] In FY 1998, the national association received just under ¥1.4 billion from the MAFF for its stabilisation activities (see Table 2.3).

The Japan Pulses Fund Association (Nihon Mamerui Kikin Kyokai) is a national organisation that exists to improve the production and distribution of pulses, to promote their consumption and to conduct public relations activities with respect to the consumption of beans. Although MAFF is its supervisory body, it receives no financial support from government. Funding comes from bean importing companies.[522]

The National Egg Price Stabilisation Fund (Zenkoku Keiran Kakaku Antei Kikin) undertakes price compensation operations in case of a drop in the price of eggs. It compensates farmers up to 90 per cent of the decrease in the egg price. The Fund's financial sources are producer groups, Zenno, local co-ops and government subsidies.[523] In FY 1998, it received more than ¥760 million in subsidies from the MAFF for price stabilisation purposes (see Table 2.3).

Other categories of public interest corporation serve a range of general agricultural sector and agriculture-related industry interests. They form part of the vast institutional infrastructure furnishing all kinds of financial, organ-isational, social, research and technical services to the farming industry as well as providing a vehicle for the maintenance and advancement of these interests in a public policy context. A cross-section of group categories and the organisations within them is listed in Table 2.5.

The National Reclamation Promotion Association (Zenkoku Kaitaku Shinkokai) is one of the groups in the agricultural infrastructure development category. It provides support and managerial guidance for agricultural settlers (i.e. those farming reclaimed land, usually for livestock). Its members are relevant agricultural cooperative organisations at each of the three

Table 2.5 Public interest corporations serving general agricultural sector and agriculture-related industry interests

---

Agricultural policy research organisations:
New Agricultural Policy Research Institute[a]
Agricultural Policy Research Association
Agricultural Policy Investigation Committee
Food and Agricultural Policy Research Centre

Other types of research groups:
Japan Agricultural Research Institute
Cooperative Union Management Research Institute
Rural Finance Research Association
Food Demand and Supply Research Centre
Food Livelihood Research Association
Japan Agricultural Engineering General Research Institute

Agricultural and rural culture promotional organisations:
Greater Japan Agricultural Association[b]
National 'Love Agriculture' Association
Japan Agriculture, Forestry and Fisheries Promotion Association
Agricultural Policy Promotion Council
Agriculture, Forestry and Fishery Industries Encouragement Association
Agricultural Industry Promotion Encouragement Association
National Agriculture, Forestry and Fishery Groups Promotion Association
National Reclamation Promotion Association
National Food Livelihood Improvement Association
21st Century Village Construction School

Various agriculture-related funds and the associations of various funds:
Agricultural Improvement Fund Association
Central Agricultural Settlers' Fund Association

Farming techniques dissemination groups:
Agricultural Techniques Association
National Agricultural Improvement Dissemination Association
National Agricultural Improvement Dissemination Works Council
National Cattle and Livestock Products Hygiene Guidance Association

---

Professional organisations:
National Agricultural Managers' Association
Overseas Agricultural Development Consultants Association
Japan Cattle Artificial Insemination Practitioners' Association

---

stages: national, prefectural and local and they provide funding for the organisation.[524]

One of the groups of the strictly promotional kind is the Japan Agriculture Forestry and Fisheries Promotion Association (Nihon Noringyogyo Shinkokai). It operates at the national level, has no members but receives contributions from other agricultural organisations including the Nokyo

Table 2.5 (continued)

Agricultural and rural welfare groups:
Agriculture and Forestry Pensions Welfare Group
Regional Society Planning Centre
National Rural Youth Education Promotion Association
National Agriculture, Forestry and Fisheries' Groups Promotion Association

Statistics and information collection and dissemination groups:
Agriculture and Forestry Broadcasting Corporation
Agriculture and Forestry Statistics Association
Japan Rural Information Systems Association

Agricultural Infrastructure Development Groups:
Land Improvement Construction Association
Agricultural Public Works Association
Japan Soil Association
Japan Agricultural Mechanisation Association
National Reclamation Promotion Association

Federations of business cooperative unions operating in broad agriculture-related fields:
National Federation of Agricultural Machinery Business Cooperative Unions
Japan Federation of Agricultural Chemical Cooperative Unions
National Federation of Agricultural Chemical Industry Cooperative Unions
National Fertiliser Business Federation
Japan Federation of Fertiliser Business Cooperative Unions
National Federation of Agricultural Mechanisation Industry Cooperative Unions

Federations of business cooperative unions and other associations operating in food processing, manufacturing and distribution:
National Federation of Food Industry Cooperative Unions
National Federation of Staple Food Collection Cooperative Unions
National Federation of Meat Industry Cooperative Unions
Japan Meat Processing Association
Japan Meat Council
Japan Milk Products Association
Food Industry Central Council

Notes:
a The Japanese titles for all these organisations can be found in Norinsuisansho Meibo, 1995, pp. 613–711.
b This group (Dainihon Nokai) is a remnant of the prewar *nokai* organisation. It was founded in 1942.

Source: *Norinsuisansho Meibo*, 1995, pp. 613–711.

keizairen. Its principal financial sponsor is, however, the MAFF. It undertakes various public relations activities designed to raise the morale of primary producers, improve agricultural techniques and management, and deepen the understanding of the general public about agriculture.[525] In collaboration with the MAFF, it sponsors special awards and prizes for farmers and holds national events including festivals and promotional campaigns for primary industries. It also sponsors prefectural events and campaigns together with prefectural governments. Its Chairman is the MAFF Minister by necessity, as it organises a farm management prize that only the MAFF Minister is permitted to award.[526] In FY 1998, the association received just over ¥53 million in subsidies from the MAFF for improving agricultural techniques and developing managerial skills in agricultural, forestry and fisheries industries (see Table 2.3).

Another such group is the Agricultural Policy Promotion Council (Nosei Suishin Kyogikai). It was established in November 1958 as a result of a proposal from Sasayama Shigetaro, Chairman of the LDP's Agriculture and Forestry Division, or AFD (Norin Bukai) of the Policy Affairs Research Council, or PARC, the party's policymaking body. The idea was for an organisation to be set up that would unite LDP agriculture and forestry Diet members and major agricultural organisations for the purpose of securing a bigger budget for agriculture. LDP Diet members were asked to join the newly-formed group as *gakushiki keikensha*. The council's membership is composed of the national offices of 24 major agricultural, forestry and fisheries organisations. Its secretariat is located in the National Chamber of Agriculture, while the staff of the secretariat are employees of the NCA and Nokyo.

In December each year at a critical stage of the agricultural budgetmaking process,[527] the council organises lobbying activities *vis-à-vis* LDP Diet members in order to reflect the views of agricultural organisations on budget policy. In turn, the Diet members articulate the views of the agricultural groups in their lobbying of the MOF. The council enhances this process by sponsoring not only the individual lobbying by Diet members who belong to the council but also coordinating them so that the LDP can appeal as a party to the government. Individual agricultural organisations in the group organise their own lobbying activities separately, but the council also coordinates their budget activities for greater impact.[528] In short, the council not only connects agricultural organisations with LDP Diet members on budget matters, it also coordinates both sides for more effective lobbying. This is done through a process of meetings held between the leaders of agricultural groups and Diet members. About two years after the establishment of the council, its members also decided to discuss agricultural policy matters as well as issues relating to the budget.

The main purpose of the council from the LDP's perspective is to maintain the support of major agricultural organisations by obtaining government funding for them. The LDP's *norin giin* wanted to exclude *norin giin* from the Opposition parties from the battle for the budget in order to give the impression that only they could secure a favourable budget for agriculture.[529]

Although the preceding discussion gives the impression that many public interest corporations are active as interest groups, in fact most of the organisations in this category are purely technical in function and have only tangential policy-related interests. A select minority, however, are highly politicised, particularly around the task of obtaining subsidies from government to fund their operations and to advance the industries and activities they represent. Levels of politicisation are also dictated by the amount of government subsidies they distribute to farmers.

Membership of the public interest corporations consists of groups that pay membership fees as financial contributions to the organisation as well as groups benefiting from their semi-administrative services (the statutory agricultural interest groups – particularly agricultural cooperative organisations – and other public interest corporations). The members of the National Egg Price Stabilisation Fund, for example, are divided into prefectural and central: prefectural members are the 48 prefectural *keizairen* and 47 prefectural governments, while its central members are Zenno, Norinchukin and ALIC. Funding comes from its producer organisation members, Zenno, local *nokyo* and from MAFF subsidies, as noted above. Zenno and local *nokyo* contribute to the fund as contract members.[530]

The members of the Compound Feed Supply Stabilisation Organisation, on the other hand, are ALIC and two other *gaikaku dantai* (the National Livestock Compound Feed Price Stabilisation Fund (Zenkoku Chikusan Haigo Shiryo Kakaku Antei Kikin) and the All-Japan Compound Feed Price Stabilisation Fund (Zennihon Haigo Shiryo Kakaku Antei Kikin)), all the Nokyo livestock-related federations (Zenno, Zenrakuren, Zenchikuren, Kaitakuren and Niyoren) as well as the Nokyo-based National Compound Feed Supply Stabilisation Fund,[531] and the private industry association representing Japanese feed makers (Cooperative Union Japan Feed Industry Association, or Kyodo Kumiai Nihon Shiryo Kogyokai).[532] Half of the organisation's funding comes from the MAFF and the other half is from Zenno and feed manufacturers. The purpose of the funding is to make up for any increase in the feed price and to stockpile fodder. Expenses used for the management of the organisation are derived from the interest earned on MAFF subsidies. In this way, the Compound Feed Supply Stabilisation Organisation forms an important channel whereby government subsidies can be paid to farmers who use livestock feed. Subsidies are disbursed through Zenno, through the *keizairen* and local co-ops to the farmers.

Clearly the membership structure of the public interest corporations can vary. Some operate only at the national level, like the Japan Agriculture, Forestry and Fisheries Promotion Association, and have no member-organisations. Others only have agricultural cooperative organisations as members, like the National Reclamation Promotion Association. Many groups have a two-stage membership structure, combining central members (from other national agricultural groups) as well as prefectural members (agricultural organisations operating at prefectural level).

The regular members of the CLA, for example, are its prefectural branches (that is, 47 prefectural livestock associations), 63 so-called 'central members' (*chuoin*) including national agricultural cooperative organisations (particularly those operating in the livestock sector), livestock-related public interest corporations such as Zenraku and Chuo Rakuno Kaigi, other public interest corporations such as the National Agricultural Mutual Aid Association and agricultural public corporations such as the Agriculture, Forestry and Fisheries Finance Corporation and ALIC. A category of 24 associate members consists mainly of associations and cooperative associations of private industry enterprises operating in the livestock processing and distribution sector. Finally a smaller category of supporting members consists of a miscellaneous group of agriculture-related associations and councils, mostly other public interest corporations.[533] The prefectural associations, in contrast to the CLA, focus almost exclusively on providing technical and management services to livestock farmers. They are not interest groups in the sense of pursuing particular policy goals.

In other cases the public interest corporations have a three-stage membership structure with prefectural and even local branches. The members of Zenraku, for example, are the prefectural federations of dairy agricultural cooperatives and prefectural dairy farmers' associations. The members of these organisations are, in turn, local dairy cooperatives.

The NBA, on the other hand, reaches right down from national to local level. At the national level, it has a dual membership structure of associate and full members. Its associate members are national organisations such as Zenno and livestock public interest corporations, the National Beef Calf Price Stabilisation Fund Association and various beef registration organisations (*nikuyogyu toroku dantai*). Full members are its prefectural associations (although they do not operate in all prefectures), prefectural Nokyo *keizairen* and prefectural livestock associations. In turn, the prefectural associations of the NBA have a membership made up of their own local branches and prefectural entities of the organisations that belong to their national-level organisation. The final unit of membership is the farmer or agricultural company, particularly Nokyo-related companies (*kanren gaisha*).[534] At each level, organisational members pay membership fees which fund the salaries of group officials, but the government also provides these organisations with subsidies[535] not only for their own operations but, as noted earlier, as a channel of disbursement to the livestock sector.

The subsidy-dependent nature of many of the public interest corporations is one of the primary reasons why they assume interest group functions. Requests for subsidies become an important part of their policy-related activities and an important reason why many of them choose LDP politicians as leaders.[536] The search for budgetary and other financial resources from government subsidy and investment sources motivates them to seek direct political representation in the Diet.[537] 'They use the politicians to get funding. These organisations want to exercise political influence and power, although sometimes a politician is placed in the top position in the group as an "honourable person".'[538] Table 2.3 indicates which groups had current or former Diet politicians in leadership positions the mid-1990s amongst the public interest corporations that received subsidies from the MAFF in FY

1998. It also describes the administrative purposes for which the subsidies were received. In total, these groups were allocated more than ¥98 billion for the various 'jobs' and 'tasks' assigned to them by government in that year.[539]

Public interest corporations also obtain subsidies from other sources. For example, the LIPC (now ALIC) disburses large amounts of subsidies to livestock-related public interest corporations under its designated assistance projects scheme – in fact, much more than these groups derive from the MAFF itself. Indeed, ALIC is the main source of subsidies for groups such as the CLA, the NBA and the National Beef Calf Price Stabilisation Fund Association.[540] A larger number of livestock-related public interest corporations receive ALIC subsidies (on average around 30) compared with the number benefiting from direct MAFF subsidies (only a few livestock *gaikaku dantai* receive subsidies from this source – four in total in FY 1998, as shown in Table 2.3). Moreover, the amounts disbursed by the ALIC are considerably larger. Given the quantity of funding involved, it would appear that a large proportion of the subsidy funding for the livestock public interest corporations comes via the ALIC subsidy budget, and therefore from the beef import trade.

For example the Central Livestock Association obtained ¥181 billion in subsidies from ALIC in FY 1997,[541] compared with the figure of ¥604 million from the central government in FY 1998 (see Table 2.3). Other groups like the National Beef Association (which obtained ¥2.1 billion in FY 1997 from ALIC[542]) and the National Beef Calf Price Stabilisation Fund Association including its prefectural branches (which received ¥22.6 billion in FY 1997[543]) *only* receive subsidies from the LIPC. These livestock-related groups were also recipients of subsidised investments from the LIPC/ALIC. For example, the National Beef Price Stabilisation Fund Association had acquired a cumulative total of ¥717 million in investments by FY 1990 and the CLA ¥650 million.[544] Both of these groups have been traditionally led by Diet politicians.

The MAFF *gaikaku dantai* – *tokushu hojin, ninka hojin* and *koeki hojin* – share and complement the activities of Nokyo and the other agricultural statutory interest groups in representing various kinds of agricultural interests in Japan. Their focus always relates to their narrow sector of activity, however, unlike Nokyo which has a very broadly based interest in agricultural policy. Furthermore, the main concern of these institutional interest groups is usually acquiring government funds to support their operations and the beneficiaries of their services. This makes the MAFF and its bureaus to which all the various categories of *gaikaku dantai* are attached a natural target for pressure in relation to subsidy and other policy matters. The beneficiaries are group members who are, for the most part, other agricultural organisations, in many cases agricultural cooperative organisations. The farmers are also beneficiaries. They are the ultimate targets of many of the subsidies, but they come at the end of a line of subsidy distribution, with the *gaikaku dantai* all taking their cut (usually for administering subsidised schemes of one sort or another) along the way.

This system builds up entrenched institutional interests in a highly regulated and administered agricultural economy. Without the regulation providing the fundamental *raison d'être* of these organisations, they would not need to exist, with loss of jobs for those whose livelihood depends on the agricultural administration industry.[545] Some of these groups, for example, are essentially welfare organisations for the officials who work in the MAFF *gaikaku dantai*. The National Agriculture, Forestry and Fisheries Groups Promotion Association (Zenkoku Noringyogyo Dantai Shinkokai) is one such body. Its members are agricultural organisations including the agricultural, forestry and fisheries cooperatives. It funds pensions for those who work for agriculture, forestry and fisheries-related organisations. Financial support for these pensions comes from its group membership.[546] In other words, it is a superannuation organisation for the salaried officials of agricultural, forestry and fisheries groups.

Nokyo plays a crucial role in many of these agricultural *gaikaku dantai*. As the universal organisation of farmers it is often the essential intermediary that allows these organisations to distribute the subsidies they administer to the farmers. This is done through their internal membership structure. Many have agricultural cooperative organisations as members.

A corporatised sector?

The fact that statutory agricultural interest groups and institutional interest groups combine public functions for government with service to and sponsorship of private interests obscures the boundaries between public institutions and private groups in the agricultural sector. Because a number of national-level Nokyo groups are also officially classed as MAFF *gaikaku dantai*, along with the national organisations of the mutual aid associations, land improvement industry groups and agricultural committee organisation, the statutory interest groups could be said to incorporate the features of a dual organisational type. At the rice roots, their members are individual farmers who have joined on a voluntary basis; at the national level, they are quasi-public groups working in close association with the government. The dual nature of these organisations is also suggestive of relatively high levels of interest group corporatism in the Japanese agricultural sector.

Corporatism occurs where 'single interest groups are licensed, recognized and encouraged by the state, enjoy the right to represent their sector of society and . . . work in partnership with government in both the formulation and implementation of policy'.[547] Corporatism thus results in 'intimate mutual penetration of state bureaucracies and large interest organizations'.[548] Another important dimension according to Keeler is that groups drawn into the public policymaking process are also 'provided by the state with certain benefits in exchange for their cooperation and their restraint in the articulation of demands.'[549]

Other definitions of corporatism, particularly those coming out of the European and Latin American fascist tradition, put more emphasis on the 'control' aspects of corporatised relations between government and groups, defining it as a system in which interest groups have compulsory membership and a state-sanctioned representational monopoly within their respective spheres, and are legally subordinated to governmental authority in leadership selection and interest articulation.[550]

Depending on which definition is employed, the agricultural interest group system in Japan conforms to a greater or lesser extent to the key corporatist criteria. If a corporatist system requires the existence of a single, large, peak interest group with compulsory membership which monopolises representation of a particular sector, then it is difficult to see how agricultural interest representation in Japan complies. While Nokyo is a large, mass membership group that dominates the articulation of farmers' interests, compulsory membership was divested with the abolition of the *nogyokai*. The latter were part of the government-controlled wartime system of incorporated groups – the Imperial Rule Assistance Association, or IRAA (Taiseiyoku Sankai) – which represented a fascist type of corporatism.[551] Indeed, as instruments of control of the Meiji, Taisho and early Showa governments respectively, all Nokyo's historical antecedents (the *nogyokai*, and, to a lesser extent, the *nokai* and *sangyo kumiai*) were far more corporatised in this respect than Nokyo.[552] Moreover, as pointed out above, Nokyo does not exercise a representational monopoly of agricultural interests and nor is it the only agricultural interest group through which the state acts to implement agricultural policy. Nokyo shares both its interest articulation and policy implementation roles with a plethora of other agricultural organisations of differing legal status, composition, functioning and focus.[553]

Indeed, the agricultural interest group system involves multiple layers of mutually reinforcing demand articulation and semi-public functioning by different groups. The livestock sector, for example, is particularly well represented by a number of different organisations. A profile of the groups involved in promoting and protecting livestock (including dairy) farming interests within Nokyo alone would include: Zenchu – the national leadership organisation of the agricultural cooperatives which concentrates on budgetary requests in relation to livestock farming, the formulation of 'demand' prices for livestock products and the sponsorship of mass mobilisation activities of farmers against market opening for livestock products;[554] Zenno – the national trading arm of the Nokyo organisation involved in all aspects of marketing and input supply for livestock farmers as well as being an end-user and distributor of imported beef;[555] Zenchikuren and Zenrakuren – the National Livestock and Dairy Nokyo Federations and their regional federations which conduct economic and other functions for their specialist cooperative members as well as channelling policy demands relating to livestock farmers; and Kaitakuren – the national Nokyo specialist federation of reclamation cooperatives, which also weighs in on livestock matters, particularly in relation to beef farming. In addition, there is Nokyo's Churaku organisation which makes claims to dairy companies on behalf of milk producers.

Non-Nokyo groups that represent livestock interests are two exclusively dairy farmers' groups: Zenraku, which provides various services for farmers as well as agricultural policy activities on their behalf; and Rakuseiren, its specialist political arm which undertakes active campaigns on the policy and electoral front on behalf of dairy farmers.

Other prominent livestock-related organisations are *gaikaku dantai* such as the LIPC (now ALIC), CLA, NBA and the National Beef Calf Price Stabilisation Fund Association. Although they are primarily administering agencies of government and not lobby groups, in relating to the MAFF on livestock matters, whether it be in connection with their own funding, disbursement of subsidies, managing the beef import trade or administering price support schemes, as noted earlier, their activities indirectly benefit the ultimate beneficiaries of these programmes – livestock farmers, livestock production groups and other agricultural organisations, such as the agricultural cooperatives.

Clearly the livestock sector, like the agricultural sector in general and its many sub-sectors, is represented by various groups of differing organisational type. The degree to which these groups are corporatised into governmental processes is one of the many possible dimensions according to which they may vary. Because the *gaikaku dantai* combine the characteristics of private group membership with the performance of public duties, because they obtain funding from a mixture of public and private sources, and because their leaders are recruited from both the bureaucracy and the political world, strongly corporatist aspects characterise their make-up and behaviour. And despite the quasi-governmental status of the *gaikaku dantai*, some of them behave like interest groups in certain contexts.

It is problematic, however, whether institutional interest groups such as these deserve to be considered interest groups in the normal sense. While it is true that they take on pressure group-type functions when they lobby for subsidies from budgetary and other sources, in almost all cases the *gaikaku dantai* have been created solely for public purposes, which are specific and narrow, and their membership is dominated by public and semi-public organisations. Their interest representational role is a by-product of their public functioning and not part of their fundamental organisational rationale.

In corporatist analysis, interest groups are usually considered to be organisations whose role is to represent the interests of a particular group of citizens. Furthermore, in the standard model of corporatism in pluralist democracies, interest groups are formally independent of government and are made up of individuals who join on a voluntary basis for the primary purpose of representing their interests to government. Such groups become assimilated into the policy formulation, negotiation and implementation processes by various formal mechanisms, but they are not necessarily subordinated to government control.

The notion of corporatism is more clearly applicable to the statutory interest groups in the agricultural sector than to the *gaikaku dantai*. Nokyo, the agricultural committee organisation, the land improvement groups and the agricultural mutual aid associations are all voluntary organisations of farmers, although the breadth of their membership varies. They act as spokespersons for these members in policy processes, and in the case of Nokyo and the agricultural committee organisation, this role is underwritten in the form of a legally-sanctioned interest articulation function. They are 'licensed' by the state to undertake a representational role.

At the same time, the statutory agricultural interest groups share many of the quasi-governmental features of the *gaikaku dantai*. Like the *gaikaku dantai*, they are sponsored by the state and are recruited into the functioning of agricultural administration 'as though they are government agencies or extension agencies in disseminating innovations and information to improve farm operations and rural life in general.'[556] In this way, their activities serve both private interests (organisational and membership interests) and public policy objectives (the government's interests). Nokyo, for example, institutionalises self-help amongst farmers at the same time as serving the official purpose of promoting agriculture, the agricultural economy and the farm household economy. As Kawagoe comments, it 'has eased the task of imposing all manner of control measures in its role as implementing agency of government policy'.[557]

Together, the statutory agricultural interest groups embody one of the most important facets of state intervention in the Japanese agricultural economy, namely the enlistment of voluntary farmers' organisations to assist in the process of agricultural administration. Their ancillary role as agents for the government was notably encouraged by the dominant element of regulation in Japanese agriculture and the strong legal underpinning of agricultural policies.[558] In this respect, corporatisation of these groups could be said to reflect the high level of government intervention in the agricultural sector.[559]

Nokyo alone amongst these groups, however, is a mass membership group with a broad span of policy interests, exemplifying the requirement implicit in corporatist analysis that policy implementation by the group will reach the entire sector because it has sufficient geographic and membership coverage. In the same way, it is sufficiently inclusionary to speak for the farming community as a whole. For these reasons, although it is possible to argue that there are corporatised aspects to the relationships between the Japanese government and the other statutory agricultural interest groups, particularly the agricultural committee organisation, Nokyo approximates most closely the corporatist concept of a sector-wide authoritative spokesperson for a particular section of society.

Nokyo also meets another essential requirement of corporatism in that its integration into governmental processes is accomplished on the basis of formal mechanisms. The mechanisms concerned are variously legal, institutional and procedural.[560] Nokyo's assignment of semi-official duties under various agricultural laws represents legal corporatisation which encompasses both the policy formulation and implementation stages.[561] With respect to policy formulation, the central unions not only enjoy the legal right to submit proposals to administrative authorities under Nokyo Law, but many other statutory provisions require the authorities to listen to the opinions of Nokyo. Under the 1980 Agricultural Land Utilisation Promotion Law for example, when a prefectural governor approves farm land utilisation promotion projects, he must listen to the opinions of the prefectural central union of agricultural cooperatives.[562] The same requirements apply in the case of several other laws: under 1954 Law Concerning the Promotion of Dairy Farming and Beef Cattle Production, the prefectural governor must listen to the opinions of those in the milk industry as well as the agricultural cooperatives and federations of agricultural cooperatives in deciding dairy farming promotion plans;[563] under the Land Improvement Law, the agricultural cooperatives and federations of agricultural cooperatives may petition prefectural governors and the MAFF to undertake certain types of land improvement activities, including proposals that the national, prefectural or municipal governments implement farm land creation projects on land that local public bodies are using;[564] under the 1966 Vegetable Production Shipment Stabilisation Law, the agricultural cooperatives and federations of agricultural cooperatives are permitted to submit their opinions to the governor when he/she determines plans for modernising the production and shipment of nominated vegetables;[565] under the Livestock Products Price Stabilisation Law, the LIPC was required to consult with the cooperatives as producer bodies before buying designated meats (beef and pork) at the central wholesale markets; and under the 1954 Dairy Farming and Beef Cattle Production Promotion Law, prefectural governors, when they wish to decide on or alter intensive dairy farming promotion plans, must listen to the opinions of milk industry groups in the region as well as agricultural cooperative federations and city, town and village agricultural cooperatives in the region.[566]

With respect to the policy implementation function, details of Nokyo's administrative tasks under agricultural legislation have already been provided. Nokyo's legal status as a statutory interest group in fact facilitates its extension into other areas nominated by law. Amongst these, the most important has been Food Control. Nokyo's designated tasks under this system constituted its core corporatist function. From an administrative perspective, Food Control was historically Nokyo's primary organisational rationale. Over time, however, Nokyo's semi-administrative roles diversified into other areas of administrative purview and control.

Apart from legal statute, the formal mechanisms by which interest groups can be drawn into the fabric of administration include the establishment and funding of quasi-governmental organisations in which interest groups form part of the executive, advisory or membership structure. Nokyo's institutional corporatisation is thus achieved through its executive, advisory, membership and financial links with the quasi-governmental *gaikaku dantai*.

For example, although LIPC (now ALIC) executives and staff members are either retired or seconded officials from the MAFF (and to a lesser extent the MOF), representatives of Nokyo are appointed by the LIPC with approval from the MAFF Minister to serve as part-time LIPC directors. Representatives from Nokyo also sit on the LIPC Board of Councillors, which functions like an advisory board.[567] This system allows for the institutionalised participation of Japanese domestic producer representatives in the administration of the beef (until 1991) and dairy product import trades.[568] In addition, Nokyo has a financial investment in the LIPC.

Other public corporations with which Nokyo is formally connected are Norinchukin (this exemplifies Nokyo's dual organisational structure as both an institutional and statutory interest group), the Agriculture, Forestry and Fisheries Finance Corporation, the Japan Central Horse Racing Association (Nihon Chuo Keibakai), the Forestry Development Corporation (Shinrin Kaihatsu Kodan), the Agriculture, Forestry and Fishery Groups Staff Members' Mutual Aid Association, the National Association of Regional Horse Racing, the Silk Thread and Sugar Price Stabilisation Corporation (like the LIPC, agricultural cooperative and federations of agricultural cooperatives could invest in the SSPSC), the Farmers' Pension Fund and the Agricultural Land Development Corporation. Nokyo executives (usually from Zenchu or Zenno) act in a variety of capacities in these organisations, usually as members of executive or advisory boards. The agricultural cooperatives are also important organisational members of groups such as the CLA and NBA.

The designation of high-level Nokyo national groups (as well as the other statutory agricultural interest groups) as *ninka hojin* or *koeki hojin* represents another form of institutional corporatisation, as does the dual organisational status of public interest corporations associated with the agricultural cooperatives and statutory agricultural interest groups, as discussed earlier. Nokyo, in particular, has a large number (over 130) of so-called 'related agricultural, forestry and fisheries groups' (*kankei norinsuisan dantai*), which are not formally part of the federated Nokyo organisation, but which come within Nokyo's official orbit.[569] Amongst these, those that are also MAFF *koeki hojin* can be officially classed as 'related' to both Nokyo and the MAFF. This common institutional linkage represents a form of institutional corporatisation.

Nokyo's procedural corporatisation is achieved through less formalised and more ad hoc mechanisms such as its representation on government advisory councils, particularly those attached to the MAFF. Nokyo sends one or more representatives to all the major MAFF advisory councils, including the RPAC, LIPAC, APAC and so on. Its main representatives are top-level officials of Zenchu, including the Zenchu Chairman, who sits on APAC for example, but other representatives also come from Zenno, Norinchukin and the general and specialist Nokyo federations. The same is true of the other statutory agricultural interest groups and the institutional interest groups.[570] The National Chamber of Agriculture is a particularly prominent member of MAFF advisory councils. Even farmers' union groups such as Zennichino are included in this kind of procedural corporatisation, with its representative traditionally sitting on the RPAC.[571] MAFF bureaucrats solicit policy advice from these groups in the formal context of government advisory councils. In fact one of the main ways in which the latter interact with government is by providing personnel to serve on agriculture-related advisory councils.[572] The statutory and institutional interest groups may also be commissioned from time to time to perform specific tasks or projects for which special financing is allocated. These commissioned reports and surveys are a speciality of the agricultural committee organisation, for example.

The balance of power: state dependence versus organisational independence

One of the key issues raised in corporatist analysis is the extent to which corporatised relations with government compromise the organisational autonomy of interest groups. According to Keeler's definition, acceptance of restraint in the articulation of demands is an integral aspect of the political behaviour of corporatised interest groups.[573] Corporatisation bestows privileged status on groups at the same time as it undermines their organisational independence. It does so by imposing legal restrictions and administrative obligations on groups whilst legitimising group participation in the policy process and granting the benefits of government patronage. Patronage is a reward for compliance in the execution of government policy.

In Nokyo's case, the question is whether the mechanisms of reward and restraint are so highly developed that they undermine its organisational autonomy and thus its ability to bargain effectively with the state on behalf of its membership. In short, does corporatisation come at the price of Nokyo's representative function? The evidence suggests that it is difficult to answer this question decisively one way or the other.

It is an undoubted fact that in exchange for undertaking various tasks as an auxiliary organ of government, Nokyo (as well as the other statutory agricultural interest groups) receive various forms of administrative and financial support.[574] The parallel administrative set-up of government and the agricultural cooperatives facilitates not only Nokyo's supervision by MAFF administrators but also its role in implementing agricultural policy and its subsidisation by government.[575] These linkages are closest in the case of the mainstream multi-purpose side of Nokyo rather than the specialist side which tends to be more independent of government.

Patronage comes in many different guises. Firstly, it comes in the form of a 'licence' to expand the range of economic activities in which the agricultural cooperatives are legitimately able to participate and from which they draw financial benefits. A number of amendments to Nokyo law and the passage of other legal provisions enabled the agricultural cooperatives to diversify their operations. As Calder points out, in 1950, the abolition of restrictions on the private distribution of stockfeed, agricultural chemicals and tools allowed the agricultural cooperatives to supply these goods to farmers. Under the Yoshida administration alone, the agricultural cooperatives were also offered 'extensive tax and regulatory benefits through six major revisions of the Agricultural Cooperatives Law'.[576] The ABL of 1961 provided for an even wider range of economic activities by the agricultural cooperatives. Article 17 states that 'the State shall formulate the necessary measures including the establishment of joint-use facilities by the agricultural cooperatives and the development and improvement of schemes for joint farm work to be carried out by the agricultural cooperatives';[577] while Article 18 permits the 'agricultural cooperatives to underwrite trust relating to the leasing and sale of farmland.'[578]

The passage of the ABL was followed by amendments to existing laws and the passage of others facilitating the adoption by the agricultural cooperatives of various government-sanctioned functions in relation to the implementation of the ABL. For example, the Nokyo Law and the Agricultural Land Law were amended and the Agricultural Modernisation Fund Assistance Law was passed to accommodate the changes introduced by the ABL. Nokyo Law was revised to permit the agricultural cooperatives to undertake agricultural land trust activities and to permit the formation of agricultural production cooperatives. The Agricultural Land Law was amended (some agricultural land ownership restrictions were abolished) in order to authorise the formation of agricultural production juridical persons, which were required for Nokyo to be able to undertake agricultural land trust activities. The Agricultural Modernisation Fund Assistance Law was passed to establish a trust fund association that would underwrite interest subsidies by the state and by prefectural governments for agricultural cooperatives and other agriculture-related organisations to provide long-term low-interest funding to farm households for the provision of barns and livestock sheds, agricultural machinery, fruit tree and other cattle facilities and so on.

Diversified activities under government sponsorship thus generated direct spin-offs in terms of Nokyo's own business expansion. Nokyo was able to seek its own business interests through the mechanism of policy implementation.[579] In assisting the government in the administration and implementation of government policy, it developed its own enterprises.

The second form of government patronage is the category of administratively-sanctioned monopolies. Because of its designated functions in the FC system, Nokyo gained instant dominance of the delivery of grain products (above all rice) to the Food Agency of the MAF. In turn, it 'was able to maintain and expand its own organization through its reliance on the Food Control System.'[580] Mitsukawa, for example, partly explains Nokyo's victory over MAF Minister Kono's FC reform plan of 1961[581] to the fact that government rice purchases from their principal collecting agencies – the agricultural cooperatives – stabilised their operations and thereby increased Nokyo's influence on politics.[582]

Moreover, as a government-designated rice collection agent, Nokyo received various direct financial benefits, such as commissions from government for collecting and storing the rice sold by farmers to the government,[583] in addition to other benefits such as interest and incentive subsidies for rice sold directly to wholesalers under the IDR system.[584] As Mitsukawa observes, Nokyo's dependence on the FC system meant that it was impossible for Nokyo to maintain its functions and management independently of agricultural administration and the LDP's *norin giin* (whose political power, Nokyo frequently harnessed to preserve the FC system).[585] In 1950, the agricultural cooperatives were also granted a monopoly over the distribution of government rations of fertilisers to farmers.[586] This laid a solid foundation for Nokyo's purchasing business.

Low-interest institutional loans to agriculture are another area where the agricultural cooperatives' position has been buttressed by the assignment of quasi-governmental functions.[587] Government-subsidised long-term, low-interest loans have been provided to the farmers through the cooperatives from the Agriculture, Forestry and Fisheries Finance Corporation,[588] the Agricultural Modernisation Fund and the Agricultural Improvement Fund. The latter provides loans to farmers at low-interest rates for purposes such as improvement of the agricultural production environment, managed crop conversion, the development of agricultural techniques and fostering the development of joint-utilisation facilities.[589] As Moore explains, while about half of all loans for farmers come from Nokyo, if government loans administered by Nokyo are added in, the proportion is closer to 70 per cent.[590]

Not surprisingly, Nokyo's auxiliary role in agricultural administration has generated vested interests in government-regulated systems involving controlled and semi-controlled products such as rice, fertilisers and low-interest loans. These were all products and services where government policies granted Nokyo the benefits of 'monopolistic franchises'.[591]

A third major category of patronage has been the government's use of Nokyo as an institutionalised mechanism for dispensing the whole array of agricultural subsidies and price support to farmers. Under the Central Bank for Agriculture and Forestry Law, Norinchukin acts as the central collection and distribution point for these subsidies and payments. For example, government payments to farmers for rice have been channelled through the cooperative financial network thereby directing what is frequently the largest source of farmers' income from agriculture through Nokyo savings accounts.[592] The same agricultural cooperative channel has been used for government deficiency payments to producers for raw milk for processing under the Provisional Measures Law for Subsidies to Producers of Raw Milk for Processing.

Another significant source of government assistance has been the direct financial support Nokyo has received from its administering body – the MAFF – for its own organisational purposes, particularly in relation to agricultural cooperative management. In the late 1940s and early 1950s, many *tankyo* and *rengokai* found themselves in dire financial straits because of a chronic shortage of working capital.[593] When local initiatives for restructuring proved ineffective,[594] the cooperatives turned to the government for help. The MAF responded with a 'reconstruction and consolidation' (*saiken seibi*) programme implemented in a series of laws pertaining to Agriculture, Forestry and Fishery Cooperative Unions' Reconstruction and Consolidation. The first of these was the *Saiken Seibiho* of 1951. With the support of this law, agricultural cooperatives suffering from large deficits laid off surplus personnel and abolished bad assets. The programme also provided for direct government assistance in the form of subsidies and technical advice to *tankyo* and *rengokai* designated as 'non-flourishing'.[595] A total of ¥3.3 million was allocated in subsidies to cover the deficits of some 2,600 agricultural cooperative organisations.[596] State grants saved many local co-ops from organisational demise, although the majority of *rengokai* failed to fulfil reconstruction plans in spite of large amounts of financial assistance.[597]

The Consolidation Promotion Law (*Seibi Sokushinho*) of 1953 was specifically designed to improve the managerial situation of the federations.[598] In addition to promoting their rationalisation, the law provided interest subsidies for *shinren* and Norinchukin investments in other federations. It also permitted favourable treatment for Nokyo in relation to juridical persons tax (*hojinzei*).[599] Marketing, purchasing, silk and agricultural processing federations were subsequently unified into economic federations, the deficits of Zenkoren and Zenhanren completely vanished by 1955, and the 44 *keizairen* designated for consolidation under this law pulled themselves out of a poor managerial situation by 1963.[600]

Still, as of March 1955, one-quarter of *tankyo* (3,300) were still in financial difficulties. What followed was the passage of the 1956 Nokyo Consolidation Special Measures Law (*Nokyo Seibi Tokubetsu Sochiho*), which was the *tankyo* version of the Consolidation Promotion Law for the *rengokai*. The main difference between the two was that the former aimed to revive *tankyo* by a merger process.[601] Taken together, the laws passed in 1951, 1953 and 1956 became known as the 'three reconstruction laws' (*Saiken Sanpo*).[602]

The combined effect of all these programmes was a perceptible shift towards agricultural cooperative dependence on government. As Asuwa comments, the process strengthened the posture of policy dependence (*seisaku izon*) of Nokyo management.[603] Because most of the recipient agricultural cooperatives were exempted from repaying the subsidies, the MAF succeeded in making these organisations indebted to the government.[604] Nokyo's relationship with the MAF tended to revert to that of a subordinate group continually petitioning for subsidies. As Ishimi points out: 'Despite the fact that Nokyo was organised as an independent organisation from the state, it relinquished its policy of independence and started relying on the government only after about five years after its formation.'[605] Thus, 'the agricultural cooperative unions which had been organized as free and democratic farmers associations after the Second World war came under the direct control and supervision of the government in return for the provision by the latter of financial assistance.'[606] Fujitani notes further that the infusion of large amounts of funds to cover co-op management deficits merely strengthened the trend of postwar cooperatives to become extensions of government administration.[607] Takeuchi and Otawara also identify broader political factors at work. As soon as the Peace Treaty was concluded between Japan and the United States in 1951, bureaucratic control over Nokyo was revived.[608] Although the agricultural cooperatives were reconstituted as voluntary farmers' organisations independent of government, by the time the reconstruction and consolidation programmes had been completed, the government's policy of non-interference had been well and truly abandoned.[609]

The second major set of structural alterations to the Nokyo system undertaken with direct governmental assistance was the programme of amalgamation (*gappei*) of the agricultural cooperatives.[610] It began in 1961 with the passage of the Nokyo Amalgamation Assistance Law (*Nokyo Gappei Joseiho*).[611] Even though Nokyo opposed sections of both the ABL[612] and the Nokyo Amalgamation Assistance Law, it compromised with the government over both policies basically because it had no choice. Amalgamations of the cooperatives were further advanced in a series of amendments to the law in 1966, 1970 and 1972. These promoted mergers of local co-ops by providing the necessary funding for guidance to agricultural cooperatives undergoing amalgamation and the expenses involved in unifying co-op facilities accompanying these mergers.[613]

Although government-subsidised amalgamations began as a policy of dealing with the slump in *nokyo* management, they continued as measures for strengthening the basis of that management.[614] The *gappei* program produced quite large reductions in the number of local agricultural cooperatives and is still progressing.[615] Between 1960 and 1970, the number of *sogo nokyo* virtually halved (from just over 12,000 to just over 6,000). By 1980 it had dwindled further to just over 4,500 and in 1990 to a little over 3,500. By 1998, the pace of amalgamation had quickened with numbers of *sogo nokyo* dropping to just over 2,000. The slide in numbers of specialist co-ops was even more rapid, slumping from nearly 17,000 in 1960 to a little over 5,000 in 1980, just on 4,000 in 1990 and a little over 3,300 in 1998. Comparable declines were registered amongst the upper level federations, where the total dropped from 1,216 in 1960, to 290 in 1998.[616]

Since the passage of the original Nokyo Amalgamation Assistance Law, the MAFF has extended the law at least nine times. It has also continued to assist the amalgamation process by providing tax reduction measures for merged *nokyo*.[617] In 1986 the law was revised to allow taxes such as the corporation tax, income tax, enterprise tax, and registration and licence fees to be reduced in situations where agricultural cooperatives merged in the period April 1986–March 1989. Government subsidies also continued to be provided to assist with the merger of agricultural cooperatives. In FY 1995, the agricultural cooperatives received around ¥470 million in subsidies from the MAFF for agricultural cooperative amalgamation purposes,[618] dipping to just over ¥414 million in 1998 (see Table 2.6). In addition, substantial amounts have been supplied by prefectural governments.[619]

The agricultural cooperatives also benefit from subsidies to carry out activities duly designated under Nokyo Law. Article 73, Clause 8 of Nokyo Law states that 'the state within the sphere of the budget can assist with a part of the necessary costs for central union activities.'[620] Since 1954 (the year of its establishment), Zenchu has received subsidies for auditing purposes, for 'federated Nokyo organisation consolidation promotion works' and for 'agricultural cooperative union mutual aid works'. In FY 1998, the amount received for these designated purposes was over ¥662 million (see Table 2.6). In FY 1995, a new subsidy for Zenchu of over ¥18 million was set up to support its guidance promotion activities.[621]

Other legislation facilitates the supply of direct government assistance to agricultural cooperatives other than the central unions or provides for other channels through which funds can be paid by government to the agricultural cooperatives from budgetary and other sources. The ABL of 1961 incorporated a number of paragraphs which provided for additional government support to the operations of the agricultural cooperatives and their federations. Under Article 12 of the law, the state was permitted to furnish direct assistance to the agricultural cooperatives for the development and improvement of cooperative marketing, purchasing, production and other facilities. It specified that 'the State shall take whatever measures are needed to develop the sales, purchasing and other activities undertaken by the agricultural cooperatives and their federations, modernise their transactions in agricultural commodities, develop their undertakings related to agriculture, and develop and improve undertakings relating to the processing of agricultural commodities or the production of agricultural requisites in which the agricultural cooperatives and their federations have invested and/or otherwise participated'.[622] In addition, Article 24 of the Law provided that the State would formulate the necessary measures for the organisational improvement of groups related to agriculture in order to elevate the position of those engaged in agriculture and ensure the development of agriculture.[623]

The last major category of patronage is represented by the subsidies that the agricultural cooperatives acquire for the various tasks they undertake on the government's behalf which are not directly related to agricultural cooperative activities per se. Zenchu, for example, receives subsidies for assisting the government in the implementation of agricultural policy

Table 2.6 Fiscal 1998–99 national budget subsidies[a] allocated by the MAFF main ministry to agricultural cooperative organisations as either primary or secondary works agents[b]

Unit: ¥'000

Nokyo organisation(s)	Amount received and year of first subsidy[c]	Main administrative purpose for which subsidy was received[d]
Agricultural Cooperative Unions	¥414,161 (1988)	Promoting the reorganisation of Nokyo federated organisations.
	¥3,022,514 (1995)	Consolidating facilities to promote efficient and planned livestock production reorganisation integrated from the production through to the processing and distribution stages.
	¥876,970 (1995)	Reorganising and consolidating regional livestock production.
	¥4,578,802 (1995)	Consolidating facilities to promote efficient and planned beef production reorganisation integrated from the production through to the processing and distribution stages.
	¥3,194,449 (1995)	Disseminating new techniques, the promotion of cattle hygiene management, and the cultivation of enthusiastic management bodies in order to promote the reorganisation and consolidation of regional production of beef.
	¥158,000 (1962)	Constructing stock farm pastures in order to cultivate high efficiency livestock management.
	¥496,000 (1991)	Grassland development works and construction of stockfarm facilities in order to cultivate high efficiency livestock management.
	¥909,000 (1989)	Improving the livelihood environment of livestock.
Zenchu	¥662,676 (1954)	Auditing that the Nokyo central unions undertake, Nokyo federated organisation consolidation promotion works and agricultural cooperative union mutual aid works.
	¥13,955 (1996)	Establishing a stable production system for rice and wheat in response to demand.
	¥18,924 (1992)	Promoting lower usage of fertilisers.
	¥21,665 (1995)	Promoting an aged persons policy in agricultural, mountainous and fishing villages and develop the capabilities of women in order to establish a partnership of men and women in agricultural and rural villages.

	¥33,410 (1995)	Guidance activities in order to achieve the advancement of a comprehensive promotion policy for strengthening an agricultural production system.
	¥100,355 (1998)	Promoting harmonisation of rice production adjustment target areas by producer groups across regions.
	¥43,094 (1995)	Guidance for promoting a comprehensive policy for livestock reorganisation.
	¥5,756 (1996)	Rice paddy management promotion.
National Nokyo Settlers' Federation	¥144,658 (1958)	Talent and technical exchange that the National Nokyo Settlers' Federation undertakes.
Zenno	¥91,475,000 (1998)	Rice demand and supply stabilisation.
	¥4,791,750 (1998)	Rice cultivation management stabilisation.
	¥20,319,980 (1998)	Achieving the harmonious transition to a new rice policy.
	¥20,950,378 (1969)	Implementing a planned distribution policy for independently distributed rice.
	¥677,670 (1989)	Providing independently distributed rice for the school lunch programme.
Total subsidies received by Nokyo	**¥153,089,167**	

Notes:

a Sources are the General Account and Special Account budgets. Only those allocations from the General Account budget by the MAFF main ministry are included. Subsidy contributions from prefectural and municipal governments and from other sources for the above administrative purposes are not included, although these may be substantial.

b A group becomes a secondary works agent when a central government budget subsidy is channelled through prefectural or local governments. Where a group is a secondary agent, the subsidy has been treated as if the total amount was allocated to the group.

c Where Nokyo organisations as well as others (including local governments) share in a subsidy, amounts have been divided equally amongst them. Amounts, therefore, must be considered as only approximate.

d In all cases the actual subsidy was used to assist with the costs incurred by the agricultural cooperative organisations in carrying out the specified function designated by government.

Source: Hojokin Soran, 1998, pp. 188–613.

objectives in a number of different areas. The 1998–99 budget figures reveal that since FY 1990, Zenchu has been given subsidies for the establishment of a stable production system for rice and wheat in response to demand; since FY 1992 for executing policies to lower the usage of fertilisers; since FY 1995 for promoting an aged persons' policy in agricultural villages, for strengthening the agricultural production system and for promoting the reorganisation and consolidation of regional livestock production; since FY 1996 for promoting rice paddy management; and since FY 1998 for promoting harmonisation of rice production adjustment target areas by producer groups across regions (details of actual amounts are provided in Table 2.6). The total amount of subsidies received by Zenchu for all purposes in FY 1998 was just under ¥900 million (calculated from figures in Table 2.6).

Agricultural cooperatives and agricultural cooperative federations also benefit from subsidies for a range of policy tasks under various laws. Under the Livestock Products Price Stabilisation Law, for example, agricultural cooperatives can get loans and subsidies channelled through the LIPC for livestock-related enterprises.[624] These continue under ALIC. Under the Provisional Measures Law for Soybean and Rapeseed Subsidies (1961), the agricultural cooperatives and federations of agricultural cooperatives are given subsidies for the rational and planned marketing of soybeans and rapeseeds in order to adjust the methods and amounts of marketing, storage and collection of these products.[625] Under the Land Improvement Law, the agricultural cooperatives pick up subsidies for undertaking various agricultural development and rural improvement activities on behalf of the government. As one Japanese agricultural policy journalist observed: 'Who has gained most from structural improvement works? – Nokyo'.[626]

Total subsidies allocated by the MAFF to agricultural cooperatives (*nogyo kyodo kumiai*) in FY 1998 amounted to ¥13.6 billion (calculated from figures in Table 2.6).[627] The subsidies were allocated for a range of purposes, but all but one were directed to livestock-related projects conducted by the agricultural cooperatives. In addition, agricultural cooperatives obtained a further ¥1.6 billion via the Hokkaido Development Agency for promoting pasture-based livestock farming, ¥9.9 billion from the Defence Agency for 'facilities environs consolidation assistance', and a total of ¥206 million from the National Land Agency for various agriculture-related activities.[628]

In 1998, a number of substantial new subsidies were introduced in connection with a new rice policy.[629] These were paid to Zenno for conducting several tasks in relation to rice distribution, supporting rice farmers' incomes, and demand and supply adjustment in order to reduce the rice surplus. The total allocation to Zenno amounted to around ¥137.5 billion[630] (calculated from the figures in Table 2.6).[631]

In sum, local co-ops as well as the national federations and central unions have continued to gain the financial benefits of their participation in the implementation of agricultural policy. They are provided with subsidies from government to support their own organisational objectives as well as public policy objectives.[632] In FY 1998, these amounted to a total of more than ¥153 billion (see Table 2.6).

Nokyo could be said, therefore, to amalgamate contradictory forces within its organisational structure. On the one hand, it is a voluntary organisation, representative interest group, agricultural policy pressure group and independent business group; on the other it is an instrumentality of the administration, facilitating the spread and penetration of government policies in areas such as Food Control, agricultural finance and agricultural subsidies into the agricultural sector,[633] and receiving large dollops of government patronage in return. On the other hand, although its twin roles as a political pressure group and subordinate organ of government policy might appear contradictory, Nokyo in its response to and dependence on policy played both roles cleverly to expand its business and organisation.[634] The result was a mutual relationship between the state and supplicant, with 'the MAFF using Nokyo to implement policies and Nokyo advancing its own interests through fulfilling that role, in many instances of . . . carrying through agricultural policy.'[635]

The way in which Nokyo has been inextricably interwoven into the whole fabric of agricultural administration and policy execution in Japan is described by Ishida as representing the 'governmentalization of interest groups, a particular type of institutionalization encountered in Japan. In this process the specific purposes of interest groups become fused with governmental purposes'.[636] In Ishida's view, although the agricultural cooperatives became the dominant force in the villages, 'they remained dependent on government control over the marketing of rice and on government subsidies, while playing their perennial role of helping government policies to be accepted in rural areas.'[637] He further argues that organisations that were not completely independent of government inevitably made concessions to the government bureaucracy[638] and that such an organisational basis resulted 'in almost overwhelming difficulties in their interest group activities . . . [with] their interest demands . . . often identified with the request for government subsidies.'[639] The concessions Nokyo was able to extract from government largely depended on the fact that the agricultural cooperatives provided a convenient link to farmers' production and livelihood.[640]

Ongoing financial support from government thus became a permanent incentive for compliance with government measures. In Ishida's view, the organisational weakness of the agricultural cooperatives made it 'impossible for these farmers' interest groups to fully develop their interest group functions.'[641] The guiding principle of Nokyo's policy-related action was the need to maintain the flow of subsidies and other government funding into and through the organisation. This became the criterion against which all agricultural cooperative strategies, both policy-related and electoral, were measured.

Thus, the corporatised nature of Nokyo's relations with government as well as state financial support compromised Nokyo's organisational independence and imposed limits on the conduct of its agricultural policy activities. As Kuwabara puts it, 'the *chuokai* which are core organisations of *nosei katsudo*, include *nokyo* which implement supplementary administrative operations of national policies such as food control. Therefore, the *nosei katsudo* of the *chuokai* naturally have limitations.'[642] Ishida goes further: 'The functions of interest representation on the part of agricultural cooperative unions . . . cannot threaten that of the economic enterprises which the farmers undertake through them . . . nor can they resort to any methods which would contradict the intentions of the government and therefore might result in the reduction of government subsidies.'[643] Nor can Nokyo impose negative sanctions like breaking off ties with the MAFF.[644]

Ishikawa concludes that although Nokyo acts as a pressure group when it mobilises several thousand representatives to undertake mass petition exercises, its agricultural policy activities can never go beyond the limitations of its functioning as a subcontracting body of the government, because it cannot adopt tactics beyond petition activities, such as strikes, which might lead its patrons in the government to discard it.[645] Asuwa makes a similar observation, arguing that because Nokyo acts as a subcontracting organ of state administration, Nokyo's *nosei katsudo* has big limits.[646] Sakurai, for example, contrasts the approach of Nokyo and the farmers' unions to the introduction of the IDR system in 1969. Both sets of groupings launched campaigns opposing it, but Nokyo as an economic organisation had no alternative in the end but to participate in it, although there was no change in its basic opposition to the idea. About 1,000 Zennichino members, on the other hand, entered the Nokyo Building in Tokyo demanding that Zenchu executives withdraw their approval of the IDR system. Given its status, Nokyo had to accommodate the reality of having to deal in independently distributed rice, something that its own agricultural policy leadership accepted as illustrating the limits to its agricultural policy activities.[647] When Zenchu canvassed the Nokyo prefectural rice headquarters chairmen, only two prefectures clearly expressed their objections to the IDR system.[648]

Thus Nokyo has had no choice but to reject 'anti-system strategies' and operate as a 'pressure group within the system' (*taiseinai no atsuryoku dantai*).[649] Its political constitution is habitually 'pro-system' or 'pro-establishment'.[650] As some observers argue, Zenchu's confrontations with the MAFF are just a sham. In fact, the MAFF expects Zenchu to apply pressure on the LDP and the MOF on its behalf.[651]

The general perception of the constraints on Nokyo's demand-making as an interest group is shared by other organisations that have a more autonomous status than the agricultural cooperatives. According to Rakuseiren leaders, Nokyo's central unions cannot represent farmers directly because they receive subsidies.[652] In a similar vein, Nakamura Yoshijiro, Zennosoren Chairman, lamented the 'limits to Nokyo's agricultural policy activities' in the early 1970s, arguing that these arose from Nokyo's activities 'within the system', which prevented it from ever really acting on its dissatisfaction with government agricultural policies.[653]

Nokyo's limitations as an autonomous farmers' organisation have been even more strongly challenged by the JCP, which argues that the ruling classes use national organisations like Nokyo to control the farmers and farm villages. In its view, Nokyo is an agent of 'monopoly capitalism' that cooperates with government agricultural policy as an 'executive group'.[654] Ono holds a similar view, asserting that from the time of its establishment, Nokyo possessed the character of a subordinate organ of state control. This was particularly effected through its monopolistic functions in relation to rice.[655] In short, Nokyo 'control' has dual aspects: it is controlled by government just as it acts as a controlling agent of government in relation to farmers.

A common thread in most of these arguments is that Nokyo's fundamental organisational identity has leaned far more in the direction of a MAFF *gaikaku dantai* than in the direction of an agricultural pressure group. As Takeuchi and Otawara put it, Nokyo's intimate relationship with government underlines its strong character as a public institution (*seido toshite no Nokyo*) rather than as a pressure group (*atsuryoku dantai toshite no Nokyo*).[656] In fusing the roles of government agent and farmers' organisation, Nokyo embodies a fundamental internal contradiction which calls into question its identity as a genuine interest group.[657]

The inbuilt curbs on Nokyo's role as an interest group are well understood and accepted by its own executive leadership. In 1974–75, in the wake of extremist action taken by some farmers in pursuit of higher producer rice prices, Zenchu conducted an internal investigation into 'the way in which the farmers' voice should be organised and Nokyo's agricultural policy activities should be carried out'. The terms of reference for the investigation stated that 'Nokyo is facing increasing demands for illegal action, for unrealistic requests and for a stance against the ruling party. This reflects farmers' dissatisfaction with policies that undermine agriculture in the wake of rapid economic growth and with the government because of abnormal rates of inflation, strikes in other industries and the spread of progressive thinking in farm villages.'[658] The report of the investigation recommended putting severe restrictions on Nokyo's political activities. It concluded: 'We are not prepared to take measures that may cause the destruction of the organisation or obstacles to Nokyo's economic activities.'[659]

On the other hand, the arguments about Nokyo's inherent organisational weakness and dependence on administrative authorities were, to some extent, challenged during the course of its organisational evolution and economic expansion in later decades. Firstly, agricultural cooperative management was gradually weaned from government subsidies for internal organisational purposes. Generally speaking, large-scale rescues of *sogo nokyo* in dire financial distress were confined to the initial period of Nokyo's development in the early 1950s.[660] The *gappei* programme that followed in the 1960s was designed to produce more viable cooperatives.[661] Amalgamation contributed greatly to the increased management efficiency of the *tankyo* and also bolstered their business operations. The agricultural cooperatives recovered from the period of management weakness and financial distress not only as a result of government support but also their own efforts.[662] By the early 1970s, over 98 per cent of all multi-purpose cooperatives were recording profits. In effect agricultural cooperative management was revived and made stronger by the financial assistance from the MAF which was seeking to promote agricultural cooperative development. In rebuilding Nokyo management, the MAF enhanced Nokyo's independence.[663]

Secondly, the expansion of Nokyo's business activities became an important source of independent organisational clout. As already noted, under the paternalistic eye of the MAF, the agricultural cooperatives were permitted to move into an ever wider range of businesses in the farm sector through successive amendments to Nokyo Law.[664] Meanwhile, national Nokyo organisations such as Norinchukin and Zenkyoren were officially encouraged to diversify their operations into ancillary businesses including financial activities in areas such as international share and bond trading, foreign exchange transactions, company development, insurance, loans to non-banking organisations and so on.[665] Agricultural cooperative groups at all levels also invested in agriculture-related industries via subsidiary companies.[666]

Nokyo's economic and financial expansion contributed to the formation of an immensely powerful, independent, economic power base. The rapid expansion of the Japanese economy supported this growth as did the rises in farm incomes resulting from the increase in the rate of part-time farming and the dramatic lifting of commodity support prices. By the late 1960s, Nokyo's expanding business operations were generating much greater organisational independence and transforming Nokyo from a *gaikaku dantai* into an *atsuryoku dantai*.[667]

During the period of rapid economic growth, Nokyo thus greatly buttressed its power as a pressure group. On those occasions when Nokyo did come into conflict with the administrative ideas of the MAF about what its legitimate activities should be,[668] it increasingly displayed a 'firm attitude' (*tsuyogoshi*) towards the government. It also positively rejected any *amakudari* by MAF officials in order to bolster its autonomy.

Although Nokyo was not able to countenance activities that threatened its legal and policy obligations and although it abrogated a certain measure of its organisational autonomy by accepting subsidies, the resulting limitations on its policy and tactical choices were to some extent counterbalanced by the tremendous expansion of its independent financial and economic power. The dimensions of Nokyo's economic operations put it on a par with some of Japan's best known business conglomerates. Nokyo became a veritable giant in a nation of economic giants.

Thirdly, Nokyo was not corporatised to anything like the same degree as its organisational antecedents. The *nokai* and the *sangyo kumiai* were commonly regarded as being 'glued' to the MAF, particularly in the late 1930s when

producer cooperative organisations merged and became centralised institutions for the collection of agricultural products. Indeed, they always existed
far more for state purposes than for articulating or promoting members'
interests to government. The *nogyokai* were even more closely controlled by
the state. They functioned mainly for the purpose of mobilising farmers to
achieve agricultural and other political objectives during the war. Even for a
short period after the war, the *nogyokai* were described as 'relatives' of the
MAF. All Nokyo's predecessors, in short, functioned primarily to achieve
state purposes in relation to the diffusion of agricultural policy, and in the
case of the *nogyokai*, importantly as controlling agencies of farmers on behalf
of the government.

Despite the tradition of government-sponsored agricultural organisations
and the fact that Nokyo inherited the basic infrastructure of the *nogyokai*
after the war, relations between government and the agricultural cooperatives
were structurally different and, according to one group of Japanese agricultural policy journalists, gradually became more distant over time.[669] The
fundamental difference between the two organisations was the MAF's
switching from direct to indirect control (i.e. administrative supervision) of
the cooperatives. Amongst other things, this was mandated by Nokyo's
internal democratisation[670] and the principle of voluntary membership.
These organisational characteristics changed the relationship between
agricultural cooperative leaders and their farmer members, circumscribing
Nokyo's powers to control farmers on behalf of the government. No longer
was the bureaucracy able unilaterally to impose its will on farmers via their
own organisations. Postwar democratisation transformed not only the
relationship between the government and agricultural groups but also
between agricultural groups and their members. Farmers' organisations were
much more autonomous and their leaders were made more accountable to
their farmer members through democratic election processes.[671] Nokyo thus
considerably boosted its rice-roots representational character based on
democratic norms,[672] which strengthened its position as an independent
farmers' pressure group.

Lastly, although the central organisations of Nokyo might act as instruments of government administration, they and the regional and local Nokyo
organisations also engage in mass mobilisation activities in support of their
policy demands[673] as well as in electoral activities.[674] Furthermore, they have
created their own organisational offshoots to get around the legal constraints
on these activities imposed by Nokyo Law and even the administrative
strictures imposed by their corporatised relationship with the MAFF.

In fact, Nokyo's expanding electoral power became an important factor
underpinning its organisational independence. Nokyo was increasingly able to
generate autonomous political power because of the strategic importance of
farm voters in the national electorate, the increasing involvement of agricultural cooperative organisations in electoral support activities at all levels of
government, the extent to which Nokyo achieved both direct and indirect

representation in the Diet, and the emerging alliance between Nokyo and conservative party politicians at the rice roots. Through its vote-collecting ability, Nokyo preserved its independence and voice.[675]

Nokyo's growing political efficacy was evident as early as 1953, when it successfully applied pressure on agricultural and forestry Diet members to raise the producer rice price.[676] Although there were compelling reasons to institute price incentives to increase output in the light of an extremely poor harvest, the actual size of the increase was widely viewed as a political victory for the agricultural cooperatives. Following the 1953 decision, the fight for the producer rice price demand became an annual event in the middle of the year.[677]

The second turning point was the planned reorganisation of agricultural groups in 1955–56 in which MAF Minister, Kono Ichiro, proposed to restrict agricultural cooperative functioning to economic activities only (not including credit functions) and to set up other agricultural organisations as farmers' interest groups.[678] This proposal, together with Kono's plan for reforming the FC system by abolishing rice control,[679] were both defeated by comprehensive counter-attacks from the entire Nokyo organisation. In relation to the latter, Zenchu established a Food Control Task Force to conduct a nationwide anti-FC reform campaign[680] and used its leverage over the LDP in view of the impending UH election in July 1956 to good effect.[681] As Dore observed, one of the morals drawn from both these disputes was that Nokyo was 'able to exert sufficient influence on rural voters to constitute an extremely strong pressure group capable of influencing government policy.'[682] The defeat of Kono's plan to reorganise agricultural organisations prevented a reversion to the traditional form of government-controlled farmers' interest groups which existed to serve state purposes and whose autonomy was strongly circumscribed.[683]

The third turning point was the successful implementation in 1958 of a pension scheme for the employees of agricultural organisations with the passage of the Agriculture, Forestry and Fishery Groups Staff Members' Mutual Aid Law (*Noringyogyo Dantai Shokuin Kyosai Kumiaiho*). According to Ishida, around 300 LH members, 'including both Conservatives and those in opposition, lent their influence to facilitate the passage of the bill by playing the role of intermediaries'.[684] Nokyo's coming of age as a pressure group dated from this period of the mid- to late 1950s, when it scored these successive policy victories.[685]

When it encountered MAF resistance, Nokyo's strategy was to outflank the bureaucracy and extract concessions from the ruling party, or use ruling party politicians to put pressure on the MAF and its minister. When, as MAF Minister in 1961, Kono made a second attempt to reform the FC system,[686] Nokyo launched a nationwide campaign to prevent the Kono plan from being realised, emphasising the likely political costs to the LDP in terms of loss of farmers' electoral support. As in 1956, Kono found himself opposed by a large section of his own party, who argued that the plan was premature, particularly in the light of the impending UH election in mid-1962. In the end, this viewpoint prevailed and the plan was shelved. In other words, Nokyo's partial dependence on the bureaucracy was counterbalanced by its political leverage *vis-à-vis* the ruling party.[687] By the late 1950s, Nokyo was simultaneously expanding its role as a pressure group and as a subordinate electoral organisation of the LDP.[688] Although Nokyo was vulnerable when it started out and had to rely on politicians, as it gained increased economic and vote-gathering power, it mobilised a strong voice that even influential Diet members could not ignore.[689]

So, while some elements of administrative control and dependence remained in Nokyo's relationship with the MAFF, Nokyo assumed a position of some leverage in relation to the government party because of its stronger political standing and its electoral value to the LDP. In short, Nokyo's political and electoral power helped to offset its organisational weakness *vis-à-vis* the bureaucracy. In this context, the analytical distinction between 'the relationships between interest groups and political parties and between interest groups and the bureaucracy'[690] is important. As Pempel and Tsunekawa observe, in the postwar democratic system, political parties and the Diet were significantly strengthened as political institutions, which 'greatly expanded the channels of influence open to . . . [the agricultural sector] and tended to counterbalance corporatist tendencies.'[691]

The extent of Nokyo's organisational autonomy is thrown into sharper relief when compared with the position of the other statutory agricultural interest groups. Although the latter share with Nokyo a number of common features – at the rice roots, each has a membership of individual farmers, each performs public functions for private benefit, each has specific policy interests that it pursues and each seeks direct and indirect representation in the Diet – there are some key differences: Nokyo is the only one whose membership extends over the entire agricultural electorate, it is the only one representing the broad collectivity of agricultural policy interests and it is the only one operating its own, independent economic and financial businesses.

The agricultural committee organisation, for example, which shares with Nokyo a legally sanctioned interest representation function, has very limited financial resources on its own account. It is largely dependent on subsidies donated by central and prefectural governments and its representation of farmers is limited and indirect. Although it conducts a representational function, it does not have a strong pressure group character. Only when it lobbies for subsidies for its own organisational purposes at budget time or joins with Nokyo in demanding increases in the producer rice price and the agricultural budget does it assume such a role. Even then, because it operates on the basis of government funding it cannot exert genuine pressure on the government.[692] The scale of its dependence on MAFF largesse is, therefore, much greater than Nokyo's and thus its function as an instrument of interest articulation more limited.[693] With its strongly developed administrative base and its weaker claim as an organisation representing farmers, the agricultural committee organisation is not in a position to mount a serious challenge to the government on policy issues. It more readily and rapidly falls into line with the MAFF's position on any issue, and this, on occasions, has been the cause of differences of opinion with Nokyo.

The agricultural mutual aid associations and land improvement groups exhibit a similar degree of dependence on government. Indeed, their very organisational rationale is to distribute subsidies for various government projects and programmes. In this respect they are subsidy-dependent and budget-parasitic organisations. This naturally politicises their interests at the same time as it undermines their organisational independence. Their only source of independent political clout is via the electoral system. Organisational membership can be tapped for votes and other electoral resources. Like Nokyo, this generates leverage *vis-à-vis* certain individual politicians, who can be deployed to political advantage within the ruling party. The potential for mobilising members at the rice roots is not as extensive as Nokyo's, however, particularly in the case of the agricultural committee organisation.[694]

Finally, corporatisation itself generates policy leverage by institutionalising Nokyo's access to the administration and by facilitating direct participation in the formation of public policy in a bureaucratic-administrative context. Paradoxically, the development towards greater economic autonomy during the 1960s and 1970s was accompanied by Nokyo's increasing corporatisation into the policymaking and policy implementation processes as legal and institutional mechanisms of incorporation multiplied. Nokyo's closer integration into agricultural administration also served to bolster rather than undermine its standing as a representative organisation for farmers. In fact, as Fujitani argues, Nokyo made efforts to extend its capacity as a semi-administrative institution in order to magnify its bargaining power as a pressure group.[695] Takeuchi and Otawara also make the similar point that Nokyo's true character was revealed through its *nosei katsudo* in which it achieved its goals as a pressure group by cosying up to the administration.[696]

In short, corporatisation accords Nokyo the right to participate in the policy process and considerably buttresses its bargaining power over policy. Nokyo is automatically consulted about major changes to policy, proposed amendments to existing legislation or the passage of new laws with which it might be associated. It is the organisation on which the government relies when it wishes to consult the agricultural world. Collaborative planning procedures and two-way consultation processes are institutionalised, maintaining permanent channels of communication between officials and Nokyo leaders.

Indeed, Zenchu benefits from an established tradition of prior consultation with both the LDP and the MAFF in the lead-up to major agricultural policy decisions.[697] It is automatically brought into the negotiation process, with the initiative coming from the government and party side. In this respect, Nokyo exemplifies the model of liberal corporatism in which the state incorporates representatives of major economic sectors into national policymaking processes.

When the Japanese government decided to phase out quotas on beef and citrus imports in June 1988, for example, Zenchu was consulted by the LDP and MAFF during the drawn-out negotiations before each round of talks with the United States.[698] According to Zenchu, while it was 'unhappy' about liberalisation, it did not feel let down by the government.[699] The same modus operandi applied to rice market opening during the Uruguay Round. The MAFF kept Nokyo closely informed of its negotiating positions and indeed discussed these with Nokyo officials in advance. The same procedure was again observed during the December 1998 rice tariffication decision, which was reached by means of a three-way consultation process involving the MAFF, LDP and Zenchu. Given Nokyo's role in domestic rice distribution, it was inevitable that it be brought into the final decisionmaking process on this issue. It is during these kinds of negotiations that various compensation schemes are worked out to appease agricultural cooperative and farming interests.[700] In this way, the government as well as the ruling party avoid the harsh reaction of the organisation and its members.

Thus, while Nokyo is subjected to a mixture of legal controls, institutional constraints, procedural norms and financial inducements which ultimately limit its powers of sanction or non-compliance with government policy, in bargaining on agricultural policy issues, its formal role in the implementation of policy means that Nokyo can extract concessions as the price of its compliance. Administrators must respond in some way to cooperative demands on agricultural policy, particularly in those areas in which the cooperatives are deeply involved: the operations of agricultural price support and distribution systems, crop incentive and acreage reduction schemes, government-sponsored alterations to the structure of agricultural production, the dissemination of advanced farming techniques and the encouragement of long-term agricultural investment. It is difficult to see how, given the extent of Nokyo's role in providing assistance to government in the implementation of these policies, the government could make decisions without close communication and consultation with representatives of the agricultural cooperatives.

As an interest group, Nokyo does not, therefore, just lobby. It sits around the table bargaining, illustrating one of the basic propositions of corporatist theory that '[m]ajor decisions . . . are made by governments after close consultations approximating to negotiations with major interest groups.'[701] As a legitimate participant in policy negotiation Nokyo's interests are considered because it delivers the necessary compliance of its membership on negotiated policies. Nokyo endeavours to 'sell' policies to the government which suit it; the price is ultimate agreement and compliance with government policies. One of the reasons why Nokyo has been such an effective pressure group is that the leadership can obtain a disciplined response from its farmer members even when it strikes a bargain at their expense.[702]

Nokyo's corporatised relationship with government does not, therefore, amount to one-sided dependence or a 'captive' relationship with the MAFF.[703] Although the balance of power remains weighted in the MAFF's favour, this does not prevent Nokyo from exercising bargaining leverage in the negotiating process. Furthermore, what Nokyo loses in terms of diminished levels of organisational autonomy and subordination to the MAFF, it can offset with political and electoral leverage over LDP politicians. Nokyo is thus very different from its organisational antecedents whose 'formal recognition and inclusion in formal policy making and implementation came at the expense of autonomous political development and articulation.'[704] Nokyo's structural dependence on the bureaucracy is counterbalanced by its political independence *vis-à-vis* the ruling party and its penetration of Diet processes.[705] This makes a final judgement on Nokyo's interest group status extremely difficult. Ultimately, Nokyo incorporates aspects of both a *gaikaku dantai* and an *atsuryoku dantai*.

Implications for the corporatist, elitist and pluralist paradigms

As the preceding analysis seeks to demonstrate, state corporatism in Japan is clearly visible in the agricultural sector. Nokyo exhibits strongly corporatist features as do the other statutory agricultural interest groups. Although no single organisation represents agriculture in the political sphere, Nokyo can claim to speak for all farmers because practically all farmers are members. In this sense, Nokyo is a peak organisation of agriculturalists.

Like the agricultural committee organisation, Nokyo is also licensed to represent the agricultural sector to administrative authorities and is formally drawn into policy implementation and formulation processes through legal, institutional and procedural mechanisms. As an agent of state authority Nokyo enjoys privileged access to government as a legitimate participant in negotiations on agricultural policy. Corporatism thus bestows influence and leverage, although ultimately Nokyo's organisational power is constrained by structural dependencies on monopoly franchises, subsidies and other benefits. State-dependency thus eliminates the option of anti-system strategies.

On the other hand, Nokyo's position in relation to both the MAFF and LDP is buttressed by its independent economic, financial and political resources, which serve to counterbalance its dependence on bureaucratic largesse and generate dependencies on the part of Diet politicians. Political resources in particular are a source of policy leverage for Nokyo when it assumes the role of a pressure group and thus help to equilibrate the mutually contradictory aspects of the Nokyo organisation in its relations with government.

Looking at the sector as a whole, corporatisation is ultimately a matter of degree depending on levels of legal, institutional and procedural incorporation amongst different farmers' organisations. Even the farmers' unions are corporatised to some extent – through Zennichino's representation on the RPAC, for example.[706] At the other extreme can be found the level of corporatisation demonstrated by Nokyo and the other statutory agricultural interest groups, which are fully corporatised through legal, institutional and procedural mechanisms. The degree of corporatisation is linked closely to levels of state recognition and access to the policy process, but it does not create exclusive categories of 'insider' and 'outsider' groups. The agricultural policymaking system is not closed in the sense of restricting participation to only those groups that have substantially corporatised relations with the state. Furthermore, the ties amongst the different farmers' organisations, both more corporatised and less corporatised, tend to be non-conflictual and non-competitive, although this does not rule out the possibility of competition and conflict with organised interests in other sectors, such as business.

On the systemic level, the present discussion of corporatisation in the agricultural sector makes no claims to cross-sectoral validity. Corporatism is not necessarily the dominant paradigm for the Japanese interest group system as a whole.[707] It is an aspect of government-group relations which needs to be investigated in each case: at the individual interest group or micro-level; at the sectoral level, and at the systemic or macro-level.[708] It is likely, for instance, that because corporatised interest groups act as instruments of regulation and because they deliver the compliance of their membership with state-sponsored initiatives, levels of corporatisation will vary from sector to sector and will be linked to levels of sectoral regulation. Corporatisation of interest groups supplements the use of other regulatory mechanisms and is highly functional in the regulatory process. It enhances state power at the same time as legitimising it in the eyes of the regulated.[709] Nokyo's ancillary role as administrative agent, for example, has been notably encouraged by the dominant element of regulation in Japanese agriculture.[710] Levels of corporatisation can also vary from group to group even within the same sector, as it does in the case of agricultural organisations, with variations in the mechanisms of corporatisation amongst different groups.

Furthermore, this analysis does not make the standard, derivative claims of corporatist theorists that power is concentrated in the hands of government elites and corporatised interest groups (government, labour and business in the Western European conception[711] and government, business and agriculture in Japan).[712] Although corporatisation bestows privileged status on some agricultural interest groups, formal connections with government are not the only source of interest group power. Indeed, in the traditional elitist conception of Japanese politics, corporatisation is regarded as a source of weakness as noted earlier. Ishida classed Nokyo as being outside the tripartite power elite of big business, bureaucrats and LDP politicians, because of 'its economic and financial weakness'.[713] In his view, Nokyo was one of the 'relatively small and weak pressure groups . . . dependent on bureaucrats for their access to government funds and various other favours', while 'the larger and more powerful employer groups manipulated and used almost at will, and could if necessary negotiate directly with, the leadership of the ruling class'.[714]

Ishida also regarded Nokyo as being in a subordinate relationship to the LDP, distinguishing between economically powerful suppliers of financial support to the government party and economically weak suppliers of votes. In his view, although Nokyo was closely tied to the ruling party, like small business it was linked in a different way to big business because it was 'dependent on government allocations controlled and used by the LDP to maintain its rule'[715] and because it served 'as an organised constituency . . . [for the LDP] at election time.'[716] Ishida argued that Nokyo's organisational weakness explained the amount of public noise it made in presenting its policy demands to government. Powerful organisations like Keidanren did not have to employ the mass, public, lobbying tactics of Nokyo, because of their innate proximity of their leaders to government, their assured access to the centres of power and the money power they exercised, which both reflected and necessitated that the exercise of their power be covert.[717]

As argued earlier, however, Nokyo's economic vulnerability and level of financial dependence on government underwent drastic alteration in the 1960s, 1970s and 1980s as the agricultural cooperatives expanded and diversified their independent business operations.[718] Historical developments in the Nokyo organisation progressively invalidated the fundamental premise of Nokyo's economic and financial weakness, its relative dependence on subsidies for organisational survival and its consequent categorisation as one of the 'weaker' interest groups. Furthermore, Nokyo developed a substantial political power base in relation to the government party, utilising its mass membership and voter mobilisation in crucial farm electorates.[719] Ishida failed to acknowledge these electoral factors as a source of reciprocal leverage on Nokyo's part, enabling it to extract policy favours from the ruling party and to use Diet members as intermediaries with the bureaucracy and the LDP leadership. Moreover, as later policy developments demonstrated, in the clash of giants (Keidanren versus Nokyo) the former has by no means been the automatic victor. In fact, when it came down to key agricultural policy decisions, Nokyo always exercised more influence on the outcome than Keidanren.[720]

The example of Nokyo can, therefore, be used to invalidate the conception of Japan as being ruled by a tripartite power elite consisting of the bureaucracy, LDP politicians and big business which dominated policymaking.[721] Patently, Japan's farm lobby has been an integral and influential actor in Japan's agricultural policymaking process. Highly corporatised groups such as Nokyo are very much 'establishment' groups and could, in this sense, be considered part of the Japanese 'power elite', but not if it is narrowly conceived along conventional tripartite lines. Including agriculture may represent a version of modified elitism (or equally, modified pluralism), with power concentrated in the ruling party, the bureaucracy and those interest groups in the agricultural sector which enjoy continuous and direct access to authoritative decision makers and considerable influence over government policies.[722] In other words, the circle of influence has been expanded to include a range of interest groups, with membership determined by levels of corporatisation as well as proximity to the LDP.

Looking at Japan's agricultural interest group system as a discrete model, it is quite clearly more pluralist than elitist in structure. A multiplicity of representational organisations participate in a wide range of electoral and policy-related activities resulting in the representation of their interests in government. This is suggestive of relatively open political processes in which a range of groups can attempt to mobilise influence.[723] On the other hand, some groups are more highly corporatised than others, resulting in inequalities of access, status and influence amongst groups and more compromised autonomy in the case of the most highly corporatised groups. In this respect, the term 'pluralist corporatism' appears to be the most appropriate because it draws attention to the range of different farm interest groups and thus the absence of sectoral monopolisation by one organisation; to the implicit hierarchy amongst groups depending on their level of corporatisation with government; to the way in which the statutory and institutional interest groups participate in public policymaking not as external pressure groups separate from the state, but rather through recognised cooperative and even collusive relationships with state actors; to the fact that the cooperation and consent of these groups is important for both economic and political management; and to the existence of a single group – Nokyo – which very closely approximates the pure corporatist model.[724] In short, the bureaucracy regulates the agricultural sector by means of a working partnership with agricultural organisations, which are contracted to the government to assist in formulating policies for and allocating resources to the agricultural economy and in implementing policy outcomes.

Conclusion

The preceding analysis has detailed the complexities of the organised representation of agricultural interests in Japan. Although Nokyo's comprehensive coverage of the farm sector suggests a hegemonic role, in fact its position as a farm interest group is supplemented by a wealth of other organisations of differing legal status, historical lineage, functional scope and interest focus. The relationships amongst these groups are generally noncompetitive. While the functions and interests of farmers' groups may vary, basically they reinforce and complement rather than compete with each other. Taken as a whole, they constitute a large interest representational network, characterised by cross-cutting organisational linkages and interlocking membership and leadership structures.

Each of the three categories of agricultural interest groups have generally undergone separate experiences of organisational development and decline. The rice-roots farmers' groups, for example, demonstrated a strong upsurge

during the early postwar period of land reform and organisational democratisation until 1947. This was followed by a decade of disunity and
stagnation particularly for the farmers' unions in the period between land
reform and the so-called 'reform of agriculture' (*nogyo kaikaku*), which began
in the late 1950s and early 1960s. After the formation of Zennichino in 1958
and with the opportunities provided by high economic growth and the
development of the ABL agricultural policy, the farmers' unions entered a
period of unification and reorganisation. Their policy-related activities
expanded, starting with the producer rice price but also extending to price
demands for other agricultural products, land problems, Food Control and
other issues. This period lasted through the 1960s decade into the early
1970s.[725] Subsequently, most rice-roots farmers' groups entered a period of
steady decline, ending up by the 1980s and 1990s pretty much on the political
periphery, except for a few exceptions such as the farmers' political leagues
attached to Nokyo and some commodity groups, particularly in the dairy
sector.

Nokyo on the other hand, began with rather shaky organisational foundations in 1947, fought off other organisational claimants to an agricultural
interest group role in the 1950s and 1960s and consolidated its position as the
farmers' paramount pressure group, the government's chief auxiliary body in
the countryside and the economic powerhouse of the agricultural economy in
the 1960s and 1970s. Throughout, its activities were complemented by those
of the other statutory agricultural interest groups which maintained their
respective positions of organisational relevance and influence. It has only
been in the late 1980s and early 1990s that Japan's policy, economic and fiscal
environment has begun to throw out a policy challenge to the statutory
agricultural interest groups in terms of their organisational relevance and
their abilities to extract benefits from government.

The institutional interest groups, although not strictly farmers' groups per
se, have played an important role as organisational intermediaries between the
government and the farmers and as distributors of largesse to this sector.
They proliferated in the 1960s and 1970s, but now face a more uncertain
future in the 1980s and 1990s as the twin pressures of deregulation and
administrative reform bear down on them. As with Nokyo and the other
organisational instruments of MAFF administrative control, their historical
and developmental peak has passed.

As the creator and sponsor of many of these organisations, the MAFF is
the core institution to which the institutional and statutory agricultural
interest groups relate, providing support in exchange for varying degrees of
supervision and compliance. For organisations centring around farmers as
mass members, however, the MAFF's powers of control have been severely
curtailed in the postwar period. Groups such as Nokyo counterbalance their
relative subordination to the bureaucracy with independently generated
economic, financial and political power. Furthermore, organisations created
on the spontaneous initiative of the farmers' such as the farmers' unions and

the farmers' political leagues lie beyond the purview of the MAFF. Japan's agricultural interest group system by no means embodies the features of the pure corporatist type; it is a hybrid of pluralist corporatism.

In the final analysis, Nokyo's dual organisational character eludes simple categorisation. A fundamental tension remains between, on the one hand, its independent power base and, on the other, its position as a beneficiary of government subsidies under the continuing supervision of MAFF bureaucrats, a representative function bestowed by law and its role as a subcontracting organ of government.

In general terms, corporatist intermediation in the Japanese agricultural sector is on a distinctly declining trend. In the late 1980s and early 1990s, the government has been reconsidering its policies of support and protection involving the relaxation of all kinds of restrictions and policy regulations. Deregulation effectively means a contracting role for Nokyo as government agent, expanding the distance between Nokyo and the administration and reducing the influence generated as a byproduct of its role in negotiating and implementing government policy. Deregulation also means less benefits and concessions of the type that regulated systems generate. Symbolised by the series of changes to the FC system, an environment is being created which is less sympathetic towards the concessionary rights that Nokyo has enjoyed and on which Nokyo management has been partially dependent. Nokyo has no choice but to proceed along the road to independence whether it wants to or not.[726]

Furthermore, the fact that a critical source of Nokyo's organisational leverage has been its capacity to generate support for ruling party politicians at the electoral level suggests that Nokyo's independence will become vulnerable if its electoral power dwindles.[727] This will upset the delicate balance maintained in recent decades and throw Nokyo increasingly on to the mercies of the MAFF.

3   Farmers' politics

In recent decades, a farmers' party in Japan has been notably absent, although this was not always the case. In the first decade after World War II, a number of fervent attempts were made by agrarian leaders and those imbued with the spirit of cooperative unionism to establish political parties to serve farmers' interests and the cooperativist cause. The following discussion documents these attempts, tracing the steps taken by agrarian leaders to establish their own party groupings and examining the activities of locally-based farmers' organisations in national politics as well as the connections between farmers' organisations and established political parties.

The analysis aims to present an overall picture of the party-political representation of the farm sector in the national Diet from the mid-1940s until the mid-1960s. Generally speaking this was a period of marked political activism when the party allegiance of farm leaders and their organisations was by no means fixed. The organisations they led generally pursued their own independent course in elections and rejected closed alliances with political parties. Variable patterns of political attachment were, however, gradually displaced by more fixed and predictable alignments as the LDP consolidated its electoral dominance in the countryside. The drive for political representation continued predominantly via the LDP, both reinforcing and reflecting the ruling party's closer ties with agricultural cooperative organisations.

The investigation of this earlier period is useful in underlining the complexities of the party-political allegiance of farmers' groups, particularly the fact that the LDP in both past and present times has never been able to lay an absolute claim on the political loyalties of farmers and their organisations. Variations in party support continue to reflect the personalised connections between politicians and farmers' groups, as well as the personal basis of support engendered by farm politicians amongst their agrarian supporters. The most basic political concern of farmers, particularly during the early postwar era, was the predisposition of politicians to support rural demands rather than the issue of party affiliation. Farmers were prepared to countenance support for politicians of different party colours provided they strongly identified with the farmers' cause.

Historical traditions of political representation and party alignment in the countryside

The connections between agricultural organisations and Diet politics in Japan have always been intimate, but at the same time complex. Mutual inter-dependence characterised the ties between political parties and rural organisations whereby politicians used farmers' groups as electoral machines in the absence of rice-roots party organisations,[1] and agricultural organisations achieved an important avenue of direct representation by helping to elect their officials to political office.[2] It was not unusual for members of political assemblies, including the Diet, to fuse the roles of politician and agricultural leader through dual office-holding. Officials of agricultural organisations were elected to municipal or prefectural assemblies or to the national Diet as members of established political parties. The institutional-isation of close ties between farm leaders and Diet politicians was partly due to the lack of alternative mechanisms for representing agrarian interests to government. Agricultural organisations were subordinate to the bureaucracy at the functional level and thus the potential for articulating the interests of farmers through administrative channels was limited.[3] The political expression of agricultural interests during the prewar period was largely conveyed through Diet representatives from rural communities (including the executives of agricultural organisations), rather than through the lobbying activity of these organisations because of their role as subordinate organs of government.[4] The members of the Diet who were from farming constituencies generally represented the interests of the land-owning class.[5] The presence of landowners in the prewar Diet was a salient feature of national politics.

Diet members who were either *nokai* or *sangyo kumiai* officials gradually increased in number from 1900 onwards. For example, the promoters and directors of the first national federation of cooperatives, the Greater Japan Central Association of Industrial Cooperatives (Dainihon Sangyo Kumiai Chuokai) established in 1905 were either Diet members of the House of Peers, or high officials of the Ministry of Agricultural and Commercial Affairs, the Ministry of Finance or the Ministry of Home Affairs.[6] The same was true of its successor organisation, the National Central Union of Industrial Cooperatives established in 1909.[7]

In terms of party affiliation, the alignments of the *nokai* and *sangyo kumiai* in the early Showa era were divided between the Rikken Seiyukai (Constitutional Friends' Association) and the Kenseikai (Constitutional Government Association) and its successor, the Rikken Minseito (Consti-tutional Democratic Party) respectively. The Seiyukai was a rural-orientated conservative party, which represented the interests of landowners (and hence the *nokai*).[8] The Minseito, which was opposed to the Seiyukai,[9] was a more urban-orientated progressive party which viewed agricultural policy from the standpoint of industrial capital.[10] Generally speaking the Seiyukai supported landed farmers, whilst the Minseito supported a strengthening of cultivation rights. In reality, however, the distinctions between the two parties were not so sharp.[11]

The representation of the industrial cooperatives in the Diet was greatly spurred on by the anti-industrial cooperative movement launched by the commercial and industrial world in the 1930s. This was a reaction against the increased competition presented by the cooperatives to private sector traders across a range of different fields including the provision of farm inputs and rice distribution. The anti-cooperative movement was led by the Japan Chamber of Commerce and Industry representing small and medium enterprises threatened by the advance of the industrial cooperatives. It forced the *sangyo kumiai* to safeguard their interests by expanding their Diet representation. By 1933, 49 officials of the *sangyo kumiai* held seats in the House of Representatives, representing 11 per cent of its total membership.[12] At the same time, *sangyo kumiai* officials occupied 39 per cent of the seats in prefectural assemblies.[13]

The anti-cooperative movement began in 1932–33, flared up in 1935 and defeated three important agricultural bills in the Diet.[14] In 1935 the political advance of the National Central Association of Industrial Cooperatives was advocated by *sangyo kumiai* leaders as a means of opposing the business campaign. A Rural Industrial Cooperative Association (Noson Sangyo Kumiaikai) was set up as a separate political body of the central association to lead the fight against the attack on cooperatives. Youth groups were strengthened[15] and the union of rural Diet members called the Noson Giin Domei was organised. It consisted of Diet members who received backing from the *sangyo kumiai* in national elections because they supported the industrial cooperatives' cause.[16] Members undertook Diet activities under the slogan of 'mobilising the farmers' political power', and as a supra-party group of Diet members, the league was active in making policy proposals relating to agriculture. The equivalent organisation at the prefectural level was the Agriculture and Forestry Promotion Diet Members' League (Norin Shinko Giin Domei) which assisted the election of supporters of the *sangyo kumiai*. Both organisations were supra-party, reflecting the producer cooperatives' official position of political neutrality.[17]

Early postwar representation of farmers' organisations

Relations between farmers' organisations and political parties during the relatively fluid period of party formation and dissolution in the first postwar decade were in an evolutionary phase and thus complex, varied and shifting. The party alignments of farmers' organisations during this period were extremely diverse, locally determined and centring very much on the career connections and personal political philosophies of individual leaders. Connections were commonly mediated by those who had established their reputations as leaders of farmers' organisations or who held both organisational and party office and thus straddled the two kinds of groupings.

In such cases a clear coincidence of interests existed between the leaders of farmers' organisations actively seeking Diet office, and political leaders who sought to centre party organisations around farmers' groups in order to gain an organisational sub-structure and rice-roots base of support. In other cases, farmers' organisations followed a course of action that was more independent of party organisation and elected their representatives as Independents or as representatives of different established parties. The first postwar decade was a period of idealism and ideological ferment when parties frequently mobilised around matters of principle and political conviction, and leaders were inspired by the desire to realise hitherto impossible political ideals.

Organisationally speaking, four main streams of farmers' political representation can be detected in the early postwar period: the farmers' unions; agrarian leaders supporting the principle of cooperative unionism; the *nogyokai* (later Nokyo); and the rural youth leagues. Each of these streams had different and complex relations with political parties, extending in some cases to the actual sponsorship of party organisations. The last three also overlapped with each other – to the point where the main division amongst the political representatives of the agricultural sector in the early postwar period fell between the farmers' union movement on the one hand, and groups associated with the agricultural cooperatives on the other. Each of these broad sets of groupings inherited a distinct historical tradition of political alignment which influenced later party affiliations: the farmers' unions with left-wing parties (the Socialists and Communists) and the rest with centre or right-wing conservative parties. The intervening wartime control situation and the unprecedented reforms instituted by the Occupation authorities interrupted but did not radically alter this basic pattern.

In comparison with the more clearly defined and predictable party attachments after 1955, however, the immediate postwar years represented a transitional period when political alignments reflected the rapidly changing contours of party organisation and also the plethora of Independent and minor party candidates who successfully contested Diet elections.[18]

The farmers' unions and the socialist party

Chapter 2 on 'Interest Group Politics' has already pointed out the apparent contradiction in the early organisational development of the farmers' unions. Firstly they traced their origins to the prewar tenants' rights movement spearheaded by left-wing politicians; and secondly, Nichino, at least in the beginning, aspired to be non-partisan. As Dore explains, it 'was to be an association of all farmers, directed toward the promotion of the farmers' economic interests and the democratization of the villages. Members were to be free to associate with any party. Thus, out of a desire for unity . . . the fiction was established that the aims and functions of the Japan Farmers' Union, though political, were somehow nonparty.'[19] In practice, however, Nichino's leaders 'were predominantly Socialist Party members, and after the elections of 1946 most of them became Socialist Diet members.[20] Equally, the agrarian experts of the Socialist Party were almost without exception prominent leaders of the Japan Farmers' Union. Hence, in the next few years there was a close integration of policy and tactics between the two organizations.'[21]

Although the farmers' unions affiliated to Nichino expanded their popular following at the rice roots, JSP Diet members continued to dominate executive leadership positions within the movement. Apart from their semi-administrative functions in the land reform programme, local farmers' union branches concentrated chiefly on providing an organisational and electoral base for the mobilisation of farmers' votes for Nichino executives affiliated to the JSP in Diet elections. As Tanimoto puts it, Nichino played a role like a political party (a farmers' party) in some areas.[22] Indeed, 'it was the union, rather than the party, which had large and active local organizations.'[23]

The dual office-holding of Nichino executives as Diet members reflected the overlap between the farmers' union movement and the JSP. In the 1946 elections, five of the seven executive members of Nichino were elected on a JSP ticket.[24] This group included the Chairman of Nichino, Sunaga Ko, and its Secretary-General, Nomizo Masaru.[25] In the 1947 House of Representatives' election, 31 of 143 JSP Diet members were reputedly either national or prefectural leaders of Nichino, and eight were members of the right-wing breakaway group led by Hirano Rikizo.[26] In the 1947 UH elections, two Nichino candidates contested the national constituency (NC), one a Socialist, the other an Independent. Together they garnered 280,000 votes, which was sufficient to elect the Socialist candidate, Okada Soji, but was considerably less than their claimed membership at the time of over one million.[27]

The membership strength and electoral involvement of large numbers of farmers' union branches campaigning on a platform of land reform undoubtedly contributed to the support shown for the JSP in rural areas in the elections of 1946 and 1947, although other factors were also involved.[28] In the 1946 elections, JSP candidates secured more than 20 per cent of the total vote in a number of agricultural constituencies,[29] and in the LH election of 1947, '50 per cent of the Socialists elected to the House had come from 69 of the most rural constituencies.'[30] As Calder notes: 'Basic damage had been done to the conservative structure of grassroots control.'[31]

The loss of membership strength by the farmers' unions following the completion of land reform, however, left the farmers' unions as little more than groups organised and dominated by Socialist party politicians, with regional branches serving as surrogate electoral organisations for Socialist candidates endeavouring to retain a hold on farmers' votes in rural electorates.[32] As Dore explains, it was often individual farmers' union politicians rather than the JSP that retained the support of local farmers. These politicians were elected largely on the basis of their personal following in the guise of a farmers' union. Their activist followers continued to sustain the Nichino and while their votes were votes for the JSP, these farm voters were motivated by personal allegiance rather than deeply held Socialist convictions.[33]

After 1947, representation of the farmers' unions in the Diet fluctuated considerably as their organisational fortunes slipped in the wake of ideological fission, including the formation of the right-wing farmers' union organisation (Zenno) and increasing divisions between the Socialists and Communists in the movement,[34] with the Socialists dominating the national leadership and the Communists 'increasingly influential in the lower echelons.'[35]

In the 1949 elections the JSP did badly[36] which, in the countryside, reflected the declining urgency of protest issues, such as the land reform and food requisitioning, and the weakening of the farmers' union movement generally.[37] The same 69 rural constituencies that had provided 50 per cent of the Socialist seats in the Lower House generated only 44 per cent of the smaller number of Socialists elected to the House.[38] The substantial dip in JSP support was reflected in only 10 farmers' union representatives being elected.[39]

The Right and Left Socialist Parties[40] picked up seats in the early 1950s, however, and representation of the farmers' unions in the Diet again surged to previous levels, with numbers multiplying until they reached 31 by 1953.[41] As Dore points out, the fact that the farmers' unions survived at all is testimony to their functional aspect in relation to mustering support for rural Socialist Diet members. From the late 1940s, the farmers' unions were 'little more than loose federations of electoral support committees for such incumbent, or would-be, members of the Diet or of prefectural assemblies. It was they who pre-empted the leadership, who directed the unions' policies, and who contributed funds for the upkeep of the unions' skeletal central offices.'[42]

Farmers' union breakaway parties

One of the by-products of the intense factionalism within the farmers' union wing of the JSP was the creation of breakaway parties both to the right and left of the Socialist party. In January 1948, 16 JSP affiliates of the right-wing farmers' union organisation Zenno defected from the JSP and formed a group called the National Farmers' Union Representatives' Club (Zennoha Yushi Giin Kurabu). They all represented agricultural constituencies and included Zenno's leader Hirano Rikizo,[43] who had been forced to resign the previous November as Minister of Agriculture and Forestry in the Katayama Cabinet.[44] They were subsequently behind the establishment in March 1948 of a new political grouping called the Social Reformist Party (Shakai Kakushinto) with 21 LH members and one UH member. The party's platform spoke of 'rejecting the extreme right and the extreme left, and fighting for the establishment of democratic politics based on cooperative socialism'.[45] However, party leader Hirano was later removed from office in the purge and the party as a whole suffered electoral decline as voters turned away from small parties in the late 1940s. The Shakai Kakushinto won only five seats in the January 1949 elections. In February 1951 it reconstituted itself as another minor party, the Social Democratic Party (Shakai Minshuto), with a de-purged Hirano as leader. The party continued to draw its representation and support from Zenno but its total Diet membership numbered only four seats in the Lower House. After many attempts by members to join forces with parties organised around the cooperative principle, in July 1952 it finally succeeded with the formation of the Cooperative Party (Kyodoto). Figure 3.1 traces the steps and stages of this evolutionary process.

The left wing of the Socialist Party on the other hand spawned a Labourers and Farmers Party[46] (Rodosha Nominto, or Ronoto) in 1948.[47] Although led by former JSP agrarian leaders operating from a base in a number of agricultural constituencies, the Ronoto never managed to escape its JSP factional origins and emerge as a farmers' party proper. Set up by the expelled pro-Communist Nichino leader Kuroda Hisao[48] in December 1948, the Ronoto secured seven seats in the Lower House in 1949. Kuroda was supported by left-wing farmers' unions in his constituency in Okayama Prefecture. In the LH poll of 1952, the party picked up four seats, five in 1953 and four in 1955.[49] In the 1950 UH elections, two Ronoto members were successful, but the party had no success in either the 1953 or 1956 UH elections. It was disbanded in 1957 and its members rejoined the Socialist fold (see Figure 3.1). The concept of a worker–farmer alliance had limited appeal in the face of a burgeoning sense of petty proprietorship amongst a majority of emancipated tenant farmers whose conservative proclivities were increasingly revealed in successive elections after 1947.

The labour-farmer cooperation observable at the electoral level in the early and middle 1950s centred around issues that united the farmers' sense of petty proprietorship and the anti-militarism of the Japanese left. In Ishikawa Prefecture, Sohyo participated in a battle over a military base in a farming and fishing village. Labour-farmer interests supported an anti-base candidate standing for the Reformist Party (Kaishinto) in a by-election in 1953. A similar battle occurred over an American airbase in Niigata with the struggle centring on the labour unions. In the Niigata gubernatorial elections of 1955, a cooperative recommendation (*suisen*)[50] by the Japan Democratic Party, Right and Left Socialists and labour-farmers' groups defeated the incumbent by a wide margin.[51]

Cooperative parties

In the initial phase of party formation following World War II, a number of political groupings were founded which catered either exclusively or mainly to agricultural interests and the principle of cooperative unionism. One of the first parties to be launched at the beginning of the Occupation in December 1945 was the Japan Cooperative Party (Nihon Kyodoto). It was the official party representing the general philosophy of cooperative unionism (*kyodo kumiai shugi*)[52] and it was based principally on the Hokkaido region. Its founder was Sengoku Kotaro, originally from Hokkaido, who had been a leading figure in the industrial cooperatives before the war[53] and Minister of Agriculture and Commerce (MAC) in the first postwar Cabinet led by Prince Higashikuni.[54] He collaborated with the so-called Hokkaido 'Butter King' and leader of a dairy cooperative, Kurosawa Torizo, in setting up the party. Kita Katsutaro, another agriculturalist from Hokkaido and a former prefectural *nokai* director became Vice-Chairman. The party had 20 affiliates at the time of its formation,[55] but many of these, including Sengoku Kotaro, fell victim to the purge of prewar and wartime leaders.[56] Other prominent members were former *nokai* directors such as Igawa Tadao and Funada Naka. Funada had strong links to the Japan Chamber of Commerce and Industry and later became Chairman of the Lower House.[57] Reflecting these broader connections, the Japan Cooperative Party was not solely a rural-based party. It also sought to encourage the support of urban, middle-class, industrial and business interests.[58] One of its central planks was the ideal of labour-management cooperation.[59] Its members were mainly farmers or those in small business.[60]

It was a specific organisational precept of the Japan Cooperative Party to 'utilize the agricultural associations to influence elections'.[61] The *nogyokai*, which had incorporated the prewar industrial cooperatives and *nokai*, shared many common interests with a party that sought to combine the spirit of cooperative unionism with agricultural and business interests. The Japan Cooperative Party fielded 94 candidates in the April 1946 general elections, although only 14 of them were elected.[62] Of the latter, nine were either *nogyokai* executives or former *nokai* leaders, or both,[63] which gave the party a strong agricultural flavour. On a platform that demanded a rice price of more than ¥500 per 150kg, the party secured much of the farm vote in the first postwar elections.[64] In January 1946, the party also proposed that the system of compulsory deliveries of rice instituted by the MAF in December 1945 be replaced with a voluntary system.[65]

Overall, however, the Japan Cooperative Party did not end up having a monopoly of the direct Diet representation of the *nogyokai*. In fact, the party affiliations of *nogyokai* leaders in the Diet were quite diverse. The 36 *nogyokai* officials elected to the Diet in 1946[66] distributed their allegiance predominantly amongst three major groupings: the Japan Cooperative Party (9), large and more established parties of the right (the Japan Liberal Party, or Nihon Jiyuto (9) and the Japan Progressive Party, or Nihon Shinpoto (10)) and Independents (6).[67] Not even Socialist affiliation was excluded: one *nogyokai* representative from Osaka was affiliated with the JSP. Table 3.1 shows the figures for *nogyokai* officials in each party (they also include a small number of former *nokai* leaders and Diet politicians who later went on to become

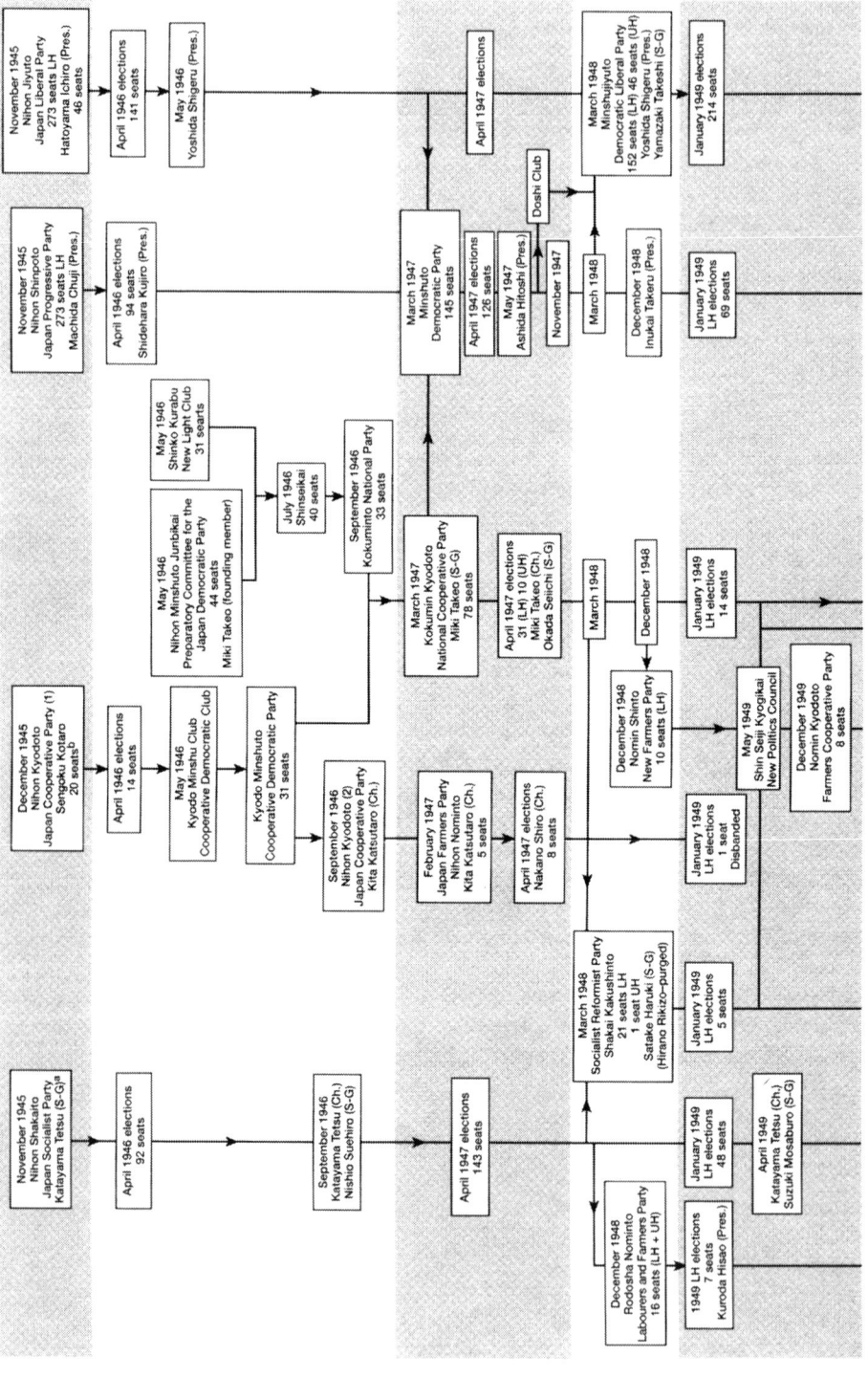

November 1945
Nihon Jiyuto
Japan Liberal Party
273 seats LH
Hatoyama Ichiro (Pres.)
46 seats

April 1946 elections
141 seats

May 1946
Yoshida Shigeru (Pres.)

April 1947 elections

March 1948
Minshujiyuto
Democratic Liberal Party
152 seats (LH) 46 seats (UH)
Yoshida Shigeru (Pres.)
Yamazaki Takeshi (S-G)

January 1949 elections
214 seats

November 1945
Nihon Shinpoto
Japan Progressive Party
273 seats LH
Machida Chuji (Pres.)[b]

April 1946 elections
94 seats
Shidehara Kijiro (Pres.)

March 1947
Minshuto
Democratic Party
145 seats

April 1947 elections
126 seats

May 1947
Ashida Hitoshi (Pres.)

November 1947

Doshi Club

March 1948

December 1948
Inukai Takeru (Pres.)

January 1949
LH elections
69 seats

May 1946
Shinko Kurabu
New Light Club
31 seats

May 1946
Nihon Minshuto Junbikai
Preparatory Committee for the
Japan Democratic Party
44 seats
Miki Takeo (founding member)

July 1946
Shinseikai
40 seats

September 1946
Kokuminto National Party
33 seats

March 1947
Kokumin Kyodoto
National Cooperative Party
Miki Takeo (S-G)
78 seats

April 1947 elections
31 (LH) 10 (UH)
Miki Takeo (Ch.)
Okada Seiichi (S-G)

March 1948

December 1948

January 1949
LH elections
14 seats

December 1945
Nihon Kyodoto
Japan Cooperative Party (1)
Sengoku Kotaro
20 seats[a]

April 1946 elections
14 seats

May 1946
Kyodo Minshu Club
Cooperative Democratic Club

Kyodo Minshuto
Cooperative Democratic Party
31 seats

September 1946
Nihon Kyodoto (2)
Japan Cooperative Party
Kita Katsutaro (Ch.)

February 1947
Japan Farmers Party
Nihon Nominto
Kita Katsutaro (Ch.)
5 seats

April 1947 elections
Nakano Shiro (Ch.)
8 seats

January 1949
LH elections
1 seat
Disbanded

December 1948
Nomin Shinto
New Farmers Party
10 seats (LH)

May 1949
Shin Seiji Kyogikai
New Politics Council

December 1949
Nomin Kyodoto
Farmers Cooperative Party
8 seats

November 1945
Nihon Shakaito
Japan Socialist Party
Katayama Tetsu (S-G)[a]

April 1946 elections
92 seats

September 1946
Katayama Tetsu (Ch.)
Nishio Suehiro (S-G)

April 1947 elections
143 seats

March 1948
Socialist Reformist Party
Shakai Kakushinto
21 seats LH
1 seat UH
Satake Haruki (S-G)
(Hirano Rikizo—purged)

January 1949
LH elections
5 seats

April 1949
Katayama Tetsu (Ch.)
Suzuki Mosaburo (S-G)

January 1949
LH elections
48 seats

December 1948
Rodosha Nominto
Labourers and Farmers Party
16 seats (LH + UH)

1949 LH elections
7 seats
Kuroda Hisao (Pres.)

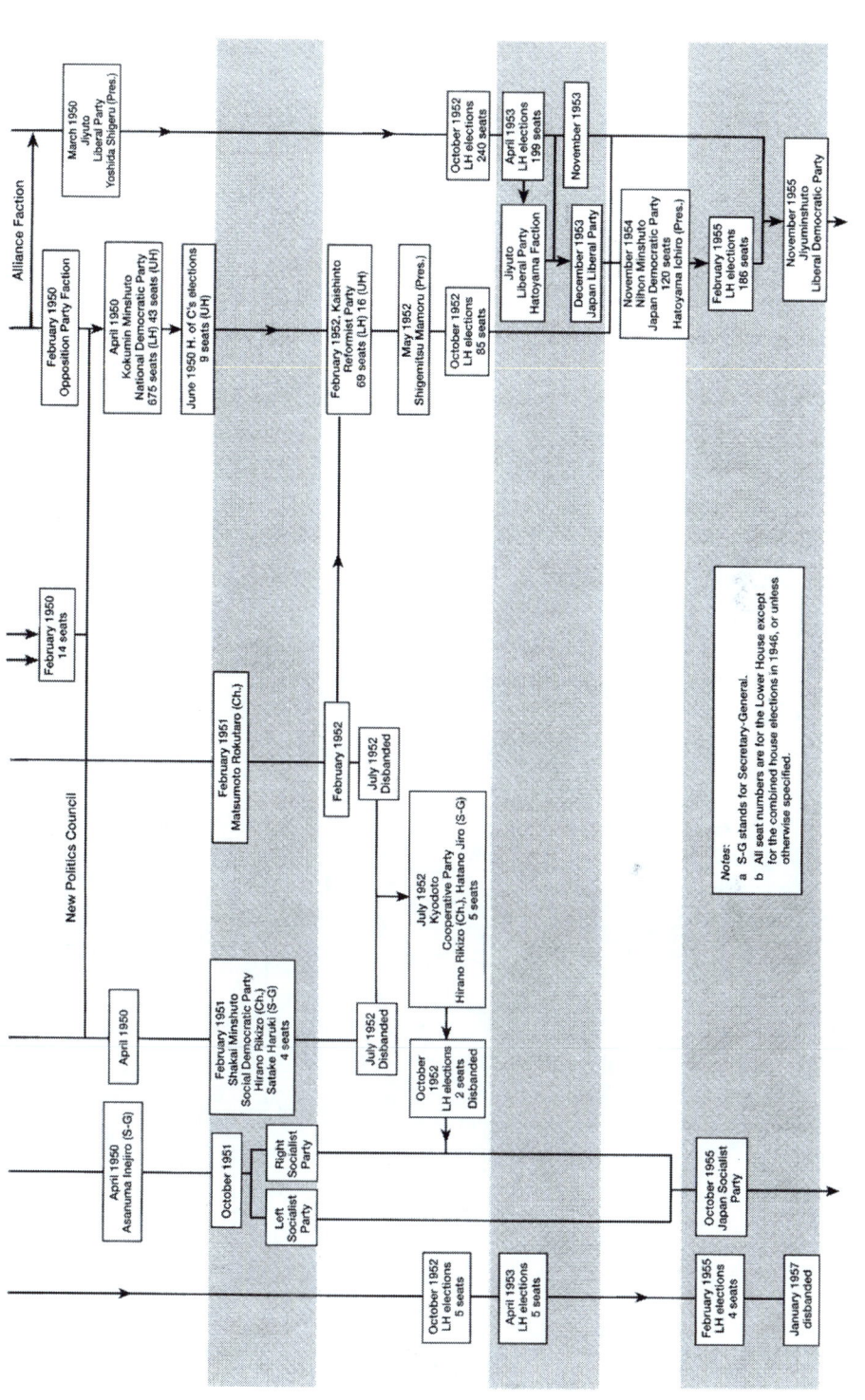

Figure 3.1 Cooperative and associated parties: evolution and dissolution, 1945–1957

Source: Gikai Seido Nanjunenshi: *Shugin, Sangin (A 70-Year History of the Diet System: House of Representatives, House of Councillors)*, Tokyo, Okurasho Insatsu Kyoku, 1961; Haruhiro Fukui, 'Japan', in Fukui (ed.), *Political Parties*, pp. 449–632.

Table 3.1 Party affiliations of Nokyo Lower House Diet members, 1946–67

Year	Numbers Affiliated By Party							Total
	Japan Progressive	Japan Liberal	Japan Socialist		Japan Cooperative	Minor Parties	Independents	
1946[a]	10	9	1		9	1	6	36
1947[a]	Democratic 4	3	2		National Cooperative 7	Japan Farmers 1		17
1949	1	Democratic Liberal 8	2		1	New Farmers 5		17
Dec.1949–Aug. 1952	National Democratic 1	8	Left Socialist 1	Right Socialist 1	1	Farmers Cooperative 5		17
1952 pre-election	Reformist 4	Liberal 7	2			Cooperative 2		15
1952 post-election	2	10	5	2				19
1953	2	13	5	3				23
1955	Japan Democratic 10	6	5	3				24
1958	Liberal Democratic 13		Socialist 11					24
1960	13		7		Democratic Socialist 1		Combined Socialist 8	21
1963	15		6		4		10	25
1967	17		8		5		13	30

Notes:

a These are the figures for current and former *nogyokai* and *nokai* executives, plus Diet members who later served in leadership roles in the agricultural cooperatives.

Sources: Author's own personal records of Japanese farm politicians based on sundry sources including Diet handbooks.

leaders of agricultural cooperative organisations). The variations in party allegiance amongst the *nogyokai* representatives not only reflected the fluidity of party organisation and the existence of several conservative parties at the time, but also the absence of a tradition of fixed party loyalties in the countryside and the candidate-specific nature of agrarian support.

From another perspective, what was notable about this election was the relatively high number of farm organisation executives who successfully acquired seats in the newly constituted Diet, underlining the continuity of the nexus between agrarian leadership and national politics, although not on a fixed party basis. This connection was quickly re-established after the war, with political parties organised around the ambitions of local agricultural leaders who wanted to influence national policy in line with their particular worldview – as in the case of the Japan Cooperative Party. In other cases, more broadly based political groupings (such as the Japan Progressive and Japan Liberal Parties) utilised agricultural groups as an organised basis of support by recruiting into their ranks aspiring politicians with strong connections to farmers. Both types of representation helped to reconstruct and consolidate channels of influence between the agricultural and political worlds in the immediate postwar period.

Above all, this was a time of organisational flux and political uncertainty, with large numbers of parties contesting the 1946 elections. An electoral system that favoured minor political groupings also assisted in this process.[68] Many candidates stood as Independents or as minor party candidates representing a conglomeration of social, political and economic interests.[69] Political parties formed, dissolved and consolidated, a phenomenon that was particularly evident amongst those groupings that endeavoured to represent the agricultural sector.

The Japan Cooperative Party, after bringing under its wing a number of small local parties, chiefly of farmers or small businessmen, changed its title firstly to Cooperative Democratic Club (Kyodo Minshu Kurabu) and then Cooperative Democratic Party (Kyodo Minshuto) in May 1946 (see Figure 3.1). Its initial Diet membership stood at 31.[70] The party took cooperative principles as the basis of its organisation. In March 1947 it amalgamated with the National Party (Kokuminto)[71] to form the National Cooperative Party (Kokumin Kyodoto) with Miki Takeo as Secretary-General and a broad ideology emphasising the cooperative spirit. This grouping claimed 78 seats in the Diet which made it one of the larger parties in the house.[72] The impetus for amalgamation came from the realisation that small parties would be penalised under the new election law due to come into effect in the April 1947 general elections.[73]

The number of agricultural officials elected in the 1947 poll was less than half the figure elected in 1946 (see Table 3.1). Nonetheless, the strong connection between the *nogyokai* and the mainstream cooperative group, the National Cooperative Party, remained evident, although the overall pattern of party affiliation remained fairly diverse, with *nogyokai* leaders affiliated to

Table 3.2 Party affiliations of Nokyo Upper House Diet members, 1947–68

Year	Numbers Affiliated By Party							Total
	Democratic	Japan Liberal	Socialist	Right Socialist	National Cooperative	GBS	Independents	
1947	1	1	0		2	7	0	11
1950		Liberal 2	Left Socialist 1	1		7	3	13
1953		5	1	1		4	2	13
1956	Liberal Democratic 7		Socialist 2			3	1	13
1959	12		2			1		15
1962	17		2				1	20
1965	15		3				1	19
1968	17		2					19

Sources: Author's own personal records of Japanese farm politicians based on sundry sources including Diet handbooks.

almost all parties, including the Democratic, Japan Liberal and Socialist parties as well as other minor parties.[74] In the UH poll, *nogyokai* officials[75] figured more prominently in the non-partisan Green Breeze Society, or GBS (Ryokufukai)[76] than in any other grouping. Two leading *nogyokai* officials who later became chairmen of national agricultural cooperative organisations, however, allied themselves to the National Cooperative Party[77] (see Table 3.2).

The original Japan Cooperative Party and the political groupings that succeeded it constituted the mainstream of the cooperative movement in national politics, but their attachment to cooperative ideology and their agrarian orientation was diluted by later amalgamation with larger political groupings that exhibited no special connection to the principles of cooperativism in terms of party label. Nor were they specifically farmers' parties.[78] This was largely because they were forced to seek more realistic ways of political survival. Although the National Cooperative Party did achieve government office in coalition with the JSP and the Democratic Party between April 1947 and October 1948, ultimately this stream of the cooperative political movement ended up in the Japan Democratic Party (via the National Democratic Party and the Reformist Party) which merged with the Liberal Party to become the LDP (see Figure 3.1). By the late 1940s it was obvious that neither an exclusively agrarian orientation nor cooperative principles were sufficient to sustain a party organisation that was to have any chance of gaining government. National Cooperative Party Diet membership peaked in the 1947 elections with 29 seats (or 6.2 per cent of the total),[79] dropping to 14 seats (or 3.0 per cent of the total)[80] in the 1949 LH poll, which was the last election the party contested.

The rural youth leagues

Another stream of agricultural representation centred around activist farmers' groups that were part of the rural youth league movement and which provided the impetus for the formation of farmers' parties. This movement was spearheaded by the prefectural branches of the National Rural Youth League (Zennoseiren) in Hokkaido (the Hokkaido Farmers' League, or Hokkaido Nomin Domei)[81] and in Fukuoka. These groupings were behind the formation of the Japan Farmers Party (Nihon Nominto) in February 1947,[82] in time to contest the first simultaneous Upper and Lower House elections.

The party began as a splinter group of former Japan Cooperative Party members who had broken away from the Cooperative Democratic Party to form a second Japan Cooperative Party founded in September 1946. It was led by Kita Katsutaro, former Vice-Chairman of the Japan Cooperative Party.[83] At the time of its founding, its total Diet membership numbered five. It sought to return to the original purpose of Sengoku's Japan Cooperative Party, which was to unite the spirit of cooperativism with agricultural interests. The change of name to Japan Farmers Party gave a clearer indication of its basic philosophy.

Only one of the original founding group of Japan Farmers Party members, Nakano Shiro, survived the purge and the 1947 LH election, and he became leader of the party.[84] He was joined by three successful Japan Farmers Party candidates in the 1947 LH election (of 12 candidates put up) and four more who joined subsequently. With eight members, the party was the second smallest in the House.[85] More than half of its membership were leaders of farmers' groups associated with the rural youth league movement, particularly the Hokkaido and Fukuoka branches, both of which took the lead in the pre-Nokyo rice-roots farmers' movement. In the Upper House, the rural youth leagues successfully sponsored the Zennoseiren Chairman, Kunii Junichi, as an Independent candidate for the national constituency.[86]

The official political philosophy of the Japan Farmers Party was by no means uniformly conservative. It was essentially a centre party that aimed to adopt a political stance independent of both left and right. Party philosophy specifically rejected 'dictatorship by left or right wing parties'.[87] It 'looked forward to the establishment of a peaceful Japan based on the principle of cooperative unionism',[88] and it recognised the need for strong representation of farmers' interests in the re-establishment of Japanese agriculture based on a rapid increase in production and improvement in the self-sufficiency ratio for food.[89] These objectives reflected the views of its sponsoring organisations in the rural youth league movement. An attempt to merge the party with the National Cooperative Party failed because of opposition from its chairman, Nakano Shiro.[90]

The fact that *nogyokai* officials in the main chose major conservative or cooperative party representation and not the more obvious preference for Japan Farmers' Party affiliation reflected not only the strong regional focus of the latter in Hokkaido and Fukuoka and its lack of major party status, but also a more fundamental political division in the embryonic agricultural cooperative movement. This set apart local agrarian activists representing rice-roots farmers' organisations, such as the rural youth leagues, from *nogyokai* officials with a long-standing tradition of close ties to established conservative parties. The former were thoroughly imbued with notions of organisational democratisation and political independence,[91] while the latter found it difficult to shake off more elitist notions of agrarian leadership and a history of infiltration by the bureaucracy.

Although the *nogyokai* were no longer politically relevant following their legal dissolution in August 1948, these two streams of the pre-Nokyo agricultural movement, one locally-based, activist and politically independent, and the other more conservative and orientated towards the central policy elites, continued to exist in different organisational locations under the broad Nokyo umbrella. The former was to be found amongst Nokyo's farmers' political leagues into which the rural youth league movement evolved and the latter amongst the central Nokyo leadership.

The failure of farmers' parties

The Japan Farmers Party continued to operate as a minor party in the Lower House until November 1948, when Zennoseiren sought to inject new impetus into the farmers' political movement by sponsoring a National Council for Mobilising Farmers' Political Power (Nomin Seiji Ryoku Kesshu Zenkoku Kyogikai). The council was united in its desire to set up a new party and the Japan Farmers Party was subsequently dissolved. In December 1948, some of its former members joined with a small splinter group from the mainstream National Cooperative Party to form the New Farmers Party (Nomin Shinto) with seven members.[92] It polled 1 per cent of the vote in the January 1949 LH elections and had 10 members in the post-election house.[93] Its membership reflected the continuing sponsorship of the Hokkaido Nomin Domei and the rural youth league in Fukuoka and was, therefore, strongly representative of Hokkaido and Fukuoka where the prefectural *noseiren* were very active.

The 1949 LH elections, however, were the first in which candidates who were also executives of the newly created agricultural cooperative organisation stood for political office. Almost half the Diet membership of the New Farmers Party were Nokyo executives or staff members.[94] They were outnumbered, however, by Nokyo leaders making their political debut as endorsed candidates of the governing Democratic Liberal Party (Minshu-jiyuto),[95] as shown in Table 3.1. The overwhelming superiority of the latter in the 1949 elections undoubtedly contributed to this pattern. As Fukui points out, 'the results of the January 1949 general elections were generally unfavourable to small parties'.[96] The balance of Nokyo representatives were fairly evenly divided amongst National Cooperative, Democratic and Socialist parties as shown in Table 3.1.[97]

The varied nature of party affiliation was a reflection not only of the fragmented party configuration in the Diet, but also of the diversity of party loyalties amongst new agricultural cooperative leaders and members. Unlike the farmers' union movement, Nokyo failed to emerge as the political appendage of any particular political party. Complicating factors were the diversity of political affiliation amongst its membership, the residual influence of progressive farmers' movements in the countryside, the candidate-specific nature of political support amongst farmers, and the fundamental division in the organisation between populist, locally orientated and more 'progressive' leaders, and more establishment-orientated conservative leaders with connections to the now defunct *nogyokai*. The dominance of the Nokyo-Democratic Liberal connection, however, can be viewed in retrospect as representing the beginning of a trend that was to be sustained without exception from 1949 onwards: the predominant allegiance of Nokyo politicians (*Nokyo giin*)[98] with the ruling conservative party and the greater chances of electoral success for agricultural politicians in the ranks of this party.

The principal policy tenet of the New Farmers Party was 'stabilisation of the national economy on the basis of cooperative union socialism' (*kyodo kumiai shakai shugi*).[99] The proximity of the party to the centre and extreme right of the socialist movement was exemplified by its participation in the New Politics Council (Shin Seiji Kyogikai) formed in May 1949. Seven members of the New Farmers Party (three members reverted to the ranks of Independents) joined this group together with the 14 members of the centre National Cooperative Party, six members of an Independent group, the Justice Club (Kosei Kurabu), and five members of the right-wing socialist group backed by Zenno, the Social Reformist Party (Shakai Kakushinto). The New Politics Council never developed beyond the stage of a temporary political alliance amongst minority parties, however, and soon dissolved into the same political factions that had given it birth.

Between 1949 and 1952, much of the effort of the small group of Nokyo politicians within the New Farmers Party continued to be directed towards finding a discrete avenue of political expression via the organisation of a separate farmers' party. An attempt was made to infuse new life into this concept in December 1949 with the dissolution of the New Farmers Party and the establishment of a Farmers Cooperative Party (Nomin Kyodoto), all previous cooperative parties having been incorporated into the Democratic, National Democratic and Reformist Party stream, as shown in Figure 3.1. It was hoped that the Farmers Cooperative Party would provide a single, united political leadership for the agricultural cooperative movement and Nokyo-associated farmers' groups. With only eight members in the Lower House, however, its status was that of a minor political grouping.[100] Its platform, like that of its predecessor, advocated the construction of a national economy based on 'cooperative socialism', an ideological position that was much more left-wing than the National Cooperative Party under Miki Takeo. Its principal goal was the establishment of a policy that emphasised increases in agricultural production.[101] It called for measures 'to strengthen the food-control system, to restrict food imports, and to encourage self-sufficiency in food production by a variety of methods, including attractive producer prices and technological improvement.'[102]

Although the party by no means had a monopoly on Nokyo's direct representation in the Diet, it deserved the label of 'Nokyo party' by virtue of its agricultural cooperative leadership and the high proportion of Nokyo officials in its ranks.[103] This was the same group that had previously been affiliated with the New Farmers Party.[104] Once again, like its predecessors, the sponsors of the Farmers Cooperative Party were mainly the Nokyo-associated rural youth movement in Fukuoka and the Hokkaido Farmers' League.[105] The party successfully elected three[106] candidates to the Upper House in 1950, which represented a minuscule 2.27 per cent of seats and 1.2 per cent of the national vote. All were affiliated to the Hokkaido Nomin Domei.[107] The party's performance in these elections merely served to under-line its inability to escape its localist origins and attract nationwide support amongst farmers. Although the Hokkaido and Fukuoka farm groups were very active, the strong regional orientations of the party[108] severely limited its capacity to attract additional members to its ranks from amongst Nokyo-based political aspirants in other localities. Moreover, a majority of Nokyo Diet members elected to the Upper House in 1950 chose either pro-conservative Independent or Ryokufukai membership (see Table 3.2).

In any event, the life span of the Nomin Kyodoto in the House of Councillors proved extremely short. Almost immediately after the election, its representatives joined a grouping of nine Independent agricultural members which included other Nokyo politicians called the No. 1 Club (Daiichi Kurabu).[109] In the Lower House, the majority of its members defected to join the newly formed Reformist Party (Kaishinto)[110] in February 1952, with the Farmers Cooperative Party disbanding the following July.

The influence of Nokyo Diet members from the Farmers Cooperative Party on the Reformist Party was apparent in the party's pro-Nokyo position in the restructuring process of the agricultural committee system which, at the time, sought to deny Nokyo a role in interest representation of the farm sector.[111] Nokyo's intensified lobbying during the Diet session of late 1952 and the tenacity of the Reformist Party in complying with Nokyo's demands resulted in significant amendments to the bill drafted to establish the prefectural chambers of agriculture and the National Chamber of Agriculture. These amendments effectively allowed Nokyo to penetrate the membership of these organisations.[112]

When the Farmers' Cooperative Party dissolved, those remaining in the party amalgamated with Hirano Rikizo's Social Democratic Party (the Shakai Minshuto which had evolved from the Social Reformist Party or Shakai Kakushinto) to form the Cooperative Party (Kyodoto) in July 1952 (see Figure 3.1). Both groups had earlier rejected a call for unification with a third group, the Right Socialist Party, preferring the alternative of a limited amalgamation between their own groupings. The Cooperative Party, which had a total Diet membership of five, was led by Hirano with a Nokyo politician and former Japan Cooperative Party member, Hatano Jiro, as Secretary General.[113] It incorporated the Farmers Cooperative Party goal of reforming the economic structure of Japan through cooperative socialism (*kyodo shakai shugi*). In practice this meant 'the establishment of a socialist society by democratic means, the democratization of private monopolies' control of key industries, and a whole range of proposals designed to improve the conditions of farmers and fishermen.'[114] One of the more notable features of the party was the fact that it had brought together 'politicians from the socialist and conservative camps . . . . What they had in common was an interest in agriculture.'[115] The 1952 elections, however, saw very few of the former Nomin Kyodoto members left in the Diet.[116] Moreover, of the 28 candidates who stood for the Kyodoto, only two survived,[117] both of whom joined the Right Wing Socialist Party, thus dissolving the Cooperative Party.

The dissolution of the Farmers Cooperative Party marked the end for the time being of attempts by Nokyo activists and leaders of associated farmers' organisations to carve out a separate niche for farmers' and agricultural cooperative interests in national politics by means of separate party organisations. The formation of the Reformist Party, the direct successor of the National Democratic Party which had National Cooperative and Democratic Party origins,[118] also heralded the end of attempts to sustain a political party based on the economic philosophy of cooperative unionism. Only the socialist rump of the original Japan Farmers Party and its successor the Farmers Cooperative Party still clung to the ideology of cooperativism as a central tenet of party organisation. This political strand, however, was also extinguished with the demise of the Cooperative Party.

The immediate cause of the Farmers Cooperative Party's dissolution was simply erosion of membership, lack of financial backing[119] and a broad base of support amongst farmers, and consequently lack of organisational viability, a process that was greatly hastened by declining public support for minority parties and the general trend towards party consolidation. To some extent, the very existence of this series of small farmers' parties in the early postwar period was symptomatic of an early transitional period of fission and fusion in Japanese party politics. As Muramatsu and Krauss observed, 'in the immediate postwar period, a broad range of values and ideologies and a rather chaotic multiparty system emerged. No party had a clear electoral mandate.'[120]

The Farmers Cooperative Party also suffered from a slide in the popularity of its national backing organisation, the Zennoseiren. After reaching a peak of 432,499 members in 1949,[121] the membership of the National Rural Youth League declined markedly after 1950. It altered its official title to the National Farmers' Federation (Zenkoku Nomin Renmei or Zennoren) in October 1950,[122] but by the end of that year, it had only 221,724 members, half the number of Zennoseiren in 1949.[123] By 1952, Zennoren's membership had dwindled even further to 148,527.[124]

A major factor contributing to the weakening of the rural youth leagues was the successful launching of the agricultural cooperative system which was one of their principal aims. The result was a shift in focus away from farmers' demands for a voluntary, democratic cooperative organisation to the desirable scope of Nokyo's activities, which also became one of the central concerns of the agricultural cooperative leadership. In 1951, a Nokyo youth division (*seinenbu*) was created to rival the rural youth leagues, which was an additional reason for the change in nomenclature to farmers' federation (*nomin renmei*). Long deliberations took place between the two organisations about the supposed connection between the old and the new youth organisations.

Cooperative executives also began to utilise the expanding Nokyo system and its universal membership structure to build their own local power bases. Other potential rivals such as the farmers' unions were organisationally too weak to present any real alternative to the farm policy leadership of the cooperatives. Likewise the agricultural committees were too limited in their farm membership and organisational independence to pose a real threat to

Nokyo as the farmers' representative organisation.[125] Zennoren was also hindered by dwindling finances derived solely from membership fees. Unlike Nokyo, it lacked economic functions so vital as a basis for membership. Moreover, during the early 1950s, the concerns of farmers began to switch to policy matters that impinged on their agricultural production and marketing activities, in other words, more 'bread and butter' issues affecting the farm household economy. Nokyo was best placed to represent farmers on these questions.

In one of its last major electoral victories, the Zennoren successfully backed its Chairman to the Upper House in 1950 for two terms as a member of the Ryokufukai.[126] Its other political representatives during this period were predominantly Socialists from Hokkaido who were also affiliated to the Hokkaido Farmers' League.[127] In the early 1950s, the Zennoren was depicted as being far closer to the progressives than to the conservatives,[128] and after 1952, its representatives were either Independents or Right or Left Socialist Party members.[129]

Although the Zennoren and its local farmers' groups now lacked a specific party organisation in the Diet, they did retain the same position on party alignment as the early activists in the Nokyo movement who advocated steering a political course between both right- and left-wing parties. What this meant in practice was greater distance from the conservative ruling party and generally more radical affiliations for their small group of representatives in the Diet from 1952 onwards, compared with the majority of Nokyo politicians elected during this period.[130]

In summary, in spite of their auspicious beginnings in the wake of land reform when farmers' expectations and interest in politics were high, small farmer and cooperative parties gradually failed for lack of voter support and organisational viability, with their surviving members moving to affiliate with larger, conservative political groupings in the process of party amalgamation. Although the cooperative parties initially had the potential to become middle-of-the-road socialist parties, most of their members later ended up in the ranks of conservative parties. One reason for this was the difficulty members of small cooperative parties faced in having a strong political voice in government without affiliating themselves to one or other of the conservative parties. Another reason was that the constituency basis of cooperative parties was in conservative agricultural villages.[131]

Nevertheless, what the early attempts to create farmers' and cooperative parties showed was that their parliamentary members occupied diverse positions on the ideological spectrum, with one stream associated with the right wing of the Socialist Party, another with more conservative political groupings, and the third a more centrist grouping, striving to represent farmers' and cooperative interests independently of both the right and left of politics.

At the organisational level, with the effective demise of the farmers' unions as groups representing rural interests, Nokyo increasingly asserted its organisational presence in the agricultural economy as well as in national politics. Furthermore, as Nokyo consolidated its membership and organisational powers, the rice-roots, active farmers' groups in the rural youth leagues gradually waned, one of their major objectives – the founding of a national agricultural cooperative organisation based on democratic principles – having been achieved. With the establishment of Nokyo's own youth division, the rural youth leagues also became increasingly redundant.

Political alignments towards the end of the first postwar decade

In the early 1950s, the trend towards party proliferation completely reversed. The number of Independents and minor parties slumped dramatically in both Houses.[132] By 1955, a conservative-progressive cleavage between major political groupings (the Liberal and Japan Democratic parties on the one hand, and the Right and Left Socialists and the Communists on the other) had replaced the multi-party configurations of the early postwar years. Against this background, Nokyo's Diet representatives were increasingly representative of one or other of the major parties as these groupings consolidated their position in national politics.

At the electoral level, the early 1950s also witnessed the conservatives gradually asserting their dominance in the countryside. In the 1952 LH election, the Liberal Party secured an impressive victory in the rural belt. As Tanaka observed, farm villages had once again become 'an impregnable fortress of conservatism'.[133] The Liberals further entrenched themselves in farming regions in the 1953 LH elections, 'eating into' the farm vote with an appeal based on 'the person rather than the party' (*to yori jinbutsu*).[134] The judicious combination of *kaban* (money), *jiban* (local base of support) and *kanban* (signboard, meaning the public 'face' or personal appeal of a candidate) ensured the party kept its place as No. 1 political grouping amongst farm voters.[135]

Nevertheless, in spite of the strong support shown by farmers for the Liberals in the 1952 and 1953 elections, the Socialists also recovered, with support expanding in rural areas in addition to the electoral advances in the cities. The progress of reformist forces in agricultural areas reflected the dissatisfaction some farmers felt towards the Yoshida government's deflationary policies, which culminated in low prices of agricultural commodities including rice.[136] In terms of the agricultural policies being advocated by the various parties, however, very little separated the conservatives from the progressives. All called for higher rice prices, relaxation of enforced rice deliveries, increases in food production, lower prices for fertilisers and so on.[137]

The primary advantage on which the conservatives were able to capitalise was incumbency. As Dore explains, conservative politicians in the early 1950s were more successful than the Socialists in building up a support base in the countryside because they were 'able to promise tangible benefits to their constituents.'[138] The two major conservative parties realised the value of electoral support from rural constituents and thus directed increasing quantities of material benefits to their core supporters in the countryside.[139] Driven partly by the need to encourage greater food production and partly by election promises, the producer rice price climbed steadily between 1951 and 1955,[140] accompanied by steady increments in production subsidies for agricultural infrastructure, farm equipment purchases and so on.[141] These included specific-purpose grants and subsidies to local authorities, and through local authorities and the agricultural cooperatives, to individual farm households. These grants and subsidies to the rural sector proved to be 'a powerful electoral weapon in the hands of government candidates.'[142] The two most important components of government policies for farmers – adjustments in prices and the distribution of agricultural subsidies – were thus subject to the direct influence of conservative politicians.[143]

In the Lower House, the conservatives (the Liberal and Reformist parties) succeeded in taking 197 rural seats (or 73 per cent of the total) in the 1953 LH election, compared with 66 seats (or 25 per cent of the total) for the Socialists. In the subsequent 1955 LH election, the Liberals and Japan Democrats[144] gained 186 rural seats (or 69 per cent of the total) compared with 75 (or 28 per cent) for the Socialists.[145] In rural electorates, the Socialists thus functioned as an alternative, albeit minority voice in opposition to the dominant conservatives.

The retention of power by the Liberal Party in the LH elections of 1952 and 1953 saw by far the largest group of Nokyo politicians in its ranks (see Table 3.1). In spite of the dominance of the Liberal Party, however, respectable numbers of *Nokyo giin* were elected in the ranks of the Right and Left Socialists – around half the number of the conservative parties as shown in Table 3.1.[146] In the 1952 election, Zenshiren categorised candidates connected to Nokyo into three groups, both conservative and progressive, and supported them directly and indirectly regardless of party. Category A consisted of those who were directly connected to Nokyo (12 candidates, who were chairmen of Nokyo prefectural organisations). Category B were candidates who had a deep understanding of Nokyo (a total of 27), while Category C were candidates who had a relatively good understanding of Nokyo (14 in total) – to make a grand total of 53 candidates. Only three out of Category A candidates were elected, whilst the majority of Categories B and C were successful.[147] All Diet members connected to Nokyo from the Right Socialist Party were re-elected in the 1953 poll except for one, as well as four who had lost in 1952 but were 'revived'.[148]

Following the assumption of power by the newly formed Japan Democratic Party in December 1954, the number of Nokyo Diet members affiliated to the Liberal Party dropped precipitously in the 1955 LH elections while the number of those in the ranks of the Japan Democratic Party surged (see Table 3.1), with some Nokyo politicians actually shifting allegiance to the Japan Democratic Party as members of a Liberal breakaway group.[149] Numbers of Nokyo Diet members affiliated to the Right and Left Socialists remained steady.

The conservative-progressive division between *Nokyo giin* was particularly pronounced in the Lower House, where the proportions were exactly two-thirds conservative to one third Right and Left Socialist in 1955. In the Upper House the picture was more diversified by the number of Nokyo Diet members who were either Independents or members of the Ryokufukai. Almost half of all Nokyo politicians in the Upper House after the 1953 elections were in this category, marginally outnumbering those belonging to the Liberal Party (see Table 3.2). After the 1956 UH election, the distribution was more or less equally divided between LDP and non-LDP Nokyo politicians: seven were LDP while of the rest, two were JSP, one was an Independent and three were members of the Ryokufukai (see Table 3.2). The relatively large non-LDP proportion reflected the numbers of co-op members, staff and executives who remained connected to the progressive side of politics.[150]

The extent of Socialist Nokyo representation constituted a fundamentally new element in the political orientation of the postwar version of legally defined, government-sponsored agricultural organisations. The landlord class had been displaced from their established positions of political leadership in the countryside.[151] The effect of land reform was to remove not only the economic and social foundations of their political power but the prime cause of class differentiation within agricultural society – namely land ownership. This factor, combined with the democratisation of agricultural organisations, meant that Nokyo incorporated within its membership the totality of a much broader and less stratified class of owner-farmers.

At the same time, this group exhibited a much greater degree of natural political variation, producing the varied strands of agrarian politics identified earlier: the farmers' unions; groups pursuing the ideology of cooperative unionism in national politics; populist democratic farmers' groups imbued with cooperative ideals associated with the rural youth movement; and leaders of establishment agricultural groups, such as executives of the transitional *nogyokai* groups (including former leaders of the *nokai* and *sangyo kumiai*) and later Nokyo.

Not surprisingly, the conservatives, although increasingly dominant in government and in rural electorates, never quite achieved a monopoly of the political representation of the agricultural cooperatives and still less of the agricultural sector as a whole. The fact that Nokyo's membership embraced all farmers and thus overlapped with those of other farmers' groups, including the left-wing farmers' unions, also militated against absolute uniformity of political alignment, inhibiting the development of an exclusive attachment by the agricultural cooperatives to conservative parties.

Farmers' political leagues

Although the attempt to organise a farmers' party and achieve independent representation of the agricultural sector in national politics had proved a failure by 1952, rice-roots political activism amongst farmers was far from extinguished. As pointed out in chapter 2, the prefectural farmers' political leagues flourished from the mid-1950s into the early 1960s, proving themselves to be effective electoral support organisations for chosen candidates. Their basic objective was to reflect the voices of farmers directly in prefectural and national policymaking on agriculture through elections. They were often vehicles for the electoral ambitions of prefectural Nokyo leaders, although their objectives were not necessarily shared by other Nokyo executives in any particular constituency. It was a matter of policy to eschew fixed relationships with particular parties and to build electoral connections with individual politicians and candidates, based on their support for the farmers' cause. This was a period when the farmers' relative income position was declining in comparison with urban workers, which magnified farmers' anxiety and dissatisfaction with government agricultural policies.

In the mid- to late 1950s, a major burst of rice-roots electoral activity amongst the farmers' political leagues occurred, centring on prefectural assembly elections and on the promotion of prefectural agricultural cooperative leaders to positions of national and prefectural political prominence. Focusing originally on successive gubernatorial elections between 1955 and 1959, these groups later set their sights on the UH elections of 1959 and 1962 and the LH elections of 1960 and 1963.

In the space of five years, six Nokyo executives were elected governors of prefectures (Ishikawa in 1955, Toyama and Miyazaki in 1956, Fukushima in 1957, Shiga in 1958 and Ibaraki in 1959). In Miyazaki for example, a prefecture-wide Agricultural Policy Reform League (Nosei Kakushin Renmei) successfully backed a Nokyo Economic Federation Chairman to the governorship in September 1956. A similar organisation in Fukushima, the Agricultural Policy Reform League (Nosei Sasshin Renmei) mobilised the necessary support to elect their Combined Nokyo Prefectural Federation Chairman to the governorship in 1957.

In July 1958, the National Nokyo Executive and Staff Members' League (Zenkoku Nokyo Yakushokuin Renmei) adopted a 'Resolution Relating to the Strengthening of Farmers' Political Power' and at the national Nokyo convention in November, prospects for a general mobilisation of farmers' political power – the old catch-cry of Zennoseiren and the Noson Giin Domei – were energetically canvassed in the light of the success of local Nokyo-affiliated political leagues in gubernatorial elections.[152] The convention adopted an explicit resolution calling for a strengthening of farmers' political power. This was based on the agenda submitted by local agricultural cooperatives which demanded the formation of political organisations centring on Nokyo along the lines of the farmers' political leagues. They were lukewarm about Nokyo's political activities and felt the need to organise independent political organisations.[153]

One of the central themes at the convention was the question whether farmers as a group should adopt the standpoint of a third political party independent of the Socialists and the LDP. At the time, it was considered likely that a farmers' party (Nominto) would be established because sub-leaders of Nokyo in prefectural and local areas wanted to unify and mobilise farmers' political power and because farmers were disappointed with the major established parties. The LDP was regarded as having broken its public pledges to the farmers and having ignored the farmers' will. In the view of many rice-roots agricultural activists, the financial and economic policies of the LDP also played down the importance of agriculture and were centred on business.[154] The leader of the Farm and Fishing Villages' Political League (Noson Gyoson Seiji Renmei)[155] pointed out that Nokyo should not get involved in politics because it was an economic organisation and, since neither political parties nor agricultural organisations reflected the desires of serious farmers and neither the LDP nor the JSP were direct representatives of farmers, members of the Diet needed to be sent directly from a political party for farmers.[156]

It was with such stimulus that the Political League for Promoting Agriculture (Kono Seiji Renmei) was launched in Ibaraki Prefecture in December 1958 which was instrumental in electing the prefectural Nokyo Central Union Chairman to the governorship the following year. The Ibaraki group, like its predecessors, took the agricultural cooperatives within the prefecture as its organisational base. It explicitly affirmed its independent political identity, however, and developed an ideology of farmers as a third political force (i.e. independent of the LDP and the JSP). This entailed recognition of the limitations of Nokyo as a political body because of the growing emphasis of the central Nokyo leadership on acquiring government subsidies which limited in practice the alternatives of party support. The Oita Prefecture Agricultural Policy Promotion League (Nosei Suishin Renmei) summarised the party-political philosophy of the movement: 'Neither the LDP, which speaks for monopoly capital, nor the JSP, which is tethered to the Sohyo organisation, are our allies.'[157]

The rejection of fixed party relations by the farmers' political leagues echoed the views of the early farmers' political leaders in their attempts to set up farmers' parties. The leagues aimed to promote the sectional interests of farmers as a distinct and separate group in society. In each case, electoral backing for Nokyo-based gubernatorial candidates embodied the principle of political independence, steering a non-committed course between left-wing and right-wing parties. Full use was made of judicious political alliances formed on the basis of electoral expediency.

With the exception of the Miyazaki gubernatorial election of 1956 where the Nokyo nominee stood on a JSP ticket, Nokyo candidates campaigned in opposition to the officially endorsed LDP candidates as Independents. The latter all presided over temporary but extremely successful alliances between breakaway LDP factions and the JSP. The Fukushima victory in 1957, for example, was the successful result of a political combination involving the progressive faction within Nokyo and organised workers.[158] It was interpreted by the Secretary-General of the LDP as a defeat not at the hands of the JSP but at the hands of the Nokyo organisation.[159]

Similar alliances produced the successes in Shiga and Ibaraki,[160] where Nokyo gubernatorial candidates benefited from divisions in conservative party prefectural federations and received joint support from LDP splinter groups and progressives. Almost a decade later in 1967, the Chairman of the Rural Construction Political League (Noson Kensetsu Seiji Renmei) in Fukui was victorious in the gubernatorial election with support from his organisation and the JSP. He remained in office for five terms.[161]

What all these governors had in common was the fact that they were leaders of agricultural organisations and they triumphed in elections over LDP candidates with support from the JSP. As Nakamura explains, although farmers were certainly conservative, they often chose to associate with the JSP in order to put their representatives into government,[162] although the series of progressive Nokyo successes was attributed more to dissatisfaction with LDP agricultural policies amongst Nokyo-sponsored political groups than to positive support for JSP farm programmes as such.[163] Nevertheless, the farmers' political leagues proved themselves capable of defeating incumbent LDP candidates in heavily agricultural prefectures by means of judicious alliances with Opposition and breakaway LDP groups.

The first LH election tackled by the farmers' political leagues was the 1958 general election, in which active campaigns were undertaken in Fukushima and Hokkaido. The Fukushima Nosei Sasshin Renmei took as its slogan 'all power to agricultural policy reform and the campaign to mobilise farmers' political power'. Its membership consisted of 53,000 farm households out of the total of 160,000 in the prefecture. It recommended three candidates – from the LDP, JSP and the prefectural 'Democracy Club' (Minshu Kurabu) – standing in one or other of the two LH electoral districts in the prefecture. This diversity of party representation embodied the league's supra-party stance based on the principle of 'free party support' and exclusion of 'political party control'. The active support of the league was credited with ensuring the victory of its LDP-recommended candidate, who had fallen out with the LDP prefectural federation over the former MAF Minister backed by the federation.

In Hokkaido, the Hokkaido Nomin Domei which organised 130,000 out of a total of 230,000 farm households, helped ensure the victories of the five candidates it recommended from the JSP.[164] Because the league's Socialist orientation attracted a good deal of criticism from its sub-branches which rejected the notion of their organisation becoming a 'subordinate organ' of the JSP in the prefecture, those candidates who received the backing of the league downplayed their JSP endorsement, preferring to present themselves more as 'local farmers' representatives'.[165] Farmers supported them under this banner, particularly those dissatisfied with LDP agricultural policies.

The first UH election tackled by the farmers' political leagues was the 1959 poll, in which they made concerted efforts to elect as many as possible of their prefectural Nokyo chairmen to Diet office, in addition to a range of other candidates who pledged their support for the agricultural cooperative cause. Their electoral targets were accomplished in the case of a majority of their supported LDP candidates,[166] but Independent and GBS candidates enjoyed a much lower success rate. Although the number of politicians without party affiliation had diminished more slowly in the Upper House than in the Lower House, the general process of party consolidation, particularly after the establishment of the two-party system in 1955, caught up with the House of Councillors when the newly amalgamated LDP obtained an absolute majority in the House, which removed the strategic advantage that Independents and GBS members had hitherto enjoyed.[167] In fact, in the 1959 UH elections, the LDP expanded its hold over the Upper House by filling former Ryokufukai seats.[168] In January 1960, the group was dissolved. The conscription of farmers' political leagues into the electoral service of a number of LDP Nokyo Diet candidates in the 1959 UH election brought the agricultural cooperative-LDP connection to the fore as a significantly new phenomenon in Japanese electoral politics at the national level.

After the patent political successes of 1959, the *noseiren* expanded their scale of organisation by setting up a national umbrella organisation, the National Farmers' Political League (Zenkoku Nomin Seiji Renmei, or Zennoseiren) prior to the 1960 LH election.[169] It operated in addition to the Zennoren which was still in existence and which was gradually assuming closer ties to the LDP.[170] The farmers' political leagues had a choice of joining either the Zennoren or the Zennoseiren. There were also personnel links at the executive level between the two organisations.[171]

The Zennoseiren officially sponsored its own candidate, Koga Ryo, in the 1960 LH elections for Saga constituency. Koga was Saga Prefecture *kenchu* and *noseiren* chairman[172] and campaigned on the *noseiren* slogan of 'mobilising farmers' political power', securing 75,000 votes and top place in the election.[173] Various prefectural *noseiren* also sponsored their own leaders in a number of other constituencies,[174] the majority with LDP endorsement, a minority with Opposition party affiliation.

Koga's rejection of any party affiliations and his nomination as a Zennoseiren-endorsed candidate was a positive reaffirmation of the organisation's support for the principle of political independence. The Zennoseiren also declared its formal independence of the agricultural cooperative system, although it acknowledged Nokyo as its organisational base. It undertook to cooperate and liaise with Nokyo, but it reserved the right to agree or disagree with Nokyo policies in the light of its own interpretation of agricultural sector interests.[175]

The expanding involvement of Nokyo and its associated farmers' political leagues in national elections was particularly evident in the 1962 UH election. In addition to the successful candidacy of a prefectural *noseiren* leader in Kumamoto,[176] the advance made by currently serving LDP-endorsed Nokyo prefectural executives in the 1959 UH elections was consolidated and extended to include five new members.[177] Altogether, the number of Nokyo politicians in the Upper House strengthened from 15 in 1959 to 20 in 1962 (see Table 3.2).

Prior to the 1963 House of Representatives' election, the amalgamation of the Zennoseiren with the Zennoren[178] produced the Zennosoren. The primary function of both the national and prefectural branches of the new Zennosoren organisation was to act as the 'advance corps' of the Nokyo electorate (*senkyo botai*),[179] which represented the strongest aspect of its activities. The Zennoren had continued to function, although increasingly less effectively, with some prefectural branches or farmers' federations (*nomin renmei*) still in existence. The functions of the Zennoren and its locally-based farmers' federations had, however, been largely taken over by the farmers' political leagues.

The 1963 LH elections marked the turning point in the national political fortunes of the farmers' political leagues as sponsors of their own political representatives. Koga Ryo was ignominiously defeated in Saga constituency, which, in retrospect, marked the end of attempts by Nokyo-based political groups to elect their own non-party affiliated candidates to the Diet. In 1964, Saga Prefecture *noseiren* changed its organisation to an all-village council and renamed itself the Agricultural Policy Countermeasures Council (Nosei Taisaku Kyogikai), which later became a more conservative organisation.[180]

The short-lived success of the Zennoseiren as an independent political force was due to its very insistence on the principle of non-party attachment at a time when the two-party system had become well established in the Diet and the popularity of Independent and minor party candidates had drastically diminished.[181] Moreover, the existence of a political grouping devoted solely to farmers' interests irrespective of party was being pre-empted by the obvious benefits of close links with the LDP. In 1960 a decade of rapid and sizeable increases in the producer rice price began, and in 1961, the Agricultural Basic Law was passed which justified increases in subsidies to meet a whole raft of new policy objectives relating to agricultural production, improvement in agricultural structure, farm incomes, farm management and rural welfare.

Even Koga Ryo had become aware of the weakness of his position in 'no man's land' in the Diet and the impracticalities of his neutral, non-party stance.[182] This prompted him to request (unsuccessfully) LDP endorsement prior to the 1963 election campaign. Lack of influence in agricultural policy-making during his brief stint in the Diet had been a severe disadvantage for Zennoseiren at the time, given the intense debate being waged in agricultural circles over the ABL proposals and the strong policy orientation of the farmers' political leagues.

The results of the 1963 election in Saga Prefecture prompted a fundamental reappraisal of prospects for setting up a non-affiliated Nokyo-sponsored political grouping in the Diet. Zennosoren rejected the standpoint of the Zennoseiren in putting up its own candidates, although it continued to espouse the principle of guaranteed support for farmers' representatives irrespective of party. Evidence of this was the tendency amongst Zennosoren-recommended candidates to stand with the endorsement of Opposition socialist parties, sometimes in competition with LDP Nokyo candidates. In 1965 for example, a two-way rivalry for Nokyo votes developed between a Zennosoren candidate and a Nokyo executive in the UH national constituency. The clash involved Nakamura Yoshijiro, the Secretary-General of the Zennosoren standing as a DSP candidate, and Okamura Fumijiro, the Chairman of Zenkyoren, who was an LDP incumbent. The Zenkyoren faction within Nokyo mustered enough nationwide support to guarantee a successful result for their leader, but the division in Nokyo votes overall was sufficient to ensure the defeat of the Zennosoren candidate who proved weaker. That this clash took place at all is evidence of a certain amount of electoral conflict and lack of co-ordination between these two organisations, particularly in view of the general acknowledgment within Nokyo that agricultural cooperative votes could only support one official Nokyo candidacy in the national constituency.[183]

The increasing dominance of the LDP–Nokyo connection

The electoral rivalry between competing Nokyo candidates in 1965 was an extreme example of the differences that were sometimes apparent in the organisational, electoral and political standpoints of various parts of the Nokyo organisation. These differences had various dimensions: an organisational dimension – the *noseiren* were generally more politically independent and flexible than the mainstream Nokyo organisation, in spite of the overlap between the two; a time dimension – Nokyo and its affiliated organisations became progressively more conservative over time; a regional dimension – in some parts of rural Japan, connections with the progressive side of politics were stronger than in others; and a centre-periphery dimension – the *noseiren* represented Nokyo's sub-leadership in the provinces which was more inclined to press hard on behalf of local farmers' demands and maximise political representation of the cooperatives by choosing candidates who offered the strongest support for the agrarian cause, regardless of party affiliation. In principle the issue of party colouring was not raised as long as the candidate professed his support and was willing to align his interests with those of the cooperatives.[184] In contrast, the central leadership of Nokyo wanted to cooperate with LDP members because that was the way to get government subsidies.[185] This priority mandated electoral strategies that would maximise Nokyo's influence within government ranks. As Hiwatari observed, the 'agricultural cooperatives . . . as a mouthpiece for mobilizing and representing the economic interests of farmers . . . opt[ed] increasingly to make use of the conservative political parties as a means of realizing their political interests'.[186] Over time, as the LDP consolidated its hold on power and the JSP's fortunes receded, these considerations also exerted a more powerful influence over the political alignments of local Nokyo leaders.

Nokyo's corporatisation into the policy process was another factor pushing it in the direction of the LDP. As Ishida points out, by acting as an agricultural policy 'permeation' organisation (*nosei shinto soshiki*), Nokyo assimilated all the more easily to the ruling party compared with the Opposition parties because the former represented the political establishment.[187]

Conversely, from the LDP's perspective, the association with agricultural cooperative organisations helped to compensate for the party's lack of an effective organisation at the rice roots.[188] As the newly founded conservative party increasingly felt the lack of a strong local organisation, it began to co-opt substitute groupings into a symbiotic relationship for the specific purpose of mobilising votes.[189] The LDP thus sought to enlist agricultural cooperative organisations as electoral sub-contractors in rural areas, exploiting them as rice-roots substitutes for mass membership organisations and as a direct link to farmers' votes. Just prior to the 1958 LH election, for example, the LDP introduced a system of pensions for officials of agricultural organisations in order to strengthen its relationship with Nokyo and to consolidate Nokyo's position as a powerful elective body on the LDP's behalf (*Jiminto no senkyo soshiki*) in the countryside.[190]

The agricultural cooperatives, together with their associated political organisations, thus gradually assumed the role of organisational sub-structures (*kabu soshiki*) for the LDP at the electoral level.[191] Agricultural cooperative organisations became the principal force behind the mobilisation of support for LDP Diet candidates amongst the farmers.[192] They were the primary mechanism allowing 'conservative politicians to bring rural communities under their sway'.[193] Indeed, in Ishida's view, Diet members from the LDP 'more frequently than not exploited . . . [farmers'] organizations.'[194]

Another important factor helping to forge closer links between Nokyo and the LDP was the 'natural' alliance between two conservatively-orientated organisations which in effect shared the same constituency. Not only were a majority of Nokyo's members LDP voters, but most of the chairmen and executives of local branches of Nokyo were conservative local figures.[195] In 1955, 52 per cent of persons working in agriculture, forestry and fisheries were LDP supporters. At the same time, they comprised the largest single bloc (43 per cent) of the party's supporters.[196] A subsequent survey of persons employed in agriculture, forestry and fisheries in the 1958 elections showed that 70 per cent of males and 61 per cent of females in this category voted for the LDP, while only 19 per cent of males and 17 per cent of females supported the JSP. In contrast, the largest category of JSP voters was the technical, white-collar class of workers, with 47 per cent of males and 37 per cent of females in this category supporting the JSP in the 1958 elections.[197] Although a minority of farmers supported the JSP, the Socialist Party was clearly drawing greater support from those in non-agricultural employment, such as white-collar workers in public and semi-public organisations who were highly unionised, including local government employees and Nokyo staff members.[198] Their unions were affiliated with prefectural labour councils and

Sohyo, which, in turn, was affiliated with the JSP. Nokyo staff members, for instance, joined unions affiliated to the National Federation of Nokyo Labour Unions (Zenkoku Nokyo Rodo Kumiai Rengokai, or Zennokyo Roren) which was generally regarded as being progressively-aligned. Their party support patterns can be contrasted with Nokyo's farmer-executive class, in which 75 per cent of female and 60 per cent of males voted for the LDP in the late 1950s.[199]

The LDP thus gradually consolidated its hold on the countryside in successive elections from 1955 onwards. The JSP remained the only viable party alternative in rural LH electorates,[200] although its support was largely drawn from public sector unionised workers and the ever-diminishing numbers of farmers still loyal to organisations such as the farmers' unions and farmers' political leagues with a more progressive orientation.

In elections in the late 1950s and early 1960s, the JSP consistently received a higher percentage of the total vote in urban rather than rural areas. On a four-point scale of population density beginning with the most densely populated and moving to the least densely populated electorate type, the JSP secured 38.51 per cent, 32.01 per cent, 28.88 per cent and 23.22 per cent of the total vote in each of these categories respectively in the 1958 LH elections (see Table 3.3). This pattern was the reverse of the LDP's cross-constituency support rate, which was highest in the least populous district type (65.39 per cent), decreasing to 63.48 per cent, 58.01 per cent and 51.38 per cent across the continuum to the most densely populated district type. The JCP obtained only 1.33 per cent of the total vote in the least populous constituencies and was clearly a marginal electoral force in rural areas.

Despite the LDP's relative bias towards electorates towards the rural end of the spectrum, however, Table 3.3 shows that the disparity in the LDP's polling rates across constituency categories in the late 1950s was not very great. The LDP did best in rural districts, but it also polled relatively well in urbanised areas, which moderated the party's rural bias to some extent. Conversely the LDP gained lower than expected support in some strongly rural prefectures such as Iwate, Fukushima, Niigata, Nagano, Yamanashi, Tottori and Kochi where the JSP performed quite strongly.[201] These were regions where JSP-affiliated farmers' union candidates and more 'progressive' candidates supported by the prefectural farmers' political leagues polled well. The JSP as a whole made significant gains in the 1958 LH elections, including rural constituencies.[202]

This can be attributed to several factors. Firstly, the Socialists in this election had a unified electoral strategy for the first time in a LH poll since the amalgamation of the Right and Left Socialists in 1955.[203] Secondly, many farmers were dissatisfied with the growing income disparities between rural and urban workers and felt the LDP was not doing enough to redress this gap. Thirdly, the disparate strands of the farmers' union movement came together with the establishment of Zennichino in March 1958. Although Zennichino did not mount an active election campaign, and although deep divisions still

Table 3.3 Electoral district type and percentage of the total vote obtained by parties (1958–67 Lower House elections)

Unit: %

Party	Electoral District Type	1958	1960	1963	1967
LDP	A (Most Populous)	51.38	50.26	44.86	34.96
	B	58.01	58.65	56.18	48.52
	C	63.48	62.74	62.29	59.50
	D (Least Populous)	65.39	66.25	62.59	66.75
JSP	A (Most Populous)	38.51	30.91	31.02	27.19
	B	32.01	27.36	28.03	28.51
	C	28.88	24.52	26.12	27.76
	D (Least Populous)	23.22	19.47	23.08	25.17
DSP	A (Most Populous)		12.00	11.79	6.19
	B		7.67	6.04	13.00
	C		7.02	3.62	2.16
	D (Least Populous)		5.61	2.87	1.44
JCP	A (Most Populous)	4.41	4.88	6.37	7.44
	B	1.90	2.08	1.82	2.67
	C	1.39	1.86	2.39	2.74
	D (Least Populous)	1.33	1.33	1.47	1.78
CGP[a]	A (Most Populous)				12.30
	B				0.96
	C				1.77
	D (Least Populous)				0.00

Notes:
a CGP stands for Clean Government Party, or Komeito.

Source: Hajime Shinohara, 'Postwar Parties and Politics in Japan', *The Developing Economies*, Vol. 6, No. 4, December 1968, p. 402.

existed between right and left camps, it recommended 116 JSP candidates in the 1958 poll. Of these, 75 were elected.[204] Amongst these were a number of farmers' union leaders who subsequently formed the Zennichino Diet Members' Group (Zennichino no Kokkai Giindan). A total of 32 Diet members were Zennichino officials in 1958.[205] A recommendation from Zennichino gave the impression that the candidates were representatives of farmers which appeared to be an effective device for gathering farmers' votes.[206] In short, farmers appeared to discount the party factor and vote for candidates who had strong agricultural connections.

Table 3.1 reveals that a greater number of JSP-aligned Nokyo politicians were swept into power in the 1958 elections than ever before (a total of 11 compared with a total of 8 Right and Left Socialists in 1955). Conversely, no increase in the number of LDP-aligned Nokyo politicians took place. In fact there was a slight reduction with only 13 LDP Nokyo-candidates winning seats in the Diet (a decline of three for the conservative party side of politics compared with the 1955 LH election).

Almost all the JSP-affiliated Nokyo Diet members had one or more of the following characteristics: they were from or were associated with the permanent staff ranks of Nokyo or of its predecessor organisations (the *nogyokai, nokai* and *sangyo kumiai*), or the staff unions of these organisations, not the elected farmer-executive class, from where the LDP Nokyo politicians were exclusively drawn;[207] they had a history as leaders in the farmers' union movement;[208] or they were associated with the farmers' political leagues affiliated with the Zennoren and its long-standing principle of political independence.[209] These organisational connections and career attributes suggest that the supporters of JSP Nokyo politicians were farmers affiliated to the farmers' unions and farmers' political leagues and Nokyo staff members. As noted earlier, the JSP drew support in the countryside from unionised clerical employees working in local government and agricultural cooperative offices. Many of the group of JSP Nokyo politicians elected in 1958 had been in the Diet affiliated with either the Right or Left Socialists since the early 1950s and were, in many respects, a hangover from the past.

A similar party support pattern also showed up in the 1960 LH election with the LDP polling relatively well in some urban districts. As Table 3.3 indicates, the LDP gained more than 50 per cent of the vote in the most populous constituencies in 1960.[210] At the same time the LDP garnered less support than might be expected in some agricultural constituencies such as Niigata, Ishikawa, Nagano, Shiga, Saga and Oita where there were pockets of Socialist support.[211] Clearly, the LDP's rural bias was not as distinct as it was to become in later years.

On the other hand, despite these relatively good performances by the JSP in some rural districts, the party was never able to make significant inroads into LDP support in the countryside. In the 1960 LH elections, the JSP's polling rate across all constituency types slipped, dropping to 19.47 per cent in the least populous constituencies (see Table 3.3). A smaller number of the same group of JSP-affiliated Nokyo Diet members (seven) were returned, all but one from those elected in 1958. A feeling that agricultural support for the JSP was ebbing was the motivation behind the formation of a JSP Agricultural Policy Diet Members' Group (Shakaito Nosei Giindan), with members drawn from politicians interested in agricultural policy, the central committee of the party and the Farmers' and Fishermen's Department of the party's Organisation Bureau (Soshiki Kyoku Nogyobu).[212] The membership of this body reached 105 across both houses of the Diet, which was equivalent to about half the total number of JSP Diet members. Its objective was to mount a 'return home campaign' (*kikyo undo*), which involved members' returning to their home villages and explaining their policies to farmers and canvassing opinions in relation to the 1961 ABL. The country was divided into nine blocks, with a manager and policy promotion unit consisting of between four and eight politicians assigned to each block. The unit's task was to collect the opinions of as many farmers as possible in each block, hold discussions with them in order to make them understand JSP agricultural policy, find activists in agricultural villages and establish strong ties with them. It was hoped that groups of discontented farmers would be established at the rice roots, which could then be organised systematically from local through to prefectural and national levels. This was seen as a way of eliciting as many votes as possible from farmers.[213] The JSP clearly saw farmers as a potentially disaffected group from whom it could gain higher levels of support, particularly in an economic environment where farmers' incomes were slipping so far behind the wages of urban workers.

During the 1960s, Zennichino remained the national body of farmers' union organisations aligned with the JSP, but its influence waned as rice-roots support amongst farmers for the union movement gradually diminished. The local farmers' union branches rapidly became moribund in many areas, although in certain prefectures where they had been traditionally more active, they continued to function as supporters' associations for JSP candidates. Zennichino's influence remained particularly strong in Northern Japan, with farmers' union candidates almost continuously representing LH districts such as Niigata (2) and (3), Miyagi (1) and (2), Akita (2),[214] Yamagata (2), Nagano (3), Aomori (1), Fukushima (2) and Hokkaido (4) from the early 1950s until the late 1970s,[215] and similarly, UH prefectural constituencies such as Niigata, Fukushima and Okayama. In Niigata Prefecture specifically, JSP support in Niigata (2) and (3) was consistently strong because farmers' votes flowed to agricultural representatives of the Socialist Party. As Sakai explains, this was a period when the JSP had candidates specialising in agricultural policies. Farmers' support for these Diet members underscored the fact that farmers voted for particular individuals in terms of their personalities and agricultural connections, rather than for political parties or for the ideologies of particular parties.[216]

Likewise, a relatively stronger progressive influence within the Nokyo organisation was detectable in a number of prefectures such as Niigata, Tottori, Shimane, Hokkaido, Chiba, Aomori and Akita. In some cases, *Nokyo giin* had served in executive posts in both the agricultural cooperatives and the farmers' unions.[217]

A major political development in the 1960 LH elections was the emergence of a separate right-wing socialist party, the DSP. The primary base of support for this breakaway group from JSP ranks was the most populous district type, reflecting the party's links with the trade union movement in the private sector. In 1960, the newly formed DSP collected 12.00 per cent of the vote in the most densely populated electorates compared with only 5.61 per cent of the vote in the least populous constituencies. As Table 3.3 indicates, its polling rate in the latter tailed off to 2.87 per cent and 1.44 per cent in the 1963 and 1967 elections respectively. The small number of LH seats the DSP managed to secure in the countryside in 1960, 1963 and 1967 were predominantly in semi-rural districts and affected LDP and JSP performance almost equally.

The establishment of the DSP also meant a fracturing of the farmers' union movement, with the formation of the DSP's own farmers' union wing, the

National Farmers' League (Zenno), which was established in August 1960 (see Figure 2.1). This gave the party some credibility amongst farm voters although it is doubtful how useful farmers' union backing for DSP candidates continued to be areas with higher concentrations of farm population. In addition, the DSP initially inherited ex-JSP Nokyo Diet members who were former agricultural cooperative staff members with close connections to employee unions. In some prefectures, candidates with strong agricultural credentials also received support from 'progressive' farmers' political leagues; in others it was successful in mobilising connections with agricultural organisations, including Nokyo, particularly in semi-rural constituencies. One DSP Nokyo politician was elected in 1960; four were elected in 1963 and five were elected in 1967 (see Table 3.1).

After the JSP split in 1960, the numbers of JSP Nokyo Diet members decreased, falling from a figure that was about the same as the LDP's in 1958 to consistently about half the number of LDP Nokyo politicians in the 1960–1967 LH elections. As Table 3.1 shows, the latter went up from 13 in 1960 to 15 in 1963 and 17 in 1967. In terms of the JSP's overall electoral performance, a general pattern of decline was also in evidence, although the party did make small gains in rural constituencies. Its voting support in the most densely populated districts slipped dramatically, while in the least populous districts, its polling rate climbed steadily, albeit marginally, from 1960 to 1967. It remained little more than a minority party in these districts, however, gaining a quarter or less of the total vote. In terms of seat acquisition rates, the JSP garnered 31.0 per cent of rural seats in the 1958 elections, 26.5 per cent in 1960 and 27 per cent in 1963.[218]

The overall impact of these trends was to generate a more evenly balanced electoral base for the party, with voting support levels that were more or less the same across all types of constituencies (see Table 3.3). The urban base of the JSP was crumbling at the same time as its rural support was expanding slightly, thus shifting its orientation from a relatively urban one to one characterised by a more or less even cross-section of electorate types. Even so, in 1967, the JSP was still securing a smaller percentage of the total vote in the least populous constituencies than in any other type (see Table 3.3).

Between 1958 and 1967, the LDP's support rate in the most populous districts steadily ebbed (it contracted to 34.96 per cent of the total vote by 1967 as shown in Table 3.3). On the other hand, the party maintained stable support in the least populous districts (see Table 3.3). In terms of rural seat acquisition rates, the same pattern is observable. The LDP secured 69 per cent of rural seats in 1958, 71 per cent in 1960 and 72 per cent in 1963.[219] For the LDP, the overall effect was a more pronounced rural bias in the character of its representation. At most it ceded only minority party status to the JSP in rural areas. As for the JCP and Komeito (which first entered national LH elections in 1967 as the political arm of the Soka Gakkai), these were clearly urban parties, particularly the latter.[220]

In the Upper House, the LDP emerged as the dominant political force in agricultural prefectures. The ruling party polled extremely well (garnering more than 50 per cent of the vote) in agricultural constituencies, gaining almost complete dominance of rural seats in the Upper House. This was partly a function of the electoral system. UH prefectural constituencies were large and populous electoral districts and the 25 two-member prefectural constituencies[221] in effect became single-member, first-past-the post districts because of the three-year half election for house membership. This type of electorate favoured strong, nationwide, majority parties – in this case the LDP. Almost half of Nokyo's UH Diet members came from single-member prefectural constituencies between 1956 and 1965.[222] These were predominantly in the more rural, agricultural regions of Tohoku, Northern Kanto, Hokuriku, Shikoku and Kyushu, although not all the prefectural constituencies in these districts were single-member electorates.

Japan's smaller Opposition parties also suffered from the increasing divisions in their ranks which split their UH votes even further. Between 1955 and 1967, the JSP (the only Opposition party to win seats in UH rural electorates) secured just 12 seats out of a total of 100 contested. Independent or Ryokufukai candidates won three and the rest were successfully contested by the LDP.[223] Electoral and party factors thus contributed to the lack of success by the JSP and Nokyo candidates with socialist affiliations in prefectural districts of the Upper House, particularly in agricultural regions.

The same LDP dominance was observable in the national constituency, where agricultural organisations supporting endorsed LDP candidates proved to be much stronger than the organisations supporting 'progressive' candidates. In the 1959 UH election, for example, seven LDP candidates with connections to agricultural and forestry organisations (including Nokyo, land improvement industry groups, tobacco growers' associations and agricultural mutual aid associations) as well as food industry groups were elected to the Upper House from the national constituency.[224] The only victorious JSP candidate received the backing of the farmers' unions and the MAF labour union, embodying the principle of worker–farmer cooperation. Two other Zennichino candidates failed to be elected.[225] It was a slightly different story in the 1962 UH poll in which Zennichino's Chairman, Nomizo Masaru won 39th place with 430,000 votes, belying expectations that because Zennichino's organisational power had waned, he would have a real fight to retain his seat.[226] Candidates with connections to agricultural and forestry labour unions were also successful.[227]

Nevertheless, the dominant connection for the vast majority of Nokyo politicians in the Upper House from 1959 onwards was with the LDP (see Table 3.2). Their number enlarged from 12 in 1959 to 17 in 1962, 15 in 1965 and 17 in 1968. Conversely, the numbers of JSP and Independent Nokyo politicians in the Upper House contracted to a small minority. This was a distinct change from the pattern that had prevailed between 1947 and 1956 when the total number of Independents, GBS and Socialist *Nokyo giin* either exceeded the number aligned with the conservatives or were approximately the same in number. It was also distinctly different from the pattern of party affiliation in the Lower House, which was more evenly balanced between ruling and combined socialist parties (see Table 3.1).

The same disparity emerged between LH and UH *noseiren* party support choices. In the prefectural constituencies of the Upper House, most prefectural *noseiren* played a role as support groups for the LDP, whereas in LH constituencies, where the multi-member districts gave candidates from minority parties a greater chance of success, a greater diversity of political allegiance amongst *noseiren*-backed candidates was in evidence.

Consolidation of the links between Nokyo and the ruling party in the Upper House was symbolised by the decision of Nokyo's UH Diet members to form their own group, the Upper House Nokyo Diet Members' Group (Sangiin Nokyo Giindan) after the 1962 election. Membership was restricted to current Nokyo executives, excluding a JSP Zenchu staff member newly elected to the House.[228] Restricting membership to Nokyo executives was designed to keep out non-LDP members, not politicians of lesser rank within the Nokyo organisation.[229] Considerable opposition had emerged within Nokyo to the JSP candidacy of a Zenchu staff member because it directly contravened the policy Zenchu had adopted of concentrating selectively on utilising government party members to influence agricultural policy.[230]

As already noted, the continuing electoral victories of the conservative party, in a circular process of reciprocal cause and effect, reflected and provided on-going justification for strengthening the connection between Nokyo and the LDP. This period in Japanese political history marked the beginning of semi-permanent LDP rule, and as the Opposition's chances of coming to power receded, the tactical advantage of an electoral strategy that advocated political neutrality or countenanced representation in the ranks of the Opposition parties correspondingly dwindled. The alliance between Nokyo and the LDP was reinforced by success, and by the enhanced prospects of government party endorsement which offered potentially greater electoral gains for candidates than endorsement by a minority Opposition grouping. Amongst candidates supported by Nokyo, those affiliated with the LDP generally had a better chance of success.[231]

This incentive was buttressed by the practical budgetary and policy advantages of alignment with the ruling party. As the party in power, the LDP was the chief distributor of political largesse.[232] It controlled the political side of the budgetary allocation process and hence the flow of subsidies, grants and price supports to farmers, the agricultural cooperatives and rural communities in general. The early 1960s saw rapid increases in the quantities of subsidies being directed to the agricultural sector in the wake of the passage of the 1961 ABL. Not only did this legislation herald the introduction of the government's farm incomes policy which produced sizeable increases in agricultural support prices, but it also produced an agricultural and rural public works bounty into which LDP election candidates could tap. A 1962 survey showed that 53 per cent of workers in primary industry supported the LDP, but by 1965 this figure had leapt to 64 per cent.[233] The distribution of material benefits to farmers was also the dominant factor underlying and reinforcing the government party–Nokyo electoral nexus. A vote for an LDP candidate could realise increased assistance to the cooperatives as well as to the farmers.[234]

Rationalising support for LDP candidates along these lines was frequently made by Nokyo leaders in pre-election speeches: 'If our representatives do not belong to the party in power, we cannot expect policies to be realised';[235] 'a vote for an opposition candidate is a dead vote';[236] 'the opposition parties have no powers of decision in either the budget or the rice price';[237] and 'to put people into the government party who understand us is to prevent policies being formulated which ignore the farmers'.[238] These considerations were often powerful enough to override virulent opposition to LDP agricultural policies coming from certain sections of Nokyo.[239]

As the LDP–Nokyo connection was cemented, progressively-aligned factions of local and central Nokyo leaders correspondingly retreated.[240] Evidence of this was the changing ratio of conservative to progressive Nokyo Diet members in the Lower House: it was 54:46 per cent in the 1958 elections, 62:38 per cent in the 1960 elections, 60:40 in the 1963 elections and 57:43 per cent in the 1967 elections (calculated from figures in Table 3.1). The trend was even more pronounced in the Upper House. As already pointed out, the more numerous LDP Nokyo group in the Upper House in fact engaged in a positive anti-JSP movement against the token force of Socialist Nokyo politicians in that house.

Trends in the political alignments of Nokyo's political representatives reflected its adjustment to the political realities of the time. The principle of political neutrality was of limited utility in a situation where one party remained continuously in office. These trends, however, raised questions about the extent to which Nokyo had placed itself under the control of the LDP and allowed its local chapters to become electoral support organisations of conservative politicians. By the mid-1960s, Nokyo had become so dependent on the LDP that it was being referred to as the 'LDP's Nokyo'.[241] According to Tanaka, Nokyo nurtured this dependence on the ruling party partly because reformist forces in the Opposition camp rarely conducted political campaigns in rural areas, except for Zennichino in prefectures like Niigata and Yamagata.[242]

Conclusion

This chapter has attempted an historical analysis of Nokyo's political representation in the Diet and the formation of farmers' and Nokyo-associated parties and political groups in the early postwar decades. In Japan, initial attempts to establish a farmers' party proved a failure. A series of embryonic political groupings appeared in the Diet between 1947 and 1952 with much of the impetus behind their formation coming from voluntary farm organisations associated in some way with the ideology of cooperativism and the agricultural cooperative movement. The political parties that emerged as a result of these efforts, however, were symptomatic of the early postwar period of party upheaval and change, and ultimately faced a choice similar to many other such temporary intra-Diet alliances: incorporation into larger political groupings or electoral extinction. As minor party organisations gradually coalesced into smaller numbers of major parties across the political spectrum, the potential viability of those representing a narrow base of farmers or cooperative unionism diminished. It became increasingly obvious that neither farmers' organisations nor the principle of cooperative unionism could separately or jointly sustain a viable national party organisation, and by 1955, agricultural organisations were consolidating themselves and their connections with the major parties.

Another important factor was electoral demographics. Farm voters in the late 1940s comprised almost half the national electorate, whereas by 1955, their numbers had edged down to just over 40 per cent, and to just under one-third by 1963 (see Table 5.1). In the early postwar decade, their greater numbers could, therefore, sustain political parties devoted principally to advancing agricultural interests in a way they could not in later years, as population began leaving rural areas for the cities in the process of urbanisation.[243]

The farmers' organisations that flourished in the early postwar period underwent a similar process of advance and decay to farmers' political parties. Farmers' unions grew markedly weaker at the rice roots, which considerably reduced their electoral value, although many of their leaders remained in the Diet as a hangover from an earlier period of greater organisational viability. Likewise, the rural youth leagues had a brief period of ascendancy amongst farmers only to be displaced by organisations spawned by the agricultural cooperatives.

With the establishment of the farmers' political leagues in the late 1950s, Nokyo's electioneering role underwent significant historical development. In the gubernatorial elections of this period, and even more in the expansion of their operations in the general elections of 1959, 1960 and 1962, the farmers' political leagues' efforts in mobilising the political power of the farmers increasingly began to bear fruit in terms of the numbers of Nokyo officials elected to public office. Furthermore, it was in the testing ground of the gubernatorial elections that concrete evidence of vote 'control' by the cooperatives began to be observed.

Ultimately, the fundamental political and ideological orientation of the Diet representatives of the agricultural cooperative movement, its associated political groups, and its leaders and members, who made up the nation's farm voters in the 1950s and 1960s, became predominantly, although not exclusively, conservative. The long-term rule of the LDP gradually undermined the variable party support pattern of the agricultural sector. Farmers were increasingly seduced by the LDP's targeted agricultural and rural infrastructure spending, which required close connections with local LDP members as a means of tapping the rewards allocation mechanism.[244] In Nokyo's case its political bias was similarly mandated by practical considerations relating to the strategic electoral and policy advantages of endorsement by the government party. The preference amongst Nokyo Diet members for alignment with the LDP was to become an enduring feature of the political affiliations of agricultural cooperative politicians.

The highly variable party affiliations of agricultural organisations in the early postwar decades, however, challenge the widespread assumption that the LDP has monopolised the agricultural 'connection' in Japan and that farmers' organisations are LDP-attached. The story as told here is in fact much more complex and nuanced.

Firstly, the farmers' unions were uniformly aligned with the Opposition socialists; they inherited a radical, anti-establishment tradition. When they weakened organisationally, their core function as rice-roots electoral organisations of socialist parties was clearly revealed. The ascription of party-attachment therefore applies in their case, but it was to the socialist and not the conservative party(ies).

Secondly, Nokyo's associated political groupings inherited a tradition of greater independence from political parties. Not only did they attempt to steer a 'third course' between government and Opposition parties, but their political orientation was, on occasions, more 'progressive' than 'conservative'. In general, their approach was largely non-ideological and highly instrumentalist: they pursued the connections that would best serve their own interests. Even when they backed candidates who had LDP endorsement, officially they maintained a position that was independent of party organisation and reserved the right to vary their party support depending on the candidate.

Likewise, many farmers were inclined to vote for those politicians who pledged their support for agricultural causes, who maintained close connections with farmers' groups and who had a good record on farmers' issues, almost regardless of party. The personal attributes and characteristics of individual candidates, including their organisational connections and their willingness to work on behalf of the local farming communities within their electorates, were often the key determinants of voter support, not the factor of party affiliation, which was, in many cases, a subordinate consideration. In the Lower House and to a lesser extent in the Upper House, such an approach was underwritten by the multi-member electoral system, which enabled voters and Nokyo organisations to focus on candidate-specific rather than party-related factors. Even in the 1960s, JSP and LDP candidates in rural constituencies were observed to emphasise in their campaign speeches that they stood as 'representatives of rural districts' rather than as 'members of political parties'.[245] This was particularly the case when the farmers were dissatisfied with government policy and looked around to send their representatives to the Diet irrespective of party.[246] As one Nokyo-based conservative politician commented in the wake of the 1962 UH election:

'Candidates who respond to farmers' demands collected their votes. What mattered for farmers was whether a candidate, regardless of whether he was LDP or JSP, understood their situation and maintained their interests.'[247]

On the other hand, the farmers' political leagues learned the hard lesson in the 1963 LH election that independent agricultural representation in the Diet could not be sustained. The failure to uphold the notion of a third force representing farmers' interests through sponsorship of an official candidate in the Diet by the national Nokyo-based political group merely served to legitimise closer ties with the ruling party. The powerlessness of Diet members who eschewed major party attachment also seriously undermined the principle of strict political neutrality. Whilst the *noseiren* retained a higher degree of political flexibility than the mainstream Nokyo organisation, they increasingly put their weight behind LDP candidates.

Indeed, the creation of the farmers' political leagues was historically significant from the point of view of the development of the electoral relationship between the agricultural cooperatives and the LDP at the rice-roots level. The leagues provided an organised context in which LDP candidates could pursue their electoral objectives amongst farmers by enlisting the support of the *noseiren* leadership in many of the prefectures in which the groups operated.

One major stream of agricultural leadership within Nokyo itself was predominantly conservative from the beginning because of Nokyo's corporatised relations with government. This group could be found in the central leadership of the mainstream Nokyo organisation, but increasingly amongst prefectural and municipal leaders also. The consolidation of Nokyo's corporatised relations with the MAFF and the institutionalisation of the agricultural policy subgovernment involving the LDP, the MAFF and Nokyo[248] ultimately undermined the viability of flexible political alignment strategies.

The LDP–Nokyo connection thus came ultimately to predominate, but never absolutely. Nokyo's formal organisational status as a statutory interest group mandated an official policy of political neutrality which precluded fixed party attachment. The connection between political parties and agricultural cooperative organisations remained one between two formally separate and independent organisations. The primary link was with individual politicians or candidates, not with political parties. Furthermore, considerations relating to the personal attributes and connections of an individual politician or candidate remained important determinants of electoral support. It was the candidate-specific rather than party-centred nature of the organised political support activity of Nokyo groupings which accounted for the more diverse patterns of party affiliation amongst these groups and the diversity of agricultural representation across the party spectrum.

4 Organisational politics

Because of Nokyo's dominant presence in the countryside, its universal membership of farm households, its all-encompassing services for agricultural producers, its semi-administrative role as an extension of the MAFF and its designated function as a farm interest group, understanding the agricultural cooperative organisation is critical to comprehending the past, present and future of Japanese agriculture and agricultural policy. Nokyo is one of the core economic, social and political institutions in Japan, and alongside the MAFF, is one of the two most important public institutions in the agricultural sector.

Nokyo also deserves attention as one of Japan's mammoth business, economic and financial groups, with interests that extend well beyond the farm sector. As an economic organisation, the development of Nokyo's business activities in the postwar period has in many respects mirrored trends in the Japanese economy as a whole. Spectacular expansion in the 1960s and 1970s was followed by slower growth in the 1980s, and the liberalisation and deregulation challenges of the 1990s. Furthermore, in recent years, many Nokyo organisations have faced a financial crunch of spectacular proportions.

From a sociological and political perspective, Nokyo is also noteworthy because its diverse operational scope encapsulates features common to many Japanese organisations. For example, like many other voluntary associations, Nokyo displays a tendency to expand the range of its organisational activity well beyond the core functions for which it was originally conceived. Nokyo is not simply the sum of its activities as defined by law and administrative rule-making. It also exists as a socio-economic and cultural system that reflects the nature of interpersonal relations, work patterns, modes of production, social relationships, cultural norms, customs and traditions in the countryside. Moreover, Nokyo has developed the means to conduct activities well beyond its capacities defined in law.[1] Many of Nokyo's political activities are derivative in this sense.

The following analysis elaborates the multifarious aspects of Nokyo's organisational character, structure and functioning. It catalogues Nokyo's organisational resources and the various ingredients in its much-vaunted economic and political power as well as illuminating the internal divisions that threaten its cohesiveness. Nokyo's organisational interests as distinct from those of its farm membership are also assessed in the light of the various benefits it extracts from the agricultural support and protection regime. Nokyo's position as a major obstacle to agricultural deregulation and liberalisation is explained together with a discussion of why Nokyo has been targeted for sustained criticism and structural reform. The study canvasses some of the difficulties currently faced by Nokyo in struggling to retain its organisational power and viability in an environment of rapid economic change and financial crisis.

Because Nokyo is in a constant process of evolution, this chapter can do no more than capture the flavour of the organisation in different phases of its development in the 50+ years since 1947. During this span of time, Nokyo Law has been amended 28 times, with 12 of these amendments being particularly significant.[2] In short, the Nokyo of the half-century mark was a far cry from the Nokyo at the turn of the twentieth century. The following description merely highlights the essential continuities as well as the more consequential aspects of this historical journey.

Nokyo's organisational 'sides' and 'faces'

Nokyo has been described as an organisation possessing a number of different 'sides'[3] or 'faces'.[4] The concept of 'sides' is a socio-economic one and derives from the reality of Nokyo's activities rather than its form as laid down in statute. Nokyo is said to have two predominant 'sides'. As well as being a 'body of enterprise' (*keieitai*), it is also a 'body of activities' (*undotai*). As an enterprise body, Nokyo is weak, in spite of its large membership. This is because its economic power, no matter how skilfully deployed, is fragile when compared to private enterprise which it confronts. As a result, Nokyo, in addition to economic business, must pursue group activities as an organisation, including *nosei katsudo*, in order to compensate for the gap in power between itself and private sector businesses, and to preserve the interests of its members.[5]

Nokyo's character as a 'body of activities' also exhibits two sides: internal and external. Internal activities involve matters like organisational strength and the promotion of business by the federated Nokyo organisation. External activities, on the other hand, take the form of activities against private capital and in relation to politics and government, and hence include *nosei katsudo*. Activities in relation to government are highly significant because of the heavy dependence of the farm sector on government agricultural policies.[6]

The concept of a 'face' encapsulates Nokyo's diverse functional aspects. Nokyo not only serves as a self-help cooperative for farmers, it also acts as a regional cooperative, a business enterprise, a voluntary association of farmers, an agricultural pressure group, a semi-administrative arm of government, a farm guidance organisation, a bank, a real estate office, a tourist organisation, a large mass media and public relations group, a welfare agency, agricultural processor, farm manager and so on.

These myriad activities can be categorised into several dominant 'faces'. The first is Nokyo's legal face as a 'cooperative organisation of farmers' (*nomin no kyodo soshikitai*), which is operated by farmers and which promotes their mutual interests.[7] Nokyo was designed as the organisational instrument by which the farmers could achieve improvement in their economic position and an elevation in their status through mutual assistance. This philosophy is embodied in the slogan: 'one man for 10,000 and 10,000 for one man.'[8]

As part of this philosophy, the cooperatives must distribute benefits amongst their members equally. Nokyo operates for the collective benefit of all its members, who receive equal consideration and who have equal decisionmaking powers within the cooperative.[9] Moreover, the cooperatives must not operate for profit-making purposes. Article 8 of Nokyo Law explicitly states that: 'A cooperative has for its object to do business in order to render its maximum services to its cooperative members and member cooperatives . . . and it shall not be allowed to do its business for profit-making purposes.'[10] In agricultural cooperative ideology, commercialism is regarded as inimical to cooperative principles. Nokyo's first principle of action is serving the interests of cooperative union members.[11] In theory, the economic benefits of cooperative action should flow back to the farmers whose interests are paramount. The cooperative directive requires that Nokyo be an organisation 'of farmers and for farmers'.[12] As Aono puts it, Nokyo's primary face is that of a farmers' organisation (*nomin no soshiki*), or alternatively an organised body of farmers (*nomin no soshikitai*), which exists first and foremost for the interests of farmers.[13]

Nokyo undertakes self-help services for its members mainly through economic enterprise – Nokyo's second and more dominant 'face'.[14] All the functions listed under Article 10 of the *Nokyoho* which agricultural cooperatives or federations of agricultural cooperatives may undertake, altogether or individually, are business activities. In terms of its primary organisational role, Nokyo is an 'economic group' (*keizai dantai*).

Direct comparison with private sector enterprise, however, is complicated by Nokyo's cooperative face and statutory origins. As pointed out above, Nokyo is not legally a company seeking profits for its share-holders (*kabushiki kaisha*). In fact, Nokyo enjoys special privileges by virtue of its status as a non-profit, mutual assistance cooperative.[15] Unlike private enterprise, it is permitted to operate virtual monopolies in many areas. Although cartels are prohibited by law, Nokyo is a kind of producers' cartel, but being a cooperative, it is exempt from the provisions of the Anti-Monopoly Law. Cooperative status bestows very real advantages in this respect.[16]

Nokyo's cooperative status also generates tax advantages. Like the postal savings system, Nokyo is regarded as a public entity and enjoys the benefits of such status, including being exempted from paying the higher corporate tax rate that private sector enterprises pay in Japan.[17] The lower rate is compensation for the fact that Nokyo's activities are limited by law and because the agricultural cooperatives (in theory) are not permitted to pursue profit.[18] Another concession is the fact that surplus dividends paid to members are treated as a loss on the income of the cooperatives in each business year under the provisions of the Juridical Persons Tax Law.[19]

Nokyo's third major 'face' is as an interest group or pressure group.[20] Nokyo's pressure group face was underpinned by its own organising law and by the government's extensive intervention in the agricultural economy, which led to Nokyo demanding price revisions and the adoption of new policies.[21] As Ishikawa explained soon after the central unions were established, 'Nokyo became a pressure group through its agricultural policy activities'.[22]

Nokyo is often lumped together with other prominent national organisations such as Keidanren, the Japan Medical Association (Nihon Ishikai), the former Sohyo and the Housewives' Federation (Shufuren) as a lobbying group representing a specific set of interests to government. Nokyo's pressure group face became more firmly etched in both the public's and policymakers' minds during the 1960s and 1970s when it became known as 'the farmers' Sohyo'.[23]

The popular image of Nokyo the pressure group stems largely from its highly publicised leadership of the annual farmers' campaign to raise the producer rice price. The campaign traditionally received extensive coverage in the media and had all the trappings of an elaborate drama 'staged' for the benefit of public and politician alike, in addition to Nokyo's own rank and file.[24] Its operations in mobilising 'legions' of the nation's farmers to 'invade' and 'occupy' government offices, to 'stand guard' and 'launch skirmishes' outside Rice Price Advisory Council hearings, and to 'surround' the Diet when farmers present petitions to Diet members, were once likened to those of the prewar Imperial Army.[25] As Nokyo's pressure group role developed and strengthened, it progressed from a 'request group-type character' (*yosei dantaiteki seikaku*) for transmitting demands to a 'pressure bargaining group-type character' (*atsuryoku kosho dantaiteki seikaku*) for winning demands.[26] As Asuwa comments, its constitution as 'fighting Nokyo' (*tatakau Nokyo*) became even stronger than before.[27]

Nokyo differs from other prominent lobby groups in several crucial respects, however. Firstly, it possesses an entirely separate and dominant economic rationale on which its membership is based, whereas other associational interest groups such as Keidanren and the Japan Medical Association are organised primarily around the principle of promoting and protecting the common interests of their members across a range of spheres. These groups do not normally conduct economic services for their members.

Secondly, Nokyo is the product of government sponsorship, not the voluntary initiative of a group of founding members. It is also subject to the statutory provisions of its own organising law and other laws. This legal status is not the norm for other voluntary interest associations, which are juridical persons (*hojin*), but are not the legal creations of government and do not operate under specific laws. Interest groups generally draw up their own constitutions, charter or articles of association and bylaws. In Nokyo's case, the content of these are specified by law. Each individual cooperative has its own articles of incorporation and bylaws, but their provision is specified in Section Four of the *Nokyoho* pertaining to the administration of the agricultural cooperatives.

The third important difference is Nokyo's role as a subsidiary organ of government in agricultural administration as a second local government (*daini yakuba*),[28] its fourth main 'face' – an organisational characteristic largely derived from its statutory and historical origins.[29] This particular face also governs the type of relationship Nokyo maintains with the bureaucracy, which extends well beyond lobbying the ministries with petitions and various kinds of 'request activities'.[30]

Strictly speaking, Nokyo does not, therefore, occupy the same organisational genre as other prominent voluntary interest associations in Japan. Farmers do not join Nokyo the pressure group. They join Nokyo the cooperative, which undertakes various kinds of economic and other services for its members. Moreover, agricultural cooperative executives and officials go out of their way to disassociate themselves from the label 'pressure group', steadfastly asserting Nokyo's identity as an 'economic group' (*keizai dantai*).[31] Their objection to the term 'pressure group' stems not only from cultural antipathy to the notion of an organisation selfishly exercising its political muscle, but also from the emphasis given in Nokyo law to economic activities. The rejection of the label 'political' by the Nokyo leadership also stems from the equation of this term with 'ideological' or 'politically partisan'. Nokyo prides itself on being formally 'non-partisan' and seeks to distinguish itself from 'political' and 'ideological' groups like the farmers' unions and trade unions which are attached to specific political parties. Accordingly, the official doctrine of Nokyo as asserted by successive leaders of Zenchu is a position of 'political neutrality' (*seijiteki churitsu*)[32] or 'equidistance' from all political parties.[33]

An internal report prepared in 1974–75 by a special committee reviewing Nokyo's political activities at the behest of the Combined Conference of National and Prefectural Central Union and Federation Chairmen clarifies the true character of the organisation as a political body. The report was precipitated by the increasingly radical action demanded by rank and file in Nokyo's producer rice price campaigns.[34] The report clearly rejected extremist action and clarified the limits of Nokyo's political activities, fearing that if it did not, misunderstanding in the organisation would result: 'Expecting the agricultural cooperatives to take action like farmers' organisations, by identifying Nokyo, which is an economic organisation, as a farmers' group that is organised for political action, will not lead to a solution to present problems.'[35]

All this is not to discount the existence of the central unions and their legitimate function of representing agricultural cooperative interests to government under Article 73(9)-2 of the Nokyo Law. This is correctly seen as a legally sanctioned core function of the agricultural cooperatives rather than as a derivative one. On the other hand, it is also true to say that the provision itself has been operationalised in an extremely broad way. On one legal provision an enormously complex set of policy-related functions have been built.

In fact, while Nokyo's agricultural policy activities primarily involve the central union organisations they are not necessarily restricted to them. Firstly, many other branches and groups within the overall Nokyo organisational system engage in *nosei katsudo* either independently or in association with other Nokyo groups.[36] Secondly, Nokyo has a large number of organisational offshoots such as the farmers' political leagues which regularly engage in all kinds of political activity. Hence, while Nokyo can claim to have a legally sanctioned interest group role, its political activities in reality extend well beyond the narrow confines of agricultural cooperative law. Thirdly, Nokyo's political activities are not limited to the activities conducted by Nokyo executives and staff members in their official capacities. Activities that could be broadly defined as political (including election campaign activities), and which commonly involve large numbers of farmer members, are frequently conducted by Nokyo officials acting in an unofficial capacity but nevertheless drawing on the authority, status, facilities, connections and leadership bestowed by their organisational attachment.[37]

A major disjunction therefore exists between Nokyo's formal and informal roles in the political sphere. Although the law bestows an interest articulation function on the central unions, the broad scope of agricultural cooperative political activity extends well beyond this legal provision. In this respect, Nokyo exemplifies the traditional, all-encompassing role of Japanese voluntary organisations, which are often not established as political organisations or interest groups but which take on these types of roles as part of a wide range of informal functions outside the specific objectives and original purposes for which they were founded. These activities are legitimised by their value in developing the total commitment, loyalty and in-group solidarity of the membership.[38] Such organisations become involved in extremely broad spheres of activity encouraged by the dominant rationale that they enhance the group itself and therefore advance its interests. While formally apolitical, these groups can be coopted for political purposes or sponsor their own political activities as a means of advancing group aims. Many Japanese participate in politics through the medium of such groups. While not set up for explicitly political purposes, the organisations they join take on political functions as part of a wide spectrum of activity.[39] Japan has a rich organisational culture of this type. It includes but is not formally restricted to what might be considered 'interest groups' in the usual sense.

In this context it is also useful to deploy one of the distinctions in the general literature on interest groups – that between the primary and secondary functions of groups.[40] Groups can be classified according to their primary functions, which in Nokyo's case is its economic function. On the other hand, its secondary function can be political. Indeed, in many other democracies the function of interest representation is not restricted to organisations that have been established specifically to promote or protect a particular cause or interest in politics. It is diffused across a range of organisations whose primary functions and purposes are non-political, such as trade unions and business corporations. As Salisbury observed of interest representation in the United States, 'most interest groups . . . are not organizations . . . dependent on mobilizing large numbers of individuals, but are organizations such as corporations which exist for some other purpose.'[41]

In Nokyo's case, it is not only the core organisation itself that takes on a much broader range of functions as defined in law, but the fact that Nokyo creates other groups such as the farmers' political leagues, which are agricultural cooperatives in all but name, through which it assumes these other roles. As we shall see below, Nokyo's organisational reach also extends in this fashion well beyond the political world into the realm of private sector business operations.

Nokyo's organisational resources

Membership

Nokyo's farming membership is its primary organisational resource. It is outstanding in three respects: its size; its extremely high organisation rate, and, considering the dramatic socio-economic changes accompanying industrialisation and urbanisation, its stability. In 1996, the regular membership of individual farmers in the mainstream *sogo nokyo* stood at 5.44 million, down from 5.78 million in 1960,[42] an overall decrease of only 5.8 per cent over more than three and a half decades. In the 1990s, the reduction in individual membership numbers has run at around 10,000 per year, in short, about the same average rate as in the 1960–96 period. In 1994, Nokyo's farm household membership was 4.75 million, down from 5.07 million in 1960,[43] a pace of decline which is commensurate with that of its individual membership.

One of the foundations of Nokyo's organised strength has been the extremely large proportion of its potential membership which it enrols. Even amongst Japanese interest groups, Nokyo has been considered 'an extreme case'.[44] Certainly, by the standards of farm organisations in other democratic systems, Nokyo has benefited from extraordinarily high membership density. Within the first three years of Nokyo's establishment, some 80 per cent of the nation's farm households had been brought into the cooperative fold, and by 1970, this proportion had risen to almost 100 per cent. In the early 1970s, Nokyo's membership coverage of Japanese farm households even began to exceed 100 per cent.[45]

Comparing individual farmer membership of Nokyo with the agricultural workforce reveals an equally impressive record. Nokyo's individual farmer membership rate climbed to 96.6 per cent of the agricultural workforce in 1975, and since that time has exceeded the workforce figure.[46] In absolute numbers, individual farmer membership of the agricultural cooperatives expanded rapidly in the early 1950s to well over 6 million, remaining fairly stable until the 1960s when it commenced a steady diminution in parallel with the decline in farm population.[47] Saeki, writing in the early 1990s, was still claiming that there were virtually no farmers who were not members of Nokyo.[48] Similarly, at around the same time, Fujitani claimed that Nokyo's membership embraced almost every Japanese farm household.[49]

A coincidence of historical, sociological, legal and economic factors accounts for this state of affairs. Firstly, the local *nokyo* rose from the ashes of the *nogyokai*, which had compulsory membership of all farmers within their areas of jurisdiction. Even though the agricultural cooperatives were reconstituted as democratic organisations with voluntary membership, they inherited the farming members of the agricultural societies.[50]

Secondly, the *sogo nokyo* were created as territorial organisations in the sense that 'virtually all farm households belong to the agricultural cooperative in their locality.'[51] The majority of local *nokyo* thus took their name from the town or village in which they were based; they included all the farm households in the local area they covered;[52] and they extended over 'all of the inhabited area of rural Japan'.[53]

This characteristic of the *nokyo* is related to the third and most important factor explaining the extraordinarily high membership rate of the agricultural cooperatives. As Ishida argued in the 1960s, Nokyo was established as a body taking the village order as its organisational basis, and farm households joined Nokyo as part of identifying themselves with their villages.[54] As he elaborates: 'The postwar agricultural cooperatives . . . inherited the prewar tendency of relying not on their consciousness of special interest but on geographic solidarity . . . The hamlet remained the natural basic unit of rural life regulating the entire existence of the farmer. The organisational structure of the new agricultural cooperatives was therefore little different from that of the prewar rural associations, despite the fact that Occupation legislation aimed at making them strictly voluntary.'[55] The members of each cooperative thus shared in a strong tradition of localism and sense of community (*kyodotai*), based on enduring personal relationships built up through frequent face-to-face encounters and kinship ties within restricted geographic areas. In Ishida's view, the agricultural cooperatives were the formal organisational expression of the natural and spontaneous feeling of solidarity which was 'shared by those living or working in the same place.'[56] He argued that amongst all the various Japanese interest groups, the inclusiveness of the agricultural cooperatives was the strongest, which could be explained by the fact that they were 'based on natural types of solidarity spontaneously developed in villages'.[57]

Two decades later, Saeki developed a similar sociological thesis to explain the basis of Nokyo's membership. As he points out, each local unit of Nokyo is based on regional principles or localism in the sense of local ties between individuals in the village. Because the natural solidarity of the village under-scores the functional solidarity of the cooperative union, a comparatively strong human union can be realised. The local *sogo nokyo* takes the village as a unit and organises it, thereby preserving its strong, internal unity.[58] This is similar to Imamura and Inuzuka view that inter-personal relationships in rural communities formed the organisational basis of the agricultural cooperatives.[59]

Nokyo thus embodies and reinforces the strong personal ties and human solidarity in village hamlets (*buraku*), which in more contemporary termin-ology are referred to as agricultural communities (*nogyo shuraku*).[60] As Asuwa puts it, the *buraku* formed the organisational basis of Nokyo's devel-opment.[61] Smaller groups based on the village hamlet or rural community also played an important role as intermediary organisations between the *sogo nokyo* and their members.[62] For example, the agricultural practice unions (*nogyo jikko kumiai*), which were sub-groupings established at hamlet level (in the general category of *buraku* organisations, or *buraku soshiki*) in which farm households cooperated for various agricultural production purposes,[63] were part of Nokyo's substructure (*kabu soshiki*) of hamlet organisations.[64]

On a similar theme, other scholars underline the fundamental importance of 'social association' (*tsukiai*) as lying at the heart of Nokyo's high member-ship rates. *Tsukiai* means maintaining harmonious relations amongst those living in rural communities and is a central part of the mutual regulation of those communities. The geographical boundaries of the *nokyo* do not merely show the co-ops' business regions or the residential boundaries of members, but the tacit agreement amongst farmers who live in those communities that all should join. A sort of consensus exists among villagers that all members of the village must join the agricultural cooperative and use its services.[65] In such a social milieu, farmers have 'virtually no alternative but to join, even though membership . . . [is] not obligatory . . . Farmers are often obliged to buy and sell their produce and raw materials through Nokyo, even if Nokyo sells fertilizer more expensive [sic.] than commercial dealers.'[66] *Tsukiai* – the maintenance of good relations within the local community and with Nokyo – 'often has priority over economic rationality.'[67]

The fact that all farmers in each agricultural village are expected to join the local Nokyo branch amounts to a form of semi-compulsory membership.[68] Although agricultural cooperative membership was legally founded on the principle of voluntarism, in reality, this is not the case.[69] In short, the decisions of individuals to join are not necessarily free. The Nokyo branch in each village is a monopolistic organisation. Those who choose to operate outside it have often found it difficult. In the end, it is much easier to be a member than not be a member, particularly if social ostracism results.[70] This factor also helps to account for the high utilisation rates of cooperative services amongst farmers.

A more extreme version of this thesis holds that Nokyo from the time of its founding assumed the character of a subcontracting organisation of state control and supported itself by acting as a channel for subsidies.[71] In these circumstances, it was natural for Nokyo to use its controlling power over farmers as part of the village order to direct them to identify themselves with the agricultural cooperatives. Nokyo's role as a force for implementing agricultural policy was one manifestation of its power to make the villages identify with it, as was its ability to gather the votes of farmers.[72] Thus, although the basic unit of the agricultural cooperatives was, formally speaking, the private individual, in reality, it was the village community. Nokyo was an organisation based on free will, but consciousness at the Nokyo substructure (i.e. at the level of the individual) was not free at all.[73]

Ono argues that it is this characteristic that distinguishes Japanese cooperatives from those in the standard Western mould.[74] Indeed, three organisational attributes – combined management of multi-purpose enterprises, geographic zoning of agricultural cooperatives and semi-compulsory membership of farmers within the zones, and functional complementarity with government administration – contrast Nokyo markedly with Western-style agricultural cooperatives which tend to be specialised by operation or by commodity producers.[75]

Whether one accepts the authoritarian explanation for Nokyo's universal membership rates or not, it is certainly true that Nokyo's farmer members often lack a clear consciousness of why they have joined the cooperative. They become Nokyo members almost automatically and have no sense of a specific individual purpose or benefit in mind when joining the organisation. Their membership is continuous by family, passed on through the generations. This is reflected in the fact that the numbers of farmer members in the *sogo nokyo* are comparatively stable.[76] In spite of immense changes in the rural environment and farm society over the past five decades, farm membership levels in the agricultural cooperatives have remained remarkably unchanging. As the above figures reveal, the total number of individual farmer members edged downwards by only 5.9 per cent over the 36 years between 1960 and 1996.

Given all these factors, Nokyo's membership is, to some extent, a given and therefore it has not had the usual problem of obtaining and sustaining membership. Consequently the 'free rider problem' simply does not have cross-cultural application in this context. Nor are 'selective economic incentives', as Olson conceives them, necessary to encourage membership.[77] Far from being 'selective benefits' provided to encourage and maintain membership, Nokyo's economic service activities are core functions of the cooperatives. Nokyo's interest group role is another core function because of its legal basis and certainly not a 'byproduct' in Olson's sense.[78]

Over the postwar decades, the socio-cultural basis of Nokyo's membership has been the secret of its growth.[79] It underlies Nokyo's much vaunted economic power because it has guaranteed membership amongst virtually all farmers and has encouraged farmers' patronage of Nokyo's businesses.

Nokyo's universal membership rate has also meant that it could legitimately claim to speak for all farmers. This has underpinned its organisational clout as well as facilitated its corporatised relations with government. At the same time, its outstanding membership attributes have provided it with an independent power base outside the administration and considerably magnified its political influence.[80] Nokyo's mass membership of farm voters means that it encompasses the entire agricultural electorate within its organisational boundaries. Social factors influencing Nokyo membership also enhance the receptiveness of farm voters to appeals from Nokyo leaders and thus reinforce the effectiveness of Nokyo's rice-roots electoral activities.[81]

The importance of the social foundations of Nokyo's membership is not to deny the relevance of economic benefits to Nokyo members, simply to say that they are not provided as the organisational means to get and keep members. In some respects – although less so in the 1990s[82] – farmers are grossly inconvenienced by operating outside the agricultural cooperative system – in addition to any social costs that have to be borne. Local cooperatives and their branches are not only ubiquitous in the Japanese countryside, but provide almost all the services an agricultural producer might logically require.[83] Moreover, the generous interpretation of Nokyo Law by successive agricultural administrators[84] and the scope for the development of Nokyo-funded business outside Nokyo Law[85] have enabled the agricultural cooperatives to move into economic and social functions relevant to the farmer (and other local residents) practically 'from the cradle to the grave'.[86] In terms of agricultural cooperative philosophy, Nokyo is an agent of protection which, given the farmers' keen awareness of their own economic vulnerability, has considerable emotional appeal as well as economic logic.

Since the early 1970s, the continuously expanding group of associate members (i.e. non-farmer members of the agricultural cooperatives) has represented an added dimension to Nokyo's organisational basis and an increasing proportion of total co-op membership in spite of their non-agricultural status. As Takeuchi and Otawara point out, one of Nokyo's distinctive features is that non-farming members can join.[87] An associate member according to Nokyo Law is 'an individual who possesses a household in the area corresponding to that which the agricultural cooperative is in charge of, and is permitted by the agricultural cooperative to use its facilities' (Article 12, Clause 1, No. 3).[88]

Once again this underscores the regional basis of Nokyo's membership. Although the boundaries of city, town and village cooperatives have continuously expanded as a result of municipal amalgamation programmes, the aim of the agricultural cooperatives has remained as a service organisation for particular localities. Those who may join an agricultural cooperative are those who have an address in the area that it services. This gives each *nokyo* fundamentally 'the character of a regional cooperative union'.[89] In essence, the co-ops are regional groups that bring together farmers and other residents living within distinct areas. Moreover, as Nokyo's agriculture-related business has contracted in relative terms, the element of regional cooperative association has come to the fore.[90]

Many associate members used to be regular members, but gave up farming, or belong to the family of a regular member but are not engaged in farming. This is because many *nokyo* allow only one individual regular member per household. The relatively small reduction in Nokyo's farming membership has been more than counterbalanced by a steady ascent of its associate membership. Between 1960 and 1996, the number of individual associate members of the cooperatives inflated from 0.76 million to 3.59 million.[91] As a proportion of Nokyo's total individual membership, this category expanded from 11.7 per cent in 1960 to 39.8 per cent in 1996,[92] which means that between one-third and one-half of Nokyo members are not farmers at all. At the same time, Nokyo's total membership has grown steadily to 9.03 million members in 1996, making it one of the largest, voluntary mass organisations in Japan. It compares with 14.14 members for Seikyo (the consumer cooperative organisation)[93] and 7.66 million members for unions affiliated to Rengo[94] (Japanese Trade Union Confederation)[95] the main union umbrella group.[96]

The steady augmentation of Nokyo's associate membership has had two main effects. Firstly, it has shifted the balance in the organisation more towards the interests of its non-farmer membership, undermining its identity as an agricultural organisation. Secondly, in spite of the contraction in agriculture's demographic base, Nokyo continues to expand in membership size. The growth in Nokyo's associate membership reflects the increasing number of non-agricultural farm households in rural areas, the expansion of urban settlement into what were once rural communities, and the convenient and competitive services that the agricultural cooperatives have been able to provide, especially in the insurance, credit and purchasing fields.[97] Over a long period, Nokyo was able to capitalise on its cooperative status to out-compete private sector credit unions on deposit interest rates. Nokyo's credit operations paid dividends to depositors at the rate of 0.5 per cent of the value of each member's deposits, giving it a significant edge over credit unions 'whose interest payments on small deposits . . . [were] fixed by law at the same level as the Nokyo's before dividend payments.'[98]

Bureaucratic superstructure

Managing Nokyo's extensive operations in all fields is a giant bureaucracy, consisting of non-elected, full-time career executives (managing directors and auditors) and large numbers of career staff personnel who run the Nokyo offices at all levels and conduct its services in all spheres. Presiding over this bureaucracy are relatively large numbers of (usually part-time) executives (chairmen, vice-chairmen, directors) who are elected by its regular farmer members.[99]

Nokyo management represents an interest group in its own right.[100]

Executives (*yakuin*) and staff members (*shokuin*) belong to the National Nokyo Executive and Staff Members' League in which the executive side tends to be dominant. Staff members also belong to unions that are affiliated to the National Nokyo Labour Union Federation (Zenkoku Nogyo Rodo Kumiai Rengokai, or Zennokyo Roren), founded in 1956.[101] The staff unions seek improvements in wage levels and working conditions in agricultural cooperatives. In addition, Nokyo staff members, like staff members of the *kankei dantai*, belong to the Agriculture, Forestry and Fishery Groups Staff Members' Mutual Aid Association, which provides pensions for members of agriculture, forestry and fishery cooperatives (in addition to other agricultural groups). Its membership in 1998 was 490,000.[102] Career executive and staff personnel constitute about 80 per cent of the total number of Nokyo executives and staff members,[103] although full-time salaried managing directors are vastly outnumbered by elected executives.

All upper-level elected executive positions are held concurrently with local level positions (that is, national chairmen, vice-chairmen and directors also hold prefectural and local co-op office simultaneously and they are also co-op members). The total size of the executive and staff structure is, therefore, somewhat difficult to calculate. Ignoring dual office-holding, total executive and staff members numbered 483,002 in 1990, with more than half of this number listed as *sogo nokyo* staff members (297,459), with relatively large numbers of prefectural federation staff members (74,734) and *sogo nokyo* executives (68,611).[104] Given that of the total number of executives and staff members, the latter constitute 82 per cent (or 394,176 in 1990), the number of staff members in Nokyo is by far the more significant figure.

Within the *sogo nokyo*, changing executive and staff ratios are also significant. As numbers of *sogo nokyo* have dropped with co-op mergers, numbers of executives have also gone down, while figures for staff members have continued to rise – at least until very recently. For example, between 1960 and 1994, the number of *yakuin* dwindled from 149,285 to 55,422, while the number of *shokuin* just about doubled from 145,642 to 300,290.[105] Growth in *sogo nokyo* staff personnel was particularly marked between 1965 and 1985, as Nokyo expanded its business operations. Only in the mid-1990s have staff numbers begun to diminish, although the decline is marginal. By 1996, local co-op staff numbers had fallen to 297,632.[106] The total in all the prefectural federations was 74,687,[107] a slight decrease on the 1990 figure.

Nokyo's 'related groups'

Nokyo has spawned a diverse array of 'related groups' (*kanren dantai*)[108] to undertake various activities that are strictly beyond the purview of the mainstream economic functions of the agricultural cooperatives and their federations. Many of these organisations have been created in concert with other agricultural groups and are *gaikaku dantai* of the MAFF.[109] This dual status means that they are under the broad supervision of the MAFF, have recognised public functions and are usually in receipt of varying amounts of government subsidies.

Some of the organisational off-shoots of Nokyo, however, are pure creations of the agricultural cooperatives. They undertake diverse subsidiary and supplementary functions that assist Nokyo and the farmers in the conduct of their agriculture-related activities. They are dominant in the areas of producer-organised and funded price stabilisation schemes. One such group is the National Compound Feed Supply Stabilisation Fund (Zenkoku Haigo Shiryo Kyokyu Antei Kikin). It has Zenchu, Norinchukin and ALIC as members of its council. Funding comes from a mixture of sources: farmers (one-third), Zenno (one-half) and the prefectural *keizairen* (one-sixth). It receives no subsidies from the MAFF. The purpose of the fund is to compensate for any increases in feed prices and to stockpile feed. Monies are paid by the organisation to Zenno which channels the payments through the *keizairen* and local agricultural cooperatives to the farmers. The fund operates in a complementary fashion to the Compound Feed Supply Stabilisation Organisation, the MAFF *gaikaku dantai*. This is because the compensation process for feed is two-layered, consisting of normal compensation and special compensation. The Nokyo group handles the special compensation and the MAFF group handles the normal compensation.[110]

A similar organisation is the National Livestock Management Stabilisation Fund Association (Zenkoku Chikusan Keiei Kikin Kyokai). Its members and sources of funds are national and prefectural Nokyo federations, Zenno, Zenchu and Norinchukin, while local agricultural cooperatives are just members. It exists to stabilise the incomes of livestock farmers, conducting mainly public relations activities to encourage local agricultural cooperatives to loan funds to livestock farmers. As a means of fostering this kind of activity, the organisation compensates for any loss of funds the local co-op might suffer if livestock farmers default on loans by going bankrupt. Although the organisation is not formally listed as a *gaikaku dantai*, the MAFF underwrites it with subsidies and is also its supervisory body. The funding flows to the local *nokyo* from the upper level agricultural cooperatives with MAFF standing behind ensuring financial resources.[111]

Other Nokyo-based price stabilisation organisations are the National Fruit Production and Delivery Stabilisation Council (Zenkoku Kajitsu Seisan Shukka Antei Kyogikai) and the National Deciduous Fruit Tree Council (Zenkoku Rakuba Kaju Kyogikai). The latter, for example, discusses technical and policy issues relating to production, distribution and sales of deciduous fruit trees. It also lobbies the government for various policy measures including subsidies for damage caused by typhoons.

Operating in yet another field is the National Agricultural Trust Fund Association Council (Zenkoku Nogyo Shinyo Kikin Kyokai Kyogikai), which has no financial relationship with the MAFF, but which is financially supported by its 47 prefectural agricultural trust fund association members. The members of these prefectural associations are, in turn, local agricultural cooperatives. This is a national organisation conducting public relations and other functions relating to the agricultural cooperative trust business. It exchanges information relating to agriculture between the MAFF and its prefectural fund associations and also negotiates between these two bodies in terms of agricultural policy demands.[112]

The Agriculture and Nokyo Problems Research Institute (Nogyo, Nokyo Mondai Kenkyujo) is a research group spawned by the national Nokyo labour union organisation. Its membership is made up of Zennokyo Roren as a group member, in addition to the chairmen of local *nokyo* and individual researchers. It conducts research requested by its members, or delegates research to other researchers or research organisations.[113]

In some calculations of the so-called staff figure for Nokyo's federated organisation, the 80,000 officials in Nokyo's *kanren dantai* are also included in the overall calculation. According to one source, this produced a total of 460,000 officials in 1993: 300,000 in the local co-ops, 80,000 in the federations and central unions (to make a total of 380,000 mainstream officials) plus the 80,000 in the *kanren dantai*.[114] However Nokyo's bureaucracy is measured, in terms of its overall personnel strength, Nokyo ranks with Japan's largest organisations (it was as big as Japan National Railways before the latter's privatisation, for example).

The nokyo 'detached corps':[115] the women's and youth divisions

Nokyo's membership is structured around the principle of one household, one member. Within these households, however, there are wives and successors of the head of the household (who is the Nokyo member). Nokyo endeavours to provide for these household members through its women's organisations (for the wife of the household) and its youth organisations (for the successor of the household).[116] These bodies are not part of Nokyo proper because they are autonomous (*jishuteki*) organisations. In fact, however, they must be considered as integral elements of Nokyo, because they support (*oen*) its business, livelihood, policy and electoral activities,[117] as well as receive subsidies from Nokyo to fund their activities. The Nokyo women's division (*fujinbu*), now officially called the JA women's organisation (*JA josei soshiki*) and the youth division (*seinenbu*), now called the JA youth organisation (*JA seinen soshiki*), are essentially promotional arms of Nokyo which function to enhance the efficiency and productivity of Nokyo's business, livelihood and agricultural policy activities by gathering together sub-groups of Nokyo's members. Takahashi calls them the 'organisational basis of Nokyo' (*Nokyo no soshiki kiban*).[118]

The women's division is organised at the rice-roots level into unit organisations which unite to form prefectural Nokyo women's division councils (*ken Nokyo fujinbu kyogikai*), with some slight variation in title from prefecture to prefecture. The prefectural councils form a National Council of Nokyo Women's Organisations (Zenkoku Nokyo Fujin Soshiki Kyogikai, or Zennofukyo), which became the JA National Women's Council, or JA Zenkoku Fujin Kyogikai (JA Zenfukyo), when Nokyo adopted the JA nomenclature. It changed its name again in May 1995 to JA National Council of Women's Organisations (JA Zenkoku Josei Soshiki Kyogikai). It brought together a substructure of 2,091 member organisations in 47 prefectures, with an individual membership of 1.1 million.[119] The majority of women residing in farm households are members of Nokyo's women's division.

The financial system of the women's division is theoretically independent of the mainstream Nokyo organisation as is its executive and membership structure, but in practice there is some degree of financial assistance from Nokyo. Activities are conducted both independently and in concert with Nokyo-sponsored campaigns, in political as well as other spheres. The emphasis in the women's division is on cultural, social and 'livelihood' activities. It also undertakes research commissioned by the MAFF on such things as the safety of imported foods.

The *seinenbu* has identical organisational characteristics to the women's division in terms of both its internal structure and relationship with the mainstream Nokyo organisation. In theory it is funded from membership fees, but in practice it is subsidised by Nokyo. *Tankyo* youth divisions come together at prefectural level in the form of 47 prefectural Nokyo youth division councils (*ken Nokyo seinenbu kyogikai*) – in some prefectures the title 'youth league' (*renmei*) is used – which federate at the nationwide level into a National Council of Nokyo Youth Organisations (Zenkoku Nokyo Seinen Soshiki Kyogikai, or Zenseikyo), now called JA Zenseikyo.

The youth division operates according to five principles laid down in 1953: it is an organisation that promotes the Nokyo movement; it is an organisation of rural youth; it is voluntary; it is an organisation of like-minded persons; and it is politically neutral.[120] The national organisation of the youth division was established in 1954. The age limit for 'youth' division members is 43 years.

Compared to the *fujinbu*, the youth division's membership rate is inferior. It organises less than half its potential membership (which mainly consists of male farmers aged between 25 and 35 years of age), has slightly more than half the total number of unit organisations (1,226) and has only one-sixteenth the number of members of the women's division (104,084 members in 1996).[121] Membership rates tend to vary markedly according to region. By far the largest numbers belong to the youth divisions in Hokkaido and Tohoku, followed by Kyushu.[122] This is not surprising considering the historical strength of the Nokyo-associated youth leagues in these areas.

The most important theme in the organisational activities of the youth division is *nosei katsudo* centring on the modernisation of agriculture and the establishment of a 'democratic' agricultural policy aiming at the stability of farmers' livelihood.[123] It is also in the forefront of Nokyo's electoral activities.

Nokyo's businesses

The decade of Japan's rapid economic growth from the mid-1960s until the mid-1970s was a period of unprecedented expansion and prosperity for Nokyo. The rapid development of agricultural cooperative enterprises was closely related to the promotion of the government's farm modernisation policy. This spurred demand for production materials, including feed, fertiliser, farm machinery and agricultural chemicals, which expanded Nokyo's purchasing business, whilst mass sales of agricultural products amplified its marketing business. In addition, the growth in part-time farming encouraged increasing reliance by farmers on mechanisation, thus enlarging Nokyo sales even further.[124] Farmers' borrowings from Nokyo to purchase farm equipment and to modernise farm facilities in turn inflated agricultural cooperative credit business.

As farm incomes and those of its associate members swelled, all Nokyo's businesses – credit and mutual aid as well as marketing and purchasing – grew rapidly, and as a result, management profits expanded.[125] Between 1965 and 1975, the business performance of the *sogo nokyo* achieved an annual growth rate of more than 10 per cent. The most outstanding increases were recorded in the trust and mutual aid sectors. In the trust area, deposits in the *sogo nokyo* increased from ¥1 trillion in 1960 to ¥6 trillion in 1970, ¥14 trillion in 1975 and ¥22 trillion in 1978.[126] Nokyo also cashed in on the real estate boom, as farmers sold off parcels of land for residential development in high-value urban areas. Not only did farmers deposit their profits into co-op bank accounts, but Nokyo moved into real estate and land sales business itself.[127] Through its real estate dealings the agricultural cooperatives assisted the urbanisation process and profited from the decline of agriculture.[128] The growth in trust business was also directly supported by local co-ops' absorbing farmers' savings from non-agricultural sources and from land sales.[129] By the early 1970s, Nokyo was being likened to a 'mammoth agricultural *zaibatsu*'.[130]

Thereafter, growth generally continued at a steady pace until the mid- to late 1980s, with favourable comparisons being made between Nokyo and other leading Japanese enterprises in their respective fields. Almost all sectors of *sogo nokyo* businesses in the 1975–85 decade were still expanding in gross turnover value, but the biggest profit generators were trust business and to a lesser extent mutual aid business.[131] In fact trust and mutual aid profits compensated for the deficits in other operations, given that most other businesses of the local co-ops including marketing, purchasing and ware-housing actually ran at a loss by the time management and other costs were subtracted from gross profits.[132] During this period, Nokyo developed what has been described as a management structure of 'dependence on trust operations'.[133]

Nevertheless, this structure was in fact stable and conducive to membership loyalty, because core (i.e. regular) members valued the growth in trust operations and the resulting stability of co-op management, which was reflected in improvements in their own agricultural management and the development of local agriculture. The high profitability of trust operations facilitated co-op investment in various agricultural facilities financed through increases in co-op funds. These same members made great efforts to cooperate with their local *nokyo* in promoting *sogo nokyo* savings and mutual aid businesses, which in turn deepened their identification with Nokyo.[134]

Meanwhile, on paper, the sheer size of *sogo nokyo* businesses were truly impressive. In 1984, total deposits in the *sogo nokyo* amounted to ¥37 trillion, compared with ¥26 trillion for the Daiichi Kangyo Bank. In the same year, the value of life insurance policies held by the *sogo nokyo* was ¥224 trillion, compared with ¥183 trillion for Nihon Seimei (Japan Life Insurance), while combined marketing and purchasing turnover was ¥11.6 trillion compared with ¥6.9 trillion for Ito Chu.[135]

Nokyo thus proved its ability to survive and grow even during a period of agricultural decline. This was done by putting first priority on expanding financial and insurance businesses and by expanding associate membership (which also supported the former goal).[136] By 1997 the value of deposits in the *sogo nokyo* had risen to ¥67.7 trillion,[137] second only to the postal savings system's ¥230 trillion,[138] and more than the combined ¥61 trillion for the Daiwa and Sumitomo Banks, which were expected to merge, creating the world's largest bank in terms of deposits.[139]

Over the corresponding period, the total value of *sogo nokyo* purchasing business registered slower growth, with the value of supplies handled rising from ¥5.1 trillion in 1983 to ¥5.3 trillion in 1993, declining marginally to ¥5.0 trillion in 1995. The 1993 turnover, however, yielded gross profits (including commissions) to the co-ops of ¥737 billion compared with ¥564 billion in 1983, while the 1995 turnover yielded gross profits of ¥694 billion.[140] The largest items by value in the *sogo nokyo* purchasing business in 1995 were petroleum (¥624 billion), general foods (¥507 billion), perishable foods (¥414 billion), agricultural machinery (¥414 billion), stock-feed (¥387 billion) and fertiliser (¥381 billion).[141]

On the marketing side, the 1995 business volume was down slightly at ¥5.9 trillion compared with ¥6.1 billion in 1983, with marketing commissions (including marketing profit) totalling ¥139 billion (a small increase on the 1983 figure of ¥131 billion).[142] The largest items in that year were rice at ¥2.0 trillion, followed by vegetables (¥1.4 trillion) and livestock products (¥1.2 trillion).[143]

Overall, the figures suggest that the volume of co-op marketing and purchasing business has more or less stabilised (or stagnated, depending on your viewpoint),[144] but that higher profits are being generated by these activities. The figures also show that rice is big business for the agricultural cooperatives – by far the largest item in any of their purchasing and marketing operations – and that the agricultural cooperatives make far higher profits from their purchasing business than they do from their marketing business.

Even though the value of *sogo nokyo* marketing exceeds the value of purchasing in total turnover, the profits from the latter are five times as great.

The patronage of co-op services by Japanese farmers has traditionally been one of the sources of Nokyo's economic strength. By far the larger part of farm output has been marketed through the cooperatives, while farmers have purchased the bulk of their farm requisites and a smaller proportion of household needs through the same channels. In the marketing field, Nokyo has enjoyed a near-monopoly of rice collection and distribution, and has been the single most important entity marketing products such as raw milk, vegetables, fruit and beef cattle.[145] In the purchasing field, Nokyo has also been dominant, supplying farmers with almost all their fertiliser needs, a relatively large proportion of their agricultural chemicals and gasoline, followed by agricultural machinery, stockfeed, cars and livelihood materials.[146] In 1995, the figures were 94.5 per cent for fertilisers, 70 per cent for agricultural chemicals and 35.5 per cent for stockfeed.[147]

The national Nokyo glamour organisations and economic powerhouses have been Zenkyoren, Norinchukin and Zenno, with financial and business operations running into astronomical figures. Their size and interlinked operations have been likened to those of a *keiretsu*, consisting of a major trading bank surrounded by a number of large industrial firms with inter-locking share-holding. Nokyo is the Mitsubishi, Mitsui or Sumitomo of the agricultural sector. In Nokyo's case, 'Zenno serves as the trading company and Norinchukin as the bank.'[148]

Zenno reputedly handles more than 1,000 different types of fertilisers, and 1,400 different kinds of agricultural chemicals. Its total purchasing and sales amounts are equivalent to those of a large general trading company (*sogo shosha*).[149] In 1988, it became Japan's seventh-largest trading company in terms of sales turnover.[150] It serves farmers through its 2,382 local cooperative and 61 federation members.[151] Through these organisations, it supplies fertiliser, agrochemicals, stockfeed, farm equipment and technologies for agricultural and livestock production, as well as daily necessities and household goods to farmers and other consumers. Zenno also collects, distributes and markets agricultural and livestock products for farmers through its own nationwide and international channels.[152] In the year ending 30 June 1995, Zenno's operations generated a turnover of ¥6.3 trillion.[153]

The patronage of Nokyo's regular and associate members has also been critical to the growth of its financial and insurance operations.[154] Nokyo has traditionally enjoyed unique advantages in these fields, offering creditors better deals on their deposits because of the legal advantages it enjoyed as a cooperative organisation.[155] The relatively high rates of interest it offered on savings enabled it to attract deposits into its credit business. With respect to insurance, Nokyo has been able to offer better deals because of the sheer size and geographical spread of the national organisation (Zenkyoren) supporting the local agricultural cooperative insurance operations.[156] For this reason,

Nokyo insurance can include earthquake insurance in its standard fire insurance policies, while private insurance companies sell this as an extra, with premium rates set depending on where in Japan insured property is located.[157] Another advantage is that Zenkyoren is the only organisation permitted to offer both life and non-life insurance policies, which ordinary insurers are not permitted to do.[158] Nokyo's insurance business is also operated outside the regulatory supervision of the MOF to which general insurance companies are subject.[159]

In the late 1980s, Zenkyoren, which reinsures contracts made by local agricultural cooperatives, became the largest insurance group in Japan.[160] It ranked ahead of Japan Life Insurance in terms of the value of its life insurance contracts, in addition to being a top-class general insurance company.[161] In 1993, it entered the 'top ten' corporate ranking (at No. 8) for the first time, with a reported income of ¥318.4 billion.[162] In 1995, the value of long-term insurance contracts held by Zenkyoren was ¥372.9 trillion.[163]

Zenkyoren is probably eclipsed only by Norinchukin, which operates as central banker for agricultural, forestry and fisheries cooperatives' savings and loans and which is one of Japan's largest banks.[164] In 1979 Norinchukin expanded its investments into high-yielding, low-risk foreign bonds because of concerns that farmers would take their deposits to higher yielding banks. US Treasury instruments accounted for about half of these foreign bond purchases.[165] By the mid-1980s, Norinchukin ranked first amongst all the banks in domestic (yen) assets.[166] It provided 'about one-fifth of the total funds in the domestic call and discount markets which . . . [supplied] Japan's commercial banks and . . . [was] one of the largest buyers of the Japanese national debt.'[167] In 1986, when Norinchukin was privatised, the *Norin Chuo Kinkoho* was revised to allow the bank to offer much the same services as Japan's other commercial banks and in 1987 Norinchukin established a securities subsidiary, Norinchukin International, in London.[168] In 1989, it was given permission to make its first investment in equity markets abroad. In the same year, it was described as 'the world's biggest bank (in terms of deposits plus debentures) and Japan's largest institutional investor, holding ¥760 billion in Japanese stock plus ¥10 trillion in bonds and debentures.[169] The amount the bank reputedly had available for investment in 1989 amounted to ¥65 trillion, the size of the Japanese national budget.[170] In 1993, Norinchukin ranked 51st in Japan's corporate rankings with an income of ¥57.6 billion (a 221.9 per cent increase on the previous year),[171] while in 1995, Norinchukin's total assets in terms of deposits, agriculture and forestry bonds and 'other' amounted to ¥43.5 trillion.[172] This sum equalled the total held by the city banks.[173]

As far as internal financial flows within the federated Nokyo trust business are concerned, deposits flow into Norinchukin from the prefectural credit federations, while the local *nokyo* pass on a portion of their members savings as deposits in the prefectural credit federations.[174] These upper level Nokyo credit institutions have benefited from the legal requirement whereby prefectural credit federations have had to deposit half their funds with Norinchukin and the *tankyo* have had to deposit two-thirds of their surplus funds with the prefectural credit federations.

As Figure 4.1 shows, in 1986, 63.9 per cent of the funds allocated by the *tankyo* were placed as deposits in the *shinren*, whilst in 1997, the figure was 62.3 per cent.[175] Viewing it from the perspective of the *shinren*, 91.9 per cent of their total income from savings and deposits was obtained from the *tankyo* in 1986, whilst in 1997, the proportion was 84.8 per cent.[176] Meanwhile, exactly 50 per cent of *shinren* funds were deposited in Norinchukin in 1986 (see Figure 4.1) and a little over this percentage in 1997 (53.1 per cent).[177] This represented 55.6 per cent of Norinchukin's total income from bonds, savings and deposits in 1986 (see Figure 4.1) and 67.0 per cent of its total income from deposits, debentures and 'other' in 1997.[178] As the system works, the upper-level banking organisations of Nokyo effectively commandeer funds from subordinate organisations simply by right. Norinchukin pays interest (called incentive money, or *shoreikin*) twice a year on the deposits of prefectural credit federations which do the same to individual cooperatives.

In the domestic sphere, Norinchukin manages its income from deposits, savings, debentures etc. by purchasing other government and public bonds, buying stocks, issuing loans and investing in companies operating in the agricultural, forestry and fisheries sector.[179] As shown in Figure 4.1, by far the largest proportion (almost one-half the total, or 48.6 per cent) in 1986 was allocated to the purchase of securities (stocks and bonds), whilst well over one-third went on loans to related industries (36.6 per cent). Other loans went to member organisations (5.7 per cent) and to financial organs (3.2 per cent). By 1997 the proportion allocated to securities had fallen to 30.6 per cent (although the absolute amount had risen from ¥10.6 trillion to ¥13.5 trillion[180]), whilst loans remained the same (36.6 per cent, or ¥16.2 trillion, almost double the 1986 amount of ¥8.6 trillion), with the balance of 32.4 per cent (¥14.3 trillion) in the miscellaneous category of 'other'.[181] These figures underline the fact that Norinchukin's domestic investment priorities are in securities and loans to related industries.

The prefectural credit federations also devote the remaining portion of the funds they receive from the unit co-ops (after allocating their obligatory 50+ per cent share to Norinchukin) to investments in stocks, bonds and loans. As Figure 4.1 shows, in 1986 just over one-third (34.4 per cent) flowed into securities and entrustment of money, with almost all the remainder allocated as loans to members (7.7 per cent), non-members (8.1 per cent) and financial organs (3.2 per cent). In 1997, 20.3 per cent of their funds were used for loans (¥20.3 trillion) and 21.4 per cent for negotiable securities (¥11.9 trillion).[182] On the income side, the vast bulk (90.9 per cent) of their income from savings and deposits in 1986 was sourced from the unit co-ops (see Figure 4.1), while in 1997, the proportion was 84.8 per cent. The remainder came from savings invested by mutual aid federations and other organisations.

The structure of the local co-ops' funds allocation is quite different from

Unit: ¥billion

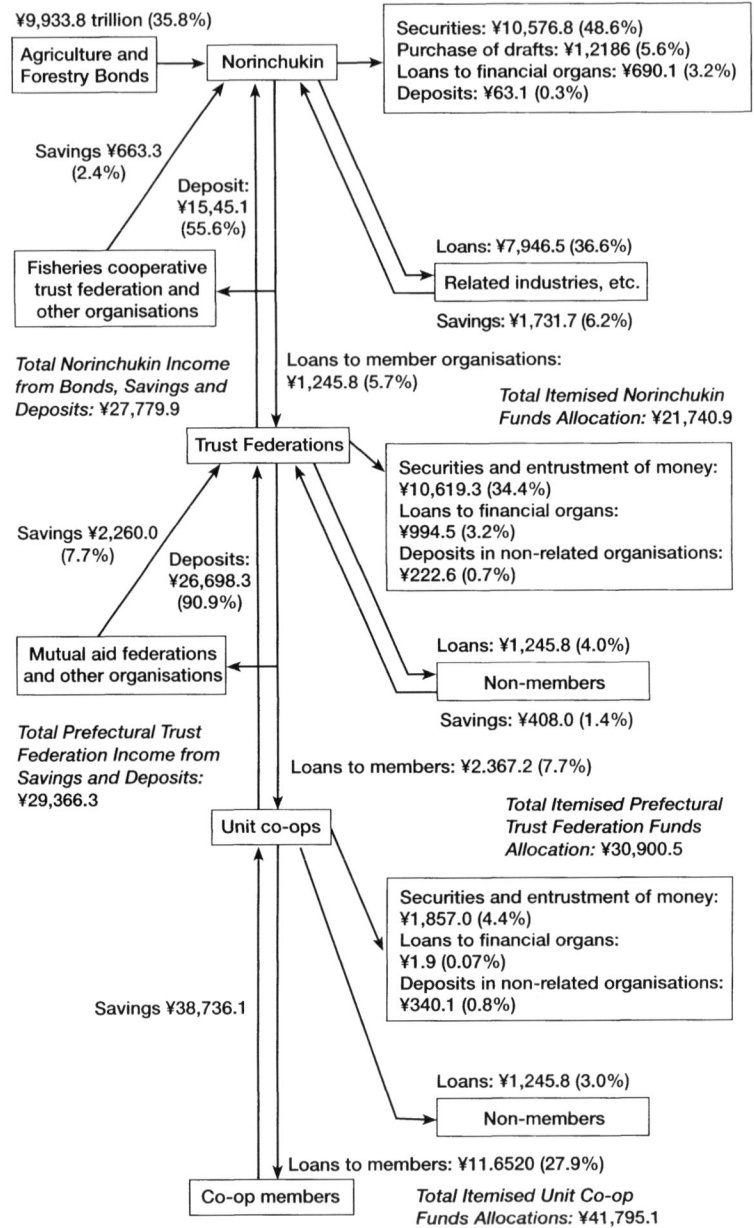

Figure 4.1 Funds flow chart of the federated Nokyo trust business (1986)
   Source: Domon Takashi, *Yoi Nokyo: 'Jiyukaga' ni Ikinokoru Senryaku*
   (*The Good Nokyo: A 'Post-Liberalisation' Survival Strategy*), Tokyo,
   Nihon Keizai Shinbunsha, 1988, p. 35, citing Somucho, *Nokyo Kansa*
   Hokokusho (*Report of the Inspection of the Agricultural Cooperative*
   Organisation).

Norinchukin and the prefectural trust federations. Because of the require-ment to pass on two-thirds of their funds to the *shinren* and because of the loans service they provide to members (which consumed 27.9 per cent of their allocation in 1986 and 20.6 per cent in 1997[183]), the funds available for investments in securities and loans to non-members are much smaller. In 1986, only 4.4 per cent of *sogo nokyo* funds, or ¥1.9 trillion, was invested in securities and entrustment of money (see Figure 4.1), while the proportion in 1997 was 6.1 per cent, or ¥4.3 trillion.[184]

Nokyo organisations in recent decades have featured quite prominently amongst the top 300 corporate income earners. In 1988, Norinchukin ranked 61st, with a declared income of ¥63.1 billion, a 58.8 per cent increase on 1987 (78th ranking in that year); Zenkyoren was 63rd (up from 69th), with a declared income of ¥61.5 billion, up 23.7 per cent on 1987; the Federation of Hyogo Prefecture Agricultural Cooperative Credit Associations was 235th (200th in 1987) with a declared income of ¥18.3 billion, up 4.4 per cent on 1987; the Federation of Shizuoka Prefecture Agricultural Cooperative Credit Associations was 265th (503rd in 1987), with a declared income of ¥15.6 billion, up 107.3 per cent on 1987; the Federation of Osaka Prefecture Agricultural Cooperative Credit Associations was 282nd (269th in 1987) with a declared income of ¥14.6 billion, up 8.7 per cent on 1987.[185]

By 1993, the ascent of the top three national Nokyo organisations had continued. Zenkyoren entered the 10 leading business entities in Japan's top 300 corporate rankings[186] for the first time with a profit of just over ¥318 billion as against the No. 1, Toyota Motor at ¥573 billion, just behind the largest bank, Mitsubishi Bank at ¥404 billion.[187] Meanwhile, Norinchukin rose to 51st in the top 300 with an income of ¥58 billion, just below the top 10 banks in Japan and a 221 per cent increase on its 1992 income of ¥18 billion.[188] Zenno came in at 278th (up from 440th in 1992) with a reported income of ¥14 billion.[189] Clearly, Nokyo's largest and most prominent economic organisations operate in the worlds of finance and insurance, rather than in just the world of agriculture.

Other significant business divisions of Nokyo include its health and medical facilities (it runs a large number of hospitals and clinics) as well as its publicity and information branches, including a daily newspaper (Japan Agri-culture Newspaper, or *Nihon Nogyo Shinbun*), and other daily and weekly publications, in addition to TV and other media businesses. As Aono argues, these 'other businesses' collectively constitute another 'face' of Nokyo.[190]

Nokyo's companies

Nokyo has broadened its business base through extensive investments in agriculture-related industries. Because legal provisions exclude Nokyo from seeking profits directly through company operations,[191] agricultural cooperative organisations have invested in private companies that undertake various businesses on their behalf. The creation of these companies has enabled Nokyo to pursue profits with greater ease and has put powers of decision over business policy mainly in the hands of full-time company executives, although some Nokyo executives (particularly from Zenno) serve concurrently as company executives. Nokyo accomplished this kind of business expansion so rapidly and so successfully that Aono likened it to a jointstock company itself: 'To launch business in the form of cooperative companies makes Nokyo a type of special jointstock company'.[192] Similarly, Nishimoto attributes the phraseology 'Nokyo Inc.'[193] to the 'promiscuous way that Nokyo capital . . . spawned private companies.'[194]

These businesses are dominant elements in what Aono calls Nokyo's massive 'extended organisation' (*gaien soshiki*),[195] which is not part of the mainstream federated Nokyo organisation but which, nevertheless, encompasses lucrative areas of economic enterprise. The companies within Nokyo's extended organisation are variously called 'cooperative companies' (*kyodo kaisha*), 'affiliated companies' (*kanren gaisha*), or 'tunnel companies'. *Kyodo kaisha* are jointstock companies or limited companies in which agricultural cooperative organisations at any level (*tankyo*, prefectural and national federations) invest share capital in varying proportions.[196] *Kanren gaisha* comprise a broader category of companies that have some relationship with Nokyo, including share ownership by agricultural cooperative organisations.[197]

Cooperative companies cover a diverse range of arm's length operations, principally in the farm input supply and processing businesses.[198] Aono categorises them into three types of operations:[199] companies that produce and process commodities that the federations supply to the unit cooperatives in their purchasing business, such as compound feed and fertiliser;[200] companies that sell to consumers items produced by the farmers as part of the cooperative marketing chain, such as processed livestock products; and companies that provide facilities for cooperative members to utilise, or from which cooperative members can make direct purchases (consumer-related cooperative businesses).[201]

Sizeable amounts of Nokyo's surplus capital generated by its insurance and credit businesses have been channelled into these kinds of profit and loss business ventures. In 1974 for instance, 2,538 *sogo nokyo* had shares in 5,574 companies worth ¥5.2 billion. Of these, 123 co-ops owned 50 per cent or more of the shares in 136 companies worth ¥1.3 billion yen.[202] More than two decades later in 1996, 1,924 *sogo nokyo* had shares in 6,308 companies worth ¥34.1 billion.[203] Of these, 274 co-ops owned more than 50 per cent or more of the shares in 310 companies worth ¥8.9 billion.[204]

Amongst companies founded by national level Nokyo organisations, the first and best known is Unicoop Japan (Kumiai Boeki KK). This company was set up in 1961 as a jointstock venture with initial capital of ¥10 million subscribed by five cooperative organisations: Zenchu, Zenkoren, Zenhanren, the National Federation of Fishery Cooperatives (Zengyoren) and the National Federation of Forestry Cooperatives (Zenshinren), along with the 'collaboration of relevant corporations',[205] which each advanced the same figure as the cooperative organisations themselves. The company was established for the purpose of importing materials for the purchasing business of the co-ops (including the import of live cattle which was liberalised in 1961) and for expanding exports of agricultural products. It is principally involved in international trading of fertilisers, feedgrains and feed ingredients, and other agricultural materials.[206] Its main shareholders are now Zenno, Norinchukin, Zenkyoren, Zengyoren, Zenshinren and Zenkoku Koseiren.[207]

The establishment of Kumiai Boeki KK was followed by the formation of other large Nokyo-related companies such as Co-op Shokuhin KK (Co-op Foods) set up by Zenhanren in 1961; Hokuso Takasaki Hamu KK (Takasaki Ham) set up by Zenkoren in 1970 after a decision to expand its business into meat processing; KK A-Co-op Rain (A-Co-op Line) founded in 1971;[208] National Nokyo Milk Direct Selling (Zenkoku Nokyo Gyunyu Chokuhan KK) formed in February 1972; and Co-op Lease (Kyodo Riisu KK) in March 1972. Other large companies in which national Nokyo organisations have invested include Co-op Chemicals[209] and Kumiai Chemical Industries.[210] By the 1990s, the number of Zenno *kanren gaisha* had risen to 150.[211] They are prominent in livestock-related activities such as meat and milk processing[212] and sales as well as the import and manufacture of farm inputs, such as feed and fertiliser.

The reason why Zenno spawned so many *kanren gaisha* was firstly because it needed to purchase large quantities of competitively priced goods of high quality (for sale to farmers) and it was restricted by law from manufacturing them itself. Secondly, as its businesses diversified, it became too difficult to handle them all within one organisation. Thirdly, fierce competition with large enterprise companies forced Zenno to establish a system incorporating production *keiretsu* in addition to purchasing to make it possible to procure cheap goods. Fourthly, private companies had the advantage in being able to react swiftly to challenges from large enterprise whereas Nokyo's businesses needed members' agreement. Finally, the federated Nokyo organisation alone could not provide officials with sufficient professional ability.[213]

The actual numbers of companies connected to Nokyo are difficult to trace because of the varying degrees of financial involvement by different agricultural cooperative organisations, the various categories of 'related companies' and 'cooperative companies', and the fact that these cooperative companies in turn spawn their own company offshoots or subsidiaries.[214] Like the proliferation of agricultural organisations in the broad categories of public, private, and semi-public/semi-private bodies, the operation and funding of Nokyo-related companies are not designed to be transparent.

The burgeoning of agricultural cooperative enterprise in the form of cooperative and affiliated companies demonstrates very clearly that the statutory basis of Nokyo's activities has not in practice proven an effective obstacle to its economic expansion and diversification. Where proposed business projects are beyond the scope of the Nokyo Law, the agricultural cooperatives have merely created 'non-cooperative' enterprises that undertake these business activities on their behalf.

Nokyo's 'affiliated companies', in spite of certain financial, managerial and personnel links with the agricultural cooperatives, cannot be considered farmers' groups. They operate outside the boundaries of the Nokyo Law and the jurisdiction of the guidance and control bodies of Nokyo – the central unions. Their political significance, however, lies in the financial resources they can generate for purposes such as political funding.[215] Furthermore, the unknown quantity of employees in Nokyo's related companies can be considered a 'plus alpha' factor on top of Nokyo's membership and leadership numbers.[216] Their total figures are unknown, but they represent a force able to be mobilised politically in terms of votes.

As these brief surveys of Nokyo's mainstream economic businesses and company investments show, it is debatable how much Nokyo has ploughed the funds and profits generated from these diverse enterprises back into agricultural modernisation and development. Surprisingly, Nokyo's most successful economic enterprises have not been a major source of loan funding for agriculture. Indeed, quite the opposite. Nokyo has functioned to channel funds out of the countryside with relatively small proportions of the huge profits and surpluses from its trust, insurance and company operations being reinvested back into the land. It is Nokyo's financial apparatus that has benefited, not the farmers.[217] The burden of agricultural investment has fallen largely to the government in the form of long-term, low-interest loans to farmers and also government-subsidised cooperative loans.[218]

Organisational cleavages

Although an integrated entity in terms of its formal structure, Nokyo is in fact an umbrella institution encompassing a complex amalgam of diverse organisational and individual member interests, not all of which are necessarily in harmony. Nokyo's all-embracing character and nationwide orientation sometimes makes unity a difficult objective to sustain. The diversity of demands from farmers (some of whom are full-time and some of whom are part-time) and the diversified activities of different agricultural cooperative organisations are becoming more and more difficult to coordinate.[219] Similarly, the diversification of agriculture over the years has multiplied the commodity interests of farmers and even produced rivalries amongst producers in different areas. This, on occasions, has made it difficult for Nokyo to maintain unity of interests amongst its membership and has sometimes required the application of concerted mediation efforts. This is particularly true when groups in different areas are competing in terms of business and market share.[220] Thus, at first sight what appears to be one of Nokyo's principal strengths – its broad spread across the entire agricultural sector – sometimes emerges as an in-built organisational weakness.

On an intra-organisational level, Nokyo executives have commented themselves that one of their hardest tasks is to overcome the mutual distrust amongst the various levels of the organisation caused by such factors as differences in business emphasis, differences in scale of organisation, and regional differences amongst agricultural cooperatives and federations of agricultural cooperatives. This requires them to strike compromises that will satisfy competing interests within Nokyo and yet be workable within the limits of existing policy and therefore acceptable to government.

A number of internal cleavages have become institutionalised within Nokyo over the years – business versus cooperativism, general versus specialist cooperative, and urban versus rural cooperative. In the face of these diverse intra-organisational pressures, Zenchu has a mammoth task of containment and adjustment to maintain organisational unity and strength in the presentation of policy demands to government. These sometimes coincide with the wishes of only certain sections of its membership.

Profits versus cooperativism

An underlying philosophical conflict has existed within the Nokyo organisation between the profit imperative and the fundamental principle of cooperativism. As early as the 1970s, members were accusing those who ran the agricultural cooperatives, particularly leaders of the prefectural and national federations, of selling their souls to the profit motive, forgetting basic principles and abandoning the spirit of mutual cooperation. As one critic put it: 'why does the capital of the Nokyo federations continue to increase steadily, although these groups do not aim to make profits as their organisational objective?'[221] An enduring concern has been the fear that Nokyo would divest itself of its cooperative character and assume the role of a normal company.

Differences over basic organisational principles have sometimes manifested themselves in the form of a centre versus periphery cleavage between the upper-level leadership of Nokyo and the rice-roots co-ops and their farming members. As Dore observed: 'The federations tend . . . to be the weakest links in the system. With some exceptions, the higher up the village-prefecture-national chain one goes the smaller the sense of responsibility to the individual Co-operative member, the greater the semi-official-enterprise character of the organization, and the weaker any conscious adherence to Co-operative principles'.[222]

Local co-op leaders tend to be more thoroughly imbued with the cooperative spirit, not only because the scale of their business and financial operations is smaller, but also because of the need to stimulate the loyalty of local farmer members by means of attachment to the idea of mutual self-help. This notion is vital for keeping the *tankyo* economically viable. Farmers have traditionally felt the greatest amount of loyalty to their local organisation, with a sharp diminution in attachment occurring the higher up the Nokyo hierarchy the cooperative operates. Once again, as Dore put it: 'The federations, indeed excite the least loyalty of all; they tend rather to be part of the 'the authorities' whose interests conflict, rather than coincide, with the farmers'.[223] Much of the criticism of the federations has come from local farmers who have objected to being treated as potential consumers of *keizairen* purchasing business and Zenkyoren insurance, rather than as agricultural managers.

The profit versus cooperativism cleavage has not manifested itself just as a centre versus periphery problem, however. It is also evident at the local level, where the perceived needs of farmers, and the imperatives and goals of local co-op management, can be at odds. Some farmers feel that a preoccupation with business and profits leads to a neglect of other services more vital to farmers, such as agricultural extension services.[224] The outstanding growth areas in Nokyo's business activities have been in finance, insurance and consumer services, not in agriculture-related services. Some cooperatives find it difficult to spare efforts and resources for purely agricultural issues. Indeed some never provide agricultural management guidance.[225]

Complaints are also made about the high-pressure salesmanship of Nokyo officials who are primarily concerned with expanding cooperative business turnover rather than the welfare of members. To many farmers, Nokyo executives are more like business salesmen than anything else.[226] Co-op staff cruise the countryside on motorcycles or bicycles to encourage and persuade farmers to deposit money into Nokyo savings accounts and to join Nokyo insurance schemes. As Sakaguchi puts it, given the way agricultural cooperative officials push business in savings and insurance on to their farming (and non-farming) clients, the pursuit of profits inevitably appears as the ultimate goal of the organisation.[227]

In many respects, the existence of a 'profit versus cooperativism' conflict within Nokyo is an inevitable by-product of the fundamental contradiction between the organisational principles of cooperativism and the need to keep co-op enterprises not only afloat but expanding by following economic principles (*keizai ronri*). In giving ostensible preference to the latter, Nokyo runs the risk of divesting itself of its primary farm cooperative character.

An historical dimension also exists to this problem. Nokyo's cooperative spirit was much stronger in the 1950s than in the 1960s and stronger in the 1960s than in the 1970s and subsequently. As Nokyo increasingly attained giant enterprise status, its primary 'cooperative' face began to take second place as an organisational objective. By the early 1970s, Nokyo had become a vast business empire whose interests and priorities no longer necessarily coincided with those of its rural clients.[228] This did not prevent appeals both inside and outside Nokyo to 'get back to basics' [*kyodo kumiai no genten ni kaere*],[229] particularly to the Rochdale spirit of cooperativism and anti-commercialism from which the first Japanese cooperative adherents took their ideological cue.[230]

Nokyo's officials have defended their economic and business priorities by pointing out that increased prosperity for the co-ops is to the greater benefit of all farmers and generates higher standards of living in the agricultural sector as a whole. The credibility of such an argument is somewhat questionable, however, for a number of reasons. Firstly, they omit to reveal the extent of their personal stake in the profitability of agricultural cooperative enterprises, which funds rising wage levels for executives and staff members by sustaining higher management costs. In fact, salary and wage increases for the Nokyo bureaucracy from the 1960s onwards forced up the management costs of the agricultural cooperatives to ever-higher proportions of their total expenses.[231] To this extent, the clash between the principles of profits and cooperativism embodies a fundamental clash between the interests of farmers and those of the Nokyo bureaucracy.

Secondly, a relatively small proportion of Nokyo's surpluses have been ploughed back into individual farm investment, as already noted. More than half of Nokyo's surplus funds have traditionally been channelled into the more lucrative fields of loans to 'related' industries and the purchase of securities.[232] Indeed, Nishimoto describes the role of the Nokyo credit institutions as 'pipes to siphon money out of the rural communities',[233] adding that the net effect was 'a growing tendency for the financial agencies to drain money from the village without replacing it'.[234] A JCP critique of Nokyo makes a similar point, although cast in Marxist terminology: 'Nokyo collects money from the farmers through its insurance business and monopoly capital uses this money. It is not well known that Norinchukin's money is used for monopoly capital. In this way, Nokyo plays an important role for monopoly capital in controlling and exploiting farmers.'[235]

The profit and loss statements for the federations in 1992, for example, revealed that Zenno's surplus was ¥3.96 billion, while the total *keizairen* surplus was ¥29.88 billion. For Norinchukin the comparable figure was ¥43.01 billion and for the *shinren* ¥71.6 billion. On the insurance side, Zenkyoren's overall profit amounted to ¥8.03 billion and the *kyosairen* ¥25.47 billion. The total for all these organisations was ¥181.94 billion.[236] As Nokyo insiders point out, only a small fraction of these 'profits' is returned to members according to the cooperative union principle.[237] The bulk is added to the capital accounts of these institutions. Indeed, the exceptionally high increases in the capital of these organisations was the result of accumulating funds that should have been returned to members as refunds or dividends on their cooperative shares.[238] The funds were kept by the local co-ops and the federations, while many farmers were burdened by bad debts and were forced to abandon farming.[239]

The solution to this problem lies with cooperative executives. They have it in their power to decide whether Nokyo's fundamental policies, including the disposal of surplus funds of the federations, are directed to members' interests. In theory their duties are to demonstrate a cooperative vision. Their stance has a crucial influence on cooperative decisions making it possible for the operational policies of Nokyo organisations to change drastically if their executives seek to defend members' interests. According to Nokyo insiders, however, the vast majority of agricultural cooperative executives do not seek to act in this way. They do not represent their members or undertake management from a members' point of view.[240] They are more inclined to identify with the business interests of the cooperative rather than the interests of individual farming members because it is the cooperative that pays their salaries. Even though they are elected by the membership, as soon as they are in the pay of the organisation, they immediately begin to identify with the official management side rather than the membership side. The incentives, therefore, are to increase the profits of the cooperative as a business rather than to pursue members' interests. Indeed, the profit-making motive puts members in the position of a group from whom to increase profits, rather than a group to whom profits should be returned. As put by one insider, a fundamental division exists within Nokyo between the executives and officials who receive money from Nokyo, and the membership who pays it.[241]

Generalist versus specialist

Within the Nokyo system, an entrenched view prevails that the *sogo nokyo* and their upper-level, multi-purpose federations represent the mainstream, while the specialist co-ops and their federations constitute a subordinate set of groupings. The question therefore arises whether the mainstream prefectural central unions and Zenchu represent the interests of the specialist co-ops within the Nokyo system.[242] The problem is partly organisational and relates to the membership composition of the *chuokai*, which leans towards the *sogo nokyo*, in spite of the formal setup of the central unions as inclusive guidance organisations. The rate of affiliation of *senmon nokyo* to *kenchu* and Zenchu is extremely low.[243] This means that the financial basis of the *chuokai* is supported by the *sogo nokyo* and their functions are naturally directed to *sogo nokyo* interests.[244] Not surprisingly, the specialist side criticises the *chuokai* for being associations for the *sogo nokyo* and not for *nokyo* in general.

For their part, the primary affiliation of the *senmon nokyo* is to their own prefectural specialist federations. As the latter are members of Zenchu, this is the only link for the vast majority of specialist *nokyo* to Zenchu. The line of affiliation is very indirect, whereas for the *sogo nokyo*, the line of affiliation is direct. The latter are members of both *kenchu* and Zenchu, an innovation that was primarily designed to facilitate Zenchu's mobilisation of farmers, rather than *sogo nokyo* input into Zenchu policymaking processes. Nevertheless, this structural arrangement has consequences for the overall balance of interests represented by central unions (including Zenchu). In addition, specialist agricultural co-ops for the most part lack financial functions and thus are forced to go to the *sogo nokyo* to request credit, which tends to compound the inferior status of the specialist side of the organisation in the Nokyo system.

On the other hand, certain features of the *senmon nokyo* endow them with strengths that the *sogo nokyo* do not possess. Firstly, the specialist co-ops vastly outnumber the multi-purpose co-ops, and as they developed their capacities in the marketing of specialist commodities, increasing numbers of them became capital-stock co-ops.[245] Secondly, as already pointed out, the *sogo nokyo* have a strong geographic focus as regional co-ops that gather together all the farmers (as well as many non-farm household associate members) within a particular area. The *senmon nokyo*, on the other hand, are product- and activity-oriented. As Nishimoto explains, their organisational basis is entirely different: 'the former enrols all farm households in a given geographic area, regardless of the crops they raise, while the latter accepts those who grow specific crops no matter where they live',[246] so the areas these different types of local co-ops service do not coincide. The tighter commodity or activity focus of the *senmon nokyo* often engenders greater organisational loyalty amongst their members, who are mainly specialist farmers, and who share this focused aspect to their farming operations. Because farmers generally belong to both types of co-op, general-purpose and special-purpose, dual membership can in theory give rise to conflicting loyalties. In practice, however, specialist full-time farmers (who are in a minority amongst Japanese producers as a whole) tend to 'rely on special-purpose cooperatives rather than general-purpose cooperatives'.[247] This is certainly the case for marketing and processing, although of course these specialist full-time farmers still need the *sogo nokyo* for things like banking and insurance services. To this extent there is an organisational division of labour. This does not prevent areas of contention between the *sogo nokyo* and *senmon nokyo*, however. In addition to issues of overlapping membership and intersecting area boundaries, real problems of competition for market share can arise, especially where both types of co-op handle the same products within a given area.

As the consumer demand for rice and the production of non-rice grain crops subsided, the *sogo nokyo* endeavoured to expand their marketing activities in other more specialist areas of Japanese agriculture. In consequence, the *senmon nokyo* felt under increasing threat of encroachment in their own specialist fields. In some localities, rivalry between the two sides of the Nokyo organisation degenerated into open competition, compounded by the resentment amongst the specialist co-ops against the tendency of the central unions to adjust conflicts of this kind by advocating the extension of multi-purpose business and the contraction of the specialist co-op share. Where rivalry between the multi-purpose and specialist cooperatives became intense over the marketing and control of a particular product in a particular area, steps were sometimes taken by both sides to get their interests represented more powerfully. In Ehime for example, the two camps actually ran separate candidates for the governorship in a bitter electoral campaign.[248]

Another related problem in the field of marketing has been the development of close ties between specialist co-ops and non-cooperative marketing and supply companies outside the Nokyo system. This has been viewed by the multi-purpose side as undermining the strength of the agricultural cooperative system. In response, they poured a substantial amount of pressure, finance and managerial expertise into developing 'regionally integrated production units', otherwise known as agricultural cooperative farm complexes (*eino danchi*),[249] which represented a major new development at the production level in the 1960s. The concept was introduced in the 1961 Agricultural Basic Law and was facilitated by later amendments to both the Nokyo Law and the Agricultural Land Law. The changes permitted agricultural cooperatives to coordinate farmers into integrated production complexes specialising in a single commodity, or to undertake the business of farm management on land leased from farmer members of Nokyo who wished to retain their lands but did not wish to work it. The schemes attracted considerable assistance and subsidisation from government. Although the *eino danchi* made no direct contribution to the objective of expanding the scale of farm management, their rationale was to strengthen and vertically integrate production, processing, marketing, distribution and retailing functions within the agricultural cooperative system in order to meet the competition from private enterprise.

The specialist versus generalist cleavage represents an institutionalised tension within the Nokyo organisation. It is built into the system through the provision of separate structural divisions catering to different interests and some degree of functional specialisation amongst the co-ops. On the other hand, the differentiation of internal structural forms can serve the constructive purpose of allowing for both the expression and containment of conflict. Competition between different sectors of the same organisation is openly acknowledged and therefore managed through legitimate channels. On balance, occasions where competition spilt over into direct confrontation between opposing groups was the exception rather than the rule. The containment of specialist versus generalist rivalry within Nokyo, however, has not always been easy for the Zenchu leadership, particularly in the political arena where the national specialist federations have assumed a growing amount of Zenchu's prerogative in the area of *nosei katsudo*.[250]

Rural versus urban

Changes in Nokyo's social and economic environment resulting from urbanisation and industrialisation have presented yet another problem of internal adjustment for the agricultural cooperatives. In addition to the absolute decline in farm numbers with the rural to urban drift in population, industry and population from the larger metropolitan areas have encroached on the countryside and thus urbanised rural areas.[251] This has given rise not only to a sharper division of interest between urban-consumer members and rural-farmer members of *nokyo*, but also to a fundamental reorientation of Nokyo towards serving the non-agriculture-related needs of heterogenous communities in urban areas.

Immediately after the formation of Nokyo in the 1950s, the proportion of full-time farmers in Nokyo's membership was 50 per cent, whilst Type II part-time farm households comprised 22 per cent and associate members 8 per cent.[252] During the period of rapid economic growth, a massive surge in the number of part-time households, especially Type II, took place, as well as substantial rises in the number of associate members. In those areas where urbanisation and industrialisation progressed most rapidly, farm income sources changed from agricultural to non-agricultural employment, and farm production declined as land was turned over to industrial and residential sites.[253]

The changes in agricultural society and the retreat of agriculture in urbanising districts directly impacted on the businesses of the agricultural cooperatives. The non-agricultural income of farmers grew as a proportion of their deposits in agricultural cooperative financial institutions, with the proportion of Nokyo savings from this source rising from 28 per cent in 1965 to 51 per cent in 1980. The high growth rate of Nokyo savings was in fact only made possible by absorbing non-agricultural incomes.[254] Meanwhile, shrinking proportions of loans were being used for purposes relating to agricultural production.[255]

The fall-off in Nokyo's agriculture-related activities in the most rapidly urbanising regions forced the agricultural cooperatives to develop their purely financial and general business operations in order to underpin management survival. Increasing numbers of agricultural cooperative executives adjusted to their new economic imperatives and adapted their cooperative services to cater to the needs of urban residents. Inevitably, urban *nokyo* began to put greater effort into credit and mutual aid business than into agriculture-related enterprise.[256] In some areas the number of farmers 'decreased to such an extent that the farm population alone . . . [was] incapable of supporting any business'.[257] In Tokyo, for example, 14 agricultural cooperative organisations continued to service its 23 wards, but the numbers of farmer members dropped precipitously.[258]

Whilst Nokyo continued to insist that it was a body that took farmers as its fundamental organisational base, agricultural cooperative management pursued a deliberate policy of increasing numbers of associate members in order to diversify business in districts where farm-related activities had contracted.[259] Some co-ops applied aggressive pressure on local residents through the development of living and cultural programmes, 'creating an image of an open *nokyo* whose membership was available to everybody in an area.'[260] As a result, the ratio of regular farmer members to associate members diminished as associate newcomers joined the agricultural cooperatives because of the convenience and benefits of Nokyo's insurance, credit, consumer purchasing and socio-cultural services.

A growing heterogeneity became apparent within the overall agricultural cooperative organisation, spanning agricultural and non-agricultural businesses, and production and livelihood-related businesses.[261] Purchasing business involving sales of living necessities to farmer members and associate members showed much higher growth rates than agricultural marketing business, which stagnated in many cooperatives.[262] The most dramatic rates of expansion, however, were recorded by Nokyo trust and insurance businesses, symbolising the transition from agricultural to non-agricultural sectors. Ventures catering to the regional population, such as gasoline stations, beauty and funeral parlours, nursery and drivers' training schools, supermarkets and jewellery shops also typified the diverse enterprises on which the *nokyo* embarked. This developmental trend was facilitated by the fact that Nokyo's enterprises were not restricted by law to strictly agriculture-related fields.[263]

Nokyo thus expanded and maintained its local management base not by grounding its operations in farm-related businesses but by transferring its operational base to non-farm ventures.[264] As Fujitani describes it, the overall emphasis in agricultural cooperative business shifted from 'production economic activities' (*seisan keizai katsudo*) targeting farm households, to 'livelihood economic activities (*seikatsu keizai katsudo*) targeting both farm households and local general households.[265] Nokyo thus changed 'from an organization overwhelmingly made up of farmers to locality-centered cooperative associations embracing a wide spectrum of local residents in all occupations.'[266] Local co-ops began to function as general community centres for all the local population.[267] Elsewhere this was described as a process of 'regional cooperativisation' (*chiiki kumiaika*),[268] with Nokyo taking on the characteristics of a '*seikyo*' (livelihood, or consumer cooperative), or a '*shinkumi*' (credit union). Because of the geographical basis of the *sogo nokyo*, they converted easily from agricultural cooperatives into multi-purpose area-based cooperatives.[269]

Nokyo's adaptation to the changing economic and social environment was reflected in differential trends in co-op numbers by district. Those in urbanised rural areas dipped comparatively slowly compared with those in genuinely rural and remote rural areas which dropped substantially.[270] The culmination of these trends was Nokyo's separation from agriculture (*Nokyo no nogyobanare*), a process of separation that enabled Nokyo to prosper, whilst Japanese agriculture continued to decline.[271] In adjusting to the immense changes in the agricultural sector, Nokyo generally displayed far greater flexibility as a business group and financial conglomerate than as an agent for agrarian interests.[272]

The local agricultural cooperative branch in South Yokohama (Yokohama Minami Nokyo) typifies the transformation of Nokyo's fundamental character in highly urbanised areas. Although this city *nokyo* is run by farmers, the bulk of its business lies in banking, insurance and real estate.[273] In JFY 1987, 70 per cent of its profits were derived from interest on loans and investments made by its credit operations, while the other 30 per cent was generated by insurance premiums.[274] A real estate subsidiary, cashing in on farmers selling their land for urban development conducted about ¥6 billion worth of business annually.[275] Its membership ratio in 1988 was 65:35 associate non-farming members to regular farming members.[276] Nevertheless, the organisation's farming members remained crucial to its organisational identity and legal status: if it converted to another type of organisation, it would lose the tax and other privileges it enjoyed as an agricultural cooperative.

Urban farmers have, therefore, remained crucial to keeping the cooperatives operating in urban areas.[277] The bifurcated nature of the agricultural cooperative's functions as a co-op to serve a dwindling number of farmers and a co-op to serve local non-farmer residents has, however, made it even harder for the *nokyo* to meet the sophisticated agricultural management needs of entrepreneurial farmers scattered in areas where urbanisation and part-time farming are prevalent. Furthermore, *nokyo* of this kind run straight up against consumer cooperatives who are also operating in these areas and even expanding into rural areas.[278]

On another dimension, the changing balance between cooperatives in highly urbanised areas, in which Nokyo exists practically as a bank-cum-insurance-cum-real-estate company, and those in remote farming areas, has produced a tremendous disparity in focus between the least urbanised and the most urbanised *nokyo*. Zenchu has the problem of adjusting the interests of vastly different organisations and of hammering out policy requests that are equally responsive to the needs of farmers operating in highly urbanised areas such as Yokohama City and those in the remote mountain villages of Fukushima. At the micro-level, the interests of farmers in the urban *nokyo* risk being ignored, while at the macro-level, the shift in managerial priorities influences the entire organisation.

Yokohama Minami Nokyo is in fact a microcosm of a nationwide trend that, as already noted, has reorientated the overall focus of Nokyo's business operations to non-agricultural enterprises. Some commentators welcome this reorientation, arguing that it is inevitable for Nokyo to refashion itself as a regional cooperative, seeing this as the salvation of the organisation.[279] At the 19th National Nokyo Convention in 1991,[280] Nokyo launched a regional policy that was basically geared to regional dwellers rather than to farmers. Primary emphasis was placed on responding to the needs of regional dwellers by strengthening the functions of the livelihood 'comprehensive centres' (*sogo sentaa*) as a basic policy direction on the livelihood side (see Figure 2.3). As Saeki points out, however, although Nokyo argues that both the agricultural and non-agricultural sides of the organisation can co-exist as 'two wheels of a cart' (that is, as an agricultural cooperative and as a regional cooperative), if the cooperative face shows the model or formal principle of Nokyo, the regional cooperative face shows its reality, or changed quality.[281] One of the risks of the excessive pursuit of commercialism is that it might lead to a neglect of the original duties of the agricultural cooperatives (i.e. cooperative activities for the benefit of farmer members, rather than profits).[282]

In some co-ops, there has been a reluctance to expand 'livelihood enterprises' stemming from members' attachment to Nokyo's identity as an agricultural organisation, their concerns about the likely success of such non-farm businesses, and their fears about agricultural cooperatives' competing with local retailers who are customers of their credit and insurance businesses.[283] In particular, concerns have surfaced about the trend for the original functions of the cooperatives relating to farm guidance and agricultural marketing and purchasing to be downgraded and even abandoned.[284] Many local cooperatives in their eagerness to expand credit or other business enterprises, have disregarded or forgotten the fundamental rationale of Nokyo which is to provide services, information and goods needed by farmers. Core functions such as agricultural guidance and marketing have gradually become limited to full-time farm households and farm households marketing agricultural products.[285] Few Nokyo staff members are employed to tackle actual problems in farming. While keen farmers continue to expect guidance and leadership in agricultural management, they are often disappointed.[286] Many co-op staff members spend their time running financial businesses, although they are not properly trained in that field either.[287] Most of them agree, however, that Nokyo emphasises its credit and insurance businesses.[288] Moreover, although the shift to regional cooperativisation has been advocated, the real operations of the *sogo nokyo* have been directed to increasing savings and mutual aid insurance.[289]

The fundamental change in the basic business orientation of the agricultural cooperatives has aggravated the division between multi-purpose and specialist cooperatives. The minority of full-time farmers now rely increasingly on specialist cooperatives rather than *sogo nokyo* whose activities and interests are being diverted from agriculture-related activities by the growth in part-time farmers and associate members. Indeed, as Goto and Imamura point out, many of the needs of part-time farmers are similar if not identical with those of urban consumers.[290] In their view, this means that: 'Farming no longer serves as an integrating theme to coordinate the activities of the cooperative members as more farm families become Class II part-time farmers'.[291]

Nokyo's vested interest in agricultural support and protection

Nokyo's economic stake in the Food Control system

As discussed in chapter 2, a number of agricultural laws integrate Nokyo into the functioning of agricultural administration and provide substantial fringe benefits for doing so. The most important of these has been the FC Law, under which the government delegated authority for rice business to Nokyo.[292] Beyond the provision of services to rice producers as co-op members, Nokyo developed its own stake in the highly regulated domestic rice market because its rice-collection and marketing businesses were subsidised by the government under the FC system.[293] As a result, maintaining 'profits' from its participation in Food Control remained a core policy interest for Nokyo.[294] The preservation of these vested rights has been consistently behind its approach to the whole question of FC reform. In essence, the FC system and Nokyo supported each other over many decades.

With respect to rice collection and marketing, the agricultural cooperatives' share under the FC system amounted to an officially sanctioned near-monopoly of the market. Local *nokyo* acted as government-designated rice collection agents, the others being rice trading cooperatives belonging to the National Federation of Staple Food Collection Cooperative Unions (Zenshuren), the national-level organisation of the rice wholesalers. Agricultural cooperatives traditionally accounted for more than two-thirds of the total number of officially designated rice collection agents, or primary collectors (4,450 out of a total of 6,170 in 1986, or 72.1 per cent, and 1,905 out of the total of 3,296 in 1996, or 57.8 per cent).[295] Although farmers had a choice of which type of designated rice collection agent to use, in practice, most were registered producers with the agricultural cooperatives (consistently 95 per cent), while Zenno's share of the total amount of rice sold to the government (*seifumai*) was close to 100 per cent,[296] and its share of the rice sold to wholesalers under the (semi-controlled) IDR system hovered at around 95 per cent.[297] The high figures reflected farmers' preference for working through the agricultural cooperatives for rice marketing. The basic pattern was for local *nokyo* to act as primary collectors of rice from farmers; for the *keizairen*, as secondary handlers, to collect rice from the local cooperatives; and for Zenno, the national collection group, to sell the rice to the government or to wholesalers.[298]

The FC system guaranteed income to the agricultural cooperative organisation from a number of functions it performed under the FC law. The cooperatives received from government, via the Domestic Rice Control Account of the Food Control Special Account (FCSA) of the national General Account budget, various subsidies from government such as delivery (i.e. collection) fees (*shukka tesuryo*), fees for storing rice in cooperative warehouses, interest subsidies on monies advanced to farmers in payment for rice, incentive and marketing assistance payments for independently distributed and 'other' rice respectively, and fees for rice inspection. Nokyo received these subsidies under the pretext of 'protecting the Nokyo organisation with scarce capital compared with general trading companies'.[299] Nokyo also obtained marketing commissions from farmers for handling the rice they sold through the agricultural cooperative system. In this way, Food Control provided the financial underpinning of Nokyo's marketing operations.

Approximate calculations of the financial benefits Nokyo reaped from the FC system are a useful measure of its vested interest in the highly regulated and subsidised rice distribution regime. For example, the total value of rice marketed by *sogo nokyo* under the FC system in 1985 was ¥2.6 trillion (government rice amounted to ¥1.3 trillion, semi-controlled rice ¥1.2 trillion and 'other rice' ¥100 billion).[300] This represented 39 per cent of the total value of agricultural commodities marketed by the *sogo nokyo* in that year, which amounted to ¥6.7 trillion.[301] A decade later the amount of rice marketed and handled by the co-ops added up to a total value of ¥2 trillion (¥375.8 billion in government rice, ¥1.5 trillion in semi-controlled rice and ¥104.7 billion in 'other rice').[302] This was 33.4 per cent of the total value of agricultural commodities marketed by the *sogo nokyo* in that year.

Much of this rice subsequently passed through the federated Nokyo system (*keizairen* and Zenno) which, like the local co-ops, received marketing commissions from farmers for handling the rice.[303] In 1985, *sogo nokyo* income from rice marketing commissions totalled ¥62.1 billion, or approximately 42.6 per cent of their total marketing commission for that year of ¥145.8 billion.[304] The *keizairen* earned ¥10.3 billion (18.2 per cent of their total marketing commission) and Zenno ¥4.9 billion (26.6 per cent of its total marketing commission).[305] This produced a grand total for the Nokyo organisation of ¥77.3 billion in commissions for marketing rice. Of this, rice for government sale represented ¥28.2 billion or 36.5 per cent of the total marketing commission from rice.[306] The figures for 1995 are equally instructive. The local co-ops earned ¥57.4 billion in commissions from rice marketing which was around 40 per cent of their total marketing commission. The *keizairen* got ¥11.5 billion and Zenno ¥5.0 billion, making a total of ¥73.9 billion for 1995.[307] Not only are the figures large, but they show that the profits from Nokyo's rice marketing business remained remarkably stable over the years.

As noted earlier, however, not only has rice been significant in Nokyo's overall marketing total, but 'the impact is much greater owing to the subsidies associated with it.'[308] Nokyo was paid ¥407.5 per 60 kg bag of rice from the Domestic Rice Control Account for collecting rice for government sale (*shukka keihi*) in 1985, producing an income of ¥34.4 billion in that year.[309] The collection fee rose to ¥414.5 in 1988, falling to ¥408.5 in 1989, where it subsequently remained.[310] In 1995, the equivalent figure was ¥18.4 billion.[311] The reduction over the 1985–95 period reflected the contraction in the quantities of rice bought by the government and the increasing diversion of rice through the IDR system.

Other benefits also accrued to Nokyo as rice collection agent. Most of the agricultural cooperative warehousing business has been taken up with storage of 'government designated commodities' – rice (including semi-controlled rice), wheat and barley – but mainly rice. The agricultural cooperatives operate more than 11,000 warehouses storing 'government designated commodities' with a total storage capacity of the equivalent of around 8 million tonnes of rice.[312] In 1985, Nokyo acquired ¥34.52 per 60 kg bag of government rice per month in storage fees paid from the Domestic Rice Control Account.[313] By 1991 this sum had climbed to ¥39.52 per month where it subsequently remained.[314] In 1985 warehousing of rice earned Nokyo ¥11.4 billion[315] (about one-third their total earnings from agricultural warehousing operations).[316] In 1995, the figure was ¥6.8 billion.[317]

The commissions from government for warehousing provided a stable income for the *nokyo*, and was one of the main sources of income paid by the Japanese government to Nokyo in the rice business.[318] Rice surpluses generated good gains for the agricultural cooperatives, particularly those operating warehouses in predominantly rice-producing areas. The profits from this business were directly linked to the amount of rice in storage; the larger the rice surplus, the more lucrative it was for Nokyo. The massive rice surpluses in the mid-1990s (over 4 million tonnes) were quite profitable for the agricultural cooperatives, as the cost of rice storage was still partially subsidised by the government.[319]

When the IDR system was introduced in 1969, the MAFF was very careful to ensure that the market share of the agricultural cooperatives under the new system would be preserved in order to obtain Nokyo's cooperation with the introduction of a partially liberalised system of rice transactions. In addition to the higher rate of marketing commission Nokyo was permitted to charge on independently distributed rice, various subsidies were provided to the agricultural cooperatives by the Food Agency for undertaking government-designated functions in relation to semi-controlled rice, principally storage and interest subsidies. These were paid to Nokyo (and other designated collectors, that is, rice wholesalers through their national organisation, Zenshuren) in the form of a marketing promotion fee (*hanbai sokushinhi*). The fee covered storage costs of the rice until it was sold, as well as interest costs on monies advanced by the agricultural cooperatives to the farmers in payment for the rice before the cooperatives themselves had received any payment from the rice wholesalers. In 1985 this subsidy averaged ¥141 per 60 kg.[320] The total cost of the marketing promotion subsidy in that year was ¥27.3 billion.[321] Of this sum, Nokyo, which had a 94.8 per cent share of the IDR collection market, was allocated the giant share of ¥25.9 billion. By 1995, the marketing promotion subsidy had fallen to ¥57 per 60 kg.[322] The total cost of providing the subsidy decreased to ¥19.0 billion, of which Nokyo collected ¥18.1 billion with its 95.1 per cent of the IDR collection market.[323]

A conservative estimate of the financial benefits for the Nokyo organisation from its rice business under the FC system in 1985 was ¥149 billion.[324] In 1995 the equivalent figure was just on ¥117 billion, with one of the most stable aspects of Nokyo's rice marketing business being the commission it was paid by farmers. The biggest reductions in benefits flowing to Nokyo registered in the amounts received from government for collecting *seifumai*, and the amounts paid to Nokyo for storing rice, both of which almost halved. The amounts allocated to the IDR marketing promotion subsidy were also reduced by the government.

Admittedly the marketing commissions, storage fees and interest subsidies that Nokyo earned from rice under the FC system accounted for only a small percentage of the organisation's total business profits,[325] which were far greater in the more lucrative purchasing,[326] insurance[327] and credit[328] areas, and in company shareholding. In addition, the sums earned from the operations of the FC system diminished as a proportion of Nokyo's total economic operations over time. Nevertheless, the above figures suggest that Nokyo retained a lucrative stake in the FC system over many years. The various subsidies received for handling rice[329] as well as marketing commissions paid by the farmers to Nokyo helped to offset the net losses that local agricultural cooperatives sustained in their overall marketing operations.[330] Moreover, as Hayami points out, Nokyo needed to exert no major effort to earn these large commissions.[331] Another consideration for the agricultural cooperatives was the fact that rice formed the core of their warehousing business which generally ran at a net loss.[332]

In addition, rice income earned by farmers was consistently a valuable source of funds for Nokyo's banking business. Government utilisation of the financial network of the cooperatives for rice payments to farmers channelled the single most important item in co-op members' agricultural income through Nokyo savings accounts. The higher the rice price, the greater the amount circulating through the cooperative banking system.[333] Norinchukin acted as the receiving agent for rice payments from government and transferred the monies to farmers through the prefectural credit associations and unit co-ops. This gave the Nokyo financial apparatus the use of substantial funds from a guaranteed source of supply, thus strengthening agricultural cooperative banking institutions, enhancing the security of their lending operations,[334] facilitating transfer payments to cooperative purchasing and insurance sections by farmers, and supplying Nokyo with funds for temporary use in other business and financial fields.[335] The value of payments for rice to farmers from Nokyo amounted to ¥2 trillion per year in the early 1990s.[336] In total, a massive amount of funds was channelled through Nokyo accounts, including not only payments for rice, but also various subsidies and commissions. These funds in turn supported other Nokyo businesses, such as marketing, purchasing, finance and insurance.

Nokyo's economic stake in the FC system accounts for a great deal of its opposition to the deregulation of the domestic rice market and the relaxation of import controls. Nokyo's concern about the effects of these developments stemmed from its anxieties about their impact on its own organisation rather than on agricultural production per se.[337] The changes that Nokyo feared the most were those that interfered with its privileged position in rice collection and distribution. Throughout the series of steps taken by the government over the years partially to deregulate the FC system,[338] the larger interest at stake for Nokyo has always been the preservation of the FC system itself. For example, Nokyo accepted the introduction of the IDR trading system in 1969 in order to avert a sudden collapse of the FC system (brought on by a buildup of rice stores and a blowout in budgetary costs). Zenhanren argued that the introduction of IDR trading was inevitable if the basic framework of Food Control were to be maintained.[339] When producer rice price freezes were introduced at the same time (in 1969 and 1970), Nokyo proposed a nationwide uniform reduction in rice production by 10 per cent.[340] The Zenchu Board of Directors had already agreed that it was necessary to reduce rice production voluntarily in order to maintain the FC system. Encouraged by the proposal, the government decided to promote rice acreage reduction (*gentan*), arguing along the same lines as Zenchu – viz., that a reduction in rice production was inevitable if the basic framework of the FC system were to be maintained.[341]

Similarly, when Nokyo was later given the task of administering the *gentan*,[342] it complied because it wanted to keep the FC system going at all costs.[343] Preservation of regulatory controls on rice distribution was more important than the burden of rice production cutbacks on many of the relatively more efficient rice farmers. Nokyo not only resigned itself to the producer rice price cuts that began in 1987, but also to the series of *gentan* policies that were applied even more severely from that time.[344] Farmers in many areas, but particularly Hokkaido (where acreage had been reduced by 44 per cent between the start of these policies and 1986, which was twice the national average) opposed these cuts for two main reasons. Firstly, they forced farmers to choose other crops to grow, which duplicated investment in machines and facilities for the cultivation of both rice and these other crops. Secondly, they reduced overall returns from production even though the producer rice price was going down, because of limited options amongst substitute crops, the high production costs of such crops, and reductions in subsidies for switching to other crops.

Zenchu's basic position, however, was that farmers should comply with the *gentan* as a means of maintaining the FC system. As it stated in 1986: 'It is necessary to reduce the cultivation area for rice in order to maintain the food control system'.[345] Zenchu had already decided on a policy of positive compliance with the next round of measures for the reorganisation of the use of rice paddies beginning in fiscal 1987 (a code phrase for the *gentan*). Nokyo was prepared to go along with the revamped rice acreage reduction policies and with the cuts to the producer rice price, both of which hurt the rice farmers, in order to maintain a system from which it benefited as an organisation. In short, Nokyo's rice price and acreage reduction policies were sacrificed to its FC preservation strategy.

Nokyo's economic stake in domestic livestock production

Remarkable growth took place in Nokyo's livestock product marketing business from the late 1960s onwards. In 1968, local agricultural cooperatives traded in rice to a value of ¥1.3 trillion and in livestock products to a value of ¥312 billion. By 1976, the respective totals were ¥2.3 trillion and ¥1.0 trillion.[346] The figures reveal that between 1968 and 1976, the relative value of the livestock marketing business by the *sogo nokyo* accelerated from one-quarter of the value of rice turnover to almost one half. In absolute terms, the value of rice turnover almost doubled, while livestock turnover more than tripled. By 1995, the value of rice turnover had slipped to ¥2.0 trillion, while livestock turnover had expanded to ¥1.2 trillion.[347]

Nokyo's economic stake in the domestic livestock industry was further expanded by the incorporation of livestock products into vast ancillary processing and farm input supply (principally feed) industries into which the

Table 4.1 Zenno-related livestock companies

Company title	Capital (¥)	Livestock-related business
Zenno Shokuhin (KK)[a]	100 million	Processing of agricultural and livestock products
(KK) Kumiai Boeki	300 million	Importing of live cattle and meat
(KK) Co-op Meat	3 million	Meat processing and marketing
Zenkoku Nokyo Chokuhan	324 million	Milk and meat sales
Zenno Takasaki Shokuniku Kako (KK)	200 million	Production and marketing adjustment amongst group production companies
Ibaraki Kyodo Shokuniku (KK)	125 million	Slaughtering and meat processing
Kyushu Kyodo Shokuhin (KK)	92.5 million	Slaughtering, meat processing and storage
Takasaki Ham (KK)[b]	150 million	Meat processing and sales
Hokkaido Nokyo Nyugyo (KK)	2.4 billion	Milk and milk products processing and sales
(KK) Hokkaido Chikusan Shinko Kosha	400 million	Cattle and pig slaughtering, meat processing, shipment and sales
Iwate Chikusan Ryutsu Senta	586.4 million	Cattle and pig slaughtering, meat processing, shipment and sales
(KK) Miyazaki-ken Chikusan Kosha	571 million	Cattle and pig slaughtering, meat processing, shipment and sales
Kagoshima Kumiai Shokuniku	50 million	Cattle and pig slaughtering, meat processing, shipment and sales
(KK) Tokyoto Shokuniku Kyokyu Kosha	1 billion	Meat storage, transport and processing
Chuo Shokuhin	151.5 million	Meat processing, packaging and marketing
Omiya Shokuniku Niuke (KK)	100 million	Carcass and fresh meat reception and marketing
Tokyo Shokuniku Shijo	600 million	Carcass and fresh meat reception and marketing
Yokohama Shokuniku Niuke (KK)	60 million	Carcass and fresh meat reception and marketing
Nagoya Shokuniku Shijo (KK)	30 million	Carcass and fresh meat reception and marketing
Kobe Chuo Chikusan Niuke (KK)	50 million	Cattle slaughtering, meat processing and sales
Nihon Rakuno Kyodo (KK)	500 million	Processing and sales of milk and milk products

Notes:
a This is also known as Co-op Shokuhin.
b This was originally known as Hokuso Takasaki Ham.

Source: Yoshihara, *Zenno o Kiru*, pp. 252–61.

agricultural cooperatives extended their business involvement. Cooperative companies launched by Zenno in the livestock sector in the mid-1970s are listed in Table 4.1. As agricultural scientists often point out, livestock products require more processing than do most other agricultural products.

Typical processes include the drying and reconstitution of milk, butter and cheese manufacture, livestock slaughter, and the packaging of meat cuts. All these need special facilities, which in turn require massive capital investment. The increasing demand for processed livestock products was an attractive proposition for capital, including surplus Nokyo funds generated in large quantities as a byproduct of its expanding financial activities in the trust and insurance areas. In the domestic beef industry, for example, Nokyo made sizeable investments in slaughter, processing and input supply industries and therefore acquired a large economic stake in local beef production.[348]

Japan's livestock producers have also been heavily dependent on factory-produced compound feed rather than pasture grass to support livestock raising.[349] Japan's expanding livestock industry provided a growing market for feed. The vast bulk of the feed consumed by livestock and poultry in Japan continues to be manufactured from imported raw materials. Nokyo is a major feed producer through its cooperative companies.

Not surprisingly Zenno objected strenuously to the entry of a Japan subsidiary of a US grain major (Cargill) into compound feed and fertiliser production in Japan in Kagoshima Prefecture in the mid-1980s. Cargill North Asia was a Japanese corporation with its head office in Tokyo but wholly owned by its US parent company. It claimed that Japanese compound feed manufacturers were selling their products at relatively high prices, although they used low-priced imported materials. Cargill aimed to challenge Zenno and other Japanese combined feed manufacturers by competing on price and quality. It declared in its application: 'We will sell our assorted feed at lower prices than Japanese products.'[350]

Zenno mounted very strong opposition to this challenge, arguing that the US company might extend its reach even into the livestock industry, using feed production as the lever.[351] From the legal viewpoint, according to the Foreign Exchange and Foreign Trade Control Law, the bid could not be rejected. Therefore, it was impossible for the MAFF to employ administrative guidance to reject the proposal. In the past the MAFF had followed a 'scrap and build policy', which maintained a fixed number of Zenno and private sector compound feed makers through administrative guidance. This had effectively protected the interests of Zenno and the other companies operating in this field, not the interests of farmers.[352] Besides Zenno, two other categories of enterprises shared the feed market: a group of 10 'majors' including Marubeni Feed, Japan Agricultural Production (Nihon Nosanko), Cooperative Feed[353] and Showa Industries; and a small group of 'other makers'. The majors had the largest marketing share (51.1 per cent in 1995), exceeding that of Zenno (30.2 per cent) and the 'others' (18.7 per cent).[354] In the end, the MAFF left it up to the local authorities in the Kagoshima Prefecture government to decide the outcome and Cargill subsequently set up its plant there.

Many local farmers, especially beef farmers in Kagoshima Prefecture, welcomed the move. A journalist covering the case reported that there was 'a welcoming atmosphere to Cargill amongst livestock-raising farm households in Southern Kyushu in spite of opposition put up by the agricultural cooperative organisation and feed manufacturers'.[355] The cost of compound feed accounted for 60 per cent of production costs in poultry farming, more than 30 per cent in hog raising, and a little less than 20–30 per cent in dairy farming. The farmers hoped that feed prices would fall as a result of Cargill's entry into the market, and that this would help to reduce their production costs. At the time, import prices of corn and kaoliang per ton were about ¥30,000 including miscellaneous costs necessary for imports. These two kinds of grain constituted about two-thirds of compound feed. Even so, Zenno's price for compound feed delivered to the farm household exceeded ¥60,000 per tonne on the weighted average of all brands of feed.[356]

Although Cargill's entry into the agricultural material supply business in Japan caused a sensation at the time, and although their products were cheaper than the corresponding Nokyo products by 15–30 per cent, they did not gain the market share they expected. Farmers' unwillingness to switch to Cargill as a supplier was explained by a number of factors. Firstly, feed bought through the Nokyo federated system and from the 10 'majors' remained eligible for price stabilisation. In 1996, for example, the Zenkoku Haigo Shiryo Kyokyu Antei Kikin outlaid over ¥30 billion in feed price subsidies.[357] Secondly, it was convenient for many farmers to continue purchasing feed and fertiliser from their local agricultural cooperative because of access to the other services offered, including credit,[358] and also the ease of combining all marketing and purchasing transactions through one bank account.

Nevertheless, episodes such as the entry of Cargill into the feed supply business in Japan highlighted the fundamental contradiction in the agricultural cooperative organisation between its role as a cooperative body operating for the benefit of farmers, and as a commercial profit-making enterprise working in its own interests. In the mid-1980s when the prices of livestock products were stagnant, and when many producers were suffering from deficit accounts and huge debts, dissatisfaction began to spread in the farming villages over the prices of compound feed.

Furthermore, compound feed is not only produced by cooperative companies forming a nationwide network of compound feed factories operating in almost every prefecture in Japan,[359] but it is marketed through the federated Nokyo system. The agricultural cooperatives sold 35.5 per cent of the total amount purchased by farmers in 1995.[360] Their share of the market for beef and dairy cattle farmers is, however, considerably higher.[361] Feed remained the No. 1 item in *sogo nokyo* purchasing business until 1990 when it was overtaken by gasoline.[362] Feed, fertiliser and fuel have traditionally been Nokyo's 'big three' in farm input sales.[363]

Nokyo's vested interests in domestic livestock production also extended into the area of *eino danchi*.[364] Its objective was to incorporate these production complexes into an integrated agricultural cooperative system of farm input supply, production, processing, distribution and marketing. The development of these projects was linked to the creation of large numbers of cooperative companies in the areas of livestock processing and input supply in the 1960s and 1970s. Cooperative farming complexes became particularly strong in the livestock and horticultural sectors, in addition to rice.[365]

Nokyo's other 'face' – not as a profit-seeking economic enterprise but as a direct recipient of government concessions and benefits – is also visible in the livestock sector. The agricultural cooperatives receive large amounts of budgetary subsidies for a variety of livestock-related projects. The actual amounts received in FY 1998 and the projects involved are listed in Table 2.6. They were valued at more than ¥13 billion in that year, and by item, exceeded in number all other types of designated projects undertaken by the agricultural cooperatives.

In addition, Nokyo is a major recipient of subsidies from the LIPC/ALIC under its designated assistance projects scheme. These subsidies are for the promotion and rationalisation of the domestic livestock industry. Organisations eligible to receive LIPC subsidies are 'agricultural cooperatives, federation of agricultural cooperatives, juridical persons for public benefit or jointstock companies in which agricultural cooperatives, federation of agricultural cooperatives, local governments or the Livestock Industry Promotion Corporation hold the majority of stocks'.[366] Provision is thus made for LIPC subsidies to be channelled directly to the cooperatives themselves, or to cooperative-related companies in which Nokyo has a direct financial stake. In 1990, for example, Zenno was the largest single recipient of LIPC subsidies for designated assistance projects (just over ¥28 billion). The total for Nokyo was more than ¥30 billion.[367]

In addition, the LIPC supplies investment funding for designated assistance projects. The recipients of these investments are, in almost all cases, Zenno's livestock companies (*chikusan kanren gaisha*), such as Hokkaido Chikusan Shinko Kosha in which Zenno originally invested ¥400 million and in which the LIPC provided a further ¥50 million worth of investment in 1970 (the company is involved in cattle and pig slaughtering, meat processing, shipment and sales). Another is the Iwate Chikusan Ryutsu Senta in which Zenno invested ¥586.4 million and the LIPC ¥307 million between 1971 and 1984 for conducting the same business as the former.[368] For Nokyo, the LIPC's domestic livestock industry subsidy scheme generated a strong vested interest in the livestock policy regime and in the LIPC's role in relation to price stabilisation for pork, beef, designated dairy products and beef calves, as well as the state trades in beef and designated dairy products.

In the light of Nokyo's extensive involvement in all aspects of the domestic livestock industry, its vehement opposition to the liberalisation of the Japanese market for livestock products is not surprising.[369] A great deal of this resistance to the entry of overseas beef and dairy products can be traced to Nokyo's substantial economic stake in this sector, not only as an organisation representing domestic livestock producers, but as a beneficiary of government

funding for livestock-related projects and as a business and commercial enterprise with substantial investment in livestock-related industries.[370]

Nokyo's vested interest in small-scale, high-cost agriculture

The vast majority of regular members of local agricultural cooperatives are
part-time farmers who derive the bulk of their income from non-agricultural
occupations and whose land holdings are too small to support efficient
agricultural production. Nokyo's own organisational interests also strongly
favour the continuation of small-scale, part-time family farming, and therefore it comes down heavily on the side of the less efficient, small-scale
land-holders on agricultural support and protection issues.[371] Some Nokyo
officials even preach an 'anti-economy of scale doctrine' that works to keep
farms small and to maximise the number of farm families.[372] Fewer farm
households raises the unwelcome prospect of fewer co-op members and therefore a depleted customer base for Nokyo's agriculture-related services such as
marketing and purchasing, particularly the latter. Furthermore, small-scale
'dependent' farmers are particularly valued customers of the agricultural
cooperatives for a number of reasons.

Firstly, part-time farm households are more reliant on cooperative services
because of the limited amount of time they have for agricultural activities and
because of the relatively limited amounts of farm produce they have for sale.
One dimension of this dependence directly affects volumes in Nokyo's
purchasing business. When it comes to the purchase of farm materials,
officials of the local co-op, not the farmers themselves, calculate the necessary
volume of inputs required by farmers by taking a look at the farm and
putting the order into the *keizairen*. The *keizairen* and Zenno, which obtain
more handling fees as the volume of materials increase, encourage the *nokyo*
to use more production inputs. This factor is held responsible, more than any
other, for the dependence of Japanese farmers on agricultural chemicals and
artificial fertilisers.[373]

Secondly, part-time farmers are not as concerned about lowering their costs
as full-time farmers endeavouring to produce commodities more competitively, because they are not making a serious living out of farming. In an
environment of full-time, entrepreneurial farm producers, the cooperatives
would have to compete more fiercely with the private sector for the business
of more efficient farmers. The larger-scale farmers might be tempted to do
business with private companies and thus bypass the agricultural cooperatives
altogether, selling farm products directly to wholesalers and retailers and purchasing farm inputs from more competitively-priced private suppliers.[374] In
fact full-time farmers' utilisation rate of co-op services has been declining for
all major farm inputs such as fertiliser, feed and agricultural chemicals.

The same trend is observable in Nokyo's marketing business. Farmers who
sell their products through the agricultural cooperative system have to pay a
certain percentage to their local *nokyo* as commission (an average of 2.4 per

cent on all commodities in 1995),[375] a somewhat smaller percentage to the prefectural economic federation (an average of 1.0 per cent in 1995),[376] and an even smaller average percentage to Zenno (an average of 0.6 per cent in 1995).[377] Bypassing the agricultural cooperative system avoids these commissions.[378] Thus if Japanese agricultural production were the predominant preserve of larger-scale, efficient farmers, the co-ops would lose members and an even greater proportion of their business.[379] Indeed, if Japanese agriculture had managed to become efficient and large scale (in spite of Nokyo), it is doubtful whether the agricultural cooperative organisation could have survived, at least in its present form.

Thirdly, small-scale, part-time farmers are more dependent on mechanised farming operations and therefore machinery sold by the cooperatives. If the number of these farmers diminished, the co-ops would lose business 'because small-scale agricultural production promotes multiple sales of farm inputs such as machinery items'.[380] Nokyo has reportedly pushed the extravagant use of farm machinery, promoting debt amongst the farmers because this represents sales for its farm purchasing business. Moreover, in encouraging debt amongst farmers, Nokyo generates further profit for its credit business in the form of interest on loans.[381]

Nokyo's dependence on the patronage of inefficient, small-scale, part-time farmers is one of the reasons why agricultural production costs remain at relatively high levels. In this sense, Nokyo bears some of the responsibility for the high-cost structure of Japanese agriculture. A by-product of the extravagant use of machinery promoted by Nokyo, for example, has been an increase in production costs. According to government data, the costs of rice production increased by 70 per cent per 10 ares between 1976 and 1986 and by about 60 to 70 per cent per 60 kilograms. This increase took place in spite of the fact that working hours in rice production were greatly reduced because of the introduction of machinery, and the fact that the amount harvested per unit area was increasing, if only gradually.[382] Rises in production costs translated into increases in the producer rice price. Farmers felt they would get their costs back in the support price. But when support prices began to deteriorate in relative terms, farmers themselves began paying the costs of Nokyo's strategy.

Nokyo is complicit in driving up the costs of Japanese agriculture in other ways. Not only have products such as rice been sold under a virtual Nokyo monopoly, but its dominance in certain sectors of the distribution chain has prevented price competition from helping to lower farmers' input costs. Hayami claims that whatever passes through Nokyo is expensive because of its distribution monopolies.[383] Lack of competition, the government-sanctioned near-monopolies it holds in some areas and even price fixing between Nokyo and private companies on farm inputs such as stockfeed enable the agricultural cooperatives to charge high prices to its members. As Higashi and Lauter allege, Nokyo's control over 'all aspects of Japanese agriculture including the distribution of credit, fertilizers, and feed-stuffs . . .

[keeps] producers cost high.'[384] Ishizuka calculated that: 'Prices of tractors and fertilizers Japanese farmers buy . . . are 30–40 per cent or even 50 per cent higher than export prices.'[385] For example, JA-affiliated manufacturers sell fertiliser to Zenno for ¥24,000 per tonne, but export the same product for ¥9,000 per tonne.[386] According to a fertiliser manufacturer not affiliated to Nokyo, a 20 kg sack of his product was at least ¥200 cheaper than one supplied by a JA-affiliated manufacturer. This is because Zenno 'takes a cut at the raw materials level. Then, prefectural federations add a margin of about 3%, and individual co-ops at the local level add another 12%'.[387] Ultimately, the 'high prices of equipment, fertilizers and feedstuffs are . . . reflected in the high prices of agricultural products.'[388] As Kano reiterates, Nokyo's purchasing business is one of the causes of the high cost of Japanese agriculture.[389]

It is difficult to avoid concluding that farmers inevitably suffer from the way in which Nokyo conducts its business, which is basically at the expense of the farmers, who are forced to purchase expensive production materials according to the logic of profits, not the logic of cooperative ideology.[390] One of Nokyo's most trenchant critics, the JCP, contends that: 'the reason why agricultural materials are so expensive in Japan is because Nokyo has a hand in buying them.'[391]

A few local agricultural cooperatives have dared to go outside the federated Nokyo organisation in order to reduce farmers' input costs and therefore the costs of production. For example, the members of Nakasatsunai village *nokyo* in Hokkaido constructed their own fertiliser factory in 1982. Setting up the business cost ¥100 million but it reduced costs for fertiliser by ¥80 million within one year. Similarly, in 1983, 22 livestock farmers in the same *nokyo* jointly constructed a feed factory because the price of feed distributed through the Nokyo system in Hokkaido was ¥15,000–20,000 per tonne more than in other prefectures. This move pressured Hokuren (the Hokkaido *keizairen*) into reducing its own feed prices. The enterprising action of one village thus resulted in assistance to all farmers in Hokkaido. One Nokyo member estimated that because of the feed factory, he was able to save ¥6–8 million annually on feed costs. A price gap existed between the feed factory and Hokuren of ¥8,000 per tonne. This gap led to a cost reduction of ¥4 million annually for farmers with 300 cows. The feed factory also received increasing orders from outside the village, signifying increasing withdrawal of farmers from Nokyo.[392] In another case, a local agricultural cooperative in Hokkaido (Koiki Nokyo) went outside the federated Nokyo system (Zenno – Hokuren) and imported fertiliser directly from Korea. It was able to supply the imported fertiliser to member farmers at a price 30 per cent lower than that of the Nokyo. Hokuren could not help but follow suit.[393]

Discontented local *nokyo* leaders have complained that Zenno has consistently failed to provide answers to the question: 'why are production materials so expensive?'[394] The losers from this system – Nokyo's farming members – do not know the answer to this question and have no means of gauging the truth.[395] As these local co-op leaders explain:

Even if co-op members ask why the price of production materials are so high, no explanation is forthcoming. Why is this? It is because Zenno's true character is to promote its own interests at the expense of members. Zenchu also sanctions Zenno's principle of secrecy. If the federations were organised on a company basis, these matters would have to be made public. Because they are cooperatives, however, there is no obligation to explain. For example, the basis on which prices are decided for agricultural chemicals, fertilisers and corrugated cardboard boxes purchased from the makers of these goods is opaque. Transactions between Zenno and the makers are far from open and transparent. Domestic fertiliser prices are three times as high as export prices; feed and agricultural chemical prices are not credible even after price reductions; and paper bags and corrugated cardboard boxes which are only purchased from designated makers are too expensive.[396]

Zenno reportedly fixes prices in collusion with makers in purchasing fertilisers and agricultural chemicals and receives huge rebates.[397] Furthermore, it has the power to control fertiliser and agricultural chemical producers through guidance of farmers by the co-ops as to usage. The rebates that Zenno receives are not refunded to members, but are accumulated as profit and used to increase its capital funds.[398] Complaints are also directed at Zenchu for its failure to tackle the price of agricultural materials, and its conniving with Zenno like a subcontracting organ.[399]

In theory, if all agricultural inputs such as fertilisers, feed and agricultural chemicals are bought by a single buyer – Nokyo – then the huge volume should generate leverage in price negotiations with makers. In short, the co-op structure is supposed to create economies of scale. For the farmers, however, Nokyo's price leverage does not make agricultural materials cheaper because the benefits are channelled to the upper level organisations.[400] Although Zenno's transaction volume amounts to a considerable share of domestic demand and should generate leverage in price negotiations with makers, in practice, all the advantages accruing to Zenno flow back into Nokyo's coffers as handling profits and not into the pockets of the farmers. For example, Nokyo makes a profit of around ¥28 billion a year on the sale of agricultural chemicals worth ¥185 billion (which amounts to around 15 per cent). This level of profit also applies to other agricultural inputs such as fertilisers, feed, corrugated cardboard boxes, paper bags and other materials. None of this is returned to farmers.[401]

Moreover, direct delivery from the factory to Nokyo should also be cheap and efficient, but, in reality, the federated organisation imposes margins of up to six times in its marketing and purchasing business.[402] Because Nokyo is a federated organisation, farm goods are bought and sold through the three stages of *tankyo*, *keizairen* and Zenno.[403] Marketing commissions are imposed at each of the six steps through the *keito soshiki* – the three steps associated with the purchasing of production materials (from Zenno to *tankyo*) followed by the three steps involved in the shipment of agricultural products (from *tankyo* to Zenno). These are all collected from farmers.[404] In the view of one local *nokyo*, for these co-op organisations to extract margins from their member farmers fundamentally contradicts the principle of cooperative unionism.[405]

Yet another criticism of the Nokyo system is that margins on farm inputs are extracted by the federations and Zenno by shuffling paper up and down the line rather than moving the goods themselves. The actual route along which production materials and agricultural products pass, does not actually follow the three-stage pattern of the federated organisation. Most agricultural commodities produced by Nokyo's members are conveyed from the *tankyo* directly to markets and wholesalers, and purchasing materials are delivered directly from makers to the *tankyo*. But invoices are conveyed through the federated system, adding handling fees at each stage. In practice, therefore, the flow of goods and money does not necessarily coincide.

Take the example of rice distributed through the IDR system. The local co-ops collect the rice and ship it to retailers via the *keizairen* and Zenno, wholesalers and other intermediaries. In reality, however, the local co-ops usually send the rice directly to wholesalers while only papers are passed from the co-op to the *keizairen* and from the *keizairen* to Zenno. The passage of paper through the federated Nokyo system costs thousands of yen for each 60 kilos. As the *Asahi* observed: 'Without such 'paper margins' farmers could sell rice at higher prices while consumers could buy it at lower prices'.[406]

Likewise, when a farmer in Hokkaido orders fertiliser, it comes directly from a fertiliser factory wholly owned by Hokuren to the *tankyo*. The invoice, however, goes from the farmer to the *tankyo*, to Hokuren and to Zenno, and Zenno places an order with the fertiliser factory which supplies it to the farmer with an invoice. The figure on the invoice grows with the addition of handling fees at each step by Hokuren and Zenno, although all they have done is move paper. No goods have passed between them. Under this system, Hokuren and Zenno reap sizeable financial benefits without doing any substantial work, which makes for an easy, profitable business. Although the ratio of handling fees differs according to the item or product, the total handling fee for gasoline is 22.4 per cent, for agricultural chemicals and agricultural machinery 15.8 per cent, fertiliser 15.2 per cent and feed 8.4 per cent.[407]

This three-tiered distribution system and the margins imposed at each step are seen as 'the root cause of the high prices of JA products'.[408] It is one of the main reasons why Japanese farmers cannot run profitable operations in spite of high agricultural product prices and why consumers are forced to purchase food at such high prices. According to the price composition of fruit and vegetables sent to market calculated by the Statistical and Information Division of the MAFF, the amount that producers receive is only 22.4 for white radishes and 12.6 for onions with the retail price at 100.[409] The money generated by the paper flow through the *keito soshiki* is reduced to the farmers by the amount equivalent to the margins that Nokyo extracts.

The appreciation of the yen in the mid-1980s exposed these paper profits to a wider public audience. Prices of farm inputs such as fuel, fertilisers and feed, for which Japan was dependent on imported raw materials, were not lowered sufficiently in spite of the high yen.[410] In particular, the decline in feed prices on the international market potentially had great significance for reducing production costs for livestock farmers,[411] but Nokyo maintained high prices even while import prices fell.[412] Responsibility for this state of affairs was sheeted home to Nokyo management and the agricultural cooperative distribution system. Because Nokyo extracted a specific percentage of the sales value as a commission, a price decrease without a demand increase meant a reduction in Nokyo's profit.[413] It took more than another decade, for example, for Zenno's compound feed prices to diminish substantially. In September 1998, they dropped by ¥2,600 per tonne, following falls in international prices of the ingredients for feed, including corn. This cut pushed down the average price of Zenno's compound feed to about ¥35,900 per tonne.[414]

Increasing divisions amongst Nokyo's farm membership

Increasing divisions are emerging in Nokyo's membership ranks between full-time farmers who want to engage in more efficient and profitable farming operations and who see Nokyo as inhibiting the structural transformation of agriculture, and small-scale, part-time farmers who are dependent on co-op services but who derive only a small proportion of their income from farming – mainly rice. Nokyo has been less and less able to meet the diversified needs of these different types of agricultural producers.

Small, part-time rice farms have been strong users of Nokyo's farm input supply services such as machinery, fertilisers, chemicals and groceries because they can use a line of credit from the local cooperative linked to the contracted payment for rice for government sale.[415] Nokyo has traditionally offered this credit at lower rates than other financial organs in the private sector. It is also easier for members to qualify for loans because they can use their rice crop or farm land as security.[416]

For these reasons, many of Nokyo's part-time members have provided little challenge to its uncompetitive practices in agri-business and are not all that concerned about the development of farming.[417] Larger-scale farmers, however, do have such concerns as farming represents their livelihood, but they lack support from their own organisation. As pointed out by Tsuboi, the structural characteristic of Nokyo's farm household membership (that is, the dominance of part-time farmers) has made it 'very difficult to implement effective measures to develop and support full-time farmers who are in the minority.'[418]

In many cases, full-time farmers have been prevented from leaving the agricultural cooperatives because of Nokyo's stranglehold on rural credit and other essential inputs such as fertilisers.[419] Those farmers who have broken away have discovered that inputs such as fertilisers and stockfeed are cheaper when bought from independent suppliers, because farmers can take advantage of volume discounts that are not available through the agricultural cooperative system. When they purchase large amounts of fertiliser and fodder from Nokyo, the price is the same as for small-scale farmers.[420] This inflexible pricing structure means that larger-scale farmers seeking to purchase agricultural materials at reduced prices by buying in bulk prefer commercial dealers to Nokyo.[421] More efficient farmers want to purchase production materials in a market where the principle of competition operates and sell agricultural products in a fair market without privilege.

The reason volume discounts cannot be obtained from Nokyo is because of the preponderance of small-scale farmers in its membership. Part-time farmers who hold ordinary jobs but cultivate small patches of land as a side business make up the regular membership of the great majority of local co-ops.[422] This group dominates their leadership and prevents such concessions to larger farmers being instituted.[423]

Member farmers of Nokyo who aim to expand farm scale and improve productivity are the ones most often in conflict with the agricultural cooperatives over prices of farm inputs and are operating more and more outside the co-op system. As a result, full-time larger-scale farmers are a shrinking minority amongst co-op members and a diminishing part of Nokyo's total business. Full-time farmers' rating of Nokyo's enterprises is, on balance, very negative. In their view, the businesses into which Nokyo puts a lot of effort do not match the needs of full-time farmers.[424] For its part, Nokyo is worried about the emergence of independent farmers who have their own ideas about farm management and who are not dependent on Nokyo and its businesses. Indeed, they are increasingly considered as rivals to Nokyo.[425]

Nokyo's attitude towards supplying credit to larger-scale farm households tends to be punitive, rejecting proposals for loans from farmers who do not purchase materials from the co-ops and who do not comply with rice acreage reduction directives.[426] Nokyo tries to hold farmers captive and dependent on the agricultural cooperative system through their credit advances for agricultural materials and through loans for expensive machinery. Farmers are sometimes forced to use Nokyo on the strength of the loan which inhibits their independent action. The subsidy system is used in the same way: it helps Nokyo control independent farmers. Although the MAFF has the authority to decide whether or not particular agriculture-related projects will be funded with government money, it often entrusts this decision to Nokyo. Considerable quantities of subsidies including from the Agricultural Modernisation Fund, the Rice Acreage Reduction Promotion Subsidy and payments under the new rice policy are allocated through Nokyo.[427] Farmers who cooperate with Nokyo are advantaged in terms of subsidy acquisition, while independent farmers who are hostile to Nokyo have their subsidy requests rejected.[428]

In relation to these kinds of actions, the Fair Trade Commission has warned Nokyo 11 times concerning possible violations of the Anti-Monopoly Law.[429]

Nokyo's actions in this respect are inevitably counterproductive. As long as it continues to behave in this way, enterprising farmers will continue to leave the *nokyo*, which will make agricultural cooperative management even harder.[430] From 1994 onwards, the MAFF began to offer special loans as working capital exclusively to farm households who were eager to expand the scale of production. The allocation of these loans was entrusted to representatives of municipal governments as well as to Nokyo in order to avoid manipulation by agricultural cooperative officials.[431]

Another increasingly common view amongst full-time, larger-scale entrepreneurial farmers is that Nokyo no longer serves their need for technical guidance. Farmers who are anxious to improve their productivity and efficiency have criticised the quality of technical expertise possessed by Nokyo staff members. According to polls taken amongst Nokyo's farmer members in 1994, an average of just under 60 per cent thought that Nokyo should strengthen its farm guidance operations, followed by an average of 47 per cent who thought Nokyo should strengthen its marketing activities.[432] Many of the better farmers are leaving the agricultural cooperatives on the grounds that they cannot rely on Nokyo for farm management guidance.[433] One Hokkaido cattle farmer described the full-time employees of his local Nokyo as 'semi-pros', 'lacking in any really useful expertise in cattle-farming but very interested in preserving their jobs.'[434] In his view, the farmers in his area existed 'for the benefit of Nokyo employees, not the other way round.'[435]

Another weakness is Nokyo's shortage of personnel familiar with farmland issues. The strength of Nokyo's farm guidance has been mainly in management and distribution and it has left agricultural land problems to other groups such as the agricultural committees, city town and village offices and the land improvement districts.[436] Part of the reason is that Nokyo retains a strong antipathy to the scale expansion of individual farm households and farm household selection. This is reflected in Nokyo's vision of the future 'bearers' of agriculture, which mainly targets regional initiatives such as the cultivation of regional agricultural management groups (*chiiki eino shudan*). Nokyo vehemently opposed the government's structural policies which focused on the creation of 'viable farms' managed by the larger-scale, more efficient farmers, because they engaged only some of its members selectively. The regional collective production units, on the other hand, included all its members and envisaged the agricultural cooperatives' playing a key role.[437] It represented a new Nokyo structural policy to promote agricultural land use adjustment and regional agricultural management groups.[438] It was also an attempt to come to grips with some of the fundamental structural problems of Japanese agriculture by devising schemes that would benefit Nokyo.

This particular proposal focused on reorganising agricultural production by converting lands from rice production to other commodities and the formation of a collective land utilisation system to deal with the problem of Type II part-time farmers making insufficient use of their agricultural lands and with whose agreement a new group utilisation system could be set in place. Under this plan, Nokyo would facilitate the mobilisation of land from part-time farm households to farm households that would take responsibility for agricultural production as so-called agricultural 'bearers'.

This was a comprehensive plan to promote the reorganisation of agricultural production and management by mobilising land and consolidating production units under Nokyo's auspices. Nokyo subsequently declared at its convention of 1988 that it planned to organise regional collective production units covering two-thirds of farm land in Japan. This was an ambitious plan, however, which has not been realised to the degree envisaged.[439]

The regional farm management collectives have become the centre of Nokyo's farm guidance activities and only in this respect have agricultural land problems become an issue. A systematic Nokyo policy for the scale expansion of individual farm management has hardly been considered.[440] What is needed is co-op personnel with knowledge of settling complicated interests amongst farmers, as well as those who can develop concrete plans to expand individual production units. Few Nokyo branches have such officials. Most of the branch executives lack strong leadership in this area.[441]

Nokyo fears that the higher class of farmers will abandon their membership of the agricultural cooperatives when the expansion of selected households progresses. Indeed, those most critical of Nokyo's agricultural management policies are full-time farmers who are engaging in scale expansion. Groups of these farmers have begun to organise commodity-specific managers' conferences of their own, demanding individual scale enlargement management through the National Chamber of Agriculture.[442] According to many farmers who wanted to expand the scale of rice production, their efforts should have received more support from the agricultural cooperatives, which no longer seemed to represent individual farmers' interests in relation to scale expansion of production.[443]

Differences also emerged amongst different types of rice producers during the 1980s with respect to the virtues and vices of the FC system. Those farmers who produced good quality rice had less to fear from partial FC reform and an increment in the share of semi-controlled rice because they could get good prices even in a more liberalised market. In high quality rice-producing areas (like Niigata, where about 90 per cent of rice was traded under the semi-controlled IDR system), there was pressure to enlarge the share of rice sold through this system. In other areas, however, the farmers and Nokyo wanted the IDR share left untouched in order to prevent the price from going down. This was the majority view in Hokkaido, for example, where the rice was of lower quality and where only about half the rice was traded under the IDR system. The same argument was used by Nokyo against liberalisation as a whole: it would drive up the prices of good quality rice to the point where only the rich could afford it, whereas the prices for poorer quality rice would drop severely.[444]

Differences amongst rice producers were reflected in internal differences within the agricultural cooperative organisation. The co-ops in areas that depended mainly on income from rice were extremely concerned about rice problems, the producer rice price and the maintenance of the FC system. Agricultural cooperatives in other areas were less so. Nokyo's virulent anti-reform posture thus began to produce divisions within its own ranks because the larger, more efficient farmers wanted some loosening of the FC system. In 1986, the All-Japan Rice Farm Managers' Conference (a gathering of full-time, larger-scale rice producers) declared that 'the FC system hinders independence in the development of business. A mechanism permitting independent production and sales by enthusiastic producers within the frame-work of the FC system should be introduced.'[445]

When the first steps towards liberalising the domestic rice collection and distribution market were taken in 1990,[446] three rice growers jointly obtained a licence to serve as rice collectors because they were dissatisfied with prices at which their local agricultural cooperative bought the rice from members.[447] The farmers' application was strongly opposed by their local cooperative 'on the grounds that it would ruin the unity of local farmers.'[448]

The debate about Nokyo (*nokyoron*)

Since the late 1980s, Nokyo's manifest organisational shortcomings have been the subject of considerable debate, with a phenomenon called '*nokyoron*' undergoing something of a 'quiet boom'.[449] According to Saeki, *nokyoron* consists of three types of critique, which are not necessarily mutually exclusive. The first focuses on Nokyo's fundamental principles and ideals, discussing how Nokyo should operate in general and abstract terms on the basis of the philosophy of cooperative unionism.[450] One critique argues that Nokyo's three pillars are its constitution as a cooperative union of farmers, the refund of surpluses (back to members) and the non-profit motive. Because the numbers of non-farm household members of Nokyo have risen, so have actions violating this fundamental precept.[451] As pointed out in chapter 2, Article 1 of the Nokyo Law stipulates that 'the purpose of this law is to promote the development of farmers' cooperative unions, and thereby to promote agricultural productivity and elevate farmers' economic and social position, as well as to promote the development of the national economy'.[452] Factors promoting the productivity of farmers, however, are reductions in costs such as the prices of agricultural materials, and a lowering of interest rates and commissions. The federations and central unions have not made efforts or produced effective results in any of these respects.[453]

Similarly, Article 8 of Nokyo Law stipulates that local cooperatives shall not conduct business for the purpose of making profit, although the *rengokai* clearly aim to generate a profit from their businesses. The federations have a volume of transactions similar to those of first class trading companies, and receive commissions from members in their purchasing and sales business.[454] The federated Nokyo organisation also has a large number of related companies, although it is contrary to the principle of cooperative unionism for them to own jointstock companies.[455]

The second stream of *nokyoron* has emerged as a result of whistleblowing by Nokyo officials and those pushing for internal reforms. Executive and staff members of the *tankyo* and *rengokai* have criticised agricultural cooperative management and tried to suggest concrete reform measures based on their own experience. Their views have also been shared by some journalist-observers of Nokyo. Much of this criticism has centred around Nokyo's lack of accountability to its rice-roots members, its costly operational and staff structure, and the burden of operational expenses borne by the Nokyo membership. According to one farmer, 'Nokyo demands that farmers engage in large-scale rationalisation and cost reductions in order to cope with liberalisation, but the *sogo nokyo* and the *keizairen* do nothing to respond to liberalisation. They should reduce their personnel numbers to lower the burden on farmers.'[456]

Funds for the activities of the *chuokai*, for example, are collected from levies imposed on their organisational members who therefore bear the burden of operational expenses. The composition of the general levies in *kenchu* is about 45 per cent from the *tankyo* and 55 per cent from the *rengokai*. The total budget for the *kenchu* and Zenchu is around ¥50 billion. The vast proportion of the budgets of these organisations is supplied from membership levies, which are paid by the *tankyo* and *rengokai*, but which ultimately come from individual farmer members. Zenchu's personnel expenses of around ¥1.4 billion, for example, are raised by the national federations, such as Zenno, Norinchukin and the prefectural federations.[457]

The *rengokai* and *nokyo* are often critical of the *chuokai*, arguing that they do not really deserve the fees they collect from the federations and lower-level organisations. At the same time, local branches still expect and demand a great deal from the central unions. This is because they are incapable of responding to the changes in the agricultural cooperative environment without support from upper-level organisations. Local branches tend to expect the central unions to deal with complicated issues before improving their own capabilities. The central unions, however, have so far failed to meet the expectations or demands of local branches and therefore the latter are becoming increasingly dissatisfied with the performance of the *chuokai*.[458]

One specific criticism is that the calculation of levies imposed on the Nokyo branches lacks transparency. Members end up paying expenses for activities with no information provided back to them by the *chuokai*. All details about how much money is used, what it is used for, the proportions in which money is allocated between co-op members and co-ops, and the proportions allocated to different businesses are completely unknown. The central unions fear that if they publish such details, they will be pressured and criticised by their members, who may subsequently refuse to pay levies. Ambiguity, in other words, is indispensable to *chuokai* interests. The result is that large amounts of money are collected from farmers in an untransparent manner.[459]

Another major criticism directed at Nokyo by its own officials centres on the three-stage distribution system of agricultural commodities and inputs which adds to farmers' production costs and reduces their income from the sale of agricultural products. The ideal method, according to these officials, is for business transactions to be made and completed within the *tankyo*, cutting out the upper-level federations altogether. Farmers need simply to pack agricultural products and have the *tankyo* ship them to markets and wholesalers. No complicated three-step marketing route is necessary to deliver agricultural products.[460] If the *rengokai* were abolished, the incomes of professional farmers would double, and more people would be attracted to farming as an occupation.[461] The main cause of Japan's 'hopeless agriculture' can thus be attributed to the three-stage structure of Nokyo, particularly the existence of the federations which undermine the interests of the farmers.[462]

The third stream of the *nokyoron* is a critique of Nokyo by scholars, journalists, management consultants and business people based on comparisons with corporate enterprise. Such appraisal often advances ideas for reforming Nokyo by taking concrete examples from successful enterprises in the non-agricultural sector. The focus of commentary is on Nokyo's outdated business characteristics and management practices.[463] Firstly, the number of personnel running agricultural cooperative businesses is well in excess of what would be permitted in a normal company. Secondly, because Nokyo operates like a commercial enterprise and has continued to expand over three to four decades, it needs personnel with appropriate managerial capabilities. In Fujitani's view, individual branches lack sufficient managerial function and therefore, Nokyo must develop capable executives for local branches. In short, the top management function of the local branches is underdeveloped. Most Nokyo executives lack sufficient managerial knowhow to run a cooperative business group.[464]

Sakaguchi, for example, has criticised the lack of specialist financial expertise in the local *nokyo*, the easy credit made available to companies and individuals without proper checks, collusive connections between Nokyo leaders and local bosses (*yuryokusha*) resulting in illegal investments and the purchase of bad real estate based on personal connections, the lack of responsibility of the *nokyo* in handling big loans, poor personnel management practices in local co-op credit operations and the resulting bad debts, improper financing, and so on.[465]

Domon, on the other hand, targets Nokyo's subsidised role in the FC system. He accuses the agricultural cooperatives of sitting with their legs crossed on subsidies and leaving their management weak.[466] He cites the example of stock control of rice by the Nokyo economic federations. Because the Food Agency took care of unsold rice by compensating for warehousing and interest costs, the *keizairen* put no real effort into marketing it.[467]

Nokyo-bashing

Nokyo-bashing is a more extreme version of *nokyoron*. It takes the form of media and public condemnation of Nokyo's modus operandi as well as open government criticism and scrutiny of the agricultural cooperatives. It reflects a marked deterioration in Nokyo's standing in government circles and amongst the public in general. It has resulted in a degree of reform to the way in which Nokyo is monitored and supervised by the government.

The first major episode of 'Nokyo bashing' occurred in 1986 and arose out of Nokyo's blatant use of political tactics in the producer rice price campaign of that year. Zenchu openly used prospective support from farmers in the impending 1986 double elections as a negotiating tool to extract a commitment from LDP Diet members to support the existing price in the face of recommendations from the MOF and MAFF that it be cut by several per cent.[468] More than 80 per cent of the LDP's candidates were induced by Zenchu to sign documents in which they pledged themselves to oppose any reduction in the producer rice price.[469]

Nokyo's tactics, and the resulting turnaround in the government's policy from a proposed reduction – in line with the government's fiscal and agricultural policy priorities – to a rice price freeze, aroused unprecedented public criticism.[470] As Sakaguchi explains, this was the first time the general public showed any real interest in agricultural issues and it was also the first time Nokyo was widely condemned in the media.[471] Nokyo was called a 'monster choking Japanese agriculture . . . This gigantic organization, which controls every aspect of Japanese agriculture from credit to fertilizers, has built itself into an empire on the foundation of the Government's agricultural policy of overprotection over the decades.'[472]

Thereafter, media criticism of Nokyo continued on a range of issues. In the late 1980s, commentators 'blamed Nokyo for holding up the modernisation of Japanese farming, and for blocking attempts by farmers themselves to adopt a more entrepreneurial approach.'[473] Other media appraisals accused Nokyo of 'disadvantaging Japanese farmers by selling farm inputs at three times their world prices and by involving itself in land speculation'.[474]

Nokyo was directly challenged by the government in the wake of the 1986 producer rice price debacle. In late 1986, Tamaki Kazuo, who was Director-General of the Management and Coordination Agency (MCA) in the Nakasone administration, lambasted Nokyo for seeking to protect its own interests at the expense of farmers, and for pursuing the business of non-farmer associate members in its insurance and banking enterprises. He attacked Nokyo for having 'strayed too far from its original objectives',[475] and for being too concerned with trying to exercise political influence and expand its financial activities. He also asserted that Nokyo was simply 'too powerful in relation to the number of farmers in Japan.'[476]

Tamaki's comments preceded an official scrutinisation of Nokyo launched by the MCA in 1987, its first-ever administrative inspection of the agricultural cooperatives. The move was interpreted as a 'pay back' for Nokyo's victory over the government in the 1986 producer rice price campaign and as displaying the government's intention to take on the agricultural cooperatives.[477] Prime Minister (PM) Nakasone, using Tamaki as his ally and the MCA as an instrument of the executive arm, was keen to capitalise on public opinion in order to undermine Nokyo's power and influence. As Kanagawa observes, the official investigation helped to 'focus public attention on the previously unchecked agricultural cooperative movement'.[478] It broke the long-standing taboo on the government's criticising Nokyo[479] and unequivocally indicated that Nokyo's status as 'a sacred organisation . . . [was] changing'.[480] To Nokyo's defenders, it was deliberately designed to give the public the impression that Nokyo was doing something very bad.[481]

As the MCA did not have the official authority to inspect Nokyo directly, the actual investigation was undertaken by the MAFF, which possessed the requisite administrative and supervisory authority. Both the MAFF and Nokyo were initially unwilling to submit relevant materials to the MCA and appealed to LDP agricultural policy leaders.[482] In spite of the appeals, the inspection went ahead as planned, looking at a total of 98 cooperatives.[483] Its objective was to scrutinise Nokyo's business operations with a view to evaluating their centrality to agricultural cooperative enterprise. If necessary it aimed to force Nokyo to cut back on some of its business operations.

The MCA report entitled *Nokyo Gyosei Kansatsu* (An Administrative Inspection of Nokyo) was released in June 1988. It criticised the way in which the local *nokyo* ran their affairs and called for tighter supervision by the MAFF.[484] It alleged that agricultural cooperative members were not properly informed about management of the *nokyo* and were unable to reflect their demands in the management of their local cooperative; that Nokyo's activities were not in keeping with the character of its original duty to contribute to members and improve agricultural productivity; that members did not receive the benefits they deserved by participating in agricultural cooperative activities; that *nokyo* management was not effective and rational and that management inspections were not properly conducted; and that the agricultural cooperatives had been neglecting farm management guidance.[485] The report found that advisers sent by the co-ops supposedly to give technical advice to farmers spent more time trying to sell them loans, insurance policies and other financial services.[486] It also noted that Nokyo charged exorbitant fees for providing goods where their near-monopoly position was underpinned by law or administrative sanction. At a more fundamental level, the report accused the agricultural cooperatives of spending too much time pursuing profits and juggling their assets in financial markets.

The results of the MCA inspection were made public in the middle of the 1988 beef and orange liberalisation negotiations with the United States. Whether or not the timing was intentional, the litany of Nokyo shortcomings it disclosed reportedly enabled the MAFF and the international faction of the

LDP's agriculture and forestry tribe Diet members (*norin zoku*)[487] to gain a tailwind for a 'soft landing' to liberalisation.[488] In any event, the protests from Nokyo were muted.[489]

In spite of the MCA report's political utility in the context of trade liberalisation, the value of the administrative inspection in rectifying Nokyo's obvious internal management deficiencies and distorted organisational objectives, was fairly limited. In the final analysis it was more a political gesture by the government than a serious attempt to reform the agricultural cooperatives. It was also weakened by Tamaki's death soon after it was launched.[490] Although another separate inquiry was launched into the workings of the cooperatives by PM Takeshita in 1988,[491] predictably, this was no more effective than the first in bringing about innovation in Nokyo's management and business practices.

Nevertheless, the idea that Nokyo should get back to its basic role as a farmers' cooperative rather than a financial conglomerate attracted support from within the LDP itself,[492] including from the head of the agricultural policy section of the LDP Secretariat, Iwakura Tomomitsu. He argued that what Nokyo needed was to ' "return to its starting point" – to stop functioning as a profit-oriented conglomerate and to rediscover its role as an organisation for helping farmers'.[493] In much the same vein, a caustic report from the MOF in early 1992 called Nokyo a self-interested, profit-seeking organisation, not a public interest organisation. In June 1992, the MAFF followed up with a more moderately critical 'Research Report Relating to the Nokyo System', which expressed the ministry's view of the undesirability of the agricultural cooperatives' continuing to increase their non-farmer associate membership simply to generate more profit.[494] Although the MAFF was generally opposed to the uncontrolled expansion of Nokyo's associate membership, the MAFF had basically closed its eyes to the associate membership system of the agricultural cooperatives because Nokyo could put powerful pressure on the MAFF.[495]

Yet another focus of Nokyo bashing in the mid-1990s was the allegedly profligate and dishonest way in which the agricultural cooperatives used government subsidies. The media reported misallocation of funding for 58 Agricultural Management Centres which were supposed to improve farm management by offering information about soil and production control to farmers. The monies reportedly ended up being deployed for the administration of Nokyo branches.[496] The Agriculture, Forestry and Fisheries Section of the Board of Audit later commented that 'Nokyo lacks managerial capabilities and thoughts of profit. It does not consider carefully whether the facilities it is planning to develop are really necessary, or if there will be enough users. Nor does Nokyo put enough effort into promoting the use of new facilities after they are established.'[497] The *Asahi Shinbun* followed with the ascerbic observation that: 'As long as the interests of the MAFF, which are needed to justify subsidies, and Nokyo, which is greedy for subsidies, are compatible, then such a system can be sustained. In an era of agricultural and fiscal reform, however, the subsidy relationship with Nokyo has become an increasing burden on the MAFF.'⁴⁹⁸

In a more recent development, the MAFF has put Nokyo under the overall supervision of a new Cooperatives Inspection Department within the MAFF Minister's Secretariat. The department is responsible for inspecting all agricultural, forestry and fisheries cooperatives, combining the functions of the inspection units that used to be located separately within the Economic Affairs Bureau (with jurisdiction over Nokyo) and the Forestry and Fisheries Agencies (with jurisdiction over the forestry and fisheries cooperatives). This administrative innovation is designed to put greater distance between groups responsible for supervision (the Nokyo Division in the Economic Affairs Bureau, for example) and inspection (the new Inspection Department) and thus improve the uniformity and efficiency of inspection.⁴⁹⁹

Nokyo's financial and management crisis

Over the past decade, the flaws in Nokyo's management practices and its crucial dependencies on highly regulated and protected markets have been exposed. Growth rates in Nokyo's businesses began to slow in the mid- to late 1980s, with the impact particularly felt by Nokyo's trust business and also by its marketing and purchasing businesses, which began to demonstrate negative growth rates in 1993.⁵⁰⁰

A number of factors have contributed to this turnaround in Nokyo's business fortunes. As Domon argues, the two main pillars of agricultural cooperative management – rice and trust business – have been exposed to three kinds of liberalisation: import liberalisation, financial liberalisation and liberalisation of the FC system.⁵⁰¹ All three liberalisations have forced Nokyo to function in a much more competitive environment. While the influence of farm trade liberalisation and FC reform has been indirect and has affected the distribution and marketing of agricultural products through the agricultural cooperative system, financial liberalisation has impacted directly on Nokyo management as a result of intensifying competition in financial markets and thus loss of profits from trust business. Many agricultural cooperative officials have complained that the speed of financial liberalisation was so fast they were not able to keep up.⁵⁰² Basically financial liberalisation undermined the stable and restricted financial order in which weak *nokyo* were able to survive.⁵⁰³

Nokyo's banking operations were hard hit by financial liberalisation for several reasons. Firstly, the liberalisation of interest on small deposits for individual customers was of crucial significance and shook Nokyo to its very foundation.⁵⁰⁴ Deregulation of interest rates meant Nokyo could no longer depend on its high interest rate strategy because of its high cost of financing relative to other private financial institutions. Its three-layered management structure was expensive and inflexible, which disadvantaged Nokyo in the interest rate war.⁵⁰⁵ Private credit unions and banks, for example, could match

Nokyo's terms to depositors. As a result of greater competition over interest rates, the long-term interest rate on deposits offered by Nokyo ended up being 0.5–1.5 per cent lower than its competitors.[506] The *sogo nokyo* thus started to experience greater difficulty in attracting large deposits in spite of their local links with members.[507] Cooperatives hurt the most were those on the outskirts of cities which relied on their financial-service business for the bulk of their earnings.[508] Part-time farmers switched to other financial organs to obtain better interest rates.

Secondly, the increased competition for both deposits and loans raised interest rates for deposits, whilst keeping rates for loans at a low and stable level, squeezing the agricultural cooperatives by contracting margins between deposit and loan interest rates.[509] Profits on credit operations dwindled as a direct result. The agricultural cooperatives were doubly disadvantaged by the fact that the interest rate they had to pay their customers on their savings was higher than the interest rate received on the deposit of their funding in the prefectural credit federations. In 1996, for example, the average annual interest rate agricultural cooperatives paid on deposits was 1.6 per cent, whilst they earned only 1.1 per cent on their deposits in the prefectural credit federations.[510]

Thirdly, as the consumption of Nokyo loans began to contract, a number of other financial agencies started to design loans targeting private customers. As a result, the deposit-loan rate (loans as a percentage of deposits) in the agricultural cooperatives declined, further cutting profits from credit business.[511] In some cases, the *sogo nokyo* were flush with funds they could not lend out.

The deterioration in the profitability of Nokyo's trust business basically turned core agricultural cooperative members, who had been good supporters of trust operations, away from this business. In short, it weakened members' links with the agricultural cooperatives.[512] In fact, Nokyo's percentage share of farm households' savings and loans had been declining steadily over the period 1975 to 1990, falling from 43.2 per cent to 34.8 per cent of farmers' savings and 58.3 per cent to 42.6 per cent of their loans respectively.[513] Other financial institutions such as the postal savings system and city banks picked up the difference. The share held by general banks of farmers' total deposits moved upwards from 21.0 per cent in 1975 to 23.8 per cent in 1990, while for loans it leapt from 10.3 per cent to 25.4 per cent over the same period.[514] In 1996, the outstanding balance of deposits in the *sogo nokyo* dropped 0.9 per cent from a year before – to ¥67,603.6 billion.[515] Financial competition was clearly making inroads into Nokyo's lending business to farmers.

The contraction in Nokyo's loan share was also attributed to the reluctance of some agricultural cooperatives to lend money to farmers because agriculture remained an unattractive target for investment, and to provide loans suitable for part-time farmers such as housing loans.[516] Another trend was for some local co-ops to become separated from their farmer members in the suburbs. When farmers sold their land, the co-ops could not supply the necessary advice about the deployment of funds.[517] Furthermore, while suburban *nokyo* were busy collecting associate members and increasing their use of agricultural cooperative services (especially banking services) in competition with private financial institutions, they were not prepared to open their books to the scrutiny of these members, unlike private companies. Even regular members were offered limited information about financial management. Because of the failure to provide both regular and associate members with the type of information that private companies provided, customers continued to shift their funds from Nokyo to other financial institutions.[518]

Fourthly, and most importantly, the contribution of financial business to overall management contracted.[519] Because agricultural cooperative management had been carried on the back of its trust business, successive waves of financial liberalisation had a profound effect on the overall financial health of the cooperatives.[520] Basically financial liberalisation did not allow the old stable structure of dependence on co-op credit operations to continue.[521] Profits from agricultural cooperative financial business kept shrinking,[522] which compelled other co-op businesses to rationalise their operations and lower their deficits to compensate. The implication was that the agricultural cooperatives could not get along if their financial business could not generate profits.[523]

As already noted, agricultural cooperative profit and loss by sector generally showed black figures in the trust and mutual aid sectors consistently supporting the deficits in other sectors, such as purchasing, marketing, warehousing and utilisation of processing facilities.[524] Over many years, this state of affairs had enabled management to post black figures overall. Cross-subsidisation meant that the co-ops could use profits from financial business to fund services and benefits to farmers which ran at a loss.

One cooperative in Kanagawa, for example, charged 40 per cent less for funerals than those arranged through funeral homes in the city. It also subsidised some of the medical expenses of its members, paid dividends of 6 per cent to its members as well as interest to depositors of 0.3 per cent above interest on ordinary accounts in banks. At the same time, the drop in the volume of farm products being shipped was making the co-ops' marketing business increasingly unprofitable. These services for members were sustainable only because they were funded by profits from the co-ops' financial and insurance businesses, which also bore the brunt of the administrative expenses of the co-op.

When the credit business of the agricultural cooperatives began to decline, however, its rate of contribution to Nokyo management (i.e. the proportion of black figures from the trust business to total management black figures) began to fall.[525] The management contribution rate of trust business dropped from 185 per cent in 1975 to 121 per cent in 1980 and 86 per cent in 1988.[526] These falls reflected reductions in trust business profits. The financial business of Nokyo thus ceased to be a reliable source of profit.

Deteriorating financial performance began to put pressure on the agriculture-related business of the *tankyo*. Quite clearly, if the financial service business collapsed, the co-ops could not continue to conduct agricultural and trading activities.[527] Although, on the surface, management looked stable, its performance was often worse than the accounts showed. In addition, the gap in performance between individual co-op branches widened, with some cooperatives in more serious financial straits than others.

Furthermore, if management rationalisation became an issue, the co-ops would inevitably take another look at functions such as farm management guidance, which had consistently been unprofitable and which would be first in line for cuts. This, in turn, would have a compounding effect on Nokyo's structural policies, such as land use adjustment and the establishment of regional agricultural management units, which consumed much time and labour power but which generated limited returns, resulting in deficits for farm guidance business. In short, structural policies were a minus for Nokyo in times of financial crisis.[528] Under the circumstances, it became difficult for cooperatives to spare energy and resources for areas with such small and indirect returns.[529]

The impact of financial liberalisation was not only to reduce Nokyo's profits, but also to increase the risks taken by management in financial business.[530] Nokyo offered more credit to various debtors in order to compete with other financial agencies. It also increased its investment in the stock market, with its associated risks. In addition, Nokyo collected relatively short-term deposits and invested them for the long term. However, in the liberated financial market, short-term and long-term interest rates did not change in tandem. When short-term interest rates increased more than long-term interest rates, the interest payments on deposits exceeded the interest gained from investment.

Finally, the collapse of the bubble economy which began in 1989 had a more critical impact on Nokyo's financial operations than on those of other private financial institutions such as the city banks.[531] The crisis also exposed all the other problems in Nokyo management: top echelons unskilled in financial matters,[532] substantial losses on the stock market and increasing amounts of bad loans,[533] including those to non-banking financial agencies.[534]

For example, the ratio of Nokyo-federated finance held in stocks and bonds increased to about 50 per cent of total assets in the early 1990s. Historically Nokyo finance had been used mainly to purchase only government bonds, financial bonds and special juridical corporation bonds, that is, government and public bonds. But in 1990 Nokyo's financial management rules were revised to permit investment in high-risk stocks which potentially yielded a high return. Unfortunately, agricultural cooperative financial officers were often not familiar with the stock market, and because of this inexperience, many Nokyo financial institutions suffered substantial losses from handling stocks. The prefectural credit federations in particular suffered considerable losses on stock exchange dealings.[535] Following the plunge in stock prices with the bursting of the economic bubble, huge losses were posted by some credit federations.[536] In the closing accounts of the 47 prefectural trust federations in March 1991, three trust federations – in Akita, Miyagi and Kagoshima – were forced to register losses – the first such losses since Tottori *shinren* registered a loss in March 1982. The three trust federations could pay neither capital dividends nor special dividends from surplus funds to their *nokyo* members.[537]

The *tankyo* also suffered from bad investments. In 1988, one particular *nokyo* in the Kanto region suffered a combined loss of ¥3.4 billion resulting from investment failures on the stock market. If this loss had been admitted in the final settlement of its accounts in that year, its liabilities would probably have exceeded its assets and it would have been forced to use reserve funds as well as members' capital.[538] Other *tankyo* recorded similar failures. Tochigi City Nokyo, for example, had been offering loans to local real estate companies for nearly 10 years, reaching a total of more than ¥10 billion. Of this amount, nearly ¥3 billion was said to be unrecoverable owing to the insolvency of the borrowers. The cooperative earned only ¥42 million in net profits in fiscal 1994. The explanation for the situation was that the screening of borrowers had been lax, partly because few managers within the *nokyo* had the necessary financial expertise.[539] A number of similar situations occurred in other cooperatives, including an incident in Ibaraki, where the co-op chairman committed suicide to take responsibility for the huge amount of bad loans caused by sloppy management.[540] Unfortunately for Nokyo, the management crisis in large numbers of *tankyo* became a management crisis in the *shinren* because of the ripple effect on all agricultural cooperatives in the prefecture in the form of a reduction in all types of bounties and investment dividends.[541]

These sorts of problems in Nokyo's financial management had been pointed out by commentators and critics before the deteriorating financial and economic conditions in Japan led to their full exposure.[542] Sakaguchi, for example, identified embezzlement by Nokyo staff members, lack of proper checking of loan applicants, and the influence of local bosses on obtaining credit from the agricultural cooperatives as constant problems in the financial management of the cooperatives.[543] There were repeated individual cases of financial mismanagement involving embezzlement and financial misappropriation by local *tankyo* executives. The frequency with which such financial scandals occurred was put down to the fact that the transactions were conducted and decided by 'men of power' and their subordinates in secret rooms. Although *kenchu* and prefectural government personnel often had knowledge of these criminal activities, they did not take action because the local *nokyo* leaders were usually influential men in their own areas. Therefore, no one, not even the prefectural governor, was prepared to raise questions about their misconduct.[544]

Within Nokyo itself, some bad loans and stock market problems were recognised and measures were taken to deal with them. However, the volume of bad loans to non-banking institutions continued to increase. In 1994, a survey by the Teikoku Data Bank put the total value of loans by agricultural cooperative financial institutions to the non-banking institutions at ¥12.5 trillion.[545] Of these ¥6.2 trillion were to housing finance companies (*jutaku senmon kinyu gaisha*, or *jusen*), a volume described as 'unusual' considering the capacity of Nokyo's financial institutions.[546] The *jusen* were one of the major categories of non-banking financial organisations set up by the banks in 1971.[547] Nokyo's financial institutions lent heavily to these housing loan companies 'in order to cash in on the lucrative home loan market.'[548] Collectively they were the largest creditor (42.2 per cent) to the *jusen*. When the 'bubble' economy collapsed, the major housing loan companies were left with bad debts.[549] As a result, credits to these companies from Nokyo became uncollectable. The increase in uncollected bills put severe pressure on financial management within the Nokyo system.[550]

The *jusen* issue both catalysed and symbolised the crisis in Nokyo's financial affairs. Norinchukin posted a ¥54 billion net loss in fiscal 1995, its first loss in the postwar period.[551] Nearly half the 47 prefectural credit federations were also estimated to have recorded net losses in fiscal 1995. A major factor in these losses was shouldering a portion of the bad loans to the *jusen*.[552] In Fukushima Prefecture, for example, the *shinren* ended up with ¥3.7 billion in bad credit to the Northern Japan Development Company which subsequently went bankrupt with a debt of ¥14.5 billion. The loan had been allocated by the *shinren* on the request of its chairman. Rumours circulated of involvement by local politicians, which, as Domon points out, was typical in these cases because of Nokyo's close involvement with politics.[553] Local politicians allegedly colluded with the *shinren* chairman to use Nokyo money to provide funds to the developers via a housing loan company (some of which, of course, may have ultimately ended up in the politicians' pockets as political donations). In fact Nokyo's financial mismanagement in real estate deals had been well known for some time, with investments made in an uncontrolled manner at the discretion of those Nokyo officials involved.[554]

According to Nokyo's financial institutions, however, they only became involved with the *jusen* 'because the finance ministry asked the agriculture ministry to secure their support.'[555] In 1990, Nokyo's credit institutions were reportedly so flush with cash that the MOF and MAFF jointly gave the prefectural credit federations special permission to extend loans to the *jusen*.[556] It was, in fact, exceptional for Nokyo's financial institutions to be permitted to make such loans.[557] Strictly speaking, their loan targets were limited to agriculture-related industries. Another excuse given by Nokyo's financial institutions for lending funds to the *jusen* was that 'they had assumed that the founding-bank shareholders stood behind the borrowings.'[559] The President of Norinchukin, Kakudo Kenichi, maintained that: 'We considered the jusen to be a kind of public financial organization and extended loans to them.'[559]

Figures relating to the total exposure of Nokyo to the *jusen* tend to vary according to source and over time. Data submitted to the Budget Committee of the Lower House revealed that the bad credit of Norinchukin and the *shinren* was ¥244.7 billion as of March 1995.[560] *The Economist*, however, reported that the agricultural cooperatives were owed a total of ¥3.4 trillion worth of non-performing loans by December 1992, while Norinchukin 'lent another ¥3 trillion or so on its own account.'[561] The *Nikkei Weekly* later claimed that prefectural Nokyo credit federations, as well as other agricultural financial institutions, accounted for ¥3.3 trillion in outstanding loans to the *jusen*.[562] The latter figure was confirmed by an *Asahi Shinbun* publication that put the *shinren* loss at ¥3.3 trillion and Norinchukin's at ¥0.8 trillion.[563] According to a MAFF source, however, Nokyo's clear loss was about ¥8 trillion, although the real loss was much more.[564] Whatever the figures, it was widely accepted that the prefectural Nokyo credit federations were the single most exposed lender to the *jusen*.[565] Moreover, they stood to lose the ¥250 billion or so a year in interest payments on their loans to these bodies.

As far as Nokyo's farm membership was concerned, precise information concerning agricultural cooperative financial matters was not made available by the central unions and federations, nor were the various financial scandals and credit problems taken up by the Nokyo-related media. Farmers were described as being in a 'complete information desert'.[566] Nokyo also lost a good deal of public credibility over the *jusen* debacle as well as sustaining criticism from a range of quarters, including the MAFF and disaffected elements within its own organisation. Moreover, the way in which the *jusen* issue was resolved further eroded Nokyo's public standing and exposed its gross financial mismanagement and lack of accountability to its members.

In the final settlement that was pushed through the Diet by the LDP coalition government, agricultural cooperative financial institutions won a big victory. Indeed, if no appropriate measures had been taken, about half of the Nokyo organisations involved would have gone bankrupt.[567] The worry was that if a number of *shinren* became insolvent, Nokyo branches would be unable to repay deposits to depositors, including farm households. Fears were also held for the Japanese economy as a whole in the event of generalised insolvency amongst Nokyo's financial institutions. Nokyo's public image was considerably tarnished by the settlement, however, because of the strong impression that the organisation had used its political power to ensure a favourable outcome for its financial institutions.[568] Although the Chairman of Zenchu, Toyoda Hakaru, resigned from his position in order to deflect public criticism, it was widely assumed that the government had to save farmers' deposits because of potential political problems arising from agricultural cooperative and farmers' losses.

The MOF draft for the resolution to the *jusen* issue proposed that the mother banks of the *jusen* would abandon loaned credit of ¥3.5 trillion and other banks ¥1.7 trillion. Nokyo-related organisations were expected to assume a total debt burden of ¥1.21 trillion (to make a total bill of

¥6.4 trillion for the first stage of the *jusen* liquidation plan). Nokyo, however, successfully deployed its massive political influence to reduce its share to only ¥530 billion.[569] Nokyo-related financial institutions insisted that this amount was the maximum burden they could carry.[570] If the outlay were distributed in proportion to lending, Norinchukin would contribute ¥78.4 billion, while the prefectural credit federations would pay ¥323.8 billion. National and prefectural mutual aid federations would throw in a combined ¥127.7 billion.[571] In practice Norinchukin assumed a large proportion of the *shinren* debt burden. The final allocation was as follows: Norinchukin (¥202.4 billion); *shinren* (¥200 billion); Zenkyoren (¥95.7 billion); and *kyosairen* (¥31.9 billion).[572]

The balance of ¥685 billion would be covered by a massive infusion of public funds (from the FY 1996 budget).[573] As the *Nikkei Weekly* observed: 'By exercising their lobbying power, agricultural financial institutions shifted to taxpayers nearly all their nonperforming loans to the *jusen*.'[574] An official of the MOF 'admitted to getting political pressure from Diet members representing the interests of farmers when the *jusen* settlement was made.'[575] Reports also surfaced of politicians bowing to the agricultural cooperatives' clout as vote-gatherers.[576]

The use of ¥680 billion in public funds to write off the massive bad lending by the *jusen* caused public outrage and focused resentment specifically on why Nokyo's financial institutions should be given preferential treatment.[577] The *Nikkei Weekly* commented: 'It was wrong to indiscriminately siphon public money to help the farm banks, on a pretext of protecting depositors and stabilizing the financial system.'[578] If the burden of unrecoverable debts were allocated according to the relative contribution rates of the lenders involved, Nokyo-related financial organisations should have carried a loss of at least ¥3.3 trillion.[579] The mother banks, on the other hand, had to write off their losses in total.

It was never made publicly clear why there was such a big difference in the treatment meted out to the mother banks compared to the Nokyo financial institutions. At the LH budget committee hearings and on various public TV programmes debating the issue, Diet members from both the ruling and Opposition parties hardly mentioned Nokyo's exposure to the *jusen*, and even when they did, they confined their remarks to various abstract comments.[580] Furthermore, although it was decided that the mother banks could receive no interest payments from the *jusen*, Nokyo's financial institutions continued to be paid interest of 4.5 per cent per annum, amounting to approximately ¥0.25 trillion in total per year.[581]

In spite of the special deal extracted from the government, Nokyo still found the figure of ¥530 billion a problem because the contributors to this share of losses had insufficient profits to absorb them. Norinchukin's profits in fiscal 1994 were ¥64.7 billion, while the prefectural credit federations earned ¥130.4 billion and the mutual aid federations ¥25.8 billion.[582] Norinchukin had the advantage of a cushion of reserves and unrealised capital gains, but the others – the prefectural credit federations, and national and prefectural mutual aid federations – each had only thin reserves which meant that liquidating *jusen* debt threatened their very existence. The MAFF estimated that approximately 20 *shinren* would fall into the red under the weight of the *jusen* crisis, with the possibility of their losses driving the entire system of local co-ops to the brink of collapse.[583]

The government subsequently announced a plan to reduce the amount of public contributions to *jusen* creditors by using the proceeds of a fund of around ¥700 billion to be established by the commercial banking community, the Bank of Japan and Nokyo. The banks, especially the founding banks of the *jusen* would put up about ¥500 billion, more than ¥100 billion would be furnished by agricultural cooperative credit institutions and the Bank of Japan would also supply around ¥100 billion. The return on fund investments would be channelled back into government coffers over a period of 15 years to cover a large part of the ¥685 billion in public money earmarked by the Diet to liquidate the *jusen* losses.

The initial MOF plan had been for Nokyo credit institutions to contribute ¥200 billion, while the coalition government plan had called on Nokyo to supply ¥150 billion over seven years through increased tax revenues gained from continued restructuring of the agricultural cooperatives. Meanwhile the cooperative credit institutions considered forgiving unpaid interest on loans extended to the *jusen* of around ¥60 billion.[584] In the end, PM Hashimoto stated that: 'Farm lenders should now think seriously of additional contributions, as they too are financial institutions.'[585]

Nonetheless, the *jusen* debacle illustrated just how cosseted and protected the agricultural cooperatives had been as state-sponsored institutions. The special accommodation given to the Nokyo over the *jusen* issue was nothing unusual in the tradition of national and prefectural governments covering for the financial failures of the agricultural cooperatives over many years. Public funds for *nokyo* mergers and the disposal of failure had been openly used in various forms.[586] What was different about the *jusen* problem, however, was the magnitude of the funds involved and the corresponding magnitude of the crisis facing Nokyo.

Unfortunately for Nokyo's public image, throughout most of the negotiations on the *jusen* issue, the organisation appeared much more devoted to extracting a special deal from the government than to developing policies to restructure its financial businesses and other economic activities in such a way that exposure to financial failure might be reduced or eliminated in the future. According to a rumour circulating in early 1993, Nokyo was even prepared to countenance rice market opening in exchange for agreement on a bail-out plan that spared them the disastrous financial consequences of their rash lending to the *jusen*.[587] Moreover, as Domon observes, the amount transferred to Nokyo from public funds (¥685 billion) might 'only serve as an emergency transfusion that keeps the patient alive somewhat longer . . . Even supposing that the co-ops find a way to dispose of their bad loans to borrowers . . . there remains the question of whether they can survive in open competition with deregulated banks and brokerages.'[588]

The *jusen* were not the only problem of bad loans facing the agricultural cooperative financial institutions. They were also left with bad loans to other non-banks.[589] Exposure was reportedly as much as ¥7.7 trillion.[590] According to financial commentators, whilst Nokyo's credit institutions might have succeeded in escaping the *jusen* problem because public money was used for the bail-out and because Norinchukin and Zenkyoren had stood behind prefectural credit federations as financial backers, as far as Nokyo's exposure to these other non-banks was concerned, it would have to assume responsibility for the bad loans itself. On this occasion Nokyo would have to spend its own money.[591] Because the other non-banks were small in comparison to the *jusen* in the financial system, agricultural cooperative and other major lenders to these institutions could not escape responsibility. As the President of Norinchukin commented: 'I do not think politicians will intervene in that problem because we made the loans at our own risk.'[592]

Although the total amount of bad credit was less than the *jusen* case, the disposal of bad loans in relation to the non-banks was still very serious for Nokyo-related financial organisations.[593] Of the 47 agricultural credit federations, 26 had lending exposure to Crown Leasing, a non-bank affiliate of Nippon Credit Bank. Hyogo *shinren*, for example, attributed almost all its bad-loan increase to the Crown Leasing failure.[594]

Meanwhile, the government's initial plan to bail out the Long-Term Credit Bank of Japan (LTCB) which was associated with one of the major non-bank lenders, Japan Leasing Corporation,[595] was criticised for unduly favouring agricultural cooperative credit suppliers.[596] The plan did not succeed in getting the agreement of the Opposition parties, however.[597] A later move by Japan Leasing to file for bankruptcy protection was calculated as likely to cause losses for about 70 agricultural cooperative financial institutions, which held a combined total of ¥340 billion in outstanding lending to the leasing firm as of the end of May 1998.[598] Depending on the amount of uncollectable loans, some credit federations were expected to post losses in their annual balance sheets, causing a further shakeout of these prefectural entities.[599] In addition to the loans to Japan Leasing, agricultural cooperative credit institutions had loans worth ¥30–40 billion to the two other troubled non-bank affiliates of the LTCB.[600]

Just how large the total problem of bad debts is in the Nokyo organisation is difficult to establish precisely. Because the cooperatives lack organisational transparency and are not subject to disclosure requirements, figures made public cannot be reliably substantiated. In March 1995, the MAFF reported to the Diet that Norinchukin and the *shinren* had bad debts of ¥244.7 billion.[601] The figure was later revised to ¥904.4 billion as of the end of March 1998, with ¥1.42 trillion the figure for Nokyo as a whole (i.e. including the *sogo nokyo*).[602] Another source put the total at ¥1.81 trillion (¥612 billion for Norinchukin and ¥1.2 trillion for lower-tier agricultural cooperatives including the *shinren*).⁶⁰³ None of these figures, however, include agricultural cooperative loans to Japan Leasing or other non-bank financial institutions, which were substantial. Total estimates of bad debts might be higher if the loan portfolios of Nokyo credit institutions were more closely scrutinised.

Prefectural governments are currently mounting massive rescue programmes for municipal agricultural cooperatives within their regions,⁶⁰⁴ and yet despite large allocations from taxpayer funds, they are not willing to press for full disclosure of the financial circumstances of troubled cooperatives, and neither have they made an effort to clarify responsibility amongst the cooperative officials concerned.⁶⁰⁵ The resort to the use of public funds to rescue cooperatives was partly the result of newly introduced financial supervision requirements based on capital-to-asset ratios which could order business improvements or even partial business shutdown of financial institutions. The assistance provided along with other measures such as management efforts or cooperative mergers⁶⁰⁶ meant that most Japanese agricultural cooperatives would be unlikely to face business suspension orders because they could meet the required capital-to-asset ratios.⁶⁰⁷

The process of administration reform, including changes to the institutional framework of financial regulation, has also caught up with Nokyo. As part of the plan for restructuring the MOF proposed in 1996, the new Financial Inspection and Supervision Agency (later retitled Financial Supervisory Agency) was given broad licensing and supervisory powers over private financial institutions under MOF jurisdiction. Supervision was also extended to include the financial activities of the *sogo nokyo* as well as those of other credit cooperatives and workers' cooperatives.⁶⁰⁸ The new entity was established in June 1998.

Intensifying competition in marketing and purchasing

Compounding the crisis on the financial front has been the assault on Nokyo's dominance of sectors such as agricultural marketing and commodity distribution. Attempts to bypass the agricultural cooperatives in marketing have been particularly evident with respect to rice. The established pattern of rice distribution under Nokyo's monopoly began to break down in the early 1990s, even prior to the more substantial reform of the FC system, which occurred with the implementation of the new Staple Food Law in November 1995. Distribution routes bypassing the federated three-stage pattern of local *nokyo* > *keizairen* > Zenno > rice wholesalers under the IDR system became operative, with direct transactions between prefectural *keizairen* and wholesalers.

This was encouraged by the Food Agency along with new entrants into the rice collection business as part of a deliberate policy to break Nokyo's near-monopoly of rice collection.⁶⁰⁹ In 1991 at the uniform renewal of rice collectors, the Food Agency permitted new entrants into the rice collection business, which spurred the spread of price competition amongst new and existing operators.[610] At the renewal, 11 dealers in nine prefectures were authorised.[611]

What was particularly disturbing to Nokyo was that 437 farmers registered with the new rice collection agents, with the overwhelming number from the category of Type II part-time farm households, in other words, those working a greater number of hours annually off the farm. In the past, Nokyo's management had been crucially supported by part-time farm households, but the consciousness that they belonged to Nokyo had obviously begun to diminish.[612] A similar incident was reported in Niigata, where a local dealer (Niigata Nosan Hanbai) who entered the rice wholesaling business in June 1991 successfully managed to wrest from the local village *nokyo* the rice collection business of 44 of its farm household members (out of a total membership of 1219). The incentive motivating farmers to register with the dealer was price. The dealer had added ¥1,000–1,500 per *koku* (60 kg) collected from farmers for the high-quality *koshihikari* from Uonuma, a basin in the southern part of Niigata. Over one ha, this made a difference of ¥100,000–150,000.[613] Such a development sent shock waves through the agricultural cooperatives in Niigata, because growers of this rice brand had traditionally sold to collectors at a uniform price set every year, displeasing rice growers in Uonuma and other areas.[614] From 1991 onwards, the number of agricultural cooperatives operating as primary collectors of rice began to fall steadily, from 70.4 per cent of the total in 1991 to 62.8 per cent in 1994 and 57.8 per cent in 1995.[615]

The Food Agency also sought to undermine Nokyo's dominance of pricing in the IDR system by introducing an auction method for sales of 20 per cent of semi-controlled rice managed by an Independently Distributed Rice Price Formation Organisation (Jishu Ryutsumai Kakaku Keisei Kiko[616]), which was established in August 1990 and which began operations in October 1990.[617] The creation of the IDR Price Formation Organisation was designed to undermine Zenno's dominance in the price formation process for semi-controlled rice and thus lead ultimately to lower rice prices. The Food Agency was concerned that if the share of government rice in the FC system continued to contract, the right to decide the rice price would shift from the Food Agency to Zenno.

Further changes consequent upon the introduction of the IDR Price Formation Organisation served to erode Zenno's near-monopoly in the market for independently distributed rice.[618] Firstly, the Food Agency created a new route through which the *keizairen* could sell rice produced in their own prefectures directly to wholesalers without entrusting the sale to Zenno. This measure aimed to diminish the influence of Zenno on the *keizairen*.

Secondly, the new system introduced more competition into the IDR market. Under the old system, Zenno (virtually as a monopoly supplier) dominated price negotiations with the wholesalers resulting in what wholesalers contended were distorted prices.[619] Prices had been rigidly determined each autumn in price negotiations between Zenno and the rice wholesalers.[620]

The negotiations set unified prices annually for the various brands of rice. This method of fixing prices was never clear and the differential scale between noted brands was almost rigidly fixed.[621]

With the establishment of the new system, the Food Agency broke Zenno's monopoly over price-setting and the system as a whole was made more transparent and diversified in terms of processes and participants. As of 1990, the auction price for commercial rice became the standard price for semi-controlled rice. This meant that independently distributed rice effectively had its price set at auction, not in negotiations between wholesalers and Zenno. Emphasis was placed on transactions centring on bidding between agricultural cooperatives at the prefectural level and wholesalers. The Food Agency even tried to exclude Zenno from the auction system altogether, but because some cooperatives still preferred to commission sales to Zenno, it remained possible for Zenno to participate in transactions, providing its sales share did not exceed 25 per cent.[622] One of the reasons why the *keizairen* continued to entrust the sale of rice to Zenno was because they feared that their direct sales to wholesalers might lead to similar direct sales by the *nokyo*. Moreover, many wholesalers were reluctant to embark on direct sales transactions with the *nokyo*, fearing retaliation by Zenno if there were a rice shortage.[623]

Reports later surfaced, however, of various kinds of price manipulations by Zenno and the *keizairen*. Shortly after the IDR Price Formation Organisation was established, Zenno and the *keizairen*, who were anxious about a fall in rice prices because of over-supply, deliberately raised rice prices by being simultaneously both sellers and buyers in the price formation market. Subsequently, the Fair Trade Commission recommended that the system in which Nokyo organisations could join the bidding as both sellers and buyers should be amended.[624] To make matters worse, reports surfaced of bid-rigging (*dango*) of rice prices in this market. According to one account, the *keizairen* were in the habit of phoning major wholesalers requesting them to put in bids at high prices. The result made a farce out of what was supposed to be genuine price competition. Prices for independently distributed rice shipped through the system in fact rose rather than fell.[625] Furthermore, the *keizairen* continued to promote the shift from low-priced government rice to high-priced quality rice shipped through the IDR system in order to inflate their commission on collection. As a result, high-priced rice varieties continued to be overproduced regardless of supply and demand.[626]

The new Staple Food Law consolidated the partial deregulation of the domestic rice distribution system,[627] permitting farmers to sell rice (so-called 'non-orderly marketed rice', or *keikakugai ryutsumai*) directly to retailers and consumers, thus bypassing the cooperatives altogether. In addition, greater diversification of distribution channels for so-called 'orderly marketed rice' (*keikaku ryutsumai*), which covered the two categories of government rice and independently distributed rice, enabled local co-ops and the *keizairen* to sell rice directly to wholesalers and retailers, thus bypassing elements of the federated Nokyo system.

With the introduction of these changes, some of Nokyo's worst fears have been realised. Although it continues to play an important role in the new food system, particularly in relation to orderly marketed rice,[628] distribution channels have been diversified, and as a consequence, Nokyo's vested rights have been substantially affected.[629] Under the new arrangements, Nokyo will not necessarily maintain its dominance over the collection of either independently distributed rice or rice for government sale.[630] Moreover, the quantity of non-orderly marketed rice has gradually increased, and, as a result, some farmers have left Nokyo because they no longer need the agricultural cooperatives to market their rice. Supermarkets and other retailers have become big buyers of rice directly from farmers. Farmers marketing their rice in this fashion sometimes also use banks as intermediaries, with savings accounts in the banks receiving the payments for rice paid by the supermarkets.[631] Farmers selling rice outside the agricultural cooperative system have found that their real income is higher because of a reduction in trading costs such as marketing commissions which they formerly paid to Nokyo. This situation has encouraged Zenno, with its large share of rice distribution under the IDR system, to increase the price of rice traded through this system in order to encourage farmers to stay in it.[632]

Together with the earlier changes to rice distribution, the reforms of the mid-1990s have forced changes in Nokyo's operating systems and threatened to deprive it of its predominant position in rice collection and distribution. The MAFF acknowledged that Nokyo would be exposed to a more competitive environment, and anticipated that this would force them to provide better service to their members. As far as the Food Agency was concerned, it regarded intensified competition in the rice market as very important and it welcomed newcomers. To this extent, it conceded that Zenno would suffer, but at the same time, it would also have a chance to do business more efficiently. 'If it has a smart idea, it can gain a lot from a more competitive market.'[633]

Rice producers were also expected to become 'more entrepreneurial in rice production and marketing'.[634] In fact, the new food system brought Nokyo into direct conflict with larger scale rice producers who opposed rice acreage reduction policies for obvious reasons (and on whose shoulders this policy mainly fell), and also because of their heavy investment in agricultural machinery. Nokyo, on the other hand, was ever more in favour of the *gentan* because it helped to prevent a significant drop in the price of rice. On these grounds, Nokyo and local governments continued to pressure more efficient rice producers because they disturbed the harmony of agricultural communities.[635]

If, however, farmers are able to sell their rice without using co-op distribution routes at all, growing numbers will inevitably turn away from the agricultural cooperatives. In this respect, the new Staple Food Law is a much greater threat to Nokyo than to farmers' incomes, because rice prices are still administratively determined to some extent. For Nokyo, on the other hand, it is a question of loss of market share which potentially hurts co-op profits not only because commissions from marketing rice have consistently been one of their main revenue sources from marketing business, but also because of a reduction in other fees and subsidies Nokyo obtained from the government under the old FC system.

These actual and potential outcomes from the new Staple Food Law have been offset to some extent by the introduction of the new rice policy in 1998, under which the government continues to underwrite Nokyo's role in a more deregulated rice distribution system.[636] Under this policy, substantial subsidies are paid to Zenno through the FCSA for a number of tasks including 'the harmonious and steady implementation of production adjustment', 'mitigating the influence which falls in the price of independently distributed rice have on rice crop management', 'paying compensation (to farmers) for falls in the price of independently distributed rice from the 1997 rice crop in order to achieve a smooth transition to a new rice policy', and 'achieving smooth deliveries and distribution of independently distributed rice from the 1997 crop following stable delivery and sales routes'.[637] As noted in chapter 2, these subsidies in 1998 amounted to well over ¥130 billion. Nokyo has thus been given substantial responsibility by the government for implementing the new rice policy.[638]

Rice, however, is not the only product where Nokyo's traditional marketing dominance is being challenged. In the 1990s, the agricultural cooperatives have been facing intensifying competition in most other sectors of marketing and purchasing as private traders have moved into their traditional agricultural product and input supply markets. Nokyo's share of these markets has, for the first time, begun to contract 'under the onslaught of non-agricultural capital'.[639]

In this more cut-throat business environment, Nokyo is hampered by several factors. First is its lack of management capability. This has made it an urgent matter for Nokyo to streamline its overall management structure and establish more businesslike operations to enable it to compete with large corporations in the private sector.[640] As Fujitani explains,

> the real Achilles' heel of Japan's nokyo is the lack of effective top management. The farmers who serve as directors in local cooperatives are complete amateurs when it comes to business. Without any expertise in business, they can elect one another to top cooperative posts and savor prestige and a sense of power, but they cannot act as responsible top management executives capable of leading the permanent staff in the endeavor to further the businesses of the cooperatives. This amateurish approach to business may have worked in the decades when nokyo were firmly guided by government, but it is less effective today, when cooperatives must return to the original objectives of the cooperative movement. It is perhaps not an overstatement to say that the survival of nokyo in the 21st century depends on whether they can successfully create a viable system of top management.[641]

The second factor is Nokyo's over-reliance on its traditional socio-cultural basis of membership. Too heavily dependent on the 'natural' organisation of individual agricultural communities and thus on its 'captive' membership base, Nokyo has made little effort to develop a modern organisation founded on rational economic incentives.[642] As traditional village loyalties have weakened, agricultural cooperative leaders have found it increasingly difficult to organise and unite their members. The result is that the very foundations of their organisations are being threatened.[643] As Fujitani puts it, Nokyo has overestimated its 'traditional organisation ability' (*dentoteki soshiki noryoku*) and made little effort to develop its 'modern organisation ability' (*kindaiteki soshiki noryoku*).[644] Nokyo's heavy dependence on the self-organising function of individual agricultural communities has made it vulnerable to the erosion of the social bonds in rural areas. In fact, the organisational ability of Nokyo and the self-organising function of local communities have declined together.[645]

The third factor is Nokyo's complex three-stage distribution system and the fourth, its high labour costs,[646] both of which push up the prices of production inputs and other commodities to farmers, and which reduce their profits from commodity sales. As a result, the organisation is increasingly seen as a structural obstacle to more entrepreneurial-type farming operations. Farmers' awareness of the need to cut production costs has been raised as a result of the growing emphasis in government policy on elevating the productivity, efficiency and international competitiveness of Japanese agriculture. Moreover, in the new more competitive, liberalised environment, full-time entrepreneurial farmers make stronger demands of Nokyo which relate directly to the profitability of their agricultural operations.[647] In the interests of reducing their overheads, many farmers are going outside the cooperatives to do better deals with private companies.

The weight of Nokyo's three-stage management structure hobbles its ability to compete with private traders in domestic agricultural product and input supply markets because it generates uncompetitive prices for goods. It is often difficult for *tankyo* to sell production materials procured from Zenno and the *keizairen* because of their general handling fees. Supermarkets that handle agricultural chemicals and agricultural materials sell them at a cheaper price. Competitive pricing is spreading to fertilisers and corrugated cardboard boxes as well. Although Zenno has been a price leader for these products in the past (which has prevented their prices from falling by much), supermarkets can sell them for less by procuring them at large volume rates directly from trading companies and wholesalers and curtailing marketing costs. In contrast, the unit co-ops' procurement price is high because it includes the handling fees of Zenno and *keizairen* in addition to Zenno's high support price. If the *tankyo* add on the general handling fees, they cannot compete with the supermarkets. In other words, while Zenno and *keizairen* extract their usual amount, it is often the *tankyo* that have to sell at a discount by reducing their handling fees.[648]

In the face of such price competition, the *tankyo* are suffering losses, not Zenno and the *keizairen*. By the early 1990s, 90 per cent of all co-ops were suffering deficits in their marketing and purchasing businesses, while Zenno and the *keizairen* remained in the black.[649] In other words, the burden of three-stage management fell on the unit co-ops, which stood between the federations, who wanted high prices, and members who were demanding cheaper prices. At the settlement of accounts in 1993, 210 *sogo nokyo* (7.7 per cent of the total) registered losses, an increase of 2.4 times over the previous year.[650]

Radical reformers within the local *nokyo* have proposed the abolition of all the federations, both prefectural and national. They maintain that the federations and central unions are nothing but impediments for independent farmers who control and manage their agricultural production activities by themselves.[651] If the federations disappear, the burden of investment in the national federations will be eliminated as will the burden of expenses of the national federations, the costs of the general conventions of the national federations, and the transfer of capital and profits from the cooperative companies. In addition, the end of the federations will block the activities of the national federations in demanding policies that it misrepresents as the collective opinions of the farmers and *nokyo*, and will abolish the manipulation of local co-op education and information activities. As a result, members' free vitality will be revived; members' and *nokyo* management will be liberalised; and because of the rice-roots democratisation of the organisation, agriculture will expand and develop. In addition, huge losses in profit caused by the cartel-like actions of the national federations will be ended; the control of the *tankyo* and their members by the prefectural federations will be weakened; and if the members control the *tankyo*, the capital of the federations will return to members and the portion allocated for the expenses of the federations will become members' income. As a result, *tankyo* capital will be halved and their expenses will be one third.[652]

In other words, getting rid of the federations would mean eliminating organisations that consume around ¥570 billion in business administration expenses each year and yield huge economic benefits to the farmers and agriculture generally.[653] According to this argument, Japanese farmers do not need the *rengokai* any longer because the federations control the *tankyo* and members, and absorb the profits of farmers. In this way they harm the farmers.[654] For all these reasons, the best option is dissolution.[655]

In fact, even without wholesale abolition of the federations, new sales routes are gradually being established which bypass them anyway, such as those between local *nokyo*, *nokyo* and consumer co-ops (*seikyo*), between *nokyo* and the fisheries co-ops (*gyokyo*), and between *nokyo* and food processors.[656] These new sales routes generate a more direct connection between producers and consumers and eliminate the giant, bureaucratic middleman – the Nokyo federations.

Organisational remedies

Vertical restructuring

One major internal response to Nokyo's financial and management crisis has been a proposal for vertical restructuring of the tri-level Nokyo system. In 1991, a Nokyo Comprehensive Advisory Committee (Sogo Shingikai), which was charged with re-examining the three-stage system, came up with concrete proposals in a report entitled 'The Future Direction and Policies for the Organisational Reform of Nokyo'. The report was later endorsed by the National Nokyo Convention held in the same year.[657] It recommended the abolition of the three-stage structure and its replacement with a two-step system with the intention of creating a more rational and efficient management and operating structure.[658] The prefectural federations would be integrated with their national federations, thus abolishing the prefectural-level organisations altogether and simplifying the overall structure of the cooperatives. The planned restructuring was scheduled for completion by fiscal 2000.

In the case of the credit function of the agricultural cooperatives, the prefectural *shinren* would be phased out (i.e. absorbed into Norinchukin), their functions would be taken over by local co-ops and Norinchukin, and the co-ops would pass a portion of their deposits directly to Norinchukin. The concept thus envisaged Nokyo's credit institutions regaining financial strength through consolidation.[659] Zenchu subsequently set up a Federated Nokyo Organisation Consolidation Promotion Headquarters (Keito Nokyo Soshiki Seibi Suishin Honbu) to advance the comprehensive restructuring plan for Nokyo.

The shift to a two-stage system, however, is potentially associated with other problems. First and foremost is the role of the prefectural federations in executing government agricultural programmes. Abolishing the prefectural federations may create difficulties with respect to the future implementation of prefectural agricultural policies. The extinction of the prefectural federations will mean the intermediary agent of prefectural agricultural policies will be lost. This will require substantial change to the management of these policies. The tradition has been for the prefectural government and the prefectural federations to implement agricultural policies cooperatively, side by side. Whether in relation to administering the FC system or the agricultural modernisation fund, these policies have been undertaken with the human and financial collaboration of prefectural federations of agricultural cooperatives. The problem may also be exacerbated by the prospect of more region-specific agricultural policies, rather than standardised national policies. In other words, the significance of prefectural agricultural policies is becoming more, not less, important, and in this agricultural policy climate, the absence of prefectural Nokyo organisations will be keenly felt.[660]

Secondly, numerous difficulties arise in relation to staffing, specifically what to do with the officials of the *keizairen, shinren, kyosairen* and other federations. For example, 8,800 personnel were employed in the *shinren* in March 1995 and 3,000 in Norinchukin. The latter only wanted personnel well versed in complex financial transactions and was not willing to accept many officials from the *shinren*. On the other hand, the *tankyo* were being forced to reduce personnel to cut costs and so could not accept them either.[661] Other problems are how functions will be split between upper- and lower-level organisations and what to do with the assets of the *rengokai*, whether they will become assets of the national federations or the *nokyo*.[662]

In addition, strong objections have been raised to the uniform abolition of powerful economic federations such as Hokuren and Nagano *keizairen* as well as weak *keizairen*. The former have countered with proposals to eliminate Zenno. One of Hokuren's executives asserted that 'Zenno is an unnecessary organisation. What Zenno has that we do not is know-how about international business. Yet, this problem can be resolved by forging business alliances with trading companies.'[663] The national average utilisation rate of Zenno services by the economic federations was around 70 per cent, and, for the more powerful amongst them, as low as 50–60 per cent, indicating a trend towards defection from Zenno. Pressures to reduce costs consequent upon liberalisation provided an additional incentive to bypass Zenno and purchase from non-co-op sources.[664]

Similar problems have emerged amongst Nokyo's credit institutions. Zenchu found that about 10 prefectural credit federations opposed the realignment proposal that called for their breakup. Protests have come from the more viable prefectural trust federations, such as Kanagawa, Aichi and Shizuoka *shinren*. The Shizuoka organisation, for example, is one of the largest prefectural organisations, handling ¥3.3 trillion in co-op deposits as of March 1996. One of its officials claimed that if Shizuoka *shinren* were abolished, co-ops would have trouble getting the kind of advice and services they had been receiving from the *shinren*.[665] Likewise, a spokesperson from Aichi *shinren* complained that it was extremely irksome for his organisation to be treated in the same way as those with bad credit in other prefectures. Other reservations were expressed about whether the national federations would pay careful attention to the *tankyo*.[666]

Relatively superior *shinren* thus have a sceptical view about the merits of the vertical restructuring programme. The bad-loan figures revealed a wide gap in the financial health of the prefectural credit federations, who reported a combined total of ¥304.3 billion in non-performing loans as of March 1998.[667] The bad loans held by *shinren* actually made the consolidation process more difficult. The President of Norinchukin, Kakudo Kenichi, said it was impossible for Norinchukin to merge with prefectural credit federations that were in serious financial difficulties.[668]

Nevertheless, it is generally anticipated that it will be easier to abolish the prefectural central unions, mutual aid federations and credit federations than the economic federations. Zenkyoren and the prefectural mutual aid federations announced in March 1998 that they would amalgamate in April 2000, bringing their combined insurance assets to around ¥30.14 trillion.[669] It is also possible that Zenno and some *keizairen* might amalgamate, such as Miyagi *keizairen* which is regarded as weak and which wants to amalgamate with Zenno.[670] Tochigi *keizairen* is in a similar position, as is Tochigi *shinren* which is in strife because of bad loans arising from the *jusen*. The Chairman of Zenchu in 1995 was also the Chairman of Tochigi *kenchu* (Toyoda Hakaru). The reasons for his resignation from the position of Zenchu Chairman arose not only from the *jusen* issue but also from the fact that his own original organisation in Tochigi (the *shinren*) was performing so badly. Organisations like Hokuren, however, will probably remain as separate cooperative entities, merging with the agricultural cooperatives in Hokkaido. Similarly, Nagano *keizairen*, which is strong in vegetable marketing, might retain its separate existence.

In spite of the objectives and reservations raised – particularly by the prefectural organisations due for abolition – the impetus for restructuring has been maintained with various high-level reform proposals emanating from Nokyo and various government bodies. In January 1996, Zenchu created a JA Reform Headquarters (JA Kaikaku Honbu), which proposed simplifying the system of the JA Group and cutting the number of personnel by shifting from the existing three-level system to a two-level system. Parallel to Zenchu's activities, the MAFF requested that its Agricultural Policy Advisory Council examine the question of Nokyo reform. In the meantime, the MAFF finalised a plan in March 1996 to dissolve the prefectural credit federations prior to the formulation of a bill to merge them with Norinchukin. Specifically the 47 prefectural credit federations would discharge their staff and unload non-performing loans over 3–5 years. Thereafter, securities and loans from the federations would be transferred to Norinchukin, and loans to local small enterprises would be passed on to individual cooperatives.[671]

In July 1996, APAC's division (*bukai*) deliberating on reform of Nokyo recommended that the existing three-tier structure of credit institutions be altered by integrating *shinren* and Norinchukin at an early date. This would be achieved by transferring *shinren* responsibilities to Norinchukin. The council stressed that the *shinren* should draw up annual plans for personnel cuts and write-offs of non-performing loans to prepare for integration. The MAFF would have to lend support to carry out this plan.[672] In August 1996, Norinchukin President Kakudo Kenichi was quoted as saying: 'We need to rationalize to survive . . . This subject is on the table again because of the jusen problem'.[673]

In December 1996, a Law Concerning the Merger of the Central Bank for Agriculture and Forestry and the Trust Agricultural Cooperative Union Federations (*Norin Chuo Kinko to Shinyo Nogyo Kyodo Kumiai Rengokai no Gappei to ni kansuru Horitsu*) was passed to realise the MAFF plan and APAC recommendation. The official objective of the law was to contribute to the improvement of the efficiency and health of the whole Nokyo credit enter-prise.[674] Even by late 1998, however, the outlook for the vertical consolidation process was still hazy. Various options were being proposed depending on the prefecture and the financial viability of the institutions involved, but the outcome was far from clear-cut or assured.[675]

Moreover, it is questionable whether vertical restructuring of the federated Nokyo organisation will solve some of its deeper financial and management problems. As Ito observes, the problems in Nokyo's financial business are fundamental and structural and cannot be solved by the shift to a two-step organisation.[676] In his view, the biggest problem is that the basis of Nokyo's financial system is collapsing because the ratio of regular members is falling. Agricultural income in total farmhouse income is as little as 18 per cent and only one out of 10 farmers is full-time. Another problem is that agriculture is too closely linked to politics in the sense that it has been under government protection and cannot accept market principles. This impedes the efficiency of financial business which is based on market principles. A further problem of the *nokyo* is that persons who are strong in elections but weak in management become heads of the organisation.[677] Nokyo leaders are not selected for their ability as managers in the way that leaders of business organisations are. Moreover, since the Public Offices Election Law (*Koshoku Senkyoho*) does not apply to the election of Nokyo leaders, corruption and bribery are not uncommon.[678] In practice, many local agricultural cooperative leaders rely on administrative guidance from upper-level Nokyo organisations without having any long-term business plans for their own organisations themselves.[679]

Agricultural cooperative mergers

One area where Nokyo's managerial crisis has resulted in more rapid struc-tural change is in the mergers (*gappei*) of local cooperatives. On the initiative of Zenchu, fresh impetus has been given to mergers since the 1991 report of Nokyo's Sogo Shingikai which suggested that it would be necessary for local branches to have more self-reliant operating systems by expanding their scale of business with an eye to improving the management of the *tankyo* and thus enhancing their overall competitive position.[680]

The immediate background to the renewed round of mergers in the early 1990s was the dip in profits from agricultural cooperative credit enterprise owing to the liberalisation of interest rates.[681] The 1991 National Nokyo Convention adopted a bold plan for amalgamating cooperatives 'serving much larger areas than individual cities, towns, or villages'.[682] Another amendment to the Agricultural Cooperative Amalgamation Assistance Law in May 1992 also strengthened measures to assist the merger process. As noted in chapter 2, the original Amalgamation Assistance Law was in fact extended nine times between 1961 and 1996.[683]

The MAFF and Zenchu have promoted agricultural cooperative mergers by stressing the advantages of 'scale merit' particularly in financial business, but also in rice marketing.[684] According to the Chairman of Zenchu, the cooperatives are now 'determined to further promote rationalization of agricultural cooperatives by, for example, accelerating mergers by and between cooperatives and reducing the work force of cooperatives through attrition and other means, with an aim to increase their total operating efficiency by 30%.'[685] This statement reflects the prevailing view that Nokyo must overcome its inefficiencies through cost reduction efforts consequent upon the merger process.[686] The fear is that the *tankyo* will not survive without the pursuit of management efficiencies through scale expansion. Furthermore, the survival of the *tankyo* is critical to the federations, because they will lose their 'daily bread' if the unit co-ops go bankrupt.[687]

Figures for *nokyo* mergers reveal an escalating programme of local co-op amalgamations in the 1990s. Between 1991 and 1996, the number of *sogo nokyo* decreased from 3,574 to 2,472.[688] By April 1998, the nationwide total had dropped further to 1,833, as 137 cooperatives in 18 prefectures across the country merged into 31 cooperatives.[689] By the year 2000, Zenchu wants to restructure the *sogo nokyo* so that their numbers will sink to just 532.[690] This would require a doubling of the current rate of mergers to 650 per year (in 1996–1998 it was about 320 per year). Meanwhile, numbers of *senmon nokyo* have been sliding steadily – from 4,023 in 1991 to 3,363 in 1998,[691] although decline of business rather than mergers is mainly involved. The number of specialist federations is dwindling for the same reason.[692] Between 1991 and 1997, the decrease in the number of federations (most of them federations of specialist cooperatives) averaged somewhere between 20–30 per year.[693] By 1998 there were 290 prefectural specialist federations and 19 national specialist federations (see Figure 2.2).[694]

A spur to the merger process has been the bad debt problem and consequent financial losses in many local *nokyo*. The number of co-ops with operating deficits increased sharply in the 1990s. In 1994, for example, 214 *nokyo*, or 10 per cent of the total, suffered losses.[695] One of the solutions to this problem was to try and merge struggling cooperatives with more viable ones.[696] As Domon explains, 'the mergers work to rescue co-ops carrying a heavy load of nonperforming loans by coupling them with healthy organizations.'[697] In addition to providing direct subsidies and tax benefits to assist the process of agricultural cooperative mergers,[698] the MAFF has also produced a plan in the form of a 'Credit Purchasing Mechanism' to remove bad credit before mergers take place. The crux of this initiative is a 'Merger Promotion Fund System', which will use funds to cover secondary losses after mergers take place. These funds will be provided by prefectural governments, either as low interest loans or as direct tax-funded subsidies.

Fund systems along these lines have been established in 20 prefectures although they were proposed by the MAFF for all prefectures. For example, a particular *nokyo* in Kanto with substantial losses was merged with one with sound finance, with compensation offered to the merged *nokyo* in the form of low-interest loans over the 1992–97 period in order to assuage the antipathy of the more successful *nokyo*.[699] Over the four years 1992–1996, the total interest subsidy cost for this programme was ¥2.5 billion.[700]

Even these provisions, however, are not proving totally effective as a solution to the bad debt problem. During the merger process that ended in March 1996, for example, 152 local *nokyo* had merged to form 27 large-scale *nokyo*. However, it was observed that co-ops in excellent economic shape were increasingly reluctant to merge with co-ops that were struggling financially. In Saitama Prefecture, Tokorozawa Nokyo backed away from a merger with Irumano Nokyo, which should have had the largest amount in savings deposits amongst all the *nokyo* as a consequence of the merger of 12 *nokyo*. The reason for Tokorozawa Nokyo's withdrawal lay in the disposal of the bad debts of ¥3 billion of one of the co-ops. A confrontation occurred between the prefectural government which claimed that the disposal would finish by the end of March 1996 and Tokorozawa Nokyo which argued that 'we do not oppose the merger but sufficient information is not available despite our repeated demands, and the management responsibility of the *nokyo* with bad loans is unclear. Accordingly our members are not happy with the current situation.'[701]

In another example, Yatsushiro City Nokyo in Kumamoto Prefecture merged with four neighbouring agricultural cooperatives in 1989. Some farmers belonging to the latter strongly objected to the merger and demanded that it be nullified because of Yatsushiro City Nokyo's record of poor management. The latter's business would have come to a complete standstill without the merger.[702]

These and other similar incidents[703] illustrate the distrust amongst the *nokyo* for mergers because of the secret disposal of bad loans. In the consolidation process, most *nokyo* with bad loans and excellent *nokyo* are merged on equal terms, with the real situation of bad credit concealed. As Kudo puts it, this means that excellent *nokyo* commit a breach of trust towards their member farmers, with the merger process facing trouble owing to members' opposition.[704] The fundamental problem is that healthy co-ops are unwilling to merge with co-ops with huge debts. Bad loans are, therefore, hindering consolidation.[705] This problem is being compounded by the widening gap in the financial conditions amongst the cooperatives. Most of the 56 cooperatives that sank into a state of net liability in fiscal 1997 were in the predominantly farming regions of Tohoku and Kyushu, compared with cooperatives in city areas which often have more favourable balance sheets. Hence, the differences in the soundness of *nokyo* balance sheets are growing amongst the prefectures.[706] In Kudo's view, there is no possibility of mergers in 111 regions, 20 per cent of the total, with the biggest impediment being the existence of bad credit.[707]

The merger programme has created a number of additional problems in its wake. Firstly, it has been assessed by sources within Nokyo as nothing but a strategy to gain breathing time for the federated Nokyo organisation to survive, not to promote the stabilisation of farmers' management.[708] Indeed, *nokyo* executives and staff members often do not understand the true objective of the mergers.[709]

Secondly, although the direction indicated by Zenchu is clear enough, cooperative unions, unlike jointstock companies, cannot conduct restructuring using a top-down method. They require a more consensual approach, with positive cooperation needed from *nokyo* members and officials. The formation of such a consensus takes time and imposes costs. Because the current merger push is proceeding without such considerations, members are losing the sense that the local *nokyo* are their own associations and so are separating from Nokyo, both psychically and physically.[710] In practice, when mergers are successful, members tend to stay with the agricultural cooperatives, but when they are not, they are more willing to leave.[711]

Thirdly, the absence of local agricultural promotion has been another reason why mergers have resulted in the withdrawal of many farmers from Nokyo, in this case, full-time farmers.[712] Associated with this is the likelihood that agricultural cooperative mergers will produce disadvantages from the perspective of Nokyo's farm management guidance (*eino shido*).[713] The limit on the number of farm households where *eino shido* functions well is 3,000. If the number of farm households exceeds 3,000 in any *tankyo*, it becomes impossible to maintain the technical level of the members at previous levels (that is, the upper of the middle level of the technical standard of farming).[714]

Fourthly, the voice of members is less likely to be reflected in the larger-scale *nokyo*, creating a disadvantageous situation for members.[715] In a Zenchu survey on the promotion of mergers, 21 prefectural federations listed members' weakened unity as one of the factors inhibiting mergers.[716] Priority is given to the interests and rights of the *nokyo* and to the areas where their executives come from rather than to farmer members. The larger in scale the *nokyo* becomes, the more democracy in the organisation retreats and the less the principle of members' participation in management is achieved. The traditionally close ties between villagers and their local cooperatives have been permanently severed in some areas. For the first time, many farmers have found themselves excluded from direct participation in the decisionmaking processes of their local cooperative.[717] As a result, *nokyo* management has inevitably moved further away from the principle of cooperative unionism.[718] Already by 1990, the proportion of small-scale *nokyo* had fallen to 30.7 per cent from 84.0 per cent in 1960 as a result of the extended merger process.[719] Zenchu currently anticipates that as a result of mergers, large-scale cooperatives will be established, each with an average of about 15,000 members, nearly 600 staff and about 40 branches.[720]

Lastly, although the necessity of implementing drastic cost reductions through mergers is widely acknowledged, amalgamations do not always lead to a reduction in *nokyo* personnel.[721] In spite of all the mergers that have already taken place, no substantial reductions in the numbers of personnel have been immediately evident. In other words, cost reductions, the major objective of mergers, have not been achieved.[722]

In March 1991, staff numbers in the co-ops exceeded 300,000, the highest ever, averaging 90 per co-op. This was more than double the figure of 145,642 staff members in March 1961.[723] By any standards, the 1991 figure constituted a bloated bureaucracy. According to Nokyo's critics, the figures show that in spite of the drop in co-op numbers and the gradual diminution in the number of regular farm members and farm household members supporting the cooperatives, restructuring of the agricultural cooperatives from the personnel aspect has not progressed at all. In fact, quite the reverse. Between 1990 and 1993, for example, the number of *sogo nokyo* staff members actually expanded from 297,459 to 300,918.[724] Only in 1994 was a slight fall in staff numbers registered and then it only amounted to 628, from 300,918 to 300,290.[725] In the light of the obvious resistance to staff reductions, one could quite legitimately ask what the process of amalgamation is actually for.[726]

Furthermore, at a total of 300,000 Nokyo staff members, one local Nokyo staff member exists for every nine commercial farm households in 1995, and one local co-op staff member for every 1.4 full-time farm households.[727] Given the continuing slippage in 'real' farm household members of Nokyo (i.e. those that are actually engaged in agriculture and which support Nokyo, rather than those who are just on the membership books), one Nokyo official existed for each eight farm household members in 1993 and one Nokyo official for each specialist farm household member.[728] In a certain *nokyo* in Tokyo, for example, there are two employees per one full-time farming household.[729]

In the light of these figures, it is commonly argued that the number of Nokyo members simply cannot support the number of Nokyo personnel.[730] Furthermore, many Nokyo employees are not particularly sympathetic to farmers' causes like the producer rice price because their main efforts are directed elsewhere – to selling insurance and savings. They know very little about agriculture. Nokyo staff members at all levels are basically white-collar office workers.

Large numbers of staff members impose a heavy burden of management expenses (which includes personnel expenses) on the agricultural cooperatives. One newspaper source, for example, reported that numbers of white-collar workers (unspecified) involved in the agricultural industry was not decreasing in spite of the decline in agriculture. In 1996 a total of 608,000 agricultural white-collar workers cost nearly ¥1 trillion every year just in personnel expenses.[731] The business management expenses of the 3,024 *sogo nokyo* in 1993, for example, amounted to just under ¥2.2 trillion. Of this, personnel expenses amounted to ¥1.24 trillion, or 56 per cent.[732] The business management expenses of the federations (*keizairen*, Zenno, *shinren*, Norinchukin, *kyosairen* and Zenkyoren) was ¥567.6 billion, while that of the central unions (the prefectural *chuokai* and Zenchu) was ¥33.4 billion.[733] Accordingly, the combined business management expenses of the federations and central unions amounted to approximately ¥601 billion, including some ¥300 billion for personnel expenses.

These huge amounts are collected from members through the *tankyo* in the form of handling fees (i.e. commissions) on purchasing and sales business, allotted charges (*buntankin*), burden fees (*futankin*), levies (*fukakin*) and expenses (*keihi*). This 'roundabout' method of collecting money from farmers is thought to be the best way of suppressing opposition from members to the charges they have to pay. The fees are hidden because farmers do not pay them directly to Nokyo. They pay them in the form of reduced amounts disbursed by the co-ops to the farmers for the farm produce they market on their behalf, or increased charges to farmers for production inputs. The burden of these charges amounts to as much as ¥3–4 million per household per year.[734] One Nokyo member commented that a farmer had to pay a commission 88 times to grow rice, including commissions on agricultural chemicals, fertiliser and agricultural machinery and ¥10 per bale (60 kg) for the rice price campaign. In his view, Nokyo charged a fee for everything and thus exploited producers.[735]

Because of the way in which Nokyo is structured, with *tankyo* established on the basis of capital from farmers and upper-level federations established on the basis of capital from *tankyo*, capital accumulates in the vaults of the national federations.[736] While the number of local unit co-ops running deficits continues to increase, the upper-level organisations run surpluses and therefore their equity capital and assets continue to inflate.[737] One set of data shows, for example, that the total capital of Zenno, *keizairen*, Norinchukin, *shinren*, Zenkyoren and *kyosairen* increased by ¥273 billion (an increase of 10.4 per cent annually) between 1985 and 1987.[738] This provided a stark contrast with the increasing cost burden for farmers whose incomes continued to shrink.[739] In short, while Nokyo flourished, farmers perished.[740]

At the 20th Nokyo Convention in 1994, one of the three main items on the agenda was 'reform of the organization of agricultural cooperatives and the streamlining of their business activities.'[741] A resolution was passed to cut Nokyo personnel numbers by one-third.[742] Subsequently, at its board of directors meeting in early July 1996, Zenchu approved a plan to cut agricultural cooperative staff by 50,000. This was in line with Zenchu's rationalisation goal targeted at the year 2000.[743] The planned restructuring was also predicated on continuing *nokyo* mergers and the shift from a three-tiered to a two-tiered federated organisation. These moves aimed to raise labour productivity by 30 per cent in terms of gross profit per employee by the year 2000.[744] It remains to be seen, however, whether such moves will achieve their targets. The rate of progress to date does not encourage optimism. Failure may, however, herald grim prospects for the cooperatives. It is anticipated that if these goals are not achieved, the co-ops' hopes of survival may be jeopardised.[745]

In spite of the difficulties and problems with the merger process, the MAFF is strongly committed to its continuation as a means of cleaning up the finances of the agricultural cooperatives. In July 1998, a further plan for sweeping, nationwide consolidation of the agricultural cooperatives was announced by the MAFF. Under the plan, prefectural governors would appoint administrators to oversee farm cooperatives that were deemed financially shaky. The functions of these administrators would be to work with existing management to find merger partners and to repair balance sheets and loan portfolios.[746]

Functional disaggregation and other proposals

A number of scholarly writers and journalists have analysed Nokyo's failings in economic and financial businesses and suggested various measures for improvement.[747] One of these, Saeki Naomi, has been a fervent advocate of Nokyo's organisational reform.[748] His main proposal has centred on the separation of agricultural businesses from non-agricultural businesses in the cooperatives and the gradual separation of credit business from the rest.[749] He argues that each of Nokyo's businesses is different in terms of regional diversification and scale of operation so that each should be restructured in a different manner. The important thing is that Nokyo's management and organisation should be reorganised to rationalise and improve the operation of individual branches. Separating businesses and making them more independent would solve conflicts among members with different interests, enable each business of the *nokyo* to specialise, and improve the overall efficiency of agricultural cooperative management.

This applies especially to the economic and managerial performance of the *sogo nokyo*. The local co-ops rely heavily on the prefectural federations, while the prefectural federations rely on the national federations for agricultural commodity marketing, the purchase of farm inputs and other goods, and the arrangement of finance. Local agricultural cooperatives are, therefore, far from self-reliant. While the functions of Nokyo branches, prefectural federations and national federations might have been complementary in the past, in the contemporary environment their functions often overlap or even compete with each other.[750]

Saeki also identifies other contradictions in the three-layered management structure. The solid vertical structure can respond flexibly to rapidly changing distribution mechanisms outside Nokyo; higher-level organisations tend to pass business risks on to lower branches; and the prevailing management system only allows local Nokyo branches to function as mere subordinate organs instead of as major units of cooperative activities. Lastly, the development of distribution and information networks outside Nokyo demand a management structure that can adjust quickly to frequent changes in markets. The Nokyo system is simply outdated.[751] Thus far, there is little evidence to suggest that any of these criticisms and suggestions have been acted on, except perhaps for vertical restructuring of the tri-level system.

In the early 1990s, Fujitani Chikuji also published a comprehensive blue-print for Nokyo's structural and managerial reform. His suggestions focused on radically improving the quality of Nokyo management, fostering Nokyo's role in guiding regional agriculture, reinforcing the basis of Nokyo businesses, redeveloping Nokyo's organisational basis as a cooperative, promoting large-scale regional mergers of agricultural cooperatives and reorganising the cooperative relationship with administrative institutions.[752] Like Saeki's proposals, the validity of Fujitani's case is self-evident, but apart from large-scale regional mergers, it is doubtful whether any of the remaining recommendations will be self-initiated by Nokyo.

Upgrading Nokyo management

In recognition of the management deficiencies of the agricultural cooperative system and the fact that lack of sophisticated managerial capabilities make it almost impossible for Nokyo to overcome its present crisis, the MAFF has stepped in with a number of innovative proposals to upgrade Nokyo manage-ment.[753] These materialised in an amendment to the Nokyo Law which came into effect in January 1997.[754] The amendment anticipates a number of alterations to the way in which Nokyo's business affairs are managed. The core of the reform is a strengthening of Nokyo's managerial and auditing sys-tems. Various provisions have been introduced to limit the side-businesses of full-time Nokyo executives managing financial activities in order make them more responsible for conducting the affairs of the agricultural cooperatives in which they are employed; to establish a managerial control committee system staffed by those with business experience who can ensure appropriate management of the cooperative and to whom the board of directors is subordinate; to enforce an auditing system staffed by external and full-time auditors as well as strengthening auditing done by the *chuokai*; and to disclose information concerning profits and losses by the cooperative in each of its business sectors.[755]

All these reforms are designed to introduce greater managerial expertise into the agricultural cooperative system, and in particular, to facilitate the transfer of management power to expert staff and to eliminate the direct involvement of farmers. Most co-op executives have traditionally been farmers; managerial experts made up only 0.1 per cent of all directors.[756]

In addition, agricultural cooperatives conducting financial business will be required to put up a minimum ¥100 million of their own capital. By establishing such a capitalisation minimum, the MAFF aims to reduce the potential damage from co-op losses. As of March 1995, more than 500 out of 2,670 co-ops had put up less than ¥100 million of their own capital. The MAFF expected mergers would be necessary for some cooperatives to reach the minimum.[757]

Conclusion

For all its much vaunted economic and political clout, Nokyo is not what it was, either objectively or in the eyes of the Japanese government, the general public and the farmers. It is proving vulnerable to the decline of agriculture and to changes taking place in domestic agricultural and other markets. In a new era of deregulation and intensified competition, Nokyo's inefficient and overlapping institutions appear inflexible, anachronistic and slow to adapt to fundamental changes in their economic and policy environment. Nokyo's financial power is eroding because of bad financial management,[758] and its economic power is diminishing because of its overall management short-comings and the liberalisation of agricultural markets and associated domestic distribution systems.

Until recently, Nokyo had the best of both worlds: it benefited from government protection, assistance and regulated markets at the same time as exploiting business opportunities for sheer profit. It built up a huge economic and financial empire which almost completely dominated Japan's agricultural economy. In the circumstances it became increasingly incongruous for Nokyo as a huge business enterprise to ask for shelter from government.[759]

Nokyo's dual identity as a commercial giant and state-protected institution was not quite so apparent during the golden era of agricultural support and protection which lasted from the late 1950s until the late 1970s, when farmers and cooperatives were able freely to extract benefits and concessions from highly regulated markets. Nor did Nokyo's selfish pursuit of advantage necessarily conflict with farmers' interests, since there were plenty of benefits to go around. From the early 1980s onwards, however, agricultural budgets have been under attack, agricultural support and stabilisation prices have been lowered, markets have been opened up to freer competition and the policy trends of the times have become much more antipathetic to the concessions and benefits being extracted by both the farmers and Nokyo. In this new and more hostile environment, Nokyo's shortcomings as a market actor, and particularly the way in which it has often benefited at the expense of the farmers in controlled markets, have increasingly been exposed. Deregulation and liberalisation have revealed all the inefficiencies and vested rights that made Nokyo the protected and pampered organisation that it was.

On the other hand, the long-standing posture of policy dependence of Nokyo management meant that state subsidies made up for any shortfall in the competitive power of the agricultural cooperatives. Not surprisingly, this bred a certain weakness in the agricultural cooperatives, whose management never developed the levels of efficiency and competence required to compete in deregulated markets. In the long run, Nokyo became a victim of its own evolutionary processes as a state-sponsored grouping that provided financial and other services to a relatively inefficient and vulnerable sector of the economy, as well as of its historical origins as a producer cooperative that helped to level the playing field between private enterprise and the farmers in the prewar period. Given this kind of organisational heritage, Nokyo should not be judged purely as a business grouping, but as an integral element of the agricultural support and protection regime. Quite clearly a different set of rules has applied to its operations when compared to private sector businesses. The upshot of this, however, is that the change in the fundamental ground rules of the financial and economic markets in which Nokyo operates brought on by deregulation and liberalisation has precipitated something of a crisis in the Nokyo organisation.

An understanding of these circumstances has not prevented relentless censure of the agricultural cooperatives in scholarly tracts as well as in the popular media and from those at the centres of power. The exposure of Nokyo's manifest deficiencies as a farmers' organisation, agricultural cooperative and market actor has provoked an outpouring of negative commentary about many aspects of Nokyo's behaviour. Perhaps the most fundamental criticism is that Nokyo began as an organisation to protect the weak but ended up as an organisation out to promote and protect its own interests, not those of the farmers.[760]

As Domon comments, the original purpose for organising Nokyo was to protect farmers from so-called 'immoral vice merchants'. Farmers who formerly suffered at the hands of such agents, however, are now suffering from Nokyo's cartel-like operations. In particular, Zenno and the economic federations, which were supposed to protect farmers, have supported the formation of cartels in order to protect their own interests.[761] They have even been prepared to sell out to the market liberationists in order to defend their business profits. In 1993, for example, reports surfaced that Zenno was considering involvement in the importation of processed rice products for which it was severely criticised by local agricultural cooperatives.[762] Likewise, even though Zenno fiercely opposed beef liberalisation, it quickly moved into the beef import business once the market was opened, saying that it was better for Zenno, which was a representative of the farmers, to deal in imported beef than to have a situation where commercial capital started dealing in beef and monopolised the market.[763]

These moves lend weight to criticism that Nokyo is 'a self-serving profit-oriented organisation, not a genuine cooperative'.[764] In Sakaguchi's view, Nokyo controls farmers politically and financially, but is not a body that represents farmers' interests.[765] In relation to farmers, Nokyo is nothing more than a superficial *tatemae* principle.[766] Even worse, it acts in a way that is contrary to the long-term survival interests of Japanese agriculture. It is being held responsible for holding down farm incomes and therefore the shortage of successors in Japanese agriculture.

Besieged by critics on all sides, both domestic and foreign, many of Nokyo's long-time friends within the government are slowly turning against it. The number of critical reports coming from various quarters are indicative of this trend. Both the MAFF and LDP are realising that reform of agriculture is impossible without reform of Nokyo. In fact, they are using Nokyo's weakness to mobilise their own political and administrative power against it.[767]

Furthermore, because the role of Nokyo in Japanese agriculture has been so pivotal, much of the criticism of Japanese agriculture is seen as actually rooted in Nokyo-related problems.[768] Nokyo 'has come to stand for the vested interests of the traditional farming community and conservative resistance to change or reform.'[769] Zenchu and Zenno have been censured for being 'part of the crisis facing Japanese agriculture. Both organisations are committed to preserving the system of small, part-time farmers [which] . . . has helped to keep Japanese farming hopelessly uneconomic.'[770] In terms of the neoclassical economic perspective, Nokyo represents an example of vested interests that have to be excised if Japanese agriculture is to flourish as a viable industry.[771]

Japanese farmers, particularly full-time farmers, are also showing increasing signs of rebellion against a system they feel has exploited them and driven up the costs of production with high-priced farm inputs. In order to survive in a more competitive agricultural market, entrepreneurial producers have found it necessary to break away from Nokyo, a development that is also influencing other farmers to weaken their links with Nokyo's operations.[772] Some part-time farm households also have little sense of belonging to Nokyo.[773] In fact, many farmers, both full- and part-time, are saying that they no longer need the co-ops, likening Nokyo to a giant parasite that feeds off its members.

The dispute that took place in 1993 over the selection of the new Zenchu Chairman, Sato Yoshinobu, is indicative of rising levels of internal dissension within the organisation as well as increased questioning of Nokyo's traditional priorities and connections by its own leaders. Sato's election to the post by the Zenchu Executives Recommendation Conference was challenged by prefectural executives who were indignant that a person was selected who was not likely to promote the abolition of the 'adhesion' of the political, bureaucratic and agricultural worlds (*seikanno no yuchaku*) in order to realise a new era for agriculture.[774]

The fact is, however, that Nokyo has always had its own interests to preserve. These were generated by its independent organisational imperatives, principally the need to pursue organisational maintenance objectives involving the promotion and protection of vested personnel and business interests. Thus, while Nokyo was first and foremost an organisation of farmers, the reality was that organisational maintenance and survival dictated that it pursue its own independent interests. Examining some of the root causes of relatively high levels of agricultural support and protection in Japan thus requires a consideration of both farmers' and Nokyo's organisational interests.

Most commentators agree that Nokyo faces severe problems unless it thoroughly reorganises its structure and operating systems. Reforms are needed to both its management structures and performance as well as to its role as a farmers' organisation. Even in the late 1960s, critics were observing that Nokyo had become bureaucratised in the sense that members' interests were being subordinated to organisational interests.[775] In Matsuzaka's view, as Nokyo became more powerful, it distanced itself from the interests of the farmers and effectively formed a second MAFF bureaucracy.[776] This perception did not change over the years. Writing in the 1990s, Kawagoe noted that Nokyo had remained 'heavily bureaucratic . . . [with] interests [that] do not always represent those of farmers.'[777] Furthermore, Nokyo's rigid bureaucratic norms and behaviours appeared to share the same basic problems recognised as endemic in the government bureaucracy as a whole: lack of transparency and accountability. This, in turn, gave rise to higher levels of internal dissension as member farmers felt greater alienation and disaffection from their own organisation and its leadership.

At some time in the future, Nokyo will have to compete in the various markets in which it operates with dwindling levels of support and protection from government. It will find this hard because of the costs imposed by its vast bureaucratic superstructure. Unless some far-reaching reforms are made, it will continue to be hobbled by its entrenched managerial methodologies, amateurish business leadership by elected cooperative officials, and a resistant mind-set on the part of its personnel. A major problem is that Nokyo's bureaucracy is fossilised and wedded to outdated practices. 'As a former Zenchu Managing Director put it, Nokyo is highly commercialised so it needs managerial capabilities to match. The reason why its power is declining is because it does not have these managerial capabilities. Nokyo expanded continuously for 30–40 years, but no one could really handle management.'[778]

The need to reform Nokyo in order to generate managerial talent enabling it to prosper in an environment of liberalisation and market principles, and to help foster independent entrepreneurial farmers, is widely recognised amongst those who are well versed in agricultural cooperative affairs and who want to see Nokyo continue to grow and flourish.[779] As Hayami observes, it is necessary to create an environment that allows several agricultural cooperatives and other organisations, such as trading companies, to compete with each other for a larger market share.[780] Nokyo officials in general, however, reject change. The critiques of Nokyo in scholarly books and in the media reportedly have almost no influence on Nokyo personnel, who do not accept the opinion of external critics because they cling to the pursuit of rights and concessions and thus the fundamental premise of closed and regulated markets.[781]

Nonetheless, the doomsayers agree that if Nokyo management fails to return to a state of health, the revival of Japan's agriculture and farmers will never be achieved.[782] Nokyo's banking system has been subjected to a particularly severe test, with commentators warning that the main threat to the survival of agricultural cooperatives is obsolete business practices in Nokyo's credit business and increasingly stiff competition from rivals who are far more skilled in handling sophisticated financial instruments.[783] A particular concern is that the cooperatives have outlived their original purpose which was to assist farmers with credit because producers had nowhere else to turn. Whether or not farmers have special financial needs requiring agriculture-specific financial institutions is now questionable. If they do not, then 'agricultural financial institutions have already lost their *raison d'être* within the financial industry'.[784] Indeed, the co-ops will not be able to survive without a new, clear-cut role, agriculturally as well as financially.[785] This includes trying harder to prove Nokyo's indispensability to farmers. The general call has gone out to execute Nokyo reform (*Nokyo kaikaku*) in order for Nokyo to survive.[786]

In this process, however, Nokyo must confront its identity crisis. In moving away from 'the principle of servicing' towards 'the principle of making a profit', Nokyo faces the disappearance of the fundamental distinction between the agricultural cooperatives and competing private enterprise. If this occurs and Nokyo is considered as just another agricultural business by its members, then it will lose its *raison d'être* as a farmers' organisation and will face even greater difficulties in retaining its farm membership. Thus, although profit-seeking management has brought rewards and was once the driving force behind Nokyo's rapid expansion, in the long run, it may turn out to be Nokyo's biggest weak point.[787]

How will Nokyo meet the challenges it faces? Unless it can adjust to new times and new policies and display an ability to compete under less regulated market conditions, its retreat will be even faster. Amongst the various businesses of the *sogo nokyo*, only mutual aid activities are healthy. Others have prospered in the past because of the government's protective policies.[788] In the future, however, this protection will diminish and there will be even greater competition in credit, marketing and supply businesses, particularly from *keiretsu* affiliates.

The solutions to Nokyo's current problems will not be easy to apply. A lot of Nokyo's organisational power has traditionally derived from its stranglehold on the distribution system for farmers, including dominance in the fields of farm credit, agricultural product marketing and input supply. Nokyo controlled a distribution oligopoly that liberalisation and deregulation are strongly challenging. Financial and agricultural trade liberalisation, deregulation of agricultural distribution systems, a weakening of domestic support within government, the increasing withdrawal of farmers from local agricultural cooperatives and the decline of agriculture are now all complicating Nokyo's future prospects.

Nokyo is thus experiencing its greatest structural crisis of the postwar period. In recognition of the magnitude of the task facing the organisation, the newly elected President of Zenchu, Harada Mutsutami, stated at a press conference following his election that: 'The current operating environment for agricultural cooperatives is the harshest ever, and many issues must be addressed. I feel a heavy responsibility.'[789]

Other developments will underscore this negative outlook. The inexorable contraction in Japan's farming population will continue to reduce Nokyo's farm membership, shrink its traditional customer base and 'undermine the markets for the services it provides.'[790] Close-knit agricultural cooperative groups will continue to break down as they are exposed to a less protected business and economic environment. This will compound the loss of farmers' interest in the agricultural cooperatives, their resistance to Nokyo's established practices and policies, and their inclination to conduct their agriculture-related activities without resort to the services and resources of the cooperatives.[791] As more and more farmers exit Nokyo, its problems will multiply, particularly efforts to stabilise the management of local organisations.

If the cooperatives lose the business allegiance of farmers, they will also lose their personal loyalty and attachment to the co-ops, and this will affect the quality of the agricultural cooperative system as a whole, including its political and electoral activities. Ono argues that one reason why Nokyo's election campaigns have not been functioning well is that Nokyo is badly managed. Because of increasing difficulties in its business, particularly its credit business, co-op members face pressure to help the agricultural cooperatives out through their patronage of Nokyo services. In the past Nokyo used to link its business to election campaigns, but in the present condition, making such a link would increase the risk to Nokyo's business.[792] Domon also reports that financial liberalisation is changing the political structure of rural areas. In the past, Nokyo officials conducted election campaign activities when they visited farmers to encourage them to deposit their funds in the co-op or take out insurance policies.[793] Such practices are now becoming less common. Young Nokyo officials avoid work relevant to election campaigns. Given fierce competition with private financial institutions, electioneering is just an added burden for them. Indeed, one cause of the increasing number of young Nokyo officials leaving their jobs can be attributed to their reluctance to engage in election activities.[794]

Compounding this trend is the fact that Nokyo is losing its farmer-centredness as it turns increasingly to providing non-agriculture-related services to a wider spectrum of local residents. The MAFF-sponsored attempt to refashion Nokyo into a more effective, efficient, transparent and accountable managerial system pushes it further in this direction. Although these reforms may improve Nokyo's business prospects in a more competitive environment, taking the management of the agricultural cooperatives out of the hands of farmers and putting it into the hands of business professionals will fundamentally alter the character of the organisation. It will weaken Nokyo's identity as a farmers' interest group because of the erosion in the executive powers of farmers within the organisation. Although Nokyo will be in a stronger economic position, it will become much more of a straight business actor in the economy, losing some of its multidimensionality as a farmers' group. Not only will it become less integral to the fabric of rural society, but ultimately, its change in organisational character will attenuate its role as a partisan pressure group for farmers.[795]

The sum of all these developments means that the pinnacle of Nokyo's organisational power has passed. Its golden age is at an end and the myth of Nokyo's 'unsinkability' is gradually being revealed as just that – a myth. Many of the factors that once made it strong – its vast economic empire built on highly regulated markets and a large bureaucracy – are now seen as major liabilities and a source of organisational weakness. These developments also have potentially important implications for Nokyo's political standing and influence. Much of its organisational independence, perceived policy clout and high public profile has rested on its massive economic and business power as well as on its organisational dominance in the agricultural sector. If these are under threat, then Nokyo will be significantly debilitated in the eyes of not only its own membership, but also the MAFF and LDP. The result will be a hastening of policy reforms challenging Nokyo's entrenched privileges.

Thus far, Nokyo's response to the changes in the demographic and economic conditions of farming, to the economic diversification of rural society and to its business environment are not promising. It has clung to an outdated image of itself as a concessionary accomplice in a highly regulated agricultural economy, rather than as an independent economic and political entrepreneur. Its major organisational response has centred on realignment of the cooperatives, through mergers and restructuring through the abolition of prefectural federations, but these moves are far from being a panacea for all of its problems. As far as the programmes themselves are concerned, the results have been patchy and highly variable depending on the region and have not produced sufficient numbers of staff cutbacks.

The purists argue that Nokyo's future as a farmers' organisation lies at the rice roots, where its fundamental roles must be to promote local agriculture and support a vigorous rural society. This means conquering the quantitative and qualitative deterioration in the agricultural workforce by 'encouraging younger, better trained people to manage farms'.[796] The problems Nokyo faces in these areas are not insignificant, but only by assisting rather than blocking the process of structural adjustment in agriculture will it ultimately help bring about a more viable, competitive farming sector and thus ensure its own future.

5 The political demography
of agriculture

The power of Japanese farmers at the ballot box has been the single most commonly cited factor in the political explanation for Japan's agricultural support and protection. As the argument goes, farming areas have formed the largest electoral support base of the LDP.[1] Politicians in the ruling party have relied on farmers' votes to win seats crucial to the maintenance of the LDP's parliamentary majorities over the many decades of its rule. Moreover, the electoral malapportionment in favour of rural areas has ensured that farmers have exercised electoral power disproportionately to their numbers. As a result, agricultural policy has been hostage to the party's concern about the potential electoral consequences of its decisions, resulting in a consistent bias towards the interests of its rural clients and resistance to any policy changes that might result in political retribution from agricultural interests.

The following discussion elucidates the two key elements in this explanation. Farmers' voting power is estimated according to a variety of different statistical measures, as is the degree of LDP dependence on the farm vote. The analysis begins by estimating the size of the agricultural and Nokyo electorates in aggregate as well as the size of particular commodity electorates. The impact on constituency profiles of changes in the socio-economic environment of agriculture is assessed along with the implications of the growth of 'mixed economies' for the determinants of voting choice in farm households. Electoral malapportionment is examined as an important factor mitigating the natural ebbing of farmers' voting power. The analysis then shifts to an investigation of the LDP as the farmers' party, its popularity amongst rural voters over time and the changing composition of its support base across the rural-urban spectrum in successive elections.

The study generally covers the period from the 1950s to the 1990s, although the main focus is on trends from the 1970s onwards.[2] The major historical issues are whether farmers' voting power has been sustained over this long period and whether electoral factors have dictated that the LDP remain as wedded to the farmers' cause in the 1990s as it was in earlier years. These questions are particularly pertinent in the light of the dramatic demographic and socio-economic transformation of the countryside associated with the twin processes of urbanisation and industrialisation, the fission and fusion amongst political parties that began in the early 1990s and the likely effects of electoral reform on the voting power of farmers.

The national agricultural electorate

One of the most crucial ingredients in farmers' electoral power has been the absolute size of the national agricultural electorate (and associated national Nokyo electorate). Because Japanese farmers have been small-holders, the countryside has remained more heavily populated than it might have been if farmland had been consolidated into large-scale plots. As *The Economist* observed in 1988, 'Japan still has a higher proportion of its people on the land than any other rich country'.[3]

A conclusive picture of trends in farm voters based on labour and demographic statistics, however, is problematic for a number of reasons. Not only do the figures vary according to which agency compiles them, but various statistical measures of so-called 'farm voters' are available, such as the agricultural workforce, persons employed in agriculture both full- and part-time, and persons resident in farm households. Depending on which of these three main statistical measures is used, the figures for so-called 'farm voters' fluctuate. Even those within single categories are not necessarily a reliable measure of the size of the agricultural electorate. These days non-farmers tend to outnumber farmers in many farm households, but if one member of the household is engaged in farming, it is still classified as a farm household providing it conforms to the MAFF's statistical definition.[4] For those not employed in agriculture, membership of a farm household is a mark of residential location rather than occupation and source of income.

Moreover, estimating the size of the national agricultural electorate is like tracking a moving target. The twin processes of urbanisation and industrialisation have slowly and inexorably shrunk the number of farm voters. Although each index is subject to differential rates of contraction, the only macro-trend to which all are subject is a downward movement, in some cases very gradual, in other cases more rapid. In recent years, the rapid aging of the farm population combined with the exodus of farming youth to the cities have exacerbated the shift in employment away from agriculture.

Urbanisation has registered in terms of the rising percentage of the population residing in cities as opposed to towns and villages. In 1950, 37.3 per cent of Japan's population was resident in cities and 62.7 per cent in towns and villages. By 1960 these figures were 63.3 per cent and 36.7 per cent respectively, demonstrating the rapid process of urbanisation during this decade. By 1990, the population resident in cities comprised 77.4 per cent of the total, with only 22.6 per cent resident in towns and villages.[5]

The same trend can be observed in the Densely Inhabited Districts (DID) scale used since the 1960 Census of Population to differentiate urban and rural population statistically.[6] DIDs are defined as census enumeration districts 'with a population density of over 4,000 per square kilometre, forming a congregation of more than 5,000 persons together with adjacent districts (DIDs). The population residing in DIDs is considered urban population.'[7] In 1960 Japan's population was divided more or less evenly between DIDs and non-DIDs (43.7 per cent and 56.3 per cent respectively). By 1985 these figures had altered to 60.6 per cent and 39.4 per cent respectively,[8] and by 1990 to 77.4 per cent and 22.6 per cent respectively. The escalation in the DID ratio was due not only to the continuous gravitation of population towards the cities but also to the consolidation of villages and towns into cities.[9]

Amongst statistics specific to agriculture, the most dramatic reductions have been recorded in the agricultural workforce. The number of persons engaged in farming as an exclusive or principal occupation is now around one-quarter of what it was more than three decades ago,[10] falling from 12.7 million in 1960 to 5.1 million in 1980, 3.3 million in 1995 and 3.15 million in 1997.[11] As a proportion of the total workforce, those employed in agriculture have shrunk from 28.7 per cent of the total in 1960 to 9.1 per cent in 1980 and 5.0 per cent in 1996.[12] However, given the prevalence of part-time farming in Japan (and particularly part-time farm households where the bulk of income is earned off the land), these labour surveys tend to undervalue the importance of farming as an occupational category. If all part-time farmers, including those who are mainly employed in non-agricultural occupations are included in the figures, the agricultural workforce roughly doubles, and while the dominant trend is still one of regression, the rate of change is slower. The number of persons engaged in farming either full-time or part-time decreased from 17.7 million in 1960 to 12.5 million in 1980 and 7.0 million in 1997.[13]

The question here is how meaningful employment statistics are as a measure of political interest and hence voting choice. The reductions that have registered in employment statistics have not been accompanied by a commensurate diminution in the electoral significance of the farm vote, which, for a number of reasons, has remained much higher than the size of the agricultural workforce might suggest.

Firstly, even in part-time farm households whose members are mainly employed in non-agricultural occupations, an interest in agriculture and agricultural policy is diluted but not necessarily negated. This type of farm household resident would retain a personal stake in the farm household economy which was not necessarily in direct proportion to their degree of engagement in farming.[14]

Secondly, many farm household residents are of advanced age and hence no longer participate in the labour market. Nevertheless, they would presumably keep a direct interest in the collective economic wellbeing of the farm household and still vote. In 1997, for example, just over two million commercial farm household residents were over the age of 70 years,[15] which was somewhat larger than the number of adults in farm households without employment.[16] This suggests that as aggregate statistics go, farm household population rather than agricultural employment is a more reliable indicator of the total number of 'stakeholders' in the farm economy and the total number of farm household voters.

This observation is related to the third point. Demographic indices for the farm sector have remained somewhat higher than the contribution of agriculture to national employment might suggest. The rate of decrease in the number of farm households has been very slow, subsiding only by a third from a peak of 6.2 million in 1950 to 4.4 million in 1985.[17] Over the last decade or so, the rate of change has accelerated somewhat, sliding by a further one million to 3.3 million in 1998.[18] Nevertheless, it has taken almost half a century for farm household figures to drop by less than half. One of the main reasons has been the reluctance of land holders to sell their land and quit farming altogether, even though their engagement in agriculture might have been minimal.

Farm household population figures exhibit essentially the same pattern. In 1950, total farm population amounted to 37.7 million, falling to 34.4 million in 1960, 26.3 million in 1970, 21.4 million in 1980, 17.3 million in 1990 and 14.8 million in 1998.[19] The rate of decline was at its most dramatic during the period of rapid urbanisation between 1960 and 1970, when farm population sank by 23.5 per cent. During the 1970s and 1980s, however, farm household population was dropping at a rate less than 20 per cent per decade. So while in 1950 almost half of all Japan's population lived on farms (45.3 per cent), by 1960 just over one-third, or 36.8 per cent were doing so, and by 1998, 38 years later, only 11.7 per cent were still resident on farms.[20] Now that farm household population is officially defined in terms of population resident in commercial farm households, the figures are superficially registering more dramatic falls. By this measure farm household population was 11.3 million in 1998.[21]

Even so, when translated into farmers' voting numbers, this has meant that the agricultural electorate (if defined as persons 20 years old and over residing in farm households) has remained a relatively significant component of the national electorate. It is certainly too large a proportion of the total eligible vote to be easily discounted in the national electoral arena. As indicated in Table 5.1, although farm household voters dwindled from 20.1 million to 15.9 million between 1960 and 1980, sliding even further to 12.0 million in 1995, this still represented 12.4 per cent of the national electorate in that year in spite of the fact that the farm vote more than halved in percentage terms between 1955 and 1979 and almost halved again between 1979 and 1995. The overwhelmingly dominant trend over these four decades was for the national agricultural electorate to shrink, although the reduction has not been particularly dramatic. Nevertheless, 1995 seems to have represented a low point in the political demography of agriculture. Since that time, the size of the national agricultural electorate has actually been amplifying both in number and as a proportion of the total voting population. It expanded marginally from 12.4 per cent of the national electorate to 12.6 per cent in 1998 (see Table 5.1) for example. It is still too early to say whether this trend will be sustained, but it reflects both the aging of the farm

Table 5.1 Farm household voters as a percentage of the national electorate

Unit: Million/per cent

Year	Population in agricultural electorate(A)	National electorate (B)	National agricultural electorate (A)/(B)
1950	20.1	42.1ᵃ	47.7
1955	20.3	49.2	41.3
1958	n/a	52.0	n/a
1960	20.1	54.3	37.0
1963	19.2	58.3	32.9
1967	19.0ᵇ	63.0	30.2
1969	17.6ᶜ	69.3	25.4
1972	17.2	73.8	23.3
1974	16.8	75.4	22.3
1976	16.5	77.9	21.2
1977	16.4	78.3	20.9
1979	16.1	80.2	20.1
1980	15.9	80.9	19.7
1983	15.6	84.3	18.5
1986	15.0	86.4	17.4
1990	13.3	90.3	14.7
1993	13.1 (10.1)ᵈ	94.5	13.9 (10.7)ᵈ
1995	12.0 (9.2)	96.8	12.4 (9.5)
1996	12.1 (9.3)	97.7	12.4 (9.5)
1998	12.5ᵉ (9.7)ᶠ	99.0	12.6 (9.8)

Notes:

(A) The number of persons living in farm households who are eligible to vote.

(B) The total number of eligible voters.

a   This is the 1949 figure, because 1950 figures were not available.

b   This figure includes farm household members over the age of 16, because of unavailability of those for 20 years and over.

c   This figure is for 1970, because 1969 figures were not available.

d   The figures in brackets are the commercial farm household figures which the MAFF began to use consistently from 1991 onwards.

e   This figure was reached by multiplying the number of eligible voters per commercial farm households in 1997 by the number of commercial and non-commercial farm households in 1998.

f   The figure for 1997 commercial farm households was used in the calculation.

Sources: *Nihon Tokei Nenkan*, annual, relevant years; *Norinsuisansho Tokeihyo*, annual, relevant years; Foreign Press Center, Japan, *The Diet, Elections, and Political Parties*, 'About Japan' Series, No. 13, January 1985, p. 104; *Yomiuri Shinbun*, 13 July 1998; *Japan Agrinfo Newsletter*, Vol. 16, No. 4, December 1998, p. 2.

household population and the Japanese economic recession. Younger members of farm households are crossing the voter threshold at the same time as being somewhat less able or inclined to leave home, hence the increment in the number of voters per household (it climbed from 3.47 in 1995 to 3.78 in 1997).[22] Meanwhile, older persons in farm households are living longer.

Nevertheless, over the entire period under examination, demographic changes in the agricultural sector have inevitably impacted on the significance of farmers as a sectoral voting bloc, both nationally and within smaller prefectural or sub-prefectural constituencies. Trends since the early 1980s can be determined from the figures in Table 5.2. In the Upper House, farm household voters constituted over 40 per cent of the total eligible vote in four (out of 47) prefectural constituencies in 1983 (Akita, Nagano, Shimane and Kagoshima). By 1989, no constituencies had farm household voters in such high proportions, although 14 districts had eligible farm voters in the 30–39 per cent range. This number halved to seven in 1992, and almost halved again to four in 1995 (Iwate, Akita, Nagano and Shimane), with the highest proportion registered by Akita at 32.0 per cent. In 1998, however, because of the small increment in the number of farm household voters, five prefectures had more than 30 per cent of voters resident in farm households (the previous four plus Tottori). Akita once again recorded the highest percentage at 34.1 per cent. Most less urbanised prefectures remained in the 20–30 per cent range.

What these proportions amount to on polling day in terms of the electoral influence of farm voters is difficult to gauge precisely. Certainly it is no longer true, as it was in the 1950s and early 1960s, that: 'Without significant support from this large sector, no party can hope to gain or keep power.'[23] Nor would it be possible to endorse unequivocally Inoguchi and Iwai's contention that the movement of farmers' votes in the mid-1980s still had a large impact on the results of elections and therefore could decide the fate of individual Diet members. In their view, the possibility of re-election was directly related to how much individual Diet members satisfied the interests of farmers.[24]

As Table 5.2 reveals, by the mid- to late 1990s, the farm vote was occupying insufficient proportions of the total eligible vote across a range of constituencies to justify such unreserved acclamations of its national electoral influence. Nevertheless, farmers' votes can still be a valuable or even decisive electoral asset for a particular candidate depending on the composition of the candidate's overall support base, the type of constituency in which he is standing and the percentage of the total vote required for victory.

Taking the last factor for example, in the 24 UH prefectural constituencies that wind up being single-member, first-past-the-post constituencies[25] – many of which are towards the more rural end of the spectrum – successful candidates in the 1995 elections obtained an average of 46.8 per cent of the cast vote.[26] The total eligible vote in farm households in those same constituencies averaged 22.1 per cent. This meant that, if they were all duly cast, farm household votes averaged around slightly less than half the required vote for victory. This was quite a large proportion for a specific sectional interest. Given that the candidate had to obtain such a high percentage of the total vote for victory, farmers might be too valuable a component of a support base to ignore, although farm voters would be courted along with a wider cross-section of other interests, and to that extent, agricultural representation would be diluted.[27]

Table 5.2 Farmers' voting strength in Upper House prefectural constituencies, 1983, 1989, 1992, 1995 and 1998 elections

Constituency	1983			1989			1992			1995			1998		
	No. of farm household voters	Total no. of eligible voters	Farm household voters as % of total eligible voters	No. of farm household voters	Total no. of eligible voters	Farm household voters as % of total eligible voters	No. of farm household voters	Total no. of eligible voters	Farm household voters as % of total eligible voters	No. of farm household voters	Total no. of eligible voters	Farm household voters as % of total eligible voters	No. of farm household voters	Total no. of eligible voters	Farm household voters as % of total eligible voters
Hokkaido	401,800	3,977,673	10.1%	356,195	4,171,987	8.5%	321,914	4,277,884	7.5%	281,025	4,444,356	6.3%	294,008	4,523,366	6.5%
Aomori	352,275	1,095,511	32.2%	324,415	1,126,981	28.8%	302,496	1,133,098	26.7%	272,714	1,159,797	23.5%	288,338	1,177,037	24.5%
Iwate	407,540	1,033,055	39.4%	387,240	1,063,280	36.4%	376,655	1,074,482	35.1%	347,940	1,103,873	31.5%	372,670	1,118,820	33.3%
Miyagi	389,970	1,498,799	26.0%	368,830	1,611,384	22.9%	350,563	1,679,137	20.9%	323,904	1,756,073	18.4%	344,925	1,813,134	19.0%
Akita	379,050	934,592	40.6%	350,875	943,213	37.2%	334,943	946,345	35.4%	307,140	959,822	32.0%	329,540	966,107	34.1%
Yamagata	340,480	925,627	36.8%	309,050	945,006	32.7%	289,325	954,774	30.3%	260,562	968,697	26.9%	277,452	979,894	28.3%
Fukushima	498,435	1,465,927	34.0%	468,440	1,533,867	30.5%	451,951	1,565,686	28.7%	416,039	1,616,529	25.7%	446,569	1,641,334	27.2%
Ibaraki	592,760	1,851,361	32.0%	553,910	2,021,966	27.4%	530,690	2,138,925	24.8%	518,004	2,244,330	23.1%	514,949	2,310,622	22.3%
Tochigi	355,530	1,282,966	27.7%	330,400	1,378,615	24.0%	318,400	1,441,933	22.1%	290,668	1,503,049	19.3%	306,407	1,546,294	19.8%
Gumma	346,500	1,325,243	26.1%	312,395	1,418,891	22.0%	287,302	1,480,324	19.4%	253,237	1,535,604	16.5%	269,060	1,571,793	17.1%
Saitama	414,680	3,768,850	11.0%	384,580	4,412,439	8.7%	358,976	4,821,596	7.4%	322,873	5,139,213	6.3%	343,451	5,343,399	6.4%
Chiba	462,455	3,379,093	13.7%	426,055	3,904,016	10.9%	406,227	4,211,535	9.6%	362,799	4,444,522	8.2%	384,691	4,604,677	8.4%
Tokyo	97,335	8,416,093	1.2%	88,655	8,991,056	1.0%	72,562	9,271,731	0.8%	60,263	9,419,153	0.6%	63,920	9,581,207	0.7%
Kanagawa	168,000	4,952,831	3.4%	155,925	5,724,909	2.7%	133,800	6,141,797	2.2%	114,330	6,421,453	1.8%	121,149	6,621,623	1.8%
Niigata	559,790	1,773,327	31.6%	514,430	1,837,989	28.0%	491,107	1,870,255	26.2%	447,286	1,923,224	23.3%	475,524	1,956,987	24.3%
Toyama	243,005	799,839	30.4%	217,910	833,377	26.1%	207,569	855,940	24.3%	187,612	881,137	21.3%	196,447	899,111	21.8%
Ishikawa	207,655	799,337	26.0%	187,530	841,380	22.3%	165,288	869,626	19.0%	145,372	903,277	16.1%	155,887	924,622	16.9%
Fukui	183,225	574,167	31.9%	171,920	599,051	28.7%	159,076	613,702	25.9%	147,617	630,314	23.4%	158,344	642,297	24.7%
Yamanashi	222,040	583,832	38.0%	208,915	626,847	33.3%	181,405	651,192	27.9%	163,975	670,785	24.4%	174,901	687,987	25.4%
Nagano	662,725	1,517,080	43.7%	635,600	1,595,169	39.8%	568,355	1,642,542	34.6%	517,301	1,693,543	30.5%	551,880	1,729,372	31.9%
Gifu	406,000	1,392,564	29.2%	381,150	1,491,296	25.6%	346,551	1,550,541	22.4%	317,279	1,607,449	19.7%	334,719	1,644,103	20.4%
Shizuoka	452,655	2,462,065	18.4%	418,670	2,652,696	15.8%	355,923	2,764,345	12.9%	318,518	2,865,153	11.1%	338,650	2,933,736	11.5%
Aichi	503,965	4,303,537	11.7%	480,970	4,716,324	10.2%	414,108	4,970,940	8.3%	368,320	5,192,353	7.1%	388,395	5,352,347	7.3%

Mie	340,795	1,224,187	27.8%	324,170	1,305,745	24.8%	289,219	1,363,643	21.2%	258,862	1,414,364	18.3%	274,655	1,449,301	19.0%
Shiga	264,005	773,255	34.1%	237,720	849,830	28.0%	210,870	902,142	23.4%	188,581	954,216	19.8%	198,148	998,288	19.8%
Kyoto	213,080	1,801,358	11.8%	198,275	1,887,971	10.5%	177,749	1,939,156	9.2%	161,858	2,003,902	8.1%	171,423	2,048,754	8.4%
Osaka	177,135	5,844,836	3.0%	165,165	6,303,707	2.6%	136,959	6,527,826	2.1%	115,815	6,732,653	1.7%	123,946	6,875,434	1.8%
Hyogo	557,515	3,642,390	15.3%	532,350	3,894,385	13.7%	479,641	4,074,782	11.8%	433,136	4,202,716	10.3%	462,256	4,302,360	10.7%
Nara	173,215	875,010	19.8%	160,825	978,991	16.4%	139,444	1,038,503	13.4%	123,417	1,094,847	11.3%	129,767	1,130,819	11.5%
Wakayama	199,465	788,134	25.3%	186,375	806,768	23.1%	164,436	828,256	19.9%	149,175	850,647	17.5%	155,660	862,447	18.0%
Tottori	174,160	445,696	39.1%	164,150	458,068	35.8%	153,289	463,808	33.1%	141,496	473,837	29.9%	150,028	481,443	31.2%
Shimane	248,185	578,901	42.9%	229,600	589,723	38.9%	207,285	589,439	35.2%	189,639	599,270	31.6%	199,206	601,504	33.1%
Okayama	459,865	1,362,556	33.8%	430,010	1,420,121	30.3%	381,377	1,458,145	26.2%	347,854	1,508,002	23.1%	366,433	1,537,670	23.8%
Hiroshima	448,770	1,956,225	22.9%	414,225	2,065,267	20.1%	356,278	2,135,435	16.7%	319,924	2,213,262	14.5%	336,080	2,259,622	14.9%
Yamaguchi	301,455	1,149,655	26.2%	276,850	1,177,700	23.5%	243,779	1,190,162	20.5%	219,602	1,217,872	18.0%	231,449	1,228,126	18.8%
Tokushima	208,705	610,835	34.2%	195,790	627,707	31.2%	177,358	637,688	27.8%	159,547	652,353	24.5%	168,134	661,092	24.4%
Kagawa	244,160	730,640	33.4%	227,360	761,263	29.9%	204,516	779,308	26.2%	187,050	802,420	23.3%	197,392	817,771	24.1%
Ehime	339,465	1,097,673	30.9%	301,175	1,137,581	26.5%	266,286	1,155,167	23.1%	238,028	1,183,611	20.1%	249,064	1,198,612	20.8%
Kochi	182,210	622,916	29.3%	168,000	634,624	26.5%	147,929	637,234	23.2%	133,102	648,873	20.5%	140,162	654,954	21.4%
Fukuoka	437,570	3,270,785	13.4%	403,200	3,465,908	11.6%	355,320	3,592,120	9.9%	313,226	3,737,034	8.4%	326,290	3,850,253	8.5%
Saga	211,540	621,089	34.1%	191,940	638,197	30.1%	172,743	648,100	26.7%	155,671	664,978	23.4%	163,107	674,596	24.2%
Nagasaki	253,540	1,103,860	23.0%	232,680	1,139,474	20.4%	191,878	1,153,033	16.6%	168,284	1,170,494	14.4%	178,378	1,185,671	15.0%
Kumamoto	416,360	1,309,156	31.8%	381,220	1,363,219	28.0%	336,895	1,386,345	24.3%	299,513	1,422,387	21.1%	312,276	1,450,143	21.5%
Oita	318,745	895,918	35.6%	290,640	922,519	31.5%	251,553	935,799	26.9%	223,624	958,877	23.3%	234,058	972,744	24.1%
Miyazaki	281,190	830,906	33.8%	258,090	860,764	30.0%	236,608	871,496	27.1%	214,675	901,074	23.8%	228,992	915,543	25.0%
Kagoshima	571,970	1,296,267	44.1%	525,175	1,341,109	39.2%	443,537	1,341,649	33.1%	384,847	1,371,988	28.1%	396,976	1,385,016	28.7%
Okinawa	155,330	735,782	21.1%	148,470	819,069	18.1%	135,291	854,877	15.8%	109,610	895,642	12.2%	114,950	936,668	12.3%

Notes:

a Calculated by the number of farm households times the average number of eligible voters per farm household in that year. For 1983 and 1989 it was 3.5; for 1992 it was 3.55; for 1995 it was 3.47; and for 1998 it was 3.78.

Sources: *Norinsuisansho Tokeihyo*, annual, relevant years; *Nihon Tokei Nenkan*, annual, relevant years; *Seikan Yoran* [*A Handbook of Politics and the Bureaucracy*], Tokyo, Seisaku Jihosha, biannual, various issues; *Asahi Shinbun*, 24 July 1995; *Yomiuri Shinbun*, 13 July 1998.

Farm votes would certainly contribute to a total package of support in some constituencies by possibly making the difference to the success or failure of a particular candidate. If well organised, the act of bestowing or withdrawing farm votes could potentially swing the outcome in either a positive or negative direction, although the farm vote alone would not be sufficient to guarantee victory.[28] Amongst the UH single-seat prefectural constituencies in the 1995 UH elections, for example, farm support was most crucial in Aomori, Iwate, Akita, Yamagata, Yamanashi, Tottori, Shimane, Tokushima, Kagawa, Kochi and Miyazaki. These were districts where the total eligible farm vote comprised more than half the votes obtained by the successful candidate.

As for the 18 two-seat UH prefectural constituencies, the required percentage for success dropped down to an average of 29.9 per cent. In these constituencies, the farm vote averaged 16.7 per cent of the total eligible vote – once again around half the required vote for victory. Amongst these electorates, farmers were a more significant component in the two-seat districts of Miyagi, Fukushima, Ibaraki, Tochigi, Niigata, Nagano, Gifu, Okayama, Kumamoto and Kagoshima.

The percentages were even more favourable in the LH electoral system prior to the 1994 reforms, because it comprised medium-sized, multi-member districts (MMDs) with a single, non-transferable vote. In LH districts, victory could be secured with as little as 10–15 per cent of the total vote, or in some cases even lower. If the same proportions of farm voters are extrapolated to LH districts,[29] this generates a much greater potential impact for farm household residents on electoral outcomes. Until the October 1996 poll, a particular voting bloc with percentages of between 10 and 30 per cent of the total number of eligible voters in any given constituency could still determine electoral victory or loss in its own right. Based on this reasoning, farm voters, if voting in a unified way, could be expected to exert a decisive influence on electoral outcomes in those LH constituencies where they still constituted more than 20 per cent of the total eligible vote. This was the case in 23 prefectures (although not necessarily in all electoral districts within these prefectures). They were Aomori, Iwate, Akita, Yamagata, Fukushima, Nagano, Tottori, Shimane, Tokushima, Saga, Miyazaki and Kagoshima. The dependence of candidates on such blocs would climb commensurately in these districts and therefore the extent of the electoral debt to farmers would expand also.

Nevertheless, most commentators agree that the main trend occurring at the electoral level has been for farmers to lose positive voting power (that is, sufficient numbers to elect a Diet member outright), but to retain considerable negative voting power (i.e. the ability to ensure electoral failure if votes are redirected away from a candidate). Where farmers' voting power has been eroded to the greatest extent has been in areas around the big conurbations of Nagoya (which shows up in Aichi), Shiga (around Kyoto), Chiba (around Tokyo) and what used to be provincial areas but which are now highly urbanised like Hokkaido, Shizuoka, Hiroshima, and to a lesser extent Shikoku and Kyushu. In contrast, farm voters can still form a large enough proportion of the total number of votes required by a successful candidate to impact on electoral outcomes in the Tohoku region of Northern Honshu (i.e. the prefectures of Aomori, Iwate, Akita and Yamagata), the Tosan region (Nagano), Chugoku (Tottori and Shimane), and to a lesser extent Northern Kanto (Ibaraki and Tochigi), Shikoku and Kyushu.

The impact of changing rural society on farm votes

The basic assumption behind using aggregate statistics as a measure of the political 'weighting' of the agricultural electorate is that farm household residents still vote as farmers. In other words, they vote on the basis of con-siderations that relate in some way to their agricultural production activities. This assumption needs further examination, however, if it is to remain valid, particularly in the face of the socio-economic transformation of rural areas in the postwar period.

The exponential rise in part-time farming has been the most dramatic change in the countryside, diversifying the occupational interests of farm households and reducing their dependence on agricultural income. Over the past few decades, more than two-thirds of Japanese farm households have become Type II part-time households, which means that they earn the greater part of their income from non-agricultural sources. Surveys of the farm household economy reveal that the ratio of non-agricultural income to agri-cultural income in the average farm household in 1970 was around two-thirds to one-third, but by 1996, this ratio had reached four-fifths to one-fifth.[30] In other words, the vast majority of farm households have become part-time with one or more of their residents engaged in non-farming occupations. Those who are defined as farm voters for purposes of this analysis thus hold an ever-declining stake in the agricultural economy.

The diversity of occupational interests within farm households is matched by a similar social and economic heterogeneity at the village (*noson*) level. A *noson* is an area where the population is less than 4,000 persons per square kilometre. Even in agricultural villages thus defined, the share of non-agricultural households accounted for more than three-quarters of all households in an average agricultural village in 1980,[31] while the population not residing in farm households expanded to 54.7 per cent in the mid-1980s.[32] Moreover, with respect to the structure of employment in farm villages, 23.1 per cent were employed in manufacturing industry, 22.0 per cent in agri-culture, 15.3 per cent in wholesaling and retailing, 15.3 per cent in service industries, 10.5 per cent in construction, and 5.4 per cent in transport and communications. In other words, employment in agricultural villages had become highly diversified, reflecting the escalation in the number of part-time farm households and the emergence of a mixed economy in rural Japan.[33]

These changes inevitably call into question concepts like the 'farm vote', which rely on statistics such as farm household population over the age of 20 years as an aggregate measure of the electoral weighting of the agricultural community. Residence in a farm household may or may not mean that the members of that household retain a substantial enough interest in government agricultural policy for their voting choices to be influenced by perceptions of how the government is responding to the needs of farmers. If farm household residence is meaningless as a determinant of voter choice, the utility of measuring the farm vote by using farm household population statistics will be considerably compromised, providing at best an exaggerated indication of just how significant a force farmers are within the total voting population.

The fundamental question, therefore, is whether farm household residence remains a significant determinant of political interest and therefore voting choice, and whether such residence is sufficient to guarantee a stake, however minor or indirect, in the farm economy and in agricultural affairs in general. In short, do part-time farm household residents think and vote as farmers or think and vote as non-farmers? Is residence in a farm household a sufficient condition for voting like a farmer? Furthermore, given the social and economic diversity of farm villages, how strong is the sense of common interest amongst farmers and how cohesive is their vote? To what extent is there a community of interest amongst rural people such that it encourages other rural dwellers to identify with agricultural interests and to support farmers with their votes and other political activities? What policy interests do rural dwellers have in common?

Direct answers to these questions are not readily available without doing surveys of the political attitudes and behaviour of farm household and rural dwellers, which is beyond the scope of this study. Nevertheless, some analysis of this subject has been done by others, although the results are somewhat inconclusive. In the early 1970s, one study observed that village communities which had functioned as organisations for collecting votes were breaking down as a result of urbanisation and an expansion in the numbers of farmers with side jobs.[34] Another study published at the same time observed that the 50/50 farmer/non-farmer mentality in the political consciousness of part-time farmers had given way to something with a much higher weighting on the non-farmer side.[35] This was because of the expansion in contact between farmers and other labourers in the course of part-time wage employment and farm migrant jobs. Indeed, one million or so *dekasegisha* in the 1960s and 1970s travelled from the colder regions of northern Japan to work in the factories and construction sites of big cities for about six months of the year. When away from their homes, these farmers adopted the views and outlook of labouring people.[36] Moreover, the JSP took on their cause and organised them through *dekasegi* associations.[37] The political effects of these developments could be seen in the 1971 UH elections in which the LDP was defeated in some one-seat prefectural constituencies because farmers were prepared to vote for labour union executives tied to the JSP.[38]

Other commentators continued to observe the political effects of rural social and economic change into the late 1970s and 1980s. In the late 1970s Atsumi noted that because rural society was gradually changing, campaign strategies designed to raise a sense of community or consanguinity were not as effective as they had been in the past.[39] The same study reported that political representatives from rural areas had previously maintained good relations with village leaders to order to secure local votes. Villagers had believed that there was a certain security in being on good terms with politicians. This was no longer the case, however. Village societies had diversified and the sense of unity in each village was gradually disappearing. Members of farm families commonly had different jobs outside agriculture and therefore did not necessarily help the head of the household with agricultural production. In many cases, farmers themselves also had side jobs.[40] A decade later much the same observations were being repeated. Saeki, for example, reported that society in rural villages had diversified and the sense of community was disappearing rapidly.[41] Even the MAFF admitted that a real problem in rural Japan was the 'disintegration of traditional community relationships'.[42]

Other studies, however, have drawn a more qualified set of conclusions. Fukutake completed a wide-ranging study of Japanese rural society in the early 1970s. He made a number of crucial observations, arguing initially against the retention of rural communitarian traditions. Firstly, he acknowledged that social changes in agricultural villages after WWII weakened the unity of agricultural communities and destroyed the landlord system.[43] Farmers no longer found it necessary to obey authoritarian power or to act in accordance with the customs of agricultural communities. Secondly, farmers were more profit-oriented and started to seek non-agricultural income. As farm households became more diversified with the expansion in part-time farming, the character of farmers began to change substantially and it became even more difficult to maintain unity and harmony in agricultural villages. Fukutake goes on to qualify these observations, however, by noting that the farmers' self-centred character did not develop into fully fledged individualism because the patriarchal system remained to some extent and agricultural communities did not disappear entirely. Critically farmers did not develop sufficient production capability to operate completely independently of traditional agricultural communities. To this extent, farmers retained their essential community character developed in the past, and hence agricultural communities still strove to uphold their principles, existence and identity. As a result, agricultural organisations like Nokyo remained as organisations for all farmers although they only served the interests of some.[44]

Writing around the same time, Fukui maintained that being employed off the farm but remaining resident in the farm household was a critical factor in inhibiting a shift in political allegiance away from the generally conservative inclinations of the farmers in the household, typically the older generation.[45] Similarly, Tanaka observed in the early 1970s that although the lifestyle of farmers had been urbanised, their political awareness displayed little change.[46] Another study in the early 1980s remarked that 'the characteristics and attitudes of traditional life in agricultural villages remain in the political behaviour and perceptions of people in these regions, even when the regions have inhabitants with diverse occupations.'[47] A similar observation was made to the effect that farmers, although changing, tended to yield to the powerful and keep feudalistic traditions.[48] Moore, writing in the mid-1980s, concluded that part-time farmers viewed themselves as 'farmers who work' rather than 'workers who farm' even though most of them made more money off the farm than on it.[49] As he pointed out: 'They view the safest and most profitable strategy to be maintenance of agricultural land rights at any cost, even if it means being over-capitalized in equipment and farming on weekends.'[50]

The general point was also argued by Goto and Imamura that although the shift to part-time farming had 'made the contribution of many farm families to agricultural output quite small (except for rice), part-time farm families are not excluded from the family farm category . . . At the village level, farming remains a way of life among part-time farmers. They usually participate in the maintenance of irrigation canals and village roads and cooperate with other farmers. While part-time farmers are often viewed as an obstacle to farm adjustment and rationalization, their role in maintaining village solidarity and practising resource stewardship is appreciated by the increasingly urbanized society.'[51]

Certainly it is a fact that administratively defined rural communities (*nogyo shuraku*)[52] are still viable sociological entities, with a long history that extends in many cases back to before the Meiji Restoration in 1868.[53] *Nogyo shuraku* were the customary basic unit of settlement 'discernible by territorial integrity and often characterized by kinship relationships.'[54] Furthermore in 'the Edo period, these rural communities served, at the same time, as a natural village and as an administrative village. The village was a unit of local autonomy, cooperation in irrigation agriculture (i.e. rice farming), and mutual help in the sphere of reproduction. The same village was used as a unit of tax collection (mainly in harvested rice), various forms of coercion and regulation by the authorities, and residence of farmers.'[55]

Kada and Goto maintain that these 'rural communities have persisted as the basic unit of rural settlement.'[56] Even though the economic foundation of most communities has 'shifted from agricultural to non-agricultural employment in adjacent cities and towns as many farmers became part-time farmers . . . [i]n many communities, the attention of community life started to shift from cooperation in agriculture to matters of mutual concern to neighbors such as festivals, garbage collection, and road improvement. However, the maintenance of agricultural land and water resources is still an important concern for most rural communities.'[57] Furthermore, farmers still had to cooperate at the level of coordinating individual agricultural operations 'including such routine activities as canal and road maintenance, communal forest care-taking, and strategic decisions such as applying for land improvement, irrigation improvement, cooperative mechanization, and other subsidized schemes for modernization and adjustment.'[58] In addition, agricultural communities form the natural social basis of the agricultural cooperatives.[59]

Those areas where rural communities have disappeared have been either in the remotest regions or on the urban fringe where they have been absorbed into urban sprawl. Nevertheless, even in 1990 there were still 140,122 officially defined rural communities.[60] This is a decline from 152,431 in 1960.[61] As Kada and Goto acknowledge, however, where change has occurred is in the internal social composition of these communities: 'On average, the share of farm households in total households of rural communities decreased from 61.4 percent in 1960, to 23.2 per cent in 1980, and to 16.0 per cent in 1990 . . . [a]lthough the average number of farm households per rural community did not decrease rapidly (39 in 1960, 33 in 1980, and 27 in 1990)'.[62] These figures suggest that the number of farm households per rural community has not diminished so much as the number of non-farm households per rural community has expanded. Even amongst non-farm households that used to be farm households, identification with agriculture may remain to some extent.

In summary, the bonds created by history, tradition, kinship, administration, agricultural organisation, the needs of farming production and the desire for viable local communities and agricultural prosperity help to maintain the sense of community amongst farm households and rural dwellers even in the face of rapid social and economic change. The fact that rural communities are economically differentiated does not necessarily signify that community bonds have become meaningless. The rural community is still a place of residence, if not occupation, and common interests relating to agriculture, the desire for local development programmes and other aspects of rural life continue to be shared amongst its members. The fact that industries have often developed in nearby urban centres to which rural residents can commute has contributed to this state of affairs.[63]

To the extent that rural dwellers retain a sense of community and share common interests with farm household residents, and to the extent that farm household dwellers retain a residual sense of collective identity as a farm household unit, then both farm households and rural communities can be considered as relatively meaningful entities from an electoral perspective. Although socio-economic changes in rural society, including continuing urbanisation and occupational diversification are inevitably complicating the economic interests of farm households and rural dwellers, residence within an agricultural production unit or within a rural community remains relevant as a determinant of electoral behaviour. Many farm voters continue to share common perceptions of policy benefits to farm households including those that are specific to agriculture even under conditions of mixed employment. Moreover, while not all members of the farm household might work in agriculture, farming would still contribute to the collective economic benefit of the farm household. The sense of solidarity amongst members of farm households irrespective of employment also perpetuates a personal stake in agriculture that is not necessarily in direct proportion to their degree of engagement in agricultural production. Even though most farm household residents cannot be called farmers in the pure sense of the word, producer subsidies remain an important and welcome component of farm household income and therefore agricultural policy.

In the case of rural communities, their significance as part of a broader phenomenon called the 'rural electorate' which shares certain common interests with agricultural producers cannot be easily dismissed. As Keeler has observed of the European case, the electoral foundation of agricultural support and protection has never rested purely on numbers of farm voters.[64] Supporters of farm interests are in fact much greater than the actual numbers of farmers might suggest. The community of interest amongst rural people generally has often meant that rural dwellers support farmers with their votes and other political activities. In other words, the broader 'rural community' exerts a politically relevant demographic 'multiplier effect', with a much larger percentage of the national electorate possessing a 'strong agricultural attribute'.[65] In reality, the 'farm vote' (*nominhyo*) should be considered the major component of an even larger 'rural vote' (*nosonhyo*).

In Japan's case this 'multiplier effect' has been reinforced by several additional factors. Firstly, both farm and non-farm household dwellers in rural areas benefit from the provision of local services and rural infrastructure. Many of the benefits from the central government distributed to rural regions are not just for agriculture but for facilities servicing the rural community as a whole, which makes it difficult to separate the interests of farmers from rural dwellers generally.[66] In this respect, farmers and non-farmers alike share common interests in the promotion of their infrastructural environment. What is good for agriculture is perceived as good for the local community regardless of the type of occupational connection of the voter with farming. In this sense, both categories of voters share a common interest that can be mobilised as the basis of shared political support. Subsidies for rural public works are just as important as agricultural public works as a determinant of voter choice in rural areas amongst both farmers and non-farmers. Moreover, both types of public works provide employment for farmers as well as rural dwellers more generally.

Secondly, farm and rural solidarity has also been reinforced by the agricultural cooperative system. The organisational structure of the agricultural cooperatives has provided an institutional overlay to farm households as cohesive units because farmers can join Nokyo as farm households, not only as individuals.[67] Furthermore, the organisational structure of the agricultural cooperatives act as a cohesive element in the rural community as a whole.[68] Because of the geographic rather than the functional basis of membership, the agricultural cooperatives both embody and strengthen local community ties. Farmers can belong only to the multi-purpose cooperative within their community, while most rural people belong to Nokyo regardless of their engagement in farming. In this way, rural communities have remained the natural units of local agricultural cooperatives, and Nokyo has both represented and reinforced traditional solidarity in rural communal life.[69]

Other relevant factors include the links many urban dwellers retain to their rural hometowns and farming relatives, with many only one generation removed from farming. Hence the pull of the rural lobby has been much greater than the simple number of agricultural workers or farm household dwellers suggest.

The national Nokyo electorate

One of the most potent sources of Nokyo's influence has been the extremely large number of votes that allegedly come within the scope of the agricultural cooperative system. In the broadest sense, agricultural cooperative membership can be considered equivalent to 'the farmers'. Because farmers can take out farm household membership of Nokyo, this automatically brings in all members of the family into the agricultural cooperative fold and gives Nokyo an organisational reach to a much larger membership base, namely total population resident in farm households. For example, a farm household membership of 5.07 million in 1960 affiliated a total of 30.93 million voters. Similarly the 4.75 million farm household members in 1994 expanded to a total affiliated membership of 16.86 million.[70]

Calculated in terms of individuals over the age of 20 years residing in farm households with agricultural cooperative membership, the national Nokyo electorate is, in fact, larger than the national agricultural electorate because of the looser definition of what constitutes a farm household in agricultural cooperative bylaws compared to the statistical definitions used in the MAFF surveys. For example, Nokyo's total farm household membership figure in 1994 exceeded the total number of farm households in Japan according to MAFF figures by more than one million (i.e. the 4.75 million farm household members of Nokyo compared with only 3.64 million farm households according to the MAFF).[71] This difference raises the proportion occupied by total Nokyo farm household voters in the national electorate several percentage points higher than farm household voters as a proportion of the national electorate (to around 16 per cent, compared to around 12–13 per cent).[72] Clearly, changes in Nokyo's farm household membership lag behind occupational and demographic changes in the farm sector (largely a definitional lag). Nonetheless, Nokyo's organisational reach remains somewhat larger than figures for farm households would suggest.

Viewed from the perspective of Nokyo's individual farmer members, the Nokyo vote comprises a smaller but theoretically 'harder' group of voters. In 1994, it represented 5.5 million votes, or 5.6 per cent of the national electorate.[73] This is not generally the measure used to gauge Nokyo's potential voting power, however, because of the solidarity within farm households. Nokyo leaders argue that their organisation can make a claim on the voter loyalties of not only their direct members but also of the family members in Nokyo-affiliated households. A career executive of Zenchu put a figure on this in 1986: 'Including the votes of Nokyo family members, the number of voters we control is around 15 to 16 million.'[74] He also laid claim to 40 out of Japan's 47 prefectures as being under Nokyo's control.[75] A decade later, the Zenkoku Noseikyo claimed that it could influence 10 million votes prior to the October 1996 elections.[76] This was essentially the individual farmer-membership of the *sogo nokyo* multiplied by two, i.e. two voters per farm household. If these figures are to be believed, they rank Nokyo alongside some of the largest Japanese interest groups in terms of voter numbers.[77]

Even casting the net this wide is not sufficient for some commentators, however. Tachibana points out that the Nokyo vote extends beyond the household to other family relations, business contacts and others,[78] while Aono argues that it should also include Nokyo's staff members, associate members and group members in addition to the 'plus alpha' or unknown number of employees in Nokyo's subsidiary companies.[79]

Aggregate figures can only provide a general indication of Nokyo's potential voting power, however. Whether or not agricultural cooperative leaders are in a position actually to influence these votes is another matter altogether.[80] Figures for the gross membership of the farmers' political leagues provides one possible indicator of the number of voters who are committed to supporting the agricultural cooperative cause with their votes. In 1979, the total number of votes that the farmers' political leagues claimed they could control was approximately 4.62 million, or 28.7 per cent of the total farm vote in that year.[81] These figures are somewhat less impressive that those cited earlier.

Continuing socio-economic and demographic changes

The future size and significance of the agricultural electorate will be negatively influenced by a number of continuing socio-economic and demographic changes in the farm sector. Undoubtedly the economic and occupational interests of farm households are now very heterogeneous with the dominant household type consisting of part-time farmers and non-farmers residing together in a form of 'mixed living'. On top of this is firstly, the rapid aging of the agricultural workforce. In 1997, 26.2 per cent of persons engaged in family-operated commercial farms were 65 years or older,[82] whilst core farmers aged 65 or above accounted for a high 42.6 per cent of the total core-farmer population. In short, nearly half the core-farming population were old people.[83] The EPA's projections for the age structure of farm employment in 2000 and 2010 puts active farmers 65 years old or older at 56.1 per cent in 2000 and 56.0 per cent in 2010 (active farmers are those who work 150 days or more in farming per year).[84]

The second major trend that has appeared in the last decade or so and which, according to some observers, is of 'crisis' proportions,[85] is the shortage of successors to take over the farm when the current generation dies or retires.[86] Large numbers of farms are without a designated successor. In this respect agriculture is a dying industry because very few young workers are taking up farming. Of school leavers amongst the children of farm households, those who take up employment in agriculture are falling in number every year. In 1992, they amounted to barely 1700.[87] The problem initially became discernible in the early 1970s, with the number of young workers taking up farming falling dramatically from 36,900 in 1970 to 9,900 in 1975.[88]

Until the recent economic crisis, the biggest cause of the reduction in the number of 'bearers' of agriculture was the expansion in employment opportunities in non-agricultural sectors consequent upon the growth of the Japanese economy centring on urban areas and the disparity in income between agriculture and other industries. Although Japan's economic recession of the mid- and late 1990s has caused some reassessment amongst young and middle-aged workers about farming as an occupation either by choice or by necessity, the hard economic facts underline the relative lack of financial attractiveness of farming as a career. In 1996 the average daily wage in non-agricultural sectors was ¥20,655, while that for agricultural workers was only ¥8,219[89] (for males, even less for females). The average commercial farm household income from agriculture in 1995 was ¥1.4 million, down 9.5 per cent on 1994.[90] It fell by a further 4 per cent in 1996.[91] Total average income per commercial farm household in 1995 (comprising farm income, income from non-agricultural sectors and income from other sources such as annuities and insurance) was also down – by 1.9 per cent on 1994. This was the first fall in 39 years.[92] It did, however, rise slightly in 1996, to ¥8.9 million, but this was due to increments in non-agricultural income and annuities etc., not to an expansion in agricultural income, which continued to diminish.[93]

Besides economic factors such as contracting income opportunities in agriculture,[94] social and cultural factors have also been responsible for the exodus of young workers from agriculture.[95] These include the attraction of urban life for young people, the more interesting job prospects available in cities, the fact that individual status is derived increasingly from modern business corporations[96] and the declining social status of farming as an occupation. Nowadays, the time-honoured sense of obligation amongst the eldest sons of farm households to take over the family farm is breaking down, and in society agriculture is widely perceived as a minor, i.e. low-level industry.[97]

According to MAFF research, only 56.0 per cent of commercial farm households had successors in 1992.[98] Of the latter, only 13 per cent were mainly working in agriculture, while employment in mainly non-agricultural jobs accounted for 58 per cent, with the balance in non-agricultural employment.[99] Five years later in 1997, the MAFF 'Survey of Trends in Agricultural Structure' revealed that of farm households with workers aged 60 and above, only 7.7 per cent had successors who were engaged mainly in farming. However, 50.4 per cent of these farm households had successors who lived in those households and who commuted to work in other industries, while engaging in farming on weekends and holidays. Although these percentages were lower than in 1992, just over half of all farm households had successors in some form or other.[100] Just how many of these successors might ultimately take over the family farm remains uncertain. The final choice will be influenced by factors such as the production structure in different agricultural areas and part-time employment opportunities outside agriculture.[101] Given the record-high unemployment in Japan in the late 1990s, there has actually been an increase in the entry into farming of workers from non-agricultural sectors as a result of corporate bankruptcies and restructuring. In 1998, for example, the number of people engaged in farming actually grew for two consecutive months year on year in April and May.[102]

Nonetheless, the overwhelmingly dominant trend is one of contraction. Farm household population and, as a consequence, the size of the national agricultural electorate are likely to shrink even more dramatically in the future because of the lack of successors in Japanese farm households. Demographic shifts mean a waning rural influence even without electoral reform. The future of farmers' electoral power is not auspicious if it relies on sheer weight of numbers. Research by the Norinchukin Research Institute in 1992 established that population in rural districts or counties (*gunbu*) with a lot of farming areas would continue to dip, with 8.2 per cent less population in 2025 compared with 1990.[103] Economic Planning Agency projections of the number of farm households in 2000 is 3.1 million and 2.4 million in 2010.[104] According to Ministry of Labour forecasts, the number of people engaged in the agriculture, forestry and fisheries sectors will slump by 47 per cent – from 4.5 million in 1990 to 2.4 million in 2010. The proportion of these workers to the total work force will contract from 7.3 per cent in 1990 to 3.8 per cent in 2010, slightly above the level of present-day United States.[105] The MAFF's own statistics also underline these future trends. It estimates that the number of people engaged in 'basic agriculture' (i.e. core farming) will decrease in 2005 to 1.8 million, about 60 per cent of totals in the 1990s – because of the retirement of the generation born between 1926 and 1934.[106]

Changing constituency classifications

Another perspective on trends in the size and importance of the national agricultural electorate can be gained from adjustments in constituency classifications over time. Kobayashi uses a seven-point categorisation system to demonstrate changes in the character of LH electoral districts from 1960 through 1980. His categories run from 'strongly rural', 'rural' and 'semi-rural' to 'average', 'semi-urban', 'urban' and 'strongly urban'.[107] In 1960, 'strongly rural' districts comprised 46.6 per cent of the total number of LH constituencies; by 1980, they comprised 0.0 per cent, with large and continuous falls occurring in the period 1960 to 1975, when urbanisation was at its most rapid. Rural districts diminished more slowly from 28.5 per cent in 1965 (their proportion actually enlarged between 1960 to 1965 with the influx from strongly rural to rural categories) to 23.4 per cent in 1970, dropping more rapidly from 13.8 per cent in 1975 to 6.9 per cent in 1980. Meanwhile the proportion of semi-urban constituencies magnified from 2.5 per cent in 1960 to 21.5 per cent in 1980, urban electorates from 4.2 per cent to 10.0 per cent and strongly urban districts from 11.0 per cent to 25.4 per cent, with the rate of increase slowing sharply for strongly urban districts between 1975 and 1980, while semi-urban districts maintained their rapid inflation. Over the entire period of two decades, these changes amounted to a wholesale reconfiguration of the Japanese electoral landscape with the combined proportion of 'rural' electorates dwindling from 79.6 per cent of the total to 21.5 per cent, while the combined proportion of 'urban' districts inflated from 17.7 per cent to 56.9 per cent. In short, by 1980, less than one-quarter of all Japanese LH electorates could be classified as having some measure of 'rural' characteristics.

Tables 5.3 and 5.4 attempt a similar sort of recategorisation exercise for both Houses of the Diet from the mid-1970s onwards, except in this case, seats rather than electoral districts across a rural-metropolitan spectrum are utilised. Table 5.3 reveals that rural seats in prefectural constituencies of the Upper House (defined as 40 per cent of the population and above resident in farm households)[108] ceased to exist in all elections after 1983, and by 1992, the number of semi-rural seats (defined as 30–39 per cent of the population resident in farm households) had fallen to only one. On the other hand, the number of metropolitan and urban seats more than doubled from 28 to 59 over the period from 1974 to 1998. The latter figure represented 65.5 per cent of all UH prefectural constituency seats in 1998. With semi-urban seats thrown in, the proportion enlarged to 96.1 per cent.

In spite of the overall thrust of these macro-trends, an interesting phenomenon has revealed itself in the 1990s. In 1995, numbers of semi-rural and semi-urban seats began to rise again. Without necessarily understanding all the complex demographic variables involved, one can speculate that the departure of non-farming population for the big cities was leaving rural areas relatively more agricultural in character. In other words, non-farm household population continued to move from rural to urban areas, leaving farm household population comprising a higher percentage of the total in semi-rural and semi-urban constituencies. This would suggest that provincial areas are becoming increasingly denuded of non-farm population, a phenomenon common to industrialised societies.

In 1998, this trend partially continued, with the number of semi-rural seats continuing to climb, while the number of semi-urban seats dropped slightly. The factor cited above may be responsible, but so may factors identified earlier with respect to the expanding size of the national agricultural electorate, namely, the increasing average number of farm household residents owing both to longer-living older persons and the Japanese economic recession keeping the younger generation on the farm.

Table 5.3 Changing categorisation of Upper House seats based on percentage of population in farm households

Election year	1974		1977		1980		1983		1986		1989		1992		1995[c]		1998	
Seat type[a]	No. of seats	% of total[b]	No. of seats	% of total	No. of seats	% of total	No. of seats	% of total	No. of seats	% of total	No. of seats	% of total	No. of seats	% of total	No. of seats	% of total	No. of seats	% of total
Rural	16	21.1	7	9.2	7	9.2	2	2.6	0	0.0	0	0.0	0	0.0	0	0.0	0	0.0
Semi-Rural	23	30.3	27	35.5	25	32.9	22	28.9	14	18.4	11	14.4	1	1.3	2	2.6	3	3.9
Semi-Urban	9	11.8	14	18.4	10	13.2	18	23.7	26	34.2	29	38.2	16	21.1	26	34.2	24	31.6
Urban	19	25.0	19	25.0	21	27.6	21	27.6	19	25.0	19	25.0	27	35.5	23	30.3	25	32.9
Metropolitan	9	11.8	9	11.8	13	17.1	13	17.1	17	22.4	17	22.4	32	42.1	25	32.9	24	31.6
Total	76	100.0	76	100.0	76	100.0	76	100.0	76	100.0	76	100.0	76	100.0	76	100.0	76	100.0

Notes:
a Seats were categorised according to the percentage of population in each prefectural constituency residing in farm households.

    Rural = 40%+
    Semi-Rural = 30–39%
    Semi-Urban = 20–29%
    Urban = 10–19%
    Metropolitan = 0–9%

b Some of the percentage columns do not add up to 100 per cent because of rounding off.

c Prior to the 1995 UH election, a seat adjustment meant that four seats changed hands, mainly amongst metropolitan and urban electorates.

Source: Calculated from figures in *Norinsuisansho Tokeihyo*, annual, relevant years.

Table 5.4 Changing categorisation of Lower House seats based on population employed in primary industry, 1976, 1980, 1986 and 1990 election years

Election year	1976		1980		1986		1990	
Seat type[a]	No. of seats	Per cent of total	No. of seats	Per cent of total	No. of seats	Per cent of total	No. of seats	Per cent of total
Rural	51	10.0	3	0.6	0	0.0	0	0.0
Semi-Rural	101	19.8	18	9.1	8	1.6	n/a	n/a
Semi-Urban	135	26.4	104	20.4	46	9.0	n/a	n/a
Urban	86	16.8	189	37.0	220	43.0	n/a	n/a
Metropolitan	138	27.0	197	38.6	238	46.5	n/a	n/a
Total	511	100	511	100	512	100	512	100

Notes:

a Seats were categorised according to the percentage of population employed in primary industry based on the census for 1975, 1980 and 1985 and the calculations of Nishihira Shigeki kindly supplied to J. A. A. Stockwin. Unfortunately, categorisation of LH seats based on the 1990 census is not available.
Rural   = 40%+
Semi-Rural   = 30–39%
Semi-Urban   = 20–29%
Urban   = 10–19%
Metropolitan = 0–9%

The equivalent table for the Lower House, which categorises seats according to the percentage of population employed in primary industry[109] (but only over the period 1976 to 1986) identifies the usual trend of falling rural and semi-rural seat, numbers and rising urban and metropolitan seat numbers (Table 5.4). In 1976 there were 51 rural seats (defined as 40 per cent of the population employed in primary industry in the constituency). This number fell to three in 1980 and zero in 1986. Likewise, semi-rural seats (defined as 30–39 per cent of the population employed in primary industry) constituted only 1.6 per cent of seats by 1986 while the urban and metropolitan categories comprised 89.5 per cent of all seat types.

Because each seat represents an individual politician, the import of these figures is that by 1986, just under 90 per cent of all LH Diet members represented constituencies with less than 20 per cent of the working population in primary industry. The figures point to stronger incentives for the vast majority of LH politicians to reorientate themselves more towards urban voters. Elections in all districts, except those in the most rural areas, have largely become contests for the votes of the non-agriculturally employed. It should be remembered, however, that agricultural employment represents only the core of the farm voting population given the prevalence of part-time farming. As argued earlier, farm household residency is a more accurate indicator of the total number of farm voters, and also potentially the attitudes that shape their voting choices.

Table 5.5 Changing categorisation of Lower House seats based on population concentration ratio 1980–90[a]

Election year	1980		1983		1986		1990	
Seat type[b]	No. of seats	Per cent of total	No. of seats	Per cent of total	No. of seats	Per cent of total	No. of seats	Per cent of total
Non-Urban (Dispersed)	89	17.4	81	15.9	76	14.8	44	8.6
Semi-Urban	205	40.1	186	36.4	167	32.6	175	34.2
Urban (Medium Concentration)	84	16.4	116	22.7	130	25.4	148	28.9
Metropolitan (High Concentration)	133	26.0	128	25.0	139	27.1	145	28.3
Total	511	100	511	100	512	100	512	100

Notes:
a The *Asahi Shinbun* ceased this categorisation system after 1990.
b The *Asahi Shinbun* categorisation system is based on a scale of population concentration.

Source: *Asahi Shinbun*, 25 June 1980, 20 December 1983, 8 July 1986 and 20 February 1990.

Yet another seat classification system for the Lower House devised by the *Asahi Shinbun* using a four-point scale based on population concentration ratios (*jinko shuchu ritsu*)[110] confirms the increasing preponderance of urban voters in the national voting population. The *Asahi* figures indicate that the number of non-urban (the equivalent of rural and semi-rural) LH seats halved (from 89 to 44) between 1980 and 1990. Metropolitan and urban seats, on the other hand inflated by one-third, with the biggest increment coming in the urban category (from 84 to 148). The data is presented in Table 5.5.

What the changes in seat classification illustrate in general terms is that very few Diet members now represent areas that could be called truly 'agricultural' or 'rural'. Indeed, in the vast majority of Japanese electorates, whether Upper House or Lower House, the population either employed in agriculture or resident in farm households has fallen to less than 30 per cent. Various factors have been involved. Some degree of attrition in the agricultural sector has occurred as farmland has been sold for residential or industrial purposes and as urban sprawl has consumed the countryside. In other cases, agricultural land ownership or usage rights have been transferred to make larger farms. Another trend has been for the sons and daughters of farmers to move to the cities to find work.

These socio-economic and demographic changes have inevitably altered the nature of political representation of these areas. All politicians could now be said to represent electorates with mixed socio-economic profiles where the significance of agriculture has been almost continuously contracting in relative terms. As a result, farm votes are becoming submerged by the sheer weight of non-farm votes in both the Upper and Lower Houses. The only qualification to this general observation is the slightly more agricultural flavour being given to some prefectural UH constituencies in the latter half of the 1990s.

Commodity constituencies

As already pointed out in chapter 1, not all farm commodities are equally important in political and therefore electoral terms. The key determinants are numbers of producers involved, their geographical dispersion and their degree of specialisation. Production geography tends to be significant in the case of commodities that are either nationally prominent or concentrated in particular regions. In the latter case, producers can exercise electoral power disproportionate to their overall numbers because of their consolidated voting power in certain districts.

The rice-farming electorate

Rice farmers constitute the largest single voting group in the farming population. They combine nationwide spread with significant regional densities in certain parts of the country. The rice-farming electorate includes all those persons 20 years and over residing in rice-producing farm households. In 1995, they numbered around 8.1 million voters,[111] or 8.4 per cent of the national electorate. This represented only a relatively small drop compared with 10 years earlier, when they numbered 10.5 million voters,[112] or just under 12 per cent of the national voting population.[113] The reduction in numbers of rice-producing households has clearly diminished the size of the rice electorate, but not significantly. The fall-off has been somewhat more dramatic when compared to the figures for 1960 when over 5 million farm households were engaged in rice production (or more than 17 million rice voters) and the national electorate was markedly smaller. In that year, rice producers comprised around one-third of the total number of eligible voters.

The size of the rice-marketing, or Food Control electorate is somewhat smaller than the rice-producing electorate. In 1995, 7.1 million voters, or a little over 7 per cent of the national electorate marketed rice.[114] This compares with 9 million voters,[115] or a little over 10 per cent of the national voting population in 1985.[116]

As a group, rice producers benefit from a number of electoral advantages. Apart from sheer numbers, they gain from the fact that rice as a crop is geographically well distributed over the entire country. Rice farmers combine this nationwide spread with significant regional clusters in Kanto-Tosan (504,000 households), Tohoku (449,000 households), Hokuriku (219,000 households) and Kyushu (347,000,000 households).[117] In these regions, single-crop rice-marketing households are numerically predominant. For example, Niigata in Hokuriku has the highest number of single-crop rice-marketing households in the country at 92,000 (this adds up to more than 300,000 voters), followed by Fukushima (70,000), Akita (65,000) and Miyagi (62,000) in Tohoku, Ibaraki in Northern Kanto (63,000), Hyogo in Kinki (56,000) and Okayama in Chugoku (42,000).[118] Tohoku has three out of the seven most prominent rice-producing prefectures in terms of numbers of single-crop, rice-marketing households, and in fact all the Tohoku prefectures except for Aomori have more than 40,000 single-crop households marketing rice (in other words, more than 140,000 pure rice voters each).[119]

The overall national figures and regional intensities of production would support the proposition that rice remains not only an important component of farm voter interest in the countryside generally, but the common and specific focus of large numbers of farmers in certain regions, particularly in northern Honshu. In these rice-dominant regions, support patterns at the party level are likely to register the impact of rice policy positions more than in other districts, while at the candidate level, they will tend to reflect the stance that individual politicians take on rice policy issues.

The livestock electorate

The electoral weighting of the dairy cattle sector has manifested dramatic slides in recent years. In consequence of rationalisation and restructuring, the number of dairy cattle farms decreased from 382,000 in 1965 to 160,000 in 1975, 82,000 in 1985, 44,000 in 1995 and 39,000 in 1997.[120] Over the 30-year period between 1965 and 1995, this represented a contraction from around 1.2 million voters to approximately 150,000 voters.[121] In 1997, the number of such voters ebbed further to around 147,000.

The pace of restructuring has been somewhat slower amongst beef cattle farms. In 1965 there were 1.4 million farms raising beef cattle. By 1975 their number had sunk to 474,000, by 1985 to 298,000 and by 1995 to 170,000.[122] Over the 1965–1995 period, this represented a reduction in voting numbers from around 4.6 million voters to just on 590,000 voters. The trend downwards continued through 1997, with figures dwindling to around 540,000 voters nationwide.[123]

The drop in the number of farm households raising dairy cattle and those raising beef cattle in the 1990s has been attributed to the aging of farmers and a shortage of successors, pressures to rationalise production for efficiency gains, continued stagnation in raw milk prices and low prices for dressed carcasses of domestic beef because of increased imports.[124] Domestic dairy beef producers have been most affected by the increased competition from beef imports, with the biggest price falls registering in this sector in the 1990s.

Political influence, however, is not purely a function of absolute numbers. One factor sustaining the effective electoral representation of livestock interests is the existence of regional concentrations of livestock producers.

Certain districts have strong and clearly identified livestock interests, particularly the beef cattle-raising regions of Kyushu and Tohoku, and the dairy cattle-raising regions of Hokkaido, Kanto-Tosan and to a lesser extent Tohoku, where livestock voters still comprise an important component in the overall composition of voter interests.

Producer specialisation is another important factor because it increases the vulnerability of farmers to price trends in the market and other factors affecting producer returns. Hokkaido, for example, is characterised by high levels of specialised dairy farming. In Hokkaido where 85 per cent of dairy farms are specialised, they generate over 40,000 votes.[125] Consideration of the likely impact of market liberalisation on Hokkaido and other dairy-producing regions such as Iwate and Kanto-Tosan, was reportedly the main factor accounting for the government's refusal to include processed milk products (such as condensed and powdered skim milk) on the list of eight miscellaneous products liberalised in February 1988.[126]

Voter numbers are even greater in beef cattle-raising constituencies such as Kagoshima (90,000 votes) and Iwate and Miyazaki (around 60,000 each).[127] Many of these farms specialise in beef production (around 40 per cent in Kagoshima for example), which, as in the case of specialist dairy producers, makes them vulnerable both to price movements on the domestic market and to market liberalisation. This is particularly the case if they run small numbers of cattle, as they do in Kyushu, for example (the average herd size in Kagoshima is 13.2 head).[128]

In electoral terms, beef and dairy products are more significant than pig or poultry farming, because numbers in the latter categories are much smaller, although numbers of head per farm are much higher. The most significant pork-producing prefectures are Ibaraki, Miyagi, Miyazaki and Kagoshima, with just over 1,000 hog-raising farm households each.[129] The highest numbers of chicken farmers can be found in Aichi, Chiba, Ibaraki and Kagoshima. In electoral terms, their smaller numbers (a national total of 7,000 farmers raising layers and 4,000 farmers shipping broilers) reduces their overall electoral magnitude. The higher numbers of poultry per farm also reflect much more efficient operations, thereby reducing the demand for support and protection.

The fruit-farming electorate

Significant numbers of specialist fruit-producing households exist in Nagano, Ehime, Yamanashi, Wakayama and Aomori. Apple and citrus growers are prominent amongst these fruit producers. Indeed, in terms of farm household numbers, fruit producers rank third after vegetable growers and rice producers as the most numerically significant (see Table 1.2)

The Japanese citrus industry (effectively Japanese mandarin, or *mikan* producers[130]), although experiencing some adjustment problems, is much more competitive than the Japanese beef, dairy or rice industries. It is in fact a modest export industry. Once again, structural adjustment in the industry has dramatically reduced the number of producer households. In the mid-1960s around 300,000 farm households produced mandarins. By 1985 their number had dropped to 187,000, by 1990 to 140,000, and by 1995 to 115,000 (see Table 1.2).[131] This translates into around 400,000 votes nationwide, although they are concentrated in a few prefectures. Around one-third of all *mikan* acreage can be found in Kyushu, somewhat less than another third is in Southern Honshu (Shizuoka, Wakayama and Hiroshima), and one-sixth in Ehime Prefecture (in Shikoku).[132] Nearly 80 per cent of *mikan* production is concentrated in 10 out of Japan's 47 prefectures. So, whilst numbers of *mikan* producers might have diminished significantly nationwide, regional densities sustain concentrated voting power in certain districts. In Wakayama and Ehime, for example, specialist fruit producers (predominantly mandarin growers), comprise around 57,000 voters and 66,000 voters respectively.[133]

It is a similar story with apples. Around 270,000 voters produce apples with a majority of them found in either Aomori or Nagano.[134] Although apple and *mikan* producers may not be able to make an electoral difference nationally, they can still make a difference in certain electorates. The Japanese apple market was officially liberalised in 1971, but quarantine restrictions effectively kept foreign apples out of Japan until the 1990s, except for small quantities of Korean imports. According to official US government assessments of the issue, technical aspects associated with fears of imported pests infecting domestic apple trees were not the real issue: the real issue was political.[135]

Individual electorates for speciality products

Even amongst minor agricultural products, regional clusters of producers can be sufficient to generate electoral significance for these commodities. For example, commercial tea growers represent around 200,000 voters nation-wide, with a good proportion of them found in Shizuoka. Farmers cultivating potatoes for starch number about 370,000 voters, with the vast majority of them found in Hokkaido, in addition to more than 235,000 votes connected to sweet potato production, most of which is concentrated in Kagoshima. Sugar beet producers are smaller in number (about 45,000 voters), but they can be found only in Hokkaido. Sugar cane growers (generating just under 60,000 votes) are predominantly located in Okinawa and in the southwestern part of Kagoshima Prefecture.

The Japanese government's omission of starch from the list of eight agricultural product categories liberalised in February 1988 was reportedly due to its importance to Hokkaido's potato growers. The decision defended a heavily subsidised potato crop in Hokkaido as well as sweet potatoes in southern Kyushu. According to the Chairman of the Hokkaido Central Union, the 'size and strength of the Hokkaido movement (compared with those of smaller prefectures further south) may have helped the prefecture to get special treatment for its farmers'.[136] Producers in Hokkaido claimed they had no other immediate means of living except for turning out potato starch and milk. Officials in the Foreign Ministry claimed it would be 'almost impossible' for Hokkaido farmers to stop growing potatoes without destroying the crop cycle that was the basis of the island's entire farming economy. Similarly, in southern Kyushu dust emitted by Sakurajima (a major active volcano) is said to make sweet potatoes one of the few viable crops.[137]

A third item on the prospective liberalisation list was canned pineapple which provided underpinning for the farm economy of Okinawa which had been 'allowed to develop a dangerously high degree of dependence on a small number of semi-tropical crops.'[138] The possible importation of canned pineapples was a highly sensitive political issue for this reason. Nevertheless, the Japanese government went ahead with liberalisation in February 1988, even though it was 'of even greater relative importance to Okinawa farmers than potatoes to Hokkaidans'.[139] One possible explanation was the differential voting weight of commodity producers (there were only around 1600 farms producing pineapples in 1988[140] and therefore just 5000–6000 votes involved).[141]

Not on the list recommended for liberalisation by the GATT adjudication panel were, however, miscellaneous beans and peanuts. Similar arguments to those advanced about the likely effect of import liberalisation of milk products and starch were presented in the case of these products. Most of Japan's peanut growers, for example, can be found in Chiba. Pockets of dependence on particular products meant that, in the event of liberalisation, farmers would be vulnerable.

In a separate episode, *konnyaku* was the target of market-opening pressure from China, but not only were *konnyaku* imports restricted (until the 1993 UR Agreement on Agriculture) but a high tariff of 40 per cent was also applied. This rate was amongst the highest of any agricultural products (see Table 1.1). *Konnyaku* remains a regional speciality, with voters linked to this product concentrated in Gumma Prefecture.

Minor products on the electoral scale

The case of wheat, barley and soybean producers is rather anomalous. Relatively larger numbers of producers are involved (149,000 farm households marketed wheat and barley in 1995, while 67,000 marketed soybeans).[142] This generated approximately 500,000 and 230,000 votes respectively, generally well distributed around the country. Very few farms specialise in the production of these crops, however. Most engage in mixed farming, particularly in combination with rice, which takes precedence as a cash crop.

In the case of Japan's raw silk producers, cocoon growers have registered dramatic declines from 248,000 in 1975 to 44,000 in 1991, 14,000 in 1995 and 8,000 in 1996.[143] The reduction has been directly attributed to the flood of finished silk goods coming into Japan from China and South Korea. The number of farm households raising silkworms even in areas where they are reasonably numerous is now hardly large enough to have anything more than a minimal electoral impact, although historically domestic silk producers have been well mobilised politically and electorally. Gumma had the greatest number with just under 3,000 in 1996, followed by Fukushima and Saitama with well under a 1,000 each.[144] Although MAFF officials bleat about protecting regional economies and the people who can grow only cocoons, the argument of regional decline hardly seems justifiable in the face of the dramatic falls in silk growers to date.

In each case, the analysis of commodity electorates treats separate products as representing a discrete group of voters, whereas in fact, many farm voters combine commodity interests because of mixed farming. Hence, adding up all the commodity votes would exceed the total number of farm household votes. This must be borne in mind when assessing the electoral weighting of particular commodities. It is unlikely that the voting choices of farmers will be based solely on considerations linked to a particular commodity interest, or even commodity-related factors as a whole. Nevertheless, commodity interests cannot be discounted as a contributory factor in electoral choice, particularly where agricultural products exhibit a dominant national presence like rice and/or a significant regional presence like livestock commodities, fruit and some speciality products. This is especially so with respect to electoral districts where alternative production choices are limited and/or where alternative non-farming opportunities are restricted.

Electoral malapportionment and farmers' voting power

Farmers' voting power measured in the aggregate has never been just a simple function of the size of the national agricultural electorate relative to the total voting population. Malapportionment has grossly privileged farmers in the electoral system by overrepresenting the least populated districts in terms of voters per seat and correspondingly underrepresenting the most densely populated constituencies. Put simply, voters in rural constituencies have been endowed with electoral power disproportionate to their absolute numbers.

The imbalance arose historically from rapid urbanisation and the failure of successive conservative governments to adjust electoral boundaries sufficiently to compensate for population movements. The boundaries of the electorates were drawn up in accordance with population distribution patterns derived from a special population survey conducted in April 1946 in time for the first comprehensive democratic elections,[145] when approximately half the population was resident in farm households.[146]

Although the causes of the unequal representation of Japanese voters were widely acknowledged over a long period, rectification of the situation was viewed as a political problem requiring solutions that were unacceptable to the ruling LDP which consistently benefited from overrepresentation of politically conservative rural areas.[147] Although the LDP's nationwide support rate remained below 50 per cent in elections, overweighted rural constituencies made a decisive contribution to LDP seat majorities in the Diet.[148]

Japan had no mechanisms for automatically adjusting electoral districts and seats to reflect population changes. A schedule attached to the Public Offices Election Law stated that such alterations were required every five years to reflect the results of the most recent national census. Implementing the provision, however, would have necessitated amending the law, which was dependent on the consent of a majority of members of parliament. Until 1993–94, this was impossible to obtain because the two largest parties in the Diet, the LDP and JSP, were both advantaged by the malapportionment[149] and would not have voluntarily contemplated such an option.

The effect of the failure substantially to reapportion Diet seats to take account of population movements produced a rural gerrymander by default, with effects over time that became more, not less, severe. Malapportionment continued to magnify the value of farmers' votes even while farm numbers continued to lessen. Metropolitan areas were severely underrepresented from the early 1950s and suburban areas were severely underrepresented from the mid-1960s.[150] In 1972, for example, it was calculated that the disequilibrium amongst LH electorates was such that 50 per cent of seats were shared amongst 38 per cent of eligible voters.[151] Another analysis of the 1972 LH election demonstrated that a JSP candidate for Tokyo (7) garnered 144,415 votes and lost, whereas an LDP candidate received 37,258 votes in Gumma (3) (the lowest number received by a winning candidate over the whole country) and still secured a seat. The former was 20th place in a ranking of candidates by total votes received. In fact seven candidates who gained more than 100,000 votes lost in this election.[152] By 1979, little had altered: rural and semi-rural voters comprised just over 20 per cent of the total number of eligible voters whilst being represented by 30 per cent of the total number of LH Diet members.[153]

In the Upper House the distortion in vote values at the extreme (the ratio of difference in the voting value between the most populous and least populous districts) magnified from 1.25:1 in 1947 to 2.39:1 in 1960 and then leapt to 5.07:1 in 1967 as a result of rapid urbanisation. Malapportionment peaked in 1992 at 6.59:1 in 1992 (see Table 5.6). A 1994 revision of the Public Offices Election Law permitted the first-ever redistribution of prefectural constituency seats to take place which made some headway towards adjusting seat numbers to population distribution (it reduced the disparity to 4.97:1 in the 1995 UH elections), but it by no means eliminated the severe distortion in vote values between less populated rural areas and densely populated urban areas.[154] As Table 5.6 reveals, by 1998, the differential had again risen to 4.98:1 in the two electorates with the greatest disparity in the value of votes. UH voters in metropolitan Tokyo with 2,395,302 voters per seat were significantly disenfranchised compared to voters in rural Tottori Prefecture with 481,443 voters per seat.[155]

Table 5.6 Differences at the extreme between voting values in the least and most densely populated electorates (1947–98)

Year	Ratio[a] in House of Councillors prefectural constituencies		Ratio in House of Representatives constituencies	
	Least densely populated constituency	Most densely populated constituency	Least densely populated constituency	Most densely populated constituency
1947	1.25 : 1		1.51 : 1	
1950	1.55 : 1		2.17 : 1	
1955	1.94 : 1		2.68 : 1	
1960	2.39 : 1		3.21 : 1	
1963			3.55 : 1	
1964			2.19[b] : 1	
1965			3.20 : 1	
1967	5.07 : 1			
1970			4.83 : 1	
1972	5.01 : 1		4.99 : 1	
1974	5.11 : 1		5.31 : 1	
1975			2.92[c] : 1	
1976	5.25 : 1		3.50 : 1	
1977	5.26 : 1		3.74[d] : 1	
1979	5.34 : 1		3.87 : 1	
1980	5.37 : 1		3.95 : 1	
1982	5.50 : 1		4.24 : 1	
1983	5.56 : 1		4.41 : 1	
1985			5.12 : 1	
1986	5.86 : 1		2.92[e] : 1	
1989	6.25 : 1			
1990	6.25 : 1		3.38 : 1	
1992	6.59 : 1		2.81 : 1	
1993			2.84[f] : 1	
1994			2.14 : 1	
1995	4.97[g] : 1			
1996			2.32 : 1	
1998	4.98 : 1		2.40 : 1	

In the Lower House, the differential was only partially rectified by insufficient and belated adjustments in seats per constituency. In spite of massive shifts in population from rural to urban sectors from 1960 onwards, the only response to the huge demographic swing was to increase the number of constituencies from 117 to 130 and to raise the number of seats from 466 to 511[156] by allotting additional seats to LH metropolitan constituencies in 1967, 1976, 1986 and 1992 during a period when the number of voters more than doubled to 95 million.

The seat adjustments were not voluntary on the part of the ruling LDP, but were compelled by a series of Supreme Court rulings. After the June 1980 general election, for example, groups of disgruntled voters challenged the

Table 5.6 (*continued*)

Notes:

a Ratios in this table were calculated by taking the numbers of voters on the electoral roll per seat in the most densely populated constituency and dividing it by the number of voters on the electoral roll per seat in the least densely populated constituency.

b The reduction in the differential in 1964 was due to the addition of 19 seats to the most densely populated districts.

c The high ratio in 1974 and its reduction in 1975 were due to the addition of 20 new seats to the most densely populated districts.

d This figure is for 1978, owing to the unavailability of figures for 1977.

e The reduced ratio in 1986 was due to the addition of 8 seats to the most populous constituencies and the subtraction of 7 seats from the least populous constituencies in May 1986, prior to the LH elections.

f The reduced ratio in 1993 was due to the addition in 1992 of another 8 seats to the most populous constituencies and the subtraction of 9 seats from the least populous constituencies.

g This figure reflects the adjustment in seat numbers that took place prior to the 1995 UH election.

Sources: *Seiji Handobukku*, annual, relevant issues; *Asahi Shinbun*, 27 June 1983; *Asahi Nenkan*, 1984, p. 103; Iwamoto Isao, *Hachiju Nendai Nihon Seiji to Sekai* [*Japanese Politics and the World in the 1980s*], Kyoto, Koyo Shobo, 1988, p. 97; *Japan Agrinfo Newsletter*, Vol. 9, No. 6, February 1992, p. 4; *Mainichi Shinbun*, 24 July 1995; *Dai-41 Shugiingiin Sosenkyo Ichiran Heisei 8-nen 10-gatsu 20 Shikko* [*The 41st House of Representatives Election Held on 20 October 1996*], Shugiin Jimukyoku, 18 March 1997, pp. 2–282; Junichiro Wada, *The Japanese Election System: Three Analytical Perspectives*, London and New York, Routledge, 1996, pp. 11–12; *Yomiuri Shinbun*, 13 July 1998; *Nikkei Weekly*, 28 December 1998– 4 January 1999.

disparity in vote values on the grounds that they contravened Article 14 of the constitution which guarantees that 'all of the people are equal under the law'. In its ruling of November 1983, the Supreme Court held that the prevailing discrepancy in vote values was unconstitutional and urged the Diet to rectify the system, although it did not declare the 1980 election results invalid. The court's ruling effectively held that the disparity must be under 3:1 for any election to maintain constitutional equality of rights granted in Article 14 of the Constitution.[157]

A subsequent Supreme Court ruling in July 1985 held that the 1983 LH election had been unlawful because house seats were distributed so disproportionately that they contravened the constitutional guarantee of equality under the law.[158] Five judges also expressed the supplemental view that if the next LH election were held without first revising the LH representation table of the Public Offices Election Law, 'the Court would nullify the election'.[159] This ruling prompted the most radical and unprecedented reshuffle of LH seats by means of the passage of a redistribution law in May 1986, prior to the July 1986 election.[160] The redistribution actually subtracted seats from the most depopulated rural constituencies (7) and allocated a slightly larger number (8) to a group of metropolitan constituencies. As a result, the maximum disparity in voting values was cut to less than 3:1. As Table 5.6 confirms, it fell to 2.92:1,[161] still large by international standards, but nevertheless within the acceptable limit set by the Supreme Court. In a subsequent judgement made in October 1988, the Supreme Court ruled the July 1986 LH election was constitutional because the gap in voting values at the extreme was under 3:1.

A somewhat larger subtraction and addition process took place prior to the 1993 elections, when nine seats were taken from less populous constituencies and eight seats were given to urban and metropolitan constituencies, along with a reduction in the number of constituencies (from 130 to 129). The entire seat reshuffling process between 1985 and 1993 reduced the differential in voting values from a peak of 5.12:1 to 2.84:1 (see Table 5.6).

Overweighting of rural districts has consistently been one of the crucial ingredients in rural voting power, in spite of the paring back of this electoral advantage by more than a third at the extreme in the Lower House between 1983 and 1993. The chief political effect of malapportionment was partially to insulate farm voters from the direct electoral consequences of demographic changes associated with the gradual contraction of the farm sector.[162] The electoral significance of the farm vote continued to translate into something more than the absolute percentage it occupied within the national electorate. In other words, farmers' demand for agricultural support and protection was made effective by electoral power considerably greater than might have been expected from an objective evaluation of agriculture's place in the economy as revealed by the usual economic, employment and demographic indicators. As Cowhey aptly puts it, malapportionment 'muted shifts in public policy associated with the rising power of urban districts (e.g., reduced protection for farmers)'.[163]

There comes a point, however, when even electoral maldistribution is unable significantly to ameliorate the political effects of reductions in farm voter numbers. As noted earlier, numbers of rural and semi-rural districts in the mid-1980s (as measured by population employed in primary industry) diminished to the point where they almost disappeared from the electoral map. Furthermore, a much more radical redistribution of voting power took place as a result of the electoral reforms of 1994.[164] These further enfranchised urban voters at the expense of their rural counterparts.

As a result of the changes, the numbers of Diet members whose voting base was in agricultural or rural areas decreased. One single-member district

(SMD) or small electorate (*shosenkyoku*) as the Japanese prefer to call it, was allocated to each of the 47 prefectures out of a total of 300, and the remaining 253 districts were distributed in proportion to population. Likewise, 200 proportional representation (PR) seats were simply allocated across 11 regional blocs according to population distribution.

Although the method of distributing seats across the 47 prefectures in the SMD system was still advantageous to less populous prefectures,[165] the number of Diet members from agricultural regions certainly fell: those from Tohoku, for example, dropped from 48 to 42; those from Shikoku from 25 to 20; and those from Kyushu from 68 to 61 (amounting to 18 in total). Zenkoku Noseikyo predicted that the number of farm politicians would decrease by 30 because of the reduction in the number of seats allocated to agricultural constituencies.[166] Sugita calculated, however, that the 260 Diet members who had previously represented rural areas such as Hokkaido, Tohoku, Kita Kanto (Gumma and Tochigi), Shinetsu, Hokuriku, Chukoku, Shikoku and Kyushu would be almost halved to 138, and thus the proportion of so-called 'regional Diet members' (*chiho giin*) would fall by a large margin.[167] Furthermore, because the new electoral system made too much of the large cities, it was a system where regional representation was difficult.[168]

Amongst the SMDs, roughly 20 seats were allocated to more urbanised prefectures, while 17 seats were extracted from less urbanised prefectures. As a result of the changes, the maximum disparity in voting values in these districts stood at 2.14:1 in 1994.[169] Although this was a reduction in the disparities that prevailed under the old system, 28 less populous districts still enjoyed more than a 2:1 advantage over the most densely populated districts.[170] The figures suggest that malapportionment has not been completely eliminated from the LH election system. Furthermore, it is widely accepted that demographic changes will continue to expand the disparities, requiring further adjustments down the track. In 1996 the disparity in voting values had risen to 2.32:1 and in 1998 to 2.40:1 (see Table 5.6). Nevertheless, the changes have enabled the impact of the diminution in farm household numbers to be more accurately reflected in vote values instead of being muted by a *de facto* gerrymander.[171]

Zenkoku Noseikyo's view of the changes was that the multiplication in Diet members from urban areas and the contraction in the number of Diet members from rural areas made it more problematic to promote agricultural policies, and the status of agriculture would inevitably be lowered in the context of national policy formulation.[172] It should not be surprising to find, therefore, that in the 1996 LH election, amongst the many candidates recommended by Zenkoku Noseikyo,[173] an unprecedented number were from constituencies within the environs of large cities such as Tokyo (13) and Kanagawa (9). The reason given was that under the new electoral system 'it had become more difficult to reflect the voice of farm households' and that 'the strength of city Diet members is growing'.[174] The National Council plumped for city Diet members because it was concerned to keep them on side on agricultural policy issues.

Farmers as LDP supporters

One of the most stereotypical observations about Japanese politics is that rural areas have been bastions of conservatism and the electoral support base (*jiban*) of the LDP.[175] With the value of rural votes inflated by mal-apportionment, farmers have contributed disproportionately to continuing LDP victories in national elections. The combination of overrepresented rural and semi-rural voters and strong support for the conservatives has ensured a high level of responsiveness from ruling LDP Diet members to their rural clients.

Over the years, survey research amongst major occupational groupings substantiates the proposition that a majority of workers in primary industries have consistently been LDP supporters. As noted in the previous chapter, the correlation between conservative votes and employment in primary industry was established in the first LH election contested by the LDP in 1958. In this poll, an average of 65.5 per cent of those employed in primary industry were LDP voters. This pattern was sustained in subsequent elections. In the 1969 poll, the LDP's support rate was 74.2 per cent amongst those who were self-supporting in agriculture, forestry and fisheries industries. The figure for 1972 was 71 per cent.[176] In addition, 69 per cent of those who professed to be members of Nokyo and other agricultural groups in the 1972 survey said that they voted for the LDP, which was higher than any of the other voluntary membership groups surveyed.[177]

A later survey conducted by Kyodo Tsushinsha in 1977 revealed that 67.2 per cent of farmers (and those employed in the fishing industry) supported the LDP, whilst public support for the LDP nationwide was only 38.4 per cent.[178] On the other hand, amongst those in the primary industry category, only 10.3 per cent supported the JSP, 0.8 per cent supported the Komeito, 1.1 per cent supported the DSP and JCP respectively, 3.8 per cent supported the New Liberal Club, or NLC (Shin Jiyu Kurabu),[179] whilst 0.4 per cent supported other parties, 9.9 per cent supported no party and 4.6 per cent did not answer.[180] Part of the explanation given for the low support rates for the Opposition parties amongst those employed in agriculture and fishing was that rural voters were not very familiar with the Opposition parties who often found it difficult even to nominate a good candidate in rural areas. Consequently, rural voters either lost interest in politics or supported the LDP's candidates who, they hoped, would represent their interests in the Diet.[181] The data demonstrates unequivocally that even in the 1970s when voter disaffection with the LDP was at its height, the traditional Opposition parties received little support from primary industry voters.

Table 5.7 indicates support rates amongst agricultural, forestry and fishery workers for the LDP and JSP respectively for the period from 1972 through

Table 5.7 Farm, forestry and fishing industry workers' party support rates in Lower House elections

Unit: %

Party	1986	1983	1980[a]	1979	1976	1972
LDP	56[a]	60	55	55	50	52
JSP	6	7	7	8	9	10
Komeito	2	2				
DSP	2	2				
JCP	1	1				
Other parties	1	0				
No parties supported	10	10				
No answer	22	18				
Total	100	100				

Notes:
a This is a composite of support rates in both the Lower House and Upper House elections.

Source: Tables 2.5 and 2.6 in Iwamoto, *Hachiju Nendai*, pp. 96, 98.

to 1986. The data reveals that LDP support rates varied from 50–60 per cent while those for the JSP hovered at 6–10 per cent. The other Opposition parties scored even lower amongst primary industry workers (at least in 1983 and 1986). The same study also established that those employed in the farming, forestry and fishing industries supported the LDP in greater proportions than did any other occupational category. In the 1986 elections, LDP support rates were 33 per cent for office and management workers, 32 per cent for workers in industry, 37 per cent for workers in commerce and 49 per cent for those self-employed in commerce and industry.[182]

Table 5.8 provides figures for LDP polling rates in elections between 1976 and 1986 according to a similar categorisation of voter occupation. The figures underline the very high proportions of primary industry workers who were supporters of the LDP, with the peak for the 1976–86 decade being the 75.9 per cent scored in 1986. Other significant groups of supporters during this decade were those employed in the commercial and service sectors (48.8 per cent in 1986) – this category would be inclusive of those self-employed in small business – and those in the liberal professions/management (48.0 per cent in 1986). Even voters in labouring occupations scored 35.0 per cent in 1986, up from 25.9 per cent in 1976. Clerical workers were the least likely to vote for the LDP of any occupational category – only 29.6 per cent in 1986. This group would doubtless be more inclined towards JSP support through their membership of white collar unions affiliated with Sohyo.

A similar set of conclusions can be drawn from Figure 5.1, which illustrates LDP and non-LDP support rates in the 1983 and 1986 elections according to more or less comparable categories of occupation. Once again, those employed in the farming, forestry and fishing industries were the most likely

Table 5.8 Percentage of the total vote from different occupational categories won by the LDP in Lower House elections, 1976–90

Type of employment	Election year 1976	Election year 1979	Election year 1980	Election year 1983	Election year 1986	Election year 1990
Agriculture, forestry and fisheries	60.7	61.1	73.9	73.2	75.9	54.5
Self-employed						42.2
Commerce/service	46.2	48.5	55.1	53.3	48.8	
Sales/service						35.6
Clerical occupation	18.6	29.5	27.6	26.3	29.6	
Clerical/technical						29.9
Administration/ management						45.1
Liberal profession						32.6
Liberal profession/ management occupation	32.1	46.2	52.6	42.6	48.0	
Skilled work						33.3
Labouring occupation	25.9	26.6	33.4	29.1	35.0	
Women at home						31.7
Unemployed women	27.7	27.9	43.2	33.4	37.9	
Other unemployed	34.8	31.7	40.8	41.7	38.2	

Source: Tables 2.7 and 5.14 in Kobayashi, *Gendai Nihon no Senkyo*, pp. 20, 130. Note the categories of employment are different for the 1990 election year.

to vote for the LDP (60 per cent in 1986, rising from 57 per cent in 1983), while the LDP also drew reasonable rates of support from management workers, industrial workers, and the self-employed in commerce and industry (the next highest after primary industry, with 51 per cent in 1986, climbing from 37 per cent in 1983).

The results of yet another survey, this one done by the *Asahi Shinbun* covering the 1975–85 period, endorse the basic patterns revealed in Table 5.8 and Figure 5.1. The research reveals that 62 per cent of primary industry workers supported the LDP in 1975, rising to 70 per cent in 1980 and 72 per cent in 1985. The figures for office workers were 34–50 per cent over the same period; for those working in management 48–66 per cent; for industrial workers 32–49 per cent; for those employed in the service industry 38–54 per cent; and for the self-employed 59–66 per cent. Some of these other non-primary industry categories quite clearly provide quite respectable levels of support for the LDP, but none are as high as farming, forestry and fishery workers.[183]

Miyake reports another useful series of *Asahi Shinbun* surveys in his analysis of the LDP's 1989 UH election defeat.[184] The research covered the

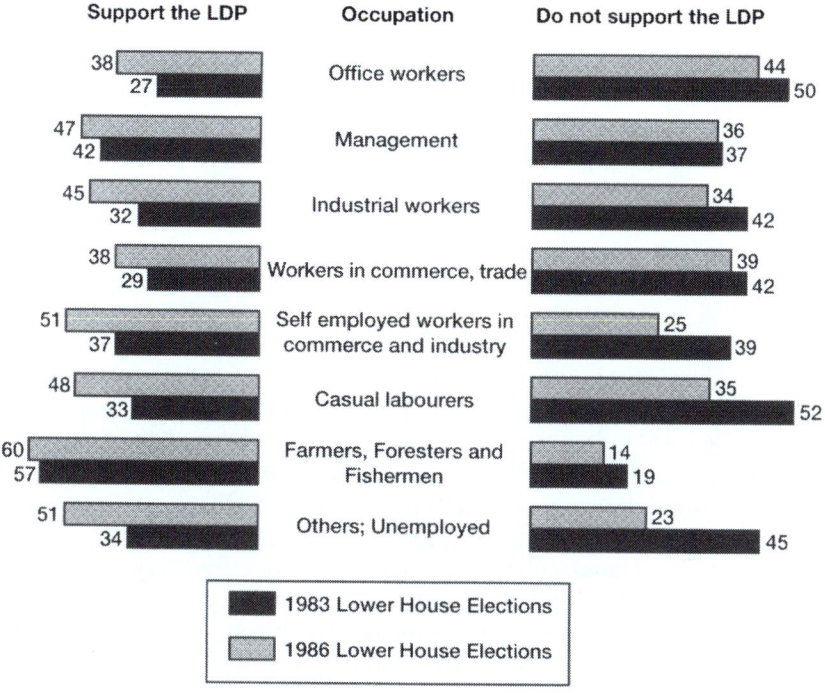

Figure 5.1 Party support rates by occupation, 1983 and 1986 Lower House Elections
Source: Ishiwata Sadao, 'Nomin to Seiji' ('Farmers' and Politics'), in
Ishiwata (ed.), *Nomin to Senkyo*, p. 12.

Upper and Lower House elections in 1972, 1986, 1989 and 1990. The range of
LDP support over this period from office and management workers was 31–34
per cent, from industrial workers 23–33 per cent, from workers in commerce
31–37 per cent, from the self-employed in commerce and industry 46–49 per
cent, and from primary industry workers 52–58 per cent. For 'others' and for
the unemployed it was 36–38 per cent. Conversely, the figures for the JSP over
the same period were 23–22 per cent for office and management workers,
28–23 per cent for industrial workers, a stable 19 per cent for workers in
commerce, 11–13 per cent for the self-employed in commerce and industry
and 10–11 per cent of primary industry workers. 'Others' and the unemployed
scored 12–20 per cent.[185] The data records both the fundamentally stable
social composition of LDP support, with farmers and the self-employed in
small business constituting the electoral backbone of the party, together with
a gradual diversification of the LDP's support base amongst other categories
of occupation, particularly amongst industrial workers and to a lesser extent
workers in commerce. The JSP, on the other hand, was no more than a minor
party for primary industry voters, while it suffered some erosion of support

amongst office and management workers as well as industrial workers. Its biggest increase in support came from 'others' and the unemployed (i.e. housewives).

The 1990 figures in the *Asahi Shinbun* survey compare with those for 1990 in Table 5.8, which uses a slightly different classificatory schema to designate occupational categories. The primary industry category, however, remains constant, although LDP support from farmers, forestry and fishery workers declined quite significantly from 75.9 per cent in 1986 to 54.5 per cent in the 1990 election.[186] This compares with an incremental rise from 56 per cent to 58 per cent in the *Asahi Shinbun* survey. Nevertheless, the 1990 rate for primary industry workers was still way ahead of any of the other occupational categories surveyed, including the self-employed at 42.2 per cent.

The data in the above tables and figure all underline the fact that farmers (albeit within the broader category of primary industry workers) comprise a particularly reliable group of supporters within the LDP's 'grand coalition of support'. Although other groups of faithful LDP adherents can also be identified, particularly the self-employed, the view that farmers are just one element of a more complex picture does not really do justice to their relative support rates compared with those in the other major occupational categories shown above. Although some non-primary industry sectors manifest respectable levels of support for the ruling party, their proportions of LDP voters are consistently somewhat lower than those in agriculture, forestry and fishing.

A number of reasons, not necessarily mutually exclusive, have been advanced to explain why farmers support LDP candidates in such high proportions. The first and most simple reason is that farmers are naturally conservative and therefore do not easily vote for progressives.[187] Furthermore, the continual drain of the young workforce from the rural villages helps to keep these villages conservative.[188]

The second and more complicated explanation is the Marxist one. It holds that Japanese farmers are not peasants according to the true Marxist definition, because after land reform, they came to belong to the middle layer of a society of bourgeoisie.[189] Although farmers belong to the labouring class, they also possess the means of production which makes them protective towards their possessions and therefore they tend to be politically conservative.[190]

Fukutake argues in much the same vein. In his view, farmers have two 'souls'. One is their soul as labourers and the other is as small-scale proprietors of land and capital goods. As petty proprietors, farmers are reluctant to support reformist parties because the latter are identified with workers' interests. In his view, only if farmers realise they are suppressed, exploited and not rewarded for their hard labour, will they rebel. They tend to remain conservative, however, as long as they are not aware of their exploitation and suppression, or when the degree of their exploitation and suppression is bearable. Furthermore, Japanese farmers would not become radicalised as long as they could maintain their inherited assets and continue agricultural production.[191]

The third factor accounting for high rates of support for the LDP amongst farmers rests on the socio-cultural traditions in farm villages, particularly their communitarian customs and habits of cooperation which encourage farmers to act in unison. As Yamamoto explains: 'Throughout history, farmers have been tied to blood and community relations because they were not covered by any social safety net when they got into difficulties. In times of adversity, they relied on their family relations. Consequently, in the postwar period, they may have been unconsciously encouraged to vote for people on whom they felt they could rely. This predisposition has been reinforced by the fact that rural communities (*shuraku*) remained subordinate elements of government administration. Once local elites became aligned with the admin-istration and the ruling party as an extension of the bureaucratic structure, the whole community tended to fall into line. In this context the farmers were susceptible to the voting directives coming from the leadership of agricultural interest groups (such as Nokyo) to which they belonged, and which, in the majority of cases, encouraged them to vote for LDP candidates.[192] In this way, it was not difficult for the LDP to place a whole village under its control.'[193]

Furthermore, farm voters living in rural communities were much more receptive to the personalistic appeals of LDP candidates than to the more programmatic appeals of Socialist (and other Opposition) candidates. While the latter tended to emphasise party and policy, the former, in the manner of village election campaigns, were more inclined to personalise the election process. In the 1986 LH election in Miyagi, for example, the LDP gained just under 680,000 votes, or 62.3 per cent of the total number of votes cast in the prefecture. In the national constituency, however, the LDP achieved only about 300,000 votes, indicating that voters centred their choices on the personal attributes of candidates (in the prefectural constituency) rather than the party factor (in the national constituency). According to the Chairman of the Miyagi Nokyo Youth League, farmers in the prefecture voted for the personalities of the LDP candidates, rather than the agricultural policies they proposed.[194] The similarities in the election pledges of LDP and Opposition party candidates on agricultural policy also encouraged farmers to focus on candidates rather than parties. Even when farmers did vote for progressive candidates, they tended to support the individual rather than the party.[195] From the 1950s until the late 1970s when the JSP had a relatively large number of agricultural specialists with close ties to the farmers' unions in its ranks, many farmers voted for these politicians, regardless of party.[196]

As Dore explains, appeals based on a candidates' personal attributes blended easily with rural social norms which personalised all aspects of life,[197] as well as echoing the predominant theme in all village social relationships which were based on the exchange of favours. Such an approach also conformed to more traditional styles of prewar electioneering when the only choice for farmers was between conservative candidates, who were, therefore, obliged to distinguish themselves in terms of their personal attributes.[198] The particular design of LH medium-sized multi-member districts from 1947 until 1994 only served to reinforce this tradition, as did the factionalised nature of the election process in which several LDP factions (represented by individual candidates) contested seats in the same constituency in the manner of independent parties.

Despite the importance of individual candidates' personal attributes as a basis of voter choice,[199] policy was not completely irrelevant. Indeed, quite the reverse. Farmers manifested a strong interest in national issues if they directly concerned their own economic position.[200] Furthermore, the predominantly personal basis of the vote meant that LDP politicians were individually accountable to their electorate for ruling party decisions on agricultural policy, which made issues relating to farmers a matter of great import to LDP Diet members from rural and semi-rural areas. Husbanding their base of support was a strong motivation for LDP politicians to mobilise in the Diet and in the party as representatives of agricultural interests.[201]

Over the years, the agricultural policy decisions of the ruling party reflected the nature of these electoral incentives both for individual Diet politicians and the party as a whole. In terms of the delivery of benefits, the LDP basically performed sufficiently well over the decades to keep agricultural producers voting for LDP candidates. When the income gap between agricultural and other industries widened in the 1950s, the government moved quickly enough to improve the standard of living in agricultural villages for farmers to continue to support the government.[202] As the years went by, the farmers made even greater income gains in comparison with average working house-holds in the cities. The fiscal pie expanded during the period of Japan's rapid economic growth, which enabled the ruling LDP to distribute even higher levels of benefits to agricultural villages by means of rising rice prices and agricultural subsidies.[203] These were the two major interest incentives engineered by the LDP to counteract the loosening of the integrity of village communities in the process of high economic growth.[204] As Okamoto puts it, the ruling classes doled out 'lollipops' to the farmers to secure them as a stable influence in society.[205] Even when agricultural policy was targeted for reform in line with government budget-cutting and other reform agendas, many farmers continued to support the LDP because they felt they had no choice but to rely on the party to shield them from radical policy change.[206]

Moreover, the LDP as the dominant ruling party has been the only party in a position to deliver desired benefits to farmers and other rural dwellers in the form of local development projects in provincial municipalities. Because the fundamental principles of agricultural support and protection were not contested between the ruling and Opposition parties,[207] the principal way in which the LDP could distinguish itself from its political rivals was the advantage it enjoyed in terms of the delivery of grants and subsidies to specific interest groups and specific localities. Farmers voted for the LDP because rural areas received economic benefits immediately prior to elections.[208] Farmers tended to consider the benefit for a small region on a short-term basis as an important factor in deciding their vote.[209] In particular, individual LDP candidates put a lot of effort into delivering patronage or pork barrel-type benefits to local farming constituents.[210] Once the benefit-distribution system was in place, farm villages became robust supporters of the LDP.[211]

Many of these benefits consisted of subsidies for agricultural public works, particularly for land improvement as well as subsidies for rural public works centring on the provision of public infrastructure and facilities to improve the quality of the farmers' (and other rural dwellers') daily lives. The fact that farming villages were initially behind urban areas in terms of social amenities made local leaders eager for subsidies to catch up with the cities. As Ishiwata explains, 'farmers need improvement both in farming and in their daily lives, which requires large amounts of government funds. In order to obtain the necessary funds, an entire village tries to keep a close relationship with a Diet member from the government party.'[212]

Moreover, social and economic infrastructure benefits in the countryside benefited the large and growing part-time farmer class as rural dwellers rather than as agricultural producers. In this respect, it was not important whether they voted as farmers or as workers in non-agricultural occupations. These people supported the LDP as the provider of local infrastructure benefits, like many of those not resident in farm households at all.

The LDP's long-time monopoly over the patronage distribution mechanism thus generated a compelling logic for voters resident in farm households and rural dwellers generally. Since members of the ruling party were in the best position to act as intermediaries between the national government and local institutions, voters in rural constituencies were much more likely to vote for the ruling party.[213] Many believed that backing an Opposition party candidate was a wasted vote because it would not be productive in terms of a return of economic favours. Only by supporting an LDP candidate was there an opportunity to communicate demands for favours and to receive them back. In short, the shared political consciousness of farmers and rural residents was shaped by their common need for local benefits.[214]

Expressed in the language of rational choice theory, farmers and other rural dwellers were voting 'according to their 'expected candidate differential,' or the relative expected utility associated with different politicians' activities during their incumbency.'[215] Once the LDP became entrenched in government, its enduring power over public expenditure was a strong disincentive for farmers and other rural voters to opt for an alternative party. The Opposition's increasingly dim chances of coming to power meant that voting for an Opposition candidate would not deliver the desired benefits. The way to influence subsidy allocation was to maintain close connections with one or more of the ruling party's political representatives in the district.

In studies of Japanese voting behaviour, such logic has been labelled 'regional egotism', 'localism' (*chiikisei*),[216] or in more contemporary analysis, 'consciousness of local interests' (*jimoto rieki ishiki*).[217] What it amounts to in practice is the desire to preserve patronage connections for selfish regional advantage. If farmers do not express support for ruling party candidates, they will jeopardise their patronage connections and thus reduce their chances of obtaining the income and lifestyle benefits flowing from LDP largesse.

Another aspect of the government-subsidised public works industry important to part-time farmers and other rural dwellers has been the employment opportunities this industry has generated in local regions. Part-time farmers relying on wages earned in the construction industry have been particularly dependent on the intervention of LDP politicians in terms of the provision of public works.[218]

The general point should be made, however, that even as ordinary wage-earners, farmers may still be LDP supporters. As the data in Table 5.8 and Figure 5.1 reveals, many non-farm workers in Japan vote for the LDP. In short, non-agricultural employment for wages and salaries does not necessarily make voters supporters of other parties, although it is clear that support rates for the LDP amongst different categories of non-agricultural workers vary, with the general trend moving upwards over time.[219]

Last but not least are the majority preferences of the leaders of agricultural organisations, including Nokyo, for the LDP for many of the same reasons that attract farmers to support the ruling party. Over the decades, agricultural group leaders have predominantly although not exclusively influenced their members to support LDP candidates.[220] As studies of partisanship amongst voters have demonstrated, organisational membership can be a force for stabilising the party identification of voters. Because 'members often internalize the ideas, interests and cultures of their organizations, members may come to consider organizational policy interests as their own political interests'.[221] Thus, to the extent that farmers' organisations, including Nokyo, are pro-LDP, farmers' identification with the ruling party has also tended to be stabilised in a pro-LDP pattern.

The ruling LDP as the farmers' party

The magnitude of the LDP's rural support base can be estimated by looking at the correlation between support for the LDP in terms of either seats or votes gained, and levels of urbanisation, industrialisation or employment in primary industry. A number of studies have demonstrated a strong correlation between the two sets of variables in this equation.

In a systematic evaluation of the LDP's performance over three elections in 1967, 1969 and 1972 relative to constituency type (that is, according to an urbanisation index of LH electorate types which divided them into metropolitan, urban, semi-urban, semi-rural and rural categories),[222] an inverse correlation was demonstrated between levels of urbanisation and levels of support for the LDP.[223] Over the three elections, the LDP gained an average of 31 per cent of metropolitan votes, 47 per cent of urban votes, 54 per cent of semi-urban votes, 57 per cent of semi-rural votes and 62 per cent of rural votes.[224] And while the LDP's support rate dipped in all categories of districts over the three elections, it fell by approximately 2 per cent in all categories except for the rural one, where it decreased by only 0.5 per cent: from 62.5 per cent in 1967 to 61.7 per cent in 1969 and to 62.0 per cent in 1972.[225] Over the course of these elections, the rural character of the party thus strengthened.[226] A similar conclusion was reached in another study which demonstrated that while the LDP's voting support rate slipped by 8.47 percentage points in rural constituencies in LH elections over the period 1960 to 1972, it was still above 60 per cent in 1972.[227]

Other research has substantiated these same basic patterns. On a four-point scale of electorates categorised into metropolitan, urban, semi-rural and rural types according to the percentage of population employed in primary industry (with rural electorates 40 per cent and above), Tanaka disclosed that in the 1969 election, the LDP obtained 64 per cent of the total vote in rural districts, with a consistent fall-off in support with the shift from rural through urban and metropolitan types. In the latter, for instance, the LDP demonstrated only a 39 per cent support rate.[228] A study of the results of the 1976 LH election using a five-point scale of electorates in terms of a 'population concentration rate' reached a similar conclusion that as the 'population concentration rate' intensified, the percentage of LDP votes dropped.[229]

Measurement of the LDP's support rate in rural and semi-rural constituencies in terms of seats rather than votes won demonstrates that the LDP consistently secured more than 60 per cent of semi-rural and rural seats in the Lower House in three spaced elections (1958, 1967 and 1972). Over the same period, the percentage of its combined dependence on these seats as a proportion of its total advanced from 55 per cent in 1958 to 57 per cent in 1967 and still further to 61 per cent in 1972.[230]

These relative support rates across constituency types partly explain why the LDP's electoral fortunes ebbed generally in the 1960s and 1970s as the process of urbanisation undermined its voting base at the same time as it failed to capture significant support amongst the growing numbers of city dwellers. In short, some of those people who used to support the LDP in farming areas left the countryside and became Opposition party supporters in the cities. Indeed, the 1979 elections was the nadir of the LDP's electoral fortunes in the first two and a half decades of its rule.

In the 1980s, however, the LDP moved into an era in which its electoral fortunes as a whole fluctuated quite markedly in elections, with those in 1980 and 1986 prominent as LDP victories, while the 1983 election was distinguished by a relatively poor performance.[231] These overall trends were reflected in basic patterns of support in all types of constituency, but it was essentially a period when the structure of LDP support was characterised by a narrowing of the gap between its support rates at the two extremes (i.e. metropolitan and rural types), particularly from the 1986 elections onwards.[232] This came about because the LDP's support rates climbed in metropolitan

Table 5.9 Percentage of the total vote obtained by the LDP in constituencies categorised according to DID percentage rates[a] in Lower House elections 1972–93

DID%	No. of constituencies	1972	1976	1980	1983	1986	1990	1993	% Point decline, 1993/ 1990
1–29%	26 (25)[b]	57.4	61.9	66.0	61.5	63.4	50.7	48.3	−2.4
30–39%	24	48.3	52.8	57.2	56.0	58.6	48.3	47.2	−1.1
40–49%	23	51.0	51.9	54.9	53.9	58.2	52.1	45.6	−6.5
50–69%	22	40.9	44.0	45.8	44.0	49.6	45.8	33.7	−12.1
70–89%	12	32.1	32.1	37.7	34.6	39.0	36.3	26.3	−10.0
90–100%	23	24.3	24.6	30.7	27.5	30.7	40.3	23.5	−16.8
Total/ Average	130 (129)[b]	41.8	44.6	47.9	45.8	49.4	46.1	36.6	−9.5

Notes:
a These percentages were based on 1985 DID rates used as a fixed base.
b In 1993, the number of Lower House constituencies was reduced with the abolition of the Amami Islands electorate.

Source: Data provided by Nishihira Shigeki and kindly supplied by J. A. A. Stockwin.

constituencies, while in other categories they remained essentially stable or tapered off marginally.

Kobayashi, for example, demonstrates that voting support for the LDP in strongly urban, urban, semi-rural and average electoral districts advanced around four percentage points between 1983 and 1986, while its voting support in semi-urban and rural electorates improved by only around two percentage points. In strongly rural districts, it slipped by around three percentage points.[233] These trends both reflected and reinforced the LDP's strengthening orientation towards urban voters and the relative weakening of its bias towards farm voters as a long-standing electoral strategy during the 1980s.[234]

Table 5.9 provides details of LDP polling rates in LH elections from 1972–1993 in constituencies categorised according to the DID scale. What the table indicates is that, in all elections except for 1990, the LDP's success rate improved uniformly in inverse correlation to the climb in the DID rate. In other words, the less densely inhabited the district, the better the LDP performed, with its popularity most marked in the least populous, rural districts. On the other hand, the differential in its popularity between the least and the most densely inhabited districts narrowed considerably during the period 1972–1990. Its support rate swelled in the least populous districts over the period 1972–1986, then retreated in the 1990 elections. Its popularity in more densely inhabited districts also improved gradually over the entire 1971–1990 period,[232] but jumped in a particularly marked fashion in the two categories of most densely inhabited districts in 1980, an advance that was generally sustained thereafter (at least until 1993). This shift underlines the fact that the LDP was acquiring expanding numbers of supporters amongst non-agriculturally employed voters in more urbanised regions over this period. By 1990 the LDP was much more of an urban party than previously, with the 1990 elections even pointing to some waning in its popularity in the least densely populated districts.[236]

Table 5.10 records the LDP's success rates across five types of LH constituency categorised according to the percentage employed in primary industry. The figures cover both percentage of seats gained and percentage of the total vote acquired in each category for the period 1976–93.[237] The table confirms that the LDP was more successful in securing seats from areas where the proportion of population engaged in primary industry was higher, although the variations amongst rural, semi-rural, semi-urban and urban categories were not very large. A gradual decline was also observable in the percentage of seats won from rural through urban categories, but the major contrast was between metropolitan constituencies and all the rest. Generally speaking, the LDP attained twice the percentage of seats in rural districts than it did in metropolitan districts. The LDP usually picked up less than a third of metropolitan seats until 1986 and 1990, when its gains in this type of district were quite marked.[238]

These trends suggest that in 1986 and to a lesser extent in 1990, the LDP began to escape its electoral dependencies on rural and semi-rural constituencies and build support across the entire range of constituencies including more urbanised districts. The 1986 elections recorded the greatest victory for the LDP over this period, but the biggest seat gains for the party in this election were recorded in metropolitan districts (+17), followed by urban (+12) and semi-urban districts (+12), rather than in semi-rural (+7) and rural (+2) ones. As Hirose points out, the LDP's *norin giin* maintained or expanded the number of votes only slightly in agricultural areas in this election. In his view, this suggested that the LDP had gained as many farmers' votes as they could through previous elections and were now making efforts to augment support in those areas that had a substantial number of floating votes, while tending to neglect the areas where they no longer expected to enlarge the number of their supporters. Based on this reasoning, Hirose predicted that the LDP would be less focused on agriculture and agricultural regions in future and would be looking for other sources of votes.[239]

The 1986 election placed at least 29 new LDP urban politicians into the House of Representatives and appeared to indicate that the LDP was at last redressing its rural bias and moving towards the large middle ground of the Japanese electorate – the 'new' urban middle class of wage and salary earners, as opposed to the 'old' provincial middle class of farmers, and small and medium business entrepreneurs.[240]

Over the entire period between 1976 and 1990, the ruling party gained one rural seat, three semi-urban seats, three urban seats and 22 metropolitan seats, whilst it lost two semi-rural seats. Until the major party defections prior to the 1993 elections, the LDP was, therefore, gradually acquiring a more urban

Table 5.10 LDP success rates in constituencies according to percentages employed in primary industry, 1976–93 Lower House elections

% Employed in primary industry[a]	Constituency type	Number of seats		
40+	Rural	51	(48)[b]	(43)[c]
30–39	Semi-Rural	101	(98)	(95)
20–29	Semi-Urban	135	(135)	(134)
10–19	Urban	86	(86)	(88)
0–9	Metropolitan	138	(145)	(151)
	Total	511	(512)	(511)

Constituency type	1976	1979	1980	1983	1986	1990	1993		1993/1990
Won by LDP									*Seat loss*
Rural	30	33	39	34	36	31	26	(30)[d]	−4
Semi-Rural	60	59	65	63	70	58	53	(59)	−5
Semi-Urban	75	75	85	74	86	78	70	(77)	−8
Urban	44	43	47	40	52	47	34	(43)	−13
Metropolitan	40	38	48	39	56	62	39	(45)	−23
Total	249[e]	248	284	250	300	275	223	(254)	−52
LDP percentage share of seats									*% point decline*
Rural	58.8	64.7	76.5	66.7	75.0	64.6	60.5	(69.8)[d]	−4.1
Semi-Rural	59.4	58.4	64.4	62.4	71.4	59.2	55.8	(62.1)	−3.4
Semi-Urban	55.6	55.6	63.0	54.8	63.7	57.8	52.2	(57.5)	−5.6
Urban	51.2	50.0	54.7	46.5	60.5	54.7	38.6	(48.9)	−16.1
Metropolitan	29.0	27.5	34.8	28.3	39.6	42.1	25.8	(29.8)	−16.3
Total	48.7	48.5	55.6	48.9	58.6	53.7	43.6	(49.7)	−10.1
% of total vote won by LDP[f]									*% point decline*
Rural	56.3	61.9	68.3	64.1	63.8	59.9	49.7	(63)[dg]	−10.2
Semi-Rural	49.3	52.2	56.7	55.3	59.5	53.0	48.2	(59)	−4.8
Semi-Urban	51.2	53.0	55.6	54.2	57.8	52.9	42.9	(51)	−10.0
Urban	44.4	48.2	49.2	47.5	53.1	53.1	36.9	(51)	−16.2
Metropolitan	25.7	26.7	31.8	29.2	32.2	33.4	24.4	(30)	−9.0
Total	42	45	48	46	49	46	37	(48)	−9

Notes:

a These percentages are based on the 1975 Census of population engaged in primary industry, used as a fixed base.

b The figures in brackets in this column register the adjustments in seat numbers per constituency in 1986.

c The figures in brackets in this column register the adjustments in seat numbers per constituency in 1992.

d The figures in brackets in this column include those who left the LDP prior to the 1993 elections.

e These totals do not include Independents with connections to the LDP.

f These percentages do not include Independents with connections to the LDP.

g These figures are the average percentage of the vote won by the LDP in this category of constituency.

Sources: Based on figures for primary industry employment by constituency provided by Nishihira Shigeki. Election results were obtained from *Seiji Handobukku*, annual, relevant issues; *Yomiuri Shinbun*, 20 February 1990; *Asahi Shinbun*, 19 July 1993; and *Asahi Nenkan*, 1993, pp. 126–131.

orientation although not at the expense of its rural voting base. While its over-all electoral fortunes might have fluctuated considerably over this period, it gained metropolitan seats consistently from 1979 until 1990.

The percentage of the total votes obtained by the LDP in each category of electoral district more or less reflects the trends in types of seats won over this period. In general, the rate of support registered increasingly lower levels with the shift across the rural-metropolitan spectrum. Between 1976 and 1990, the LDP polled 56.3–63.8 per cent of the total vote in rural districts, 49.3–59.5 per cent in semi-rural electorates, 51.2–57.8 per cent in semi-urban districts, 44.4–53.1 per cent in urban constituencies and 25.7–33.4 per cent in metro-politan electorates (see Table 5.10).

The same characteristics of LDP performance thus stand out. Firstly, the party was more popular in rural electorates than in any other, although in rural, semi-rural, semi-urban and urban districts its support rates generally converged over time. Secondly, the primary contrast was between these four categories of electoral district and the metropolitan category where the LDP generally gained only one-third or less of the total vote, although it did gain ground in metropolitan constituencies over time. Indeed, until the party defections of 1993, the LDP was becoming a distinctly more urban party with a rather more evenly balanced support base across seat type. In fact the variations in its support rates from rural through urban categories were not all that marked, suggesting that the LDP not only had solid support in the countryside but in the regional cities as well.

Table 5.11 summarises trends in LDP support rates for all LH elections between 1958 and 1993 in terms of the correlation coefficient between the proportion of farm household voters in the total eligible vote and the per-centage of votes collected by the LDP.[241] The strong statistical association between the two categories is clearly evident over the entire period, although it was sustained at its highest levels between 1963 and 1986. The slightly lower level between 1958 and 1960 was due to the LDP's rather more even support rates across the rural-urban spectrum in those years,[242] and the relatively high polling rates for JSP candidates in some rural areas where the farmers' unions remained viable electoral organisations in the late 1950s and early 1960s.[243] From the late 1960s onwards, however, the LDP's rural character strength-ened quite markedly.

Table 5.12 makes clear the association between support for the LDP (measured in terms of the percentage of seats and total vote won) and the percentages of farm voter (measured in terms of the proportion of the total population residing in farm households in a constituency) in UH elections between 1977 and 1998. During the LDP's unbroken incumbency from the late 1970s until 1992, it secured 70–86 per cent of rural, semi-rural and semi-urban seats, compared with a little over 40 per cent of urban seats and 22–33 per cent of metropolitan seats, except for the 1989 elections in which farmers registered their strong disapproval of government agricultural policy, including rice policy and the beef and citrus liberalisations of 1988.[244]

Table 5.11 Correlation coefficient of farm voters and LDP support rate

Election year	Correlation coefficient
1958	0.509
1960	0.469
1963	0.633
1967[a]	0.694
1969[b]	0.601
1972	0.710
1976	0.672
1979	0.678
1980	0.723
1983	0.736
1986	0.679
1990	0.596
1993	0.511

Notes:
a Figures for 1966 farm household voters were used because of the unavailability of those for 1967.
b Figures for 1970 farm household voters were used because of the unavailability of those for 1969.

Sources: Figures for eligible voters residing in farm households were calculated from data in *Norinsuisansho Tokeihyo*, annual, relevant years. Election figures were obtained from *Nihon Tokei Nenkan*, annual, relevant years.

These seat acquisition rates reflected the LDP's relative polling rates in each category of constituency, with voting support for the party tending to lessen from rural through metropolitan categories. Between 1977 and 1992 (apart from the anomalous elections in 1989), the range for rural districts was 50–76 per cent; for semi-rural districts 50–57 per cent; and for semi-urban districts 46–55 per cent. The lack of marked variation in these constituency types suggests that the LDP drew support not only from farmers but also from the non-farming population in regional areas.

On the other hand, a stark contrast is evident between these categories and the LDP's support rates in urban and metropolitan electorates where its polling rates were consistently lower (35–47 per cent in urban districts, and 16–26 per cent in metropolitan districts). Nevertheless, the LDP's support rates in fact lifted in all categories except the semi-urban one over the 15-year period. The LDP was gaining ground amongst urban and metropolitan voters at the same time as it was retaining the support of rural, semi-rural and semi-urban voters. By the 1992 UH poll, the LDP's rural base was stronger than ever, at the same time as the party was obviously advancing in urban and metropolitan regions.

Table 5.12 LDP success rates in constituencies according to percentages residing in farm households, 1977–98, Upper House elections

	% residing in farm households[a]	Constituency type	Number of seats[b]
	40+	Rural	7
	30–39	Semi-Rural	27 (29)
	20–29	Semi-Urban	14
	10–19	Urban	19 (16)
	0–9	Metropolitan	9 (10)
	Total		76

Constituency type	1977	1980	1983	1986	1989	1992	1995	1998	1998/1995
Won by LDP									
Rural	5	6	6	6	1	6	2	5	+3
Semi-Rural	19	22	20	20	8	23	15	15	0
Semi-Urban	11	10	12	12	4	10	6	8	+2
Urban	8	8	8	9	6	8	5	3	−2
Metropolitan	2	2	3	3	2	3	3	0	−3
Total	45	48	49	50	21	50	31	31	0
LDP percentage share of seats									*% point rise/decline*
Rural	71.4	85.7	85.7	85.7	14.3	85.7	28.6	71.4	+42.8
Semi-Rural	70.3	81.5	74.1	74.1	29.6	85.2	51.7	51.7	0.0
Semi-Urban	78.6	71.4	85.7	85.7	28.6	71.4	42.9	57.1	+14.2
Urban	42.1	42.1	42.1	47.4	31.6	42.1	31.3	18.8	−12.5
Metropolitan	22.2	22.2	33.2	33.3	22.2	33.3	30.0	0.0	−30.0
Total	59.2	63.2	64.5	65.8	27.6	65.8	40.8	40.8	0.0
LDP's percentage share of total vote									*% point increase*
Rural	48.5	52.5	48.4	52.3	34.9	53.4	17.2	30.2	+13.0
Semi-Rural	49.1	59.9	57.5	56.0	39.1	54.6	32.3	37.9	+5.6
Semi-Urban	53.6	54.6	55.5	55.6	40.3	52.3	30.9	43.4	+12.5
Urban	35.3	39.0	45.0	35.2	24.1	38.0	23.6	27.8	+4.2
Metropolitan	18.4	15.6	21.1	24.8	20.6	26.3	17.6	18.6	+1.0
Total	41.0	44.3	30.6	30.4	31.8	43.0	25.4	30.8	+5.4

Notes:

a These percentages were based on farm household figures for 1977, used as a fixed base.

b The figures in brackets register the changes in seat numbers per constituency with the redistribution of UH seats prior to the 1995 elections.

Sources: Farm household population figures were obtained from *Norinsuishansho Tokeihyo*, annual, relevant issues. Election results were from *Seiji Handobukku*, annual, relevant issues; *Nihon Tokei Nenkan*, annual, various issues; *Asahi Nenkan*, annual, various issues; and *Yomiuri Shinbun*, 24 July 1995; 13 July 1998.

The figures for the percentage of the total vote obtained by the LDP not surprisingly exhibit a similar pattern, with no great distinctions between rural, semi-rural and semi-urban categories, where its polling range was uniformly between 48 and 57 per cent (excluding the 1989 elections), whereas its vote tally in urban and metropolitan constituencies, particularly in the latter, ranged from 18–45 per cent. Even so, the LDP's performance generally improved in metropolitan districts over time.

The main observations arising from the above statistical data are firstly, that the LDP's maintained its rural voting base over the entire period under scrutiny in spite of wholesale socio-economic changes arising from urban-isation and industrialisation;[245] and secondly, that the LDP, while far from jettisoning its farm supporters, nevertheless garnered much higher levels of support from non-farm urban voters beginning in the 1980s, which inevitably reorientated the party more towards city districts at the macro level. The entire story is not told, however, until the LDP's relative dependence on different constituency types is factored into the equation. This is attempted in the following section.

LDP dependencies on constituency types

The LDP's relative dependence on different categories of electorate is one of the most important influences shaping its responsiveness to the interests of voters across the rural-metropolitan spectrum. This can be discerned in a number of different ways. Table 5.13 utilises a six-point DID scale to reveal the percentage of the LDP's total vote coming from each category of electoral district for LH elections between 1972 and 1993. Less populated districts occupy the lower percentage end of the DID scale (from 1–49 per cent), compared to the more densely populated (50–100 per cent). What the table bears out is that the four categories at the lower end of the DID scale (1–69 DID percentage rate) each provided 17–21 per cent of the LDP's total vote tally, but the two categories in the 70–100 per cent range generated only around 10–11 per cent of the LDP's total vote. In other words, the ruling party acquired around 80 per cent of all its supporting votes from constituencies in the 1–69 per cent DID range, which included not only farming electorates, but also semi-rural, semi-urban and even more urbanised districts such as regional cities. In fact, the LDP recorded its highest proportional dependence on constituencies in the mid-range of 40–49 per cent on the DID scale, suggesting solid support from non-farm interests in provincial areas.

With respect to changes over time, the party's dependency ratios remained remarkably stable except for the most densely industrialised district category which varied by more than four percentage points between 1972 and 1990 (from 9.8 per cent to 14.2 per cent). The figures confirm the same general trends identified in the earlier analysis. Until the party defections of 1993, the LDP was gradually lowering the differentials in its support rates across constituency types. In this sense, it was becoming relatively less reliant on

Table 5.13 Percentage of the LDP's total vote supplied by electoral districts categorised according to the DID percentage rates[a] in Lower House elections, 1972–93

DID%	No. of electorates	1972	1976	1980	1983	1986	1990	1993
1–29%	26 (25)[b]	20.5	21.5	19.9	19.8	18.9	20.0	18.3
30–39%	24	17.9	19.3	18.5	19.2	18.4	18.1	19.6
40–49%	23	21.0	20.7	19.8	20.5	20.5	20.2	21.0
50–69%	22	18.5	19.0	17.8	18.4	18.9	17.5	17.2
70–89%	12	10.7	9.7	11.3	10.9	11.6	10.0	11.4
90–100%	23	11.3	9.8	12.7	11.3	11.7	14.2	12.5
Total	130 (129)[b]	100.0	100.0	100.0	100.0	100.0	100.0	100.0

Notes:
a These percentages were based on 1985 DID rates used as a fixed base.
b In 1993, the number of Lower House constituencies was reduced with the abolition of the Amami Islands electorate.

Source: Data provided by Nishihira Shigeki and kindly supplied by J. A. A. Stockwin.

rural support and acquiring a more balanced electoral support profile across the spectrum of constituency types. Indeed, some of its biggest gains were being made in highly urbanised and metropolitan districts. This lends further evidence to support the proposition already advanced that the LDP was scoring ever-greater numbers of votes from the new urban, salaried and wage-earning middle class, even in the more densely populated cities.

The picture of relative LDP electoral dependencies drawn by Table 5.13 are confirmed by Tables 5.14 and 5.15. These undertake a similar exercise for LDP seat dependency ratios in Lower and Upper House constituencies categorised according to percentage of population employed in primary industry and percentage of population resident in farm households respectively. Table 5.14 demonstrates that firstly, while rural, semi-rural and semi-urban constituencies contributed just over half the number of seats in the Lower House, they generated around two-thirds of the total number of seats acquired by the LDP. The party was thus disproportionately dependent on seats gained in constituencies where the percentage of population employed in primary industry was higher. In 1976, the proportion from these three categories was 66.3 per cent, in 1979 it was 67.3 per cent, in 1980 66.5 per cent, in 1983 68.4 per cent, in 1986 64 per cent and in 1990 60.7 per cent.

Secondly, LDP seat acquisition rates in rural, semi-rural and semi-urban districts were remarkably stable over time, although a downwards trend could be observed between 1976 and 1990. This suggests some reorientation of the party away from agriculture towards non-agricultural voters, a shift confirmed even more by the third point, namely that the LDP began to gain a greater percentage of its seats in metropolitan constituencies over time (16.1 per cent

Table 5.14 LDP dependency rates on constituencies according to percentages employed in primary industry, 1976–93 Lower House elections

% Employed in primary industry[a]	Constituency type	Number of seats		
40+	Rural	51	(48)[b]	(43)[c]
30–39	Semi-Rural	101	(98)	(95)
20–29	Semi-Urban	135	(135)	(134)
10–19	Urban	86	(86)	(88)
0–9	Metropolitan	138	(145)	(151)
	Total	511	(512)	(511)

Constituency type	1976[d]	1979	1980	1983	1986	1990	1993	1993/1990
Percentage of total seats won by LDP[e]								*% point rise/ decline*
Rural	12.0	13.3	13.7	9.7	12.0	11.3	11.7	(11.8)[f] +0.4
Semi-Rural	24.1	23.8	22.9	25.2	23.3	21.1	23.8	(23.2) +2.7
Semi-Urban	30.1	30.2	29.9	29.6	28.7	28.4	31.4	(30.3) +3.0
Urban	17.1	17.3	16.5	16.0	17.3	17.1	15.2	(16.9) −1.9
Metropolitan	16.1	15.3	16.9	15.6	18.7	22.5	17.5	(17.7) −5.0
Total	100.0	100.0	100.0	100.0	100.0	100.0	100.0	(100.0)

Notes:
a These percentages are based on the 1975 Census of population engaged in primary industry, used as a fixed base.
b The figures in brackets in this column register the adjustments in seat numbers per constituency in 1986.
c The figures in brackets in this column register the adjustments in seat numbers per constituency in 1992.
d All percentages in these columns have been rounded off.
e These totals do not include Independents with connections to the LDP.
f The figures in brackets in this column include those who left the LDP prior to the 1993 elections.

Sources: Based on figures for primary industry employment by constituency provided by Nishihira Shigeki. Election results were obtained from *Seiji Handobukku*, annual, relevant issues; *Yomiuri Shinbun*, 20 February 1990; *Asahi Shinbun*, 19 July 1993; and *Asahi Nenkan* 1993, pp. 126–131.

in 1976 compared with 22.5 per cent in 1990). This represented the biggest movement of all in its seat dependency ratios.

Trends in the Upper House (Table 5.15) are a little more complicated because of LDP seat losses in the 1989 elections. Discounting this atypical result and reserving the 1995 and 1998 election results for discussion below, it is clear that the LDP's seat dependency ratios tracked in a fairly narrow band in each category: for rural constituencies, it was 11–12 per cent; for semi-rural constituencies it was 40–46 per cent; for semi-urban constituencies it was 19–24 per cent; for urban constituencies it was 16–17 per cent; and for metro-

Table 5.15 LDP success rates in constituencies according to percentage of population residing in farm households, 1977–98 Upper House elections

	% residing in farm households[a]	*Constituency type*	*Number of seats*[b]
	40+	Rural	7
	30–39	Semi-Rural	27 (29)
	20–29	Semi-Urban	14
	10–19	Urban	19 (16)
	0–9	Metropolitan	9 (10)
		Total	76

Constituency type	*1977*[b]	*1980*	*1983*	*1986*	*1989*	*1992*	*1995*	*1998*	*1998/1995*
Percentage of total seats won by LDP									*% point rise/decline*
Rural	11.1	12.5	12.2	12.0	4.8	12.0	6.5	16.1	+9.6
Semi-Rural	42.2	45.8	40.8	40.0	38.1	46.0	48.4	48.4	0.0
Semi-Urban	24.4	20.8	24.5	24.0	19.0	20.0	19.4	25.8	+6.4
Urban	17.8	16.7	16.3	18.0	28.6	16.0	16.1	9.7	−6.4
Metropolitan	4.4	4.2	6.1	6.0	9.5	6.0	9.7	0.0	−9.7
Total	100.0	100.0	100.0	100.0	100.0	100.0	100.0	100.0	

Notes:

a These percentages were based on farm household figures for 1977, used as a fixed base.

b The figures in brackets register the changes in seat numbers per constituency with the redistribution of UH seats prior to the 1995 election.

Sources: Farm household population figures were obtained from *Norinsuisansho Tokeihyo*, annual, relevant issues. Election results were from *Seiji Handobukku*, annual, relevant issues; *Nihon Tokei Nenkan*, annual, relevant issues; and *Yomiuri Shinbun*, 24 July 1995, 13 July 1998.

politan constituencies it was 4–6 per cent. Over the entire period (1977–1992), the ratio of the LDP's dependence on constituency types heightened marginally with respect to rural and semi-rural electorates, slipped marginally with respect to semi-urban and urban electorates and lifted marginally with respect to metropolitan districts. The variations are not sufficiently significant, however, to disturb the essentially stable structure of LDP seat dependencies.

Moreover, while semi-urban, semi-rural and rural constituencies represented just under two-thirds of the total number of seats in the Upper House over this period, they produced approximately three-quarters or more of the LDP's prefectural constituency seats (except for 1989). The LDP obtained 77.8 per cent of its UH seats in rural, semi-rural and semi-urban districts in the 1977 elections, 79.2 per cent in 1980, 77.6 per cent in 1983, 76.0 per cent in 1986, 61.9 per cent in 1989 and 78.0 per cent in 1992.

Once again, the stability of these shares in the LDP's overall support profile underlines a fundamental point about the nature of the LDP's performance in the face of the twin processes of urbanisation and industrial-isation. All the tables indicating LDP electoral performance and dependencies use a fixed base on which their constituency categories are organised. They do not, therefore, record the effects of demographic and employment changes on the makeup of electoral districts, because constituencies remain fixed in the categories across the rural-metropolitan or DID continuum. The advantage of holding the statistical basis of categorisation constant is that it reveals LDP performance in the same constituencies over time. Given that this was remark-ably stable over the space of two decades or so, it suggests that the LDP successfully maintained its support rates in the various constituencies in spite of the changes attendant upon industrialisation and urbanisation. The socio-economic transformation of electorates did not appear to alter basic patterns of support for the conservative party. The LDP retained the electoral loyalties of farmers whilst winning support amongst other occupational categories in urban areas to supplement the declining numbers of farm voters. In other words the party was as successful in garnering votes from the swelling numbers of urban dwellers and non-agricultural workers as it had been from farm voters. This general comment accords with the elevating trend of pro-LDP support in more urbanised electorates of the Lower House between 1986 and 1990. While the LDP might have started out as a predominantly rural party, and while it remained the party of the farmers and rural voters, by 1990 it did not end up with such a clear-cut agrarian orientation.

These observations are supported by research analysing the changing nature of the LDP's support base relative to voters' occupational category from the mid-1970s onwards. One study argued that until about the mid-1970s, the major cause of the diminution in the LDP's support rate was the rapid drop in the numbers of persons engaged in agricultural, forestry and fishing industries.[246] Other evidence certainly lends credence to the fact that primary industry workers were contracting as a proportion of the LDP's support in the 1960s and 1970s. Although they were the largest single supporting bloc for the LDP over the period 1955–75, primary industry workers declined from 43 per cent of LDP supporters in 1955 to 34 per cent in 1962, 29 per cent in 1965 and 19 per cent in 1975.[247]

On the other hand, according to Iwamoto, support for the LDP began to spread amongst non-primary industry workers after 1976.[248] He maintains that between 1976 and 1986, the LDP's support rate climbed eight percentage points because of a rise in support from industrial workers, office workers, those in service industries and the self-employed, indicating that not only was the LDP making great strides into the voting base of the JSP, but that the LDP was significantly broadening its support base. According to Iwamoto's figures, the escalation in support for the LDP was greatest amongst industrial workers over this period.[249]

Similar conclusions have been reached as a result of other survey research which verifies that office, management, labouring and service workers all expanded incrementally as a proportion of the total LDP support constituency over the period 1975–85, thus eating into the predominance of the LDP's two major electoral substructures – primary industry and the self-employed (i.e. small business). Between 1975 and 1985, office workers climbed from 19 per cent to 23 per cent of the total number of LDP supporters; management from 7 to 10 per cent; industry labourers from 11 to 12 per cent, and service workers from 14 to 16 per cent. In contrast, those employed in primary industry contracted from 19 per cent to 15 per cent in 1980 and 13 per cent in 1985; and the self-employed from 25 per cent in 1975 to 23 per cent in 1980 and 19 per cent in 1985.[250] In short, by the mid-1980s, the LDP's distribution of supporters by occupation was exhibiting a much more dispersed pattern across the whole range of occupational categories, demonstrating unequivocally that farmers and small business were not nearly as predominant and therefore as important to the LDP as they had been in the past.[251]

The following two tables endeavour to capture these trends at constituency level by showing changes in LDP seat dependency ratios consequent upon the changes in the socio-economic profiles of electoral districts. This exercise is designed to give a more accurate picture of shifts in the LDP's relative dependencies on farm voters. Using a statistical categorisation system that illustrates the changing employment composition of LH electorates, Table 5.16 reveals that the LDP garnered 12.0 per cent of its seats in the rural category in 1976, but only 0.8 per cent in 1983 and 0.0 per cent in 1986.[252] Likewise, its tally of semi-rural seats slumped from 24.1 per cent to 2.3 per cent between 1976 and 1986, while semi-urban constituencies slipped from 30.1 per cent to 11.7 per cent over the same period. On the other hand, its seat dependency rate on urban constituencies expanded from 17.7 per cent to 48.3 per cent, and in metropolitan constituencies from 16.1 per cent to 37.7 per cent. In other words, by 1986, the LDP was acquiring 86 per cent of all its LH seats from urban and metropolitan constituencies – as defined by the percentage employed in primary industry.

The same exercise is repeated for the Upper House in Table 5.17. LDP rural seats disappeared by 1986, while the party's dependence on semi-rural seats dropped from 39.5 per cent in 1974 to 2.0 per cent in 1992. Its proportional dependence on semi-urban and urban constituencies, on the other hand, amplified from 14.0 per cent to 26.0 per cent and 7.0 per cent to 46.0 per cent respectively over the same period. By 1992, the majority of LDP seats were being acquired in constituencies where farm household population amounted to less than 20 per cent of the total population.

Table 5.17 underlines the fact that, firstly, the LDP was becoming less dependent on the farm vote over time in the sense that farmers made up ever-diminishing proportions of its total voting support in any particular election. Secondly, the LDP was gaining support from non-farm voters who comprised an expanding proportion of the national electorate, which compounded the decline in the relative importance of the farm vote for the LDP.

A number of general conclusions can be drawn from the trends identified in the above tables with respect to the LDP's inclination to respond to the

Table 5.16 Changing composition of LDP electoral base by constituency type in the Lower House, 1976–93

	% Employed in primary industry[a]	*Constituency type*					
	40+	Rural					
	30–39	Semi-Rural					
	20–29	Semi-Urban					
	10–19	Urban					
	0–9	Metropolitan					
		Total					
No. of seats by constituency type							
Rural	51	51	3	3	0	0	0
Semi-Rural	101	101	18	18	8	n/a	n/a
Semi-Urban	135	135	104	104	46	n/a	n/a
Urban	86	86	189	189	220	n/a	n/a
Metropolitan	138	138	197	197	238	n/a	n/a
Total	511	511	511	511	512	512	511
Won by LDP							
Rural	30	33	3	2	0	0	0
Semi-Rural	60	59	13	12	7	n/a	n/a
Semi-Urban	75	75	71	67	35	n/a	n/a
Urban	44	43	116	105	145	n/a	n/a
Metropolitan	40	38	81	64	113	n/a	n/a
Total	249	248	284	250	300	275	223
% of total seats won by LDP							
Rural	12.0	13.3	1.1	0.8	0.0	0.0	0.0
Semi-Rural	24.1	23.8	4.6	4.8	2.3	n/a	n/a
Semi-Urban	30.1	30.2	25.0	26.8	11.7	n/a	n/a
Urban	17.7	17.7	40.8	42.0	48.3	n/a	n/a
Metropolitan	16.1	15.3	28.5	25.6	37.7	n/a	n/a
Total	100.0	100.0	100.0	100.0	100.0	100.0	100.0

Notes:
a This classification system is the same as that used for Table 5.4. Unfortunately, categorisation of LH seats based on the 1990 census (for the 1990 and 1993 elections) is not available.

Sources: As for Table 5.10.

demands of farmers and their organisations in terms of policy benefits. In the 1960s, Ishida claimed that 'the majority of the Diet members from the Conservative Party ... [were] elected because of their [the farmers'] support .... This makes the Conservative Party unable to say 'no' to the demands of farmers'.[253] Two to three decades later, such a proposition would be insupportable. The electoral data presented in the tables suggest a political inclination on the LDP's part that was inevitably diminishing, although it was far from extinguished because farmers remained such a stable core of voting support. Electoral strategy thus continued to dictate that the LDP agree to

Table 5.17 Changing composition of LDP electoral base by constituency type in the Upper House, 1974–98

	% Residing in farm households[a]	Constituency type
	40+	Rural
	30–39	Semi-Rural
	20–29	Semi-Urban
	10–19	Urban
	0–9	Metropolitan
		Total

Type of constituency	1974	1977	1980	1983	1986	1989	1992	1995	1998
No. of seats by constituency type[a]									
Rural	16	7	7	2	0	0	0	0	0
Semi-Rural	23	27	25	22	14	11	1	2	3
Semi-Urban	9	14	10	18	26	29	16	26	24
Urban	19	19	21	21	19	19	27	23	25
Metropolitan	9	9	13	13	17	17	32	25	24
Total	76	76	76	76	76	76	76	76	76
Won by LDP									
Rural	11	5	5	2	0	0	0	0	0
Semi-Rural	17	19	20	16	10	3	1	1	2
Semi-Urban	6	11	10	16	22	8	13	13	16
Urban	6	8	9	10	11	6	23	10	10
Metropolitan	3	2	4	5	7	4	13	7	3
Total	43	45	48	49	50	21	50	31	31
% of total seats won by LDP									
Rural	25.6	11.1	10.4	4.1	0.0	0.0	0.0	0.0	0.0
Semi-Rural	39.5	42.2	41.7	32.7	20.0	14.3	2.0	3.2	6.5
Semi-Urban	14.0	24.4	20.8	32.7	44.0	38.1	26.0	41.9	51.6
Urban	14.0	17.8	18.8	20.4	22.0	28.6	46.0	32.3	32.3
Metropolitan	7.0	4.4	8.3	10.2	14.0	19.0	26.0	22.6	9.7
Total	100.0	100.0	100.0	100.0	100.0	100.0	100.0	100.0	100.0

Note:
a This classification system is the same as that used for Table 5.3.

Sources: As for Tables 5.3 and 5.12.

policies that were basically designed to retain farmers' support, but nevertheless more consciously reorientate the party towards urban voters employed in a range of non-primary industry occupations. In other words, the changing demographic and occupational profiles of electorates meant that the LDP had to seek a much broader base of support over time, increasingly take urban, consumer issues into account (in spite of the relatively devalued urban vote), and actively seek urban support by appealing to a wider range of non-agricultural interests – although not necessarily at the expense of the farmers.

In summary, the LDP's electoral report card illuminated here basically endorses the well-known stereotype of the ruling party. Throughout the period of its unbroken rule from 1955 until 1993, the LDP remained the farmers' party and preserved its rural voting base, although the balance of interests within the party gradually shifted in relative terms away from rural voters towards urban voters, particularly in the 1980s. Moreover, while the LDP remained the party of the farmers, it was never just a farmers' party. Clearly, its electoral base extended well beyond farm voters to a range of other interests, which gradually gained more weighting within the party as its farm support base contracted.

The impact of party defections

In 1993, the LDP went into the LH election fighting three new parties, the Japan New Party, or JNP (Nihon Shinto), the New Party Harbinger, or NPH (Shinto Sakigake) and the Renewal Party, or RP (Shinseito).[254] Figure 5.2 tracks the complicated party developments of this period. Shinto Sakigake and Shinseito were splinter groups whose members defected from the LDP in 1993. In 1995, the LDP contested the UH election against the New Frontier Party, or NFP (Shinshinto) as the major Opposition grouping, as well as the partners in its own coalition, namely the Shinto Sakigake and the Social Democratic Party, or SDP (Shakai Minshuto), a reincarnated version of the old JSP.

The onset of party fluidity in 1992–93 did not alter the basic structure of the LDP's traditional support base. Indeed, the party's rural core was strengthened in relative terms. Table 5.9, for example, indicates that while support for the LDP decreased in all LH constituencies categorised according to the DID rate, the percentage falls were greatest in the most densely industrialised constituencies (a slide of 16.8 percentage points) and least in constituencies at the lowest end of the DID scale (a drop of 2.4 percentage points).

This represented something of a reversion to the LDP's standard pattern of relative support across constituency types, which suggests that the inverse correlation between the degree of population density and percentage of the total vote obtained by the LDP was once again reestablished. As noted earlier, this basic structure was starting to break down in the late 1980s because of the increasing popularity of the LDP in more densely populated areas. In the 1993 LH elections, however, the LDP ceded the most votes to defectors and other Opposition party candidates in the more densely inhabited districts. Its polling rate in the least populous districts according to this scale (48.3 per cent of the total) was more than twice the rate in the most densely inhabited districts (23.5 per cent).

The strong association between support for the LDP on the one hand and, on the other, low population densities and primary industry employment in the 1993 elections is confirmed by Table 5.18. It provides the correlation

Table 5.18 Correlation coefficient between party support rates and the ratio of population concentration/shares of primary, secondary and tertiary industries in the 1993 Lower House districts

Party	LDP	SDP	JCP
Population Concentration Ratio	−0.618	−0.281	0.696
Primary Industry	0.516	0.295	−0.574
Secondary Industry	0.089	−0.062	−0.128
Tertiary Industry	−0.489	−0.190	0.568

Source: Nishihira, 'Shosenkyoku Bunrui', p. 2.

Table 5.19 Opposition party support rates in the 1993 Lower House election

| DID rate(%) | No. of constituencies | Per cent | | | | | | |
		SDP	Komeito	JCP	DSP	Nihon Shinto	Shinseito	Shinto Sakigake
Over 90	23	10.9	15.1	13.6	2.7	13.1	9.1	3.1
70–90	12	15.2	15.2	11.6	2.9	14.0	10.0	1.0
50–70	22	17.9	5.6	7.4	4.2	6.0	12.1	1.8
40–50	23	16.4	3.2	4.7	5.6	4.7	10.0	1.2
30–40	24	16.1	2.8	4.5	1.9	4.0	11.1	2.2
0–30	25	15.7	1.1	4.1	0.9	2.4	11.3	3.4

Source: Calculated from data kindly supplied by Nishihira Shigeki. Election results were obtained from *Asahi Shinbun*, 19 July 1993.

coefficient between voting support for three parties (the LDP, SDP and JCP) and district population concentration ratios, and for the same three parties and population employed in primary, secondary and tertiary industries respectively. The correlation coefficient between the number of votes obtained by the LDP in the 1993 general election and the percentage of the total population employed in primary industry was in the positive range (0.516), compared to secondary industry (0.089) and tertiary industry (−0.489). This performance contrasted strongly with that of the JCP which was negatively correlated with primary industry (−0.574). The SDP, on the other hand, was positively correlated with primary industry (0.295), although this figure was considerably lower than the LDP's. Conversely, the LDP's correlation coefficient with the population concentration ratio was −0.618, while that for the SDP was −0.281 and the JCP's was 0.696. These figures register the fact that the share of votes obtained by the LDP was elevated in areas where rates of primary industry employment were high, while the association for the SDP was also positive but weaker. The JCP, on the other hand, was unequivocally an urban party with very little support in agricultural regions.

Table 5.19 provides an indication of where support for parties other than the LDP lay in the 1993 LH election. The SDP, Shinseito and Shinto Sakigake polled relatively evenly across constituency types categorised according to the

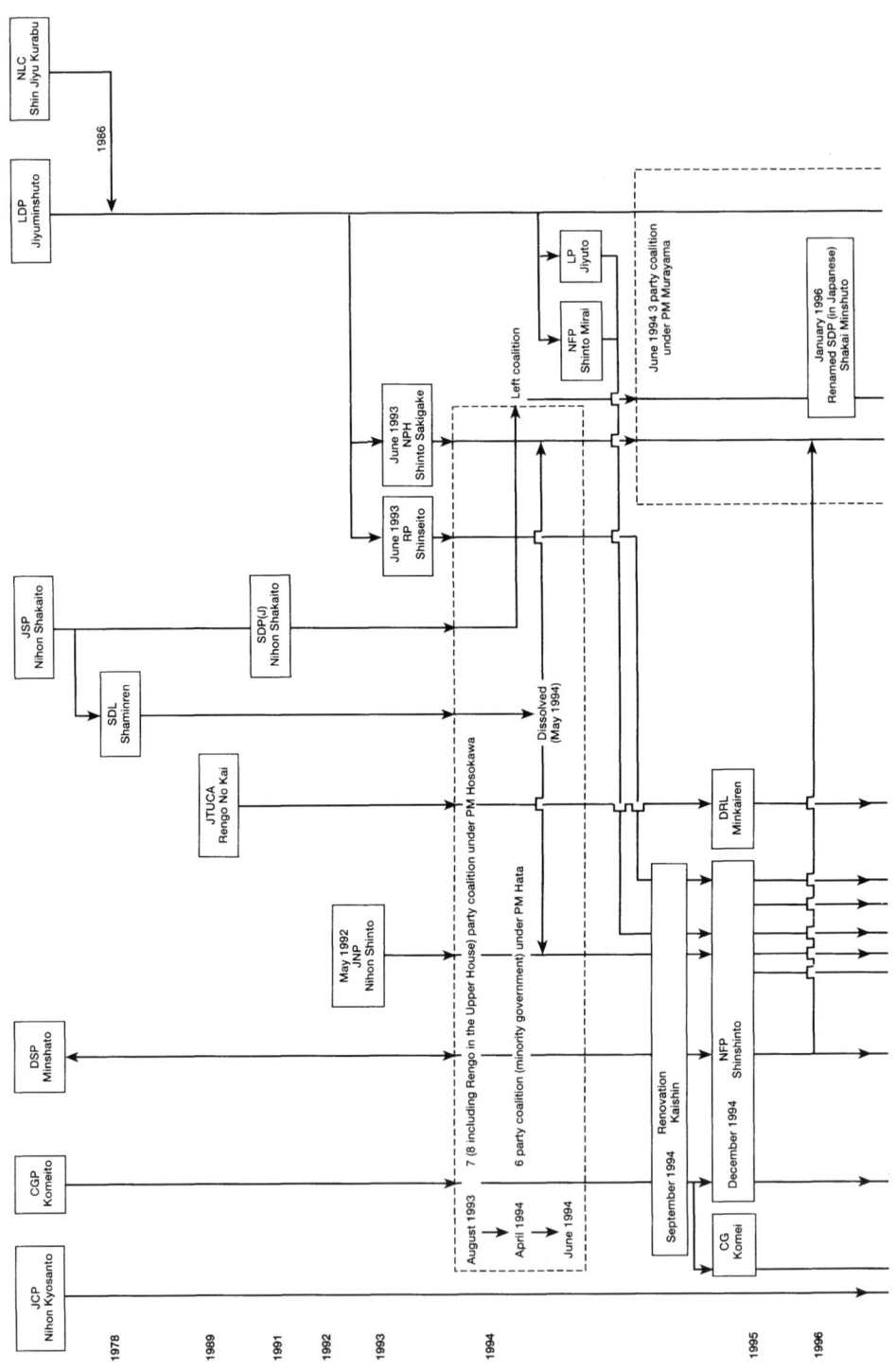

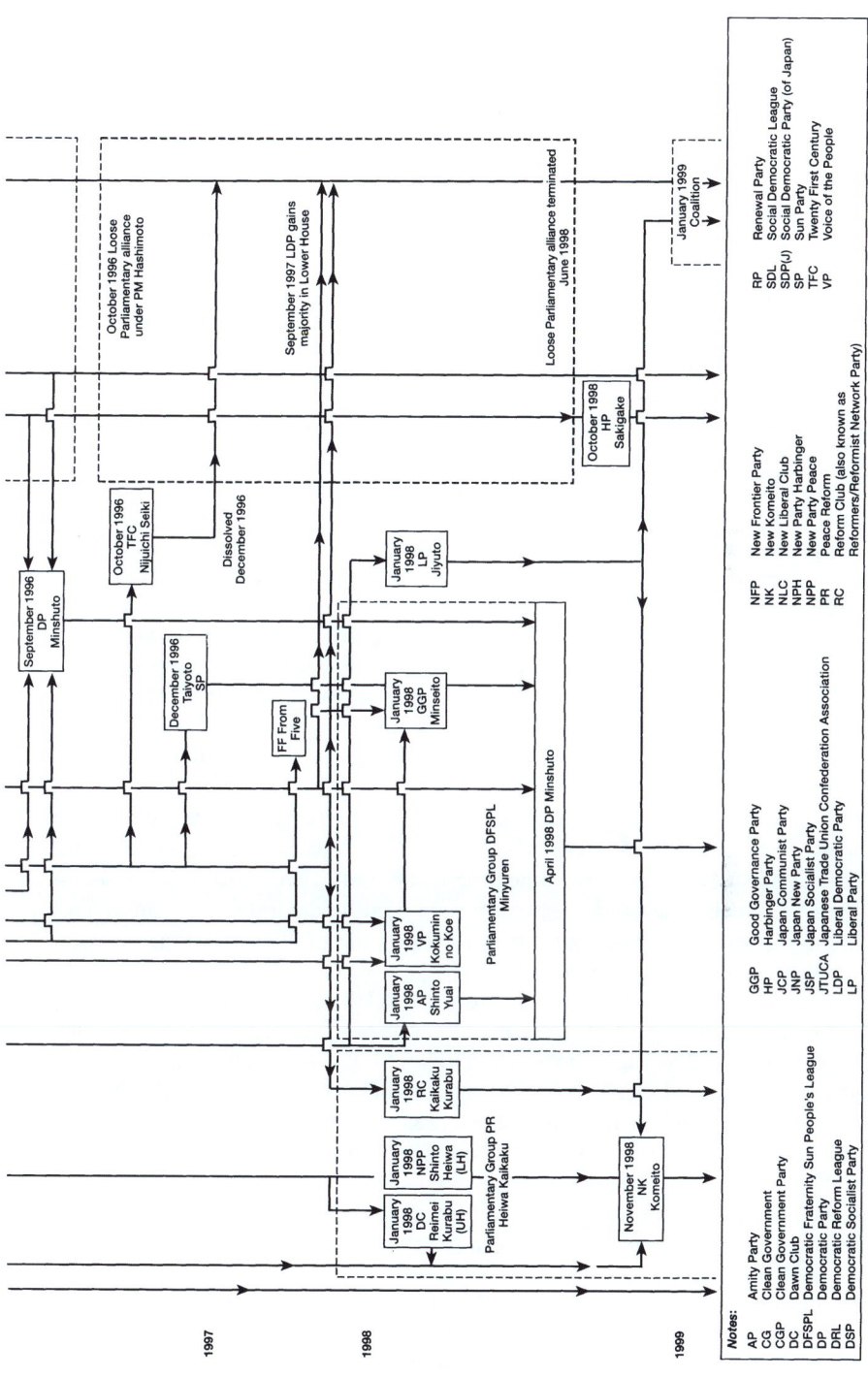

Figure 5.2 Changing party configurations in the Japanese Diet, 1978–99

DID scale. If anything these parties were slightly more orientated towards the less-urbanised end of the spectrum. In the case of the Shinseito and Shinto Sakigake, this is not surprising, given the origins of many of their members in the LDP itself, although their popularity in more urbanised electorates was also in evidence. The Komeito, JCP and JNP, on the other hand, were patently urban parties, with by far the largest number of their votes drawn from constituencies in the 70 per cent plus range on the DID scale. The DSP, while demonstrating a relatively even spread of support, bulged in the mid-range.

In contrast, the figures in Table 5.10 provide further evidence to support the contention that the LDP retained and indeed strengthened its connection with rural and farm voters in the process of party fragmentation. In the 1993 LH elections, the LDP once again reasserted its predominance in farming areas in spite of the defections to the Shinseito. The LDP secured 60.5 per cent of rural seats, 55.8 per cent of semi-rural seats and 52.2 per cent of semi-urban seats, while the proportion for urban seats and metropolitan seats was only 38.6 per cent and 25.8 per cent respectively.

Furthermore, in spite of its relatively lacklustre performance in this election compared to the 1990 elections, the LDP lost far more seats in metropolitan and urban districts (13 and 23 respectively) compared with rural and semi-rural districts (five in each). This pattern underlines the degree to which the party reverted to its traditional scale of relative performance across con-stituency types in this election. The LDP gained two-thirds (66.8 per cent) of its total seat tally from rural, semi-rural and semi-urban districts in spite of the fact that the total number of these seats comprised only just over half the house.

Altogether, party defections cost the LDP four rural seats, six semi-rural seats, seven semi-urban seats, nine urban seats and six metropolitan seats. Clearly the LDP was most vulnerable to ex-party rival candidates in semi-urban and urban seats and less so in semi-rural and rural seats. Conversely, those Diet members more likely to defect from the LDP were politicians with weaker ties to rural and agricultural interests.

Focusing on the actual areas where the LDP lost the most support to Shinseito and Shinto Sakigake defectors in urban and semi-urban seats, the regional cities of Miyagi, Tochigi, Shizuoka, Shiga, Aichi, Hyogo, Hiroshima and Kyushu stand out.[255] On the other hand, where it lost to the Nihon Shinto, a party of all new candidates, was in the metropolitan districts of Hokkaido, Saitama, Chiba, Tokyo, Kanagawa, Aichi, Osaka and Hyogo.[256] In terms of the percentage of the total vote won across constituency types, the LDP lost across the board, with the biggest falls coming in urban districts (a loss of 16.2 percentage points in polling performance), and the least in semi-rural districts (a loss of 4.8 percentage points). This confirmed the strength of the new parties in city areas, rather than in strictly metropolitan areas.

Table 5.11 reveals a small reduction in the correlation coefficient between support for the LDP and farm household voters in the 1993 LH elections (from .596 to .511). This was mainly due to the LDP's comparatively poor showing in some key constituencies with relatively high rates of farm household voters (such as Iwate, Nagano and Kumamoto) because of the influence of Ozawa Ichiro, Hata Tsutomu and Hosokawa Morihiro respectively, and high levels of support in some key prefectures where the farm household residency rate was only in the 10–20 per cent range (such as Gumma, Gifu, Okayama, Ehime, Nagasaki and Kagoshima). In other words, where the LDP lost support in constituencies with higher concentrations of farm household voters, it was largely due to the personal influence of key politicians who had defected from the LDP. As emphasised by a Zenkoku Noseikyo official, because rural voters follow particular politicians rather than a political party, voters in Iwate, Nagano and Kumamoto now supported the Shinshinto because prominent politicians in those areas had moved from the LDP to the Shinshinto.[257]

At the same time, the LDP as a whole continued to poll well in a few relatively urbanised regional areas as well as in rural areas generally. Certainly, survey research amongst farmers after the party resumed power in 1994 demonstrated that, at least amongst Nokyo's farmer members, support for the LDP was as robust as ever. In two polls conducted in August–September 1994, an average of more than 65 per cent of respondents acknowledged that they supported the LDP, whilst an average of around 10 per cent supported the SDP. The remaining parties scored extremely low percentages. As expected, the next highest average percentage was the Shinseito (3 per cent), while all other parties registered 1–2 per cent, except for the Nihon Shinto and Komeito at less than 1 per cent.[258]

In terms of the LDP's voting dependencies, Table 5.13 discloses a continuation of the relatively stable distribution of dependency ratios of previous years. The LDP's reliance on voters in the least densely industrialised districts lessened marginally (by 1.7 per cent), registering the losses in the key rural constituencies noted above). The same proportional decline took place in the most densely industrialised districts. Basically, however, the traditional scale of dependency reasserted itself, with the increment in the percentage figures for the metropolitan category between 1986 and 1990 being partially reversed.

The LDP's relative dependencies in terms of seats gained in the Lower House as illustrated in Table 5.14 underline the party's reversion to its established scale of relative performance even more strongly. The figures confirm that rural, semi-rural and semi-urban constituencies reasserted their importance to the party (the share of these categories rising by 0.4 per cent, 2.7 per cent and 3.0 per cent respectively), while urban and metropolitan constituencies diminished somewhat in importance (falls of 1.9 per cent and 5.0 per cent respectively). The biggest shift was in the last category, once again signalling an amplification in the LDP's relative dependency on rural areas.

However it is measured, the LDP's performance in the 1993 LH elections indicates that, after the party's fracturing of the early 1990s, the LDP lost more support in urban and metropolitan districts, areas where it had been previously gaining ground, than in rural and semi-rural districts. The escalation in the LDP's urban rate of support was, therefore, truncated by the splintering of the party, with new political groupings emerging as conservative and centrist options for urban voters. These trends facilitated the LDP's reversion to predominantly provincial party status, with its stronghold in less urbanised districts. The tables also point to the emergence of a rural-urban divide between the LDP and the post-1993 Opposition parties, whether old or new. A rural bias was apparent in none of the Opposition parties; in fact their support was distributed either evenly across constituency categories or firmly orientated towards urbanised areas.

Table 5.12 provides details of the LDP's performance in the two UH elections since the onset of party fluidity in 1993. It records percentages of seats and votes gained across the rural-metropolitan spectrum. In the 1995 poll, the Shinshinto and other non-LDP Diet candidates began to eat into the LDP's seat tallies more severely across the board. The LDP lost four out of the six rural seats it normally won, which accounted for its extremely low percentage share of rural seats in this election (28.6 per cent compared to 85.7 per cent in the 1992 UH election). This loss can be explained by the dramatic reduction in its support rate in these constituencies (from 53–17 per cent, a drop of 36 percentage points). Nevertheless, apart from the rural category where particular causal factors applied (as explained below), the LDP's polling rate and percentage share of seats still climbed with the number of voters resident in farm households. Indeed, as polling by Japan's NHK bore out, in the week prior to the 1995 UH elections, the LDP's support rate amongst voters connected to agriculture was 52.8 per cent, as opposed to 11.6 per cent for the NFP, 9.8 per cent for the SDP, 1.4 per cent for NPH, 1.5 per cent for the JCP and 14.2 per cent for Independents.[259]

In the case of rural seats, two went to Shinshinto candidates in the prefectures of Iwate and Nagano, where the most prominent Shinshinto leaders, Ozawa Ichiro and former Prime Minister Hata held their LH seats and where electoral outcomes in the Upper House were undoubtedly influenced by the standing of these two politicians in national politics. The other two rural seats lost by the LDP went to conservative Independents, not to members of other parties. The small number of seats in the rural category also helped to produce the large fluctuation in the percentage of these seats obtained by the LDP.

In semi-rural electorates the LDP fared somewhat better in relative terms (acquiring 55.6 per cent of seats compared to 85.2 per cent in 1992 and almost a third of the vote, compared with more than half in 1992). Of the eight seats it lost in this category, three went to the Shinshinto (although one was in Kumamoto, the home prefecture of former PM Hosokawa, who was prominent in the Shinshinto as the ex-leader of the Japan New Party), two went to Independent candidates, and one each to the SDP, Shinto Sakigake and the Democratic Reform Party, or DRP (Minshu Kaikaku Rengo, or Minkairen), the successor organisation to Rengo[260] in the Upper House.

A similar kind of redistribution was evident in semi-urban electorates where only two of the four seats the LDP lost went to the NFP, while the other two went to the SDP and an Independent respectively. The LDP's percentage point slide in voting support was similar to that in semi-rural electorates, at a little over 20 per cent. In urban electorates, all three of the seats lost by the LDP went to NFP candidates, while in metropolitan electorates the LDP's seat tally remained unchanged at three.

These trends do not support the proposition that the main conservative Opposition party at the time, the Shinshinto, was advancing into the LDP's rural and semi-rural support base. Excluding prefectures where powerful party leaders exerted a strong influence, the NFP's advance was clearest in urban electorates, although it took seats from the LDP across the board. At the same time, from the LDP's perspective, its loss of support in proportional terms was greatest in rural electorates and diminished thereafter across the spectrum from semi-rural through to metropolitan districts. This was indicative of some disaffection amongst farmers with the LDP.

This trend was confirmed by 1994 polls amongst Nokyo's farmer members. An average of only about 40 per cent of respondents in two polls claimed that they intended to continue to support the LDP in the future. Which party alternative, if any, they were entertaining, however, was far from clear. The proportion that claimed that they would vote for the SDP in the future (an average of 5 per cent) was about half previous rates of SDP support amongst farmers, whilst DSP support also fell and Komeito support remained exactly the same at less than 1 per cent. Shinseito supporters recorded the largest increase (from an average of just over 3 per cent to an average of just over 8 per cent). Most other parties (NPH, JNP, JCP) recorded minor increases only, suggesting the absence of any clear alternative for those farmers dissatisfied with the LDP. Most farm voters in this category appeared to lapse into not supporting any party at all. Their numbers multiplied from an average of just over 12 per cent of the total to just over 18 per cent, whilst the remainder were uncertain about which party they would support (also just over 18 per cent).[261] The same surveys did disclose, however, that two-thirds of respondents supported an administration with the LDP either as a mono-ruling party, or in coalition with the SDP, or in a conservative coalition of some kind.[262]

Despite the deterioration in the LDP's electoral performance in the 1995 elections, the party retained its relative dependence on seats towards the rural end of the spectrum as demonstrated in Table 5.15. The LDP still gained more than half its prefectural constituency seats (54.9 per cent) in just two categories of rural and semi-rural districts; and almost three-quarters (74.3 per cent) of its seats in semi-urban, semi-rural and rural constituencies, even though these categories represented just under two-thirds of the total number of seats in the Upper House (63.2 per cent). In fact, the proportions in the semi-rural, semi-urban and urban categories in 1995 were little different from those recorded since the late 1970s (apart from the anomalous 1989 elections).

If the constituency classification system in Table 5.17 is used, a different picture emerges. According to the data presented in this table, the LDP was most affected by seat losses in urban and metropolitan categories in that order. Comparing the 1992 and 1995 election results, the LDP retained all its semi-rural and semi-urban seats, but lost 13 seats in the urban category and six seats in the metropolitan category. The figures underline the LDP's reversion to its standard pattern of electoral performance. All the seat losses that the LDP suffered in 1995 were in urban and metropolitan districts, dramatically altering its relative dependencies across constituency categories. In 1992, the LDP acquired almost three-quarters of its total seats from urban and metropolitan districts; in 1995, it obtained only just over one-half. Furthermore, in 1995, the LDP picked up almost half of its total seats from the semi-rural and semi-urban categories, although these seats made up just over one-third of the total number of prefectural district seats.

As far as the new parties were concerned, the data presented in the tables underlines the fact that they performed best in urban and metropolitan districts. The composition of the electoral support base of parties such as the Japan New Party, which had strong support from urbanites, was reflected in the relatively negative orientation of the 1993–1994 coalition government towards agricultural protection issues.[263] Nokyo, for example, attributes the failure of its agricultural policy activities over the rice importation issue to the fact that the Hosokawa regime came to power.[264] For a brief period under coalition rule, the administration displayed a more overt urban-consumer orientation, except for the SDP, which was an ill-fitting partner in this enterprise and whose subsequent defection brought about the coalition's downfall in June 1994.

With the subsequent emergence of the Shinshinto as the conservative party of the Japanese cities, a rural-urban cleavage in Japan's conservative politics appeared to be developing. An executive of Zenkoku Noseikyo stated that his organisation regarded Shinshinto as basically a party for city dwellers.[265] Similarly, a Zenchu official described the younger members of the Shinshinto as much more interested in urban issues, which meant that Nokyo had to watch closely developments in Nagata-cho.[266] The urban character of the party was doubtless reinforced by its incorporation of the Komeito, whose support base lay unequivocally in the cities. The Shinshinto thus represented the beginnings of a conservative, centrist, mainstream alternative to the LDP.

The 1995 UH election also witnessed the national appearance of a new farmers' party, the so-called Farmers' Alliance (Nomin Rengo). This political grouping was established in the wake of the Hosokawa Cabinet's decision to allow minimum access for foreign rice as part of the UR settlement and arose out of dissatisfaction with the existing political parties as representatives of farming interests.[267] Nomin Rengo parties formed in a number of agricultural districts, including Kyushu, North Shinetsu, Tokyo and Northern Kanto. In the local elections of April 1995, Yamaji Mitsugu, the first candidate from the Nomin Rengo gained only 1,142 votes, which was the least amongst the six candidates in his constituency for the local assembly in Kochi Prefecture.[268] In the 1995 UH poll, Nomin Rengo targeted seats in the national constituency because it wished to avoid competing directly with LDP candidates in prefectural constituencies.[269]

The experiment was hardly a resounding success in terms of rallying widespread support from farmers. The total vote for the Nomin Rengo was so low that the party failed to get any of their members elected, winning only 141,274 votes or 0.35 per cent of the total number of votes cast, not many more than the UFO party. In the opinion of one farmer: 'It is inevitable to support the LDP, or the ruling party, which is still the main representative of the interests of rural voters'.[270] This is despite the fact that in the 1994 survey of Nokyo's farmer members, an average of more than 40 per cent agreed that there was a need for an independent farmers' party and almost two-thirds said they would vote for it, either 'without fail' or 'probably'.[271]

The outcome of the bid to register a strong protest vote against what farmers' perceived as unsatisfactory agricultural policy decisions and to secure independent agricultural representation in the Diet merely confirmed farmers' attachment to the existing alternatives and particularly their support for LDP candidates. In fact, some concerns were raised within Nokyo about how the new farmers' party would be funded and how the other established parties, especially the LDP, would react. In the words of a Zenchu official, if a new farmers' party were organised, Nokyo's lobbying could not be 'efficient' in relation to existing parties, especially the LDP.[272]

In general terms, the LDP's performance in the 1993 and 1995 Diet elections in the face of an unprecedented party realignment process indicated that it not only remained the national political entity most representative of agricultural interests, but that it had also reverted to a more standard pattern of orientation towards the rural end of the electoral spectrum (except for some key rural seats dominated by Shinshinto leaders). Far from escaping its rural dependencies, the LDP managed to retain them in spite of the upheavals that began in 1993.

The impact of Lower House electoral reform

The rules of the electoral game in Japan finally changed in November 1994 with the enactment of four electoral reform laws, which established a new electoral system for the Lower House and significantly altered the legal boundaries of political funding for politicians and political parties.[273] The existing multi-member, medium-sized district system (*chusenkyoku seido*) with a single non-transferable vote was replaced with a combination of 300 SMDs and 11 regional bloc constituencies electing 200 candidates using a PR system, called *heiritsusei* (parallel, or 'standing abreast' system).

Although it is hard to predict with any certainty over the medium to long term how the changes to the LH electoral system will impact on dominant elements of agrarian power, such as the farm vote and the LDP as the farmers' party, a number of effects have already manifested themselves (in addition to the reduction in electoral malapportionment discussed earlier). Others may become apparent in the future.

Firstly, because constituency boundaries were redrawn, the new boundaries did not always optimise the location of all Diet members' existing voting bases and local support networks. For some, their *jiban* were preserved, but for others, their supporters were partially relocated outside the new district they had to contest in the LH elections of 1996.[274] On balance this affected those who benefited most in the past from 'stable' votes based on closely knit local interests, the kind of power base LDP politicians had traditionally nurtured in their provincial strongholds. Under the new system, some of the voting blocs that regularly returned LDP Diet members were rendered less effective for reasons that explained their past electoral utility: the more or less 'fixed' ties politicians cultivated over many years amongst their rural supporters in specific localities.[275]

Compounding the impact of boundary changes was the reduction in seat numbers in rural areas with the electoral redistribution. This intensified competition amongst existing LDP Diet members for the seats that were available and sometimes made it difficult for whomever obtained LDP endorsement in a particular constituency to take over the loyal supporters of a former rival. LDP rural Diet members were, therefore, more vulnerable to the constituency reshuffling than urban Diet members, who had received proportionally less of a stable vote in the past and who were less dependent on localism and personalistic ties as the basis of voter support.

From the voters' perspective, the redrawn electoral boundaries were equally dislocating insofar as they disrupted long-standing relationships with particular Diet members and thus lessened their interest and participation in politics. According to a questionnaire survey conducted by Zenkoku Noseikyo at the time of the October 1996 poll, one of the reasons why farmers' interest in the election dimmed was because the altered electoral boundaries meant that the candidate whom these voters had supported in the past was now standing in another electorate, even though the party remained the same.[276] Other farmers complained that because of the single-member electorates, there was no candidate for whom they wanted to vote.[277]

Secondly, one of the most significant changes wrought by reform has been the contraction in the size of the sub-prefectural constituencies. The new, small-sized SMDs contain fewer eligible voters compared with the larger, medium-sized electorates of the past. In theory, this should mean that electoral districts will become more clearly differentiated than under the old system. A significant proportion of districts will contain less of a rural-urban mix because their boundaries have shrunk and they comprise fewer voters (about one-third the previous number). The socio-economic make-up of the new districts will, therefore, become more distinct and thus more easily identifiable on the rural-urban spectrum. In theory, this should make for a more efficient allocation of electoral resources by farm organisations, and the deployment of more effective electoral strategies by political parties and election candidates. The districts in which farmers can make a difference should be more obvious.

On the other hand, any of the advantages farm voters and election candidates might draw from the clearer differentiation of electorates is diminished by two countervailing factors. The SMD system in practice tends to homogenise the electoral appeal of candidates, because they have to maximise their vote across entire electorates, rather than pitch their appeal to small segments of them.[278] The 'electoral niche marketing' of the multi-member districts is quite clearly inappropriate under the new system. No longer is there any question of different candidates from the LDP slicing up the electorate into smaller parcels from which they draw their main support. The result is to reduce the policy differences amongst the parties rather than to accentuate them.[279] Farmers complained in the Zenkoku Noseikyo survey, for instance, that under the new system, they could not understand the differences between the parties on agricultural policy, which was another reason why they lost interest in politics.[280]

The other of these countervailing factors is, in practice, the small proportion of the total number of new SMDs taken up by constituencies with a significant rural component. As Table 5.20 indicates, when categorised according to percentage of workers employed in primary industry,[281] only one constituency has 30 per cent and above in primary industry, while only 25 have 20–29 per cent. At the other end of the spectrum, the vast majority (198 electorates) have 0–9 per cent employed in primary industry. In other words, the share of primary industry employment has sunk to such low levels in most electorates that 'rural' electorates, thus defined, hardly exist. This accords with trends observed under the old system, except that the redistricting has accentuated their effects by redistributing seats more accurately to reflect population distribution. The result is that both farm voters and election candidates are obliged to operate in most cases in electorates with mixed occupational and economic profiles, and in which the farm vote is a relatively small element (albeit in varying proportions) in the overall picture.

Other classification systems of the new SMDs underline the diminution of the significance of farm voters amongst the nation's eligible voters. On a population concentration scale, Table 5.20 discloses that 126 SMDs have a population concentration ratio of under 50 per cent, while a larger number (174 districts) have a population concentration ratio of more than 50 per cent. The majority of Japanese voters, in other words, now live in highly urbanised districts.

Another schema that mixes population concentration and industrialisation rates produces seven categories of SMDs, in which electorates with higher numbers of farm voters are in a distinct minority (see Table 5.21). A total of 27 seats have been designated as semi-rural (27),[282] while 63 are classified as depopulating,[283] 33 as residential/commercial/densely populated,[284] 48 as industrial/densely populated,[285] 42 as large cities and their environs,[286] 37 as regional cities,[287] and 50 as semi-industrial.[288] Semi-rural electorates thus

Table 5.20 Composition of single-member districts in the new electoral system, according to voter employment characteristics and population concentration ratios

Industry category	Constituency numbers with 0%+	Constituency numbers with 10%+	Constituency numbers with 20%+	Constituency numbers with 30%+	Constituency numbers with 40%+	Constituency numbers with 50%+	Total
Primary industry	198	76	25	1	–	–	300
Secondary industry		7	98	135	57	3	300

Industry category	Constituency numbers with 30%+	Constituency numbers with 40%+	Constituency numbers with 50%+	Constituency numbers with 60%+	Constituency numbers with 70%+	Constituency numbers with 80%+	Total
Tertiary industry	2	78	79	97	41	3	300

	Constituency numbers with 10, 20%	Constituency numbers with 30, 40%	Constituency numbers with 50, 60%	Constituency numbers with 70, 80%	Constituency numbers with 90%+	Constituency numbers with 100%	Total
Population concentration ratio	63	63	51	42	56	25	300

Source: Table 2 in Nishihira, 'Shosenkyoku Bunrui', p. 4099.

Table 5.21 LDP success rates in single-member districts according to constituency type, 1996 Lower House election

Constituency type	Number of seats
Semi-rural	27
Depopulating	63
Semi-industrial	50
Regional city	37
Large city & environs	42
Industrial/densely populated	48
Residential/commercial/densely populated	33
Total	300

Constituency type	1996	
Won by LDP		
Semi-rural	20	(23)[a]
Depopulating	47	(59)
Semi-industrial	31	(38)
Regional city	22	(30)
Large city & environs	20	(27)
Industrial/densely populated	12	(22)
Residential/commercial/densely populated	17	(19)
Total	169	(218)
LDP percentage share of seats		
Semi-rural	74.1	(85.2)
Depopulating	74.6	(93.7)
Semi-industrial	62.0	(76.0)
Regional city	59.5	(81.1)
Large city & environs	47.6	(64.3)
Industrial/densely populated	25.0	(45.8)
Residential/commercial/densely populated	51.5	(57.6)
Total	56.3	(72.7)
Percentage of LDP's total seats/votes		
Semi-rural	11.8	12.1
Depopulating	27.8	30.5
Semi-industrial	18.3	21.3
Regional city	13.0	12.4
Large city & environs	11.8	10.1
Industrial/densely populated	7.1	5.5
Residential/commercial/densely pPopulated	10.1	8.2
Total	100.0	100.0

Notes:

a The figures in brackets in this column include members of the Shinshinto who used to be members of the LDP.

Sources: The seat categorisation system was obtained from Nishihira, 'Chosenkyoku Bunrui', p. 4101. Election results were obtained from *Asahi Shinbun*, 21 October 1996.

comprise only 9 per cent of the total, which, together with depopulating electorates (21 per cent) make a total of 30 per cent at the rural end of the spectrum. The vast majority (70 per cent) are classified as either highly urban, commercial, industrialised or densely populated, or varying degrees of some or all of these characteristics.

The 1996 and 1998 general elections

The October 1996 LH election results confirmed the LDP's strength in rural areas and underlined its weakness in the cities. Table 5.21 utilises the new categorisation of seat types based on population density and industrialisation ratios to demonstrate this fact. According to the new classification system, the number of seats won by the LDP receded along the industrialisation and population concentration spectrum. The further along the scale of industrialisation and population density the districts were placed, the fewer seats the LDP collected, with the exception of residential/commercial and densely populated districts in which the LDP gained more than 50 per cent of seats. This compares with only 25 per cent of industrial and densely populated seats, just under 50 per cent of seats in large cities and their environs, just under 60 per cent of regional city electorates, just over 60 per cent of semi-industrial seats and more than 74 per cent of depopulating and semi-rural seats.[288]

In terms of its seat dependencies, the LDP quite clearly continues to rely disproportionately on seats that are more strongly rural in character, securing just under 40 per cent of its total seat tally in the semi-rural and depopulating categories, although these districts constitute only 18 per cent of the total number of seats. As Table 5.21 indicates, the same pattern is evident with respect to the party's dependencies in terms of voting support, with 12.1 per cent of its votes obtained in semi-rural constituencies and 30.5 per cent in depopulating constituencies, to make a total of 42.6 per cent from these two categories alone. Adding voting support in semi-industrial districts produces an overall proportion of 63.9 per cent, signifying that nearly two-thirds of LDP votes were collected in seats towards the rural and less populated end of the industrialisation/population density spectrum. These figures compare with 5.5 per cent of LDP votes acquired in industrial/densely populated constituencies and 8.2 per cent in residential/commercial and densely populated constituencies. Clearly, rural areas, traditionally a bastion of LDP support, continue to carry disproportionate weight for the party under the new system, while the new suburbs of large urban areas, usually less likely to vote LDP, carry the lowest weighting.

Looking at the LDP's performance by region, the SMDs where it scored complete victories were Niigata, Toyama, Yamanashi, Gifu, Okayama, Yamaguchi, Shimane, Ehime, Kagawa, Miyazaki and Kagoshima – 11 in total and all rural prefectures. Furthermore, it almost controlled 11 others of the same type: Aomori, Akita, Gumma, Tochigi, Ibaraki, Ishikawa, Tottori,

Hiroshima, Kochi, Saga and Nagasaki. The only exceptions to this general pattern were the prefectures where NFP heavyweights had their political strongholds, such as Iwate (Ozawa), Nagano (Hata) and Kumamoto (Hosokawa).[289]

In terms of seats won, the NFP in contrast, manifested a distinct bias towards more urbanised areas. The proportion of NFP seats climbed as industrialisation and population concentration rates intensified. The party acquired four, or 14.8 per cent of semi-rural seats, 13, or 20.6 per cent of depopulating seats, 13, or 26.0 per cent of semi-industrial seats, 11, or 29.7 per cent of regional city seats, 17, or 38.1 per cent of large city and environs seats and 30, or 48 per cent of industrial/densely populated seats. The only exception was the party's relatively poor showing in the residential/commercial/ densely populated category, where it secured only eight, or 24.2 per cent of the total number of seats (in a reversal of fortune with the LDP which managed to secure 51.5 per cent).

Bearing in mind that the NFP collected 62.5 per cent of seats in the industrial/densely populated category, the figures reveal that the party performed well in the big industrial centres with large populations of predominantly private sector workers, particularly those employed in factories. The NFP, for example, acquired almost all the single-seat districts in Osaka (15), while the LDP picked up only three. Similarly, the NFP did exceedingly well in other districts in this category in the prefectures of Aichi, Hyogo, Kanagawa and Saitama, compared to the LDP. On the other hand, the LDP fared better in districts that were densely populated but primarily residential and commercial such as Chiba and Tokyo, in other words, where white collar, public and private sector employees reside. Similarly, the NFP did poorly in depopulated and semi-rural constituencies: in fact all but one of the NFP candidates who won seats in the depopulated and semi-rural categories were ex-LDP members. Amongst these were the constituencies of NFP luminaries like Ozawa, Hata and Aichi Kazuo (Miyagi).

The NFP's urban bias was not altogether surprising given some of the parties from which it was originally composed: the former Opposition Komeito and DSP, and the newer JNP with its strong base in urban districts. Furthermore, a number of private-sector unions affiliated to the Japanese Trade Union Confederation, such as Zenkin Rengo, a 330,000-member machinery and metal trades union and Zensen Domei, which represents 610,000 textile, distribution, food and service workers, strongly supported Shinshinto.[290] These unions were formerly affiliated to the DSP. Likewise, strongholds of the Soka Gakkai which traditionally provided the Komeito's largest support base can be found in highly urbanised regions such as Osaka and Hyogo.[291]

The SDP and the newly established Democratic Party, or DP (Minshuto), which was formed just prior to the October 1996 elections by defectors from Shinto Sakigake and the SDP, also performed better in more urbanised districts. The DP fared particularly well in Hokkaido, no doubt owing to the strong support for its leader (Hatoyama Yukio) in this northern region, and the popularity of a former Hokkaido governor, Yokomichi Takahiro, who ran as a DP candidate, along with the absence of the SDP as an option for voters at the polls.[292]

The 1996 election results confirm the observations made earlier: the NFP's emergence as the major conservative Opposition force in Japanese cities; the contrast between the LDP with its rural electoral base and all the other parties; and thus the emergence of a rural/urban cleavage in Japanese party politics. This observation has not been qualified by the continuing process of fission and fusion amongst Japanese political parties (see Figure 5.2) since that time. Indeed, farmers demonstrated little interest in the reorganisation of political parties that took place in 1997–98. This is because a large number of new political parties formed with unclear policies on agriculture, farm villages and the development of local areas. Hata Tsutomu of the Sun Party and Kano Michihiko of the Voice of the People, both leading figures in early 1998 in the loose grouping of Opposition parties entitled the Democratic Fraternity Sun People's League (Minshu Yuai Taiyo Kokumin Rengo, or Minyuren), were former MAFF Ministers in LDP governments and were, therefore, unlikely to be indifferent to agricultural causes. The main parties in the grouping (see Figure 5.2), however, were urban-based: the DP, which formed the core of the Minyuren and its largest grouping; the Amity Party – formerly the DSP; and From Five, which consisted of remnants of Hosokawa's Japan New Party. Furthermore, a spokesperson for the Minyuren acknowledged that it was difficult for the grouping to present a clear policy on agriculture because of the different political backgrounds of the various parties within it.[293] This made it equally difficult for the Minyuren to gain sufficient support from farming areas, particularly as it would, in any election, be competing with the LDP and its record on agriculture. In the view of Zenkoku Noseikyo, the lesson learned by the former NFP was ominous for this new political grouping. The NFP was unable to take up the reins of government because it did not receive support from local regions, even though it gained sufficient support from urban areas.[294] In general, Nokyo groups hesitated to support NFP candidates, and the farmers themselves, rather than cast a vote in favour of Shinshinto candidates, were inclined either to abstain from voting or to cast blank ballots.[295] The various political groupings within the Minyuren also lacked strong regional organisations based around local politicians who were the foot soldiers of Diet members' personal support machines.[296]

By the 1998 UH elections, party configurations in the Diet had altered once again (see Figure 5.2), with a new and expanded version of the Democratic Party replacing the Shinshinto (and the Minyuren) as the main Opposition alternative.[297] The NFP, after several major defections, finally fractured on 31 December 1997, with its core grouping led by Ozawa Ichiro reincarnating itself as a small conservative grouping called the Liberal Party, or LP (Jiyuto).[298] Meanwhile, the rump of the SDP and NPH lingered on to face diminishing electoral prospects and to depart the loose parliamentary alliance with the LDP prior to the 1998 election.

Table 5.12 illustrates the LDP's performance in the various categories of seats across the metropolitan-rural spectrum in this election. The vast majority of its seats (28 out of a total of 31, or 90 per cent) were acquired in rural (5), semi-rural (15) and semi-urban (8) prefectural constituencies. In rural and semi-urban districts, the LDP augmented its seat tally to levels which compared with its performance in the 1977–92 period, certainly restoring almost all the fall-off in its performance in 1995. In the semi-rural category its seat tally was on a par with the 1995 elections, although still down on the 1992 elections. On balance, however, the results unequivocally demonstrated the ruling party's reassertion of its identity as a party of the provinces rather than as a party of the cities.

In terms of its percentage share of seats, the LDP garnered more than 70 per cent of the small number of seats in the rural category, just over half the total in the semi-rural category and heading towards two-thirds of the total number of semi-urban seats. In contrast, the LDP's performance in urban and metropolitan electorates was dismal: its seat tally in the urban category slipped by two compared with the 1995 elections (down to less than 20 per cent of the total), while it lost all its metropolitan seats, a level of performance unmatched over the period recorded in Table 5.12 (1977–98).

The LDP's electoral failure in the cities can be directly attributed to Japan's economic crisis which rapidly narrowed the ruling party's support base in more highly urbanised areas.[299] In short, the LDP's reversion to type was in a sense by default. It lost support amongst voters in more densely populated areas and thus fell back on its core supporters in the towns and counties of regional Japan. This is despite the fact that the party's support rate in aggregate actually amplified across all constituency types compared with its 1995 performance, including both urban and metropolitan districts, although not by sufficiently large amounts in the latter for the party to perform well in the seat acquisition stakes. The biggest advances were recorded in rural districts, followed by semi-urban and semi-rural electorates (see Table 5.12).

By region, the main pockets of support for the LDP (as measured by seat acquisitions) were in the rural areas of Tohoku (Akita, Yamagata and Fukushima), Kanto (especially Gumma – a prefecture where it won both seats), Chubu (Toyama, Fukui and Nagano), Chukoku (Tottori, Shimane), Shikoku (Kagawa, Ehime and Kochi), Kinki (Shiga) and Kyushu (Kumamoto, Oita, Miyazaki and Kagoshima – another prefecture where it picked up both seats).

On a more general level, however, the LDP's performance in prefectures with relatively large numbers of rural voters was mixed. Looking at LDP support rates on a district-by-district basis rather than on an aggregate basis, seven single-member prefectures – Yamanashi, Toyama, Fukui, Tokushima, Ehime, Ishikawa and Kagawa – were amongst the top ten prefectures where the LDP's votes contracted compared with the 1995 UH elections. All had significant rural sectors. On the other hand, the LDP did better than in 1995 in prefectures such as Hokkaido, Fukushima and Kumamoto. So while it is clear that in the cities, floating votes flowed in an anti-LDP direction, what happened to rural votes remains somewhat more obscure. On the one hand, large numbers of LDP rural representatives were re-elected, but on the other, notable defeats also occurred like Urata Masaru in Kumamoto – a Nokyo executive, who was also Chairman of Kumamoto Farmers' Political League, Chairman of the Kyushu Land Improvement Council and an agricultural policy heavyweight in the LDP and in the Diet; Sato Shizuo in Fukushima – an adviser to the prefectural federation of land improvement industry groups and also a 'big power' in the agricultural policy field; and Endo Kaname in Miyagi who usually received the support of the prefectural farmers' political league and prefectural land improvement political league.

Nevertheless, looking at the LDP's performance as a whole, the party's relatively poor showing in the cities meant that it ended up registering an increase in its dependence on rural and semi-urban districts, whilst its dependence on semi-rural constituencies remained stable and its dependence on urban and metropolitan districts fell markedly (see Table 5.15). Much the same pattern is evident in Table 5.17, which records the effects of socio-economic changes on seat type. LDP dependence on metropolitan seats slumped dramatically from 22.6 per cent in 1995 to 9.7 per cent in 1998, while its dependence on semi-rural seats expanded from 3.2 to 6.5 per cent and semi-urban seats, from 41.9 per cent to 51.6 per cent. Moreover, even though semi-rural and semi-urban seats comprised just over one-third of the seats in the Upper House, they constituted well over one-half (58.1 per cent) of the LDP's seat total tally.

The results of the 1998 UH election generate a dual message for the LDP. Whilst on the one hand they underscore the party's continuing support in the provinces even in the face of Japan's worst economic conditions in decades, on the other, they also deliver a loud message to the party that without more successful seat acquisition rates in the cities, they will not win a majority in the Upper House. On balance, this may prompt some reconfiguring of the LDP's electoral priorities *towards* rather than *away from* urban areas.[300]

At the same time, the election results also underline the fact that no other party is in danger of encroaching on the LDP's strong rural base of support. Although the newly united Democratic Party presented a coherent alternative for urban and metropolitan voters in Saitama, Tokyo, Kanagawa, Aichi and Hyogo where the DP won seats in the prefectural constituencies, it was impossible for the party to find sufficiently attractive candidates in rural areas to defeat sitting LDP incumbents.[301] No DP candidates stood in the 14 semi-urban seats, only nine contested the 29 semi-rural seats, while four DP candidates contested the seven rural seats.[302] In the election itself, only one rural seat in Nagano fell to a DP candidate.[303] Moreover, although the DP secured seven semi-rural seats, all were in prefectures with substantial regional cities or close to dense urban centres, such as Miyagi, Ibaraki, Tochigi, Gifu, Okayama and Kumamoto.

These electoral outcomes suggest that little prospect exists of any of the new Opposition political groupings presenting a serious alternative to the LDP in rural areas. The new political parties that generate such a confusing picture on the Japanese political scene are all basic variants of urban parties, as emphasised earlier. In fact, one of the most striking features of the 1998 UH election was the relatively large number of Independent candidates (20) who carried off prefectural constituency seats, underlining the shift away from both old and new parties by Japanese voters and the fact that a substantial and reliable personal base of support can still be sufficient for success in Diet elections.

At the same time it should be pointed out that the majority (12) of the successful Independents were not genuine Independents, but were refugees from established political parties, especially the NFP. Amongst this group the figures for those who had previously been affiliated with the Shinshinto and various combinations of the Shinshinto and other parties were as follows: ex-NFP (3); ex-LDP/NFP (2); ex-DSP/NFP (1), ex-JNP/NFP (1), ex-Komeito/ NFP (2). Of the rest, two were ex-LDP and one was ex-JSP. In short, these politicians already had substantial records as party-endorsed representatives in particular prefectures and could trade on this in the 1998 election.

Another striking aspect of the group of Independents was the relatively large number (7) who were previously from the Lower House but who had failed to win seats in the new SMDs in 1996. Amongst this group, former NFP members or members from NFP combinations were again prominent. Of the seven genuine Independent candidates, apart from the 'talent candidates', representatives of organised interests, including agricultural interests were noteworthy.[304]

Conclusion

Some of the most crucial ingredients in farmers' electoral power have been the absolute size of the national agricultural electorate (and the associated national Nokyo electorate), the magnitude of the electoral bias in favour of farm votes and the extent to which the LDP has been dependent on farmers' votes. The enduring nature of the LDP-farmer electoral connection is critical to an understanding of the political influence of agrarian interests in national politics. It has enabled large numbers of LDP politicians to put together the string of electoral successes that allows them, under the entrenched seniority system, to progress to ever-higher positions in the party and in the government.[305] This in turn permits those politicians to wield ever-greater influence over policy, advantaging the agricultural sector with powerful representation.

Over the years, however, social, economic and political changes have impacted directly on the main ingredients in farmers' electoral power. The number of farm votes continues to shrink reducing the importance of this sector in the LDP's electoral calculus, while electoral reform has partially rectified those distortions in the electoral system which used to advantage

378 *The politics of agriculture in Japan*

rural voters over their urban counterparts. Fundamentally speaking, the political demography of agriculture no longer works in the farmers' favour: the dominant features of the farming population are an aged workforce, lack of successors and steadily declining numbers. The MAFF has predicted that the number of farm households will drop 30 per cent from 1995 levels to 2.46 million by 2010.[306] If current trends continue, Japan's farming population will be halved in 15 years.[307]

On the other hand, the decline in farmers' political power is a very gradual process. The extensive electoral data presented in this chapter underlines the fact that farmers continue to be a core element in the political substructure of the LDP, which remains the party most representative of electoral districts towards the rural end of the spectrum. Despite shrinking numbers, farmers in the short to medium term will remain a stable component of the LDP's voting base. Farmers are manifesting no real signs of mass defection from the LDP in favour of one or other of the plethora of new party alternatives. Indeed, it is the stability of farmers' support which makes them so valuable to the LDP.

As the LDP weathered the storms of party defections and reformations in the early to mid-1990s and then the LH election under the new electoral system, its rural orientation was in fact reasserted because the new parties occupied ground mainly in urban districts. The recent affirmation of the LDP's political identity as the majority party of the farmers means that it is unlikely to undercut a group of core supporters by withdrawing largesse from rural areas or by allowing farm incomes to fall drastically. This is despite the fact that in the mid- to late 1980s, the LDP was clearly expanding its support levels in urban areas, thus altering the relative import of its rural support component.

In the future, the LDP is unlikely to escape its partial electoral dependency on the farm bloc over the short term, which will help to sustain the agricultural support and protection regime. The LDP cannot afford to neglect one of its solid blocks of voting support, particularly if the party's Diet position is not strong. Its retention of the provinces is a necessary (although not a sufficient) condition of its continuing electoral victories. The LDP will, therefore, continue to pay careful attention to policies that impact on blocs of organised supporters, such as farmers.[308] If the LDP remains in government, either ruling on its own or in coalition, it will preserve its strong rural connection with appropriate policies.

Furthermore, although Japan's voting population is now predominantly urbanised necessitating greater LDP orientation towards attracting the votes of city dwellers, policies targeting urban residents do not guarantee increases in the number of votes for the LDP in urban constituencies, partly because there is no political organisation (like Nokyo) to direct the salaried vote.[306] Rural votes are organised and therefore more reliable than the floating votes of urban dwellers.[310] Thus, while it has long been anticipated that the gradual contraction of the agricultural sector will have a number of inevitable political and electoral consequences which have been hastened by electoral reform, these consequences will inevitably be delayed or muted by the continuing reliability of farm voters and the salience of agrarian electoral organisations.

The only possible challenge to this general prediction will come from an LDP calculating that higher levels of support from city voters are absolutely crucial to its future electoral prospects and that an expanding city vote cannot be garnered without redirecting largesse away from rural areas to the cities. Such concerns emerged in the wake of the 1998 UH election in which the LDP's poor performance in metropolitan areas translated into a significant loss of seats overall. If the LDP decides that urban votes need to be more deliberately and consciously courted, this may undermine its long-standing policies of redistributing income from metropolitan to rural areas through measures such as farm income support and rural public works. An effort will be made to redirect more financial resources into urban areas, something already visible in the prominence of requests for spending on 'urban' projects by ministries in the FY 1999 national budget.[311] Furthermore, an unfavourable economic climate and any associated budgetary constraints will impose a zero sum imperative rather than a positive sum calculus on such distributive choices.[312]

Ultimately the changing demography of agriculture and the declining agricultural workforce will make the task of restructuring agriculture and distributing public resources more evenly between rural and urban areas easier as time goes by. Because the electoral basis of agrarian support in Japan has been an important factor in creating and sustaining the agricultural support and protection system, its demise will contribute to the creation of a political environment in which withdrawing benefits from farmers and rural dwellers will become a more feasible proposition for the ruling party. It is unlikely that such policy shifts will occur in a dramatic fashion, however. They will be gradual and will demonstrate a lagged effect, with socio-economic and demographic movements as well as political and electoral developments gradually registering on the strategic calculations of LDP politicians.

6   Electoral politics

Not only have Japanese farmers represented a significant proportion of the electorate strategically located in overweighted rural constituencies, but they have also been a highly organised vote. A key aspect of agrarian power has been the ability of agricultural organisations to mobilise the votes of their members on behalf of chosen candidates. Like almost all Japanese political parties, the LDP lacks a grass-roots mass membership base that supplies funds, organises local constituency support for election candidates and preselects candidates. In rural areas, the LDP's 'fragile base of organized support'[1] has enabled agricultural groups to fill the breach by furnishing votes, serving as a source of active campaign workers and in some cases providing financial backing missing as a result of lack of membership fees and contributions from party members. In this way, agricultural groups have become the *jiban* of conservative power[2] and an LDP voting base.[3]

The relationship between LDP politicians and Nokyo groups as electoral support organisations was established very early in the ruling party's post-1955 Diet history. From the late 1950s onwards, the LDP successfully penetrated rural districts by linking up with Nokyo and *noseiren* executives in each prefecture.[4] Indeed, the LDP's use of Nokyo as a vote-gathering machine is seen as one of the defining characteristics of the 1955 political system.[5]

Conversely, the kind of political resources Nokyo mobilised in its relationship with the ruling party provided one of the primary sources of its influence over agricultural policy.[6] The basis of Nokyo's political power was widely regarded as residing in its vote-gathering ability.[7] Having control over farmers' votes enabled Nokyo to pressure farm politicians within the LDP to meet Nokyo's demands.[8] As Kawagoe describes it: 'It was a concrete political system which was based on mutual dependence between Nokyo, acting as a political pressure group to protect profits in the agricultural sector and further its own interests, and the ruling party, which relied on Nokyo's vote garnering strength.'[9]

The historical tradition of vote-gathering in rural areas

The electoral connection between farmers' groups and Diet politicians was built on a strong tradition of rural areas delivering votes to their chosen candidates via an intermediary who directed the votes of farmers. In prewar Japan, agricultural organisations such as the *nokai* and *sangyo kumiai* as well as landlords acting in the role of influential local notables (*kenryokusha*) functioned as rice-roots substitutes for local party organisations. Leaders of farm groups gathered votes amongst their members and sometimes used these organisations to gain a foothold in national politics. Landlords also used their influence amongst the local farming community to collect votes for election candidates (they often served simultaneously in the leadership structures of farm organisations, particularly the *nokai*). It was customary for landlords to instruct their tenant farmers and influence other small owner-farmers as to which candidate to support. As Fukutake points out, ordinary farmers rarely voted on an independent basis before the war. Even after they were given voting rights, their votes were almost always collected by landowners or prominent local figures and allocated to candidates whom these local leaders recommended.[10]

An important facilitating mechanism in this context was the *buraku*, or small residential hamlet,[11] which was the primary social unit in the country-side. The geographic concentration of rural society into individual hamlets created closely-knit farming communities. These often tied landowner and tenant together in a shared community of interest that transcended class- and property-based divisions. True, agrarian social structures were hierarchical, with rich landlords who owned large tracts of agricultural land at the top and lowly tenants at the bottom, but hamlet solidarity was a strong force in rural communities. The ability of the larger landowners to gather the vote and commit it to certain candidates was one facet of their total leadership role within the hamlet. Landlords also dominated executive positions in the wide range of *buraku* cooperative associations,[12] some of which were also sub-contracting organs of municipal administration and which, at election time, performed the function of rounding up the vote (and committing it to conservative parties).[13] The landlords' powers rested on the internal cohesive-ness of the *buraku*, and the social pressures and forces of consensus that sustained it. The traditions of social unity and cooperative activity within the hamlet upheld motivations to act for the good of the local community, whether the issue at hand related to farming, road building, irrigation or politics. These same predispositions assisted the vote-gathering activities of *nokai* and *sangyo kumiai* leaders, who also operated through the *buraku* and their sub-groupings. In most cases the leaders of the agricultural organisations were either landlords or owner-farmers and therefore, as already noted, served in executive positions in the *buraku* associations. Personal connections were everything; Diet members were linked to farm householders through a chain of personal connections mediated by key individuals and groups.

Postwar reforms instituted by the Occupation eliminated the landlord class, abolished existing rural organisations and democratised the villages and farmers' groups. In particular, land reform dispossessed landlords of their role as local authority figures and political brokers by undermining the economic basis of their authority.[14] The tradition of local influential persons (*yuryokusha*)[15] continued, however, with new authority figures recruited in some cases from the ranks of former landlords, but more importantly, from newly emerging rural elites, such as mayors and members of village, town and city assemblies, and elected leaders of major rural and other local organisations, such as members of education committees, the chiefs of fire-fighting groups, and leaders of women's associations and youth organisations.[16]

Agricultural cooperative executives, along with the leaders of the farmers' unions, members of agricultural committees, and executives of the land improvement districts became important elements of this new rural leadership structure.[17] Although farmers no longer automatically voted for candidates recommended by former landlords, they could still be influenced by prominent local figures, particularly by agricultural cooperative leaders.[18] For politicians, to connect with Nokyo and its mass membership of farmers meant forging a link with Nokyo executives as leaders of the rural community.[19] The agricultural cooperatives became core institutions in rural villages, with Nokyo leaders playing the crucial role of intermediaries between farmers and election candidates, and associated groupings such as the Nokyo's women's and youth divisions and farmers' political leagues acting as spearhead organisations of agricultural cooperative involvement in election activities.[20] Nokyo groups quickly and easily assumed the role of an organised voting base for rural politicians. Their effectiveness as tools for 'grabbing' farmers' votes[21] and their involvement in election activities of all kinds were reflected in the increasing number of Nokyo officials holding political office in the Diet and in prefectural and municipal assemblies in the 1950s, 1960s and 1970s.[22]

The evolution of rice-roots mechanisms of vote-gathering

In the early postwar period, the influence of local men of power including the leaders of agricultural cooperative and other organisations in rural communities was still largely transmitted through the *buraku* in the villages, which remained the smallest social unit in the village and the lowest fundamental unit of both local government and agricultural groups. Under the so-called *buraku* recommendation system (*buraku suisensei*), village hamlet leaders would recommend a particular candidate to members, who would agree by a process of group consensus to support a certain candidate. In this way, the *buraku* delivered the vote as a cohesive unit in response to requests coming from local community leaders including agricultural cooperative officials. As Ono explains, group executives and staff members were thus connected to the rice roots of administrative and agricultural cooperative organisations through the process of *buraku* recommendation.[23] In turn, these group leaders were connected through their political networks to municipal and prefectural assembly politicians, Diet politicians and political parties.

Even in the late 1950s, the system of *buraku* recommendation was still functioning 'as an important method of voting and vote-getting.'[24] Farmers' voting choices were often based on *buraku* recommendations, particularly in local elections.[25] Farmers asked to vote for a certain local politician would justify their decision with the response: 'because he is a *buraku yuryokusha*', or 'because we borrow farm implements from him'.[26] According to research done in Shimane Prefecture in 1959, *buraku* and village *yuryokusha* and organisational recommendations were acknowledged by 25–30 per cent of respondents.[27]

Such a system of mobilising votes was recognised as delivering a 'hard vote' (*koteihyo*), meaning a reliable or 'fixed' vote for a certain politician based on enduring considerations such as communal or personal loyalties.[28] The system was basically hierarchical with the directives (or requests) coming down through the pipeline of intermediary power brokers, including the leaders of local organisations such as the agricultural cooperatives, via the hamlet to the voter. At the bottom of the hierarchy was the head of the farm household who directed the votes of its members. In the late 1950s, votes from families which followed the lead of the head of the farm household were still significant.[29]

The system began to break down, however, with the rapid outflow of rural population, the growth in part-time farming and the increase in those leaving farming when workers from farm families found jobs in factories and offices in towns and cities. These socio-economic trends wrought great changes at both the *buraku* and family levels. Amongst farming youth, parental and local community pressures became less and less effective,[30] whilst changes in the structure of employment and occupational diversification in rural areas gradually worked to undermine the delivery of votes based on the *buraku* recommendation system. When many rural district heads were no longer able to deliver the anticipated number of votes, the system started to unravel. In general terms, increasing class and vocational divisions in regional society weakened the hold of *buraku* leaders on farmers.

As the effectiveness of the *buraku* recommendation system diminished, the influence of local leaders (*chigen yuryokusha*) expanded. As already noted, this group included the heads of local organisations such as the agricultural cooperatives, youth groups, chambers of commerce and industry, educational and fire service associations, local government groups and so on. They worked to gather the votes of their members for those standing in elections and played a particularly important role in mobilising the vote for LDP candidates.[31] Nevertheless, as Fukutake argues, although farmers were susceptible to the influence of locally prominent figures, they did not blindly follow their recommendations without considering their own interests or those of their villages. It was important for candidates to explain how they could benefit farmers and rural villages in their constituencies during election campaigns. This automatically inclined farmers and local leaders to support the ruling party which controlled the budget.[32] The LDP thus consolidated its support base in the countryside by delivering subsidies to local executives through organisations such as the agricultural cooperatives and local governments.[33]

Conservative candidates also started to organise personal support organisations (*koenkai*) as vote-gathering machines in the late 1950s.[34] These provided an organisational locus in which to establish and maintain connections with local elites including the leaders of local groups. Many interest group leaders joined the *koenkai* and mobilised their membership behind their favoured politicians. Group leaders provided not only votes, but also rank and file activists (*katsudoka*) and campaign workers (*undoin*) from amongst their staff and members. Candidates also collected votes outside their *koenkai* through direct contacts with the leaders of interest groups such as Nokyo, one of several large national organisations that became prominent in this regard.[35]

In this way, organised groups and their members figured in varying degrees in the formation of a candidate's *jiban*. Within the *jiban*, human relationships and group connections that could mobilise 'fixed' or 'hard' votes held the central position above all other factors.[36] The core element in the *jiban* were 'connections' (*kankei*) – kinship, geographical, occupational, organisational, obligatory and so on. As Flanagan explains, these 'operate to join diverse groups and individuals to a particular candidate through chains of personal relationships which claim the individual's loyalty quite apart from considerations of public policy.'[37] Connections centring on Nokyo thus became important elements in the *jiban* of many Diet politicians from rural and semi-rural electorates.

Nokyo's *senkyo katsudo*

Nokyo's electoral and associated activities need to be treated in terms of three separate categories or types: the electoral support activities in which agricultural cooperative leaders, staff members and farmer members engage personally and unofficially; the electoral support activities in which agricultural cooperative organisations qua Nokyo organisations become involved unofficially; and the electoral support activities that agricultural cooperative organisations, qua Nokyo organisations, conduct officially. The last category is the most restricted because the agricultural cooperatives are not permitted to become directly involved in election campaigning. If, for example, a co-op chairman were arrested on a charge of electoral irregularities, the agricultural cooperative in question might be disqualified from collecting rice.[38]

In practice the distinction between official and unofficial activity is difficult to maintain. The various forms of *senkyo katsudo* are often simultaneous, highly interrelated and largely indistinguishable, whether on a personal or organisational level. When references are made to Nokyo's electoral activities, any or all of these practices can be inferred.

In addition, Nokyo in this context can extend to its organisational offshoots, such as the farmers' political leagues, youth divisions (and their offshoots – the youth leagues), cooperative companies and so on. Because the latter are not agricultural cooperatives as such, they do not operate under the same legal strictures as the mainstream organisations in elections. They can, therefore, openly provide electoral resources and organised backup without the same restrictions applying. These groups are, however, Nokyo organisations in fact, if not in name.

Unofficial electoral activities: individuals

Unofficial involvement by Nokyo leaders, staff members and farmer members in elections consists of a number of different types of activity. As already noted, one of the the most important is the role of agricultural cooperative leaders as local bosses or *yuryokusha*. In this capacity, Nokyo leaders become integrated into the political networks that often extend from individual Diet members down to the rice roots through prefectural and local politicians. The function of Nokyo leaders in this context is to gather votes amongst their members as a bloc of organised support on behalf of election candidates. The vote is gathered on the basis of the personal obligations and relationships that voters have with the local leader, whose role is that of an intermediary. He is the pivot of an interlocking network of personal contacts and reciprocal obligations linking local bosses at city, town and village level to prefectural politicians, who in turn have closer connections with members of the Diet. Nokyo's leaders in the 1950s and 1960s, for example, were often the specialist farmers with time and money who became elected executives of Nokyo as influential members of the local community and whose connections extended to the political centre through municipal and prefectural assembly members.[39]

Flanagan describes this type of network as 'a system of multiple hierarchies . . . which links faction leaders and Dietmen to the local yuryokusha (men of influence) at the grass roots'.[40] Prominent leaders at the local level are recruited by Diet members as core organisers of their personal support base. They are the crucial intermediaries at the rice roots who can mobilise blocs of voting support. Each aspiring politician aims to build a 'network of personal acquaintanceship with large numbers of prominent persons in the villages each of whom is in a position to influence a larger number of votes personally himself.'[41] The local influence and political connections of Nokyo leaders are considered invaluable as a means of forging electoral links with farmers and opening up channels for effective voter mobilisation.

As *yuryokusha*, Nokyo leaders thus facilitate political connections, massage networks of interpersonal relations, help create and sustain local bases of support, commit their own core of supporters to election candidates, and mobilise votes and campaign workers through their extensive contacts with other executives, staff members and farmer members of the Nokyo organisation and associated groups including cooperative companies. These connections are an important political resource, as are the organisational standing of these leaders and the ties of personal loyalty and obligation of those whose votes they gather.

One of the reasons why agricultural cooperative leaders readily accede to a crucial role as intermediaries between voters and LDP candidates is because of Nokyo's own position as a channel for government subsidies to farmers, particularly specific-purpose subsidies for local projects such as improved rice seedbeds or livestock facilities. Farmer members of Nokyo are likely to vote for their leaders' chosen candidates because it might return specific benefits through the cooperative to the farmer. If the local co-op leader delivers the vote and thus helps to ensure the victory of the candidate, then it is likely the reward will follow in the form of the desired subsidy.[42] Indeed, there are strong incentives on all sides to make the connection subsidy-productive.[43]

Nokyo leaders may also become formal party members and officials of prefectural and local party organisations[44] (which are important institutions for determining party endorsements), as well as politicians in prefectural and municipal assemblies. The latter positions place them directly within the regional networks of Diet politicians, and enable them to commit the votes of their own supporters to those politicians with whom they are connected.

Ties between Diet politicians and Nokyo leaders are most likely to be nurtured and maintained through *koenkai*. The primary locus of electoral activity at the rice-roots level is the *koenkai* of individual candidates, and it is through the medium of these personal support groups that a great deal of electoral activity connected to the agricultural cooperatives is channelled. Nokyo executives frequently become leaders, 'advisers' and 'officials' of *koenkai*, with their involvement sought as an indispensable part of a campaign strategy aimed at reaching a multitude of farm voters and tapping into other electoral resources.[45]

Participation in the *koenkai* is not limited to the Nokyo executive class. It is one of the principal means whereby not only agricultural cooperative leaders but also staff members and farmers as well as those affiliated with associated organisations such as the farmers' political leagues and youth divisions unofficially engage in *senkyo katsudo*. The latter can be mobilised within a *koenkai* context as Nokyo's election campaign workforce. The *koenkai* also provide an organisational setting in which primary political connections can be established between Nokyo leaders and members, and where both these categories of Nokyo-affiliated voters can form a common purpose, rather than Nokyo members just uncritically accepting the directions of their leaders transmitted through other channels.

In the two polls conducted amongst Nokyo's farmer members in 1994, around 50 per cent of respondents claimed that they were involved in *koenkai* activities. This compares with 10 per cent for the nation as a whole[46] and underlines the importance of the *koenkai* as a locus of *nokyo* members' political and electoral activity. It also underscores the candidate-specific nature of farmers' political support, a characteristic of their electoral behaviour which has been emphasised in earlier chapters. Other data from the same poll indicated that factors relating to individual candidates (as opposed to policies or parties and other influences) were the primary determinant of farmers' voting choices in around 40 per cent of cases.[47] The salience of farmers' connections to individual politicians might help to explain why farmers were so self-evidently reluctant to support the single-purpose farmers' party option in the 1995 UH election.[48]

Unofficial electoral activities: organisational

Unofficial electoral activities also extend to the involvement of agricultural cooperative organisations qua Nokyo organisations. Nokyo executive and staff members collect votes amongst co-op members (and even the employees of subsidiary companies) under the pretext of other kinds of legitimate agricultural cooperative activities. In this context, vote-gathering amongst the farmers by Nokyo officials is very subtle and indirect, using regular meeting and consultation procedures already operating in other fields. These may be technical and related to farm guidance activities or part of the conduct of Nokyo business, whether buying or selling farm products or inputs, or selling other services such as insurance or loans. The Kagoshima Farmers' Political League, for example, had a reputation for conducting a lot of house calls in the name of savings and purchasing. Candidates consider it very crucial to use the influence of Nokyo on farmers' daily production and livelihood in the elections.[49]

In the course of this type of legitimate interaction, Nokyo officials offer a detailed exposition of the merits of certain candidates who have received the endorsement of the organisation, without issuing actual and direct instructions about whom to support. Nevertheless, established discussion, communication and contact channels in these types of contexts are used to publicise and promote the names of certain politicians who have received the official stamp of approval of a particular Nokyo group.

Unofficial operations may sometimes take on a large-scale political machine-like character, extending to a phenomenon known as 'conducting an election from an organisational base' (*soshiki senkyo*).[50] In these circumstances the campaign becomes an intra-organisational crusade with a cross-section of the more highly motivated Nokyo executives, staff members and farmers recruited to work in the campaign. As already noted, agricultural cooperative leaders often muster staff members as campaign workers in the service of particular candidates. The major campaigners in local areas are often employees in the prefectural and local organisations. The latter become part of the volunteer force of campaign workers for particular candidates under the guidance of Nokyo leaders. As Kobayashi, Shinohara and Soma point out, Nokyo offers an electoral support base particularly through the command of rice-roots activist campaign workers.[51] In the main, however, these organisationally-centred campaign activities are concentrated in the candidate's *koenkai*, in which Nokyo officials and members participate and which they organise as if it were a Nokyo-led operation.

In practice, large-scale, Nokyo-centred campaigns are most common in the case of agricultural cooperative officials seeking Diet office, particularly when they centre their *jiban* on the Nokyo organisation. Such candidates are called 'persons from the ranks of Nokyo' (*Nokyo no shusshinsha*). A good example is the campaign conducted by Okamura Fumijiro for a NC seat in the UH elections of 1965. The handling and organisation of Okamura's campaign was typical of an election based on organisationally generated support (*soshiki senkyo*). Because he was Chairman of Zenkyoren, Okamura's *koenkai* and campaign organisations were staffed predominantly by executives and staff members of Zenkyoren. His election office leaders were the Zenkyoren Information Section Chief and the Office Chief of the group of Nokyo-affiliated Diet members, the Nosei Kenkyukai (Agricultural Policy Research Association, or APRA).[52] Other section heads of Zenkyoren, prefectural *kyosairen* staff and Zenchu managers were also involved, producing posters and handbills and organising local electioneering tours. Okamura's *koenkai* office chief was a Zenkyoren manager, and staff workers of Zenkyoren toured the *tankyo* in Kagawa Prefecture, making calls on each cooperative, and conducting Zenkyoren business and electoral support activities simultaneously amongst co-op union members.

Another example is the campaign conducted by Nokyo in the Kagoshima prefectural constituency in the UH elections of 1977. The Kagoshima Prefecture Nokyo organisation extensively used its employees and members to support the candidacy of LDP-affiliated Tahara Takeo, who was Chairman of the prefectural *keizairen* and Director of Zenno. There were about 20,000 regular members of agricultural cooperatives in the prefecture, making Nokyo the largest organisation in Kagoshima. In addition, staff personnel in the four Nokyo federations and in the 116 co-ops numbered around 8,000 and they were actively mobilised in the campaign. Before the election was publicly announced, they engaged in electoral support activities for Tahara by recruiting potential voters to join the candidate's *koenkai*. After the announcement, male *nokyo* employees walked around rural villages collecting votes in the guise of undertaking co-op business such as giving technical advice, collecting deposits and so on. Female employees were requested to take holidays to go home and collect votes from their family members and relatives. As a result of this committed support from the Nokyo organisation, Tahara garnered an unexpectedly large amount of votes in the election – as much as 47,000 in Kagoshima City for example.[53]

A very important and often underrated type of unofficial electoral support activity is political funding. Although Nokyo has never been publicly prominent on the list of financial donors to political parties, factions and politicians,[54] it has been able to use its enormous economic and financial power to good effect in the electoral funding business. As Sakaguchi claims, Nokyo knows how to control Diet members by scattering political contributions.[55]

Concrete details regarding Nokyo's political funding are not, however, easy to collect. More often than not, they emerge as part of the disclosed circumstances of election and other scandals involving breaches of the Political Funds Regulation Law. These scandals have exposed some of the details with respect to Nokyo's direct financial contributions to politicians, although it is probable that they represent only the tip of the iceberg.[56]

In 1957, the Zenkoren bribery scandal brought to light for the first time hard evidence of financial contributions from agricultural groups being lavished on MAF officials and Diet members.[57] The money came from a secret supply of election funds (*jinchu mimai*), comprising ¥7,000,000 as so-called hidden funds (*ura shikin*) and ¥1.1 billion as so-called secret funding (*kakushi riekikin*) for electoral activities.[58] Political donations of approximately ¥1–3 million per head were allegedly distributed to 20–40 Diet members in order to pass two fertiliser bills.[59] At the time, the scandal brought Nokyo's political standing into severe disrepute,[60] although such practices were not eliminated.

Other instances of illegal donations continued to surface from time to time. In 1965 Okamura Fumijiro was charged with violating the Political Funds Regulation Law. His *koenkai* received a formal donation from Zenkyoren after a conference of executives, in addition to a certain sum in the form of concealed donations (*tsutsumigane*) not officially reported in the expenses of his electoral office. The money was distributed amongst various national Zenkyoren and prefectural *kyosairen* officials and staff members for campaign purposes. The result was that a number of Zenkyoren and prefectural *kyosairen* officials who were linked to Okamura's election campaign were arrested as was the Office Chief of APRA. The total number of people found guilty of electoral violations amounted to around 50, but the gross amount of money involved was relatively small. The upshot was that Okamura resigned from this chairmanship of Zenkyoren but evaded prosecution. He died three years later.[61]

In April 1976, Kimura Morio won his fourth term as governor of Fukushima Prefecture in a comprehensive victory over a candidate from the progressive camp. He was later convicted of accepting illegal campaign donations from local construction contractors. The investigation by the prosecutor's office in Fukushima revealed that part of the money was given to Saito Shoshiro, Chairman of the Nokyo Five Federations and head of Fukushima Prefecture's Agricultural Policy Reform League (Nosei Sasshin Renmei). The purpose of the transaction was to get Nokyo to act as a vote-gathering machine in the gubernatorial election. A total of ¥10 million was distributed to permanent executives in the Nokyo federations and to *tankyo* chairmen and management staff to cover campaign spending. With the funds from Kimura, the Nosei Sasshin Renmei went into action as a vote-collecting machine. In addition to Saito, all those holding executive positions in the organisation were Nokyo executives, while the branch chairmen were *tankyo* chairmen. In short, Nokyo and the Nosei Sasshin Renmei were one and the same organisation. The federation having already decided earlier to recommend Kimura divided the prefecture into six districts in order to stage the election campaign. Nokyo officials called on members to bolster support for Kimura who won a landslide victory. Saito and eight permanent officials of Nokyo were later found guilty of corruption. Saito kept silent about how the money was actually distributed in order to protect the Nokyo organisation from prosecution.[62]

In spite of these disclosures, the amount of political contributions from Nokyo to politicians continued to increase in the 1960s and 1970s and became organised on a more systematic basis. One of the reasons for the increasingly liberal use of money in Nokyo's election campaigning was the declining reliability of vote control in the villages. As Ono puts it, 'votes could not be squeezed out as in the past'.[63] Farmers were being more flexible in their voting decisions and as a result, the Nokyo vote-collection machine no longer functioned efficiently without money.[64] The suggestion is that money was being used to grease the wheels of Nokyo campaign organisations and possibly even to bribe voters. The 1977 gubernatorial election campaign in Fukushima was a good example of Nokyo acting as a 'hired gun', possibly soliciting votes from amongst its membership in exchange for payment.

In most instances, however, the money was flowing in the opposite direction – from Nokyo into the campaign funds of politicians for their own uses. Specialist 'tunnel' organisations for collecting and distributing political funding to election candidates were in fact established at a national level by Zenchu and other central Nokyo organs (*chuo kikan*) soon after the Zenkoren scandal of 1957. Nokyo entered the 1958 electoral campaign with an energetic programme of activities. Zenchu, Zenkoren and Zenhanren established the Agricultural Problems Research Association, or Nogyo Mondai Kenkyukai as an organisation to pool election funds. Its Chairman was a Zenchu Managing Director. The body was duly registered as a political association (*seiji kessha*) under the Political Funds Regulation Law. Nokyo provided funds through this organisation in accordance with candidates' respective contributions to agricultural policies.[65] Altogether the association reportedly collected ¥15–20 million from Nokyo-related groups and offered a maximum of ¥500,000 to 110 candidates from the LDP and JSP in the 1958 elections, of which 103 were elected. In the UH election in the following year, the same group supplied a total of around ¥10 million yen to 30 candidates from both the LDP and JSP. Zenchu staff members also undertook direct support activities for the most important candidates from amongst those who had been recommended by Nokyo.

The basic reasons for establishing a separate and official political funding organ at the time was, firstly, to channel political donations through a formal route, abandoning contributions through the type of back door accounting revealed in the Zenkoren affair; secondly to support candidates who cooperated with Nokyo in the introduction of a pension system for officials of agriculture-related organisations and on rice price issues, and to obtain further cooperation from them; and thirdly, to respond to the need for organisational support by Diet members who were cooperative with Nokyo.[66]

The Nogyo Mondai Kenkyukai later changed its name to Agricultural Policy Research Association (Nogyo Seisaku Kenkyukai, or Noseiken). Noseiken operated a 'dual structure' (*niju kozo*) system of political funding in concert with another organisation: the National Nokyo Council (Zenkoku Nogyo Kyodo Kumiai Kyogikai, or Zennokyo). Zennokyo was a 'society' or 'association' (*kessha*) that had its headquarters in the building that housed the Nokyo publications' association: the Ie no Hikari Kaikan in Tokyo. It was a juridical person (*hojin*), composed of members who belonged to the full-time managing director (*jimu riji*) class of Nokyo central organisations, such as Zenno, Zenchu, Zenkyoren and Ie no Hikari Kyokai. Funds gathered from Nokyo sources by these officials in Zennokyo were transferred to Noseiken which operated out of the office of the National Agricultural Tax System Research Association within the Nokyo Building in Tokyo. This amounted to a division of labour between the collection of money and its distribution.[67]

Noseiken was a political group (*seiji dantai*) registered under the Political Funds Regulation Law. It could, therefore, legally distribute money to election candidates. It had, however, the same members as Zennokyo, but they were operating in a different legal capacity. It was composed of 25 Nokyo officials who were full-time managing directors of the central Nokyo organs: Zenchu, Zenno, Zenkyoren etc. These executives created the Noseiken, and operated within it in a private capacity. Staff members of the National Agricultural Tax System Research Association transported the money directly to politicians. As for how much was to be distributed to each Diet member, a committee of Noseiken members decided the amount depending on a Diet member's service to agricultural policy.[68]

In terms of actual figures, donations amounted to ¥56.9 million in 1969 and ¥95.6 million in 1972 for the LH elections in those years; and ¥18.8 million in 1968 and ¥23.3 million in 1971 for UH elections in those years.[69] For example, prior to the 1971 UH election, the ¥23.3 million was contributed by Zennokyo to Noseiken, and ¥95.6 million in the following year prior to the 1972 UH election. Noseiken, as the official 'window' for Nokyo's political funding operations, redirected the money to 48 and 179 LDP, JSP, DSP and Independent candidates respectively in the elections.[70] The lowest figure per candidate in the Lower House was ¥100,000 and the highest was ¥4 million;[71] whilst in the Upper House, the highest amount was ¥2 million.[72] The most prominent recipients were Nakagawa Ichiro[73] (¥1.7 million), Kuraishi Tadao[74] and Narita Tomomi[75] (¥1 million each), and Hashimoto Tomisaburo,[76] Fukuda Takeo, Nakasone Yasuhiro and Ohira Masayoshi (¥500,000 each).[77]

The sum donated by Noseiken to LDP candidates in the 1972 LH election (¥95.6 million) compared not unfavourably with some of the larger donations made by Japanese business and industrial groups to the LDP through its official election funding organisation, the People's Association (Kokumin Kyokai).[78] The Noseiken was essentially modelled on the Kokumin Kyokai as a specialist political fund-gathering organisation manned by Nokyo officials. The extent of the funding by Nokyo challenges the stereotypical distinction between big business as the primary source of funding for the LDP and rural areas as the primary source of votes. Clearly, not only big business but also agriculture was making substantial contributions to LDP (and other parties') election funds from time to time.

The activities of Zennokyo and Noseiken and the extent of their financial backing for election candidates came to light in 1973 as part of what became known as the Zenno 'black mist' scandal (*Zenno kuroi kiri jiken*). Not all the activities of the participants in these groups were strictly legal. Details revealed as a result of the scandal highlighted extensive involvement by full-time Zenno executives in covert election funding (*ura shikin*). Large sums were allegedly collected from Zenno's related companies and reported in the Zenno accounts as 'miscellaneous income'.[79] The fact that Nokyo executives frequently serve concurrently as *kanren gaisha* executives facilitates this sort of fund collection.[80]

Moreover, the way in which the 'incident' was dealt with officially was suggestive of a large-scale political cover-up. The official of the National Tax Administration Bureau who investigated the affair suddenly changed his mind about calling for the resignation of the three Zenno Managing Directors involved after the head of the bureau was pressured by influential Diet members who had been lobbied by other Zenno executives and a Zenchu Managing Director. The latter was very close to Zenchu Chairman, Miyawaki Asao, who in turn, was very close to the MOF Minister at the time, Ohira Masayoshi.[81] Furthermore, Diet members who received money from Nokyo did not want to become involved in Nokyo's money problems. Even Opposition party members sought to avoid touching Nokyo issues.[82]

In the wake of this scandal, Zennokyo and Noseiken were dissolved, only to reappear prior to the 1974 elections in the form of two new organisations called the International Economics Research Association (Kokusai Keizai Chosakai) and the Resource Economics Research Association (Shigen Keizai Kenkyukai), names that had no connection whatsoever with Nokyo or agriculture. Their donations in the 1974 UH election amounted to ¥3.3 million.[83]

In 1976 during Miki Takeo's administration, the Political Funds Regulation Law was significantly tightened to exclude organisations like Nokyo, as a recipient of subsidies from the state, from legally making political donations in connection with elections.[84] Article 22 (3-1) of the Political Funds Regulation Law prohibited donations from organisations that received subsidies (*hojokin*), obligatory shares (*futankin*), interest supplementary compensation (*rishi hokyukin*) and other kinds of benefit payments (*kyufukin*)[85] from the national government (excluding grants related to research, surveys and national disaster relief expenditure etc.) for one year from the date the benefit allocation was decided. Article 22 (3-4) of the same law also prohibited political donations from organisations that received similar subsidies and benefits from local governments. The prohibited donations included those to Diet members, prefectural and local assembly members, candidates for public positions and also organisations that supported or opposed these people.[86] After the passage of the amendments to the law in 1976, the International Economics Research Association and Resource Economics Research Association were both dissolved.

The more restrictive law in practice, however, did not prevent agricultural cooperative organisations from continuing to make political and electoral donations illegally and covertly. It is widely acknowledged by Nokyo insiders that illicit political donations to Diet politicians remain an established practice within the organisation. As Tachibana reports, 'if you travelled to regional areas, it was not unusual to hear voices in Nokyo prefectural organisations saying, "we wrap the money for a secret supply of election funds in sealed letters" '.[87] In 1985, a political funds report kept by the Chiba Prefecture election administration committee disclosed that Chiba Nokyo Chuokai was making political donations. The report clearly recorded the fact that Chiba *kenchu* donated ¥1,000,000 to the LDP Chiba Prefectural Federation. The same kind of illegal donation was made in Hiroshima.[88] More than a decade later, LDP agricultural heavyweight and possible future LDP Prime Minister Kato Koichi was said to have received ¥100 million as a secret donation from Shizuoka *shinren*, one of the major lenders to the *jusen*.[89]

Another type of channel for political funding takes the form of organisations with dual membership comprising Diet politicians on the one hand, and national Nokyo organisations on the other. The membership fees paid by the national Nokyo organisations effectively wind up as political donations to the Diet politicians who are individual members of the group. One such organisation was the Association to Protect Farmers' Health (Nomin no Kenko o Mamoru Kai). In its heyday in the 1970s and 1980s, it had around 200–250 members who were Diet members. Money flowed into the organisation from Nokyo in the form of membership fees. The association's basic function was to act as a pooling organisation for political funds (*kenkin puuru kikan*) from the agricultural world. Its secretariat was located inside Zenchu's headquarters in the Nokyo building in central Tokyo.[90]

Another organisation with the same structure of membership was the Nosei Kenkyukai, or APRA. APRA was an organised grouping of Nokyo's Diet supporters. According to its organisational charter, its membership was divided between individual Diet members and agricultural groups (*nogyo dantai*).[91] National Nokyo organisations such as Zenchu, Zenno and Zenkyoren made up these agricultural groups. The executive office of APRA was located on the 8th floor of the Nokyo Building in Ohtemachi.

APRA had two main functions: on the surface, its job was to lobby political parties (both government and Opposition) on agricultural policy matters.[92] Politicians who were members undertook to pursue Nokyo's interests in Diet affairs. APRA's covert function was to raise election funds.

In fact Nokyo raised the funds, and APRA did the administrative work in parcelling them out. Its membership consisted of Diet members who had received electoral backing from agricultural cooperative organisations. In a questionnaire survey of APRA members done by the author, membership of APRA was coincident with some form of support from Nokyo groups in elections for nearly all respondents.[93]

Most of these Nokyo-sponsored organisations have not survived into the 1990s. Indeed, all are now largely defunct. APRA was dissolved in 1994 when its long-time secretary died. Even in the mid-1980s, it was described as a 'sleeping organisation' because its members were getting old and tending to fall asleep in meetings. The Nomin no Kenko o Mamoru Kai also virtually ceased to exist by the early 1990s.

From the late 1970s onwards, another method of political funding which violated the spirit if not the letter of the Political Funds Regulation Law became popular. This method centred on unofficial political donations to Diet politicians by means of cheer groups (*hagemasukai*), which exploited a loophole in the legislation. Each of these cheer groups had a different name. Nokyo politician Niwa Hyosuke, for example, had a cheer group called the Biotechnology Organisation. The role of cheer groups was to sell tickets to fund-raising social functions. The Diet member's faction leader frequently made a speech at these functions. Each ticket cost ¥20–30,000, with national Nokyo organisations, especially Zenchu, commonly buying anything up to 2,000 tickets. Because only two to three rather than 2,000 Nokyo representatives attended, the politicians made a large profit (it usually cost only around ¥5,000 out of the ¥20,000 ticket price to fund the party). The balance represented a political donation. Zenchu and the other national federations were selective in whose *hagemasukai* they bought tickets for. The location of the social function varied depending on the politician's status. If he were a minister, a big party would be held in a Tokyo hotel. If he had more power in rural areas, the party would be organised in a rural town.[94] LDP politicians were not the only ones holding *hagemasukai*. Diet members from the Opposition parties, except for the Komeito and JCP, also resorted to this fund-raising method.

When Zenchu made political donations to cheer groups, the money was not sourced from Zenchu. Zenchu collected the money from various sources such as the *kanren gaisha* and then channelled it as financial contributions to particular politicians. Strictly speaking this was illegal, but it was also an open secret that such donations were made. As pointed out by a Nokyo source, everyone knew in general terms what went on.[95] A lot of the funds gathered from cooperative companies were also channelled directly into politicians' *koenkai*. Zenno's Managing Director in 1986, for example (Yamaguchi Iwao), was chief of the Tokyo branch of the *koenkai* of Nokyo Diet member, Eto Takami. Yamaguchi exercised 'big power' over Zenno's *kanren gaisha* and gathered funds from them.[96] His prominence is symptomatic of the key role of full-time Zenchu executives in liaising between Nokyo and the political world, and also the fact that Nokyo's most significant source of political funding has been the large number of 'cooperative companies'. As observed by Smith, 'companies associated with the Nokyo's varied . . . enterprises can and do spend money to influence the views of politicians.'[97] These companies maintain close financial, managerial, and personnel links to their parent Nokyo organisations, whose executives often serve simultaneously in extremely well paid positions as company directors. Such officials are ideally placed to divert company profits and use them for political purposes.[98]

Political funding of politicians by Nokyo organisations continues, including the use of *hagemasukai*. If organised by politicians supported by Nokyo, then Nokyo representatives still attend, but the number of social functions is declining because, under the new political funding law, parties are eligible for government subsidies for electoral purposes. Furthermore, it pays to keep Nokyo's political funding activities, both legal[99] and illegal, in perspective. In the words of an *Asahi Shinbun* journalist, 'for politicians, it is more important to collect votes through local Nokyo organisations than to get money from *kanren gaisha*.'[100] At the same time it would be foolish to assume that public subsidies for parties' campaign expenses will necessarily eliminate so-called 'money politics'. It is highly probable that politicians will devise innovative methods of raising funds in the new regulatory environment and that agricultural groups, including Nokyo will be involved.

Official electoral activities

Officially, Nokyo's electoral operations are conducted by the farmers' political leagues. In some cases, the prefectural *noseiren* functions like a *koenkai* for the Diet candidate, particularly if he happens to be its chairman.[101] In fact, three main types of connections prevail between prefectural *noseiren* and election candidates with respect to the use of personal support groups. In the first type, the local *noseiren* establishes a *koenkai* for the candidate it recommends. This often occurs when a particular candidate has a very close relationship with the prefectural *noseiren*. The *noseiren* will establish a *koenkai* for the candidate (who may be, for example, a former chairman of the *noseiren*, or someone who occupies a very high position in the *noseiren*). In the second type, the local organisation supports the activities of the candidate's *koenkai*; and in the third type, the local organisation does not have much to do with the candidate's *koenkai*.[102]

In contrast to the *noseiren*, Nokyo cannot officially engage in electoral campaigning because legislative provisions restrict the range of functions the agricultural cooperatives may conduct. Nokyo, *qua* Nokyo, is barred from overt operations in support of politicians and so, in theory, these should be conducted through the relevant branch of the farmers' political league organisation.

The relationship between Nokyo and the *noseiren* on electoral matters, however, has remained complex and varied. Formally speaking the two organisational streams are quite separate, but in practice, a great deal of overlap exists between the two. While the farmers' political leagues cannot be classed as agricultural cooperatives per se, they are very much Nokyo-based and Nokyo-sponsored organisations.

Moreover, in practice, neither Nokyo Law nor the existence of the *noseiren* has proven an obstacle to the widespread and deep involvement of agricultural cooperative leaders, staff members and farmer members in a whole range of political and electoral endeavours over the years. The electoral activities of Nokyo might be performed on the surface through the farmers' leagues as organisational *tatemae*, but the reality, or *honne*, is that Nokyo conducts these activities covertly under the camouflage of its other legitimate operations. The artificial division between the two formal organisations – Nokyo and the *noseiren* – disappears when it comes to the actual conduct of campaigning and associated political activities at the rice-roots level. The fiction can be maintained, however, because the *noseiren* sit almost perfectly on top of the Nokyo organisation, forming a dual structure, with a transposition of leadership positions from one organisation to the other. The *noseiren* head offices are located in the relevant main branch of Nokyo (the prefectural headquarters of the farmers' political leagues are in the prefectural Nokyo central union); the *noseiren* branches and sub-branches are located in Nokyo branch offices and sub-branch offices; their leaders down the organisational hierarchy are the group leaders of the Nokyo organisation; league supporters are co-op union members and staff members,[103] and the two organisations have pretty much the same intra-organisational hierarchy for decisionmaking.[104] Agricultural cooperative members in varying proportions become *noseiren* members (although on a strictly voluntary, individual basis). In many cases, national and prefectural Nokyo organisations offer guidance in policy activities. Close liaison is maintained between *noseiren* executives and executives of Nokyo prefectural federations and central unions in the form of regular roundtable discussions, attended by prefectural assembly politicians who have received organisational backup from these groups. When held in Tokyo, these discussions are also attended by a selection of Diet politicians. The result is that it is almost impossible to differentiate the political activities of the two organisations because the same people are involved, the same facilities are used, and Nokyo organises, guides and subsidises the activities of its political arm.[105] Some finance for the *noseiren* also derives from members' subscriptions, but generally speaking, the agricultural cooperatives provide the bulk of the funding.

The official forms of support undertaken by Nokyo are extremely limited. In this context, making 'recommendations' (*suisen*) is the most publicly visible form of electioneering, and also a widely accepted practice amongst a whole range of voluntary organisations that do not exist primarily for political purposes. For national organisations like Zenchu, its recommendation(s) is/are publicised nationally and represent an official statement of position. Zenchu recommends candidates in all LH and UH elections (in fact Zenchu,

Zenkyoren, Zenno etc. all recommend the same people). In elections to the national constituency of the Upper House, Zenchu's recommendation (like the National Council's) has generally only gone to one candidate in recent years.[106]

Regional and local Nokyo organisations in the individual electorates also officially recommend to their members that they vote for a certain candidate or candidates. Posters of the candidate(s) are put up in Nokyo offices. The custom is for the chairmen of agricultural cooperative organisations in the prefecture to hold a meeting (*ken Nokyo chokai*) to decide whom they will recommend in the election. After that decision, the agricultural cooperative organisations in the prefecture will move spontaneously to support that person.[107] Prefecturally-based executive bodies such as the combined executives meeting (*Nokyo kakuren yakuinkai*), which consists of the leaders of all the Nokyo federations within the prefecture plus those of the central union may also issue recommendations. In earlier years, the prefectural Nokyo *yakushokuin renmei* also got involved. It usually endorsed the decision of the *ken Nokyo chokai* and then acted as a spearhead of the agricultural cooperatives within the prefecture in the election campaign.[108]

According to Flanagan, the mechanism of group recommendation performs the function of mobilising the vote in the same way as traditional local leaders once did. He attributes the strength of this type of voter direction to the weakness of the Japanese party system and the consequent lack of identification between voter and party. As he explains, the 'Japanese voter identifies with a primary or secondary group which then directs his voting decision by means of the *suisensei* (recommendation system).'[109] Recommendation is a form of non-coercive voting direction between organisational leaders and their members.

Official recommendations of agricultural cooperative organisations are made known on campaign posters, signboards and handbills distributed to candidates' electoral offices. These are put up on public display in these offices together with similar recommendations from other organisations for the candidate concerned. The names of recommended candidates may also be publicised by internal Nokyo public relations activities, a purpose for which the agricultural cooperative communications system – its newspapers, TV programmes, noticeboards, telephone networks, pamphlets and other publications – can be put to good use.

Another form of official activity can be broadly described as 'electoral public relations'. It encompasses the sponsorship of special political discussion meetings using the facilities – telephones and transport – of the agricultural cooperatives, and so-called 'meet the candidate' gatherings, where candidates are invited to present their views to the assembled Nokyo leaders and members. These meetings, which may be held at prefectural, city, town or village level, sometimes precipitate decisions about which candidates should receive an organisational recommendation.

These activities are replicated by the national, prefectural and local organisations of the farmers' political leagues. The Zenkoku Noseikyo and the *noseiren* extensively publicise their recommended candidates, for example, in the *Nihon Nogyo Shinbun* and the official journal published by the Zenkoku Noseikyo. The National Council follows up its official recommendations with supporters' signature activities. The local *noseiren* hold seminars, conferences and assemblies where they introduce the recommended candidates and explain why they are the most suitable to represent farmers' interests in the Diet. Direct contact between farmers and candidates is thus often coordinated by the *noseiren*, but the national organisation also sends people to provide support and backup to the *noseiren* in organising such meetings. The National Council also organises symposia in Tokyo where representatives of all the parties are grilled on how they view major agricultural policy issues of the day. One of the National Council's functions is to provide information on Diet members to farmers, particularly on which Diet members work well for agricultural interests.[110]

Yet another form of public relations activity is to send questionnaire surveys to Diet candidates and party headquarters asking them to explain their policies on a range of agricultural issues. This has become a staple item in Nokyo-led election campaigns. It was done by Zenchu prior to the 1986 LH elections, for example, with explicit questions on politicians' views of the producer rice price question. Just before the 1992 and 1995 UH elections, Zenkoku Noseikyo also presented the major parties with a list of four basic questions on agricultural policy. The responses were published in the *Nihon Nogyo Shinbun* in the form of public election promises. This newspaper also published statements on agricultural policy from the candidates recommended by Zenkoku Noseikyo.

Such a tactic for pressuring candidates into making public commitments on agricultural policy is not confined to national Nokyo organisations. In the 1986 double elections, for example, almost no candidate in Miyagi Prefecture discussed agricultural policies in concrete terms. Although some candidates raised the producer rice price issue and the question of agricultural trade liberalisation, none of them proposed concrete measures for agricultural policy or any new blueprints for agriculture. Most of the successful candidates, however, made comments on the desirable level of the producer rice price and future agricultural policies when they answered the questionnaire distributed by the prefectural Nokyo youth league and the prefectural Nokyo women's division. The youth league subsequently proposed asking these candidates to fulfil what they had promised in their replies to the questionnaire.[111]

Political funding is also an official form of electoral activity undertaken by *noseiren*. Although illegal funding has continued, the *noseiren* have been utilised as official channels for transferring political funds to election candidates. Where *noseiren* undertake these kinds of activities, they are registered as political associations or political groups under the Political Funds Regulation Law. Indeed, political funding by Nokyo is now largely channelled through the farmers' political leagues, which continue to make donations to politicians and parties. A total of 26 prefectural farmers' political leagues are currently registered as political groups under the Political Funds Regulation Law.[112] This enables them legally to make political donations, which are still possible under the new electoral financing regime, which reformed the political funding system to allow individual politicians to designate one fundraising body to receive donations from enterprises and groups.

Although the *noseiren* registered as political groups are not formally part of the Nokyo organisation, the money still originates from Nokyo sources, and in this sense Nokyo is *de facto* making the donations, despite the fact that it receives subsidies and other financial benefits from taxpayers.[113] In total amount, however, it is likely that the sums are declining because of the relative downturn in Nokyo's business operations. In this respect, the new Political Parties Assistance Law was as welcome to Nokyo as it was to private enterprise feeling the burden of political funding operations in a time of considerable economic adversity.

Distinctive features of Nokyo's electoral activities

Apart from differentiating Nokyo's *senkyo katsudo* in terms of official and unofficial types of conduct, other consistent and distinctive features of these activities can be identified. Firstly, Nokyo does not operate as a unified body in elections.[114] At no time, for example, have the activities of the *noseiren* been controlled as a national movement from the centre, and nor have their policy and electoral objectives been necessarily endorsed by the central Nokyo leadership. An official position within the cooperatives has not been an automatic guarantee of *noseiren* electoral support, nor is leadership or Diet representation of the political leagues dependent on an official role within the agricultural cooperative organisation. Farmers' political groups have often steered their own independent course, making a virtue out of their distinctive perspectives, eschewing closed relationships with particular parties and pursuing their own causes often linked to regional issues.

Electorally speaking Nokyo is an amalgam of large numbers of separate agricultural cooperatives and associated groupings extending throughout Japan. These bodies conduct electoral activities as discrete entities. Each Nokyo organisation and its corresponding political association decides for itself whom it will support and in what type of support activity it will become involved. This does not prevent cooperation, coordination and collective agreements amongst the individual groups to achieve a common goal. In some cases, a full-scale mobilisation of the various branches of the Nokyo organisation within a prefecture may ensue, with staff and co-op members acting as campaigners and the women's and youth divisions fully engaged, as well as pressure placed on the customers, business connections and clients of the marketing and purchasing arms. In other cases, conflict can arise internally amongst Nokyo groups in a given region. Splits have occurred from time to time within groups and between groups in relation to particular candidates in particular elections.[115]

Nokyo's electoral support activities thus represent the sum total of the whole range of different types of *senkyo katsudo* in which different organisations and individuals participate according to their own independent decisions and motivations. There is no coordination from the centre or by any single group. In practice, each agricultural cooperative organisation is a self-governing body or self-contained unit. It may or may not choose to go along with other agricultural cooperative groups in the pursuit of specific electoral objectives. In this respect, Nokyo is far from being monolithic in an electoral context. As the umbrella organisation for the entire farming sector, it encompasses a wide range of agricultural interests and political viewpoints amongst its leaders, staff and members. Furthermore, not only is Nokyo divided horizontally into the three levels of federated organisation, it is also divided vertically into general/specialist cooperatives in addition to encompassing a vast extended organisation including its primary spearhead groups in elections – the *noseiren*.

Although the *noseiren* represent the official political arm of the agricultural cooperatives, they do not monopolise electoral activities within the organisation. In some regions they are not very active at all. Where they take place, their operations should be viewed as complementary to the wide-ranging unofficial and official engagement by the agricultural cooperatives in election activities, an additional organisational mechanism whereby farm voters can be mobilised in support of candidates with links to Nokyo. At the same time, it should be emphasised again that it is fundamentally difficult to separate the two organisations in practice. For all intents and purposes, Nokyo and its political organisations are but one body in the sense that one set of groups (the *noseiren*) are superimposed on the other (Nokyo).[116]

The second major characteristic of Nokyo's electoral activities is related to the first. Geographically speaking, something of a division of labour exists between different levels of organisation. This division is mainly between the types of *senkyo katsudo* conducted by the central and prefectural organisations and those at the rice roots. In the latter context, election campaigning by agricultural cooperative leaders and organisations centres around the mobilisation of farmers' votes. Historically the most important organisations in this context have been the lowest units of the agricultural cooperatives based on the farming villages.[117] In these days of induced amalgamations, however, small village cooperatives have been gobbled up by larger branches. Nevertheless, the closer to the rice roots the agricultural cooperative organisation is, the more involved it is in actual vote-gathering. Nokyo bodies with an organisational membership such as the central unions, the other national federations, Zenkoku Noseikyo and even the prefectural *noseiren*, concentrate on organisational recommendations and the supply of funding. In particular the national organisations do not undertake campaign activities of the mass mobilisation kind.

Zenkoku Noseikyo describes its formal functions as recommendation, political funding and providing backup for the prefectural groups, whilst the *noseiren* and their branches provide recommendation and political funding. As a Zenkoku Noseikyo official described it, local organisations that have the ability to collect votes take care of support activities during the campaign with the central organisation providing backup.[118] It is at the lowest level of organisation – local chapters (*bunkai*) of the *noseiren* sub-branches (*shibu*) – where farmers come into direct contact with electoral influences from the group and so this is a primary locus of vote-gathering. Meanwhile, *noseiren* leaders at all levels engage in campaigning on behalf of recommended candidates as do some farmer members. Connections with *koenkai* and candidates' offices are restricted to prefectural and local organisations, however. National organisations such as Zenkoku Noseikyo do not get directly involved with *koenkai*.

Zenkoku Noseikyo recommended 34 candidates in the 1995 UH election, as did the prefectural *noseiren* (more or less the same list).[119] In the 1996 LH election, Zenkoku Noseikyo recommended 225 candidates: 201 in the single-member districts and 24 in the PR districts. These candidates were also recommended by the prefectural *noseiren*, in addition to more than 20 others who were only recommended by the prefectural *noseiren*.[120] The figures for 1996 are a big jump on those for 1990, when only 88 LH candidates were recommended by the National Council, and those for 1989 – its first year of operation – when only 80 UH candidates were recommended. The fact that the number of recommended candidates is multiplying underlines the National Council's increasing activism at the electoral level. Rather than gearing down, it is gearing up. The list of recommended candidates is decided by the National Council's Board of Directors, which includes the Chairman of Zenkoku Noseikyo, plus its Vice-Chairman (the Vice-Chairman of Zenno),[121] in addition to various other prefectural Nokyo central union and federation chairmen to make a total of seven.

When it comes to vote-gathering, therefore, Nokyo's electoral activities are in fact highly decentralised and in fact very much a rice-roots enterprise. Most vote-collection associated with the agricultural cooperatives is directed by leaders of prefectural and municipal agricultural cooperative organisations and takes place at the local level. According to Miyake, what frequently happens is that the Nokyo organisation in the prefecture or the constituency issues an 'across-the-board' (*sobanateki*) recommendation and leaves the rest up to the *tankyo*. As a result, the candidates who have been recommended approach unit *nokyo* relying on their respective connections, and the agricultural cooperatives must lay on support individually.[122] Moreover, *tankyo* leaders often know the farmers in their area best so they can more easily advance their political activities.[123] Vote-mobilisation in this context is primarily mediated through personal connections between politicians and Nokyo leaders within the prefecture and in turn between local Nokyo leaders and the farmer members of the *tankyo* and *noseiren* sub-units. In terms of the election campaign itself, candidates' *koenkai* also assume importance as hub organisations, with campaign workers from the agricultural cooperatives focusing their activities around these bodies.

One of the reasons for electoral decentralisation of this type is because an important influence on the formation of a *jiban* centring on Nokyo and other agricultural groups is regionalism or localism.[124] As applied to farmers' votes as well as rural votes more generally, consciousness of local interests generates demands for agricultural policies that respond to particular regional circumstances as well as demands for distributive largesse for local projects, some of which are channelled through the agricultural cooperatives.[125] It is a generally accepted fact that in provincial areas of Japan, electoral activities often take place within blocs that have a regionally unified character. Election candidates respond to voters' consciousness of local interests because they believe this factor is an important determinant of voting choice.[126] Candidates supported by agricultural cooperative organisations take advantage of these kinds of parochial considerations to win political allegiance and voting support. As Miyake affirms, the vote-gathering of unit agricultural cooperatives is largely a mobilisation of regional groupings.[127]

The third major characteristic of Nokyo's *senkyo katsudo* is the focus on individual candidates. As put by a former Zenchu Managing Director, 'Nokyo supports individual politicians, not political parties. Since the LDP has enjoyed a long regime, Nokyo has been in a way close to the LDP, but generally it supports individual politicians.'[128] Each prospective candidate is evaluated by agricultural cooperative organisations on his merits, with party-related considerations one of a composite set of factors including connections to the cooperatives and other agricultural organisations.[129] According to national research reported by Miyake, agricultural, forestry and fisheries groups scored higher than any of the other categories of functional groups surveyed (the others were labour unions, religious groups, commerce and industry groups and citizens' movements) in electoral support for individuals rather than for political parties. Although Nokyo's party inclinations were clear (namely with the LDP), the connections with candidates were far more individually-based than party-based.[130] The candidate-specific focus of Nokyo's electoral activities was one reason why splits and rivalries sometimes occurred within the Nokyo organisation in any given area when the leaders of some agricultural cooperative groups supported one candidate and other leaders backed another.

The particular construction of the 1947–94 LH election system and the UH election system in some constituencies has also supported a candidate-centred focus because it has promoted intra-party, inter-candidate competition and thus encouraged support organisations to focus on candidates rather than political parties. Consequently, the relationship between individual politicians and voters has been much stronger than that between voters and political parties.

In the case of the electoral support activities of Zenkoku Noseikyo and the *noseiren*, for example, when politicians have moved from one party to another (from the LDP to the NFP for instance), some local organisations have continued to recommend the same individuals regardless of the change in party affiliation.[131] So, while the local organisations of the Zenkoku Noseikyo are generally pro-LDP, in the 1995 UH elections, Shinshinto candidates were recommended by the *noseiren* in Iwate, Shizuoka and Hiroshima.[132] This was a direct result of the shifting party allegiances of the politicians in question. The enduring connection remained the personal one, centred on the individual. This aspect of Nokyo's *senkyo katsudo* reflects predominant patterns of voting behaviour. As Miyake observes, although interest in politics and elections is generally low, voters undertake political participation centring on individuals, submitting to the mobilisation of entities such as *koenkai*, functional groups to which they are attached, and society in their local neighbourhoods.[133]

Case study of a Nokyo politician's electoral support base

The patterns of political support evident in agricultural cooperative electoral behaviour: private, unofficial campaigning and vote mobilisation, combined with formal recommendation and organised support through Nokyo-based political groups, were exemplified in the six LH election campaigns of Nokyo Diet member Someya Makoto for a seat in Chiba (4) district over the period 1972–90. Someya was a typical local-turned-national politician and Nokyo-backed candidate.[134] He held positions in several agricultural organisations. At various times he was the prefectural Nokyo Central Union Chairman, Zenchu Director, Chairman of the prefectural Chamber of Agriculture (Chiba-ken Nogyo Kaigi), member of the National Chamber of Agriculture and Chairman of the prefectural Agricultural Residential Association (Chiba-ken Noju Kyokai). Earlier in his political career, he had been chairman of the prefectural assembly, and secretary-general of the LDP's prefectural federation.

When interviewed, Someya, as a Nokyo politician, identified his main organisational backers as 'agricultural groups' (*nogyo dantai*), 'land improvement groups' (*tochi kairyo dantai*) and 'social welfare councils' (*shakai fukushi kyogikai*). He also claimed a special link with dairy farmers through the Dairy Farmers' Political Federation of Japan. He disclosed that his *koenkai* centred on Nokyo and agricultural groups in general and that his main electoral strategy focused on activities conducted by his personal support group (*koenkai katsudo*). Nokyo members, staff and leaders, he claimed, participated in his election campaign through membership of his *koenkai*. He characterised *koenkai* activities as the principal avenue of electoral participation by the agricultural cooperatives.

Although representative of an urban electorate, Someya acknowledged that given his primary organisational links, his campaign naturally emphasised rural interests. He endeavoured to balance this, however, with a general appeal aimed at the whole electorate in the light of the contraction of rural areas and the shrinkage in farm population. In elections he regularly received more than 50 formal recommendations (*suisenjo*) from different organisations and their leaders. These recommendations were posted up on the walls of his campaign headquarters.[135] Someya described his interests as essentially a combination of agricultural and social welfare interests. As a former wounded soldier he also took particular care of returned soldiers' groups, handicapped groups, health centres (*hokenjo*) and groups concerned with food nutrition. He regarded his Diet member's duties as consisting chiefly of acting as an intermediary for his constituents with two ministries: the MAFF and the Ministry of Health and Welfare (MHW).

Someya confirmed the variation in electoral support activities relative to organisational level within Nokyo. At prefectural level and below, agricultural cooperative election activity involved the supply of mass membership resources: votes and campaign workers (*undoin*), including assistance from Nokyo leaders in nurturing a *jiban* and mobilising votes. These were primarily locally orientated activities where personal political and organisational connections could be utilised. Moreover, it was chiefly at the *tankyo* level that agricultural cooperative leaders had face-to-face contact with the farm voter.

On the other hand, the task of prefectural federations, prefectural central unions and national level organisations was to furnish formal recommendations for candidates. Because prefectural Nokyo organisations incorporated the *tankyo*, it was unnecessary for each agricultural cooperative within these larger groupings to issue their own recommendation. Recommendation from national level federations or Zenchu, on the other hand, carried a great deal of significance and prestige, and were valued by candidates for this reason. Someya also acknowledged that he received assistance from the cooperatives in the form of political funds (*seiji kenkin*). He categorised the types of organisational support he received from Nokyo in the following terms: from Zenno, recommendation and political funds; and from prefectural-level Nokyo organisations, recommendation, political funds and campaigners as Chairman of Chiba Prefecture Nokyo Central Union.[136]

Electoral activities of other agricultural organisations

Nokyo's prominence in electoral activities stems from a number of key organisational advantages: its command of electoral resources; its reach into the villages, cities and towns where farm voters reside; its universal membership rate; and the fact that Nokyo leaders constitute important elements of rural political and social elites. Because the ensuing electoral profile of Nokyo is so high, it is often assumed that Nokyo is a monopoly player in agrarian electoral politics. This is not in fact the case.

Like the agricultural cooperatives and their associated groups, other agricultural organisations also provide various kinds of electoral backing for Diet candidates. The statutory agricultural interest groups, for example – the agricultural committee system, the agricultural mutual aid associations and the land improvement groups – are all actively involved. As Kobayashi, Shinohara and Soma point out, agricultural groups such as the agricultural committees and land improvement districts and their federations are not only a source of political funds, they all play an important role as electoral voting bases (*jiban*) of individual politicians.[137] The significance of electoral activities for the land improvement groups is indicated by their organisation of political leagues to specialise in electoral operations. Also engaged in electoral support activity are the various rice-roots farmers' organisations, including the commodity groups and the farmers' unions, as well as some institutional interest groups attached to the MAFF.

The activities of these other agricultural groups should be seen as supplementary to those of the agricultural cooperatives. Non-Nokyo groups become immersed in much the same kinds of electoral support functions as do Nokyo groups and with much the same focus on individual candidates. None, except for the farmers' unions and the *dekasegi* organisations, are party-attached. Most offer at least 'recommendation' of candidates; some are led by political 'bosses', playing key roles in political and electoral networks; some have leaders, staff and individual members who join politicians' *koenkai*; some provide campaign workers; and some are also involved in political funding. Not only Nokyo but every agricultural group, including the institutional interest groups, are asked to buy tickets to politicians' *hagemasukai*. In fact, something of a division of labour exists amongst agricultural organisations as to which politician they will support. Each organisation only backs a few politicians.[138]

The degree of involvement by non-Nokyo groups in elections varies considerably, however. Some mobilise nationally in only a very sporadic fashion. Others like the land improvement federations and their political leagues, conduct campaigns at the national and prefectural levels continuously as a full-time endeavour.[139] The same is true of the Dairy Farmers' Political Federation of Japan (Rakuseiren), the full-time specialist political organisation representing Japan's dairy farmers.[140] One of its main functions is to provide backing for sympathetic politicians in elections. Although its members (and sometimes its leaders) overlap with agricultural cooperative organisations,[141] decisions on electoral backing are made independently and candidates are chosen on the basis of their ability to promote specialist dairy interests. The federation selects its own candidates for support and has special links with Diet members from dairy farming constituencies. It offers recommendation, campaign support and also a modest amount of financial backing. The emphasis in the federation's electoral activities is on collecting votes rather than providing money, although it is registered as a political group under the Political Funds Regulation Law. Prefectural branches of the federation engage in support for selected candidates in particular electorates. Although for prime candidates the central organisation sends people in to assist, most campaigns are conducted by the local members. Because the federation, unlike Nokyo, receives no subsidies, it claims to be a very independent organisation politically and electorally. It can say no to any particular requests for support.[142]

As already noted in the case of Rakuseiren, the picture of farm group electoral activities is complicated by overlapping leadership and membership structures – with Nokyo and also with each other. For example, the local farmer members of the land improvement districts will also be members of the local *nokyo*. They may also be members of the local branch of the land improvement political league and the *noseiren* as well as the local Nokyo youth division. Any or all of these groups may be mobilised at election time and farmers might get involved in campaign activities in any or all of these different organisational contexts.

Similarly, the leaders of these groups may hold multiple positions in different organisations and undertake electoral activities in a number of different organisational locations. In the 1980s, for example, the head of Tochigi Prefecture's *noseiren* was also a Nokyo prefectural federation chairman, a powerful figure within the prefectural *rakuno seiji renmei* and the head of LDP politician Watanabe Michio's *koenkai*.[143]

The electoral activities of different agricultural organisations, however, are fundamentally discrete. They take place under separate organisational umbrellas with distinct organisational objectives in view. These groups do not conduct their *senkyo katsudo* 'as one body', although temporary alignments between and amongst groups have occurred from time to time depending on the connections amongst candidates and organisational leaders, and on the election in question.[144]

In each case, the scale of electoral activity of the non-Nokyo groups reflects their particular organisational make-up and the size and nature of their particular membership body. For example, the agricultural committee system is not a mass-membership organisation like Nokyo. The local agricultural committees have limited, indirect membership amongst farmers (although over the entire country this amounts to many thousands of farmers' representatives[145]) and therefore, these groups are not in a position to mobilise voters on a mass basis across a spectrum of different electorates. Nevertheless they can make a valuable contribution to the organised support base of agricultural politicians through formal recommendations (*suisen*) to their members and political funding.

Some groups compensate for their limited membership by mobilising around a highly concentrated national interest and providing funding resources, like some institutional interest groups. Organisations such as the Central Livestock Association and the National Beef Association, for example, lack a mass membership base of individual voters that is effective across a range of electorates and so concentrate on political funding.

On the other hand, those farmers' organisations with larger, direct memberships amongst the farmers are more likely to engage in vote-gathering. The *sine qua non* of successful vote-mobilisation is mass membership of some kind because this determines the vote-gathering potential of the group. Indeed, the larger the rice-roots individual membership of the group, the greater the likelihood that it will actively engage in collecting votes amongst its members.

Political funding varies according to the financial power of the group, which in turn is linked to the quantities of government subsidies flowing through the group. The land improvement organisations are renowned for their financial as well as their voting power, as are the agricultural mutual aid associations, although to a lesser extent. Technical staff of the land improvement districts and the veterinary surgeons attached to the mutual aid associations who have regular contacts with farmers as well as co-op chairmen have a significant influence over vote collection amongst farmers.[146] Rumours persist that a certain proportion of the large quantities of government subsidies flowing through these groups are recycled back into politicians' pockets. Furthermore, the land improvement industry is lucrative for the private companies involved in land redevelopment who employ farmers as labourers. They also make donations to politicians and mobilise the votes of their farmer-labourers.

The capacities of the non-Nokyo groups to mobilise votes and the kinds of electoral resources they can offer thus vary from group to group. Their organisational structures differ, as does their available 'manpower' and 'vote power', and their potential to provide electoral funding. Those that have political leagues signal their involvement in rice-roots vote-gathering activity, such as the land improvement groups and the *rakuno seiji renmei*. In the 1995 UH election, for example, the chairman and vice-chairman and other executives of the Rakuseiren visited local constituencies, organised talks, travelled around all areas within different constituencies and tried to gain support for particular candidates.

Like the agricultural cooperative organisations, the electoral activities of non-Nokyo farmers' groups may be, but are not necessarily, conducted in a cooperative manner, either amongst themselves or in combination with Nokyo. Certainly it is true that these groups generally do not operate at the electoral level in a unified, coordinated fashion. Although their numbers are smaller than the agricultural cooperatives, they often represent a more concentrated political interest, and as such, can offer a reliable and organised vote from amongst their members. The land improvement groups, for example, are renowned for their strength and effectiveness in offering backup to politicians with close links to the land improvement industry.

In 1990 the author conducted a questionnaire survey of Japanese politicians broadly identified as 'agricultural representatives'[147] to determine the nature of the support they received from Nokyo and other farmers' groups.[148] A total of 321 agricultural representatives were surveyed, with 77 replies.[149] The following types of electoral support from non-Nokyo farmers' groups was acknowledged:

• agricultural mutual aid organisations: recommendation, campaign assistance and political funds;

- land improvement organisations: recommendation and campaign workers;[150]
- agricultural committee organisations: recommendation and campaign workers;
- livestock, dairy, settlers' and forestry associations – recommendation and campaign workers;
- Zennichino, its prefectural federations and local unions: recommendation and campaign workers;
- Nichino, its prefectural federations and local unions: recommendation;
- Zenno and its prefectural federations: recommendation;
- charcoal, farm migrant workers, feed rice and tea industry organisations: recommendation;
- tobacco cultivators' groups: recommendation and political funds;
- labour-farmer councils: recommendation and campaign workers.

Criteria of electoral support

Election candidates supported by agricultural organisations including the cooperatives and their associated political groups receive backing for a multitude of different reasons and according to a diverse set of criteria. The variables on which agricultural organisations base their decisions about electoral support and what kind of support they will provide, include historical, personal, career, business and organisational connections between the candidate(s) and the group; factors relating to party affiliation and positions on certain agricultural policy issues; influence over agricultural policymaking and subsidy acquisition processes; level of standing in government, in the Diet and in the party; attitudes and sympathies towards farmers and agricultural organisations; degree of willingness to work on behalf of farmers in the Diet, in government and in the party; and last but not least, the politician's record in terms of delivering local projects and other promised benefits. Sometimes these factors may reinforce each other and sometimes they may cancel each other out. The party alignment of candidates can in some instances be set aside in the face of other candidate attributes, such as historical and organisational connections, degree of commitment to farmers' interests and so on. Quite clearly, many of these factors are linked. Because an important criterion of electoral backing is the extent to which politicians can be relied on as brokers and representatives working on behalf of their supporting interests within Parliamentary and government circles,[151] other factors also become important such as positions in government, in the Diet and in the party, and thus whether or not the candidate is a member of the ruling party.

The basis of choice can also depend on the circumstances of an election. In 1993, for example, the most weighty issue was liberalisation of the rice market, and so Zenkoku Noseikyo asked each candidate what approach they would take on this issue and gauged their decisions on recommendation accordingly. Similarly, in the 1995 UH election, Zenkoku Noseikyo asked what each candidate was going to do to promote agriculture after the ratification of the UR agreement. Individual local organisations requested election promises from each candidate and then judged them on their merits. For example, the Shimane Prefecture Agricultural Policy League (Nosei Domei) made a special election pact with LDP candidate Kageyama Shuntaro before they decided to recommend him.[152] This obligated him to a certain course of action once he was re-elected.

In 1996, a Zenkoku Noseikyo questionnaire of branch organisations about the basis on which their decisions to recommend candidates were made, was revealing of the criteria at work in this LH election – bearing in mind that it was contested under the new electoral system. The questionnaire permitted multiple answers, and the results were as follows. By far the most important criterion was 'the past record (*jisseki*) of the candidate up until now' at 71.7 per cent. The second most important criterion was 'party attachment' (52.2 per cent); the third was 'the candidate's prospects' (26.1 per cent), and the last was 'the candidate's election promises and policy' (19.6 per cent).[153] Quite clearly, the candidate's record and his party affiliation were the two most important factors determining a formal organisational recommendation. Equally clearly, policy issues took a back seat relatively speaking, as did the future potential of the candidate.

The following sections provide evidence from various studies, including questionnaire surveys, about the types of electoral support bestowed on election candidates according to some of the variables identified above, such as organisational connections and party affiliation. The aim is to see whether the quality of electoral support differs consistently in relation to these variables

Direct and indirect organisational connection

Diet members supported by farmers' organisations fall into two categories depending on the presence or absence of an official leadership connection between the politician and the group. These connections determine the nature of the representation in the Diet of the organisation in question. Groups obtain direct representation when politicians hold or have held formal leadership positions in the organisation. Indirect representation arises when politicians pledge their support for group interests and those of their members and in return receive electoral assistance from them. Support is provided in the expectation that the politician will advance the interests of the group in parliamentary, party and government circles.[154] In both cases a relationship of reciprocal interdependence underlies the electoral linkage between the politician and the group: candidates use farmers' groups as an organised platform in their bid for elective office and to provide much needed electoral resources; interest groups use politicians to gain access to policymaking processes in which their interests may be advanced.[155]

Tanaka linked relationship to Nokyo, party affiliation and type of electoral support received from the agricultural cooperatives into a classification of Nokyo-connected diet members.[156] Category I is where Nokyo nominates its own candidates (to the national constituency of the Upper House). Party affiliation is not a decisive consideration in this case. Category II is where Nokyo gives its all-out support (*zenmenteki oen*) for candidates from the conservative party who are current Nokyo executives, whether chairmen or full-time directors.[157] Such candidates often use Nokyo as a foothold to obtain LDP endorsement to stand for election. The electoral campaigns of these candidates take on the appearance of organisationally-based elections (*soshiki senkyo*) involving a range of cooperatives from prefectural level downwards. On these occasions, Nokyo demonstrates its power as a provider of an organised voting base in support of a clearly identifiable Nokyo candidate.[158] Once elected, the politicians in both Category I and Category II are clearly identifiable as Nokyo Diet members (*Nokyo giin*).[159]

Category III is that of positive backing for specific candidates from the conservative party, where there are no direct connections to Nokyo,[160] but where, as Diet members sympathetic to Nokyo (*Nokyo shinpa giin*), electoral support is given in expectation of policy favours.[161] Tanaka maintains that this category represents by far the most common type of electoral bargain struck between Nokyo and LDP candidates. Diet members in this category of conservative, pro-Nokyo sympathisers vastly outnumber those in the category of current Nokyo officials.

Category IV is common in constituencies where there are no specific connections or agreements between candidates and Nokyo. In this situation all-round recommendations are given to candidates who are connected to agriculture and forestry regardless of party, but in this case, Nokyo's backing tends to be formal. Nevertheless, as expected, Nokyo renders relatively strong assistance to candidates from the ruling party.[162] In single-member UH prefectural constituencies, for example, where one-to-one battles between conservatives and progressives have been common, Nokyo's backing has customarily gone to LDP candidates. Tanaka emphasises that in this category, no instances of JCP or Komeito candidates having received the recommendation of Nokyo have been recorded.[163] He estimates that this type of electoral backing is comparatively less common than Categories II and III.

One of the key distinctions incorporated in Tanaka's classification of Nokyo-supported Diet members is that between current Nokyo officials on the one hand and politicians with more indirect ties to the cooperatives, including those who have previously held executive or staff positions, on the other. In Tanaka's estimation, it is the former group that receives the full-scale backing of the agricultural cooperatives in elections. He indirectly discounts one-time service in the ranks of agricultural cooperative leaders as being as vital a qualification for electoral support as current employment.

Results of the questionnaire survey of APRA members by the writer do not generally support this proposition.[164] No marked variation in agricultural cooperative support emerged relative to the status of current or former Nokyo official, or to the presence or absence of an official connection to the cooperatives, although maybe the full story lay in the detail which the survey answers did not reveal. All current and former Nokyo officials amongst APRA respondents claimed to have received some form of electoral support from the cooperatives. The very small number who gave 'no support' replies claimed no leadership connection to Nokyo either before or after entry into the Diet.

Furthermore, past and present Nokyo officials and those without official leadership connections to the cooperatives scored exactly equal in the receipt of recommendation from the cooperatives, although the latter group did register a lower percentage for campaign assistance and an even lower percentage for political funds in combination with other forms of support. No significant differences, however, were observed between former and current Nokyo officials. The most one could say was that the quality of Nokyo assistance was marginally lower for those without career connections to the agricultural cooperatives. The combinations of types of support were also more variable for this group.

The only major area of difference between Nokyo officials and non-Nokyo officials concerned the origins of electoral support relationships. Respondents were asked whether they were offered Nokyo support, or whether they had requested it. Most of the Nokyo officials group replied that they had received electoral backing from the cooperatives without asking for it directly. Amongst the group of non-Nokyo officials, this was true in only a small number of cases, and even here, special Nokyo connections were observed, either as former co-op members (*kumiaiin*), or as special members of the group of UH Nokyo-connected politicians, the Nokyo Issues Roundtable Conference (Nokyo Mondai Kondankai),[165] or as former officials of Norinchukin. Most of the non-Nokyo officials had to request Nokyo's electoral support. The results suggested that politicians who occupied executive or staff positions in the agricultural cooperatives, or who had held such positions, were virtually assured of Nokyo's backing, whereas for other candidates, the situation was more open to negotiation.

The author's questionnaire survey of farm politicians in 1990 also unequivocally supports the proposition that the agricultural cooperatives do not restrict their electoral support to past or present Nokyo officials or staff members, or even to those with leadership connections to agricultural organisations. More than two-thirds (or 55 out of 77) of the politicians who responded to the survey admitted having received electoral support from the agricultural cooperatives, while a majority, or 54 per cent of respondents, received some form of electoral support from the farmers' political leagues. Almost half (47 per cent) of those who claimed to have received electoral backing from the agricultural cooperatives were neither Nokyo officials nor leaders of other agricultural organisations, as shown in Table 6.1.

Table 6.1 Agricultural group affiliations of Diet members supported by the agricultural cooperatives in elections

Agricultural group leaders	Number	Proportion of total supported by Nokyo	Proportion of category receiving Nokyo support
Nokyo leaders	11	20%	85%
Agricultural group leaders	18	33%	64%
Non-Nokyo or agricultural group leaders	26	47%	63%
Total supported by agricultural cooperatives	55	100%	–
Total Number of Respondents	77		

Source: Author's 1990 questionnaire survey.

Table 6.1 also indicates that past or present executive or staff ties to Nokyo are no guarantee of support, although it does make it more likely. The vast majority (85 per cent) of the Nokyo leaders in the questionnaire survey admitted having received electoral support from the agricultural cooperatives, whilst for other agricultural group leaders the proportion was 64 per cent, and for those not holding leadership positions in farm organisations at all, it was 63 per cent. Clearly, a career history that included an official position in an agricultural organisation was neither a necessary nor sufficient condition for Nokyo support, but nor was it a guarantee of it either.

Taken together the figures suggest that the agricultural cooperatives are not only prepared to support their own current or past leaders and the leaders of other agricultural organisations, but also politicians with no formal leadership ties to agricultural groups. This reveals a strategy of maximising parliamentary representation regardless of organisational connection.

In terms of the quality and range of support offered, a more marked distinction is observable between the leaders of agricultural organisations (including those from Nokyo) and politicians with no official leadership connection to agricultural organisations. The quality of support varies only moderately between Nokyo Diet members and the leaders of other agricultural organisations (see Table 6.2). The percentage receiving recommendation only was approximately the same; the biggest difference was in the percentage of Nokyo leaders receiving recommendation and campaign workers (almost two-thirds) compared with agricultural group leaders (almost one-half). A slightly higher percentage of agricultural group leaders reported funding support from Nokyo in concert with recommendation and political funds. The most common types of support for agricultural cooperative leaders were recommendation and campaign workers, while amongst agricultural group

Table 6.2 Variations in the quality of agricultural cooperative support according to agricultural group leadership role

Type of support	Percentages of agricultural and non-agricultural group representatives receiving type of support		
	Nokyo leader	Agricultural group leaders	Neither
Recommendation	27	29	83
Recommendation and campaign workers	64	47	13
Recommendation, campaign workers and political funds	9	12	0
Recommendation and political funds	0	6	4
Campaign workers	0	6	0
Total	100	100	100

Source: Author's 1990 questionnaire survey.

leaders, the various types of support seemed to be offered more independently of each other.

In the case of politicians without leadership ties to agricultural organisations, support appeared to be largely restricted to recommendation. A mere 13 per cent received electoral backing in the form of recommendation and campaign workers, whilst the figure for political funding was even lower. Only 4 per cent admitted to having received political funds (along with recommendation) from the agricultural cooperatives.

According to the information obtained from the questionnaire survey, types of electoral support furnished by the *noseiren* were similar to the agricultural cooperatives. Recommendation was the most common form of support, but in some cases it was also accompanied by campaign assistance and political funds. A total of 41 per cent of those who admitted accepting electoral support from the *noseiren* claimed to have received recommendation only; 2 per cent received campaign assistance only; 21 per cent received recommendation and campaign assistance; 10 per cent received recommendation and political funds; 2 per cent received recommendation, campaign assistance and political funds; and 2 per cent received recommendation and 'support'. The remaining respondents did not specify what type of support they were given. One of those surveyed acknowledged that the political funds he had obtained from the *noseiren* amounted to ¥300,000.

The questionnaire survey also confirmed that *koenkai* are an important institutional medium through which agricultural cooperative electoral support activities are conducted. Almost all respondents to the questionnaire survey had *koenkai*, and of this group, all but three had some form of participation from leaders, staff members or farmer members of Nokyo. This information confirmed earlier research which reported that, amongst a group of Nokyo's Diet supporters, of those who reportedly had *koenkai*, the vast majority acknowledged that Nokyo leaders, staff members and *kumiaiin* were all members of their personal support groups.[166]

Amongst the non-Nokyo groups, the questionnaire survey revealed a much greater focus on providing support for group leaders as direct representatives rather than a range of direct and indirect representatives like Nokyo. This may be due to the fact that these groups have a tighter organisational focus, perform a more limited range of functions, pursue a more well-defined set of interests and have a much narrower membership base. Zennichino from the time it was founded, for example, imposed three conditions on the provision of support for candidates in national elections. The candidate needed to be an executive of the Zennichino head office, or be a member of Zennichino's Diet members' group (Zennichino no Kokkai Giindan), or be associated with the farmers' movement, continue to be associated, and become a member of Zennichino's Diet members' group.[167] Over the years, the reduction in the number of those who qualified under these criteria was a measure of the deterioration in the farmers' union movement. In 1958, as already noted in chapter 3, 116 candidates were endorsed by Zennichino, in 1969 the figure was 51, and in 1983 it was only 43.[168] This trend can be explained by the fact that political representatives of the farmers' union movement were much more vulnerable to falls in the numbers of farm voters, particularly full-time farmers, because they lacked support from other sources, unlike LDP candidates. Demographic and economic changes in the countryside made it much more difficult for candidates to win elections by relying solely on the farm vote. Moreover, farmers could no longer provide sufficient donations to support the campaigns of farmers' union representatives because of the escalation in campaign costs.[169] Ishida and George reported that one of the reasons why JSP candidates accepted the support of the agricultural cooperatives in elections was because of the weakness of their own affiliated Zennichino organisation and the effectiveness of electoral support from the cooperatives.[170]

Of those respondents to the questionnaire survey who claimed to have received backing from agricultural organisations other than Nokyo (almost half, or 47 per cent of the total), the vast majority (83 per cent) had or were holding official positions in the group(s) from which they obtained the support. A leadership position in one agricultural group also made it quite likely that other agricultural groups would also provide support (almost one-third of the leaders of agricultural organisations also received support from other agricultural groups).

According to the questionnaire survey, the most common form of electoral support provided by agricultural organisations for their own leaders was recommendation and campaign assistance. In almost all cases, recommendation was received (in slightly less than half, recommendation only was received); in other cases recommendation was given in combination with campaign assistance and political funds.

Party affiliation

The second key distinction incorporated into Tanaka's classification of Nokyo-supported Diet members was that between politicians affiliated to the LDP (Categories I, II and III, and most of Category IV) and those affiliated to the Opposition parties, with the degree of electoral support and mobilisation diminishing across these categories. In fact, as emphasised elsewhere, affiliation with the LDP has never been a necessary condition for Nokyo's backing in elections. Indeed, the party affiliation of the candidates who receive the support of farmers' organisations, including Nokyo, has always been much more of an open question than is assumed by the stereotype of agricultural groups as the *jiban* of the LDP.

The party-political preferences of agricultural organisations have varied according to organisational history, organisational level (whether national, prefectural, or municipal), regional particularities, differences in group management (*dantai kanbu*), the nature of connections with the bureaucracy, and the personal political connections and preferences of group executives. At the aggregate level, patterns of party support have varied amongst different organisations, whilst patterns of party support even within the same organisation have also varied over time.

The main distinction is between MAFF institutional and statutory interest groups (except for Nokyo) and all the rest. The *gaikaku dantai* only back LDP candidates because ruling party politicians are required to act on their behalf in the quest for subsidies. In fact, many of these candidates are in fact ex-MAFF officials because this positions them advantageously in the pursuit of subsidies.[171] The institutional and statutory interest groups in this category include organisations like the Central Livestock Association, the National Beef Association, the land improvement groups, the mutual aid associations and the agricultural committee system. The National Chamber of Agriculture, for example, is almost always represented in the Diet by a former MAFF bureaucrat and has an exclusive relationship with the LDP, which is mediated by the Agricultural Policy Promotion Council, the MAFF *gaikaku dantai* established under the leadership of the Chamber in 1958 and housed within the Chamber itself.[172]

In the case of farmers' organisations including Nokyo, the picture is much more diverse. Firstly, as elaborated at some length in chapter 3, during the early postwar period, the leaders of farmers' organisations (the farmers' unions, rural youth groups, farmers' political leagues and agricultural cooperatives) displayed a variety of party affiliations: conservative, Independent and so-called 'progressive' (meaning socialist). Indeed, as pointed out, many preferred to organise their own party groupings rather than align with existing parties.

Secondly, there remained sub-groupings within the agricultural cooperative organisation which were much less tightly 'adhering' (*yuchaku*) to the LDP than the mainstream Nokyo organisations and their executives. The farmers' political leagues which became active from the late 1950s onwards, for example, had a history of countenancing alliances with, and support for, Independent and socialist candidates as well as those from the LDP.[173] In 1969,[174] the Fukushima Prefecture Agricultural Policy Promotion League proclaimed: 'We are not a sub-contracting organisation of the LDP, so let us recommend candidates connected with the progressives as well'.[175]

The political configurations that emerged amongst the various *noseiren* operating in different prefectures in the 1969 LH election tend to bear out this view. Nokyo-based farmers' political leagues recommended a total of 33 candidates over the whole country. The overall distribution amongst the parties was as follows: LDP – 14, JSP – 11, DSP – seven, and one Independent, with the proportion of conservative to progressive candidates differing from prefecture to prefecture. The Hokkaido Nomin Domei did not recommend any LDP candidates at all. Of the seven candidates nominated over the whole prefecture, six belonged to the JSP and one was a DSP member. Miyagi and Nagano Prefecture *noseiren* recommended the same number of government and Opposition party candidates each, the Fukushima Prefecture group recommended all nine LDP candidates (in spite of its rejection of the notion that its relationship with the LDP was one of a sub-contractual organisation), the Saga Prefecture Nosei Kyogikai recommended all four LDP candidates after a conscious decision to exclude support for Nakamura Yoshijiro, who was Secretary-General of the Zennosoren, because he was standing on a DSP ticket (unlike the Nokyo youth division within the same prefecture[176]). The farmers' political leagues in Akita, Nagano and Yamagata avoided making recommendations for any candidates, but active elements within the leagues gave positive backing to candidates connected to the progressives.

In the 1971 UH election, the Fukui prefecture *noseiren* decided on an anti-LDP stance, while the *noseiren* in Miyazaki and Kagawa promoted JSP candidates, indicating that farmers' discontent with the government's rice price and acreage reduction policies went very deep.[177] In some local Nokyo offices, posters of LDP candidates were torn down by farmers. The Chairman of Zenchu, Miyawaki Asao (who himself had long-standing Socialist connections) stood up in the middle of the Nokyo producer rice price convention (which also happened to be held in the middle of local elections) and said: 'To think that the Nokyo organisation and the farmers always follow the LDP is absolutely absurd. Let us express our opposition to the LDP's agricultural policy by abstaining from voting in the House of Councillors' elections which are due.'[178]

Splits sometimes occurred between the conservative executive class of Nokyo, who were pro-LDP, and young, disaffected farmers in the farmers' political leagues and Nokyo youth divisions. The latter had a reputation for being much more inclined to vote for progressive candidates in protest against LDP agricultural policies. In 1969, for example, the Ishikawa Prefecture

Nokyo youth division made good its threat to withdraw collectively from the LDP in protest against the government's decision to defer a producer rice price increase. In response to its pressure for Nokyo members to leave the party as a group, more than 300 left the LDP in that prefecture.[179] The move was made all the more serious by the fact that a full-time director of the Ishikawa Prefecture Nokyo Central Union was running for election at the same time with the endorsement of the LDP.[180] In the same election in Saga Prefecture, the youth division made a point of supporting DSP candidate Nakamura Yoshijiro because of its desire to assert its independence from the mainstream Nokyo organisation and its executives.

Amano also reports that small groups of young farmers in Kumamoto in the late 1970s criticised the LDP's agricultural policy and Nokyo's commercialism, which made them less reliable members of the hitherto entrenched alliance between the LDP prefectural federation and the Nokyo prefectural organisations. More recently, the 1989 election 'revolt' by Nokyo was effectively led by the *seinenbu* across a whole host of prefectures.[181]

The political independence of the youth division has only been qualified by its financial dependence on the mainstream agricultural cooperative organisation. Around 80 per cent of the campaign budgets of the youth division derive from funds allocated by the agricultural cooperatives. This contributes in general to youth division support for conservative candidates, in spite of support for the progressives from time to time as an anti-LDP protest.

The All-Japan Settlers' League incorporating members of the specialist reclamation agricultural cooperatives is another organisation within Nokyo's orbit regarded as being inclined towards the progressives. The same is true of the Nokyo staff class. The conservative-progressive division within Nokyo, so far as it has ever existed, has tended to follow the fundamental divide between the executive and staff members of the organisation. Evidence of this lies in the uniform endorsement of former staff members-turned-politicians by socialist parties,[182] support for the socialist parties from Nokyo staff members,[183] and the progressive alignment of Zennokyo Roren.[184]

Thirdly, divisions and splits have sometimes occurred within the mainstream agricultural cooperatives over which candidate(s) to support because of conflicting interests within the Nokyo organisation itself. In 1960 Nokyo was described as an organisation finding it difficult to achieve organisational unity because of the increasing diversification of farming and the growth of divisions amongst farming classes.[185] As Kobayashi, Shinohara and Soma point out, the organisational power of the agricultural cooperatives and their organisational directions were not the same.[186] It was not unusual for Independents, socialist and LDP Diet members to be supported by agricultural cooperatives as rival Diet candidates. In some cases, political confrontations involved cohorts of agricultural cooperative groups lined up in conservative versus progressive electoral battles. In the 1971 UH election, for example, the Miyagi Nokyo Political League recommended the endorsed LDP candidate but did not take any major action to support the candidate. This was because the various *nokyo* in Miyagi were divided into those that supported the LDP and those that supported Opposition party candidates.[187]

Political divisions within Nokyo also occurred in regions such as Akita and Yamagata, where the influence of the farmers' unions remained strong, even within the agricultural cooperatives. In fact, the progressives actively sought the support of Nokyo because candidates were given an advantage in that their campaigns connected with Nokyo became easier to conduct.[188]

These electoral divisions were often attributed to regional differences in economic development, agricultural production structure[189] and farm organisations, which led to regional confrontations and rivalries.[190] The confrontation between Tohoku and Western Japan, between the Japan Sea side and Pacific side, or the numerous confrontations between prefectures or between blocs within prefectures in the form of east versus west, south versus north, were often expressed in terms of political confrontations such as conservative versus progressive and others.[191]

Over time, the pattern of party support amongst candidates supported by agricultural cooperative organisations gradually stabilised into a stable majority-LDP, minority-Opposition party configuration. Most of those who received Nokyo support were from the LDP, but Opposition party politicians (from the JSP, DSP and NLC) and some Independents also received backing from Nokyo organisations. It was sometimes useful for Nokyo to provide backing for Opposition party politicians, because it meant that they could call on them from time to time to embarrass the LDP on agricultural policy issues. Likewise, it represented something of an insurance policy for Nokyo to have some allies within the Opposition parties in case a coalition of Opposition groupings came to power.[192]

The membership of APRA as an organisation of recipients of Nokyo's electoral support illustrated the majority LDP-minority Opposition socialist proportions quite consistently over time. Between 1973 and 1977, 65 per cent of APRA members in the Lower House were from the LDP; 23 per cent were from the JSP, 12 per cent were from the DSP and the remainder were Independents or from minor parties. In the Upper House, 86 per cent of APRA members were from the LDP, 10 per cent were from the JSP; 2 per cent were from the DSP and 2 per cent were Independents or from minor parties.[193] The difference in the relative party proportions between each House was partly a reflection of the differences in their respective electoral systems, particularly the LDP's predominance in UH prefectural constituencies for the reasons explained earlier.

In spite of its formal status as a statutory interest group, Nokyo was able to exercise flexibility in the choice of which party candidates to support because of its greater economic independence from government and because it was a non-ideological, mass membership organisation. Which candidate would receive the backing of agricultural cooperative organisations was something their leaders and farmer members decided for themselves in each case. Not surprisingly, the results across different organisations, regions and elections were not totally uniform.

Results of the questionnaire survey of APRA members by the writer[194] showed that agricultural cooperative electoral backing was remarkably similar for candidates of the LDP and JSP[195] in terms of recommendations, campaign assistance and political funds. Amongst this group of Nokyo's Diet supporters, the issue of party affiliation ranked even lower than type of connection with Nokyo as a criterion for political backing.

An examination of the list of candidates who received political funding from Noseiken in the 1971 UH election and the 1972 LH election confirms this general thesis.[196] Party affiliation was not the decisive factor. In fact what really counted was how useful the politician was likely to be in a policymaking context. As noted above, Noseiken's financial contributions to LH candidates ranged from a maximum of ¥4 million to a minimum of ¥100,000. Amongst UH candidates it varied from ¥2 million to ¥100,000. A total of 203 LH candidates received support, while only 18 UH candidates were recipients of funding.[197] Almost all members of both groups were elected. The emphasis on establishing close links with LH members dictated Nokyo's priorities in guiding the bulk of Noseiken's contributions to LH candidates. The Lower House as the house of government (and its dominance in passing the annual budget bill) was clearly regarded as a key target of pressure,[198] as were LH Diet members because of the more influential positions they were likely to hold.

The criteria of electoral support which emerged from a grading of the recipients according to the amount they received illustrated Nokyo's distinct preference for supporting agricultural policy leaders from the various political parties. This appeared to be the single most important principle guiding the quantity of Noseiken political funding, not official connections to Nokyo, although this figured as a second-ranking criterion. Party considerations were not crucial either, although the relative proportions of majority LDP-minority Opposition Socialist (JSP and DSP) were apparent. No funds were donated by Noseiken to either Komeito or JCP candidates.[199]

The top-ranking recipients of Noseiken funds had in common proven experience and influence over agricultural policy-making in relevant party decisionmaking structures (LDP, JSP and DSP) and/or in prominent agriculture-related Cabinet and Diet agricultural policy positions, such as former MAF Ministers and Chairmen and Directors of the Diet Agriculture and Forestry Committees. A large proportion of this group had also held the Chairmanship or Vice-Chairmanship of the LDP's Norin Bukai and its Comprehensive Agricultural Policy Investigation Committee, or CAPIC (Sogo Nosei Chosakai) within the PARC, or the JSP and DSP equivalents: the JSP Farmers' Office (Nomin Kyoku) and its PARC Agriculture and Forestry Committee (Norin Iinkai); and the DSP's Agriculture, Forestry and Fisheries Industries' Policy Committee (Norinsuisangyo Seisaku Iinkai) and its PARC Agriculture, Forestry and Fisheries Division (Norinsuisan Bukai) and Special

420   *The politics of agriculture in Japan*

Table 6.3 Party affiliations of Diet members supported by the agricultural cooperatives

Party[a]	Number supported by the agricultural cooperatives	Proportion of the total supported by the agricultural cooperatives	Proportion of the total respondents from the same party
LDP	37	67%	76%
JSP	15	27%	65%
Independents	2	4%	100%
DSP	1	2%	100%
Komeito	0	0	0
Rengo	0	0	0
Total	55	100%	–

Note:
a These were the only parties whose agricultural representatives responded to the questionnaire survey.

Source: Author's 1990 questionnaire survey.

Committees on Livestock Policy and Food Policy (Chikusan Seisaku/ Shokuryo Seisaku Tokubetsu Iinkai).

A total of 23 recipients in the LH group received ¥1 million or more, and of these, 16, or 70 per cent, had been either chairmen or vice-chairmen of party agriculture and forestry committees. The remainder were important either as Nokyo politicians, former MAF Ministers, or leaders of prominent Nokyo-connected organisations.[200] This group averaged a donation of ¥1.4 million each against an average of ¥470,000 per candidate over the whole group.

The second-ranking criterion was a long-standing and high-level position in the Nokyo organisation. Twenty-six current or former Nokyo officials (or 15 per cent of the total number supported by Noseiken) received a total of ¥20.9 million. This was 23 per cent of the total amount given, or an average of approximately ¥800,000 each, which was considerably higher than the average over the whole group. Amongst these politicians, no significant variation in amounts given were observed relative to party affiliation. Two-thirds were LDP members and the remaining third JSP and DSP.[201] JSP Nokyo candidates averaged ¥1.1 million each, which was higher than the overall average of the Nokyo group. LDP Nokyo candidates averaged ¥760,000 each, while DSP Nokyo recipients averaged ¥660,000 each. As Sakaguchi has observed, Nokyo's political donations to Opposition party candidates was the real reason why these parties did not speak out clearly about agricultural policy (i.e. to oppose agricultural support and protection).[202]

Table 6.3 reports the responses of politicians supported in the elections by the agricultural cooperatives in 1990. LDP, JSP, DSP and Independent Diet members acknowledged that they had received support from the agricultural cooperatives.[203] The differences between the Opposition parties and the

Table 6.4 Variations in the quality of agricultural cooperative electoral support according to party

Type of support	Percentages of total party respondents receiving type of support			
	LDP	*JSP*	*DSP*	*Independent*
Recommendation	58	54	100	0
Recommendation and campaign workers	30	38	0	50
Recommendation, campaign workers and political funds	6	0	0	50
Recommendation and political funds	6	0	0	0
Campaign workers	0	8	0	0
Total	100	100	100	100

Source: Author's 1990 questionnaire survey.

LDP was a matter of degree. Support was more likely to be given to an LDP member (of whom three-quarters received Nokyo backing) than a JSP member (of whom almost two-thirds received backing). Clearly, however, Nokyo did not offer its support exclusively to LDP candidates.

Amongst recipients of electoral support from the agricultural cooperatives, 'quality' of support did not vary significantly relative to party affiliation either,[204] except that no JSP Diet member reported support in the form of political funding (see Table 6.4). Comparing the figures in Tables 6.2 and 6.4, it would appear that the difference in the quality of Nokyo support was determined less by party affiliation than by a leadership connection to an agricultural organisation.

Although the party situation changed in the 1990s, politicians who received recommendation from Zenkoku Noseikyo in the 1990, 1995, 1996 and 1998 elections still included those from outside the ranks of the LDP.[205] Amongst the 88 candidates supported by the National Council in the 1990 LH elections, nine were from the JSP while two were from the DSP (the balance, or 87.5 per cent were LDP candidates).[206] Figures for the 1995 and 1996 elections demonstrate a similar pattern, with non-LDP candidates in a small minority. In the 1995 UH elections, of the 32 candidates recommended in prefectural constituencies by the Zenkoku Noseikyo, 26, or 81 per cent, were members of the LDP. The balance belonged to the SDP (two), DRP (two), NFP (one) plus one Independent. In the national constituency, one was an LDP candidate, the other was from the SDP.[207] Similarly, of the 32 prefectural constituency candidates who received recommendations from *noseiren*, 26 were from the LDP, three from the NFP, two from the SDP and one from the DRP. Likewise, in the national constituency, one was LDP, the other SDP.[208] In both cases, this represented an overall LDP candidate support rate of just under 84 per cent.

In the 1996 LH elections, the distribution of support was even more in favour of LDP candidates. Of the 225 candidates with Zenkoku Noseikyo and prefectural *noseiren* recommendation, 181 or 91 per cent, were members of the LDP, nine (or 4 per cent) were from the NFP, four were Independents, three each were from the Democratic Party and Shinto Sakigake, and two were from the SDP.[209] The Chairman of Sagami Nokyo in Kanagawa Prefecture appealed to *noseiren* members that only the LDP could solve the current problems of Japanese agriculture and therefore the prefectural *noseiren* needed to strengthen the support system for the LDP.[210] In Fukui Prefecture, however, one *noseiren* leader bemoaned the fact that even though his organisation backed an LDP candidate in Fukui (2) and a Democratic Party candidate in Fukui (3), both of whom were successful, there used to be three LDP Diet members from Fukui constituency, which meant that the new election results diminished the opportunity to have local farmers' opinions reflected in policy.[211] In the 1998 UH elections, 52 candidates were recommended by Zenkoku Noseikyo and the prefectural *noseiren*. A total of 49 (94 per cent) were from the LDP, with one each from the DP and SDP, and one Independent.

These figures underline the proposition argued in the previous chapter that the LDP came through the period of party fissure and fusion in the 1990s as the overwhelmingly dominant party representing farmers. Although the NFP included many former LDP members, and although commentators were predicting that each agricultural cooperative would become much more independent in its choice of which candidate to support,[212] in fact the agricultural cooperatives' electoral preferences remained predominantly in favour of LDP candidates.

The weight of evidence, both historical and contemporary, however, is against the stereotype of Nokyo as an exclusive appendage of the LDP. In this respect, Nokyo is very different from the farmers' unions in terms of the nature of its party alignment. In spite of early differences in the farmers' union movement when pro-Socialist and pro-Communist groupings were formed, the political orientation of the movement was exclusively progressive, and predominantly Socialist for a large part of its history. Indeed, the farmers' unions effectively operated closed alliances with socialist parties. Instances of Nichino or Zennichino leaders affiliating with the LDP in the Diet were rare.[213] These exclusive party ties were generated by a top heavy Diet and local assembly leadership. The farmers' unions were essentially party-parasitic groupings with virtually no independent non-party leadership. They helped mobilise electoral support for Opposition socialist candidates amongst the farmers. Membership of the farmers' unions carried with it a vote for the JSP or DSP. As already noted the JCP described the close ties between Zennichino and the JSP as the former having become the 'private property' (*shibutsuka*) of the JSP.[214] Zennichino recommended only JSP candidates in elections. Also, many of the prefectural farmers' union federations linked to Zennichino were effectively JSP Diet politicians' *koenkai*.[215] The JCP's resented Zennichino's politicisation by the JSP and accused Zennichino of totally abandoning its function and duty as a national centre of the farmers' movement.[216]

Nokyo on the other hand, although it has been a semi-administrative arm of government, or perhaps because of it, at no stage assumed the characteristics of an organisational appendage of the LDP. As emphasised elsewhere, it is formally apolitical and non-ideological in terms of its party alignment. It encompasses a national membership of farmers of all political persuasions and therefore must eschew formal and fixed party attachments. In 1973, Zenchu Chairman Miyawaki Asao in an interview professed that Nokyo maintained a policy of equidistance from all political parties.[217] Nokyo's electoral support activities serve as an extension of its official objective which is to conduct cooperative activities for the benefit of the farming community. First and foremost, it has always sought to further its own organisational aims. These are defined by its own leadership and not by the LDP. Decisions on how Nokyo leaders and members are to align themselves politically are kept strictly as a matter for the individuals themselves and are not predicated on the adoption of agricultural cooperative membership or leadership. In each case, the relationship between political parties and their candidates, on the one hand, and agricultural cooperative organisations, on the other, is one between two separate and independent organisations.

The relationship between Nokyo and the LDP at the electoral level is not, therefore, a given in the sense of fixed on ideological premises that automatically exclude all other party alternatives. Group affiliation is not an automatic predictor of party support. Nokyo and the LDP have a mutually interdependent relationship based on a fundamentally pragmatic rationale: farmers' preferences for conservative party candidates and the preference of farm organisations to be on the side of the party in power so they can get their demands more effectively realised. Choice of LDP candidates is thus based on pragmatic self-interest, not ideological considerations. This means that in practice an affiliation with the LDP is likely to be the dominant party characteristic of election candidates supported by agricultural cooperative organisations. As Muramatsu and Krauss sensibly point out, interest groups like Nokyo, choose 'to gravitate to the LDP because it . . . is the only party capable of formulating policy'[218] and because of the LDP's ability, as the ruling party, to reward those groups within its social coalition.[219]

Furthermore, as emphasised earlier, a key aspect of the conduct of electoral activities by different agricultural cooperative organisations is their decentralised, regionally-focused and locally activist nature, which prevents exclusive party attachment and inhibits uniformity of political affiliation. This is buttressed by the candidate-specific focus of electoral support from these groups. Agricultural cooperative organisations support individual Diet politicians, not political parties although a distinctive party-support pattern may be observable in the aggregate. Because the LDP enjoyed a long, unbroken period in government, Nokyo naturally drew closer to the LDP, but in principle, support was always directed towards individuals, not parties.

Indeed, survey research on Japanese pressure groups reveals that agricultural groups are not in fact amongst those most steadfastly affiliated to the LDP in the sense of uniformity of party alignment. Those closest to the LDP are 'professional (medical, legal, and the like), educational, and administrative (e.g. local government and public corporation groups). These are followed by agricultural groups. Then come large business and financial groups, and finally, with the least close relationship, labor and civic and political groups.'[220] Moreover, agricultural groups acknowledge quite high levels of contact with the JSP and DSP (certainly higher than economic groups and administrative groups).[221] In policymaking terms, this has meant that Nokyo has been able to keep open the lines of communication with the Opposition parties, particularly the JSP and DSP. As already noted, this was both an insurance policy in the event of the Opposition parties ever coming to power and as a means of encouraging the Opposition parties to outflank and embarrass the LDP on agricultural issues.[222] The same research also established that the relationship between the LDP and agricultural interest groups was based primarily on pragmatic exchange relationships as opposed to common values (i.e. ideology), although the latter were not entirely absent. The reasons given by agricultural interest group leaders for the support their organisations received from politicians were votes, 'long trust relationship' and 'sympathy with group aims and goals'.[223]

Evaluating Nokyo's vote-gathering powers

The particular strength of agricultural cooperative organisations as electoral support groups has been their potential to collect farmers' votes via the thousands of branches (*sogo nokyo*) all over Japan.[224] Not only has Nokyo's geographic coverage of the country been total, but it has captured almost all farm households within its membership structure.

On the other hand, the fact that farmers and Nokyo members are virtual equivalents does not necessarily mean that the agricultural cooperatives are in a position to command the votes of all farmers. Nokyo has strongly influenced farmers' daily lives and agricultural production activities, but whether this translates into power to shape their voting behaviour is another matter. In the first place, Nokyo's diversity is one factor that potentially creates difficulties for the organisation in influencing farmers' votes sufficiently.[225] Nokyo is a mass organisation encompassing a heterogenous membership with differing values and political opinions.

Secondly, it is very difficult to make blanket judgements about Nokyo's vote-gathering powers, because evidence suggests that it varies widely from region to region, constituency to constituency, and election to election. In some cases, the 'Nokyo vote' can virtually deliver a candidate into the Diet. In Kagoshima, for example, Nokyo in alliance with its auxiliary arm specialising in political and electoral activities, the prefectural *noseiren*, comprises the largest vote-collecting machine in the prefecture. In other areas, the so-called 'Nokyo vote' is barely in existence, insufficient in number, ill-coordinated and even divided. The result can be electoral failure and organisational impotence. Thus, to estimate whether or not Nokyo has the vote-gathering ability to make good its threat that 'it will confront the LDP government in the election' is simultaneously both true and false.[226] Evidence exists to support both sides of the argument.

Certainly in theory – in terms of the potential size of Nokyo's aggregate vote and a host of other organisational, socio-cultural and political factors – Nokyo should be able to exercise formidable voting power. Interrelated aspects of organisational culture as they impact on voting behaviour, traditional patterns of voting behaviour in rural society and specific characteristics of the Nokyo system have provided a strong basis for the vote-gathering capacities of agricultural cooperative organisations.

Firstly, group norms have predisposed members towards conformity with leadership directives. These have put co-op leaders in a position to deliver the votes of their members who have been motivated by loyalty to the generally agreed objectives of the group.[227] The system whereby agricultural cooperatives (and their associated organisations) have mobilised votes in the farm villages has been essentially patterned on the older-style *buraku*-recommendation and *yuryokusha* systems already described. Leading figures in the village harness community loyalties and their own powers of patronage as well as ties of personal loyalty and obligation to influence the votes of village dwellers. Indeed, one of Nokyo's great organisational qualities and the secret of its powers of mobilisation in economic, electoral and policy-related activities has been strong membership loyalty derived from the local community base of the agricultural cooperatives and the tight human networks in the farm villages on which the agricultural cooperatives were founded.[228] At the *tankyo* level, each farming community has formed the core of agricultural cooperative membership, with firm bonds of community interest reinforced by loyalty to a common group.

This is particularly the case when a candidate with close connections to the agricultural cooperatives is standing for election. Miyake reports that when Nokyo puts a candidate up for election from amongst its 'friends' and 'relatives', it demonstrates vote-collecting ability to an extraordinary degree.[229] Where a solid relationship exists between the local *nokyo* chairman and the local *nokyo* members, election battles have sometimes been very 'severe', involving blood relations, community relations, and all other relations with friends and acquaintances.[230]

Agricultural cooperatives also work through, or in concert with, other leading figures in the villages (the mayor, chairman of the local agricultural committee, the chairmen of land improvement districts and so on) to collect the votes of entire villages. These other local leaders often share a feeling of responsibility for their villages' prosperity and consider it important to unite villagers behind a common cause. This has meant cooperating with Nokyo to achieve a consensus amongst villagers at election time.[231]

A second and related point is the fact that agricultural cooperatives have been distinctly advantaged in their electoral support activities by being territorial organisations.[232] The *tankyo* have membership coverage of all the farm houses in the district, which has meant that Nokyo *suisen* and the local recommendation (*chiiki suisen*) have often been one and the same thing. Furthermore, the coincidence of operational zones between Nokyo's regional and municipal branches and administrative units such as cities, towns and villages[233] has enabled the agricultural cooperatives to mobilise the 'locality consciousness' of members within these clearly defined geographic areas and administrative sub-regions as an instrument of vote-mobilisation.[234] The consciousness of regional interests is something that can be engaged not only at village level, but also across the larger geographical zones that agricultural cooperative organisations encompass – prefectural and municipal. Supplementing locality consciousness have been the specialist Nokyo groups, the *senmon nokyo* and specialist prefectural federations, which have formed their own electoral *jiban* around particular commodity or farming interests, such as the reclamation, livestock, horticultural and sericultural cooperatives.[235]

Thirdly, Nokyo is closely linked to farm households in various respects through commodity handling[236] and because officials of the local co-ops know each farm household in detail from subsidy-related activities. In the latter case, the agricultural cooperatives have established intimate relationships through the different subsidised works they administer on behalf of the government. As Hirose points out, the close relationships established by Nokyo officials through different *hojo jigyo* (subsidy projects) and grants are ties that help in elections.[237] A similar factor operates with respect to Nokyo's leadership of *nosei katsudo*. The producer rice price, for example, has been cited as playing the principal role in underpinning Nokyo's vote-collection mechanism.[238] As Ono puts it, Nokyo's strategy has been 'to organise farmers' energy into votes for the LDP by utilising the political impact of the rice price decision.'[239]

Finally, a number of organisational intermediaries exist through which political ties between Nokyo leaders and members can be forged. These include the farmers' political leagues, the youth divisions and the *koenkai* of individual candidates, which all provide a locus in which a common voting choice and collective political view can be formed and reinforced amongst agricultural cooperative members. These groups also furnish an appropriate medium through which effective political public relations activities can be conducted by Nokyo activists with the aim of influencing the votes of the general membership.

In spite of all these advantages, the image of Nokyo leaders issuing directives to co-op members in the way that former landlords did to their tenants is totally anachronistic. Influencing votes often takes more subtle forms. It is 'in the air' in rural areas, with the electoral influences emanating from Nokyo leaders and various branches of the organisation being hard for farmers to escape. According to the 1994 poll amongst Nokyo's farmer members,[240] when asked whether they attached importance to the information coming from Nokyo-related persons when they voted, 12.8 per cent said they attached a great deal of importance, whilst 41.1 per cent said it was quite important, making a total of just over half of all respondents (53.9 per cent). The remainder (46.1 per cent) claimed that information from Nokyo-related persons was not important at all in determining their vote.[241] These results are about 50:50, suggesting that Nokyo's influence is far from negligible, but at the same time, far from overwhelming. At most, one can say that the 'Nokyo vote' is a partially cohesive entity able to be moved in blocs by agricultural cooperative leaders.

It is certainly true, as pointed out earlier, that the extent to which agricultural cooperative votes can be reliably delivered to candidates varies from region to region and election to election. Table 6.5 lists the numbers of votes which the farmers' political leagues claimed were under their direction in various prefectures in 1979. They ranged anywhere from 14.3 per cent of the total farm vote in Tochigi to 104.3 per cent in Kanagawa (suggesting at least in this case that the claims of the league were exaggerated). In most prefectures, the leagues laid claim to between one-half and two-thirds of the total farm vote, with the figures endorsing the observation that the vote-gathering powers of agricultural cooperative organisations varied considerably from prefecture to prefecture. And if Kumamoto is anything to go by, time does not appear to have diminished by very much the volume of votes potentially able to be mobilised by the prefectural farmers' political league. In 1979, it was 120,000; in 1998 it was 112,000.[242]

Moreover, in different respects, the voting figures for the *noseiren* may both understate and overstate their ability to influence farmers' votes. According to the figures in Table 6.5, the *noseiren* in Miyagi can collect 100,000 votes, but another source claims that the same organisation can influence the votes of 100,000 farm households which translates into more than 300,000 votes.[243] If this is the case, it suggests that all the figures in Table 6.5 need to be multiplied several times over (by the average number of voters per farm household), expanding considerably the vote-collection powers of these groups.

On the other hand, even comparing gross figures for different farmers' political leagues can be misleading. For one thing, the prefectural totals are a compound of many different smaller groups. As already pointed out, the vote-gathering ability of the agricultural cooperatives is at its most potent at the rice-roots level via the individual *tankyo* (and the local sub-branches of the farmers' political leagues) working in association with the candidates' *koenkai*. Cooperative units such as these do not necessarily undertake campaigns on instructions from above, even in prefectures with strong farmers' political leagues, although they may become part of a district- or prefecture-wide consensus in favour of a certain candidate or candidates.

Table 6.5 Self-proclaimed vote-collection capacities of farmers' political leagues as a percentage of the total farm vote

Constituency	Prefectural Farmers' Political League(s)	No. of farm household voters[a]	Professed vote-collection capacity of farmers political league	Farmers' political league members as % of total eligible farm vote[c]
Hokkaido	Nokyo Political League; Farmers' Federation	404,635	250–260,000	61.8–64.3%
Aomori	People's Political League	375,406	n/a	n/a
Iwate	Politics and Economics Roundtable Conference	434,881	n/a	n/a
Miyagi	Nokyo Political League	435,262	100,000	23.0%
Akita	Nokyo Political League	389,585	250,000	64.2%
Fukushima	Farmers' Political League	554,819	200,000	36.0%
Ibaraki	Political League for Promoting Agriculture	623,613	370,000	59.3%
Tochigi	Political League for Promoting Agriculture	385,178	50–60,000	14.3%
Gumma	Political League for Promoting Agriculture	373,239	150–200,000	46.9%
Saitama	Farmers' Political Association	480,653	180,000	37.4%
Kanagawa	Agricultural Policy Promotion League	191,703	200,000	104.3%
Toyama	Agricultural Policy League	258,908	150,000	57.9%
Fukui	Rural Construction Political League	189,925	150,000+	79.0%
Yamanashi	Agricultural Policy League	204,821	n/a	n/a
Nagano	Agricultural Policy Friends' Association	629,784	150,000	23.8%
Shizuoka	Agricultural Policy Countermeasures Council	491,165	n/a	n/a
Aichi	Agricultural Policy League	547,690	200,000	36.5%
Shiga	Political League for Promoting Agriculture	277,274	200,000	72.1%
Hyogo	Agricultural Policy Promotion Council	547,434	450,000	82.2%
Wakayama	Farmers' Political League	184,200	100,000 (UH) 50,000 (LH)	40.7%

Shimane	Agricultural Policy League	227,169	Practically none	n/a
Okayama	Farmers' Political League	420,593	300,000	71.3%
Yamaguchi	Nokyo Agricultural Policy Promotion League	261,463	n/a	n/a
Tokushima	Agricultural Policy Council	206,409	n/a	n/a
Ehime	Agricultural Policy Comrades' Association	314,658	200,000 (UH) 100,000 (LH)	47.7%
Fukuoka	Farmers' Political League	463,458	350–400,000	80.9%
Saga	Agricultural Policy Council	237,029	n/a	n/a
Nagasaki	Farmers' Political League	283,394	n/a	n/a
Kumamoto	Farmers' Political League	432,451	120,000	27.7%
Oita	Nokyo Agricultural Policy Council	286,922	50–100,000	26.1%
Miyazaki	Farmers' League	264,882	170,000	64.2%
Kagoshima	Farmers' Political League	439,405	270,000	61.4%

Notes:

a Calculated by the percentage of persons 20 years and over living in farm households in 1979 (over the entire country it was 73.2 per cent).

b The figures are for 1979.

c Where a range of voting figures are given, the mid-point in the range is taken to calculate the percentage.

Source: Tachibana, *Nokyo*, pp. 320–322.

A similar absence of top-down authority on electoral support matters exists in the relationship between the prefectural and national levels of the Nokyo organisation. At the national level, almost no powers of control operate. Although Nokyo might have a national political arm (Zennosoren, now Zenkoku Noseikyo), not all farmers' political leagues are affiliated with it (although the latter has a higher rate of affiliation amongst prefectural groups than the former did). Unaffiliated groups conduct their *senkyo katsudo* as they choose at prefectural level and through their branches. Even the affiliated groups do not necessarily obey orders from the centre. As far as electoral activities are concerned, sub-prefectural and prefectural-level activities are the core (the latter particularly in UH prefectural constituencies), and no national organisation, including Zenchu, gives orders on electoral matters. Of course, national Nokyo leaders do travel around making campaign speeches on behalf of various candidates supported by the agricultural cooperatives, but how effective these activities are in influencing farmers' votes is questionable, because the latter are much more powerfully determined by local influences, relationships and connections.[244] Nokyo's vote control thus diminishes drastically at the national level, and operates much more reliably within smaller geographical areas such as prefectural constituencies of the Upper House, or the prefectural sub-regions of LH medium-sized constituencies – which after 1994 were converted into the small-sized SMDs.[245]

The weakness of Nokyo as an electoral actor at the national level is clearly illustrated in elections to the national constituency of the Upper House. Amongst Nokyo's direct organisational representatives (i.e. *Nokyo giin*), prefectural constituency politicians almost completely monopolised its UH membership during the period from 1950 to 1983, the first election in which candidates no longer contested NC seats as individuals but as members of a party list elected on a proportional representation basis. As Table 6.6 indicates, except for 1950 when two Nokyo officials were elected, no more than one Nokyo leader won a seat in the national constituency.[246] Moreover, from the 1971 election onwards, no Nokyo officials contested NC seats. Even during the 1950–68 period when there was always at least one Nokyo candidate, Nokyo had to do its utmost to get them elected.[247] The fact that Nokyo was a nationwide organisation of farmers by no means guaranteed victory for Nokyo leaders in NC elections. Even electing one representative sometimes proved a difficult task.[248] Nokyo's vote mobilisation capacity as a national organisation was clearly much less than has been commonly supposed.[249] It did not function as a unifying electoral force in national constituency polls. The majority of farmers' votes in the national constituency were distributed amongst various LDP candidates.[250]

Thus in an electoral arena where Nokyo's size, nationwide spread and all-encompassing role in the agricultural sector should have proved valuable assets, they turned out to be electoral liabilities. Basically Nokyo was too complex and unwieldy an organisation to be able to formulate a comprehensive electoral strategy suitable for NC elections and to operate efficiently on a nationwide scale for electoral purposes. The competition between Okamura Fumijiro and Nakamura Yoshijiro for the NC 'Nokyo' seat in 1965 was a good illustration of this lack of co-ordination as a national electoral machine. Okamura and Nakamura represented different branches of the agricultural cooperative organisation, but it was generally acknowledged within Nokyo at the time that, going on previous NC experience, only one official Nokyo candidate could successfully stand. Nakamura's campaign for a Diet seat as the Zennosoren representative was regarded as a break with precedent because it meant two Nokyo candidates competing for the agricultural cooperative vote. Although a vote-splitting arrangement of sorts was agreed between the two candidates, it was insufficient to prevent competition for the Nokyo vote in some districts. Okamura as Zenkyoren Chairman agreed to utilise the backing of the insurance and trust federations, while the Nakamura faction chose to base its campaign on the economic federations. This was practicable as far as it went in terms of the assistance and support of the executive and staff of the national and prefectural branches of these organisations, but when the campaign reached the level of the rice-roots farm voter, there was an unavoidable clash of interests because of the concentration of these agricultural cooperative activities within the same units – the *tankyo*. Zennosoren, similarly, was the national political leadership organisation of *tankyo* members, creating yet another intra-organisational cleavage. As noted in chapter 3, Okamura and Nakamura ended up splitting the agricultural cooperative vote and Nakamura lost. Furthermore, Okamura's election victory was shrouded in scandal relating to illegal electoral donations.[251]

The Okamura–Nakamura election struggle exemplified an additional impediment preventing Nokyo from deploying a cohesive, well co-ordinated, national electoral strategy. As a group representing the farmers in toto, Nokyo necessarily encompasses a wide range of political convictions, connections and party alignments among its members. Membership of the agricultural cooperatives does not carry with it uniform party affiliation as it does in the case of the farmers' unions or trade unions affiliated to Sohyo; nor does Nokyo ever operate closed electoral alliances with political parties. The Okamura–Nakamura rivalry was, therefore, reinforced by political divisions: between LDP-aligned Nokyo leaders and members supporting Okamura on the one hand, and DSP-aligned leaders and members supporting Nakamura on the other. Nakamura was clearly identified within Nokyo as a progressive and as a representative of the Zennosoren, which traditionally had rather more radical orientations than its parent organisation.[252] He was also known as a spokesman for the younger generation of Nokyo leaders. Okamura on the other hand, was equally well known as a conservative oldguard Nokyo leader. He was in his seventies and had until 1965 stood with conservative party endorsement.

As emphasised earlier, the national farming electorate embraces diverse economic, commodity, and regional interests. Generally speaking separate agricultural cooperative organisations exist for each of these interests. Hence, the multitude of groupings operating under the agricultural cooperative umbrella and the divisions amongst them are a potential source of electoral as well as organisational conflict. Intra-group loyalties can and often do contribute to successful agricultural cooperative campaigns in elections, but they can have the reverse effect when, in national constituency elections under the old system, Nokyo needed to operate as a single, closely-knit, unified organisation. The Nokyo vote in the national constituency clearly revealed internal divisions and differences of interest. They surfaced not only in the 1965 in the Okamura–Nakamura debacle, but also earlier in 1956, when Okamura was making his second bid for election.[253]

Another difficulty Nokyo continues to face in NC elections is the multitude of different organisational claims on the farm vote. Although, as noted in chapter 2, farmers' organisations have not characteristically been rivalrous in terms of competition for government largesse, it is customary for a number of agricultural candidates to represent smaller, more specialised sub-divisions of the agricultural electorate, under both the old and new electoral systems in the national constituency. Former MAFF officials, for example, specialise in representing statutory and institutional interest groups in the Diet.[254] They tend to choose organisations with which they have had close dealings in the course of their careers and in whose fields of interest they have some expertise.[255] In almost every case, a strong link exists between former administrative background and current organisational representation.[256]

During the 1950s and 1960s, these ex-MAFF candidates competed directly with Nokyo representatives for a seat in the Upper House as NC members.[257] In the 1971 poll, in which no officials from Nokyo contested NC seats, the agricultural field was made up of three successful ex-MAF representatives from the National Federation of Land Improvement Industry Groups (Zendoren), the National Food Livelihood Improvement Association (Zenkoku Shokuseikatsu Kaizen Kyokai)[258] and the MAFF labour union (Zennorin Rodo Kumiai).[259]

The success of these candidates in the national constituency was in no small part due to the fact that they represented national groups organised around more concentrated interests.[260] By focusing on a single interest nationwide, they combined the advantages of geographical breadth with unity of focus. Such groups called upon the more easily identifiable and limited concerns of their membership as a basis for support. Their smaller total membership was not a disadvantage in this situation, but quite the opposite. A narrower, more concentrated interest could be more effective in mobilising votes in support of national representatives than a massive nationwide membership encompassing a diversity of interests.[261]

Success for Nokyo leaders in the national constituency generally required a combination of two types of votes: organisationally-generated votes, which derived from official positions in national agricultural cooperative organisations (this represented a vertical campaign strategy); and locality- (*jimoto*) or commodity-generated votes, which appealed to closer, more meaningful interests and connections within the Nokyo system (this formed the horizontal campaign strategy which utilised direct regional and/or commodity loyalties). Okamura's successful election in 1959 (in which he received 350,000 votes), rested on a voting base organised around the Nokyo mutual aid business and the Hokkaido-based dairy industry (he was Director of Snow Brand Milk Industries). The latter reputedly contributed 150,000 votes to his total. Even this combination, however, provided no guarantee of success for other Nokyo candidates in later years, although without it, failure was guaranteed.[262]

A number of other factors also worked to remove Nokyo's direct representation from the UH national constituency from the early 1970s onwards. Firstly, the national constituency registered without distortion the expanding size of the national electorate and the diminishing size of the total farm vote as a proportion of that electorate. According to the Executive Secretary of the Zenkoku Noseikyo, the number of Nokyo's farming members decreased to the point where Nokyo executives simply could not get enough support.[263] This factor, along with the diminishing number of candidates in the NC poll, raised the number of votes required for victory (i.e. the top 50 places) from 144,000 in 1950 to 642,554 in 1980. Combined with Nokyo's reduced efficiency as an electoral machine at the national level, these developments gradually made victory for Nokyo officials more difficult.

A second factor was the issue of party affiliation. Nokyo leaders standing in the national constituency were traditionally Independents in order to symbolise Nokyo's official position of political neutrality and the status of its candidates as distinctive Nokyo representatives.[264] In practice, however, lack of party endorsement, particularly by the LDP, reduced their chances of victory compared with prefectural constituency candidates, who were almost invariably endorsed by the ruling party.[265] For example, when Mori Yasoichi was endorsed by the LDP for the first time in 1968, he recorded his highest vote tally ever, although it was also his first election as Zenchu Chairman (see Table 6.6). Nevertheless, the number of so-called 'Diet members from Nokyo' (*Nokyo no shusshinsha*) in the national constituency slumped to zero with his departure in 1974.[266] From that time on, all *Nokyo giin* represented UH prefectural constituencies and LH districts, with the agricultural cooperative interest in the UH national constituency subsumed within a bloc of so-called general agricultural votes (as opposed to land improvement votes) represented by an ex-MAFF bureaucrat-turned LDP politician.[267] Indeed, overall agricultural representation in the national constituency was reduced to a total of two Diet members.

Nokyo's electoral strength is not, therefore, evident on a national scale as a specific-purpose, organisationally-centred interest. It lies in the regional localities and is generated very much by community-based connections between politicians and the agricultural cooperatives as territorial organisations. This is the main reason, for example, why most *Nokyo giin* are politicians who have built up a strong support base in local politics and moved up the scale of national political office over time. It is also the reason why

Table 6.6 Success rates of national constituency Nokyo candidates, 1950–80

Election	Nokyo candidate	Official position(s) in Nokyo	Party	Votes received	Placing
1950	Ishikawa Seiichi	Kamikawa Nokyo Chairman / Zennoseiren Vice-Chairman / Hokkaido Nomin Domei Chairman	Farmers' Co-op Party/Independent	238,339	25[a]
	Mori Yasoichi	Zenhanren Manager	Green Breeze Society	150,244	51[b]
	Kuroda Shinichiro	Zenkoren Vice-Chairman	Independent	102,548	63 Lost
	Hirao Ujiro	Zenshiren Manager	Independent	42,771	172 Lost
	Okita Tadayoshi	Zenhanren Vice-Chairman	Independent	11,039	285 Lost
			Total	544,941	
1953	Sekine Kyuzo	Zenyoren Chairman	Liberal	164,701	49
	Okamura Fumijiro	Zenyoren Chairman	Progressive	151,859	59 Lost
			Total	316,560	
1956	(Ishiguro Tadayuki)[c]	Zennoren Chairman	Independent	283,469	37
	Mori Yasoichi	Zenhanren Manager			
		Aichi *kenchu* Chairman	Green Breeze Society	259,010	46
	Okamura Fumijiro	Zenkyoren Chairman	LDP	222,737	60 Lost
	Mori Masao	Former Hokkaido *kenchu* Vice-Chairman	JSP	152,437	93 Lost
			Total	634,184	

Year	Name	Position	Party	Votes	Result
1959	Okamura Fumijiro	Zenkyoren Chairman	LDP	350,124	35
	Takemasa Soichiro	Saitama *kenchu* Chairman	LDP	158,792	72 Lost
			Total	508,916	
1962	Mori Yasoichi	Zenchu Director	Independent	536,727	19
		Aichi *kenchu* Chairman	Total	536,727	
1965	Okamura Fumijiro	Zenkyoren Chairman	Independent	565,000	25
	(Nakamura Yoshijiro)	Zennosoren Secretary-General	DSP	273,000	67 Lost
			Total	838,000	
1968	Mori Yasoichi	Zenchu Chairman	LDP	720,000	13
			Total	720,000	
1971	—		—	—	—
1974	—		—	—	—
1977	—		—	—	—
1980	—		—	—	—

Notes:

a According to Tanaka, Ishikawa received 228,010 votes, and was placed 24th. *Nihon no Nokyo*, p. 43.

b Tanaka puts Mori Yasoichi in 50th place. *Nihon no Nokyo*, p, 436.

c Those candidates whose names have been entered in brackets were standing as representatives of farmers' political leagues affiliated to Nokyo and therefore they should be considered recipients of a certain proportion of the Nokyo vote.

Source: Vote tallies: *Asahi Nenkan*, relevant years; *Asahi Shinbun*, 6 June 1950.

Nokyo provides support not only for its own officials who enter politics, but for sympathetic politicians in general. The pattern of Nokyo's electoral support contrasts with the other statutory interest groups and the institutional interest groups which focus on assisting their own leaders almost exclusively. Many of these are not politicians with careers in local politics at all, but with former careers in the national bureaucracy. This bureaucratic connection generates a specific value when it comes to the subsidy acquisition process.[268]

It is also true that the vote-gathering powers of the agricultural cooperatives have waned over time. This general observation applies not only with respect to the performance of Nokyo leaders in the national constituency of the Upper House, but across the board with respect to all Nokyo-backed candidates in all types of constituencies. In 1974 for example, Zenchu Chairman Miyawaki Asao felt confident enough to claim that if a prefectural Nokyo federation chairman were selected as a candidate to run for electoral office, he would seldom fail to achieve this goal. Similarly, in a gubernatorial election, a Nokyo-recommended candidate would win in nine cases out of 10.[269] Few Nokyo leaders would dare to make such claims these days. In fact, by the mid-1980s, analysts were reporting that although in some regions agricultural cooperatives could still control farmers' votes and win a seat for their favoured candidate, in general, farmers' votes were becoming less and less effectively organised by Nokyo.[270] In 1990, the Kumamoto Farmers' Political League admitted that all the candidates it had recommended in the LH election that year had failed, requiring a fundamental reform of the league and a change of title.[271]

On the other hand, the 1990 questionnaire survey undertaken by the author revealed that, amongst the Diet members who responded, a majority (or 56 per cent of cases) had requested the backing of agricultural cooperative organisations as opposed to 28 per cent of cases where it was offered rather than requested (the remainder did not answer). The fact that candidates were more likely than the agricultural cooperatives to take the initiative in seeking support suggests that agricultural cooperative electoral backing was valued by candidates.

Furthermore, almost all respondents who received agricultural cooperative support regarded it as useful to their election (94 per cent of cases). Estimates of just how useful varied, however. The majority had no idea; others maintained that the proportion of their total vote owed to the agricultural cooperatives was anything from 0.5 per cent to 60 per cent.[272] When asked how they evaluated this support in general terms, most respondents had a healthy respect for the electoral power of the agricultural cooperatives. A total of 57 (or 74 per cent) of respondents agreed that Nokyo wielded considerable electoral power; 11 or 14 per cent disagreed; the remainder either did not know or did not answer the question.[273]

Generally speaking what has persisted is the perception that Nokyo's voting power is much greater in a negative rather than a positive sense.

Negative voting power means that the agricultural cooperatives can prevent a particular candidate from being elected by withdrawing their support, but they do not have sufficient power to guarantee the success of a chosen candidate. As a Zenchu official explains: 'It is often said that while we can't give enough votes for a candidate to be elected, we can pull him from power if he fails to act profitably for us.'[274] Former Zenchu Chairman, Horiuchi Tomotsugu, was also quoted as saying that 'even if we cannot get specific Diet members elected, we can ensure their defeat'.[275]

Although these comments have been interpreted as symbolising the retreat of Nokyo's power to influence votes,[276] Nokyo's reputed negative voting power has tended to linger on in the belief amongst farm politicians that 'to harm Nokyo leads to certain political death'.[277] The actions and motivations of rural Diet members appear to be very much influenced by their belief that 'if one should lose the sympathy and support of the agricultural cooperative unions, one would be sure to lose the elections'.[278] Even negative voting power can be a substantial power because of the view that 'even if LDP politicians cannot get themselves elected with farm support only, a concerted effort by Nokyo can easily ruin someone's career.'[279] One Nokyo executive was quoted as saying: 'I don't know if one can honestly say whether a politician that Nokyo is promoting will be elected for sure. But, if Nokyo decides that a candidate will lose, then he'll lose all right.'[280]

Objectively speaking, these views also have some basis in fact as Table 5.2 and the associated discussion suggest. If organised, the so-called 'Nokyo vote' can still be a substantial force in some districts. Diet members standing in rural seats cannot afford to lose the farmers' votes under the influence of agricultural cooperative leaders and Nokyo knows this very well.[281] To some extent, therefore, politicians have remained afraid of Nokyo because of the large number of potential votes under its organisational umbrella and its reputed powers of vote control. Even if they want to criticise Nokyo, they cannot openly do so for this reason.[282] Given these considerations, Nokyo's threat to use its vote mobilisation power may be sufficient to bring politicians standing for election in rural and semi-rural constituencies into line.

Demonstrations of farmers' and Nokyo's voting power

The power of farmers' votes, and particularly the power of votes organised by Nokyo and its associated groupings can be demonstrated in two ways: by providing evidence of their having made a positive contribution to the successful election of Diet candidates, and conversely, by providing evidence of their having contributed to the electoral failure of Diet candidates. On the positive side, electoral backing from the agricultural cooperatives was, for example, reputedly the decisive factor ensuring victory for 18 candidates in the LDP, six in the JSP and two Independent candidates in the 1958 LH election.[283]

Another example from the late 1970s provides a useful illustration of

Nokyo's vote-gathering capacities when it was at the height of its electoral powers. In the 11th UH election in July 1977, the two-seat Kumamoto district witnessed a savage contest amongst three candidates (two endorsed by the LDP and one from the JSP). One of the conservative candidates was Miyoshi Shinji, a former MAFF Vice-Minister who was backed by agricultural organ- isations and the other was a young Hosokawa Morihiro, who had moved from the national constituency and was well-known as the descendent of the Hosokawa clan. Nokyo set up election campaign workforces (*sentai*) all over the prefecture in order to stage the campaign for Miyoshi, who was not well- known in the district, despite his former career as Vice-Minister. Nokyo deployed a strategy of infiltrating rice-roots rural communities, establishing an election campaign workforce in each school district to recommend its candidate and also obtaining the recommendation of local executives and officials (of prefectural government and other organisations in the local community) who were recruited as surrogate campaigners. As a result, Miyoshi obtained the most votes in almost all districts and won one of the seats. Hosokawa won the other and the JSP candidate lost the seat which the party had held for years.[284]

These days, one possible test of Nokyo's vote power is the success rate of candidates recommended by Nokyo's political organisations. In 1995, Zenkoku Noseikyo recommended 34 candidates (most of whom were also recommended by prefectural farmers' political leagues in the relevant con- stituencies): 29 were successful, representing an 85 per cent success rate. It also placed Nokyo-backed politicians in 27 of the 76 prefectural constituencies in the Upper House (or more than a third of the total), and two in the national constituency. In the 1996 LH elections, of the 225 candidates recommended by Zenkoku Noseikyo, 180 were successfully elected (an 80 per cent success rate), 160 in the single-member districts and 20 in the PR districts. In addition, another 22 candidates recommended only by the prefectural *noseiren* were also elected.[285] In the 1998 UH election, the success rate of candidates recommended by Zenkoku Noseikyo reflected the LDP's relatively poor performance at the polls, given that all but three of the recommended candi- dates were from the LDP. Of the 52 endorsed by the National Council, only 27 (or just over a half) won seats in the UH (one for the national constituency; all the rest for prefectural constituencies), and all of these were from the LDP.

As far as the farmers' and Nokyo's negative voting power are concerned, the evidence is both weightier and somewhat clearer. At various times, the farmers have reacted at the polls to unpopular agricultural policies by with- drawing their support for LDP candidates. Nokyo organisations have been behind some of the revolts against LDP candidates leading to their electoral failure.

The fact that farmers take agricultural policy considerations into account when deciding their vote has been substantiated by the two polls conducted amongst Nokyo's farmer-members in 1994. Amongst those who responded to the survey, some 80 per cent reported that they attached great or fair importance to agricultural policy in voting.[286] From time to time, the Japanese media have also revealed that the government's agricultural policies were spreading widespread mistrust and dissatisfaction amongst the agricultural population.

The fundamental question is, however, whether such dissatisfaction rebounds to the disadvantage of the LDP in the polls. Historical evidence in later years suggests that it takes a lot to shift the political allegiance of farmers from LDP to non-LDP candidates. The main fear amongst farmers and agricultural organisations is that if they do not vote for ruling party candidates, they will have no representatives in the Diet who can speak for the interests of farmers and farmers' organisations, particularly in policymaking contexts. As Yanagida explains, farmers cling to the idea that they must send someone to the Diet who can represent their interests effectively, although they criticise the LDP's agricultural policies.[287]

These fears, however, are not always sufficient to prevent small- to large-scale defections from LDP candidates to those affiliated with other parties, particularly the JSP. Signs of disaffection amongst farmers with LDP policies and their electoral consequences have surfaced in numerous elections over the years.[288] Trends in LDP support rates in some rural constituencies have dwindled following unpopular agricultural policy decisions, failures and 'shocks' of various kinds, such as freezing and lowering agricultural support prices (particularly the producer rice price), market opening moves, insufficient alleviation of farm debt, rice acreage reduction directives and so on. The following analysis provides a number of examples where farm votes have shifted from LDP candidates to those from other parties in response to this disaffection, although the picture is far from conclusive over time.

Ono argues that LDP performance in rural electorates in both the 1969 and 1974 general elections was significantly affected by LDP rice policies. He claims that in the 1969 LH elections, the LDP's share of votes dipped in all prefectures in Tohoku except for Iwate and Miyagi because of the producer rice price freeze and the unpopularity of the *gentan* amongst rice farmers.[289] Prior to this election, Nokyo in the name of the combined conference of the National and Prefectural Nokyo Rice Policy Headquarters' Chairmen, made a representation to the LDP to the effect that 'we cannot help but confront the LDP through the election'.[290] This was the first time Nokyo had explicitly threatened to use the electoral weapon against the ruling party.[291] In the 1974 UH election, the LDP won only seven more seats than the Opposition parties and thus equilibrium between the ruling and Opposition parties in the Diet (*hokaku hakuchu*) ensued. According to Ono, this was because of the LDP's electoral failure in rice-producing areas, which gave rise to farmers' dissatisfaction with government rice price policies.[292]

Okamoto makes similar observations about the 1971 UH election. Not only did the LDP's support rate drop in the cities in this election, it also flagged in rural areas. He attributed the LDP's 'defeat' to the poverty of its agricultural policies symbolised by the rice acreage reduction policy (*gentan seisaku*), but also including the rice price freeze and the liberalisation of agricultural products, particularly grapefruit. The former saw support for the LDP fall amongst the rice-producing prefectures of Akita, Miyagi, Fukushima, Ibaraki, Niigata, Fukui, Kumamoto and Oita. The latter saw a reduction in the LDP vote in the fruit-producing belt extending from Ehime, Yamanashi, Shizuoka, Shimane, Hiroshima and Yamaguchi to Oita and Kumamoto. What is more, votes critical of the LDP flowed into the progressive camp.[293]

In another example, the Socialist candidate reportedly overwhelmed the LDP candidate in some agricultural areas in Yamagata Prefecture in the 1977 UH election because farmers were dissatisfied with the agricultural policy of the LDP.[294] At the same time, another observer of developments in the Tohoku region commented that, while agricultural villages were no longer a stable source of votes for the conservatives, this did not mean that farmers had switched their support to the Opposition parties. Although farmers were dissatisfied with LDP agricultural policies, they did not believe the 'flowery words' of the Opposition parties either.[295]

A later study analysed the results of the 1983 LH elections in rural constituencies in the light of a series of agricultural policy 'shocks' sustained by farmers in the early 1980s. These included the freezing of the producer rice price, sustained rice acreage cutbacks and the impending US–Japan agreement on expanding the import quota for beef and citrus. The study concluded that the 1983 election results provided no clear indication of a rural backlash against the LDP. On the one hand, the ruling party did not increase seats in any constituencies in Hokkaido and Tohoku where farming regions were prominent. On the other hand, in other farming regions such as Niigata, Nagano, Wakayama, Kagawa and Tottori, the LDP gained an additional seat in each prefecture.[296] These observations were supported by more systematic analysis of the LDP's polling rate in the 1983 LH election in the 23 prefectures with 30 per cent or more of the total eligible voters residing in farm households. The LDP's support rate decreased in 13 of these prefectures but increased in 10. Moreover, it expanded in five out of the top seven agricultural prefectures (Nagano, Akira, Iwate, Tottori and Yamanashi).

The lack of uniformity in voting trends across different regions underscores the fact that the farm vote is not monolithic and farmers in each district have their own interests.[297] It also indicates that farmers' votes are tied in the first instance to particular individuals rather than particular parties. Local, personalistic factors, relationships of patronage and the nature of the connections between farmers' organisations and individual politicians can counterbalance and even neutralise the electoral effects of agricultural policy decisions.

The absence of uniformity is consistent with particularistic rather than general factors, and region-specific rather than national (i.e. government agricultural policy) factors being critical to the performance of individual LDP candidates in rural areas. The political consciousness of the farmers is defined not only by their response to the government's agricultural production, price support and trade policies at a general level, but also by their ties to individual politicians, particularly as these embody the need for subsidies for agricultural and public works which benefit local regions.[298] This suggests that whatever decision the LDP may make in agricultural policy, its electoral effects can be mitigated by special arrangements and deals over subsidies in particular constituencies.[299] In the event of unpopular policy decisions, arrangements can be made for political compensation, meaning agricultural and public works projects that the LDP funds in particular regions. This represents a form of vote-buying par excellence.[300]

This argument also suggests that because of fixed ties between farm interests and candidates based on personalistic considerations and those relating to patronage and 'regional egotism', electoral threats from the farmers to cast their votes for alternative candidates lack credibility. Voting for an Opposition party candidate yields no potential gains because of the historically slim chance of Opposition parties acquiring power over subsidy distribution. The farmers and agricultural cooperatives have been inexorably tied to LDP candidates through the binds of patronage politics, personalised connections and obligations built up over a long period.

In some cases, however, the continuous operation of such a system over many decades is not sufficient to override widespread disaffection amongst the farmers with LDP agricultural policies. The 1989 UH elections provides the best example in recent times of a full-scale, Nokyo-led farmers' electoral revolt against the LDP. Farmers' support for the LDP sank from 74 per cent in 1985 to 59 per cent in 1989.[301] In retrospect, the ground was laid by the series of policies the ruling party launched in the years preceding the election which struck at the very heart of Japan's agricultural support and protection system. Indeed these were described by the JCP as an LDP attack on its own support base.[302] The writing was already on the wall in a 1987 by-election for an UH prefectural seat in Iwate, in which farmers' dissatisfaction with the LDP manifested itself in a JSP victory.[303]

For rice farmers, no relief could be found from the rice acreage reduction policies which, by the late 1980s, averaged 27 per cent nationwide and which hit the larger-scale, more efficient rice farmers harder than the small-scale, inefficient producers. In 1985 and 1986 the producer rice price was frozen, then in 1987 and 1988 it was actually cut – by 5.95 per cent in 1987 and 4.6 per cent in 1988. These measures impacted on small-scale, inefficient producers more than on the larger-scale, more efficient producers who channelled a lot of their product through the IDR system. The 1987 decision to lower the producer rice price was particularly unpopular because it was the first reduction in 31 years, and because it exited fears about what it symbolised for rice farmers generally.[304] Furthermore, a new basis for calculating the producer rice price was devised by the MAFF and approved by the LDP in which farm households owning more than five ha of farm land would become the standard for calculating production costs. This category of farm household was more efficient that the average rice-producing farm household but comprised less than 1 per cent of farm households. Accordingly, the proposal was viewed as an attempt to change the formula so that further cuts in the producer rice price could be facilitated.[305]

In consequence of this series of policy decisions, farmers felt squeezed between rice acreage reduction policies that increased the costs of rice production (because they reduced economies of scale), and the policy of holding down or lowering the producer rice price which reduced their margins even further. Furthermore, given the text of the April 1989 agreement reached at the UR Mid-Term Review,[306] which stated that member countries would 'put into effect gradually large scale cutbacks in protection and support to agriculture', it became clear in the eyes of Japanese rice farmers that an opening of the Japanese rice market was inevitable.[307]

Other unpopular decisions by the LDP around this period were the 1986 decision to lower the guaranteed price of raw milk for processing for the first time (although only marginally), trade liberalisation for a group of eight miscellaneous agricultural product categories in February 1988,[308] and the June 1988 agreement to liberalise beef and citrus in 1991.[309] Beef liberalisation in particular anticipated a further lowering of livestock support prices at a time when, according to results of a survey conducted by Zenchu and made public in 1986, around 60 per cent of livestock enterprises in the country were depressed and burdened with huge debts.[310] Following the government's size expansion policy, livestock farmers had installed modernised cattle-raising facilities at great cost with borrowed money only to be hit by stagnation in the market prices of their products.[311] Low prices, in turn, were due to the unrelenting expansion in the beef quotas as a result of both the 1984 and 1988 beef import agreements. The biggest rise in Japan's agricultural imports in 1988 over 1987 was in beef – amounting to a 20.2 per cent increment to 265,000 tonnes with the value of the imports standing at $1.19 billion (a 49.2 per cent increase).[312] Moreover, cattle prices were predicted to fall even further with the quota abolition and tariffication due on 1 April 1991.[313]

Farmers' opposition to the government's agricultural policies clearly registered in the disastrous performance of the LDP in the 1989 UH election. A severe erosion of the LDP's farm support base took place with a wholesale revolt of the agricultural cooperatives against LDP candidates in some key rural constituencies. Looking at the national trends, the LDP's percentage share of rural and semi-rural seats collapsed from 85.7 per cent to 14.3 per cent and from 74.1 per cent to 29.6 per cent respectively. The percentage vote won by the LDP in rural and semi-rural constituencies collapsed from 52.3 per cent to 34.9 per cent and from 56.0 per cent to 39.1 per cent respectively (see Table 5.12).

The dissatisfaction amongst farmers with the LDP was profound, particularly in areas where specific commodity producers were being hard hit by the changes in government policy. For example, in the rice-producing regions of Niigata, where good quality rice was grown for distribution through the IDR system and where farmers tended to be specialist rice producers working larger than average plots of land, the prospects for rice liberalisation at the GATT and the liberalisation of beef and citrus created a strong sense amongst so-called 'core farmers' that farming was an occupation without a future. They felt considerable anxiety about whether they would have to relinquish agriculture altogether.[314] At the centre of the anti-LDP movement were the *seinenbu* whose members comprised many of these core farmers who were concerned with the present and future of agriculture. In some cases, they revolted against the Nokyo bosses who had strong ties with the LDP.[315]

According to one Niigata rice farmer who produced good quality rice (*koshihikari*) on five or so ha of land, farmers were worried about how far the rice price would fall, whether agricultural land would be expanded and whether farmers would be able to live on agricultural income alone. He described the general attitude of Niigata farmers towards the LDP in the following terms: 'There are feelings of distrust towards the LDP's agricultural policies. Apart from the House of Representatives where you write down an individual's name on the ballot paper, in the proportional representation constituency, there is resistance to writing down the name of the LDP'.[316]

The Recruit scandal and the imposition of the 3 per cent consumption tax hardened the attitudes of the farmers even further, particularly part-time farmers whose major source of income was non-agricultural occupations and who were as much consumers as producers.[317] According to the local secretary of a Niigata LDP Diet member: 'the farmers were compelled to put up with the government's policy, then the Recruit scandal broke out like another bad blow. This was double trouble: the LDP's unpopular farming policy and the Recruit scandal. The LDP might lose voters if they do not think of the farmers. To be honest, I would like to get rid of the name plate of the LDP'.[318]

The LDP's electoral difficulties in rural areas manifested themselves in the defections of agricultural cooperative organisations from LDP candidates in a number of key farming constituencies. As observed by the Chairman of the JCP's Farmers' and Fisherpersons' Bureau in 1988: 'One special feature of the situation in rural areas is that Nokyo management (*kanbu*) has also begun to have doubts about the LDP's agricultural policy'.[319] The press also reported that: 'The farmers have become so hostile to the LDP that one-third of their local organisations have declared that they no longer support the party.'[320] The JSP claimed that their candidates were invited to talk to Nokyo youth division meetings and Nokyo members were happy to hear the talks. At the time it was considered a big change for people in agricultural regions to come to hear the views of other political parties on agriculture.

The LDP began a direct dialogue with the farmers in an attempt to stem the tide of defection by agricultural cooperative organisations. It launched a series of regional pilgrimages to the countryside in the lead-up to the elections in order to try and promote discussions directly between LDP agricultural leaders and dissatisfied farmers. This counter-strategy, however, failed to halt the LDP's sliding support amongst farmers. The elections were marked by active and widespread campaigning against LDP candidates by the *seinenbu*, sufficiently angered by the government's agricultural policies to challenge their organisations' customary support for conservative candidates. The Chairman of the Niigata Prefecture Nokyo Youth League, which had 5,000 members, declared his organisation's position in March 1989: 'No support for LDP candidates in the national and prefectural constituencies of the Upper House', complaining that the league 'had gone past the stage of asking the LDP about such matters as the cuts in the rice price and rice liberalisation. The feelings of the farmers who are at their wits end have exploded.'[321] As it happened, the LDP retained its customary Niigata seat, although the LDP candidate traded places with the JSP candidate for first place in the polls.

In Iwate Prefecture, where many middle-scale rice-producing farmers had suffered from cold weather damage in 1988, the prefectural Nokyo Youth Organisation Council (with 5,281 members) decided for the first time to 'divorce' the LDP, advising its members: 'Don't support the LDP in the proportional representation electorate, and in the prefectural constituency, vote how you like – it is an independent vote'.[322] When the resolution was taken not to give voting direction to farmers, the chairman of the organisation said: 'The feeling is that it is no longer possible to produce rice. The LDP's policy really does not consider the farmers. The LDP at any rate thinks that Nokyo young people are only making a fuss. But this is not only the feeling of the farmers. The roots are very deep.'[323] In response to LDP Diet members' earlier expressions of support for agricultural trade liberalisation, the Nokyo women's division in Iwate declared: 'We cannot cooperate with a party that has members who make such rash statements', and demanded a split with the party in the prefectural assembly.[324]

Press reports cited many other cases of defection from the LDP by Nokyo groups, notably the agreement by the Kagoshima Prefecture Central Union and the prefectural farmers' political league (with 130,000 members) to back an Independent, the former governor Kamada Kaname, as their own candidate. In fact, the two LDP-endorsed candidates, the former Director-General of the MCA and the Kagoshima LDP Prefectural Federation Youth Bureau Chief, ended up withdrawing their candidacies because of opposition from Nokyo-based groups.[325] In the end, the LDP's endorsement went to Kamada who emerged the biggest vote-winner in the election.

Similar defections occurred in other parts of rural Japan. In Aomori the prefectural *noseiren* and other Nokyo groups put forward their own Independent candidate; in Iwate Prefecture, the Kitakami City Nokyo youth division (191 members) decided not to support LDP candidates in national, gubernatorial and prefectural elections, only in city elections; in Miyagi the prefectural Nokyo youth league (7,300 members) decided not to support the LDP in the national constituency and the Ozaki district Nokyo youth liaison council decided not to support LDP candidates in the local constituency; in Akita the prefectural Nokyo youth division council (6,200 members) decided not to recommend the LDP, thus giving members a 'free vote' in both the national and prefectural constituencies and the prefectural *noseiren* (to which 120 agricultural cooperatives belonged) decided on a 'free vote' in the prefectural constituency; in Yamagata the prefectural Nokyo youth organisation council (5,600 members) decided not to support the LDP in the national constituency and endorsed their own candidate in the prefectural constituency;[326] the Niitsu City Nokyo in Niigata (1,440 households) decided not to vote for LDP candidates, and the Niitsu City Nokyo General Representatives' Council decided not to support the LDP after the UH election; in Fukuoka the prefectural Nokyo youth division council decided not to support the LDP in the national constituency, as did the prefectural Nokyo youth division council in Saga Prefecture; in Nagasaki, the *noseiren* decided to allow a 'free vote' in the national constituency; and in Oita the prefectural Nokyo youth organisation council (310 members) decided not to support the LDP in the national constituency and to allow a 'free vote' in the prefectural constituency.[327]

Another 31 agricultural cooperative organisations in 17 prefectures passed resolutions on the selection of their own candidates or non-support for the LDP.[328] The 'free vote' advocated by the *seinenbu* in many districts was a direct criticism of the LDP, but from another perspective, it was also a criticism of Zenchu and its acceptance of government policy changes.[329] In some constituencies, the *noseiren* tried to organise support for the LDP, but the youth divisions decided to support other candidates. According to one report, the *noseiren* tried to rally votes by referring to the LDP's decision not to lower the rice price, but their political power amongst farmers was weakened by the latter's disillusionment with LDP agricultural policy.[330] The success rate of Zenkoku Noseikyo and prefectural *noseiren*-recommended candidates was only fair. A total of 15 prefectural agricultural policy organisations recommended 17 candidates, who were subsequently endorsed by the National Council in an official statement of recommendation.[331] Of the 17 recommended candidates, only six were elected.[332] One source within Nokyo claimed that lower-level members ignored Nokyo leaders' commands in the election campaign and acted independently in their towns and villages.[333]

The drastic reduction in support for the LDP in rural constituencies quite clearly contributed to the loss of the party's UH majority in this election, particularly in the single-member prefectural constituencies most of which were agricultural prefectures. In these districts, the LDP recorded three wins and 23 losses.[334] Media commentary summed up the cause and effect as follows: 'Full-time farmers, young members of the agricultural cooperatives and other voters in the rice-growing areas of the Tohoku region, in the major mandarin-producing areas of Shikoku and in the livestock-and citrus-producing areas of Kyushu cast their ballots against the LDP to punish the party in this election.'[335] The LDP lost six out of seven seats in Tohoku, all four in Shikoku, and eight out of 11 seats in Kyushu.

By prefecture, the LDP lost to the JSP the single-member rural constituencies of Iwate and Akita and the semi-rural constituencies of Miyagi and

Fukushima (a two-member constituency where the LDP lost one seat to the JSP). All were in prominent rice-producing regions. It also lost to the JSP the semi-rural seats of Kagawa in Shikoku (a citrus-producing region) and Miyazaki (a beef-producing region) in Kyushu. In fact an LDP candidate did not even contest this seat.

Elsewhere the ruling party lost to Rengo a rural seat in the rice-producing prefecture of Yamagata, and six semi-rural seats in Fukui, Yamanashi, Gifu, Mie, Shiga and Tokushima (a *mikan*-producing area of Shikoku).[336] Other rural seats went to Independents (in Tottori and Shimane)[337] and amongst semi-rural seats, two in the beef-producing region of Kumamoto.[338] Amongst semi-urban seats with key agricultural areas, two were lost in the key *mikan*-producing areas of Ehime (to a Rengo candidate), Kochi (to a JSP candidate) and Shizuoka (to an Independent candidate), the two seats in Ishikawa and Yamaguchi (to Rengo and JSP candidates respectively), one seat in Gumma (to a JSP candidate) and in Kyushu, the seat of Nagasaki also to a JSP candidate. The biggest falls in the LDP support rate came in the rice-producing regions of Northern Japan (in Miyagi and Iwate prefectures where the LDP's vote slumped by 24.2 per cent and 21.8 per cent respectively), in the mandarin-producing prefecture of Ehime (where it fell by 23.6 per cent) and in the beef- and fruit-producing prefecture of Nagasaki (where it slipped by 24.9 per cent).[339]

LDP Diet members against whom specific campaigns by agricultural cooperative organisations were conducted and who were defeated in the election were the following: in Mie Prefecture, Mizutani Tsutomu, the incumbent MAFF Parliamentary Vice-Minister lost his seat held since 1983; in Ehime, Higaki Tokutaro, a senior adviser to the LDP's CAPIC, and former Director-General of the Food Agency and MAFF Vice-Minister,[340] was supported by the prefectural *noseiren* and the prefectural Fruit Political League, but lost the support of fruit growers and their 4,000-member association in the southern part of the prefecture;[341] in Tohoku, the youth divisions of the agricultural cooperatives largely decided not to support the LDP and the LDP candidate Hoshi Choji (a former MAFF Parliamentary Vice-Minister and Chairman of the LDP's Fisheries Division) lost a Miyagi Prefecture seat. In Yamagata Prefecture, Furuya Keiyu, chairman of agricultural structural and rural projects within the LDP also lost his seat. In Aomori Prefecture, the LDP candidate Matsuo Kanpei, a Nokyo politician, lost the seat to JSP-backed Independent candidate Mikami Takao, who was Secretary-General of the Aomori Prefecture Nomin Seiji Renmei. He won a seat for the first time on a platform opposing nuclear power plants in the region and the LDP's agricultural policies.

Other key agricultural candidates who were defeated included Miyajima Hiroshi, the former Chairman of the Nagasaki Prefecture Nokyo Credit Federation; Urata Masaru, Chairman of Kumamoto Prefecture Agricultural Policy Promotion Association (the prefectural *noseiren*); Soeta Masutaro, the former Chairman of the National Sericulture Nokyo Federation and

Fukushima Prefecture Sericulture Nokyo Federation; and Kamenaga Tomoyoshi, former MAFF Vice-Minister, in Tokushima Prefecture.[342]

These failures were of two main types: candidates who were associated with the government's agricultural policy (Mizutani-Mie, Higaki-Ehime, Hoshi-Miyagi, Furuya-Yamagata and Kamenaga-Tokushima) and those who were traditional Nokyo representatives in the Diet (Matsuo-Aomori, Miyajima-Nagasaki, Urata-Kumamoto and Soeta-Fukushima). Most of these failures were attributable to the direct campaigns against these candidates by farmers and farmers' groups, especially Nokyo youth groups.

In the case of Urata from Kumamoto, for example, the Kumamoto Nokyo Seisonenbu (the Youth and Middle-Aged Division) with 12,000 members protested against the LDP's agricultural policy and bossy control of agricultural organisations and tried to field its own candidate. The attempt failed, however, because of counter-pressure from the LDP prefectural federation and Nokyo executive leaders. When Urata, who was the LDP candidate and who was officially recommended by the Kumamoto Prefecture Nomin Seiji Renmei, visited each *nokyo* in the prefecture, he was even asked to leave the LDP. Many Nokyo members said that they did not want to vote for the LDP. Some *seisonenbu* organised panel discussions with all candidates including the JCP candidate, which was very unusual in conservative Kumamoto. Just before the official notice of the UH election, the Kumamoto Nokyo Seisonenbu finally decided to leave it to members to decide by themselves whom they would vote for. Urata's failure was attributed not only to dissatisfaction with the LDP's agricultural policy but also the readiness of local Nokyo leaders to ignore commands from the top to put pressure on members to vote for the LDP candidate because of insecurity over their own positions if they ignored members' anti-LDP feelings.[343]

In the case of Higaki, he was regarded as one of the party's top agricultural policy experts, who had served 18 years as an UH member initially for the national constituency and then for Ehime Prefecture. His loss after three consecutive wins ended the LDP's domination of this *mikan*-growing region. Opposition to the LDP in this prefecture became apparent from mid-April, with the most vocal criticism coming from young mandarin farmers in the Nanyo district via its Fruit Tree Comrades' Association. In April 1989, this group with 3,600 members decided not to support the LDP and specifically Higaki in the UH election, whereupon the LDP prefectural federation put pressure on eight vegetable and fruit *nokyo* through their league (*seika renmei*) to support Higaki. Only one of these confirmed its support for Higaki.[344] At the executive committee of Ehime *noseiren* in April, a *kenchu* leader's request for support for Higaki was not accepted. In the same month, at the general meeting of the Ehime Nokyo Youth and Middle-Aged League (Seisonen Renmei), 48 representatives (from various *seisonen renmei* around the prefecture) decided that their organisation would be politically neutral in the election.[345] By the end of June, the youth division of the Shuso cooperative in the rice- and wheat-growing areas of the prefecture announced its support for Ikeda Osamu of Rengo.

The campaign indicated that conflicting decisions were being made within Nokyo groups in the prefecture about whom they should support and that commands from the top were not necessarily accepted.[346] The final result also showed that young farmers' discontent with the government's decision to liberalise the citrus market was even greater than anticipated. Unlike the situation with beef, no measures were introduced to compensate farmers for prospective liberalisation of this market. The Vice-Chairman of the Hizuchi Fruit Growers' Cooperative youth division said: 'The decision to liberalize imports of oranges has awakened young people to politics. The concrete action that they chose to take was to seek a sense of balance. Liberalization was decided without any explanation and without any vision. The dissatisfaction with and concern about relying on the ruling party outweighed the need to depend on Mr. Higaki.'[347]

Even though Ehime *kenchu* decided to support Higaki, its chairman commented: 'There was too much feeling against the LDP. Not only was there distrust of the party's agricultural policies, but there was also dissatisfaction with the consumption tax. The LDP should humbly accept the fact that the dismay with its earlier agricultural policies came to a head in this way.'[348] The Vice-Chairman of the Hizuchi Fruit Growers' Fellowship Association described the feeling in the area just before the government decided to liberalize oranges: 'In competition with the other local orange-producing areas, we were confident of our superiority, but there was a growing fear about the aggression from outside the country and about what was in store for us in the future.'[349] He added: 'In many of the past elections, farmers voted according to what their organizations decided, but this time, they voted according to their conscience.'[350] His remark was indicative of a certain disregard amongst farmers for what their own organisations were recommending in some cases.

As noted earlier, although many Nokyo and *noseiren* executives still supported the LDP, the *seinenbu*, *fujinbu* and others who were the actual working force in the election campaign rebelled. In particular, the main actor in the rebellions was the *seinenbu* whose activities influenced the *fujinbu*.[351] Although these groups organised only about 10 per cent of Nokyo members, they were the chief instruments of vote-collection and their influence on voting was very strong.[352] One reason for this was that the younger generation in the Nokyo *seinenbu* led discussions about agricultural policy as well as other issues at home and thus influenced their family members' voting.[353] They also had a good network of liaison and contacts all over Japan.[354]

The electoral support profile of the agricultural sector thus changed significantly in 1989, with the unravelling of the supportive relationship between the LDP and its traditional allies in the countryside as 'betrayed' farmers avenged themselves on the party. The LDP paid the political price of its moves to liberalise Japanese agriculture from its protective embrace. Both the farmers and groups within Nokyo in farming regions demonstrated that they were capable not only of threats but also effective action to direct their political allegiance away from LDP candidates in order to register a protest against government policy. For the first time, many farmers voted against the party they had supported for 30 years. They did not like the LDP's agricultural policy and they wanted to deliver a strong message.

A public opinion poll conducted by NHK just prior to the election revealed the extent of the downturn in support for the LDP amongst voters in the agriculture, forestry and fisheries sector.[355] Of the 67.7 per cent of this category that supported the LDP, only 18.7 per cent 'strongly supported' the ruling party (compared with 30.2 per cent in 1986), while 32.1 per cent 'generally supported' the LDP (compared with 40.4 per cent in 1986). The remainder (16.9 per cent) 'did not give much support'.[356] It was the contraction in the 'strongly supportive' group which suggested that core supporters of the LDP had withdrawn their vote in the 1989 elections. This sentiment translated into an unwillingness to become actively involved in election campaigns on behalf of LDP candidates, which was one of the main factors contributing to the LDP's defeat in agricultural regions in the election.[357]

On a prefectural basis, the survey recorded a particularly marked fall in support for the LDP in Tohoku (by 18 per cent in Miyagi and 10 per cent in Akita compared with 1986). In Fukushima, by contrast, LDP support fell by only 3 per cent, where significantly, Nokyo did not rebel against the LDP. But in the other Tohoku prefectures such as Aomori, Iwate, Miyagi, Akita and Yamagata, Nokyo did not support the LDP, but instead supported the JSP or Rengo, except for Aomori where Nokyo supported a progressive Independent candidate.[358]

Out of the total of 18 rural and semi-rural seats the LDP ceded to non-LDP candidates, farm household dwellers ranged from a maximum of 38.9 per cent of the total eligible vote in Shimane to 22.9 per cent in Miyagi. And yet, as final electoral outcomes indicated, those candidates whom the farmers and agricultural cooperatives would have normally backed lost in almost all areas where they were opposed. Quite clearly, the 20–30 per cent proportion of eligible voters added up to considerable negative voting power on election day, particularly as many of the votes were organised and directed away from the LDP by agricultural cooperative groups, such as the *seinenbu.*

From the farmers' perspective, however, they were primarily casting a protest vote against the LDP rather than positively supporting any other particular party such as the JSP. Certainly, no single party emerged as the saviour of the farmers. Many farmers voted for Independents rather than for candidates from one or other of the established Opposition parties. Many did not think Opposition policies on agriculture were realistic or particularly convincing, but at the same time, were determined to express their unhappiness with the ruling party.[359] The feeling amongst beef farmers, for example, was divided. Some were very concerned about the future of beef farming, were very critical of the LDP and were prepared to change their vote for that reason. Others thought that liberalisation would not bring such drastic changes because they were reassured that the LDP's beef liberalisation countermeasures (such as support price measures for beef calves) would be adequate. Furthermore, they would not support Opposition parties because these parties did not have any measures against liberalisation. The situation was somewhat different for citrus farmers, however. In this case, the government had not implemented compensation measures for farmers, and for this reason anti-LDP feeling ran very high amongst this particular group.

Some farmers were generally disaffected from the agricultural policies of all parties. A Director of the Hakodate Branch of the Hokkaido Central Union of Agricultural Cooperatives said: 'The contentions of all parties and candidates do not reflect a convincing theory of how to maintain Japanese agriculture in an age of internationalisation. In what way should agriculture and fisheries, which are in a period of transition, be revived? Farmers and fishermen are casting particularly critical eyes on politics'.[360] The JCP, for example, was generally derided as offering nothing but criticism of the LDP's policy.

Similarly, one Nokyo youth leader in Yamagata stated: 'When we invited different candidates to hear their opinions, I did not think progressive (*kakushin*) candidates understood the realities of agriculture'.[361] As Takabatake subsequently commented: 'For many farmers like him, there was no real alternative to the LDP. They would rather turn in a blank ballot paper than vote for an Opposition party.'[362] Another Nokyo youth leader in Kumamoto, like the one in Yamagata, said he 'was not likely to vote for the Opposition even if he thought the LDP agricultural policy was wrong. He regarded the JSP's proposed new Agricultural Basic Law (*Nogyo Kihonho*) bill,[363] which it suddenly announced before the election, as paying lip service to farmers and wished there had been another conservative party that could accept farmers' opinions.'[364] This was demonstrated by a sign that the Miyagi *seinenbu* put up saying 'Goodbye LDP, Hello OO Party'.[365]

The LDP's mistake was its strategic miscalculation about the electoral effects of its series of unpopular agricultural policy decisions and its need for farmers' voting support. It thought that, since most of Japan's farm households were part-time with agricultural income constituting a small percentage of their income, they would not have such a direct material interest in policies that eroded some of the main pillars of agricultural support and protection. The farmers' strong rejection of the LDP at the polls suggests that their identification with the fate of agriculture remained strong regardless of their actual level of engagement in production activities and that the apparently dim prospects agricultural policies held for farmers at the time turned them away in droves from the party. Producers voted on the basis of their fears about the future of Japanese agriculture in general and their own farms in particular.

One electoral study, however, drew a distinction between the voting behaviour of full- and part-time farmers. It reasoned that full-time farmers, who made up the leadership of the *seinenbu* but who were in a minority amongst farmers in general, and who strongly opposed the government's agricultural policy, did not easily shift their allegiance towards the JSP. Part-time farmers, on the other hand, had no future. In particular, part-time farmers who were producing only rice were threatened by prospective import liberalisation and they constituted the majority of farm votes.[366] Votes that flowed to the JSP in the 1989 elections were from farmers in this category.[367] Certainly the JSP's support rate expanded in agricultural regions in the 1989 elections, which would suggest that it gained support from former LDP farm voters.[368] The JSP won 24.4 per cent of votes in these regions, compared with 19.5 per cent in 1983 and 17.2 per cent in 1986.[369] According to one report, farmers' votes in fact flowed not only to the JSP but also to the JCP.[370]

Indeed, the Opposition JSP and JCP saw the late 1980s in the countryside as their big opportunity to capitalise on the disaffection of farmers and move into traditional LDP electoral territory themselves.[371] The consumption tax was the political means in the urban areas, and the government's agricultural policies were the means in the countryside. The JCP described the 1989 elections as a political turning point in rural areas.[372]

As noted earlier, however, farmers' opposition to the LDP did not necessarily translate into a major shift in support to any single Opposition party as a viable alternative. In spite of farmers' profoundly negative evaluation of LDP agricultural policies and a strong desire to punish the ruling party, support for the traditional Opposition alternatives was not particularly marked, and certainly not sufficient to justify the heady optimism of some commentators in the JSP and JCP. Amongst the 18 rural and semi-rural seats the LDP ceded to non-LDP candidates in the 1989 elections, the greatest beneficiary was the right-wing trade union party (Rengo) which gained seven of these seats. The JSP came in next with six seats, but five went to Independents.

With the benefit of hindsight, the results of the 1989 election were an aberration that did not herald a sustained swing on the part of farmers away from the LDP towards the Opposition parties. Farmers just wanted to cauterise the LDP with moxa – to punish the LDP for its wrongdoings – but not to defect permanently from a long-established relationship.[373] The revolt was not repeated in the Lower House in 1990, although the LDP's performance did suffer to some degree in farming constituencies.[374] Three party agricultural heavyweights – Yamanaka Sadanori, Eto Takami and Horinouchi Hisao – lost their seats in what the press interpreted as a farmer backlash against agricultural trade liberalisation exemplified by the LDP's earlier decision to open up Japan's beef and orange markets.[375]

Furthermore, the LDP's polling rate deteriorated in all 14 prefectures with 30 per cent or more of the total eligible voters residing in farm households except one – Tottori.[376] The 1990 LH election, like the 1983 LH election, followed an LDP 'great victory' in the previous election (that is, in 1980 and 1986), and therefore some fall-off from the earlier 'high' could have been expected. Because, however, this did not occur in any consistent fashion in rural electorates in 1983, it is doubtful whether such a factor could explain the across-the-board falls in the 1990 elections. The results suggest the lingering effects of farmer disaffection with the ruling party. The fact that a local co-op chairman in Hokkaido (5) supported a candidate from an Opposition party was considered indicative of continuing dissatisfaction with the LDP's agricultural policies amongst farmers at the time.[377] Moreover, one JSP Diet member claimed that it was easier to mount an election campaign in agricultural regions in the 1990 election, and that JSP candidates were invited to talk to Nokyo *seinenbu* meetings. Previously, even hiring a public hall had been difficult for the party.[378]

Generally speaking, however, wholesale disaffection amongst farmers with the LDP was not evident in the 1990 LH election. An NHK survey in the aftermath of the 1989 UH election reported that support for the LDP was recovering in agricultural areas, with the ruling party's overall support rate rising from 68 per cent at the time of the 1989 election to 76 per cent, whereas support for the JSP was falling dramatically from 15 per cent at the time of the 1989 elections to 6 per cent.[379] Other research confirms this general trend, with LDP support amongst primary industry workers recovering from 41 per cent in 1989 to 58 per cent in 1990, while support for the JSP amongst the same occupational group dropped from 17 per cent to 11 per cent – only 1 per cent higher than in 1972 – hardly much of an advance for a party with such enduring aspirations to expand its support amongst farmers.[380]

Nevertheless, the ruling party gained a new appreciation of the electoral power of the agricultural cooperatives in the 1989 election and made an effort to deflect attention from the issue of rice import liberalisation and the future of the FC system in the lead-up to the 1990 LH election. In fact, on key agricultural issues the platforms of each party were virtually indistinguishable. All promised to continue support for agricultural prices and to oppose rice liberalisation.[381] Although the Opposition parties' promises on agricultural policy were, as usual, somewhat more generous to farmers than those of the LDP, they lacked a certain element of credibility.[382] Farmers were suspicious of the fact that the Opposition parties espoused mutually contradictory objectives such as cheaper consumer prices for food (to appeal to trade union members) and higher agricultural support prices.[383] As Kobayashi comments, what this amounted to for farmers was a 'negative choice' between the LDP and JSP as to which one represented the 'least worst' option.[384]

Other factors also counted against the Opposition parties in the 1990 election. The JSP continued to present itself in ideological terms which, at Cold War's end, did not appeal to farmers. It also suffered from the lack of a well-organised generational shift of agriculture and forestry Diet members. Whereas there was no shortage of aspiring farm politicians in the ranks of the LDP – many of whom were recruited from amongst former officials of the MAFF and agricultural organisations – there was a dearth of viable rice-roots farm organisations attached to the Opposition parties which could provide a fertile recruiting ground for Opposition-affiliated farm politicians. Almost all the JSP and DSP farmers' union officials in the Diet in the 1980s and 1990s were relics from the 1950s, 1960s and 1970s and no new blood was entering these parties from that particular quarter.[385] In fact, when the agricultural policy experts of the JSP elected to constituencies like Niigata (2) and (3) were replaced by candidates from labour unions, farmers swung their support to LDP candidates, a shift that was reinforced by the latter's pledges to attract more agricultural subsidies and improve social infrastructure in rural areas.[386]

Such a trend highlighted the fundamental weakness of the Opposition parties in the eyes of farmers: their inability to obtain subsidies. Many farmers had conflicting feelings towards the LDP because they were dissatisfied with government agricultural policy, but they were still hoping to keep a reliable *sensei* in the sense of a representative able and willing to deliver subsidies and other benefits back to the constituency.[387] There was a big difference between registering a protest vote in an UH election and rejecting the LDP as the party of government in the Lower House with political and legislative control over the budget. Electoral contests in rural areas were normally between different LDP members competing in terms of their ability to deliver policy benefits to particular localities rather than on matters of agricultural policy where all shared the same view as members of the same party. This is what made the 1989 elections so distinctive. Farmers and the agricultural cooperatives protested against the LDP's very unpopular agricultural policies. Many farmers were genuinely concerned about their future prospects as agricultural producers in the face of the liberalisation of the beef and citrus sectors and the possibility of rice liberalisation in combination with cuts in agricultural support prices.

After the election debacle of 1989 and the diminution in support for the LDP in agricultural regions in the 1990 LH elections, the rice market-opening issue still showed itself to be capable of inducing a protest vote from farmers. The prospect of rice liberalisation attracted an anti-LDP protest vote in the 1992 March by-election for the Upper House in Miyagi Prefecture. The decision was taken by the Nokyo prefectural organisation to allow members to vote as they wished, following a formal decision by the prefectural Nokyo youth league not to work for LDP candidate Onodera Nobuo.[388] 'The farmers have been continually betrayed by the LDP' according to the Vice-Chairman of the prefectural Nokyo youth league.[389]

In the subsequent election the LDP candidate was defeated by a narrow margin by the Rengo candidate. The *Nikkei* reported that this LDP defeat was linked to statements from LDP politicians in favour of rice liberalisation. Deputy Prime Minister Watanabe Michio had declared that there should be a discussion of methods of rice market opening, including the proposed tariffication system, while PM Miyazawa had indicated his agreement with Watanabe's statement. The *Nikkei* also reported that in the Miyagi by-election, the Rengo candidate won more votes than the LDP candidate in Furukawa City, the centre of an area that produces top-grade *sasanishiki* rice, and gained a considerable number of votes even in the north of the prefecture, another major rice-producing area and traditionally a conservative stronghold. These results were interpreted as a criticism by farmers of the government's agricultural policies translating directly into anti-government votes.[390] In the same month, another by-election was held in Gumma Prefecture in the Lower House. Both seats were won by LDP candidates from a field of four candidates. One of the explanations given was that Gumma Prefecture was far less dependent on rice production than Miyagi Prefecture.[391]

Throughout the UR negotiations, however, the prospect of an electoral backlash from farmers in specific elections (particularly in the 1990 and 1992 general elections) was widely regarded as the main political factor preventing the Japanese government from acceding to various market opening proposals. As early as late 1988, Zenchu was warning the LDP that it could lose up to 80 seats in the Lower House if it liberalised rice,[392] and the results of the 1989 and to a lesser extent the 1990 elections offered credible evidence to the ruling party that they should not take this threat too lightly. Not surprisingly, the election timetable directly affected the tenor of comments by government and LDP spokespersons on this issue.[393] Fears that a UR agricultural trade agreement might be sabotaged by LDP politicians beholden to farm interests, and the aspirations of Opposition parties anxious to move in on the LDP's traditional bailiwick, prompted one policy advisory group to warn in the lead-up to the 1992 election that: 'If both the ruling and Opposition parties take action to prevent the UR agreement because they are concerned about movement in Nokyo organisational votes in the next House of Councillors' election, it will be a criminal act towards the Japanese people and the majority of farmers. Even though the legislative amendments accompanying the tariffication of rice are politically difficult, politicians who cannot manage that have no right to be in power.'[394]

As the UR talks progressed into their final year, however, farmers became more resigned to the prospect of rice liberalisation.[395] In fact, many farmers preferred a 'realistic' policy that countenanced the possibility of rice market opening and which made preparations to ease its impact on farmers, to a 'blanket' policy of rejecting rice imports devoid of concrete counter-measures.[396] Although publicly it was holding the line, the Nokyo organisation was also privately resigned to the prospect of some degree of liberalisation.[397]

In post-UR Japan, the LDP has restored its relations with its farming constituents and the agricultural cooperative organisations, both national and local. It has been able to gain electoral advantage from the fact that it was not directly responsible for the decision to allow foreign rice access to the Japanese market which the Hosokawa coalition government agreed to as part of the UR Agreement on Agriculture in December 1993. Nevertheless, as late as 1995 it was being acknowledged that the once rock-solid support the LDP had once enjoyed from the farmers had softened. The November 1995 UH by-election in Saga worried the LDP, particularly after the prefectural *noseiren* declared before the campaign that its individual members would be left to decide which candidate to vote for. In the event, the LDP need not have been so concerned with its candidate romping home ahead of the NFP candidate.[398]

Nokyo's diminishing powers of vote control

Although the 1989 UH election provides perhaps the clearest and most unequivocal demonstration of the ability of agricultural cooperative organisations to influence the votes of their members in recent times, many interrelated factors have worked inexorably to diminish Nokyo's vote-gathering powers in elections. The first of these is the shrinking number of Nokyo's primary farming clientele, a demographic trend elaborated in detail in chapter 5.

A powerful offsetting factor has been the extent to which the farm vote remains an organised vote in any particular electoral district. If the farm vote moves in a unified fashion, the fact that it comprises ever-smaller proportions of the total vote does not necessarily reduce its impact to the same degree. As Arimitsu explains, even if the ratio within a Diet member's constituency is 20 per cent rural and 80 per cent urban, if that 20 per cent is a 'hard vote' and the 80 per cent is a 'scattered vote', then in order to protect that 20 per cent, the Diet member will still feel obliged to become an agricultural and forestry Diet member.[399] In short, much still depends on the continuing reliability of Nokyo's vote control.

This is where other negative factors come into play. The relationship between Nokyo and its members is being influenced by socio-economic trends in farming areas.[400] Miyake reports that Nokyo's powers of vote mobilisation are showing some weakening because of the changes accompanying the transition of rural villages to mixed societies owing to the growth in part-time farming.[401] Similarly, Yamaguchi Ichimon, a retired Nokyo executive of 28 years' standing, argues that the consciousness of cooperation amongst farmers is flagging because of the large proportion of farm household income derived from work outside agriculture. This is also altering the attitude of farmers towards their own farming work and the land. The younger generation are inclined to work in non-agricultural fields, reducing their opportunities to acquire farming knowledge and skills and urbanising their attitudes towards life. They also have the opportunity to participate in other life-protection organisations such as the trade unions. This makes older people who are mainly engaged in farming feel that they are the last generation of farmers and therefore they tend to treat the land as a saleable object.[402] In short their commitment to farming and to the land is being degraded along with their perceptions of a stake in agriculture. Nokyo has had problems in dealing with these changes in farmers' thinking and their way of life.[403]

The bonds between farmers and Nokyo are also fading because the social associations or *tsukiai* that formed a natural basis for agricultural cooperative membership are starting to break down. The deterioration in the human relationships in farm villages is helping to dilute the membership solidarity that provided a foundation for Nokyo's vote 'control'. When farmers' sense of belonging to their village weakens, it automatically affects their attachment to Nokyo. The ability of Nokyo leaders to organise votes, which was based on the sense of local community and social order in the villages, is thus diminishing.[404] These developments have inevitably undermined the capacity of local Nokyo leaders to deliver the votes of entire villages. Ono reports that public works contractors, instead of Nokyo, are collecting farmers' votes and that this sector had replaced the agricultural cooperatives as the political base of the LDP in rural areas.[405]

In recent times, another increasingly important aspect of the socio-economic transformation of rural areas has been the restructuring of Japanese agriculture and the emergence of new modes of agricultural production and farm labour. The farm sector is witnessing a burgeoning number of farms under corporate-style enterprise management. Because of the shortage of successors in farm households, an expanding number of producers are switching family farming operations to a more business-orientated corporate set-up. These innovations in farm enterprise do not come without certain costs. Expanding the scale of production management by encouraging joint operation of farms through leasing or through outright sale and transfer of land entails the slow destruction of *nogyo shuraku*, which will 'shake the social stability of rural Japan'.[406] The agricultural cooperative leadership is aware of the implications of farm corporatisation and has opposed expansion in the scale of farm management by these means, preferring an approach that puts emphasis on providing farmers with management services and guidance rather than encouraging farmers to sell their lands or to lease them to other farmers.

Another facet of the farm restructuring process is the shift from hereditary agriculture to occupational agriculture. The number of farm work contractors – such as those ploughing farmland and drying husks – is steadily rising. Their service coverage is expanding from the small village to the prefectural level. While this is apparently related to the ongoing mergers among agricultural cooperatives across the country, it also suggests that changes are occurring in the narrow, traditional concept of the farming community.[407]

An even more profound change is in the offing with the impending entry of private business into agricultural cultivation. One of the proposals emerging from the government's advisory council on administrative reform in December 1995 was a recommendation to allow joint-stock corporations to own farmland.[408] This option was also examined by the Prime Minister's Food, Agriculture and Rural Areas Basic Problems Investigation Committee in 1997–98 and later received qualified approval from the MAFF and LDP. Nokyo has been virulently opposed to this form of 'privatising' agriculture through the sale or lease of agricultural land to private business firms.[409] As Higashi and Lauter point out, although corporate farming will result in more efficient and internationally competitive units where modern production methods and equipment can be applied, it will also 'mean the end of the rural socioeconomic structures which have existed for centuries and which form the basis of the rural communities throughout the country.'[410]

These changes to the social face of agriculture consequent upon the agricultural restructuring process will continue to undermine the ability of local agricultural cooperative organisations to capitalise on the sense of community within farm villages for political purposes. Nokyo's local community base which generated such a strong sense of collective identity over many decades is slowly being eroded, which bodes ill for its future capacity to organise and direct votes in the farming sector.

These developments cannot be separated from the erosion in the ties of farmers to the agricultural cooperatives on membership and business as well as other levels. As noted in chapter 4, private sector enterprises are advancing into rural areas, increasing competition for the patronage of farmers, particularly those who find the high-cost structure of Nokyo's goods and services unhelpful in their efforts to reduce production costs.[411] In the circumstances, the agricultural cooperatives are finding it difficult to retain their prior claim on the loyalties of their members and, in some cases, even to retain them at all. Reports have surfaced of Nokyo executives 'chasing members of the agricultural cooperatives, begging for their support'.[412] Such a development suggests that co-op members are not satisfied with what Nokyo can offer in terms of economic and other services. A 1994 poll revealed that two-thirds of Nokyo members were rather dissatisfied or completely dissatisfied with Nokyo activities whilst only one-third were completely satisfied or rather satisfied.[413] The failure of Nokyo's businesses to attract and satisfy members of the agricultural cooperatives both reflects and reinforces its declining competitiveness compared with private sector enterprises.[414] As Saeki notes, the tendency of members to 'leave Nokyo' is especially strong amongst the younger generation.[415] The fall-off in membership is absolutely critical for Nokyo because it 'poses the threat of "losing its teeth"'[416] as an economic, political and electoral organisation. As Fujitani puts it, Nokyo is undergoing a process of 'hollowing out' as 'an organised body of activities' (*soshiki undotai*).[417]

In addition, the continuing mergers of Nokyo branches have compounded the erosion of agricultural cooperative solidarity, putting even greater distance between Nokyo members and executives.[418] For example, the average membership per cooperative has risen from 1,256 in 1980 to 2,200 in 1996.[419] Many farmer members of newly merged cooperatives complain that: 'The personnel have become unfriendly and their attitude is businesslike'.[420] In other words, the mergers of *tankyo* have disrupted the local human relationships on which they were based, and the sense of togetherness between the *nokyo* and their members is disappearing. This also encourages members to move their business elsewhere.[421] The increasing distance between Nokyo's members and their organisation has, therefore, potentially direct consequences for Nokyo's capacities at the electoral level. In 1990, for example, it was reported that more and more members were disobeying commands from the top people in Nokyo.[422]

The anticipated structural conversion of the federated three-stage system of Nokyo into a two-stage system will compound these developments. The removal of prefectural Nokyo federations will undermine broader regional consciousness within the prefecture, which in turn will make it harder for the *noseiren* to operate effectively as coordinating bodies for electoral operations across prefectures. The *noseiren* are quintessentially prefectural organisations. Their branches are composed of the agricultural cooperatives in each prefecture and they undertake active support campaigns in the prefectural constituencies of the Upper House.[423]

In more recent years, farmer dissatisfaction with Nokyo's waning policy effectiveness is also impacting on its powers of vote mobilisation. From the late 1980s onwards, Nokyo's spectacular failure in campaigns to pressure the government into resisting concessions on critical agricultural market access questions capped off by its capitulation to the UR agreement were critical developments in this regard. Nokyo's farmer members have become particularly disillusioned with the central unions, whose job it is to represent agricultural cooperative and farmers' interests to government. As a former Zenchu Managing Director commented, 'Nokyo is losing its power to control its members in telling them how to vote because it is losing its power to intervene in agricultural policymaking. This factor, along with the decline in the number of farmers are the two reasons why Nokyo's political power is becoming weaker.'[424]

In Fujitani's view, the contraction in Nokyo's electoral power can already be discerned in its changing strategies as an interest group. Nokyo is being compelled to put increasing emphasis on lobbying Diet members directly in its policy campaigns, rather than influencing Diet members through the process of electoral representation. As he reasons, this is because candidates have become more concerned with the opinions of general voters (i.e. non-farmers) than with farmers' views.[425]

The impact of LH electoral reform[426]

The electoral reforms of 1994, providing Japan does not undergo yet other rounds of reform, will inevitably have an impact on the organised electoral influence of the agricultural cooperatives, although it is still too early to state definitively whether the overall effect of the new electoral rules will be positive or negative. What one can say without doubt is that the electoral environment has altered dramatically, with the changes suggestive of several possible developments.

Firstly, because many farmers customarily based their vote on considerations relating to individual candidates, any reforms that loosened personalistic ties between individual politicians and their farm supporters potentially undermined this traditional voting nexus. By redrawing the boundaries of local districts and contracting constituency size, electoral reform created possibilities for individual politicians in particular regions to be geographically separated from their long-standing supporters amongst the farmers and Nokyo.[427] Likewise, the transference of politicians into the larger regional PR blocs as candidates on a party list generated even greater distance between politicians and their former supporters. Such changes particularly affected politicians and interests that had previously been bound together by 'hard' votes generated by the forces of localism and closely knit ties to supporters in particular regions – the kind of relationship LDP members customarily maintained with farmers and Nokyo in their conservative rural strongholds. In some cases, the effect of this was to lower the interest of farmers in the 1996 LH election because they had lost their *sensei* and because the alternatives on offer did not appeal.[428]

Secondly, depending on the location of the new district boundaries and consequently the altered socio-economic profile of the new electorates, the vote-mobilisation capacities of farmers' organisations were enhanced in some districts and diminished in others. This was because the redrawn electorates were more clearly delineated as agricultural, partially agricultural or non-agricultural, as noted in chapter 5.[429] The restructuring of electoral districts enabled farmers' organisations to target their resources in a more strategic and concentrated fashion, focusing their energies on those constituencies where their influence had been magnified and downgrading their efforts in those districts where agricultural interests had become more 'diluted'. Equally, it was clearer for those standing in the new constituencies which interests were worth cultivating and which were not, depending on the makeup of the electorate.[430]

Thirdly, a specific consequence of the contraction in constituency size was the change in emphasis from large to smaller groups, making the national campaign more like those for local elections.[431] Smaller collections of agricultural cooperative organisations within particular districts were now asked to support particular candidates. This did not present a problem for Nokyo, which operates in parallel fashion to the administrative units of government, or the prefectural *noseiren* with their networks of branch federations consisting of local units in towns and cities. In fact, however, the new electoral districts occasioned a new strata of organisational hierarchy to develop, insofar as the prefectural *noseiren* established branches specifically for each of the new LH single-member districts. In short, both Nokyo and its associated political groups mobilised flexibly in the new system.

Take the Fukui *noseiren* for example. Fukui was previously a single prefectural constituency that elected four LH members. Eight *noseiren* branches (*shibu*) which divided the prefecture into eight districts (*chiku*) shouldered the burden of election activities. Each of these *shibu* was formally registered as a political group. The branches operated out of the amalgamated large-scale *nokyo* in the prefecture, and, in turn, divided into 119 chapters with smaller *nokyo* branch managers (*shitencho*) in charge. In the 1996 election, however, a new structure was needed, with the *noseiren* setting up three headquarters in each of the three new electorates. These groups were the prime movers in the election contest. The Fukui *noseiren* claimed that in creating campaign organisations for each new district, command systems and responsibility were clarified, and a framework emerged for mobilising undispersed power in the small-district system.[432]

The reason for the new framework was, in the words of the prefectural *noseiren* office chief, that in order to have the farmers' voice reflected in national policy, the organisation recommended a candidate in each of the single-member districts, and also decided to engage in election activities that mobilised the power of the farmers across the entire prefecture. The three constituency headquarters, in addition to having their own sub-branches (*shibu*) and local chapters (*bunkai*), also operated under the Fukui Prefecture Farmers' Political League Election Policy Headquarters Chief and the Election Policy Council which included *noseiren* executives, executives of the five Nokyo federations and others. These bodies were located in the *noseiren* head office, which also engaged in liaison and 'adjustment' with the recommended candidates' offices.[433]

Likewise, the agricultural cooperatives had more or less elastic vote-gathering power in the larger PR regional blocs, where Nokyo-connected votes could be gathered as a compound of many smaller agricultural cooperative and *noseiren* branches within the larger constituency. Nevertheless, the multiplication of electoral units generally made it more difficult for organisations like the Zenkoku Noseikyo to make decisions about whom to recommend as the national organisation, and to coordinate these decisions with the multiplicity of group recommendations at the rice-roots level.

The fourth and perhaps most important change under the new system has been the fact that successful candidates now have to obtain a much higher proportion of the total vote to win a seat. This is because of the change-over from a multi-member to a single-member district system. Because candidates could previously scrape in with as little as 10–15 per cent (or even less) of the total vote, politicians needed the strong backing of only a small portion of the district's voters – perhaps Nokyo, or a labour union or a chamber of commerce and industry.[434] Small groups of well-organised supporters could thus ensure the election of their chosen candidate. They could make a real difference to electoral outcomes.

Under the new system, candidates need to cultivate a much broader base of support, at least 30 per cent of the total vote, probably more, depending on the number and relative strength of the candidates. In the 1996 elections, for example, the vast majority of successful candidates garnered voting support in the 30–50 per cent range, with a few as low as 25 per cent and some as high as 83 per cent. Logically enough, the percentage of the total vote obtained by the winning candidates appeared to be a function of the total number of candidates standing in the electorate, which meant that those competing in densely urbanised electorates generally won lower proportions of the total vote because the number of candidates contesting the seat was greater, whereas candidates in rural electorates generally obtained higher proportions of the total vote because the number of candidates was lower.[435]

The larger proportion of the total vote required for victory inevitably reduces the electoral impact of the farm vote because it amounts to a smaller proportion of the total number of votes obtained by the winning candidate and therefore a smaller element in the electoral strategies of candidates generally. Under the old system, any single interest could represent a larger share of a politician's support base, which expanded the potential influence of decisions by interest groups to bestow or withdraw their support. The new system, however, diminishes the electoral effectiveness of organisations such as Nokyo, because agricultural cooperative organisations within a given district will be markedly less able to swing the outcome in any direction, negative or positive. For a given interest group, the votes at their command will be relatively less important to the final outcome because they amount to a smaller proportion of the candidate's total vote. As Nokyo's voting power has already largely shifted from positive to negative, the changes potentially undermine its electoral influence even further.

The new system thus requires candidates to build a much broader base of support from a cross-section of groups, which means less commitment to any single group overall. The traditional 'division of interests' that used to occur in the MMDs amongst contending LDP candidates has been completely negated in the new SMDs. In a sense, everybody is now competing for the same blocs of votes. Under the old system, a premium was placed on identifying particular candidates with particular blocs of voters because of the need to carve up the constituency so that each LDP candidate could be elected without competing for support with other LDP candidates, and hopefully the number of seats extracted from any given constituency could be maximised.[436] Under this system, candidate A would draw his main support from agriculture and forestry, candidate B would do likewise from commerce and industry, while candidate C would target the construction industry, and so on and so forth across the electoral districts of the nation. The combinations differed depending on the electorates, but the principle remained the same. This carve-up was one of the main factors reinforcing the close nexus between individual candidates and client interest groups.

The new system, however, negates this 'structural' need to build a personal support base around an exclusive set of special interests and replaces it with a compelling requirement to combine support from as wide a range of interests as possible. In this respect, the SMDs inevitably generate more generalist than special interest politicians, which dilutes the relative importance of any single sectional grouping like farmers, reduces the capacity of interest groups to influence individual candidates and weakens the dependency of particular politicians on particular interests. As a result, interest representation by politicians is inevitably less narrowly focused and, conversely, less potential exists for special interests to dominate the individual loyalties of Diet members. In the new electoral system politicians are obliged to be more inclusive and less tied to specific interests. They have to become what Sugita calls 'all round players'.[437] Farmers complained in the 1996 elections, for example, that with one person standing in a constituency, candidates had to appeal to everybody, and thus the focus on agricultural policy issues waned.[438]

The new electoral system thus appears to diminish the electoral power of agricultural interests and further undermine the nexus between individual politicians and farming communities. In some respects it also makes picking candidates much harder for groups like the *noseiren*, because no contestant is willing to fly strong enough agricultural colours for them to be easily identified as sympathetic. This is potentially a recipe for more chaotic and less clear-cut choices for farmers' organisations and farm voters, with greater potential for disagreement amongst groups and equally greater potential for farm votes to be split.[439]

On the other hand, the effect of this particular change on agrarian electoral power may, to a certain extent, be mitigated by other factors. In those constituencies where farmers represent an electorally significant proportion of the total eligible vote, their voting power may be magnified relative to interests represented by smaller numbers of voters, although such districts are now in a distinct minority. On the other hand, in districts where farmers are less numerous, the electoral leverage of the farmers and agricultural cooperatives will be substantially diminished. Candidates will be much less dependent on their vote as a proportion of the total required for electoral success.

In general, the requirement for most candidates to appeal to a wider cross-section of interests will tend to reduce the electoral leverage of special interest groups. The result will be fewer genuine interest representatives in the Diet and thus fewer clearly identifiable farm politicians.[440] Even amongst those with electoral ties to agricultural interests, their allegiance will be diluted by a more diverse range of connections to other groups. The sense of ownership of, and close identification with, particular politicians encapsulated in the term 'our *sensei*' will be diminished. Take the newly elected LDP member for Kanagawa (12), Sakurai Ikuzo, for instance. He is a member of the Fujisawa City Agricultural Committee, but also Vice-Chairman of the Atsugi Base Policy Council, Chairman of the Fujisawa City Public Hospital Management Council and Secretary-General of Fujisawa City Defence Cooperation Association.[441]

On balance, the ultimate effects of the need for successful candidates to win a higher proportion of the total vote may be contradictory. While the new system will weaken the allegiance of particular politicians to particular organisations, competition for the support of interest groups that can offer reliable blocs of votes is likely to increase. The small-sized electorates in fact intensify competition between the candidates representing different parties because of the need to win a plurality. This will mean that any given group or voting bloc is likely to be courted by more candidates, which may have the effect of partially restoring group leverage if it chooses to play one candidate off against another. Increased competition amongst candidates should, therefore, empower organised interests in principle, particularly as support from blocs of voters will remain attractive to candidates in the absence of effective grass-roots organisations amongst the political parties (with a few exceptions such as the Komeito, or new Komeito, and the JCP). Large and powerful groups with sizeable numbers of votes to mobilise, the ability to provide good organ-isational backup and access to other electoral resources such as finance, will be courted much more assiduously than smaller, weaker groups. In the past, smaller groups could make a difference to a candidate because they represented a greater proportion of the total vote the candidate needed for victory. Under the new system, as noted earlier, their value will be greatly reduced.

Generally speaking this factor should benefit the agricultural cooperatives. In gross terms, not only do Nokyo voters compare favourably with other large organisations,[442] they also command other advantages such as nationwide spread, high organisation rates, access to economic and other organisational resources and a long tradition of vote-gathering at the rice roots. In other words, the agricultural cooperatives may remain too big and too strong for candidates to ignore in some SMDs, although in others, it may end up being a relatively minor interest.

In general, the prediction made by the agricultural cooperatives themselves prior to the October 1996 elections was that their influence over Diet deliber-ations would be strengthened because of the requirement for candidates to obtain a higher proportion of the vote to win under the new SMD system.[443] They reasoned that the intensified competition amongst candidates for a plurality would force the contestants to seek votes from whatever quarter they could, and this would enhance the value of votes linked to the agricultural cooperatives. In short, candidates could not afford to alienate any voting blocs because this might make the difference between winning and losing. The newly introduced electoral system thus increased the vulnerability of candi-dates in the SMDs to small shifts in support. In accordance with this theory, agricultural cooperative organisations were encouraged to flex their electoral muscles on some policy issues, threatening to use their vote-mobilisation power against the ruling party if it did not come up with the right policy goods.

At the same time, agricultural cooperative organisations were under pressure to decide their candidate choices more carefully because of the more extreme confrontation in the SMDs between the parties and their candidates on each side.[444] In the past, Nokyo's backup organisations could issue cross-candidate and cross-party recommendations based on candidates' demonstrations of understanding and support for farmers' causes. As there were more seats to go around within a given electorate, greater flexibility could be shown with respect to choice of candidate(s). Moreover, several candidates could be supported whilst still aligning only with the LDP. In the new system, such an approach became less flexible in accommodating a range of opinions and political loyalties within the agricultural cooperative organisation as well as requiring cross-party backing, including non-LDP candidates. The harder choices on whom to support risk greater dissension within the organisation and the likelihood that members will disregard the recommendations of farmers' groups. In the 1996 LH election, some *noseiren* organisations avoided issuing recommendations because of their fear that making a choice between candidates from different parties would split their organisation, and because recommending only one candidate would leave an unpleasant feeling. In fact there were many blank spaces amongst the 300 SMDs where no candidates were recommended by the *noseiren*. Only 24 prefectures had all the constituencies covered by such recommendations.[445] According to several reports issued by individual *noseiren* in January 1999, uniform disorder emerged in the selection of recommended candidates in the 1996 LH election because of the changeover to the SMD system, in which there was a choice of party, from the MMD system in which recommendations were allocated depending on a candidate's personality and views. It was acknowledged that the new system required unity of purpose within organisations as well as a need to strengthen branch activities.[446]

On the other hand, the power of nationally organised interests like Nokyo and the Zenkoku Noseikyo can make itself felt through the party list system in the PR regional blocs, which places a premium on the abilities of interest groups to mobilise their members reliably across the larger constituencies. Candidates representing particular sectors and organisations that offer access to large numbers of votes and other kinds of electoral resources are assured of placings towards the top of the party list in order to help secure those electoral benefits for the party and to reward candidates for bringing such benefits. This will tend to underwrite candidates' special connections with organised blocs of voters rather than detract from them, which the SMD system tends to do. Politicians from the PR regional constituencies will have greater leeway to pursue specialist policy themes. Indeed, the new regional districts create a tendency for a clearer differentiation of interests and allotment of roles amongst candidates standing on the party ticket.[447] The PR system will operate very much as the current NC system does in the Upper House. In those regional PR constituencies that are more rural in character, candidates with agricultural connections will remain an attractive electoral proposition as a means of harnessing the farm vote. Zenkoku Noseikyo's Vice-Chairman Kumagai Ichio, for example, was elected from the Tohoku PR bloc in the No. 3 slot in the 1996 elections.

The prospects for organising a farmers' party in the PR constituencies remain distant, however. Although the option has been canvassed in the context of the new LH electoral system, and was briefly implemented in the 1995 UH election to the national constituency,[448] *noseiren* executives acknowledge that they are not capable of successfully forming and sustaining a farmers' political party. This is partly because of the requirement that registration as a party requires at least five successful candidates, which would require *noseiren* organisations to collect most of the farmers' votes within given electorates. Victory might be a possibility in Tohoku and Kyushu where the percentage of farmers is relatively higher, and it might be possible to send a farmers' party representative to the Diet if more than half the farmers' votes could be reliably collected, but in either case, large quantities of election funds would be needed, which might not be forthcoming.[449]

The preference of Zenkoku Noseikyo and the *noseiren* in the circumstances is to pursue the tried and true option of providing backing for election candidates standing for the established parties (LDP candidates in the majority of cases), who are connected in some way to the agricultural cooperatives and their associated organisations, and/or who have demonstrated themselves through policy activities to be effective brokers on behalf of their farming constituents and/or who show sympathetic understanding of agriculture and farming villages. Whilst not abandoning altogether the option of running their own farmers' party candidates, the *noseiren* and Zenkoku Noseikyo recognise that in the meantime, the best alternative is to establish their own Diet members' league on the basis of policy agreements with the politicians for whom they provided support.[450]

Overall, it is difficult to reach definitive conclusions about how effectively the agricultural cooperatives will be able to translate their vote-gathering powers to the two new constituency sizes. The SMDs are a geographic contraction and the PR regional districts a geographic expansion of the former MMDs. In the past agricultural cooperative organisations have performed flexibly enough in both the prefectural constituencies of the Upper House and the smaller districts of the Lower House and, therefore, the 1994 reforms do not present insurmountable obstacles from an organisational perspective. Because Nokyo has never operated as a coordinated electoral body nationally, however, and because the vote mobilisation capacities and political connections of the agricultural cooperatives have been highly localised at prefectural level and below, the agricultural cooperative organisation may not represent such an effective electoral entity on a larger region-wide basis. To some extent this was confirmed by the nature of recommendations from the Zenkoku Noseikyo in the 1996 LH elections. The vast majority (89 per cent) were directed towards candidates in the SMDs. Some *noseiren* leaders also expressed unease with the larger regional bloc system because the forces of localism could not be harnessed as effectively, particularly if the party list in question contained no one from the prefecture and also because the candidate's home prefecture became the centre of election activity.[451] On the other hand, as already pointed out, Zenkoku Noseikyo's candidate was successfully elected to the Tohoku PR bloc suggesting that national organisations can successfully put their candidates forward in the larger regional districts.

On balance, however, the long history of electoral involvement by Nokyo and its associated organisations suggests that such groups are likely to operate far more effectively in the SMDs than the regional PR blocs. Candidates in the SMDs will continue to rely on local interest groups to help gather the vote (although a wider cross-section of groups will be needed) and will still tend to focus their appeal around local issues. Those with strong connections at the grass-roots level will also do much better in this type of seat. This may create a division in the recruitment patterns of politicians, with former local politicians (such as those with rice-roots support from co-op members) pre-dominating in the SMDs, while those following other career paths such as former bureaucrats and politicians' secretaries (and those identified with national organisations with good and reliable vote distributions in larger regional areas) will prefer to stand in the PR districts. The divergence between these two types of Diet representatives already appears to have been realised in the contrasting makeup of successful SMD and PR bloc candidates in the 1996 elections.

Finally, perhaps one of the most momentous structural changes in Japanese politics potentially consequent upon electoral reform may work to diminish Nokyo's influence. This change relates to the stronger party profiles that are possible in the absence of the need to differentiate candidates from within the same party in both the SMDs and PR districts. In theory this should also diminish the need for *koenkai* as the primary vote-mobilising bodies for candidates and thus undermine one of the major mechanisms by which the LDP mobilised strong rice-roots support in the countryside. Because of the role of *koenkai* as important loci of farmer and interest group-leader partici-pation in electoral politics, the new system may loosen the nexus between individual politicians and their supporters in farming communities. Instead, greater emphasis may be placed by candidates on local party chapters as the core organising force in electoral districts and by voters on party policies as the basis of support rather than the personal attributes of particular candi-dates. Parties may become less collections of successful individual candidates and more organisations with greater internal coherence and control over their candidates.[452] In other words, the new system may change organisational strategies at the electoral level and thus 'change incentives about how to run for office because positions on issues not only would become compatible with a strategy to win a parliamentary majority, but also they would become desirable.'[453]

In this scenario, candidate success or failure will be tied much more to party resources and party considerations, with the latter linked more closely to national leadership considerations and perceptions acquired through the mass media. In short, party choice will be sufficient for voter choice in a way that it was not in the past. Candidates are able, to some extent, to free-ride on the party vote and therefore do not have to go out and collect it so assiduously for themselves. This, in turn, will reduce their need for back-up from personal support organisations. Candidates will be more concerned that their party is popular and therefore that it has the right policies. Overall, there will be much more concern with party identity, party principles and party policies with stronger competition taking place between parties in terms of both national and local policies.

The big question is whether such a scenario will ever be played out in Japan. Certainly it is further encouraged by the party lists in the PR regional constituencies. A shift towards parties as primary actors on the electoral stage also fits with the overall design of the electoral reformers who aimed to promote competition amongst parties on the basis of their platforms and, over the longer term, induce a system that would see an alternation of power between two main parties.[454]

To some extent, however, the outcome depends on the parties themselves. At present they remain loosely organised groups of like-minded politicians, with only nuanced differences in policy positions and often with internal divisions that are more striking than their differences with their electoral rivals.[455] The organisational and electoral viability of the Opposition grouping called the Minyuren, in which the dominant elements were the Democratic, Sun and From Five parties, rightfully remained in question during the short period of its existence. The issue now is whether its replacement – the Democratic Party – can develop into a large and viable enough political grouping with a sufficiently distinguishable policy position to enable it to become the main Opposition and potential alternative government.

In this context, Nokyo's electoral threats to certain LDP candidates may or may not have less credibility than under the old MMD system because changing support now means switching to another party (i.e. a non-LDP grouping), rather than just switching candidates. In the past, as Sakaguchi points out, a Diet member who wanted to fight Nokyo had to have considerable courage, because he knew how Nokyo would react against his rebellion. It would field another rival candidate in his constituency.[456] In the new system, Nokyo may have less credibility in threatening to withdraw its backing for an LDP candidate, unless it is really serious about doing business with an Opposition party candidate. The potential utility of this option rests on the likelihood of a particular Opposition group (or groups) coming to power. The threat of vote-switching is certainly one that has arisen as a somewhat more viable course of action when electoral competition in the SMDs takes place along party rather than along candidate lines. At the same time, failure to operate strategically *vis-à-vis* different parties may serve just to underline how durable and entrenched Nokyo's electoral connection to the LDP is.

To the extent that party identification becomes a primary determinant of voter choice, organised interests will have less leverage because voters will be less likely to cross party lines in compliance with organisational guidance. As a general rule, party identification disempowers groups in the same way that it disempowers voters because the credibility of vote-switching and therefore voter leverage is reduced.

Logic also dictates that if electoral competition increasingly takes place along party lines, parties will need to delineate much more clearly what they stand for in order to distinguish themselves from rival groupings. The effect of this may, to some extent, be contradictory. In developing more clearly identified interests in order to locate themselves in the voting market, parties may solidify links between themselves and interest groups, such as Nokyo and the LDP. On the other hand, if parties become too closely identified with certain interests, this may alienate other groups and make it harder for parties to maximise their votes. In this case, electoral strategy dictates that parties obscure rather than illuminate their differences,[457] thus militating against rigid and closed relationships with particular interests. The concomitant effect will be to reduce the leverage of special interests because parties will normally try to stand for a range of interests and as well as having the capacity to speak for more diffuse community-wide interests such as taxpayers and consumers.

In practice, the effect on party behaviour on the hustings may be highly variable depending on the socio-economic profile of the constituency. Stronger party identities will tend to increase the distance between the LDP and the farmers in those constituencies where agriculture is more of a marginal interest, and reduce the distance between farmers and other parties in those constituencies where agriculture is a more dominant interest. In general, each party will endeavour to maximise its vote by building a solid core of supporters without sacrificing its chances to compete for non-aligned voters.

In summary, to the extent that the LDP maintains and consolidates its reputation as the party of the farmers under the new system, this will decrease the leverage of the agricultural cooperatives at election time because it will reduce the credibility of any electoral sanction threatened by the farmers and Nokyo groups against the LDP. Under the old system, the agricultural cooperatives could withdraw support from a particular candidate and give it to another without having to change party affiliation, or at least give it to an Independent who stood a greater electoral chance than under the new system. Depending on the solidity of ties between the LDP and the farmers in the future, such an electoral strategy may be less effective in the SMDs, although it might still be applicable in the PR blocs where non-LDP candidates have a greater prospect of success.

If, however, a viable two-party system emerges in Japan with parties alternating in government,[458] this will tend to increase the distance between organised groups and political parties because of the need for interest groups to work with whichever party is in power. Furthermore, if the two main parties are the LDP and the Democratic Party, or its successor organisations, and the latter can develop sufficient rural links to be a credible alternative to the farmers and agricultural cooperatives, then swinging support from one conservative/centrist party to the other might become a viable electoral strategy for Nokyo organisations.

Ultimately the impact of electoral reform on the organised electoral power of the farmers and Nokyo is very difficult to assess because of so many counterbalancing factors. Indeed, many of the likely effects of the new system may cancel each other out. In some respects candidates will be less dependent on individual groups, which will reduce the number of Diet members predominantly identified with farming interests. The micro-political incentives will be for politicians to appeal to a greater range of interests and to stand for broad principles with the widest voter appeal.

On the other hand, the greater homogeneity of electorates will tend to encourage alignment with dominant interests in any particular constituency, and the need to win a plurality in the SMDs will make candidates willing to seek the endorsement of large, well-mobilised groups that can offer reliable voting support. Nokyo stands to gain from this need because of its size and reputation at the hustings. If national party identification takes over as a primary determinant of voter choice, however, this will tend to reduce the influence of all groups, although if a viable two-party system develops, Nokyo may be able to exert electoral leverage by threatening to support candidates from an alternative party.

It is, therefore, difficult to state categorically whether the power of the farm vote and Nokyo's vote-mobilisation capacities will, in practice, be magnified or diminished by the changes to the LH electoral system. Undoubtedly, the reforms will, to some extent, serve further to undermine the electoral incentives for Japanese governments to protect farmers. On the other hand some features of the new system will work to retain the electoral leverage of the farm bloc. The optimism that sees Japan's economic liberalisation, including substantial cuts in agricultural support and protection, as inevitably consequent upon electoral reform may not be so well founded.[459]

The outlook for agrarian electoral power will likely be further modified as the changes work through the system and political actors adjust their behaviour to the new rules of the electoral game – providing the electoral reforms stick. The structural reforms to the system call for adaptive strategies from parties, candidates and supporting interests. Over time, the changes will educate participants into new patterns of behaviour. Pressure from organised interests such as the farmers and Nokyo will continue to be applied, although it may be channelled in different ways and be felt at different points.

The 1996 LH election

One LH election has occurred since the reforms – in October 1996. Based on what was observed in this election, it is clear that in the SMDs, electioneering still relied heavily on traditional support networks mobilised through *koenkai*. This was undoubtedly due to the intensified competition amongst candidates and the premium placed on each candidate maximising the proportion of votes won in order to obtain a plurality. As predicted by an LDP politician prior to the election: 'Contrary to the original intention, the introduction of the single-seat system will enhance voters' inclination to select a candidate based on personal appeal rather than the policy goals of political parties'.[460] The fact that the LDP performed markedly better in the SMDs than in the regional blocs suggests that personal support organisations embodying long-standing connections with interest groups and personal ties to local elites were still major factors in bringing out the vote for LDP candidates. This is despite the fact that in some cases, politicians were dispossessed of their customary voting base, the reforms put an end to fierce intra-party competition between candidates, and parties traditionally without a strong mass membership providing crucial electoral resources, such as the LDP, had branches organised in each single-member district. These local branches in fact extended the reach of the party organisation further down to the rice roots than the party prefectural federations had ever done. Even so, they did not displace the *koenkai*, nor electoral contests based primarily on the personal attributes and connection of politicians.

A concomitant of this was the notable absence of strong party identification. Indeed, a distinct trend towards de-alignment was apparent, in spite of, or perhaps because of the new electoral system.[461] Voters displayed increasing disenchantment with political parties overall. Public opinion polls revealed that rising numbers of Japanese voters, particularly in the cities, favoured no political party at all, which explained more volatile voting patterns. Party identification was certainly not sufficient to neutralise voters' predisposition to base their choice on candidates' personal attributes and Diet records, or to interfere with particularistic connections and support networks, although voters did respond more to issues, especially in the cities. Nevertheless, both the NFP and LDP seemed to disregard disaffected voters and instead relied heavily on their traditional support groups to win votes.

The old-style politics drawing on a web of social duties, obligations and responsibilities certainly remained the key to success in country areas. In Hokkaido (13), for example, both the LDP and NFP based their campaigns on small-scale meetings to which supporters could invite friends and colleagues to meet the candidate. The small number of unaffiliated voters meant that the new DP fared worse than either of the major parties.[462] In city districts, the LDP and NFP both fought to win favour with conservative voters, centring their campaigns on candidates' *koenkai* as well as on the interest groups that operated in the cities, such as doctors, veterans and some business and industry groups,[463] in short the special interests on which the LDP had traditionally relied in more urbanised areas. The NFP's main supporting groups were those that previously voted for two of the parties it amalgamated: the Soka Gakkai (Komeito) and private-sector trade unions (the DSP) within Rengo, plus those groups that had previously voted for former LDP members. Only the DP worked to exploit voter disenchantment with the mainstream and developed an appeal based on the political principles for which the party stood. Some observers noted that Diet members with close connections to specific interest groups were less active than before,[464] postulating that being too active as a lobbyist on behalf of one group clearly ran the risk of endangering relations with other potential groups of supporters.

Nevertheless, electoral competition in the form of a party-dominated, policy-focused contest did not really materialise in the first elections held under the new LH electoral system. As revealed by the Zenkoku Noseikyo questionnaire of their branch organisations, candidates' election promises and policies were germane to *noseiren* recommendation decisions in only 19.6 per cent of cases.[465]

At a more general level, political parties failed to alter their fundamental character as weak, loosely organised groupings, with only an amorphous identity on policy issues. Indeed, the pursuit of the 'median voter' in the SMDs drew most parties closer together and blurred their differences rather than accentuating any contrasts. This was as predicted by an SDP Diet politician, who postulated that the SMD system meant that candidates had to appeal to a majority of voters. As a result, policies espoused by candidates would be general, and in some, cases, policy debates would be avoided entirely.[466] Although it was possible to differentiate the policy positions of the parties on popular issues of the day like tax and administrative reform, the differences were so nuanced as to be immaterial. In terms of their fundamental organisational characteristics, political parties remained predominantly groups of like-minded individual politicians, bound together by personal loyalties, connections and political aspirations rather than ideological or policy-based commonalities. Furthermore, at the grass roots, other organisations such as interest groups and *koenkai* continued to step into the breach to compensate for the lack of strong, viable mass-based, local party groupings.

Conclusion

One of the crucial elements in Japanese farmers' voting power has been the ability of agricultural cooperative and other farm organisations to organise and direct farm votes. For most of the postwar period, farmers' groups (particularly Nokyo and its associated groupings) have been an important organisational ingredient in the voting base of a majority of Diet members elected from constituencies where farmers constitute an important element in the voting populace. The role of farmers' organisations in Japanese elections certainly supports the long-standing contention that the weak foundations of Japanese political parties at the grass roots have strengthened the power of organised interest groups as electoral actors.

Agricultural organisations have, in the majority of cases, supported candidates from the LDP, although Nokyo and its associated groups have maintained an in-principle stance of independence from political parties. This enables them to 'use' political parties to protect agriculture and farmers[467] and involves focusing their electoral decisions on the merits of each candidate. In reality, however, Nokyo's pro-LDP bias has been clearly in evidence. For

most of the past four to five decades, the dominance of the LDP in government and the conservative leanings of a majority of farm voters has
undermined any sustained anti-LDP movement within the organisation.
Although some socialist candidates with agricultural connections scored
relatively well amongst farmers in certain districts in the 1950s, 1960s and even
1970s, and although protest votes from time to time have demonstrated the
renowned capacities of agricultural cooperative organisations to ensure the
electoral failure of candidates, examples of the latter were generally confined
to particular organisations in particular elections in particular constituencies
at particular times. Furthermore, they were most notably deployed as a
concerted strategy in extreme circumstances such as the 1989 UH election,
and not as a standard electoral strategy.

Nokyo grew increasingly reliant on the LDP as the ruling party's power to
dispense distributive largesse through the national budget became more and
more pervasive. Nokyo and its associated organisations chose to 'use' the
political power of the LDP to support agriculture and raise the standard of
living of farm households.[468] Political demands after 1955 quite clearly
exemplified 'agricultural policies of dependence on the government party'.[469]
The reciprocal aspect of this relationship was Nokyo's emergence as a
subordinate agent of the LDP at the electoral level.

The relationship of reciprocal interdependence between Nokyo and the
LDP was based on a delicate balance of power. On the one hand, the LDP
could not afford to serve Nokyo as a mere tool because of the many competing claims on its generosity. On the other hand, LDP candidates remained
wary of Nokyo's retaliation in the elections if they took a strong stand against
the agricultural cooperatives and farmers' interests. In public, they often
spoke differently from what they really thought (in short, they used *tatemae*
to disguise *honne*).[470] Although reports surfaced from time to time that some
Diet members were increasingly disregarding Nokyo,[471] in fact they were
paying less heed to Zenchu's demands, not necessarily considerations relating
to individual agricultural cooperatives and their members at the rice roots.
Disregarding the latter risked abandoning one's constituency and thus
endangering one's political life.[472]

The early 1990s saw a partial and temporary destabilisation of the long-
standing interdependency relationship between Nokyo and the LDP, with the
latter's departure from the government's ranks. In the elections since, however,
the LDP has benefited from a resounding affirmation of Nokyo's support
with any temptation to back non-LDP candidates resisted under strong
pressure from the ruling party. It remains a fact of electoral life in rural areas
that Nokyo's involvement in LDP *jiban* is strong. Moreover, the agricultural
cooperatives still operate as if their voting power is hardly diminished,
seeking to exercise leverage over the ruling party by citing their ability to
control votes. In October 1997, for example, explicit threats were made by
prefectural Nokyo executives against the LDP in the 1998 UH election if the
party did not accede to Nokyo's demands for a new rice policy.[473] According

to one executive from Aomori Prefecture: 'Although the national financial situation is tight, this is an issue that is directly related to our lives. If you cannot support us and the establishment of a new rice policy, we will have to change the political party we are currently supporting'.[474] Similarly, an executive from Kumamoto Prefecture stated: 'We strongly ask for the strong support of LDP Diet members for this system. In return, we are going to support you in the next UH election'.[475] In a subsequent meeting of CAPIC's Sub-Committee for Agricultural Basic Policy (Nogyo Kihon Seisaku Shoiinkai), and in the presence of Zenchu Chairman, Harada Mutsutami, LH Diet politician Imamura Masahiro from Saga (2) district argued strongly for the new rice policy by pointing out that 'Nokyo said that if we will not do anything for the establishment of the new rice policy, they are not going to support us in the next UH election'.[476] Similarly, Matsuoka Toshikatsu (an 'old boy' of the MAFF and a previous chairman of the LDP's Agriculture and Forestry Division) said that 'this issue is related to the future of the LDP. We are going to put maximum effort into realising this system.'[477] Both politicians exemplified the typical response of LDP Diet politicians fearing the pressure of votes that Nokyo could bring to bear. Closer to the election in March 1998, Zenkoku Noseikyo chimed in with a campaign to mobilise the political power of farmers (*nogyosha seiji ryoku kesshu*), echoing the battlecry of earlier generations of Nokyo organisations as far back as the 1930s.

In the lead-up to the July 1998 UH elections, agricultural cooperatives also used their vote power to pressure the LDP on the issue of permitting the introduction of corporate farming in Japan.[478] A group of co-ops in a Tohoku prefecture wrote to the LDP prefectural headquarters saying that their support for the LDP in the elections depended on the party's stance on the issue.[479] Nokyo's national political organisation was also very conscious of the fact that the politicians elected in the 1998 UH election were going to be directly involved in the WTO negotiations, and therefore it was very keen to establish cooperative arrangements with those candidates recommended by the Zenkoku Noseikyo in order to lock them into supporting the protectionist cause.[480]

While these examples provide some evidence of the continuing credibility of Nokyo as an electoral force, its powers of vote collection are inevitably undergoing some deterioration in terms of a gradual loss of capacity to influence the votes of its members. This is due to a loosening of the bonds between farmers and their ubiquitous and all-powerful organisation and other changes taking place in rural society, as elaborated above. In the future, it is possible to envisage some politicians cutting their ties with Nokyo because of the declining importance of farmers' votes and the reduced efficacy of the agricultural cooperative-directed vote in elections. To some extent, the outcome depends on the political capacities and activism of the younger generation in agricultural regions and whether they can assume the mantle of their predecessors.

7 Representative politics

Extensive engagement by agricultural organisations in electoral activity and the voting power of their farm membership leads to representation in the Diet by politicians who can articulate agricultural interests from within the policy process. The following analysis of agricultural representation reviews the common labels for particular groups of politicians related to agricultural affairs and constructs a more systematic set of categories into which they can be classified. Past and present trends in different forms of agricultural representation are charted, together with a cross-sectional and time-series analysis of politicians who can be broadly termed 'agriculture-related Diet members' (*nogyo kankei giin*). The nature of their connections to farm interests is assessed as well as the linkage between electoral support from the agricultural sector and policy positions.

The picture that emerges of the Diet representation of agrarian interests is that it is far from exclusive. Most politicians identify with a range of different interests and can rarely be labelled 'single interest politicians', agricultural or otherwise. Furthermore, politicians maintain varying degrees of loyalty and obligation to farm voters and organisations depending on their reliance on rural support and the strength of their connections to agricultural groups. Nevertheless, over the period under investigation, agricultural representation at the aggregate level was sustained, and even in the face of party turmoil in the 1990s, displayed relatively strong continuities in terms of party alignment.

Categories of agricultural representation

Many terms are in common usage to describe Diet members with links to agriculture. They include 'farm politicians' or 'rural Diet members' (*noson giin*), 'rice Diet members' (*kome giin*), 'Nokyo Diet members' (*Nokyo giin*), 'livestock Diet members' (*chikusan giin*) and 'agricultural and forestry Diet members' (*norin giin*). Such labels are not confined to politicians with connections to agricultural interests. Other terms of a similar nature also spring to mind such as 'construction politicians' (*kensetsu giin*), postal politicians (*yusei giin*) and so on. Diet politicians are frequently tagged according to the interests (and even interest groups) they are considered to represent.

Labelling is generally based on several standard indicators: the characteristics of Diet members' constituencies, the composition of their electoral *jiban*, the nature of their connections to interest groups and their predominant policy concerns as demonstrated by Diet and party office-holding. None of the terms used are mutually exclusive and nor are politicians necessarily limited to one particular category. Many politicians are identified with several different sets of interests at the same time and many shift from one category to another over time.

Because multiple terms are used in the case of agricultural representatives, a more systematic analysis of what these various terms mean is needed to clarify a rather confused mix of labels. The generic category is that of 'agriculture-related Diet member'. It includes all those politicians with some connection, whether close or peripheral, to agricultural interests and agricultural policy issues. Thie link can be established by examining the career backgrounds, organisational connections and policy positions of Diet members. Agricultural policy interest can be elicited by a record of relevant office, such as current or past MAFF Ministers and Vice-Ministers, members of the Agriculture, Forestry and Fisheries Committees of both houses, members of party committees on agriculture, and members of the LDP's *norin zoku*. Diet members with leadership connections to agricultural organisations also belong to this group. Others are Diet members whose biographical details register some connection with agriculture through educational, career, organisational or electoral ties, or who have an expressed interest in agricultural policy.

The catch-all category of 'agriculture-related Diet member' can be divided into several sub-categories. The most clearly identifiable is the category of 'Nokyo Diet member'. This group is defined stipulatively as politicians holding parliamentary office who have at one time held an official position within the Nokyo organisation (executive or staff), including the post of adviser (*komon*).[1] It does not include those who have been co-op members (*kumiaiin*), but it does incorporate those who hold Diet office concurrently with Nokyo positions (*Nokyo geneki*) and those who have held such positions prior to entry into Parliament.[2] The number of Nokyo officials in the Diet at any one time will be smaller than the total number of Nokyo Diet members thus defined, because a certain proportion relinquish their agricultural cooperative leadership roles on entry into national politics.

This definition does not take into account individuals who took up Nokyo positions after entering the Diet, nor officials of the 100 or so Nokyo-related groups with which the agricultural cooperatives maintain connections of one sort or another. The value of defining *Nokyo giin* restrictively is that it enables the researcher to reach finite conclusions about the political character of Nokyo politicians as a group as well as changes in the direct representation of the Nokyo organisation over time.

Among other sub-categories of *nogyo kankei giin*, *noson giin* is a term commonly used to refer to politicians who represent agricultural constituencies, but can also be used to refer to politicians known to be associated with various locally-based farmers' groups. On the other hand, labels such as *norin giin* and 'agriculture and forestry-related Diet member' (*norin kankei giin*) are perhaps the most common. They refer to politicians from rural districts who attempt to exert influence over agricultural policy through Diet and party activities. *Norin giin* reputedly have a number of features: firstly rural districts are their native places or electoral bases; secondly, they receive electoral support from agricultural groups like Nokyo; and thirdly, policies on agricultural products important to their native place or electoral base are directly related to votes.[3]

It has been said that all politicians from rural prefectures are *norin giin*.[4] For example, when it comes to the producer rice price, all Diet members, except those from Tokyo and Osaka, deserve the label *norin giin* because rice is not only Japan's staple food but is a farm product grown nationwide.[5] Furthermore, Diet members who benefit from the votes of farmers have to call themselves *norin giin*, since to do otherwise might invite an electoral backlash from farmers.[6] In other words, self-labelling is frequently used by Diet members as a political expedient to obtain farm votes, a tag they tend to hang on themselves when they visit rural areas in order to appeal to their farming constituents.[7]

In this sense, the political opportunism of Japanese politicians can exaggerate the strength of farm representation in the Diet, given the inclination of Diet candidates to employ convenient labels if it advantages them electorally. Although the number of self-styled *norin giin* as a proportion of the total number of Diet members from a given prefecture roughly correlates with the proportion of farm population in the total population,[8] even in circumstances where electorates are 80 per cent urban and 20 per cent rural villages, politicians tend to label themselves *norin giin* for strategic reasons. It is done to secure even a relatively small proportion of their total vote, particularly if it makes the difference between winning and losing an election. As Arimitsu has commented, politicians would call themselves a *norin giin* even if one vote depended on it.[9] This explains the alleged surplus of *norin giin* in spite of the decline in the number of farmers.[10] The attachments in practice, however, may only be superficial. Furthermore, the political price of such self-labelling is minimal, given the generally favourable disposition of urban dwellers towards farmers.[11]

Norin giin can also refer to a more specific sub-category of former bureaucrats from the MAFF who successfully attain Diet office, and of politicians with connections to agricultural organisations on the list of MAFF *gaikaku dantai*. In addition, it can denote a politician with some kind of agricultural policy interest and expertise, and therefore it is often used to refer to members of the Diet Committees on Agriculture, Forestry and Fisheries, members of party agricultural and forestry policymaking bodies (such as the LDP's Norin Bukai) and supporters of informal Diet groupings centring on more specific agricultural policy issues or commodity interests – the so-called Diet members' leagues (*giin renmei*). The leagues are informal policy caucuses of Diet members in which special interest backbenchers cluster as a means of advancing the interests with which they are most closely identified. The leagues actively lobby the party leadership on behalf of their rural supporters. Although designated as Diet members' leagues, they function by and large within parties,[12] those in the LDP being the most dominant and the most active on agricultural matters. In order for Diet members to become real *norin giin*, they have to join three to four Diet members' leagues in agricultural affairs.[13]

The members of formal party agricultural committees and informal Diet members' leagues can also be referred to as 'agricultural policy Diet members' or *nosei giin*. The special label of agricultural and forestry tribe Diet member (*norin zoku*) is reserved for those who are part of the LDP's inner circle of specialist agricultural policymakers who are well connected to outside interests in the agricultural world.[14]

Within the categories of *noson giin* or *norin giin* are commodity-based sub-categories such as rice politicians, livestock politicians, 'dairy politicians' (*rakuno giin*), 'fruit Diet members' (*kudamono giin*) and so on. In the 1960s and early 1970s, the most notorious commodity sub-grouping was the group of LDP rice Diet members known as *betokon giin* (rice Vietcong).[15] Other labels can be more specific and individual. Nakasone Yasuhiro, when he was Chairman of the LDP's Executive Council in 1971, was known as a *konnyaku giin* because of the importance of *konnyaku* production in Gumma Prefecture and because he was Chairman of the Nihon Konnyaku Kyokai (see Table 2.3).

As pointed out earlier, these categories and sub-categories are not mutually exclusive. Not only would it be possible for Diet members to belong to all categories simultaneously, but the labels are not used with any great precision in general commentary, particularly in the Japanese media. For purposes of this analysis, however, the first category on this list – that of *Nokyo giin* – is defined restrictively. It requires a distinct and direct leadership connection to the agricultural cooperatives. *Noson giin* is also used to designate specifically those politicians representing rural/agricultural regions.

Numbers of agriculture-related Diet members

Over the course of several decades of scholarly and journalistic analysis, many general observations have been made about the number of politicians who represent agricultural interests. One, for example, suggested that for most of the LDP's uninterrupted period in government, the leading members of the party, including faction leaders,[16] were closely linked to rural districts.[17] In other cases, actual figures have been suggested for the number of politicians representing agricultural interests. In 1966 an agricultural journalist reported that there were some 200 Diet members in the LDP 'with a *'noringiinteki'* character, 110–120 of which were under the strong influence of Nokyo'.[18] At the other extreme was a 1968 assessment which argued that amongst 486 members in the Lower House, less than 30 members (about 20 LDP, 5 JSP, 3 DSP) were playing an active role as *norin giin* (including seven ex-bureaucrat members in the LDP). In the Upper House, not more than 25 politicians out of 250 members (about 20 in the LDP and four in the JSP) were *norin giin*. Of these, six from the LDP were ex-MAF and two from the JSP were from the MAF union.[19]

Two decades later in 1988, the farm lobby could reputedly still count on the votes of about 200 of the 445 LDP members of parliament.[20] Indeed, throughout the 1980s, around 200 Diet members regularly attended Nokyo's rallies in Tokyo protesting the prospects of agricultural trade liberalisation. In 1986, Ito Kenzo, a career executive of Zenchu went as far as to assert that: 'Of the 390 Liberal-Democratic party members [in the Diet], 320 support Nokyo'.[21] Based on this figure, Ito claimed that 'we are clearly strongly opposed to any change in agricultural policy and [are] in a position to block change . . . . Of the present Cabinet, 12 Ministers support Nokyo and have our support, therefore 80 to 90 per cent support our policies. In that sense, we have established control.'[22] Ito's figure was exceeded by another estimate which maintained that prior to the 1989 election, around 350 or 70 per cent of Diet members from the LDP could be referred to as *norin zoku* with connections to rural areas. This group represented the largest internal force of the LDP's Diet members'.[23]

Evaluating the magnitude of Diet representation of agricultural interests can depend on the nature of linkages between the Diet members and the agricultural world. If the emphasis is placed on a politician's voting base and supporting interests, then the figure for agricultural representatives tends to be large. On the other hand, if a close funding connection is the determining criterion, then the number shrinks. In Arimitsu's view, the relationship between farm votes and so-called agricultural representatives is not close or direct because it does not encompass political funding. If politicians represent groups that provide money for their elections, then the number of *norin giin* is small. Even though around 200 members of the LDP are considered to be *norin giin*, if a funding connection is the decisive criterion, the figure of 200 shrinks to around 30. In fact, as Arimitsu contends, the large number of so-called *norin giin* in fact impedes the genuine representation of farmers, which might have been possible if the figure were 30 from the start. In his opinion, roughly 30 politicians in the LDP genuinely represent farmers' interests, but they are vulnerable in elections because they lack election funds.[24]

Arimitsu's argument discounts those of other informed observers such as Sakaguchi who maintains that if you throw a stone blindly at the Diet, you will hit a politician who is receiving a donation from Nokyo because so many politicians are doing so.[25] Furthermore, as the evidence of various scandals and other disclosures reveals, large numbers of politicians are in receipt of political funding from the agricultural cooperatives, and in some cases relatively large sums are involved.[26] Arimitsu also underrates the value of farmers' voting support to candidates from rural and semi-rural areas. Voting and funding are the two wheels of a Diet politician's electoral cart. Remove one, and the cart falls over.

Measuring agricultural representation in the Diet

The ideal definition of an 'agricultural representative' is a Diet politician who relies on farmers for a sizeable proportion of his voting support and has close connections with agricultural organisations. The problem with this definition, however, is that it is very difficult to substantiate empirically across 763 (now 752) Diet members. Furthermore, one has to keep in mind the caveat about trying to quantify what is essentially a very subjective phenomenon: whether or to what extent a politician feels motivated to act on behalf of agricultural interests in the Diet and in party policymaking contexts.

In all cases, the number of 'agricultural representatives' depends on the definitional basis that is employed. One could count as *noson giin*, for example, the total number of Diet members representing rural and semi-rural areas (also defined arbitrarily). Using the figures for rural and semi-rural seats in Tables 5.14 and 5.15, 172 Diet members could be defined as farm politicians in 1993 (prior to the changes in the LH electoral system), not counting NC representatives in the Upper House. One problem with this definition is that it does not differentiate the type of support base each politician has and the proportion of farm votes within that support base. Not all *noson giin* thus defined would represent agricultural interests equally, but more importantly, some representatives from these constituencies might have marginal support from farmers and farm organisations. In this case, they could not be considered to be truly 'agricultural representatives'.

An investigation of the nature of rural and semi-rural Diet members' links to agricultural organisations might make this definition more reliable, but the difficulty in this case is determining the nature and extent of the connections between farm groups and politicians. The representation of agricultural organisations in the Diet is a composite of current and previous executives of these groups (direct representatives) plus an indeterminate group of indirect representatives (those who have received electoral support from these organisations). Connections based on direct representation can be clearcut, but they are less so in the case of indirect representation where politicians have received varying degrees of electoral support from agricultural groups. In the latter case, information is available publicly only in a small minority of cases.

Approaching from another direction, the number of *norin giin* could be considered to be the sum total of all members of Diet and party agricultural committees. In the LDP's case, the two main agricultural policymaking committees are the AFD and CAPIC. Not counting those politicians who belonged to both, the total membership of these two committees in 1987 was 290; in 1997 it was 230. The combined membership of 290 in 1987 was 65.5 per cent of the party's total Diet membership; in 1997, it was 65.9 per cent.

The problem with this method is that politicians rotate their memberships around different policy committees at different times (in addition to holding several committee memberships simultaneously), and even those very closely identified with agricultural interests are not always sitting on one or other of the relevant Diet or party committees. Conversely, not all the members of these committees qualify as *norin giin* or farm politicians on other grounds such as constituency or interest group connections, but are sitting on these committees in order to gain experience across a range of policy areas. In other words, the fact that a Diet member is or has been a member of an agricultural committee does not necessarily make him an agricultural representative, although it makes it likely, particularly if membership is sustained over a long period of time.

Moreover, as LDP Diet members rise to the top of the party and policy hierarchy, they tend to move beyond positions that reflect their representational interests into higher office in the party (such as Secretary-General) or in government (such as Chief Cabinet Secretary, or Cabinet office unrelated to their long-standing field of policy expertise). Watanabe Michio, for example, was a leading *norin zoku*, but subsequently became Minister of Welfare, Minister of International Trade and Industry, Minister of Finance and Minister of Foreign Affairs. In the last position, he appeared to adopt a policy stance that was quite antipathetic towards agriculture on trade issues, reflecting his role as spokesperson for the Foreign Ministry.[27]

The attempt in this chapter to quantify different categories of agricultural representatives begins by casting the net as widely as possible, without necessarily assuming anything about the quality of agricultural representation on the part of those caught up in the net. For these purposes, the broadest category of all is used: that of 'agriculture-related Diet member'. These politicians can be defined according to a range of criteria which identifies most if not all politicians with some connection, whether central or peripheral, to agricultural interests and agricultural policy issues. The criteria are:

a) Agricultural policy interest: past or present MAFF Ministers and Parliamentary Vice-Ministers; members of parliamentary Agriculture, Forestry and Fisheries Committees; past or present members of the LDP's AFD and CAPIC; officials of the LDP's Agriculture, Forestry and Fisheries Office (Norinsuisan Kyoku), members of the LDP's *norin zoku*; and past or present executives of opposition parties' agricultural policy committees who are Diet members.[28]
b) A leadership connection with an agricultural organisation: past or present executive or staff members of an agricultural organisation including Nokyo; past or present members of APRA, Nokyo's group of Diet supporters.
c) General connection with agriculture: Diet members whose biographical

details as recorded in Diet handbooks or as known to the author from a range of other sources reveal some connection with agriculture through educational, career, organisational or electoral ties or an expressed interest in agricultural policy.

The limitations of this classification system is that it is very broad and will include politicians who have simply sat on agricultural committees in the Diet or in their parties at one time or another. As noted earlier, such a move is commonly made by politicians merely to gain experience across a range of policy fields. These politicians are not necessarily all 'agricultural representatives', meaning politicians whose electoral and organisational connections motivate them actively to work on behalf of farmers' interests in national politics. Such connections can be more reliably gleaned from characteristics such as organisational ties, the constitution of Diet members' *koenkai* and the holding of leadership positions in agricultural committees. Nevertheless, the catch-all category of 'agriculture-related Diet member' indicates the maximum number of politicians with some connection to agriculture or experience in the field of agricultural policy.

A cross-sectional analysis of this group was undertaken by the author for 1990 by means of a sample and questionnaire survey.[29] The numerical strength of *nogyo kankei giin* thus defined was 426, or 56 per cent of total Diet membership, indicating that around one-half of the Diet at the time had a known connection with agriculture and agriculture-related policy matters.

Predictably a large majority (78 per cent) of LH Diet members from constituencies designated as 'rural' were agricultural representatives.[30] For semi-rural districts the proportion of agricultural representatives was 73 per cent, for semi-urban districts 59 per cent, for urban districts 45 per cent and for metropolitan districts 13 per cent.[31] The fact that almost two-thirds of politicians from semi-urban districts were agricultural representatives and almost half the total of urban Diet members were also agricultural representatives can be attributed to several possible factors. Most importantly, the factor of land-use geography dictates that few purely urban districts exist in Japan. Agriculture is interspersed with residential, industrial and commercial areas in almost all electorates, although the ratio of farming areas to non-farming areas varies considerably across the metropolitan-rural spectrum. As noted earlier, even candidates from urban districts may cultivate the few farm votes they have in their electorates because these votes tend to be more reliable and organised.

Secondly, Diet members may retain residual connections with agriculture even when their districts undergo urbanisation because of well-established electoral support relationships particularly with groups like Nokyo which survive the urbanisation process. The sample survey picked up both historical and current ties to agriculture, although it did not distinguish between committed and uncommitted agricultural representatives.

Thirdly, for politicians from urban and metropolitan electorates to

Table 7.1 Number of Diet members with agricultural
connections 1986–98

1986	Lower House	284
	Upper House	117
	Total	401
	Proportion of total Diet membership	52%
1989	Lower House	284
	Upper House	122
	Total	406
	Proportion of total Diet membership	53%
1990	Lower House	302
	Upper House	124
	Total	426
	Proportion of total Diet membership	56%
1992	Lower House	302
	Upper House	123
	Total	425
	Proportion of total Diet membership	56%
1993	Lower House	296
	Upper House	123
	Total	419
	Proportion of total Diet membership	55%
1995	Lower House	296
	Upper House	133
	Total	429
	Proportion of total Diet membership	57%
1996	Lower House	302
	Upper House	135
	Total	437
	Proportion of total Diet membership	58%
1998	Lower House	295
	Upper House	91
	Total	386
	Proportion of total Diet membership	51%

Sources: Author's sample survey of Diet members with agricultural connections; *Seikan Yoran*, relevant issues; listings of LDP
agricultural policy committees supplied by MAFF officials.

acknowledge a policy or other connection to agriculture is not regarded as an
electoral liability in the sense of potentially alienating non-agricultural voters.
As noted earlier, the decision to speak for farmers or urban consumers has
not generally been perceived electorally as a 'zero sum game'. Both broad
categories of voter can be represented because of the shared interests
identified by their respective interest groups and because the basic public
policy philosophy underlying policies of agricultural support and protection
emphasises the national interests advanced by such policies.[32]

Lastly, those who show an interest in agricultural policy may not in fact all be 'agricultural representatives' in the sense of politicians who work on behalf of farmers' interests in Diet politics. Some of the politicians from urban and metropolitan electorates in the survey, for example, represented urban-consumer and women's groups and showed an interest in agricultural policy out of a concern for food prices and other consumer-related issues connected with agriculture, such as food safety or food security. In other words, they were interested in agricultural policy issues, but not as representatives of the farmers. Their presence on committees concerned with agricultural and food, however, meant that they were caught up in the definitional net utilised in the sample survey.

Nevertheless, amongst the total group of agriculture-related Diet members, it should be emphasised that, overall, Diet members from urban and metropolitan constituencies are in a distinct minority. More than three quarters (or 77 per cent) were from semi-urban, semi-rural and rural constituencies. The results of the author's follow-up questionnaire survey revealed an even stronger connection between agricultural and constituency representation. In this case, the great majority, or 74 per cent of respondents classified their constituencies as either rural or semi-rural,[33] indicating that almost three quarters of this group saw themselves essentially as 'farm politicians'.

Table 7.1 depicts trends in numbers of agriculture-related Diet members over the years 1986–1998. Any possible reduction in the power of the farm vote should have registered in a downward trend in agricultural representation. The results do not confirm this proposition. Indeed, the time series analysis indicates remarkable stability in the proportion of agricultural representatives in both houses of the Diet, in spite of the continuing decline in agriculture in both economic and demographic terms. The political voice of the farm sector in the national Diet has clearly been sustained at between 50–58 per cent of its total membership over this period.[34] Although a relatively sharp fall can be detected between 1996 and 1998, agriculture may take a while to become a minority interest in the years ahead. Sheer weight of numbers has always been one of its main strengths. This is only a fraction less true in 1998 than it was in 1986.

The party alignment of agriculture-related Diet members in 1990

An examination of the party alignment of agricultural representatives in 1990 confirms the close nexus between farmers and the LDP. A majority of politicians with agricultural connections were affiliated to the ruling party. The figures for agricultural representation by party varied somewhat between the two Houses of the Diet, with the LDP recording 83 per cent of agriculture-related Diet members in the Lower House (Table 7.2) and 72 per cent in the Upper House (Table 7.3).[35] A total of 341 Diet members or 80 per cent of all agriculture-related politicians in the 1990 Diet belonged to the LDP (Table 7.4).

Table 7.2 Lower House agriculture-related Diet dembers by party, 1990–98

Party	1990 — Number of agricultural representatives in Lower House	1990 — Percentage of agricultural representatives in that house[d]	1995[a] — Number of agricultural representatives in Lower House	1995 — Percentage of agricultural representatives in that house[d]	1996[b] — Number of agricultural representatives in Lower House	1996 — Percentage of agricultural representatives in that house[d]	1998[c] — Number of agricultural representatives in Lower House	1998 — Percentage of agricultural representatives in that house[d]
LDP	252	83	215	73	225	75	231	78
JSP/SDP	34	11	20	7	8	3	8	3
Shinto Sakigake			8 (7)[e]	3	2 (2)[e]	1	2 (2)[e]	1
Ind.	5	2	4 3)[f] (3)	1	7 (5)	2	8 (7)	3
Shinseito			31) (26)					
Komeito	4	1	5)				3[g]	1
DSP	4	1	4)					
Nihon Shinto			4)					
Shaminren	1	0	1)					
Shinshinto[h]			48 (29)	16	49 (26)	16		
Minshuto[i]					8	3	26 (8)	9
Jiyuto							11 (6)	4
Kaikaku Kurabu[j]							3 (1)	1
JCP	2	1	1	0	3	1	3	1
Total	302	100	296	100	302	100	295	100

Notes:

a 1995 has been chosen because of the complexity of party changes in the 1992–94 period. The 1993 election results were analysed then converted to 1995 figures.

b The figures in this column do not show the Sun Party, formed in December 1996, and other defections from the Shinshinto in 1997 (see Figure 5.2).

c 1998 has been chosen because of the complexity of party changes in the 1996–98 period.

d The percentages in these columns have been rounded off.

e The figures in brackets in this column are those who are ex-LDP members.

f The figures in half brackets in this column give the party breakdown for the Shinshinto figure below.

g These are figures for the New Komeito formed in November 1998 (see Figure 5.2).

h The Shinshinto amalgamated the Shinseito, Komeito, DSP and Nihon Shinto in December 1994. Some of the Shaminren members as well as Independents also joined (see Figure 5.2).

i The Minshuto was formed predominantly of members of the SDP and Shinto Sakigake in September 1996; in April 1998, it absorbed several other newly formed parties (see Figure 5.2).

j The Kaikaku Kurabu is a small party grouping that formed in January 1998 in the wake of the dissolution of the Shinshinto (see Figure 5.2).

Sources: Author's sample survey of Diet members with agricultural connections; *Seikan Yoran*, relevant issues.

Table 7.3 Upper House agriculture-related Diet members by party, 1990–98

	1990	1990	1995	1995	1996[a]	1996	1998	1998
Party	Number of agricultural representatives in Upper House	Percentage of agricultural representatives in that house[b]	Number of agricultural representatives in Upper House	Percentage of agricultural representatives in that house[b]	Number of agricultural representatives in Upper House	Percentage of agricultural representatives in that house[b]	Number of agricultural representatives in Upper House	Percentage of agricultural representatives in that house[b]
LDP	89	72	97	73	99	73	63	69
JSP/SDP	19	15	13	10	11	8	4	4
Ind.	3	2	3 1)[c]	2	3	2	3 (1)[d]	3
Shinseito			2)					
Komeito[e]	4	3	2 3)	2	2	1	4	4
DSP	1	1	0)					
Nihon Shinto			0)					
Shaminren	0	0	0)					
Shinshinto			14 (1)[d]	11	14 (1)[d]	10		
Minshuto					2	1	9 (2)	10
Jiyuto							3	3
JCP	2	2	3	2	3	2	4	4
Rengo/ Minkairen	4	3	1	1	1	1		
Minor parties	2	2	0	0	0	0	1 (1)	1
Total	124	100	133	100	135	100	91	100

Notes:
a 1996 is included because of the party reshuffling that was going on at that time.
b The percentages in these columns have been rounded off.
c The figures in half brackets in this column give the party breakdown for the Shinshinto figure below.
d The figures in brackets in this column are ex-LDP members.
e Those Komeito members who did not join the Shinshinto in December 1994 were known as Komei in the Upper House. In November 1998 they rejoined the New Komeito (see Figure 5.2).

Source: Author's sample survey of Diet members with agricultural connections; Seikan Yoran, relevant issues.

Table 7.4 Total number of agriculture-related Diet members by party, 1990–98

	1990 Total in both houses	1990 Percentage of agricultural representatives in both houses[a]	1995 Total in both houses	1995 Percentage of agricultural representatives in both houses[a]	1996 Total in both houses	1996 Percentage of agricultural representatives in both houses[a]	1998 Total in both houses	1998 Percentage of agricultural representatives in both houses[a]	1990 Percentage of total members in the Diet from that party[b]	1995 Percentage of total members in the Diet from that party[b]	1996 Percentage of total members in the Diet from that party[b]	1998 Percentage of total members in the Diet from that party[b]
LDP	341	80	312	73	324	74	294	76	80	95	93	80
JSP/SDP	53	12	33	7	19	4	12	3	36	32	43	44
Shinto Sakigake			8 (7)c	2	2 (2)c	0	2 (2)c	1		35	40	40
Ind.	8	2	7 4)d (3)	2	10 (5)	2	11 (8)	3	33	21	36	31
Shinseito			33) (26)	0								
Komeito	8	2	2 8)		2	0	7	2	11	18	18	12
DSP	5	1	4)						15			
Nihon Shinto			4)									
Shaminren	1	0	1)						25			
Shinshinto			62 (30)	14	63 (27)	14				26	31	
Minshuto					10	2	35 (10)	9			16	25
Jiyuto							14 (6)	4				27
Kaikaku Kurabu							3 (1)	1				25
JCP	4	1	4	1	6	1	7	2	10	14	15	14
Rengo/Minkairen	4	1	1	0	1	0			33	50	25	
Minor parties	2	0	0	0	0	0	1 (1)	0	25	0	0	50
Total	426	100	429	100	437	100	386	100	–	–	–	–

Notes:

a The percentages in these columns have been rounded off.

b The total LDP Diet membership in 1995 includes not only those elected as LDP candidates in the 1993 elections, but also Independents and members of other parties (e.g. the Shinshinto) who rejoined the LDP.

c The figures in brackets in this column are those who are ex-LDP members.

d The figures in half brackets in this column give the party breakdown for the Shinshinto figure below.

Sources: Author's sample survey of Diet members with agricultural connections; *Seikan Yoran*, relevant issues.

Amongst the Opposition parties, the JSP far outnumbered all the other parties in the number of its agricultural representatives, although the figure was relatively small compared to the LDP (34, or 11 per cent of LH agricultural representatives and 19, or 15 per cent of UH agricultural representatives), making a total of 53, or 12 per cent of agriculture-related Diet members in both Houses.

Figures for the other parties were very low in comparison. Moreover, a closer look at the career details and policy interests of those in the Komeito, JCP and the Tax Party disclosed that their main qualification for inclusion in the category of 'agriculture-related Diet member' stemmed from experience in the Agricultural, Forestry and Fisheries Committees of the Diet, where membership is customarily allotted in proportion to the total number of seats each party has in the house. Under this system, parties such as the Komeito and JCP would be expected to supply members for these committees regardless of their particular connections to or interest in the agricultural sector. All the Opposition Diet members in question were from metropolitan or urban districts and in some cases had strong connections with urban-consumer and women's groups. Their interest in agricultural issues, as explained earlier, would primarily originate in a concern for food issues rather than a self-perception as farmers' representatives.[36]

The general point from the figures for 1990 in Tables 7.2–7.4, however, is that the LDP, although overwhelmingly dominant, did not have a monopoly of agricultural representation. The average over both houses was 80 per cent, underlining the general pattern of majority-LDP, minority-Opposition party configuration demonstrated with respect to politicians supported in elections by the agricultural cooperatives – including the members of APRA and recipients of Nokyo funding.[37] As already noted, the JSP was by far the most significant Opposition party in terms of the number of agricultural representatives within its ranks.

Table 7.4 also shows the 'weight' of agricultural interests in each party, with the LDP once again out-ranking all other parties. The great majority of the ruling party's Diet membership were agriculture-related Diet members. At the other extreme were the Komeito and JCP which scored very low in terms of the proportion of agricultural representatives in their Diet membership (11 per cent and 10 per cent respectively). The DSP was not much higher at 15 per cent. Agricultural representatives in the JSP, on the other hand, comprised more than a third (36 per cent) of its Diet membership. Rengo and Independents were only slightly behind at 33 per cent. Some of the Independents, and certainly most Rengo members, benefited from the farmers' protest vote in the 1989 UH election. Rengo did particularly well in some areas where farmers rejected their long-standing political representatives, such as in Yamagata, Ishikawa, Yamanashi, Gifu, Mie, Shiga, Tokushima and Ehime, but were not prepared to vote for JSP candidates.[38] Rengo's performance in 1989 was not repeated, however, in subsequent elections.

The implications of the cross-party figures for the overall profile of these parties in agricultural policymaking is significant. They undoubtedly confirm the LDP's majority orientation towards agricultural interests. On the other hand, the conservatives do not exclusively dominate the category of agriculture-related politicians; they share this category with the Opposition parties. The JSP, particular, registered a not insignificant level of agricultural representation within its Diet membership, as did Rengo as well as Independents. This factor helps to account for the resistance of some Opposition Diet members to cutbacks in subsidies and protection for farmers.[39]

On the other hand, the figures also help to explain why a party such as the Komeito, with a low agricultural representation rate, explored rice liberalisation options in the early 1990s.[40] In contrast, the JCP – a party with an equally low agricultural representation rate – has demonstrated unwavering support for the principle of agricultural protection, which, at first glance, appears irrational as an electoral strategy. This stance, however, can be explained in terms of the JCP's electoral practice of standing a candidate in every constituency, and its politically opportunistic strategy of using all means to try to expand its extremely small political support base in rural areas.[41]

The impact of party defections

In spite of shifting party-political ground which began with the formation of the Japan New Party in June 1992, and which was followed by the breakup of the LDP in 1993 and the defections of a number of LDP farm politicians to the Renewal Party and later the New Frontier Party in 1994, the political alignment of the farm sector remained basically unaltered. The LDP still contained the majority of Diet politicians with agricultural connections in 1996. Trends in agricultural representation by party in LH and UH elections over the 1990–96 period are contained in the data in Tables 7.2–7.4. As a proportion of the total number of Diet members with agricultural connections, the LDP retained its dominance amongst all the parties. Tables 7.2 and 7.3 depict the breakdown in LDP proportions for each house: from 83 to 75 per cent of the total number of agricultural representatives in the Lower House over the period 1990–96, and from 72 to 73 per cent in the Upper House over the same period. For both houses, the decline was from 80 per cent to 74 per cent (see Table 7.4).

In 1996, the LDP still, therefore, comprised just under three-quarters of the total number of Diet members with agricultural connections in the Lower House, while only 14 per cent were members of the Shinshinto, with somewhat less than half of these being former LDP members and not new Shinshinto members (see Table 7.4). In this respect, the connection to agriculture in Shinshinto's case was partly an inherited link. If LDP defectors are subtracted, only 36 of the 286 Diet members with agricultural connections, or 8 per cent, were Shinshinto Diet members without a previous affiliation to the LDP.

Furthermore, shifting to the Shinshinto (and other parties such as Shinto Sakigake) proved to be a fatal move for a number of former LDP farm politicians in the 1996 elections[42] and also for first-term agricultural representatives in the Shinshinto and other parties, such as Shinto Sakigake, who had been elected to the Lower House in 1993. A number of the JSP/SDP's long-standing agricultural representatives were also swept aside by the anti-SDP tide in the 1996 poll, reducing its percentage of agricultural representatives for both Houses from 33 per cent in 1995 to 19 per cent in 1996 (see Table 7.4).

The parties that later made up the Shinshinto did not, therefore, elect sizeable numbers of new agricultural politicians in the 1993 LH elections,[43] nor did the Shinshinto elect sizeable numbers of new members with agricultural connections in the 1995 or 1996 Upper and Lower House elections respectively. This reflected the Shinshinto's predominantly urban support base. While consisting of a rump of ex-LDP politicians, it also incorporated the urban-based Komeito and DSP as well as the new party of the cities, the Nihon Shinto.[44] Consequently, it is not surprising that, given the nature of the political groupings it comprised and the relatively more successful performance of its candidates in urban areas, the Shinshinto made up such a small proportion of the total number of politicians with agricultural connections.

Nor did the wholesale defections from the LDP fundamentally alter the ruling party's agricultural character. Indeed, in the period under examination, this solidified in relative terms. The total proportion of agriculture-related Diet members in the party rose from 80 per cent in 1990 to 93 per cent in 1996 (see Table 7.4). The continuing high rates of agricultural representation in the LDP reflected two characteristics of the ruling party: first, the fact that most members of the LDP in the Diet, apart from those representing city areas, showed an interest in agricultural policies;[45] and second, the fact that at some time in their Diet career, most LDP politicians served on CAPIC or the AFD. Indeed, like some members of urban-based Opposition parties, some LDP politicians from city areas from time to time joined agricultural committees as a way of voicing the consumer viewpoint on food issues.

In contrast, Shinshinto's agriculture-related Diet members comprised only 31 per cent of the party's total membership in the Diet in 1996, which was lower than the SDP at 43 per cent, Shinto Sakigake at 40 per cent and Independents at 36 per cent. The figure for Independents was quite high because in rural and semi-rural electorates they were often conservative politicians who had failed to gain LDP pre-selection. Nevertheless, they could still garner support from farmers' organisations and maintain good connections with them in order to 'harden' their support base. Given the SDP and Shinto Sakigake figures, however, it seems that agreement on agricultural policy matters during the ruling coalition that lasted from June 1994 until October 1996 was facilitated by the relatively high orientations of its three component groupings – the LDP, SDP and Shinto Sakigake – towards political representation of the agricultural sector. Shinto Sakigake almost entirely inherited this legacy from the LDP (see Table 7.4).

In 1998, following the UH elections, neither the character of agricultural representation in the Diet, nor the relative orientation of each party towards agriculture changed dramatically. Perhaps the most striking development was the fall in the number of LDP agricultural representatives in the Upper House, from 97 in 1995 to 63 in 1998, which represented more than a third (see Table 7.3). This was only exceeded by the SDP, whose agricultural representatives fell in number from 11 to four (see Table 7.3).

These results probably reflect the general decline in the electoral performance of both these parties, rather than a reorientation away from agricultural representation. Reviewing the LDP across both houses of the Diet, 80 per cent of its total Diet membership were agricultural representatives in 1990 just as they were in 1998 (see Table 7.4). This is even more so in the case of the JSP/SDP where 36 per cent were agricultural representatives in 1990 while 44 per cent were in 1998. In short, if anything, the party that played the role of the major Opposition party to the LDP in the postwar period became even more orientated towards agricultural interests over the period of its electoral decline in the 1990s. The JCP and Komeito also exhibited a slight reorientation in the direction of agricultural representation, although the numbers were so small it is difficult to attach any particular significance to them.

As far as the new Opposition parties are concerned, adding Minshuto and Jiyuto agricultural representatives together as the successor parties to the Shinshinto produces a slight fall in the number of their UH agricultural representatives (from 14 in 1995 to 12 in 1998) as shown in Table 7.3. Nevertheless, in 1998, about one-quarter of these parties' Diet membership still had links to agricultural interests (see Table 7.4). This is higher than other Opposition parties like the JCP and Komeito and undoubtedly reflects the LDP roots of some of their Diet members.

In terms of party proportions of the total number of agricultural representatives in the Upper House, the LDP suffered only a slight decline over the 1990–98 period, from 72 per cent to 69 per cent (see Table 7.3). The JSP/SDP, however, fell from 15 per cent in 1990 to 4 per cent in 1998, reflecting its transition to minor party status, rather than any dramatic reorientation away from farm interests, as noted earlier. Meanwhile the Komeito and JCP demonstrated a slight shift in the direction of greater agricultural representation, although as already pointed out, statistically this is not large enough to suggest any fundamental refocusing in these parties away from their traditional bailiwick in the cities. Rengo/Minkairen, which began so strongly in 1989, faded into insignificance (it was absorbed into the Minshuto in April 1998), while Minshuto itself was a paler version of the old Shinshinto in terms of its agricultural representation (see Table 7.3).

Taken together, the data over the period 1990–98 in Tables 7.1–7.4 endorse a number of the observations made in the two preceding chapters. The LDP remains the party most strongly aligned with agricultural interests notwithstanding the period of party fracture and fusion between 1993 and 1998, while the main conservative Opposition party – the Shinshinto until its breakup in January 1998, and more latterly the Minshuto – is emerging as the major alternative party in the Japanese cities, although a residual hangover from the past still exists in the form of its 10 ex-LDP agricultural representatives which make up almost one-third of its total number of agricultural representatives (see Table 7.4). The Jiyuto, meanwhile, is a conservative force which more closely approximates the LDP in terms of the composition of its membership (and more latterly its policies as the LDP-Jiyuto coalition of January 1999 signifies). More than half of the LP's agricultural representatives in the Lower House are former LDP members (see Table 7.2). Neither the LP nor the DP are, therefore, in a position to reject their agricultural roots or alienate farm voters entirely. Some of their most prominent leaders (in particular Ozawa Ichiro of the LP and Hata Tsutomu of the DP) come from agricultural regions. Hata, in particular, is a former LDP MAFF Minister and *norin zoku*. Nevertheless, the overall orientation of the Minshuto, in particular, is towards urban areas, which predisposes it towards supporting consumer rather than agricultural producer interests.

Factional affiliation of agriculture-related Diet members

In the Japanese commercial and industrial world, which is both broad and heterogeneous, it has not been unusual for different industrial sectors to become associated with different factions of the LDP (for example, what was formerly the Tanaka faction had close links to construction interests; the former Takeshita faction was similarly aligned with construction and financial interests; the former Miyazawa faction had close ties to financial interests; and the former Nakasone faction had good connections to telecommunications interests and so on).

In contrast, the factional variable appears to be largely irrelevant to the representation of agricultural interests. According to the 1990 sample survey, no one LDP faction or even group of factions had a monopoly on agricultural representation. Substantial numbers of agriculture-related Diet members were present in all the LDP factions at that time. Essentially the differences amongst them amounted to one of degree: in some factions agriculture-related Diet members made up between two-thirds and three-quarters of the total factional membership (the Miyazawa, Abe[46] Komoto[47] and Nikaido factions), while in others (the Watanabe and Takeshita factions), they represented about half. No obvious factors accounted for the variations. Abe Shintaro was an agricultural representative as was Nikaido Susumu. On the other hand Watanabe Michio was the most prominent agricultural representative amongst all the faction leaders and a *norin zoku*, and yet his faction had the lowest proportion of agricultural representatives. Generally speaking, amongst all the LDP factions at the time, the Abe faction (and to a lesser extent, the Miyazawa faction) were known to have relatively large numbers of *norin giin* in their ranks. When the producer rice price was being decided in 1986, for example, the *norin giin* within the Abe faction exerted strong pressure on the party executive leadership to support the maintenance of the existing price.[48]

Data obtained from the 1990 questionnaire survey also confirmed that the factional variable was irrelevant to agricultural representation in the JSP.[49] Most JSP respondents reported no factional affiliation at all. Those that did, claimed affiliation to a number of different factions. As for the other Opposition parties, respondents either asserted no factional affiliation or disclaimed the existence of factions in these parties.

Direct representation of agricultural organisations

Many agricultural organisations are directly represented in the Diet by politicians who hold or have held official positions in these groups. Muramatsu's research on Japanese pressure groups, for example, revealed that agricultural groups represented the highest percentage of the types of groups (the others were welfare, educational and economic) that allowed membership to Diet politicians.[50] The 1990 sample survey by the author showed that 90 of the 403 agricultural representatives or just under one-quarter were, or had been, associated with agricultural organisations in an official capacity.[51] This number constituted 12 per cent of total Diet membership and compared with 113 politicians or 15 per cent of the Diet who had held office in trade unions.[52] On these grounds, trade unions appeared to be a more significant category of extra-Parliamentary group with direct Diet representation. In 1990, they exceeded in outright numbers those representing agricultural organisations.

A straight numerical comparison, however, can be misleading. An important qualifying factor is party affiliation. More than two-thirds of the agricultural representatives with experience in leading agricultural groups were members of the LDP (62 were members of the LDP, 24 were members of the JSP, two were DSP and the same number were Independents). All the trade union representatives, on the other hand, were members of the Opposition parties at the time: the JSP, DSP, JCP and Rengo, or were Independents.[53]

Furthermore, agricultural group representatives represented more than one organisation in several cases, thus multiplying the number of agricultural organisations directly represented in the Diet. A politician like Yamanaka Sadanori, for example, who is LDP member for Kagoshima (5), is not only a Nokyo politician, but holds a variety of leadership positions in agricultural organisations. He is Chairman of the National Beef Association, Vice-Chairman of the Central Livestock Association, Chairman of the National Beef Calf Price Stabilisation Fund Association, Chairman of the Japan Artificial Insemination Practitioners' Association, Chairman of the Bee-keeping and Honey Association, and Vice-Chairman of the Japan Light Horse Association. These are all MAFF *gaikaku dantai*.

Other politicians who hold, or have held, multiple positions in agricultural organisations are Ono Matsushige, LDP member for Saitama (9) in the Lower House, Higaki Tokutaro, former LDP member for Ehime in the Upper House,[54] Niwa Hyosuke, former LDP member for Aichi (2) in the Lower House, and Oishi Buichi, former member for Miyagi (2) in the Lower House. Because of multiple group representation by individual politicians, the 90 politicians in 1990 with leadership connections to agricultural organisations ended up representing well over 100 separate groups.

The distribution of agricultural group representatives corresponded roughly to the proportional membership of each house. In 1990, there were 58 agricultural group leaders in the Lower House and 32 in the Upper House, or 64 per cent and 36 per cent respectively of the total number of agricultural group representatives (in 1990, the Lower House had 67 per cent of total Diet membership and the Upper House 33 per cent). These figures challenge the widely held view of the Upper House (particularly before the introduction of the proportional representation in the national constituency in 1982) as being the 'house of groups' and significant for its 'vocational representation', a perception reinforced by studies implying that direct representation of interest groups was significant only in the Upper House and not in the House of Representatives.[55]

By 1996, the figures for agricultural group representation had declined to 54, which was 14 per cent of agriculture-related Diet members and 7 per cent of Diet membership.[56] Like the 1990 figures, these agricultural group representatives were distributed between the two houses of the Diet almost exactly in proportion to their membership, with 35 in the Lower House (or 65 per cent of the total) and 19 in the Upper House (35 per cent of the total). In 1996, LH membership made up 66 per cent of total Diet membership, while UH membership constituted 34 per cent.

The representation of agricultural groups falls into the major categories of agricultural organisations identified in chapter 2: statutory interest groups (Nokyo, the agricultural committee organisation, agricultural mutual aid associations and land improvement groups), institutional interest groups (the MAFF *gaikaku dantai*), and a miscellaneous category of so-called rice-roots farmers' organisations, including those centring on specific commodities and the farmers' unions.[57]

Nokyo's direct representation

As the above analysis suggests, the agricultural sector as a whole is represented by a diverse range of politician-cum-group leaders and is not confined to Nokyo. The difference between Nokyo and all the other agricultural organisations is a question of number. Just as farmers' organisational votes centre on Nokyo, so the direct representation of the agricultural sector centres on Nokyo Diet members. Of any agricultural organisation, Nokyo has been by far the most prominent in terms of its organisational presence in the Diet. One of its main political strategies as an interest group has been to promote its own leaders and officials to Diet office, continuing a tradition that began with the *nokai* and *sangyo kumiai*.

Even greater numbers of Nokyo leaders have successfully obtained positions in local government. Research on 5,408 cooperatives conducted by the MAF in August 1969 revealed that 140 prefectural assembly members were serving concurrently as agricultural cooperative chairmen: 900 city, town and village assembly members as co-op chairmen or full-time officials; and 73 city, town and village mayors as co-op chairmen.[58] The current Chairman of Zenchu is Harada Mutsutami, President of the Hiroshima Prefectural Central Union of Agricultural Cooperatives, who was elected to the Zenchu post in 1996. He had served as a Hiroshima prefectural assembly member for 24 years from the age of 38, and is a member of the Liberal Democratic Party.[59]

With so many Nokyo officials either politicians in their own right holding electoral office as prefectural, city, town or village mayors, governors, assembly members or chairmen, or with extremely close connections to these various branches of local government, the dividing line between Nokyo activity and political activity becomes almost indistinguishable. Local government and Nokyo office often becomes fused in one and the same individual.[60] In 1995, around 50 agricultural cooperative officials still occupied seats in prefectural assemblies.[61]

Table 7.5 shows trends in Nokyo's Diet representation since 1949, the first year in which politicians with direct leadership connections to the agricultural cooperatives contested Diet office. Their numbers rose steadily in the 1950s and 1960s until they reached a peak of 51 in 1971. Indeed, during the 1970s the number of LDP Nokyo Diet members in the Upper House was large enough for them to form the distinct sub-grouping of UH Nokyo Diet members called the Nokyo Mondai Kondankai. All members were required to belong to the LDP and hold executive positions within the Nokyo organisation.[62] Just how influential the group was in policy terms is difficult to establish, although it did hold meetings on issues that directly affected the agricultural cooperatives. Basically, it was too small a grouping to have any decisive impact on policy apart from presenting a united front on certain issues and acting as a kind of informal lobby group. It had 17–18 members and its representative (*daihyosha*) was Nokyo UH Diet member, Inoue Kichio from Kagoshima. He was chairman of a city agricultural cooperative and a director of a prefectural Nokyo federation.

The Nokyo Mondai Kondankai was later replaced by the Agricultural Reconstruction Policy Research Association (Nogyo Saiken Seisaku Kenkyukai). As the number of *Nokyo giin* has fallen, membership has been widened to include Diet members who have received the support of agricultural cooperative electoral organisations, such as the *noseiren* and Zenkoku Noseikyo. Around the time of the 1995 UH election, calls went out from the *noseiren* to form an agricultural policy Diet members' league made up of politicians who had received recommendation from the *noseiren* and who had signed policy agreements with them reflecting their deep understanding and

Table 7.5 Upper and Lower House distribution of Nokyo Diet members, 1946–98

Election years	Upper House	% of Upper House	% of both Houses	% of Lower House	Lower House	Total of both Houses
1946 (Joint House)						36[a]
1947	11/250	6.4	5.9	5.6	17/467	28[b]/717
1949			4.6	3.6	17	33
1950	13	5.2	4.2	3.6	17	30
1952			4.5	3.2	19	32
1953	13	5.2	5.0	4.9	23	36
1955			5.2	5.1	24	37
1956	13	5.2	5.2			37
1958			5.2	5.1	24	37
1959	15	6.0	5.5			39
1960			5.2	4.5	21	36
1962	20	8.0	5.7			41
1963			6.3	5.3	25	45
1965	19	7.6	6.1			44
1967			6.7	6.2	30/486	49/736
1968	19	7.6	6.7			49
1969			6.8	6.4	31	50
1971	20/252	7.9	6.9			51/738
1972			6.6	5.9	29/491	49/743
1974	18	7.1	6.3			47
1976			5.5	4.7	24/511	42/763
1977	20	7.9	5.8			44
1979			5.8	4.7	24	44
1980	23	9.1	6.2	4.7	24	47
1983	18	7.1	5.1	4.1	21	39
1986	17	6.7	4.5	3.3	17/512	34/764
1989	13	5.2	3.9	3.1		30
1990			3.7	2.9	15	28
1992	7	2.8	2.9			22
1993			2.6	2.5	13/511	20/763
1995	6	2.4	2.5			19
1996			2.5	2.6	13/500	19/752
1998	3	1.2			12/500	15

Notes:

a The majority of these were *nogyokai* executives, including former *sangyo kumiai* leaders. The rest were former *nokai* leaders and a small number who later became executives of the agricultural cooperatives.

b These are all *nogyokai* executives.

Sources: Author's card system of Japanese farm politicians, 1949–98; *Seikan Yoran*, relevant issues.

passion for agriculture and rural areas. Such a grouping was subsequently set up in October 1995 in the form of a Japan Agricultural Policy-Nokyo Diet Members' League (Nihon Nosei-Nokyo Giin Renmei) amongst LDP UH members. It comprised those Diet members who had successfully contested the UH election with support from Zenkoku Noseikyo and the *noseiren*. The league represented a special new Diet members' group which supported Nokyo's policies (in addition to the *Nokyo giin renmei*, a body already in existence, but not a strong grouping) and which would be supported by Nokyo's member organisations in the elections.[63]

From the 1971 peak, the total number of Nokyo Diet members has steadily fallen, almost halving by 1990 and slipping further to 15 in 1998. The rate of reduction increased dramatically in the 1990s. For the four decades from the 1950s to the 1980s, Nokyo politicians averaged somewhere between 5 and 6 per cent of total Diet membership. The percentage figure in 1998, however, was less than half this, at 2.0 per cent, the lowest since 1949 when Nokyo leaders first appeared in the postwar Diet. Although the electoral power of the agricultural cooperatives is still in evidence, Nokyo's Diet profile has receded dramatically over the past 20 years.[64] The reduction in Nokyo's direct representation undoubtedly reflects the gradual decline in the farm vote and the associated erosion of Nokyo's vote-gathering capacities.

The party alignment of Nokyo's Diet politicians is shown in Tables 7.6 and 7.7 (which continue on from Tables 3.1 and 3.2). The figures confirm the persistent attachment of the majority of Nokyo's parliamentary representatives to the LDP, although the figures should provide additional evidence to dispel the myth that Nokyo is exclusively aligned with the conservative ruling party. Some variation is apparent in the ratios of party support between houses. In the Upper House, the majority in favour of the LDP has been consistently higher than in the Lower House, where the range of party affiliations has been greater and more evenly balanced between LDP and non-LDP, although the two-thirds LDP to one-third socialist pattern was dominant until 1990.

The variations in the proportions of each party's Nokyo Diet members in each House corresponds roughly to the relative seat acquisition rates of the LDP and JSP in rural and semi-rural districts over these decades. Not surprisingly, a greater variation in the party representation of Nokyo politicians was evident in the Lower than in the Upper House where the LDP, as the largest party, traditionally dominated the single-member prefectural constituencies that are to be found in more rural areas.

Since 1993, the party affiliations of Nokyo Diet members have become more complex because of party formations, defections and dissolutions. The breakaway Shinseito and Shinshinto parties effectively divided up the party affiliations of conservative *Nokyo giin* in the Lower House, resulting in more or less evenly balanced numbers between LDP and non-LDP members. In 1996, the ratio was seven LDP to six (three NFP, one SDP, one DP and one Independent) and in 1998, seven LDP to five non-LDP (four DP and one Independent). A similar distribution pattern also emerged amongst UH Nokyo Diet members with three LDP members balanced by one Minkairen and one Shinshinto member in 1995, while in 1998 the split was two LDP and one Liberal Party.

Table 7.6 Party affiliation of Nokyo Lower House Diet members, 1969–98

Numbers affiliated by party

Year	Liberal Democratic	Socialist	Democratic Socialist	Independents	New Liberal Club	Total
1969	22	5	4			31
1972	19	6	4			29
1976	15	4	3	1	1	24
1979	18	4	2			24
1980	20	2	1		1	24
1983	17	3	1			21
1986	16	1				17
1990	10	4		1		15

Year	Liberal Democratic	Renewal / New Frontier	Social Democratic	Japan New / Democratic	Independents	Total
1993	6	2 (Renewal)	4	1 (Japan New)		13
1995	6	3 (New Frontier)	3		1	13
1996	7	3 (New Frontier)	1	1 (Democratic)	1	13
1998	7			4 (Democratic)	1	12

Sources: Author's card index of Japanese farm politicians, 1949–98; *Seikan Yoran*, relevant issues.

Table 7.7 Party affiliation of Nokyo Upper House Diet members, 1971–98

Year	Numbers affiliated by party					Total
	Liberal Democratic	Socialist			Independents	
1971	15	4			1	20
1974	14	3			1	18
1977	19	1				20
1980	22	1				23
1983	17	1				18
1986	16	1				17
1989	13					13
1992	7					7
			Democratic Reform	New Frontier		
1995	3		1	1		5
				Liberal		
1998	2				1	3

Source: Author's card index of Japanese farm politicians, 1949–97; *Seikan Yoran*, relevant issues.

Nokyo Diet members from parties with strong union backing such as the JSP/SDP, DSP and Minkairen have almost always emanated from the staff rather than the executive side of the organisation. The 1995 group in the Diet, for example, included Kunii Masayuki, Minkairen member in the Upper House for Tochigi who was Tochigi *keizairen* Personnel Section Chief; Horigome Ikuo, JSP-turned-Independent (later Shinshinto) member in the Lower House for Nagano (2) (later Hokuriku-Shinetsu PR district), a staff member of Nagano Prefecture *keizairen*; Hachiro Yoshio, JSP-turned-Democratic Party member in the Lower House for Hokkaido (3)/(8), who was former head of the Farm Management Guidance Section and later Manager of Imagane Nokyo; and Tanaka Tsunetoshi, JSP/SDP member in the Lower House for Ehime (3), former Chief of the *kenchu* General Planning Room and Vice-Chairman of Ehime Prefecture Labour-Farmer Council and leader of 'farmers' campaigns' (*nomin undo*), a codephrase for farmers' union-based activities. Nokyo staff candidates get strong support throughout their electorates from other Nokyo staff members who amount to some thousands of voters, and who constitute a strong union-based grouping in the National Nokyo Labour Union Federation. Accordingly it is not unusual for these Nokyo Diet members also to have close and official connections to labour union organisations.[65]

The data in Table 7.8 includes a list of the names and positions of Nokyo's Diet members in 1995. The table illustrates several main representational characteristics of these politicians. Firstly, some have held multiple positions in Nokyo organisations, in certain cases, centring around specific commodity interests, such as livestock or fruit growing. Secondly, the Nokyo Diet members are predominantly executives of prefectural and municipal agricultural cooperatives, with national leadership positions being in the minority.[66] This

Table 7.8 Agricultural cooperative organisations represented by Nokyo Diet members, 1995–98

Name of politician	Party	Type/name of organisation	Main position held
		A. Nokyo	
1. Aino Koichiro	LDP/NFP	Kashima Nokyo	Chairman
		Kagoshima Prefecture Nokyo Economic Federation	Director
		Saga Prefecture Economic Federation	Director
2. Eto Takami	LDP	Livestock Nokyo	Director
3. Hachiro Yoshio	JSP	Imakane Nokyo	Secretary
4. Hagiyama Kyogon	LDP	Takaoka City Nokyo	Director
5. Horigome Ikuo	JSP/Ind.	Nagano Prefecture Economic Federation	Staff Member
6. Horinouchi Hisao	LDP	Tojo City Nokyo	Executive/Adviser
7. Kohata Kodo	JNP/NFP	Fukushima Prefecture Nokyo Youth League Secretariat	Chief
8. Kyuma Fumio	LDP	County Nokyo	Director
9. Mitsubayashi Yataro	LDP	Saitama Prefecture Nokyo Guidance Federation	Management Section Chief
		Local Nokyo	Executive
10. Tanaka Tsunetoshi	JSP	Ehime Nokyo Central Union	General Planning Room Chief
11. Tsuji Kazuhiko	JSP	National Nokyo Settlers' Federation	Part-Time Adviser
12. Watanabe Kozo	LDP/NFP	Tajima Nokyo	Chairman
13. Yamanaka Sadanori	LDP	Kagoshima Prefecture Nokyo Central Union	Director
		Kagoshima Prefecture Nokyo Economic Federation	Director
14. Asoda Kiyoshi	NFP	Kumamoto Prefecture Central Union	Director
		Kumamoto Prefecture Nokyo Fruit Federation	Director
15. Inoue Kichio	LDP	Kagoshima Prefecture Nokyo Federation	Chairman
		Shussui Nokyo	Chairman
16. Kunii Masayuki	DRP	Tochigi Prefecture Nokyo Economic Federation	Personnel Affairs Section Chief
17. Otsuka Seijiro	LDP	National Central Union of Agricultural Cooperatives	Director
		Japan Fruit Juice Nokyo Federation	Chairman
		Japan Horticultural Nokyo Federation	Chairman
		Saga Prefecture Nokyo Horticultural Federation	Chairman
		Saga Prefecture Nokyo Central Union	Chairman
18. Suzuki Seigo	LDP	National Nokyo Livestock Federation	Director
		Fukushima Prefecture Nokyo Livestock Federation	Chairman
		Town Nokyo	Chairman

Name	Party	Organisation	Position
19. Urata Masaru	LDP	Prefectural Nokyo	Chairman
		Local Nokyo	Chairman
B. Nokyo's Farmers' Political Leagues			
1. Otsuka Seijiro	LDP	Saga Prefecture Farmers' Political League	Secretary-General
2. Urata Masaru	LDP	Kumamoto Prefecture Farmers' Political League	Chairman
C. Other Statutory Agricultural Interest Groups[a]			
1. Inoue Kichio	LDP	Shussui Land Improvement Group	Director-General
2. Suzuki Seigo	LDP	Fukushima Prefecture Agricultural Council	Chairman
3. Urata Masaru	LDP	Kumamoto Prefecture Land Improvement Council	Chairman
D. Gaikaku Dantai (National or Prefectural Level)			
1. Eto Takami	LDP	Japan Cattle Business Association	Chairman
		Cattle Trading Fund Association	Chairman
2. Yamanaka Sadanori	LDP	National Beef Association	Chairman
		National Beef Calf Price Stabilisation Fund Association	Chairman
		Central Livestock Association	Chairman/Vice-Chairman
		Japan Artificial Insemination Practioners' Association	Chairman
		Japan Light Horse Association	Vice-Chairman
		Japan Beekeeping and Honey Association	Chairman
3. Otsuka Seijiro	LDP	Central Fruit Production and Delivery Stabilisation Fund Association	Chairman of Board of Directors
4. Suzuki Seigo	LDP	Japan Fruit Juice Association	Chairman
		National Beef Association	Vice-Chairman
		Fukushima Prefecture Livestock Association	Chairman
		National Cattle and Livestock Products Hygiene Guidance Association	Chairman
5. Urata Masaru	LDP	Kumamoto Prefecture Land Improvement Council	Chairman
E. Other Agricultural Organisations			
1. Eto Takami	LDP	Miyazaki Prefecture Cattle Registration Association	Chairman
		Miyazaki Prefecture Cattle Improvement Association	Chairman of Board of Directors
2. Horinouchi Hisao	LDP	Miyazaki Prefecture Cattle Registration Association	Director
3. Mitsubayashi Yataro	LDP	Saitama Prefecture Horticulture Association	Chairman

Table 7.8 (continued)

Name of politician	Party	Type/name of organisation	Main position held
		F. Sundry Farmers' Groups	
1. Horinouchi Hisao	LDP	Miyazaki Prefecture Agricultural Pension Recipients' League	Chairman
2. Tanaka Tsunetoshi	JSP/SDP	Ehime Prefecture Farm Migrant Workers Federation	Chairman
		G. Farmers Unions/Labour–Farmer Councils	
1. Horigome Ikuo	JSP/Ind.	Nagano Prefecture Labour–Farmer Council	Secretary-General
2. Tanaka Tsunetoshi	JSP/SDP	Ehime Prefecture Labour–Farmer Council	Vice-Chairman
		Zennichino Prefectural Federation	Vice-Chairman

Note:
a Even though the national level organisations of the statutory agricultural interest groups (like Nokyo) are formally listed as *kankei dantai* in the MAFF Officials' Register, they are considered a separate type of grouping for purposes of this analysis.

Source: Card index of Nokyo politicians compiled by the author.

suggests that regional (as opposed to national) positions are the most productive in electoral terms with Nokyo Diet members drawing on a support base centring on regional areas, especially prefectural.[67] From a vote-gathering point of view, it is clearly important to have a prominent 'face' in regional and local agricultural cooperatives so that organisational loyalties amongst the individual farmer members can be mobilised.[68]

Three other indicators also confirm the general locality-orientation of Nokyo Diet politicians: the percentage with a career background in local politics;[69] the relatively high proportion with a role in local party organisations;[70] and the frequency with which some have become strongly identified with commodity interests in specific regions. Of the Nokyo politicians listed in Table 7.8, more than three-quarters had also been prominent in local politics, particularly in prefectural assemblies, as well as in local party politics, with the post of chairman of the (LDP) party prefectural federation being common.[71] Nokyo politicians belong almost exclusively to one of the two dominant career streams leading into the Diet – the category of former local politicians (as opposed to retired bureaucrats).

Thirdly, around half of the Nokyo Diet members listed in Table 7.8 also act as leaders of other kinds of agricultural organisations (other statutory agricultural interest groups, MAFF *gaikaku dantai* and various farmers' associations, particularly commodity groups). Those who represent the JSP/DSP have close ties to farm migrant workers', farmers' union organisations and the labour-farmer councils, in other words, farmers' groups sponsored by socialist parties. The leadership connections of politicians with Nokyo are not, therefore, necessarily exclusive.

Nokyo and other agricultural interest groups regard their representatives as 'fixers' and 'policy brokers' on their behalf and jealously guard their relations with their direct representatives, particularly those from the ruling LDP. Nokyo asks their representatives in prefectural and municipal assemblies and the Diet to fulfil the demands of farmers in exchange for farm votes.[72] Conversely, LDP Diet members have found it necessary to hold executive positions in Nokyo and to support Nokyo during the budget compilation and other agricultural policymaking processes in order to secure farm votes.[73]

In 1988, a much publicised verbal clash took place between a female representative of the Kagoshima Prefecture Minseikyo (People's Consumer Cooperative – a JCP-affiliated consumer group) and an LDP *Nokyo giin* from that prefecture, Yamanaka Sadanori, at an 'Emergency Combined Assembly of Agricultural Cooperative and *Noseiren* Branch Chairmen to Oppose the Liberalisation of Agricultural and Livestock Product Imports' sponsored by the Kagoshima Prefecture Nokyo Central Union. The Chairman of the Kagoshima Prefecture Nokyo Central Union apologised for asking the Minseikyo representative to leave, explaining: 'Yamanaka Sensei is our director and looks after us'.[74] Even though many Nokyo leaders and rank-and-file at the assembly agreed with the Minseikyo representative's criticism of LDP policy on agricultural trade liberalisation, the relationship between the

Nokyo organisation and Yamanaka was considered by the prefectural Nokyo leadership as ultimately too valuable to endanger. Likewise, Yamanaka was indignant that such a JCP-affiliated representative had been allowed in their midst.

In a similar example, the 1994 Zenchu Chairman, Toyoda Hakaru, who along with a group of *norin giin*, received the final LDP compensation package for farmers in October 1994 resulting from the UR Agreement on Agriculture, was clearly satisfied with the work done on his membership's behalf by the group. He commented: 'I will explain to the Nokyo members how hard you politicians work for us and I will make them fully understand that.'[75] Although Nokyo objected to the GATT UR agreement of late 1993, Toyota's observation about how hard the agriculture-related Diet members had worked signified that Nokyo would accommodate the agreement, however reluctantly. Demonstration of effort on the part of *norin giin* to get benefits for Nokyo, even if not always fully successful, is critical to Nokyo's acceptance of unpopular decisions taken by the government. The activities of rural backbenchers in this way facilitates the political process. It is intentions, efforts and displays that count, not necessarily favourable outcomes.

Categories of Nokyo representation

The category of *Nokyo giin* represents only the core of Nokyo's Diet representatives. A much greater number of politicians owe some degree of electoral debt to the cooperatives than those who hold or have held executive or staff membership positions in the organisation. This is because Nokyo has always extended its electoral support activities well beyond its own leadership ranks, as pointed out in chapter 6.

As with farm politicians and agricultural and forestry Diet members, many figures have been put on the number of politicians who are considered to represent Nokyo's interests in the Diet. Specific examples of the actual numbers of Diet candidates supported by the agricultural cooperatives were given for individual elections in the 1950s. Zenshiren reputedly recommended 53 Nokyo-connected candidates (*Nokyo kankei kohosha*) in the 1952 LH election.[76] Similarly, it was reported that in the 1958 poll Zenchu put up 110 candidates for election[77] and that there were 30 Nokyo-connected candidates in the 1959 UH election.[78] Almost two decades later in the early 1970s, one writer asserted that 'Nokyo claims the loyalty of all dietmen from rural constituencies'.[79] At about the same time, the number of Diet members who owed some sort of electoral debt to Nokyo was estimated at around 150.[80] Other figures can also be advanced such as the membership of APRA, or the lists of those who received electoral funding from the Noseiken in the early 1970s.

In general, it is difficult to put a precise figure on the number of Diet members who are connected to Nokyo, either directly or indirectly, because of the complexities of the relationships involved. Nokyo-connected Diet members (*Nokyo kankeisha*) fall into three main categories which are largely organisationally-based and correspond to the closeness of Diet members' affiliations to Nokyo and other agricultural groups.

Type I consists of *Nokyo giin*, Diet members with direct connections to Nokyo by virtue of their formal positions in the agricultural cooperative organisation. Type II and Type III are categories of Nokyo sympathisers (*Nokyo shinpa*):[81] politicians with no career background in agricultural cooperative organisations, but who wish to undertake activities supportive of Nokyo in the Diet in exchange for Nokyo's organised support outside it. Type II is a category of politician 'with a deep understanding of Nokyo'. It is made up of Diet members with indirect connections to the agricultural cooperatives, a group that falls into two fairly distinct types. One is the Diet member with a specialist expertise in agricultural policy as a result of long career experience – retired MAFF bureaucrats or *norin giin*. The other is the Diet member with connections to agricultural groups other than Nokyo mainstream organisations, such as the MAFF *kankei dantai*, the statutory agricultural interest groups and rice-roots farmers' organisations like the farmers' unions. Type III is made up of farm politicians (*noson giin*) with no formal leadership connections to Nokyo or other agricultural organisations (i.e. no career or organisational role in agricultural groups or institutions), but who nevertheless possess 'a relative understanding of Nokyo'[82] and a strong constituency-dictated interest in agricultural policy as representatives of rural electorates.

Nokyo organisations strive to keep the channels of communication open between their 'sponsored' Diet members and agricultural cooperative group leaders in between elections, as well as just prior to national polls. This is done by various means. Firstly, Nokyo institutionalises connections by means of a specific body created for this purpose. The Nosei Kenkyukai, or APRA, is the best known in this regard. All the above categories of politician could be found in this group of Nokyo-sponsored Diet members, although Types I and II made up the bulk of its membership.[83]

APRA was the main extra-parliamentary Diet members' grouping directly connected to the Nokyo organisation, although not all *Nokyo giin* in any one year were members. Nor did it contain all Diet members who received electoral backing from the agricultural cooperatives.[84] Membership of APRA signified a politician's need to have his name entered on a list of Nokyo 'sympathisers', although this might or might not be accompanied by regular attendance at APRA meetings or an activist approach to the policy discussions sponsored by APRA.

APRA originated as a defensive group of Diet members with connections to the *sangyo kumiai* in reaction to the anti-industrial cooperative movement in the prewar Diet which began in 1932–33 and which was led by business interests and their political representatives.[85] When the group was initially formed in 1937, it was known as the Rural Diet Members' League.[86] At the time, it functioned literally as an agricultural policy research organisation, because this function had not matured within the political parties themselves.

As soon as the war ended, some agricultural and forestry Diet members took part in planning the formation of the Japan Cooperative Party in December 1945. Amongst them was an array of former members of the pre-war Noson Giin Domei but all were purged and thus barred from standing in the April 1946 elections. Nevertheless, 17 Diet members with connections to agriculture and forestry were elected from the Japan Cooperative Party,[87] all of whom, including Kita Katsutaro from Hokkaido, had in fact been closely connected to members of the Noson Giin Domei before the war. When under the leadership of Miki Takeo and others, the Japan Cooperative Party ended up going in another direction (see Figure 3.1), this group played a central role in reconstituting the Noson Giin Domei as the Nosei Kenkyukai in 1947. It was formed along the lines of its predecessor as a supra-party organisation of Diet members with connections to agriculture and forestry quite separate from the Japan Cooperative Party. Its establishment received backing from the 1947 national Nokyo convention, which issued a request for strong support from a group of Diet members.[88]

APRA's distinctive features were its exclusive membership of agriculture and forestry-related politicians and its suprapartisan (*chotoha*) character.[89] The latter reputedly made APRA activities more vigorous. At the time, there was a saying amongst the membership of the organisation that 'we will absolutely not let pass legislation not in the interests of the farmers'.[90] APRA provided the organisational means by which Nokyo leaders could mobilise their Diet sympathisers in support of desired policy objectives.

One of the main rice-roots activities of the group was the holding of regional agricultural policy roundtable conferences. At these conferences, reports were furnished on matters such as how the Diet was deliberating on agricultural policy problems; and secondly, as background for the next round of Diet activities, information was collected on agricultural policy problems in local areas, thus helping communication on agricultural policy issues between the rice roots and agricultural leaders in the Diet.

These regional agricultural policy roundtables were held nationally two or three times a year during Diet recesses. The organisation and management of these meetings were undertaken voluntarily by agricultural groups, particularly Nokyo and the agricultural committee organisation as well as prefectural government officials. The first regional agricultural policy round-table conferences were held in 1951 in Shizuoka, Aichi and Mie, with representatives from APRA attending. The conferences helped to secure mutual understanding of agricultural policy issues between the localities and the political centre. Each region was covered nationally with matters heard at the regional conferences being picked up and transmitted by APRA members to the MAF. The MAF's replies were relayed back to those attending the next regional conference.

Besides the regional roundtable conferences, APRA put effort into policy formulation and held frequent meetings to discuss important items. Its main organisational objective as set down in its formal charter was to undertake joint research and investigation into agricultural policy problems. Agreements were reached at APRA meetings on agricultural policy issues, followed by suggestions for policy realisation and policy proposals to the relevant ministers, beginning with the MAF and MOF Ministers, and to each party's representatives. It was the job of the APRA chairman to explain the proposals and accompany the APRA delegation. To some extent, APRA's policy research function was later displaced by the development of a similar function amongst the political parties themselves, as well as by Diet activities such as the agriculture and forestry standing committees. Over time, therefore, APRA's policy proposal activities became fewer and fewer.

In practice APRA served as a pipeline between Nokyo and its political supporters in the Diet, enabling Zenchu and other key national agricultural cooperative organisations to present Nokyo's policy demands to the government and to the LDP, particularly in relation to the MAFF budget. APRA also provided a means for Diet members to obtain Nokyo's perspective on current agricultural problems in order to facilitate more effective performance of activities within the Diet and political parties on Nokyo's behalf.[91]

In the early postwar period, APRA regularly maintained a membership of around 100 Diet politicians, but as the years passed, its membership slowly declined. In addition, some of its more prominent members such as Mori Yasoichi (UH member for the national constituency from 1950–74) eventually decided to leave the Diet. However, the role of APRA as a group promoting the policies requested by organisations related to Nokyo remained unchanged.[92]

Between 1963 and 1977, APRA membership averaged 94 members in the Diet, 63 in the Lower House and 31 in the Upper House. This was an average of 13 per cent of Diet membership over the period, with comparatively balanced representation between both Houses relative to their total membership. In the 1977–87 decade, its membership declined to an average of 72, and by 1990 to a total of 45: 33 in the Lower House and 12 in the Upper House.[93] By 1994, the organisation was officially defunct, although many of its former members remained in the Diet.

The party affiliations of APRA members generally reflected the breakdown of party affiliation amongst Nokyo Diet members as a whole. In the Lower House, two-thirds were members of the LDP, with the balance on the so-called 'progressive' side of politics: most were JSP, a few were DSP and one or two were Independents. In the Upper House, over 85 per cent were LDP members, with the remainder attached to the JSP, DSP, Independents and minor parties.[94] The kind of Opposition party members that were asked to join the organisation were representatives of rural constituencies, those prominent in farmers' organisations such as the farmers' unions and those sympathetic to the farmers' point of view as shown in their Diet and party activities.

In view of APRA's virtual demise, agricultural cooperative organisations are now pursuing more ad hoc arrangements, nevertheless recognising the importance of keeping open the channels of communication with Diet members. In organised activities involving the leadership of the *noseiren*, constant reference is made to the need to strengthen the 'pipe' between themselves and political representatives at all levels of government in order that the opinions of farmers and the agricultural policy campaign organisations are reflected in politics and policies. In the words of the Fukui *noseiren*, it endeavours to main a 'fat pipe' (*futoi paipu*) with Diet members through various kinds of meetings and gatherings.[95] In January 1999, Zenkoku Noseikyo held a 'research assembly' (*kenkyu shukai*) entitled 'Strengthening the Bonds with Recommended Diet Members and Aiming for the Establishment of an Organisational System in Response to Small-Sized Electoral Districts'.[96] The gathering of 27 prefectural *noseiren* secretariat chiefs and officials emphasised the urgent need to expand the opportunities for consultation with Diet representatives in order to engender the understanding and cooperation of these Diet members with Nokyo's agricultural policy campaigns.[97]

Direct representation of other agricultural organisations

The most striking feature of the direct representation of agricultural organisations in the Diet is the enormous variety of organisations involved. The 1990 sample survey revealed that well over 80 separate agriculture-related organisations (some of them prefectural and local branches of the same national organisation) were represented in the Diet by politicians who were or had been executive or staff members of these groups (some politicians were leaders of more than one). A list of these organisations is provided in Appendix A.

In 1996–97, information was obtained on the direct representation of around 60 agricultural groups (not including the agricultural cooperatives). The breakdown was as follows: statutory agricultural interest groups: land improvement groups (seven), agricultural mutual aid associations (eight), agricultural committee organisation (five); institutional interest groups (16); and others (20), including the farmers' unions (six) and miscellaneous commodity organisations. The combined figures for the non-Nokyo statutory interest groups are suggestive of quite effective vote-gathering and political fund-generating power, although their direct representatives number around half or less of the Nokyo total.

Overall, representatives of non-Nokyo groups vary in terms of both numbers and actual organisations in any particular Diet. Groups can go for a period without direct representation. The politician-advisers to the prefectural tobacco cultivators' associations are not on the 1996–97 list for example, nor are tea Diet members such as executives and advisers to the Japan Tea Industry Central Union and its prefectural associations. This is because of the retirement/defeat of their Diet representatives. Table 7.9, however, provides a comprehensive listing of MAFF *gaikaku dantai* (statutory and institutional interest groups) traditionally led by LDP Diet politicians. It includes only national-level groups, although as Appendix A reveals, many prefectural and local branches of these groups are represented by politicians (sometimes by the same Diet member acting in both capacities). The groups are subdivided into *tokushu hojin* (effectively only the National Association of Regional Horse Racing, although a few politicians who have worked in Norinchukin have been elected to the Diet from time to time);[98] the *ninka hojin* (effectively only the National Chamber of Agriculture, because Zenchu's representatives come under the Nokyo listing); and the public interest corporations (*koeki hojin*), which can be sub-categorised into their respective areas of interest, such as 'general agricultural', 'land improvement and agricultural engineering', 'commodity-related' and 'food-related' groups. In total, these groups number 48, not including their prefectural and local branches (where they have them).

As explained in chapter 2, all of these organisations function partially or wholly by means of public funding, hence the utility of direct connections, through ruling party politicians, to government. This explains why their representatives are always members of the LDP, because it is the only party that, with the exception of a few months in 1993–94, has wielded concerted political power over the budget.

The politician-leaders of the *gaikaku dantai* are co-opted into organisational office as 'men of influence' (*kenryokusha*). They are not full-time executives of these organisations, but nominal political figureheads mobilised when necessary for the policy-related purposes of the group. Outside the Diet, they play no continuously active role in leading these organisations. In short, they are not part of internal organisational functioning on a day-to-day basis. A position in the group merely signifies that they are prepared to act as lobbyists on its behalf when asked. Full use is made of their name, standing and political influence to augment the group's leverage in government and to represent their interests in policymaking contexts. Politician-leaders make direct representations on the group's behalf with MAFF officials, for example. Such contacts are, in some cases, facilitated by personal connections with the ministry itself as one of its retired members. Their most critical role is to intercede on behalf of their organisations in budgetary negotiations, in particular to obtain subsidies from the MAFF budget and from other administrative sources such as the LIPC. From this point of view, retired bureaucrats with connections to their former ministry can be especially effective in exerting influence over incumbents making the micro-allocation decisions on MAFF subsidies. Indeed, former bureaucrats-turned-politicians combine the best of both worlds. They have automatic access to currently serving bureaucrats who were previously their juniors in the ministries and who remain susceptible to their former superiors' influence and persuasion. Furthermore, as politicians, they can also mobilise the power that is generated

Table 7.9 MAFF *gaikaku dantai*[a] customarily led by Diet members or former Diet members

---

Special Corporations (Tokushu Hojin)
*   1. National Association of Regional Horse Racing (Chiho Keiba Zenkoku Kyokai)

Approved Corporations (Ninka Hojin)
*   1. National Chamber of Agriculture (Zenkoku Nogyo Kaigisho)

Public Interest Corporations (Koeki Hojin)
*   1. Japan Agriculture, Forestry and Fisheries Promotion Association (Nihon Noringyogyo Shinkokai)
   2. Agricultural Policy Promotion Council (Nosei Suishin Kyogikai)
*   3. Agriculture, Forestry and Fisheries Encouragement Association (Norinsuisan Shoreikai)
*   4. Agriculture and Forestry Broadcasting Corporation (Norin Hoso Jigyodan)
*   5. International Agricultural and Forestry Industries Cooperation Association (Kokusai Noringyo Kyoryoku Kyokai)
   6. Japan–China Agriculture, Forestry and Fisheries Exchange Association (Nichu Norinsuisan Koryu Kyokai)
*   7. Overseas Agricultural Development Consultants Association (Kaigai Nogyo Kaihatsu Konsarutantsu Kyokai)
*   8. National Agricultural Mutual Aid Association (Zenkoku Nogyo Kyosai Kyokai)
*   9. National Federation of Land Improvement Industry Groups (Zenkoku Tochi
**   Kairyo Jigyo Dantai Rengokai)
* 10. National Land Improvement Fund Association (Zenkoku Tochi Kairyo Shikin Kyokai)
* 11. National Agricultural Public Works Techniques League (Zenkoku Nogyo Doboku Gijutsu Renmei)
* 12. 21st Century Village Construction School (Nijuisseki Murazukuri Juku)
* 13. Japan Soil Association (Nihon Dojo Kyokai)
* 14. Japan Agricultural Engineering General Research Institute (Nihon Nogyo Doboku Sokenkyujo)
* 15. Japan Rural Information Systems Association (Nihon Noson Joho Shisutemu Kyokai)
* 16. Farmland Agriculture Promotion Association (Hatachi Nogyo Shinkokai)
 17. National Agricultural Improvement Dissemination Association (Zenkoku Nogyo Kairyo Fukyu Kyokai)
 18. National Agricultural Improvement Dissemination Works Council (Zenkoku Nogyo Kairyo Fukyu Jigyo Kyogikai)
 19. Central Fruit Production and Delivery Stabilisation Fund Association (Chuo Kajitsu Seisan Shukka Antei Kikin Kyokai)
 20. Japan Fruit Juice Association (Nihon Kaju Kyokai)
 21. Japan Fruit Tree Seeds and Seedling Association (Nihon Kaju Shubyo Kyokai)
* 22. Japan Konjak Association (Nihon Konnyaku Kyokai)
 23. Japan Tea Industry Central Association (Nihon Chagyo Chuokai)

Table 7.9 (*continued*)

---

*   24. Japan Agricultural Mechanisation Association (Nihon Nogyo Kikaika Kyokai)

*   25. Japan Rose Association (Nihon Barakai)

** 26. Cattle Trading Fund Association (Kachiku Torihiki Kikin Kyokai)

    27. National Cattle and Livestock Products Hygiene Guidance Association (Zenkoku Kachiku Chikusanbutsu Eisei Shido Kyokai)

    28. National Riding Horse Club Promotion Association (Zenkoku Joba Kurabu Shinko Kyokai)

** 29. National Beef Association (Zenkoku Nikuyogyu Kyokai)

** 30. National Beef Calf Price Stabilisation Fund Association (Zenkoku Nikuyo Koushi Kakaku Antei Kikin Kyokai)

    31. National Hog Raising Association (Zenkoku Yoton Kyokai)

    32. National Dairy Farming Association (Zenkoku Rakuno Kyokai)

** 33. Central Livestock Association (Chuo Chikusankai)

    34. Japan Cattle Business Association (Nihon Kachikusho Kyokai)

** 35. Japan Cattle Artificial Insemination Practitioners' Association (Nihon Kachiku Nyuko Juseishi Kyokai)

    36. Livestock Trading Fund Association (Kachiku Torihiki Kikin Kyokai)

    37. Japan Race Horse Association (Nihon Kyosoba Kyokai)

** 38. Japan Light Horse Association (Nihon Keishuba Kyokai)

*   39. Japan International Dairy Farming Federation (Nihon Kokusai Rakuno Renmei)

    40. Japan Hog Registration Association (Nihon Shuton Toroku Kyokai)

*   41. Japan Livestock Facilities and Machinery Association (Nihon Chikusan Shisetsu Kikai Kyokai)

    42. Japan Poultry Association (Nihon Yokei Kyokai)

    43. Japan Holstein Registration Association (Nihon Horustain Toroku Kyokai)

** 44. Japan Beekeeping and Honey Association (Nihon Shokuho Hachimitsu Kyokai)

    45. Horse and Livestock Hall (Baji Chikusan Kaikan)

*   46. National Association of Dairy Farming Helpers (Rakuno Herupaa Zenkoku Kyokai)

*   47. Food Demand and Supply Research Centre (Shokuhin Jukyu Kenkyu Sentaa)

*   48. National Food Livelihood Improvement Association (Zenkoku Shokuseikatsu Kaizen Kyokai)

Notes:

a This listing does not include Nokyo organisations or the prefectural and local branches of the *gaikaku dantai*, although they are represented by Diet members in many cases as shown in Appendix A.

* Stands for those groups normally represented by retired MAFF bureaucrats-turned politicians.

** Stands for those groups also represented by Nokyo Diet members in some cases.

Sources: *Seikan Yoran*, 1990, First Half Year Issue, pp. 30–424; *Norinsuisansho Meibo*, annual, various issues; card index of farm politicians compiled by the author.

by Diet office. They embody the so-called 'iron triangle' of LDP politicians, bureaucrats and interest groups in the agricultural sector.[99] They bridge the gap between the bureaucracy and interest groups as former ministry officials and they also cement the relationship between the ruling LDP and the bureaucracy.

The standing of a Diet member within agricultural policymaking circles, his influence and the quality of his connections are, therefore, the decisively important criteria for selection to a group leadership position. Most of the politicians in question have been prominent *norin giin*, with executive positions in Diet and formal and informal party agricultural policy groupings. Many of them are retired MAFF bureaucrats (see Table 7.9). A little over half of the national-level *gaikaku dantai* have retired-bureaucrats-turned-politicians in their top posts, particularly in the category of general agricultural organisations, and those connected to the land improvement industry.

Examples include agricultural policy 'heavyweights' such as Okawara Taiichiro, Chairman of the Japan Agriculture, Forestry and Fisheries Promotion Association and Adviser to the Central Livestock Association. During his MAFF career, he rose to the position of Livestock Bureau Director, Director-General of the Food Agency and MAFF Vice-Minister. In this role, he was dubbed the 'Godfather', because of his considerable influence over agricultural policy and his dedication to the mission of protecting agriculture and related industries against the onslaught of liberalisation pressure. On entering to the Diet, he quickly assumed key positions in agricultural policymaking within the LDP and became MAFF Minister in 1995.

Another good example is the now-retired Higaki Tokutaro, chairman of a whole host of MAFF *gaikaku dantai*, such as the Agriculture and Forestry Broadcasting Corporation, the 21st Century Village Construction School, the National Agricultural Improvement Propagation Works Council, the Japan Agricultural Mechanisation Association, the Japan Rural Information Systems Association, the Japan Livestock Facilities Mechanisation Association and the Japan International Dairy Association, and Vice-Chairman of the Central Livestock Association, the National Association of Dairy Farming Helpers and the Japan International Dairy Farming Federation. Like Okawara, he was also a former Director-General of the Food Agency and MAFF Vice-Minister and executive leader of LDP agricultural policy committees.

Politician-leaders of agricultural groups like Okawara and Higaki receive electoral and financial backing from these organisations in exchange for acting as their direct representatives in the Diet and in the LDP, although what is offered varies according to the group in question. Accepting a leadership position is designed to signify a politician's commitment to the interests of the group and to acting politically on their behalf, thereby generating voting support from the membership. The group provides the vital institutional link which leverages the loyalty of its membership for electoral purposes. This will be formally acknowledged in the group's recommendation for the politician at election time in addition to other forms of support. The latter includes, in many cases, something akin to outright influence-buying whereby the politician acts on the group's behalf to obtain subsidies in exchange for political funding.

Not all *gaikaku dantai* are led by politicians. Indeed, the majority of agricultural institutional interest groups receiving subsidies from government do not have politicians as leaders. They are led by ex-bureaucrats outside the Diet. In some cases, these retired bureaucrats can be just as informed, influential and well-connected with bureaucratic incumbents as the politicians. The most important category of leader is the former MAFF Vice-Minister. The second most important is the ex-Director General of a MAFF Bureau. These former officials have influence over current officials in the ministries. When it comes to the budget, for example, the *amakudari* bureaucrats can be as effective as the politicians in influencing the ministry to outlay subsidies to these groups. In particular, because of the parallel structure of *gaikaku dantai* and the ministry bureaus, they have a direct line of communication into the initial draft of budgetary demands within the bureaus.

Furthermore, a majority of MAFF *gaikaku dantai* have mainly technical functions, and when this is the case, it is more appropriate for them to be staffed and led by retired bureaucrats who have the detailed knowledge of agricultural administration that is required. During the period of fiscal retrenchment in the 1980s when it became more difficult to extract agricultural subsidies from the government, bureaucrats became more popular than politicians, because many had friends in the administration. The bureaucrats also knew all the various ways and means of getting money. Because of the government deficit, less money became available, which weakened politicians' power on budgetary matters. As one MAFF bureaucrat explained, if a politician has no power over government, he has to apologise to the group's members: 'I have no money now', with the result that members lose confidence in the politician.[100] Conversely, politicians become less interested in being a leader of a *gaikaku dantai* if their money is not flowing. Retired bureaucrats-turned-politicians, of course, combine the best of both worlds.

Having a politician in the top post says a lot about the group as well as the politician. If Diet members are appointed to leadership positions, this indicates that votes are attached to the organisation's membership as well as political funding, possibly in the form of recycled subsidies. It also signifies that the group is concerned with highly politicised areas of agricultural administration and is able to mobilise electoral resources.

Groups that are rich in terms of the amounts of subsidies they receive from government, or those that have a clearly defined and motivated voter clientele are, therefore, more likely to have politicians in their leadership positions. As one MAFF official observed, groups have to be rich to get a Diet member as chairman because they have to contribute money to the politician.[101] He nominated the land improvement and livestock groups as outstanding in this regard. In his view, groups in the land improvement area receive substantial

514 *The politics of agriculture in Japan*

amounts of subsidies from the government and consist of organisations that obtain a lot of money from their membership. The data in Table 2.1 confirms the point about government subsidies. It shows that the land improvement industry groups are allocated sizeable quantities of subsidies from the central government (around ¥260 billion in 1995).

Land improvement industry groups

Not only Zendoren, but the prefectural federations of land improvement industry groups and the land improvement districts are well represented in the Diet by their own politician-leaders, as revealed in the details in Appendix A. In the 1990 Diet, three politicians were either former or current leaders of Zendoren; six were current or former leaders of prefectural federations of land improvement industry groups; one admitted a leadership connection to a federation of land improvement districts; two were associated with individual land improvement districts; one with a city land improvement group; and one with a land improvement association.

Table 7.10 provides a list of the leading land improvement politicians in the Diet from the early 1960s onwards, the positions they formerly held in the MAFF (where relevant), their official connections to land improvement organisations and, where details could be obtained, other agricultural organisations that provided them with electoral support. Amongst this group, ex-MAFF bureaucrats, particularly former officials of the Structural Improvement Bureau, have been prominent. Seven of the 19 listed were from the Structural Improvement Bureau of which Zendoren is a *gaikaku dantai*. In short, these politician-leaders had been involved in land improvement projects before being elected to the Diet and are later chosen as leaders of local, prefectural and national land improvement organisations. Because subsidies are the life blood of the land improvement industry,[102] who better to secure these subsidies than former bureaucrats from the bureau in charge of land improvement who have entered the political world with support from those with a vested interest in this industry?

The number and type of representatives suggest that land improvement industry votes convert into an effective political force at election time. Because former officials of the MAFF Structural Improvement Bureau have access to a lot of political funding from the land improvement industry, they tend to be successful in elections.[103] Not surprisingly, land improvement industry bureaucrats have retained their position in the top 10 of the LDP's party listing in the UH national constituency, where candidates are ranked in order of their vote-getting and fund-generating ability.[104] In 1983, Kajiki Matazo was placed 3rd on the LDP NC party list; in 1980, Okabe Saburo won 8th place on the list of top vote-getters and so in 1986 he was placed 10th and then 5th in 1992; in 1989 Sudo Ryutaro (a new ex-MAFF Structural Improvement Bureau candidate who replaced Kajiki Matazo) was placed 7th and then 10th in 1995; in 1998, Sato Akio who replaced Okabe was placed 8th.

In general, given the priority placed on vote acquisition and funding considerations, the top NC rankings on the LDP's party list are allocated to those candidates who are backed by powerful nationwide groupings such as the dentists, doctors, pharmacists, veterinarians, postmasters, police, school, college and university presidents, small business groups and other organisations such as the right-wing political grouping Seicho no Ie (House of Growth) as well as the Japan War Bereaved Political League (Nihon Izoku Seiji Renmei) and the Japan War Veterans' Association (Nihon Gunonren). They also include former bureaucrats (who may overlap with the first category) tied to national subsidised industries such as land improvement and public works construction. Prominent amongst these representatives in the top 10 party listing are ex-bureaucrats from the 'ministries of patronage': the MAFF and the Ministry of Construction, plus the other large distributors of subsidies such as the MHW, Ministry of Education and the Ministry of Home Affairs.[105] These all rank above so-called 'talent' candidates because they attract money and votes as well as bringing in policy expertise into the party. From the candidates' perspective, as policy experts from the bureaucracy, they have traditionally been assured of block votes from vested interest groups and business corporations.[106]

The significance of the land improvement industry as a source of votes and funds is also indicated by the fact that land improvement industry politicians fill one of the two positions reserved for agricultural representatives amongst the top 10 on the LDP's NC party list. In every election one land improvement industry representative is listed as well as one agricultural policy expert to represent the rest of agriculture. The qualification for the latter position has customarily been the rank of former MAFF Vice-Minister, the most elevated position in the agricultural bureaucracy, which commands the necessary national significance and weight to be elected to the national constituency. In 1986 and 1992, for example, it was Okabe Saburo for land improvement, while Okawara Taiichiro, former MAFF 'Godfather', represented the balance of agricultural interests.

Importantly in 1980, Okabe and Okawara's vote-getting ability was almost exactly the same – Okabe received 1,162,000 votes (which placed him 8th amongst the top 50 candidates successfully elected in the national constituency), while Okawara got 1,129,936 votes (which placed him 10th). This was almost an exact repeat of the 1968 UH election in which Mori Yasoichi, Zenchu Chairman who had successfully defended his Diet seat over four UH elections, got 720,000 votes which ranked him in 13th place, while Kobayashi Kuniji, who was standing for the election as an unknown 'new face' but as an ex-MAFF agricultural works engineering official, won 780,000 votes and 6th place, upsetting election forecasts. Kobayashi successfully collected the votes of those connected with agricultural engineering and also received the backing of the land improvement political leagues. As Tanaka points out, the land improvement industry differs from Nokyo in terms of its concentrated focus

Table 7.10 Profile of land improvement industry group leaders in the Diet

House	Constituency	Name	Former major position(s) in MAFF	Agricultural Policy Positions	Positions in land improvement and other agricultural organisations	Other agricultural supporting organisations
UH	National	Sato Akio (1998–)	Structural Improvement Bureau Assistant Director	Member, AFF's Committee	Adviser, National Federation of Land Improvement Industry Groups	National Land Improvement Political League
UH	National	Sudo Ryutaro (1989–)	Structural Improvement Bureau Assistant Director, Construction Department Chief	MAFF Parliamentary Vice-Minister; Vice-Chairman, AFD; member, CAPIC	Adviser, National Federation of Land Improvement Industry Groups	Unknown
UH	National	Okabe Saburo (1980–98)	Structural Improvement Bureau Assistant Director	Chairman, Diet AFF's[a] Committee; Assistant-Chief, LDP's Agriculture and Fisheries Bureau; Vice-Chairman, AFD; member, CAPIC	Director/Adviser, National Federation of Land Improvement Industry Groups; Chairman, Overseas Agricultural Development Consultants' Association	National Land Improvement Political League, Hokkaido Land Improvement Political League, Land Improvement Construction Association, Agricultural Public Works Association; All-Japan Settlers' League; National Agricultural Mutual Aid Association
UH	National	Kajiki Matazo (1971–89)	Structural Improvement Bureau Construction Department Chief	Member, AFF's Committee; Chief, LDP's AFF's Bureau; Vice-Chairman, AFD; member, CAPIC	Chairman, National Federation of Land Improvement Industry Groups; Chairman, National Land Improvement Fund Association; Adviser, National Agricultural Public Works Techniques League; Chairman, National Land Development Chubu Region Committee	National Agricultural Mutual Aid Association; All-Japan Settlers' League

	Region	Name (years)	Position	Committee roles	Organisations	Affiliation
UH	National/Tottori	Kobayashi Kuniji (1968–80, 1980–86)	Structural Improvement Bureau Construction Department Chief; Director of MAF Hokuriku Agricultural Policy Bureau	Chairman, AFF's Committee; Vice-Chairman, AFD	Vice-Chairman, National Federation of Land Improvement Industry Groups; Chairman, Japan Agricultural Engineering General Research Institute; Chairman, Farmland Agriculture Promotion Association; Adviser, Agricultural Land League	Unknown
UH	National	Shigemasa Yotoku (1953–71)	Chief of Okayama Agricultural Land Office	Chairman, AFF's Committee	Vice-Chairman, Zendoren Chairman, Agricultural Public Works Techniques League	Land improvement organisations
UH	Kagoshima	Inoue Kichio (1974–)	–	Chairman, AFF's Committee; Chairman, AFD; Vice-Chairman, CAPIC; *norin zoku*	Director-General, Shussui City Land Improvement Group; Chairman, Shussui City Nokyo; Director, Kagoshima Prefecture Nokyo Federation	Forestry cooperatives
UH	Fukushima	Sato Shizuo (1992–98)	(Prefectural Office, Agricultural Affairs Department Chief)	Director, AFF's Committee; Vice-Chairman, AFD	Adviser, Fukushima Prefecture Federation of Land Improvement Industry Groups	Unknown
UH	Kumamoto	Urata Masaru (1983–89, 1992–98)	–	Chairman, AFF's Committee; Vice-Chairman, AFD; Assistant Chief, LDP AFF's Bureau	Chairman, Kyushu Land Improvement Council; Chairman, local agricultural cooperative; Chairman, Kumamoto Farmers' Political League	Zenkoku Noseikyo
UH	Fukuoka	Oma Kei (1989–95)	Structural Improvement Bureau Planning Department Chief	Member, AFD and CAPIC	–	Zenkoku Noseikyo

Table 7.10 (continued)

LH	Saitama (9)	Ono Matsushige (1996–)	–		Vice-Chairman, Furokawa Land Improvement District; Director, Saitama Prefecture Federation of Agricultural Mutual Aid Associations; Chairman, Irima Agricultural Mutual Aid Association	Zenkoku Noseikyo
LH	Tochigi (2)	Nishikawa Koya (1996–)	–	Member, Regional Administration Committee	Chairman, Prefectural Land Improvement Political League	Zenkoku Noseikyo
LH	Ibaraki (3)(1)	Akagi Norihiko (1990–)	Minister's Secretariat Planning Counsellor; Forestry Agency Planning Section Chief	Member, AFF's Committee; Chairman's Representative, AFD	–	Federation of Land Improvement Industry Groups; Ibaraki Prefecture Nokyo Political League
LH	Hyogo (3)(4)	Inoue Kiichi (1986–)	Structural Improvement Bureau Director; Minister's Secretariat Counsellor; Shizuoka Prefecture Agriculture and Fisheries Department Chief	Director, Special Committee on Land	–	Hyogo Prefecture Farmers' Political League
LH	Akita (1)(2)	Norota Hosei (1983–)	–	MAFF Minister; MAFF Parliamentary Vice-Minister; Member, AFF's Committee	Director, Akita Prefecture Federation of Land Improvement Industry Groups	Zenkoku Noseikyo
LH	Tochigi (1)	Watanabe Michio (1963–95)	–	MAFF Minister; MAFF Parliamentary Vice-Minister; Chairman, AFD; Vice-Chairman, CAPIC, *norin zoku*	Chairman of Directors, Nasunogahara Land Improvement District	Nokyo; land improvement organisations

LH	Fukushima (2)	Ito Masayoshi (1963–93)	Agricultural Land Bureau Director; Vice-Minister	Member, AFF's Committee; Vice-Chairman, AFD and CAPIC; Chairman, LDP's Mountain Village Development Committee	Chairman, Japan Soil Association; Vice-Chairman, Chairman, Fukushima Prefecture Federation of Land Improvement Industry Groups; Chairman, National Agricultural Mutual Aid Association	Japan National Land Research and Surveying Association
LH	Aichi (2)	Niwa Hyosuke (1955–93)	Director-General, National Land Agency; MAFF Parliamentary Vice-Minister; Chairman, AFF's Committee; Chairman, AFD and CAPIC; *norin zoku*	Vice-Chairman, National Federation of Land Improvement Industry Groups; Chairman, Aichi Prefecture Federation of Land Improvement Industry Groups; Chairman, National Mountain Village Promotion League; Director, local Nokyo; Chairman, Aichi Prefecture Federation of Agricultural Mutual Aid Associations; Director, Agricultural Mutual Aid Fund	Aichi Prefecture Nokyo Central Union
LH	Nagano (1)	Kosaka Zentaro (1949–83)		Member, AFF's Committee; Member, CAPIC	Chairman, National Federation of Land Improvement Industry Groups	Unknown

Note:

a AFF's stands for Agriculture, Forestry and Fisheries.

Sources: Seikan Yoran, relevant issues; *Norinsuisansho Meibo*, 1991, pp. 615–772; 89 *Gendai Seiji Joho: Shusan Hyoin Giin Paanaru Deeta Banku [1989 Current Politics Report: Upper and Lower House Diet Members' Panel Data Bank*], Tokyo, Seikai Jihosha, 1991; personal card index of farm politicians compiled by the author; author's questionnaire survey of Diet members with agricultural connections; 'Dai 41-kai Shugiin Giin Sosenkyo: Zenkoku Noseikyo Suisen Tosen Giin Ichiran [The 41st House of Representatives Election: List of Successful Diet Members Recommended by the National Agricultural Policy Council]', *Nosei Undo Jyaanaru*, No. 10, November 1996, pp. 19–22.

and vote-collection power, whereas in Nokyo's case, the field is basically too wide and the votes unexpectedly difficult to collect.[107]

In the 1980 UH election, Okawara reputedly benefited from a 'grand alliance' on an unprecedented scale amongst forestry, food and general agriculture-connected organisations, but that is what it took to rival the total collected by Okabe, whose power base centred first and foremost on the land improvement industry. He was a retired land improvement bureaucrat, a former Assistant Director of the Structural Improvement Bureau of the MAFF in charge of land improvement works. Table 7.10 provides details of his formal organisational affiliations to land improvement groups and those groups that provided electoral support for his candidacy. He served as both Director and Adviser of the National Federation of Land Improvement Industry Groups and received support from the National Land Improvement Political League, the Hokkaido branch of the league and other land improvement-related groups such as the Agricultural Public Works Association and the All-Japan Settlers' League.

Like other land improvement representatives such as Kajiki Matazo, Ito Masayoshi and Niwa Hyosuke, however, Okabe supplemented land improvement industry representation with connections to, and support from the agricultural mutual aid organisations. These organisations are similar to the land improvement groups in the extent of their subsidisation by the government which provides the bulk of money paid to farmers for crop and other damage caused by natural disasters. Okabe also gained support from the construction and civil engineering fields.

Okabe's election promise in 1986 claimed that he would 'advance the consolidation of the land improvement industry and the rural livelihood environment, and that he would aim for bountiful agriculture and livable villages'.[108] As before, Okawara's support base spread across the balance of agricultural interests. As former Director of the Livestock Bureau he also had a special connection to livestock farmers, hence his role as Adviser to the Central Livestock Association.

In the 1986 election Okabe was allocated 10th place on the LDP's party list in his first election under the new PR system, while Okawara gained 4th place on the LDP's party listing. The combination of one slot for land improvement and one for the rest of agriculture in the LDP's top ten party listing thus survived the changeover to the new system. In 1992 Okabe was placed 5th while Okawara was switched to 10th.

In 1989 the two new MAFF candidates were Ishikawa Hiroshi, former Director of the Livestock Bureau, Director-General of the Food Agency and Vice-Minister (the same career positions as Okawara) who was placed 6th, while Sudo Ryutaro (who was replacing Kajiki Matazo) was placed 7th. In 1995 Sudo was put in 10th place while Ishikawa Hiroshi was placed 8th. The latter was an ex-MAFF Vice-Minister of the same genre as Okawara Taiichiro.

As these candidates' standing in the national constituency reveal, the agricultural world appears to be divided politically into two sectors as far as the national electorate is concerned: general-agricultural (which includes Nokyo) and land improvement-related. Both are slots for former MAFF bureaucrats, one representing overall agricultural policy and the other representing the specialist land improvement industry. In the 1995 UH election, the Dairy Farmers' Political Federation of Japan, Zenkoku Noseikyo and the prefectural *noseiren* supported Ishikawa Hiroshi.[109] In the 1998 UH election, the agricultural policy candidate was Hide Eisuke, replacing Okawara. In a break with tradition, he had not previously been the former MAFF Vice-Minister although he had occupied various elevated administrative positions within the ministry, the last one being Director of the Agriculture, Silk and Horticulture Bureau. His career history also included a position as Director of the Agriculture, Forestry and Fisheries Finance Corporation. Rumour had it that the LDP found it difficult to field an ex-MAFF candidate to replace Okawara in this election to the national constituency. It failed to pick a replacement for the retiring Okawara from possible candidates in the MAFF by the 25 June 1997 deadline. Some likely candidates declined the offer; others seemed to lack the ability to hammer out the necessary compromises with various factions and interest groups. As a result, the LDP had to cast the net wider in search of a suitable candidate.[110] Hide was, however, strongly recommended by Zenkoku Noseikyo. In the land improvement slot, as noted earlier, Sato Akio, former MAFF Structural Improvement Bureau Assistant Director, Adviser to Zendoren and recommended by the National Land Improvement Political League, replaced Okabe.

It is significant that just two representatives in the national constituency are now considered the maximum number the national agricultural electorate can reliably elect. What is more, the general agricultural representatives and those representing the land improvement industry are all former MAFF officials. The category of bureaucrat-turned-politician appears to have NC representation for the agricultural sector sewn up. It is certainly a less diverse picture than four decades previously. In the 1959 UH elections, for example, a wide array of agriculture-related candidates were elected to NC seats. They included Okamura Fumijiro with his voting base in the Hokkaido-based dairy industry and Nokyo mutual aid organisations;[111] Shigemasa Yotoku, Vice-Chairman of Zendoren and Chairman of the Agricultural Public Works Techniques League (see Table 7.10); the Chairman of Meiji Milk Industries; an ex-MAFF candidate who was Chairman of the National Federation of Food Industry Cooperative Unions (Zenshokuren), the organisation representing rice and wheat traders; and a politician with a voting base amongst the tobacco growers' associations who was Adviser to the National Central Union of Tobacco Cultivation Associations.[112] All these candidates were from the LDP. In addition, a JSP candidate who was a former MAFF official and who had voting base in the Zennorin Rodo Kumiai and the farmers' unions was successful.[113]

522   *The politics of agriculture in Japan*

These were the successful candidates in a much broader field of aspiring agricultural politicians who also included (from the LDP) an ex-MAF Agricultural Improvement Bureau Director who was Chief of the National Chamber of Agriculture's Secretariat; the Chairman of the Saitama Nokyo Prefectural Central Union (see Table 6.6); an Independent who was recommended by the Agricultural, Forestry and Fisheries Industries Political League and the International Agricultural Supporters' Association;[114] and two JSP candidates, one a vet and Zennichino adviser, and the other who was Fukushima Prefecture Zennichino Federation Vice-Chairman and who also received the backing of Kaitakuren.[115]

The key to the continuing electoral success of the NC land improvement representatives (Sudo, Okabe, Kajiki, Kobayashi *et al.*) is the fact that they are 'dedicated' representatives. Land improvement is powerful enough to generate votes and support equivalent to all the other agriculture-related interests put together. This is because land improvement votes can be reliably mobilised on a nationwide basis and represent a highly politicised and concentrated interest. Significantly also, the land improvement groups are powerful enough financially to 'buy' politicians in their own right. They are operating in a field awash with government subsidies.[116] Their representatives might have a fairly narrow support base, but one that seems particularly reliable in terms of producing votes on a national scale.[117]

In the Lower House, however, the picture is somewhat different. Here politicians' links to the land improvement industry are part of a much broader cross-section of support from other agricultural interests as well as non-agricultural interests. Niwa Hyosuke, who represented the land improvement industry in Aichi (2) from 1955–93, for example, was also a Nokyo Diet member with strong connections to various livestock industry groups and agricultural mutual aid groups and was famous as a '*betokon giin*'. In addition he was supported by the Nihon Izokukai and local construction industry. This suggests that in regional constituencies, land improvement votes represent too narrow a support base to ensure electoral success and need to be supplemented by votes from a cross-section of other agricultural and non-agricultural groups.

Nevertheless, in terms of their electoral performance, land improvement representatives in the Lower House are more often than not the top vote-getter in their districts. Niwa Hyosuke, for example, ranked No. 1 in all elections from 1980 onwards, except for 1990 (his last), when he came second to a Socialist (on the wave of support spreading from the 1989 UH elections). Ito Masayoshi was the top vote getter in 1980 and 1990, and No. 2 in 1983 and 1986. Inoue Kiichi was No. 1 in 1986 and No. 2 in 1990. Kosaka Zentaro was No. 1 in 1980, but lost his seat in 1983. Akagi Norihiko ranked third in 1990 and 1993. His connection with the land improvement industry was more tenuous, as he had held no MAFF positions connected with this field and had no direct leadership connections to land improvement industry groups.

Other statutory agricultural interest groups

As noted earlier, the agricultural mutual aid organisations also receive relatively large amounts of government subsidies each year (just under ¥75.5 billion in FY 1998) and hence are also relatively popular with politicians. In 1996, six Diet members represented eight agricultural mutual aid organisations, most of which were prefectural federations of agricultural mutual aid associations. The agricultural mutual aid organisations are a clearly identified interest around which farmers' votes and the votes of those associated with the agricultural disaster relief industry can be mobilised.

Other organisations, for instance, general agricultural policy groups such as the National Chamber of Agriculture, while they receive smaller amounts of subsidies compared to the land improvement and agricultural mutual aid groups, often choose bureaucrats-turned-politicians as leaders because of the latter's career experience in agricultural administration and their expertise in agricultural policy issues. The subsidy dependence of these organisations requires that they appoint *kenryokusha* to leadership positions.

Given the stature of the National Chamber of Agriculture as a nationwide agricultural organisation, its chairman has traditionally been a politician who was previously MAFF Vice-Minister. In the late 1990s, Higaki Tokutaro remains in the post in spite of the fact that he has retired from politics. This does not apparently affect his standing or influence amongst his former colleagues in the MAFF or the LDP.[118]

At the sub-national level, however, the picture can be different. Politicians with links to prefectural chambers of agriculture and city, town and village agricultural committees often begin their careers in local politics, using the agricultural committee organisation (along with other locally-based organisations) as the core of a support base at the constituency level. In 1996, five LDP politicians claimed a career history in the agricultural committee organisation: three from city agricultural committees and two from prefectural chambers of agriculture. One of these, Tanaka Shoichi, a new LDP member in the Lower House for Chiba (4) in 1996, built his support base around Funabashi City Agricultural Committee, a post he claimed awakened his consciousness to politics and got him started in local politics. These rice-roots elective positions, like similar *nokyo* positions and other positions in local farmers' organisations often provide valuable experience in the electoral process at the constituency level. The support amongst voting members of these groups which is engendered as part of an internal organisational process can be used as the basis on which to build loftier political ambitions.

Groups within the agricultural committee organisation can offer votes from their individual farmer membership in spite of the fact that they do not represent a mass-based farmers' grouping like Nokyo. Being generalist organisations they have more broadly defined interests than the land improvement or agricultural mutual aid organisations, although historically they have been concerned with agricultural land matters, particularly land ownership issues. They can also offer some political funding, possibly originating from their group members (including Nokyo), or recycled government subsidies.

Institutional interest groups in the livestock sector

Livestock-related *gaikaku dantai* are particularly well represented by politicians as detailed in Table 7.9 and Appendix A. They have well organised votes attached to their membership and also deal in very large amounts of subsidies which are a source of both political need and political power. Politicians consistently figure as leaders in the national and prefectural branches of the Central Livestock Association and the National Beef Association, for example.

As pointed out in chapter 2, livestock-related groups have secured most of their subsidies via the LIPC (a total of ¥31.6 billion in direct subsidies in 1990 from this source alone). The Central Livestock Association received ¥7.5 billion in direct subsidies from the LIPC in 1990 with an additional cumulative total of ¥650 million in subsidised investments; the National Beef Association obtained ¥730 million in direct subsidies, the National Beef Calf Price Stabilisation Fund Association ¥3.7 billion in direct subsidies and a cumulative total of ¥717 million in subsidised investments; the National Hog Raising Association ¥402 million and the National Cattle and Livestock Products Hygiene Guidance Association ¥41 million.[119]

In the case of some of these institutional interest groups, financial donations to their politician-leaders and to other influential Diet members comes in the form of recycled subsidies, and in this respect, the financial connections involved are allegedly both illegal and corrupt. A portion of the profits generated by the LIPC's state trade in imported beef, for example, was converted into financial donations to LDP politicians in exchange for services rendered in the form of pressure on government to protect the interests of domestic livestock producers.[120] A number of livestock politicians were named in this connection, including the Chairmen of both the NBA and CLA which were identified as the principal organisational channels involved (that is, they recycled some of the subsidies they received from the LIPC into the politicians' pockets as political donations). Other Diet members representing livestock-producing constituencies with Nokyo connections were also included on the list of beneficiaries of LIPC subsidies.

Diet and group office

For subsidy-dependent statutory and institutional interest groups, their politician-leaders must hold group and Diet office concurrently. The questionnaire survey of agriculture-related Diet members undertaken by the author in 1990 revealed that a total of 30, or 39 per cent of the 77 respondents claimed leadership connections to agricultural organisations and all were holding executive positions simultaneously with Diet office.

For the agricultural cooperatives the figures varied markedly the other way. Thirteen out of the 77 respondents, or 17 per cent of the questionnaire sample, reported executive or staff links to an agricultural cooperative prior to becoming a Diet member; only three retained this executive connection after entering Diet office. This suggests that a Nokyo executive or staff position is a career office that entails an active commitment to conducting the affairs of the agricultural cooperative. Nokyo leaders are not nominal but real leaders, and time constraints and work commitments make it more difficult for them to undertake the roles of Diet member and agricultural cooperative leader simultaneously. This contrasts with the other statutory agricultural interests groups and the institutional interest groups.

Nokyo politicians tend to be long-serving agricultural cooperative officials, who have worked in the organisation over many years in an executive (or staff) capacity and who have built a voting base around the organisation's membership and connections. They are 'bottom-up' leaders. The agricultural *gaikaku dantai* on the other hand, particularly the national-level bodies, invite politicians into their leadership positions once they have gained Diet office. They do not have a career record of working for the group. They come in at the top after they attain Diet office.

The fact that simultaneous office-holding by Diet members in the agricultural cooperatives is limited does not necessarily signify a reduced commitment to the agricultural cooperative cause. It is quite likely that experience in career positions in Nokyo will continue to exert an influence even after the office has been relinquished. Furthermore, in most cases, the connection is reinforced by the extensive involvement of agricultural cooperative organisations in electoral activities, including support for their own past and present officials.

Commodity representation

Commodity representation frequently cuts across other categories of agricultural representation. Diet members closely associated with particular agricultural products often exhibit a number of distinctive characteristics: constituency-related commodity interest, organisational (including agricultural cooperative) connection with a range of commodity interest groups, and activity in Diet and party groupings concerned with particular commodity issues.

Commodity representatives will, therefore, strongly reflect the production profiles of their electorates. Their *jiban* or native place (*shusshinchi*) will be an important area for the production of a particular commodity or set of commodities (e.g. livestock products). In addition, they will have, in most cases, leadership connections to specific commodity groupings. They will have been members of, or have served as leading executives of, Nokyo organisations at the national level (both general and specialist), Nokyo prefectural federations (particularly the specialist federations organised around particular commodities), unit agricultural cooperatives (often specialist co-ops), or Nokyo-associated groups such as commodity political associations (for example, the Dairy Farmers' Political Federation of Japan); and/or they hold or have held executive posts in relevant *gaikaku dantai* or their prefectural branches.[121] Thirdly, they will be members of party sub-committees concerned with commodity policy as well as Diet members' leagues organised along commodity lines (see Appendix B). Of all these representational characteristics, the critical one is constituency interest: commodity representation is primarily driven by the dominance of a particular agricultural industry in an electorate. Other characteristics tend to flow from that.

Rice is somewhat unusual insofar as it does not have commodity-based organisational representation, but, given its centrality to Nokyo's interests and the identification of rice farming with agriculture generally, a host of agricultural organisations provide cover for rice interests. Rice Diet members tend to be identified by their constituencies (all *kome giin* come from predominantly rice-growing prefectures), their activities within the party (in policymaking committees and groups), and their membership of Diet members' leagues that mobilise around rice issues. The best known is the LDP's Diet Members' Council for Promoting Farming Villages (Noson Shinko Giin Kyogikai, or Noshinkyo).[122] Noshinkyo has been described as a gathering of rice Diet members within the LDP responding to farmers' power.[123]

With respect to other commodities, producer interests are represented at the group level by national and prefectural Nokyo specialist federations, but importantly also by the *gaikaku dantai* (both national and prefectural level organisations), and by rice-roots farmers' groups. As indicated by Tables 7.8 and 7.9 and also by Appendix A, politicians are leaders of all these kinds of groups representing special commodity interests. They pursue these interests in the various Diet and party agricultural committees, but also in the Diet members' leagues. In almost all instances, the leadership positions of these politicians in agricultural organisations are dictated by their constituency interests. Some commodity-related *gaikaku dantai* are represented by *Nokyo giin* (see Table 7.9).

The main commodity representation categories are *chikusan giin*,[124] which includes sub-categories of beef representatives (*gyuniku giin*) and *rakuno giin*,[125] and *kudamono giin*.[126] There are also smaller categories, such as tobacco Diet members (*tabako giin*). The best-known beef politicians, for example, come from constituencies in the beef-producing regions of Kyushu and Tohoku such as Kagoshima, Miyazaki, Kumamoto, Iwate, Miyagi and Fukushima. Similar regional ties are also evident amongst dairy politicians from Kanto, Hokkaido and Tohoku.[127] Likewise, politicians representing constituencies with strong beef and dairy interests demonstrate their support for their farming constituents by engaging in Diet members' activities on livestock-related issues. They become prominent members of the Diet Members' League for Promoting Livestock Farming (Chikusan Shinko Giin Renmei). Where they have sought to exercise greatest influence is in the LDP policymaking committees and sub-committees on livestock issues. They dominate the membership of these committees.

Commodity-related groups maintain close connections with these leagues. The fruits of the electoral support activities of the Dairy Farmers' Political Federation of Japan in 1995 was reportedly a group of politicians in the Diet belonging to the Rakuseikai (Dairy Policy Association), a Diet members' group (*giin dantai*), supportive of dairy farmers. The job of the Rakuseikai was to influence the MAFF to maintain the guaranteed price of industrial milk and to keep the costs of feed down. It also lobbied the ministry to get more subsidies for dairy farmers.[128] Membership of the group was restricted to the LDP (140) and the NFP (30). No other parties were represented. The NFP was included because these members originally came from the LDP, so were effectively the same from the federation's perspective.[129] The federation's leadership maintained contact with SDP politicians, but did not include them in the Rakuseikai membership because, although the SDP was sympathetic to farmers, it did not have enough power to influence the bureaucrats and the government. According to a federation spokesman, bureaucrats do not care what SDP members think. Even when the party belonged to the ruling coalition, the bureaucrats did not listen to them. Everything was still decided by the LDP.[130]

Agricultural representation and electoral reform

In spite of the potentially negative developments for agricultural representation consequent upon electoral reform canvassed in the previous chapters, the new system appears to have had minimal short term impact on this form of representation in the Japanese Diet – at least in quantitative terms. For example, as far as Nokyo's direct representation in the Lower House is concerned, six Diet members representing the PR constituencies and seven representing the SMDs were elected in October 1996, to make a total of 13 *Nokyo giin*, the same number as after the 1993 LH election. The distribution across the two types of districts also suggests that the restructuring of the electoral system has had a neutral effect and that, contrary to predictions, an agricultural cooperative base is sufficiently flexible to generate votes at either a small district level or a wider regional district level. In the case of the PR bloc constituencies, it would also tend to indicate that the LDP and other parties are sufficiently confident of the vote-pulling power of agricultural cooperative candidates to place them high enough on their party lists to guarantee election.

Nevertheless, qualitatively speaking, it is undoubtedly true that the *Nokyo giin* elected from the SMDs have been compelled to broaden their support bases to encompass a wider cross section of the voting community, and thus the significance of a 'label' like *Nokyo giin* may be a less reliable indicator of a politician's identification with special interests than it used to be. Whether or not this will impact negatively on the policy positions of these Diet members is difficult to say. On the one hand, the alignment with agricultural interests is not as strong as in the past because the picture is more complicated by other loyalties; on the other hand, there is a more compelling need for SMD representatives to avoid alienating any particular sectional group because this could mean political life or death at the next election.

Moreover, some prefectural *noseiren* report that because of the changeover to one Diet member per constituency in the SMDs, they have sharpened their scrutiny and follow up of recommended Diet members' activities. In becoming a constituency-type election (*senkyoku senkyo*), discussions between the candidates and the farmers' political leagues have naturally intensified in the process of selecting just one candidate, as have post-election activities. These have taken concrete form with the publication of prefectural and national policy reports distributed as news bulletins to *noseiren* members, the holding of liaison meetings with governors, Diet members' secretaries and prefectural office chiefs, and the organisation of agricultural policy report meetings and roundtable conferences which Diet members attend as do *noseiren* executives and prefectural and municipal Nokyo leaders. These activities have broadened the regular communication 'pipe' and exchanges of opinion between the *noseiren* and their political representatives – prefectural governors and Diet members from both houses. Nokyo and *noseiren* leaders use these occasions as opportunities for making direct policy demands to Diet members.[131]

The concept of broadening or 'thickening' the pipe between recommended Diet members and their *noseiren* supporters is one frequently reiterated in *noseiren* reports. It basically involves engaging in greater direct and indirect communication between the two sides in the exchange relationship. Report meetings, for example, have become much more common. The purpose of these meetings is to hear about the activities of those Diet members who were recommended by the *noseiren* and have them listen to the demands of the members of the *noseiren*. In short, in some respects, the new SMD system has strengthened the connections between interest groups and their representatives, offsetting somewhat the lack of the highly personalised linkages that were the hallmark of ties between individual politicians and their supporters under the old MMD system. In this respect, the notion of national politicians as representatives or political brokers on behalf of outside interests in the Diet has certainly been maintained, if not reinforced,[132] as has accountability on the part of Diet members to rice-roots interests.

As far as the non-Nokyo statutory interest groups are concerned, their focus of electoral activity and zone of vote mobilisation under the new LH electoral system have tended to be confined to the SMDs. Politicians with official leadership connections to the land improvement, agricultural mutual aid and agricultural committee organisations are almost all elected from this type of constituency. A similar bias, but not as strong, is evident amongst agriculture-related Diet members as a whole. An overall majority elected to the Diet in October 1996 were from SMDs, rather than from the PR regional constituencies. This is suggestive of strong local support structures working to sustain these politicians and the fact that votes attached to these groups were reliably engendered at a small-district level. From the SMD candidate's perspective, it also indicates that agricultural connections are still regarded as an important component of their support base.

Of the agricultural representatives elected from the PR blocs, three distinct sub-types stand out. The first is the group of representatives, albeit a relatively small number, from the smaller Opposition parties like the SDP, DP and Shinto Sakigake, not surprising given their higher chances of electoral success in a PR system. The second sub-type is the elder statesman, such as former PM Nakasone or former MAFF Minister Sakurauchi Yoshio. The LDP has tended to relegate to the PR blocs politicians with a well-known public 'face' that extends beyond local constituencies. The third sub-type, as predicted, is the category of ex-bureaucrats who have not built up a sufficiently resilient voting base at the rice roots through careers in local politics and local organisations for them to have a good enough chance of scoring an SMD seat. This is particularly true of agriculture-related Diet members with a previous history in the MOF who are almost uniformly PR constituency representatives. In the case of the 10 ex-MAFF politicians, six stood in the PR blocs (whereas the distribution should have been the reverse to support the argument that constituency type had a 'neutral' effect on ex-bureaucratic representation). The fact that four ex-MAFF candidates successfully contested SMDs, however, indicates that MAFF candidates have often had close contact during their official careers with well organised interests that can mobilise funds and votes at the constituency level.

Dilution of Agricultural representation

While direct and indirect representation of interest groups may be prevalent in Japanese national politics, it is rarely exclusive. The agricultural sector has been able to exercise sheer strength of numbers in the Diet and make strong claims on the loyalties of politicians because of the importance of the farm vote, but the degree to which a Japanese Diet member identifies with the farming sector is always relative. At one extreme are agricultural representatives who are virtually single-cause politicians. In such cases, the politician centres his entire support base around his farming constituency and associated agricultural interest groups, some of which he will represent directly. These agricultural interests become the main focus of his Diet and party activity. A good example is Kumagai Ichio, LDP member in the Lower House for Tohoku PR district. He is Chairman of Miyagi Nokyo Political League, Vice-Chairman of Zenkoku Noseikyo and chairman of a local *nokyo*.

Although his home base is Miyagi Prefecture, he entered national politics as a self-proclaimed representative of the farmers' voice. His slogan was 'national development balanced with cooperative living' and his professed political objective is to create policies for realising the stable supply of food, the technical development of agriculture and the formation of rural regional society from the farmers' standpoint.[133] Kumagai acts simultaneously as a Zenkoku Noseikyo lobbyist *vis-à-vis* the LDP's agricultural policy leadership as well as a LH Diet member in his own right. In March 1997, for example, he led a Zenkoku Noseikyo delegation to the office of Tamazawa Tokuichiro, who was CAPIC Chairman at the time, on the matter of support and stabilisation prices for livestock products. He is a key intermediary between Nokyo and agricultural decisionmakers. Described by Zenkoku Noseikyo as a representative of agricultural policy organisations in national policy circles, it is his job to report back to the Nokyo organisation on agricultural policy matters under consideration by the government. He furnishes these directly to high-level policy meetings within the Nokyo organisation, where they can influence the composition of Nokyo demands. One of his most important tasks is to elucidate broader government policy priorities, often relating to fiscal policy, thus helping Nokyo policymakers to locate an appropriate level of demand within a general policy context. In particular, he is able to explain what current party thinking is on an issue and thus indicate what is a potentially viable set of policy requests and what is not.[134]

The example of Kumagai as a direct and active representative on behalf of the farm sector contrasts with the much greater number of politicians whose connections to the agricultural sector are only nominal. In such cases, a Diet member's main support base will lie elsewhere, but there will be some obligation to register an interest in agricultural affairs because of electoral or other factors. Most agriculture-related Diet members will probably fall somewhere between the two extremes because pressures of constituency and party politics as well as electoral strategy will demand that they represent a range of interests. Too much devotion to a single cause can mean a limited network of supporting groups with the possibility of defeat at the polls.

In particular, the gradual contraction of the farming electorate associated with the decline in Japanese agriculture has required most farm politicians to broaden their support base beyond traditional rural interests. The category of 'pure' agricultural representative is fast disappearing because agriculture has become too narrow a support base to guarantee electoral success. Diet members representing rural and semi-rural areas may rely on farm votes but only as part of a package of support from a range of different groups and interests. As Matsuzaki commented, their 'supporters consist of people with diverse interests. To get elected, politicians cannot represent specific interest groups. They have to balance interests. This skill is the most important required of politicians.'[135] As far as their representational function is concerned, the vast majority of politicians are pluralistic in their interest orientation.

Saito Juro, for example, began his Diet career as LDP member in the Upper House for Mie Prefecture in 1968. A former official in the MHW, he became a member of the welfare policy tribe (*kosei zoku*) and one-time MHW Minister. Nokyo leaders and members, however, were prominent members of his *koenkai* and he also joined both CAPIC and the AFD. His constituency support base extends to a total of 140 organisations, including prefectural agriculture and forestry-related groups of all types, as well as environmental, livelihood-related groups, the war bereaved association and war veterans' association.[136]

The tendency to combine representation of a range of interests has been reinforced by the introduction of SMDs in the Lower House, which requires that candidates obtain a much larger percentage of the total vote for victory than under the old system.[137] Representation of multiple interests does not necessarily generate a conflict of policy choice; if conflict does occur, then the outcome can be one of relative emphasis, a temporary re-ordering of priorities and compromise rather than a complete sacrifice of one interest for another. As Inoguchi and Iwai observed, since most members of the LDP represent various interests, they are able to make mutual concessions over a number of issues in which they all have a stake.[138] As noted earlier, this is one of the skills of a successful politician. Furthermore, in the case of agriculture, conflict with other sectors is not necessarily a zero sum game. Advancement of agricultural interests is often perceived by voters even in city areas as in their own interest for reasons of food security or other non-economic considerations.[139]

The general point about pluralistic interest representation by Diet politicians can be illustrated by examining the range of interest groups that Nokyo Diet members represent directly in national politics. Even *Nokyo giin*, as the most obvious, direct representatives of farming interests, have wider associations than just their own agricultural cooperative organisations. For example, Aino Koichiro, LDP/NFP member for Saga/Kyushu PR district in the Lower House from 1972, built the core of his support base around not only the agricultural cooperatives but also Saga Prefecture Trucking Association (of which he was Chairman) and the Japan Bus Association (to which he acted as Adviser). Similarly, Hagiyama Kyogon, LDP member in the Lower House for Toyama (2)/Hokuriku–Shinetsu PR district from 1990, professed enthusiasm for all local industries in Toyama Prefecture and the need to promote the cultivation of high quality rice, the fishing industry and local industry generally. Likewise, Mitsubayashi Yataro, LDP member for Saitama (4)/(14) constituency in the Lower House from 1967–76 and from 1979 also drew support from horticultural, river improvement and volley ball associations for which he acted as an executive. Another example is Tsuji Kazuhiko, JSP member for Fukui/Fukui (3) in the Lower House from 1983 who professed interest in agricultural policy, but also claimed that his main support base centred around prefectural youth groups and the Japan Youth Group Council.[140]

Amongst socialist party Nokyo Diet members, trade union affiliations also tend to be important. Horigome claimed a special interest not only in Nokyo campaigns (*Nokyo undo*) and in the reconstruction of agriculture, but also in labour campaigns (*rodo undo*) and the bridging organisation between the two, illustrating a dual support base centring on Nokyo staff members on the one hand, and unions associated with the prefectural labour federation on the other.[141]

Amongst the agriculture-related Diet members in the author's 1990 sample survey, those with exclusive ties to agricultural interest groups constituted only 15 per cent of the total. Slightly more than one-third were also direct representatives of non-agricultural organisations. Of this group, one-quarter had formal links to both agricultural and non-agricultural groups and the rest had leadership ties only to non-agricultural groups. Amongst the latter, the entire range of interests was encompassed, from business to labour, citizens and religious organisations etc. (these are listed in Appendix C). Although the leaders of non-agricultural groups qualified as agriculture-related Diet members according to the specified criteria, they clearly represented other sorts of interests as well (in some cases their direct organisational interest lay outside agriculture). These factors would inevitably dilute the strength of their attachment to agricultural causes,[142] suggesting that just as more dedicated farm politicians spread their support base across a range of organised interests, so politicians who are primarily dedicated to other causes extend their range of interests to include agricultural affairs in order to stake a claim to support from that sector.

The sample survey also established that half of all agricultural representatives had no leadership ties to any organisation, agricultural or otherwise. The main career tracks not associated with interest group office were the bureaucracy, service as Diet members' secretaries, and employment in companies or banks, in the media, as academics or teachers, lawyers or party officials.[143] The absence of group office did not preclude support from agricultural interest groups, however.

As noted earlier, electoral support from interest groups is not necessarily dependent on direct leadership ties between politicians and groups. Agricultural cooperative organisations provide electoral backing for Diet members who do not hold and have not held official positions in their groups. They spread their support widely across a large number of politicians whose ties to agriculture are not immediately obvious. Other agricultural organisations tend to be much more tightly focused on providing support only for their group leaders. Nevertheless, information gained from the questionnaire survey showed that agriculture-related Diet members, whether agricultural group leaders or not, were often supported by a range of groups, agricultural and non-agricultural alike. Amongst respondents, a majority acknowledged that they had received support in their election campaigns from agricultural organisations as well as from other groups, while just under one-third reported support from agricultural groups alone. A small number received electoral backing only from non-agricultural organisations and an equally small number reported no support from any organisation.

In summary, most agriculture-related representatives receive electoral backing from some interest group source, and, for a majority, this comes from an agricultural organisation, either alone or in combination with other groups. While many agricultural representatives are dependent on support from agricultural organisations, many of them also rely on non-agricultural organisations. And while Diet members with direct ties to agricultural organisations might tend to specialise in leading agricultural groups, agricultural representatives as a whole maintain diverse attachments to different interest groups both at the leadership and electoral level.

This suggests that, for a majority of agriculture-related Diet members, successful election requires a more broadly based combination of supporting groups than agricultural interests alone can provide. The questionnaire survey revealed that JSP agricultural representatives commonly combined support from both the farmers' unions and the trade unions, with Nokyo, citizens' and women's groups also figuring strongly. LDP agricultural representatives, on the other hand, drew support from a variety of agricultural organisations and non-agricultural groups, including professional associations, business associations and so on (the supporting groups of respondents to the questionnaire survey are listed in Appendix D).

Amongst agricultural representatives as a whole, there are, therefore, degrees of identification with the farmers' cause not only as measured by the range of direct leadership connections they maintain with agricultural and non-agricultural groups, but also by the electoral support they receive from a range of groups. 'Pure' agricultural representatives are in a minority. Politicians classified as agriculture-related Diet members for purposes of the survey would also qualify in many cases as representatives of some other interest or combination of interests. It would seem that most so-called farm politicians have broadened their range of organisational connections beyond traditional rural interests.

An institutional framework of interest group politics

Direct and indirect representation of the agricultural sector in the Diet is symptomatic of a very broadly based phenomenon in Japanese politics whereby interest groups act as surrogate local party organisations, supplying all kinds of electoral resources and organisational backup to candidates seeking national political office. The pattern of interest group representation in the Diet exemplified by agricultural organisations is not, therefore, confined to this sector. Although agricultural interest groups have excelled in this area because of their vote-gathering capacities, the promotion of group leaders to national and local government office as representatives of specific sectional interests is standard practice amongst Japanese organisations.[144] The phenomenon operates across all sectors where votes can be mobilised and electoral funds can be generated.

One of the fundamental goals of interest groups in supplying support to their direct and indirect representatives is to achieve access to the policy-making process. As Truman put it, access is 'the facilitating intermediate objective of political interest groups'.[145] Whether or not interest groups are successful in attaining their policy objectives can depend on the quality of access they enjoy to the various branches of government, primarily the Parliament, the bureaucracy, the ruling party and its executive, and also the government executive. Muramatsu, Ito and Tsujinaka's research on Japanese pressure groups revealed that agricultural groups enjoyed the best access of any broad category of organisation amongst those surveyed.[146] Moreover, agricultural groups' contacts with the LDP registered a higher percentage than any other category of pressure group.[147]

A related survey of Japanese interest groups established that organisations close to the LDP 'clearly had direct access to the top party officials and to the internal policy-making body of the dominant party (the Policy Affairs Research Council)'.[148] Further, 'the closer the relationship with the dominant party, the more frequent a group's contact with the government bureaucracy, especially at the highest levels of prime minister, minister, and vice-minister.'[149] The same study also showed that agricultural organisations scored quite highly on their self-perceptions of influence over the LDP, which was a direct function of the closeness of their relationship with the dominant party.[150]

The difference between the custom of direct and indirect representation in the Japanese Diet and what is observed in Western democratic systems is essentially one of scale and intensity.[151] Firstly, many Japanese organisations seek national political representation in this manner, and a relatively large proportion of Japanese Diet politicians maintain explicit organisational ties.[152] Research has shown that few Diet members are without connections to interest groups, and that in many cases politicians hold simultaneous office in the Diet and in outside groups.[153]

Secondly, aspects of the Japanese political environment have made relationships between politicians and interest groups particularly salient. As already pointed out, party organisations have been generally deficient at the grassroots level, requiring candidates to rely on non-party sources (including interest groups) to provide the means for electoral success, such as campaign workers, funds and the machinery for collecting votes. Moreover, the existence of multi-member constituencies in the Lower House and in slightly less than half the prefectural constituencies of the Upper House has forced candidates from the LDP, and in some cases the JSP, to compete against each other for votes. In these circumstances, candidates for Diet office have been compelled to build a support base outside their parties by relying on personal attributes and connections.

In spite of the introduction of a new electoral system in the Lower House, the strong tradition of interest group involvement in supplying electoral resources in order to secure political representation means that interest groups will remain an important non-party source of such connections and voting support. The introduction of SMDs in the Lower House will not convert Japanese political parties into mass-based organisations overnight, if at all. Although political parties have organised branches in the new electoral districts, the *koenkai* of individual candidates have not been displaced.[154]

What is particularly marked about the relationship between interest groups and politicians in the Japanese case is the prevalence of direct representation. This realises access from within the policy process by politicians who have a dual role as both interest group leader and Diet member. Even amongst indirect representatives, quality of access can often be ensured by the degree of dependence of the politician on interest group support. In both cases, the relationship between the interest group and the politician is closer and the obligations more compelling than in other democratic systems because of the electoral and party-organisation factors described above.

In this respect, the Japanese case, and the agricultural sector in particular, fundamentally modify the standard preconception of the relationship between interest groups and political institutions in democratic systems, particularly the notion of a 'lobby'. Interest groups are usually assumed to operate outside the policymaking process; their role is to lobby political actors. The orthodox model thus conceptualises government (which includes the legislative, executive and administrative bodies) and interest groups as two autonomous structures, each impinging on the other, but remaining largely self-contained.

What the above analysis shows, however, is that in the case of Japanese interest groups (and particularly agricultural interest groups), quite considerable overlap occurs between the legislative and executive branches on the one hand and 'outside' groups on the other. Role-sharing or functional overlap occurs: interest group leaders are not limited to the function of interest articulation but are also involved in the functions 'normally' associated with government, namely the legislative and policymaking roles. This is the functional equivalent of the corporatist mode of government-interest group interaction[155] in which the latter also assumes public administration roles. Indeed, interest group leaders are not only incorporated into the policymaking process as a by-product of their participation in agricultural administration, but they directly penetrate the policymaking process on the ruling party and parliamentary side of government.

Positions of influence in policymaking

The realisation of interest group demands requires not only access to the policymaking process but also the exercise of influence. One of the main reasons why interest groups seek direct and indirect representation in the Diet is to place their supporters in positions where they can influence the decisions of government. Once in the Diet, agricultural representatives gravitate into positions in the Diet, government executive and political parties, particularly in the LDP, where they can exert influence over agricultural policy outcomes. The role of the LDP's *norin giin*, for example, has been described as 'pipe for "pressuring petitions"' (*'atsuryokuteki chinjo' no paipu*).[156]

A number of policy-related contexts are important. In the government executive, the most influential position is that of MAFF Minister. In the Diet, the relevant formal positions are executive and ordinary memberships of Diet standing committees on agriculture, forestry and fisheries and Parliamentary Vice-Ministerships for agriculture, forestry and fisheries. The standing committees, for example, consist of agricultural experts from the major parties.[157] The informal Diet members' leagues organised around specific agricultural policy issues or commodity interests also attract large numbers of farm politicians (see Appendix B). Acting as individual Diet members, politicians can also attempt to exert influence over ministry officials, particularly in relation to the allocation of subsidies for specific projects in specific localities.[158]

In the parties themselves, the formal agricultural policymaking machinery and informal groups of party politicians focused on agricultural policy issues are critical entities. As soon as Zenkoku Noseikyo Chairman Kumagai was elected to the Lower House in October 1996, for example, he started his Diet member's activities (*giin katsudo*), which in his case meant grappling with rice policy centring on the rice price and attending his first meeting of the LDP's Norin Bukai.[159] As Table 7.10 also indicates, the land improvement politicians commonly occupy senior agricultural policymaking positions in the LDP (in CAPIC and AFD) and in the Diet (Parliamentary Vice-Minister and membership of Agriculture, Forestry and Fisheries Committees). In the LDP, the *norin zoku* are by far the most influential, but informal group.

The job of direct and indirect representatives alike is to act as lobbyists inside the policy process and to exert influence directly on agricultural policies and draft legislation on behalf of their supporters. This internal policy function does not replace but complements the various kinds of public and private lobbying activities in which interest groups and their non-Parliamentary leaders engage from outside the policy process.

As pointed out in chapter 6, a key criterion of electoral backing from the agricultural cooperatives, for example, is how much potential influence a politician can exert on agricultural policymaking. A distinctive feature of Nokyo's group of Diet supporters, APRA, was seniority in the ranks of Diet members and experience in party agricultural and forestry leadership positions. Nokyo gave electoral support to politicians who could exercise influence over agricultural policy from a powerful vantage point. APRA members from the LDP occupied a disproportionately large number of positions of power in the government executive. In the period 1972–74, almost one-quarter of this group had at one time held the position of minister, including that of MAF Minister. About the same number had been Parliamentary Vice-Ministers of Agriculture and Forestry and Chairmen of Diet Agriculture, Forestry and Fisheries Committees.

They were outnumbered, however, by the even greater number who had been prominent in LDP policy committees on agriculture and forestry. More than one-third of the LDP's APRA membership in this period had been chairmen or vice-chairmen of PARC agriculture and forestry committees. These proportions were repeated in JSP and DSP agricultural committees. One quarter of the JSP membership had been PARC Agriculture and Forestry Division Chairmen (Norin Bucho) and almost one-third had been party Farmers' Division Chairmen (Nomin Bucho) or Vice-Chairmen. The same proportion (one-quarter) had been Chairmen or Vice-Chairmen of the DSP Policy Committee on Agriculture, Forestry and Fisheries (Noringyogyo Taisaku Iinkai).

These figures support APRA's self-professed identity as a supra-party, policy-orientated organisation whose membership was dominated by those occupying important positions in party agricultural policymaking organs. The constitution of APRA's membership also testifies to the strong connection between Nokyo and influential party agriculture, forestry and fishery leaders. Amongst the remnants of APRA's membership in the Diet in 1995 (30 in the Lower House and six in the Upper House), most were very senior LDP politicians with a record of high government office, all had a history of activity in agricultural policymaking contexts, most had connections with agricultural organisations including Nokyo, and most had occupied leadership positions in party (particularly the LDP) agricultural policymaking committees.

The 1990 sample survey endeavoured to establish the extent to which agriculture-related Diet members occupied positions of influence over agricultural policy in their party, in the government and in the Diet. Table 7.11 identifies the policy positions held by these politicians. The figures reveal that the party committee (in a majority of cases this was the LDP agricultural committee[160]) was the most common position. More than three-quarters had served on party agricultural committees compared with one-third for the Agriculture, Forestry and Fisheries Committees of the Diet.

A number of possible factors account for the fact that agricultural representatives gravitate to party policy committees rather than the relevant Diet policy committee. Firstly, agricultural representatives can crowd into the LDP's policy committees which are voluntary and which, therefore, have large accommodating memberships, unlike Diet committees which are restricted in number (40 in the Lower House and 21 in the Upper House) with a membership allotted on a strictly rotating basis. Diet members may join up to three *bukai* and even non-members may attend the discussions of these committees and join in if they wish. Members of Diet standing committees, on the other hand, are appointed by the Diet Speaker or President as recommended by the parties and apportioned according to each party's numbers in the house. Every Diet member must serve on at least one standing committee.

Table 7.11 Relevant agricultural policy positions of agriculture-related Diet members

Minister[a]		Parliamentary Vice-Minister[a]		Diet committee executive		Diet committee member		Diet committee total		Party committee executive		Party committee member		Party committee total		Diet leagues	
No.	%	No.	%	No.	%	No.	%	No.	%	No.	%	No.	%	No.	%	No.	%
12	5	21	8	48	14	67	19	115	33	77	22	185	54	262	76	56[b]	73

Notes:
a LDP only.
b This figure is based on information gained from the questionnaire survey.

Source: Author's sample survey of Diet members with agricultural connections.

In the Lower House, the 18 standing committees alone require a total of about 570 members so that, in order to fill all these committees and the several special committees as well, some representatives must serve on up to three committees. The same is true of members of the Upper House and its committees.[161]

Secondly, there is a strong perception that PARC committees of the LDP facilitate a much more influential policy position. In the view of many LDP politicians, the most effective post for exerting influence over agricultural policy is from the vantage point of a party policy committee. The chair of a Diet standing committee is regarded as requiring some specialisation, but the post is not permanent, and is often filled according to political factors relating to factional and party considerations as well as the seniority system.[162] As Izumi points out: 'Compared to committee chairmen, the numerous directors of the Liberal Democratic party's Policy Affairs Research Council enjoy far greater prestige and influence. This difference results from the fact that key officials of the LDP are directly involved in the actual legislative process, intervening and guiding government officials, whereas committee chairmen are often no more than moderators of debates between the LDP and the opposition parties.'[163] The party committee is, therefore, a much more powerful actor in determining government policy than the standing committee of the Diet whose task is to deliberate on pending legislation and other matters, but not to make policy.

Thirdly, because Japanese policymaking procedures emphasise informal negotiations rather than formal procedures, career development in each division of the PARC is generally more important for LDP members than Diet committees.[164] On the other hand, the importance of participating in formal policymaking processes should not be totally dismissed, especially in the Diet where the importance of forms and ceremonial events is stressed.[165] With respect to the *zoku*, Inoguchi and Iwai pointed out that, in addition to experiences in each LDP PARC division, so-called policy tribe members of the LDP developed their careers by participating in Diet committees. As a general rule also, LDP members of standing committees of the Diet are automatically members of the corresponding PARC division.

Fourthly, Diet committees are much smaller than party committees and entail a major investment in terms of time and energy. A Diet committee has regular business to conduct and requires a commitment from its members to study the policy and legislative matters placed before it. Inoguchi and Iwai noted that the Agriculture, Forestry and Fisheries Committees had a relatively high degree of commitment from Diet members, with nine members remaining on the committee for more than 10 years.[166]

In contrast, an LDP Diet member can stay on a party committee indefinitely and do very little in terms of making a real contribution. Unlike the leadership positions of these committees, rank and file membership requires as large or as small an investment of time and energy as a Diet member chooses to make. In many cases it involves a nominal commitment but attracts a high political value in symbolic terms in the electorate, which makes it an attractive choice under conditions where committee memberships are voluntary. In these circumstances, membership amounts to little more than putting one's name on a list. It need not necessarily signify that a Diet member is active or influential in agricultural policymaking. Many agriculture-related Diet members join these committees to earn credit points with their agricultural constituents and supporting groups; most of the real business of the committees is done by others, particularly the committee executives and bosses of the LDP's *norin zoku*, who either hold or have held leadership positions in these committees.[167]

The informal Diet members' leagues also appear to be an important venue in which politicians can demonstrate their support for particular interests. Amongst respondents to the questionnaire survey, 73 per cent were members of informal Diet leagues of members concerned with agricultural policy, a percentage that was only slightly less than the proportion of those who had served on agricultural committees of their party. These groupings are purely voluntary and politicians can gain easy credit by enlisting as members in order to show solidarity for a particular cause. In fact this is one of the main ways in which a politician can display activism on behalf of his supporters, particularly as the leagues rally at decision points and thereby attract a great deal of publicity. Forming a new league around a particular issue is also designed to indicate a high level of dedication on the part of an agricultural representative. Because these groups are highly informal, they can have a transient existence, with new groups forming and older ones dissolving from time to time. A group that formed specifically amongst younger Diet members to fight rice imports in 1992 was the Special Action Diet Members' League to Protect Japanese Agriculture (Nihon no Nogyo o Mamoru Tokubetsu Kodo Giin Renmei). Yet another new group that formed in 1997 was the Diet Members' League for Countermeasures Against Bird and Animal Damage to Agriculture, Forestry and Fisheries (Norinsuisangyo Higai Choju Taisaku Giin Renmei).

Intra-Diet and intra-party lobbying through the leagues provides an opportunity for special interest politicians to use sheer weight of numbers and mob tactics in order to achieve a particular policy goal.[168] The leagues are, however, ephemeral groupings with a shadow membership and no real activities. They mobilise spontaneously around particular issues but their chief function is to serve as a badge of identity with certain interests, not to play an active role in the determination of policy. They align far more with the demands of their interest group backers than with the dominant view of the formal policymaking committees of the party.

The position of MAFF Minister was not particularly significant for agriculture-related Diet members in the sample survey. Only 5 per cent of agriculture-related Diet members had held this position. This is not only a reflection of the limited opportunities to hold this position, but the fact that, like all ministerial positions, the MAFF Minister has traditionally been a factionally-appointed post based on seniority ranking within the LDP. This is still the case even though the party factions were formally dissolved in December 1994. In 1996, PM Hashimoto appointed his Cabinet using this traditional methodology, for example. This means that no particular policy aptitude, specialism or connections are necessarily part of the qualifications for the MAFF Minister's job.

The MAFF Minister in Hashimoto's second-term 1996–97 Cabinet was Fujimoto Takao, a former MHW Minister and not an agriculture-related Diet member. His background was in securities (Nomura Securities) and Denden Kosha (Nippon Telephone and Telegraph, or NTT), entering politics after his father retired. He freely admitted that he was not well versed in agricultural policy, but claimed that with support from his Parliamentary Vice-Minister and *norin zoku jitsuryokusha*, Hori Kosuke, he would grapple with the job.[169] Fujimoto can be contrasted with PM Obuchi's first appointee, Nakagawa Shoichi (son of Nakagawa Ichiro), who is a well-known farm politician and LDP agricultural committee executive.

The other side of this coin is the fact that agriculture-related Diet members get appointed to the full range of Cabinet positions. Horinouchi Hisao, for example, was appointed by PM Hashimoto as Minister of Posts and Tele-communications in the post-October 1996 LH Cabinet. He is a Nokyo Diet member, former member of APRA, a *chikusan giin*, former MAFF Minister, former Chairman of CAPIC and the LH Committee on Agriculture, Forestry and Fisheries, and former Vice-Chairman of the AFD – in other words, a *norin zoku*.[170] At the government level, agriculture-related Diet members do not specialise; it is at the party level and to a lesser extent at the parliamentary level that they specialise in particular policy issues in order to represent the interests with which they are aligned.

Using information gained from the questionnaire survey, Table 7.12 indicates the agricultural policy positions held by direct representatives of agricultural organisations and by Diet members who had received electoral support from Nokyo or other agricultural organisations. Three committee situations were tested: past or present membership and executive office in the Diet's Agriculture, Forestry and Fisheries Committees, party agricultural committees, and leagues of Diet members concerned with agriculture. Once again the importance of the party agricultural committee was underlined with the highest scores being registered for this committee by agricultural leaders and non-agricultural leaders alike.

Major differences, however, could be discerned between the committee attachments of agricultural group leaders and non-agricultural group leaders. The results generally emphasise the difference being a Nokyo official or agricultural group leader makes. Nokyo leaders scored highest for member-ship of all committees except for the Diet members' leagues where agricultural group leaders were the most numerous. The next highest scores overall were those for agricultural group leaders. Non-agricultural group leaders had low scores for the Diet standing committees, moderately high scores

Table 7.12 Agricultural committee positions of agricultural representatives
according to leadership and electoral support connections to agricultural groups

Unit: %

Committee position	Executive or member of Diet committee	Executive or member of party committee	Member of Diet League
Type of agricultural representative			
Agricultural cooperative leader	77	92	69
Agricultural group leader	61	90	74
Non-agricultural group leader	32	78	63
Supported by agricultural group(s) in election campaign	48	85	71
Not supported by agricultural group(s) in election campaign	40	80	53

Source: Author's questionnaire survey of Diet members with agricultural connections.

for party agricultural committees (but still significantly lower than Nokyo and other agricultural group leaders) and relatively lower scores again for the Diet members' leagues. The direct representatives of agricultural organisations clearly target policymaking contexts in which they can exert their influence.

This is supported by other research that rated LDP *norin giin* amongst other things according to their membership of and leadership positions in a range of agricultural committees (PARC committees, Diet members' leagues etc.) and their attendance at meetings such as Nokyo's 'demand' conventions for the rice price and the agricultural budget, and meetings held by the rice and fruit farming Diet members' leagues. Those *norin giin* with by far the highest scores, for both membership and attendance, were *Nokyo giin*. Grouped according to prefecture, the *Nokyo giin* almost uniformly scored the highest numbers of combined membership and attendance points amongst the *norin giin*.[171] The *norin zoku* also tended to score high points in the membership category, although not necessarily consistently in the attendance category.[172] Indeed, for most *norin giin*, membership of various policy committees was not matched by their attendance at high profile Nokyo-sponsored gatherings or meetings of the Diet members' leagues. It was, generally speaking, the *Nokyo giin* who showed up the most dutifully at these gathering and meetings.

The questionnaire survey revealed, however, no great differences in the agricultural committee memberships of those Diet members who claimed support from agricultural organisations (including the cooperatives) and those who did not. While the percentages of the latter group were lower than the former, they were not significantly lower, except for the Diet members' leagues. Clearly other considerations can determine committee memberships apart from support factors relating to outside groups, such as expertise generated by past career experience (in the bureaucracy for example), constituency factors (although these had not materialised in the form of electoral support from agricultural groups), and an interest in agricultural policy from an urban-consumer perspective. On the other hand, league membership would tend to signify the receipt of some form of electoral backing, hence the need to 'make efforts' on behalf of supporting interests in a way that would attract publicity.

The most important conclusion that can be drawn from the figures in Table 7.12 is that agricultural group leadership results in a high probability of membership of all types of formal and informal agricultural committees. This factor appears to be more important than whether or not the support of an agricultural group was received in the election.

Finally, it should be emphasised that Diet members customarily belong simultaneously to a number of Diet and party committees in reflection of their diverse constituency and organisational interests and consequently their policy interests. It is not unusual, for example, for an LDP politician to belong at the same time to up to four Diet committees (although the usual number is two to three), anywhere from three to six PARC divisions, and up to 12 investigation committees, totalling up to 20 committees extending across a whole range of policy sectors and interests. Over the longer term, the number of divisions, investigation committees and Diet committees to which an LDP Diet politician has belonged may amount to quite a considerable number – as many as 20 investigation committees, 10 divisions and seven Diet committees.

Moreover, even membership of an agricultural committee is not necessarily an infallible sign that a Diet politician really represents agricultural constituents. For example, when members were being enlisted in the LDP's Rice Price Committee during the producer rice decision season and politicians from Tokyo districts were propositioned, the majority of them joined.[173]

It is, in fact, possible to quantify the performance of LDP *norin giin* according to their 'willingness' (*iyokuten*) and their 'attendance' (*shussekiten*) in relation to agricultural policy committees.[174] The former can be measured by the number of agricultural committees agriculture and forestry Diet members belong to: the AFD and CAPIC within the PARC; APRA, the Agriculture Reconstruction Policy Research Association and the Association to Protect Farmers' Health as Nokyo-sponsored Diet members' groups; and various Diet members' leagues such as the Diet Members' Round Table Conference for Promoting Vegetables (Yasai Shinko Giin Kondankai), the Diet Members' Roundtable Conference for Promoting Flowering Plants (Kaki Shinko Giin Kondankai) and the Diet Members' League for Promoting Livestock Farming. For each of these committees, membership generates one point for the Diet member. In addition, an executive position and/or membership of either the UH or LH Agriculture, Forestry and Fisheries Committees carries with it another half-point, in order to differentiate more influential *norin giin*.

In terms of the points for attendance, one point is awarded to each *norin giin* who attended Nokyo's rice price convention (*beika taikai*) during the previous year's rice price campaign, a half-point was allocated each time the Diet member attended meetings of Noshinkyo, one point was awarded for those who attended Nokyo's Unified Demand Assembly (Nokyo Toitsu Yosei Shukai) during the budget campaign, and for those who participated in the general meeting of the Nomin no Kenko o Mamoru Kai, and the general meeting of the Diet Members' League for Promoting Fruit Farming.

Although the point system was crudely quantitative rather than qualitative (it could not measure the amount of influence exerted on agricultural policy decisions by party or government leaders, for example, other than through their formal positions on agricultural policy committees or their attendance at various Nokyo gatherings), it did pick up those Diet members who deserved the label of *norin giin* from those who were only nominally *norin giin*. If a Diet member's score was below five, or if the attendance score was zero, then these Diet members were simply *norin giin* in name only. In total, this group added up to 211 politicians. On the other hand, Diet members with a score greater than 10 numbered only 16 in total, suggesting that the farm lobby in the Diet was more mirage than substance, or at least, only a hard core of *norin giin* did the real work of representing agricultural interests in the Diet.

Moreover, Diet members' scores tended to correlate well with prefectural scores recording the numbers of *norin giin* as a proportion of the total number of LDP politicians from that prefecture, the number of farm house-holds as a proportion of the total number of households in that prefecture and the dependency rate of farm households on agricultural income. In short, the higher the prefectural scores, the higher the scores of Diet members from that prefecture. Numbers of genuine *norin giin* fell along with the gradual contraction in the various statistical indices relating to agriculture in the prefecture.[175] As Tachibana suggests, the widespread phenomenon of self-styled *norin giin*, which these figures underline, merely reflects the fact that a majority, although they cannot depend positively on farm votes, are reluctant to let them go and run the risk of being labelled an enemy of the farmer. Such nominal agricultural representatives even constitute a majority in the LDP.[176]

Diversity of interest representation

The above discussion underlines the point made earlier that almost no poli-ticians are single-interest representatives; most have backing from diverse groupings, although they may develop a closer association with a particular interest and gain influence and expertise in the relevant policy area over time. It would appear that ultimately all Diet members wear many hats as representatives of constituencies, groups, interests and factions, and operate simultaneously in a number of decisionmaking contexts. They may stay on particular committees for a period of years, but not continuously over the course of their Diet careers. They chop and change to acquire a range of policy expertise. These figures make it impossible to conclude that any Diet members are exclusively representative of a particular interest. Even those LDP members who end up closely identified with special interests such as the *zoku* are not exclusively associated with these interests.

This point is well illustrated by the highly variable career tracks of agriculture-related Diet members. The policy interests of these Diet members, as illustrated by the formal Diet and party policy positions that they hold, can be quite varied. In some cases they include agriculture, but they are not necessarily centred around it. These Diet members display several basic patterns of linkage between interest representation and policy activity, two of which were identified earlier.

The first pattern is the politician who has a limited connection to agriculture either in organisational terms or in terms of Diet or party activity, because his main interests centre elsewhere in terms of his major support base and constituency connections. He joins relevant agricultural committees on a sporadic basis, merely to take advantage of a nominal alignment with agricultural interests. Around 30 per cent of agriculture-related Diet members fall into this category.

At the other extreme is the farm politician who specialises narrowly in agricultural affairs, has strong constituency-based interests in agriculture and close connections to agricultural organisations. At one time or another this Diet member occupies all the relevant, leading positions on agricultural policy in the Diet and in the party: as an executive of the Agriculture, Forestry and Fisheries Committee and party agricultural committees and bureaus, and as Parliamentary Vice-Minister of Agriculture, Forestry and Fisheries. This politician has no other discernible interest. He is almost exclusively dedicated to representing agricultural interests. This category of Diet member is a small minority and is becoming smaller.

The third pattern is demonstrated by a politician who holds some agricultural policy positions because of constituency-dictated interests, but his other interests begin to take precedence over time. Agriculture-related activity is followed up by greater dedication to another field, including high policy and government office in that particular area. In this case, the function of agricultural representation recedes into the background; it becomes an historical connection. A small number of agriculture-related Diet members fall into this category.

In the fourth pattern, the politician shows a more consistent policy interest in agricultural affairs but this is balanced by activity in other policy areas. This is usually a reflection of the composition of his support base and organisational connections. Most agricultural representatives fall into this category. They are members of several committees including agriculture, and pursue several sets of interests in an even-handed fashion. A good example is Yamanaka Sadanori who has been a prominent agricultural politician but who has become strongly identified with another area of policy specialisation – taxation affairs.

The last pattern is the politician who is an expert in agricultural-policy related issues and holds all the top party and Diet agricultural policy related positions, has close connections to agricultural organisations and represents a farming constituency. This politician begins with the post of Parliamentary Vice-Minister for Agriculture, Forestry and Fisheries and membership of the Diet Committee on Agriculture, Forestry and Fisheries and the party agricultural policymaking committees (CAPIC and the AFD in the case of the LDP). He then moves up the ladder into executive positions in these committees and, if he is a member of the LDP, becomes a *norin zoku*.

This pattern in the case of the LDP further divides into two sub-categories. For a relatively small number of agriculture-related Diet members, their role as *norin giin* is modified by advancement into higher government office. This is because once farm politicians get to higher levels of seniority in the party, they become eligible for Cabinet positions. Examples of this type are Inoue Kichio, Eto Takami and Suzuki Seigo. Each became a minister in areas other than the MAFF. They can retain their agricultural policy leadership functions, however, after their turn in ministerial positions is over.

The second sub-category is the LDP *norin giin* who attains some of the highest posts in the party and the government. In some cases, party-based specialism in agricultural affairs is left behind for more senior party executive and government posts (for example, LDP Secretary-General, PARC Chairman and Executive Council Chairman) and, in the government, Cabinet positions, the Deputy Prime Ministership and even the Prime Ministership. Only one of these high executive posts is related to agriculture – that of MAFF Minister. Examples are Watanabe Michio, Hata Tsutomu and Kato Koichi. All were *norin zoku*, but all went beyond this into higher political office. Of this group, only Watanabe and Hata have been Minister of Agriculture, Forestry and Fisheries. All have held diverse ministerial office, high executive posts in the LDP and in government, and in the case of Hata, the Prime Ministership.

Conclusion

The preceding analysis has cast the net wide to gauge the maximum number of Diet politicians with a connection to agriculture and agricultural policy issues. This provides a general, though indirect and necessarily imprecise tool for measuring the political influence of the farm lobby in parliamentary and party circles. Clearly political representation of the farm sector remains strong at the national level as estimated by a number of different indices.

It would be useful for comparative purposes to evaluate these numbers against other major economic interests such as the construction lobby, the small retailers and so on, but such an exercise is beyond the scope of this study. Moreover, absolute numbers are not necessarily an indication of actual influence. As noted earlier, the trade unions have consistently sponsored relatively large numbers of their officials into Diet politics, but their influence does not correlate particularly well with the figures for their Diet representation. In terms of sectoral influence, the factor of gross Diet membership can be enhanced by the party alignment of Diet representatives (as it is in the case of agriculture), or it can be diminished, as in the case of the trade unions. Furthermore, the influence of some interests such as large enterprise, for example, is not easily measurable in these terms, since it is exercised in a different kind of way.[177]

The examination of the Diet profiles of representative organisations in the agricultural sector suggests that one of the reasons why agrarian power has not been severely eroded by the declining importance of the farm sector in the national economy is the structural overlap between political institutions and agricultural interest groups. The agricultural and political worlds directly intersect at the legislative levels, with the leaders of farm groups strategically positioned in the Diet (and in local assemblies). Dual office-holding by farm politicians enables the agricultural sector to penetrate the centres of Japanese power and exert influence where it can be most effective – in the agricultural policymaking machinery of the ruling party. Although a contraction is evident in the number of direct agricultural representatives, the farm sector remains well represented in the Diet not only by current or previous office holders in agricultural organisations but also by politicians whose *jiban* include farm organisations, farmers' groups and MAFF *goikaku dantai*, reflecting the relative weight of the national agricultural electorate and the utility of these bodies as electoral support groups.

The way in which the agricultural sector is represented in national politics provides strong support for the general proposition that interest representation is institutionalised in the Japanese Diet.[178] Politicians are elected for the purpose of furthering the interests of the special interest groups with which they are allied. From this perspective, the Diet becomes a collection of special interest representatives with a relatively high degree of dependence on outside interests for crucial political resources. This dependence creates policy obligations that are difficult to ignore. Politicians become identified with particular interests and articulate these interests in various policy-related spheres. One of their primary roles is to act as internal party and Diet lobbyists in formal and informal decisionmaking contexts.[179]

The Japanese case thus implies a high degree of allegiance on the part of interest group representatives to their original organisation and therefore much stronger definition of policy by outside interests. Diet members carry a degree of policy 'debt' that exceeds that normally observed amongst politicians in other systems of representative democracy. Organisational definition of policy demands is consequently much greater. This characteristic derives not only from the custom amongst Japanese Diet members of combining professional roles in outside organisations with Parliamentary careers, but also from the extent of their reliance on organised group backing for votes and other critical electoral resources. The relationship between interest groups and Diet politicians is characterised by a high degree of inter-dependence, extending in some cases to duality of function. Interest group leaders become members of the Diet, acting as representatives of their original organisations at the same time as they undertake policy-related functions in Diet and party contexts. In some cases, penetration becomes mutual with interest groups functioning primarily as appendages of political parties and existing almost entirely for party-political purposes.[180] A good example in the agricultural sector is the farmers' unions.

The extent of direct and indirect representation of interest groups in the Diet provides solid evidence for the pluralist model of interest group politics in Japan. Interest groups effectively penetrate Diet and party policymaking processes, suggesting that the political system is open and accessible to a range of organised interests that make inputs into the policy process and exercise leverage in different policy areas.[181] On the other hand, the analysis does not endorse the notion implicit in the pluralist thesis that all groups necessarily enjoy more or less equal access. In Nokyo's case, for example, it has been able to gain an inestimable advantage from its ties to the LDP in power over a long period. For groups desiring budget subsidies like Nokyo, logic has dictated close ties to the LDP as the party of patronage. Groups affiliated to the traditional Opposition parties have enjoyed more limited access to the policy-making process. The continuous period of one-party rule by the LDP has had the effect of elevating the political support patterns of interest groups to a critical determinant of policy access and therefore influence.

As the evidence in this chapter showed, however, the degree of identification between politicians and particular sets of interests can be highly variable and is rarely exclusive. The nature of the connections differs and hence so does the quality of representation by politicians. Some Diet members have vital connections to particular interest groups (one-quarter of agricultural representatives in the 1990 survey, for example, had official leadership ties with agricultural organisations); for others the connections are looser and are shaped by constituency interests and voting support. In the end, most politicians are highly pluralistic in their representational characteristics, putting together a composite support base from a variety of different interests and displaying a range of different intensities of connection with these interests. In some cases, attachments can be fairly nominal. Belonging to a party agricultural policy organ or an agricultural Diet members' group, for example, supposedly demonstrates a community of interest with the farmers, but in reality, for many such self-styled *norin giin*, it is only a matter of having their names put on a list, with little real commitment in practice. If there are potential electoral gains to be made, politicians habitually behave opportunistically in relation to different interests. In this respect, their loyalties may be superficial. On the other hand, groups like the LDP's *zoku* should be viewed as ready-made collectivities enabling particular groups of politicians to be more reliably identified with particular sets of interests.

The dominant role of Japanese politicians as interest intermediaries also illuminates a fundamental aspect of party organisation in Japan. Political parties are defined more by the interests with which they are connected than the ideological principles for which they stand. In essence, the LDP is an organised collection of individual politicians representing a cross-section of societal and economic interests. LDP Diet members act like freelance interest representatives and lobbyists, each supported by a range of groups whose interests they endeavour to promote and protect in national politics. While Opposition parties like the JSP and DSP have been seen as spokespersons for organised labour, the LDP's interest-based character is much broader and extends across agricultural, small business, professional and conservative social groups, such as the war bereaved associations. The LDP ends up as a loose federation of interest representatives, with the strongest binding element within the parliamentary party being the common clientele interests of its members and their desire to retain power so they can reward their supporters with acts of political patronage and by interceding with policymakers. As Fukunaga puts it, 'the party is a 'policy department store', responding to the demands of each interest group and trying to offer policies to suit each and every one of them. When interests conflict, the party works as a coordinator, seeking to find compromises acceptable to all parties.'[182]

Broad stereotypes about the identity of particular interests with particular parties sometimes mask a more complex reality. In the case of agriculture, for example, although a majority of farm politicians can be found within the LDP where they form a vocal pro-farmer lobby, agricultural interest representation in the Diet reveals a suprapartisan character. The Diet Agriculture, Forestry and Fisheries Committees, for example, have been described as committees of friends (*nakayoshi iinkai*), in spite of the differing party affiliations of members. This reflects the tradition of bipartisan agreement on agricultural policy issues. Agriculture is a case where, in dealing with policies that relate to specific interests, politicians may end up having more in common with those representing the same interests in other parties, than they do with other kinds of interest representatives in their own party.

The penetration of Diet and party policymaking processes by outside interests via their politician-representatives helps to explain the immobilism of the Japanese policy process.[183] The political process is highly penetrated by a range of societal interests which in many cases helps to block change because of the obligations felt by politicians to their supporters. The phenomenon of direct representation, in particular, explains why the parameters of policy change are set so tightly in Japan. Such politicians are keenly sensitised to the implications of changing policy initiatives for the interests they represent.

Immobilism has been compounded by the conflation of interest representative and policymaking roles by leading politicians, particularly those clustered in the *zoku*. Big payoffs accrue for interest groups that achieve this level of penetration of the policy process. The more elevated the position the politician holds, the better for the affiliated interest group. This explains the tendency of organisations like APRA to select and back prominent Diet politicians as their members. It is only in the later stages of a Diet member's career that some politicians manage to divest themselves of the ties of interest group capture.[184]

The dominant interest representational characteristic of Diet membership was entrenched by the previous LH electoral system. The construction of the new electoral system, which requires politicians to pitch their appeals to a broader cross-section of the voting population, will serve to weaken the special interest connections of Japanese politicians. This will gradually alter the dominant modes of political behaviour of Diet politicians and will ultimately strengthen their party identity at the expense of their interest-representational identity.

Appendix A
Agricultural interest groups represented in the Diet by their leaders in 1990 (excluding Nokyo)

[Unless otherwise indicated, the Diet representatives of these groups are members of the LDP. The number of Diet members who are or have held leadership positions in these groups is listed in brackets ( )].

A. Statutory Agricultural Interest Groups:

Agricultural mutual aid organisations:
National Federation of Agricultural Mutual Aid Associations (1)
Prefectural Federation of Agricultural Mutual Aid Associations (5)
Local Agricultural Mutual Aid Associations (2)

Agricultural committee organisations:
Prefectural Agricultural Councils (3)
National Chamber of Agriculture (1)

Land improvement organisations:
National Federation of Land Improvement Industry Groups (3)
Prefectural Federations of Land Improvement Industry Groups (6)
Federation of Land Improvement Districts (1)
Land Improvement District (2)
City Land Improvement Group (1)
Land Improvement Association (1) (JSP)

B. MAFF Gaikaku Dantai (National or Prefectural/Local Level)

Public Corporations:
Agriculture, Forestry and Fisheries Finance Corporation (1)
National Association of Regional Horse Racing (1)

Individual commodity organisations:
Livestock
Central Livestock Association (2)
Prefectural Livestock Associations (2)

Prefectural Livestock Promotion Associations (2)
National Beef Association (1)
National Cattle and Livestock Products Hygiene Guidance Association (1)
Prefectural Hog Raising Association (1)
Japan Poultry Association (1)
Japan Holstein Registration Association (1)
Dairy Farming Association (1)
Crops
Japan Tea Industry Central Association (1)
Prefectural Tea Industry Council (3)
Japan Konjak Association (1)

General Agriculture and Food:
Japan Agriculture, Forestry and Fisheries Promotion Association (1)
Agricultural Policy Promotion Council (1)
International Agriculture and Forestry Cooperation Association (1)
Food Demand and Supply Research Centre (1)
Prefectural Foodstuffs Hygiene Association (1)
National Feedrice Research Association (1) (JSP)
Japan–China Agriculture, Forestry and Fisheries Exchange Association (1)

C. Farmers' Groups:

Commodity Organisations:
Prefectural Horticultural Association (1)
Prefectural Apple Association (1) (JSP)
Mushroom Production Association (1)
Tobacco Cultivation Union (1)
Prefectural Leaf Tobacco Cooperative Struggle Council (1) (JSP)
Cattle Business Cooperative Association (1)

Farmers' Political Leagues:
Dairy Farmers' Political Federation of Japan (1)
National Tobacco Cultivators' Political League (1)

Farmers Unions:
All-Japan Farmers' Union Federation (Zennichino) and its prefectural
federations (5) (JSP)
Prefectural Farmers' Union Federations (5) (JSP)[185]
Japan Farmers' Union (Nichino) (3) (JSP)
Prefectural Farmers' Unions (3) (JSP)[186]
National Farmers' League (Zenno) (1) (DSP)
Prefectural Labour-Farmer Councils (6) (JSP)

Sundry:
Japan–China Agriculture and Farmers' Exchange Cooperation Prefectural Association (1)
Reclamation Association (1)
National Mountain Village Promotion League (1)
Farm Migrant Workers' Association (1)
Prefectural Farm Migrant Workers' Federation (1) (JSP)
National Federation of Farm Migrant Workers' Associations (2) (JSP)

Appendix B
Diet members' leagues listed by respondents to the questionnaire survey

[Unless otherwise stated, these leagues operate within the LDP. The number of respondents claiming membership of the league is given for each one.]

1. Diet Members' Council for Promoting Farming Villages (Noson Shinko Giin Kyogikai, or Noshinkyo) (includes one JSP, and one Independent): Total 23.
2. Diet Members' League for Promoting Livestock Farming (Chikusan Shinko Giin Renmei) (includes one JSP, and one Independent): Total 20
3. Diet Members' League for the Promotion of Fruit Farming (Kaju Nogyo Shinko Giin Renmei): Total 9
4. New Agricultural Policy Vision Research Association (Shinnosei Bijiyon Kenkyukai): Total 6
5. Agricultural Policy Diet Members' Group (Nosei Giindan) (exclusively JSP): Total 4
6. Organic Agriculture Promotion/Research Diet Members' League (Yuki Nogyo Suishin/Kenkyu Giin Renmei): Total 4
7. Forests, Forestry and Forestry Industry Activisation Promotion Diet Members' League (Shinrin, Ringyo, Rinsangyo Kasseika Suishin Giin Renmei) (includes 1 JSP and 1 DSP): Total 4
8. Expansion of Rice Consumption and Genuine Rice Price Promotion Diet Members' League (Beishohi Kakudai Junbeika Suishin Giin Renmei) (includes 1 JSP and 1 DSP): Total 3
9. Flower Industry Diet Members' League (Furawaa Sangyo Giin Renmei): Total 2
10. Dairy Policy Association (Rakuseikai): Total 2
11. Pig and Poultry Promotion Diet Members' League (Yoton, Shokucho Shinko Giin Renmei): Total 2
12. Shiitake Promotion Diet Members' League (Shiitake Shinko Giin Renmei): Total 2
13. Agriculture and Forestry Pension Policy Diet Members' League (Norin Nenkin Taisaku Giin Renmei): Total 2
14. Japanese Agricultural Policy Reform Comrades' Association (Nihon Nosei Sasshin Doshikai): Total 3 (This has also been formally translated

as 'Group of Those Interested in Renewal of Japanese Agricultural Administration'. It is a group of LDP Diet members involved in rice issues.)

15. Dairy Farming Diet Members' League (Rakuno Giin Renmei): Total 1
16. Agriculture Diet Members' League (Nogyo Giin Renmei) (JSP): Total 1
17. Agriculture and Forestry Policy Committee (Norin Seisaku Iinkai) (JSP): Total 1
18. Forestry Policy Promotion Diet Members' League (Rinsei Suishin Giin Renmei): Total 1
19. Flight Agriculture Promotion Research Association (Furaito Nogyo Shinko Kenkyukai): Total 1
20. Diet Members' Round Table Conference for Promoting Vegetables (Yasai Shinko Giin Kondankai): Total 1
21. Domestic Animal Business Diet Members' League (Kachikusho Giren): Total 1
22. Tea Industry Comrades (Chagyo Doshikai): Total 1
23. Mushroom Comrades (Shiitake Doshikai): Total 1
24. Diet Members' League for Promoting Mountain Villages (Sanson Shinko Giin Renmei): Total 1
25. Diet Members' Conference for the Promotion of Propagation Enterprises (Fukyu Jigyo Suishin Giin Kondankai): Total 1
26. Agriculture and Forestry Promotion Economics Council (Norin Shinko Keizai Kyogikai]): Total 1
27. Fruit Tree Division (Kaju Bukai): Total 1
28. Rice Policy Diet Members' League (Kome Taisaku Giin Renmei): Total 1
29. Forestry Industry Policy Diet Members' League (Ringyo Taisaku Giin Renmei): Total 1
30. Agricultural Policy Basic Problems Research Association (Nosei Kihon Mondai Kenkyukai): Total 1
31. Land Improvement Diet Members' League (Tochi Kairyo Giin Renmei): Total 1
32. Silkworm Round Table Conference (Kaiko Kondankai): Total 1
33. Agricultural Problems Research Council (Nogyo Mondai Kenkyu Kaigi) (DSP): Total 1
34. Food Self-Sufficiency and Environmental Preservation Diet Members' League (Shokuryo Jikyu/Kankyo Hozen Renmei) (JSP): Total 1
35. Urban and Rural Research Association (Toshi to Noson Kenkyukai): Total 1
36. Horticulture Promotion Diet Members' League (Engei Shinko Giin Renmei): Total 1

Appendix C
Non-agricultural interest groups with which agricultural representatives have leadership ties

[Numbers of Diet members associated with each group is given in ( ).]

LDP Representatives:

Prefectural Flood Control Association (3)
Japan Rivers' Association (1)
Prefectural Rivers' Association (2)
Prefectural River Improvement Association (1)
National River Erosion Control Association (1)

National Federation of Commerce and Industry Associations (2)
Prefectural Federation of Commerce and Industry Associations (2)
Prefectural Chamber of Commerce and Industry (1)
Local Chamber of Commerce and Industry (1)
National Commerce and Industry Association (1)
Prefectural Managers' Association (1)
Prefectural Construction Industry Association (3)
All-Japan Real Estate Association (1)
Prefectural Sake Brewing Association (1)
Prefectural Knitwear Cooperative Union (1)

Lions Club (1)

Japan Chamber of Youth (6)
Prefectural Chamber of Youth (2)
Local Chamber of Youth (1)
Prefectural Youth Group (1)
Youth Groups (2)
Local Youth Association (1)
Youth Culture Centre (1)
Youth Culture Association (1)
Prefectural Youth Fellowship Group (1)

International Study and Training Association (1)
Sports Boy Scouts' Council (1)
City Boys Scout Liaison Council (1)

Prefectural Central Trust Association (1)

Prefectural Welfare Promotion Association (1)
Prefectural Welfare Association (1)
Prefectural Federation of War Bereaved Associations (1)

All-Japan Piano Coaching Association (1)
Japan Cycling Association (1)
Prefectural Volley Ball Association (1)
Prefectural Softball Association (1)
Prefectural Handball Association (1)
Prefectural Motor Boat Association (1)
Japan Gateball League (1)
Prefectural Canoeing Association (2)
Prefectural Physical Education Association (2)
City Physical Educational Association (1)
Prefectural Swimming League (2)
Prefectural Weightlifting Association (1)
Prefectural Curling Association (1)
Skiing League (1)
Prefectural Soccer Association (1)
Local Athletics Association (1)
Prefectural Baseball League (1)
Prefectural Hunting Supporters' Association (1)
Prefectural Rifle Association (1)
Japan Rifle Shooting Association (1)
Prefectural Kendo League (2)
Prefectural Sumo Federation (1)
Sumo Federation (1)
Prefectural Karate Federation (1)

Japan Freight Transport Cooperative Union Federation (1)
Japan Bus Association (2)
Prefectural Trucking Association (2)
City Passenger Car Association (1)
Japan Roads Association (3)
Oil League (1)

National Federation of Statistical Associations (1)

Prefectural Defence League (1)

National High School PTA Association (1)
International Child Association (1)
Japan Teachers' Union (1)
Prefectural Private Kindergarten Support Federation (1)
Prefectural Private Kindergarten Association (1)

All-Japan Haiku Federation (1)
National Radio Music Broadcasting Association (1)
Prefectural Winning Move Association (1)
Prefectural Smokers' Federation (1)
Alcoholics Anonymous (1)

Prefectural Federation of Dangerous Articles Safety Association (1)

Lawyers' Association (1)
No. 1 Tokyo Lawyers' Association (1)

National Association of Prefectural Assembly Chairmen (1)
National Town and Village Association (2)
Kanto Governors' Association (1)
National Mayors' Association (1)
Prefectural Association of·City Mayors (1)
National Association of Prefectural Assembly Chairmen (1)
National City, Town and Village Officials' Mutual Aid Association (1)
National Association of Special Post Office Chiefs (1)

Youth Asian Association (1)
Japan–Korea Friendship Association (1)

City Fire Services Group (1)
Fire Service Association (1)
Prefectural Fire Service Association (1)

Religion and Politics Research Association (1)
World Salvation Faith (1)

Undersea Development Technology Association (1)

Prefectural Federation of People's Health Insurance Groups (1)
Japan Medical Association (1)

JSP Representatives:

Labour Unions (15)
Prefectural Workers' Welfare Council (1)

City Commerce and Industry Federation (1)
National Small and Medium Commerce and Industry Federation (2)
Town Commerce and Industry Association (1)
Prefectural Small and Medium Industry Affairs Association (1)
Japan Lawyers' Federation (2)
Prefectural Lawyers' Federation (1)
Local Lawyers' Association (1)
Japan Judiciary and Barristers' Federation (1)
Sohyo Lawyers' Group (1)

Japan Youth Group Council (1)
Youth Group (2)

Parent–Teachers' Association (2)
Japan Teachers' Union (1)
Prefectural Teachers' Unions (4)

Prefectural Public Council for the Revival of Japan–China Exchange (1)

Prefectural Federation for the Protection of the Constitution (1)

Japan–China Friendship Society (1)
Japan–China Agricultural Exchange Association (1)
Prefectural Japan–China Friendship Society (1)

Storytelling Association (1)
Entertainment Association (1)

Prefectural Weightlifting Association (1)
Prefectural Table Tennis Association (1)

Prefectural Anti-Nuclear Association (1)

Independents:

Hakodate Region Politics and Economics Research Centre (1)
Okayama Lawyers' Association (1)
Labour Union (1)

JCP Representatives:

Japan Teachers' Union (1)
New Japan Women's Association (1)
Prefectural Mothers' Convention Liaison Council (1)
City Anti-Nuclear Council (1)

City Youth Group Council (1)
City Federation of Small and Medium Enterprise Groups
Democratic Lawyers' Federation (1)
Sohyo Lawyers' Group (1)
Free Judges' Group (1)

DSP Representatives:

Labour Unions (2)

Rengo Representatives:

Labour Union (1)
Youth Group (1)

Komeito Representatives:

Japan Housewives' League (1)

Appendix D
Interest groups providing electoral support for respondents to the questionnaire survey

[This list does not include agricultural cooperative organisations or the agricultural groups in which the respondents held office – both of which were examined in another section of the questionnaire. The figures in ( ) refer to the number of respondents who claimed to have received support from the category of group in their election campaigns. Most respondents reported support from several categories and types of groups.]

1. Labour Union Organisations:
   Labour Unions (unspecified) (13)
   Prefectural Labour Councils (6)
   Forestry Unions (3)
   – National Forests and Fields Workers' Union
   – National Agricultural and Forestry Workers' Union
   – Forestry unions (unspecified)
   Manufacturing Unions (3)
   – Iron and Steel Workers Union
   – Electrical Industries Workers' Union
   – Automobile Workers General Federation
   – All-Japan Metal Workers' Federation
   Service Unions (2)
   – National Water Service Workers' Union
   – National Construction Workers' Union
   – Port Labourers Workers' Union
   – Transport Workers' Union
   National Labour Federation (1)
   – Japan Confederation of Labour
2. Agriculture and Forestry:
   Farmers Unions (4)
   Prefectural Farmers' Federation (1)
   Livestock-related groups (3)
   – Dairy or livestock-related groups
   – Hokkaido Dairy Farming Association
   Land improvement groups (2)

Agricultural Mutual Aid Association (1)
Tobacco Growers' Association (1)
Forestry groups (unspecified) (4)
Agriculture and Forestry Political Leagues (2)
– Forestry Industry Political League
– Livestock Political League

3. Fisheries:
Fisheries Cooperatives (2)
Fishery groups (unspecified) (2)

4. Business:
Commerce and Industry groups (9)
– Political League of the Youth Division of the Commerce and Industry Association
– Commerce and industry groups (unspecified)
– Commerce and Industry Political League
– Youth Division of the Commerce and Industry Association – Commerce and Industry Association
Small and Medium Enterprise group (1)
Small and Medium Enterprise Political League (2)
Construction Industry groups (5)
– Construction industry groups (unspecified)
– Construction Industry Association
Real Estate group (1)
– Real Estate Dealing Industry Group
Trucking Association (1)
Enterprise Groups (unspecified) (2)

5. Education:
Educational Associations (7)
– Education groups (unspecified)
– Middle School Alumni
– University Alumni
– Alumni Association
– High School Alumni
– School Alumni

6. Health:
Medical Associations (Doctors/Dentists/Pharmacists/Nurses) (12)
– Nurses League
– Medical Association
– Dentists Association
– Pharmaceutical Association
Medical Insurance Group (1)

7. Social
Women's groups (8)
– Women's groups (unspecified)
– Housewives' groups

   – Mothers' League
   – Family Wives
   Youth groups (3)
   – Youth Council
   – Chamber of Youth (JC)
   Sports groups (3)
   Religious Groups (2)
 8. Military
   Ex-Soldiers Group (1)
   Veterans' Association (1)
   Veterans' Pensions League (1)
 9. Professional
   Tax Accountants Association (3)
   Lawyers' group (1)
   – Japan Judiciary and Lawyers Federation
10. Welfare:
   Retired People's Groups (1)
   National Detainees' Compensation Council (1)
   Welfare groups (unspecified) (4)
   War Bereaved Association (7)
   Funeral Association (1)
   Pensioners' Groups (2)
   Retired Public Servants Federation (1)
   Buraku Liberation League (1)
11. Grass-Roots Political:
   Citizens' groups (5)
   Environmental groups (1)
12. Consumer:
   Consumer Groups (2)
   – Consumer Cooperative
   – Consumer group (unspecified)

8 Policy campaigning

Much of the discussion in the preceding chapters has focused on identifying the key organisational, electoral and representational dimensions of agrarian power. The following analysis examines how this power is mobilised by Nokyo across a range of agricultural policy issues, including support and stabilisation prices, market liberalisation and the agricultural budget. Nokyo is chosen because it has dominated the conduct of rice-roots agricultural policy campaigns in the postwar period and because it is widely regarded as one of Japan's most powerful pressure groups, 'as influential in lobbying as the *zaibatsu* corporations.'[1] A lot of public attention that Nokyo receives stems from this aspect of its activities.[2]

Nokyo's political leadership of the farm sector is based on several factors. Firstly, its extremely high organisation rate and comprehensive range of services underlines its mass mobilisation capacities and its claim to speak for all agricultural producers.[3] Secondly, Nokyo's all-encompassing interests and farm membership enable Zenchu to operate as a 'peak' farmers' organisation, a function buttressed by the formal designation of a policy representational role to the central unions. Thirdly, Nokyo's corporatised status grants privileged access to administrators as well as automatic consultation on all policy matters of importance.[4] Fourthly, Nokyo has vital interests of its own in systems of agricultural regulation including support and stabilisation price regimes. Fifthly, Nokyo has a vastly superior full-time professional bureaucracy when compared to other farmers' groups. This administrative apparatus is well geared to the formulation of demands across the entire span of agricultural policies. Last but not least, Nokyo's huge economic apparatus comprises a formidable economic power base from which to influence government. Indeed, alongside its business activities, Nokyo's *nosei katsudo* form one pillar of the two pillars of the agricultural cooperative system.[5]

Hence, by all the standard measures of interest group capabilities, it is not surprising that Nokyo is the only farmers' group that has organised and led mass, public campaigns by farmers on a continuous basis. In fact Nokyo has regularly mobilised its leaders and members en masse to advance its demands. It is the most public leader of agricultural policy campaigns; other farmers' groups and agricultural organisations tend to work behind the scenes through their influential intermediaries. Furthermore, unlike groups such as the farmers' unions, Nokyo's close ties to LDP politicians enable it to gain ready access to the agricultural policy committees of the ruling party, where it makes regular representations on a wide range of issues.

All aspects of Nokyo's *modus operandi* as a pressure group are investigated in this study: its internal structures and processes for demand formulation and decisionmaking; its various strategies as a farm pressure group; and the key political actors it targets within its policy network. The first part of the study reviews the various steps and stages of Nokyo's major public campaigns. It focuses on how Nokyo goes about advancing policy claims through a range of agricultural policy activities. The second part takes up the substance of these campaigns. It evaluates the kinds of demands Nokyo advances and the tactics it follows, and how these reflect its understanding of optimal strategies for success. It also examines how Nokyo has adjusted the nature and tenor of its demands to a policy environment more antipathetic to agricultural support and protection in recent years.

Nokyo's *nosei katsudo*

Nokyo's agricultural policy activities act as a pipe linking the farmers to government. Nokyo concentrates farmers' demands and then acts as a channel transmitting them to political and administrative authorities.[6] *Nosei katsudo* are conducted within parameters set by Nokyo's organising legislation and by its corporatised status in relation to agricultural administration. These bestow certain advantages as well as setting certain limits to the kinds of leverage and tactics it can deploy in bargaining agricultural policy outcomes with the MAFF and the LDP.[7] Agricultural policy activities encompass all internal organisational procedures leading to the formulation of policy demands and their subsequent presentation to government. Demands are issued as requests (*yosei*), resolutions (*ketsugi*), declarations (*seimei*), statements of opinion (*ikensho*) and petitions (*chinjo*).

Nokyo's lobbying is officially conducted by means of 'request campaigns' (*yosei undo*) targeting various aspects of agricultural policy. In practice, a wide variety of activities are countenanced: formal representations to MAFF advisory councils dealing with agricultural policy matters, to LDP agricultural policy committees and Diet Agriculture, Forestry and Fisheries Committees; formal representations as well as personal appeals to the MAFF Vice-Minister, LDP executives such as the PARC Chairman and the executives of party agricultural policy committees and sub-committees, the Prime Minister and Cabinet ministers (particularly the MAFF Minister, but also the MOF Minister on budgetary matters and other ministers depending on the issue); behind-the-scenes informal consultations between Nokyo (mainly Zenchu and Zenkoku Noseikyo) leaders and LDP agricultural policy leaders (*norin zoku* and the executives and former executives of LDP agricultural policy committees); presentation of members' petitions (including the products of signature campaigns) to MAFF officials and the ruling party; discussions between Nokyo executives and members of the LDP's agricultural policy committees and Diet members' leagues; face-to-face meetings and discussions between Nokyo leaders and MAFF officials;[8] general lobbying by means of visits to the Diet offices of members of all parties on an individual basis; and last, but not least, the mobilisation of mass public rallies, demonstrations, assemblies and conventions of farmers and Nokyo representatives in Tokyo and other provincial cities.[9]

Nokyo's basic approach is to supplement large-scale public action with behind-the-scenes negotiations, which may be either formal (with LDP executives and Cabinet Ministers, for example)[10] or informal. Nokyo not only approaches its targets directly, but also indirectly, enlisting sympathetic politicians to act as agents of influence within the policy process.[11] One of its main strategies has been to pressure MAFF bureaucrats through the LDP.[12] In some cases, Nokyo sets up organisations for the express purpose of maintaining lines of direct communication with sympathetic Diet members, such as APRA, but the latter has not been the only vehicle for undertaking such action. The Diet members' leagues, particularly the most recently established *noseiren*-backed Nihon Nosei-Nokyo Giin Renmei is important in this context.[13]

Nokyo's major policy campaigns are highly centralised in their implementation, with the organisational impetus coming not from individual agricultural cooperatives but from the prefectural and national organisations, especially Zenchu and *kenchu*.[14] The main campaigns are spearheaded by the various policy central headquarters (*taisaku chuo honbu*) within Zenchu, which have been set up to focus on specific policy issues,[15] such as rice and livestock prices and agricultural trade liberalisation. The exact titles of these headquarters have changed over the years, but they include the Rice Policy Central Headquarters (Beikoku Taisaku Chuo Honbu), the Livestock Policy Central Headquarters (Chikusan Taisaku Chuo Honbu), the Livestock and Horticulture Policy Central Headquarters (Chikusan Engei Taisaku Chuo Honbu), the Urban Agricultural Policy Central Headquarters (Toshi Nosei Taisaku Chuo Honbu), the Agricultural Policy Promotion Central Headquarters (Nogyo Taisaku Suishin Chuo Honbu), the Paddy Field Agriculture Policy Central Headquarters (Suiden Nogyo Taisaku Chuo Honbu), the Agriculture, Forestry and Fishery Products Import Liberalisation Prevention Policy Central Headquarters (Nosanbutsu Yunyu Jiyuka Soshi Taisaku Chuo Honbu) and the Rice Market Opening Prevention Policy Central Headquarters (Beishijo Kaiho Soshi Taisaku Chuo Honbu).[16] These headquarters each consist of approximately 20–30 Nokyo executives: prefectural central union chairmen from each of the main producing prefectures and representatives (executives) of the national federations, as well as Zenchu. Sometimes the *honbu* set up smaller working committees to decide policies.

The central headquarters are replicated within the prefectural central unions and the *sogo nokyo*, and facilitate the process of 'accumulating' (*tsumiageru*) or transmitting demands from the bottom of the Nokyo organisation to the top. Their main tasks are to make representations to the government (e.g. the MAFF Minister) and to the LDP, as well as sponsor mass activities of Nokyo leaders and members in Tokyo.

Rank and file participation in Nokyo's *nosei katsudo* most often takes the form of executive-sponsored exercises such as the mass conventions and assemblies of Nokyo leaders and members together with those associated with the farmers' political leagues. Agricultural policy activities on a mass scale graduate to the level of agricultural policy campaigns (*nosei undo*) or farmers' campaigns (*nomin undo*). When large numbers of Nokyo officials and members travel to Tokyo to attend rallies, they are almost always subsidised by the agricultural cooperatives. Mass action provides a chorus to the demands that are delivered more directly by Nokyo leaders to agricultural policymakers.

In its public campaigns, Nokyo has the advantage of being able to mobilise a powerful public relations machine that uses its mass media power to support chosen causes. For example, the organisation's interest in rice production and the maintenance of the FC system has caused it to be worried about the fairly precipitous decline in rice consumption in Japan over a number of decades.[17] Zenchu has responded with a series of campaigns over many years to halt the decline of rice consumption amongst Japanese.[18] Nokyo's public relations powers have also been exercised to the full in the campaign against agricultural trade liberalisation. This was part of an attempt to win the hearts and minds of the Japanese people in the battle over market access questions. A special focus has been placed on engendering public support for agricultural protection on food security grounds.[19] This approach has become more appropriate as public perceptions of the farmers' privileged position has become more apparent, and consumers have become more aware of food price differentials between Japan and abroad.[20]

As a target of Nokyo lobbying, LDP Diet members are a crucial focus of *nosei katsudo*. Until the formation of the LDP in 1955, Nokyo was in a position to exploit the antagonism between the two rural conservative parties. It used this tactic to great effect in its producer rice price demands, demonstrating the advantages of a stance of 'political neutrality' and 'equidistance from all political parties'.[21] A change in these tactics was rendered inevitable, however, by the amalgamation of the Liberals and Democrats in 1955, which called for the establishment of a more fixed relationship with LDP politicians.

Within the LDP, the most important sub-groupings are the *norin zoku* and executives of PARC agricultural policy committees and sub-committees (committee executives are automatically *norin zoku*). PARC agricultural policy committees are the target of Nokyo's formal policy representations to the party, underlining the role of the PARC as an important channel through which interest groups can bring their policy appeals to the attention of the ruling party.[22] The executives of these groups are the crucial figures, however, as convincing the agricultural policy leadership of the party is the key to bringing the committee rank and file into line.[23]

Although non-LDP politicians are not a primary target for policy persuasion, Nokyo engages in a lot of *ad hoc* lobbying of Diet members from all parties in order to build a broad base of cross-party support for its policy demands. This also reflects the awareness of the central leadership that co-op members are of diverse political persuasions and therefore both the ruling and Opposition parties must be targets of pressure.[24] This helps particularly in the context of discussions held in Diet committees on pending agricultural legislation. Diet members (mostly from the LDP) also attend Nokyo's mass gatherings to show solidarity with farmers' policy demands and to provide a direct channel of communication into party policymaking processes. It has been customary for large numbers of LDP Diet politicians (sometimes several hundred), including leading figures in the government and even the Prime Minister, to attend rallies and assemblies of farmers organised by Zenchu. As Muramatsu observes, this typifies the behaviour of LDP politicians wishing to consolidate their ties with interest groups: 'LDP Diet members attend the national conventions of their constituents' interests groups. Farmers' rice price organizations continue to campaign seeking support from locally and nationally elected officials, especially LDP Diet members. When asked to attend the national farmers' convention for the rice price in Tokyo in 1979, of a total of 763 Diet representatives, 319 members (mostly LDP) including some substitutes attended.'[25] Those who most reliably attend on a regular basis are, however, *Nokyo giin*.

Although Ishida argues that the more inclined a group is to undertake direct action like mass rallies, the less influential it is,[26] in agriculture's case, the underlying purpose is to impress on the LDP the sheer weight of farmers' votes. Zenchu openly claims that its power of influence over politicians derives directly from Nokyo's ability to influence votes in elections.[27] In later years, however, the aim has been to present Nokyo's case to the public at large. Muramatsu and Krauss observe that such tactics can be an effective tool of protest, forcing the government to revise unpopular policy proposals, an outcome surely not lost on interest groups like Nokyo.[28] Attendance at Nokyo rallies and conventions has often numbered in the thousands, although figures have been slowly declining over the years. The usual procedure at the conventions is for Nokyo leaders and farmers to push for certain demands and to remind the attending Diet members to show their support by helping to get Nokyo's demands realised.[29]

Every three years Zenchu sponsors a national Nokyo convention in Tokyo. This brings together Nokyo chairmen from all over the country. The purpose is to try and unify their views concerning basic problems in the Nokyo movement (*Nokyo undo*) as a whole, including *nosei katsudo*. The focus is on basic problems in the organisation itself, Nokyo's future, and long-term issues relating to Japanese agriculture and agricultural policy. At these conventions resolutions are passed relating to things such as promoting a basic plan for agriculture (sometimes called a 'Nokyo vision'), strengthening the Nokyo movement (including matters such as possible amendments to the Nokyo Law, long-term organisational planning and restructuring,[30] and improving agricultural cooperative management) and promoting the education of executives and staff members.[31] Resolutions sometimes have an explicit policy focus like agricultural trade liberalisation or the producer rice price. At the 14th national Nokyo convention held in October 1976, for example, the major resolution was entitled 'Achieving the Positive Development of Agricultural Policy Activities and Looking to the Establishment of a Basic Agricultural Policy that Lays Emphasis on the Measures Listed Below' (it was accompanied by nine basic agricultural policy demands). The 20th national Nokyo convention held in late 1994 and attended by PM Murayama and about 5,000 agricultural cooperative representatives issued a demand for the government to take adequate domestic measures to deal with issues arising from the agreement reached at the UR.[32] The convention also adopted resolutions on the restructuring of Japanese agriculture, reorganising the agricultural cooperatives and reforming the FC system towards the twenty-first century.[33]

Although Nokyo's mass meetings and associated campaigns represent the most publicly visible face of Nokyo, in fact the crucial connections on agricultural policy matters often entail the utilisation of informal, interpersonal networks, based on long histories of face-to-face contacts, working relationships and friendships amongst individuals – politicians, MAFF officials, Zenchu's managing directors (whose role is to act as full-time lobbyists) and elected executives – in short, the establishment elites in Tokyo. These are the primary actors in Nokyo's policy network. Zenchu's managing directors, for example, have regular, routine meetings with MAFF bureaucrats which may become more frequent, even daily, depending on the agricultural policy decision in the offing. They have all had long experience in dealing with agricultural policy issues and are the equivalent of senior bureaucrats within the MAFF. The bureau chiefs of the MAFF are often seen going in and out of the Nokyo building and vice versa.[34] Resolution of contentious issues is usually left to closed negotiations, discussions and consultations of a more informal type. For example, Nokyo's accession to the UR settlement on agricultural trade was handled by Zenchu's Managing Director, Ishikura Teruka, and the head of the Food Agency, Tsuruoka Toshihiko.[35]

Table 8.1 provides a sample of the daily round of activities conducted by one Zenchu Managing Director, Matsumoto Tokuo. His programme centred around meetings with MAFF bureaucrats, attendance at various policy meetings within Nokyo, participating as a Nokyo delegate in the *hagemasukai* of LDP politicians, and visits to the Diet offices of politicians, the LDP and Opposition included. In other words, the actual day-to-day lobbying of politicians and the MAFF is done by key members of the Zenchu executive leadership and staff. Sometimes local Nokyo leaders join in, especially for issues such as the producer rice price. Zenchu calls up the leaders of primary

Table 8.1 Weekly round of activities of a Zenchu lobbyist

Week day	Lobbying activity
Monday	Phone calls to the MAFF and attendance at two meetings: the first was with the staff of the MAFF Livestock Bureau in order to consult on the 'realisation' of livestock demand prices; the second was a political fund-gathering party for LDP Diet member Yamamura Shinjiro, former MAFF Minister two years previously.
Tuesday	Attendance at two meetings: the first was in the MAFF Livestock Bureau in order to discuss the support price level for dairy products; the second was in the new Nokyo Kajitsu Seisan Chosei (Fruit Production Adjustment) organisation which targeted apples and grapes. This was another new, small organisation in Tokyo, established by Nokyo in addition to Kajuren, Nichienren and Zenno for purposes of marketing and lobbying pressure.
Wednesday	Consulted with Diet members about livestock products. Also attended the National Conference of Nokyo Division Heads (Zenkoku Tanto Bucho Kaigi). Issues discussed included change in the direction of basic agricultural policy activities, adjustment of rice production and the future outlook for the FC system in the context of the trade liberalisation problem. Also fielded many phone calls about the livestock problem and had an interview with the *Nikkei Shinbun*. In the evening attended a Diet member's party for the purpose of gathering political funds.
Thursday	Meetings continued on the previous day's problems. Attended another meeting of the Egg Price Stabilisation Fund Council, of which Zenchu was a member, in order to discuss the 1986 stabilisation price for eggs. In the afternoon attended a Zenchu Board of Directors meeting as a member of the staff of that board. In the evening, attended a fund-raising party for a *noson giin*. After the party, discussed agricultural policy issues with members of the House of Representatives.
Friday	Visited the offices of six *norin giin* separately to consult on livestock policy prices (best way to get their real views). In the afternoon, attended Zenchu's annual general meeting involving members' representatives: the chairmen of each federation, national level and prefectural level, and 500 *tankyo* chairmen. They discussed Zenchu's business plan and budget.

Source: Author's personal interview with Zenchu Managing Director, Tokyo, March 1986. The author accompanied the Managing Director on various missions to the Diet offices of politicians.

agricultural cooperatives on certain dates and they visit the offices of Diet members and press them to support Nokyo's demands.

Deciding demands

The quality of Nokyo's internal democracy is difficult to evaluate precisely. On matters relating to Nokyo's interest articulation functions, it is a question of the extent to which the 'proposals to administrative authorities on matters concerning the cooperatives' presented to the government reflect the will of the farmers.[36] On matters relating to Nokyo's predominant role as an economic group, it is a question of the accountability of co-op leaders and executives to Nokyo rank-and-file members. Both these aspects of the Nokyo organisation come down to the procedures for democratic elections within the cooperatives and thus the representative qualities of Nokyo leaders as well as the provision of communication and consultative channels between leaders of Nokyo organisations at all levels and rice-roots members. Nokyo is at least in theory run along democratic lines. In this respect, it differs markedly from its organisational predecessors. Its fundamentally democratic character was shaped by its postwar re-establishment as a cooperative organisation by farmers and for farmers.[37]

Organisational democratisation was one of the key reforms instituted by the Occupation authorities. On 25 December 1945, an amendment to the Agricultural Groups Law mandated democratic elections of agricultural group executives. This principle was later enshrined in articles of the Nokyo Law itself relating to voting rights (*tohyoken*) and election rights (*senkyoken*) of agricultural cooperative members. The crucial legal provision was Article 16 which provided that 'each member shall have one voting right and one right to elect the executives or officers [*yakuin*] of agricultural cooperatives and representatives [*sodai*].'[38]

In the *tankyo*, voting and election rights are limited to full or regular members: individual farmer members, farm household members, farmers' group corporations (*noji kumiai hojin*) undertaking farm management,[39] and other types of juridical persons (*hojin*) undertaking farm management. They elect the executive leadership of the *tankyo* from amongst the regular membership in hotly contested polls. The executive leadership consists of co-op chairmen (*kumiaicho*), vice-chairman, directors (*riji*) and auditors (*kanji*). The highest executive authority is vested in the co-op's board of directors (*rijikai*), which consists of the chairman, vice-chairman and ordinary directors, and which meets monthly.[40] The *kumiaicho* is elected from amongst the directors.[41] The role of these executives is firstly, to direct the activities (i.e. businesses) of the cooperatives, secondly, to maintain and improve the ability to organise members and thirdly, to represent the membership.[42]

Regular members also exercise resolution rights (*giketsuken*) in the supreme decisionmaking organ of each cooperative: its ordinary general meeting (*sokai*) which, according to Article 34 of Nokyo Law, cooperative executives must convene at least once per business year.[43] The *sodai* are members' delegates to the general meetings, although some cooperatives eschew a system of members' delegates and invite all regular members to attend.[44] The general meeting is also the principal procedural mechanism providing for the accountability of the cooperative leadership to its members. At this meeting, the co-op chairman, vice-chairman, directors and auditors are elected for a period of not more than three years.[45]

Associate membership of Nokyo carries no voting or election rights, excluding this category of member from basic decisionmaking as well as from the election of executives.[46] In spite of the rapid growth of this form of membership, executive control of the agricultural cooperatives remains firmly in the hands of Nokyo's farming members. Built-in safeguards in Nokyo Law guarantee the supremacy of farming over urban interests within the organisation. Article 30 Paragraph 10 of Nokyo Law states that 'at least three-quarters of the established number of the directors of a cooperative shall be of its membership (excluding associate members).'[47] Nokyo's internal democratic procedures thus embody a form of structural discrimination against its associate members, particularly given the fact that they comprise around 40 per cent of the total individual membership. Although the legal provisions guarantee that Nokyo's basic character as a cooperative association for farmers is preserved,[48] in view of the changing balance of members in the organisation, Nokyo's internal election system is fundamentally undemocratic and therefore does not conform to the cooperative ideal.[49] Associate members are treated not as part of the agricultural cooperative organisation, but merely as customers for its purchasing, banking and insurance businesses.

Article 44 of Nokyo Law lists the items that must be put to the resolution of general meetings. They include all matters pertaining to the cooperatives' internal operations, such as finance, business and their federation, amalgamation or membership of other cooperatives. The function of the annual general meeting is to make resolutions in connection with these matters. Decisions are taken by a majority of votes, and, according to Nokyo Law, the duties of directors include observing 'resolutions adopted at general meetings'.[50]

Democratic procedures involving voting and election rights are replicated at the upper levels of the Nokyo organisation where the unit cooperatives are members of federations of agricultural cooperatives and central unions. 'Members' with the same kind of voting and election rights in upper level Nokyo federations and central unions are limited to regular member cooperatives only. The only difference here is that adjustment is made for variations in the membership size of member cooperatives.[51] The executives of the federations and prefectural central unions are elected by their agricultural cooperative membership, that is, by one or more executives representing each member cooperative. Three-quarters of the executives of a cooperative must come from its membership, and therefore, at least this proportion of upper level national and prefectural cooperative leaders must at the same time be executives of *tankyo*.

The system of annual general meetings also operates within upper level organisations. The business of these meetings is not only to elect directors and auditors, but also to take votes on resolutions affecting the operations of the cooperative concerned. The most fundamental organisational principle of Nokyo is that procedure, membership and structural aspects of the cooperatives are virtually identical throughout the entire system – both vertically and horizontally.

Where regular membership of a cooperative exceeds 500, direct democracy becomes impracticable, and so Nokyo Law makes provision for a system of indirect participation in general meetings and executive elections through the mechanism of representative members (*sodai*). A meeting of representative members (*sodaikai*) then replaces the general meeting of regular members. Nokyo Law thus provides for rank and file participation, either direct or indirect, in the decision-making of local cooperatives pertaining to their management, finance and business and in the election of their leaders. As a general principle, the system of representation becomes more indirect the greater the number of members of a cooperative, and the higher up the organisational ladder a cooperative operates.[52]

The internal organisational management of the *noseiren* essentially follows the same pattern. Members (called 'staunch friends', or *meiyu*) belong to one or other of the many local branches (*shibu*), which each have their general meetings (*sokai*) or meetings of representatives (*sodaikai*), branch chairmen and vice-chairmen. These branches are members of the general branches (*soshibu*), which are organised on a larger regional basis. These in turn are members of the prefectural *noseiren*, which has a committee (*iinkai*), chairman and vice-chairman. These report to the general meeting (*sokai*), which is really a delegates' meeting (*daigiinkai*), on which large numbers of delegates (usually 100–200) of the individual members sit.[53]

By allowing regular member cooperatives of the prefectural central unions to become members of Zenchu, Nokyo Law provides a mechanism for the participation of rice-roots Nokyo organisations in the national leadership and policymaking body for the entire cooperative system. They do this through the elections of representative members to the general meeting of Zenchu, which is its 'supreme decision-making body'.[54] Matters that must be submitted for resolution at the general meeting of representatives are concerned wholly with internal matters relating to executive elections, membership, management, business and finance of Zenchu. The same functions and focus of business are evident in the content of general meetings/general meetings of representatives at all levels of Nokyo. They are not directly concerned with matters relating to the agricultural policy activities of the agricultural cooperatives.

As elected officials, Zenchu has one chairman and not more than three vice-chairmen (it currently has two) and 15 elected directors (*riji*) as well as three auditors and one or two advisers, or *komon* (previous Zenchu chairmen) in addition to three non-elected, full-time managing directors (one *senmu riji* and two *jomu riji*).[55] The *kenchu* usually have one elected chairman and vice-chairman, plus a non-elected managing director, possibly one or more auditors and a secretary (*sanji*). Article 73-19 of Nokyo Law states that 'The chairman shall represent the central union and shall have charge over its business'.[56] In Zenchu's case, the supreme executive decisionmaking group is its board of directors to which the chairman reports and which he heads. Both report in the ultimate sense to the Zenchu general meeting of representatives which is very large, reflecting Zenchu's membership size (in 1997, its regular members consisted of 2,672 *tankyo*, 308 *rengokai*, 47 *chuokai* and 15 executives of central groups (*chuo dantai*) which were unspecified; and 12 associate members (also unspecified).[57] The *sodaikai* of Zenchu elects its board members, which in turn selects the chairman and vice-chairmen etc.[58]

Control exercised by Nokyo rank and file over their leaders in this sphere is only through executive accountability. In this sense, the general meeting or meeting of representatives of each Nokyo organisation and of Zenchu in particular is the supreme decisionmaking organ of the agricultural cooperatives. These meetings provide a forum in which executive decisionmaking is submitted to the final arbitration of the membership through the medium, primarily, of executive elections. Participation of the rice-roots membership in the actual process of executive decisionmaking is, therefore, only very indirect.

Moreover, what often happens at the *tankyo* level is that a few prominent branch members dominate the management of the co-op. As Saeki observes, this is totally against the one-person, one-vote principle and the democratic management ideology of Nokyo.[59] Another factor limiting the power of the membership over the running of the cooperatives is the fact that the management of all agricultural cooperative organisations on a day-to-day basis is often largely in the hands of its full-time paid directors (*jomu riji* and *senmu riji*).[60] This means that often the elected board of directors does not fully play a decisionmaking role in the *nokyo* although this is its duty.[61]

The fact that Nokyo is characterised by such a high level of corporatisation also fundamentally challenges the principle of its democratic management because corporatisation constrains organisational options. Asuwa, for example, argues that in strengthening its management posture of policy dependence,[62] Nokyo neglected its principle of democratic management as a mass organisation of farmers.[63] Yamaguchi takes the argument further, reasoning that Nokyo's role as a 'subcontractor' for the government is fundamentally incompatible with its constitution as a democratic organisation. Under such a setup, the fact that the investors, managing bodies and users of *nokyo* are all farmers is inevitably forgotten. The notion that the organisation and its constituent members are but one body is replaced by the concept of members being a third party, acted on by the management who are in the thrall of government. In these circumstances, Nokyo has become bureaucratic and 'run away together with government policies'. The term 'democratic management' is just a customary epithet: the intentions of the members are not reflected in it.[64]

When it comes to deciding what policy demands the Nokyo organisation is going to make, procedures are somewhat different, although not necessarily any more democratic. Policy demands are not processed through the mechanism of general meetings of the agricultural cooperatives. The business of these meetings impinge only very indirectly on matters relating to agricultural policy activities. In spite of legal guarantees of democratic executive elections and democratic vote-taking at annual general meetings or meetings of representatives, the opportunity for rank-and-file farmers members to influence the actual policy demands pursued by Nokyo's leaders is, therefore, limited through this route.

In theory, the decisions relating to Nokyo's policy demands take into account the opinions of individual agricultural cooperatives (and indirectly their farmer members). This is achieved by means of a so-called 'bottom-up' procedure of 'accumulating demands' which Nokyo leaders are fond of referring to as the means by which rice-roots requests reach the top. On producer prices, Zenchu describes the process as being one of 'piling up the price demands of the producer farm households, which are then concentrated by Zenchu'.[65]

In practice, however, direct participation by rank-and-file *nokyo* members in the process of 'accumulating' or 'piling up' demands is limited. The role of Nokyo's farmer members is primarily to be mobilised by their leaders after decisions have been made. Generally speaking the executive leadership assumes the initiative at all levels with actual decisionmaking primarily an area of executive responsibility at prefectural level and above.

Yamaguchi in fact contends that farmers have generally been passive about policy and have never played a central role in Nokyo.[66] He develops this point by describing the process of organisational decisionmaking with respect to policy demands. In terms of actual steps and stages, the process begins at the centre with a Zenchu policy draft which is then distributed to prefectural Nokyo organisations where it is decided on (i.e. basically ratified) by representatives from the prefectural federations and central unions. It is then subject to the decisions of the conference of *nokyo* chairmen from all the prefectures.[67]

Other Nokyo sub-units that sometimes also get involved are the policy headquarters' committees (both within Zenchu and *kenchu*), the conferences of central union chairmen and the conference of central union and federation chairmen. Matters that are dealt with by the conferences of central union and federation chairmen are the more important ones.[68] Of course, the process of manufacturing policy requests is not always a matter of 'whole organisation' perusal and decisionmaking. The less important requests and those that need emergency treatment are decided by Zenchu's Board of Directors and receive ratification from the separate sets of Nokyo decisionmakers afterwards.

These procedures suggest that at least at the organisational level the process is relatively decentralised, allowing for wide consultation amongst the elected leadership at all levels. As Zenchu itself elaborates: 'Nokyo's *nosei katsudo* involve a process in which discussion is undertaken at the various levels of Nokyo relating to the actual demands that will be presented. These are organised at the prefectural level, and then at the national level, with the demands converted into a Nokyo policy that is an expression of the united will of the entire organisation.'[69] The formalities of nationwide consultation and consensus-building are thus observed although they are restricted to Nokyo leaders, not members. At no stage of the internal decisionmaking process is there anywhere where farmers' requests can actually be embodied into Nokyo policy demands.[70]

Throughout this entire process Zenchu and the *kenchu* assume policy leadership, which Nokyo Law places squarely on their shoulders.[71] Policy initiative is concentrated particularly in the hands of Zenchu's executive leadership (a majority of its elected directors are simultaneously *kenchu* and co-op leaders) by virtue of the national responsibilities of the organisation. Nokyo executives, particularly those in Zenchu, also have access to the research facilities, expertise and intelligence of their own secretariats. This is a particularly valuable resource given that Zenchu is officially charged with drafting proposals and suggestions to administrative authorities relating to the agricultural cooperatives.

Zenchu maintains a bureaucratic superstructure centring on its Agricultural Policy Department (see Figure 2.3) enabling it to research policy demands and formulate them in a coherent and comprehensive manner. The Noseibu develops and fleshes out the proposals that are ultimately translated into demands, representations, requests etc. that are presented to government. Officials within the Noseibu replicate the work of MAFF bureaucrats, who are charged with the mechanics of drawing up ministerial recommendations (*shimon*) to the advisory councils on agricultural prices and other aspects of agricultural policy formulation.[72] The professional staff of Zenchu thus operate like a parallel agricultural bureaucracy. The complexity of the issues involved, the administrative procedures entailed and the fiscal and statistical knowledge required in the formulation of concrete policy submissions demand a level of expertise that can only be gained from executive experience and staff training. Technical expertise injects an element of intellectual respectability into Zenchu's policy demands which need to be backed up by facts and figures if they are to present a convincing case. In fora such as the RPAC, technical expertise can also be a valuable source of influence.

From another perspective, however, the bureaucratic juggernaut that Nokyo has become is regarded as more of a liability than an asset. The JCP has lambasted Nokyo for its lack of democratic representation of the farmers particularly on policy-related matters, arguing that although the directors that sit on the Nokyo boards are elected in a democratic way, they are incapable of responding to farmers' demands. It argues that Nokyo executives should act more like local politicians, linking up with mass struggles and forming farmers' organisations that can support executive activities in board meetings.[73] This is essentially a criticism of the centralised nature of Nokyo's internal decision-making process leading to the formulation of agricultural policy demands. The JCP puts the case for a much more rice-roots orientated method, with greater influence being wielded by the farmers themselves.

Certainly, the local membership often feels that Zenchu leaders are closer to the central authorities than they are to the *tankyo* members and are, therefore, out of touch with the rice roots. On many policy issues, farmers feel very distant, isolated and alienated from their central leadership, whom they sometimes accuse of collaborating with administrative authorities to preserve the organisation's interests, rather than the interests of its farming members. The outcome of internal policy debates within the Nokyo organisation is not always a common measure of producer demands nationwide, but more a policy that Zenchu leaders calculate the governing LDP can be persuaded to accept or which can be successfully negotiated with MAFF officials. This is not always positive from the rank and file's point of view.

Disaffected farmers are not hesitant to embarrass Nokyo leaders in front of their political allies and to reject their organisation's stance on policy issues. In one such example, the Nokyo producer rice price rally in 1974 was stormed by a group of farmers from Tohoku. The stage was occupied and Miyawaki Asao, Zenchu Chairman, was spat at. Farmers later picketed in front of Nokyo's stores in various prefectures in Tohoku and Hokuriku and stopped the shipment of rice.[74]

Nokyo, however, has explicitly rejected the option of operating as a mass political movement of farmers organised along democratic lines. The terms of reference of the special investigation committee into Nokyo's political action in 1974–75 stated: 'There are gaps in thinking between actual farmers and Nokyo leaders regarding Nokyo's agricultural policy activities . . . If no action is taken to deal with this problem, Nokyo's political activities will become disunited.'[75] In spite of the recognition that a problem existed, the final report of the committee underlined the authority of the Zenchu Board of Directors and rejected any mass movement aspect to Nokyo's political activities. Instead, it supported the view that Nokyo's *nosei katsudo* constituted a movement organised by a small group of leaders.[76]

On the other hand, the fact that the elected chairman, vice-chairmen and directors of Zenchu are chosen from amongst the prefectural Nokyo central union chairmen[77] and that these individuals are, in turn, also *tankyo* chairmen means that regional and local viewpoints are, to some extent, transmitted through the organisation to the very top. Indeed, one of the criticisms of the Zenchu secretariat is that it is under the control of the prefectural central unions. This is because *kenchu* chairmen become directors of Zenchu and in this way control officials in the secretariat. This allegedly poisons the atmosphere and stifles free discussion, particularly on problematic issues where accommodation that challenges the rigidly protectionist views of the prefectural leaders is required.[78] Chiba *kenchu*, for example, successfully petitioned for the resignation of the chief Zenchu negotiator on the UR rice deal (Ishikura Teruka), when the terms and conditions of the deal became known and were widely viewed as unacceptable.[79]

Last but not least, the quality of Nokyo's internal democracy can be raised with respect to its ability to represent full- as opposed to part-time farmers.

The interests of the minority of full-time farmers as opposed to the majority of part-time farmers are almost entirely ignored or glossed over by Nokyo. Certainly they are not expressly catered to in the way that specialist non-rice farmers receive recognition in the structural division between *sogo nokyo* and *senmon nokyo* (although the part- versus full-time farmer division to some extent overlaps with the rice versus non-rice specialist farmer division). In fact, as already pointed out, Nokyo's membership, operations and management have been biased in favour of small-scale part-time family farms, and thus very real questions can be raised about Nokyo's ability to represent farmers whose interests in some respects conflict with the main body of its membership.[80] After all, farmers who harbour aspirations to become more efficient and competitive by expanding their scale of operations are obstructed by inefficient part-time farmers who are supported by the sort of agricultural policies pushed by Nokyo. In the absence of generous subsidies and protection, these farmers would more seriously consider leasing or selling their land to more efficient producers. Furthermore, entrepreneurial full-time farmers often want to see deregulated distribution systems for both agricultural products and farm inputs and thus their economic interests clash directly with Nokyo's.[81]

Sharing the policy representation function

In theory, Zenchu functions as the political headquarters for the entire agricultural cooperative movement and even more broadly for farmers' groups as a whole.[82] It is the peak organisation of the cooperatives, and the only national Nokyo organisation on whom an interest group function has been bestowed. The public requests, demands, statements of opinion and proposals emanating from Nokyo are, therefore, almost all formally issued under the imprimatur of Zenchu, sometimes in concert with its policy central headquarters, Zenno, the Chairman of Zenchu (by name), combined conferences of national and prefectural central union and federation chairmen, national Nokyo representatives' assemblies and conventions focusing on particular agricultural policy issues, and the National Chamber of Agriculture. Lists of demands often run to multi-page documents, particularly budget requests.

This is not to say, however, that Zenchu exercises a monopoly of Nokyo's policy representation function. It occupies a position that is more 'first among equals' than the sole channel for all policy-related demands. Zenchu's activities have always been complemented by the actions of other Nokyo groupings, not only in the hierarchical *tani nokyo* > *kenchu* > Zenchu direction, but also in the horizontal one, that is, Zenchu in the company of national Nokyo federations. Zenchu's predecessor, Zenshiren, for example, shared the policy representation function to some extent with Zenhanren and Zenkoren in the early 1950s, and even after Zenchu was founded in 1954, Zenhanren and Zenkoren reportedly continued their policy-related activities, although unlike in the days of Zenshiren, they were structurally subordinate to Zenchu in these matters.

The partial division of labour between Zenchu and other national Nokyo federations was to some extent an inevitable consequence of the sheer size of the Nokyo organisation and the difficulties it faced in coordinating internally the interests of such a vast organisation and its membership. Over the years Nokyo continued its octopus-like spread over the entire agricultural economy and greatly expanded its volume of business. This was partly facilitated by the passage of additional laws and amendments that allowed the agricultural cooperatives to assume a greater variety of functions.[83] The number of policy-related problems on which Zenchu was required to make representations multiplied dramatically and proved too vast in range and complex in content for Zenchu to be able to handle alone.

The outcome was an expansion into the area of *nosei katsudo* by other Nokyo national organisations. The rationale was that each of these bodies should conduct agricultural policy activity that related solely to its own business, on the grounds that inside knowledge of its own affairs best enabled it to represent its own interests. Policy-related activities were thus incorporated into the range of operations and even internal structural forms of other top Nokyo organisations, such as Norinchukin, Zenno and Zenkyoren, 'which depending on the issue come into action independently as well as being mobilised by Zenchu.'[84] Norinchukin, for example, maintained contact with the relevant ministries (the MOF and MAFF) and other financial policy authorities and issued policy requests.[85] The other mainstream national Nokyo organisations developed the habit of making representations to government on issues of specific concern to them as well as lending their support to Zenchu's policy representations by jointly sponsoring policy demands with Zenchu. This was done without encroaching on the traditional spheres of central union activity, such as the sponsorship of national conventions and other types of mass action. The other national organisations also ceded leadership to Zenchu on matters relating to support and stabilisation prices (for all products), agricultural market opening, the agricultural budget and any other matters relating to agricultural policy as a whole such as basic laws, agricultural structure, taxation[86] and pensions, as well as policies for specific sectors (fruit and livestock for example) and the agricultural cooperative organisation itself, such as mergers.

The leaders of all prefectural and national federations also represented their organisations and participated in the joint chairmen's conferences that became an integral feature of Nokyo's *nosei katsudo*. These meetings issued policy demands, requests and submissions, but they were always collective affairs and were in many cases under the guidance of the *chuokai* executives present. Such combined action, however, did not prevent the federations functioning in policy roles as separate and individual groupings on their own behalf instead of being represented by Zenchu via their membership of that body. Most often they were concerned with issues that related to them specifically as organisations, leaving matters of policy representation relating to the farmers to Zenchu.

In reality, therefore, Nokyo as a whole has been a somewhat less integrated and unified organisation in the conduct of *nosei katsudo* than would appear from a reading of Nokyo Law, which places the leadership of *nosei katsudo* so squarely on the shoulders of the central unions. Nokyo's policy leadership at the national level is not confined to the activities of Zenchu, but involves other executive structures within Nokyo providing additional and complementary policy leadership for specific interests within the agricultural cooperative organisation.

In the 1960s and 1970s, the national organisations of specialist agricultural cooperatives also became important in the conduct of *nosei katsudo* under the broad Nokyo umbrella. What is more, Zenchu did not always have harmonious relations with these groups, as they not only pursued agricultural policy activities independently, but also rivalled Zenchu as representative bodies for specialist (particularly full-time) farmers.[87]

From the perspective of the specialist side of the organisation, Zenchu failed to seek a balanced appreciation of what was satisfactory to specific branches of the farming industry and tended to act as spokesperson for certain selected and entrenched interests within the agricultural cooperative movement, particularly the rice-related interests of the *sogo nokyo*. The specialist side criticised Zenchu for centring its main agricultural policy interests on rice (and to a lesser extent wheat in the early days),[88] and questioned the traditional emphasis of Zenchu's *nosei katsudo* on maintaining the FC system and fighting for ever-higher producer rice prices. The latter, in addition to the poor rate of affiliation of specialist *nokyo* to the central unions, led to a conviction amongst specialist co-ops that they must assume responsibility for their own policy-related activities.

Zenchu, on the other hand, found it easier to integrate agricultural cooperative interests when rice cultivation was dominant than when producer interests became more diversified.[89] The regionalisation of agricultural production and the diversification of farmers' demands actually made the conduct of farmers' campaigns more difficult. Nokyo's obstruction of government proposals for policy change affecting the agricultural cooperatives was often the consequence of a massive three-layered organisation trying to establish a consensus amongst a large number of its members.[90] Zenchu did make some structural innovations in the 1970s allowing other specialist federations to take on the job of representing the more concentrated interests of their membership. The result was a greater measure of sharing of the policy leadership role by Zenchu with some key national specialist federations.

The specialist federations that expanded most vigorously into *nosei katsudo* were those operating in what were the growth sectors of Japan's farm industry identified for selective expansion under the 1961 ABL, particularly livestock (including dairy farming) and horticulture. This development was substantially assisted by the passage of laws relating to specific commodities as the agricultural support system was extended to include greater numbers of products.

Another reason for the increasingly conspicuous policy activities of the national specialist federations was the emergence of an anti-liberalisation movement amongst Japanese farmers in the face of the growing trend in the 1960s and early 1970s for freer access to the Japanese market for agricultural imports.[91] The national federations representing those farm industries facing competition from imports (particularly the livestock, dairy and citrus sectors) became actively and openly involved in agricultural policy activities. Their motivation was essentially defensive, a feeling that the specialist interests of their members had to be protected at a particularly vital time. In the course of agricultural trade liberalisation campaigns, the national specialist federations began to work more harmoniously in coalition with Zenchu.

The push towards agricultural trade liberalisation in the 1960s and early 1970s took place at the same time as positive de-controls were instituted in the FC system. These accompanied even more sensitive changes in rice policy such as the producers' rice price freeze (1969 and 1970)[92] and rice production cutbacks. Zenchu and Zenno responded to these policy changes with a strategic concentration of energies into policy activities opposing changes in Food Control.[93] They laid themselves open to the accusation from the specialist co-ops that their overwhelming concern with rice led them to neglect the vital concerns of specialist farmers.

Initially, Nokyo's anti-agricultural trade liberalisation campaign was led separately by Zenchu and the relevant national Nokyo specialist federations. In December 1968, for example, a council of Nichienren chairmen issued a resolution opposing the liberalisation of citrus fruit, but it took until July 1971 for Zenchu and Nichienren successfully to hold a combined assembly of 2,200 producers 'for getting over the crisis in fruit agriculture'. Insofar as Zenchu and Nichienren jointly organised the assembly, it was exceptional given their past history of poor relations.[94]

Another political technique developed more keenly by the specialist arm of Nokyo was the formation of close ties with LDP Diet members' leagues which were often organised around specialist farming interests (see Appendix D in chapter 7), and whose membership was dominated by politicians from constituencies in which certain types of farming were concentrated. Some of the strongest campaigns mounted by these internal LDP lobby groups were launched on behalf of farmers and Nokyo organisations opposing trade liberalisation.[95]

The farmers' political leagues have also been important instruments of *nosei katsudo*, acting as 'ginger groups' for the entire Nokyo organisation and spearheading more activist rice-roots campaigns by co-op leaders and members. Their activities are often aimed as much at the farmers themselves and at raising their level of political consciousness and engagement as they are at politicians and administrators. The activities of the farmers' political leagues should be seen as complementary to those of Zenchu and the other mainstream Nokyo organisations, although in the early days they were an outlet for local grievances not only against the government but also against the central leadership, particularly when it placed more importance on maintaining good relations with the MAFF and LDP than on advancing the interests of local farmers. Essentially, however, the function of the *noseiren* and their branches has been to mobilise farmers around particular causes and to act as a convenient mechanism for policy campaigns to be directly linked to rice-roots election campaigns. Just as the national Nokyo leadership targets Diet politicians, *noseiren* leaders in the prefectures target prefectural assembly politicians, holding joint seminars and discussion meetings to exchange opinions on agricultural policy issues of the day.

With the formation of Zenkoku Noseikyo in 1989, *noseiren* agricultural policy activities became much more efficiently and professionally led at the national level. Every year, the National Council holds an ordinary general meeting at which it decides, amongst other things, its 'Agricultural Policy Campaign Basic Plan', as well as issuing resolutions on agricultural policy matters of the day.

The Nokyo women's and youth divisions, particularly the latter, also assist the mainstream Nokyo organisation in the conduct of *nosei katsudo*. They supplement the activities sponsored by Nokyo executives as well as operating on their own initiative, thereby contributing to the weight of agricultural cooperative pressure on government. The activities of the women's division, for example, are conducted both independently and in concert with Zenchu-sponsored campaigns, in political as well as other fields. The women's division regularly holds assemblies and conventions in the Nokyo building in Tokyo. Its overall political colouring is reputedly conservative. In 1977 its programme of campaigns included movements 'to strengthen its organisation', 'to protect agriculture' and 'livelihood protection activities'.[96] The women's division also participated in the 1977 rice price campaign by means of a 'rice price demand car relay' which began in all parts of the country and terminated at the 'National Nokyo Convention for Realising the Demanded Rice Price'. In later years, it focused on questions such as food security and self-sufficiency, and pursued common cause with consumer groups on these issues.[97]

Political activities conducted by the *fujinbu* are determined by means of autonomous decision-making procedures within the division itself. Whether or not these demands coincide or conflict with those formulated in the mainstream Nokyo organisation is a matter for their own determination. In practice, Zennofukyo/JA Zenfukyo has not been known publicly to disagree with the policies and demands put forward by the national executive leadership. Generally speaking, the women's division supplements and reinforces Zenchu-led campaigns.

The same cannot be said for the Nokyo youth division, which gives much more substance to its organisational independence. From time to time it adopts a confrontationist posture with both the Zenchu leadership and the ruling LDP. It has a reputation for being the most pro-active grouping of any of Nokyo's organisations in both *nosei katsudo* and *senkyo katsudo*. It is the first to object to deals done between Nokyo and the government (the MAFF and LDP), to threaten discord both within Nokyo ranks and in Nokyo's primary relationships with these bodies, to make the most vocal, outspoken threats against LDP candidates in elections (and in many cases to put them into effect),[98] and to forge ties with socialist candidates. As a result, the *seinenbu* long ago earned the label 'progressive' (*kakushinteki*). At its inception, it formally adopted a posture of political neutrality, which in Nokyo-speak usually means reserving the right to support non-LDP candidates in elections.[99]

The youth division has been strongest in Northern Japan, in prefectures where the left-wing farmers' unions were historically active – Hokkaido, Akita, Niigata, Yamagata and Nagano – and in Kyushu (particularly in Kumamoto, Fukuoka, Saga and Miyazaki). Kyushu and Hokkaido were also former strongholds of the National Rural Youth League. The Nokyo youth division usurped many of the functions of this organisation.

The *seinenbu* puts much greater effort into its agricultural policy activities than the *fujinbu* does, and is also more inclined to engage in active political lobbying of Diet representatives. It incorporates agricultural policy divisions within its internal organisation. It has rice, urban agriculture, livestock, dairy farming, and fruit and vegetable policy councils which parallel the commodity and policy headquarters of Zenchu, *kenchu* and the *sogo nokyo*. The *seinenbu* councils perform the same function as those within the mainstream Nokyo organisation, although on a smaller scale. They 'accumulate' or 'pile up' the opinions and demands of their membership and translate them into constructive policy proposals and campaigns at the national level.

Each year, the youth division is active in holding numerous meetings, rallies and assemblies on various issues and concerns. Like the *fujinbu* and Zenchu, it holds its own annual national convention with an average of around 1,000 in attendance. Prefectural youth divisions that are individually strong engage in similar activities at a regional level: organising conventions and assemblies around certain agricultural policy issues, setting up specialist commodity divisions, undertaking budget requests to prefectural assemblies and making representations to national and local public officials. The *seinenbu* also joins in a programme of cooperative activities with the *fujinbu*.

On occasions the youth division has been more successful than the mainstream organisation in extracting what it wants because of its propensities for direct action. In 1961, a milk price war took place in Saku county of Nagano prefecture. The youth division of the local dairy *senmon nokyo* led the struggle in the form of a popular movement. The shift in the leadership of the campaign from the executives of the dairy cooperative (who had maintained close connections to the dairy manufacturers) to the youth division led to a successful rise in the price of milk paid to the farmers by the manufacturers.[100]

In 1977 *nosei katsudo* conducted by the youth division involved a series of activities along much the same lines as the women's division. A rice price car relay was organised during the rice price campaign and, after the Nokyo Rice Price Convention, the permanent executive leadership of Zenseikyo took the lead in holding three 'request assemblies' (*yosei shukai*) and 'all-party demand assemblies' (*toitsu seito yosei shukai*), at which Diet politicians from each party met face-to-face with youth division delegates. Like the *fujinbu*, the youth division also participated in the 'Campaign on Livestock Product Prices', and the permanent executive leadership launched a special campaign on this issue which included holding 'Assemblies to Present Requests to Political Parties'.[101]

By 1993–94, the agricultural policies targeted for campaigns by the *seinenbu* had changed but the principle of active involvement remained the same. When the deal crafted between MAFF and US government negotiators for settling the rice market access issue was announced (it had also been tacitly accepted by the Zenchu leadership), youth division leaders called for the resignation of the Zenchu executives involved in the negotiations between the MAFF and Zenchu.[102] Zenseikyo and the Hokkaido and Tohoku region youth and women's divisions joined forces in demonstrations at Tokyo Station and in the Ginza to secure the maintenance of a domestic policy that emphasised the importance of food self-sufficiency for consumers and for the nation.

The youth division also joined in demonstrations as part of a special campaign directed at the government and political parties on agricultural reconstruction and reform of the FC system, including expressing opposition to the contents of the UR Agreement on Agriculture. The youth division held four conferences and discussions with MAFF Secretariat Planning Section officials as part of the Nokyo-sponsored 'Agricultural Reconstruction and Food Control System Reform Special Campaign'. Meetings of *seinenbu* chairmen published resolutions on protecting regional agriculture and on maintaining solidarity with consumers; on promoting campaigns for the establishment of agricultural policy and FC reform; and on food self-sufficiency and safety.[103] As part of this campaign, the youth division organised a meeting to encourage government party Diet members (*yoto hagemasukai*) attended by 42 Diet members designed to check the final round of negotiations between the ruling party and the government on the compensation package for the agricultural sector arising from the UR agreement. Unlike previous *hagemasukai* at which requests and petitions were presented, *seinenbu* delegates expressed their views directly to the Diet members. Three days after these activities took place, the compensation package was announced. Together with JA Zenfukyo, the youth division issued a joint declaration in response to the government's decision which emphasised the need to undertake the reconstruction of agriculture 'by their own hands' in order to raise the self-sufficiency rate, preserve agriculture and so on.[104]

The main foci of Nokyo's *nosei katsudo*

The range of issues on which demands and requests emanate from Nokyo covers diverse policies impacting on the interests of the agricultural cooperatives, the farmers and the agricultural sector in general. As already noted, the number and variety of policy demands have expanded over the years as Nokyo's functions have diversified and as agricultural policy itself has altered direction and become more complex. Of those policies specifically concerning the farmers as agricultural producers, the main ones are agricultural production and pricing policies, agricultural trade policies, land policies, budget policies, farmers' pension policies and tax policies.

Each year, a formal list of the 'JA Group's Main Resolutions, Requests and Declarations' is published.[105] It is divided into several categories: basic agricultural policy and budget policy (which is further sub-divided into 10 major areas including one for each of the main commodity categories); agricultural trade policy; rice and wheat policy, including matters relating to the FC system and rice diversion and acreage reduction policies; livestock and dairy policies; soybean, potato and starch policies; taxation policy; and 'other'.[106]

Amongst the diverse agricultural policy issues covered by Nokyo's *nosei katsudo*, four have stood out as the main focus of its energies and the subject of concerted public campaigns: agricultural support and stabilisation prices, questions of agricultural market access, rice production and marketing issues (i.e. matters such as rice production adjustment and reform of the FC system), and securing agricultural subsidies from the budget. In this respect, Nokyo does not treat all agricultural policy issues equally. In Kuwabara's view, it has concentrated its main energies on pricing policies.[107] For example, its *nosei katsudo* have been more focused on pricing matters relating to specific commodities, than on issues relating to the actual structure of the production of these commodities. In this sense, the priorities of Nokyo's *nosei katsudo* are not necessarily the same as the farmers. Although subsidies for land improvement projects are crucial for improving farm production and are of vital concern to many farmers, Nokyo does not undertake concerted *nosei katsudo* in relation to these subsidies even though they amount to around half the agricultural budget,[108] and even though Nokyo itself receives large quantities of subsidies to conduct agriculture-related projects.[109] Nokyo's budget demands include the categories of 'Structural Policy' and 'Rural Mountain Village and Regional Revitalisation Policies', but these are subsumed within its larger budget campaign as a whole.

Several factors are at work here. The first is that Nokyo shares the lobbying for structural improvement subsidies with the land improvement organisations. These groups are particularly well mobilised, highly focused, politically effective and rich.[110] They concentrate their efforts on behind-the-scenes connections with well-placed politicians and bureaucrats.

Secondly, because public works projects are region-specific, they do not lend themselves to large-scale public mobilisations of farmers with a representative sprinkling of agricultural cooperative officials and members from around the country – as do issues like the producer prices and import liberalisation. In fact, as explained by a Zenchu official, Zenchu's budget campaign is not in charge of promoting budgets for individual projects. These projects are recommended by prefectural governments which consult with local *nokyo* and members of prefectural assemblies. Sometimes Diet members will join that coordination, and then those Diet members will pressure the MAFF (for items such as country elevators or land adjustment projects, for example). Zenchu, on the other hand, is concerned with the total amount of spending for each major policy – either to increase it or maintain the current level of expenditure.[111] The methodology of requesting particular subsidies for particular projects in particular regions is thus different from Nokyo's agricultural policy campaigns. This kind of lobbying does not, strictly speaking, come within the ambit of *nosei katsudo* which focus on macro-policy issues affecting large groups of farmers.[112]

Thirdly, Nokyo's *nosei katsudo* are very much skewed towards farmers' incomes and associated with this, the business profits of the agricultural cooperatives. This explains the heavy emphasis not only on agricultural commodity prices in general, but on rice and FC matters in particular. In fact, as Ishikawa argues, the real motivation behind Nokyo's intensive efforts on rice price issues, which form one of the main pillars of its agricultural policy campaigns, is to keep farmers' trust in the agricultural cooperatives as their rice marketing agent. Thus the impetus is to collect as much rice as possible, to gain as much in the way of handling and other fees and commissions as possible, and to absorb the farmers' rice payments into Nokyo savings accounts.[113]

Nokyo's agricultural policy campaigns have traditionally observed a yearly timetable of national conventions and assemblies of farmers and co-op representatives. The producer rice price campaign has been held in July, that on livestock support and stabilisation prices in March, the agricultural budget in December, prevention of agricultural trade liberalisation of various farm products timed to coordinate with major trade negotiations, and maintenance of the FC system whenever FC reform is on the policy agenda.

Of these major policy sub-sectors, Nokyo's agricultural price campaigns have long occupied a central place in its *nosei katsudo*. Zenchu submits price requests with respect to all agricultural products subject to government intervention. Its price-related pressure group activities go back a long way. In addition to its early producer rice price activities,[114] Nokyo demanded and got a price stabilisation law for agricultural products in 1953.

Table 8.2 shows the commodity items that have been subject to 'administered' prices, the support price target for farmers and Nokyo, the different price calculation methods used, the price advisory council involved, and the scheduling of the pricing decision during the year. Not only are the methods of calculating these prices different but also the ways in which they are decided. The MAFF Minister exercises the final power of decision for each price, but in some cases this decision is taken after receipt of a report from an advisory council, while for others the decision is automatic according to a specific formula (those calculated according to the 'Parity Method', except for wheat, for example). Where the decision is automatic it might be thought that there would be little sense in Nokyo's launching agricultural policy campaigns, but in fact, associated incentive payments for particular crops can be subject to political pressure at the time of the pricing decision.[115]

The timing of the decisions also varies for each product. Depending on their respective harvest period, agricultural commodities have special annual seasons: the rice year begins in November, the soybean year in October, the potato year in September and so on, with their prices decided at the beginning of the production year or at the end of the preceding production year. In March, milk and meat prices are decided, in April cocoon prices, in June wheat and rapeseed prices and in July (now November) rice prices. In other words, administrative pricing decision periods last throughout almost the entire year. Nokyo launches its agricultural policy campaigns in relation to these prices in the months preceding the decision. The result is that its agricultural price campaigns go on throughout the whole year without respite. Whatever the price issue is, Nokyo decides its own price demand beforehand.[116] Only two commodity price sectors, however, have engaged Nokyo in mass public campaigns: the producer rice price and livestock stabilisation prices.

The producer rice price campaign

The *seisansha beika* (the price paid by the government to farmers for so-called government rice) has been a pivotal focus of Nokyo's activities as a pressure group from the earliest period of its organisation. Not only has the producer rice price traditionally been the annual agricultural policy 'event' of the year, but Nokyo's *beika undo* has been the summit of all its agricultural policy activities, attracting more publicity than any other Nokyo policy campaign through various mass mobilisation exercises such as conventions, assemblies, petitions, marches, media advertisements and general 'human wave tactics', all under the aegis of Zenchu.

Although lobbying for higher producer rice prices went back beyond the time of the establishment of the RPAC in 1949,[117] Nokyo began organising its producer rice price campaign as a mass movement – such as holding large rallies and picketing in front of LDP headquarters – in the early 1960s.[118] The first national Nokyo representatives' convention for accomplishing the demanded rice price was held in July 1961 (and annually thereafter).[119] The pattern of Nokyo's rice price campaigns was established at this time and proved highly successful.

In 1960, Nokyo won a changeover from the 'Parity Method' for calculating the producer rice price (which took into account general price movements) to a 'Production Cost and Income Compensation formula' which compensated

Table 8.2 Main support price targets, price calculation standards and decision seasons

Product	Support Price Target for Farmers/Nokyo	Price Calculation Formula	Price Advisory Council	Decision Season
Rice for government sale	Government purchase price	Production cost and income compensation[a]	RPAC	July (November)[b]
Wheat Barley and naked barley	Government purchase price	Parity;[c] production cost of core farmers (from 1987)	RPAC	June
Raw milk for processing	Guaranteed price (i.e. producers' sale price); ceiling quantity to receive the deficiency payment	Production conditions; the demand and supply situation and other factors in the economic situation[d]	LIPAC	March
Designated dairy products	Stabilisation indicative prices	State of production, supply/demand situation and consumption stability[e]	LIPAC	March
Beef	Japanese beef and other beef upper stabilisation (ceiling) price and standard stabilisation (floor) price; from 1988 – upper stabilisation price of beef and standard stabilisation price of beef	Production conditions; the demand and supply situation and other factors in the economic situation[d]	LIPAC	March
Pork	Upper stabilisation price (ceiling) and standard stabilisation (floor) price	Production cost[d]	LIPAC	March
Beef calves	Guaranteed standard price	Production cost[f]	LIPAC	March
Sweet potatoes, potatoes (for materials)	Standard price	Parity		September
Sugar beet and sugar cane	Lowest producer price	Parity		September
Soybeans	Standard price	Parity		September

		Parity		June March
Rapeseed	Standard price			
Silk cocoons	Standard price	Production cost		Silk Thread Price Advisory Council
Vegetables	Stabilisation Fund			
Eggs	Stabilisation Fund			
Fruit for processing	Stabilisation Fund			
Broilers	Stabilisation Fund			
Miscellaneous beans	Stabilisation Fund			
Feeder hogs	Stabilisation Fund			

Notes:

a This applied from 1960–95. This formula not only takes producer costs into account but also seeks to provide financial returns to rice producers which are on a par with urban factory workers. After 1980 demand and supply conditions were also *de facto* taken into account. After the passage of the 1994 Staple Food Law, the government's buying price had to reflect trends in the supply and demand of rice, especially the price of independently distributed rice, and also took into account production conditions, commodity prices and other economic factors, and the need to ensure the continuous production of rice. Later changes to price setting are not included in this table.

b Since the implementation of the Staple Food Law in 1995, the government's purchasing price of rice has been decided in November.

c The parity formula is one that reflects the extent of price rises over the year in living expenses and production inputs, and compensates farmers for increases in these costs. In the case of wheat, a production incentive payment was incorporated into the support price from 1977 onwards. The table does not encompass the proposed alteration to the domestic wheat marketing system, in which the Food Agency will shift to a free market, combined with compensation to wheat growers for a possible decline in their income.

d Production costs are also taken into account in determining the price paid to farmers.

e The table does not encompass the changes to the marketing of dairy products with the establishment of a new trading centre for dairy products in 1999, or the anticipated changes to the deficiency payment scheme for manufacturing milk which will come into effect in FY 2001, under the reform programme for the dairy and milk sector decided in December 1998.

f This also included past price trends and other relevant factors.

Sources: Based on Table 5 in Tachibana, *Nokyo*, p. 335; ABARE, *Japanese Agricultural Policies*, p. 125; *Livestock Industry Promotion Corporation: Corporate Profile*, 1996, pp. 1–6; The Food Agency, *An Outline of the Staple Food Law: The Law for Stabilization of Supply-Demand and Price of Staple Food*, January 1995, p. 19.

farmers for increases in the wages of urban workers. The general economic situation had changed dramatically in the latter part of the 1950s, with the rapid boost in the incomes of urban wage earners as Japan underwent accelerated industrial growth. Farm incomes, constrained by the limits of a small-holding system of agriculture, began to lag considerably behind those in industry. Farmers simply could not achieve productivity increases at a rate that matched those in industry and were thus unable to attain the rising wage levels of urban workers. The new formula not only took producer costs into account but also sought to provide financial returns to rice producers which were on a par with urban factory workers.

With the principle of income equality further enshrined in the 1961 ABL, the government fell back on the convenient mechanism of the producer rice price as a means of providing across-the-board increases in income to the largest group of Japanese agricultural producers. The result was the producer rice price rose at an average of just under 9.0 per cent a year between 1960 and 1968 (from ¥10,405 per *koku* (150 kg) to ¥20,672). This was practically a 100 per cent rise in less than a decade. Although burgeoning FC costs and a rice surplus virtually froze producer rice prices in 1969 and 1970, they subsequently rose again at an average of 11.0 per cent per year between 1971 and 1977.[120]

In the heyday of these price campaigns in the 1960s and 1970s, the average Nokyo representatives' convention (*taikai*) mustered 10,000–15,000 participants. Every summer, central Tokyo was besieged by large numbers of headband-wearing farmers, demanding a sizeable increase in the producer rice price. Over the years this campaign took on a ritualistic quality, an elaborate drama stage-managed by Zenchu. As Sakaguchi describes it:

> The actors are always the same, they repeat the same words every year. The event is just like a play in a country town theatre, which never shows anything new. Poor audiences are shown a play almost like a farce. On top of that, consumers will get the big bill after the curtain comes down. There is no way consumers can enjoy the event. On the other hand, the rice price campaign is an important stage for Zenchu which is an actor in the show, and which can show its talent. It is also an important ceremony for Nokyo members to raise their morale as producers and strengthen their cooperative spirit.[121]

The rice price season traditionally began simultaneously within the parallel bureaucracies of the MAFF and Nokyo some months prior to the actual decision itself as each organisation began the technical and political input into a 'recommended price' (MAFF) and a 'demand price' (Nokyo). In measuring producer cost variables and doing the relevant calculations, Zenchu drew on the professional expertise of its Noseibu, which conducted parallel surveys to the MAFF's on items such as production cost – the most frequently challenged factor input into the government's recommendation. It then produced the Nokyo demand price (*yokyu beika*). Nokyo's independent production cost survey targeted a national sample of 1,500 farm households. Without these kind of preparations, the negotiations with the government on the price would have been reduced to a mere 'fight over principles'.[122]

Like the MAFF-recommended price (*shisan beika*), the Nokyo demand price was ultimately the product not only of such economic data-gathering, but also the application of an 'objective' statistical formula and political judgement. Behind the scenes, the formulation of Nokyo's demand price involved a very careful series of statistical calculations and political assessments. Where the MAFF and Nokyo differed was not in the mechanics of applying a statistical formula to a set of indices to produce a final price, but in the manipulation of the various economic variables fed into the calculation in the first place, and in the actual selection of which particular formula to apply. Both the MAFF and Nokyo flexibly changed the factors used to calculate the producer rice price[123] according to their own perspectives and economic trends in Japan.[124] Differences over which cost estimates to take into account and over which formula to apply produced differences in the final price, the latter being determined in the last resort by calculations about what was politically feasible at the time. If the formula in question did not yield the desired result, Zenchu was not above changing the method of calculating the price.[125] Despite the overtones of statistical objectivity, both the MAFF-recommended price and the Nokyo demand price were, therefore, essentially the outcome of a process that could be manipulated to produce the desired result.

Also like the MAFF-recommended price, the Nokyo demand price was formally submitted to the RPAC. Preceding this formal presentation in early July, advance discussions were held between Zenchu executives and MAFF officials from about the middle of May in order to get a 'feel' of both sides' advance positions on price, and to enable each side to make an input into the other's calculations. These discussions would proceed through four rounds up until the time when the RPAC began its sittings.[126]

Although the technicalities were left to Noseibu staff, the political decisions that influenced the final demand price were taken by Zenchu's Rice Policy Central Headquarters after extensive consultation and canvassing of national and prefectural central union and federation leaders and the executives of prefectural rice policy headquarters. This was a process of consensus decision-making within the Nokyo organisation itself. It began at the periphery (rice policy headquarters were also set up in a majority of city, town and village *sogo nokyo*) and moved towards the centre and was designed to elicit the agreement of the entire organisation with the final demand price. The latter did not, however, always end up with the blessing of the wider Nokyo organisation. In 1977, for example, Zenchu demanded a relatively small increase in the producer rice price to a level that was lower than its demand for the previous year. This caused division among the Nokyo branches in rice-producing regions and in other areas.[127]

Once the Nokyo demand price had received the final stamp of approval of the Zenchu Board of Directors, it would become the focus of a nationwide mobilisation campaign led by the Rice Policy Central Headquarters. Headquarters membership was dominated by Zenchu executives and the chairmen of other national federations directly involved in rice handling such as Zenno. The campaign would also seek to engage local, prefectural and national politicians directly. Local activities involved members of prefectural assemblies and local government mayors in request activities and discussion meetings (*taiwa shukai*), as well as mass rallies. At the hamlet level, each *sogo nokyo* organised rallies in its own district and sent delegates to prefectural and national rallies.[128] The levy on rice sales by farmers provided the funds for sending delegates to prefectural capitals and to Tokyo. Zenchu exacted a contribution from farmers of ¥10 per bale of rice to fund the campaign. The local rallies required mandatory attendance from co-op members. As Moore explains: 'This is due to the goal of the rice price rally which is to apply pressure on local politicians by ensuring representation by each hamlet at the prefectural demonstrations and by each township at the national demonstrations. The implicit threat to the politicians is that the hamlet and township group being represented will vote against them if they do not support the Nokyo policy.'[129] The rice price conventions held simultaneously in each prefecture were attended by the Diet members elected from those particular regions.

These activities would culminate in mass demonstrations, rallies, conventions and gatherings of farmers in Tokyo. About 400–500 representatives from each of the main rice-producing prefectures (and lower numbers of people from the less significant rice-producing prefectures) would travel to the capital. Their primary targets were politicians elected from their own areas, which was the standard technique of Nokyo's *nosei katsudo*. Diet members (sometimes numbering in the hundreds) would attend the farmers' rallies, and following these, smaller groups would gather by prefecture with their local Diet members in 'request gatherings' and discussion meetings in order to make 'resolutions' with respect to the demand rice price.

The rallies were timed to coincide with sittings of the RPAC. Indeed, the opening sessions of the RPAC in July each year were traditionally the starting signal for the launching of Nokyo's *beika undo* or 'rice price battle' (*beika toso*) in Tokyo. The campaign was directed from a 'base' set up in the Zenkyoren building in Hirakawamachi near to both the LDP's headquarters and the Diet. Zenchu's Chairman undertook the formal presentation of Nokyo's rice demand price to the RPAC, although Zenno (as the main seller of rice to the government) was also represented on the RPAC at least until the 1990s. Producer rice price demands put forward by Zenchu's Chairman at council sessions were supplemented by more unruly demonstrations of pressure by Nokyo rank and file outside the council's meeting chambers. Human wave tactics were also deployed against the MAFF building in Kasimigaseki, other relevant ministries like the MOF, political party headquarters and the Diet.

Increasingly over the years, Nokyo targeted the public directly, advertising in the media,[130] organising speeches by Nokyo executives in the streets of Tokyo, handing out agricultural products to passers-by and undertaking interviews on television. Nokyo also sought to improve the understanding of consumer organisations and local governments on rice issues.

In addition, Zenchu executives handled the official representations to government agencies (the MAFF and the MOF), parliamentary committees and LDP and other party committees conducting their own investigations into rice price policy. Their approach was multifocused, ignoring no section of government, the Diet, or political parties which was in any way connected to the issue. They worked particularly closely with LDP politicians and supporting groups such as Diet members' leagues, which would lobby party agricultural committees, LDP executives, and the MOF and MAFF Ministers on their behalf. The primary intra-party lobbyists were LDP rice Diet members (*kome giin*),[131] who, as Sakaguchi put it, 'worked hard and with almost irresistible force to give favour to Nokyo.'[132] During the 1960s and 1970s, for example, if the Chairman of the LDP's rice price committee, called the Rice Price Round Table (Beika Kondankai, or Beikon)[133] were from the anti-mainstream faction, rice prices would increase sharply, while only small increases would be achieved when the Beikon Chairman was from the mainstream faction. As Arimitsu contends, this implied that while Nokyo's pressures were effective to some 80 per cent, the remaining 20 per cent depended on negotiations within the party.[134]

Nokyo evaluated the performance of these political allies by the enthusiasm they showed for attending the rallies it sponsored and for supporting the resolutions that were passed at these mass meetings, and by politicians' membership of and participation in relevant party committees.[135] Zenchu compiled reports on the activities of *norin giin* in relation to rice price demands, particularly their response to farmers' petitions.[136] The results of these observations were published in the media such as the *Nihon Nogyo Shinbun* (40,000 printed daily).[137] In the face of such tactics, even the MOF Minister when pressed, was inclined to avow support for farmers' demands, only to turn around later and say how dissatisfied he was with the result.[138]

Nokyo endeavoured to use the timing of elections to good effect in its producer rice price campaign, particularly when the RPAC deliberations more or less overlapped with election day. In 1977, for example, Nokyo used its putative vote mobilisation power in the UH election as a very effective bargaining weapon to extract an addition to the government-recommended price. It amounted to a relatively high ¥246 per 60 kg or 4.0 per cent.[139]

All Nokyo's efforts in its producer rice price campaign were directed towards achieving an increase in the producer rice price which the MAFF was prepared to offer. Although the amount of increase varied from year to year, pressure from Nokyo and the farmers as well as from their political allies in the Diet was specifically catered to in the form of a so-called 'political addition' (*seiji kasan*) to the MAFF-recommended price. The political addition was a reflection of farmers' power as transmitted through the LDP. In those years when price increases were not forthcoming, various kinds of subsidies to rice farmers which could substitute for an actual price increase were instituted. In 1970, for example, the standard producer price of rice was frozen, but ¥23.8 billion was allocated as subsidies to producers for high quality rice.[140] Thereafter supplementary subsidies for encouraging the production of higher quality rice, for rice acreage control and for promoting the IDR system were commonly allocated at the time of the producer rice price decision.[141]

Nokyo's livestock price campaign

Livestock policy issues were amongst the first around which the Nokyo actively organised in the early 1950s. In December 1952, Zenshiren, Zenkoren and Zenhanren made strong representations on the issue of promoting dairy farming. In 1954, Zenshiren and Zenrakuren held their first National Dairy Farmers' Convention and in the same year, the Law Concerning the Promotion of Dairy Farming and Beef Cattle Production (*Rakuno oyobi Nikuyogyu Seisan no Shinko ni kansuru Horitsu*) was passed. The major statute passed relating to livestock prices, however, was the 1961 Law Concerning Price Stabilisation for Livestock Products (*Chikusanbutsu no Kakaku Antei to ni kansuru Horitsu*). The first Zenchu-sponsored national Nokyo representatives' meeting for demanding the price of livestock products was held in March 1966.

Deciding support and stabilisation prices paid to farmers for beef, beef calves, pork and raw milk for processing, as with the producer rice price, has been the MAFF Minister's responsibility, taking production costs into consideration (see Table 8.2). When the Livestock Products Price Stabilisation Law was being drafted, the MAFF stipulated that prices for beef and raw milk would be calculated taking into account production conditions, demand and supply trends and economic conditions. Zenchu strongly objected, arguing that these prices should be decided using the production cost and income compensation method just as in the case of rice. The entire Nokyo organisation (the federated Nokyo organisation as well as the *senmon nokyo*) demanded that the government apply the production cost and income compensation formula. The MAFF resisted the idea because of the likely financial burden, as in the case of rice, and because production costs would be based on existing production conditions which would impede the rationalisation of livestock management.[142] Zenchu was successful, however, in getting the government to take production costs into account, although not explicitly in the legislation.

Livestock price policymaking subsequently became institutionalised along much the same lines as the producer rice price. The MAFF's calculations, using the required input data, emerge as a series of 'recommended' prices which the minister submits to LIPAC, which in turn deliberates on the different prices. As part of this process, an ancillary concern for producers is the ceiling quantity on raw milk for processing which is eligible for the deficiency payment. This is also a matter for the MAFF Minister to decide after receiving the LIPAC report.

LIPAC is similarly constituted to the RPAC. It is made up of 'OBs' from MAFF *gaikaku dantai* operating in the livestock sector, academics, directors of cooperative associations of meat processing companies, Nokyo directors, including those from specialist livestock federations, journalists, a few livestock farmers, technical experts and so on. LIPAC also breaks up into various divisions, such as a dairy production division, a meat division and a poultry division, with smaller numbers of the members sitting on each.[143]

Producer spokespersons easily dominate in terms of numbers of representatives on the council. Out of a total of 46 members on the 1980 membership list, livestock farmers were represented by 17 delegates: five Nokyo officials (from Zenno, Zenrakuren, Zenchikuren, Norinchukin and the National Settlers' Nokyo Federation; seven officials from livestock *gaikaku dantai* (the Central Livestock Association, the National Beef Association and the Hokkaido Dairy Association); four officials from statutory agricultural interest groups (including the National Chamber of Agriculture); and (at least) one official from a MAFF public corporation, in this case the Agriculture, Forestry and Fisheries Finance Corporation. Other categories of representation were livestock industry wholesalers and processors (10); academics with a specialist knowledge of Japanese agriculture and agricultural economics (eight); representatives from the mass media (four); representatives from local government (two); and other peripheral groups (three). There was one representative from the consumer cooperative organisation, the Japan Federation of Livelihood Cooperative Unions (Nihon Seikatsu Kyodo Kumiai Rengokai, or Nisseikyo).[144]

Like the RPAC, LIPAC provides a useful forum in which producer spokespersons from Nokyo can formally present their demand prices to the MAFF and its minister. These are calculated along similar lines to the MAFF-recommended prices, but, as with the producer rice price, manipulation of key variables in the statistical calculation invariably produces prices that are higher than those of the ministry.

LIPAC sessions, together with public demonstrations of farmers timed by Nokyo to coincide with council hearings, have traditionally attracted a good deal of press and public attention. The day before LIPAC's general meeting is held, the Nokyo organisation intensifies its focus on livestock policy, holding meetings of representatives (Nokyo chairmen), both national and local, and publicising its demands. These have been formulated by the usual process of 'accumulation' through the different levels of the organisation, culminating in decisions taken by Zenchu executives within the special campaign headquarters. Nokyo representatives hold gatherings (*shukai*) in the Zenkyoren building, Zenchu lobbyists then visit the offices of politicians from each of the parties (including the Opposition), as well as the MAFF, presenting to each a page of resolutions (*ketsugi*) passed by the organisation, plus pamphlets issued by Zenchu on its livestock policy and livestock policy price demands. The main political targets are, however, LDP politicians, particularly those from livestock-producing regions.

At the Diet members' offices, secretaries take down details of livestock price calculations from Zenchu lobbyists and listen to explanations about what will happen to dairy and livestock farmers if prices are not maintained or increased, or if expanded imports come in from the United States, Australia or New Zealand. On these occasions, Diet members secretaries frequently take the opportunity to ask Nokyo lobbyists for political funds for their *sensei*. Meanwhile the Zenchu Chairman, accompanied by other Nokyo representatives, calls on the MAFF Minister, while the Chairman of the Livestock Policy Central Headquarters presents Nokyo's demands directly to the Livestock Commodity Prices Subcommittee of the LDP's Norin Bukai. Zenkoku Noseikyo executives also target other LDP agricultural policy leaders, such as the CAPIC Chairman.

As part of its annual March campaign, Zenchu's Livestock Policy Central Headquarters (now the Agricultural Policy Promotion Central Headquarters) calls for all dairy-related organisations including the *rakuno seiji renmei* to decide a unified demand on the guaranteed price as well as policies relating to dairy production. The central headquarters generally decides what the collective demand will be, except for the *rakuno seiji renmei* demand, which the latter decide for themselves. Each local league also has a campaign headquarters and conducts separate campaigns. They are the only groups that have a separate campaign headquarters from Nokyo. Other dairy-related organisations are all under Zenchu's umbrella. The non-dairy livestock industries as well as those for fruit juice, wheat and rice are also very dependent on Zenchu. In the local campaign arena, dairy farmers' leagues conduct joint activities with the *sogo nokyo* to increase the guaranteed price for raw milk for processing.

The reason for the separate dairy farmers' leagues is mainly historical. Special dairy cooperatives were set up exclusively for dairy farmers and were very strong and successful, in spite of the fact that the *sogo nokyo* tried to involve themselves with dairy farmers. Furthermore, dairy farmers felt that they could not rely on Zenchu to represent their interests, because its main interest was rice. In the dairy farmers' view, Zenchu put so much emphasis on rice it did not pay sufficient attention to other products. Indeed, Zenchu would do anything for rice, while not paying much attention to dairy products at all.[145]

As with the producer rice price, an important focus pressure from Nokyo and livestock farmers' groups has been the 'political addition' to livestock prices achieved through direct intervention from LDP agricultural representatives at the urging of their producer constituents.[146] From about the late 1970s onwards, however, livestock commodity support and stabilisation prices became a less and less productive target for pressure in terms of the size of the political concession able to be extracted from the government. This was due to a shift in fiscal and agricultural policy priorities away from an emphasis on price policies towards the structural adjustment of production in anticipation of market liberalisation.[147] Political additions to beef stabilisation prices and for the guaranteed manufacturing milk price became a thing of the past by the late 1970s, and in the 1980s, price trends for these commodities gradually entered freeze and reduction modes.[148]

At this point in time, livestock policy campaigns have refocused on limiting the extent of any cuts in support prices proposed by the MAFF, seeking other kinds of subsidies that would compensate for lowered price supports, pressuring for assistance to ameliorate the impact of market liberalisation on domestic livestock producers, and resisting any form of deregulation of the domestic dairy market. As with the subsidies allocated as part of the producer rice price decision, these government payments may be distributed to farmers or, in some cases, to Nokyo itself.

Other price campaigns

Other price campaigns have followed much the same procedures and processes as the rice and livestock price campaigns, although on a smaller scale. In the case of the guaranteed price (i.e. the government's buying price) for wheat, for example, a demand price is decided by a subcommittee of Nokyo's Agricultural Policy Central Headquarters, which consists of Nokyo executives from wheat-growing regions. The level of this demand is invariably higher than the existing price. It is then communicated to various *norin giin* (particularly those from wheat-producing areas), the Chairman of CAPIC and the Director-General of the Food Agency. Zenchu representatives from the Agricultural Policy Central Headquarters explain the farmers' demand to the Wheat Policy Sub-Committee of CAPIC which meets around the same time as the RPAC whose job it is to deliberate on the government-recommended wheat price. The National Nokyo Representatives' Council also gathers to report to delegates on the basic attitude of the LDP and government to Nokyo's demand price, and they then decide how to conduct various demand activities to achieve their objectives covering the period in which the RPAC meets and government–party negotiations on the wheat price are held.

Nokyo's budget campaign

Along with the producer rice price campaign, Nokyo's budget acquisition struggle (*yosan kakutoku toso*) has been one of the two main pillars of Nokyo's *nosei katsudo*.[149] In fact, as increases in the producer rice price became more modest over the years, Nokyo's principle of focusing all its energies on the *beika undo* gave way to greater emphasis on its budget acquisition campaign.

The budget campaign has traditionally followed a fairly uniform, structured sequence, in which virtually the same steps and stages are observed by the same actors year after year, and which are coordinated with the government's own budgetary decisionmaking sequence. The process involves three major elements: firstly, the formulation of budgetary demands within the federated Nokyo organisation; secondly, the presentation of these demands to government and to the Diet; and thirdly, pressure group activity including lobbying to back up these demands.

Step one begins when Zenchu executes an 'Agriculture-Related Policy–Budget Demand Accumulation Campaign' (*Nogyo Kankei Seisaku – Yosan Yokyu Tsumiage Undo*), although the title varies slightly from year to year. This is a bottom-up exercise whereby various budgetary-related requests are passed on up the line from lower-level organisations and from different regions to be collected by the prefectural federations and central unions and then passed on to the central collecting organisation, Zenchu. A lot of the work at the prefectural level is undertaken by the *kenchu noseibu*, which formulate various budgetary proposals as part of the process of piling up demands. Zenchu also consults with the other central organs such as Zenno and Norinchukin. Nokyo thus gathers demands at the prefectural level and then finalises them at the national level.

The process of accumulating demands normally begins anywhere from February through to April, just as ministry and agency officials are beginning the process of formulating the MAFF's draft budget estimate (*gaisan yokyu*) for the following fiscal year. Nokyo basically takes its cue from this process. Thus, while the budget formulation process is being conducted within government, it is also taking place in parallel fashion within Nokyo. As in the case of producer prices, Nokyo replicates governmental policy formulation sequences within its own organisation.

Step two involves a meeting of the Zenchu Board of Directors in June or July to make the final decision on Nokyo's budgetary demands, having received the report of the results of the campaign to accumulate demands. The Zenchu Board of Directors finalises a list of requests which varies from eight to 13 items. The task of the accumulation and subsequent decision-making process is to concentrate the various demands into a number of big items which are then subject to a distillation and concentration process until they fit under a series of main headings. The actual list of demands is headed up 'A Statement of Requests Concerning the Year's Agriculture-Related Priority Measures and the Establishment of Agricultural Basic Policy' (*Nogyo Kihon Seisaku no Kakuritsu narabi ni Showa/Heisei . . . Nendo Nogyo Kankei Juten Shisaku ni kansuru Yoseisho*). This is a bulky document in which the main headings are amplified with additional lists and headings and explanations underneath.

The contents of Nokyo's 'Statement of Requests' exhibit strong continuities in core policies from one year to the next. For example, the main agricultural products are always covered in some form: rice, livestock and dairy products, vegetables, fruit and fruit juice, upland field products, special products and local foods. Similarly, requests are consistently issued in relation to welfare policy for rural areas, agricultural finance, promoting urban agriculture and agricultural disaster policy.[150]

On the other hand, adjustments are made for changing circumstances and the shifting emphasis in government agricultural policy. Nokyo's budget demands reflect the main thrust of government policy at the time and thus what Nokyo leaders judge to be politically feasible and appropriate. Nokyo does not pursue the impossible, which would lead to certain failure and risk the dissatisfaction of its members. It is pragmatic in its approach. Taking the 1980–81 budget, for example, Nokyo emphasised price supports, controlling imports, maintaining self-sufficiency, setting production targets, strengthening a demand and supply adjustment policy for agricultural products (which continued until 1983–84 budget), and maintaining the FC system (which continued until 1986–87 budget). In the increasingly antipathetic environment towards rice and Food Control in the late 1980s, however, the request to preserve the FC system was replaced with a demand for a rice and wheat production and distribution policy, which envisaged various subsidies for rice and wheat farmers, and which was designed to head-off some of the proposed changes to the distribution systems for these products.

Similarly, requests for allocations relating to structural policy and consolidating the agricultural base began with the 1984–85 budget and later expanded to requests for biotechnology funding, as this branch of agricultural science began to take off. In the 1993 budget, a new focus was the so-called 'new farm policy' announced by the government in June 1992, which aimed to expand by the scale of rice production in anticipation of some form of market opening for rice.[151] Because the MAFF used the policy to insert new demands into the fiscal 1993 budget, Zenchu compiled corresponding countermeasures in its own budget request.

Step Three of Nokyo's budget campaign encompasses the presentation of its budget request to the government and to the Diet. In this case, the government means the MAFF Minister and the MAFF, the MOF and the MHW (for matters relating to farmers' pensions, for example), while the Diet means the LDP (including the *norin zoku* and formal party agricultural committees) and other political parties. This usually takes place at the end of July and mostly targets the final stages of the budget drafting process within the MAFF and the examination of this draft by the AFD.

These Zenchu-led 'request activities' are not mass mobilisation exercises but largely take the form of submissions undertaken by Zenchu officials. Staff members of Zenchu's Noseibu put pressure on the section chiefs in the MAFF, while Zenchu executives lobby at the bureau chief and vice-minister level. The MAFF listens to the various budget proposals from Nokyo and weaves them into its draft budget.[152] At the same time, Zenchu executives also put pressure on LDP *norin giin* which involves frequent formal and informal contact by Zenchu middle-ranking staff members as well as by executive management. At the same time, LDP politicians led by the *norin zoku* lobby the MAFF on Nokyo's behalf. Roundtable discussions are frequently held involving LDP politicians, MAFF officials and Zenchu officials.

Step Four encompasses the launching of Nokyo's large-scale budget campaign targeting the MOF's draft of the agricultural, forestry and fisheries budget (*norinsuisan yosan*), which is released in late December, or even as late as mid- to late January. The budget draft gives the MAFF, the LDP and Zenchu a glimpse at what the government is prepared to offer. Zenchu receives a copy of the MOF draft and examines it in detail. The period between the release of the draft budget and the final determination of the government budget presents an opportunity for the MAFF, the LDP and Zenchu to launch a last ditch attempt at achieving their political and policy objectives. It is a time when items of expenditure removed or cut back in the MOF draft can be 'revived' in order to appease political interests. Intensive four-party negotiations take place involving the MAFF, the MOF, the LDP and Zenchu.

Most of Nokyo's budget campaign is targeted at this final stage of the budget process – during the few days between the release of the MOF draft and the final decision on the government draft budget in Cabinet – usually right at the end of December, although it can be delayed until mid- to late January. Zenchu calls it a 'special campaign' (*tokubetsu undo*). There is a big difference in scale between the earlier request activities focusing on the MAFF and the Diet and this larger scale mass movement targeted at the revival negotiations, which is conducted at a public level and involves a national mobilisation of Nokyo representatives. This is when Nokyo's budget campaign reaches its climax.

On the same day or just before the MOF draft is released, Zenchu sets up an 'Agriculture-Related Budget Countermeasures Headquarters' (Nogyo Kankei Yosan Taisaku Honbu) in the Zenkyoren building near the Diet, which provides close access to targeted Diet members. The Nokyo Budget Policy Headquarters receives a copy of the MOF draft budget, and immediately launches its request activities, listing important items. Just as in the rice price battle, groups of representatives come up to Tokyo from all over Japan. They hit the streets in mass mobilisation-type exercises, and over the space of about one week, launch large-scale demand activities. Everyday a programme of pressure activities is organised. These are repeated every year and involve combined conferences of central organisation chairmen and the chairman and vice-chairmen of the various Zenchu commodity headquarters, an assembly of Nokyo representatives and a conference of executive office chiefs.

When the special campaign reaches a peak, Nokyo's request items are concentrated into 'super priority' requests (usually 12 items down to three, although as much as 24 items down to five), behind which Nokyo galvanises an even more vociferous campaign. Sometimes an 'Agricultural Budget Nokyo Unified Assembly' (Norin Yosan Nokyo Toitsu Shukai) – a mass assembly to which supporting Diet members are invited – is held and various requests are presented to the many Diet members present.[153] The assembly represents the climax of the Zenchu-led budget campaign. It involves hundreds of Nokyo representatives who lead groups of petitioners to the LDP Diet members' offices and to the MAFF and MOF.

As Tachibana points out, the difference between the MAFF's budget total and Nokyo's budget total is as little as 0.2 per cent (with the latter higher than the former). This effectively means that Zenchu and the farmers act as a 'cheer group' (*oendan*) for the MAFF in supporting the ministry's budget requests *vis-à-vis* the MOF. In his view, no other ministries have budget acquisition support groups that are as reliable as Nokyo and its cohorts of officials and farmers. This is because around 60 per cent of the budget is absorbed by farmers in the form of subsidies, and therefore it is inevitable that Nokyo plays a positive role when the government is engaged in the budgetmaking process.[154]

The outcome of Nokyo's budget campaign in combination with the exertions of pro-agriculture politicians in the LDP is a 'political addition' to the agricultural, forestry and fisheries budget, just as in the case of the producer rice price. The political addition usually amounts to only a small increase on the original MOF draft offer. In the 1992 *norinsuisan yosan*, for example, the difference was only 0.6 per cent, or ¥19.5 billion.[155]

Nokyo's anti-agricultural trade liberalisation campaign

Nokyo's campaigns against market opening for farm commodities have been conducted in two main phases. The first phase began in 1960 and intensified in the late 1960s and early 1970s as pressure from agricultural exporting countries for the abolition of Japanese import restrictions intensified and as domestic producers rallied under Nokyo's leadership to launch their own counter-offensive.

Zenchu made its first strong representations to the Diet and to government about the liberalisation of trade in early 1960 after voices were raised in favour of liberalisation at the GATT general meeting in Tokyo in October 1959. The most significant items on the government's early market opening list were soybeans (liberalised in July 1961), and lemons (liberalised in May 1964). Lemon production was a viable farm industry virtually destroyed by import liberalisation,[156] whereas soya bean production was already in decline at the time of liberalisation. It was only in connection with the former that significant opposition was aroused amongst the farmers. In 1964 Nokyo held a national convention for demanding the revocation of lemon liberalisation. The experience of lemon growers in Southern Japan, although they constituted a small, select group of farmers, provided farmers and the agricultural cooperatives with the evidence they needed of the destructive power of liberalisation. It spurred a renewed campaign against the government's much more extensive market opening proposals formulated in the late 1960s. The liberalisation dispute during this latter period centred chiefly around citrus fruit, particularly grapefruit.

The government's intention to liberalise grapefruit became known as a result of the Japan–US negotiations on abolishing residual import controls which opened in Tokyo in spring 1968. Nichienren's anti-liberalisation activities began at this point. It launched a vocal campaign opposing the government's schedule for grapefruit liberalisation at the conference of Nichienren member chairmen in December 1968. Resolutions were passed at this conference arguing against grapefruit liberalisation because of the likely effects of US imports on summer orange and *mikan* producers in Japan.

In spite of domestic producer opposition, however, the government's positive attitude towards grapefruit liberalisation was confirmed at the 7th Japan–US Trade and Economic Joint Committee in July 1969. MAF Minister Hasegawa Shiro also included grapefruit on a list of 25 articles for liberalisation under the jurisdiction of the MAF presented to the Cabinet Council for the Promotion of the Liberalisation of Trade and Exchange in September 1969. This coincided with the first 'National Nokyo Representatives' Conference for the Prevention of the Liberalisation of Agricultural and Livestock Products' hosted by Zenchu in September 1969. Zenchu's interests at the time extended beyond grapefruit to agricultural items such as rapeseed, pork, live cattle and pigs. In February 1971, Zenchu orchestrated a 'National Nokyo Chairmen's Conference for the Prevention of the Liberalisation of Pork and Other Items'.

The first half of 1971 saw the anti-liberalisation movement centring on grapefruit gaining momentum as the date for the scheduled liberalisation in April 1971 drew nearer. During the local elections in the same month, farmers' conventions protesting liberalisation were organised on a scale not seen before in Shizuoka, Ehime and Fukuoka.[157] A vigorous public campaign was also launched by Nichienren largely through the medium of conventions of fruit producers. Nichienren executives paid official visits to the MAF, particularly to the Fruit and Flowers Division of the MAF Sericulture and Horticulture Bureau. In April, Nichienren held a 'Grapefruit Liberalisation Prevention Convention' and in July, the largest Nokyo convention to be held up to that point on the liberalisation issue was organised in Tokyo. Called the 'National Producers' Convention for a Policy to Overcome the Crisis in Fruit Farming' (Kaju Nogyo Kiki Toppa Taisaku Zenkoku Seisansha Taikai), as noted earlier, it represented a break with precedent insofar as Zenchu, Zenhanren and Nichienren, as national organisations representing fruit farmers, came together for the first time in the management of a convention. These groups had not previously agreed on such combined action. Zenchu Chairman Miyawaki Asao delivered a strongly worded anti-government speech to the 2,200-strong gathering of Nokyo representatives.

The convention produced a joint Zenchu–Nichienren 'Combined Committee for a Policy to Overcome the Crisis in Fruit Farming' (Kaju Nogyo Kiki Toppa Taisaku Godo Iinkai). Nokyo and citrus farmers lost the battle, however, when the government went ahead with the liberalisation in June 1971, just after the UH elections.[158] Protests 'after the fact' against grapefruit liberalisation became incorporated into a heightened anti-liberalisation campaign involving other citrus products such as oranges and citrus juice which were the subject of sustained pressure from the United States. The 'Combined Committee to Overcome the Crisis in Fruit Farming' acknowledged in its public statements that fruit farmers had suffered a great blow from the liberalisation of grapefruit and presented a number of 'Demands Relating to the Prevention of the Liberalisation of Oranges and Fruit Juice'. The committee requested the government not to carry out its plan to liberalise these products, and 'to institute emergency policies for the fundamental constitutional improvement of Japan's fruit farming in order to enable it to cope with international competition'.[159]

The campaign escalated in the wake of the 8th Round of the Japan–US Trade and Economic Combined Committee in September 1971 in which MAF Minister, Akagi Munenori, announced that an additional number of agricultural items would be liberalised in 1972. Protests from citrus farmers became incorporated into a general anti-liberalisation campaign involving a range of products: beef, pork, flour, beans, live cattle, sugar products and edible cherries. It was at this point that the two sides of the Nokyo anti-liberalisation movement, mainstream and specialist, joined forces, and the precedent established with the first joint Nichienren–Zenchu convention was followed up with additional activities organised along similar lines.

In December 1971, Zenchu in partnership with a number of other agricultural groups including Zenhanren and Nichienren, sponsored a 'National Producers' Convention for the Prevention of the Liberalisation and Expansion of Imports of Oranges, Fruit Juice, Beef, Miscellaneous Beans etc.' This was supplemented by additional pronouncements from Zenchu and its Chairman, Miyawaki. These activities represented a significant development in the fruit producers' campaign insofar as the national Nokyo lobbying body had taken up the specific cause of oranges and fruit juice, and this trend was to continue. Zenchu and its leaders began to play a much more active role in relation to fruit interests than they had done in the past. In March 1973 and May 1974, Zenchu organised a 'National Nokyo Representatives' Convention for Preventing the Import Liberalisation of Oranges, Fruit Juice and Other Products'. In the event, these products came through the liberalisation rounds of 1973–74 unscathed.[160] The campaign was, however, lost over a number of items that were not the target of such sustained producer opposition such as pork, ham, bacon, live cattle and pigs.

The second phase in the anti-agricultural trade liberalisation campaign began in the late 1970s and accelerated in the early to mid-1980s as the United States stepped up the pressure for bilateral market access for key products such as beef, oranges and citrus juice, and began applying pressure specifically on agricultural markets through the UR of the GATT.[161] In concert with other agricultural, fisheries and forestry groups, Zenchu launched a campaign to 'Halt Quota Expansion and the Liberalisation of Imports of Agricultural Products' in October 1981.[162]

The groups identified as the three main opponents of farmers in this campaign were those favouring liberalisation in the LDP government, *zaikai*, and the US government.[163] In March 1982, a general mobilisation of farmers, forestry and fisheries groups took place and 19 agriculture, forestry and fishery groups established the Agriculture, Forestry and Fishery Products Import Liberalisation Prevention Policy Central Headquarters within Zenchu. The headquarters was designed to spearhead the nationwide campaign to prevent quota expansion and agricultural import liberalisation in much the same way as the Rice Policy Central Headquarters did for rice.

The central headquarters aimed to appeal to all classes and interests and mobilise them against agricultural trade liberalisation, beginning with the government and the Diet, but also including local government and assemblies, consumers', women's, youth, labour, economic and other groups as well as the mass media. In addition, it petitioned the US government, Congress and agricultural groups, thus launching a very broadly based campaign.[164] Because the headquarters requested support from consumer organisations, agricultural import liberalisation was launched as an issue for consumers and the mass media.[165]

As part of its campaign of direct action, the headquarters launched 'general uprising conventions' of approximately 10,000 primary producers nationwide. Altogether it held 13 national conventions in 1982–83. In addition, it organised more than 10 special campaigns; a 10 million signature campaign which by the end of December 1982 had gathered 9,070,000 signatures opposing agricultural trade liberalisation; and the dispatch of one million letters and telegrams to the United States. It also undertook questionnaire surveys of candidates in two LH and UH elections requesting favourable pledges against market opening for farm products and sent six million postcards and telegrams to the government and the Diet in a campaign the scale of which had never been seen before.[166] Its signature campaigns opposing market opening were especially targeted at government party members. One campaign succeeded in collecting signatures of 376 out of 391 Diet members opposing agricultural market opening for beef and oranges.[167] According to one of the organisers, the effectiveness of such campaigns was reflected in the resolutions passed on preventing the liberalisation and quota expansion of agricultural products in the Diet in April 1982. Furthermore, because of pressure from the central headquarters, resolutions opposing agricultural trade liberalisation were passed in the LH and UH Agriculture, Forestry and Fisheries Committees in May 1982, in addition to a number of similar resolutions passed within the government and Opposition parties. In the LDP, two resolutions were passed in combined conferences of CAPIC, the AFD and the Forestry Policy Committee.[168] Similarly, resolutions opposing agricultural trade liberalisation and quota expansion were passed by Noshinkyo and the livestock and fruit Diet members' leagues. The 356 LDP Diet politicians who supported these resolutions comprised more than 90 per cent of all LDP Diet members.[169] Amongst the JSP and other Opposition parties as well, headquarters were established to deal with issues of agricultural trade liberalisation and a wide range of special policies were formulated.

Prior to the US–Japan leaders' talks in January 1983, the central headquarters mobilised over 10,000 agricultural cooperative leaders and members in a national representatives' convention. A number of politicians were in attendance including Nikaido Susumu, Secretary-General of the LDP, Hirabayashi Takeshi, the Secretary-General of the JSP, as well as the secretaries general of other political parties. All affirmed their stand against agricultural trade liberalisation and quota expansion.[170] The central headquarters also met with the PM Nakasone a couple of times and gained a commitment from him that the government would not agree to liberalise trade in an arbitrary fashion. In addition, the Zenchu Chairman, along with representatives from the 19 agricultural, forestry and fisheries organisations participating in the central headquarters, and 11 representatives of the LDP's Agricultural Products Import Liberalisation Problem Liaison Council (Watanabe Michio later took over as Chairman from Nakagawa Ichiro) undertook last minute collaboration to present a request to the PM not to liberalise just prior to his departure for Washington.[171]

In March 1988, more than 1,600 Nokyo representatives attended a rally to protest American demands for an end to all Japanese restrictions on beef and citrus fruit imports. In front of huge banners declaring 'We Will Firmly Block the Liberalisation of Beef, Oranges, and Orange Juice Imports', Nokyo leaders and the 210 Diet members present stood up to denounce American demands as 'completely unfair' and 'provocative'.[172] The declaration of the rally read: 'We hereby strongly demand that the Government and the Diet reject, with unflinching resolve, the US Government's outrageous demand for liberalisation'.[173] It also called on farmers, consumers and politicians to join in a nationwide movement to oppose any concessions that the Japanese government might offer to the US side. The rally was timed just before the expiry of the prevailing four-year US–Japan agreement on Japan's quotas on beef and citrus fruit imports.

Zenchu also staged a movement against rice market opening for the duration of the UR which lasted slightly more than seven years (in fact seven years and three months). In the wake of the June/July 1988 settlements on beef and citrus fruit and the earlier February agreement liberalising access for eight miscellaneous agricultural items, Nokyo established a Central Headquarters for Measures to Prevent Rice Market Opening (Kome Jiyuka Soshi Taisaku Chuo Honbu) headed by the Zenchu Chairman in October 1988. The headquarters devoted itself to strengthening the campaign to stop market opening under the slogan of 'Preventing Rice Market Liberalisation'.[174]

The campaign had four main objectives: to promote study activities for gathering and analysing information concerning the Uruguay Round; to develop a national movement to gain fair public understanding of agriculture and its important multifunctionality in the face of intensifying 'agriculture-bashing' and ever-mounting moves to build up popular support for opening the rice market; to file strong and repeated petitions with local public entities, the government and the Diet requesting that government-sponsored proposals be accepted at GATT talks in strict accordance with Diet resolutions; and to promote activities designed to gain foreign countries' understanding and support for the position of Japanese farmers by organising an international movement of farmers for the protection of family farming.[175]

The campaign featured numerous rallies and meetings, with the largest gathering in the nation's agricultural history held in July 1991 at the Tokyo Dome. Organised by Zenchu it was called the 'Emergency National Rally to Protect Rice'. About 50,000 rice farmers, representatives of affiliated agricultural cooperatives, political leaders from both government and Opposition parties, citizens' groups and others participated in the rally, protesting against any motion to allow rice imports. In late December 1992, when PM Miyazawa Kiichi intimated that he was prepared to concede on the issue of rice tariffication, Zenchu staged street demonstrations and a protest assembly of 10,000 farmers wearing headbands reading: 'Absolutely stop the opening of the rice market'.[176]

Zenchu also mounted an appeal to the Diet and prefectural assemblies to pass resolutions against the opening of the rice market and to regard and maintain past Diet decisions (that is, the resolutions on rice self-sufficiency passed in 1987).[177] It organised a campaign to send questionnaires to political parties and a campaign to collect signatures from Diet members. For example, the majority of general election candidates from each party were canvassed in the lead-up to the July 1993 LH elections, with the intention of circulating their responses throughout the farming community.[178] Other activities included a direct appeal to the GATT headquarters in Geneva, an extensive distribution of GATT-related information, study activities using a variety of video cassettes and the holding of a Tokyo summit of farmers in July 1993. These actions were directed by the central headquarters.[179]

Zenkoku Noseikyo also weighed in with its own activities, holding national assemblies of representatives, demanding the rejection of proposals to tariffy import barriers and conducting signature campaigns amongst members of both houses of the Diet. One of these produced a total of 606 signatures from politicians who opposed tariffication of the Japanese rice market (407 from the Lower House and 199 from the Upper House – that is, just under 80 per cent of the membership of both Houses). Efforts were also put into a campaign for getting the farmers' message across to the Japanese public and to consumers about the need to protect Japanese food and agriculture.[180] In the 1991 LDP presidential election, Zenkoku Noseikyo canvassed the three candidates – Miyazawa Kiichi, Watanabe Michio and Mitsuzuka Hiroshi – with respect to their policies on the establishment of a basic policy for agriculture and rural areas and on rice market opening. Their answers were published in Nokyo's newspaper outlet, the *Nihon Nogyo Shinbun*.

Nokyo's strategies as a pressure group

Nokyo's demands are never formulated in a policy vacuum because the agricultural cooperative organisation is cognisant of the general policy trends that shape its campaign environment. It routinely adjusts its approach to accommodate these changing policy trends as well as the political atmosphere in which it is operating. Although these adjustments may at times be insufficient and belated, running effective policy campaigns mandates a close reading of contemporary trends in both politics and policies.

The following section reviews the types of policy demands advanced by Nokyo over the years and how they reflected its calculations of their likely success in response to shifting political and policy parameters. The discussion also reviews Nokyo's flexibility in terms of campaign tactics. The analysis is designed to illustrate Nokyo's political nous as a pressure group, particularly its ability to interpret 'the signs of the times', to gauge the receptivity of politicians and the MAFF to its demands, and to adjust its claims in response to the government's evolving policy priorities. One of the most important tasks of the Nokyo leadership is to estimate what is possible in any given political and policy environment and what will prove to be the most fruitful approach, and to transmit their understanding of these factors to local leaders and co-op members in the provinces, who can usually see little further than their own immediate interests.

Nokyo's producer price strategy

Although the tactics Nokyo has deployed in its producer price campaigns present a picture of an organisation hell-bent on achieving its objectives at all cost, in fact the agricultural cooperative leadership has endeavoured to gauge very carefully the political feasibility of its demand prices. Several considerations have been important. Firstly, too high a demand price leads to inflated expectations amongst farmers and the failure that would follow such an unrealistic target risks creating disaffection amongst the membership. Secondly, given that Japanese political culture evaluates the pursuit of self-interest negatively, Nokyo (in contrast to the Zennichino, for example) keeps its demands within realistic, although generous limits, presenting at least the appearance of considering the public interest. Thirdly, a fine line is drawn between satisfying members on the one hand and keeping faith with the MAFF and the LDP agricultural policy leadership on the other, particularly in relation to the prices that can be justified within broader bureaucratic (the MOF especially), party (the LDP executive leadership) and government (Cabinet) circles.

For all these reasons, Nokyo is not immune to the general policy environment in which producer prices are being decided at any particular time, including demand-supply conditions, fiscal constraints, food processors' concerns about the cost of domestically-produced inputs, and public attitudes towards subsidised producer prices as they are reflected in the price of food and as they compare with international prices.

During the period of rapid economic growth which coincided with the 1961 Basic Law agricultural policy, emphasis was placed on improving the gross productivity of agriculture. Accordingly, the green light was given for a fairly rapid inflation of the rice and other producer prices. Nokyo claims that its agricultural policy activities really took off at this time.[181] The focus of its agricultural policy activities centred on demand campaigns relating to agricultural prices along the lines of its rice price demand and milk price 'struggles'.[182]

During this period Nokyo effectively mobilised its members to lobby farm politicians from the ruling party. As the rice surplus expanded, however, Nokyo's producer rice price campaigns began to stagnate and its lobbying became less effective.[183] In the late 1970s, the rice surplus together with the deteriorating fiscal situation (in which the size of the FCSA deficit became less administratively justifiable and politically viable) forced Nokyo on to the defensive for the first time. Zenchu leaders revised their expectations downwards of what producer price levels were achievable and an element of realism was apparent in their demands which was never present during the 1960s and early 1970s. In 1977 Zenchu took the unprecedented step of demanding a producer rice price that was lower than its demand for the previous year. Indeed, its demand remained lower than the 1976 producer rice price level until 1981.

Subsequently in the lead-up to its 1982 producer rice price campaign, Nokyo announced a new policy outline in which it acknowledged a change in emphasis from a price support policy incorporating higher producer rice prices to a structural policy for raising productivity. This was an adjustment to the long-term shift in emphasis in agricultural assistance policies away from a reliance on price support instruments towards measures to encourage greater productivity and efficiency in agriculture.[184] Other important factors in the early to mid-1980s were the fiscal deficit leading to tighter constraints on budgetary spending as a whole and the appreciation of the yen in the mid-1980s which exposed price differentials for food between Japan and its major trading partners. In this policy context, state-guaranteed prices of major agricultural commodities such as rice (and livestock products) were suppressed.[185]

As a demonstration of its own policy adjustment, Zenchu called for an historically low increase in the producer rice price in 1982 (2.8 per cent), and followed this up in 1983 with an even lower 2.3 per cent demand increase. In 1984 and 1985, only moderate rises were requested. These unprecedented steps in recommending lower increases in support prices reflected an effort on Nokyo's part to 'opt for a more realistic price level and a wide-ranging agricultural improvement programme in a bid to enlist public support'.[186]

In 1986 a reduction in the producer rice price was almost unavoidable for a number of reasons: a 6.6 per cent reduction in production cost of rice that year; a tacit agreement within the government (i.e. between the MAFF and the MOF) that a reduction in the producer price of rice from the following year was unavoidable; a report from the RPAC endorsing a freeze in the producer rice price for three years from 1984; a statement issued by the government's budget-cutting committee[187] supporting restraint on producer rice price rises; a recommendation in the report of a blue-ribbon government advisory committee (the Maekawa committee[188]) to reduce the gap in prices between domestic rice and imported rice; and an estimate by the MAFF, after negotiations with the LDP, that the price would need to be reduced by 3.8 per cent.[189]

Nokyo's concession to these factors in the general policy environment was to request 'a decision to raise the price above current price' without indicating any actual price level. This was interpreted to mean the maintenance of the existing producer rice price. Initially it had said that the producer rice price should be raised by some 6 per cent but sensed that this would outrage those inclined towards a reduction and invite a backlash. Nevertheless, this was the first time in its history that Nokyo had effectively asked for a producer rice price freeze.[190] It represented a drastic change from its usual approach, which was consistently to demand an increase. The request was accepted.

In fact a number of problems were present in the Nokyo organisation surrounding this unusual decision. Unit co-ops located in agricultural areas where the incomes of farm households largely depended on rice vehemently opposed Zenchu's decision and organised an independent campaign to demand an increase. Individual farmer members of the co-ops were also strongly pushing for a rise. When Zenchu decided effectively to request the same price as in the previous year, dissatisfaction surfaced in Tohoku and Hokuriku. The Niigata Prefectural Central Union Chairman said: 'There is no stable job to take the place of agriculture in farming villages. The rice price is the same as our wages. We cannot consent to not increasing the rice price, when wages and commodity prices are going up. It is because of Zenchu's weak posture that the government began to talk about lowering the rice price.'[191]

Given the push for an actual cut in the producer rice price, Nokyo mounted a highly directed political campaign prior to the joint elections of 1986. It lobbied LDP election candidates aiming to obtain their support for the maintenance of the producer rice price. It offered votes in exchange for an expression of 'understanding' of the agricultural cooperatives' position. In a questionnaire circulated by Zenchu amongst LDP candidates in both the Upper and Lower Houses, it canvassed election candidates by asking them whether they supported Nokyo's demand for 'more than the existing price' (*genko beika ijo*).[192] It managed to extract a supportive response from 337,[193] which was 80 per cent of all candidates, and 95 per cent of successful candidates. LDP party executives recalled that the questionnaire was really effective, because the signature of each politician was immediately transformed into an official election promise.[194]

After the LDP's overwhelming victory, Nokyo immediately started to push successful candidates to fulfil their election promises[195] and substantial pressure was put on LDP agricultural policy leaders. Nokyo presented a pamphlet to the rice price negotiation table with photographs of the candidates who had answered Nokyo's questionnaire as evidence of the LDP's support for maintaining the current rice price. At a gathering of Nokyo representatives and the Diet secretaries of *kome giin* in the lobby of the LDP headquarters building, words of encouragement and applause were given to the Diet members going in and out. One of the Nokyo leaders spoke to the group saying: 'You must not demand an increase in the rice price without providing money and cooperating with the election. Persons who offered money and conducted election activities are qualified to demand an increase. Please take a close look at who made efforts (in the party) until late at night and publish the details in the constituency'.[196]

Zenchu's various tactics were credited with changing the LDP and government's attitude from one of support for a rice price reduction to a decision for no change over the previous year. But to some extent the outcome was a pyrrhic victory. The use of blatant pressure tactics caused an explosion of media attacks on the agricultural cooperative organisation.[197] MAFF Minister Kato Mutsuki even wanted to resign because of Zenchu's so-called 'inconsiderate enforcement' of its point of view on the government. As Sakaguchi points out, Nokyo had demonstrated its outstanding power by showing its strength 'from the edge of the ring of the producer rice price decision'.[198] In his assessment, because the government easily changed its decision under pressure from Nokyo, Zenchu was clearly more powerful than the government.[199]

One of the main reasons why the government finally accepted the proposal for a freeze in the producer rice price in 1986 instead of the planned reduction was because Zenchu threatened to withdraw its cooperation from the *gentan* policy which was due to be strengthened in the following year.[200] For the MAFF in particular, smooth implementation of the next phase of the *gentan* was an important consideration since rice acreage reductions underpinned the FC system.[201]

Nokyo's hard lobbying may have succeeded in achieving a freeze in the producer rice price, but the outcome did not come without its costs. The most serious was the rising level of antagonism amongst consumers towards the cooperatives and the loss of public support for agricultural causes at a time when the public was becoming increasingly aware of the differentials in food prices between Japan and overseas.[202] On the other hand, the fact that the focus of the issue in 1986 became a choice between a reduction or a price freeze was significant in the evolution of producer rice price decisionmaking. Compared with the past when the issue essentially concerned the rate at which the producer rice price should rise, the events of 1986 completely changed the character of the issue. Thereafter Nokyo was forced to unite farmers under the slogan of 'preventing a reduction in the producer rice price'.[203]

In 1987, the year of the first reduction in the producer rice price for 31 years, Zenchu presented no producer rice price demand at all because its leaders realised and accepted even before the season was under way that a cut was inevitable, and in such circumstances, no one within the organisation was prepared to take the responsibility for asking for a price that was lower than in the previous year. An increase or even a freeze, given the political climate, was unrealistic and would be criticised as irresponsible. Even before the government's producer rice price decision was made, Zenchu gave its approval for a lower price.[204] It issued a statement that it accepted the government's plan to lower the rice price. It did not say so specifically, but in effect Zenchu accepted the reduction. It made no demand providing that 'the government's buying price for 1987-produced rice would achieve income guarantees [to farmers] and continuing production, along with reform of the variables in the calculation formula'.[205]

Following its experience of the 1986 producer rice price debacle, Nokyo was sensitised to the need to gauge the public mood more accurately and to estimate the limits of their resistance. Given that continuing agricultural support and protection partly depended on public tolerance, it needed to evaluate carefully what appeared to be a more reasonable request against one that might alienate large sections of the populace.

The producer rice price demands of 1986 and 1987 also reflected the fact that both the Nokyo leadership and the farmers were more or less resigned to inevitable declines in the rice price and held a rather depressed view of the future of Nokyo's rice price struggles. When asked about the latter, the Chairman of Iwamizawa Nokyo said: 'Among the organisations of producers, there is a growing view that it is unavoidable that the basic rice price is kept at the present level. So, the failure of the rice price struggles is in sight'.[206] As some commentators subsequently pointed out, the decline in the producer rice price campaigns in the late 1980s reflected the low morale of rice producers.[207]

The role of Nokyo in representing farmers in the producer rice price struggle was also increasingly being called into question. According to one agricultural cooperative leader: 'It is no longer possible to act like a pressure group in the rice price movement'.[208] Pressure for a review of Nokyo's conventional tactics in pursuing the rice price campaign spread amongst farmers in 1986. The outlook for rice farming in the light of the acreage cutbacks was equally dim. In all respects, the environment around rice growing was seen as increasingly hard, particularly in the light of requests for liberalisation of the rice market.

In bowing to the inevitable and accepting a producer rice price cut in 1987, the agricultural cooperative organisation effectively began to engineer its own decline, earning criticism from both good and bad farmers for its impotence. The risk of this development for Nokyo was that if it could no longer fulfil its traditional role of fighting for higher producer prices, it would lose its relevance for farmers and lose credibility as their representative organisation. The 1987 producer rice price failure was assessed as the beginning of the end of Nokyo's agricultural policy leadership.

In subsequent years, much of the intensity in Nokyo's campaigns on this issue dissipated, particularly as the producer rice price was either reduced or frozen each year thereafter. In 1988, Nokyo's demand conference was cancelled and switched to a joint consumer–farmer symposium, because of popular demands for a reduction in the rice price.[209] This reflected an increasing acceptance amongst the farmers and Nokyo that they had to coexist with consumers.[210] It was also a tactical retreat and showed the government's enforcement of producer rice price reductions. Equally it revealed a decline in Nokyo's influence over setting the price. In retrospect, it proved to be a turning point in Nokyo's *nosei katsudo*, with a massive scaling down of the producer rice price campaign thereafter and with Nokyo shifting very much on to the defensive rather than the offensive.[211] In 1992, Zenchu demanded an increase in the producer rice price for the first time in seven years. It did not, however, specify a margin for the increase.[212] The rise was requested because Zenchu had calculated that the cost of rice production exceeded the existing basic producer price.

The reductions in the government's buying price for rice from 1987 onwards also affected the price for independently distributed rice, insofar as the former was the benchmark for the latter. In this respect, the ramifications for farmers of a cut in the producer rice price were much more widespread than first appeared in spite of the MAFF's argument that because 70 per cent of all rice was shipped through the IDR system, the influence of rice price reductions on farmers was small compared with the past.[213]

For all producer prices, the early 1990s marked the beginning of a period in which Zenchu abandoned producer price demands incorporating concrete figures. Its requests to the government were to improve prices if that were feasible, or to maintain existing prices if pressure for reductions were strong. Basically Nokyo had resigned itself to the fact that producer price trends were inexorably heading in a downwards direction.[214] In relinquishing a specific target price, however, Nokyo eliminated a lot of the impetus from its producer price campaigns, because of the lack of a concrete focus for farmers' action.

Nokyo's anti-agricultural trade liberalisation strategy

The special feature of the campaigns against agricultural trade liberalisation and particularly rice market opening has been their intensity, their mass mobilisation power and the predilection of farmers to resort to direct action. Various displays of anger at the United States have been engineered by farmers such as wrecking an American-made tractor and gate-crashing the American consulates in Fukuoka and Hokkaido to engage in direct debates and discussions, activities that were hitherto unseen in farmers' struggles. In Kumamoto, angry farmers took to the streets and smashed a Japanese car draped in a US flag with a sledge hammer.[215] Even Nokyo officials observed that these activities were different in breadth and depth from the type of campaigns organised on rice price issues hitherto. One difference was that the farmers were highly motivated by consideration of the issues themselves,[216] and sometimes acted unilaterally without direction and orchestration from Nokyo.

Another feature of the anti-agricultural trade liberalisation campaign has been their wide scope, including the formation of coalitions with non-agricultural groups. Nokyo's traditional policy campaigns and particularly the producer rice price campaign had, until the early 1980s, always been carried out by agricultural groups alone, but with the policy to prevent the liberalisation of beef and orange imports, a wider range of agricultural, forestry and fishery organisations got involved. The campaign began under Zenchu's leadership involving prefectural Nokyo groups and the *sogo nokyo* and *senmon nokyo*, but it later extended to the National Chamber of Agriculture and then Zengyoren and Zenshinren. These groups launched their own special campaigns and conventions which mobilised a broad range of agricultural, forestry and fishery organisations nationally.

The length and breadth of the anti-agricultural trade liberalisation campaign was styled by Nokyo as a 'hundred years war' (*hyakunen senso*)[217] meaning a long-term campaign. Furthermore, there was an attempt to convert it into a truly national campaign by involving a broad cross-section of non-primary sector groups, and by appealing directly to the public in order to garner broad support for farmers' objectives.

As part of its increasingly high-gear campaign against agricultural trade liberalisation in the early to mid-1980s, agricultural groups launched a campaign that involved acting in concert with other types of organisations such as cultural associations, trade unions and consumers groups, beginning with Seikyo,[218] and emphasising the need for guarantees of safe food and stability of food supply. This campaign established connections with 42 consumers' groups in the Tokyo district alone, including regional women's associations and housewives' associations as well as chambers of commerce and industry, local government organisations and labour unions in a cross-sectoral alliance against import liberalisation. Many national and local organisations of these non-farm interest groups came out in support of Japanese agriculture. Nokyo held joint activities such as civic conferences on agriculture which these groups attended. In April 1982, the central headquarters met with leaders of the nation's major consumer organisations to seek their understanding of and support for the producers' position on agricultural trade. Subsequently, several meetings and debating sessions were held with leaders of various consumer organisations.[219] Consumer groups, as well as women's, youth and cultural associations also launched their own anti-liberalisation campaigns.[220]

In June 1984, the central headquarters hammered out a four-year action programme. It decided to establish a national council for protecting the nation's domestically produced food and its agriculture, fishery and forestry industries. The council, to be joined by consumers, housewives, youth leaders and union members, was designed to help shape economic policies that would mitigate economic friction with the country's major trading partners. In addition, the headquarters planned to step up information gathering and public relations activities by conducting opinion polls both in Japan and the United States and on-the-spot surveys abroad.[221]

The tactics of Nokyo's anti-agricultural trade liberalisation campaign thus emphasised the need to focus not only on policymakers but on the general public, particularly consumers, and on forming a united front with other key interest groups behind concerted publicity campaigns and other combined activities. In particular, Nokyo sought to establish coalitions with consumer groups. In a questionnaire survey of Nokyo chairmen regarding groups that Nokyo federations had lobbied on the issue of agricultural liberalisation, 63 per cent of respondents answered that they had lobbied consumer groups. This was the fourth highest on the list after the LDP (86 per cent), MAFF (80 per cent) and LDP local politicians (68 per cent).[222]

Nokyo deliberately orchestrated a strategy of forging a 'community of interest' between urban consumers and rural producers through roundtable discussions, conventions, national publicity campaigns and joint activities as well as the collection of millions of signatures on petitions opposing liberalisation. This strategy extended its mode of public campaigning around the producer rice price. An important part of these campaigns from the time RPAC deliberations began had always been the use of the mass media, including newspapers and TV, 'to deepen the understanding of consumers regarding the producer rice price'.[223] Furthermore, the goodwill of consumer organisations had always been necessary within the RPAC because of their representation on this council. For farmers, consumers were potent supporters. In addition to repeated petitions to the government and related agencies, the Central Headquarters for the Prevention of the Liberalisation and Quota Expansion of Agricultural Imports targeted publicity directly to consumers and wage-earners in order to obtain their understanding of the problem.

In this joint campaign, Nokyo played on consumer fears of the dangers of food additives and agricultural chemicals in imported foods and on anxieties about commodity shortages if Japan were to become too reliant on food imports. As Vogel reported, producer groups deliberately 'attempted to take advantage of the public's concern about health and safety in order to generate political support for continued restrictions on imports'.[224] Agriculture-related organisations, including Nokyo, disseminated a large number of publications on this topic, both the unscrupulous and the more respectable.[225]

During the beef and citrus negotiations in early 1988, Zenchu produced a videotape claiming that chemical preservatives in imported American food were making Japanese children ill.[226] The video was called 'You Still Eat That Stuff?' It showed American oranges and grapefruit being heavily doused with insecticides and toxic preservatives as well as rice being treated with dioxin prior to shipment overseas. The video depicted widespread public health problems, purportedly caused by US foodstuffs treated with toxic chemicals. Even more dramatically, it linked images of deformed human foetuses, children with strange diseases and citrus decaying on the docks with imported food from the United States.[227] The film's narrator noted that 'children's diseases are increasing in tandem with the rapid increase of imported foods and food additives'.[228] He asked rhetorically: 'Can this really be a simple coincidence? If Japanese consumers are being poisoned, is it good to have open trade with the United States?'[229]

The videos were ordered from Zenchu by agricultural cooperatives, labour unions, consumer groups, women's groups and schools. The total sold reached 4,000 copies, while another 40,000 pirated copies were believed to be in circulation. As Vogel reported: 'Encouraged by the films' popularity, Zenchu began to work with interested consumer and women's groups to arrange to have the film shown throughout Japan. Their campaign apparently struck a responsive chord among much of the Japanese public. One Western journalist noted in 1988, 'The fear of foreign food has taken hold of Japanese consumers, and like the rice issue, is growing beyond the reach of reason.'[230] Nokyo thus managed to turn the consumer debate into an issue of food safety rather than food prices.

Vogel also noted that in 1990, the Central Council of Dairy Farmers[231] ran a series of full-page ads in a number of Japanese newspapers expressing concern about the safety of 'Foreign-made Food' and arguing that 'domestic milk is safe.'[232] This campaign was provoked by a decision of the MAFF to import 3,000 tons of butter as an emergency measure.

Local Nokyo groups also formed some strange alliances in the late 1980s in the process of endeavouring to mobilise all means to resist agricultural trade liberalisation. In addition to seeking unprecedented relations with JCP-allied consumer cooperatives, they also held discussions with JCP members. For example, with the prospect of the liberalisation of citrus in the late 1980s, the Ehime Nokyo leaders and the JCP Prefectural Committee undertook a 'Roundtable Conference to Overcome the Crisis in Agriculture'.[233] There were also reports of farmer groups giving donations to consumer groups opposed to deregulation of rice imports.'[234]

Joint action was also reported between farmers' unions and consumers in western Japan over the government's decision to allow the import of frozen sushi from California. In October 1992, the government allowed the 'Sushi Boy' fast food chain, which operated 44 cut-price sushi restaurants in Osaka, to import less costly frozen American-made sushi. The farmers in question were the Osaka branch of Zennichino along with 20 local consumer groups. They sent telegrams to the importer and the MAFF and MOF urging them to stop the imports. According to a Zennichino spokesperson: 'Sushi is Japan's traditional delicacy. We would expect a restaurant which respects Japanese good tradition to not make a breakthrough for foreign rice imports . . . Consumers in Osaka are worried about the hygienic aspect of such imported food. Under the current law, consumers can't tell where the products are from and how safe the products are. Consumers are now more concerned about food safety rather than cost'.[235]

The anti-agricultural trade liberalisation campaign led by Nokyo was less productive in its approaches to labour organisations. The central head-quarters conferred with leaders of the nation's major labour groups, namely Sohyo, the Japanese Confederation of Labour (Domei) and the Federation of Independent Unions (Churitsu Roren).[236] Cooperation with labour groups, however, was more limited as some labour groups criticised agriculture.[237]

The approach to small business was more successful, because of the argument that agriculture was an essential industry for regional development. The chambers of commerce and industry in regional areas were responsive to calls for collaborative action, seeking as they were close cooperation and supportive solidarity with agriculture as an industry that was indispensable to the development of regional economies.[238]

Nokyo also regarded it as important to get the understanding of foreign organisations, beginning with agricultural groups in other countries. In the 1980s and early 1990s, a number of missions from the central headquarters were sent to GATT headquarters, OECD headquarters, EC headquarters and to the United States, Australia and New Zealand where they met represen-tative groups. The central headquarters also invited representatives of agricultural associations from the United States to Japan to promote their understanding of Japanese agriculture and to gain their support for the prevention of agricultural import liberalisation. In addition, farm groups came to Japan for negotiations and to deepen their understanding of Japanese agriculture.[239] At one point, Nokyo tried to engineer direct economic retaliation on American farm interests. In 1988 Zenno contracted to buy 500,000 tonnes of feed grains from non-US suppliers as a first retaliatory step against US pressure on Japan to liberalise food imports.[240]

Perhaps the most important dimension of the campaign was directed at winning the hearts and minds of the general public. At its national convention in October 1982, Nokyo set itself the task of publicising 'accurately the role and position of the agricultural cooperatives with the aim of obtaining the support and cooperation from people in every walk of life and undertaking informational activities designed to shape desirable public opinion concerning the importance of domestic agriculture and production.'[241]

Campaigns directed at the general public included a signature-collection drive staged nationwide in 1987 called the 'National Signature Campaign for Protection of Japan's Food and Preservation of Land'. It garnered more than three million signatures on a petition declaring opposition to agricultural trade liberalisation. The central headquarters also conducted active publicity campaigns involving mass gatherings of farmers in street marches nation-wide,[242] speeches on the streets by Nokyo leaders and the distribution of pamphlets and handbills. In July 1982 the central headquarters set up a mini-paddy field in Tokyo's Ginza to remind the people of the important role agriculture plays in the security of food.[243]

Nokyo and the farmers also sought the 'understanding' of urban dwellers to their plight by inviting them to sample the rice planting process and other agricultural activities. In 1990, a 'From Rural-to-Urban-District Message Campaign' was carried out, in which more than two million farmers mailed postcards to residents in urban regions asking for their understanding of agriculture's multifaceted role in society and the economy. In 1990, Zenchu issued a 'People's Statement Pondering Food and Agriculture in the 21st Century' to which 5,600 personalities and celebrities from various circles expressed their support. As explained by Zenchu, 'our long-term struggle gave top priority to the activities to obtain understanding and support from people in all walks of life for the position of farmers and the objectives of their movement.'[244] One of Zenchu's main organisers of the campaign against agricultural trade liberalisation in the 1980s, Ito Kenzo, noted in the introduction to his book that 'we must win national agreement [in support of Japanese agriculture in the face of American pressure for agricultural trade liberalisation]'.[245] In targeting the Japanese public, Nokyo was acknowledging the importance of maintaining public support for agricultural protection and tolerance of its costs.

It was clearly important for the case for agricultural protection to be argued on public interest grounds because this would automatically find much greater public acceptance than arguments based on farmers' self-interest. Zenchu thus tried to make the agricultural trade liberalisation issue a question of the survival of Japanese agriculture, equating market opening with the destruction of the farm economy. The mission of the central headquarters was depicted as taking 'the initiative in organizing a national campaign to ensure the survival of Japanese agriculture.'[246] The Nokyo campaign also laid stress on identifying issues of self-interest for other groups by citing national causes such as food security, food safety, preservation of Japan's national cultural heritage and environmentalism.[247] Nokyo developed an elaborate ideological justification of Japan's agricultural support and protection regime on these kinds of public interest grounds.[248]

The verbal reaction from Zenchu to the partial liberalisation of the Japanese rice market alleged, for example, that the government's decision amounted to 'the abandonment of the policy of self-sufficiency of food, and consequently the foundations of Japan's existence as a nation for now and the future.'[249] As one cynical commentator observed: 'The myth of the sanctity of agriculture – symbolised by the veneration accorded to rice – has been skilfully exploited for the past 40 years by Japan's powerful farm lobby.'[250]

What was unprecedented about the agricultural trade liberalisation campaign was its attempt to unite a broad cross-section of interested groups and the consuming public in a way that Nokyo's price and budget campaigns generally could not, given their narrow focus on the economic self-interest of farmers. Nokyo's mass media machinery operated in high gear throughout the anti-agricultural trade liberalisation campaign because of the importance placed on winning the widest possible public support for the agricultural protectionist cause. Because of Nokyo's skilful identification of the public interest aspects of agriculture, such as food self-sufficiency, food security and food safety, other groups, such as consumer organisations, saw their interests as also being engaged on the question of market opening and were thus mobilised alongside the agricultural cooperatives on an unprecedented scale. Opposition to agricultural trade liberalisation was a uniting force amongst these groups. Nokyo very skilfully manipulated and exploited the common ground that it was able to identify between farmers and other groups, striking a familiar chord with consumer organisations on issues such as food safety and playing on the fears of consumers generally.[251]

This strategy continued into the late 1990s. Although Zenchu acknowledged that it lost the fight on agricultural trade liberalisation, it credits itself with having gained sufficient public support from its anti-agricultural trade campaigns to mould 'a national consensus for the reconstruction of agriculture and the revitalization of rural communities.'[252] One of the main items on the agenda for the national convention of agricultural cooperatives in late 1994 was 'the strengthening of agricultural cooperative activities, such as the formation of friendly ties between cooperatives and consumers'.[253]

In the post-UR period, as cheaper food imports have penetrated the Japanese market, Nokyo has been aware that public consciousness of the relatively high prices of domestically produced food would rise, hence the need to keep the consumers aware of the farmers' position, and of their endeavours to lower costs. It remains one of Zenchu's objectives 'to develop a nationwide campaign to think about food issues in the 21st century.'[254]

Nokyo's policy influence

The political impact of Nokyo's policy campaigns and therefore its effectiveness as a pressure group can only be indirectly inferred from trends in government agricultural policy.[255] At any particular point in time, the factors actually influencing the government's agricultural pricing, budget and trade policy decisions are both complex and cross-cutting, and include not only political calculations relating to the farmers and Nokyo, but also macroeconomic and fiscal considerations, shifting priorities in agricultural policy and so on.[256] Moreover, when it comes to agricultural trade decisions, external pressure, particularly from the United States, is all-important.[257]

In other words, no general conclusions about the efficacy of Nokyo's policy campaigns can necessarily be drawn from short-run trends in agricultural support and stabilisation prices, from budgetary expenditure on agriculture or from government decisions on market access. Downward movement in agricultural support prices, for example, needs to be explained with reference to shifting government policy and budget priorities and does not necessarily indicate a commensurate decline in Nokyo's political influence.[258] The producer rice price, for example, was frozen in 1969 and 1970, just as it was in the late 1980s. Likewise, the government has executed various deregulatory moves with respect to the FC system over the years, in each case, overriding the strenuous objections of the agricultural cooperatives. In fact, when the introduction of IDR system was approved by the LDP in 1969, this decision rocked the Nokyo lobbyists, who had been feverishly pressuring members of the LDP. A rice-roots electoral revolt was also threatened by local Nokyo leaders and youth divisions in the provinces. Journalists at the time concluded that, as Nokyo depended to such a large extent on the ruling party, its objections no longer had any influence on the party, except when the LDP and the MAFF were at loggerheads over a particular issue.[259] Such a comment, however, takes no account of the various compensatory gestures that have been made towards Nokyo on each occasion FC reform was instituted.[260]

It is equally difficult to reach any conclusive observations about long-term trends in Nokyo's political influence from government decisions on agricultural trade policy. Although the liberalisation of beef in 1988 was widely interpreted as a symbol of the decline in Nokyo's power, the government embarked on as many if not more market opening moves in the mid- to late 1960s and early 1970s as it did in the late 1980s and early 1990s.[261] Similarly, the agricultural budget cuts of the early to mid-1980s were followed by increases in the late 1980s and early 1990s, and then the reinstitution of reductions in the mid-1990s.[262]

These twists and turns in government agricultural policy make it difficult to reach any definitive conclusions about Nokyo's effectiveness as a pressure group. The only consistent pattern over time is the ruling party's propensity to make decisions highly favourable to farmers and Nokyo when general elections are in the offing. On these occasions, political considerations seem to carry far greater weight than on occasions when elections are a more distant prospect.[263]

The empirical data from Muramatsu, Ito and Tsujinaka's study of Japanese pressure groups offers some indication of how agricultural organisations rated themselves in terms of policy influence. Although not confined to agricultural cooperative organisations, 83 per cent of the agricultural groups in the survey claimed that they had succeeded in influencing policy implementation, while 39 per cent claimed that they had successfully blocked certain policies.[264] About half (52 per cent) claimed that they were well known, were generally influential (48 per cent) and that their existence was essential (61 per cent).[265] On the basis of these figures, the authors concluded that agricultural groups had 'more or less strong influencing power'.[266] This was very much in line with Muramatsu's earlier analysis of Japanese pressure groups which reported that 43.5 per cent of agricultural groups evaluated their influence as 'fairly big', whilst 39.1 per cent rated it as 'big to a certain extent'. Only 8.7 per cent of agricultural groups thought their influence was 'very big', while an equally small proportion considered their influence to be 'not very big at all'.[267] These self-ratings by agricultural groups, although not confined to agricultural cooperative organisations, were well below administrative, educational and professional groups, and even below welfare groups, but slightly higher than economic groups.[268]

Perhaps the most useful measure of Nokyo's policy influence is to compare the content of its demands with actual policy outcomes. Evaluated in this way, Nokyo's record of success in extracting what it wants from government has been mixed. In almost all cases, not surprisingly, it has failed to achieve exactly what it was asking for. On the other hand, in almost all cases it has achieved some measure of what it was asking for, even if this only amounted to a delay in the execution of an unpopular government proposal.

In addition to these rather limited generalisations, several more specific observations can be volunteered. Nokyo lost the early rounds of agricultural trade liberalisation in the 1960s and early 1970s (the 1971 grapefruit liberalisation, for example, occurred in the face of strong opposition from Nokyo) and it failed to prevent the producer rice price freezes of 1969 and 1970. On the other hand, in most years until the late 1980s, the government awarded the farmers increases in the producer rice price, and from the early 1970s until the late 1980s, it refused to countenance any further liberalisation of agricultural markets. In the late 1980s and early 1990s, however, Nokyo conspicuously failed to win some high profile public battles over liberalisation and producer prices, which shifted to a predominantly freeze/decline mode.[269] Nokyo's 'success' was confined to extracting what it could from a deteriorating policy environment. With respect to the producer rice price, for instance, Nokyo was a significant player in the conversion of cuts into price freezes in the early 1990s. This is despite the fact that production costs of rice continued to fall.[270]

Over time, the general policy environment towards agricultural support and protection also became more antipathetic and hence Nokyo's demands were interpreted much more negatively in policy as well as public circles. Nokyo sustained rising levels of criticism for the conduct of its *nosei katsudo* (epitomised by the 1986 producer rice price campaign) as well as for the nature of its demands. In more recent times, these have been widely depicted as blatantly self-interested, shortsighted and failing to come to grips with the urgent need for structural adjustment in a declining sector. Critics have pointed to the traditional emphasis in *nosei katsudo* on demands for higher prices, subsidies and border protection rather than on constructive policies that would deal with the real problems facing farmers and which would work towards developing a more independent, viable farming sector. One disaffected group in Hokkaido argued: 'The same demands are repeated every year. In fact the central unions should be demanding that the agricultural administration make efforts to reduce production costs rather than demanding higher prices which invites opposition from consumers.'[271]

The public image of Nokyo has changed from one of an all-powerful colossus to a rather incompetent and ineffectual organisation whose past mistakes are catching up with it. In this context, Nokyo's agricultural policy failures have been just one more manifestation of the general crisis besetting the organisation. Opinion surveys show that whilst the Japanese public in the majority support food self-sufficiency, the advancement of agriculture and agricultural protection,[272] their perceptions of Nokyo are much more negative. The typical image that urban residents have of Nokyo is that it is a selfish and closed-minded organisation lacking in concern for consumer issues. In short, the consciousness of urban Japanese is pro-agriculture and anti-Nokyo.[273]

Signs of serious dissatisfaction are also emerging in the ranks of Nokyo members. Some criticisms are specifically directed towards the central unions – for their alleged failure of leadership on key agricultural policy issues including rice market opening, and for their inability to deal constructively with the new and more difficult policy environment in which Nokyo now operates. The central unions are also charged with being unable to meet the technical and policy needs of farmers facing the challenges of liberalisation. As one insider comments, 'what members expect is information on how to cope with internationalisation, changes in agricultural production, marketing, processing and market structure, trends in farm material prices, the agricultural price support system, agricultural technology and administration. The *chuokai* should deliver such information in an objective fashion. At the moment, however, the central unions only offer information that suits them and the federations.'[274] This criticism repeats the ever-more widely held view that Nokyo works in its own interests, rather than those of its members or the long-term interests of farmers.[275]

The result is increasing discontent amongst Nokyo's own membership with the conduct of *nosei katsudo* and consequently a growing sense of distance or 'separateness' between the farmers and their own organisation. Nokyo's ability to represent its core constituency is under challenge, with calls being made for farmers to get behind voluntary farmers' groups (*jishuteki nomin soshiki*) and farmers' campaigns (*nomin undo*).[276] Co-op members are particularly suspicious of the central unions' costly agricultural policy campaigns that are funded from levies on the sale of products handled by the co-ops. Many members do not know, for example, how their contributions to Zenchu for the *beika toso* have been used.[277] The morale in the 'rice price battle' which in the past used to unite Japanese farmers in a nationwide movement, inexorably diminished, making it difficult for Zenchu's Rice Policy Central Headquarters to issue directives to each prefecture to organise its own rice price convention. In the late 1980s and 1990s, some prefectures did not bother, and even amongst those that did, attendance was, in some cases, less than 100 farmers. The attitude of many Nokyo members was that the *beika toso* was only for growers in the main rice-producing prefectures, and if Nokyo could not get a rice price increase, then Nokyo's rice campaign levy should be lowered.[278]

The resentment towards the levies imposed by the upper echelons spread more generally, with some local agricultural cooperatives refusing to pay levies to the *chuokai* to fund their operations. They accused the central unions of supporting the profit principle of the *nokyo* and *rengokai* and of inflicting an unnecessary burden on farmers. According to one Nokyo source: 'Without the *chuokai*, the *tankyo* would be able to avoid huge levies and get a true agricultural policy for the farmers through the conduct of independent *nosei undo*.'[279]

Sakaguchi points out that few opportunities exist for regular co-op members to feel involved in relation to agricultural policy issues.[280] In his view, many members are abandoning Nokyo's policy activities and are not interested in Nokyo's support for political parties.[281] In 1983 in the wake of the quota expansion of beef and citrus imports, farmers in Ehime were asked what their attitudes were to Nokyo as a means of representing their interests. Only 35.5 per cent replied positively.[282] The 1994 polls amongst Nokyo's farmer members revealed an even greater decline in members' faith in their own organisation. An average of only 22.6 per cent of respondents thought that Nokyo should strengthen its agricultural policy activities.[283]

In this respect, Nokyo's failure to prevent the government's acceding to the UR Agreement on Agriculture was a watershed. Losing the battle over agricultural trade liberalisation at the UR demonstrated that, in a direct confrontation between external pressures and domestic resistance, Nokyo was compelled to accept government concessions each time.[284] The unsuccessful campaign against rice imports, more than any other single agricultural policy development, generated the greatest danger of Nokyo's losing the trust of its members.[285] From the farmers' perspective, it signalled the dwindling effectiveness of their representative organisation.

> For seven years from 1986 until 1993 Zenchu's member cooperatives had contributed to a special fund for the campaign against rice imports. After the 1993 rice market opening, it became more difficult to collect such donations from member organisations. Imports also affected rice farmers emotionally. The economic damage was difficult to calculate, but the psychological impact was great because farmers found it impossible to gauge the future of the rice market. Although Japanese farmers were expected to expand the scale of production, without a promising future for rice production, only a handful were prepared to invest money in purchasing new farmland or leasing it. The situation was not dissimilar to beef producers or vegetable producers because of rapidly increasing farm imports from China and SE Asia, especially fruit and vegetables.[286]

The 1993 rice market opening debacle gave Nokyo pause for reassessment of its pressure group tactics. A January 1994 document circulated by Zenchu amongst prefectural organisations as a basic agenda for organisational discussions contained a section entitled 'Issues Left by the Rice Market Liberalisation Prevention Campaign and Points to be Reflected'. In this section, Zenchu acknowledged a string of failures: that there was a limit to the lobbying activities of Nokyo and that it was unsuccessful in preventing the government from making the undesirable decision; that Nokyo had failed to respond flexibly to political changes (that is, the formation of the coalition government and the difficulties of targeting it on agricultural policy activities when it consisted of eight parties); that Nokyo was remiss in not investigating the truth of the statement by the PM and others that they would guarantee to 'maintain existing policies'; that Nokyo was inadequate in dealing with the anti-agriculture influence on public opinion of business circles and the mass media; that Nokyo failed to reinforce campaigns to prevent trade liberalisation for agricultural products other than rice; and that Nokyo had no comprehensive ideology that supported the protection of family farming systems all over the world.[287] Elsewhere, Zenchu also acknowledged that it 'failed to put up effective opposition to the tide of opinions favoring agricultural liberalization because it had no negotiating power.'[288]

In a similar vein, Nokyo executives argued that the reason why Nokyo failed to defend Japan's agricultural protection in the UR was because it relied too much on the LDP to communicate with the coalition government (on whose authority the ultimate decision rested). Although Nokyo made an effort to obtain information on the GATT agricultural negotiations from the ruling coalition parties, it was difficult for Nokyo, which had always supported the LDP, to develop a close relationship with the new ruling parties. In short, Nokyo was hobbled by its long history of close relations with the LDP regime.[289] In its own estimation, it was also disadvantaged by the widespread perception that Japanese agriculture had a large external impact because agricultural protection policies had become an international issue.[290]

In a more general assessment of Nokyo's pressure group tactics, Fujitani describes its *nosei katsudo* as too old-fashioned in their dependence on petitions and on the lobbying of Diet members. Even Nokyo's media activities aimed at engendering public support lacked a strong theoretical basis employing logical arguments about the impact of food imports on international agricultural trade and the public good that agriculture as an industry serves.[291] Furthermore, as a former Zenchu Managing Director observed, it was difficult for Nokyo to show a future vision of Japanese agricultural policy. After liberalisation, prevailing trends in agricultural policy and what Nokyo wanted were on a diverging course. It insisted on upholding the current system of support and protection, but agricultural policy had changed.[292]

As the tide slowly turned in favour of liberalisation and deregulation in the early 1990s, Nokyo became both more defensive and more realistic in pressing its case. The Managing Director of Zenchu acknowledged in 1993 that it was 'unrealistic to assume that the government in financial difficulties will continue costly agricultural subsidy schemes and maintain high producer rice price indefinitely. The only option left for Japanese agriculture is to increase the scale of production in order to reduce the cost of production.'[293]

Subsequently, in the lead-up to the 1994 national Nokyo convention, Zenchu Chairman, Toyoda Hakaru, admitted in an interview that further opposition to rice liberalisation was futile and possibly even counter-productive insofar as it might jeopardise the sort of compensation deal the government would negotiate on behalf of the rural sector. He acknowledged that 'agricultural cooperatives should concentrate on more realistic demands.'[294] This response was endorsed by the interviewer who commented that the activities of the agricultural cooperatives had 'shifted considerably to a more realistic line'[295] in order to gain and keep the understanding of the general public. In particular, Nokyo needed to secure the continuing understanding of consumers.

Nokyo's changing relationship with the MAFF and the LDP

The factors contributing to the slow decline in Nokyo's influence as a pressure group are also affecting its relationship with key actors in the government. The core of Nokyo's influence has been its economic and political power, but as this is assailed by a multitude of unfavourable developments, Nokyo has become more vulnerable in its relations with both the MAFF and the LDP. Given Nokyo's traditionally 'strong dependence on politics',[296] the potential shift in the delicate balance of power between Nokyo and these two major institutions is a critical development.

In relation to the MAFF, Nokyo has had to throw itself increasingly on to the mercies of its administrative supervisor, but at the same time, in order to retain its influence, trade more of its vested rights. Evidence of Nokyo's lower standing can be seen in the reduction of its traditional functions in, and associated benefits from the FC system. By the late 1980s, the Food Agency was seeking to reform the FC system, not only in order to save the associated costs, but also to be able to retain those elements that would protect its position and which were viable in an era of impending liberalisation. The collection power of Zenno, however, with its 95 per cent share of the IDR market, had become an obstacle to the Food Agency's plan. Zenno's basic demand was to keep the right to decide the price of semi-controlled rice because it had begun to have a sense of crisis about the future of its rice marketing business. Its preponderant share was sustained by the FC system and the uniform rice acreage reduction policy. Rice market deregulation threatened both these policies because it encouraged a shift from a uniform *gentan* policy to selective production adjustment. If the latter were adopted, local co-ops and the farmers would have independent ideas about rice production and marketing, abandoning the trust of rice sales to Zenno.[297]

Discord between Zenno and the Food Agency became serious after the establishment of the IDR Price Formation Organisation in 1990.[298] Two main areas of conflict emerged. One was the creation of a new route through which the *keizairen* could sell rice directly to wholesalers without entrusting it to Zenno, and the other was over the rules for the new rice market for independently traded rice. The permissible price range in this market was the biggest issue. When the market opened in late 1990, Zenno opposed the price-bidding range that was accepted (10 per cent).[299] Under pressure from Zenno, the Food Agency finally adopted a bidding rule that limited price variations to a 7 per cent range.[300] Nevertheless, the Food Agency became increasingly frustrated with Nokyo and continued to argue for the introduction of market mechanisms into rice sales. In 1992, it began gradually to reduce the subsidies for the operation of the IDR system including those outlaid to the agricultural cooperatives. In spite of opposition from Nokyo, the amount of subsidies allocated to the agricultural cooperatives for market promotion of independently distributed rice in 1995 fell to half the 1985 level.[301]

Nokyo also opposed the proposals for FC reform in 1994, because reducing controls would introduce unwanted competition into a lucrative market.[302] Agricultural cooperative groups led by Zenchu launched a special campaign to reflect their demands on the issue of FC reform, threatening to prevent the ratification of the GATT agreement if their opinions were not reflected in the new arrangements. One of Nokyo's principal objections was to the 'uncontrolled' entry of new players into the rice collection market. The response from some MAFF officials was unsympathetic. In their view Nokyo had to be less dogmatic and more realistic in its requests in relation to this issue.[303]

During the negotiations over the new system, it was consistently clear where Zenchu's priorities lay. Its foremost imperative was to protect Nokyo's vested interests in rice collection and marketing, and in particular, the three-stage federated system of rice distribution involving the *nokyo*, *keizairen* and Zenno. Zenchu responded unfavourably to farmers' demands for direct sales to wholesalers and retailers, arguing that 'direct sales by producers would lead to increases in grains out of control'.[304] It wanted at all costs to avoid direct sales by farmers and *nokyo* to wholesalers and retailers, thus bypassing the *keizairen* and Zenno. What Zenchu feared on this issue was pressure from Zenno and the *keizairen*. Zenchu's policies throughout the rice marketing reform process aimed to maintain the interests of Zenno and the *keizairen* because these organisations were the major economic powerhouses standing behind Zenchu. At the same time, Zenchu was in favour of a policy that would allow direct sales of rice by Nokyo.[305] In the final analysis, Zenchu's opposition to the changes in the FC system suddenly melted when it was offered agricultural and rice distribution subsidies. The delivery of this funding would follow the customary three-stage Zenno > *keizairen* > *nokyo* route, as before. Nokyo's key representative in negotiating this outcome as part of the deal for the new food system was a Zenno Managing Director.[306]

Nevertheless, FC reform was substantially less than a total victory for Nokyo.[307] With its passage, the 1994 Staple Food Law amounted to a direct attack on Nokyo's dominance of the rice collection and distribution market. Some commentators even argued that the new Food Law could be interpreted as the equivalent of an Agricultural Cooperative Reform Law.[308] Under the new system, farmers were no longer obliged to use the co-ops as their primary collectors; they could bypass them and sell so-called 'free-market rice' directly to consumers and retailers in what amounted to a legalisation of the 'black market' sales route. Moreover, the rice distribution system was substantially opened up to other participants in addition to the agricultural cooperatives.

The new law permitted private companies to register as rice collectors, whole-salers and retailers in order to encourage greater competition in rice collection and marketing. The government preserved some aspects of Nokyo's privileged position in IDR and government rice channels sufficiently to secure its continuing cooperation with rice acreage reductions. Since 1987, Nokyo had been integrated into the rice paddy diversion scheme as means of encouraging farmers' compliance with planned rice acreage production cutbacks,[309] and from Nokyo's perspective, as a means of increasing its bargaining power as a pressure group on rice issues.[310] Because of mounting rice stockpiles in the 1994–96 period, rice acreage set asides rose as high as 700,000 hectares in 1995 and 800,000 hectares in 1996.[311]

On a more general level, deregulation of the FC system symbolised the increasing trend towards liberalisation of many aspects of the agricultural support and protection regime in Japan and thus anticipated a declining role for Nokyo as a corporatist intermediary in the policy implementation process. This potentially affected Nokyo's position in relation to the agricultural administration and its role in agricultural policies, which posed a long-term threat to its standing as a key actor in the agricultural policymaking process. As Fujitani puts it, deregulation of rice reduced Nokyo's role as a semi-administrative arm of government, which undermined its capacity as a pressure group.[312] Just as Nokyo increased its bargaining power with the government by playing a crucial role in the administration of agricultural policies, this bargaining power came under challenge from a contraction in this role.

Nokyo's relationship with the LDP, on the other hand, has been vulnerable to a reassessment in the value of the farm vote to the ruling party and the party's perception of Nokyo's declining capacities to collect votes. Tanaka in fact traces Nokyo's dependence on the LDP back to the late 1950s and the beginning of the LDP's long-term rule, which forced Nokyo to abandon its principle of political neutrality. He argues that a crucial weak point in Nokyo's *nosei katsudo* is its 'weakness' *vis-à-vis* the ruling party and its 'capture' by the party at the electoral level. He attributes Nokyo's compliance with the introduction of the IDR system in 1969 to this weakness, observing that Nokyo's objections to proposed policies meant nothing unless the government and the ruling party confronted each other or there was internal conflict in the ruling party over a particular issue. In the case of the intro-duction of IDR system, a majority of LDP Diet members felt that they had no choice but to agree to the system given the continuing expansion in the rice surplus, and hence Nokyo had to fall into line.[313]

Ono, however, traces the crucial turning point in the balance of power between Nokyo and the LDP back to 1970 and the introduction of rice acreage reduction cutbacks. He argues that because many farmers gave up rice growing and no longer welcomed agricultural subsidies which imposed additional loan burdens on the farmers themselves (for land improvement, for example), Nokyo's vote-collecting power declined. Rice prices and agricultural subsidies were no longer political goods desired by these farmers. This precipitated a gradual process of Nokyo's subordination to the LDP.[314]

It was in the 1980s, however, that the electoral value of the farmers' vote underwent much more significant reassessment in LDP circles because of the rise in support for the party in urban areas.[315] It was in this context that PM Nakasone (1982–87) made a concerted attempt to undermine Nokyo's power as well as the FC system. He was also behind Tamaki Kazuo's criticism of Nokyo.[316] The series of decisions expanding agricultural import quotas for beef and citrus in 1983, followed by the producer rice price cut in 1987 and the agricultural trade liberalisation moves in the late 1980s, were clearly influenced by electoral trends, symbolising the changing relationship between the LDP and Nokyo. This has made it more difficult for Nokyo to rely on its traditional political allies in the LDP to undermine any reformist impulses within the MAFF which might reduce levels of benefits to Nokyo.

Uneasiness in the LDP–Nokyo relationship surfaced at the September 1983 Nokyo's representatives' convention 'To Prevent the Liberalisation of Agricultural Imports and the Expansion in Import Quotas' held under the auspices of Zenchu. At this meeting, a local co-op leader from Ibaraki criticised Nokyo's 'timid' campaign against import liberalisation and proposed that the LDP should not be supported in the forthcoming election. Those 80 LDP *norin giin* in attendance reacted extremely negatively to this suggestion. In particular it incurred the wrath of Eto Takami, Chairman of CAPIC and Nakao Eiichi, Chairman of the AFD's Agricultural, Forestry and Fisheries Products Import Liberalisation Problem Sub-Committee who stood up shouting 'What are you talking about?'[317] The LDP delegation to the convention promptly walked out. After the incident, the Zenchu Board of Directors immediately expressed official regret, agreed not to permit such an incident to happen again and confirmed Nokyo's 'moderate approach'. Iwamochi Shizuo, Zenchu Chairman, also apologised at a joint meeting of the LDP's agricultural committees the following day. Two official apologies were carried in the *Nihon Nogyo Shinbun*, with the newspaper calling the LDP's *norin giin* comrades.

These acts of contrition made a mockery out of Nokyo's principle of 'political neutrality'. Nokyo reacted as if it were the LDP's subordinate organisation, obliged to apologise for daring to contemplate another political alternative. As Ono explains, the behaviour of the LDP *norin giin* was explicable in one of two ways: a sense of isolation in the party because their involvement in agriculture, forestry and fisheries was not carrying much weight in the party; or a feeling of crisis over the unreliability of Nokyo as a vote-gathering machine, despite their commitment to agricultural policy.[318] In the subsequent LH election, the LDP's performance suffered in rural areas, with its share of the vote rising in the cities and falling in rural areas (see Table 5.10).

Friction again arose during the 1984 producer rice price campaign when Iwamochi and Ishibashi Masashi, JSP Secretary-General, met to discuss the issue. The LDP *kome giin* in the Noshinkyo criticised Nokyo over the meeting, accusing it of trying to curry favour with the Opposition and 'relying on the JSP'.[319] Once again, Zenchu executives were forced to apologise for their behaviour in order to placate their primary allies within the ruling party. Clearly the balance of power in the relationship had changed, with some erosion of electoral value on Nokyo's part resulting in a derogation of its position *vis-à-vis* the LDP, thus compelling a more conciliatory approach. As Ono put it, given its declining ability to collect votes. Nokyo needed to sidle up to the government party in a humble manner.[320]

Henceforth, Nokyo's subordinate posture *vis-à-vis* the LDP was visible in almost every aspect of its agricultural policy activities.[321] Nokyo traded significant concessions in 1986, for example, in exchange for the LDP's engineering the freeze in the producer rice price. The first of these concessions was that Nokyo would not complain even if the rice price formula which should have reduced prices by 6.6 per cent in 1986 were adopted in 1987. In fact, as noted above, the producer rice price ended up being cut by 5.7 per cent in 1987. Secondly, Nokyo would promote the rice acreage reduction policy responsibly, in spite of the fact that the total acreage set-aside was expanded and subsidies supporting the policy were largely curtailed owing to administrative reform.[322]

Likewise in the sales tax debacle of 1987, Nokyo supported the Nakasone initiative to introduce a sales tax on the condition that agriculture-related materials would be exempt. This allied Nokyo with its arch enemy – large-scale enterprise – which was causing friction in the US–Japan relationship and generating American pressure for agricultural trade liberalisation. Although the farmers were due to be severely hit by the sales tax, Nokyo persisted in endorsing it because it feared that if it did otherwise, the LDP would abandon it.[323] Ono argues that Nokyo's subordination to the LDP accelerated the loss of its initiative towards MAFF bureaucrats. For example, it became customary for Zenchu to consult with the MAFF about draft resolutions to be presented to the Nokyo convention held every three years, including the usage of particular words.[324]

After the 1989 UH election debacle and the LDP's subsequent loss of power in the early 1990s, farmers' votes regained much of their previous value, but at the same time, objective estimates of this value remain subject to demographic trends as well as to electoral system restructuring. In this new political environment, Nokyo's relationship with the LDP may again start to weaken, particularly if the party responds to the increasing need to cultivate voters in city areas. For example, an important actor in the development of proposals for FC reform in 1994 was Matsuoka Toshikatsu, an ex-MAFF official first elected to the Lower House for Kumamoto in 1990.[325] His proposals, which he had developed with some of his Diet colleagues, were first announced in April 1994. The Kumamoto Prefecture Nokyo Central Union was stunned by Matsuoka's actions, because only four months previously, he had strenuously objected to the liberalisation of rice imports alongside the major Nokyo organisations. Nevertheless, in justifying his move, Matsuoka said: 'The increase in rice traded on the black market makes the FC system a dead letter. I do not intend to destroy Nokyo, but it is difficult to say that I will support and protect Nokyo in the future. I understand the situation in domestic agriculture very well, so I have developed a reform plan.'[326]

Matsuoka's proposals were interpreted as part of a strategy of advantageous positioning in the new electoral system in which he would have found it difficult to gain a majority of votes in his new single-member electorate of Kumamoto (3) by relying solely on Nokyo-related votes. A reorientation towards attracting votes from consumers was called for. Matsuoka's approach suggested that LDP–Nokyo cooperation, which had for so long guaranteed the LDP a large proportion of farmers' votes and which in return had produced a number of agricultural policies in favour of farmers, had begun to change.[327]

These developments occurred alongside Nokyo's increasing dependence on its political connections. From Nokyo's perspective, the severe situation for agricultural cooperative business and financial management and the more antipathetic policy environment for agricultural support and protection meant a rise in the number of occasions in which Nokyo organisations needed to rely on political power in order to realise their agricultural policy demands. This situation was a strong spur to rice-roots political activities such as *nosei katsudo* and *senkyo katsudo* amongst the farmers. In short, it became even more important to support those Diet and prefectural assembly members who were able to reflect the demands of farmers and Nokyo in policymaking contexts.[328]

Given these strengthening imperatives, the question of where Nokyo's major party allegiance lay also became more crucial. The fluid party situation of the early 1990s has more latterly stabilised into a new status quo with the LDP continuing to dominate government ranks. The question facing Nokyo, however, is whether its strategy of working through the LDP will remain viable for the foreseeable future, or whether it might be more advisable to pursue a strategy of 'equidistant diplomacy' in relation to the LDP and the new centrist Opposition parties.[329]

Policy demands for a new era

In the wake of across-the-board agricultural trade liberalisation measures mandated by the UR Agreement on Agriculture, Nokyo mounted a concerted campaign to extract the largest possible compensatory settlement for farmers. The campaign was led by Zenchu's Emergency Agriculture and Rural Policy Headquarters set up for this express purpose. Because the final deal in the form of a UR countermeasures policy[330] amounted to the enormous sum of ¥6.01 trillion, Zenchu sought to repair the damage done to Nokyo's popular image by placing renewed emphasis on gaining the understanding and agreement of the people with the farmers' and agricultural cooperatives' position.

The countermeasures policy was widely perceived as exceedingly generous and a blatant concession to farmers' interests prior to the 1996 LH elections under the new electoral system.[331]

As ruling party politicians became more susceptible to fiscal considerations in the wake of the election,[332] however, indications emerged of a possible revision and contraction in the government's total expenditure commitment to the UR countermeasures policy. Nokyo responded by mobilising energetic 'demand activities' to secure the entire expenditure framework of the UR-related countermeasures policy during the first half of 1997 as part of its annual budget campaign. Led by Zenchu and Zenkoku Noseikyo, it targeted a whole range of key government and LDP leaders (including the MOF Minister, the MAFF Vice-Minister, the Chairman of the PARC and the Chairmen of the AFD, CAPIC and LDP's Fiscal Reform Committee) as well as the LDP's Uruguay Round-Related Policy Implementation Promotion Sub-Committee (a sub-committee of the AFD).[333]

In association with the launching of the original UR countermeasures policy, Zenchu had also set in motion a publicity campaign justifying the level of expenditure in terms of agriculture's role in supplying food to the nation and also its multifaceted role in the lives of the people.[334] This subsequently evolved into a campaign to promote the establishment of a New Agricultural Basic Law, led by Zenchu in cooperation with the Zenkoku Noseikyo. This was initiated partly to help overcome the disappointment of farmers with the acceptance of the GATT trade agreement. The UR countermeasures policy stipulated that the MAFF would set to work to formulate a New ABL. The new law was seen as laying down the basic philosophy whereby agriculture would continue to receive support from the government and as establishing the basic goals of agricultural policy. It would also provide the philosophical underpinnings of the government's stance at the next round of global farm trade liberalisation talks under WTO auspices due to start in 1999/2000.[335] Zenchu was intent on using the opportunity of revising the law to prevent any further fall in the self-sufficiency rate. This effectively meant preventing any decline in budget support and subsidies for farmers.

After implementation of the new Staple Food Law, Nokyo was also forced to adjust and refocus its demands in relation to rice. It ceased issuing its annual rice price demand and developed a new 'rice strategy' (*kome senryaku*), concentrating on requests for a 'new rice policy'. This involved budgetary expenditure for 'sufficient' production adjustment measures, the preservation of orderly marketed rice (an area where Zenno retained dominant control over distribution) and a price policy (i.e. continuing rice price support) in the interests of stabilising rice crop management.[336] Each of these areas required budget support: subsidies for rice production adjustment, subsidies associated with the operation of the IDR system and subsidies for producer prices.

Just prior to the government's announcement of its new rice policy in November 1997, Zenchu and Zenkoku Noseikyo held a 'National Assembly of Representatives for the Establishment of a Rice Policy and for the Stabilisation of Rice Crop Management', with approximately 1,200 representatives from local agricultural cooperatives attending as well as a number of LDP *norin zoku*. This was followed by another 'National Assembly of Representatives To Demand A Source of Revenue for the Establishment of a Rice Policy', attended by 1,300 Nokyo representatives and *norin zoku*, held immediately prior to the government's decision. Zenchu and the Zenkoku Noseikyo also held a separate national demand assembly for the purpose of presenting rice policy-related requests to the SDP and the Shinto Sakigake as participants in the loose governing alliance. In addition, Zenkoku Noseikyo executives held a rice policy roundtable conference with LDP agriculture and forestry committee executives (*norin kanbu*), who consisted of the CAPIC Chairman, the AFD Chairman, the Chairman of the LDP's Rice Price Committee (a joint sub-committee of CAPIC and the AFD) and three other prominent LDP agricultural policy leaders. Nokyo representatives subsequently met with the Japan Agricultural Policy-Nokyo Diet Members' League to demand the realisation of a new rice policy and guarantees of sufficient funding for its implementation.

Noseiren affiliated to Zenkoku Noseikyo also issued requests to their local Diet members for the establishment of a rice policy. Local members were invited to assemblies held in Tokyo for this purpose by the organisations in each prefecture. Finally, Zenkoku Noseikyo and Zenchu sponsored a mass rally of Nokyo representatives 'to break through the rice crop management crisis' at LDP headquarters in order to present last minute demands to the LDP for the establishment of a new rice policy. In short, no political target was left untouched by the blanket campaign. As the movement showed, however, the traditional focus on the producer rice price had been finally replaced with a broadly based demand for a multifaceted rice policy that included pricing matters but was not fixated on them.

Nokyo congratulated itself that its energetic campaign for a new rice policy was rewarded with the allocation by government of ¥610.1 billion as a source of revenue for the policy over two years beginning in fiscal 1998. It consisted of three elements: production adjustment, stabilisation of rice production management (under a new income compensation system for rice farmers) and improvement in the management of orderly marketed rice. The bulk of subsidies to achieve these goals would be channelled through Zenno.[337] The policy was mainly to compensate rice farmers who agreed to limit paddy cultivation to help ease the rice surplus that had reached 3.7 tonnes by October 1997. Under the new income compensation system, farmers would be indemnified for a possible drop in their incomes whenever the market price fell below the 'standard price', to be officially calculated using the average market price of rice over the previous three years. Compensation would be limited to independently distributed rice produced by farmers who met their production adjustment targets. Farmers would be compensated for 80 per cent of the difference between the two prices.[338] This group had been hardest hit by the fall in the prices of independently distributed rice since 1995 (it dropped from just over ¥20,000 in 1995 to just over ¥17,000 in late 1997).

In the overall outcome on the new rice policy, Nokyo nevertheless had to trade some key concessions: a cut in the producer rice price by 2.5 per cent for 1998 rice; total cooperation with the *gentan* (in 1995–96, Nokyo had said it was willing to buy rice even from those farmers who did not obey the *gentan* policy, thus encouraging farmers not to follow the policy); an expanded area for production adjustment in fiscal 1998 (which it had previously opposed, wanting to keep both price supports and acreage); a limit set on the volume of rice purchased by the government to ensure appropriate rice stocks (a maximum of two million tonnes); a review of the policy of maintaining rice prices by keeping rice reserves off the market; abolition of subsidies for rice marketed through non-government channels; and introduction of the income compensation scheme in lieu of price supports for farmers who cut back rice acreage.[339] The latter was a radical departure from the previous rice price support system because of the shift to an income compensation scheme funded jointly by farmers and the government.

The 1997 policy followed hard on the heels of a similar set of trade-offs in November 1996. A cut in the government purchasing price for rice for the first time in six years was achieved by keeping the targeted amount for rice production adjustment at the same level. In three-way discussions involving Zenchu, the LDP and the MAFF, a ¥10 billion subsidy linked to the achievement of the *gentan* policy was also successfully negotiated. Zenchu demanded an improvement in relief measures for the negative effects of the *gentan* policy in exchange for its enforcement and the cut in the government rice price. As the savings in the producer rice price amounted to less than half that figure (¥3.5–4.0 billion), the government came out of the deal an obvious loser. It was not absolutely clear to whom the *gentan* subsidy would be paid, however. In theory, if it were linked to the achievement of rice acreage reduction, it should have been paid to farmers, but it appeared as if it would be paid to distributors, the majority of whom were agricultural cooperatives. This was because management of the agricultural cooperatives had become much more difficult owing to the departure of many of their farmer members.[340]

The scoreboard for Nokyo's policy campaigns in the 1998–99 period records its continuing acquisition of concessions from the government on some key issues, although it has been obliged to trade benefits in some instances. Even more importantly it has been compelled to accommodate changes to some of the bedrock premises on which agricultural policy has been formulated over the past three to four decades.

On an issue that is central to Nokyo's interests, the government has continued to deregulate the rice market even beyond the changes introduced by the new Staple Food Law, with further changes to the operations of the IDR price-setting centre.[341] In a move endorsed by Zenchu, the Food Agency in June 1998 announced that it would convert the centre into Japan's first fully fledged rice exchange to enable prices directly to reflect supply and demand conditions and to encourage more flexible price setting. All limits on price fluctuations to protect the farmers and the co-ops were scrapped and the tradeable volume of rice was reviewed as well as the frequency of bidding. Rice varieties passing through the exchange were expanded as was the range of market participants. Henceforth, the Agency permitted the new exchange to receive payments previously handled by Zenno.[342]

In contrast, the LDP's tax reform package for fiscal 1998 was a clear and unequivocal victory for the agricultural cooperatives. They sought and obtained cuts in the tax rate imposed on agricultural cooperatives which matched the reductions in corporate tax rates. Initially, the plan did not include any tax rate cuts for the co-ops, but a visit en masse by Nokyo officials together with supportive LDP *norin zoku* to the LDP tax panel considering the reforms, as well as a deluge of faxes calling for a lighter tax burden, resulted in a lowering of the tax rate on agricultural and other cooperatives by two percentage points.[343]

Nokyo's major campaign in 1998–99, however, has focused on the New ABL. Early in the piece Zenchu established a special recommendation committee to discuss what kind of new basic law should be worked out. The committee subsequently announced a series of proposals and requested Diet members and the MAFF to support them.[344] Zenchu's demands in relation to this law centred on the need for continuing recognition of agriculture's role in the stable supply of food (in particular specifying target self-sufficiency rates that would justify the maintenance of agricultural support and protection for certain products); on the multifaceted functions of agriculture and rural areas; and on promoting environmentally sustainable agriculture and the food industry. It also stressed the need to maintain a price and incomes policy for farmers, a comprehensive land utilisation policy for agricultural production, a basic policy for the revitalisation of disadvantaged areas such as mountainous regions, as well as new agricultural trade rules that respected agricultural production for food security and environmental purposes.[345]

The campaign concentrated on gaining the support of the Japanese public for these objectives by launching a signature-collection drive aimed at obtaining the signatures of 10 million people on a petition requesting the establishment of a New ABL. The collection campaign (supported by the *kenchu*, the prefectural *noseiren*, local agricultural cooperatives, the National Council of Nokyo Women's Organisations, the National Council of Nokyo Youth Organisations, the National Chamber of Agriculture, prefectural chambers of agriculture and local agricultural committees) was conducted in 1997–98 throughout Japan, including the centre of Tokyo, where consumers (salarymen and 'OL' – office ladies) were directly targeted and small packages of high quality rice were given out. The sign boards read 'Food and agriculture are a topic for the whole nation. Please cooperate by signing this petition'. Nokyo recognised that national understanding was absolutely crucial for the success of its campaign. It aimed for a national agreement on the law that would be understood and supported by those who were engaged in agriculture as well as by the general public, especially consumers and city dwellers.

The petition requested that the government clarify a domestic production plan in order to supply safe food in a stable fashion; establish measures to stabilise agricultural management; ensure and train farm successors based on family farming; implement an appropriate agricultural pricing policy and a policy to support the income of farmers; preserve the total amount of agricultural land and promote its effective and continuous usage; prohibit jointstock companies from owning farmland; establish a basic policy for supporting the revitalisation of disadvantaged areas such as mountainous regions and provide favourable living conditions for farmers who live in such places; seek new agricultural trade rules that respect the continuous agricultural production of each nation for food security and protection of the global environment.[346]

The final tally of signatures collected by January 1998 was 10,565,008. Nokyo was particularly pleased that its campaign attracted support from consumer cooperatives, from the food industry and rice traders, and from city dwellers in metropolitan areas, which it took to indicate that the movement was supported and understood by a wide range of classes. The signature campaign also provided an opportunity for Nokyo groups to expand their exchanges with consumer groups and labour unions. In Hiroshima Prefecture, for example, the breakdown of supporting signatures was as follows: agricultural cooperatives within the prefecture – 445,611; Nokyo federations – 93,786; passers-by – 15,492; people connected to the prefectural agricultural committee (including the agricultural mutual aid associations, land improvement federations and agricultural development public companies) – 28,589; prefectural forestry cooperative federations – 333; prefectural fisheries federations – 970; prefectural consumers' associations – 150; the Hiroshima consumers' cooperative – 45,577; the prefectural Labour Union Council and the prefectural People's Council – 22,647, making a total of 653,605.[347]

The list was sent to the Prime Minister, the MAFF Minister, the Chairman of the PM's special investigation committee charged with coming up with a blueprint for the New Agricultural Basic Law (the Food, Agriculture and Rural Areas Basic Problems Investigation Committee) and other relevant persons. Backed up by their petition containing 10 million signatures, in December 1997 the leaders of Nokyo and Zenkoku Noseikyo demanded the establishment of the new law from PM Hashimoto, MAFF Minister Shimamura Yoshinobu, LDP Secretary-General Kato Koichi, Chief Secretary of the Cabinet Muraoka Kanezo and the Chairman of the PM's Food, Agriculture and Rural Areas Basic Problems Investigation Committee. Follow-up meetings with the new MAFF Minister, Nakagawa Shoichi, including a delegation of the Zenkoku Noseikyo executive, was organised after the Obuchi government came to power.

Throughout the period of deliberation on the content of the new law, Zenchu continued to galvanise farmers and Nokyo officials in assemblies, meetings, rallies and other kinds of gatherings to which leading agricultural politicians from the LDP were invited.[348] Some of these gatherings were held in cooperation with the NCA, Zenshinren and Zengyoren. Nokyo was eager to put its imprint on the final draft of the new legislation, because the New ABL, like its predecessor, would lay down the ideological principles and legal foundation not only for other agricultural laws, but also for agricultural policy in general, agricultural trade policy specifically and the annual agricultural budget into the new millennium. It would be a new agricultural policy constitution.

Three crucial issues for resolution in the debate over the New ABL were whether jointstock companies would be able to purchase farmland (for purposes of corporate enterprise farming), whether the government should shift to a direct incomes policy for farmers (*chokusetsu shotoku seisaku*) in place of the long-standing price support policy, and what food self-sufficiency ratios should be set for individual products. Nokyo's position on the first was that the family farm formed the basis of agricultural production and it opposed the rights of jointstock companies to own and cultivate farmland.[349] From Nokyo's perspective, farming by such companies would encourage speculation in farmland, risk the termination of the agricultural operations of these companies and the disposal of agricultural land for other purposes if they became unprofitable,[350] erode traditional human relations within rural communities and spell the end for small farmers. Nokyo's real concern was that the basis of its membership and of the patronage of its services – the farm household – would be destroyed if private enterprise entered the picture. In particular Nokyo feared the establishment of direct channels by trading companies and restaurant chains with agricultural production companies, thus bypassing Nokyo and undermining its customer base.[351] The final report of the Basic Problems Investigation Committee in September 1998, however, recommended that farms be allowed to form themselves into jointstock companies and that outside companies could own stakes in farming concerns.

With respect to a direct income support policy, Nokyo pressed for a new income compensation policy to be incorporated into the new law in order to prevent a negative impact on farmers from the increased introduction of market principles to agriculture. On the other hand, it maintained that Japan could not easily institute direct income support and therefore an income compensation policy appropriate to the Japanese agricultural situation should be pursued.

In its final set of recommendations on the New ABL in September 1998, the PM's investigation committee resorted to familiar exhortations about the need to make further use of market principles in setting prices for farm products in order that they accurately reflect trends in demand and the market's evaluation of product quality.[352] The report called for subsidies to lessen the impact on farmers' incomes. If prices tumbled and caused a major dent in farmers' incomes, then the government should compensate for the losses.[353] On the question of setting a clear numerical target for food self-sufficiency for which Nokyo was pressing (it called for the overall ratio to be set at 50 per cent), the Committee took refuge in the vague conclusion that: 'Based on understanding from the public, setting a target for Japan's food self-sufficiency ratio is valuable as a production and consumption guideline'.[354] This amorphous statement committed itself to the need for some sort of guideline, but only one that was supported by a national consensus that would include both consumers and producers. Nokyo's demand, however, was for a clear target ratio to be set in the legislation. If this subsequently became a production target, it would justify a call for subsidies and other forms of support to enable farmers to achieve the target. This would uphold the basic premise of the agricultural support and protection regime and run counter to the basic thrust of government reforms which aimed to reduce levels of support and make Japanese farmers more competitive.[355]

The new law (called the Food, Agriculture and Rural Areas Basic Law) introduced into the Japanese Diet in March 1999 and passed in July conceded on some of the points at issue but not on others. On the plus side, it emphasises food security and environmental conservation as fundamental agricultural policy values and proposes financial support to farmers in mountainous regions where production conditions are severe. Direct subsidies will be paid to farmers working under difficult conditions in hilly and mountainous areas. On the minus side, jointstock companies will be permitted to own farmland although under certain conditions,[356] while the government will adopt agricultural trade policies that conform to global trading rules adopted by the WTO. Somewhere in between the plus and minus sides is a provision that will see the government drawing up a basic policy framework every five years which will include a target for food self-sufficiency. Policy targets for the nation's food self-sufficiency rate will thus be set.[357] Even more important is the 'thoroughgoing' introduction of market principles into agricultural pricing and thus the abandonment of direct price supports.[358] This is, however, counterbalanced by a commitment to direct income subsidies for farmers.[359] Support prices for certain commodities will be replaced by income-support programmes to protect farmers from price declines.[360]

The bill submitted to the Diet in March 1999 thus envisages some radical adjustments to agricultural policy at the same time as inserting several critical guarantees that policy fundamentals will not change.[361] Translating the bill's provisions into agricultural policy initiatives has been accomplished by an 'Agricultural Policy Reform Outline' and accompanying this, an 'Agricultural Policy Reform Program', which fleshes out the detail of the policy initiatives contained in the outline together with an implementation schedule lasting until 2003. The Agricultural Policy Reform Outline defines Japan's basic posture for the WTO negotiations beginning in November 1999 as resting on the twin pillars of food security and the multi-functionality of agriculture.[362] Just prior to the final round of negotiations with the MAFF and LDP on the new law and associated policy documents, Zenchu and Zenkoku Noseikyo issued a final, comprehensive statement of requests in two parts: part one emphasised the need for a food policy that aimed to preserve stable supplies of food based on domestic agricultural production, while part two focused on the establishment of an agricultural policy aiming for the lasting development (of agriculture).[363]

The impending WTO round of agricultural trade liberalisation talks also emerged as a conspicuous theme in Nokyo's *nosei katsudo* in the late 1990s.[364] In fact Nokyo adopted two major strategies for the second half of the decade. The first was to lobby the Japanese government to make the New ABL; the second was to improve the existing UR farm trade agreement. It proposed to request new agricultural trade rules within the framework of the WTO and to continue its efforts to make the Japanese government take the initiative in international lobbying to establish new rules that would be fairer to food-importing countries like Japan, as well as enabling each country to have a sustainable agriculture. The latter was a key point from Nokyo's perspective. It was very important for Japanese farm organisations to realise these two requests in order to obtain the support of non-farm sectors, such as consumers and business as well as political parties. Zenchu labelled this approach the *kokumin undo* (the people's campaign). The real focus of the movement was to engender more collaboration with consumer groups, based on common concerns about food security and environmental issues. At the prefectural level, 30–35 *kenchu* joined forces with consumer groups to promote the *kokumin undo* at the grass-roots level. Through such activities, Nokyo hoped to get the support of consumer groups for Nokyo's demands, especially for the new basic law and fairer farm trade rules. The campaign also included providing information on the food and agricultural situation around the world to various consumer groups and Diet members through an 'International Agriculture and Food' newsletter, in order to engender 'correct understanding' on food, population and environmental issues. Zenchu acknowledged that its seven-year campaign against rice imports at the UR had not been successful because of its lack of a *kokumin undo*. This was, therefore, a necessary adjunct to its regular lobbying activities.[365]

By and large, however, market opening issues after the termination of the UR talks in late 1993 remained off the domestic policy agenda as well as the international trade negotiating agenda, except for the odd gripe made by countries such as Australia and the United States with respect to individual items such as rice and apples, as well as intermittent appearances on the discussion schedule of annual APEC meetings.[366] Periodically Zenchu and Zenkoku Noseikyo organised gatherings of like-minded groups spanning the entire primary industry sector in Japan, taking advantage of the targeting by APEC of forestry and fisheries products to protest APEC's trade liberalisation and tariff removal goals. Prior to the 1998 APEC gathering in Kuala Lumpur, Zenkoku Noseikyo got eight agricultural, forestry and fisheries groups together in a convention under the banner of 'protecting Japan's agricultural, forestry and fishing industries'.[367]

The main game, however, remained the WTO because of its significance for the Japanese rice market. The project team that Zenchu organised to support the establishment of the New ABL was also charged with preparing for the WTO negotiations. Nokyo acknowledged that its agricultural policy campaign was not well organised during the UR negotiations and so it aimed to be better prepared in relation to the WTO round beginning in 2000. Each prefecture set up a separate organisation with the aim of establishing a nation-wide system in which every small constituency had a local agricultural policy campaign organisation to lead a popular mass movement against liberal-isation. In December 1998, Zenchu issued a request for the government to impose a tariff of up to 1,300 per cent on imported rice as part of an early tariff plan to reduce the amount of rice coming into Japan from 758,000 tonnes under the minimum access agreement to 682,000 tonnes in the year 2000.[368] Although the idea was predicated on an early shift to tariffication and thus the abolition of quantitative controls on rice imports, the move to tariffy rice was designed to have the effect of actually reducing the amount of rice coming into Japan. According to WTO rules, tariffication allowed Japan to slow down the growth of rice imports compared to the quota system.[369]

Tariffication was an option extensively debated by prefectural agricultural cooperative organisations, a majority of which ended up favouring it, providing a high tariff was imposed. This view was communicated in a report compiled by Zenchu and subsequently discussed by its special policy promotion committee. Zenchu and Zenkoku Noseikyo also conferred extensively. The Zenchu Board of Directors then endorsed the proposal for tariffication,[370] although the final decision on whether to accept it was left to Zenchu Chairman, Harada Mutsutami.[371] What followed were intensive negotiations involving the LDP, the MAFF and Zenchu. In the end, the government eschewed the idea of imposing a tariff rate at 1,000+ per cent of the value of imported rice in favour of a fixed rice tariff of ¥351 per kilogram.[372] This was designed to achieve the same objective of shielding Japanese rice growers from the threat of cheaper imports.[373] The alternative tariff system was agreed by the LDP and MAFF and then approved by the Zenchu Chairman.[374]

The MAFF also announced a plan to abolish in FY 2000 the *gentan* which is no longer mandatory since rice imports had been tariffied. Under WTO trading rules, quantitative controls on imports are only permitted in circum-stances where production controls are operating domestically. In place of the rice acreage reduction programme, the MAFF proposed to develop a stability fund, supported by contributions from both the government and farmers, which would compensate farmers for 80 per cent of their loss in the event of declines in rice prices.[375] The aim is to encourage more competitive rice farmers practising extensive rice-field cultivation to take over the lands of small farms that are comparatively inefficient and managed by part-time farmers.[376]

As this series of policy outcomes in the late 1990s indicate, Nokyo has been forced to contemplate some fairly radical adjustments in the operations of the domestic market for agricultural products, most of which directly affect its own operations and economic prospects. Nevertheless, the days when Nokyo could extract concessions in its own and the farmers' interests by exercising political influence do not yet appear to have ended. Although on some issues Nokyo has been restricted to negotiating at the margins of policy decisions taken in the interests of deregulation and continuing liberalisation, it still takes its place as a legitimate participant in the policy negotiation process. In this way, Nokyo injects its views and demands directly into the policy process and helps to shape policy outcomes.

Conclusion

For annual decisions like support and stabilisation prices and the agricultural budget, a distinct policymaking sequence has been followed year after year, with Nokyo coordinating its agricultural policy activities to intersect with this sequence at the most advantageous points. This synchronised process is suggestive of a policymaking ritual, with only the individual players and issues changing from time to time, but the system itself enduring decade after decade.

Over the years, Nokyo evolved set procedures and tactics across a range of prominent issues on the agricultural policy agenda. It was only in the mid-1990s that new foci of policy campaigning replaced the traditional producer rice price campaign. The 1994 Staple Food Law broke the cycle of producer rice price decisionmaking. With the decision shifted from July to November each year and concerning only about 15 per cent or less of the total quantity of rice marketed, most of the heat has dissipated from this key item on Nokyo's public campaign agenda. It is significant, however, that in order to engender real change on the issue, the government had to alter the timing of the decision from July to November. This was because Nokyo's whole agricultural policy campaign structure had been locked into a fixed campaign schedule timed to coincide with government decisions, which made it difficult to change the policies themselves.

In more recent times the government's decision on its buying price for rice has been complicated by linkage to the *gentan* policy under the new Staple Food Law whereby the government purchased rice only from farmers who participated in this programme. Hence, the producer rice price came to be decided along with rice acreage reductions, which allowed trade-offs between the two decisions. The key change, however, was the greater injection of market forces into the price-determination process for rice. Prices for independently distributed rice, which reflect demand and supply conditions, became the basic yardstick for the producer price of rice, although a minimum price was still set in order to stabilise overall rice prices.[377] Moreover, the gradual transformation of the rice distribution system embodied a very real and sustained attack on the core of Nokyo's administrative privileges and forced Nokyo to cope with some fairly unpalatable reforms. This is not to say, however, that Nokyo has been excluded from the new distribution system. It is still used as a channel for rice-related subsidies to producers as well as retaining a key role in this system.

Nonetheless, as far as the producer rice price is concerned, only remnants of the old system remain. To the extent that the producer price of rice is still investigated by the RPAC, it is questionable whether it is possible to eliminate altogether pressure from the agricultural cooperatives in the rice price decision process, although Nokyo's demand price and the producer rice price campaign as a public, mass mobilisation exercise have clearly been abandoned.[378] A distinct shift in the pricing stance of the RPAC is also observable. In 1997 it submitted a unanimous draft report to the government suggesting that the price of government-bought rice be lowered by 2.5 per cent.[379] Producer rice prices are clearly on a continuously declining trend,[380] in spite of the fact that Zenno is not above manipulating the independently distributed rice market by other means. The final end to the producer rice price campaign will come with the abolition of the RPAC as part of a basic plan to rationalise advisory councils which was passed into law in June 1999.

In the livestock and other agricultural commodity sectors, Zenchu still pursues its price campaigns very much in the traditional mould. Officially it continues to issue demand prices for livestock and other products, but many of these prices have become irrelevant since tariffication of imports and in some cases, such as dairy products, in view of the impending deregulation of the domestic marketing system.[381] As a Zenchu official commented, after the UR agreement it became very difficult to improve price support systems. Even to maintain current producer price levels was becoming problematic.[382] Zenchu continues to go through the motions of issuing a standard demand to maintain the existing prices, knowing full well that there will be virtually irresistible pressure for reductions. One concession to the trends of the times has been the abolition of the product divisions amongst Zenchu's official lobbyists. They have now been amalgamated under the authority of one person.[383]

The underlying question is how productive Nokyo's policy campaigns will remain in the new environment of liberalisation, deregulation and policy innovation. Nokyo is now facing the most antipathetic policy environment it has ever encountered. Although the organisation's leaders can be astute in gauging the political feasibility of their demands, they sometimes cling to outmoded tactics and to policy expectations that are out of touch with changing policy trends. At the same time, Nokyo's bargaining room has been drastically curtailed: it is caught between the demands of its members, who are increasingly questioning its performance across a whole range of areas, and the inclinations of the MAFF and LDP who are less favourably disposed towards the cooperatives and protecting their vested interests.

For all these reasons, Zenchu is far from being an omnipotent organisation on agricultural policy issues. The question is whether in the light of recent developments, Nokyo's effectiveness as the spearhead of farmers' policy campaigns is diminishing to the point where it signals the eventual demise of farmers as a powerful sectoral interest in Japan. On the available evidence, it is difficult to reach a definitive judgement on this issue. Several negative developments, however, portend potentially serious consequences for Nokyo as a farmers' pressure group.

In addition to the burden of all-encompassing *nosei katsudo*, Zenchu and the Nokyo organisation as a whole have had increasingly to tackle many other problems that are inevitably leading to a fragmentation of the organisation's limited energies.[384] These include the weakening linkages between the agricultural cooperatives and their members, the viability or lack of it of the federated Nokyo system, merger difficulties and the deficits of unit co-ops, not to mention the financial crunch hitting many of Nokyo's credit institutions in recent years. The costly managerial failures in some agricultural cooperatives and Nokyo's outdated practices as an economic and financial organisation are reducing its standing in the eyes of its members and reinforcing its irrelevance to their needs.[385]

Although Nokyo continues to wage public campaigns on a whole spectrum of issues, these activities are on a distinctly diminishing scale than in previous decades. In the 1960s, Nokyo's mass mobilisation exercises regularly drew more than 10,000 participants; by the mid-1980s, they had downsized to much smaller 'request' assemblies of farmers representatives; and by the late 1990s they are lucky to attract even modest numbers of around 1,000–2,000 participants (although the lists of names on Nokyo's petitions seems to be getting longer). Demonstrations of farmers' power thus lack the mass mobilisation capacities of earlier years. In the past when the legitimacy of Nokyo's political demands was in question, it could rely on its sheer organisational size which lent credibility to its public rallies and reputed voting power. These days, demonstrations of mass membership power are less feasible and acceptable as a means of wielding influence. Nokyo is sensitive to media criticism of its public campaigns, which has made it difficult to mount large-scale mass rallies. Even the MAFF thinks Nokyo has 'gone quiet'.[386] The agricultural cooperative organisation has thus been forced on to the defensive, not only in relation to the LDP and the MAFF but also in relation to its membership and the general public.

The increasing divisions amongst Nokyo farm membership and the transfer of business by larger-scale farmers to private sector enterprises are also eroding the homogeneity of farmers' policy preferences. Full- and part-time farm households are assuming very different approaches to agricultural policies, with larger-scale farmers having quite dissimilar policy needs from small-scale farmers. This makes it ever more difficult for Nokyo to conduct uniform lobbying activities to achieve the common goals of all farmers.[387] If this is a fundamental precondition for the policy representation of members,[388] then doubts may be raised about Nokyo's claim to speak for all farmers and consequently its representativeness of farmers' interests.

Furthermore, the future for Japanese agriculture lies in corporate farming, either as collective entities of farm households or as private companies investing in agricultural production in the interests of their shareholders. Nokyo, however, cannot represent the interests of either of these groups because it is an organisation representing small, family-operated and mostly part-time agricultural production units that are both economically inefficient and dependent on agricultural cooperative services. Newcomers to agriculture will inevitably forge ties outside the agricultural cooperative system. An owner of one farming corporation predicted, for example, that trading houses that are well acquainted with the kind of high-tech agricultural machinery that the increasing number of agricultural corporations are using will expand their presence in Japan's agricultural machinery market because the agricultural cooperatives, which have hitherto dominated this market, are losing their influence.[389]

For all the reasons outlined, agricultural cooperative policy campaigns have reached a critical stage: Nokyo's organisational solidarity as well as its relevance as a farmers' pressure group is on the line. It may be that the era of Nokyo as a frontline pressure group is over. Its current and future campaigns, whilst retaining some of their traditional aspects, are fraught with unprecedented difficulties. The altered policy environment means that what Nokyo can realistically expect and demand from government has changed considerably. The emphasis in government policies is now uniformly on lowering production costs and endeavouring to make Japanese farming more efficient and in less need of government resources and protection.[390]

The declining case for government handouts, however, does not mean farmers and the agricultural cooperatives will readily part with their long-held benefits. Both are fighting a rearguard action to hold on to what they have got. Nokyo is certainly not about to surrender; it has a good many policy battles left in it yet. As the imposition of high tariffs on rice in December 1998 demonstrated, the question of access to the Japanese rice market certainly retains its potential for galvanising Nokyo into action.

On the other hand, the political picture has been complicated by the LDP's poor performance in the 1998 UH elections and the fact that its numbers in the Upper House now fall short of a majority. The situation may herald a new era that has some unwelcome parallels with the period after the Hosokawa coalition came to power in 1993, when Nokyo was no longer able to make cosy deals with the LDP or rely on them to exert pressure on the MAFF. This in turn substantially weakened its influence, to which the Hosokawa government's acceptance of the UR agreement attests.

For the LDP, the loss of its majority in the Upper House in 1998 means working in coalition (with the Liberal Party and later the New Komeito), but for Nokyo it means having to deal with more than just its traditional political ally. Even after the LDP resumed government in coalition in June 1994, Nokyo found it more difficult to influence LDP policymakers directly, because the coalition government had a coordination committee on agricultural policy and the LDP had to spend more time coordinating with other parties in the ruling coalition. As recounted by a Zenchu official, in the circumstances Zenchu was forced to make an equal approach to each party, but some prefectures within the Nokyo organisation had never had any experience in dealing with the JSP/SDP. Zenchu had to keep the NFP warm too, because it was dangerous to say 'goodbye'. Even so, Nokyo had mainly to deal with and support the LDP because more of its members were still interested in agriculture and because the ruling party 'realised things'.[391]

The resumption of certain elements of a coalition system may prompt a new approach in which Nokyo targets both ruling and Opposition parties issue by issue, endeavouring to find common ground amongst all the parties on food, agricultural and rural issues, emphasising that these issues are fundamental national questions for all parties.[392] Nokyo is conscious of the rising strength of urban-based parties such as the DP, New Komeito and the JCP, and the fact that the LDP will want to cultivate greater support amongst urban-dwellers in order to expand its narrow support base beyond regional areas where there are greater concentrations of farmers.[393]

Nokyo's instinctive reliance on the LDP, however, may prove difficult to eradicate. It will be especially troublesome for Nokyo to rid itself of the legacy of the 1955 political regime from within its own ranks.[394] As one Zenchu official commented, 'it is problematic for Nokyo to change its strategy drastically. It still has to depend on a lobbying system through the LDP.'[395] Habits established over decades of LDP monopoly rule will not be easy to eliminate. They could pose a real dilemma if a combination of new Opposition parties comes to power.

Whatever the party situation in government, Nokyo will be forced to appeal to the public and attract greater public support for its causes. One of the pledges offered by the Chairman of Zenkoku Noseikyo with respect to the New ABL in late 1998 was to 'mobilise the political power of the farmers against the background of the formation of a national consensus, with a view to the next round of WTO agricultural negotiations and securing the necessary financial resources to achieve the realisation of a policy for raising the food self-sufficiency rate and for a new ABL system'.[396] In fact Nokyo labelled its campaign strategy with respect to the new law as one based on 'symbiosis with the people' (*kokumin kyosei*), translated into English as Joint! Action![397]

It may be that the success of Nokyo's *nosei katsudo* now depends largely on the power of its social appeal (*shakaiteki apiiru ryoku*). This puts a premium on the individuals selected to be top executives of Zenchu, and Nokyo's capacity to utilise the media to full effect by presenting convincing policy arguments.[398] Although Nokyo is endeavouring to preserve its position as a legitimate participant in agricultural policymaking, exercising influence in the future will require a less blatant attempt to secure the protection of special interests and a more self-conscious articulation of policy demands that serve the broader interests of the agricultural sector, and the national interest in the continuing viability of Japanese farming. In relation to both the MAFF and the ruling party, because Nokyo's capacity for applying political pressure has declined, it requires a change in tactics from 'pushing with strong power' to cooperation and conciliation.[399]

What Nokyo also needs for 2000 and beyond is a realistic vision of agriculture over the medium to long term and the development of agricultural policy demands to achieve that vision. This means promoting agriculture as an element of regional economic development, establishing border measures that are in line with the trend towards internationalisation, and establishing systems that adjust supply and demand for agricultural products, particularly rice.[400] This is in addition to the much-needed development of Nokyo's ability to operate as a market actor in a more competitive and deregulated financial, distribution and marketing environment. In short, Nokyo's agricultural policy campaigns and managerial capacities will have to be adjusted to the situation as it is in Japan today and in the future.

9 Conclusion

Agriculture is a highly politicised industry in Japan and agricultural policies the quintessential expression of the political power of Japanese farmers. No explanation of Japanese agricultural support and protection is complete without due account being taken of political factors, particularly the primacy of electoral and interest group politics in this sector of state policy. Agriculture is one area where political forces in economic policymaking have been remarkably salient and where the political intrusiveness of interest groups has had a large impact on the agricultural policy formation process. The agricultural sector has been too electorally powerful, too highly organised, too visible publicly and too well represented in the Diet and in the ruling party for the government to ignore the political ramifications of any major decision on agricultural policy. The political strength of agriculture has undoubtedly contributed to the distinctly pro-rural, anti-urban bias of the ruling LDP, and thus to the general neglect of urban consumer interests in the policies of postwar Japanese governments. To this extent, the Japanese state has been captive of agrarian interests.

The interest in this subject, however, is not limited to elucidating the multi-dimensional aspects of farmers' political power and the nature of agricultural politics in Japan. A broader analytical objective has been to locate this subject in its wider political context. To begin with, a dominant feature of postwar politics has been the long-term, stable rule of a single party. In providing the LDP with one of its strongest power bases, farmers and their organisations have been a crucial factor in the ruling party's longevity in power and thus one of the core elements of the so-called '1955 political system'.[1] The failure to rectify distortions in the electoral system, which benefited both rural voters and the LDP, also helped to perpetuate this system.

Secondly agricultural organisations exemplify a distinctive system of interest group politics certain aspects of which may be generalised across other sectors in Japan. The organised representation of farm interests is multilayered and includes a diverse array of groups. In terms of the proliferation of farmers' organisations and their access to political institutions, the system is strongly pluralist. Although one grouping, Nokyo, provides comprehensive coverage for the entire sector, it is one of a number of agricultural groups that penetrate deeply into parliamentary and party structures through direct and indirect representation, and the dependency of politicians on electoral and other resources of external organisations. Agricultural groups act as the primary mediators of connections between farmers and rural politicians, taking advantage of strong community-based loyalties and the coincidence of organisational boundaries with social collectivities in the countryside. Amongst other things, the large number of agriculture-related Diet members attests to the resilience of interpersonal connections between individual politicians and agricultural interest groups.

Interest group penetration of political institutions is counterbalanced by bureaucratic penetration of interest groups through corporatist modes of interaction, with varying degrees of state sponsorship and interest group capture. Some farmers' organisations, notably the farmers' unions and some commodity-based groups, are independent of the government bureaucracy, but they are in the minority. Most are integrated into the functioning of agricultural administration in varying degrees. Their existence, activities and, in some cases, the prosperity of their businesses depend on trends in agricultural policy and economic and social conditions in Japan.[2] The core groups are the statutory agricultural interest groups – Nokyo, the agricultural committee system, land improvement groups and agricultural mutual aid associations – which operate within legal strictures that confer a range of administrative burdens and benefits. Taken together, these groups constitute a highly corporatised system of interest intermediation. The nature of this regime is encapsulated in a description of the structures and norms of interest inter-mediation in the French agricultural sector: 'Through this system, a set of organisations has enjoyed a prominent, statutorily-mandated role in the web of institutions that implement . . . agricultural policy, and a well-entrenched, [formal and] informal consultative privilege with state officials at the national and local levels.'[3] In this respect, Japan typifies the corporatist mode of inter-action that prevails, or has prevailed, between governments and agricultural groups in other developed democracies – not only in France, but also in the United Kingdom, the United States, Canada, Australia and New Zealand.

The duality of function by state-sponsored agricultural interest groups – their penetration of political institutions and simultaneous co-option into agricultural administration – presents no contradiction in practice. Indeed, in many respects, it continues a historical tradition of agricultural organisations seeking to counterbalance their weakness *vis-à-vis* state bureaucracy with representation through Diet and party channels. While administrative co-option might impose costs in terms of a lack of organisational independence, agricultural groups counterbalance their subordination to the bureaucracy by providing electoral and organisational backup to politicians, thus harnessing the influence of their political allies as group operatives and interest brokers in the policy process. Agricultural representatives typify the role of Japanese politicians as lobbyists, acting on behalf of special interests from strategic positions in the Diet and in political parties.

Institutional interest groups – the agricultural *gaikaku dantai* – are even closer to government. They were created for bureaucratic purposes and could not operate without an administrative rationale and government largesse. Their functioning as interest groups is secondary and derivative of their administrative roles. However, insofar as once established these bodies strive to defend and expand their activities, powers and budgetary claims, their role as interest groups is important. What is more, their specific organisational purpose coincides with the interests of those in the agricultural sector who ultimately benefit from their services (farmers, agricultural organisations and associated industries). In this respect, the institutional interest groups represent a much wider group of beneficiaries, further entrenching the interests of multiple claimants on agricultural subsidies and other benefits such as regulated distribution systems.

The existence of large numbers of statutory and institutional interest groups, each performing specified duties in a highly administered and controlled farm sector, provides an organisational bulwark against significant deregulation of the agricultural economy. These bodies have acquired vested interests in those parts of the regulatory and distributive regime in which they are involved. In this sense, agricultural support and protection in Japan is highly institutionalised, which increases the degree of difficulty faced by reformist elements seeking to dismantle key regulatory and distributory elements of the agricultural policy system. Market liberalisation, deregulation and cuts in subsidies will require devolution of function by these organisations and possibly even their disestablishment. This is likely not only to present formidable administrative obstacles to reform but also to amplify the political costs of any attempts by the government to loosen administrative controls over the agricultural sector. As Lowi observed some decades ago, programmes of subsidies for established interest groups tend to 'freeze the political system in the status quo, retard policy innovation and lessen the influence of newly emerging interests'.[4]

Furthermore, farmers' organisations like the agricultural cooperatives and their offshoots, as well as the agricultural committees and the land improvement districts, are institutions that not only embody rural social structures, but also the dominant mode of agricultural production centred on small-scale family farms. The organisational foundations of agricultural support and protection are thus woven into the very fabric of rural society and agricultural economy. For this reason, they have a permanence and a resilience that will prove very difficult to eradicate. Future changes to the traditional socio-economic structure of farming will only come with the corporatisation (*hojinka*) of agricultural production and the increasing penetration of private companies into the farming sector.

The 1990s have seen many facets of the political power of Japanese farmers and their organisations coming under greater challenge. The LDP has a less secure grasp on government; farmers' electoral clout is diminishing; Nokyo is under siege from the economic, financial and policy environment as well as its own membership; reform of the LH electoral system has altered the incentives for politicians in relation to organised interests; and stronger calls are being made for agricultural policy reform and deregulation of agricultural administration as well as for dismantling the institutional instruments of control. Because the rice-roots power of farmers and a highly regulated farm sector are defining elements of the Japanese politico-economic system, the developments that are taking place in relation to agriculture both contribute to and reflect those taking place in Japan's political economy as a whole.

In particular, what is happening to Nokyo represents an example of the impact of liberalisation and deregulation on an administratively cosseted institution and the need for restructuring and greater efficiencies in the new, less protective climate these shifts in policy impose. Nokyo's altered status has been symbolised by Standard & Poor's downgrading of their long-term rating on Norinchukin to single-'A'-plus (from double-'A'), and the short-term rating to 'A-1' (from 'A-1'-plus) in late 1998. The grounds for the altered rating included the deteriorating quality of assets held not only by Norinchukin but also by its lower-tier institutions stemming from the worsening economic conditions in Japan,[5] as well as Norinchukin's negative prospects in a more challenging operating environment requiring it to cope with increasing competition and further deregulation of financial markets.[6]

The abolition of the FC system, which has been attacked as a symbol of the nation's outdated institutions, and its replacement with a more market orientated set-up, are also part of the process of fundamental politico-economic reform, as is the rewriting of the Agricultural Basic Law. One of the most radical innovations introduced by the new Food, Agriculture and Rural Areas Basic Law has been the phasing out of government-guaranteed sales prices for agricultural products and the substitution with a system subjecting growers to market principles, in which the government directly compensates farmers for lost income based on production costs.[7]

The reform in slow motion that is taking place in domestic marketing and distribution systems represents a real threat to Nokyo's cartelisation of the agricultural economy. Because of its cooperative status, Nokyo profited from government-sanctioned near-monopolies in a number of its businesses. What is more, it entrenched its position with the connivance of the MAFF because the arrangement supported the ministry's regulatory and subsidy goals – all at the expense of the Japanese consumer.

Nokyo has yet to resolve its fundamental identity crisis arising from the combination of its cooperative and semi-governmental status along with its profit-seeking business interests. In an economic environment that increasingly demands a more competitive business profile modelled on private enterprise, Nokyo will find it difficult to resist pressure to divest itself of cooperative obligations and traditional management structures dominated by farmers. Where this leaves Nokyo the interest group is difficult to say. Although its business activities have generated independent economic clout, Nokyo's political standing has rested very much on the loyalty of its farming members based on cooperative customs and social ties in rural communities as well as on its corporatised status as an administrative arm of government. The key to Nokyo's survival in the future will be its ability to develop stronger account-ability mechanisms and to meet the needs of entrepreneurial farming entities, both of which will put a higher priority on quality management at all levels of the organisation along with a lower priority on concession-seeking and associated political activities. In the meantime, a premium will be placed on the efficacy of cooperative mergers and rationalisation of staff numbers. Whether this will take place at the required pace remains to be seen.

The agricultural cooperative leadership is aware that it is not fulfilling the expectations of its members and is revamping its member-centred philosophy as a result. At the same time, it pleads the imperative of prioritising manage-ment issues in the light of the difficulties it faces in the current economic climate. Above all it is realising that it can no longer take membership loyalty for granted and that it will need to provide competitive services in order to retain its membership strength. In dealing with its first major crisis of organ-isational power, Nokyo is hampered by its multifunctionality and its dual public/private face, which are no longer concordant. Indeed, they have become discordant.

There is no doubt that the ebbing of Nokyo's fortunes and the economic and social decline of agriculture are leading over the long term to an erosion of the political significance of the farm sector and thus a repositioning of this sector in Japan's domestic power structure. Agriculture in Japan is in a transitional phase from a dominant, well organised and electorally powerful majority interest, to a less well organised minority interest. Although farmers remain a core constituency of the LDP, the relative importance of this 'core' has declined over the years. Many of the changes in the political demography of agriculture have not been sudden, but are the culmination of trends that have been occurring over some decades and which will continue inexorably into the future. The changes in the demographic indices of agriculture – the agricultural population, the number of farm households, the agricultural labour force and the aging structure of the farm population – are significant not only in themselves but also because of their political fallout. Farm household population continues to diminish, and as a result, the national agricultural electorate continues to shrink. In future such contraction may be even more dramatic as the lack of successors for family farms results in a more rapid reduction in farm household numbers. According to Zenchu's former Managing Director, Ishikura Teruka, Japanese agriculture is facing four critical problems: less than 1,800 new graduates take up farming each year (lack of successors), abandoned agricultural land now amounts to more than 220,000 hectares (increasing areas of non-utilised farmland), regional agri-cultural resources are poorly maintained owing to the decline of rural societies (urbanisation and income diversification in rural areas) and the aging of the population in rural areas is progressing much faster than in urban areas.[8] The political effects of these socio-economic changes have been ameliorated in the past by the overweighting of rural districts in the electoral system, but as the changing classification of Upper and Lower House constituencies shows, all districts are now more or less urbanised and the electoral advantages traditionally bestowed on farmers have been further eroded by electoral reform.

The established pattern of agricultural influence is thus under threat. Although constantly evolving, its heyday lasted from the 1960s until the early to mid-1980s. Since then, it has been gradually weakening. In some respects, however, it remains tenacious and formidable, not the least because the contraction in farmers' political power is an incremental rather than a sudden process and because farmers are still highly organised to defend their economic and political interests (particularly when compared to urban consumers). Their skills in running public campaigns, although not on the grand scale of the 1960s and 1970s, have been honed over many decades. Moreover, out in the prefectures, 'provincial conservatism, and provincial support for the LDP cultivated over many years, remain as strong as ever'.[9] Nokyo's involvement in LDP *jiban* in rural areas and the *koenkai* of LDP election candidates is still very evident. Contrary to some reports,[10] farmers are not yet electorally marginalised.

All this means that the process of reducing agricultural support and protection will continue to engage many domestic political sensitivities. Farmers still demand all kinds of benefits and concessions from the government and expect their representative organisations and political allies to lobby successfully for them. In the past this has worked considerably to stymie policy change. Agrarian reform has often been foiled by organised agricultural interests and the politicians who serve them. For this reason, it is quite possible that the new Food, Agriculture and Rural Areas Basic Law will go the same way – emasculated or turned into schemes for new subsidies.[11]

On the external front, the question of opening Japan's agricultural market has clearly not disappeared from the international trade negotiating agenda. In recent years it has figured in APEC meetings and is currently the focus of WTO negotiations launched in November 1999. Even the September 1998 report of the Food, Agriculture and Rural Areas Basic Problems Investigation Committee carefully dodged the issue of which stance Japan should take in the WTO negotiations on rice market opening.[12] When the government did grasp the nettle in December 1998 and moved to tariffy rice imports, it did so in order to reduce the obligatory quantity of foreign rice coming into Japan. Furthermore, the extremely high fixed tariff of ¥351.17 per kilo on imported rice was designed to penalise foreign rice in the domestic market. The outcome of this decision and the manner in which it was reached suggest that the power of Japan's farm lobby has not been extinguished and that agricultural import barriers remain well defended in a domestic political context. Amongst the bilateral trade problems involving Japan and countries like Australia and the United States, agriculture is one of the last great hurdles to overcome.

Finally, interest in the political power of farmers extends beyond its continuing influence on agricultural policy to a consideration of the changing nature of the Japanese political system as a whole. Agriculture is a prime example of how this system has been captive of special interests. The selective advantages that politicians, organised interests and favoured minorities have been able to draw from public policy have come at the cost of Japan's wider publics – the consumers, the taxpayers, the urban salary and wage earners – who have footed the bill for agricultural patronage, suffered the rigours of administrative over-regulation and the inequitable distribution of public resources. In the wake of Japan's financial and economic crisis, risks of a major rural–urban confrontation over the distribution of these resources are rising. For the politico-economic superstructure of agricultural support and protection, and the wider system of which it is such a crucial element to undergo real transformation, the political and bureaucratic forces that have sustained it will also have to change.

Notes

1 Introduction

1 Y. Iwahashi, 'Why Do Farmers Have Such Great Power?', *Tokyo Business Today*, May 1986, p. 48.

2 Using two variables to represent the comparative advantage of agriculture, a labour-productivity ratio and a factor-endowment ratio, Honma and Hayami demonstrated extremely low labour-productivity and factor-endowment ratios for Japanese agriculture over the period 1955 to 1980. See Table 4.1 in Masayoshi Honma and Yujiro Hayami, 'The Determinants of Agricultural Protection Levels: An Econometric Analysis', in Kym Anderson and Yujiro Hayami *et al.*, *The Political Economy of Agricultural Protection: East Asia in International Perspective*, Sydney, Allen & Unwin, 1986, pp. 40–41. Goto and Imamura reached a similar conclusion about productivity rates in agriculture: 'In spite of efforts to improve the infrastructure and adopt labor-saving technologies, the labor productivity of agriculture compared to non-agricultural sectors continued to decline and was approximately 25 percent in 1988.' Junko Goto and Naraomi Imamura, 'Japanese Agriculture: Characteristics, Institutions, and Policies', in Luther Tweeten, Cynthia L. Dishon, Wen S. Chern, Naraomi Imamura and Masaru Morishima (eds), *Japanese & American Agriculture: Tradition and Progress in Conflict*, Boulder, CO., Westview Press, 1993, p. 17. On a comparative scale, labour productivity in Japanese agriculture (at 100) has remained considerably lower than in a selected range of countries such as the United States (312), West Germany (152), Sweden (228), and Australia (210). It is only higher than in South Korea (71). It is also the lowest of any sector in Japan. See Japan Productivity Center for Socio-Economic Development, *International Comparison of Labour Productivity*, Tokyo, September 1995, pp. 5, 10.

3 In fact the 1997 figure was 13.3 per cent. Norinsuisansho, Tokei Johobu, *Poketto Norinsuisan Tokei* [Pocket Agriculture, Forestry and Fisheries Statistics], Tokyo, Norin Tokei Kyokai, 1999 (hereafter known as *Poketto*), p. 16. The physical characteristics of Japanese agriculture will not be elaborated further except to point out that Japan has fertile soils and a favourable climate, which is particularly suited to rice growing.

4 A part-time farm household is defined as one that has one or more household members engaged in jobs other than farming. A Type II part-time farm household is defined as one in which more farm household income is earned from non-agricultural occupations than from farming, whilst in Type I part-time farm households, the reverse is the case. The number of part-time farm households as a percentage of the total has been over 80 per cent since 1970. In 1980 it was 85.7 per cent and in 1997, 83.1 per cent. In 1997, Type II part-time farm

households amounted to 67.1 per cent, a proportion that is rising not falling. Norinsuisansho, Tokei Johobu, *Dai 73-ji Norinsuisansho Tokeihyo Heisei 8nen–9nen* [Statistical Yearbook of the Ministry of Agriculture, Forestry and Fisheries 1996–1997], Tokyo, Norin Tokei Kyokai, 1998 (hereafter known as *Norinsuisansho Tokeihyo*), p. 9. Type II part-time farm households own the bulk of the agricultural land in Japan. Okuyama Taro, 'Hojokin 4-cho En Nosei wa Kuni o Horobosu' ['The ¥4 Trillion Agricultural Policy That is Damaging the Country'], *Shukan Daiyamondo*, 8 February 1986, p. 36.

5 Average farm size increased from 1.07 ha in 1960 to 1.37 ha in 1990. By 1998, average farm size had grown to 1.490 ha. *Poketto*, 1999, p. 103. These figures compare with around 15 ha in Europe and around 175 ha in the United States. Richard Moore, *Japanese Agriculture: Patterns of Rural Development*, Boulder, Co., Westview Press, 1990, p. 200.

6 The agricultural workforce fell from 17.4 million (or 48.7 per cent of the total workforce) in 1950, to 12.0 million in 1960 (25.1 per cent of the total), 5.1 million in 1980 (or 9.1 per cent of the total), 3.3 million in 1995 (5.1 per cent of the total) and 3.15 million in 1997 (4.8 per cent of the total). See E. A. Saxon, *Farm Production in Japan: Determinants, Performance and Prospects*, Bureau of Agricultural Economics (BAE), Occasional Paper No. 35, Canberra, Australian Government Publishing Service, 1976, p. 14; JA Zenno Sogo Kikakubu Kikaku Chosaka (ed.), *JA Guruupu Keizai Jigyo Kiso Tokei* [JA Group Basic Economic Business Statistics], 1997, Tokyo, Zenno Sogo Kikakubu Kikaku Chosaka, 1997 (hereafter known as *JA Guruupu Keizai Jigyo Kiso Tokei*), p. 1; *MAFF Update*, No. 265, 26 June 1998, http://www.maff.go.jp; *Poketto*, 1999, p. 19.

7 In the early 1960s, total agricultural planted areas exceeded 8 million ha while total arable land areas exceeded 6 million ha. Since that time, both indices have continued to drop annually at a rate of about 100,000 ha and 30,000–40,000 ha respectively. In 1995, total agricultural planted areas stood at 4.92 million ha, which was the first drop below the five million ha level since the government began surveys in 1955. Total arable land, on the other hand, fell to 5.04 million ha in the same year, down 45,000 ha from the 1994 figure owing to increases in fallow land, as well as continuing conversion of agricultural land to other purposes. By 1997, total agricultural planted areas had contracted to 4.72 million ha and total arable land to 4.95 million ha. Both this figure and that for total arable land are predicted to drop further. *Japan Agrinfo Newsletter*, Vol. 14, No. 2, October 1996, p. 2; *Poketto*, 1999, p. 103; *MAFF Update*, No. 270, 31 July 1998, http://www.maff.go.jp. In the past, total agricultural planted areas have usually exceeded the total area of arable land because of double cropping, although the above figures show that the rate of double cropping has fallen precipitously. In fact, total agricultural planted areas are now lower than the total area of arable land, indicating that some arable land is no longer being utilised for agricultural purposes. As Goto and Imamura point out, 'the ratio of idle farmland to cultivated farmland is increasing at a phenomenal rate. The total area of idle farmland increased between 1985 and 1990 by about 60 percent . . . In some regions, the ratio of idle land to total farmland reached as high as one-tenth.' 'Japanese Agriculture', p. 19.

8 For instance, the share of agriculture, forestry and fisheries income in national income declined from 30 per cent in 1946 to 17 per cent in 1954, continuing downward to 11 per cent in 1960. By 1996, it had slumped even further to less than 1 per cent. *Poketto*, annual, relevant years. The share of agriculture in gross domestic product (GDP) declined in parallel fashion, contracting from around 10 per cent in 1960 to 7.4 per cent in 1965, 2.4 per cent in 1980 and 1.4 per cent in 1995. *Poketto*, annual, relevant years.

9 The mixture of economic, social and biological reasons for its decline have been extensively discussed in the relevant literature. Amongst the factors most commonly cited are the transfer of agricultural land to non-agricultural uses, the long-standing structural obstacles to an expansion in the scale of Japanese farming operations and the lack of so-called 'successors' (*kokeisha*) in Japanese farm households.

10 Fixed capital formation in agriculture declined as a proportion of total domestic fixed capital formation from 4.8 per cent in 1980 to 3.7 per cent in 1995. *Poketto*, 1999, p. 100.

11 Kenji Horiguchi, 'Issues for a Country Dependent on Imported Foodstuff to Consider: Implications of Recent Structural Changes in Farm Products Trade', unpublished manuscript, n.d., p. 3.

12 See Saxon, *Farm Production in Japan*, p. 9; *Japan Agrinfo Newsletter*, Vol. 16, No. 4, December 1998, p. 2. The exact figure for 1998 is 3,291,000. The figure for commercial farm households is lower (2,522,000 in 1998). Commercial farm households (*hanbai noka*) are farm households that either cultivate crops on farmland of 30 ares (0.74 acres) or more, or sell farm products worth ¥500,000 or more a year.

13 Saxon, *Farm Production in Japan*, p. 10.

14 Total farm household population (as opposed to commercial farm household population) is no longer provided in the official statistics compiled by the MAFF. This last figure was, therefore, calculated informally by multiplying the average number of persons per commercial farm household by the number of farm households, commercial and non-commercial. Commercial farm household population in 1998 was 11.3 million. The figures were obtained from *Japan Agrinfo Newsletter*, Vol. 16, No. 4, December 1998, p. 2. The shrinkage in both farm household numbers and farm household population is currently around 1–2 per cent per annum.

15 Other factors have also contributed, such as the increase in land values during the period of Japan's economic growth, which encouraged farmers to maintain their land as part of their assets. Ishimi Takashi, *Nokyo: Sangyo no Showa Shakaishi* [Nokyo: The Social History of Industries in the Showa Period], Tokyo, Nihon Keizai Kyoronsha, 1986, p. 220.

16 'Protection' in this book normally means only border, or import protection. Economists use the term 'protection' to encompass what is being referred to here as 'agricultural support and protection'. This is because they define 'protection' broadly to mean 'policies to increase agricultural output and income through government intervention into agricultural product and input markets'. Yujiro Hayami, *Japanese Agriculture Under Siege*, London, Macmillan and St Martin's Press, 1988, p. 51.

17 This phenomenon has been extensively analysed by agricultural economists. See, for example, Kamiya Mitsugi and Korenaga Tohiko (eds), *Nogyo Hogo to Nosan Butsu Boeki Mondai [Agricultural Protection Policies and Agricultural Trade Issues]*, Research Monograph No. 105, Tokyo, Nogyo Sogo Kenkyujo, 1985; Anderson and Hayami *et al.*, *The Political Economy of Agricultural Protection*; and Yujiro Hayami and Saburo Yamada *et al.*, *The Agricultural Development of Japan: A Century's Perspective*, Tokyo, University of Tokyo Press, 1991.

18 Calder, however, argues that patterns of agricultural support in Japan diverge in important respects from those in other industrialised nations since WWII. See Kent Calder, *Crisis and Compensation: Public Policy and Political Stability in Japan, 1949–1986*, Princeton, Princeton University Press, 1988, pp. 232–233.

19 In a comprehensive evaluation of the macro-economic costs of agricultural support and protection, one study noted that: 'The large transfers to agriculture

also have significant repercussions for the overall macroeconomic performance of industrial and developing countries. Studies undertaken by the Organisation for Economic Cooperation and Development (OECD) showed that agricultural support is wasteful of resources, impairs competitiveness of manufacturing, and may reduce total employment and discourage the development of efficient agriculture. Moreover, a number of analyses quantifying these effects shows the macroeconomic impact of farm support to be extremely significant.' *Reforming World Agricultural Trade: A Policy Statement by Twenty-nine Professionals from Seventeen Countries*, Washington D.C., Institute for International Economics, Canada, The Institute for Research on Public Policy, May 1988, pp. 5–6.

20 Criticisms directed at the European Community's Common Agricultural Policy (CAP) could equally apply to Japanese agricultural policy, viz., 'excessively burdening consumers and taxpayers, stimulating surplus production, and wreaking havoc on world markets through price distortions'. See John T. S. Keeler, 'Agricultural Power in the European Community: Explaining the Fate of CAP and GATT Negotiations', *Comparative Politics*, Vol. 28, No. 2, January 1996. See also Alex F. McCalla and Timothy E. Josling, *Agricultural Policies and World Markets*, New York, Macmillan, 1985.

21 The Spanish agricultural subsidy scheme which helped to maintain the ruling Socialists in power for twelve years, for example, came under attack in 1994 for being corrupt and preserving feudal farming conditions in southern Spain. *Reuter Textline*, Reuter News Service – Western Europe, 27 April 1994.

22 Russian President Boris Yeltsin, for example, promised import duties (and also cheap credit and debt forgiveness for the farm sector) while on a stumping tour of an agricultural region prior to the June 1996 Presidential election. *Reuter Textline*, Reuter News Service – CIS and Eastern Europe, 18 April 1996.

23 A good example is President Clinton's promises in Iowa in April 1995 not to hurt price supports and to continue to send billions of dollars to farmers in the form of subsidies in the lead-up to the new farm policy law of 1995 and foreshadowing his 1996 election campaign. *Reuter Textline*, Reuter News Service – United States, 25 April 1996.

24 The French government promised to present a bill in late 1994 to this effect prior to the European Parliament elections in 1994. *Reuter Textline*, Reuter News Service – Western Europe, 10 June 1994.

25 Taiwan's President Lee Teng-hui, for example, pledged in the 1996 election campaign to create a Taiwan $100 billion (US$3.8 billion) fund to subsidise farmers after Taiwan's entry into the WTO. *Reuter Textline*, Bangkok Post, 7 June 1995.

26 In May 1994, a Ukrainian farmers' organisation offered to support a particular candidate in the presidential elections if he implemented a programme of land reform. Reuter Textline, BBC Monitoring Service: CIS, 5 May 1994. In June 1995, farmers in Northeast Thailand belonging to the Assembly of Small-Scale Farmers vowed to support any politician who promised to solve rural problems. *Reuter Textline*, Reuter News Service – Far East, 28 November 1995.

27 For example, political action committees for US farm groups donated US$15.5 billion to congressional candidates in the 1994 election. Those House members who signed letters urging that agriculture be spared budget cuts received an average of US$13,636 from farm political action committees in 1993–94, which was more than twice the average for the whole House. The figure was even higher for members of the House Agriculture Committee who received an average of US$18,341 each. *Reuter Textline*, Reuter News Service – United States, 13 June 1995.

28 Brian Reading, *Japan: The Coming Collapse*, London, Weidenfeld & Nicolson, 1992, p. 214.
29 Carlisle Ford Runge, 'The Assault on Agricultural Protectionism', *Foreign Affairs*, Vol. 67, No. 1, Fall 1988, p. 146.
30 Goto and Imamura, 'Japanese Agriculture', p. 23.
31 Bureau of Agricultural Economics (BAE), *Japanese Agricultural Policies: An Overview*, Occasional Paper, 98, Canberra, Australian Government Publishing Service, 1987, p. 1. In another comparative study done in the 1980s, however, Japan ranked a little below other major world economies. According to the United States Department of Agriculture (USDA), US government intervention in the agricultural sector was found to be as large as that of other industrialised countries over the period 1982–87. The USDA's calculation of comparative government intervention in agriculture (the ratio of total transfers to total producers' value, 1982–87 average) showed a rate of 0.63 for Japan, 0.69 for the United States, 0.71 for the EC countries and 0.92 for Canada. USDA, Estimates of Producer and Consumer Subsidy Equivalents: Government Intervention in Agriculture, 1982–1987, cited in Akira Inoue, *The Widening Gap between U.S. and Japanese Agricultural Policies and Its Implications for Agricultural Production*, USJP Occasional Paper 95-04, Program on U.S.–Japan Relations, Harvard University, 1995, p. 25. By the mid-1990s, however, Japan was outranking all these other countries. According to an OECD report on agricultural policies in member countries, Japan ranked second only to Switzerland in terms of the producer subsidy equivalent (PSE) in 1996. Japan's percentage PSE was 71, compared to Switzerland (78). This was much higher than the EU (43), the United States (16) and Canada (22). OECD, *Agricultural Policies in OECD Countries: Measurement of Support and Background Information 1997*, Paris, OECD, 1997, p. 31. The OECD defines the PSE as 'an indicator of the value of the monetary transfers to agriculture resulting from agricultural policies in a given year. Both transfers from consumers of agricultural products (through domestic market prices) and transfers from taxpayers (through budgetary or tax expenditures) are included' (p. 21). PSE figures can be expressed as the total value of support (i.e. total PSE), or as a percentage PSE (i.e. what percentage government support amounts to in the value of what farmers produce). The Australian Bureau of Agricultural and Research Economics defines the PSE as 'the payment that would be required to compensate agricultural producers for the loss of income resulting from the removal of that policy. This payment may be measured either in money terms or as a percentage of the value of production at producer prices'. Australian Bureau of Agricultural and Resource Economics (ABARE), *Proposed Strategies for Reducing Agricultural Protection in the GATT Uruguay Round: A Synthesis and Assessment*, Discussion Paper, 90.6, 1990, p. 13.
32 Shiraishi Masahiko, 'Gyunyu' ['Milk'], in Ouchi Tsutomu and Kajii Isao (eds), *Nokyo Yonjunen – Kitai to Genjitsu* [*Forty Years of Nokyo: Expectation and Reality*], *Nihon Nogyo Nenpo*, Vol. 36, Tokyo, Ochanomizu Shobo, 1989, p. 158.
33 This was phraseology used by Japan's Minister of Agriculture, Forestry and Fisheries at the time, Nakagawa Shoichi, in launching the new agricultural policy reform outline and schedule in December 1998. '21 Seki o Tenbo Shita "Nosei Kaikaku"' ['"Agricultural Policy Reform" With A View to the 21st Century'], *Nosei Undo Jyaanaru*, No. 23, February 1999, p. 3.
34 The average income tax burden for farm households, for example, was about 80 per cent of that for workers' households between 1965 and 1983. ABARE, *Japanese Agricultural Policies: A Time of Change*, Policy Monograph No. 3, Canberra, Australian Government Publishing Service, 1988, p. 85. In another study Ishi established that over the period 1970–78, the ratio of income captured

as taxable by the tax office to real taxable income was only 20–30 per cent for farmers, as opposed to 60–70 per cent for the non-farm self-employed and 90–100 per cent for employees. Hayami, *Japanese Agriculture Under Siege*, p. 61, citing Ishi Mitsuhiro, 'Kazei Shotoku Hosokuritsu no Gyoshukan Kakusa' ['Inter-Occupational Differences in the Rates of Capturing Taxable Income'], *Kikan Gendai Keizai*, Vol. 42, 1981, pp. 72–83. Similarly, Honma established that the tax rate on agricultural income in 1983 was only one-half the rate on non-agricultural income within farm households. Honma Masayoshi, *Nihon no Nogyo to Zaisei Kozo* [*Japan's Agriculture and Financial Structure*], Tokyo, Seisaku Koso Fuooramu, January 1987, pp. 11–14. See also Calder, *Crisis and Compensation*, pp. 242–244.

35 With respect to land tax, for example, the fixed property tax rate on agricultural land has been maintained at one-tenth the rate on residential land. *Asahi Shinbun*, 22 April 1990. If agricultural land were in a district zoned for urban development, it was subject to a municipal urban-planning tax. Differential tax rates on residential as opposed to agricultural land, however, ensured that the taxes on farm land were as low as 2–3 per cent of those on an adjacent housing lot, even if the land were valued at the same amount. Chihiro Nakajima, 'A Peaceful End to Urban Farming', *Economic Eye*, March 1987, p. 19. From 1982 onwards, taxation on farmland at a rate comparable to residential land was introduced on farmland valued at more than ¥30,000 per 3.3 square metres (that is, in the three major metropolitan areas of Tokyo, Osaka and Nagoya). If, however, there were an intention to continue farming on land of more than 900 square metres for more than ten years, the tax was waived. A total of 86 per cent of the 44,000 hectares targeted for this tax was thus exempted under this provision, with the farmers owning this land only paying the agricultural land tax rate. In addition, the inheritance tax on agricultural land is waived if the successor continues farming for twenty years. *Asahi Shinbun*, 22 April 1990. Moore reported that in the 23 wards of Tokyo, the tax rate on residential land was 80 times that of agricultural land. *Japanese Agriculture*, p. 281.

36 Established in 1970 the farmers' pension fund system (*nogyosha nenkin seido*) established a pension for farmers from 60–65 years, after which it could be supplemented from the national pension system. Moore, *Japanese Agriculture*, p. 294. The way in which the agricultural pension system operates provides supplemental monies to farmers in addition to the national old age pension. Farmers can receive supplemental pensions from the farmers' pension fund under certain terms and conditions, some of which are designed to encourage farmers to leave the land and thus assist the restructuring of Japanese agriculture. ABARE, *Japanese Agricultural Policies*, pp. 313–315. Because pension levels are too low to achieve this objective effectively, the benefits paid end up as just another form of subsidy to farm households (p. 315).

37 Kawasaki Isonobu, *Shokuryocho-dono: Watashi Wa Yamigomeya Desu* [*Mr Food Agency: I Am Running A Black Market Rice Shop*], Tokyo, Gendai Shorin, 1992, p. 16. As one Western cynic explained: 'The bulk of Japan's "farmers" are not farmers. They are merely part-time or weekend folk who put in the odd hour to collect the subsidies that go with agriculture'. Roger Buckley in a letter to *The Economist*, 23 July 1988.

38 See the statistics above for part- and full-time farmers, particularly for Type II part-time farmers who make up the majority.

39 Minami Tetsuo, 'Jiminto no Nogyo Seisaku' ['The LDP's Agricultural Policy'], in Nosei Jyaanarisuto no Kai (ed.), *Tatoka Jidai no Nosei* [*Agricultural Policy in the Era of Party Proliferation*], Nihon Nogyo no Ugoki No. 44, Tokyo, Norin Tokei Kyokai, 1977, p. 29.

40   S. Kobayashi, J. B. Morison and P. Riethmuller, 'A Review of Recent Developments in Japanese Agriculture and Agricultural Policy', *Review of Marketing and Agricultural Economics*, Vol. 59, No. 3, December 1991, p. 220. Houck also comments that 'trade policies and other decisions by national governments are almost always extensions of domestic agricultural and food policies'. James P. Houck, 'Agricultural Trade: Protectionism, Policy, and the Tokyo/Geneva Negotiating Round', *American Journal of Agricultural Economics*, Vol. 61, No. 5, December 1979, p. 863. Saeki writes that trade can be restricted in two ways: by border adjustment measures that impact directly on the inflow of products and services into domestic markets; and secondly, by specific domestic policies that have an indirect effect on international trade. See Saeki Naomi, 'Nogyo Kosho no Tenkai to Kiketsu' ['The Development and Results of the Agricultural Trade Negotiations'] in Ouchi Tsutomu and Saeki Naomi (eds), *GATTO Nogyo Kosho to Nihon Nogyo* [*The GATT Agricultural Negotiations and Japanese Agriculture*], Nihon Nogyo Nenpo 37, Tokyo, Norin Tokei Kyokai, 1991, p. 4. According to Korenaga, agricultural protection influences agricultural imports by changing the relationship between domestic demand and supply, whether this is done by means of price supports or direct payments such as deficiency payments. Korenaga Tohiko, 'Senshinkoku Nosei no Tenkai to Nosan Boeki Mondai' ['The Development of Agricultural Policy in Advanced Countries and Agricultural Trade Problems'], in Kamiya and Korenaga (eds), *Nogyo Hogo*, p. 11.

41   David N. Balaam, 'Self-Sufficiency in Japanese Agriculture: Telescoping and Reconciling the Food Security–Efficiency Dilemma', in William P. Browne and Don F. Hadwiger (eds), *World Food Policies: Toward Agricultural Interdependence*, Boulder, CO., Lynne Rienner Publishers, 1986, p. 99.

42   In some years, rice and the general category of livestock products have changed places. In 1991, for example, rice generated only ¥2.92 trillion in gross output value, or 25.5 per cent of the total. Production of meat and dairy products in that year, on the other hand, expanded to ¥3.11 trillion in gross output value, or 27.1 per cent of the total. This was the first time since the end of WWI that rice had been dislodged from its pre-eminent position as the nation's No. 1 product. *The Japan Times*, 14 January 1993.

43   These include Japanese radishes (*daikon*), carrots, edible burdocks, lotus root, taros, Chinese cabbages, cabbages, onions etc.

44   Beef farming in Japan has traditionally been divided into two main sub-sectors: cattle raising for meat (*nikuyogyu*) and dairy cattle farming (*nyuyogyu*) producing both meat and milk. Most beef cattle farms raise Japanese native cattle (*wagyu*), while the cattle raised by dairy farmers (for both meat and milk) are almost all the Western species of Holstein.

45   See the OECD and ABARE definitions above.

46   *Poketto*, 1999, pp. 126, 181.

47   *Poketto*, 1999, pp. 126, 181.

48   Pig breeding, like poultry farming, has flourished in Japan because of the development of intensive breeding and rearing techniques which are inapplicable to cattle farming.

49   These figures are for 1999. *Poketto*, 1999, p. 188.

50   *Norinsuisansho Tokeihyo*, 1996–97, pp. 404–405.

51   *Daily Yomiuri*, 8 January 1993.

52   *Norinsuisansho Tokeihyo*, 1996–97, p. 11.

53   *Norinsuisansho Tokeihyo*, 1996–97, p. 11.

54   *Norinsuisansho Tokeihyo*, 1996–97, pp. 11, 124.

55   *Poketto*, 1994, p. 232.

56 *Norinsuisansho Tokeihyo*, 1996–97, pp. 64, 66, 82, 89, 90.
57 *Norinsuisansho Tokeihyo*, 1996–97, pp. 81, 107.
58 Pincus advances a similar view in relation of industry, arguing that geographic concentration positively correlates with the ability to lobby successfully for protection, because of the greater ease of communication and coordination amongst the firms involved. J. J. Pincus, 'Pressure Groups and the Pattern of Tariffs', *Journal of Political Economy*, Vol. 83, No. 4, 1975, pp. 757–778.
59 Between 1989 and 1997, for example, these households declined from 57,230 to 6,310. *Poketto*, 1997, p. 267; *Poketto*, 1999, p. 272.
60 Hasegawa Hiroshi, 'A Petition to Open the Rice Market', *Japan Quarterly*, Vol. 34, No. 1, Jan.–March 1987, p. 72.
61 *Norinsuisansho Tokeihyo*, 1996–97, p. 10.
62 *Norinsuisansho Tokeihyo*, 1996–97, pp. 186–187.
63 *Norinsuisansho Tokeihyo*, 1996–97, pp. 186–187.
64 *Norinsuisansho Tokeihyo*, 1996–97, pp. 186–187.
65 Ito Kenzo, *Nosanbutsu Yunyu Jiyuka Mondai to Nihon Nogyo* [*The Problem of Liberalising Imports of Agricultural Products and Japan's Agriculture*], Tokyo, Tsukuba Shobo, 1984, p. 22.
66 *Norinsuisansho Tokeihyo*, 1996–97, pp. 10–11.
67 *Heisei 8-Nensan Hatasakumotsu Kakaku no Kettei ni tsuite* [*About the Price Decisions for Dry Field Products in 1996*], MAFF Home Page, http://www.maff.go.jp.
68 A viable farm is one that can generate 'income per full-time farm worker at a level equivalent to the average income of non-farm workers without relying on government protection'. Hayami, *Japanese Agriculture Under Siege*, p. 76.
69 Kobayashi, Morison and Riethmuller, 'A Review', p. 216.
70 *Poketto*, 1999, p. 181.
71 *Poketto*, 1996, p. 178.
72 *Poketto*, 1999, p. 181.
73 Sadako Nakayasu, 'Japan's Agricultural Structure: Characteristics and Changes', in The Committee For the Japanese Agricultural Session, XXI ICAE Conference (ed.), *Agriculture and Agricultural Policy in Japan*, Tokyo, University of Tokyo Press, 1991, p. 144, quoted in Kobayashi, Morison and Riethmuller, 'A Review', p. 216.
74 Domon Takeshi, 'Kome Gyosei: Kengyo Noka o Mamori, Shokuryocho o Mamotta?' ['The Administration of Rice: Protection for Part-Time Farmers and the Food Agency?'], *Ekonomisuto*, 22 November 1994, p. 47. In his view: 'Apart from a small minority of serious rice cultivators, the majority of Japan's "farmers" are growing rice on a part-time basis, mainly to preserve the extremely low tax valuations on their "farmland"'. Takashi Domon, 'MAFF Fiddles While Taxpayers Burn: Rice Market Opening Close at Hand', *Tokyo Business Today*, January 1994, p. 20. Yamaji and Ito also make the point that 'operators have a strong feeling that they would be shamed and lose face if they left their farms barren. In other words, it is a tradition of shame culture that makes them grow rice despite an economic loss.' Susumu Yamaji and Shoichi Ito, 'The Political Economy of Rice in Japan', in Tweeten *et al.* (eds), *Japanese & American Agriculture*, p. 357.
75 *Poketto*, 1999, p. 229.
76 *Poketto*, 1997, p. 276.
77 *Poketto*, 1999, p. 280.
78 *Poketto*, 1999, p. 281.
79 Boonekamp, *Agriculture in Japan*, p. 6.
80 OECD, *Agricultural Policies, Markets and Trade*, p. 160.

81 OECD, *Agricultural Policies, Markets and Trade*, p. 160.
82 OECD, *Agricultural Policies, Markets and Trade*, p. 99.
83 *Nihon Keizai Shinbun*, 31 July 1986.
84 Yamaji and Ito, 'The Political Economy of Rice', p. 361.
85 Michael Donnelly, 'Setting the Price of Rice: A Study in Political Decision-making', in T. J. Pempel (ed.), *Policymaking in Contemporary Japan*, Ithaca and London, Cornell University Press, 1977, p. 199.
86 Personal communication, Norinchukin Research Institute, April 1998.
87 It has also been translated in English language materials as 'agricultural cooperative association' (the dictionary translation for '*kumiai*' is either 'union' or 'association') or 'agricultural cooperative society', or simply 'agricultural cooperative'.
88 Various translations of Nokyo are used in the English, including Agricultural Cooperative Association, the National Association of Agricultural Cooperatives, the Agricultural Cooperative Society or the Union of Agricultural Cooperatives.
89 Takeshi Ishida and Aurelia D. George, 'Nokyo: The Farmers' Representative', in Peter Drysdale and Hironobu Kitaoji (eds), *Japan and Australia: Two Societies and their Interaction*, Canberra, ANU Press, 1980, p. 202.
90 Tanaka Toyotoshi, *Nihon no Nokyo [Japan's Nokyo]*, Tokyo, Tokyo, Nokyo Kyokai, 1971, p. 424.
91 Nagao Satoru, 'Nihon no Seiji Taisei to Kome no Jiyuka Mondai' ['Japanese Political Institutions and the Rice Liberalisation Issue'], *Outlook*, No. 10, Fall 1990, p. 30.
92 The LDP was in a governing coalition between June 1994 and October 1996 and in a loose Parliamentary alliance between October 1996 and June 1998, despite its regaining a Lower House majority in September 1997. After the Upper House elections of July 1998, the LDP initially required Diet members from other Opposition parties to help pass its legislation in that house. It later entered into coalition agreements with other parties.
93 The JSP renamed itself the Social Democratic Party (of Japan) or SDP(J) in English in January 1991, and then changed its Japanese title in January 1996, when it became the Social Democratic Party, or SDP (Shakai Minshuto).
94 This general point has also been made elsewhere. See Michio Muramatsu and Ellis Krauss, 'The Conservative Policy Line and the Development of Patterned Pluralism', in Kozo Yamamura and Yasukichi Yasuba (eds), *The Political Economy of Japan*, Vol. 1, Stanford, Stanford University Press, 1987, p. 521.
95 Muramatsu and Krauss, 'The Conservative Policy Line', p. 520.
96 Toshihiko Kawagoe, 'The Origins of Protectionism in Japanese Agriculture', Seminar, Department of Economic History, Australian National University, September 1996, p. 18.
97 In 1976 the Ministry of Agriculture and Fisheries (MAF) altered its title to Ministry of Agriculture, Forestry and Fisheries (MAFF). The MAF was reestablished immediately after the war, having been abolished and replaced during the war by the Ministry of Agriculture and Commerce (MAC), or Nososho.
98 This is the gist of Article 1 of the MAFF Establishment Law which sets out the purpose of the legislation. 'Norinsuisansho Setchiho' ['Ministry of Agriculture, Forestry and Fisheries Establishment Law'], in Norinsuisansho (ed.), *Nogyo Roppo [A Compendium of Agricultural Laws]*, Tokyo, Gakuyo Shobo, 1993 (hereafter *Nogyo Roppo*), p. 13.
99 In 1998 a total of 121 agricultural laws were listed on the statute books, although the actual number in any particular year can vary slightly. This total does not include laws administered by the Forestry Agency or the Fisheries Agency of the MAFF.

100 Kajii Isao, 'Nogyo Kosho no Zasetsu to Nihon Nogyo no Saihensei' ['The Failure of the GATT Agricultural Trade Negotiations and the Reorganisation of Japanese Agriculture'], in Ouchi and Saeki (eds), *GATTO Nogyo Kosho*, p. 124.

101 Matsushima Masahiro, 'Kome Zenmen Jiyuka wa Mondai' ['Total Liberalisation of Rice is a Problem'], *Asahi Shinbun*, 17 March 1990.

102 'Nogyo Kyodo Kumiaiho' ['Agricultural Cooperative Union Law'], in *Nogyo Roppo*, 1993, p. 108. For a thorough exposition of all aspects of this law, see Zenkoku Nogyo Kyodo Kumiai Chuokai, *Shinpan: Nogyo Kyodo Kumiaiho [New Publication: Agricultural Cooperative Union Law]*, Tokyo, Ie no Hikari Kyokai, 1995.

103 This is a translation of Article 1 of the 'Tochi Kairyoho' ['Land Improvement Law'] in *Nogyo Roppo*, 1993, p. 460.

104 Hiroshi Yamauchi, 'Analytical Institutional Economics of Japanese Agricultural Policy', Seminar, Research Institute for Asian Development, University of Hawaii, May 1993, p. 9.

105 Article 1 of the 'Nochiho' ['Agricultural Land Law'], in *Nogyo Roppo*, 1993, p. 255.

106 Goto and Imamura, 'Japanese Agriculture', p. 22.

107 This objective was met through the 'selective expansion' provision which held that farmers expand production of commodities subject to growing consumer demand such as livestock commodities and fruit. The other side of this coin was the abandonment of agricultural products that competed with foreign imports (such as wheat and soybeans). Such production rationalisation would also have extended to rice had the government followed the provisions of the law to the letter.

108 Article 1 of the 'Nogyo Kihonho' ['Agricultural Basic Law'] in *Nogyo Roppo*, 1993, p. 3.

109 Somucho, Gyosei Kanri Kyoku, *Shingikai Soran [A Compendium of Advisory Councils]*, Tokyo, Somucho, Gyosei Kanri Kyoku, 1996 (hereafter *Shingikai Soran*), pp. 1–10. By 1998 their number had fallen to 211.

110 Masahiko Aoki, 'The Japanese Bureaucracy in Economic Administration: A Rational Regulator or Pluralist Agent?', in J. Shoven (ed.), *Government Policy Towards Industry in the United States and Japan*, Cambridge, Cambridge University Press, 1988, p. 286.

111 This was established as an advisory organ to the Prime Minister, MAF Minister and relevant ministers by the ABL of 1961. It was charged with investigating and deliberating on important matters relating to the implementation of the ABL. It had three separate divisions (for planning, trends and Nokyo) and its membership was set at not more than fifteen persons.

112 Others are the Agriculture, Forestry and Fisheries Statistics Observation Advisory Council, the Agriculture, Forestry and Fisheries Insurance Investigation Council, the Irrigation and Drainage Advisory Council, the Agriculture Mechanisation Advisory Council, the Agricultural Materials Advisory Council, the Veterinary Affairs Advisory Council, the Food Distribution Advisory Council and the Agriculture and Forestry Commodities Standards Research Council. *Shingikai Soran*, 1996, p. 6.

113 *Shingikai Soran*, 1996, pp. 6–8.

114 An examination of the RPAC's recommendations on the producer rice price over twelve years from 1975 to 1986 revealed that on seven occasions, the council endorsed the price recommendation of the MAFF, on two occasions, it put two dissenting views in the report (that is, support for and against a producer rice price rise or freeze), and on three occasions, the report was abandoned. *Tokyo Shinbun*, 10 August 1986.

115 Diet members were removed from the RPAC in 1968. See Aurelia George, *The Strategies of Influence: Japan's Agricultural Cooperatives (Nokyo) as a Pressure Group*, unpublished doctoral dissertation, Australian National University, 1980, pp. 322–324.

116 Sakurai Makoto, *Beika Seisaku to Beika Undo* [*Rice Policy and the Rice Price Campaign*], Tokyo, Zenkoku Nogyo Kyodo Kumiai Chuokai, 1977, p. 39. Calder claims that the RPAC in 1949 was 'dominated by officials sympathetic to producer price increases'. *Crisis and Compensation*, p. 258.

117 These are almost always former officials of the MAFF (i.e. 'old boys' or 'OBs'), who have retired into executive positions in MAFF *gaikaku dantai*.

118 Okurasho Insatsu Kyoku (ed.), *Shokuinraku* [*List of Staff Members*], 1987, Tokyo, Okurasho Insatsu Kyoku, 1986, p. 1300. The maximum number of RPAC members is 25.

119 *Shingikai Soran*, 1996, pp. 327–328.

120 This was true until 1998–99 when the abolition of 121 of the existing 211 advisory councils was mooted, including several attached to the MAFF.

121 Viz.: 'Electoral rules amplify the importance of blocs of votes and hence delay decisions that could hurt any group of constituents'. Frances McCall Rosenbluth, 'Comment', to Ito Takatoshi, 'U.S. Political Pressure and Economic Liberalization in East Asia', in Jeffrey Frankel and Miles Kahler (eds), *Regionalism and Rivalry: Japan and the United States in Pacific Asia*, Chicago, University of Chicago Press, 1993, p. 421; and: 'Given the importance to LDP members of personal support networks and of campaign financing to nurture these blocs of votes, the party leadership faces ferocious opposition from within the party's own ranks to policy measures – trade liberalization, for instance – that alienate groups of supporters.' 'Comment', p. 422.

2 Interest group politics

1 Fujitani Chikuji, 'Nokyo at a Crossroads', *Japan Quarterly*, Vol. 39, No. 3, July–September 1992, p. 376.

2 Mitsukawa Motochika, *Nogyo Dantai Hattenshi* [*A History of the Development of Agricultural Groups*], Tokyo, Meibun Shobo, 1972, p. 97.

3 The profits from the sale of rice and wheat were converted into deposits in the *nogyokai* credit division. These deposits were then loaned to farmers to purchase fertiliser and other farm inputs.

4 *Nogyo Dantai Hattenshi*, p. 101.

5 See chapter 8 on 'Policy Campaigning'.

6 These organisations are also called 'mutual cooperatives', 'mutual cooperative unions', 'cooperative unions' and 'industrial guilds'.

7 According to Havens, this law was 'directly concerned with economic activity, especially interest rates and loans, for smaller cultivators'. T. R. H. Havens, *Farm and Nation in Modern Japan*, Princeton, Princeton University Press, 1974, p. 78. The *sangyo kumiai* achieved the removal of commercial and other high interest rate capital from the villages. Zenkoku Nogyo Kyodo Kumiai Chuokai, *Shinpan: Nogyo Kyodo Kumiaiho*, p. 4.

8 Zenkoku Nogyo Kyodo Kumiai Chuokai, *Shinpan: Nogyo Kyodo Kumiaiho*, p. 4.

9 In 1903, there were 870 cooperatives nationwide, 549 of which were credit cooperatives. The Institute for the Development of Agriculture Cooperation in Asia, *Agricultural Cooperative Movement in Japan*, n.d., p. 15.

10 Fujitani, 'Nokyo at a Crossroads', p. 376. These functions were, however, conducted in specialised *sangyo kumiai* such as credit cooperatives (*shinyo kumiai*), marketing cooperatives (*hanbai kumiai*), utilisation cooperatives (*riyo*

kumiai) and purchasing cooperatives (*kobai kumiai*), and in this respect, the *sangyo kumiai* were more akin to the postwar specialist agricultural cooperatives. Takeuchi Tetsuo and Otawara Takaaki, *Asu no Nokyo: Rinen to Jigyo o Tsunagu Mono* [*Tomorrow's Nokyo: The Connection Between Principle and Enterprise*], Tokyo, Nosangyoson Bunka Kyokai, 1994, p. 28. See also below.

11 *Agricultural Cooperative Movement*, p. 16. This comparatively low rate of membership is regarded by Takeuchi and Otawara as a sign of low organising ability on the part of the *sangyo kumiai*. *Asu no Nokyo*, p. 28.

12 Takeshi Ishida, 'Interest Groups in Japan', unpublished monograph, n.d., p. 21.

13 This was the Central Bank for Industrial Cooperatives Law (*Sangyo Kumiai Chuo Kinkoho*) passed in 1923. At the time of its establishment, half of its capital was supplied by the government. Personal communication, Norinchukin Research Institute, March 1998.

14 Gilbert C. George, 'Japan's Post-War Agricultural Cooperative Movement', M.Econ. Thesis, Hitotsubashi University, Tokyo, 1976, p. 6.

15 Ishimi, *Nokyo*, pp. 16–22. See also below.

16 See chapter 3 on 'Farmers Politics' for a discussion of the organisational and political mobilisation of the industrial cooperatives against the anti-industrial cooperative movement of private merchants in the 1930s.

17 Ishida, *Interest Groups*, p. 22.

18 Havens, *Farm and Nation*, p. 74.

19 Havens, *Farm and Nation*, p. 74.

20 Funding was also derived from membership fees.

21 Kuwabara Masanobu, 'Nogyo Kyodo Kumiai no Nosei Katsudo' ['The Agricultural Policy Activities of Nokyo'], in Nogyo Kaihatsu Senta (ed.), *Nokyo Undo no Genjo Bunseki* [*Analysis of the Current State of Nokyo's Activities*], Gendai Nogyo Kyodo Kumiai Soshikiron 2, Tokyo, Ie no Hikari Kyokai, 1974, p. 257.

22 Kuwabara, 'Nogyo Kyodo Kumiai no Nosei Katsudo', p. 257.

23 Havens, *Farm and Nation*, p. 74.

24 Takekazu B. Ogura, *Can Japanese Agriculture Survive?*, Tokyo, Agricultural Policy Research Centre, 3rd Edition, 1982, p. 270.

25 Ogura, *Can Japanese Agriculture Survive?*, p. 308. Ogura classifies their activities into three types: 'The first was the guidance and encouragement of farming; the second was the study and research of agriculture, and the third was activities concerning agricultural policy, which consisted of recommendations and reports to the authorities and also concerned lobbyism'.

26 Kuwabara, 'Nogyo Kyodo Kumiai no Nosei Katsudo', p. 258. In one text for political science students in Japan, the *nokai* are classified as agricultural policy organisations. See Muramatsu Michio, Ito Mitsutoshi and Tsujinaka Yutaka, *Nihon no Seiji* [*Politics in Japan*], Tokyo, Yuhikaku, 1992, p. 209.

27 Mitsukawa, *Nogyo Dantai Hattenshi*, pp. 259–263. See also chapter 6 on 'Electoral Politics' for a discussion of the vote-mobilisation role of prewar landlords.

28 Ronald P. Dore, *Land Reform in Japan*, London, Oxford University Press, 1959, p. 293.

29 Fujitani, 'Nokyo at a Crossroads', p. 376.

30 These were the livestock cooperatives (*chikusan kumiai*), sericulture cooperatives (*yosan kumiai*) and tea industry cooperatives (*chagyo kumiai*).

31 The *nogyokai* organisation consisted, at the national level, of the Central Association of Agriculture (Chuo Nogyokai) which undertook guidance activity, the National Economic Association of Agriculture (Zenkoku Nogyo Keizaikai) which conducted economic business, and Norinchukin which performed financial business. At the prefectural and municipal levels there were prefectural

associations of agriculture and city, town and village associations of agriculture respectively. The *nogyokai* organisation was thus modelled on a three-stage pattern of municipal, prefectural and national organisations. Zenkoku Nogyo Kyodo Kumiai Chuokai, *Hayawakari JA no Subete* [*An Easy Guide to All of JA*], Tokyo, Ie no Hikari Kyokai, 1994, pp. 138–139.

32 For details of their role in land reform, see Ronald P. Dore, 'The Socialist Party and the Farmers', in Allan D. Cole, George O. Totten, and Cecil H. Uyehara (eds), *Socialist Parties in Postwar Japan*, New Haven and London, Yale University Press, 1966, pp. 370–391; Tadashi Fukutake, *Japanese Rural Society*, Ithaca and London, Cornell University Press, 1972, pp. 189–201; and Ito Toshio, 'Nokyo to Seiji Katsudo' ['Nokyo and Political Activities'], in Kondo Yasuo (ed.), *Nokyo Nijugonen: Sokatsu to Tenbo* [*Twenty Five Years of Nokyo: Summary and Outlook*], Nihon Nogyo Nenpo Vol. 22, Tokyo, Ochanomizu Shobo, 1973, p. 149. Ito makes the point that Nokyo made little or no contribution to this 'great reform of the century' (p. 149).

33 The first Nichino was established in 1922. For a detailed history of the farmers' union movement in the prewar period see Nomin Mondai Kenkyukai (ed.), *Nomin Undo to Kyosanshugi Katsudo* [*The Farmers' Movement and Communist Activities*], Tokyo, Nikkan Rodo Tsushinsha, 1962.

34 This figure was taken from Kyoto Daigaku Bungakubu Kokushi Kenkyu Shitsu (eds), *Nihon Kindaishi Jiten* [*A Dictionary of Modern Japanese History*], Tokyo, Toyo Keizai Shinposha, 1964 (hereafter *Nihon Kindaishi Jiten*), Furoku No. 36.

35 At this convention, Nichino's platform included a revision of the Farm Land Adjustment Law (the land reform law), the development of large-scale farm land by the government, the expansion of the agricultural insurance system and the implementation of an Agricultural Union Law (*Nogyo Kumiaiho*). Another objective was the establishment of a democratic way of life and culture in farm villages. Nomin Kumiai Goju Shunen Kinensai Jikko Iinkai (ed.), *Nomin Kumiai Gojunenshi* [*A Fifty-Year History of the Farmers' Unions*], Tokyo, Ochanomizu Shobo, 1972, pp. 250–267.

36 *Nihon Kindaishi Jiten*, Furoku No. 36.

37 Mitsukawa, *Nogyo Dantai Hattenshi*, p. 182.

38 Mitsukawa, *Nogyo Dantai Hattenshi*, p. 68.

39 Dore, 'The Socialist Party', pp. 378–391.

40 Ishida, *Interest Groups*, p. 46.

41 Ishida, *Interest Groups*, p. 46.

42 Dore, *Land Reform in Japan*, pp. 471–472.

43 As Tanaka explains, Nichino aimed to increase the share of its representatives in Nokyo's management in order to ensure the complete dissolution of the *nogyokai*, centre the agricultural cooperatives on small-scale farmers and establish agricultural cooperatives that would be independent of the landed class and prominent farmers. *Nihon no Nokyo*, pp. 14–15.

44 These are discussed below.

45 Dore, 'The Socialist Party', p. 386. Nishida also reports that a 'large number of farmers' movement leaders launched themselves into public positions such as mayors, town and village headmen, members of municipal councils and the prefectural assembly, members of the National Diet, officials of agricultural cooperatives, and members of the local agricultural committees, thereby forming a channel through which to represent the interests of farmers in the political arena.' Nishida Yoshiaki, *The Rise and Decline of the Farmers' Movement and Transformation of the Rural Community in Postwar Japan*, Occasional Papers in Labor Problem and Social Policy, No. 19, Institute of Social Science, University

of Tokyo, September 1994, p. 38. Nishida mounts a strong challenge to the orthodox thesis that the accomplishment of land reform deprived the farmers' union of their main purpose and was thus the primary factor responsible for their organisational decline. He argues, firstly, that farmers participated in the farmers' unions in order to strengthen and develop their farming operations and not simply to lobby for land reform, and therefore the completion of land reform did not necessarily remove the rationale for farmers' membership of these groups. One of the failures of the farmers' union movement was their inability to meet these production and economic concerns of farmers. Nishida emphasises 'the general lack of capability on the part of the union organizations to deal squarely with matters of urgent need for farming operations – e.g., food delivery, taxation, land improvement, procurement of agricultural implements, and the maintenance of farm product prices' (p. 21). This argument also endorses the point made earlier – that it was the agricultural cooperatives that stepped in to meet this need by performing economic service functions for farmers and by assuming an interest representational role on policy issues germane to the farm household economy.

46 Dore, 'The Socialist Party', p. 386.
47 Dore, 'The Socialist Party', p. 383. See also chapter 3 on 'Farmers' Politics'.
48 Mitsukawa, *Nogyo Dantai Hattenshi*, p. 60.
49 Hirano Rikizo had previously led the right wing of the prewar Nichino.
50 Nihon *Kindaishi Jiten*, Furoku No. 36.
51 Mitsukawa, *Nogyo Dantai Hattenshi*, p. 183.
52 *Nihon Kindaishi Jiten*, Furoku No. 36.
53 *Nihon Kindaishi Jiten*, Furoku No. 36.
54 *Nihon Kindaishi Jiten*, Furoku No. 36.
55 *Nihon Kindaishi Jiten*, Furoku No. 36.
56 Mitsukawa, *Nogyo Dantai Hattenshi*, p. 545.
57 *Nihon Kindaishi Jiten*, Furoku No. 36. According to Mitsukawa, the Zennoseiren increased its supporters from 700,000 to 1 million between 1946 and 1947. *Nogyo Dantai Hattenshi*, p. 69.
58 *Nihon Kindaishi Jiten*, Furoku No. 36.
59 Mitsukawa, *Nogyo Dantai Hattenshi*, p. 69.
60 Mitsukawa, *Nogyo Dantai Hattenshi*, p. 69.
61 Mitsukawa, *Nogyo Dantai Hattenshi*, p. 61.
62 Executives of the *nogyokai* were associates of the leagues.
63 Mitsukawa, *Nogyo Dantai Hattenshi*, p. 70.
64 Tanaka, *Nihon no Nokyo*, p. 73.
65 This replaced the Central Association of Agriculture and the National Economic Association of Agriculture which were dissolved just before the end of the war. Zenkoku Nogyo Kyodo Kumiai Chuokai, *Hayawakari JA no Subete*, p. 139.
66 From Nichino's perspective, the purpose of the agricultural revival movement was to improve agricultural productivity, ensure food supplies and construct democratic farming villages. Nomin Kumiai Goju Shunen Kinensai Jikko Iinkai (ed.), *Nomin Kumiai Gojunenshi*, pp. 298–300.
67 Tanaka, *Nihon no Nokyo*, p. 74. See also below.
68 Tanaka, *Nihon no Nokyo*, pp. 74–75. See also below.
69 Ishida, *Interest Groups*, pp. 47–48.
70 Ishida, *Interest Groups*, p. 48. As Tanaka points out, although GHQ forbade *nogyokai* executives from becoming involved in the establishment of the agricultural cooperatives, they managed to take the lead in this process through the Agriculture Reconstruction Council. *Nihon no Nokyo*, p. 11. See also below.

71 Taguchi Fukuji, 'Pressure Groups in Japanese Politics', *The Developing Economies*, Vol. VI, No. 4, December 1968, p. 478.

72 The agricultural policy objectives of the Party Preparatory Committee of the Socialist Party in 1945, for example, included development of the agricultural cooperatives and fundamental reform of the land tenure system. Dore, 'The Socialist Party', p. 375.

73 There seems to be some confusion in Calder's analysis of agricultural organisations at this time. He notes, for example: 'On December 15 1947, it [the government] succeeded in passing a major revision of the old Agricultural Cooperative Association Law. This revision decreed abolition of the conservative agricultural associations, or *nokai*, which had dominated the Japanese countryside on behalf of landlords and the state since the mid-Meiji period.' *Crisis and Compensation*, p. 76. It would seem that Calder has confused dates as well the organisational genealogy of the *nokai*, *sangyo kumiai* and *nogyokai* which he has rolled into one and called *nokai*. In fact the Nokyo Law was promulgated on 19 November 1947 and executed on 15 December 1947. Accompanying the enactment of the Nokyo Law was the promulgation of legislation relating to the reorganisation of agricultural groups, called the Agricultural Groups Reorganisation Law (*Nogyo Dantai Seiriho*), under the terms of which the *nogyokai* were to be dissolved by August 1948. Zenkoku Nogyo Kyodo Kumiai Chuokai, *Hayawakari JA no Subete*, p. 139. The legal dissolution of the *nogyokai* is officially recorded as being on 14 August 1948.

74 Ogura, *Can Japanese Agriculture Survive?*, pp. 287, 288.

75 Mitsukawa, *Nogyo Dantai Hattenshi*, p. 132. Calder gives different figures: from 892 in March 1948 to 27,819 by the end of the year. *Crisis and Compensation*, p. 252.

76 'Nenpyo: Nokyo 25-nen' ['A Chronology: The 25 Years of Nokyo'], in Kondo (ed.), *Nokyo Nijugonen*, p. 437.

77 Ishida, *Interest Groups*, p. 35.

78 Mitsukawa, *Nogyo Dantai Hattenshi*, p. 132.

79 This section of the book draws heavily on George, *The Strategies of Influence*, pp. 10–67.

80 For a detailed explication of each of the businesses of the agricultural cooperatives, see Zenkoku Nogyo Kyodo Kumiai Chuokai, *Shinpan: Nogyo Kyodo Kumiaiho*, pp. 66–113.

81 These joint-use facilities (*kyodo riyo shisetsu*) include rice mills, rice centres, country elevators, high speed sprayers, vegetable and fruit markets, breeding facilities, egg selecting facilities, joint pastures, milk collection facilities, cooler stations, cold storage facilities, unpacked feed collecting stations and agricultural machinery service stations. For the numbers of joint-use facilities and the numbers of agricultural cooperatives involved, see Norinsuisansho, Keizai Kyoku Nogyo Kyodo Kumiaika, *Sogo Nokyo Tokeihyo* [*Statistics on Agricultural Cooperatives*], Tokyo, Norin Tokei Kyokai (hereafter *Sogo Nokyo Tokeihyo*), annual.

82 This function did not involve the agricultural cooperatives engaging in farm management directly. They were only permitted to undertake farmland trust (*nochi itaku*), agricultural management trust (*nogyo keiei jutaku*) and adjustment of utilisation rights as a corporation for the rationalisation of farmland possession (*nochi hoyu gorika hojin toshite no riyoken chosei*). Kajii Isao, 'Nokyo no Nogyoteki Katsudo no Kyoka to Hoseidoteki Kadai' ['Strengthening Nokyo's Agriculture-Related Activities and Legal System Themes'], *Nogyo to Keizai*, Vol. 58, No. 3, March 1992, p. 17.

83 For a complete and detailed list of agricultural cooperative businesses, see Article 10 of 'Nogyo Kyodo Kumiaiho' in *Nogyo Roppo*, 1998, pp. 158–160.

Under other laws Nokyo also conducts agricultural warehousing business, post office and national health insurance business, proxy duties for the Agricultural Trust Fund Association and the Farmers' Pension Fund, and business relating to the acquisition of prior rights and mortgages over agricultural movables. See Aono Bunsaku, *Nokyo: Soshiki to Hito to Senryaku* [*Nokyo: Organisation, People and Strategies*], Tokyo, Daiyamondosha, 1976, p. 8; Zenkoku Nogyo Kyodo Kumiai Chuokai, *Hayawakari JA no Subete*, pp. 44–45. For details of the laws under which these functions are conducted, see Zenkoku Nogyo Kyodo Kumiai, *Shinpan: Nogyo Kyodo Kumiaiho*, pp. 107–113. See also below.

84 Article 10 was amended six times between 1947 and 1972 alone: in 1950, 1951, 1954, 1962, 1970 and 1972. The principal changes incorporated in these amendments were the addition of Paragraphs 2–12.

85 This amendment was passed in 1993. A full description of this business and the terms and conditions under which it is conducted is given in Zenkoku Nogyo Kyodo Kumiai, *Shinpan: Nogyo Kyodo Kumiaiho*, pp. 106–107.

86 Nokyo, for example, is one of a few institutions that offers educational services in rural areas. Nagata Shozo and Saito Misao, *Nokyo no Hanashi* [*Story of Nokyo*], Tokyo, Tokyo Keizai Shinposha, 1982, p. 163.

87 Zenkoku Nogyo Kyodo Kumiai Chuokai, *Hayawakari JA no Subete*, p. 48.

88 Imamura Naraomi and Inuzuka Akiharu, *Seifu to Nomin* [*Government and the Farmers*], Shokuryo Nogyo Mondai Zenshu No. 10, Tokyo, Nosan Gyoson Bunka Kyokai, 1991, p. 73. This does not mean that every cooperative carries out the full range of businesses. Each branch coordinates their businesses according to members' needs, which often differ from region to region. According to one study, the diversification of agricultural cooperative businesses took place as a result of the attempt by Nokyo to meet the diversified needs of its members rather than the mere pursuit of profits. Nagata and Saito, *Nokyo no Hanashi*, p. 162. Takahashi categorises *sogo nokyo* into one of four types: the first type is the agricultural cooperative union; the second is the real estate cooperative union (these co-ops mainly operate in large urban centres and their surrounding areas and the main income sources of members are from the management of rental houses, apartments and car parks, although the main operations of the co-ops themselves are credit and mutual aid); the third type is the livelihood activity *nokyo*, whose operations are focused on supplying members' everyday life needs; and the fourth type is the rural industry co-op, where the *nokyo* has developed into a major conglomerate in the rural economy, and has gained influence over the regional cattle breeding industry, agricultural product processing industry and so on. Takahashi Goro, ' "Kyodo Kumiainai Shijo Genri" to Nokyo no Soshiki Saihen' [' "Market Principles in Cooperative Unions" and the Reformation of the Nokyo Organisation'], in Ouchi and Kajii (eds), *Nokyo Yonjunen*, pp. 231–234.

89 Fujitani, 'Nokyo at a Crossroads', p. 377. As Masuda elaborates, the comprehensive business management system of Nokyo was a response to the economic character of postwar owner-farmers. The system was an attempt to satisfy farmers' every demand from agricultural management to daily living, in line with their two dominant characteristics: the farm operated as a family business in which farm management and family living were inseparably united; and the combination of rice production (as a basic commodity) with other crops. Therefore, each operational section of the multi-purpose Nokyo (i.e. credit, mutual aid, sales, utilisation etc.) was managed in a highly integrated fashion as an inevitable response to the management process (i.e. purchasing, production, sales and raising funds) of owner-farmers. Masuda Yoshiaki, 'Nokyo no Keiei Bunseki' ['An Analysis of Nokyo's Management'], in Ouchi and Kajii (eds), *Nokyo Yonjunen*, p. 58.

90 See also below.

91 These are production-level, joint-use organisations that use facilities and machinery on a cooperative basis and/or which engage in cooperative management of farmland and marketing of products. They are groups directly related to agricultural production and their establishment is authorised under Nokyo Law (in fact by an amendment to the law in 1962 designed to promote cooperative agricultural production). Nagata and Saito, *Nokyo no Hanashi*, p. 22. Their functions are described on pp. 29–31. See also Tanaka, *Nihon no Nokyo*, p. 18.

92 For a clarification of the generic term juridical person (*hojin*), see Zenkoku Nogyo Kyodo Kumiai Chuokai, *Shinpan: Nogyo Kyodo Kumiaiho*, pp. 24–25.

93 Zenkoku Nogyo Kyodo Kumiai Chuokai, *Nogyo Kyodo Kumiai Nenkan* [*The Yearbook of Agricultural Cooperatives*], Tokyo, Zenkoku Nogyo Kyodo Kumiai Chuokai (hereafter *Nokyo Nenkan*), annual, various issues, and Nihon Nogyo Nenkan Kankokai (ed.), *Nihon Nogyo Nenkan* [*Japan Agricultural Yearbook*], Tokyo, Ie no Hikari Kyokai (hereafter *Nihon Nogyo Nenkan*), annual, various issues. *Nokyo Nenkan* ceased publication in 1993, and its contents (in dramatically reduced form) were incorporated into *Nihon Nogyo Nenkan* from 1994 onwards.

94 These were the figures as of 31 March 1998. *Norinsuisansho Tokeihyo*, 1998, p. 578. The reductions in the numbers of *tankyo* over the decades is due to the ongoing amalgamation programme, which is accelerating. Approximately 40 per cent of *sogo nokyo* are located in town and village areas and around 25 per cent in cities or areas larger than cities, but these proportions are changing constantly because of co-op amalgamations which are reducing numbers of village and town cooperatives by grouping them into larger units. See below and chapter 4 on 'Organisational Politics'.

95 Yamamoto Osamu, 'Sogo Nokyo to Senmon Nokyo' ['Multi-Purpose Agricultural Cooperatives and Special-Purpose Cooperatives'], in Ouchi and Kajii (eds), *Nokyo Yonjunen*, p. 245. Yamamoto provides a comprehensive list of the differences between *sogo nokyo* and *senmon nokyo* (pp. 245–246).

96 Each *nokyo* is able to do business with other business organisations outside its area of membership, however. Nagata and Saito, *Nokyo no Hanashi*, p. 9.

97 The number of *senmon nokyo* that run credit operations is very limited. Yamamoto, 'Sogo Nokyo', p. 246.

98 A breakdown of the types and numbers of special-purpose agricultural cooperatives operating in 1998 was as follows: sericultural – 328; livestock – 295; dairying – 387; poultry – 204; pasture management – 785; horticultural – 458; rural manufacturing – 185; agricultural broadcasting – 55; 'ordinary' – 411; plus another 205 unspecified agricultural cooperatives to make a total of 3,363. *Norinsuisansho Tokeihyo*, 1996–97, pp. 578–579. 'Ordinary' or 'general' (*ippan*) *nokyo* are not, strictly speaking *senmon nokyo*. Their activities cover those relating to the production of various crops and products (like the *sogo nokyo*), but they do not conduct financial business. Nagata and Saito, *Nokyo no Hanashi*, p. 8.

99 Yamamoto, 'Sogo Nokyo', p. 246.

100 Saeki Naomi, *Nokyo Kaikaku* [*Reform of Nokyo*], Tokyo, Ie no Hikari Kyokai, 1993, pp. 155–156.

101 Yamamoto, 'Sogo Nokyo', p. 245.

102 In 1990, for example, the 13 fruit juice cooperative federations operating in prefectures such as Ehime, Kumamoto, Saga and Wakayama produced about 50 per cent of the *mikan*-based juices and blended orange and *mikan* beverages sold by beverage and food companies in Japan. *Daily Yomiuri*, 15 August 1991.

103 See also below.

104 Fujitani, 'Nokyo at a Crossroads', p. 371.

105 Saeki, *Nokyo Kaikaku*, p. 29. He lists the four distinctive features of the *sogo*

nokyo: they are based on regional human relationships and they have three layers of management, diversified business activities and a strong dependence on politics (see pp. 27–34).

106 They also have a variety of associate members. Associate members of the federations are cooperative organisations established under different laws which conduct similar activities to the agricultural cooperatives (such as fishery, forestry, credit, agricultural mutual aid, and small and medium enterprise cooperatives, and land improvement districts), and juridical persons (*hojin*) which mainly consist of Nokyo branches (*tankyo*) or cooperative organisations established under different laws, or whose major contributors are these kinds of organisations. Nagata and Saito, *Nokyo no Hanashi*, p. 49. Some of these organisations – the agricultural mutual aid and land improvement groups – are discussed below. See also Zenkoku Nogyo Kyodo Kumiai Chuokai, *Shinpan: Nogyo Kyodo Kumiaiho*, pp. 129–131.

107 In 1977, for example, 4,329 local agricultural cooperatives nationwide became directly affiliated members of Zenno. Zenno's Home Page, http://www.zennoh. or.jp/

108 Nagata and Saito, *Nokyo no Hanashi*, p. 55.

109 Two horticultural federations are the only ones now operating at combined prefectural levels.

110 Saeki, *Nokyo Kaikaku*, p. 120. Saeki gives the example of the specialist dairy co-operatives whose fresh milk marketing functions terminate at the prefectural dairy federations. Only the national organ has processing and liaison adjustment functions. Similarly, with respect to the specialist horticultural cooperatives, the marketing function involves the unit co-ops and the prefectural federations, whilst the national federation performs no more than a liaison-adjustment role. What this means is that when compared with the multi-purpose cooperatives, the specialist cooperatives operate from a one-to-two stage structure businesswise and the functions of the federations are limited.

111 Settlers are farmers who have moved on to land which has been made suitable for agricultural purposes, such as reclaimed land.

112 *Nihon Nogyo Nenkan* 1997, p. 368.

113 These figures were calculated from those given in *Norinsuisansho Tokeihyo*, 1998, pp. 580–581.

114 This is short for Zenkoku Nogyo Kyodo Kumiai Rengokai.

115 This is short for Zenkoku Kyosai Nogyo Kyodo Kumiai Rengokai.

116 It is also the national banking institution for fishery and forestry cooperatives. Nagata and Saito provide a very good description of the multi-dimensional aspects of Norinchukin's functioning. See *Nokyo no Hanashi*, p. 76.

117 This is short for Zenkoku Kobai Nogyo Kyodo Kumiai Rengokai. It was established in October 1948.

118 This is short for Zenkoku Hanbai Nogyo Kyodo Kumiai Rengokai. It was established in October 1948.

119 See also chapter 4 on 'Organisational Politics'.

120 Kyosanto Bukkuretto, *Gaiatsu no Naka no Nihon no Shokuryo, Nogyo* [*Japan's Food and Agriculture Under Foreign Pressure*], Tokyo, Nihon Kyosanto Chuo Iinkai, 1988, p. 31.

121 This figure is for 1995. *JA Guruupu Keizai Jigyo Kiso Tokei*, 1997, p. 89.

122 This figure is for 1995. *JA Guruupu Keizai Jigyo Kiso Tokei*, 1997, p. 95.

123 This figure is for 1995. *JA Guruupu Keizai Jigyo Kiso Tokei*, 1997, p. 86.

124 This figure is for 1995. *JA Guruupu Keizai Jigyo Kiso Tokei*, 1997, p. 92. In the case of both marketing and purchasing, all figures have gradually trended downwards over time.

125 See chapter 4 on 'Organisational Politics', especially Figure 4.1. This general analysis is taken from Saeki, *Nokyo Kaikaku*, p. 120. The term 'system capital' (*seido kinyu*) refers to funding from government sources, such as the Agriculture, Forestry and Fisheries Finance Corporation, the Agricultural Modernisation Fund, the Agricultural Trust Fund Association and the Agricultural Improvement Fund. See also below.

126 Saeki, *Nokyo Kaikaku*, p. 120.

127 Economic activities in the broader sense mean all businesses conducted by Nokyo except for credit and insurance businesses. However, it generally refers to only the sales of agricultural commodities and the supply of producer inputs as well as daily necessities. Nagata and Saito, *Nokyo no Hanashi*, p. 135.

128 See below and chapter 8 on 'Policy Campaigning'.

129 See also chapter 4 on 'Organisational Politics'.

130 This describes the process under the now defunct FC system. See below and chapter 4 on 'Organisational Politics'.

131 Nagata and Saito, *Nokyo no Hanashi*, p. 137.

132 Yamamoto claims that in comparison with the multi-purpose side of the organisation, the *senmon nokyo* do not necessarily have their own federated organisations because their three-stage systems are imperfect, because they lack self-sufficiency and because of cross-cutting organisational memberships. 'Sogo Nokyo', p. 246.

133 Zenrakuren was established in 1949 as the national federation of specialist dairy co-operatives. There is, therefore, a division of labour between Zenrakuren and Zenchikuren: Zenrakuren is concerned with commodities produced by dairy cattle – milk and beef. Zenchikuren covers all livestock interests.

134 In 1993 there was a third sericultural national federation called the National Dried Cocoon Marketing Nokyo Federation (Zenkoku Kanken Hanbai Nogyo Kyodo Kumiai Rengokai, or Zenkanren). It was subsequently abolished.

135 Kyodo Kumiai Tsushinsha, *Nogyo Kyodo Kumiai Rengokai Yakushokuin Meibo* [*Executive and Staff Members' Register of the Agricultural Cooperative Union Federations*], 1995, Tokyo, Kyodo Kumiai Tsushinsha, 1994 (hereafter *Nokyoren Yakushokuin Meibo*), p. 2. Each of the shortened titles of these organisations now has 'JA' in front.

136 Zenkoku Nogyo Kyodo Kumiai Chuokai, *Hayawakari JA no Subete*, p. 80.

137 Zenkoku Nogyo Kyodo Kumiai Chuokai, *Hayawakari JA no Subete*, p. 80.

138 Tanaka, *Nihon no Nokyo*, p. 75.

139 Sakurai, *Beika Seisaku*, p. 38.

140 Tanaka notes, however, that the government ignored the recommendation of the RPAC until 1968. *Nihon no Nokyo*, p. 76. This had a lot to do with the eviction of politicians, producer and consumer representatives in that year. In 1969, producer and consumer representatives returned, although they never re-established their former levels of membership.

141 See below.

142 See Mitsukawa, *Nogyo Dantai Hattenshi*, pp. 223–269. These rival organisations consisted not only of the farmers' unions but also the agricultural committee organisation founded in 1951. See below.

143 See below.

144 Ishida and George, 'Nokyo', p. 202.

145 Ishida and George, 'Nokyo', p. 209.

146 Ishida and George, 'Nokyo', p. 202.

147 Tanaka, *Nihon no Nokyo*, p. 75.

148 Tanaka, *Nihon no Nokyo*, p. 46.

149 See also below.

150 Dore, 'The Socialist Party', p. 387.
151 See also below.
152 Zenkoren, for example, raised funds for lobbying activities to abolish the Fertiliser Distribution Corporation which controlled the distribution of fertiliser. Tanaka, *Nihon no Nokyo*, pp. 28–30. See also below.
153 Kuwabara, 'Nogyo Kyodo Kumiai no Nosei Katsudo', p. 258. Nagata and Saito argue that the *shidoren* were not organised as bodies for representing the interests of farmers, hence the need for a solid managing organisation that could also coordinate not only the agricultural cooperatives but also agricultural policy activities. *Nokyo no Hanashi*, p. 23.
154 Sakaguchi Takashi, *Kyodai Nokyo no Sugosa [The Power of Massive Nokyo]*, Tokyo, Ginko Jihyosha, 1987, p. 21. Part of the urgency was due to the rival claims to this role from the agricultural committees. See Mitsukawa, *Nogyo Dantai Hattenshi*, pp. 223–269. See also below.
155 This organisation has also been referred to as the 'Central Union of Agricultural Cooperatives', or CUAC, without the insertion of 'National'. It now calls itself JA-Zenchu.
156 'Nogyo Kyodo Kumiaiho', in *Nogyo Roppo*, 1993, p. 125.
157 Fujitani Chikuji, *Nokyo Daikakushin [Revolution in Nokyo]*, Tokyo, Ie no Hikari Kyokai, 1994, p. 127.
158 This does not include Norinchukin as shown in Figure 2.2. See also the discussion on Nokyo's internal democracy in chapter 8 on 'Policy Campaigning'.
159 Ishimi, *Nokyo*, p. 215.
160 'Nogyo Kyodo Kumiaiho', in *Nogyo Roppo*, 1993, p. 126.
161 Kuwabara, 'Nogyo Kyodo Kumiai no Nosei Katsudo', p. 254. Kuwabara also argues that in addition to Article 73 (9)-2, the clause in Article 10 of the law where it states that the agricultural cooperatives may undertake 'any other business incidental to the foregoing items' is also interpreted as providing legal authority for the agricultural cooperatives to conduct *nosei katsudo* (p. 254).
162 Kuwabara, 'Nogyo Kyodo Kumiai no Nosei Katsudo', p. 260. See also the discussion below in relation to the agricultural committees.
163 Central Union of Agricultural Cooperatives, *Central Union of Agricultural Cooperatives*, 1972, p. 6.
164 The role of these executives is discussed at greater length in chapter 8 on 'Policy Campaigning'.
165 Kobayashi Naoki, Shinohara Hajime and Soma Masao, *Senkyo [Elections]*, Tokyo Iwanami Shoten, 1960, p. 79.
166 Aono, *Nokyo*, p. 23.
167 Michael Donnelly, 'Conflict Over Government Authority and Markets: Japan's Rice Economy', in Ellis S. Krauss, Thomas P. Rohlen, and Patricia G. Steinhoff (eds), *Conflict in Japan*, Honolulu, University of Hawaii Press, 1984, p. 343.
168 Aono, *Nokyo*, p. 16. An exception is the American Farm Bureau Federation which had quite a close relationship with government at its formation, particularly with respect to state and federal funding. The Farm Bureau was a cross between the *nokai* (in its role in agricultural extension) and the *sangyo kumiai* (cooperative purchasing). See O. M. Kile, *The Farm Bureau Movement*, New York, Macmillan, 1921, and O. M. Kile, *The Farm Bureau Through Three Decades*, Baltimore, Waverly Press, 1948.
169 In Europe for example, farmers founded cooperatives on their own independent initiative, and only after that was there legislation recognising them. The contrast between this and the Japanese situation is pointed out by Aono, *Nokyo*, p. 16. It should be noted that shortly after the agricultural cooperatives were established by law, consumer and fisheries cooperatives were established in the same way in

July and December 1948 respectively, followed by the forestry cooperatives in June 1951.

170 Prototypes of cooperative organisations set up by farmers on their own initiative did exist prior to 1900 and the passage of government legislation setting up the *sangyo kumiai*, but they were only scattered embryonic organisations with limited membership and limited functioning.

171 Ishida also points out that *nogyokai* leaders were dominant over the representatives of other farmers' groups in the organisational activities of the Agriculture Reconstruction Council which led to the formation of the agricultural cooperatives. *Interest Groups*, p. 48.

172 Tanaka, *Nihon no Nokyo*, p. 11.

173 Fujitani, 'Nokyo at a Crossroads', p. 377.

174 Yamaguchi Ichimon, *Ima Nokyo o Do Suru Ka* [*What Should be Done About Nokyo?*], Tokyo, Ie no Hikari Kyokai, 1987, p. 55.

175 Fujitani, 'Nokyo at a Crossroads', pp. 376–377. Tanaka also makes the point that in spite of the democratisation of agricultural organisations, the lack of strong, independent initiative among member farmers made it difficult to democratise Nokyo as much as expected. *Nihon no Nokyo*, p. 12. See also chapter 4 on 'Organisational Politics'.

176 There is an interesting story attached to this process. According to Ogura, the 'MAF wanted to establish the new agricultural cooperative as much as possible on the basis of the organization and assets of the wartime system of agricultural organization as well as on the basis of ideas of the free and democratic cooperative. But the Occupation Forces laid stress on the latter point . . . [and so] . . . a compromise was reached. The agricultural cooperative would be established independently from the Municipal Association of Agriculture, but a new agricultural cooperative satisfying certain conditions could consult with the Municipal Association of Agriculture regarding the future of the assets and holdings.' In practice, this meant a transfer of the latter virtually intact to the agricultural cooperatives. *Can Japanese Agriculture Survive?*, p. 286.

177 'The Origins of Protectionism', pp. 14, 19.

178 Ishida, *Interest Groups*, p. 48.

179 See above.

180 Tanaka, *Nihon no Nokyo*, p. 12. Nokyo also inherited the *nogyokai* labour union (p. 484). Mitsukawa refers to a survey undertaken in 1948 which showed that former executives of the *nogyokai* accounted for 22.4 per cent of the executives of Nokyo branches. Tenants and owner-farmers accounted for 20 per cent and 66 per cent respectively, while the share of landowners was only 11 per cent. *Nogyo Dantai Hattenshi*, p. 144. Many *nogyokai* leaders were prohibited from holding positions of authority in the new agricultural cooperatives because of the purge of public officials instituted by the Occupation authorities.

181 Tanaka, *Nihon no Nokyo*, p. 36.

182 Ishida Takeshi, 'The Development of Interest Groups and the Pattern of Political Modernization in Japan', in Robert E. Ward (ed.), *Political Development in Modern Japan*, Princeton, Princeton University Press, 1968, p. 302. See also below.

183 Ishida, 'The Development of Interest Groups', p. 302.

184 Ishida and George, 'Nokyo', p. 209.

185 Fujitani, 'Nokyo at a Crossroads', p. 377.

186 Mitsukawa, *Nogyo Dantai Hattenshi*, p. 93.

187 Fujitani, 'Nokyo at a Crossroads', p. 377.

188 Yamaguchi, *Ima Nokyo o Do Suru Ka*, p. 55.

189 Saeki, *Nokyo Kaikaku*, p. 122. Takeuchi's view is that Nokyo's federated three-

stage system was established in parallel to the administrative zoning of the government because the Occupation forces during the immediate postwar period intended Nokyo to play the role of an economic control institution. Administrative zoning was quite effective for this purpose. Takeuchi Tetsuo, 'Keito Sandankaisei no Saihen' ['Reorganisation of the Federated Three-Stage System'], in Ouchi and Kajii (eds), *Nokyo Yonjunen*, p. 208.

190 In fact, as Asuwa points out, the guiding concept of the establishment of the cooperatives was the principle of 'one town or village, one *nokyo*'. Asuwa Shinzaburo, *Nokyo no Genjo to Kadai* [*Nokyo's Present Condition and Themes*], Tokyo, Toyo Keizai Shinbunsha, 1979, p. 109.

191 Saeki, *Nokyo Kaikaku*, p. 168.

192 These points were made by Yamauchi, 'Analytical Institutional Economics', p. 10.

193 Otawara Takaaki, 'Nokyo no Ichi to Yakuwari' ['Nokyo's Position and Role'], in Ouchi and Kajii (eds), *Nokyo Yonjunen*, p. 16.

194 As Saeki explains, whether it be agricultural modernisation facilities or system finance, these are usually implemented with the close cooperation of administrative organs and federated agricultural cooperatives side-by-side (i.e. cooperation between the same level of organisation on both sides: the *tankyo* with city, town and village governments, the prefectural federations with prefectural government, and similarly with the national organisations and national government). *Nokyo Kaikaku*, p. 122.

195 *Nokyo Kaikaku*, p. 122.

196 'Tochi Kairyoho', in *Nogyo Roppo*, 1993, p. 491.

197 Japanese agricultural economist, Yuize Yasuhiko, quoted in the *Far Eastern Economic Review*, 17 November 1988, p. 25.

198 'Nogyo Kindaika Shikin Joseiho', in *Nogyo Roppo*, 1993, p. 84. See also below.

199 'Nogyosha Nenkin Kikinho', in *Nogyo Roppo*, 1993, p. 366.

200 'Chikusanbutsu no Kakaku Antei to ni kansuru Horitsu', in *Nogyo Roppo*, 1993, p. 770.

201 'Tokutei Nochi Kashitsuke ni kansuru Nochiho to no Tokurei ni kansuru Horitsu', in *Nogyo Roppo*, 1993, p. 317. See also below.

202 'Nogyo Shinko Chiiki no Seibi ni kansuru Horitsu', in *Nogyo Roppo*, 1993, p. 322.

203 Ishida, *Interest Groups*, p. 68. See also below.

204 Saeki, *Nokyo Kaikaku*, p. 168.

205 Kawagoe, 'The Origins of Protectionism', p. 18.

206 Yamauchi, 'Analytical Institutional Economics', p. 10.

207 See also chapter 8 on 'Policy Campaigning'.

208 See above.

209 As Dore elaborates, the agricultural committees were created as an amalgam of three semi-administrative bodies: the land committees (whose *raison d'être* had been removed by the land reform), the food adjustment committees (which apportioned government crop-delivery quotas) and the agricultural improvement committees (in charge of measures to improve and diffuse agricultural techniques). Ronald Dore, *Land Reform in Japan*, 2nd edition, London, The Athlone Press, 1984, p. 425.

210 The National Chamber of Agriculture, *The National Chamber of Agriculture: Its Organization and Activities*, March 1982, pp. 2–3.

211 Mitsukawa, *Nogyo Dantai Hattenshi*, p. 624.

212 *Land Reform*, 2nd edition, p. 427.

213 The content of this dispute in the early 1950s, its revival in 1955–56 under MAF Minister, Kono Ichiro, and the various proposals advanced for restructuring agricultural organisations are discussed in Mitsukawa, *Nogyo Dantai Hattenshi*,

pp. 223–227, 362–398, and Dore, *Land Reform*, 2nd edition, pp. 425–431. See also below.

214 The National Chamber of Agriculture, *The National Chamber of Agriculture*, pp. 8–10. See also the relevant legislation on the agricultural committee organisation in 'Nogyo Iinkaiho', *Nogyo Roppo*, 1993, pp. 50, 58, 61. The reporting function, however, was distinctive to the agricultural committee organisation, compared with the agricultural cooperatives. Kuwabara, 'Nogyo Kyodo Kumiai no Nosei Katsudo', p. 259.

215 Tanaka, *Nihon no Nokyo*, pp. 50–52.

216 See also below.

217 Ishimi, Nokyo, p. 204. Kono's objective was also to establish agricultural organisations that would provide a strong basis of support for the conservative party by collecting farmers' votes. In addition, it has been speculated that he wanted to have an agricultural organisation that would support his policies and drive a wedge into the gigantic agricultural bureaucracy. Mitsukawa, *Nogyo Dantai Hattenshi*, pp. 390–391.

218 Tanaka, *Nihon no Nokyo*, p. 58.

219 Tanaka, *Nihon no Nokyo*, p. 59.

220 Tanaka, *Nihon no Nokyo*, p. 59.

221 Tanaka, *Nihon no Nokyo*, p. 59.

222 Dore, *Land Reform in Japan*, 2nd edition, p. 428.

223 Tanaka, *Nihon no Nokyo*, pp. 62–63. See also below.

224 The National Chamber of Agriculture, *The National Chamber of Agriculture*, p. 3.

225 The National Chamber of Agriculture, *The National Chamber of Agriculture*, p. 9.

226 The National Chamber of Agriculture, *The National Chamber of Agriculture*, p. 10.

227 Mitsukawa, *Nogyo Dantai Hattenshi*, p. 622.

228 Donnelly, 'Setting the Price of Rice', p. 155. See also Nagata and Saito, *Nokyo no Hanashi*, p. 27.

229 If the Nokyo prefectural federations are abolished under the new organisational restructuring plan (first promulgated in 1991), this could have serious implications for the agricultural committee organisation, as well as for other agricultural organisations of which Nokyo is a member. This question is examined in Saeki, *Nokyo Kaikaku*, pp. 173–175. The issue of Nokyo's restructuring is taken up in chapter 4 on 'Organisational Politics'.

230 These details were obtained from The National Chamber of Agriculture, *The National Chamber of Agriculture*, p. 7.

231 The National Chamber of Agriculture, *The National Chamber of Agriculture*, p. 8. In law, its duties (besides the interest articulation function) are listed as follows: providing education and publicity services regarding agriculture and the farmers; conducting surveys and research of agriculture and the farmers; providing guidance and liaison activities in connection with duties performed by the prefectural chambers of agriculture; and performing other duties necessary to the fulfilment of the objectives of the National Chamber of Agriculture (p. 8).

232 The National Chamber of Agriculture, *The National Chamber of Agriculture*, p. 8. The duties of the prefectural chambers are formally listed as follows (in addition to the interest articulation function): performing duties assigned by the Agricultural Land Law, the Law Promoting Utilisation of Agricultural Land, the Land Improvement Law, and other laws and ordinances; providing education and publicity services regarding agriculture and the farmers; conducting surveys and research of agriculture and farmers; organising training course and programmes

for agricultural committee members; cooperating with agricultural committees in performing specified duties; and performing all duties incidental to any of the above items (pp. 8–9).

233 The National Chamber of Agriculture, *The National Chamber of Agriculture*, p. 9.

234 The actual functions of the agricultural committees under these laws are spelled out in the text of the laws themselves.

235 Nagata and Saito, *Nokyo no Hanashi*, p. 28.

236 Under the Agricultural Land Law, when proprietary rights of farming and grazing land are transferred, the parties must obtain permission from the relevant agricultural committee. Under the Land Improvement Law, when those who engage in farm work or stock raising request the exchange, division or merger of farm land, the agricultural committees determine the plan for the exchange, division of the land concerned if they approve the request.

237 Until 1986 the agricultural committees of the respective cities, towns and villages also managed farmland banks, which recorded cases where the right to use or lease land between farmers was established. In 1986, the MAFF firmed up a plan to strengthen the activities of the farmland banks from 1987 onwards, which would make it possible for these banks to start businesses such as establishing the right to use agricultural land and offering good offices in leasing farmland, with a view to stepping up the expansion in the scale of agricultural enterprise. According to the plan, the functions of farmland banks would be expanded, with the agricultural committees charged with collecting information concerning those who wanted to lease farmland and offering to render their good offices by holding talks among such farmers.

238 'Nogyo Iinkai to ni kansuru Horitsu', in *Nogyo Roppo*, 1993, pp. 49–50. The list also includes the interest articulation function of the agricultural committees referred to earlier.

239 Mitsukawa, *Nogyo Dantai Hattenshi*, p. 628.

240 The National Chamber of Agriculture, *The National Chamber of Agriculture*, p. 11.

241 Mitsukawa, *Nogyo Dantai Hattenshi*, p. 629.

242 Mitsukawa, *Nogyo Dantai Hattenshi*, p. 636.

243 See chapter 4 on 'Organisational Politics' and also George, *The Strategies of Influence*, pp. 317–362.

244 Mitsukawa, *Nogyo Dantai Hattenshi*, p. 645.

245 Nosei no Shoten II [Focus on Agricultural Policy II], 'Sanjiko no Koso o Megutte' ['Concerning the Third Structural Plan'], in Nosei Jyaanarisuto no Kai (ed.), *Tatoka Jidai no Nosei*, p. 225. For other examples, see The National Chamber of Agriculture, *The National Chamber of Agriculture*, pp. 11–13.

246 This was the shorthand title for 'New Policy Directions for Food, Agriculture and Rural Areas' (*Atarashii Shokuryo, Nogyo, Noson Seisaku no Hoko*).

247 Personal interview with NCA personnel, Tokyo, July 1995.

248 Saeki, *Nokyo Kaikaku*, p. 175.

249 For example, beginning in 1985, the national and prefectural chambers of agriculture promoted a campaign called 'Don't You Want to Try Farming?' which was designed to encourage new entrants into the field of agriculture. It was managed under the title of 'New Farm Employed Guide Business'.

250 The *nogyo iinkai*, according to agricultural commentators, 'are not organisations based on farmers. Their administration is supported by funds from the central government. Subsidies from the central government, however, are insufficient to cover the cost of employing their officials and therefore they depend for a considerable portion of their funding on municipal governments. In addition, officials representing the *iinkai* are municipal government officials, such as the

head of the economic department or the agriculture and forestry department. They undertake their *iinkai* work as officials of municipal governments rather than as officials of the *iinkai*. As a result, the *iinkai* are buried in municipal government organisation. Nosei Jyaanarisuto no Kai, *Chiho Gyosei to Noson* [*Regional Administration and Agricultural Villages*], Kikan Nosei no Ugoki, 19, Tokyo, Nokyo Kyokai, 10 October 1962, p. 40.

251 See chapter 6 on 'Electoral Politics'.

252 See below.

253 'Nogyo Saigai Hoshoho', in *Nogyo Roppo*, 1993, p. 191.

254 'Nogyo Saigai Hoshoho', in *Nogyo Roppo*, 1993, p. 220.

255 *Nogyo Roppo*, 1993, p. 192.

256 *Nogyo Roppo*, 1993, p. 192.

257 'Nogyo Kyosai Kikinho', in *Nogyo Roppo*, 1993, p. 231.

258 See chapter 3 on 'Bureaucratic Politics' in my forthcoming volume, *Politicians and Bureaucrats: Agricultural Politics and Policymaking in Japan.*

259 At the local level there are also unions (*tochi kairyo rengo*). Zenkoku Tochi Kairyo Jigyo Dantai Rengokai [National Federation of Land Improvement Associations], Pamphlet, n.p.g. In prewar Japan, there were similar organisations called irrigation unions (*suiri kumiai*), but after the war, the 1949 law was passed under the authority of GHQ to put the activities of such groups into legislative form. Furthermore, the *tochi kairyoku* were modelled on California districts. Personal interview with Zendoren official, Tokyo, July 1995.

260 See above.

261 Personal interview with Zendoren official, Tokyo, July 1995.

262 Although farmers initially establish the idea for a project and all the farmers in the group agree to go ahead with construction, in fact farmers agree first only formally. In many cases, officials (MAFF and prefectural and municipal government officials) persuade farmers to initiate a particular land improvement project. Personal interview with ex-MAFF official, Tokyo, July 1995. See also chapter 4 on 'Patronage Politics' in my forthcoming volume, *Politicians and Bureaucrats.*

263 *Nogyo Roppo*, 1993, p. 501.

264 Personal interview with Zendoren official, Tokyo, July 1995.

265 In the 1983 preliminary MAFF budget for example, the amount designated for land improvement expenses was ¥745.9 billion, or 25.5 per cent of the total budgetary allocation to agriculture. This made it the largest single item of expenditure in the budget. Norinsuisansho Daijin Kanbo Chosaka (ed.), *Nogyo Hakusho Fuzoku Tokeihyo* [*Statistical Supplement to the White Paper on Agriculture*], Tokyo, Norin Tokei Kyokai, 1982, p. 14. See also the extensive discussion on land improvement administration, politics and expenditure in the chapter 3 on 'Bureaucratic Politics', chapter 4 on 'Patronage Politics' and chapter 5 on 'Budget Politics' in my forthcoming volume, *Politicians and Bureaucrats.*

266 A Zendoren official actually distinguished amongst three different types of land improvement projects: national projects, prefectural projects and land improvement projects. National projects take around 10 years for completion, with the government supplying about two-thirds of the funding. Prefectural projects take four to five years for completion, with the prefectural government providing one-half of the funding. Land improvement projects take about one year with national and prefectural governments providing one-third the funding, although this depends on the type of project. Specific projects have specific subsidy volumes. No land improvement projects are 100 per cent funded by government. In 1995, there were approximately 100 national projects going on, such as the Hachirogata project. Personal interview, Tokyo, July 1995.

267 Personal interview with Zendoren official, Tokyo, July 1995.

268 Moore, *Japanese Agriculture*, p. 164.
269 Moore, *Japanese Agriculture*, p. 164.
270 Moore, *Japanese Agriculture*, p. 289.
271 Personal interview with Zendoren official, Tokyo, July 1995.
272 Zenkoku Tochi Kairyo Jigyo Dantai Rengokai, n.p.g.
273 *Hojokin Soran*, 1998, p. 613.
274 *Hojokin Soran*, 1998, pp. 24–77; 354.
275 These organisations are not to be confused with the rural youth leagues (*noson seinen renmei*, or *noseiren*) discussed earlier.
276 Ono Kazuoki, 'Nokyo to Senkyo' ['Nokyo and Elections'], in Ishiwata Sadao (ed.), *Nomin to Senkyo: Nomin no Seiji Ishiki to Hyo no Yukue* [*Farmers and Elections: The Political Consciousness of Farmers and Trends in the Farm Vote*], Tokyo, Ochanomizu Shobo, 1984, p. 87.
277 Ono, 'Nokyo to Senkyo', p. 87.
278 See chapter 3 on 'Farmers' Policies' and chapter 7 on 'Representative Politics'.
279 Nagase Meitoku, 'Nosei Kyogikai no Kaiso to Nosei Domei no Kessei' ['The Reorganisation of the Agricultural Policy Council and the Formation of the Agricultural Policy League'], *Nogyo Kyodo Kumiai*, Vol. 19, No. 2, February 1973, p. 54. This article describes in detail the activities of the Agricultural Policy Council in Shimane Prefecture. Major policies of this council related to price policies for agricultural products and opposition to undesirable changes to the FC system and to the liberalisation of agricultural trade and so on. The council's approach centred around petitions and demands. It also followed political activities initiated by Nokyo. The council tried to strike a balance between policy activities related to local farmers' needs and interests, and national-level, unified activities such as the rice price demand and the agriculture-related budget which were actively undertaken at Nokyo's initiative and in which the full range of Nokyo organisations participated. It acknowledged, however, that the council was too dependent on Nokyo with which it had maintained a very close relationship and on whose initiative it relied in agricultural policy activities, thus failing to satisfy various local demands from farmers. It concluded that in order to realise farmers' demands, a solid political organisation mobilising farmers' political power should be established as an independent body from Nokyo, the economic organisation. On this basis, the council transformed itself into a new organisation, the Agricultural Policy League (Nosei Domei), which claimed to be a political association that mobilised farmers' power; a core organisation pursuing the development of agriculture in Shimane Prefecture; an organisation that promoted demands for policies and moves for their realisation; and a voluntary organisation where members were free to join or secede. The main organisers were core farmers who were no longer dependent on central organisations (i.e. the MAFF and Zenchu). The primary unit of association was based on municipalities rather than districts or the prefecture in order to focus on so-called 'daily activities' of the farmers i.e. local agrarian interests (pp. 55–58).
280 See chapter 3 on 'Farmers' Politics'.
281 Kobayashi, Shinohara and Soma, *Senkyo*, p. 79.
282 This was called the Ibaraki Prefecture Political League for Promoting Agriculture (Ibaraki-ken Kono Seiji Renmei).
283 The views of the Ibaraki Prefecture Political League for Promoting Agriculture can be found in Soma Masao, *Nihon no Senkyo Seiji* [*Election Politics in Japan*], Tokyo, Aoki Shoten, 1963, p. 152.
284 Midoro reports that by 1956 farmers' political leagues were operating in 33 prefectures. Midoro Tomiyuki, *Rodosha Nomin Undoron* [*A Treatise on Workers' and Farmers' Movements*], Tokyo, Tsukuba Shobo, 1994, p. 18.

285 Nagase, 'Nosei Kyogikai', p. 53.
286 See below.
287 *Nogyo Dantai Hattenshi*, p. 555.
288 Mitsukawa, *Nogyo Dantai Hattenshi*, p. 555.
289 See below.
290 Nosei Jyaanarisuto no Kai, *Hanjutsu Hatten to Keiei Kakushin: Atarashii Nominzo o Motomete* [*The Development of Marketing Techniques and Management Reform: Searching for a New Farmers' Image*], Kikan Nosei no Ugoki, 7, Tokyo, Kyodo Kumiai Kyokai, 30 June 1959, p. 92.
291 This is not to be confused with the National Rural Youth League, which also contracts in Japanese to Zennoseiren.
292 The number of prefectural groups that joined the Zennoseiren varies according to source. The above figure was taken from Tanaka, *Nihon no Nokyo*, p. 452, but in Okamoto, 29 prefectural groups are reported as joining. Okamoto Matsuzo, 'Nomin Dantai no Genjo to Undo no Tokucho' ['The Current State of Affairs Amongst Farmers' Groups and the Special Features of their Campaigns'], *Nogyo Kyodo Kumiai*, Vol. 19, No. 2, 1973, p. 44.
293 Soma, *Nihon no Senkyo Seiji*, p. 153.
294 Takeshi Ishida, 'Organizations and Symbols in Contemporary Politics: A Political Scientist's View of Postwar Japan', *Annals of the Institute of Social Science*, No. 20, 1979, p. 129.
295 See chapter 3 on 'Farmers Politics'.
296 Kobayashi, Shinohara and Soma, *Senkyo*, p. 77.
297 The organisational genealogy of this group is discussed in chapter 3 on 'Farmers' Politics'.
298 At the time of its establishment, Zennosoren consisted of 46 groups in 26 prefectures and was said to have had 700,000 supporters. Its Chairman was the former Chairman of the Zennoseiren. Okamoto, 'Nomin Dantai no Genjo', p. 44.
299 Soma Masao, *Kokumin no Sentaku: 1972-nen Sosenkyo no Bunseki* [*The People's Choice: An Analysis of the 1972 General Election*], Tokyo Sanichi Shobo, 1974, p. 124.
300 See chapter 3 on 'Farmers' Politics'.
301 Okamoto, 'Nomin Dantai no Genjo', p. 45.
302 The Common Forestry and Grassland Modernisation Law was passed in 1966. It was designed to promote the effective utilisation of commonages for the purposes of forestry and agricultural modernisation, particularly managed grassland for cattle. It aroused local opposition in a number of areas. Ogura, *Can Japanese Agriculture Survive?*, pp. 328–329.
303 As Ogura notes, the land boom during the last years of high economic growth caused the loss of land owned by rural communities as well as farmers. *Can Japanese Agriculture Survive?*, p. 329.
304 Okamoto, 'Nomin Dantai no Genjo', p. 45.
305 Okamoto, 'Nomin Dantai no Genjo', p. 44.
306 See also Table 6.5 and associated discussion.
307 Okamoto, 'Nomin Dantai no Genjo', p. 44.
308 See chapter 6 on 'Electoral Politics'.
309 This is sometimes translated as National Council of Farm Policy Organisations.
310 The 23 prefectural league members were the Iwate Prefecture Nokyo Political League, the Miyagi Prefecture Nokyo Political League, the Akita Prefecture Nokyo Political League, the Fukushima Agricultural Policy Reform League, the Ibaraki Prefecture Political League for Promoting Agriculture, the Tochigi Prefecture Political League for Promoting Agriculture, the Gumma Prefecture

Political League for Promoting Agriculture, the Tokyo Prefecture Agricultural Policy Promotion League, the Nagano Prefecture Farmers' League, the Fukui Prefecture Rural Construction Political League, the Shizuoka Prefecture Agricultural Policy Countermeasures Council, the Aichi Prefecture Agricultural Policy League, the Shiga Prefecture Political League for Promoting Agriculture, the Wakayama Prefecture Agricultural Policy League, the Shimane Prefecture Agricultural Policy League, the Hiroshima Prefecture Nokyo Agricultural Policy Council, the Tokushima Prefecture Nokyo Agricultural Policy Council, the Kagawa Prefecture Nokyo Agricultural Policy Countermeasures Council, the Fukuoka Prefecture Farmers' Political League, the Saga Prefecture Agricultural Policy Council, the Nagasaki Prefecture Farmers' Political League, the Miyazaki Prefecture Farmers' League, and the Kagoshima Prefecture Farmers' Political League (cf. table 6.5). *Kenchu* chairmen were, in the majority of cases, chairmen of these prefectural farmers' leagues. According to the establishment agreement of the National Council, its prefectural member organisations were formed from farmers and people with connections to agricultural and other 'similar' or 'equivalent' groups. See *Nokyo Nenkan*, 1990, p. 148.

311 *Nokyo Nenkan*, 1993, p. 85.

312 *Nokyo Nenkan*, 1990, p. 148.

313 The role of Zenchu's policy central headquarters is discussed in chapter 8 on 'Policy Campaigning'.

314 *Nokyo Nenkan*, 1990, p. 148.

315 See chapter 6 on 'Electoral Politics' and chapter 8 on 'Policy Campaigning'.

316 A Zenkoku Noseikyo official laid claim to 45 prefectural associations, including 26 formal branches in 1995. Personal interview, Tokyo, July 1995. The formal register of Zenkoku Noseikyo's regular members in the same year, however, listed *noseiren* under various titles in 40 prefectures, plus another group consisting of four *kenchu* and one *kenchu* agricultural policy department. The Chiba *noseiren* has been the latest to join the Zenkoku Noseikyo (in 1997). Those prefectures without farmers' political league branch members of Zenkoku Noseikyo are Hokkaido, Yamanashi, Toyama, Mie, Okinawa and Kanagawa (no branch at all). This does not mean, however, that farmers' political leagues do not exist in these prefectures. The Hokkaido Nokyoren Seiji Renmei operates in Hokkaido, for example.

317 Some of the new groups prefer the title 'Agricultural Policy Council' to the previous titles 'Political League' or 'Political Federation' in recognition of the new title of the national organisation.

318 'Noseikyo no Ugoki' ['Activities of Agricultural Policy Councils'], *Nosei Undo Jyaanaru*, No. 1, Inaugural Issue, 1995, p. 33.

319 The amalgamations of agricultural cooperatives and the restructuring of the *noseiren* within prefectures occasioned by the new LH electoral system have altered the complementary aspects of the Nokyo and *noseiren* organisations within prefectures somewhat. See below, chapter 4 on 'Organisational Politics' and chapter 6 on 'Electoral Politics'.

320 Personal interview with Zenkoku Noseikyo Secretariat Chief, Tokyo, July 1995.

321 'Noseikyo no Ugoki', p. 33.

322 See chapter 8 on 'Policy Campaigning'.

323 See chapter 3 on 'Farmers' Politics' and chapter 6 on 'Electoral Politics'.

324 Personal interview with Zenkoku Noseikyo Secretariat Chief, Tokyo, July 1995. See also chapter 6 on 'Electoral Politics'.

325 Yamaguchi Hiroshi, 'Nyuka Funso to Rakuno no Tachiba' ['The Milk Price Dispute and Dairy Farmers' Standpoint'], *Ekonomisuto*, March 1967, p. 48.

326 See chapter 4 on 'Organisational Politics' and chapter 8 on 'Policy Campaigning'.
327 This is despite the fact that they were acknowledged as 'backward' by one dairy industry leader in the late 1960s. See Yamaguchi, 'Nyuka Funso', p. 48.
328 A good description of the origins of this movement can be found in Midoro, *Rodosha Nomin Undoron*, pp. 33–39.
329 Document of the Dairy Farmers Political Federation of Japan, supplied to the author in July 1995.
330 Document of the Dairy Farmers Political Federation of Japan, supplied to the author in July 1995.
331 Document of the Dairy Farmers Political Federation of Japan, supplied to the author in July 1995. According to this document, there were 44,247 dairy farming households in 1995.
332 Personal interview with federation executives, Tokyo, July 1995.
333 But see also the comments on this issue in chapter 4 on 'Organisational Politics'.
334 Document of the Dairy Farmers Political Federation of Japan, supplied to the author in July 1995.
335 See table 2.3 and below.
336 This is a Nokyo organisation. See below.
337 See table 2.3.
338 Document of the Dairy Farmers Political Federation of Japan, supplied to the author in July 1995.
339 Interview with league executives, Tokyo, July 1995.
340 See chapter 3 on 'Bureaucratic Politics' in my forthcoming volume, *Politicians and Bureaucrats*.
341 Document of the Dairy Farmers Political Federation of Japan, supplied to the author in July 1995.
342 The tobacco cultivation association organisation was established under its own legislation and along the same lines as Nokyo in 1958.
343 Kobayashi, Shinohara and Soma, *Senkyo*, p. 77.
344 There seems to be some difference of opinion as to whether this group is called the National Land Improvement Political League or the National Land Improvement Industry Political League (Zenkoku Tochi Kairyo Jigyo Seiji Renmei). This writer has opted for the former.
345 Okamoto, 'Nomin Dantai no Genjo', p. 45.
346 Personal communication with league official, September 1997.
347 Okamoto, 'Nomin Dantai no Genjo', p. 45.
348 Longworth, *Beef in Japan*, p. 58.
349 See Dore, *Land Reform in Japan*, p. 466.
350 See below.
351 His Diet career lasted from 1958 until 1969, and then from 1976 to 1979.
352 See below.
353 Tanimoto Takashi, 'Nomin Undo to Senkyo Toso' ['The Farmers' Movement and Election Struggles'], in Ishiwata (ed.), *Nomin to Senkyo*, p. 98.
354 Okamoto, 'Nomin Dantai no Genjo', p. 46.
355 Nationwide, their numbers were around 600,000. Okamoto, 'Nomin Dantai no Genjo', p. 46.
356 See below.
357 Okamoto, 'Nomin Dantai no Genjo', p. 46.
358 Socialist representative for Akita (2), Kawamata Kenjiro, also combined a history of Nichino leadership with an executive position in the *dekasegi* federation. His political career spanned 1969–79 and 1980–93.
359 At the time of its establishment, Zennichino's membership figure was announced

publicly at 250,000. Its actual membership strength was, however, only a third of this figure. See Kobayashi, Shinohara and Soma, *Senkyo*, p. 84.

360 At the time of its establishment convention in 1958, Zennichino declared that it would never be split. The JCP also committed its unconditional support for this declaration. The JCP secured nine seats in Zennichino's standing committee to establish a footing for its future activities within the organisation. It saw the unification of the farmers' union movement as very important politically, because it could become the starting point of political unification of the left, including the JSP and JCP. Nomin Mondai Kenkyukai (ed.), *Sengo Nihon no Nomin Undo*, pp. 200–201.

361 Mitsukawa, *Nogyo Dantai Hattenshi*, p. 545.

362 Mitsukawa, *Nogyo Dantai Hattenshi*, pp. 560–561.

363 In fact ¥1.2 million out of the total Zennichino budget of ¥7.2 million in 1958 was contributed by political parties. Nomin Mondai Kenkyukai (ed.), *Sengo Nihon no Nomin Undo*, p. 202.

364 Nosei Jyaanarisuto no Kai, *Nogyo Kihonho no Soten* [*Points at Issue in the Agricultural Basic Law*], Kikan Nosei no Ugoki, 14, Tokyo, Nokyo Kyokai, 15 May 1961, p. 156.

365 Kyosanto Bukkuretto, *Gaiatsu no Naka no Nihon*, p. 42.

366 Kyosanto Bukkuretto, *Gaiatsu no Naka no Nihon*, p. 43.

367 Kobayashi, Shinohara and Soma, *Senkyo*, p. 84.

368 Okamoto, 'Nomin Dantai no Genjo', p. 43.

369 Okamoto, 'Nomin Dantai no Genjo', p. 43.

370 Yamaguchi Taro, 'Nihon Shakaito no Nogyo Seisaku' ['The Japan Socialist Party's Agricultural Policy'], in Nosei Jyaanarisuto no Kai (ed.), *Tatoka Jidai no Nosei*, p. 46.

371 Ono Kazuoki, *No to Shoku no Seiji Keizaigaku* [*The Political Economy of Agriculture and Food*], Tokyo, Ryokufu Shuppan, 1994, p. 65.

372 Both Zennichino and Zenchu were using the 'Production Cost and Income Compensation' formula to calculate their producer rice price demands (Nokyo began using this particular formula in 1956). It conceived of farmers as workers and saw the producer rice price as a means of equalising wages between urban workers and farmers. Nokyo, however, used the average cost of labour for manufacturing enterprises with more than five employees, whereas Zennichino insisted on using that for enterprises with more than thirty employees. Tanaka, *Nihon no Nokyo*, p. 95.

373 Ono dates the separate campaigns from 1960 as does Sakurai, *No to Shoku*, p. 65; *Beika Seisaku*, p. 124. Nevertheless, Mitsukawa dates the separate campaigns from 1959 (*Nogyo Dantai Hattenshi*, p. 561), while Tanaka also dates the separate campaigns from 1959. *Nihon no Nokyo*, p. 94.

374 Mitsukawa, *Nogyo Dantai Hattenshi*, p. 561.

375 See chapter 8 on 'Policy Campaigning'.

376 Ono, *No to Shoku*, p. 65. He regards this development as being highly significant politically insofar as it enabled a new conservative rural control system to be established via Nokyo's links to the LDP (p. 66).

377 In Niigata, for example, the farmers' unions mobilised rice producers in Sannoichinakakanbara region by means of a rice-producing farmers' council. Farmers protested against low rices prices in 1964 and 1966 by delaying the shipment of the early crop of rice, while in 1973 and 1974, they went as far as stopping the shipment of rice. Basically Nokyo in Sannoichinakakanbara was under the control of the rice-producing farmers' council. Tanimoto, 'Nomin Undo', p. 97.

378 Tanaka, *Nihon no Nokyo*, p. 95.

379 Dore, 'The Socialist Party', p. 400. Elsewhere it was reported that Labour-Farmer Councils were established in 32 different areas. See Nosei Jyaanarisuto no Kai, *Nogyo Kihonho no Soten*, p. 40.

380 Nosei Jyaanarisuto no Kai, *Nogyo Kihonho no Soten*, p. 40. See also chapter 3 on 'Bureaucratic Politics' in my forthcoming volume, *Politicians and Bureaucrats*.

381 In 1961 for instance, Zennichino adopted a policy of promoting a labour-farm alliance to 'crush' the government's proposed Agricultural Basic Law policy. The JSP draft law was touted as reflecting the 'intention' of farmers and workers. Nosei Jyaanarisuto no Kai, *Nogyo Kihonho no Soten*, p. 39.

382 It progressed further in Hokkaido than in many other districts. The local farmers federation (*nomin renmei*) conducted election campaigns by setting up a separate organisation called the Association to Protect Farm Villages (Noson o Mamoru Kai). Trade unions cooperated with this organisation and they campaigned for farmers' representatives from progressive parties. As a result they got elected five progressive candidates (from the JSP and DSP). Two farmers' representatives were elected in one constituency. Nakamura Yoshijiro, 'Nominhyo no Pawaa' ['The Power of the Farm Vote'], in Ishiwata (ed.), *Nomin to Senkyo*, pp. 120–121. See chapter 3 on 'Farmers' Politics' for a discussion of the *nomin renmei*.

383 Kobayashi, Shinohara and Soma, *Senkyo*, p. 85.

384 Nosei Jyaanarisuto no Kai, *Nogyo Kihonho no Soten*, pp. 168–169.

385 In Japanese this was the Zenkoku Nokyo Rodo Kumiai Rengokai, or Zennokyo Roren, which organised staff members of Nokyo. See chapter 4 on 'Organisational Politics'.

386 Okamoto, 'Nomin Dantai no Genjo', p. 43.

387 Dore reports that at the time of the split, it was estimated that there were only about 1,200 farm members in the JSP. 'The Socialist Party', p. 401.

388 Okamoto 'Nomin Dantai no Genjo', p. 43.

389 Okamoto 'Nomin Dantai no Genjo', p. 43.

390 Okamoto 'Nomin Dantai no Genjo', p. 44.

391 Kyosanto Bukkuretto, *Gaiatsu no Naka no Nihon*, p. 43.

392 Personal interview, Tokyo, March 1986. The organisation in question was the Agricultural Policy Research Association discussed in chapter 6 on 'Electoral Politics' and chapter 7 on 'Representative Politics'.

393 Kyosanto Bukkuretto, *Gaiatsu no Naka no Nihon*, p. 42.

394 Kyosanto Bukkuretto, *Gaiatsu no Naka no Nihon*, p. 42.

395 Kyosanto Bukkuretto, *Gaiatsu no Naka no Nihon*, p. 36.

396 In Fukushima Prefecture, for example, there were only 400 people in farmers' unions affiliated with Zenkokukon, although the JCP claimed that Toyama and Fukui were the only prefectures that did not have affiliated prefectural federations. According to the JCP, both of these prefectures were intensifying their efforts to create prefectural centres. It anticipated that Fukuoka and Osaka which had not joined but would shortly become members.

397 Kyosanto Bukkuretto, *Gaiatsu no Naka no Nihon*, p. 43.

398 Kyosanto Bukkuretto, *Gaiatsu no Naka no Nihon*, p. 36.

399 Kyosanto Bukkuretto, *Gaiatsu no Naka no Nihon*, p. 36.

400 Kyosanto Bukkuretto, *Gaiatsu no Naka no Nihon*, p. 36.

401 Kyosanto Bukkuretto, *Gaiatsu no Naka no Nihon*, p. 36.

402 Kyosanto Bukkuretto, *Gaiatsu no Naka no Nihon*, p. 73.

403 Kyosanto Bukkuretto, *Gaiatsu no Naka no Nihon*, p. 42.

404 Kyosanto Bukkuretto, *Gaiatsu no Naka no Nihon*, p. 42.

405 Zadankai, 'Seiji no Gekido to Nogyo, Noson no Shinro' ['Dramatic Movements in Politics and the Direction of Agricultural and Farming Villages'], *Zenei*, June 1989 pp. 63–64.

406 In Muramatsu, Ito and Tsujinaka's study of Japanese pressure groups, 57 per cent of the agricultural groups surveyed replied that they had not had any conflict over differing interests and opinions, while 35 per cent reported that they had (45 per cent of this group claimed their conflict was with other agricultural groups). Muramatsu Michio, Ito Mitsutoshi and Tsujinaka Yutaka, *Sengo Nihon no Atsuryoku Dantai* [*Pressure Groups in Postwar Japan*], Tokyo, Toyo Keizai Shinposha, 1986, pp. 136–137.

407 The issue of interest group pluralism is discussed more fully below.

408 Muramatsu, Ito and Tsujinaka, S*engo Nihon no Atsuryoku Dantai*, p. 136.

409 Muramatsu, Ito and Tsujinaka, for example, reported that agricultural groups who replied to their questionnaire acknowledged cooperation almost exclusively with other agricultural groups, rather than with organisations representing other non-agricultural interests. *Sengo Nihon no Atsuryoku Dantai*, p. 107.

410 The author has been unable to elicit relevant information about this particular organisation, although the word 'liaison' is commonly used when farmer, labour and consumer groups come together to form temporary alliances around a particular policy issue.

411 Nosei no Shoten I [Focus on Agricultural Policy I], 'Kotoshi no Beika Undo no Tokucho' ['Special Features of This Year's Rice Price Campaign'], in Nosei Jyaanarisuto no Kai (ed.), *Nihon Nogyo ni Mirai Wa Aru Ka* [*Does Japanese Agriculture Have a Future?*], Nihon Nogyo no Ugoki No. 23, August 1971, p. 160.

412 In 1960, for example, Nokyo, the NCA, Zennoren and the *kaitakusha renmei* demanded a producer rice price of ¥11,400, whereas Zennichino was pressing for ¥12,700. Each of these groups mounted their own separate campaigns. Sakurai, *Beika Seisaku*, p. 124. In 1965, Zenchu demanded a 26.56 per cent increase in the producer rice price while Zennichino demanded a 50 per cent increase; in 1976, Zenchu demanded a 30.9 per cent increase, while Zennichino demanded a 62.4 per cent increase. See also chapter 5 in George, *The Strategies of Influence*, pp. 288–370.

413 See chapter 4 on 'Organisational Politics'.

414 Nokyo is, of course, biased towards the economic, production and other needs of part-time farm households. See below and chapter 4 on 'Organisational Politics'.

415 Personal interview with NCA personnel, Tokyo, July 1995.

416 Mitsukawa, *Nogyo Dantai Hattenshi*, p. 596.

417 Mitsukawa, *Nogyo Dantai Hattenshi*, pp. 598–599. This is a theme that has been revisited since. See the discussion in chapter 4 on 'Organisational Politics'. It is also an issue in the framing of the New Agricultural Basic Law.

418 These fears were raised at the same time as Nokyo acknowledged that the ABL would provide a rationale for demands for agricultural modernisation funds, the entrusting of farmland to the cooperatives, promotion of agricultural groups and so on. Nosei Jyaanarisuto no Kai, *Nogyo Kihonho no Soten*, pp. 36–37.

419 *Nokyo Kaikaku*, p. 174.

420 Otawara, 'Nokyo no Ichi to Yakuwari', p. 24.

421 This contrasts with the case in Britain for example where the National Farmers' Union exercises such a monopoly. See Graham K. Wilson, *Interest Groups*, Oxford, Basil Blackwell, 1990, p. 20.

422 Muramatsu, Ito and Tsujinaka, *Sengo Nihon no Atsuryoku Dantai*, p. 107.

423 In Muramatsu, Ito and Tsujinaka's study, exactly half of all the agricultural groups referred to cooperation with Zenchu. This may have something to do with the fact that half of the organisations surveyed were either Nokyo organisations or structurally connected to Nokyo. *Sengo Nihon no Atsuryoku Dantai*, p. 107 and Appendix, p. 21.

424 See chapter 4 on 'Organisational Politics'.

425 The farmers' unions conceived of farmers as an exploited rural labouring class, demanding higher producer rice prices as 'wages' for farm 'workers'. Intrinsic to agricultural cooperative ideology, on the other hand, was the rejection of a narrow, class-based view of farmers' interests.

426 Okamoto, 'Nomin Dantai no Genjo', p. 43. Okamoto also called it the 'united mother of 'class-based' farmers' unions' (*kaikyuteki nomin kumiai no toitsu botai*) (p. 43).

427 In this category Miyake includes groups aiming at the achievement of mutual objectives through collective action, such as industry associations, shopkeepers' associations, labour unions, religious and war bereaved associations. See Miyake Ichiro, *Tohyo Kodo* [*Voting Behaviour*], Tokyo, Tokyo Daigaku Shuppankai, 1989, p. 50.

428 Miyake, *Tohyo Kodo*, p. 51. See also chapter 6 on 'Electoral Politics'.

429 Zenkoku Nogyo Kyodo Kumiai Chuokai, *Hayawakari JA no Subete*, p. 80.

430 See chapter 3 on 'Farmers' Politics'.

431 See chapter 3 on 'Farmers' Politics' and chapter 6 on 'Electoral Politics'.

432 See chapter 6 on 'Electoral Politics'.

433 See chapter 7 on 'Representative Politics'.

434 See chapter 7 on 'Representative Politics'.

435 See chapter 3 on 'Farmers' Politics' and chapter 6 on 'Electoral Politics'.

436 See chapter 3 on 'Farmers' Politics' and chapter 6 on 'Electoral Politics'.

437 The official title is *Norinsuisansho Meibo* [*Ministry of Agriculture, Forestry and Fisheries Officials' Register*], Tokyo, Norin Shuppansha, annual (hereafter *Norinsuisansho Meibo*).

438 This label is usually restricted to the *tokushu hojin*.

439 But see also the comments in chapter 3 on 'Bureaucratic Politics' in my forthcoming volume, *Politicians and Bureaucrats*, which explain other ministry imperatives behind the formation of these groups.

440 For a more extensive discussion of these organisations operating in all policy areas in Japan, see Chalmers Johnson, *Japan's Public Policy Companies*, Washington, DC, American Enterprise Institute for Public Policy Research, 1978.

441 Jun Fukuda, Shigeki Kakinuma and Hiroshi Fukunaga, 'When in Doubt, Cut it Out: Trimming Useless Organs of the Bureaucracy', *Tokyo Business Today*, June 1994, p. 4.

442 As one Japanese official explained, 'the government asks these groups to do the same thing as it would do itself, but it does not have the manpower, so it pays the organisation to do the same job. The money comes from the budget.' Interview with MAFF official, Canberra, May 1995.

443 See chapter 3 on 'Bureaucratic Politics' in my forthcoming volume, *Politicians and Bureaucrats*.

444 See chapter 4 on 'Patronage Politics' in my forthcoming volume, *Politicians and Bureaucrats*.

445 *Norinsuisansho Meibo*, 1991, pp. 649–772.

446 Muramatsu's research on Japanese pressure groups showed that agricultural groups were very keen to have retired bureaucrats as part of their organisational structure. According to his survey data, 75 per cent of agricultural groups who responded had retired bureaucrats as 'members'. This compared with 68 per cent for economic groups, 40 per cent for educational groups and 37 per cent for welfare groups. He conducted research on 23 agricultural groups (unspecified, although they included MAFF *gaikaku dantai*). Muramatsu Michio, 'Nihongata Atsuryoku Dantai no Kenkyu' ['Research on Japanese Pressure Groups'], *Shukan Toyo Keizai*, 2–9 May, 1981, p. 80.

447 Shigeki, Kakinuma and Fukunaga, 'When in Doubt', p. 5.
448 Shigeki, Kakinuma and Fukunaga, 'When in Doubt', p. 5.
449 Shigeki, Kakinuma and Fukunaga, 'When in Doubt', p. 5.
450 Shigeki, Kakinuma and Fukunaga, 'When in Doubt', p. 5.
451 The three accounts of the national government are the General Account, the Special Account and the Government Affiliated Agencies Account. See chapter 4 on 'Patronage Politics' and chapter 5 on 'Budget Politics' in my forthcoming volume, *Politicians and Bureaucrats*.
452 See chapter 4 on 'Patronage Politics' and chapter 5 on 'Budget Politics' in my forthcoming volume, *Politicians and Bureaucrats*.
453 This means 'descend from heaven'. See chapter 3 on 'Bureaucratic Politics' in my forthcoming volume, *Politicians and Bureaucrats*.
454 Shigeki, Kakinuma and Fukunaga, 'When in Doubt', p. 5.
455 In fiscal 1992, subsidies to loss-making special corporations totalled some ¥2 trillion. Shigeki, Kakinuma and Fukunaga, 'When in Doubt', p. 5.
456 See below.
457 Nosei Jyaanarisuto no Kai, *Nogyo Kihonho no Soten*, p. 118.
458 Nosei Jyaanarisuto no Kai, *Nogyo Kihonho no Soten*, p. 119.
459 Under Article 21 of the 1965 Provisional Measures Law for Subsidies to Producers of Raw Milk for Processing, the government furnishes 'exceptional subsidies' from the budget to the LIPC in order to provide the necessary funding revenue for the LIPC's business in relation to this task. *Nogyo Roppo*, 1993, pp. 789–790.
460 *Livestock Industry Promotion Corporation: Corporate Profile*, 1996, p. 4.
461 The LIPC imported on average around 75–80 per cent of all beef imported into Japan (or 90 per cent of what was known as the general quota). See Aurelia George, *Japan's Beef Import Policies 1978–84: The Growth of Bilateralism*, Pacific Economic Papers, No. 113, July 1984.
462 *Livestock Industry Promotion Corporation, LIPC*, 1975, p. 4. This activity is now undertaken under the new 1996 Agriculture and Livestock Industry Corporation Law (*Nochikusangyo Shinko Jigyodanho*).
463 *Livestock Industry Promotion Corporation, LIPC*, 1975, p. 8. In 1997, these designated assistance projects focused on reducing costs of livestock production, strengthening the production base and the 'constitution' of livestock management, realising 'unconstrained' management, reorganising and rationalising the processing and distribution system, preserving the livestock environment, promoting sanitation and preventing epidemics, recovering and expanding the demand for livestock products and so on. Chikusan Shinko Jigyodan, *Chikusan Shinko Jigyodan Nenpo, 1997 [Livestock Industry Promotion Corporation Annual Report, 1997]*, Tokyo, Chikusan Shinko Jigyodan (hereafter *Chikusan Shinko Jigyodan Nenpo*), 1998, n.p.g. See also chapter 3 on 'Bureaucratic Politics' in my forthcoming volume, *Politicians and Bureaucrats*.
464 Under Article 54 (2) of the 1961 Livestock Products Price Stabilisation Law, the government can supply 'exceptional subsidies' from the budget for supplying the revenue source of the necessary expenses for the business of the LIPC. *Nogyo Roppo*, 1993, p. 774.
465 Designated assistance projects are: management or storage aimed at rationalising the distribution of major livestock products; guidance in livestock management or technology; rationalisation of beef production; and other projects that can contribute to the promotion of the livestock industry. *Livestock Industry Promotion Corporation: Corporate Profile*, 1996, p. 11.
466 *Livestock Industry Promotion Corporation, LIPC*, 1975, p. 14.

467 The tariff revenue on imports comes via the MAFF.
468 *Hojokin Soran*, 1998, p. 397. For a more detailed discussion of this policy, see chapter 8 on 'Policy Campaigning' and chapter 4 on 'Patronage Politics' in my forthcoming volume, *Politicians and Bureaucrats*.
469 *Hojokin Soran*, 1998, p. 399.
470 For a discussion on aggregate totals of LIPC beef import profits and subsidy allocations see chapter 5 on 'Budget Politics' in my forthcoming volume, *Politicians and Bureaucrats*.
471 Shigeki, Kakinuma and Fukunaga, 'When in Doubt', p. 7.
472 *Hojokin Soran*, 1995, p. 389.
473 *Hojokin Soran*, 1995, p. 388.
474 *Hojokin Soran*, 1998, p. 397.
475 *Hojokin Soran*, 1995, p. 392.
476 *Hojokin Soran*, 1998, p. 398. This is according to Article 37 of the new ALIC Law of 1996.
477 Fukuda, Kakinuma and Fukunaga, 'When in Doubt', p. 5.
478 *Hojokin Soran*, 1998, p. 228.
479 *Hojokin Soran*, 1998, p. 207.
480 *Hojokin Soran*, 1995, p. 205; *Hojokin Soran*, 1998, p. 207.
481 *Hojokin Soran*, 1995, pp. 205, 370–371; *Hojokin Soran*, 1998, pp. 206, 374–375.
482 *Hojokin Soran*, 1995, p. 401; *Hojokin Soran*, 1998, p. 409.
483 The law establishing this organisation was actually passed in December 1952.
484 'Noringyogyo Kinyu Kokoho' ['Agriculture, Forestry and Fisheries Finance Corporation Law'], *Nogyo Roppo*, 1993, p. 76. See also below.
485 See chapter 5 on 'Budget Politics' in my forthcoming volume, *Politicians and Bureaucrats*, where the proposed abolition of most of these corporations is also discussed.
486 *Hojokin Soran*, 1995, p. 401; *Hojokin Soran*, 1998, p. 409.
487 See chapter 5 on 'Budget Politics' in my forthcoming volume, *Politicians and Bureaucrats*.
488 Shigeki, Kakinuma and Fukunaga, 'When in Doubt', p. 7.
489 Shigeki, Kakinuma and Fukunaga, 'When in Doubt', p. 7.
490 *Hojokin Soran*, 1995, p. 237.
491 See chapter 5 on 'Budget Politics' in my forthcoming volume, *Politicians and Bureaucrats*.
492 See chapter 3 on 'Bureaucratic Politics' in my forthcoming volume, *Politicians and Bureaucrats*.
493 *Hojokin Soran*, 1998, pp. 189, 232. Additional subsidies are allocated by the Hokkaido Development Agency (¥3.3 billion) and by the Okinawa Development Agency (¥3.7 billion). *Hojokin Soran*, 1998, pp. 24, 54.
494 *Hojokin Soran*, 1995, p. 201.
495 *Hojokin Soran*, 1998, pp. 198–199.
496 In the mid-1980s, the wave of deregulation in the Japanese economy and financial system under the rubric of 'internationalisation' began, and Norinchukin had to make an effort to adjust to this situation, hence the privatisation. Personal communication, Norinchukin Research Institute, March 1998. See also chapter 4 on 'Organisational Politics'.
497 The main objective of this organisation is to compensate farmers for the difference in price if vegetable prices go below a certain level. Price stabilisation extends to 32 vegetables. The fund is accumulated from budgetary sources (national and prefectural governments) as well as vegetable producers. Subsidies allocated to the fund from the FY 1998 budget amounted to more than ¥5.1 billion. Hojokin Soran, 1998, pp. 318–319.

498 Others are the Ocean Fisheries Resources Development Centre (Kaiyo Suisan Shigen Kaihatsu Sentaa), the Fishing Boat Insurance Central Association (Gyosen Hoken Chuokai), the Biologically-Related Designated Industries Technology Research Promotion Organisation (Seibutsukei Tokutei Sangyo Gijutsu Kenkyu Suishin Kiko) and the Agricultural and Fisheries Industries Trust Fund (Nosuisangyo Shinyo Kikin).

499 In the case of the agricultural committee organisation, the prefectural chambers of agriculture are also *ninka hojin.*

500 A *shadan hojin* has members i.e. *sha* means society, or members' system.

501 *Zaidan* means accumulation of assets, thus *zaidan hojin* accumulate assets.

502 See chapter 7 on 'Representative Politics'.

503 See chapter 7 on 'Representative Politics'.

504 For a listing of these groups and their current executive and staff members, see the annual issue of *Norinsuisansho Meibo.*

505 *Norinsuisansho Meibo,* 1995, pp. 613–678.

506 More details of the constitution and activities of this group and the mechanisms of drinking milk price negotiations can be found in George, *The Strategies of Influence,* pp. 429–432.

507 Zenkoku Nogyo Kozo Kaizen Kyokai, *Zenkoku Nogyo Kozo Kaizen Kyokai no Goannai* [*A Guide to the National Agricultural Structural Improvement Association*], 1997, p. 2.

508 Zenkoku Nogyo Kozo Kaizen Kyokai, *Zenkoku Nogyo Kozo Kaizen Kyokai no Goannai,* 1997, pp. 2, 4–5.

509 In FY 1998, for example, it received more than ¥480 million in subsidies from the MAFF (see Table 2.3).

510 Personal communication with association official, September 1997.

511 Zenkoku Kaitaku Shinko Kyokai Pamphlet, 1997.

512 In the FY 1995 budget, however, it received almost ¥82 million to conduct lectures for middle management and staff members. *Hojokin Soran,* 1995, p. 214.

513 Personal communication with association official, September 1997.

514 Personal communication with association official, September 1997.

515 Personal communication with association official, September 1997.

516 Longworth, *Beef in Japan,* p. 68.

517 Shadan Hojin Chuo Chikusankai, *Yoran* [*Outline*], p. 3.

518 See also the discussion below on subsidies to the CLA from the LIPC/ALIC.

519 Haigo Shiryo Kyokyu Antei Kiko, *Haigo Shiryo Kyokyu Antei Kiko no Gaiyo* [*Outline of the Compound Feed Supply Stabilisation Organisation*], 1997, p. 3.

520 *Activities of the Dairy Farmers' Association of Japan,* Pamphlet, p. 1.

521 Personal communication with association official, September 1997.

522 Personal communication with association official, September 1997.

523 Personal communication with fund official, September 1997.

524 Personal communication with association official, September 1997.

525 Interview with association officials, Tokyo, July 1995.

526 Personal communication with association official, September 1997.

527 See chapter 5 on 'Budget Politics' and chapter 6 on 'The Politics of Agricultural Policymaking' in my forthcoming volume, *Politicians and Bureaucrats.*

528 Personal interview with NCA personnel, Tokyo, July 1995.

529 Mitsukawa, *Nogyo Dantai Hattenshi,* p. 513.

530 Personal communication with association official, September 1997.

531 See chapter 4 on 'Organisational Politics'.

532 Haigo Shiryo Kyokyu Antei Kiko, *Haigo Shiryo Kyokyu Antei Kiko no Gaiyo,* p. 3.

533 Chuo Chikusankai, *Kaiin Meibo* [*Membership Register*], August 1997, pp. 1–16.

534 See chapter 4 on 'Organisational Politics' for a discussion of these companies.
535 These are channelled through the LIPC/ALIC. See below.
536 In contrast, politicians never become leaders of *tokushu hojin* or *ninka hojin*.
537 See chapter 7 on 'Representative Politics'.
538 Personal interview with *ninka hojin* official, Tokyo, July 1995.
539 The figures exclude the *tokushu hojin*.
540 This is the national association of prefectural beef calf price stabilisation fund associations. It administers the deficiency payments scheme for feeder calves. Its members are its own prefectural stabilisation fund associations, prefectural Nokyo livestock-related federations (Zenno, Zenchikuren, Zenrakuren and Kaitakuren), the National Beef Association and the LIPC. The members of the prefectural price stabilisation associations are local governments (prefectural, city and town), relevant agricultural cooperative groups (prefectural federations and unit co-ops of both specialised and multi-purpose co-ops), other producer groups and the LIPC. Longworth, *Beef in Japan*, pp. 214, 216.
541 The bulk of this was for making available low-interest loans for livestock-related development. The figures were obtained from *Chikusan Shinko Jigyodan Nenpo*, 1997, pp. 1–81.
542 This sum was shared with Nokyo – agricultural cooperatives and their federations. *Chikusan Shinko Jigyodan Nenpo*, 1997, pp. 1–81.
543 *Chikusan Shinko Jigyodan Nenpo*, 1997, pp. 1–81.
544 *Chikusan Shinko Jigyodan Nenpo*, 1990, pp. 247–298. No later information on cumulative investment figures by recipients has been obtainable by the author.
545 See chapter 3 on 'Bureaucratic Politics' in my forthcoming volume, *Politicians and Bureaucrats*.
546 Personal communication with association official, September 1997.
547 Wilson, *Interest Groups*, p. 23. This definition is very close to Lehmbruch's classic notion of corporatism as 'an institutionalized pattern of policy-formation in which large interest organizations cooperate with each other and with public authorities not only in the articulation . . . of interests, but . . . in the "authoritative allocation of values" and in the implementation of such policies.' Gerhard Lehmbruch, 'Liberal Corporatism and Party Government', *Comparative Political Studies*, Vol. 10, No. 1, April 1977, p. 94.
548 Lehmbruch, 'Liberal Corporatism', p. 94.
549 John T. S. Keeler, *The Politics of Neocorporatism in France*, Oxford, Oxford University Press, 1987, p. 9.
550 Schmitter, for example, defines corporatism as 'a system of interest representation in which the constituent units are organized into a limited number of singular, compulsory, noncompetitive, hierarchically ordered and functionally differentiated categories, recognised or licensed (if not created) by the state and granted a deliberate representational monopoly within their respective categories in exchange for observing certain controls on their selection of leaders and articulation of demands and supports'. Philippe Schmitter, 'Still the Century of Corporatism?', in Philippe C. Schmitter and G. Lehmbruch (eds), *Trends Toward Corporatist Intermediation*, London and Beverly Hills, Sage Publications, 1979, p. 13. Keeler also equates the more fully developed types of corporatism with a system of interest intermediation in which there is a single state client group. *The Politics of Neocorporatism*, p. 9. See also the definition offered by Ishimi in his study of Nokyo. He defines 'neo-corporatism' as 'a collective body of centrally controlled interest groups'. *Nokyo*, p. 6.
551 The IRAA united under a monolithic organisational umbrella the compulsory and government-controlled representative organisations in each sector. This

period of Japan's interest group history most clearly exemplified 'corporatism' as defined by Schmitter.

552 Calder, although he confuses the *nogyokai*, *nokai* and *sangyo kumiai*, regards prewar agricultural organisations as quintessentially corporatist groups. He claims that: 'Corporatist agricultural associations . . . were a central feature of the Japanese countryside from the 1880s through World War II'. *Crisis and Compensation*, p. 260. The type of corporatism that prevailed in the prewar period was closer to the model of corporatism in which interest groups are officially sanctioned, have compulsory membership and are subsidised by the government, which also exercises various controls over leadership selection and other internal matters. As noted earlier, half the funding for the Central Bank for Industrial Cooperatives was provided by the government which also appointed its senior executives, which meant that the government had strong control over the bank. See Ishimi, *Nokyo*, p. 21. See also the bureaucratic-authoritarian model of corporatism advanced by Pearl T. Robinson, in 'Niger: Anatomy of a Neo-traditional Corporatist State', *Comparative Politics*, Vol. 24, No. 1, October 1991, pp. 3–4.

553 This point directly challenges one of the key assumptions made in Pempel and Tsunekawa's corporatist analysis of Japan, which argues that the agricultural sector is corporatised through Nokyo alone. See T. J. Pempel and K. Tsunekawa, 'Corporatism Without Labour: The Japanese Anomaly', in Schmitter and Lehmbruch (eds), *Trends Toward Corporatist Intermediation*, p. 245.

554 See chapter 8 on 'Policy Campaigning'.

555 Longworth, *Beef in Japan*, p. 58.

556 Goto and Imamura, 'Japanese Agriculture', p. 19.

557 Kawagoe, 'The Origins of Protectionism', p. 18.

558 Muramatsu, Ito and Tsujinaka's study revealed very high levels of contact between administrative authorities and agricultural groups through such mechanisms as subsidies, permissions and approvals, legal regulations, administrative guidance, membership of advisory councils, 'cooperation and support', exchanges of opinion, conference requests and membership by former officials. Amongst all the categories of group surveyed (in addition to agricultural groups, the other categories were welfare, economic, labour, administrative i.e. local government, education, professional, citizens' and political, and 'other' groups), agricultural groups scored highest on legal regulations (71 per cent) and administrative guidance (81 per cent). See table 4.17 in *Sengo Nihon no Atsuryoku Dantai*, p. 204.

559 See also below.

560 The various mechanisms of interest group incorporation in Japan are discussed in Aurelia George, *The Comparative Study of Interest Groups in Japan: An Institutional Framework*, Pacific Economic Papers, No. 95, Canberra, Australia–Japan Research Centre, December 1982, revised and reprinted as 'Japanese Interest Group Behaviour: An Institutional Approach', in J. A. A. Stockwin *et al.*, *Dynamic and Immobilist Politics in Japan*, London, Macmillan, 1988, pp. 106–140.

561 The same is true of the agricultural committee organisation.

562 'Nochi Riyo Zoshinho', in *Nogyo Roppo*, 1993, p. 305.

563 'Rakuno oyobi Nikuyogyu Seisan no Shinko ni kansuru Horitsu', in *Nogyo Roppo*, 1993, p. 762.

564 'Tochi Kairyoho', in *Nogyo Roppo*, 1993, p. 481.

565 'Yasai Seisan Shukka Anteiho', in *Nogyo Roppo*, 1993, p. 976.

566 'Rakuno oyobi Nikuyogyu Seisan no Shinko ni kansuru Horitsu', in *Nogyo Roppo*, 1993, p. 762.

567 In 1973, for example, of the 23 members of the board, five were from Nokyo organisations: the Director of Ibaraki Prefecture *keizairen*, a Norinchukin Director, the Head of Zenno's Livestock and Dairy Department, the Vice-Chairman of Zenrakuren and Chairman of Kanagawa Prefecture Poultry Federation. *Chikusan Shinko Jigyodan Hyogiin Meibo* [*List of LIPC Councillors*], 7 December 1973.

568 Aurelia George, 'The Japanese Beef Import Controversy', *New Zealand International Review*, Vol. 3, No. 2, March/April 1978, p. 22. See also Aurelia George, 'Politics of Agricultural Protectionism in Northeast Asia: The Japanese Experience', in Kym Anderson and Aurelia George (eds), *Australian Agricultural and Newly Industrialising Asia: Issues for Research*, Canberra, Australia–Japan Research Centre, 1980, pp. 49–50.

569 These are listed in *Nokyoren Yakushokuin Meibo*.

570 In 1996, for example, the RPAC included six representatives from these categories of groups, including the National Chamber of Agriculture, the Greater Japan Agricultural Association, the People's Livelihood Centre and the Agricultural, Forestry and Fisheries Finance Corporation. APAC had representation from the National Chamber of Agriculture, the Agricultural Policy Investigation Committee and the Greater Japan Agricultural Association. *Shingikai Soran*, 1996, pp. 288–289, 327–328.

571 See also above.

572 Calder makes the general observation that: 'Government officials . . . [o]ften . . . engage in extensive formal consultation with social groups, using corporatist advisory mechanisms'. *Crisis and Compensation*, pp. 131–132.

573 See above.

574 Yamauchi, 'Analytical Institutional Economics', p. 10.

575 Saeki, *Nokyo Kaikaku*, p. 168.

576 *Crisis and Compensation*, p. 260.

577 Agricultural Basic Law, unofficial translation, n.d., p. 8.

578 Agricultural Basic Law, unofficial translation, n.d., p. 8.

579 Kawagoe, 'The Origins of Protectionism', p. 18.

580 Kawagoe, 'The Origins of Protectionism', p. 19.

581 See below.

582 Mitsukawa, *Nogyo Dantai Hattenshi*, p. 622.

583 According to Ishikawa, Nokyo management in the 1960s was dependent on handling fees as subcontracting bodies of the government. Ishikawa Hideo, 'Nogyo Kyodo Kumiai no Mitsu no Kao' ['The Three Faces of the Agricultural Cooperative Unions'], in Usui Yoshimi (ed.), *Kanryo, Seito, Atsuryoku Dantai* [*Bureaucracy, Political Parties, Pressure Groups*], Gendai Kyoyo Zenshu, Vol. 21, Tokyo, Chikuma Shobo, 1960, p. 249.

584 These are spelled out in detail along with calculations of the actual financial benefits extracted in chapter 4 on 'Organisational Politics'.

585 *Nogyo Dantai Hattenshi*, p. 322.

586 Hayami, *Japanese Agriculture Under Siege*, p. 46. Tanaka explains in detail how Nokyo got into the purchasing business for fertiliser. The Nokyo purchasing network effectively replaced the abolished Fertiliser Distribution Corporation as the major distributor of fertilisers to farmers. See *Nihon no Nokyo*, pp. 28–30.

587 Hayami, *Japanese Agriculture Under Siege*, pp. 46–47.

588 As Hayami points out, around 20 per cent of capital formation in agriculture is financed from institutional loans. These institutional loans consist of low-interest loans from the Agriculture, Forestry and Fisheries Finance Corporation and 'loans from the credit departments of the agricultural cooperatives for which a

part of interest is subsidized by the government'. *Japanese Agriculture Under Siege*, p. 58. See also above.

589 Moore, *Japanese Agriculture*, p. 304. See also above.

590 Moore, *Japanese Agriculture,* p. 154. Nokyo's own loans to farmers tend to be for purposes like houses, cars, agricultural materials and farm machinery, rather than for agricultural development and modernisation purposes. See also chapter 4 on 'Organisational Politics'.

591 Asuwa, *Nokyo no Genjo*, p. 57. This issue is also taken up at greater length in chapter 4 on 'Organisational Politics'.

592 The advantages of this system for Nokyo are spelled out in greater detail in chapter 4 on 'Organisational Politics'.

593 Calder asserts that in 1949, 70 per cent of the new agricultural cooperatives had operating losses, 'despite their monopoly on rice collections'. *Crisis and Compensation*, p. 252. These figures vary from those provided by Zenchu which claims that 43 per cent of co-ops were in the red between the autumn of 1949 until the end of 1951. Zenkoku Nogyo Kyodo Kumiai Chuokai, *Hayawakari JA no Subete*, p. 141. Zenchu's figures are close to those of Tanaka, who reports that by the end of 1950, 43.1 per cent of *tankyo* were in the red. *Nihon no Nokyo*, p. 23.

594 Nokyo's managerial crisis is considered to have originated in the organisational setup of many agricultural cooperative organisations at the time. Too many *tankyo* were operating in one area; gross investment levels in these co-ops were inadequate; co-op executives were not sufficiently experienced to run the cooperatives; too many federations were operating in one area; and Nokyo executives did not have a clear concept of the principles of cooperative unionism. GHQ issued guidelines for the restructuring of agricultural cooperative organisations on their own independent initiative, and accordingly the cooperatives responded with campaigns to increase investment and other proposals, but to no avail. Takeuchi and Otawara, *Asu no Nokyo*, p. 37. Tanaka lays the blame on the so-called 'Dodge Line' deflationary policy which reduced public investment in agriculture at the same time as raising taxes on farm households. Another factor was the import of surplus agricultural products from the United States resulting in price declines for many agricultural commodities, which was also in accordance with the Dodge Line policy. He also agrees that because Nokyo Law allowed any fifteen farmers to set up a cooperative, many were formed which later proved non-viable. *Nihon no Nokyo*, pp. 23–24. Asuwa, on the other hand, argues that the root cause of the problem was because the development of agricultural cooperative businesses had run ahead of advances in agricultural production and farm household management. *Nokyo no Genjo*, p. 57. Ishimi is another writer who provides a comprehensive list of the reasons why the newborn agricultural cooperatives experienced this management crisis. See *Nokyo*, pp. 187–191. See also Zenkoku Nogyo Kyodo Kumiai Chuokai, *Hayawakari JA no Subete*, pp. 141–142.

595 See also Dore, *Land Reform*, 2nd edition, p. 294.

596 Ishida, *Interest Groups*, p. 67. According to Takeuchi and Otawara, a total of 2,480 local cooperatives became 'designated' cooperatives, which was 18.7 per cent of the total. *Asu no Nokyo*, p. 36. Tanaka records the same figure of 2,480 local co-ops and 141 *rengokai*, which amounts to some 2,600 organisations in total. *Nihon no Nokyo*, p. 37.

597 Tanaka notes that owing to government financial assistance, 70 of the *tankyo* designated for assistance made substantial progress. *Nihon no Nokyo*, p. 37.

598 The full title of this law was Federations of Agriculture, Forestry and Fishery Unions Consolidation Promotion Law (*Noringyogyo Kumiai Rengokai Seibi Sokushinho*). The basis of financial problems in the federations is extensively

examined in Tanaka, *Nihon no Nokyo*, pp. 24–27. He also lists the specific provisions under the law on pp. 42–43.

599 Ishimi, *Nokyo*, p. 194. See also chapter 4 on 'Organisational Politics'.

600 Ishimi, *Nokyo*, pp. 193–194. Tanaka notes that the restructuring promotion plan made great progress in the reform of the *rengokai*, many of which successfully recovered earlier than expected. In addition to the plan, consecutive good harvests of rice accelerated their recovery. Rises in farm household income owing to employment outside agriculture and expanding markets for livestock and other commodities also contributed. *Nihon no Nokyo*, pp. 42–43.

601 Tanaka, *Nihon no Nokyo*, p. 45.

602 Tanaka, *Nihon no Nokyo*, p. 45.

603 Asuwa, *Nokyo no Genjo*, p. 57.

604 Tanaka, *Nihon no Nokyo*, p. 37.

605 Ishimi, *Nokyo*, p. 183.

606 *Interest Groups*, p. 50.

607 'Nokyo at a Crossroads', p. 377. Takeuchi and Otawara also make the point that as soon as the Peace Treaty was concluded between the United States and Japan in 1951, bureaucratic control over the agricultural cooperatives was revived. *Asu no Nokyo*, p. 43.

608 *Asu no Nokyo*, p. 40.

609 Ishida and George, 'Nokyo', p. 209.

610 In fact the number of local agricultural cooperatives began to decline after 1950. In that year they totalled 13,314, falling to 12,221 in 1960. Asano Naonobu, 'Jigyo, Soshiki Kaikaku no Hoko to Kadai' ['Directions and Issues of the Reform in Business and Organisation'], *Nogyo to Keizai*, Special Issue, Vol. 61, No. 2, 1995, p. 60.

611 This practically doubled the farm household membership of individual agricultural cooperatives between 1960 and 1965, from 471 households to 885 households, and multiplied the individual farmer membership of agricultural cooperatives by about the same amount from 537 members to 981 members. Asuwa, *Nokyo no Genjo*, p. 106.

612 See above.

613 Nosei Jyaanarisuto no Kai, *Nogyo Kihonho no Soten*, pp. 165–166.

614 Hokkaido Koiki Nogyo Kyodo Kumiai and Kajiura Yoshimasa, *Datsu Nokyo: Nihon Nogyo Saisei e no Michi* [*Getting Out of Nokyo: The Road to the Revival of Japanese Agriculture*], Tokyo, Daiyamondosha, 1995, p. 47.

615 The more recent, accelerated programme of *nokyo* mergers in the 1990s is discussed in chapter 4 on 'Organisational Politics'.

616 *Nihon Nogyo Nenkan*, 1995, p. 387; *Poketto*, 1997, p. 317; Figure 2.2. See also chapter 4 on 'Organisational Politics'.

617 Domon Takeshi, *Nokyo ga Tosan Suru Hi* [*The Day that Nokyo Goes Bankrupt*], Tokyo, Toyo Keizai Shinposha, 1992, p. 150.

618 *Hojokin Soran*, 1995, p. 196.

619 Details of the amounts of public funds being provided for *nokyo* mergers in 1995, the *nokyo* that received them, and the exact purpose for which the funds were received is provided in Kudo Taishi, 'Nokyo Hatan de Hisoka ni Tsukawareta "Koteki Shikin"' ['"Public Funds" Secretly Used for Nokyo Failures'], *Kinyu Bijinesu*, July 1996, p. 13.

620 *Hojokin Soran*, 1998, p. 195.

621 *Hojokin Soran*, 1995, pp. 208–209.

622 Agricultural Basic Law, unofficial translation, n.d., p. 6.

623 Agricultural Basic Law, unofficial translation, n.d., p. 9.

624 See chapter 4 on 'Organisational Politics'.

625 'Daizu Natane Kofukin Zentei Sochiho', in *Nogyo Roppo*, 1993, p. 753.

626 Kaiin Toron, 'Norin Kanryo Ikigai to Kikikan' ['The Agriculture and Forestry Bureaucracy's Meaning of Life and Sense of Crisis'], in Nosei Jyaanarisuto no Kai (ed.), *Norin Kanryo o Kaibo Suru* [*Dissecting the Agriculture and Forestry Bureaucracy*], Nihon Nogyo no Ugoki No. 11, Tokyo, Nihon Norin Keikaku Kyokai, January 1968, p. 105. See also above.

627 According to other data sources, total subsidies received by the *sogo nokyo* rose from ¥13.4 billion in 1968 to ¥38.1 billion in 1974, ¥83.8 billion in 1988 and ¥97.0 billion in 1992. *Sogo Nokyo Tokeihyo*, annual, various issues. Saxon claims that subsidy allocations to agricultural co-ops and others recorded a growth from ¥17.9 billion in 1960 to ¥152.6 billion in 1976. He does not explain, however, the sources of these subsidies, the exact recipients amongst the agricultural cooperative organisations or the purposes for which the subsidies were put. E. A. Saxon, *Recent Developments in Food Consumption and Farm Production in Japan*, Bureau of Agricultural Economics, Occasional Paper No. 43, Canberra, Australian Government Publishing Service, 1978, p. 76.

628 *Hojokin Soran*, 1998, pp. 14–78.

629 See chapter 4 on 'Organisational Politics' and chapter 8 on 'Policy Campaigning'.

630 This is a very conservative figure because Zenno in practice would have received the bulk of these subsidies which were shared (equally in the case of the above calculation) with other rice trading entities. The latter are discussed in chapter 4 on 'Organisational Politics'.

631 The subsidy listed as beginning in 1969 was actually only paid to Zenno in FY 1998 for rice produced in 1997. *Hojokin Soran*, 1998, p. 527.

632 Kaiin Toron, 'Norin Kanryo', pp. 105–106.

633 Takeuchi and Otawara, *Asu no Nokyo*, p. 238. As they explain, although the concept of Nokyo derived from its own organising legislation rejected the notion of Nokyo as an 'institution' (*seido*) and conceived of it as an independent and democratic cooperative for farmers, many factors in postwar society forced Nokyo to function as an institution, and a gap appeared between the idea and reality of Nokyo's operations (p. 49).

634 Saeki, *Nokyo Kaikaku*, p. 30.

635 Kawagoe, 'The Origins of Protectionism', p. 19.

636 Ishida, 'The Development of Interest Groups', p. 297.

637 *Interest Groups*, p. 35.

638 Calder, who also has a strongly corporatist conception of the agricultural cooperatives would agree with this view. He argues that corporatised interest groups 'are in normal circumstances, somewhat vulnerable to state pressure, which has successfully incorporated many of them through institutionalized compensation arrangements such as those long prevailing between agricultural cooperatives and the government.' *Crisis and Compensation*, p. 187.

639 Ishida, *Interest Groups*, p. 50.

640 Ishikawa, 'Nogyo Kyodo Kumiai', p. 254.

641 *Interest Groups*, p. 36.

642 *Nokyo Undo*, p. 260.

643 Ishida, *Interest Groups*, p. 68.

644 According to a source inside Nokyo, one of the reasons why the agricultural cooperative federations have been able to expand their business enterprises has been by violating Nokyo Law as well as other laws (the Civil Code, the Penal Code and the Anti-Monopoly Law). Because MAFF is well aware of these violations, it can put pressure on the federations at any time. (Kawasaki also points out, for example, that the Food Agency was well aware of Nokyo's black market trading in rice but looked the other way because they wanted to protect their own vested

rights and interests in the FC system. *Shokuryocho-dono*, p. 23.) For this reason, the federations simply cannot afford to quarrel with the administration. The central unions, which receive large amounts of money from the federations in the form of levies, are also put in the position of being complicit in the violation of the Nokyo Law by the *rengokai*. Hokkaido Koiki Nogyo Kyodo Kumiai and Kajiura, *Datsu Nokyo*, p. 36, *passim*.

645   Ishikawa, 'Nogyo Kyodo Kumiai', p. 254.
646   N*okyo no Genjo*, p. 252.
647   Sakurai Makoto, 'Nokyo no Nosei Katsudo' ['Nokyo's Agricultural Policy Activities'], *Nogyo Kyodo Kumiai*, February 1972, p. 65. Sakurai was the head of Zenchu's Agricultural Policy Department at the time. Tanaka advances a similar argument, noting that under the circumstances, Nokyo had no choice but to assume the leadership in implementing the new system, although it continued to oppose the idea in principle. *Nihon no Nokyo*, pp. 213–214. See also chapter 8 on 'Policy Campaigning'.
648   Tanaka, *Nihon no Nokyo*, p. 241.
649   Tanaka, *Nihon no Nokyo*, p. 46. Muramatsu, Ito and Tsujinaka's study, for example, revealed that agricultural groups, unlike professional groups, did not exercise their veto against administrators. *Sengo Nihon no Atsuryoku Dantai*, p. 204.
650   Saeki, *Nokyo Kaikaku*, p. 163.
651   Kaiin Toron, 'Norin Kanryo', p. 104.
652   Interview with federation executives, Tokyo, July 1995.
653   'Nokyo no Nosei Katsudo to Sono Genkai' ['Nokyo's Agricultural Policy Activities and Their Limits'], *Nogyo Kyodo Kumiai*, February 1973, pp. 47–49.
654   Kyosanto Bukkuretto, *Gaiatsu no Naka no Nihon*, pp. 29–30.
655   *No to Shoku*, pp. 67–68.
656   Takeuchi and Otawara, *Asu no Nokyo*, p. 252.
657   See also the arguments in Asuwa, *Nokyo no Genjo*, Ch. 3, pp. 57–72.
658   Ono, 'Nokyo to Senkyo', p. 86.
659   Ono, 'Nokyo to Senkyo', p. 87.
660   The picture was complicated, however, by differential dependencies of the federations of agricultural cooperatives and the *tankyo*. By the late 1950s, the national and prefectural federations had successfully completed organisational reconstruction and consolidation, and had entered an era of strong management. The *tankyo*, on the other hand, continued to 'hang their heads' to bureaucrats in order to get subsidies for organisational reconstruction and consolidation.
661   This was not 100 per cent successful in all cases, leaving some co-ops in weak, dependent states.
662   Mitsukawa, *Nogyo Dantai Hattenshi*, p. 622.
663   Matsuzaka Shojiro, 'Koritsuka Suru Norin Kanryo' ['The Increasingly Isolated Agriculture and Forestry Bureaucracy'], in Nosei Jyaanarisuto no Kai (ed.), *Norin Kanryo o Kaibo Suru*, p. 14.
664   See above.
665   See chapter 4 on 'Organisational Politics'.
666   See chapter 4 on 'Organisational Politics'.
667   Matsuzaka, 'Koritsuka Suru Norin Kanryo', p. 13.
668   'Toron' ['Discussion'], in Saito Makoto, 'Shimeikan no Henshitsu wa Tozen' ['It is Natural that the Nature of the Mission Has Changed'], in Nosei Jyaanarisuto no Kai (ed.), *Norin Kanryo o Kaibo Suru*, p. 44.
669   'Toron', in *Saito*, p. 44. This view is not necessarily shared by others. One commentator in the same volume argued that Nokyo's basic characteristics had not changed even before or after the war. Kaiin Toron, 'Norin Kanryo', p. 105.

670 See chapter 8 on 'Policy Campaigning'.
671 See chapter 8 on 'Policy Campaigning'.
672 But see also the comments on the basis of Nokyo's membership in chapter 4 on 'Organisational Politics' and the reference to the effects of Nokyo's corporatisation on internal processes of democracy in chapter 8 on 'Policy Campaigning'.
673 See chapter 8 on 'Policy Campaigning'.
674 See chapter 6 on 'Electoral Politics'.
675 Ono, 'Nokyo to Senkyo', p. 76.
676 Matsuzaka, 'Koritsuka Suru Norin Kanryo', p. 13.
677 Matsuzaka, 'Koritsuka Suru Norin Kanryo', p. 13. See also chapter 8 on 'Policy Campaigning'.
678 See above.
679 See George, *The Strategies of Influence*, pp. 292–294 and Mitsukawa, *Nogyo Dantai Hattenshi*, pp. 488–513, 606–612. Kono wanted to introduce a new system for rice marketing and distribution whereby the government would continue to purchase rice from farmers who had contracted to do so, with the purchasing price determined by the need to guarantee reproduction with consideration given to the costs of production, commodity prices and economic conditions. On the other hand, producers would also be able to sell rice freely, while consumers could purchase rice freely in addition to rationed rice. The government would retain the right to prevent rice prices from being raised unfairly and to stop hoarding of rice. If necessary, the government would set the maximum price of rice traded freely. The changes to the FC system that ended up being introduced involved the replacement of the compulsory rice delivery (i.e. quota) system for rice farmers with a voluntary pre-contract system, under which farmers could decide for themselves how much rice they would sell to the government.
680 Mitsukawa, *Nogyo Dantai Hattenshi*, p. 609.
681 The National Chamber of Agriculture and prefectural chambers of agriculture also weighed in, along with the Opposition parties, labour unions, other farmers' organisations and consumer groups. Factors responsible for the defeat of the FC reform plan included not only the strong opposition to it led by Nokyo, but also the fact that the producer price of rice plus the administration costs of FC were catching up with or were higher than the consumer rice price so there was little possibility that rice could be traded freely, and the fact that the government was not determined enough to enact FC reform. Mitsukawa, quoting Ogura Takekazu, in *Nogyo Dantai Hattenshi*, p. 612.
682 *Land Reform in Japan*, p. 431.
683 Nokyo's victory on this issue, however, came at the price of a lower producer rice price in 1956, which was seen as the government's revenge for Nokyo's blocking the reform of agricultural organisations. Tanaka, *Nihon no Nokyo*, pp. 87–88.
684 *Interest Groups*, p. 69.
685 Taguchi, 'Pressure Groups in Japanese Politics', p. 479.
686 The 'Kono Plan' envisaged 'flexible' reforms of the management of FC while maintaining the basis of the system: that is, the government would continue to buy unlimited quantities of rice from the farmers and the distribution system to consumers would be maintained; but the plan also canvassed the idea of opening up new ways for farmers to sell rice freely. In other words, what had hitherto been 'black market' rice, would be formally channelled into a free distribution system. Nokyo saw this as the beginning of the end of the FC system. Asahi Shinbunsha (ed.), *Asahi Nenkan [Asahi Yearbook]*, Tokyo, Asahi Shinbunsha, 1962 (hereafter *Asahi Nenkan*), p. 93.
687 See chapter 4 on 'Organisational Politics'.

688 Nosei Jyaanarisuto no Kai, *Tenki ni Tatsu Norin Kinyu* [*Agricultural and Forestry Finance at a Turning Point*], *Kikan Nosei no Ugoki*, 3, Tokyo, Kyodo Kumiai Kyokai, 25 June, 1958, p. 59. See also chapter 3 on 'Farmers Politics'.

689 Sakaguchi, *Kyodai Nokyo no Sugosa*, p. 97.

690 Ishida, 'The Development of Interest Groups', p. 299.

691 'Corporatism Without Labor', p. 258. At the same time, they also argue that '"democratization" policies after WWII did little to change the basic structure of the interest associations in the agricultural and the small-business sectors nor their relationships with the state bureaucracy . . . paternalistic control over the peasantry by the state bureaucracy, through the cooperatives, continued' (p. 259). The evidence presented here, however, suggests that this was not the case.

692 Nosei Jyaanarisuto no Kai, *Teimei Suru Nosei Undo*, p. 26. As Eda Saburo of the Left Socialist Party said as early as 1954: 'It would be impossible for the agricultural committees to represent the interests of farmers and agricultural cooperatives if it were funded by the government.' Mitsukawa, *Nogyo Dantai Hattenshi*, p. 291. On the other hand, they were effective in playing off one conservative party against another prior to the formation of the LDP in 1955. They managed to prevent a cut to their funding in 1955 by lobbying the Liberal Party against the ruling Democratic Party (p. 342).

693 Ishida cites the example of the National Chamber of Agriculture which openly requested an increase in budgetary support from the government 'in return for the adoption of a resolution pledging their support and loyalty to the Conservative government'. *Interest Groups*, p. 59.

694 This is less true of the land improvement groups, which are particularly effective on an electoral level. See chapter 6 on 'Electoral Politics' and chapter 7 on 'Representative Politics'.

695 Fujitani, *Nokyo*, p. 9.

696 *Asu no Nokyo*, p. 252.

697 See also chapter 6 on 'The Politics of Agricultural Policymaking' in my forth-coming volume, *Politicians and Bureaucrats*.

698 *Far Eastern Economic Review*, 7 July 1988.

699 *Far Eastern Economic Review*, 7 July 1988.

700 See also chapter 8 on 'Policy Campaigning' and chapter 4 on 'Patronage Politics' in my forthcoming volume, *Politicians and Bureaucrats*.

701 Wilson, *Interest Groups*, p. 35.

702 The author is grateful to Ronald Dore for making this point.

703 Much of the discussion of the relationship between interest groups and govern-ment in Western democracies has focused on the reverse phenomenon of agency 'capture', whereby government agencies become 'clients' of particular interests because of the extent to which interest groups become institutionalised into the policymaking process and because of agency dependence on interest groups for critical information, political intelligence or support for particular policy positions. See the discussion in Jeffrey M. Berry, *Lobbying for the People: The Political Behavior of Public Interest Groups*, Princeton, Princeton University Press, 1977, pp. 280–284. Although there are some parallels in the MAFF–Nokyo relationship, Nokyo's fundamental relationship with the MAFF is primarily as a subordinate client group petitioning for favours.

704 Pempel and Tsunekawa, 'Corporatism Without Labour', p. 250.

705 See chapter 7 on 'Representative Politics'.

706 In the 1940s, of course, the farmers' unions' role in land reform represented another instance of corporatisation of these groups. Zennichino's procedural incorporation illustrates why Pempel and Tsunekawa's claim that Japan rep-resents 'corporatisation without labour' is fundamentally incorrect. The labour

union movement has been corporatised through formalised consultation processes with government including representation on advisory councils. Furthermore, contrary to Pempel and Tsunekawa's argument, neither business nor agriculture is represented by a single, monolithic organisation (see also below). Both sectors are pluralist in their representational structures. Keidanren, moreover, is not licensed by the state to represent business interests; Nokyo's closest parallel in the business world is the Japan Chamber of Commerce and Industry (Nissho), established under the same kind of legislation as Nokyo.

707 Calder makes one such systemic claim. He argues that the Japanese government utilises corporatist modes of interaction with interest groups and that in general, Japanese interest groups have a dual relationship with the state, flowing from their large size and relatively strong organisation as well as the broad range of administrative and compensatory dealings with government in which they are engaged. The predominance of this type of system is due to what he labels the 'technocratic response'. In other words, the bureaucratic-technocratic elite seeks to depoliticise policy which 'fits well with corporatism's organic view of the state. This view seeks to replace interest-group-oriented mass politics with harmonious, integrative interest articulation under the auspices of a technocratic elite. Private groups are 'chartered' by the state to assume representational and often administrative functions in place of central authority'. *Crisis and Compensation*, p. 131. See also Pempel and Tsunekawa, who posit that the political system is populated with 'generally monolithic associations all receiving varying degrees of official state recognition and policymaking roles'. *Corporatism Without Labour*, p. 245. As this chapter argues, however, in the case of agriculture, the monolithic character of interest organisation is more apparent than real. Although Nokyo has practically universal membership amongst farmers, it does not have a representational monopoly in the agricultural sphere.

708 Wilson talks about corporatised relations between government and groups existing 'at the "meso" level at which individual industries interact with government'. *Interest Groups*, p. 110. Because agriculture in Japan is a homogeneous industry, the sectoral level is more relevant.

709 See Dunleavy and O'Leary, for example, who argue that: 'Strong state elites may pursue corporatist modes of policymaking because they recognise that their capacity to steer the modern expanded state is enhanced if they can incorporate the expertise and legitimacy available from major functional blocs.' Patrick Dunleavy and Brendan O'Leary, *Theories of the State: The Politics of Liberal Democracy*, Houndmills, Macmillan, 1987, p. 196.

710 Based on his work on agricultural organisations in France, Keeler argues that the particularities of agriculture amplify the state's incentives to corporatise agricultural interest groups. The 'peculiar economic aspects of agriculture – the long time lag in shifting supply to meet new demand, the inelasticity of consumer demand for food products, and the existence of multiple, small units of production which make co-ordinating daunting – all tend to promote extensive state intervention in agriculture. In addition, the imperative of food security and the political overrepresentation of farming interests common to most advanced industrial democracies . . . compel politicians to support the farming sector. The political economy of agriculture thus enhances the state's incentives to establish a neo-corporatist system: the potential for social destabilisation increases with the political sensitivity of the sector, and the existence of dispersed units of production increases the difficulty of complex intervention schemes.' Quoted in Pepper D. Culpepper, 'Organisational Competition and the Neo-Corporatist Fallacy in French Agriculture', *West European Politics*, Vol. 16, No. 3, July 1993, p. 298.

711 This is the predominant view of the European situation advanced by authors in Schmitter and Lehmbruch (eds), *Trends Towards Corporatist Intermediation* and S. D. Berger, *Organizing Interest in Western Europe: Pluralism, Corporatism, and the Transformation of Politics*, New York, Cambridge University Press, 1981.

712 Pempel and Tsunekawa, 'Corporatism Without Labor', pp. 231–270.

713 Ishida, *Interest Groups*, p. 67.

714 Haruhiro Fukui, 'Studies in Policymaking: A Review of the Literature', in T. J. Pempel (ed.), *Policymaking in Contemporary Japan*, Ithaca and London, Cornell University Press, 1977, p. 25, quoting from Ishida Takeshi, 'Waga Kuni ni okeru Atsuryoku Dantai Hassei no Rekishiteki Joken to sono Tokushitsu' ['The Historical Conditions and Characteristics of the Origins of Pressure Groups in Japan'], in Nihon Seiji Gakkai (ed.), *Nihon no Atsuryoku Dantai [Pressure Groups in Japan]*, Tokyo, Iwanami Shoten, 1960, p. 33.

715 This is a summary of Ishida's view in Michio Muramatsu and Ellis Krauss, 'The Dominant Party and Social Coalitions in Japan', in T. J. Pempel (ed.), *Uncommon Democracies: One Party Dominant Regimes*, Ithaca, Cornell University Press, 1990, p. 286.

716 Muramatsu and Krauss, 'The Dominant Party', p. 286.

717 Takeshi Ishida, 'Interest Groups Under A Semipermanent Government Party: The Case of Japan', *Annals of the American Academy of Political and Social Science*, Vol. 413, May 1974, pp. 1–10.

718 Ishida himself pointed out that conditions relating to the 'weakness of autonomy' which characterised Japanese interest groups varied 'depending on the strength of their financial bases'. See 'The Development of Interest Groups', p. 299.

719 See chapter 6 on 'Electoral Politics'.

720 See chapter 5 on 'The Role of Business' in my forthcoming volume, *The Challenge to Vested Interests: Contesting Agricultural Power in Japan*.

721 The traditional 'power elite' conception of Japanese politics argued that Japan was ruled by a triad of bureaucrats, ruling party politicians and big business. See George, *The Comparative Study of Interest Groups*, p. 1.

722 This conclusion is supported by Muramatsu's work on Japanese pressure groups. Based on his research, he concluded that Japanese politics conformed to the type called 'pluralism' in modern liberal democratic countries. At the same time, he identified a two-fold structure in the Japanese political process (this was first presented in his work on the postwar Japanese bureaucratic system). The 'inner structure' or 'policy process' comprised the LDP, bureaucracy and what he identified as 'mainstream (*honkeiretsu*) pressure groups' such as agricultural, economic, administrative, professional and educational organisations, which were characterised by a high level of contact with the LDP and which influenced the policy process. The 'outer structure' or 'ideological process' comprised 'alternative (*betsukeiretsu*) groups', namely the Opposition parties such as the JSP and JCP, and groups associated with them such as labour, citizens' and political groups. These groups criticised the existing ideological basis of the policymaking process. The *honkeiretsu* and *betsukeiretsu* pressure groups had different kinds of relationships with the bureaucracy: mainstream pressure groups accepted retired bureaucrats as staff members, they had connections associated with acquiring permissions and approvals, they accepted administrative guidance, they cooperated with administrative policy, they had consultative-type relations with bureaucrats, they exerted strong pressure on budget formation and they had a high level of trust towards administrative policy. The alternative pressure groups, on the other hand, did not have these kinds of relations with bureaucrats. They exerted little influence on budget formation and had low levels of trust towards administrative policy. Muramatsu still identified the interest group system as

pluralistic, however, because in his survey, so-called 'alternative' pressure groups did not necessarily see themselves as weaker pressure groups and in general pressure groups of all kinds believed that they played an important role in Japanese politics. He reasoned that this confidence was possibly due to the fact that they had some policy successes in the past. 'Nihongata Atsuryoku Dantai', pp. 77–78, 82.

723 This theme is pursued further in chapter 7 on 'Representational Politics'.

724 Ishimi argues that the history of Nokyo in the Showa era is a history of conflict between neo-corporatism and pluralism, defining pluralism as systems in which power is decentralised and neo-corporatism as systems in which power is centralised. *Nokyo*, pp. 6–8.

725 Okamoto, 'Nomin Dantai no Genjo', p. 42.

726 Saeki, *Nokyo Kaikaku*, p. 32.

727 See chapter 6 on 'Electoral Politics'.

3 Farmers' politics

1 For example, politicians such as Hara Takashi (who was leader of the Seiyukai Party after WWI and Prime Minister in the first party Cabinet in Japan 1918–21) used the agricultural associations 'as a basis for their political parties through the policy of "penetration of party influence into the Farmers' Associations"'. See Keito Nokaishi Hensankai, *Nokai no Kaiko* [*Agricultural Associations in Retrospect*], pp. 11, 12, quoted in Ishida, Interest Groups, p. 22.

2 The concepts of 'direct' and 'indirect' representation of agricultural organisations are explored in chapter 7 on 'Representative Politics'.

3 See chapter 2 on 'Interest Group Politics'.

4 Ishida, *Interest Groups*, p. 10.

5 Ishida, *Interest Groups*, p. 21.

6 Ogura, *Can Japanese Agriculture Survive?*, pp. 269–270. As noted in chapter 2, in the early period of the development of these organisations, leadership by bureaucratic officials was standard practice. Control over executive appointments was one of the primary means whereby the agricultural bureaucracy supervised and controlled these groups.

7 Ogura, *Can Japanese Agriculture Survive?*, p. 270.

8 As noted earlier, Hara Takashi urged his party members to establish strong ties with farming communities because he considered it essential to gain strong support in agricultural villages in order to develop party politics in Japan. Following his advice, members of the Seiyukai developed close relations with the *nokai*. Mitsukawa, *Nogyo Dantai Hattenshi*, pp. 259–269.

9 Ogura, *Can Japanese Agriculture Survive?*, p. 285. Ishimi, *Nokyo*, pp. 124–125.

10 Ishimi, *Nokyo*, p. 125.

11 Ishimi, *Nokyo*, p. 125.

12 Amongst this group, Diet members connected to the Seiyukai were overwhelmingly numerous (73.5 per cent), while only 20.4 per cent were affiliated with the Minseito. Ishimi, *Nokyo*, p. 125.

13 Ishida, *Interest Groups*, p. 22. This group was split more or less evenly between those connected to the Seiyukai and those affiliated with the Minseito. Ishimi, *Nokyo*, p. 125. He concluded that the prominence of *sangyo kumiai* representatives in prefectural assemblies compared with the national Diet meant that they exercised little political power at the national level (p. 126).

14 One was the Rice and Grains Self-Control Bill that would have allowed the industrial cooperatives to trade in rice within a certain standard price range. Not surprisingly, rice merchants took action to scrap the bill. Ishimi, *Nokyo*, p. 127.

15 Ogura, *Can Japanese Agriculture Survive?*, p. 285. See also chapter 2 on 'Interest Group Politics'.

16 The Noson Giin Domei chose for its representative, Tasukawa Keishiro, the father of LH member for Fukushima (2), Tasukawa Ryohei, who was first elected as a *nokyo* chairman to the Lower House for the Liberal Party in 1953 and again in 1955, and who then became a member of the LDP from 1955–58.

17 This followed the beliefs of one of the founders of the movement, Sengoku Kotaro, who adhered to the principle of no political favouritism followed by the Rochdale Pioneers in Britain (on which the *sangyo kumiai* were partly modelled). Ogura, *Can Japanese Agriculture Survive?*, p. 285. Ishimi, however, notes that Sengoku was connected to the Minseito, *Nokyo*, p. 125. See also below.

18 In the first general election after the war in 1946, Independents polled 20.4 per cent of the total vote and minor party candidates 11.7 per cent. In 1947, these figures were 5.8 per cent and 5.4 per cent respectively. See Kobayashi, Shinohara and Soma, *Senkyo*, *Furoku*, p. 4.

19 Dore, 'The Socialist Party', p. 377.

20 The JCP was initially against the formation of Nichino, arguing that the farmers' movement had to be conducted by its own farmers' committees (*nomin iinkai*), which were the party's organisations handling all issues relating to farm villages. Nevertheless, the JCP participated in the formation of Nichino by withdrawing this stipulation. In this sense, Nichino began as an organisation in which the JSP and JCP jointly collaborated. See Nomin Mondai Kenkyukai (ed.), *Sengo Nihon no Nomin Undo*, pp. 58–64.

21 Dore, 'The Socialist Party', p. 377.

22 The example he cites is Niigata. 'Nomin Undo', p. 97.

23 Dore, 'The Socialist Party', p. 377.

24 Dore, 'The Socialist Party', p. 379.

25 Nomizo Masaru, long-time leader in the farmers' union movement, became a Minister and Chairman of the Local Finance Commission in the 1947 coalition government in which the JSP participated. He was criticised for proposing legislation exempting farmers producing staple foods such as rice, barley, wheat etc. from enterprise taxes because of his past professional representation of farmers' organisations.

26 Dore, 'The Socialist Party', p. 381. Scalapino and Masumi reported that 44 Socialist Party Diet members were farmers' union leaders or affiliated members in the 1947 Lower House. See Robert A. Scalapino and Junnosuke Masumi, *Parties and Politics in Contemporary Japan*, Berkeley and Los Angeles, University of California Press, 1962, p. 164.

27 Dore, 'The Socialist Party', p. 381.

28 According to Dore: 'It was probably a widespread feeling among such voters, as it appears to have been throughout the country, that the time had come for a change, which explains the increase in the Socialist vote in rural, as in urban, areas.' 'The Socialist Party', p. 382.

29 According to Dore, these were the predominantly agricultural constituencies of Tochigi, Gumma, Yamanashi, Shiga, Kagawa and Shimane prefectures. 'The Socialist Party', p. 378.

30 Dore, 'The Socialist Party', pp. 378–379 and p. 386. These constituencies had less than 30 per cent of their population in urban areas.

31 Kent Calder, *Crisis and Compensation*, pp. 75–76.

32 Dore, 'The Socialist Party', p. 391.

33 Ronald Dore, unpublished comments, 1980.

34 The JCP did not abandon the platform of its own farmers' committees, which advocated the confiscation of mountains, forests, fields and land and their free

redistribution. It started attacking the JSP in order to change the Nichino into an organisation serving the farmers' committees. The JCP and JSP also competed for the leadership of Nichino – hence the split between Nichino's JSP and JCP-dominated factions. Nomin Mondai Kenkyukai (ed.), *Sengo Nihon no Nomin Undo*, pp. 84–88.

35 Dore, 'The Socialist Party', p. 382.
36 The JSP secured only 48 seats in the 1949 LH elections, after winning 143 seats in the 1947 elections. Scalapino and Masumi, *Parties and Politics*, p. 159.
37 Dore, 'The Socialist Party', p. 386. A more general factor, of course, was the Socialists' chequered record in the coalition government of 1947–48. Dore analysed the JSP's policy statements at the time, which advocated cooperative forms of land use. This offended the emerging sense of petty proprietorship amongst the expanding class of small land-holders and was hardly a vote-catcher (p. 389).
38 Dore, 'The Socialist Party', p. 386.
39 Scalapino and Masumi, *Parties and Politics*, p. 165.
40 The Left and Right Socialist Parties resulted from the 1951 split of the JSP. They contested the 1952, 1953 and 1955 elections until their amalgamation into the Japan Socialist Party in October 1955.
41 Scalapino and Masumi, *Parties and Politics*, p. 166.
42 Dore, 'The Socialist Party', p. 391.
43 Hirano had a prewar history of support for the tenants' movement, agrarian fascism and national socialism of the radical right. Dore, 'The Socialist Party', p. 374.
44 One of the reasons for his dismissal was his 'spirited advocacy of the agricultural interests in the face of different cabinet priorities'. Haruhiro Fukui, 'Japan Socialist Party-2', in Haruhiro Fukui (ed.), *Political Parties of Asia and the Pacific*, Westport, Connecticut, Greenwood Press, 1985, p. 528.
45 Haruhiro Fukui, 'Social Reformist Party', in Fukui (ed.), *Political Parties*, p. 620.
46 This is sometimes called the Worker Farmer Party.
47 The idea of joining labourers and farmers under one party umbrella had an extensive prewar history, going back to the formation of the Farmer Labour Party (Nomin Rodoto) by the prewar Nichino in 1926 and the Labour Farmer Party (Rodo Nominto) in 1927. See Ishimi, *Nokyo*, pp. 117–119.
48 Kuroda was a Marxist who had been imprisoned in 1937.
49 Scalapino and Masumi, *Parties and Politics*, p. 159.
50 On the involvement of agricultural organisations in recommending candidates to their members in elections, see chapter 6 on 'Electoral Politics'.
51 Kobayashi, Shinohara and Soma, *Senkyo*, p. 84.
52 *Asahi Nenkan*, 1946, p. 109.
53 He is described by Ogura as a 'a pioneer of "industrial-cooperative-ism"', working first in the *nokai*, but later transferring to the industrial cooperatives. He was employed in the Central Association of Industrial Cooperatives in Tokyo for about twenty-five years, finally ending up as Chairman. *Can Japanese Agriculture Survive?*, pp. 272–273. Sengoku's prewar ideology of cooperative unionism aimed to promote the social autonomy of the industrial cooperative sector by ending the suppression of the middle and working classes by the capitalist class which controlled the market; make landowners who controlled the agricultural villages politically and socially stabilise the cultivation rights of the tenants, improve the status of tenant and owner farmers, and promote rural renovation based on egalitarian human relationships; and establish the autonomy of the industrial cooperatives against control of agricultural villages by agricultural bureaucrats. For all these reasons, Sengoku advocated the involvement in politics of the

industrial cooperatives. During this period, he was connected to the Minseito. Ishimi, *Nokyo*, pp. 124, 125.

54 During his term, the MAF replaced the MAC. Sengoku was Minister for less than 50 days, having to resign with the general resignation of the Cabinet. Ogura, *Can Japanese Agriculture Survive?*, p. 285.

55 Ishimi puts the figure at 30. *Nokyo*, p. 171.

56 Haruhiro Fukui, 'Japan Cooperative Party-1', in Fukui (ed.), *Political Parties*, p. 514.

57 Fukui, 'Japan Cooperative Party-1', p. 514.

58 Harold S. Quigley and John E. Turner, *The New Japan*, Minneapolis, University of Minnesota Press, 1956, p. 85.

59 Fukui, 'Japan Cooperative Party-1', p. 514.

60 Fukui, 'Japan Cooperative Party-1', p. 514.

61 Quigley and Turner, *The New Japan*, p. 85.

62 This represented 3 per cent of the total number of seats in the newly constituted Diet. Scalapino and Masumi, *Parties and Politics*, p. 159.

63 In fact, many *nogyokai* leaders had previously been executives of *nokai*.

64 Nakamura, 'Nominhyo no Pawaa', p. 112, Tanaka, *Nihon no Nokyo*, p. 429. The government's decision was in fact, ¥550 per 150 kg (p. 429).

65 Ishimi, *Nokyo*, p. 251.

66 Six members of this group were later to take up executive positions in Nokyo. Three subsequently became Nokyo Diet members, holding concurrent office in both the national Parliament and the agricultural cooperative organisation. The remaining three were to relinquish national politics for careers as Nokyo leaders.

67 Some of these are named along with their organisational connections, including later positions in Nokyo in Tanaka, *Nihon no Nokyo*, p. 429.

68 In fact there were 363 parties in 1946.

69 A total of 81 Independents won seats in the 1946 Diet (17.4 per cent of the total), while 38 represented 'miscellaneous' parties (8.2 per cent of the total). Scalapino and Masumi, *Parties and Politics*, p. 159.

70 Haruhiro Fukui, 'Cooperative Democratic Party', in Fukui (ed.), *Political Parties*, p. 475.

71 This was a relatively small, moderate centre party formed in September 1946 with a particular interest in educational issues. See Haruhiro Fukui, 'National Party', in Fukui (ed.), *Political Parties*, p. 581.

72 Shortly after the merger, however, 15 members left the party and joined the newly established Democratic Party. Haruhiro Fukui, 'National Cooperative Party', in Fukui (ed.), *Political Parties*, p. 576.

73 Fukui, 'Cooperative Democratic Party', p. 475.

74 One of these was the Japan Farmers Party (Nihon Nominto), which is discussed below. See also Tanaka, *Nihon no Nokyo*, p. 431.

75 This group included Yanagawa Sozaemon, Chairman of the National Association of Agriculture (Zenkoku Nogyokai), who attained second position in the list of successful NC candidates with over 4 million votes (compared with the combined total of 280,000 votes for the two Nichino candidates). He was later disqualified as a Diet member under the purge and also resigned as Chairman of the National Association of Agriculture. Altogether seven prefectural *nogyokai* chairmen were elected to UH prefectural constituencies in this election. Tanaka, *Nihon no Nokyo*, p. 433.

76 This was a loose grouping which formed in May 1947 amongst UH members. It had no particular fixed political line and its members included both conservatives and progressives. Haruhiro Fukui, 'Ryokufukai-1', in Fukui (ed.), *Political Parties*, p. 611. This group of GBS politicians included Shimamura Gunji elected

from Okayama who later became Chairman of Zenshiren. Tanaka, *Nihon no Nokyo*, p. 433.

77 These were Yonekura Tatsuya, Chairman of Nagano Prefecture Association of Agriculture, who became the first Chairman of Zenchu and Okamura Fumijiro, Chairman of Hokkaido Prefecture Association of Agriculture who later succeeded to the position of Zenkyoren Chairman. See also chapter 6 on 'Electoral Politics' for further discussion of Okamura.

78 Ishida and George, 'Nokyo', p. 203.

79 Scalapino and Masumi, *Parties and Politics*, p. 159. Fukui puts their seat tally in the April 1947 elections at 31, with 10 seats obtained in the UH election. 'National Cooperative Party', p. 576.

80 Scalapino and Masumi, *Parties and Politics*, p. 159.

81 This organisation was reportedly launched in 1947 to act as Nokyo's 'detached corps'. It subsequently undertook energetic campaigns in elections to all levels of government to get farmers' representatives elected. Nosei Jyaanarisuto no Kai, *Tenki ni Tatsu Norin Kinyu*, p. 55.

82 A party of the same name led by Hirano Rikizo had been established in 1926 by the right wing of the prewar Nichino. According to one assessment, it 'was the only prewar Japanese proletarian party that was based entirely on the support of country people, mainly tenant farmers'. Haruhiro Fukui, 'Japan Farmers Party-1', in Fukui (ed.), *Political Parties*, p. 515. The party disbanded in 1928.

83 Kita Katsutaro had been expelled from the Cooperative Democratic Party for insisting on the cooperative principle in negotiations with the New Politics Society (Shinseikai), a progressive group formed in July 1946, which attempted unsuccessfully to merge with the Cooperative Democratic Party, later changing its name to the National Party. Haruhiro Fukui, 'Shinseikai-1', in Fukui (ed.), *Political Parties*, p. 617.

84 Nakano Shiro was the political representative of a local farmers' organisation in Aichi Prefecture.

85 Apart from Nakano, its members were: Kawaguchi Yoichi from Hokkaido (2), member of the Hokkaido Nomin Domei, who became Secretary-General of the party in November 1947; Kota Jiro from Hokkaido (4) and Takakura Sadanori from Hokkaido (5), both agriculturalists; Kato Yoshitaro from Fukui, Tsunejima Masaoki from Nagasaki (2), later Chairman of the successor group to the National Rural Youth League, the National Farmers' Federation (Zenkoku Nomin Renmei, or Zennoren); Nakamura Torata from Fukuoka (1), who was Secretary-General of Zennoseiren, and Terasaki Kaku from Fukuoka (3), who was an executive member of the Fukuoka Prefecture Rural Youth League.

86 Kunii Junichi was the Founding Chairman of Zennoseiren.

87 *Asahi Nenkan*, 1948, p. 165.

88 *Asahi Nenkan*, 1948, p. 165.

89 *Asahi Nenkan*, 1948, p. 165.

90 Haruhiro Fukui, 'Japan Farmers Party-2', in Fukui (ed.), *Political Parties*, p. 516.

91 Once again this accorded more closely with the spirit of cooperativism and no political favouritism of the Rochdale Pioneers.

92 This split was over the Katayama coalition government's enforced rice deliveries from farmers. The National Cooperative Party was one of the three parties in this coalition.

93 On this basis it deserves classification as a minor party, although this was only one seat less than the Ronoto which has attracted a great deal more attention from scholars. It was also one more than Zenno's leader, Hirano Rikizo's socialist splinter group, the Social Reformist Party. New Farmers Party members were: Kawaguchi Yoichi, Hokkaido (2), ex-Nihon Nominto; Matsumoto Rokutaro,

Hokkaido (1), formerly National Cooperative Party; Kodaira Tadashi, Hokkaido (4), who stood on a Nomin Shinto ticket and was newly elected to the House; Kita Jiro, Hokkaido (2), ex-Nihon Nominto; Takakura Sadanori, Hokkaido (5), ex-Nihon Nominto; Iida Yoshishige, Hokkaido (5), former National Cooperative Party member and prefectural *nokai* executive; Hatano Jiro, Oita (1), who joined the party having been elected as an Independent; Nakamura Torata, Fukuoka (1), ex-Nihon Nominto; Terasaki Kaku, Fukuoka (3), ex-Nihon Nominto; and Mizuno Hikojiro, Shizuoka (1), who later reverted to non-party alignment.

94 These were Kawaguchi Yoichi, Chairman of the National Agricultural Cooperative Union Liaison Council in 1948 and later Hokkaido Purchasing Nokyo Federation Chairman; Matsumoto Rokutaro, Chairman of the Hokkaido Guidance Nokyo Federation; Hatano Jiro, who was Chairman of Oita Prefecture Marketing Nokyo Federation; and Kodaira Tadashi, also from Hokkaido, who had a considerable history in the producer cooperative movement as a prewar staff member of the National Purchasing and Marketing Federation (Zenkohanren) of the *sangyo kumiai*, as a wartime staff member of the National Association of Agriculture, and after the war, as a Managing Director of the Hokkaido Production Federation (Seisanren), an interim agricultural cooperative-type organisation. Kodaira was described as a 'true-blue cooperative man' by Tanaka, *Nihon no Nokyo*, p. 435.

95 During the Ashida Cabinet in 1948, the Democratic Liberal Party often enlisted minor parties such as the Social Reformist Party and the Japan Farmers Party in an anti-government alliance. Haruhiro Fukui, 'Democratic Liberal Party', in Fukui (ed.), *Political Parties*, p. 481.

96 'Social Reformist Party', p. 620.

97 Amongst this group, the so-called 'progressive triumvirate' consisted of Ashika Kaku, the Chairman of Tottori Prefecture Marketing Nokyo Federation with a history of association with the farmers' unions, Yamasaki Tsune, the Chairman of Zenhanren from Kagawa, and Fujishima Iwao from Akita. Tanaka, *Nihon no Nokyo*, p. 434.

98 The concept of Nokyo Diet members (*Nokyo giin*) is elaborated in chapter 7 on 'Representative Politics'.

99 *Asahi Nenkan*, 1950, p. 303.

100 This was, nonetheless, more than double the membership of the Ronoto or the Shakai Kakushinto.

101 *Nihon Kindaishi Jiten*, p. 496.

102 J. A. A. Stockwin, 'Farmers Cooperative Party', in Fukui (ed.), *Political Parties*, p. 496.

103 The first leader of the Farmers Cooperative Party was Matsumoto Rokutaro, Chairman of the Hokkaido Guidance Nokyo Federation and later Vice-Chairman of the National Guidance Nokyo Federation. He was followed as leader in June 1950 by Kawaguchi Yoichi, a leading Hokkaido Nokyo official. Other members were Kodaira Tadashi, Hatano Jiro, Iida Yoshishige, Takakura Sadanori, Terasaki Kaku, Nakano Shiro and Nakamura Torata, a majority of whom were Nokyo officials.

104 They were Kawaguchi Yoichi from Hokkaido (2), Kodaira Tadashi from Hokkaido (4), Matsumoto Tokutaro from Hokkaido (2), Iida Yoshishige from Hokkaido (5) and Hatano Jiro from Oita (1).

105 The party's Secretary-General was Nakamura Torata, also Secretary-General of the Zennoseiren. Another member, Terasaki Kaku, was an executive of the Fukuoka Rural Youth League. Kawaguchi Yoichi and Kodaira Tadashi were affiliated with the Hokkaido Nomin Domei.

106 These are listed in *Gikai Seido Nanajunenshi: Shugiin, Sangiin [A 70-Year History of the Diet System: House of Representatives, House of Councillors]*, Tokyo, Okurasho Insatsu Kyoku, 1961, p. 956. Another source puts its Upper House membership at four. See *Nihon Kindaishi Jiten*, p. 496.

107 These were Matsuura Sadayoshi, Chairman of the Hokkaido Nomin Domei Prefectural Committee, Azuma Takashi, previously elected to the Diet in 1946 as a Japan Cooperative Party candidate and Managing Director of Hokkaido Prefecture Agricultural Association, and Ishikawa Seiichi, Chairman of the Hokkaido Nomin Domei, a Nokyo Federation Chairman and Vice-Chairman of Zennoseiren. Ishikawa stood in the national constituency and gained 24th place, but a majority of these votes were from Hokkaido Prefecture. The Hokkaido Nomin Domei also basically elected Matsuura and Azuma to Hokkaido prefectural constituency seats. Tanaka, *Nihon no Nokyo*, p. 436.

108 In addition to its three Hokkaido representatives in the Upper House, of its members in the Lower House, six represented Hokkaido electorates and two Fukuoka.

109 This group included Okamura Fumijiro and Mori Yasoichi, who was to become the best known and longest standing Nokyo figure in the Diet, with a joint Parliamentary and Nokyo career lasting from 1950 to 1974, during which time he served as Chairman of Zenchu.

110 This group included Kawaguchi Yoichi, leader of the party, Nakamura Torata, Takakura Sadanori, Terasaki Kaku, Nakano Shiro and Iida Yoshishige.

111 See chapter 2 on 'Interest Group Politics'.

112 Mitsukawa, *Nogyo Dantai Hattenshi*, pp. 259–269.

113 Hatano Jiro joined the Kyodoto together with Kodaira Tadashi, who later became a Right Socialist Party member. Both lost their seats in the 1952 elections.

114 J. A. A. Stockwin, 'Cooperative Party', in Fukui (ed.), *Political Parties*, p. 476.

115 Stockwin, 'Cooperative Party', p. 476.

116 These were Nakano Shiro, Takakura Sadanori and Nakamura Torata, who left the Kyodoto to join the Kaishinto.

117 These were Hirano Rikizo and Oishi Yoshie.

118 When the National Democratic Party was formed, the Democratic Party provided the largest contingent (with 47 LH and 36 UH members). The National Cooperative Party provided 14 members and the New Politics Council five. One member of the Social Reformist Party also joined. Haruhiro Fukui, 'National Democratic Party', in Fukui (ed.), *Political Parties*, p. 578.

119 Farmers provided election campaign funds, but could not provide sufficient funds to maintain the party. Nakamura, 'Nominhyo no Pawaa', p. 113.

120 Muramatsu and Krauss, 'The Conservative Policy Line', p. 522.

121 *Nihon Kindaishi Jiten*, *Furoku* No. 36.

122 This organisation and its prefectural bodies called farmers' federations (*nomin renmei*) are sometimes classed as farmers' unions. See Dore, *Land Reform in Japan*, p. 466. According to Dore, Zennoren was 'the least political of the farmers' unions and . . . concentrated chiefly on price issues, its branches working as ginger groups to stimulate Co-operatives, or organizing their own collective bargaining' (p. 466).

123 *Nihon Kindaishi Jiten*, *Furoku* No. 36.

124 *Nihon Kindaishi Jiten*, *Furoku* No. 36.

125 See chapter 2 on 'Interest Group Politics'.

126 This was Ishiguro Tadaatsu, who had had a long career in agricultural affairs as a former Chairman of the Zenkoku Nogyokai, Vice-Minister of Agriculture and Forestry, Minister of Agriculture and Forestry just before the outbreak of WWII and Minister of Agriculture and Commerce in the final stages of the war. The

only former member of the rural youth league organisation left in the Diet after 1952 was Nakamura Torata, who later joined the LDP.

127 One of these was former Japan Cooperative Party member Matsuura Sadayoshi from Hokkaido (5), who was a Zennoren adviser (*komon*), and Haga Mitsugu, from Hokkaido (2), a member of Zennoren's Central Committee.

128 Dore, 'The Socialist Party', p. 391. The attribution of farmers' unions to the *nomin renmei* reflected their politically more 'progressive' orientation.

129 These were: Haga Mitsugu, Left Socialist, then JSP member in the Lower House from 1952; Azuma Takashi, Right Socialist, then JSP member in the Upper House from 1950; Yasui Yoshinori, JSP member in the Lower House from 1958; and Matsuura Sadayoshi, also JSP member in the Lower House from 1958.

130 The Zennoren did, however, undergo a process of 'creeping conservatism' after 1955 until its amalgamation with Zennoseiren in 1963 to form the Zennosoren (see chapter 2 on 'Interest Group Politics'). See also below.

131 Ishimi, *Nokyo*, pp. 177–178. See also the comments below.

132 Independents in the Lower House secured 20.4 per cent of the total vote in 1946. Their polling rate slumped to 5.8 per cent in 1947 and by 1955, to 3.3 per cent. The same was true of minor parties. In 1946, minor party candidates gained 11.7 per cent of the vote. This figure was more than halved in 1947 and 1949, and diminished progressively after that until it reached 0.4 per cent in 1953. In the 1955 elections it was 1.3 per cent. See Kobayashi, Shinohara and Soma, *Senkyo, Furoku*, p. 4.

133 Tanaka, *Nihon no Nokyo*, p. 438.

134 Tanaka, *Nihon no Nokyo*, p. 439.

135 Tanaka, *Nihon no Nokyo*, p. 439.

136 Tanaka, *Nihon no Nokyo*, p. 439. In fact the producer rice price rose from ¥2,820 per 60 kg in 1951 to ¥3,000 in 1952 and ¥3,384 in 1953. *Nihon Nogyo Nenkan*, 1996, p. 44. See also chapter 2 on 'Interest Group Politics'.

137 Tanaka, *Nihon no Nokyo*, p. 439.

138 *Land Reform in Japan*, 2nd edition, p. 416. Dore rates this factor as the most important in accounting for the support which the conservatives drew from the farmer. See chapter 17 in the 2nd edition, pp. 405–418.

139 Dore, 'The Socialist Party', p. 392.

140 See above. It rose from ¥3,384 per 60 kg in 1953 to ¥3,704 in 1954, and ¥3,902 in 1955. *Nihon Nogyo Nenkan*, 1996, p. 44.

141 Dore, 'The Socialist Party', pp. 392–393. See also the analysis of this period in chapter 2 on 'The Economists' Explanation' in my forthcoming volume, *The Challenge to Vested Interests*.

142 Dore, *Land Reform in Japan*, 2nd edition, p. 416.

143 See also chapter 5 on 'The Political Demography of Agriculture'.

144 In the 1955 LH elections, the newly formed Japan Democratic Party was the largest vote-winner nationally and retained government (which had been formed in December 1954 when a breakaway group of Liberals joined up with the Reformist Party to form the Japan Democratic Party).

145 This compares with 23 seats in urban areas and 87 in semi-urban areas. Dore, *Land Reform in Japan*, p. 406. These same figures are reported in Arimitsu Reimin, 'Seito to Beika Seisaku' ['Political Parties and Rice Price Policy'], in Nosei Jyaanarisuto no Kai (ed.), *Beisaku no Shintenkai* [*New Developments in Rice Cultivation*], Nihon Nogyo No Ugoki No. 5, Tokyo, Kyodo Kumiai Kyokai, April 1966, p. 105. Another study showed that the Liberals and Democrats acquired 90 seats (or 72 per cent of the total) in the 33 rural constituencies in the 1955 LH elections, while the combined Right and Left Socialist tally was 32 seats

or 26 per cent of the total. The seats were categorised according to a typology derived from Okino Yasuharu, *Showa 30 Nendai ni Okeru Toshika, Kogyoka to Tohyo Kodo Henka* [*Urbanisation, Industrialisation and Changes in Electoral Behaviour, 1955–65*], Tokyo, Minshushugi Kenkyukai, 1966, pp. 18–19.

146 As Tanaka puts it, in fact in both the 1952 and 1953 elections, rural areas became the biggest support base of the conservative party, but the Right and Left Socialists also advanced little by little. *Nihon no Nokyo*, p. 442.

147 Tanaka, *Nihon no Nokyo*, p. 437.

148 Tanaka, *Nihon no Nokyo*, p. 440.

149 This breakaway group of anti-Yoshida Liberals which included Hatoyama Ichiro and Kono Ichiro actually formed the Democratic Party by amalgamating with the Kaishinto. Tanaka, *Nihon no Nokyo*, p. 441. See above also.

150 See also below.

151 See chapter 6 on 'Electoral Politics'.

152 Nagase, 'Nosei Kyogikai', p. 53.

153 Nosei Jyaanarisuto no Kai, *Teimei Suru Nosei Undo*, p. 8.

154 Nosei Jyaanarisuto no Kai, *Teimei Suru Nosei Undo*, p. 13.

155 This was a local farmers' political league, but no further information is available about the prefecture in which it operated.

156 Nosei Jyaanarisuto no Kai, *Teimei Suru Nosei Undo*, p. 14.

157 Nosei Jyaanarisuto no Kai, *Hanjutsu Hatten to Keiei Kakushin*, p. 87.

158 In this election the LDP candidate was defeated by Sato Zennichiro, the Nokyo candidate, who was a former LDP Lower House Diet member. He broke from the party, making Nokyo, in which he was a prefectural central union chairman, his main back-up organisation. He cooperated on policy matters with the JSP and stood as an Independent candidate with JSP recommendation.

159 Soma, *Nihon no Senkyo Seiji*, p. 151.

160 In the Ibaraki election, Nokyo candidates managed a successful alliance of one section of the LDP (in the main, prefectural assembly members who had split from the incumbent LDP faction), agricultural cooperatives, farmers' unions and youth groups. These were all mobilised into the Kono Seiji Renmei. At the time it was regarded as a victory for a joint farmer-labour struggle.

161 Nakamura, 'Nominhyo no Pawaa', p. 115.

162 Nakamura, 'Nominhyo no Pawaa', p. 115.

163 Nosei Jyaanarisuto no Kai, *Hanjutsu Hatten to Keiei Kakushin*, p. 92.

164 Nosei Jyaanarisuto no Kai, *Tenki ni Tatsu Norin Kinyu*, pp. 54–55. By the late 1950s, this organisation supported Socialist principles and therefore recommended candidates from the JSP. Although it originally provided the basis for the Farmers Cooperative Party, in the process of party reformation it shifted to the right wing of the Socialist Party, and from there to the Socialist Party (p. 56).

165 Nosei Jyaanarisuto no Kai, *Tenki ni Tatsu Norin Kinyu*, pp. 56–57.

166 This group included Nagasaki Prefecture Nokyo Central Union Chairman and incumbent Diet member, Fujino Shigeo; and amongst the newly elected group, Hyogo Prefecture Nokyo Trust Federation Chairman and Director of the Central Cooperative Bank for Agriculture and Forestry, Aota Gentaro, and Kagoshima Prefecture Nokyo Economic Federation Chairman and Chairman of the National Nokyo Transport Federation, Taniguchi Keikichi. Two prefectural Nokyo chairmen supported by farmers' political groups who stood as Independents lost. The activities of these groups were not confined to providing backup for Nokyo executives. The Ibaraki Kono Seiji Renmei did not formally recommend any candidates, but it did give informal support to a member of the Ryokufukai whose supporters' association had thrown its weight behind the Nokyo aspirant for the prefectural governorship in the same year, in addition to a JSP candidate who had

a good record on agricultural policy matters. Farmers' political leagues also recommended Ryokufukai candidates in Shiga and Oita prefectures.

167 Haruhiro Fukui, 'Ryokufukai-1', p. 612.

168 The only Ryokufukai Nokyo Diet member left in the Upper House after 1959 was Mori Yasoichi. He was one of only eleven members.

169 See also chapter 2 on 'Interest Group Politics' for a discussion of this organisation.

170 Tsunejima Masaoki, former Japan Farmers Party and Liberal Party member in the Diet between 1947 and 1949, and from 1952 onwards, succeeded Ishiguro Tadaatsu as Chairman of Zennoren. In 1955 he joined the LDP. In 1959, the Chairman of the Miyazaki Prefecture *nomin renmei*, Nukumi Saburo, a Nokyo executive, was elected to the Upper House for the LDP.

171 The Chairman of Zennoseiren was the Miyagi Prefecture Nokyo Central Union Chairman; the three Vice-Chairmen were from Hyogo, Ibaraki and Fukuoka Prefectures; and Chief of its Secretariat was Nakamura Yoshijiro, who was serving concurrently as Secretary-General of the Zennoren. Tanaka, *Nihon no Nokyo*, p. 453.

172 Saga Prefecture's *noseiren* was the No. 3 strength in the prefectural assembly with six members. Its membership stood at 60,000. Tanaka, *Nihon no Nokyo*, p. 453.

173 Soma, *Nihon no Senkyo Seiji*, p. 153.

174 In Miyagi (1) for example, the prefectural Nosei Kakuritsu Renmei (League for the Establishment of an Agricultural Policy) elected its adviser (and also Nichino adviser) Nishimiya Hiroshi to the Lower House as a JSP candidate. The same group was also behind his election in 1963. Nishimiya successfully contested every election until 1972 (he was revived in 1976–79). In 1980 he stood as an Independent and lost.

175 Soma, *Nihon no Senkyo Seiji*, p. 153.

176 This was Sonoda Kiyomitsu who stood on an LDP ticket. He represented Kumamoto Farmers' Political League (Nomin Seiji Renmei) founded in 1961. It later changed its name to Farmers' Political League (Nogyosha Seiji Renmei).

177 This group included Mori Yasoichi, the Chairman of Aichi *kenchu* and later Chairman of Zenchu. In this election, he was endorsed by the Doshikai (formerly GBS).

178 The only remaining Zennoren member in the Upper House, its Chairman Ishiguro Tadaatsu, did not stand for re-election in 1962.

179 Okamoto, 'Nomin Dantai no Genjo', p. 44.

180 Tanaka, *Nihon no Nokyo*, p. 458.

181 In 1955, Independent and minor party candidates obtained only 1.7 per cent of seats, in 1958 2.8 per cent, in 1960 1.3 per cent, and in 1963, 2.6 per cent.

182 The same realisation prompted five of the six *noseiren* representatives in the Saga prefectural assembly to desert to the LDP.

183 See chapter 6 on 'Electoral Politics'.

184 Ishida, *Interest Groups*, p. 70.

185 Ishida, *Interest Groups*, p. 70.

186 Hiwatari Nobuhiro, *Sengo Nihon no Shijo to Seiji* [*The Market and Politics of Postwar Japan*], Tokyo, University of Tokyo Press, 1991, p. 162, quoted in Nishida, *The Rise and Decline of the Farmers' Movement*, p. 32.

187 Ono, *No to Shoku*, p. 67, quoting from Ishida Takeshi, *Gendai Soshikiron* [*Discourse on Contemporary Organisation*], Tokyo, Iwanami Shoten, 1961.

188 Nosei Jyaanarisuto no Kai, *Hanjutsu Hatten to Keiei Kakushin*, p. 92.

189 As Muramatsu and Krauss observe, 'Japan's conservatives had to create their own

organizational and electoral support. Interest groups began to lay a major role in conservative politics at this time. Nokyo was a useful social organization such as a labour union or a religious organization to penetrate the society and mobilise support. The conservatives' . . . lack of a rice-roots party organization made many conservative politicians turn increasingly to *nokyo* [agricultural cooperatives] for support.' 'The Conservative Policy Line', p. 521. See also chapter 6 on 'Electoral Politics'.

190 This and other policy victories for Nokyo in the 1950s are discussed in chapter 2 on 'Interest Group Politics'.

191 Nosei Jyaanarisuto no Kai, *Hanjutsu Hatten to Keiei Kakushin*, p. 92. The relationship between the *noseiren* and the agricultural cooperatives at the electoral level is discussed in chapter 6 on 'Electoral Politics'.

192 Scalapino and Masumi claim that the agricultural cooperatives were 'undoubtedly the most vital affiliation for the conservatives at the mass level'. *Parties and Politics*, p. 90.

193 Nishida, *The Rise and Decline*, p. 32, quoting Hiwatari, *Sengo Nihon no Shijo*, chapter 4.

194 Ishida, *Interest Groups*, p. 69.

195 Fukutake Tadashi, *Nihon no Noson [Japan's Agricultural Villages]*, Tokyo, Tokyo University Press, 1971, p. 230.

196 These figures were obtained from figure 3.1a in Miyake, *Tohyo Kodo*, p. 88.

197 Scalapino and Masumi, *Parties and Politics*, p. 177. Their data was sourced from the Election Bureau, Ministry of Home Affairs, *Sosenkyo no Jittai [The Actual Conditions of the General Election]*, December 1958, pp. 54–55. This was a survey of 3,000 voters. The same research was also reported in Kobayashi, Shinohara and Soma, *Senkyo*, p. 93. See also chapter 5 on 'The Political Demography of Agriculture'.

198 According to the Secretary-General of the JSP, one of the main supporting groups of the Socialist Party in the countryside was that of agricultural cooperative staff employees, along with school teachers, postal and railway workers, and the ever-increasing numbers of part-time farmer wage earners who had joined unions. Personal interview with Ishibashi Masashi, Canberra, December 1975.

199 Midoro, *Rodosha Nomin Undoron*, p. 19.

200 Nishida disputes the argument that farmers rapidly became supporters of conservative parties in the aftermath of land reform which turned them into smallholders. He ties the growth in farmers' support for the LDP to the rise of part-time farming, particularly expansion in the numbers of farm households earning a greater proportion of their income from non-agricultural occupations. Indeed, according to his thesis, those prefectures with the highest rates of farm household residence and the highest proportion of full-time farmers showed rates of support for progressive parties which were higher than national averages. His empirical evidence, however, tends to support the old adage that statistics can be somewhat misleading. Using his own figures, Nishida was able to demonstrate that in the seven prefectures with the lowest percentage of farm households with greater non-agricultural than agricultural incomes (in other words, with the highest numbers of full-time farmers) the average support rate for the LDP in the 1967 LH election was 59.3 per cent; while in the seven prefectures with the highest proportion of farm households with greater non-agricultural than agricultural incomes, the average support rate for the LDP was 55.3 per cent (not a dramatic difference). Nevertheless, he argues that those prefectures with higher numbers of Type II part-time farmers were, on average, less likely to support the LDP (and conversely more likely to support the progressives) than

those prefectures with lower numbers of farm households in this category. Nishida contends that in the 1950s and 1960s, many full-time farmers supported progressive candidatess because of their critiques of the LDP's agricultural policies. He cites the LDP's increasing opening of the agricultural market to imports (although this was minimal in the 1960s with liberalisation concentrated in the early 1970s), and argues that farmers really only started to support the LDP in greater numbers in the 1970s and 1980s when they became part-time and agricultural policy issues became less important for them. According to Nishida, this group began to value the local pork-barrel projects brought to the district by LDP politicians which provided non-agricultural employment opportunities and which improved their livelihood environment. See *The Rise and Decline of the Farmers' Movement*, pp. 27–38. While the latter argument certainly helps to explain why farm households supported the LDP in the 1970s and 1980s, it underestimates the importance of agricultural subsidies (price and agricultural infrastructure subsidies) for all classes of farmers from the 1950s onwards. These benefits were delivered by conservative parties (and later by the LDP) and were one of the principal factors behind farmers' support for conservative candidates in the 1950s and subsequently. Nishida's thesis also contradicts the surveys of farmers' party support preferences, which unequivocally demonstrate preference for the conservative parties/LDP. See also the analysis below, which offers alternative explanations for why the JSP retained residual support in some rural prefectures in the 1958 LH election.

201 The author established a correlation coefficient between percentage of voters resident in farm households and LDP polling rates in the 1958 elections by prefecture. Although LH constituencies were sub-prefectural, all LDP votes were added up in each prefecture and calculated as a percentage of the total cast vote. The figures were obtained from Somucho, Tokei Kyoku, *Nihon Tokei Nenkan* [*Japan Statistical Yearbook*], Tokyo, Somucho, Tokei Kyoku (hereafter, *Nihon Tokei Nenkan*), 1958, p. 449. The overall correlation coefficient between these two factors in this election was 0.509. Table 5.11 shows the correlation coefficient for all elections from 1958–93.

202 According to public opinion polls taken at the time, voting support for the Socialists expanded amongst the farmers from 15 to about 20 per cent during the late 1950s. Dore, 'The Socialist Party', p. 410. Soma also noted that compared with 10 years previously, the progressives had increased their voting support in so-called 'agricultural prefectures' by the late 1950s. They received 20 per cent or less of the vote in no agricultural prefectures in 1958 compared with three in 1947 (Aomori, Chiba and Kagoshima), and received between 20 and 40 per cent in 11 rural prefectures in 1958 (Yamagata, Chiba, Yamanashi, Shizuoka, Toyama, Ishikawa, Fukui, Ehime, Saga, Kumamoto and Kagoshima) compared with seven in 1947. *Nihon no Senkyo Seiji*, p. 130.

203 There was a similar surge in JSP popularity in the 1956 UH elections, which was the first held after unification.

204 Kobayashi, Shinohara and Soma, *Senkyo*, p. 84.

205 Nomin Mondai Kenkyukai (ed.), *Zengo Nihon no Nomin Undo*, p. 202.

206 Kobayashi, Shinohara and Soma, *Senkyo*, p. 84.

207 My earlier research established that over the three decades from the late 1940s to the late 1970s, all Nokyo staff members who had successfully contested Diet seats had sought the endorsement of socialist parties. This laid the basis of a conservative-executive, progressive-staff cleavage within Nokyo. See George, *The Strategies of Influence*, p. 278.

208 This accords with Nishida's earlier observation that large numbers of farmers' union leaders launched themselves into public office including positions as

agricultural cooperative officials in order to represent the interests of farmers in the political arena. *The Rise and Decline of the Farmers' Movement*, p. 38.

209 These details were obtained from the author's records of Japanese farm politicians, 1949–99.

210 The correlation coefficient between farm household voters and LDP support was marginally lower in the 1960 LH elections at 0.469. See table 5.11.

211 In Niigata, for example, where the farmers' unions were historically strong, 29.9 per cent of votes went to the JSP. Sakai Yoshiaki, ' "To yori Hito" o Jissho Shita Nominhyo' ['Farmers' Votes Demonstrated "The Man Rather Than The Party" '], in Nosei Jyaanarisuto no Kai (ed.), *Senkyo, Beika, Nokyo* [*Elections, the Rice Price and Nokyo*], Nihon Nogyo no Ugoki No. 79, Tokyo, Norin Tokei Kyokai, October 1986, p. 95.

212 Nosei Jyaanarisuto no Kai, *Nogyo Kihonho no Soten*, p. 156.

213 'Shakaito no Nosei Giindan Kessei', pp. 156–157.

214 In Niigata (2) and Akita (2), two JSP candidates (a former Zennichino Chairman and an activist in the farmers' union movement) continuously held two seats from the 1950s until 1980. The representative from Niigata (2), for example, was Ishida Yuzen who first stood in national elections in 1946. In 1955 he was successful.

215 Sakai showed, for example, that the JSP obtained 28.9 per cent of farmers' votes in Niigata (2) in 1976, and 25.3 per cent in Niigata (3). In 1980, the figures were 28.9 per cent and 20.0 per cent respectively. ' "To yori Hito" ', p. 99.

216 ' "To yori Hito" ', p. 99.

217 George, *The Strategies of Influence*, pp. 274–276. Tanaka also reports that the Opposition parties held superiority in the agricultural belt in Hokkaido, Nagano, Niigata, Toyama and Tottori. *Nihon no Nokyo*, p. 470.

218 The LDP and JSP percentages were derived from data based on the classification system in Okino, *Showa 30 Nendai ni Okeru Toshika*, pp. 18–19.

219 These percentages were derived from data based on the classification system in Okino, *Showa 30 Nendai ni Okeru Toshika*, pp. 18–19.

220 The JSP's crumbling urban base was undoubtedly due to the fact that 'new' Opposition parties (the DSP and Komeito) were gaining ground at the expense of the JSP in these areas.

221 Their number increased to 26 in 1971 with the addition of Okinawa.

222 George, *Strategies of Influence*, p. 186.

223 George, *Strategies of Influence*, p. 186.

224 See chapter 6 on 'Electoral Politics' and chapter 7 on 'Representative Politics'.

225 Nosei Jyaanarisuto no Kai, *Hanjutsu Hatten to Keiei Kakushin*, p. 89. According to this source, these two candidates were from the right and left wings of Zennichino respectively, which split the Zennichino vote. Zennichino also gave its backing to the candidate representing worker-farmer cooperation and the MAF labour union.

226 Nosei Jyaanarisuto no Kai, *Chiho Gyosei*, p. 89.

227 The authors do not specify how many they were. Nosei Jyaanarisuto no Kai, *Chiho Gyosei*, p. 89.

228 This was Watanabe Sadayoshi, elected for the Iwate prefectural constituency who had been Chief of Zenchu's Agricultural Policy Department. Watanabe's success was regarded as victory for JSP organisational votes plus Nokyo and farmers' votes. Tanaka, *Nihon no Nokyo*, p. 454.

229 Tanaka, *Nihon no Nokyo*, p. 454.

230 According to Fukutake, however, the dominance of the Nokyo executive-LDP connection prevented Nokyo from demanding that the government make fundamental changes in agricultural policies. *Nihon no Noson*, p. 232.

231 Soma, *Nihon no Senkyo Seiji*, p. 147.

232 See chapter 4 on 'Patronage Politics' in my forthcoming volume, *Politicians and Bureaucrats*.

233 Figure 3-1a in Miyake, *Tohyo Kodo*, p. 88.

234 As argued in a seminal work on postwar Japanese pressure groups, 'agricultural groups which still had a close relationship with the JSP until the 1950s were led into the LDP's camp. This is even more apparent if we see that the LDP attracted not only agricultural groups but also small and medium size industrial groups and even welfare organisations by introducing new budgets including grants . . . It was also clear that agriculture itself was a declining sector . . . The weaker agriculture became, the more subsidies of the structural kind they required, and thus the more closely they had to relate to the LDP . . . Thus agricultural groups as sectoral groups changed into policy beneficiary groups, with group members lobbying for bigger budgets and better rice prices.' Muramatsu, Ito and Tsujinaka Yutaka, *Sengo Nihon no Atsuryoku Dantai*, pp. 85–90.

235 Tanaka, *Nihon no Nokyo*, p. 475.

236 Tanaka, *Nihon no Nokyo*, p. 428.

237 Tanaka, *Nihon no Nokyo*, p. 428.

238 Tanaka, *Nihon no Nokyo*, p. 428.

239 In the face of the producer rice price freeze instituted by the LDP in 1969, for example, there emerged a threat by the Ishikawa Nokyo youth division to instigate a mass withdrawal of its members from the LDP. The prefectural Nokyo leadership, however, argued that although voting for the LDP might mean compromising the Nokyo stance, without representatives in the government party, the rural voice within the LDP would diminish and inevitably the farmers would be disadvantaged. Tanaka, *Nihon no Nokyo*, p. 428.

240 Tanaka, *Nihon no Nokyo*, p. 443.

241 Tanaka, *Nihon no Nokyo*, p. 190.

242 *Nihon no Nokyo*, p. 425.

243 See chapter 5 on 'The Political Demography of Agriculture'.

244 See chapter 4 on 'Patronage Politics' in my forthcoming volume on *Politicians and Bureaucrats*.

245 This phenomenon was observed in the 1962 UH elections. See Nosei Jyaanarisuto no Kai, *Chiho Gyosei*, pp. 89–90. For the mid-1960s, see Kaiin Toron Kai [Members' Debate], 'Goto-Zaikai no Nogyokan o Ryori Suru' ['Examination of the Views on Agriculture Among Five Parties and Zaikai'], in Nosei Jyaanarisuto no Kai (ed.), *Yuki Zumaru Nokiho* [*The Agricultural Basic Law At A Standstill*], Nihon Nogyo no Ugoki No. 6, August 1966, p. 119.

246 One year after the passage of the 1961 ABL, for example, there were reports that farmers' expectations were not being met by agricultural policy which was failing to close the income gap between agriculture and other industries and the regional gap between rural and urban areas, and which was fostering anxiety about the future of agriculture. Farmers' disappointment only strengthened their tendency to support representatives of farmers rather than the party. Nosei Jyaanarisuto no Kai, *Chiho Gyosei*, p. 90.

247 Nosei Jyaanarisuto no Kai, *Chiho Gyosei*, p. 89.

248 See chapter 6 on 'The Politics of Agricultural Policymaking' in my forthcoming volume on *Politicians and Bureaucrats*.

4 Organisational politics

1 Fujitani, *Nokyo*, pp. 4–5.

2 Zenkoku Nogyo Kyodo Kumiai Chuokai, *Shinpan: Nogyo Kyodo Kumiaiho*, p. 7. This volume analyses in detail the 12 amendments of note (pp. 7–15).

3 Kuwabara, 'Nogyo Kyodo Kumiai no Nosei Katsudo', p. 255.
4 The metaphorical use of 'face' to describe different aspects of agricultural cooperative activity was first used by Ishikawa in 'Nogyo Kyodo Kumiai', pp. 247–255. See also Onodera Yoshiyuki, *Janbo Nokyo no Sugao [The Unpainted Face of Jumbo Nokyo]*, Tokyo Jutaku Shinposha, 1970; Aono, Nokyo, pp. 9–11; and Takeuchi and Otawara, *Asu no Nokyo*, pp. 21–24.
5 Kuwabara, 'Nogyo Kyodo Kumiai no Nosei Katsudo', p. 255.
6 Kuwabara, 'Nogyo Kyodo Kumiai no Nosei Katsudo', p. 255.
7 Fujitani, *Nokyo*, p. 6.
8 Aono, *Nokyo*, p. 5. The slogan is one of the mottos of the F. W. Raiffeisen cooperatives, which, together with the Rochdale cooperatives, provided the models for the *sangyo kumiai*. See also below.
9 Fujitani, 'Nokyo at a Crossroads', p. 370.
10 'Nogyo Kyodo Kumiaiho', in *Nogyo Roppo*, p. 108. According to Nagata and Saito, this means that agricultural cooperatives should not conduct businesses for the purpose of generating profits for themselves. This does not mean, however, that agricultural cooperatives are not allowed to generate any profits from their activities. The purpose of this article is to prohibit agricultural cooperatives from conducting businesses unnecessary to their members. Accordingly, they talk in terms of Nokyo's multi-dimensional character: as an agricultural organisation (i.e. which represents the interests of farmers), as a cooperative of farmers and as a profit-seeking economic organisation. *Nokyo no Hanashi*, pp. 6, 14–15.
11 Aono, *Nokyo*, p. 26.
12 Aono, *Nokyo*, p. 26.
13 Aono, *Nokyo*, p. 10.
14 Aono lists this as Nokyo's first 'face'. In its economic enterprise division, it has the face of a mammoth trading company (*shosha*). *Nokyo*, p. 9.
15 *Far Eastern Economic Review*, 11 November 1988.
16 According to Article 9 of Nokyo Law, Nokyo is exempt from the application of the Anti-Monopoly Law (which was itself amended in 1997 to allow the use of holding companies, as part of Japan's financial 'big bang').
17 The agricultural cooperatives pay 'juridical persons tax' or 'corporate tax' (*hojinzei*) at a rate of 27 per cent, which is considerably less than the effective rate of 49.98 per cent paid by business corporations (this figure combines national and local taxes). In proposals outlined by Minister of Finance Miyazawa in August 1998, the effective rate of taxes levied on corporations would be lowered to about 40 per cent. *Nikkei Weekly*, 2 November 1998.
18 Personal communication, Kobayashi Shinichi, Nihon University, 17 August 1997.
19 See Article 6 of 'Nogyo Kyodo Kumiaiho', in *Nogyo Roppo*, 1993, p. 109. In spite of the concessions, this does not prevent Nokyo organisations from trying to cheat the tax system. In March 1999, Zenno was nabbed in a tax scam in which faked transactions were made to reduce its profits and thus avoid income tax payments. It was subsequently ordered to pay ¥300 million in penalties and taxes. *Asahi News*, 24 March 1999.
20 Much ink has been spilled in the course of definitional debates about the differences between interest groups and pressure groups. This author has no intention of getting bogged down in semantics. Suffice it to say that Nokyo is described and analysed in the literature as both an interest group and a pressure group.
21 Kuwabara, 'Nogyo Kyodo Kumiai no Nosei Katsudo', p. 267. See also chapter 2 on 'Interest Group Politics'.
22 Ishikawa, 'Nogyo Kyodo Kumiai', p. 249.
23 Aono, *Nokyo*, p. 3.

24 Tanaka, *Nihon no Nokyo*, p. 424.
25 Nishimoto Koichi, 'Nokyo: Pressure from the Co-ops', *The Japan Interpreter*, trans. by V. Dixon Morris, Vol. 7, Nos 3–4, Sum.–Aut. 1972, p. 321; Ito, 'Nokyo to Seiji Katsudo', p. 146.
26 Asuwa, *Nokyo no Genjo*, p. 253.
27 *Nokyo no Genjo*, p. 253. See also chapter 8 on 'Policy Campaigning'.
28 This is a phrase used by Otawara, 'Nokyo no Ichi to Yakuwari', p. 16.
29 See chapter 2 on 'Interest Group Politics'.
30 Takeuchi and Otawara argue that Nokyo has three faces: as an economic cooperative, as an administrative assistance organisation and as a pressure group. *Asu no Nokyo*, pp. 21–24. In their view, its first and second face is supported by its third face.
31 Personal interviews with Nokyo officials, Tokyo, January 1977.
32 Aono, *Nokyo*, p. 10.
33 See the interview with the Chairman of Zenchu, Miyawaki Asao, in *Sankei Shinbun*, 5 June 1974.
34 See also chapter 2 on 'Interest Group Politics'.
35 Ono, 'Nokyo to Senkyo', p. 86.
36 See chapter 8 on 'Policy Campaigning'.
37 See chapter 6 on 'Electoral Politics'.
38 Ishida, 'The Development of Interest Groups', pp. 331–332. This characteristic is not only exemplified by the political functions of groups. Nokyo, for example, sponsors member organisations such as working groups, youth groups, women's groups, mutual assistance groups, pension groups, my-car clubs, local volunteer organisations, fishing clubs, travel clubs, cultural clubs etc. Zenchu Home Page, http://www.rim.or.jp/ci/ja/ejahome.html. See also below for a discussion of Nokyo's women's and youth divisions.
39 This is representative of a broader phenomenon in Japan in which high participation rates in civic groups are combined with low participation rates in political groups. As Calder has pointed out, 'Japan, although not a society of explicitly political organizations is an extraordinarily organized society at the grassroots level.' *Crisis and Compensation*, p. 183. In other words, it has a rich proliferation of voluntary associations, very few of which are organised explicitly for political purposes. According to one survey, 72 per cent of those polled belonged to some organisation, while a strikingly low proportion were members of explicitly political groups. Calder, *Crisis and Compensation*, pp. 183–184.
40 Norman J. Ornstein and Shirley Elder, *Interest Groups, Lobbying and Policy-making*, Washington, D.C., Congressional Quarterly Press, 1978, p. 31.
41 This is Wilson's summary of Salisbury's argument in *Interest Groups*, p. 25. The latter's original thesis can be found in Robert H. Salisbury, 'Interest Representation – The Dominance of Institutions', *American Political Science Review*, Vol. 78, No. 1, 1984, pp. 64–76.
42 Nokyo Pamphlet, *Kumiaisu to Kumiaiinsu oyobi Shokuinsu* [*Numbers of Cooperatives, Cooperative Members and Staff Members*], 1998; *Nihon Nogyo Nenkan*, 1997, pp. 369, 613. A very small number (0.1 per cent) of the regular membership in 1960 was made up of juridical persons, or *hojin* (i.e. group members), rather than individuals.
43 *Nihon Nogyo Nenkan*, 1997, p. 369.
44 Ishida, 'The Development of Interest Groups', p. 332.
45 There are, in fact, more farm household members of agricultural cooperatives than there are farm households in Japan. Nokyo's organisation rate averages around 112 per cent. For example, in 1984 there were 4.9 million farm household members of Nokyo, while there were only 4.4 million farm households. In 1994

Nokyo's organisation rate was 130 per cent, with 4.8 farm household members of Nokyo and 3.6 farm households. This anomaly stems from the definitional variations between 'farm household' in MAFF surveys and individual agricultural cooperative by-laws, which set lower standards for farm size and employment in agriculture as a qualification for membership. Many of the Nokyo 'farms' that qualify for regular membership of an agricultural cooperative would not engage in any commercial marketing activity. The figures cited above were obtained from *Nokyo Nenkan*, 1987, p. 153; *Poketto*, 1995, p. 116; *Nihon Nogyo Nenkan*, 1997, p. 613. See also Moore, *Japanese Agriculture*, p. 142, and chapter 5 on 'The Political Demography of Agriculture'.

46 *Poketto*, annual relevant years; *Nokyo Nenkan*, annual, relevant years.
47 Nokyo's individual members and household members overlap. Children and/or the wives of farm owners who are engaged in farming are qualified as farm household members, but it is usually the case that the head of the farm household also joins Nokyo as an individual member.
48 *Nokyo Kaikaku*, pp. 27–28.
49 'Nokyo at a Crossroads', p. 371.
50 See also chapter 2 on 'Interest Group Politics'.
51 Goto and Imamura, 'Japanese Agriculture', p. 19.
52 Saeki, *Nokyo Kaikaku*, p. 161.
53 Goto and Imamura, 'Japanese Agriculture', p. 19. See also chapter 2 on 'Interest Group Politics'.
54 As reported in Ono, 'Nokyo to Senkyo', p. 76.
55 'The Development of Interest Groups', p. 321.
56 Ishida, *Interest Groups in Japan*, p. 70. He contrasted the top level of the Nokyo, which he regarded as 'characterized by a well-developed bureaucratic mechanism, with the bottom level where the whole organization rested on the human solidarity of the villages' (p. 70). Dore also wrote: 'Japan is traditionally a co-operating rather than an individualistic society – the multiplicity of forms of co-operation found in the Tokugawa village are proof of this . . . Traditional forms of co-operation were built into small face-to-face groups.' *Land Reform in Japan*, p. 292.
57 *Interest Groups*, p. 36.
58 Saeki offers the following explanation: 'The production units in Japanese agriculture were small farm households. Division of labour for higher productivity did not progress very far. Agricultural policies were designed to target villages as production units. Cooperatives were formed by villages and supported by the existing human relationships in each village.' *Nokyo Kaikaku*, p. 31.
59 *Seifu to Nomin*, p. 73.
60 See chapter 5 on 'The Political Demography of Agriculture' for a discussion of the use and meanings of the terms *buraku* and *nogyo shuraku*.
61 *Nokyo no Genjo*, p. 83.
62 Yamamoto, 'Sogo Nokyo', p. 245. A whole research literature is devoted to discussing the relationship between Nokyo and the *nogyo shuraku*. See, for example, Noson Soshiki Kenkyukai (ed.), *Mura to Nokyo: Sogo Toron [Villages and Nokyo: General Debate]*, Tokyo, Nihon Keizai Hyoronsha, 1979. The *nogyo shuraku* were also part of the substructure of the agricultural mutual aid unions, land improvement districts and other agricultural groups, as well as of city, town and village offices as administrative units. Takeuchi and Otawara, *Asu no Nokyo*, p. 243.
63 Fukutake writes that according to the 1960 Census, 95 per cent of village hamlets had an agricultural practice union, the actual activities of which varied from hamlet to hamlet. A good many of them were 'little more than organizations for

passing round circulars received from the village Agricultural Co-operative. The range of communal activities that they organize is often very restricted and it would be true to say that there has been a decline in the extent to which hamlet members co-operate for farming purposes, though on the other hand post-war developments in the use of pesticides have created a new need for communal spraying. Some 84 per cent. of hamlets spray their lands together collectively, and in 80 per cent. of these cases the Agricultural Practice Union is the body which organizes it. In other cases hamlets own machinery in common or jointly use pieces of agricultural equipment.' *Japanese Rural Society*, p. 92. Takeuchi and Otawara make the point that co-op members invariably participate in the agricultural practice unions. They were originally cultivated as a substructure of the *nokai* and later used to strengthen the industrial cooperatives. In the postwar period, they have been commonly spoken of as the 'fourth level of the federated Nokyo' (*keito yondankai*). Takeuchi and Otawara also quote census figures as to the average number of times in the year the agricultural practice unions held meetings in 1980. It was 4.3 times nationally, with the highest number of meetings per year held in Hokkaido. *Asu no Nokyo*, p. 243.

64 Takeuchi and Otawara, *Asu no Nokyo*, p. 243. In addition to *nogyo shuraku* and *noji jikko kumiai*, they designate Nokyo's substructure as also consisting of production divisions (*seisan bukai*) and production organisations (*seisan soshiki*), and the youth division (*seinenbu*) and women's division (*fujinbu*) – for the latter two organisations, see also below. Participation in the *nogyo jikko kumiai* is based on the entire membership of each *shuraku*, whilst the production divisions are organised by commodity on a supra-*shuraku* basis. They are organisations of interested persons (*yushi*) engaged in cooperative production planning (on average there were about eight *seisan bukai* per *nokyo*). Production organisations, on the other hand, are engaged in cooperative production enterprise, particularly joint use of machinery and facilities. (pp. 242–250) Asuwa provides a diagrammatic representation of the relationship amongst Nokyo, *buraku* organisations and local government. He distinguishes Nokyo and its *buraku* practice unions, local government and its administrative *buraku*, and the *nogyo shuraku*. At the rice roots, *nogyo shuraku*, *gyosei buraku* and *buraku jikko kumiai*, to which farmers belong, are separate but overlay each other. *Nokyo no Genjo*, p. 83.

65 Nagata and Saito, *Nokyo no Hanashi*, pp. 171–172.

66 Kawagoe, 'The Origins of Protectionism', p. 18.

67 Kawagoe, 'The Origins of Protectionism', p. 18.

68 The human solidarity based on regional ties which is a feature of Nokyo contrasts with other cooperative-type organisations in Japan, such as the livelihood (consumer) cooperatives (*seikyo*) whose membership is truly voluntary and based on the pursuit of self-interest. Unlike Nokyo, the *seikyo* must, therefore, keep members satisfied, otherwise they may withdraw.

69 Saeki, *Nokyo Kaikaku*, p. 28. According to Saeki, this is the big difference between the character of the membership of the *sogo nokyo*, on the one hand, and the *senmon nokyo* and *seikyo* on the other.

70 It was reported in the late 1960s, for example, that a farmer was condemned by his fellow villagers for wanting to go outside the agricultural cooperative system to sell his rice. Ishida and George, 'Nokyo', p. 199.

71 See chapter 2 on 'Interest Group Politics'.

72 Ono, 'Nokyo to Senkyo', p. 76. See also chapter 2 on 'Interest Group Politics' and chapter 6 on 'Electoral Politics'.

73 Ono, *No to Shoku*, p. 67, quoting from Ishida, *Gendai Soshikiron*.

74 *No to Shoku*, p. 67.

75 Otawara, 'Nokyo no Ichi to Yakuwari', pp. 17–18.

76 Saeki, *Nokyo Kaikaku*, p. 161.
77 See Mancur Olson, *The Logic of Collective Action: Public Goods and the Theory of Groups*, Cambridge, Mass., Harvard University Press, 1965, pp. 50–51.
78 Nor does Nokyo's corporatised status provide purposive and material incentives in Keeler's sense. Although Nokyo enjoys 'biased influence' with policymakers and benefits from substantial material advantages by virtue of its receipt of government patronage – both of which accrue from its corporatist relationship with government – neither of these attributes are needed to overcome the usual problem of free-riding in Nokyo's case. See Keeler, *The Politics of Neo-corporatism*, pp. 13–15.
79 Saeki, *Nokyo Kaikaku*, p. 31.
80 See chapter 2 on 'Interest Group Politics'.
81 See chapter 6 on 'Electoral Politics'.
82 See below.
83 This is not to say, however, that they necessarily provide them at competitive rates. See below.
84 See chapter 2 on 'Interest Group Politics'.
85 See below.
86 Nishimoto, 'Nokyo', p. 322.
87 Takeuchi and Otawara, *Asu no Nokyo*, p. 171.
88 Quoted in Sakaguchi, *Kyodai Nokyo*, p. 189.
89 Onodera, *Janbo Nokyo no Sugao*, p. 71.
90 This point is discussed more extensively below.
91 *Kumiaisu to Kumiaiinsu oyobi Shokuinsu*, 1998; *Nihon Nogyo Nenkan*, 1997, pp. 369, 613.
92 *Kumiaisu to Kumiaiinsu oyobi Shokuinsu*, 1998; *Nihon Nogyo Nenkan*, 1997, pp. 369, 613.
93 This is the 1990 membership figure.
94 This is the 1996 membership figure. *Nikkei Weekly*, 30 September 1996.
95 Rengo was set up in 1987 with the merger of private-sector trade unions. Sohyo, the national federation of predominantly public sector trade union organisations, merged with Rengo in late 1989.
96 In 1996, Rengo's members represented 61 per cent of all union members. *Nikkei Weekly*, 4 August 1997.
97 Goto and Imamura, 'Japanese Agriculture', p. 19.
98 *Far Eastern Economic Review*, 17 November 1988.
99 There is some overlap between Nokyo's executive leadership and its membership because of Article 30 (10) of Nokyo Law, which states that at least three-quarters of the established number of directors of a cooperative shall be elected from its regular members (excluding associate members and members who are juridical persons). 'Nogyo Kyodo Kumiaiho', in *Nogyo Roppo*, 1976, p. 118.
100 Reading, *Japan*, p. 216.
101 Takeuchi and Otawara report that 1,979 local co-ops had labour unions in 1983 which accounted for 46 per cent of the total. Furthermore, most prefectural and national federations also had labour unions, with the joining rate 67 per cent of all personnel in the prefectural federations and 64 per cent in the national federations. *Asu no Nokyo*, p. 225. See also chapter 13 in Tanaka, *Nihon no Nokyo*, pp. 482–502, and Asuwa, *Nokyo no Genjo*, pp. 94–100.
102 In 1998, this organisation decided to combine its funds with the national welfare pension system by 2001 because agricultural cooperative mergers might result in large cuts in co-op staff and the consequent membership drop might make independence too difficult. *Comline News Service*, 24 June, 1998. See also the discussion on agricultural cooperative mergers below.

103 This group consists almost entirely of university graduates at national and prefectural organisation levels.
104 The balance was made up of specialist *nokyo* executives (15,731), specialist *nokyo* staff members (11,233), national federation staff members (6,319), prefectural central union staff members (4,253), prefectural federation executives (3,964), national federation executives (313), prefectural central union executives (182), Zenchu staff members (178) and Zenchu executives (25). *Nokyo Nenkan*, 1991, pp. 188–191; *Nokyo Nenkan*, 1993, pp. 151–156. This was the last year in which this particular breakdown of the Nokyo executive and staff membership structure was available in the official yearbook.
105 *Nihon Nogyo Nenkan*, 1997, p. 371.
106 *Kumiaisu to Kumiaiinsu oyobi Shokuinsu*, 1998.
107 *Kumiaisu to Kumiaiinsu oyobi Shokuinsu*, 1998.
108 These are listed in the *Nokyoren Yakushokuin Meibo* as 'related agricultural, forestry and fisheries groups' (*kankei norinsuisan dantai*).
109 See chapter 2 on 'Interest Group Politics'.
110 Personal communication with fund official, September 1997.
111 Personal communication with fund official, September 1997.
112 Personal communication with council official, September 1997.
113 Personal communication with institute official, September 1997.
114 Hokkaido Koiki Nogyo Kyodo Kumiai and Kajiura, *Datsu Nokyo*, p. 48. The actual groups are not specified, but they would include those referred to in chapter 2 on 'Interest Group Politics'.
115 This description (*betsudotai*) is used by Aono, *Nokyo*, p. 47. Midoro has used the term *gaikaku dantai* (affiliated associations). See *Rodosha Nomin Undoron*, p. 18. Takeuchi and Otawara, on the other hand, consider these groups as part of Nokyo's subordinate organisation (*kabu soshiki*), along with the agricultural practice unions (*noji jikko kumiai*), organising all the farmers in each *nogyo shuraku* within a *nokyo* area, and the production divisions (*seisan bukai*), in which producers collaborate to make a production or marketing plan. See *Asu no Nokyo*, pp. 242–250. See also above.
116 Zenkoku Nogyo Kyodo Kumiai Chuokai, *Hayawakari JA no Subete*, p. 88.
117 Aono, *Nokyo*, p. 47.
118 Takahashi, 'Kyodo Kumiainai Shijo Genri', p. 234.
119 Almost 20 years earlier in 1976, the figures were 3,971 member organisations, with an individual membership of 2.6 million. *Nihon Nogyo Nenkan*, 1997, p. 373; and *Nokyo Nenkan*, 1978, p. 100.
120 Zenkoku Nogyo Kyodo Kumiai Chuokai, *Hayawakari JA no Subete*, p. 88. See also chapter 8 on 'Policy Campaigning'.
121 *Nihon Nogyo Nenkan*, 1997, p. 374. Just under twenty years earlier in 1976 it had 161,122 members in 1,849 organisations. *Nokyo Nenkan*, 1978, p. 100.
122 Kurihara Rumi, 'Nogyo Ninaite Mondai' ['The Agricultural Bearers' Issue'], in Ouchi Tsutomu and Gomi Kenkichi (eds), *Nogyo Ninaitezo no Hikari to Kage* [*The Lights and Shadows of Pictures of Agricultural Bearers*], Nihon Nogyo Nenpo 38, Tokyo, Norin Tokei Kyokai, 1992, p. 66.
123 Zenkoku Nogyo Kyodo Kumiai Chuokai, *Hayawakari JA no Subete*, p. 88. See also chapter 8 on 'Policy Campaigning'.
124 Takeuchi and Otawara, *Asu no Nokyo*, p. 45.
125 Saeki, *Nokyo Kaikaku*, pp. 38–39.
126 Sakaguchi, *Kyodai Nokyo*, p. 66.
127 The majority of *sogo nokyo* are designated to undertake residential land supply business; a smaller number are licensed to conduct real estate transactions. See also chapter 2 on 'Interest Group Politics'.

128 Ishida and George, 'Nokyo', p. 198.

129 Masuda, 'Nokyo no Keiei Bunseki', p. 58.

130 Nishimoto, 'Nokyo', p. 321. Ishida defined *zaibatsu* as 'monopolistic cliques based upon extended family relations'. See 'The Development of Interest Groups', p. 296.

131 See table 3, in Masuda, 'Nokyo no Keiei Bunseki', p. 60.

132 See below.

133 Masuda, 'Nokyo no Keiei Bunseki', p. 59. The ratio of profits from trust business to the net profits of the *nokyo* was 300 to 100 (p. 59).

134 Masuda, 'Nokyo no Keiei Bunseki', p. 59.

135 See table 9 in Aguri Fuooramu, 'Nokyo Shinjikeeto' ['The Nokyo Syndicate'], in 'Tokushu: Nihon no Kome' ['Special Report: Japanese Rice'], *Chuo Koron*, Vol. 102, No. 2, February 1987, p. 89.

136 See also below.

137 Norinchukin Research Institute, *Funding and Investment of Agri. Coops Credit Institutions of Three Levels*, as of 31 March 1997, p. 1. More detailed comments can be found below on trends in Nokyo's trust business in the 1990s.

138 *Jiji Press Newswire*, 4 August 1997. In the early 1980s, funds held on deposit by the agricultural cooperatives amounted to approximately half those in the postal savings system, suggesting that the latter rapidly moved ahead of Nokyo in the following decade.

139 *Nikkei Weekly*, 25 December 1995–1 January 1996. In fact the merger never took place.

140 *Sogo Nokyo Tokeihyo*, 1983, p. 128; *Sogo Nokyo Tokeihyo*, 1993, p. 146; *JA Guruupu Keizai Jigyo Kiso Tokei*, 1997, p. 146.

141 These figures were for 1995. *JA Guruupu Keizai Jigyo Kiso Tokei*, 1997, p. 85.

142 *JA Guruupu Keizai Jigyo Kiso Tokei*, 1997, pp. 88, 90; *Sogo Nokyo Tokeihyo*, 1983, p. 164.

143 *JA Guruupu Keizai Jigyo Kiso Tokei*, 1997, p. 88.

144 More detailed comments on trends in Nokyo's marketing and purchasing businesses in the early 1990s can be found below.

145 In 1969, in addition to Nokyo's monopoly of rice and wheat sales, the cooperatives handled over 80 per cent of potatoes, sweet potatoes, vegetables and fruit, milk, silk cocoons and rapeseeds, and between 70–80 per cent of beans, eggs, beef and pork. See Haruhiro Fukui, 'The Japanese Farmer and Politics', in Isaiah Frank (ed.), *The Japanese Economy in International Perspective*, London and Baltimore, Johns Hopkins University Press, 1975, pp. 154–155. These percentages differ markedly from those in Asuwa who presents MAFF statistics on Nokyo's share of the market for produce sales and production inputs. According to Asuwa, Nokyo's share of rice rose from 59.9 per cent in 1955 to 81.5 per cent in 1970, wheat from 58.4 per cent to 64.0 per cent, silk cocoons from 38.2 per cent to 62.4 per cent, potatoes from 25.0 per cent to 48.9 per cent, and vegetables from 12.7 per cent in 1960 to 26.8 per cent in 1970, fruit from 26.2 per cent to 49.0 per cent and beef from 32.6 per cent to 43.2 per cent. Meanwhile its share of the egg market slipped from 24.8 per cent to 23.8 per cent during the 1960–70 period. See Table 3.3 in *Nokyo no Genjo*, p. 62. For figures over the period 1975–1983, see table 4-5 in Takeuchi and Otawara, *Asu no Nokyo*, p. 159. In 1984, the figures for raw milk and vegetables were just under 60 per cent; for fruit, 55 per cent; and for beef cattle, just under 50 per cent. See Table 10 in Aguri Fuooramu, 'Nokyo Shinjikeeto', p. 89. In 1990, Nokyo handled 52.5 per cent of vegetables, 20.0 per cent of beef, and 53.2 per cent of fruit. *Yomiuri Shinbun*, 4 March 1992. Clearly in some areas Nokyo's share of the market has been declining. In 1998,

the MAFF reported that more than 80 per cent of fresh fruit and vegetables were collected from farmers and taken to the agricultural cooperatives, which selected and categorised collected produce by size and destination and then shipped it to wholesale markets in urban areas, where it was purchased at auction by floor brokers and retailers from market traders contracted by the cooperatives. *MAFF Update*, No. 262, 5 June 1998, http://www.maff.go.jp. See also below.

146 According to Asuwa, Nokyo's share of the fertiliser market rose from 66.0 per cent in 1955 to 82.6 per cent in 1970, feed from 32.3 per cent to 42.5 per cent and agricultural chemicals from 60.0 per cent to 69.2 per cent, while its share of the consumer goods market (in the farm villages) fell from 5.9 per cent to 5.8 per cent. Table 3.3 in *Nokyo no Genjo*, p. 62. Fukui claims that in 1969, Nokyo sold over 90 per cent of the stockfeed purchased by farmers, as well as over 70 per cent of fertilisers, agricultural machines, packing materials, agricultural chemicals, oil and gasoline. Consumer goods such as clothes, cars and household appliances were somewhat lower at around 50 per cent. 'The Japanese Farmer', pp. 154–155. For figures over the period 1975–83, see Table 4–5 in Takeuchi and Otawara, *Asu no Nokyo*, p. 159. In 1984, for fertilisers the figures were almost 100 per cent; agricultural chemicals, around 70 per cent; gasoline, just under 60 per cent; agricultural machinery, just under 50 per cent; stockfeed, 45 per cent; cars, just over 20 per cent; and livelihood materials (consumables), around 15 per cent. See table 10 in Aguri Fuooramu, 'Nokyo Shinjikeeto', p. 89. In 1990, Nokyo reportedly handled 39.9 per cent of feed and 92.3 per cent of fertiliser. *Yomiuri Shinbun*, 4 March 1992.

147 *JA Guruupu Keizai Jigyo Kiso Tokei*, 1997, pp. 224, 241, 248. See also below.

148 Moore, *Japanese Agriculture*, p. 154.

149 Hokkaido Koiki Nogyo Kyodo Kumiai and Kajiura, *Datsu Nokyo*, pp. 65–66. In 1995, they amounted to a trading volume worth just on ¥6 trillion.

150 *Far Eastern Economic Review*, 11 November 1988. Kajii claimed it was fourth after Sumitomo in its gross sales. Kajii Isao, 'Ima Naze Nokyo Ka' ['Why Nokyo Now?'], in Ouchi and Kajii (eds), *Nokyo Yonjunen*, p. 9.

151 The 61 federation members consisted of 48 prefectural economic federations, 10 specialist federations and three national federations. The figures were for 1995 and were taken from Zenno's Home Page, http://www.zennoh.or.jp/

152 Zenno's Home Page, http://www.zennoh.or.jp/

153 Zenno's Home Page, http://www.zennoh.or.jp/

154 The utilisation rate of Nokyo credit amongst farmers in 1969 was more than 70 per cent, and the deposit rate nearly 40 per cent. Fukui, 'The Japanese Farmer', pp. 154–155. Ogura reported that in 1975, some 60 per cent of farmers' deposits and loans were with the cooperatives. *Can Japanese Agricultural Cooperatives Survive?*, p. 734. This declined to 54 per cent by 1983. Takeuchi and Otawara, *Asu no Nokyo*, p. 159.

155 According to Reading, neither Zenkyoren nor Norinchukin pay any tax. *Japan*, p. 215.

156 *Far Eastern Economic Review*, 17 November 1988.

157 *Far Eastern Economic Review*, 17 November 1988.

158 Reading, *Japan*, p. 215.

159 Takeuchi and Otawara, *Asu no Nokyo*, pp. 221–222.

160 *Far Eastern Economic Review*, 17 November 1988. See also above.

161 Aono, *Nokyo*, p. 9. Kajii reported that Zenkyoren had 2.5 times more contracts than Nihon Seimei, and it was therefore presumed to be the largest insurance company in the world. 'Ima Naze Nokyo Ka', p. 9.

162 'The TBT 300: 1994 Corporate Ranking', *Tokyo Business Today*, September 1994, p. 21.

163 Nokyo Pamphlet, *JA Guruupu no Jigyoryo* [*The Quantity of Business of the JA Group*], 1998.

164 According to Reading, it is Japan's sixth largest bank. *Japan*, p. 215. Moore claimed that in 1985, Nokyo ranked 4th amongst Japanese financial institutions in holdings of personal savings deposits (behind the postal savings system, the city banks and regional banks), but second in terms of personal lending (behind the city banks). *Japanese Agriculture*, p. 155.

165 Norinchukin has remained one of the biggest investors in US Treasury bonds and also in the World Bank. Personal communication, Norinchukin Research Institute, July 1999.

166 Kajii claimed that Norinchukin possessed the largest quantity of funds (*shikinryo*) of any bank in Japan, exceeding the Daiichi Kangyo Bank. 'Ima Naze Nokyo Ka', p. 9.

167 Moore, *Japanese Agriculture*, p. 154.

168 *The Economist*, 8 April 1989. In addition to London, Norinchukin now has branches in Singapore, Beijing and New York.

169 *The Economist*, 8 April 1989.

170 *The Economist*, 8 April 1989.

171 'The TBT 300', p. 26.

172 Personal communication, Norinchukin Research Institute, February 1998. By 1998, the total had risen to ¥52 trillion. *PR Newswire*, 4 September 1998.

173 Ito Momoko, 'Soshiki Nidankaika mo Saisei no Kimete de wa nai' ['The Shift to the Two-Step Organisation is Not a Decisive Measure of Revival'], *Kinyu Bijinesu*, July 1996, p. 17.

174 As the President of Norinchukin Bank explains: 'Co-ops are engaged in many activities. While they are responsible for each area of business, they cannot handle all the deposits . . . they collect. That is why they pass a portion of their deposits . . . to the prefectural credit federation.' *Nikkei Weekly*, 15 August 1996.

175 Norinchukin Research Institute, *Funding and Investment of Agri. Coops Credit Institutions*, p. 1.

176 Norinchukin Research Institute, *Funding and Investment of Agri. Coops Credit Institutions*, p. 1.

177 Norinchukin Research Institute, *Funding and Investment of Agri. Coops Credit Institutions*, p. 1.

178 Norinchukin Research Institute, *Funding and Investment of Agri. Coops Credit Institutions*, p. 1.

179 Amongst the Japanese corporations listed on the first sections of the Tokyo, Osaka and Nagoya stock exchanges (1,302 companies as of October 1993), Norinchukin's percentage holdings were listed in the fishery, agriculture and forestry, food, and textiles and apparel sections as follows: Kyokuyo (Japan's 4th largest fishing company), 4.9 per cent; Nichiro (which ranked 3rd in the fishing industry), 4.9 per cent; Maruha (2nd largest fishing company), 3.3 per cent; Nippon Flour Mills (oldest and 2nd largest flour miller in Japan), 3.6 per cent; Nitto Flour Milling (medium-standing flour miller), 1.5 per cent; Showa Sangyo (integrated food processor), 4.5 per cent; Nippon Beet Sugar Manufacturing (largest beet sugar maker, dependent on agricultural policy to protect domestic sugar and also involved in the refining of imported sugar, and medium class sugar refiner), 4.9 per cent; Meiji Seika (a leader in the confectionery industry), 2.6 per cent; Meiji Milk Products (2nd largest producer of dairy foods), 3.3 per cent; Snow Brand Milk Products (largest manufacturer of dairy products (butter and cheese) and also ranks top in drinking milk) 8.9 per cent; Morinaga Milk Industry (3rd largest manufacturer of dairy products), 1.5 per cent; Prima Meat Packers (3rd largest company in processed meat), 3.2 per cent; Marudai Food

(ham and sausage maker) 2.7 per cent; Sapporo Breweries (3rd ranking beer brewer), 2.7 per cent; Asahi Breweries (2nd largest beer brewer), 2.2 per cent; Takara Shuzo (top maker of *shochu* – distilled spirit), 4.4 per cent; Godo Shusei (medium sized maker of alcoholic beverages) 4.5: Honen (ranking 2nd in market share of edible oil and top in soybean oil), 3.9 per cent; Fuji Oil (largest manufacturer of palm oil and coconut oil), 3.0 per cent; Nichirei (general food processing company) 1.7 per cent; Yokohama Reito (2nd largest cold storage company), 4.9 per cent; Toyo Suisan (major maker of instant noodles), 3.7 per cent; Nagatanien (top manufacturer of Japanese-style instant foods), 3.9 per cent; Katakura Industries (one of the top silk spinning companies), 5.0 per cent; and Shinyei (trader and wholesaler of foodstuffs and clothing), 4.1 per cent. *Japan Company Handbook*, Tokyo, Toyo Keizai Inc., 1993, pp. 39–42, 162–220 and 1997, pp. 199–260.

180 This figure does not include Norinchukin's foreign accounts.

181 Norinchukin Research Institute, *Funding and Investment of Agri. Coops Credit Institutions*, p. 1.

182 Norinchukin Research Institute, *Funding and Investment of Agri. Coops Credit Institutions*, p. 1.

183 Norinchukin Research Institute, *Funding and Investment of Agri. Coops Credit Institutions*, p. 1.

184 Ito, 'Soshiki Nidankaika', p. 15.

185 'Japan: The Top 300', *Tokyo Business Today*, June 1988, pp. 26–31.

186 The explanation for this was the relatively small number of large-scale calamities such as typhoons during 1993, which enabled the company's reported income to rise by 55.4 per cent from ¥105 billion. *Tokyo Business Today*, September 1994, p. 22.

187 'The TBT 300: 1994 Corporate Ranking', p. 21.

188 'The TBT 300: 1994 Corporate Ranking', p. 26.

189 'The TBT 300: 1994 Corporate Ranking', p. 29.

190 *Nokyo*, p. 10. See also pp. 39–42.

191 Nishimoto, for example, explains that: 'The reason that Nokyo has invested in so many firms is partly that the Nokyo Law prevents it from going directly into business for itself in several fields.' 'Nokyo', p. 330. Ohara agrees that one of the crucial origins of these companies was to evade restrictions under the *Nokyoho*, such as limitations on non-member use, regional limitations on business, restraints on business affairs, and restraints on the number of non-member executives (less than one-quarter). Nokyo also sought entry into new businesses. Ohara Junichi, 'Kyodo Kaisha no Genjo Bunseki' ['Analysis of the Current State of Cooperative Companies'], in Nogyo Kaihatsu Senta (ed.), *Nokyo Undo*, p. 384.

192 Aono, *Nokyo*, p. 46.

193 Nishimoto, 'Nokyo', p. 329.

194 Nishimoto, 'Nokyo', p. 330.

195 As part of Nokyo's *gaien soshiki,* he also includes Nokyo's publishing and health and welfare businesses. See *Nokyo*, pp. 37–49.

196 According to Kuranishi Tsutomu, *kyodo kaisha* are defined as companies with five requirements: basic management policies aim primarily to support farmers' economic interests and their management is directly controlled by Nokyo; Nokyo-affiliated organisations hold 100 per cent or more than 50 per cent of the company shares; Nokyo representatives make up the majority of company executives; company dealings are directly linked to the federated Nokyo organisation; and company capital is totally dependent on Nokyo finance. Quoted in Ohara, 'Kyodo Kaisha', p. 380. See also the MAFF definition of *kyodo kaisha* recounted in Asuwa, *Nokyo no Genjo*, p. 163.

197 Sometimes *kyodo kaisha* and *kanren kaisha* are used interchangeably. According to an official of the Norinchukin Research Institute, a cooperative company is a company that the JA group owns. In Norinchukin, 'related enterprises' (*kanren kigyo*) or companies with which it has 'business connections' (*kanren torihikisaki*), on the other hand, are companies that operate in fields related to agriculture, fisheries, or forestry (e.g. food companies, agricultural machinery companies etc.) to which Norinchukin lends money. Personal communication, April 1998.

198 As Yoshihara explains, most *kanren gaisha* were originally related to the former Zenkoren. Yoshihara Shizuo, *Zenno o Kiru* [*I Criticise Zenno*], Tokyo, Nisshin Hodo, 1975, p. 51.

199 Aono, *Nokyo*, pp. 45–46.

200 About 70 per cent of domestically sold fertiliser, for example, is supplied by so-called JA-affiliated makers, which get their raw materials from JA, while JA group factories make around 30 per cent of domestically produced feed. *JA Guruupu Keizai Jigyo Kiso Tokei*, 1997, pp. 218, 236 (see also below). According to Hayami, the import duties on mixed feed and individual feed grains were set at levels that discouraged on-farm feed mixing and thus protected domestic feed mills, many of which were owned by Nokyo. *Japanese Agriculture Under Siege*, p. 55.

201 Zenno, for example, runs the thousands of supermarkets called A-Coops. In 1998 it announced a radical plan to restructure its A-Coop stores in order to make them more competitive with supermarkets. *Nikkei Weekly*, 27 July 1998.

202 *Sogo Nokyo Tokeihyo*, 1974, pp. 22–23.

203 *Sogo Nokyo Tokeihyo*, 1996, p. 67.

204 These figures are for 1993. *Sogo Nokyo Tokeihyo*, 1993, pp. 58–59. Equivalent figures are no longer provided for later years.

205 'Cooperative Trade and Unicoop Japan', *Japan Agricultural Coop News*, Vol. 13, No. 2, July 1972, p. 21.

206 Zenno's Home Page, http://www.zennoh.or.jp/

207 *Nokyo, Kanren Kigyo Meikan, 1995* [*The Directory of Agricultural Cooperatives and Related Corporations, 1995*], Tokyo, Nokyo Kyokai, 1995, p. 488.

208 This was established with capital of ¥300 million from Zenkoren. *Nokyo, Kanren Kigyo Meikan*, 1995, p. 549. It is involved in transporting and warehousing. Zenno's Home Page, http://www.zennoh.or.jp/

209 This company was launched in 1983; 12 per cent of its capital is supplied by Nokyo groups, and it supplies fertiliser to farmers through Zenno and agricultural cooperatives. It is described as integrated into the purchasing business of the agricultural cooperative organisation. *Nokyo, Kanren Kigyo Meikan*, 1995, p. 339. Its major shareholder is Zenno, followed by Norinchukin in sixth place. Nihon Keizai Shinbunsha (ed.), *Kaisha Nenkan 1996* [*Annual Corporation Reports, Trust Business 1996*], Tokyo, Nihon Keizai Shinbunsha (hereafter *Kaisha Nenkan*), 1995, p. 791.

210 Zenno, Shizuoka Prefecture Economic Federation and Norinchukin are the No. 1, 2, 3 shareholders in this company. *Kaisha Nenkan 1996*, p. 1144. See also below.

211 Hokkaido Koiki Nogyo Kyodo Kumiai and Kajiura, *Datsu Nokyo*, p. 38. According to Aono, Zenno *kanren gaisha* are those in which Zenno has more than a 50 per cent share or an appropriate level of shares, and where it exercises guidance rights over management. *Nokyo*, p. 43. But see also Yoshihara's analysis of the four kinds of Zenno *kanren gaisha*. *Zenno o Kiru*, p. 5. Zenno's 138 *kanren gaisha* as of June 1974 are listed in Appendix II (pp. 252–262). Zenno's major affiliated companies as of 1999 are listed on its home page, http://www.zennoh. or.jp/

212 See also below and table 4.1.

213 Yoshihara, *Zenno o Kiru*, pp. 51–52.
214 To demonstrate the complexity of connection and construction of the agricultural cooperative companies, Aono cites the example of the 'top maker' of agricultural chemicals, Kumiai Chemical Industries (Kumiai Kagaku Kogyo). This company has capital of ¥1.8 billion and 4,974 employees. Zenno's investment share is 38 per cent, Shizuoka Prefecture Economic Nokyo Federation 4.4 per cent and Norinchukin 2.7 per cent. As Aono points out, the company has 11 subsidiaries, but the names of these other companies are not recorded in his listing. He asks whether when one is looking into Nokyo's extended organisation companies, one should only take into account Kumiai Kagaku Kogyo, or its subsidiaries as well. See *Nokyo*, p. 45.
215 See below.
216 Aono, *Nokyo*, p. 21. Numbers of employees in Nokyo's cooperative companies have, in fact, been declining in the last decade (in Zenno's subsidiary companies, for example, they have fallen from about 4,000 to 3,000). One reason is that cooperative companies have been shifting functions to subsidiaries.
217 Ishida and George, 'Nokyo', p. 197. See also below.
218 See chapter 2 on 'Interest Group Politics'.
219 Takeuchi and Otawara, *Asu no Nokyo*, p. 252.
220 Muramatsu, Ito and Tsujinaka, *Sengo Nihon no Atsuryoku Dantai*, pp. 137–138.
221 Hokkaido Koiki Nogyo Kyodo Kumiai and Kajiura, *Datsu Nokyo*, p. 55.
222 Dore, *Land Reform*, pp. 291–292.
223 Dore, *Land Reform*, p. 291.
224 One farmer in Fukushima Prefecture, for example, said 'the cooperatives have become mere sellers, with business-like mind-sets. They have other roles to play, such as creating opportunities for farmers and consumers to exchange opinions'. Another Niigata farmer said: 'If the cooperatives have the money to pay the farmers who switched to different crops than rice, they should spend it for long-term projects such as land maintenance'. *Daily Yomiuri*, 11 March 1992.
225 Sakaguchi, *Kyodai Nokyo*, p. 133. In fact Nokyo looks to the national and prefectural governments to provide subsidies for the organisation of farm management guidance personnel. Kurata Jun, *Nogyo Kyodo Kumiairon* [*A Discourse on Nokyo*], Tokyo, Zenkoku Nogyo Kyodo Kumiai Chuokai, 1985, p. 266. A good critique of the shortcomings in Nokyo's guidance activities and some of the reasons behind it can be found in Fujitani Chikuji, 'Eino Shido' ['Agricultural Management Guidance'], in Ouchi and Kajii (eds), *Nokyo Yonjunen*, pp. 84–86. See also below.
226 Yamaguchi, *Ima Nokyo o Do Suru Ka?*, p. 74.
227 *Kyodai Nokyo*, p. 37.
228 *Far Eastern Economic Review*, 17 November 1988.
229 Arai Yoshio, 'Kyodo Kumiai Genten Rongi no Yukue' ['Where the Debate Stands on the Fundamentals of Cooperative Unionism'], *Norin Keizai*, 28 June 1973, pp. 2–7. See also Otawara, 'Nokyo no Ichi to Yakuwari', pp. 15–16.
230 The cooperative movement is often described as beginning in the town of Rochdale, England, in 1844. A group of 28 weavers formed a society to raise capital and organise a store of their own to supply their principal daily needs. The cooperative model soon spread to continental Europe and later to Japan. See Kile, *The Farm Bureau*, p. 54.
231 Ishida and George, 'Nokyo', p. 201.
232 Nishimoto, 'Nokyo', p. 328.
233 Nishimoto, 'Nokyo', p. 328.
234 Nishimoto, 'Nokyo', p. 328.
235 Kyosanto Bukkuretto, *Gaiatsu no Naka no Nihon*, p. 31.

236 Hokkaido Koiki Nogyo Kyodo Kumiai and Kajiura, *Datsu Nokyo*, pp. 55–56.
237 Hokkaido Koiki Nogyo Kyodo Kumiai and Kajiura, *Datsu Nokyo*, pp. 55–56.
238 Hokkaido Koiki Nogyo Kyodo Kumiai and Kajiura, *Datsu Nokyo*, pp. 55–56.
239 Hokkaido Koiki Nogyo Kyodo Kumiai and Kajiura, *Datsu Nokyo*, pp. 55–56. See also below.
240 Hokkaido Koiki Nogyo Kyodo Kumiai and Kajiura, *Datsu Nokyo*, p. 57.
241 Hokkaido Koiki Nogyo Kyodo Kumiai and Kajiura, *Datsu Nokyo*, pp. 57–58.
242 This question is pursued in relation to Nokyo's *nosei katsudo* in chapter 8 on 'Policy Campaigning'.
243 Only about 2 per cent of the *tankyo* members of *kenchu* and Zenchu are specialist agricultural co-ops.
244 Kameya Sho, 'Nokyo Chuokai no Genjo Bunseki' ['Analysis of the Current State of the Nokyo Central Unions'], in Nogyo Kaihatsu Senta (ed.), *Nokyo Undo*, p. 409.
245 This has been one of the main differences between *sogo nokyo* and *senmon nokyo*. The latter were generally not capital-stock cooperatives, while all the *sogo nokyo* were. Those not capital-stock cooperatives did not need guidance and auditing by *kenchu* and Zenchu.
246 'Nokyo', p. 326.
247 Goto and Imamura, 'Japanese Agriculture', p. 19.
248 Nishimoto, 'Nokyo', p. 327.
249 These are explained as follows: in order to attain the income targets of member farm households, individual or plural agricultural cooperatives organise member farm households on a production scale to possess market competitive power, with planned production and marketing of agricultural and livestock products undertaken through the Nokyo and at the same time, they are production areas (*sanchi*) created in order to stabilise Nokyo management. Saeki, *Nokyo Kaikaku*, pp. 194–195.
250 See chapter 8 on 'Policy Campaigning'.
251 Ishida and George, 'Nokyo', p. 196.
252 Takeuchi and Otawara, *Asu no Nokyo*, pp. 172–173.
253 Takeuchi and Otawara, *Asu no Nokyo*, pp. 172–173.
254 Kajii, 'Ima Naze Nokyo Ka', p. 11.
255 Nagata and Saito, *Nokyo no Hanashi*, pp. 170–171.
256 Takeuchi and Otawara, *Asu no Nokyo*, p. 154.
257 Nishimoto, 'Nokyo', p. 323.
258 It should be pointed out, however, that agriculture inside Tokyo provides 10 per cent of all the vegetable consumption of Tokyo residents. The productivity of urban agriculture is in fact very high. Takeuchi and Otawara, *Asu no Nokyo*, p. 85.
259 Saeki, *Nokyo Kaikaku*, pp. 184–185.
260 Yamamoto, 'Sogo Nokyo', p. 260.
261 Saeki, *Nokyo Kaikaku*, p. 185.
262 Nagata and Saito, *Nokyo no Hanashi*, p. 171. This same point is made by Kajii who comments that growth in the purchasing of livelihood necessities contrasted with stagnation in the purchasing of agricultural production materials, indicating a shift within Nokyo from agricultural to non-agricultural businesses. Kajii, 'Ima Naze Nokyo Ka', p. 11.
263 Takeuchi and Otawara, *Asu no Nokyo*, p. 172.
264 Kajii, 'Ima Naze Nokyo Ka', p. 11.
265 *Nokyo*, p. 52.
266 Fujitani, 'Nokyo at a Crossroads', p. 374.
267 Yamamoto, 'Sogo Nokyo', p. 262.
268 Saeki, *Nokyo Kaikaku*, p. 181.

269 Goto and Imamura, 'Japanese Agriculture', p. 19.
270 According to Takeuchi and Otawara, the number of local co-ops in purely rural areas declined from 69 per cent in 1960 to 51 per cent in 1982. On the other hand, the number of local co-ops in urban areas increased from 14 per cent in 1960 to 34 per cent in 1982. *Asu no Nokyo*, p. 177.
271 Nagata and Saito, *Nokyo no Hanashi*, pp. 177–178.
272 Ishida and George, 'Nokyo', p. 197.
273 *Far Eastern Economic Review*, 17 November 1988.
274 *Far Eastern Economic Review*, 17 November 1988.
275 *Far Eastern Economic Review*, 17 November 1988.
276 Calculated from figures given in *Far Eastern Economic Review*, 17 November 1988.
277 *Far Eastern Economic Review*, 17 November 1988.
278 Yamamoto, 'Sogo Nokyo', p. 263.
279 Fujitani, *Nokyo*, pp. 67–78, pp. 97–98. Nagata and Saito argue that through *seikatsu katsudo*, Nokyo is contributing to the improvement and 'rationalisation' of daily life as well as the preservation of tradition in agricultural villages in Japan. *Nokyo no Hanashi*, p. 163. The MAFF, however, is reported as not being inclined to support the transition of agricultural cooperatives to regional cooperatives, but as aiming gradually to expand their capacities as regional cooperatives by partial amendments to Nokyo Law (p. 174).
280 See chapter 8 on 'Policy Campaigning' for the organisational status of these conventions.
281 Saeki, *Nokyo Kaikaku*, p. 179.
282 Nagata and Saito, *Nokyo no Hanashi*, p. 175. See also above.
283 Fujitani, *Nokyo*, pp. 68–69. Kajii also comments that the 12th National Nokyo Convention way back in 1970 declared 'A Livelihood Basic Plan' (*Seikatsu Kihon Koso*) which pointed to Nokyo's new direction – a shift from a farmers' organisation to a local cooperative organisation of farmers and non-farmers. The requisite legislation to support such a development, however, never eventuated, and no Nokyo organisations encouraged discussions on such a new direction. He reasoned that this was because Nokyo had *de facto* moved in that direction anyway and to acknowledge such a development openly might bring on a clash with private enterprise. 'Ima Naze Nokyo Ka', pp. 12–13.
284 Saeki, *Nokyo Kaikaku*, p. 180.
285 Saeki, *Nokyo Kaikaku*, p. 221.
286 Orio Yoshiharu, *Dame na Nokyo, Genki na Nokyo no Kenkyu* [*Research into Good and Bad Nokyo*], Tokyo, Yell Books, 1992, p. 12.
287 Sakaguchi, *Kyodai Nokyo*, p. 96.
288 Fujitani, *Nokyo*, p. 95.
289 Ono, *No to Shoku*, p. 80.
290 'Japanese Agriculture', p. 19.
291 'Japanese Agriculture', p. 19.
292 *Yomiuri Shinbun*, 2 November 1994.
293 Fujitani, 'Nokyo at a Crossroads', p. 377.
294 Kawasaki, *Shokuryocho-dono*, p. 16.
295 See Zenno Sogo Kikakubu Kikaku Chosaka (ed.), *Keito Keizai Jigyo Kiso Tokei* [*Federated Economic Business Basic Statistics*], 1987, Tokyo, Zenno Sogo Kikakubu Kikaku Chosaka (hereafter *Keito Keizai Jigyo Kiso Tokei*), 1987, p. 236; *JA Guruupu Keizai Jigyo Kiso Tokei*, 1997, p. 130.
296 The figure in 1985 was 95.2 per cent, while the figure in 1995 was 98.5 per cent. *Keito Keizai Jigyo Kiso Tokei*, 1987, pp. 233–234; *JA Guruupu Keizai Jigyo Kiso Tokei*, 1997, p. 129.

297 It was 94.8 per cent in 1985 and 95.1 per cent in 1995. *Keito Keizai Jigyo Kiso Tokei*, 1987, pp. 233–234; *JA Guruupu Keizai Jigyo Tokei*, 1997, p. 129.

298 Domon, *Nokyo ga Tosan Suru Hi*, p. 83. It should also be noted that some of the rice collected by the *sogo nokyo* and handled by the *keizairen* gets diverted to Zenshuren.

299 Domon, *Nokyo ga Tosan Suru Hi*, p. 70.

300 The rice is collected by the local co-ops and then marketed up the line through the *keizairen* and Zenno.

301 *Sogo Nokyo Tokeihyo*, 1985, p. 162.

302 *JA Guruupu Keizai Jigyo Kiso Tokei*, 1997, p. 88.

303 For example, in 1985, the *sogo nokyo* earned 1.9 per cent in marketing commissions on rice sold to the government. *Keito Keizai Jigyo Kiso Tokei*, 1987, p. 94. By 1995 it had risen to 2.4 per cent. In 1995, the *keizairen* earned 0.3 per cent, and Zenno 0.08 per cent. *JA Guruupu Keizai Jigyo Kiso Tokei*, 1997, pp. 89, 96, 100.

304 *Sogo Nokyo Tokeihyo*, 1985, p. 162.

305 These figures and percentages were calculated from data in *Keito Keizai Jigyo Kiso Tokei*, 1987, pp. 100, 103, 107, 108.

306 Sources as for previous footnote.

307 Calculated from figures in *JA Guruupu Keizai Jigyo Kiso Tokei*, 1997, pp. 88, 89, 94, 96, 99, 100.

308 Moore, *Japanese Agriculture*, p. 154.

309 Calculated from figures in Shokuryocho, *Beika ni kansuru Shiryo* [*Materials Relating to the Rice Price*], hereafter *Beika ni kansuru Shiryo*, June 1995, p. 166. This source provides the total amount the government spends on collection fees in any given year, of which Nokyo picks up 95 per cent, according to a former Zenno staff member.

310 This was the figure at least until 1996. See *JA Guruupu Keizai Jigyo Kiso Tokei*, 1997, p. 131.

311 *JA Guruupu Keizai Jigyo Kiso Tokei*, 1997, p. 121.

312 *JA Guruupu Keizai Jigyo Kiso Tokei*, 1995, p. 101.

313 *Keito Keizai Jigyo Kiso Tokei*, 1987, p. 236. This figure remained constant between 1983 and 1986.

314 *JA Guruupu Keizai Jigyo Kiso Tokei*, 1997, p. 128. The monthly storage charge is calculated at twice the rate per period (¥19.76). Personal communication, Zenno official.

315 Personal communication, Zenno official, and calculated from FCSA figures supplied by Zenno official, of which Nokyo received 51.4 per cent.

316 These amounted to ¥35.0 billion in 1985. *Sogo Nokyo Tokeihyo*, 1985, p. 62.

317 *JA Guruupu Keizai Jigyo Kiso Tokei*, 1997, p. 121. The total outlay on storage fees by the government in that year was ¥18.5 billion. Nokyo's share of rice stocked in warehouses was 37 per cent. The others were warehousing companies (58 per cent), rice collection merchants (2 per cent) and government warehouses (3 per cent). Personal communication, former Zenno staff member, May 1998.

318 Personal interview with Zenchu official, Tokyo, July 1995.

319 This occurred under the new food system. See below.

320 *Keito Keizai Jigyo Kiso Tokei*, 1987, p. 232. This is over four different types of rice.

321 *JA Guruupu Keizai Jigyo Kiso Tokei*, 1991, p. 227.

322 *JA Guruupu Keizai Jigyo Kiso Tokei*, 1997, p. 127. By 1995 it was called an 'orderly marketing promotion fee'.

323 *JA Guruupu Keizai Jigyo Kiso Tokei*, 1997, pp. 128, 129.

324 This figure was calculated by adding together marketing commissions on government and semi-controlled rice for all three levels of the Nokyo organisation,

collection and storage fees on government rice and the marketing promotion subsidy on semi-controlled rice. As certain assumptions were built into the figures in some cases (e.g. the percentage of the total amount allocated to Nokyo for various tasks from the Domestic Rice Control Account), the total must be considered as approximate only. Not all subsidies have been included as the figures are not easily obtainable. See below also.

325 Total business profits of the local agricultural cooperatives in 1985, for example, amounted to ¥2.1 trillion. *Sogo Nokyo Tokeihyo*, 1985, p. 62. In 1995, they were ¥2.5 trillion. *Sogo Nokyo Tokeihyo*, 1995, p. 79.

326 Total business profit on the local agricultural cooperatives' purchasing operations in 1985 was ¥577 billion. *Sogo Nokyo Tokeihyo*, 1985, p. 62. In 1995, it was ¥657 billion. *Sogo Nokyo Tokeihyo*, 1995, p. 79.

327 Total business profit on the local agricultural cooperatives' insurance business in 1985 was ¥345 billion. S*ogo Nokyo Tokeihyo*, 1985, p. 62. In 1995, it was ¥572 billion. *Sogo Nokyo Tokeihyo*, 1995, p. 79.

328 Total business profit on the local agricultural cooperatives' credit operations in 1985 was ¥885 billion. *Sogo Nokyo Tokeihyo*, 1985, p. 62. In 1995, it was ¥932 billion. *Sogo Nokyo Tokeihyo*, 1995, p. 79.

329 Including those already nominated such as collection fees and interest subsidies, there were others such as the new subsidy introduced in 1993. Allocated under the Special Policy for Demand/Supply Equilibrium By System and By Usage, it paid varying amounts per kilo to producers and to primary collectors of rice (i.e. the *nokyo*). Domon Takeshi, *Shinshokuryoho de Nihon no Okome wa ko Kawaru* [*The New Food Law Changes Japanese Rice in This Way*], Tokyo, Toyo Keizai Shinposha, 1995, pp. 86–87.

330 The average net loss per local agricultural cooperative on marketing business in 1986 was ¥13 million. *Keito Keizai Jigyo Kiso Tokei*, 1987, p. 78. The average net loss in 1995 was over ¥38 million. *JA Guruupu Keizai Jigyo Kiso Tokei*, 1997, p. 77. The net loss takes into account not only direct business expenses associated with marketing, but also business administration expenses, including wages and salaries, as well as juridical person tax (*hojinzei*) and residential taxes etc. See also the discussion below.

331 *Japanese Agriculture Under Siege*, p. 71.

332 In 1995, the *sogo nokyo* averaged a net loss of just under ¥9 million in their ware-housing operations. *JA Guruupu Keizai Jigyo Kiso Tokei*, 1997, p. 77.

333 Moore, *Japanese Agriculture*, p. 155.

334 Dore, *Land Reform in Japan*, p. 295.

335 Norinchukin for example, makes use of the surplus of cooperative funds at harvest time by supplying the general financial market with funds by means of call loans and short-term loans to commercial banks. George, *The Strategies of Influence*, p. 308.

336 *Yomiuri Shinbun*, 2 November 1994.

337 'Nihon Nogyo Ikinokori e no Michi – Ogura Takekazu-kun ni Kiku' ['The Road to Survival for Japanese Agriculture – Listening to Takekazu Ogura'], in Ouchi and Saeki (eds), *GATTO Nogyo Kosho*, p. 187.

338 See chapter 3 on 'Bureaucratic Politics' in my forthcoming volume, *Politicians and Bureaucrats*.

339 Mitsukawa, *Nogyo Dantai Hattenshi*, p. 636. See also George, *The Strategies of Influence*, pp. 317–362. See also below.

340 In fact the proposal came directly from Zenchu Chairman, Miyawaki Asao. Tanaka, *Nihon no Nokyo*, p. 242. Zenchu's approach to the whole issue is discussed in detail by Tanaka on pp. 242–249.

341 Mitsukawa, *Nogyo Dantai Hattenshi*, p. 636.

342 Nokyo tells the farmers to grow or not to grow rice in a plan organised on municipal basis. The *keizairen* develop a prefectural plan from the municipal plans. Personal interview with Food Agency official, Tokyo, July 1995.

343 As Ono explains, 'in 1969 the government stated that a decrease in rice production by 1.5 million tonnes would be necessary in 1970 to maintain a balance between demand and supply. Nokyo faced a choice of whether to keep the FC system or accept the *gentan* policy. Nokyo decided to cooperate with the government in promoting the *gentan* policy.' 'Nokyo to Senkyo', p. 84.

344 See chapter 3 on 'Bureaucratic Politics' in my forthcoming volume, *Politicians and Bureaucrats*.

345 *Nihon Keizai Shinbun*, 1 August 1986.

346 George, 'Politics of Agricultural Protectionism', p. 46.

347 Calculated from figures in *JA Guruupu Keizai Jigyo Kiso Tokei*, 1997, p. 88.

348 William T. Coyle, *U.S.–Japan Agricultural Trade Issues in Perspective*, Economic Research Service, United States Department of Agriculture, 1983, p. 27.

349 For poultry it has been around 100 per cent, pigs 95 per cent, beef cattle 85 per cent and dairy beef 62 per cent. Otani Tetsumaru, *Nokyo no Ryutsu Senryaku* [*Nokyo's Distribution Strategies*], Tokyo, Nihon Keizai Shinbunsha, 1973, p. 82.

350 *Daily Summaries of the Japanese Press*, US Embassy, Tokyo, 4 March 1986.

351 *Daily Summaries of the Japanese Press*, US Embassy, Tokyo, 4 March 1986.

352 Domon, *Yoi Nokyo*, p. 70. There was similar cartelisation of the fertiliser market. Fertiliser makers (one of which is the Nokyo company, Co-op Chemicals) set a cartel price in order to avoid competition amongst themselves, which was legally permitted under the Fertiliser Stabilisation Law (*Hiryo Anteiho*), for the law was exempted from the provisions of the Anti-Monopoly Law. It was Zenno, however, through its systematic purchasing operations that actually supported and even reinforced the stability of the cartel price, for Zenno had a near-monopoly share of fertiliser purchasing – an 80 per cent share of ammonium sulfate purchase and 85 per cent of urea. Naturally, such legally permitted cartelisation of prices was against the interests of buyers (farm households). For this reason, the Fertiliser Stabilisation Law was originally given a time limit of five years, but Zenno and Zenchu repeatedly requested the extension of the law whenever the end of the time limit drew near. See Suzuki Saichiro, 'Kobai Jigyo' ['Purchasing Business']. In Ouchi and Kajii (eds), *Nokyo Yonjunen*, pp. 98–104.

353 This does not appear to be a cooperative company. It is listed in the statistics amongst the 10 majors who are classed as *shokei*, which is short for *shoninkei*, meaning 'connected to merchants', that is, non-Nokyo companies.

354 *JA Guruupu Keizai Jigyo Kiso Tokei*, 1997, p. 214.

355 *Daily Summaries of the Japanese Press*, US Embassy, Tokyo, 4 March 1986.

356 *Daily Summaries of the Japanese Press*, US Embassy, Tokyo, 4 March 1986.

357 *JA Guruupu Keizai Jigyo Kiso Tokei*, 1997, p. 220.

358 These purchases were often made on credit, with the cooperatives taking payment from the proceeds of farmers' marketing activities.

359 Yoshihara supplies a comprehensive list of these feed production companies. *Zenno o Kiru*, pp. 252–261.

360 *JA Guruupu Keizai Jigyo Kiso Tokei*, 1997, p. 224.

361 Aono, *Nokyo*, p. 154.

362 *Nihon Nogyo Nenkan*, 1997, p. 607.

363 Hayashi Nobuaki, 'Shijo Kaiho – Endaka no Nihon Nogyo' ['Market Opening and Japan's Agriculture under High Yen Conditions'], in Ouchi Tsutomu and Gomi Kenkichi (eds), *Keizai Masatsuka no Nihon Nogyo* [*Japanese Agriculture Under Economic Friction*], Nihon Nogyo Nenpo 34, Tokyo, Ochanomizu Shobo, 1986, p. 130.

364 See also above.
365 They began in the livestock sector – dairying, pig and poultry farming – and spread into rice, vegetable and fruit farming. By 1976, there were 32 *danchi* producing rice and wheat, 39 engaged in vegetable and fruit farming and 234 in livestock-raising (118 in beef cattle, 73 in pigs, three in dairy, 21 in eggs and 19 in poultry) in 1976. These cooperative farming complexes shipped 872,000 pigs, 400,000 head of beef cattle, 8,000 tonnes of fresh milk, 560,000 tonnes of eggs and 701,000 tonnes of poultry to Zenno. This represented 54 per cent of its total turnover in pork, 30 per cent of its beef, 4 per cent of its fresh milk, 14 per cent of its eggs and 47 per cent of its poultry. *Nokyo Nenkan*, 1978, p. 48.
366 *Livestock Industry Promotion Corporation*, 1975, p. 8.
367 *Chikusan Shinko Jigyodan Nenpo*, 1990, pp. 247–259. The figures for 1997 are a bit more difficult to determine because in each case, Nokyo shared subsidy allocations with other recipient groups. Dividing the sums equally put Nokyo at around ¥12.5 billion. *Chikusan Shinko Jigyodan Nenpo*, 1997, pp. 1–81.
368 *Chikusan Shinko Jigyodan Nenpo*, 1990, pp. 247–298.
369 See chapter 8 on 'Policy Campaigning'.
370 To a lesser extent, the same comments can be made about Nokyo's investment in the fruit juice sector, in which its specialist federations and other Nokyo companies produced *mikan* and other juices which were threatened by orange and citrus juice liberalisation in 1991 and 1992. In fact this liberalisation inflicted fatal damage on Nokyo-owned fruit juice factories as the restriction on mixing domestic juice with imported juice which provided Nokyo factories with exclusive advantage in fruit juice production was lifted. Wakabayashi Hideyasu, 'Mikan-Kaju' ['*Mikan*-Fruit Juice'], in Ouchi and Kajii (eds), *Nokyo Yonjunen*, p. 140. See also below.
371 See chapter 8 on 'Policy Campaigning'.
372 *Far Eastern Economic Review*, 17 November 1988.
373 Hokkaido Koiki Nogyo Kyodo Kumiai and Kajiura, *Datsu Nokyo*, p. 29.
374 *Far Eastern Economic Review*, 17 November 1988.
375 *JA Guruupu Keizai Jigyo Kiso Tokei*, 1997, p. 89.
376 *JA Guruupu Keizai Jigyo Kiso Tokei*, 1997, p. 96.
377 *JA Guruupu Keizai Jigyo Kiso Tokei*, 1997, p. 100.
378 *Far Eastern Economic Review*, 17 November 1988.
379 Reading, *Japan*, p. 216.
380 One reporter wrote that the 'extravagant use of money stands out, when one walks through major rice production areas. Machinery and the costs for its repair account for one-third of the total costs of rice production. It may be that farmers cannot but purchase a whole set of machinery in spite of the small cultivation area in many cases, so that they can engage in farming in between other jobs.' *Asahi Shinbun*, 8 August 1986.
381 Chikara Higashi and G. Peter Lauter, *The Internationalization of the Japanese Economy*, Boston, Kluwer Academic Publishers, 1987, p. 127. The downside of this for farmers was a spiralling level of debt. Those farmers unable to manage their debts continued farming under Nokyo's supervision, whilst those who refused to allow Nokyo to manage their farm were cut off from cooperative credit, technical advice and farm inputs such as fertiliser. As a result, they ended up bankrupt. See Nozoe Kenji, 'Trade-Friction Scapegoat in the Paddy Field', *Japan Quarterly*, January–March 1988, pp. 63–64.
382 *Asahi Shinbun*, 8 August 1986.
383 Hayami Yujiro, 'Kaikaku no Keiki Nogasu Kome Kanzeika Kaihi' ['Japan May Lose The Opportunity of Reform if it Avoids Rice Tariffication'], *Nogyo to Keizai*, Vol. 60, No. 6, June 1994, p. 36.

384 Higashi and Lauter, *The Internationalization of the Japanese Economy*, p. 127.
385 Masahiko Ishizuka, 'Black Hole in Japanese Economy', *Japan Economic Journal*, 13 September 1986, p. 6.
386 Jun Fukui, 'Japan Agriculture on the Ropes', *Tokyo Business Today*, December 1994, p. 28.
387 Fukui, 'Japan Agriculture on the Ropes', p. 28.
388 Ishizuka, 'Black Hole', p. 6.
389 Kano Yoshikazu, 'Hojokin Sakugen, Noka "Senbetsu" De Shijoka Isogu' ['Reducing Subsidies and ' "Selecting" Farm Households for the Introduction of the Market Mechanism'], *Ekonomisuto*, 22 November 1994, p. 83. Kano was an expert on agricultural issues and Chairman of the National Institute for Research Advancement (NIRA). According to another source, other factors driving costs have been the spread of agricultural methods requiring large quantities of insecticides, chemical fertilisers and energy, the high unit prices of subsidised projects and the fact that much time is required for farm work in some places, since the farm land is scattered over a wide area. *Asahi Shinbun*, 8 August 1986.
390 Hokkaido Koiki Nogyo Kyodo Kumiai and Kajiura, *Datsu Nokyo*, p. 77.
391 Kyosanto Bukkuretto, *Gaiatsu no Naka no Nihon*, p. 31.
392 Hokkaido Koiki Nogyo Kyodo Kumiai and Kajiura, *Datsu Nokyo*, p. 75.
393 Kano, 'Hojokin Sakugen', p. 83.
394 Hokkaido Koiki Nogyo Kyodo Kumiai and Kajiura, *Datsu Nokyo*, p. 60.
395 Hokkaido Koiki Nogyo Kyodo Kumiai and Kajiura, *Datsu Nokyo*, p. 60.
396 Hokkaido Koiki Nogyo Kyodo Kumiai and Kajiura, *Datsu Nokyo*, p. 59.
397 Nokyo produces 71 per cent of all the fertiliser shipped in Japan, whilst private manufacturers produce 29 per cent. However, the bulk of this privately produced fertiliser actually passes through the Nokyo system. As a result, farmers purchase 94.5 per cent of their fertiliser from the local agricultural cooperatives. *JA Guruupu Keizai Jigyo Kiso Tokei*, 1997, pp. 236, 241. Agricultural chemicals are all produced by private manufacturers (in which, however, Nokyo groups have a range of investments which makes price collusion easy). Of the total agricultural chemicals produced, 45 per cent goes to Zenno and 5 per cent to the *keizairen*. The balance of 50 per cent is shipped to wholesalers, who ship 20 per cent on to the *nokyo* and 30 per cent to retailers. As a result, farmers end up buying 70 per cent of their agricultural chemicals from Nokyo. *JA Guruupu Keizai Jigyo Kiso Tokei*, 1997, p. 248.
398 Hokkaido Koiki Nogyo Kyodo Kumiai and Kajiura, *Datsu Nokyo*, p. 38.
399 Domon, *Yoi Nokyo*, p. 95.
400 Hokkaido Koiki Nogyo Kyodo Kumiai and Kajiura, *Datsu Nokyo*, pp. 29–30.
401 Hokkaido Koiki Nogyo Kyodo Kumiai and Kajiura, *Datsu Nokyo*, p. 60.
402 Hokkaido Koiki Nogyo Kyodo Kumiai and Kajiura, *Datsu Nokyo*, p. 60.
403 The average utilisation rate of cooperative channels (i.e. the *keito riyo ritsu*) by the *sogo nokyo* in their purchasing business in 1995 was 73.5 per cent; the average for marketing was 92.7 per cent. *JA Guruupu Keizai Jigyo Kiso Tokei*, 1997, pp. 86, 89.
404 Hokkaido Koiki Nogyo Kyodo Kumiai and Kajiura, *Datsu Nokyo*, p. 68.
405 Hokkaido Koiki Nogyo Kyodo Kumiai and Kajiura, *Datsu Nokyo*, p. 69.
406 *Asahi Evening News*, 15 September 1991.
407 These figures are for 1995. The *sogo nokyo* collect 18.8 per cent on gasoline, 12.4 per cent on fertiliser, 10.5 per cent on agricultural chemicals and 10.3 per cent on agricultural machinery and 4.8 per cent on feed; the *keizairen* collect 4.0 per cent on agricultural machinery, 3.8 per cent on agricultural chemicals, 2.8 per cent on feed, 2.6 per cent on gasoline and 2.2 per cent on fertiliser; Zenno extracts 1.5 per cent on agricultural chemicals and agricultural machinery, 1.0 per cent on

gasoline, 0.8 per cent on feed and 0.6 per cent on fertiliser. *JA Guruupu Keizai Jigyo Kiso Tokei*, 1997, pp. 86, 92, 100.

408 Fukui, 'Japan Agriculture on the Ropes', p. 28.
409 Hokkaido Koiki Nogyo Kyodo Kumiai and Kajiura, *Datsu Nokyo*, p. 68.
410 *Asahi Shinbun*, 8 August 1986.
411 Imported feed accounts for about 20–40 per cent of the production cost in the case of Japanese dairy farming, beef cattle raising and hog raising, and 60–70 per cent in the case of egg and broiler production.
412 Zenno's sales prices of compound feed in 1986 were more than 20 per cent lower than in the first half of 1984. *Asahi Shinbun*, 1 June 1986. The yen, however, underwent a 50–70 per cent rise in value.
413 *Asahi Shinbun*, 1 June 1986. The JCP reported that because (with a few exceptions), the commission on agricultural materials and products was fixed at a certain ratio to the buying and selling prices, a fall in prices reduced Nokyo's income. As a result, a proposal was put within Nokyo that if prices for farm materials fell, the commission rate should be raised. Kyosanto Bukkuretto, *Gaiatsu no Naka no Nihon*, p. 31.
414 *Reuters*, 22 September 1998.
415 Moore, *Japanese Agriculture*, p. 152.
416 Moore, *Japanese Agriculture*, p. 152.
417 Nobuhiro Tsuboi, 'Appendix: Limitations and Potential of Family Farmers in Japan: Can Japanese Family Farms Survive?', in Tweeten, Dishon *et al.* (eds), *Japanese & American Agriculture*, p. 67.
418 Tsuboi, 'Appendix', p. 67. Another factor that must be considered is the reluctance of full-time farmers to accept nomination as Nokyo executives because they are too busy. As a result, those who are not as familiar with agriculture tend to be elected as officials. Takeuchi and Otawara, *Asu no Nokyo*, p. 241. See also chapter 8 on 'Policy Campaigning'.
419 *Far Eastern Economic Review*, 28 June 1990. See also above.
420 Hayashi Nobuaki, *Nogyo wa Nihon no Onimotsu Ka* [*Is Agriculture a Burden to Japan?*], Tokyo, Ie no Hikari Kyokai, 1987, p. 54.
421 *Domon, Nokyo ga Tosan Suru Hi*, p. 11. Hayami also points out that because Nokyo applies the same unit price for fertiliser regardless of the volume of purchase, this often leads large-scale agricultural producers to distance themselves from Nokyo. 'Kaikaku no Keiki', p. 35.
422 Fukui, 'Japan Agriculture on the Ropes', p. 29.
423 *Far Eastern Economic Review*, 17 November 1988.
424 In a survey of how full-time farmers rated Nokyo's individual enterprises, the figures revealed that they evaluated Nokyo's supply of production materials and fuel quite highly, whilst their view of Nokyo's agricultural machinery and stock-feed supply business was low. Similarly, their estimation of Nokyo's marketing enterprise was also low. As far as Nokyo's credit and mutual aid operations were concerned, full-time farmers still rated these as useful and convenient, but they objected to the way in which Nokyo had pushed these aspects of its business. This survey was reported in Takeuchi and Otawara, *Asu no Nokyo*, pp. 156–157.
425 Domon, *Nokyo ga Tosan Suru Hi*, p. 9.
426 Domon, *Nokyo ga Tosan Suru Hi*, p. 11.
427 *Asahi Shinbun*, 24 June 1994. See also chapter 2 on 'Interest Group Politics' and chapter 4 on 'Patronage Politics' in my forthcoming volume, *Politicians and Bureaucrats*.
428 Hokkaido Koiki Nogyo Kyodo Kumiai and Kajiura, *Datsu Nokyo*, p. 35. One example was the case of three farmers in Nagano Prefecture whose application for an interest-free loan from the Agricultural Modernisation Fund was rejected in

1993 on the grounds that Kawakami Nokyo in Nagano was reluctant to be responsible for organic lettuce production by the three farmers who had earlier left Nokyo in order to sell their products directly to supermarkets and other retailers. The Nokyo branch put negative comments on their plan to establish a compost facility, because it was concerned that popularity of the organic lettuce would eventually reduce its profits from collecting commissions on marketing and sales of fertiliser and pesticide. The three farmers appealed to the local Nagano Prefecture Agricultural Policy Bureau of the MAFF, which agreed to reconsider their application. *Asahi Shinbun*, 24 June 1994.

429 *Asahi Shinbun*, 24 June 1994.
430 Domon, *Nokyo ga Tosan Suru Hi*, p. 11. According to a survey reported in Takeuchi and Otawara, full-time farmers evaluate Nokyo's economic services very negatively because the enterprises into which Nokyo puts a lot of effort does not match the needs of full-time farmers. *Asu no Nokyo*, p. 158.
431 *Asahi Shinbun*, 24 June 1994.
432 Respondents were given a choice of two items. See Iwai Tomoaki, 'Nogyosha no Seiji Ishiki ni kansuru Chosa Hokoku' ['Survey Report on Farmers' Political Consciousness'], *Nosei Undo Jyaanaru*, Vol. 1, July 1995, p. 9. These two polls were conducted as a nationwide survey of 3,760 respondents (100 each in 3–4 agricultural cooperatives in 10 selected prefectures) and a 'fixed point' survey of 1,080 respondents from 15 agricultural cooperatives in the Kanto region. The results of the nationwide survey are reported in English in Tomoaki Iwai, 'Japan's Agricultural Politics At A Turning Point', in Purnendra Jain and Takashi Inoguchi (eds), *Japanese Politics Today: Beyond Karaoke Democracy?*, South Melbourne, Macmillan, 1997, pp. 186–205.
433 Domon, *Yoi Nokyo*, p. 230.
434 *Far Eastern Economic Review*, 17 November 1988.
435 *Far Eastern Economic Review*, 17 November 1988.
436 Saeki, *Nokyo Kaikaku*, pp. 224–225.
437 Saeki, *Nokyo Kaikaku*, pp. 220–221.
438 Saeki, *Nokyo Kaikaku*, pp. 199–201.
439 Saeki, *Nokyo Kaikaku*, pp. 210–214.
440 Saeki, *Nokyo Kaikaku*, pp. 222–223.
441 Saeki, *Nokyo Kaikaku*, pp. 224–225.
442 Saeki, *Nokyo Kaikaku*, pp. 222–223.
443 *Daily Yomiuri*, 11 March 1992.
444 Yamaguchi Iwao, 'Don't Push Our Farmers Too Far', *Japan Echo*, Vol. XIV, No. 1, Spring 1987, p. 24.
445 *Nihon Keizai Shinbun*, 1 August 1986.
446 See chapter 3 on 'Bureaucratic Politics' in my forthcoming volume, *Politicians and Bureaucrats*.
447 *Asahi Evening News*, 15 September 1991.
448 *Asahi Evening News*, 15 September 1991.
449 Saeki, *Nokyo Kaikaku*, p. 3.
450 A number of treatments of this problem can be found in the literature. They basically advocate that Nokyo should 'get back to basics' and return to its original ideological foundations of cooperative unionism. See for example, Sakizaki Chihiro, *Yomigaere Nokyo [Come Back to Life Nokyo]*, Tokyo, Zenkoku Kyodo Shuppan, 1991.
451 Hokkaido Koiki Nogyo Kyodo Kumiai and Kajiura, *Datsu Nokyo*, p. 36.
452 'Nogyo Kyodo Kumiaiho', in *Nogyo Roppo*, 1993, p. 108.
453 Hokkaido Koiki Nogyo Kyodo Kumiai and Kajiura, *Datsu Nokyo*, p. 37.
454 Hokkaido Koiki Nogyo Kyodo Kumiai and Kajiura, *Datsu Nokyo*, p. 38.

455 Hokkaido Koiki Nogyo Kyodo Kumiai and Kajiura, *Datsu Nokyo*, p. 38.
456 Domon, *Yoi Nokyo*, p. 98.
457 Domon, *Yoi Nokyo*, p. 95.
458 Fujitani, *Nokyo*, pp. 126–127.
459 Hokkaido Koiki Nogyo Kyodo Kumiai and Kajiura, *Datsu Nokyo*, pp. 62–63.
460 Hokkaido Koiki Nogyo Kyodo Kumiai and Kajiura, *Datsu Nokyo*, p. 69.
461 Hokkaido Koiki Nogyo Kyodo Kumiai and Kajiura, *Datsu Nokyo*, p. 77.
462 Hokkaido Koiki Nogyo Kyodo Kumiai and Kajiura, *Datsu Nokyo*, p. 72.
463 Saeki, *Nokyo Kaikaku*, pp. 3–4.
464 *Nokyo*, p. 14, pp. 51–52. He proposes that the reformed management body of the agricultural cooperatives should have organisational representative directors (*soshiki daihyo riji*), that is, representatives of Nokyo members, and directors who have practical management experience and knowledge (*gakushiki keiken riji*). At present, these two roles are confused (p. 214).
465 Sakaguchi, *Kyodai Nokyo*, pp. 104–107.
466 Domon, *Nokyo ga Tosan Suru Hi*, p. 70.
467 Domon, *Nokyo ga Tosan Suru Hi*, pp. 70–71.
468 Saeki, *Nokyo Kaikaku*, p. 3.
469 See chapter 8 on 'Policy Campaigning'.
470 *Far Eastern Economic Review*, 22 July 1987.
471 Sakaguchi, *Kyodai Nokyo*, p. 116.
472 Ishizuka, 'Black Hole', p. 6.
473 *Far Eastern Economic Review*, 11 November 1988.
474 The media criticism cited was an editorial in *Tokyo Business Today*, February 1987, referred to in ABARE, *Japanese Agricultural Policies*, p. 93.
475 ABARE, *Japanese Agricultural Policies*, p. 92.
476 ABARE, *Japanese Agricultural Policies*, p. 92. Tamaki's actual statement was as follows: 'Nokyo was originally created in order to serve farmers and to protect their livelihood mainly through guiding agricultural management. As Nokyo also stipulates that "Nokyo must not seek profits", Nokyo was created to serve only farmers. However, what is the situation of Nokyo now? It is neglecting its main role of guiding agricultural management at the same time as it is expanding its operations from running supermarkets to dealing in financial capital, credit, and insurance business. Now we have the impression that Nokyo is giving priority to making profits. I am saying to Nokyo not to forget its original mission of serving farmers. Another problem is that today's Nokyo has become too fat. Please think about this. There is nobody but Nokyo that deals in various kinds of businesses by itself such as banking, non-life insurance, life insurance and so on. As a result, the number of Nokyo staff has reached roughly 500,000. As farm population is a little over 7 million including part-time farmers, this means that one Nokyo staff is supported by 13 farmers.' Quoted in Kajii, 'Ima Naze Nokyo Ka', pp. 4–5.
477 Sakaguchi, *Kyodai Nokyo*, p. 101.
478 J. Kanagawa, 'Agricultural Reform: An Introduction', *Japanese Research*, Tokyo, Hoare Govett, April 1987, quoted in ABARE, *Japanese Agricultural Policies*, p. 92.
479 *Far Eastern Economic Review*, 17 November 1988.
480 Hemmi Kenzo, 'Agricultural Reform Efforts in Japan: Political Feasibility and Consequences For Trade With the United States and Third Countries', in D. G. Johnson (ed.), *Agricultural Reform Efforts in the United States and Japan*, New York, New York University Press, p. 41, quoted in ABARE, *Japanese Agricultural Policies*, p. 92.
481 Hayashi, *Nogyo wa Nihon no Onimotsu ka*, p. 52.
482 Domon, *Yoi Nokyo*, p. 24.

483 Somucho, Gyosei Kansatsu Kyoku, *Nokyo no Genjo – Somucho no Gyosei Kansatsu Kekka Kara Mite* [*Nokyo's Present Situation Viewed From The Results of the Prime Minister's Office Administrative Inspection*], cited in Saeki, *Nokyo Kaikaku*, p. 57. According to Domon, the administrative inspection was conducted on the MAFF, 26 prefectures, Zenchu, Zenno, Zenkyoren, Norinchukin, 26 prefectural central unions, trust federations, mutual aid federations and economic federations, and 124 *sogo nokyo*. *Yoi Nokyo*, p. 27.

484 *Far Eastern Economic Review*, 11 November 1998.

485 Domon, *Yoi Nokyo*, pp. 27–28.

486 *Far Eastern Economic Review*, 18 June 1988.

487 See chapter 7 on 'Representative Politics'.

488 See chapter 2 on 'Party Politics' in my forthcoming volume, *Politicians and Bureaucrats*.

489 This is the reasoning offered in Nagao, 'Nihon no Seiji Taisei', p. 30.

490 Sakaguchi, *Kyodai Nokyo*, p. 103.

491 *The Economist*, 20 February 1988.

492 It was, for example, advanced by Oshima Tadamori, an LDP Diet member representing a rural electorate.

493 *Far Eastern Economic Review*, 17 November 1988.

494 At the same time, the report underlined the need to promote the participation of non-farmers in the agricultural cooperatives in order to promote regional development, including agricultural production. The terminology used was the 'activisation' (*kasseika*) of regions and agriculture. Quoted in Saeki, *Nokyo Kaikaku*, p. 183.

495 Saeki, *Nokyo Kaikaku*, p. 184.

496 *Asahi Shinbun*, 25 June 1994.

497 *Asahi Shinbun*, 25 June 1994. This criticism is rather ironic given the flack Nokyo has taken for being too profit-orientated in its mainstream economic and financial businesses.

498 *Asahi Shinbun*, 25 June 1994.

499 *MAFF Update*, No. 232, October 1997, http://www.maff.go.jp.

500 The volume of transactions in Nokyo's economic business declined in 1993 on the 1992 figures. In marketing, transactions declined 5 per cent in the *sogo nokyo*, 3.9 per cent in the *keizairen* and 8.6 per cent in Zenno; in purchasing, transactions declined 0.3 per cent in the *sogo nokyo*, 0.7 per cent down in the *keizairen* and 0.3 per cent down in Zenno. *Nokyo, Kanren Kigyo Meikan*, 1995, p. 8. The gradual contraction in Nokyo's purchasing business continued in 1994, whilst the value of turnover in marketing rose slightly. See *Nihon Nogyo Nenkan*, 1997, pp. 606–607; 608–609. As far as individual items in the *sogo nokyo* purchasing business are concerned, the turnover in most items declined in the 1991–95 period, with the biggest falls registered in the value of turnover in feed, fertiliser, rice, perishable food and general food. Small growth registered in agricultural chemicals and gasoline. Declines also registered in most marketed agricultural commodities over the same period, except for rice, potatoes, tea and fresh milk. *JA Guruupu Keizai Jigyo Kiso Tokei*, 1997, pp. 85, 88. The volume of transactions in other businesses grew, but in general, at a low rate. The annual increase in *sogo nokyo* savings in 1993, for example, was 3.9 per cent, an historically low rate. The same was true of insurance business, up only 3.4 per cent on the previous year, but at a lower rate than in the previous year. The gross business revenue of the *sogo nokyo* in 1993 was 4.7 per cent down on the previous year. *Nokyo, Kanren Kigyo Meikan*, 1995, p. 4. See also above.

501 Domon, *Nokyo ga Tosan Suru Hi*, p. 40. See also Orio, *Dame na Nokyo*, p. 105. Elsewhere Domon describes these as the liberalisation of agricultural

imports, the liberalisation of marketing and financial liberalisation. *Yoi Nokyo*, p. 229.

502 Domon, *Nokyo ga Tosan Suru Hi*, p. 124.

503 Ono, *No to Shoku*, p. 168.

504 Domon, *Yoi Nokyo*, p. 31. The liberalisation of interest rates on deposits began with large denomination time deposits in 1985 and continued on for the next 10 years so that by 1997, all interest rates on any sort of deposits were no longer subject to interest rate controls. Personal communication, Colin McKenzie, Osaka University, 17 August 1997.

505 Aguri Fuooramu, 'Tokushu: Nihon no Kome' ['Special Report: Japanese Rice'], *Chuo Koron*, Vol. 102, No. 2, February 1987, p. 88.

506 Domon, *Nokyo ga Tosan Suru Hi*, p. 149.

507 Masuda, 'Nokyo no Keiei Bunseki', p. 64.

508 *Nikkei Weekly*, 8 April 1996.

509 Orio reports that the margin of profits on deposits and loans fell from above 3 per cent to just over 2 per cent between 1982 and 1991. *Dame na Nokyo*, p. 19.

510 *Nikkei Weekly*, 14 September 1998.

511 Domon, *Yoi Nokyo*, p. 32.

512 Masuda, 'Nokyo no Keiei Bunseki', p. 64. There was also a generational dimension to this issue insofar as those farmers born in the 1920s and 1930s strongly supported Nokyo management, but as they aged, Nokyo was faced with converting new generations to Nokyo users. This proved a difficult task because the younger the generations were, the less frequently they used Nokyo's banking services and the more frequently they used other banks. Tsuboi Nobuhiro, 'Keito Shinyo Jigyo' ['Federated Trust Business'], in Ouchi and Kajii (eds), *Nokyo Yonjunen*, pp. 179–181. As Yamamoto explains, Nokyo's conventional method of recruiting members i.e. 'one member from one household system' was replaced with a 'multiple members from one household system' method in order to encourage the younger generations to join as well as women. 'Sogo Nokyo', p. 260.

513 Saeki, *Nokyo Kaikaku*, p. 41.

514 Saeki, *Nokyo Kaikaku*, p. 41.

515 *Jiji Press Newswire*, 25 November 1996.

516 Domon, *Nokyo ga Tosan Suru Hi*, p. 142.

517 Domon, *Nokyo ga Tosan Suru Hi*, p. 145.

518 Domon, *Nokyo ga Tosan Suru Hi*, p. 161.

519 Saeki, *Nokyo Kaikaku*, pp. 43–44.

520 Saeki, *Nokyo Kaikaku*, p. 44.

521 Masuda, 'Nokyo no Keiei Bunseki', p. 64.

522 Net profits from *sogo nokyo* trust business more than halved in the early 1990s, from an average profit per cooperative of over ¥120 million in 1990 to an annual profit of just over ¥45 million in 1993. Over the same period, average profit per cooperative in mutual aid business rose from just over ¥88 million to just on ¥113 million. *JA Guruupu Keizai Jigyo Kiso Tokei*, 1995, p. 77. By 1995 the average net profit of the co-ops from trust business had recovered (to just under ¥130 million), while the net profit on insurance business also grew substantially to just over ¥150 million. *JA Guruupu Keizai Jigyo Kiso Tokei*, 1997, p. 77.

523 Ito, 'Soshiki Nidankaika', p. 18.

524 Economic business (marketing and purchasing), for example, was always in deficit. Kajii dates the first loss in *sogo nokyo* sales operations back to 1956 and purchasing operations to 1972. 'Ima Naze Nokyo Ka', p. 11. The average loss on *sogo nokyo* purchasing in 1986 was ¥22.9 million. Suzuki, 'Kobai Jigyo', p. 90.

525 Saeki, *Nokyo Kaikaku*, pp. 5–7.

526 Saeki, *Nokyo Kaikaku*, p. 44.
527 *Nikkei Weekly*, 8 April 1996.
528 Saeki, *Nokyo Kaikaku*, pp. 222–223.
529 Domon, *Nokyo ga Tosan Suru Hi*, p. 42.
530 Saeki, *Nokyo Kaikaku*, pp. 44–55. Cargill has made the general point that 'Japan's financial and regulatory structure was poorly designed for liberalization. The regulatory structure was incapable of monitoring risk-taking in the merging liberalized environment in which no meaningful financial disclosure framework existed'. Thomas F. Cargill, *Asia's Financial Crisis and Japan*, Briefing Paper, Japan–U.S. Friendship Commission in Cooperation with Japan Information Access Project, 15 December 1997, p. 2.
531 Domon, *Nokyo ga Tosan Suru Hi*, p. 125.
532 Fujitani, 'Nokyo at a Crossroads', p. 374. Tachibana, for example, warned as early as 1980 that although Nokyo was proud to be No. 2 in Japan in terms of its trust business, because of a lack of experience and appropriate checking procedures, Nokyo's trust business lost more than ¥100 million every year. *Nokyo*, p. 236. Sakaguchi also argues that there are always big risks in Nokyo's business because everyone, including co-op chairmen are amateurs in credit business. *Kyodai Nokyo*, p. 105. Tsuboi points out that *tankyo* directors, for example, are not chosen because of their skills in management, but for other reasons, such as regional balance and obligations of one sort or another. He adds that such a method might be fine when management faces no problems, but when decision-making based on a tight management strategy is what is required under conditions of intensifying competition, then such a method of electing management staff is hopelessly inadequate. He adds that Nokyo clearly lacks sufficiently competent staff to deal with intensifying competition and that it has demonstrated an unwillingness to invest in developing the competence of its management. 'Keito Shinyo Jigyo', pp. 181–184.
533 According to Saeki writing in the early 1990s, each Nokyo branch had bad loans and uncollected bills in its portfolio, totalling an average of ¥130 million and ¥13 million respectively per cooperative. On an individual level, this was largely due to over-investment in the livestock industry during the previous 20 years. Because of fierce competition in the livestock market, livestock producers expanded the size of their production units requiring large investments in capital goods. Many of these livestock farmers could not meet interest payments, let alone repayments. In addition, some loans to non-agricultural businesses, and for housing and living expenses turned into bad debts. See *Nokyo Kaikaku*, pp. 56–63.
534 See the following section.
535 See *Nokyo Kaikaku*, pp. 63–71.
536 *Nikkei Weekly*, 29 January 1996.
537 Domon, *Nokyo Ga Tosan Suru Hi*, p. 125.
538 Kudo, 'Nokyo Hatan', p. 11.
539 *Nikkei Weekly*, 25 December 1995–1 January 1996. See also the many examples of other bad loans and Nokyo losses in Domon Takeshi, 'The Inside Story of the Troubled Farm Co-ops', *Japan Echo*, Vol. 23, No. 2, Summer 1996, pp. 21–24.
540 *Nikkei Weekly*, 25 December 1995–1 January 1996. In fact, Nokyo directors are required under Article 33 of the Nokyo Law to compensate the cooperative personally for losses owing to their negligence.
541 See Saeki, *Nokyo Kaikaku*, pp. 63–71.
542 See the above discussion on *Nokyoron*.
543 He quotes a local businessman who said: 'It is hardest to borrow money from city banks. We cannot borrow from them if we cannot satisfy their credit conditions. City banks conduct very tough examinations of our credibility and also take a

long time to reach a decision on a loan. Trust banks and credit unions are more flexible, but even then, you need to have good business records and be a good credit risk. Nokyo is the easiest. You do not even need to be an associate member to apply for a loan. You only have to join when you get the loan. And if a local boss puts in a good word for you, you can borrow money even when your qualifications are not satisfactory. What is more, Nokyo does not take time in granting the loan. *Kyodai Nokyo*, p. 105.

544   Orio, *Dame na Nokyo*, p. 43. See also the analysis in Domon, 'The Inside Story', pp. 21–26. A case that came to light in late 1998 which revealed that Chiba Nokyo failed to report four cases of embezzlement by employees that cost it ¥45 million. *Mainichi Daily News*, 29 November 1998.

545   *Asahi Shinbun*, 17 November 1994.

546   *Asahi Shinbun*, 17 November 1994.

547   As Cargill explains, the *jusen* 'were created in the mid-1970s as subsidiaries of banks, securities firms, and life insurance companies that initially provided consumer credit but moved more heavily into real estate lending in the second half of the 1980s. *Jusen* were dependent on funds from banks, credit cooperatives, and other institutions since they had no deposit base. In 1991–92, the Ministry [of Finance] was aware of a serious non-performing loan problem in the *jusen* industry but failed to move to close down what was obvious to many was an insolvent industry . . . Non-performing loans in the *jusen* industries increased by 75 percent in the following four years.' 'Asia's Financial Crisis', pp. 2–3.

548   Gavan McCormack, 'Afterbubble: Fizz and Concrete in Japan's Political Economy', *JPRI Working Paper*, No. 21, June 1996, p. 2.

549   According to Cargill: 'In August 1995, the MOF conducted a special audit of the *jusen* and found that of the total ¥13 trillion of *jusen* assets, non-performing loans were estimated at ¥9.6 trillion, of which ¥6.4 trillion was considered unrecoverable and ¥1.2 trillion was considered a possible loss.' 'Asia's Financial Crisis', p. 3.

550   Saeki, *Nokyo Kaikaku*, pp. 71–82.

551   *Nikkei Weekly*, 5 August 1996.

552   *Nikkei Weekly*, 5 August 1996.

553   Domon Takeshi, 'Jusen Kokkai ni Katte Kinyu Senso ni Yabureru' ['Nokyo Won the *Jusen* Diet But Was Defeated in the Financial War'], *Kinyu Bijinesu*, July 1996, p. 25.

554   Tachibana, *Nokyo*, p. 237.

555   *The Economist*, 20 February 1993.

556   *Nikkei Weekly*, 25 December 1995–1 January 1996. This would seem to suggest that Nokyo's involvement with the *jusen* was also driven by its need to find places to invest. The author is grateful to Jennifer Amyx for this point.

557   According to Domon: 'For years the nokyo institutions had dreamed of being able to invest in real estate. Starting from the first boom in land prices . . . they had seen how the commercial banks were raking in cash from land development financing. But because the Agriculture Ministry wouldn't let them lend to developers, they could only twiddle their thumbs. Then, near the end of the bubble period in 1989, the ministry finally relaxed its restraints on large-scale loans and lending to borrowers other than co-op members.' 'The Inside Story', p. 23. Ichikawa Hiroya, formerly of Keidanren, noted that there were no restrictions imposed on *jusen* and agricultural cooperative lending for real estate because of the lack of MOF guidance. Public presentation, Canberra, January 1999.

558   *The Economist*, 20 February 1993.

559   *Nikkei Weekly*, 5 August 1996.

560   Of this figure, the exposure of the *shinren* amounted to ¥155.6 billion. According

to Domon, however, the figures do not reflect the real management of the *shinren*. In his opinion, this data was fabricated to hide the real amount of bad credit. 'Jusen Kokkai', p. 23.

561 *The Economist*, 20 February 1993.
562 *Nikkei Weekly*, 16 October 1995. The figure reported by Domon was ¥5.6 trillion. 'The Inside Story', p. 21.
563 'Daremo Iwanai Nokyo no Judai Sekinin' ['No one Says Anything About Nokyo's Huge Responsibilities'], *Aera*, No. 8, 26 February 1996, p. 7.
564 Personal interview, Tokyo, November 1994.
565 *Nikkei Weekly*, 25 December 1995–1 January 1996.
566 Domon, *Nokyo ga Tosan Suru Hi*, 1992, p. 35.
567 Personal interview with MAFF official, Tokyo, November 1994.
568 *Nikkei Weekly*, 5 August 1996.
569 According to Domon, setting the figure at ¥530 billion meant that only three prefectural trust federations (Miyagi, Tochigi and Saitama) would suffer from excess debts, whereas at ¥1.21 trillion, one-third of all prefectural trust federations would suffer from excess debts. 'Jusen Kokkai', p. 20.
570 This was despite the fact that a sum exceeding ¥685 billion (¥750 billion) had already been paid by the ailing *jusen* as interest to Nokyo's financial institutions between 1993 and 1996. Domon, *The Inside Story*, p. 21.
571 *Nikkei Weekly*, 29 January 1996.
572 *Asahi Nenkan*, 1997, p. 233. This source elaborates in detail the financial impact of the large debt burden on each of these organisations/groups of organisations.
573 Domon, 'Jusen Kokkai', p. 20. About ¥685 billion from the national budget was allocated to covering *jusen* losses by the end of 1996. *Nikkei Weekly*, 30 December 1996–6 January 1997.
574 *Nikkei Weekly*, 3 March 1997.
575 *Nikkei Weekly*, 29 January 1996.
576 *Nikkei Weekly*, 24 June 1996.
577 *Nikkei Weekly* Editorial, 29 January 1996.
578 *Nikkei Weekly*, 3 March 1997.
579 'Daremo Iwanai Nokyo', p. 8.
580 MOF Minister in the Obuchi government, Miyazawa Kiichi did, however, later admit the political influences on the outcome of the *jusen* issue in relation to Nokyo's financial institutions.
581 'Daremo Iwanai Nokyo', p. 9.
582 *Nikkei Weekly*, 29 January 1996.
583 *Nikkei Weekly*, 29 January 1996.
584 *Nikkei Weekly*, 10 June 1996.
585 *Nikkei Weekly*, 27 May 1996.
586 Kudo, 'Nokyo Hatan', p. 11. See also chapter 2 on 'Interest Group Politics'.
587 *The Economist*, 20 February 1993.
588 'The Inside Story', p. 27.
589 These were very small financial institutions in general lending, particularly in leasing and credit card businesses. Some of them got involved in real estate financing, and it was these that got into trouble.
590 Mamiya Atsushi, 'Kongo wa Nogarerarenai! Nonbanku Shori no Arashi' ['This Time It Is Impossible to Escape! The Storm of Non-Bank Credit Disposal'], *Kinyu Bijinesu*, July 1996, p. 6.
591 Mamiya, 'Kongo wa Nogarerarenai!', p. 7.
592 *Nikkei Weekly*, 5 August 1996.
593 Mamiya, 'Kongo wa Nogarerarenai!', p. 8. Mamiya's argument suggests that the unofficial MAFF figure of ¥8 trilllion+ for Nokyo's *jusen* exposure was closer to

the correct amount than officially published figures or those revealed in the media.
594 *Nikkei Weekly*, 13 July 1998. In November 1996, however, a plan was revealed whereby the Nippon Credit Bank had provided a signed memorandum in 1994 to financial institutions linked to the agricultural cooperatives effectively guaranteeing repayment of about ¥240 billion in loans that were originally made to its troubled affiliate, Crown Leasing Corporation. Such a memorandum was not provided to other creditors of Crown Leasing Corporation and was designed to appease farm-linked lenders although a spokesperson for the Bank denied allegations of preferential treatment for farm lenders. *Reuters Business Information News*, 13 November 1996, from *Jiji Press Newswire*.
595 Agricultural cooperatives, their federations (*shinren* and *kyosairen*) and Norinchukin accounted for half of the financial institutions dangerously exposed to this non-bank. *Nikkei Weekly*, 14 September 1998.
596 Under this scheme, only creditors with loans of more than ¥100 billion would need to give up their loans to LTCB non-bank affiliates, thus favouring smaller agricultural cooperative organisations. *Reuters*, 29 September 1998. Another source claimed that the plan favoured agricultural cooperative organisations because they were expected to constitute half of the financial institutions that would escape being forced to write off all their loans to Japan Leasing Corporation. *Asia Pulse*, 11 September 1998.
597 This was due to the government's lack of a majority in the Upper House following the July 1998 election.
598 *Asia Pulse*, 29 September 1998.
599 *Asia Pulse*, 29 September 1998. A Norinchukin spokesperson put the number of agricultural cooperative organisations involved at 67 and their outstanding credits at ¥350 billion. He did not foresee the bankruptcy filing as likely to cause serious management problems at Norinchukin, although there might be some agricultural cooperative organisations that fell into the red. *Reuters*, 29 September 1998.
600 *Reuters*, 29 September 1998.
601 Domon, 'The Inside Story', p. 27.
602 *Reuters*, 29 September 1998.
603 *PR Newswire*, 9 September 1998. The figure is for the end of March 1998.
604 In 1998, 10 prefectural governments extended a total of ¥23.8 billion to various *nokyo* saddled with massive bad debts. *Yomiuri Shinbun*, 29 April 1998. According to another source, 20 prefectural governments planned to spend some ¥30 billion in fiscal 1998 on support to ailing agricultural cooperatives to help them dispose of non-performing loans and strengthen their management base. Some of this money was provided as loans to funds established for promoting mergers of the cooperatives. *Financial Times*, 28 April 1998. See also below.
605 *Yomiuri Shinbun*, 29 April 1998.
606 See below.
607 *Financial Times*, 28 April 1998.
608 *Nikkei Weekly*, 9 December 1996.
609 Domon, *Nokyo ga Tosan Suru Hi*, p. 83.
610 *Asahi Evening News*, 15 September 1991.
611 Domon, *Nokyo ga Tosan Suru Hi*, p. 86.
612 Domon, *Nokyo ga Tosan Suru Hi*, p. 86.
613 Domon, *Nokyo ga Tosan Suru Hi*, pp. 84, 86.
614 *Asahi Evening News*, 15 September 1991.
615 *JA Guruupu Keizai Jigyo Kiso Tokei*, 1997, p. 130.
616 This has also been translated as the Price Determining Organization (PDO)

for Indirect-Government-Controlled Rice – see Yamaji and Ito, 'The Political Economy of Rice', p. 353; Rice Trade Board – see Kenji Ozawa, 'A New Phase for Rice in Japan: Production, Marketing, and Policy Issues', in Tweeten, Dishon *et al.* (eds), *Japanese & American Agriculture*, p. 369; and 'independent distribution rice exchange' – *Mainichi Daily News*, 1 November 1990.

617 See chapter 3 on 'Bureaucratic Politics' in my forthcoming volume, *Politicians and Bureaucrats*.

618 See also the discussion in chapter 8 on 'Policy Campaigning'.

619 Yamauchi, 'Analytical Institutional Economics', p. 26.

620 Yamauchi, 'Analytical Institutional Economics', p. 26.

621 *Mainichi Daily News*, 1 November 1990.

622 *Mainichi Daily News*, 1 November 1990.

623 Domon, *Nokyo Ga Tosan Suru Hi*, p. 75.

624 Domon, *Shinshokuryoho de*, pp. 150–151.

625 *Nihon Keizai Shinbun*, 19 January 1993.

626 *Nihon Keizai Shinbun*, 2 January 1993.

627 See chapter 3 on 'Bureaucratic Politics' in my forthcoming volume, *Politicians and Bureaucrats*.

628 Zenno, for example, effectively controls the distribution of independently distributed rice under its IDR plan which it draws up. Independently distributed rice is bought and sold according to this plan, which is also designated by the MAFF Minister, and thus the Food Agency ultimately controls all the distribution of independently distributed rice. Personal interview with Food Agency official, Tokyo, July 1995.

629 *Yomiuri Shinbun*, 2 November 1994.

630 The collection of orderly marketed rice has been opened up to private companies, including rice wholesalers, retailers and other large private corporations such as Mitsubishi and Mitsui. While these private companies cannot be designated by the Minister as 'voluntarily marketed rice distribution corporations', which prepare the IDR plans as well as engaging in rice collection (i.e. Zenno and Zenshuren), they can be registered as so-called 'first-type shippers' to collect rice from the farmers. Personal interview with Food Agency official, Tokyo, July 1995. See also The Food Agency, *An Outline of New Food Systems: Based on the Law for Stabilization of Supply-Demand and Price of Staple Food*, March 1996, pp. 8–19.

631 *Asahi Shinbun*, 31 October 1995. According to this report, the Sumitomo, Fuji and Mitsubishi banks moved quickly into the rice distribution business as intermediaries between farmers and retailers. The new law permitted farmers to use accounts with commercial banks to receive monies from the sale of rice, rather than its being uniformly deposited in Nokyo bank accounts.

632 *Asahi Shinbun*, 5 November 1996.

633 Personal interview with Food Agency official, Tokyo, July 1995.

634 East Asia Analytical Unit, Department of Foreign Affairs and Trade, 'Agriculture and Food', Draft chapter 11, in *Japan At the Crossroads: Strategies for the 21st Century*, n.d., p. 25, quoting the *Nikkei Weekly*, 30 October 1995.

635 Domon Takeshi, 'Shinshokuryoho de Toku o Suru no wa Ittai Dare' ['Who Will Profit From the New Food Law?'], *Ekonomisuto*, 7 November 1995, p. 82.

636 See also chapter 8 on 'Policy Campaigning'.

637 *Hojokin Soran*, 1998, p. 527.

638 Zenno also managed to persuade the Food Agency to provide subsidies for rice stockpiling under its IDR plan as a designated voluntarily marketed rice distribution corporation. Personal interview with Food Agency official, Tokyo, July 1995.

639 Saeki, *Nokyo Kaikaku*, pp. 41–42.
640 Fujitani, 'Nokyo at a Crossroads', p. 379.
641 'Nokyo at a Crossroads', p. 380.
642 Fujitani, *Nokyo*, p. 11.
643 Saeki, *Nokyo Kaikaku*, p. 32.
644 *Nokyo*, p. 12.
645 Fujitani, *Nokyo*, p. 12.
646 Aguri Fuooramu, 'Tokushu: Nihon no Kome', p. 89.
647 Masuda, 'Nokyo no Keiei Bunseki', p. 64.
648 Hokkaido Koiki Nogyo Kyodo Kumiai and Kajiura, *Datsu Nokyo*, pp. 70–71.
649 Orio, *Dame na Nokyo*, pp. 21, 24.
650 Hokkaido Koiki Nogyo Kyodo Kumiai and Kajiura, *Datsu Nokyo*, pp. 70–71.
651 Hokkaido Koiki Nogyo Kyodo Kumiai and Kajiura, *Datsu Nokyo*, p. 80.
652 Hokkaido Koiki Nogyo Kyodo Kumiai and Kajiura, *Datsu Nokyo*, p. 73.
653 Hokkaido Koiki Nogyo Kyodo Kumiai and Kajiura, *Datsu Nokyo*, p. 76.
654 Hokkaido Koiki Nogyo Kyodo Kumiai and Kajiura, *Datsu Nokyo*, p. 77.
655 Hokkaido Koiki Nogyo Kyodo Kumiai and Kajiura, *Datsu Nokyo*, p. 80.
656 Hokkaido Koiki Nogyo Kyodo Kumiai and Kajiura, *Datsu Nokyo*, p. 77.
657 The four major resolutions of this conference are listed in Zenkoku Nogyo Kyodo Kumiai Chuokai, *Hayawakari JA no Subete*, p. 41. They also included a plan for co-op mergers. See below.
658 Saeki, *Nokyo Kaikaku*, p. 118. This issue is taken up in detail on pp. 132–153 and pp. 169–175 of Saeki's book.
659 *Nikkei Weekly*, 5 August 1996.
660 Saeki, *Nokyo Kaikaku*, pp. 173–174.
661 Ito, 'Soshiki Nidankaika', p. 16. The particular difficulties surrounding the position and functioning of Norinchukin is explained on pp. 16–18.
662 Domon, *Nokyo ga Tosan Suru Hi*, p. 164.
663 Domon, *Nokyo ga Tosan Suru Hi*, p. 164.
664 Fukui, 'Japan Agriculture on the Ropes', p. 29.
665 *Nikkei Weekly*, 5 August 1996.
666 Ito, 'Soshiki Nidankaika', p. 16.
667 *Nikkei Weekly*, 13 July 1998.
668 *Nikkei Weekly*, 5 August 1996.
669 *Reuters*, 11 March 1998.
670 In 1998, Miyagi *keizairen*, along with Shimane and Tottori *keizairen* did, in fact, amalgamate with Zenno. Personal communication with Kobayashi Shinichi, Nihon University, December 1998.
671 *Nikkei Weekly*, 22 January 1996.
672 *Jiji Press Newswire*, 2 July 1996.
673 *Nikkei Weekly*, 5 August 1996.
674 Norinsuisansho, Noseibu Keizaika, 'Nokyo Kaikaku Niho no Kaisei Gaiyo' ['An Outline of Amendments to Two Laws Relating to Nokyo Reform'], http:// www.maff.go.jp.
675 *Nikkei Weekly*, 14 September 1998.
676 Ito, 'Soshiki Nidankaika', p. 18.
677 Ito, 'Soshiki Nidankaika', p. 18.
678 Domon, *Yoi Nokyo*, p. 232. There is an election committee in each district, and it recommends the chairman and directors from amongst the local members. Over time the salary of the elected executives rose and more and more people showed an interest in the position.
679 Domon, *Yoi Nokyo*, p. 235.
680 Fujitani, *Nokyo*, p. 17.

681 *Nihon Keizai Shinbun*, 28 March 1993.
682 Fujitani, 'Nokyo at a Crossroads', p. 379. This plan is outlined in detail in Zenkoku Nogyo Kyodo Kumiai Chuokai, *Hayawakari JA no Subete*, pp. 41–42.
683 Asano, 'Jigyo, Soshiki Kaikaku', p. 60.
684 Domon, *Nokyo ga Tosan Suru Hi*, 1992, p. 42.
685 *Japan Agrinfo Newsletter*, Vol. 12, No. 4, December 1994, p. 6.
686 Domon, *Nokyo ga Tosan Suru Hi*, p. 149.
687 Hokkaido Koiki Nogyo Kyodo Kumiai and Kajiura, *Datsu Nokyo*, p. 72.
688 *Poketto*, 1997, p. 317.
689 This figure is slightly lower than that given for 31 March 1998 in chapter 2 on 'Interest Group Politics' for the reason given. For example, 20 cooperatives in Akita merged into the Akita Obako Agricultural Cooperative; 12 cooperatives in Kochi merged into the Kochi-Hata Agricultural Cooperative; and five cooperatives in Sapporo, Hokkaido, merged into the Sapporo Municipal Agricultural Cooperative. *Japan Agrinfo Newsletter*, Vol. 15, No. 10, June 1998, p. 3.
690 *Japan Agrinfo Newsletter*, Vol. 15, No. 10, June 1998, p. 3. Elsewhere the target figure has been given as 567 by the year 2000. Kudo, 'Nokyo Hatan', p. 12.
691 *Norinsuisansho Tokeihyo*, 1996–97, p. 578.
692 Fruit juice cooperative federations, for example, dwindled to only four – those in Ehime, Kumamoto, Saga and Wakayama – because of competition in the fruit juice market from imported fresh orange juice and concentrated orange juice which expanded dramatically after liberalisation. See also above.
693 Calculated from figures given in *Poketto*, 1997, p. 317.
694 *Norinsuisansho Tokeihyo*, 1996–97, p. 580–581.
695 Kudo, 'Nokyo Hatan', p. 12.
696 Kudo, 'Nokyo Hatan', p. 11.
697 'The Inside Story', p. 26.
698 See chapter 2 on 'Interest Group Politics'.
699 Kudo, 'Nokyo Hatan', p. 11.
700 Kudo, 'Nokyo Hatan', p. 13.
701 Kudo, 'Nokyo Hatan', p. 12.
702 Domon, *Nokyo ga Tosan Suru Hi*, 1992, p. 28.
703 Domon lists several others. See 'The Inside Story', p. 27.
704 Kudo, 'Nokyo Hatan', p. 12.
705 Saeki Naomi quoted in *Nikkei Weekly*, 14 September 1998.
706 Saeki Naomi quoted in *Asia Pulse*, 9 September 1998.
707 Kudo, 'Nokyo Hatan', p. 12.
708 Hokkaido Koiki Nogyo Kyodo Kumiai and Kajiura, *Datsu Nokyo*, p. 73.
709 Kudo, 'Nokyo Hatan', p. 12.
710 Shiraishi Masahiko, 'Kyodo Katsudo Senryaku no Tenkan ni yoru Chiiki Shakai Zukuri no Shintenkan' ['The New Development of the Formation of the Regional Society By Revising the Strategy of Cooperative Activity'], *Nogyo Kyodo Kumiai*, Vol. 61, No. 2, 1995, p. 54.
711 Asano, 'Jigyo, Soshiki Kaikaku', p. 61. Asano reports the results of a nationwide survey on the merits and demerits of *nokyo* mergers in this article.
712 Orio, *Dame na Nokyo*, p. 30.
713 In a Zenchu survey of Nokyo activities, merged cooperatives were asked what were the most important issues to deal with after the merger. Only 35.5 per cent of them replied that they had to improve efforts to guide members, or to give them agricultural management advice. Zenchu Home Page, http://www.rim.or.jp/ci/ja/ejahome.html.
714 Domon, *Nokyo ga Tosan Suru Hi*, p. 42.

715 In the Zenchu survey of Nokyo activities, most of the cooperatives (61.3 per cent) answered that they had to reflect members' opinions in their management as the most important issue to deal with after mergers. Zenchu Home Page, http://www. rim.or.jp/ci/ja/ejahome.html.
716 Zenchu Home Page, http://www.rim.or.jp/ci/ja/ejahome.html.
717 Ishida and George, 'Nokyo', p. 201. See also chapter 8 on 'Policy Campaigning'.
718 Hokkaido Koiki Nogyo Kyodo Kumiai and Kajiura, *Datsu Nokyo*, p. 73.
719 *Nihon Keizai Shinbun*, 22 March 1992.
720 Zenchu Home Page, http://www.rim.or.jp/ci/ja/ejahome.html.
721 Domon, *Nokyo ga Tosan Suru Hi*, p. 151.
722 Hokkaido Koiki Nogyo Kyodo Kumiai and Kajiura, *Datsu Nokyo*, p. 73.
723 Hokkaido Koiki Nogyo Kyodo Kumiai and Kajiura, *Datsu Nokyo*, pp. 47–48.
724 *Nihon Nogyo Nenkan*, 1997, p. 370.
725 *Nihon Nogyo Nenkan*, 1997, p. 370.
726 Hokkaido Koiki Nogyo Kyodo Kumiai and Kajiura, *Datsu Nokyo*, p. 48.
727 There were 2,647,000 commercial farm households in Japan in 1995, and 427,000 full-time farm households. *Poketto*, 1996, p. 122.
728 Hokkaido Koiki Nogyo Kyodo Kumiai and Kajiura, *Datsu Nokyo*, p. 49.
729 Sakaguchi, *Kyodai Nokyo*, p. 121.
730 Domon, *Yoi Nokyo*, 1988, p. 23.
731 'The Summary of Nikkei Business: Cover Story – No More Need for Nokyo's', http://www.nikkeibp.com/News/9604/nb0429.html. This figure may have included white-collar workers in the agricultural bureaucracy.
732 Hokkaido Koiki Nogyo Kyodo Kumiai and Kajiura, *Datsu Nokyo*, p. 49.
733 Hokkaido Koiki Nogyo Kyodo Kumiai and Kajiura, *Datsu Nokyo*, pp. 49–50.
734 Hokkaido Koiki Nogyo Kyodo Kumiai and Kajiura, *Datsu Nokyo*, p. 51.
735 Sakaguchi, *Kyodai Nokyo*, p. 131.
736 Hokkaido Koiki Nogyo Kyodo Kumiai and Kajiura, *Datsu Nokyo*, p. 54.
737 Hokkaido Koiki Nogyo Kyodo Kumiai and Kajiura, *Datsu Nokyo*, pp. 53–54.
738 Hokkaido Koiki Nogyo Kyodo Kumiai and Kajiura, *Datsu Nokyo*, p. 54.
739 Hokkaido Koiki Nogyo Kyodo Kumiai and Kajiura, *Datsu Nokyo*, p. 54.
740 Hokkaido Koiki Nogyo Kyodo Kumiai and Kajiura, *Datsu Nokyo*, p. 53.
741 *Japan Agrinfo Newsletter*, Vol. 12, No. 4, December 1994, p. 6.
742 Kudo, 'Nokyo Hatan', p. 12.
743 *Japan Agrinfo Newsletter*, Vol. 14, No. 1, September 1996, p. 2.
744 *Japan Agrinfo Newsletter*, Vol. 14, No. 1, September 1996, p. 3.
745 *Nikkei Weekly*, 5 August 1996.
746 *Nikkei Weekly*, 27 July 1998.
747 See, for example, the special issue of *Nogyo to Keizai*, Vol. 61, No. 2, 1995. See also the series of structural reform proposals to streamline the agricultural cooperatives and improve their competitive operations advanced by Kano Yoshikazu in the *Daily Yomiuri*, 13 March 1992.
748 See also the discussion on Nokyo in Kajii, 'Nogyo Kosho', p. 128 and Domon, *Nokyo ga Tosan Suru Hi*.
749 *Nikkei Weekly*, 14 September 1998. A similar proposal was advanced by Oshima Tadamori, who suggested that Nokyo's banking activities should be separated from its other business activities. The notion of hiving off Nokyo's credit activities to a separate organisation has a long history going back to the 1950s. See Dore, *Land Reform in Japan*, p. 429. It has been criticised as only viable if *nokyo* economic business becomes efficient at the same time, because without injections from the financial side of the organisation, the other businesses will have to stand on their own feet. Ito, 'Soshiki Nidankaika', p. 18. When interviewed in 1996, the President of Norinchukin, Kakudo Kenichi was opposed to the idea of the *sogo*

nokyo evolving into credit cooperatives. His reasons were: 'We would not be able to prosper if we were to separate the credit business from other businesses of co-ops'; [and] 'other financial institutions, such as regional banks and credit associations, could not do businesses in the agricultural areas because it does not pay. This is what we are for.' *Nikkei Weekly*, 5 August 1996.

750 Saeki, *Nokyo Kaikaku*, pp. 120–121.
751 Saeki, *Nokyo Kaikaku*, pp. 124–126.
752 See *Nokyo*, especially chapter 9, pp. 153–231.
753 These were largely based on the recommendation of APAC in its August 1996 report on Nokyo.
754 A 1992 amendment also effected some changes to the executive/management side. See Zenkoku Nogyo Kyodo Kumiai Chuokai, *Shinpan: Nogyo Kyodo Kumiaiho*, pp. 194–195.
755 These are the main provisions only. See 'Nokyo Kaikaku Niho', http://www.maff. go.jp.
756 *Nihon Keizai Shinbun*, 30 July 1996.
757 *Nihon Keizai Shinbun*, 30 July 1996.
758 Personal interview with former Zenchu Managing Director, Tokyo, July 1995.
759 Sakaguchi, *Kyodai Nokyo*, p. 169.
760 Ogura Takekazu, for example, alleges that Japan does not have any agricultural organisations purely for farmers. While the United States and EU have agricultural organisations that pursue the interests of agriculture, Nokyo appears to be operating solely for its own sake, not for farmers. Quoted in 'Shinpojiumu "Kokusaika Jidai ni Okeru Nogyo", Noson Mondai' ['Symposium on "Agriculture and Farming Villages in an Era of Internationalisation" '], *Nogyo to Keizai*, Vol. 55, No. 5, 1989, p. 49.
761 *Yoi Nokyo*, p. 58.
762 'Shokkan Seido o Nokoshita Kanzeika wa Kiken: Chikazuku Kome Shijo no Kaiho' ['It is Dangerous to Introduce Tariffication Without Abolishing the Food Control System: The Liberalisation of the Rice Market is Approaching'], *Shukan Toyo Keizai*, 20 November 1993, p. 12.
763 'Kanzeika to Shokkan Seido Wa Ryoritsu Shinai' ['Tariffication and the Food Control System are Incompatible'], *Shukan Toyo Keizai*, 20 November, 1993, p. 12. Zenhanren made the same sort of response to the introduction of the IDR system in 1969. In order to preserve the basic framework of the FC system, it faced reality and decided to deal in *jishu ryutsumai*, and in fact to control all of it. Tanaka, *Nihon no Nokyo*, pp. 227–230. See also above.
764 *Far Eastern Economic Review*, 17 November 1988.
765 Sakaguchi, *Kyodai Nokyo*, 1987.
766 Hayami, 'Kaikaku no Keiki', p. 36.
767 Kurata, *Nogyo Kyodo Kumiairon*, p. 267.
768 Many Nokyo officials and supporters are unrepentant in the face of the increasing barrage of criticism. As two of its supporters claim, Nokyo's interests have never been synonymous with Japanese agriculture because it is an organisation of farmers, who stand as agents between Nokyo and agriculture. This explains why Nokyo could continue to expand its businesses as the economy of farm households improved whilst agriculture itself declined. Nagata and Saito, *Nokyo no Hanashi*, pp. 3–4.
769 Fujitani, 'Nokyo at a Crossroads', p. 369.
770 *Far Eastern Economic Review*, 17 November 1988.
771 Hayami, 'Kaikaku no Keiki', p. 36.
772 Matsuda, 'Nokyo no Keiei Bunseki', p. 65.
773 *Asahi Shinbun*, 25 June 1994.

774 'Zenkoku Nokyo no Toppu Jinji ni Irei no Zohan' ['An Unusual Anti-Establishment Move in National Nokyo's Top Personnel'], *Aera*, 27 July 1993, p. 21.
775 Kaiin Toron, 'Norin Kanryo', p. 91.
776 'Koritsuka Suru Norin Kanryo', p. 14.
777 'The Origins of Protectionism', p. 18.
778 Personal interview, Tokyo, July 1995.
779 See Orio, *Dame na Nokyo*, and Domon, *Yoi Nokyo*, as well as the works of Saeki Naomi and Fujitani Chikuji.
780 Hayami, 'Kaikaku no Keiki', p. 35.
781 Personal interview with former Zenchu Managing Director, Tokyo, July 1995.
782 Domon, *Yoi Nokyo*, p. 230.
783 *Nikkei Weekly*, 25 December 1995–1 January 1996.
784 *Nikkei Weekly*, 25 December 1995–1 January 1996.
785 This is the view of Okamoto Matsumi, a free-lance writer on agricultural policy, quoted in *Nikkei Weekly*, 25 December 1995–1 January 1996.
786 Orio, *Dame na Nokyo*, p. 105.
787 Otawara, 'Nokyo no Ichi to Yakuwari', pp. 26–27.
788 Domon, *Yoi Nokyo*, p. 230.
789 *Japan Agrinfo Newsletter*, Vol. 14, No. 1, September 1996, p. 2.
790 *Far Eastern Economic Review*, 11 November 1988.
791 Fujitani, 'Nokyo at a Crossroads', p. 369.
792 'Nokyo to Senkyo', p. 91.
793 See chapter 6 on 'Electoral Politics'.
794 Domon, *Nokyo ga Tosan Suru Hi*, p. 149. Orio also reports that in a more competitive environment, increasing pressure is being put on middle management of the agricultural cooperatives to expand the number of loan contracts through the imposition of individual quotas. Many of them quit because of the burden this imposes. *Dame na Nokyo*, p. 20.
795 Fujitani, 'Nokyo at a Crossroads', pp. 374, 378.
796 Fujitani, 'Nokyo at a Crossroads', p. 378.

5 The political demography of agriculture

1 Tanaka, *Nihon no Nokyo*, p. 424.
2 The earlier period was covered in chapter 3 on 'Farmers' Politics'.
3 *The Economist*, 20 February 1988.
4 The definition of a farm household is one where the area of cultivated land is 10 a or more (a household managing 5 a or more of cultivated land in Western Japan until 1989), or a farm household whose area of cultivated land is below 10 a but whose sales of agricultural products amount to ¥150,000 or more per annum.
5 These figures were obtained from Table 3.9 in Ryohei Kada and Junko Goto, 'Present Issues of Sustainable Land Use Systems and Rural Communities in Japan', in Tweeten *et al.* (eds), *Japanese & American Agriculture*, p. 44.
6 Kada and Goto, 'Present Issues of Sustainable Land Use Systems', p. 43.
7 Kada and Goto, 'Present Issues of Sustainable Land Use Systems', p. 44.
8 Table 3.9 in Kada and Goto, 'Present Issues of Sustainable Land Use Systems', p. 44.
9 Nishihira Shigeki, 'Shosenkyoku Bunrui Kijun no Teian' ['A Proposal for a Classification System for Single-Member Constituencies'], *Chuo Chosaho*, No. 449, March 1995, p. 1.
10 At first glance, aggregate data on the agricultural workforce indicates a dramatic

deterioration in agriculture's contribution to national employment because the most commonly quoted statistics relating to the agricultural labour force aggregate the number of persons engaged in farming as an exclusive or principal occupation. When a person has two or more occupations, only the occupation in which he/she spends the greater number of hours is taken into account in the collection of these statistics as part of the Labour Force Survey done by the Statistics Bureau of the MCA.

11 These are the MCA figures. See *Poketto*, annual, relevant years and *MAFF Update*, No. 265, 26 June 1998, http://www.maff.go.jp.

12 *Poketto*, annual, relevant years.

13 *Poketto*, annual, relevant years. This is the official category of 'persons engaged in own-farming' (*jiei nogyo jujisha*), which refers to farm household members over 16 years of age who are engaged in their own household's agricultural production activities, no matter how limited that engagement is. The 1997 figure covers only those employed either full- or part-time in 'commercial farm households'. From 1991 onwards, the MAFF farm household employment census only covered commercial farm households.

14 See also the discussion below.

15 *Poketto*, 1998, p. 141.

16 This figure was 1,811,000. *Poketto*, 1998, p. 142. It compared with 2,014,000 aged persons over 70 years.

17 Saxon, *Farm Production*, p. 9; *Poketto*, 1995, p. 16.

18 *Japan Agrinfo Newsletter*, Vol. 16, No. 4, December 1998, p. 2.

19 Saxon, *Farm Production*, p. 10; *Japan Agrinfo Newsletter*, Vol. 16, No. 4, December 1998, p. 2, but see also the comments on this particular statistic in chapter 1 'Introduction'.

20 Saxon, *Farm Production*, p. 10; *Japan Agrinfo Newsletter*, Vol. 16, No. 4, December 1998, p. 2; Poketto, 1998, p. 18.

21 *Japan Agrinfo Newsletter*, Vol. 16, No. 4, December 1998, p. 2.

22 Calculated from the figures in *Norinsuisansho Tokeihyo*, 1996–1997, pp. 4, 18–19.

23 Dore, 'The Socialist Party, p. 370.

24 Inoguchi Takashi and Iwai Tomoaki, '*Zoku Giin' no Kenkyu* [*Research on 'Tribe Diet Members'*], Tokyo, Nihon Keizai Shinbunsha, 1987, p. 188.

25 This is because in prefectural constituencies with two seats, only one seat is contested in any given UH election.

26 Calculated from figures in *Mainichi Shinbun*, 24 July 1995.

27 This issue is explored below and in chapter 6 on 'Electoral Politics' as part of the examination of the possible effects of electoral reform on Nokyo's electoral and interest group influence.

28 One analyst reasoned that even if a Diet member obtained 80 per cent of his/her support from urban dwellers and 20 per cent from rural areas, that 20 per cent could make the difference between success and failure. Arimitsu, *Seito to Beika Seisaku*, p. 108.

29 In practice, of course, because prefectures were divided up into a number of different LH districts, the prefectural percentage of farm votes would not translate evenly across LH electorates. They would be higher in some and lower in others depending on the location of the geographical boundaries of the constituencies in relation to relative concentrations of farm population.

30 *Poketto*, 1998, p. 156.

31 Nagata and Saito, *Nokyo no Hanashi*, p. 6. Elsewhere they note that agricultural households dipped from 44 per cent of the total in an average agricultural village in 1965 to 23 per cent in 1980 (p. 168).

32 Kyosanto Bukkuretto, *Gaiatsu no Naka no Nihon*, p. 28.

33 Kyosanto Bukkuretto, *Gaiatsu no Naka no Nihon*, p. 28. This development was hastened by the relocation of manufacturing industry to rural areas as Japan's economy grew.

34 Nosei no Shoten V [Focus on Agricultural Policy V], 'Saninsen ni Miru Nominhyo no Doko' ['Movement of Farmers' Votes in the Upper House Election'], in Nosei Jyaanarisuto no Kai (ed.), *Nihon Nogyo ni Mirai Wa Aru Ka?*, p. 184. See also the discussion in chapter 6 on 'Electoral Politics'.

35 Okamoto Matsuzo, 'Nomin no Seiji Ishiki no Henka' ['Changes in the Farmers' Political Consciousness'], *Gijutsu to Fukyu*, Vol. 8, No. 10, September 1971, p. 21.

36 Okamoto, 'Nomin no Seiji Ishiki', p. 22.

37 See chapter 2 on 'Interest Group Politics'.

38 Okamoto, 'Nomin no Seiji Ishiki', p. 23.

39 Atsumi Shigeyuki, ' "Tohoku Kessen" de Nani ga Kawatta ka' ['What Has Changed in the "Tohoku Showdown"?'], in Nosei Jyaanarisuto no Kai (ed.), *Tatoka Jidai no Nosei*, p. 175.

40 Atsumi, "Tohoku Kessen", pp. 179–181.

41 Saeki, *Nokyo Kaikaku*, p. 32.

42 Kada and Goto, 'Present Issues of Sustainable Land Use Systems', p. 456.

43 See also chapter 6 on 'Electoral Politics'.

44 *Nihon no Noson*, p. 244.

45 Fukui, 'The Japanese Farmer', p. 158.

46 *Nihon no Nokyo*, p. 425.

47 Yamamoto Eiji, 'Sengo Nosonhyo no Rekishiteki Bunseki' ['An Historical Analysis of the Farm Vote in the Postwar Period'], in Ishiwata (ed.), *Nomin to Senkyo*, p. 23.

48 Nakamura, 'Nominhyo no Pawaa', p. 111.

49 Moore, *Japanese Agriculture*, p. 209.

50 Moore, *Japanese Agriculture*, p. 209.

51 Goto and Imamura, 'Japanese Agriculture', pp. 12–13.

52 The MAFF definition is 'naturally occurring regional societies, in which households are linked by locality and by blood, and which are the fundamental regional units of social activities that have formed around all types of groups and social relations.' *Poketto*, 1997, p. 116. The term *nogyo shuraku* is used in the agricultural census and in official statistics because it is preferred to the term *buraku* (village hamlet) given the pejorative connotations of the latter. The problem is that *buraku* has two meanings: the first is a natural hamlet within larger villages (*mura*) in which members are closely tied through kinship and locational affinity. The second meaning is a community or hamlet of outcaste people who were removed from the village registry and thus excluded from the four social classes of warriors, farmers, artisans and merchants (*shinokosho*). These outcastes became the Japanese 'untouchables' called *burakumin* (other terms to describe these people were *eta* meaning 'abundant filth' and *hinin* meaning 'non-human'). Excluded from society, they assumed occupations involving matters of the flesh, such as burying the dead, slaughtering animals, leather-making, meat-handling and so on. The descendants of these people are severely discriminated against in Japanese society today, and so use of the term *buraku* is avoided. People who live in the countryside, however, often use the term *buraku* to refer to their own villages. The author is grateful to Kawagoe Toshihiko, Shimizu Tetsuro and Arthur Stockwin for their views on *buraku* and *nogyo shuraku*. See also chapter 4 on 'Organisational Politics' and chapter 6 on 'Electoral Politics'.

53 Kada and Goto, 'Present Issues of Sustainable Land Use Systems', p. 42.

54 Kada and Goto, 'Present Issues of Sustainable Land Use Systems', p. 42.

55 Kada and Goto, 'Present Issues of Sustainable Land Use Systems', p. 42.

56 Kada and Goto, 'Present Issues of Sustainable Land Use Systems', p. 42.
57 Kada and Goto, 'Present Issues of Sustainable Land Use Systems', pp. 42–43.
58 Kada and Goto, 'Present Issues of Sustainable Land Use Systems', p. 47. Ishida and George comment, however, that changing methods of agricultural production including the introduction of cultivators and harvesters and other farm machinery reduced the need for cooperation at the village level. 'Nokyo', p. 199.
59 See chapter 4 on 'Organisational Politics'.
60 *Poketto*, 1998, p. 118.
61 Kada and Goto, 'Present Issues of Sustainable Land Use Systems', p. 45.
62 Kada and Goto, 'Present Issues of Sustainable Land Use Systems', p. 45.
63 As Kada and Goto point out: 'More than 75 percent of rural communities and rural households are less than one hour away from nearby urban centers'. 'Present Issues of Sustainable Land Use Systems', p. 46.
64 Keeler, 'Agricultural Power', p. 130.
65 Keeler, 'Agricultural Power', p. 130.
66 See chapter 1 'Introduction' and chapter 6 on 'Electoral Politics'. See also chapter 4 on 'Patronage Politics' in my forthcoming volume, *Politicians and Bureaucrats*.
67 Dore argued the case strongly in the 1950s that the strength of kinship ties within farm families was such that farm households could rightly be considered cohesive membership units of Nokyo. In his early work on the agricultural cooperatives as part of his larger study of land reform in Japan, he noted that in the agricultural cooperative system 'the effective members are households'. See *Land Reform in Japan*, p. 278. These days, a farm can hold both types of membership. Although only one regular individual member used to be permitted per farm household, this was later changed to multiple members. See chapter 4 on 'Organisational Politics'.
68 See chapter 4 on 'Organisational Politics' and the discussion below.
69 Ishida, *Interest Groups*, p. 11.
70 These figures were calculated by multiplying the average number of persons 20 years and over residing in farm households in that year by the number of regular membership households in the *sogo nokyo*.
71 *Poketto*, 1995, p. 116, and *Nihon Nogyo Nenkan*, 1997, p. 613. According to one Nokyo source, however, the figure of 4.8 million agricultural cooperative farm household members in 1993 included farm households that were close to abandoning agriculture as well as those who had actually left agriculture, but they remained on the books as regular member households. The number of farm households that were actually engaged in agriculture and supported Nokyo was lower at 3.69 million (in other words, just above the MAFF figure). Hokkaido Koiki Nogyo Kyodo Kumiai and Kajiura, *Datsu Nokyo*, pp. 48–49.
72 The percentage for the Nokyo voting electorate was obtained by taking the number of eligible voters residing in farm households with Nokyo membership in 1994 (calculated in the same way as the national agricultural electorate) as a percentage of the total number of eligible voters in Japan in 1995 (see Table 5.1).
73 This percentage was obtained by using Nokyo's individual farmer membership figures for 1994 (5.45 million) as a percentage of the total national electorate in 1995. In 1996, the percentage was still 5.6 per cent (5.44 million individual farmer members of Nokyo in 1996 out of a total national eligible voting population of 97.7 million in the same year).
74 Ito Kenzo, quoted in the *Australian Financial Review*, 27 February 1986.
75 *Australian Financial Review*, 27 February 1986.
76 *Nikkei Weekly*, 30 September 1996.
77 For example, the neo-Buddhist sect Soka Gakkai which has traditionally

provided the grass-roots voting base for the Clean Government Party, or CGP, has 10 million members and the Japanese Trade Union Confederation (Rengo) has 7.66 million. *Nikkei Weekly*, 4 August 1997.

78 He argues that while the basis of Nokyo elections is the hard votes of members, Nokyo also extends its vote-gathering tentacles outside the organisation to include co-op members' relatives, acquaintances, shops where members go to buy goods, school teachers through their children and customers (clients and business connections) of Nokyo. *Nokyo*, p. 315.

79 Aono's computation of Nokyo's potential voting power is as follows: (all figures were for 1973, although he incorrectly states that they were for 1975): 5,818,249 regular members in co-ops (individuals 5,818,336 and groups 4,913); 1,720,166 associate members in co-ops (individuals 1,674,330 and groups 45,836); executive and staff members in general-purpose co-ops 352,264 (this is in fact the total figure for staff members in the entire Nokyo organisation); in specialist co-ops 28,879; in prefectural federations 62,918; and in national federations 6,419; plus an unknown quantity of those employed in Nokyo's 1,000 or more 'related companies'. *Nokyo*, p. 21.

80 But see also comments in chapter 2 on 'Interest Group Politics' and chapter 6 on 'Electoral Politics'.

81 These figures are based on research done by Tachibana Takashi and reported in *Nokyo*, pp. 346–348. It should be noted that farmers' political leagues did not operate in all prefectures, and that in some prefectures, Tachibana was unable to put a figure on the self-proclaimed vote-collection capacity of the leagues (see Table 6.5). The 4.62 million, therefore, represents only a minimum figure in this respect. Where the figures for some prefectural farmers' political leagues varied over a range, the mid-point in the range was taken.

82 *Japan Agrinfo Newsletter*, Vol. 15, No. 5, January 1998, p. 2. The proportion in 1998 was 27.1 per cent. *Japan Agrinfo Newsletter*, Vol. 16, No. 4, December 1998, p. 2.

83 *Japan Agrinfo Newsletter*, Vol. 15, No. 6, February 1998, p. 7.

84 These figures were taken from Naraomi Imamura, Nobuhiro Tsuboi and Tokumi Odagiri, 'Japanese Farm Structure: Trends and Projections', in Tweeten *et al.* (eds), *Japanese & American Agriculture*, p. 60. MAFF's own projections in 1998 estimated that one-half of persons engaged in agriculture (or 740,000) would be 65 years old or older by 2010. *Nikkei Weekly*, September, 1998. This is despite the fact that the number of people entering farming directly after graduating from school is recording quite significant increases in the late 1990s. It increased by 10 per cent to 2,200 in 1998 for example. *Japan Agrinfo Newsletter*, Vol. 16, No. 4, December 1998, p. 2.

85 Suda Toshihiko, 'Nihon Nogyo Saisei no Joken o Kangaeru' ['Considering Conditions for the Revival of Japanese Agriculture'], *Keizai Zeminaru*, Tokyo, Nihon Hyoronsha, December 1993, p. 17.

86 As Goto and Imamura point out, the meaning of 'successors' is very ambiguous: 'It refers to those who take responsibility as the next family head of the particular household (which happens to be a farm household) and does not necessarily mean that they commit themselves to farming. Thus the real successors of farming are few in number.' 'Japanese Agriculture', p. 21.

87 Domon puts the figure at 1800. *Nokyo ga Tosan Suru Hi*, p. 219.

88 Domon, *Nokyo ga Tosan Suru Hi*, p. 219.

89 *Poketto*, 1998, p. 23.

90 *Japan Agrinfo Newsletter*, Vol. 14, No. 2, October 1996, p. 3. One of the reasons given was competition from farm imports. *Nikkei Weekly*, 22 April 1996.

91 *Norinsuisansho Tokeihyo*, 1996–97, pp. 172–173.

92 *Japan Agrinfo Newsletter*, Vol. 14, No. 2, October 1996, p. 3.
93 *Norinsuisansho Tokeihyo*, 1996–97, pp. 172–173.
94 According to a survey undertaken by the MAFF in October 1995, one of the reasons why the sons and daughters of farmers work mainly in other industries is because they 'cannot make a living with income only from farming' (42 per cent of those surveyed). *Japan Agrinfo Newsletter*, Vol. 14, No. 2, October 1996, p. 3.
95 See also the social and economic factors discussed in Tsuboi, 'Appendix', pp. 63–69.
96 Tsuboi, 'Appendix', p. 66.
97 Suda, 'Nihon Nogyo Saisei', p. 18.
98 Norinsuisansho, *Nogyo Hakusho* [*Agricultural White Paper*], 1992, Tokyo, Norin Tokei Kyokai, 1993 (hereafter *Nogyo Hakusho*), p. 176. According to a Nokyo survey of farm households in July 1991, only 25.8 per cent of respondents answered that they had a successor either now or in the near future, while nearly 60 per cent answered that they did not. Domon, *Nokyo ga Tosan Suru Hi*, p. 220.
99 *Nogyo Hakusho*, 1992, pp. 176–177.
100 *Japan Agrinfo Newsletter*, Vol. 15, No. 6, February 1998, p. 7.
101 *Nogyo Hakusho*, 1992, p. 176. Other factors cited are 'price stabilisation of farm products' and 'acquisition of farmland to expand farm management'. *Japan Agrinfo Newsletter*, Vol. 14, No. 2, October 1996, p. 3.
102 The trend, however, was especially apparent among people aged 65 or above, especially women. *Japan Agrinfo Newsletter*, Vol. 16, No. 1, September 1998, p. 2.
103 *Asahi Shinbun*, 22 April 1992.
104 These were quoted in Imamura, Tsuboi and Odagiri, 'Japanese Farm Structure', p. 59.
105 *Japan Agrinfo Newsletter*, Vol. 9, No. 10, June 1992, p. 2.
106 Zenchu Home page, http://www.rim.or.jp/ci/ja/ejahome.html.
107 The basis of categorisation of these electoral districts is unknown. See Kobayashi Yoshiaki, *Gendai Nihon no Senkyo* [*Contemporary Japanese Elections*], Tokyo, Tokyo Daigaku Shuppankai, 1991, p. 14.
108 This is a different basis of calculation from that used in Table 5.2 which uses farm voters as a proportion of the total number of eligible voters in the prefecture. Table 5.3 uses farm household population as a percentage of the total population residing in the prefecture, which in fact understates somewhat the weight of the farm vote.
109 The definition of primary industry employment (i.e. in terms of hours worked per week etc.) used as the basis of this table is unknown.
110 This is defined as the share of the population residing in population-concentrated zones in the total population of villages, towns and cities. According to the definition used in the national census since 1960, a 'population concentrated zone' is an area where several census units, which have a population density higher than 4,000 per square kilometre, are adjacent, and the total population exceeds 5,000. The ratio of population concentration in each electorate indicates the percentage of the population living in highly populated zones in the total population of the electorate. In other words, the degree of urbanisation in each electorate is measured in terms of population concentration. Nishihira, 'Shosenkyoku Bunrui Kijun no Teian', pp. 4097–4098.
111 This figure was calculated by multiplying the average number of persons 20 years and over in farm households (3.47) in 1995 by the number of commercial farm households producing rice in the same year (2.35 million). The latter figure was obtained from *Poketto*, 1998, p. 179.
112 This figure was reached in the same way as the comparable 1995 figure. The average number of persons 20 years and over in farm households in 1985 (3.5) was

multiplied by the number of farm households producing rice in 1985 (3.0 million). The latter figure was obtained from *Poketto*, 1996, p. 178.

113 The number of total eligible voters in 1986 was used to make this calculation.

114 This figure was reached by multiplying the average number of persons 20 years and over in farm households (3.47) in 1995 by the number of commercial farm households marketing rice in the same year (2.04 million). The latter figure was obtained from *Poketto*, 1998, p. 179.

115 This figure was reached by multiplying the average number of persons 20 years and over in farm households in 1985 (3.5) by the number of farm households marketing rice in 1985 (2.6). The latter figure was obtained from *Poketto*, 1996, p. 178.

116 The figure for the national electorate in 1986 was used to make this calculation.

117 These figures are for 1995 and are for rice-producing households. Rice-marketing households are somewhat less in number. *Poketto*, 1998, p. 179.

118 These figures are for 1997 and have been rounded. *Norinsuisansho Tokeihyo*, 1996–97, p. 10.

119 *Norinsuisansho Tokeihyo*, 1996–97, p. 10.

120 *Poketto*, 1997, p. 276; *Norinsuisansho Tokeihyo*, 1996–97, p. 122. See also Table 1.2.

121 These figures were calculated by multiplying the number of farm households raising dairy cattle in 1965 by the average number of voters per farm household in that year, and doing the same thing for 1995.

122 *Poketto*, 1997, p. 277.

123 These voting figures were calculated in the same way as voting numbers for dairy cattle-raising farmers.

124 The Annual Report on Agriculture compiled by the MAFF and reported in *Japan Agrinfo Newsletter*, Vol. 13, No. 11, July 1996, p. 4.

125 These figures are for 1996 and have been calculated in the same way as for rice votes. Producer household numbers were obtained from *Norinsuisansho Tokeihyo*, 1996–97, p. 118.

126 See chapter 8 on 'Gaiatsu Politics' in my forthcoming volume, *The Challenge to Vested Interests*.

127 These figures are for 1996 and have been calculated in the same way as for rice votes. Producer household numbers were obtained from *Norinsuisansho Tokeihyo*, 1996–97, p. 119.

128 *Poketto*, 1997, p. 281.

129 *Norinsuisansho Tokeihyo*, 1996–97, p. 120.

130 Other citrus include the two categories of summer *mikan* (*natsu mikan*), and 'others' such as grapefruit and navel oranges, but these categories are relatively small in numbers of households involved. In 1995 they numbered 16,000 and 68,000 respectively. *Poketto*, 1998, p. 227.

131 *Poketto*, 1995, p. 220; *Poketto*, 1998, p. 227.

132 Calculated from figures in *Poketto*, 1998, p. 228. These calculations are for 1997.

133 These figures are for 1997 and were calculated in the same way as those for other commodities above. Figures for specialist fruit growers were obtained from *Norinsuisansho Tokeihyo*, 1996–97, p. 10.

134 These figures are for 1995 and were calculated in the same way as for other commodities. Unless otherwise specified, Table 1.2 is the source for numbers of farm households marketing this product and those discussed below.

135 James Parker, US official responsible for agricultural affairs at the US Embassy in Japan, quoted in the *Daily Yomiuri*, 3 May 1993.

136 *Far Eastern Economic Review*, 17 November 1988.

137 *Far Eastern Economic Review*, 17 December 1988.

138 *Far Eastern Economic Review*, 17 December 1988.
139 *Far Eastern Economic Review*, 17 December 1988.
140 This is, in fact, the 1985 figure. *Poketto*, 1989, p. 205.
141 Other factors may have also been involved, such as the central government's discriminatory policies across the board for Okinawans.
142 *Poketto*, 1998, pp. 201 and 221. See also Table 1.2.
143 *Poketto*, annual, relevant years; *Norinsuisansho Tokeihyo*, 1996–97, p. 107.
144 *Norinsuisansho Tokeihyo*, 1996–97, p. 107.
145 George, *The Strategies of Influence*, p. 146.
146 Ross Smiley in fact notes in his comprehensive study of Japanese electoral distribution that at the time of the special population survey of April 1947, the number of city dwellers amounted to only 33 per cent of the population. 'Japanese Electoral Distribution and Its Political Consequences 1947–1990', MA Thesis, University of Sydney, 1990, p. 48.
147 Smiley, 'Japanese Electoral Distribution', 'Abstract', n.p.g.
148 Tanaka, *Nihon no Nokyo*, p. 424. As Smiley points out, 'since 1967 the LDP . . . won an average of only 15 seats because of malapportionment. Even so, this margin was sufficient at three elections (1976, 1979 1983) to preserve the LDP from coalition or opposition, and thus perpetuate its rule' 'Abstract', n.p.g.
149 Smiley notes for example that the JSP gained an average of three additional seats in every election after 1967. 'Abstract', n.p.g.
150 Smiley, *Japanese Electoral Distribution*, 'Abstract', n.p.g.
151 In 1972 there were 247 rural and semi-rural seats out of a total of 491 (50.3 per cent). These contained 27,941,165 eligible voters out of a total of 73,770,000 (or 37.8 per cent) in the same year. These figures were calculated from data on the ratio of population in each electorate living in cities as opposed to counties (*shigunbu hiritsu*) found in Miyagawa Takayoshi (ed.), *Seiji Handobukku [A Handbook of Politics]*, Tokyo, Seiji Koho Senta, 1972 (hereafter *Seiji Handobukku*), pp. 203–264. All electorates were ranked by the author from 1 to 124 on an urbanisation continuum with the lower two quartiles classed as semi-rural and rural and the upper two quartiles classified as urban and metropolitan respectively. Categorised in this manner 'semi-rural' falls between 55.95 and 67.48 per cent of population living in cities, and 'rural' between 12.84 and 55.48 per cent.
152 Soma, *Kokumin no Sentaku*, pp. 117–119.
153 In that year, there were 152 seats in rural and semi-rural districts (or 29.75 per cent), with a combined total of 17,302,136 eligible voters (21.7 per cent of the total national electorate of 79,642,680). The categorisation of rural and semi-rural districts was based on Nishihira Shigeki's categorisation of population employed in primary industry according to the 1975 Japanese national census. In rural electorates 40 per cent and above were employed in primary industry; in semi-rural electorates 30–39 per cent were employed in primary industry. Nishihira's data was kindly supplied to the author by J. A. A. Stockwin.
154 Difficulties face legal challenges to disproportionate voting values in electorates to the Upper House. The first is the fact that the house is never dissolved, and therefore could not be dissolved as a result of a Supreme Court ruling that an election was invalid. The second is the view that the house is something akin to a 'states' house' in the Japanese context, meaning that it has a regional representation dynamic that leans more towards equality of prefectural representation rather than voter representation. See Smiley, 'Japanese Electoral Distribution', p. 133. See also below.
155 A number of political parties have drawn up plans to reduce the size of the Upper House by 5–10 per cent. The LDP's plan proposes to cut UH membership by 10, with Kagoshima, Ibaraki and Okayama targeted for reductions. This will

ameliorate some of the worst aspects of the current distortions in voting values in the UH electoral system and thus help to rectify the rural-urban imbalance. The plan is to introduce the new system by the time of the next UH election in 2001. Although the seat reduction idea has wide cross-party support, it is a different story for the various proposals to reorganise the UH election system.

156 It was 512 between 1986 and 1992. Prior to the 1993 LH election, the number of constituencies was reduced by one to 129, and the number of seats by one to 511 with the abolition of the Amami Islands electorate.

157 The Supreme Court has shown itself unwilling to make a comparable resolution in relation to the Upper House. It issued a judgement in September 1998 rejecting voters claims that the disparity of 4.97:1 in the 1995 UH election was unconstitutional. Its ruling stated that the inequality in voter representation between regions was 'not so great that it cannot be overlooked'. It justified its stance on the basis of the 'special nature' of the Upper House, in particular the election of Diet members more or less as representatives of each prefecture. *Nikkei Weekly*, 7 September 1998.

158 Smiley, 'Japanese Electoral Distribution', p. 136.

159 Smiley, 'Japanese Electoral Distribution', p. 136.

160 Smiley, 'Japanese Electoral Distribution', pp. 136–137.

161 The constituencies in question were Kanagawa (4) with 304,673 voters per seat and Nagano (3) with 104,170 voters per seat. See *Seiji Handobukku*, 1987, pp. 212–254.

162 As Curtis correctly points out, they also of course, cushioned the LDP against the impact of these same demographic changes. Gerald Curtis, *The Japanese Way of Politics*, New York, Columbia University Press, 1988, p. 51.

163 Peter F. Cowhey, 'Domestic Institutions and The Credibility of International Commitments: Japan and the United States', *International Organization*, Vol. 47, No. 2, Spring 1993, p. 317.

164 These are explored further below.

165 As Wada explains: 'The Lower House slipped in a rule that is advantageous for less populous prefectures. It provided one seat for each prefecture at first, and after that the rest of the seats are assigned by the method of largest remainders. Because of this rule, if we add the single-member district parts to proportional representation parts, the Minami-Kanto proportional representation area (Chiba, Kanagawa and Yamanashi) has fewer representatives than the Tokai area (Gifu, Shizuoka, Aichi and Mie), although its population is higher. *The Japanese Election System*, p. 4.

166 Personal interview with Zenkoku Noseikyo Secretariat Chief, Tokyo, July 1995.

167 See below for a further discussion of the strength of agricultural representation in the new LH electoral system.

168 Sugita Yuji, 'Seiji Kiban no Henka to Nosei no Hoko o Do Miru Ka' ['How Should We view Changes in the Basis of Politics and Directions in Agricultural Policy?'], *Nogyo to Keizai*, Vol. 63, No. 4, March 1997, p. 8.

169 *The Japan Times*, 12 August, 1994.

170 Albert L. Seligmann, 'Japan's New Electoral System: Has Anything Changed?', *Asian Survey*, Vol. 37, No. 5, May 1997, p. 414. Expressed in another way, voters in Shimane (3), the least populous district, enjoyed a greater than 2:1 advantage over voters in some 60 of the most densely populated electorates (which comprised 20 per cent of the total). *Asahi Shinbun*, 12 January 1996.

171 The new electoral legislation makes provision for regular reviews of seat boundaries to reflect demographic changes.

172 'Nogyosha Nosei Undo no Kongo no Arikata' ['What Farmers' Agricultural Policy Campaigns Should Be in the Future'], *Nosei Undo Jyaanaru*, Vol. 1, p. 15.

173 See chapter 6 on 'Electoral Politics'.
174 Sugita, 'Seiji Kiban no Henka', p. 9.
175 Iwamoto, *Hachiju Nendai*, p. 92; Tanaka, *Nihon no Nokyo*, p. 424; Nishihira, 'Chosenkyoku Bunrui Kijun no Teian', p. 4097.
176 This is based on research conducted by the Clean Elections League and reported in Soma, *Kokumin no Sentaku*, pp. 128–135.
177 Soma, *Kokumin no Sentaku*, pp. 131–132.
178 This poll was reported in Nakamura Yasutsugu, 'Kaifuku Shita Jiminto Shiji: Noringyogyosha no Seiji Ishiki' ['Recovery of the LDP's Popularity: The Political Consciousness of Farmers, Foresters and Fisherfolk'], in Nosei Jyaanarisuto no Kai (ed.), *Tatoka Jidai no Nosei*, p. 203.
179 This was a small splinter group from the LDP which broke away in 1976 because of the Lockheed scandal. It was led by Kono Yohei who subsequently rejoined the LDP in 1986.
180 Nakamura, 'Kaifuku Shita Jiminto Shiji', p. 203.
181 Nakamura, 'Kaifuku Shita Jiminto Shiji', pp. 205–207.
182 Iwamoto, *Hachiju Nendai*, p. 96.
183 See Table 3-1a in Miyake, *Tohyo Kodo*, p. 88.
184 Miyake Ichiro, '89-Nen Sangiin Senkyo to "Seito Saihensei"' ['The 1989 Upper House Election and "Party Realignment"']. *Rebuaiasan*, Vol. 10, Spring 1992, pp. 32–61. See also chapter 6 on 'Electoral Politics'.
185 See Table 1 in Miyake, '89-Nen Sangiin Senkyo', p. 36.
186 See chapter 6 on 'Electoral Politics'.
187 Nakamura, 'Nominhyo no Pawaa', p. 116. Iwamoto also cites the 'traditional conservatism in villages' along with other factors (see below). *Hachiju Nendai*, pp. 93, 97.
188 Tanaka, *Nihon no Nokyo*, p. 425.
189 Ishiwata, 'Nomin to Seiji', pp. 14–15.
190 Yamamoto, 'Sengo Nosonhyo', p. 41.
191 *Nihon no Noson*, p. 245.
192 See also chapter 6 on 'Electoral Politics'.
193 Yamamoto, 'Sengo Nosonhyo', p. 41. This same argument is advanced by Ono, in *No to Shoku*, pp. 66–68.
194 Okazaki Isamu, 'Seiken Seito no Jikkoryoku ni Kitai o Kaketa ga' ['Placing Hopes on the Ruling Party's Ability to Take Action'], in Nosei Jyaanarisuto no Kai (ed.), *Senkyo, Beika, Nokyo*, p. 85.
195 See also Nakamura, 'Nominhyo no Pawaa', p. 116.
196 See chapter 3 on 'Farmers' Politics'.
197 Dore, *Land Reform in Japan*, 2nd edition, p. 413.
198 Dore, *Land Reform in Japan*, 2nd edition, p. 413.
199 See also chapter 6 on 'Electoral Politics'.
200 Fukutake, *Nihon no Noson*, p. 229. As noted in chapter 1, the agricultural policy issues that concern farmers most at electoral level are those that impact on farm incomes such as support and stabilisation prices, taxation, agricultural trade liberalisation, and concessional loans and subsidies for various agricultural development schemes.
201 See chapter 7 on 'Representative Politics'.
202 Fukutake, *Nihon no Noson*, p. 248.
203 Ono, *No to Shoku*, p. 79.
204 Ono, *No to Shoku*, pp. 68–69.
205 'Nomin no Seiji Ishiki', p. 23.
206 Ikeyama Kiyomi, 'Sengo Seiji no Sokessan ni Jishin Tsuyomeru Nakasone Shuso' ['Prime Minister Nakasone's Strengthening Confidence in Settling the Postwar

Political Accounts'], in Nosei Jyaanarisuto no Kai (ed.), *Senkyo, Beika, Nokyo*, p. 19.

207 See chapter 4 on 'Opposition Party Politics' in my forthcoming volume, *The Challenge to Vested Interests*.

208 Iwamoto, *Hachiju Nendai*, pp. 93, 97.

209 Fukutake, *Nihon no Noson*, p. 248. See also the discussion on locality conscious-ness as a voting determinant in chapter 6 on Electoral Politics'.

210 See chapter 4 on 'Patronage Politics' in my forthcoming volume, *Politics and Bureaucrats*.

211 Yamamoto, 'Sengo Nosonhyo', p. 39.

212 Ishiwata, 'Nomin to Seiji', p. 11.

213 Fukutake, *Nihon no Noson*, p. 230.

214 The national election study in Japan established that LDP voters were much more likely to base their vote on considerations relating to the candidates who made efforts on behalf of local interests than were Opposition party supporters. In the 1969 elections it was 37 per cent rising to 51 per cent in 1986. Miyake, *Tohyo Kodo*, p. 62. The national election study referred to here was compiled as part of the Japan Election Study, or JES.

215 Masaru Kohno, 'Rational Foundations for the Organization of the Liberal Democratic Party in Japan', *World Politics*, Vol. 44, No. 3, April 1992, p. 382.

216 Kobayashi, Shinohara and Soma, *Senkyo*, p. 78.

217 See Miyake, *Tohyo Kodo*, pp. 58–64. See also chapter 6 on 'Electoral Politics'.

218 Sakai points out that one of the reasons for the popularity of Tanaka Kakuei amongst farmers was the fact that during election campaigns, construction companies that depended on Tanaka's political power, made every effort to attract the votes of part-time farmers, who earned a substantial part of their income from part-time jobs in the construction industry. '"To yori Hito"', pp. 102–104. See also chapter 4 on 'Patronage Politics' in my forthcoming volume, *Politicians and Bureaucrats*.

219 Miyake reports that in 1965, 27 per cent of industrial workers were LDP supporters, but by 1985, this proportion had risen to 49 per cent, which rep-resented 12 per cent of the total number of LDP supporters. *Tohyo Kodo*, p. 88. See also below.

220 This issue is examined in detail in chapter 6 on 'Electoral Politics'.

221 Ikuo Kabashima and Yoshito Ishio, 'The Instability of Party Identification Among Eligible Japanese Voters', *Party Politics*, Vol. 4, No. 2, April 1998, p. 164.

222 Soma, *Kokumin no Sentaku*, pp. 249–253.

223 Soma demonstrated the opposite to be largely true of the JCP, the DSP and the Komeito, with the Komeito and JCP more dependent on metropolitan and urban votes than any of the other parties. The distribution of support for the JSP, he found, was remarkably evenly balanced across all types of electorates. *Kokumin no Sentaku*, pp. 249–253.

224 Soma, *Kokumin no Sentaku*, p. 263.

225 Soma, *Kokumin no Sentaku*, p. 263. This is not to say that the LDP did uniformly well in all rural constituencies in all elections. See the discussion in chapter 6 on 'Electoral Politics'.

226 Soma, *Kokumin no Sentaku*, p. 263.

227 Taguchi Fukuji, 'Sosenkyo to Nominhyo no Yukue' ['General Elections and Trends in Farmers' Votes'], *Nogyo Kyodo Kumiai*, February 1973, pp. 16–17. He borrowed heavily from some of Shinohara's work published in the *Asahi Jyaanaru*, December 1972.

228 *Nihon no Nokyo*, p. 424.
229 See Nishihira Shigeki, 'An Anatomy of the 1976 Election', *Japan Echo*, Vol. IV, No. 2, 1977, pp. 67–76.
230 See Table 11 in J. A. A. Stockwin, *Japan: Divided Politics in a Growth Economy*, London, Weidenfeld & Nicolson, 1975, p. 100.
231 This point has been taken up by Kabashima who argues that the marked variations in LDP performance over this period were largely due to money politics scandals affecting the party (e.g. the 1983 elections), and the impact of what he calls 'buffer players', that is voters who punish the party for its corrupt transgressions in particular elections but who then return to the LDP fold in later elections. Kabashima Ikuo, *Kokusaika to Nihon no Seiji [Internationalisation and Japanese Politics]*, Tokyo, Zenkoku Noseikyo, 1997, pp. 11–12.
232 The 1993 election is considered a special case and will be discussed below.
233 *Gendai Nihon no Senkyo*, p. 18.
234 See chapter 2 on 'Party Politics' in my forthcoming volume on *Politicians and Bureaucrats*.
235 The election in 1993 was complicated by the fragmentation of political parties and will be discussed below.
236 See also the commentary on the 1990 elections in chapter 6 on 'Electoral Politics'.
237 This table deliberately does not take account of the slide in the numbers employed in primary industry between 1975 (the year in which the census figures for employment were compiled) and 1993, because its purpose is to demonstrate LDP performance in the same categories of constituencies over time.
238 The more recent 1993 results will be examined below.
239 Hirose Michisada, 'Dojitsu Senkyo ni Miru Nominhyo no Ugoki' ['The Movement of Farmers' Votes Seen in the Double Elections'], in Nosei Jyaanarisuto no Kai (ed.), *Senkyo, Beika, Nokyo*, p. 27.
240 This distinction is highlighted in Otake Hideo, 'Forces for Political Reform: The Liberal Democratic Party's Young Reformers and Ozawa Ichiro', *Journal of Japanese Studies*, Vol. 22, No. 2, 1996, pp. 269–294.
241 The total LDP vote in all constituencies within prefectures was added up and taken as a percentage of the total cast vote.
242 See Table 3.3.
243 See chapter 3 on 'Farmers Politics'.
244 See chapter 6 on 'Electoral Politics'.
245 This is the conclusion that Kobayashi also reached on the basis of his electoral data for the period 1958–86. See *Gendai Nihon no Senkyo Table 2-4*, p. 15 and also p. 93.
246 Over the elections between 1955 and 1976, the LDP support rate fell steadily from 63 per cent to 42 per cent, while the number of agricultural, forestry and fishery workers fell from 38 per cent of the workforce to 13 per cent. See Figure 2-7 in Iwamoto, *Hachiju Nendai*, p. 98.
247 Figure 3-1a in Miyake, *Tohyo Kodo*, p. 88.
248 Iwamoto, Table 2-6, *Hachiju Nendai*, p. 99.
249 Table 2-6, *Hachiju Nendai*, p. 99. This point also relates to my earlier argument about farmers not necessarily abandoning the LDP even when they took on part-time employment in labouring occupations. See also the other comments in this chapter about rising levels of support for the LDP over time amongst ordinary wage and salary earners.
250 See Figure 3-1a in Miyake, *Tohyo Kodo*, p. 88.
251 The only factor qualifying this observation was the extra-loading that voters enjoyed in constituencies with lower levels of population because of electoral malapportionment.

252 Categorisation of LH districts on the basis of the 1990 census is not available, and hence percentage figures for the 1990 and 1993 elections cannot be supplied.

253 *Interest Groups*, p. 69.

254 The LDP lost 32 of its Diet seats to defectors in the Shinseito and Shinto Sakigake in these elections.

255 *Asahi Nenkan*, 1993, pp. 126–130.

256 *Asahi Nenkan*, 1993, pp. 126–130.

257 Personal interview, Tokyo, July 1995.

258 Iwai, 'Nogyosha no Seiji Ishiki', p. 10.

259 Reported in 'Kore Kara no Seikyoku o Do Miru Ka' ['How Does the Political Situation Look After This'], *Nosei Undo Jyaanaru*, No. 2, September 1995, p. 5.

260 Rengo was short for Rengo No Kai, the Japanese Trade Union Confederation Association (JTUCA), the political arm of the Rengo. It burst on to the Japanese electoral scene in the 1989 UH elections. Its main goal was to strengthen the unions' influence on government. Initially it eschewed politics, but in the end decided that given the growing influence of Rengo, the labour organisation, it could not fulfil its responsibility if it stayed out of politics. It later changed its name to Rengo Sangiin (Rengo Upper House).

261 Iwai, 'Nogyosha no Seiji Ishiki', p. 11.

262 Iwai, 'Nogyosha no Seiji Ishiki', p. 12.

263 See chapter 4 on 'Opposition Party Politics' in my forthcoming volume, *The Challenge to Vested Party Interests*.

264 Fujitani Chikuji, 'Keito Nokyo no Nosei Katsudo wa Naze Shippai Shita Ka' ['Why Did The Agricultural Policy Activities of the Nokyo Fail?'], *Nogyo to Keizai*, Vol. 60, No. 4, April 1994, p. 51.

265 *Nikkei Weekly*, 30 September 1996.

266 Personal interview, Tokyo, July 1995.

267 According to a Zenchu official, Zenchu requested some member farmers to organise a new farmers' party. Personal interview, Tokyo, July 1995.

268 *Asahi Shinbun*, 12 April 1995.

269 *Asahi Shinbun*, 12 April 1995.

270 *Asahi Shinbun*, 12 April 1995.

271 Iwai, 'Nogyosha no Seiji Ishiki', p. 13.

272 Personal interview, Tokyo, July 1995. See also chapter 6 on 'Electoral Politics'.

273 Two of these new laws were regarded as amendments to the Public Offices Election Law (*Koshoku Senkyoho*). One was the Law on the Introduction of the Small Electorate and Proportional Representation Parallel System in the House of Representatives (*Shugiin Shosenkyoku Hirei Daihyo Heiritsusei no Kuwariho*) and the other was the Corruption Prevention Law (*Fuhai Boshiho*). The other two laws related to political funding: the Law Concerning the Juridical Person Status to be Granted to Political Parties and Associations Receiving Government Subsidies (*Seito Hojinkaku Fuyoho*) and the Political Parties Assistance Law (*Seito Joseiho*). The latter provided for government subsidies to be paid to parties under certain conditions. The Political Funds Regulation Law (*Seiji Shikin Kiseiho*) was also amended in 1994 although it was not included in the electoral reform laws.

274 According to Reed: 'Eight of the new districts were previously two- or three-member districts with unchanged boundaries, and two old districts needed parts from other districts to create a new single-member district, 250 new districts are fragments of old districts and 40 are combinations of parts from more than one old district.' Steven Reed, 'The Nomination Process for Japan's Next General Election: Waiting for the Heiritsu-sei', *Asian Survey*, Vol. 35, No. 12, December 1995, p. 1077.

275 In some cases, LDP rural politicians affected by this reshuffling were compensated by dual candidacies in the local electorate and on the party list in the regional PR districts, with the latter providing a parachute in the event of failure in the former.

276 This questionnaire is reported in Sugita, 'Seiji Kiban no Henka', p. 7.

277 Sugita, 'Seiji Kiban no Henka', p. 7.

278 See also chapter 6 on 'Electoral Politics'.

279 See also chapter 6 on 'Electoral Politics'.

280 Sugita, 'Seiji Kiban no Henka', p. 7.

281 The definition of what constitutes 'employment in primary industry' is unknown.

282 In these electoral districts, primary industry employment is 20 per cent and above. In fact Nishihira lists only 26 SMDs in his category of 'semi-rural', omitting Kagoshima (4) even though the percentage employed in primary industry in that district was 20.0 per cent. For purposes of this analysis, it has, therefore, been included in the semi-rural category.

283 In these electoral districts, the ratio of population concentration is below 50 per cent.

284 In these electoral districts, the ratio of population concentration is over 90 per cent.

285 In these electoral districts, the ratio of population concentration is over 90 per cent, and more than 30 per cent of the population is employed in secondary industry.

286 In these electoral districts, the ratio of population concentration is between 70 and 90 per cent, and more than 40 per cent of the population is employed in secondary industry.

287 In these electoral districts, the ratio of population concentration is between 50 and 70 per cent.

288 In these electoral districts, more than 40 per cent of the population is employed in secondary industry and the population concentration ratio is lower than 70 per cent.

289 Sugita, 'Seiji Kiban no Henka', p. 8.

290 *Nikkei Weekly*, 4 August 1997.

291 Sato Seizaburo, 'LDP Redivivus: The Failure of Electoral Reform', *Japan Echo*, Vol. 24, No. 1, Spring 1997, p. 24.

292 Keiko Tabusa, 'The 1996 General Election in Japan', *Australian Quarterly*, Vol. 69, No. 1, 1997, p. 24. An SDP candidate did stand in the PR regional district, gaining 3.8 per cent of the total vote.

293 'Zento Tanan na Yato Shuketsu' ['The Road Ahead is Full of Difficulties for the Opposition Parties' Concentration'], *Nosei Undo Jyaanaru*, No. 17, January 1998, p. 1.

294 'Zento Tanan na Yato Shuketsu', p. 1.

295 These are the words of a local Nokyo youth leader and political activist prior to the 1995 by-election in Saga Prefecture. *Asahi Shinbun*, 12 November 1995. Cf. above.

296 *Nikkei Weekly*, 2 February 1998.

297 After the LDP it was the second largest seat winner in this election, securing 15 prefectural seats and 12 NC seats, for a total of 27. After the elections, its UH total reached 47 members, the second largest party after the LDP's 103.

298 The LP won only one prefectural constituency and four NC seats, for a total of five seats. After the elections, its UH total was 12.

299 Takeshi Sasaki, Professor of Political Science, University of Tokyo, quoted in *Nikkei Weekly*, 3 August 1998. According to one Diet member, 'the LDP lost in

metropolitan regions in the Upper House election because they neglected the problems related to urban issues'. *Asahi Shinbun*, 18 December 1998. It is not correct, however, to attribute LDP losses in the major cities to its 'overt rural pork-barrel focus'. T. J. Pempel, *Regime Shift: Comparative Dynamics of the Japanese Political Economy*, Ithaca and London, Cornell University Press, 1998, p. 166.

300 See also below.

301 *Nikkei Weekly*, 2 February 1998.

302 This categorisation of seats is taken from Table 5.15.

303 This was partially a result, no doubt, of the Hata factor in Nagano – as in the 1995 UH election.

304 See chapter 7 on 'Representative Politics'.

305 Iwahashi, 'Why Do Farmers Have Such Great Power?', p. 49. Iwahashi pointed out, for instance, that almost all Japanese Prime Ministers have come from rural constituencies.

306 *Nikkei Weekly*, 7 September 1998.

307 *Nikkei Weekly*, 17 November 1997.

308 Sone Yasunori and Kanazashi Masao, *Nihon no Seiji* [*Japanese Politics*], Tokyo, Nihon Keizai Shinbunsha, 1989, p. 118.

309 Sone and Kanazashi, *Nihon no Seiji*, p. 118.

310 But see also the remarks of Hirose quoted above in which he claims that Diet members commonly make efforts to increase support in areas that have a substantial number of floating votes, while tending to neglect areas where they feel they can no longer expect to increase the number of supporters.

311 *Nikkei Weekly*, 7 September 1998.

312 Pempel, *Regime Shift*, p. 216. Mizuno Kiyoshi, Chairman of the LDP's commission on administrative reform in 1996, predicted that if the LDP espoused a policy that benefited only agriculture, it would alienate city voters and lose the October 1996 election. His prediction was right, if premature. See *Nikkei Weekly*, 23 September 1996.

6 Electoral politics

1 Fukui, 'The Japanese Farmer', p. 156.

2 Arimitsu, *Seito to Beika Seisaku*, p. 105.

3 Kobayashi, Shinohara and Soma, *Senkyo*, p. 77.

4 See chapter 3 on 'Farmers' Politics'.

5 Nagao, 'Nihon no Seiji Taisei', p. 28.

6 Ishida, 'The Development of Interest Groups', p. 300.

7 Tachibana, *Nokyo*, p. 314. See also chapter 2 on 'Interest Group Politics'.

8 Tanaka, *Nihon no Nokyo*, p. 424.

9 Kawagoe, 'The Origins of Protectionism', pp. 19–20.

10 *Nihon no Noson*, p. 225.

11 See also the discussion on *buraku* and *nogyo shuraku* in chapter 5 on 'The Political Demography of Agriculture'. The term *buraku* was still used by scholars in the 1950s and 1960s, and that is why it is used here, given that scholarly analysis of the period in question was done by prominent scholars of this era. See for example the works by Ishida, Dore and Fukutake.

12 The most important of these was the *noji jikko kumiai* (agricultural practice union). See chapter 4 on 'Organisational Politics'.

13 Okamoto, 'Nomin no Seiji Ishiki', p. 21.

14 Calder, for example, notes that: 'In many villages during the late 1940s, former landlords could no longer play as authoritative a role in mobilizing electoral

support for the conservatives as they had previously done'. *Crisis and Compensation*, p. 251.

15 Dore defines a *yuryokusha* as 'owners of largish holdings with experience of office whose opinions carry weight among their neighbours.' *Land Reform*, p. 339. Another term used for 'a person of power and influence' is *jitsuryokusha*.

16 Ono calls this group the 'executive and staff classes of all types, who upheld the authority of the village'. *No to Shoku*, p. 67.

17 As Ishida points out: 'Because of the land reform, it had become impossible for the politicians of the Conservative Party to count on the big landowners and influential families, who used to control the villages, for constant support in elections, as they had done before the war. The officers of the agricultural cooperative unions have become extremely important personalities in rural areas'. *Interest Groups*, p. 69. See also Ono, *No to Shoku*, p. 67.

18 Fukutake, *Nihon no Noson*, p. 227.

19 Ishikawa, 'Nogyo Kyodo Kumiai', p. 253.

20 Ishida and George, 'Nokyo', p. 204.

21 Midoro, *Rodosha Nomin Undoron*, p. 18.

22 See chapter 7 on 'Representative Politics'.

23 Ono, *No to Shoku*, p. 67.

24 Masashi Kasuga, 'The Transformation in the *Chiku Suisen* (District Recommendation) System in Postwar Japan', Paper presented to the Seventh Japanese Studies Association of Australia Conference, 11–13 July 1991, p. 9. His period of research covered 1947–1989.

25 See the discussion in Gerald Curtis, *Election Campaigning Japanese Style*, New York, Columbia University Press, 1971, pp. 35–41, 44, 54, and Kasuga, 'The Transformation', pp. 1–9.

26 Kobayashi, Shinohara and Soma, *Senkyo*, p. 95.

27 Kobayashi, Shinohara and Soma, *Senkyo*, p. 95

28 As Curtis explains, these personal connections underlying the 'hard' vote might be direct (i.e. between the candidate and the voter), or indirect (i.e. between a supporter of the candidate and the voter). *Election Campaigning*, p. 38.

29 Kobayashi, Shinohara and Soma, *Senkyo*, p. 96.

30 Kobayashi, Shinohara and Soma, *Senkyo*, p. 96.

31 Kobayashi, Shinohara and Soma, *Senkyo*, p. 96.

32 *Nihon no Noson*, p. 228.

33 Ono, 'Nokyo to Senkyo', p. 81. See also chapter 4 on 'Patronage Politics' in my forthcoming volume, *Politicians and Bureaucrats*.

34 Kobayashi, Shinohara and Soma, *Senkyo*, p. 89.

35 Sone and Kanazashi, *Nihon no Seiji*, p. 113.

36 According to Kobayashi, Shinohara and Soma, a *jiban* is an area of strong voting support, a region in which a candidate has good connections with organisations that gather supporting votes. It is normally the area where a candidate comes from – a native place – where there are many followers with strong personal connections to the politician and for whom the politician and his family (including political predecessors) have done services over a long period. A voting base is formed by means of such connections and relationships. At election time, those under this sort of obligation provide the 'silent' or 'hard votes' for a candidate. Such votes are automatic and are not tied to such things as policies and assertions of candidates. *Senkyo*, pp. 69–70.

37 Scott Flanagan, 'The Japanese Party System in Transition', *Comparative Politics*, Vol. 3, No. 2, January 1971, pp. 238–240.

38 Nakamura, 'Nominhyo no Pawaa', p. 119.

39 Arimitsu, *Seito to Beika Seisaku*, pp. 105–106.

40 Flanagan, 'The Japanese Party System', p. 233.
41 Dore, *Land Reform in Japan*, p. 414.
42 As Dore explains: 'A promise may be made to . . . Co-operative leader . . . The . . . Co-operative leader passes the word around that he is supporting X because he has promised to get the village such and such subsidy . . . and indicates that the village's interest requires that as many votes as possible should go to X – not simply to ensure his election, but even more to demonstrate the village's support and so make it difficult for him to go back on his promise.' *Land Reform*, pp. 417–418.
43 See also chapter 4 on 'Patronage Politics' in my forthcoming volume, *Politicians and Bureaucrats*.
44 The Chairman of the Iwate *kenchu*, for example, was a one-time Secretary-General of the LDP prefectural federation.
45 For example, Miyawaki Asao, Zenchu Chairman in the 1970s, was the head of Ohira Masayoshi's *koenkai* (both came from Kagawa), and the Chairman of Hokuren (the Hokkaido *keizairen*) was the one-time head of the *koenkai* of Nakagawa Ichiro, LDP member and farm politician from Hokkaido (5) from 1963 until he committed suicide in 1985. See also below.
46 Iwai, 'Nogyosha no Seiji Ishiki', p. 10.
47 Iwai, 'Nogyosha no Seiji Ishiki', p. 10. Also see chapter 4 on 'Patronage Politics' in my forthcoming volume, *Politicians and Bureaucrats*.
48 See chapter 5 on 'The Political Demography of Agriculture'. Iwai also indirectly makes this point in 'Japan's Agricultural Politics', p. 202.
49 Ishikawa, 'Nogyo Kyodo Kumiai', p. 253.
50 Tanaka, *Nihon no Nokyo*, p. 426.
51 Kobayashi, Shinohara and Soma, *Senkyo*, p. 78.
52 See below and chapter 7 on 'Representative Politics' for details of the history, functions and changing Diet membership composition of this organisation.
53 Yamashita Juntaro, 'Nezuyoi Hoshu-Kyoto Isshiki' ['Strongly-Rooted Conservatism-Local Party Consciousness'], in Nosei Jyaanarisuto no Kai (ed.), *Tatoka Jidai no Nosei*, p. 198. Van Wolferen also relates the example of the agricultural cooperatives in Mujazaki Prefecture which can reputedly mobilise 3,000 campaign workers 'free of charge'. Karel van Wolferen, *The Enigma of Japanese Power: People and Politics in a Stateless Nation*, London, Macmillan, 1989, p. 64.
54 In the early period after the war, agriculture and forestry Diet members reputedly obtained political funds from companies importing food into Japan, and later from companies manufacturing sugar and fertiliser. Funding from such agriculture-related industries, however, dried up by 1960. Kaiin Toron, 'Norin Kanryo', p. 109.
55 Sakaguchi, *Kyodai Nokyo*, p. 38.
56 In personal interviews with the author over a number of years, Nokyo executives have repeatedly denied that their organisation is involved in political funding. Other researchers have been told the same thing. See, for example, Fukui, 'The Japanese Farmer', p. 157, footnote 55. In recent years admissions of such activity have been made more readily.
57 The scandal involved officials of Zenkoren, who 'were found to be involved in corrupt relations with fertilizer manufacturers, government officials, and members of the Diet.' Dore, *Land Reform*, p. 291. See also Mitsukawa, *Nogyo Dantai Hattenshi*, pp. 515–519.
58 Kobayashi, Shinohara and Soma, *Senkyo*, p. 76.
59 Mitsukawa maintains that as no one was charged, the details of the case were not revealed. Moreover, he argues that there was no evidence that Zenkoren made political donations in order to get the bills it wanted passed, although Zenkoren

did contribute to Diet politicians from both the ruling and Opposition parties at the time of the general election. *Nogyo Dantai Hattenshi*, p. 516.

60 There were other internal management scandals at this time involving Zenkoren officials, both directors and staff members, embezzling and misappropriating public funds. Mitsukawa, *Nogyo Dantai Hattenshi*, pp. 515–516.

61 The details of this election scandal are extensively related in Tanaka, *Nihon no Nokyo*, pp. 458–461.

62 Ono, 'Nokyo to Senkyo', p. 78.

63 Ono, 'Nokyo to Senkyo', p. 79.

64 Ono, 'Nokyo to Senkyo', p. 79.

65 They were ranked into ABC categories. See Tanaka, *Nihon no Nokyo*, p. 450.

66 Nosei Jyaanarisuto no Kai, *Tenki ni Tatsu Norin Kinyu*, p. 53.

67 Tachibana, *Nokyo*, p. 333.

68 Tachibana, *Nokyo*, p. 333.

69 Tachibana, *Nokyo*, p. 333.

70 Yoshihara, *Zenno o Kiru*, p. 62. His Appendix I, however, lists 203 candidates as recipients of funds in the 1972 LH election, and only 18 candidates as recipients in the 1971 UH elections (pp. 247–251). See also below.

71 According to Tachibana, this was Nakanishi Ichiro, former MAFF Kanbo Chokan (Director-General of the Minister's Secretariat) who became Director of the Food Demand and Supply Centre (Shokuhin Jikyu Sentaa). Nakanishi, however, stood in a 1972 by-election for a Hyogo seat in the Upper House. He was not a candidate in the December 1972 General Election, although he was listed as receiving ¥4 million. Yoshihara, *Zenno o Kiru*, p. 50.

72 The latter went to the Chairman of the Akita Prefecture five Nokyo federations, who lost. See Tachibana, *Nokyo*, p. 333.

73 Nakagawa, LDP member from Hokkaido (5) was a prominent agricultural policy Diet member, holding positions such as MAFF Minister, Chairman of the LH Agriculture, Forestry and Fisheries Committee, Chairman of the LDP's Agriculture and Forestry Division and member of the informal group called the rice Vietcong (see chapter 7 on 'Representative Politics'). He was particularly well known as a representative for dairy farming, given the nature of agricultural production in his constituency.

74 Kuraishi from Nagano (1) held the position of MAF Minister in the 1960s.

75 Narita was a JSP member, whose political record in the party included posts such as Secretary-General and Chairman.

76 Hashimoto, LDP member for Ibaraki (1), was a *Nokyo giin* – a Director of the Ibaraki Prefecture *shinren*. During his career he also held posts such as Minister of Construction and Transport, and LDP Secretary-General.

77 Yoshihara, *Zenno o Kiru*, p. 63. See also below.

78 The sum of ¥30 million was generally considered as qualifying a political group as one of the larger contributors to LDP election funds in the early 1970s. A true comparison is, of course, impossible, because of the need to rely on official figures, such as those reported by the Kokumin Kyokai and Noseiken.

79 Yoshihara, *Zenno o Kiru*, p. 40.

80 In 1969, for example, 1,947 Nokyo executives served concurrently as executives of *kyodo kaisha*, whilst 98 out of 306 cooperative companies drew 20–50 per cent of these executives from Nokyo. Ohara, 'Kyodo Kaisha', p. 391.

81 See above.

82 Yoshihara, *Zenno o Kiru*, pp. 70, 227–230.

83 Tachibana, *Nokyo*, p. 334.

84 General political funding not connected with elections was not prohibited.

85 The law uses the formal terminology of the Japanese subsidy system. See

chapter 4 on 'Patronage Politics' in my forthcoming volume, *Politicians and Bureaucrats*, clarifies these terms.

86 Sakaguchi, *Kyodai Nokyo*, p. 102.
87 *Nokyo*, p. 318.
88 Sakaguchi, *Kyodai Nokyo*, p. 103.
89 *Nikkei Weekly*, 10 June 1996.
90 Interview with Nokyo official, Tokyo, July 1995. Its most prominent leader during the 1980s was Nokyo politician, Niwa Hyosuke. The existence of this organisation is currently in doubt, although the Chairman's representative in 1997 was Miyaji Kazuaki, former MAFF official and LDP Diet member in the Lower House from Kyushu PR district.
91 Nosei Kenkyukai, 'Nosei Kenkyukai Kaisoku' ['The Constitution of the Agricultural Policy Research Association'], *Kaiin Meibo* [*Membership List*], 1972.
92 See chapter 7 on 'Representative Politics'.
93 In response to the question: 'Have Nokyo groups (for example, Nokyo leaders and members) supported your election campaigns?' 88.5 per cent of those who replied responded in the affirmative. For details, see George, *The Strategies of Influence*, pp. 243–246.
94 Personal interview with former Zenchu Managing Director, Tokyo, July 1995.
95 Personal interview with former Zenchu Managing Director, Tokyo, July 1995.
96 By 1995, Yamaguchi had lost his power as an old man. Furthermore, his highly protectionist political ideology was no longer in tune with the times.
97 *Far Eastern Economic Review*, 17 November 1988.
98 The Zenno Chairman in 1974, Mihashi Makoto, for example, was president (*shacho*) of 13 Zenno-related companies, chairman of the board of directors of four more, chairman (*kaicho*) of a further five, and director of two others. The same was true of other Zenno managing directors (*jomu riji*). See Yoshihara, *Zenno o Kiru*, p. 50.
99 See below.
100 Personal interview, Tokyo, July 1995.
101 This was the case for Sonoda Kiyomitsu, LDP member in the Upper House for Kumamoto from 1962 to 1986. He was Chairman of the Kumamoto Prefecture *noseiren*, which acted like his *koenkai*.
102 Personal interview with Zenkoku Noseikyo Secretariat Chief, Tokyo, July 1995.
103 Tachibana, *Nokyo*, pp. 316–318. See also chapter 2 on 'Interest Group Politics'.
104 See chapter 8 on 'Policy Campaigning'.
105 Ono, for example, describes the *noseiren* as organisations for Nokyo's election campaigns which are, in fact, identical with Nokyo (*Nokyo to ittai no mono de aru*). 'Nokyo to Senkyo', p. 77.
106 See below and chapter 7 on 'Representative Politics' for a discussion of Nokyo and NC elections, particularly the division of agricultural interests in this election and which candidate Nokyo customarily supports.
107 Personal interview with Nosei Kenkyukai Secretary, Tokyo, March, 1990.
108 See George, *The Strategies of Influence*, p. 280.
109 Flanagan, 'The Japanese Party System', p. 239.
110 Personal interview with Nosei Kenkyukai Secretary, Tokyo, March, 1990.
111 Okazaki, 'Seiken Seito', p. 88–92.
112 This was the figure as of 1995. Personal interview with Zenkoku Noseikyo Secretariat Chief, Tokyo, July 1995. The rest he called 'voluntary groups' (*nini dantai*).
113 Sakaguchi, *Kyodai Nokyo*, p. 103.
114 Tachibana, *Nokyo*, p. 318.

115 In the 1977 UH election, for example, it was reported that the Miyagi Nokyo Seiji Renmei, which supported an LDP candidate, could not function in the election campaign. The reason for 'suspending business' was that actually mounting the campaign might cause an irrevocable breakdown in the organisation, and reaching agreement on which candidate to support was as much as they could do. Ono, 'Nokyo to Senkyo', p. 80.

116 Miyake, *Tohyo Kodo*, p. 54.

117 Nakamura, 'Nominhyo no Pawaa', p. 120. See also below.

118 Personal interview with Zenkoku Noseikyo Secretariat Chief, Tokyo, July 1995.

119 Not all prefectural *noseiren* necessarily make recommendations. Sometimes they cannot agree on who to recommend. In the 1990 elections in Fukui, the prefectural organisation tried to recommend six candidates, but because there were only four seats, it became a bit of a nonsense.

120 Personal communication with Zenkoku Noseikyo official, September 1997. The normal procedure is for the prefectural *noseiren* to make their recommendations first, then the national organisation follows up with the same recommendation. Sometimes, however, prefectural *noseiren* make recommendations without applications to Zenkoku Noseikyo. In the 1996 election, for example, four prefectures made independent recommendations – Ibaraki, Osaka, Hyogo and Okinawa. Six prefectures made no recommendations at all (Aomori, Fukushima, Niigata, Ishikawa, Mie and Tottori). Of these, all but Ishikawa had made recommendations in the previous election, but this time around they were happy to wait and see. Sugita, 'Seiji Kiban no Henka', p. 9.

121 It is no accident that the Vice-Chairman is from Zenno, given its funding capacities generated by the *kyodo kaisha*.

122 *Tohyo Kodo*, p. 54.

123 Kobayashi, Shinohara and Soma, *Senkyo*, p. 77.

124 See chapter 5 on 'The Political Demography of Agriculture'.

125 See chapter 2 on 'Interest Group Politics', but especially chapter 4 on 'Patronage Politics' in my forthcoming volume, *Politicians and Bureaucrats*.

126 See chapter 5 on 'The Political Demography of Agriculture'.

127 *Tohyo Kodo*, p. 54.

128 Personal interview, Tokyo, July 1995.

129 See below.

130 *Tohyo Kodo*, pp. 52–54. The national research data referred to was compiled as part of the JES. Miyake discusses at length the role of functional groups in influencing voting behaviour on pp. 50–55.

131 A former Managing Director of Zenchu made the similar observation that because Nokyo supported individual politicians, not political parties, it was still supporting the same people regardless of party in spite of the political upheavals of 1993–1995. Personal interview, Tokyo, July 1995.

132 Personal interview with Zenkoku Noseikyo Secretariat Chief, Tokyo, July 1995. But see also below and the comments on this issue in chapter 5 on 'The Political Demography of Agriculture'.

133 *Tohyo Kodo*, p. 62.

134 See chapter 7 on 'Representative Politics'.

135 These were from:
   1. Chiba Prefecture Nokyo Central Union
   2. Chiba Prefecture Nokyo Chairmen's Association
   3. Chiba Prefecture Nokyo Economic Federation
   4. Chiba Prefecture Nokyo Insurance Federation
   5. Chiba Prefecture Nokyo Trust Federation
   6. Chiba Prefecture Nokyo Women's Division Council

    7. Chiba Prefecture Agriculture, Forestry and Fisheries Groups' Liaison Council
    8. National Chamber of Agriculture
    9. Dairy Farmers' Political Federation of Japan
   10. Chairman of the Central Livestock Association – Akagi Munenori
   11. Agricultural Policy Promotion Council (Nosei Suishin Kyogikai)
   12. Japan Dentists' Political League
   13. Chiba Prefecture Dentists' Political League
   14. Chiba Prefecture Dental Technicians' Political League
   15. Hospital Nurses' Political Association
   16. Chairman of the All-Japan and Chiba Prefecture Pharmaceutical League
   17. Association to Protect Farmers' Health
   18. All-Japan Environmental Sanitation Service Traders' Association
   19. Japan Doctors' League
   20. Chiba Prefecture Doctors' League
   21. National Social Insurance Promotion League
   22. Japan Private Kindergarten Federation
   23. Chiba Prefecture Kindergarten Association
   24. Chiba Prefecture Specialist Schools' Association
   25. Japan League of Nurseries
   26. Chiba Prefecture Federation of Private School Groups
   27. Japan Federation of Handicapped and Retarded Groups
   28. Japan Wounded Soldiers' Political League
   29, Wounded Soldiers' Wives' Association
   30. President of the Japan Bereaved Families' Association
   31. International Anti-Communist League
   32. The House of Growth (Seicho no Ie)
   33. Shinto Political League
   34. World Salvation Army Organisation
   35. Japan Retired Government Officers' Political League
   36. All-Japan Land Agents' Political League
   37. Chiba Prefecture Accountants' Political League
   38. National League of the Self-Employed
   39. National Seaweed and Shells Cooperative Union
   40. Chiba Prefecture Public Bath Owners' Political League
   41. National Public Bath Owners' Political League
   42. Chiba Prefecture Small and Medium Enterprise League
   43. Matsudo City Industrial Federation
   44. Chiba Prefecture Branch of the National Oil Political League
   45. LDP Secretary-General
   46. Someya's factional leader – Shiina Etsusaburo
   47. Governor of Chiba Prefecture – Kawakami Kiichi
   48. Member of the House of Councillors – Saito Esaburo
   49. Member of the House of Councillors – Kashima Toshio
   50. A former member of the House of Councillors
   51. A Chiba Prefectural Assembly member
   52. Kashiwa City Mayor
   53. Nagareyama City Mayor
   54. Former Chief, Bureau of Rivers, Construction Ministry
136 Personal interview with Someya Makoto, Tokyo, December 1976.
137 Kobayashi, Shinohara and Soma, *Senkyo*, p. 76.
138 Personal interview with Nokyo official, Tokyo, July 1995.
139 Kobayashi, Shinohara and Soma, *Senkyo*, p. 77.

140 See chapter 2 on 'Interest Group Politics'.
141 The *noseiren* and *rakuno seiji renmei* overlap in Hokkaido, for instance. Elsewhere there is not much overlap between the two.
142 Personal interview with federation executives, Tokyo, July 1995.
143 Interview with Tochigi *kenchu* personnel, March 1986.
144 Kobayashi, Shinohara and Soma, *Senkyo*, p. 78.
145 See chapter 2 on 'Interest Group Politics'. Over 3,100 local agricultural committees have an average of 15 members each, amounting to an approximate total of 46–47,000 farmer-representative members.
146 Nakamura, 'Nominhyo no Pawaa', p. 118.
147 The definition of 'agricultural representative' is explained in chapter 7 on 'Representative Politics'.
148 For a comprehensive discussion of the results of this survey and the associated sample survey of 'agricultural representatives', see Aurelia George, 'The Politics of Interest Representation in the Japanese Diet: The Case of Agriculture', *Pacific Affairs*, Vol. 64, No. 4, Winter 1991–92, pp. 506–528.
149 This represents a response rate of 24 per cent, which comes within the average response rate to mailed questionnaire surveys in Japan which is somewhere between 15 and 30 per cent.
150 Note that politicians with ties to the land improvement groups failed to acknowledge the most significant and valuable resource they received from these organisations – political funding.
151 See chapter 7 on 'Representative Politics'.
152 Personal interview with Zenkoku Noseikyo Secretariat Chief, Tokyo, July 1995.
153 The results of this questionnaire were reported in Sugita, 'Seiji Kiban no Henka', p. 9.
154 See chapter 7 on 'Representative Politics'.
155 Reciprocal interdependence defines the mutual dealings of politicians and interest groups much more accurately in this context than does the uni-directional principal-agent approach favoured by rational choice theorists. See chapter 1.
156 *Nihon no Nokyo*, p. 437.
157 *Nihon no Nokyo*, pp. 425–426.
158 Tanaka was able to cite only one instance in the period he surveyed (from 1949 to 1969) of a current Nokyo official being defeated at the polls in a general election. *Nihon no Nokyo*, p. 426.
159 The Japanese term is formally defined in chapter 7 on 'Representative Politics'.
160 *Nihon no Nokyo*, p. 426.
161 *Nihon no Nokyo*, pp. 425–426.
162 Tanaka, *Nihon no Nokyo*, p. 426.
163 There are a few examples, however, of JCP candidates being recommended by Nokyo organisations (for example, Tsukawa Takeichi, JCP candidate in Aomori in the 1976 elections).
164 A questionnaire was distributed by the writer to Diet politicians who were members of APRA in December 1976, and again in May 1977 to those who had not replied. Out of a total of 84 members, 35 replies were received (i.e. a 41 per cent reply rate). More detailed results of this survey are reported in George, *The Strategies of Influence*, pp. 243–247.
165 See chapter 7 on 'Representative Politics'. In the 1970s, this succeeded the Sangiin Nokyo Giindan formed in 1962. See chapter 3 on Farmers' Politics.
166 George, *The Strategies of Influence*, p. 225.
167 Tanimoto, 'Nomin Undo', p. 93.
168 The figures for 1969 and 1983 were obtained from Tanimoto, 'Nomin Undo',

p. 93. He contrasts this situation with the labour unions, whose Diet representation rose in number of this period.

169 Tanimoto, 'Nomin Undo', pp. 94–95.

170 'Nokyo', p. 205.

171 See chapter 2 on 'Interest Group Politics' and chapter 7 on 'Representative Politics' and associated tables.

172 See chapter 2 on 'Interest Group Politics'.

173 Independent, later DSP politician Nakamura Yoshijiro, Chief of the Zennoseiren Secretariat and Secretary-General of Zennoren, and Inatomi Takato, another DSP member who held a seat in the Lower House for the constituency of Fukuoka (3) virtually from 1953 to 1977. He was the first Chairman of the DSP-attached Zenkoku Nomin Domei, and before that he was a prominent leader in the Right Socialist Party farmers' union movement. He fought the 1972 elections with a voting base in the Fukuoka Prefecture farmers' political league, one of the historical strongholds of the movement.

174 See also the discussion of this election below.

175 Tanaka, *Nihon no Nokyo*, pp. 474–475.

176 See below.

177 Okamoto, 'Nomin no Seiji Ishiki', p. 21.

178 Okamoto, 'Nomin no Seiji Ishiki', p. 21. The fact that so many farm votes went to the progressives in this election, however, was interpreted as less a positive choice for the progressives than an abandonment of the conservatives because of farmers' discontent with LDP agricultural policy. In this sense, it was a transient phenomenon that might not necessarily be repeated unless support for the progressives took root amongst the farmers. In any battle over farmers' political loyalties, however, the progressives were handicapped by their lack of ruling power (p. 23).

179 Ishida and George, 'Nokyo', p. 208.

180 See George, *The Strategies of Influence*, p. 281.

181 See below.

182 See chapter 3 on 'Farmers' Politics'.

183 See chapter 3 on 'Farmers' Politics'.

184 Tanaka reported, however, that in spite of occasional clashes and differences of political opinion within Nokyo along conservative-executive, progressive-staff lines, on the question of which candidate(s) to support in elections, conservative factions usually carried the day: 'In a majority of the electorates in which current Nokyo officials stand for election, the conservative influence is overwhelmingly strong, and opposition progressive groups within Nokyo and its federated organisation hardly become a problem.' *Nihon no Nokyo*, p. 426.

185 *Senkyo*, p. 78. They cited the example of Western Japan where they identified class divisions and crop divisions, particularly the advance of commercial agricultural products.

186 Kobayashi, Shinohara and Soma, *Senkyo*, p. 78.

187 Atsumi, "Tohoku Kessen", pp. 175–176.

188 Kobayashi, Shinohara and Soma, *Senkyo*, p. 80.

189 Agricultural production factors included problems associated with regional variations (the Tohoku region, for example, with its background as a single-crop rice production belt). It was noted that within one division of Nokyo in Western Japan, agricultural class and crop divisions were marked. Kobayashi, Shinohara and Soma, *Senkyo*, p. 78.

190 Kobayashi, Shinohara and Soma, *Senkyo*, p. 78.

191 Kobayashi, Shinohara and Soma, *Senkyo*, p. 78.

192 Ishida and George, 'Nokyo', p. 205.

193 See Table 4.1 in George, *The Strategies of Influence*, p. 216.
194 More detailed results of this survey are reported in George, *The Strategies of Influence*, pp. 246–247.
195 There was only one respondent from the DSP. He received recommendation and campaign assistance.
196 See the Appendix in Yoshihara, *Zenno o Kiru*, pp. 247–251.
197 The figures being used here are taken directly from Yoshihara's list of politicians' names. They vary slightly from the figures noted above.
198 This point was emphasised by Someya Makoto. He stated that in order to make basic agricultural policy, it was indispensable to be a member of the Lower House because it was the superior legislative body, although it was generally thought that Nokyo's support functioned better in UH elections. Personal interview, Tokyo, January 1977.
199 A comprehensive analysis of Noseiken's funding in these elections and the criteria that appeared to be operating is undertaken in George, *The Strategies of Influence*, pp. 248–252.
200 The only one without an obvious connection to agricultural interests was Narita Tomomi, Secretary-General of the JSP.
201 The recipient of the largest sum given to a Nokyo politician (¥2.5 million), also the second highest recipient overall, was a JSP candidate with a long association with the Nokyo movement and close connections to Zenno. This was Nakazawa Moichi, Diet member for Nagano (1) from 1952 to 1955, and 1958 to 1976. He was a former Secretary to Yonekura Tatsuya (the first Chairman of Zenchu and Diet member), permanent consultant to the Nokyo-based prefectural farmers' league, and a part-time staff member of the prefectural branch of Nagano Prefecture *keizairen*.
202 Sakaguchi, *Kyodai Nokyo*, p. 103. See also chapter 4 on 'Opposition Party Politics' in my forthcoming volume, *The Challenge to Vested Interests*.
203 As only one Rengo and Komeito member respectively responded to the questionnaire, the sample is too small to draw any conclusions as to agricultural cooperative support for politicians from these parties.
204 'Quality' is graded in the following way: recommendation alone is the lowest form of support; the combination of recommendation and campaign workers is a better form of support; and the triad of recommendation, campaign workers and political funds is the highest form of support.
205 With respect to the NFP, a Nokyo source interviewed in 1995 argued that Nokyo still supported the same people regardless of party. In other words, a shift to the NFP did not necessarily ruin a politician's electoral relationship with Nokyo. On the other hand, see the comments of a Nokyo activist on this subject in chapter 5 on 'The Political Demography of Agriculture'.
206 Private data collected by a Nosei Kenkyukai official.
207 Zenkoku Noseikyo, *Saninsen Taisaku Shiryo* [*House of Councillors' Election Policy Materials*], June 1995, p. 6.
208 'Noseiren Suisen no Sangiingiin Ichiran' ['List of Upper House Diet Members Recommended by the Noseiren'] *Nosei Undo Jyaanaru*, No. 2, September 1995, p. 32.
209 Personal communication, Zenkoku Noseikyo Secretariat official, September 1997.
210 'Suishin Giin to Meiyu no Paipu o Futoku' ['Thickening the Pipe between Recommended Diet Members and Supporters'], *Nosei Undo Jyaanaru*, No. 15, September 1997, p. 21.
211 'Hatsu no Shosenkyokusei Senkyo ni Mitsu no "Chiku Honbu" Sosetsu de Taio' ['Coping with the First Small-Constituency System Election with the

Establishment of the Three "District Headquarters"'], *Nosei Undo Jyaanaru*, No. 22, December 1998, p. 29.

212 This was the prediction of Rei Shiratori, Professor of Political Science at Tokai University in September 1996, and reported in the *Nikkei Weekly*, 30 September 1996.

213 According to Scalapino and Masumi, there were two farmers' union Diet representatives belonging to the Democratic Party in 1947, one in 1949, another belonging to its successor, the Progressive Party in 1953, and one in the ranks of the LDP in 1958. *Parties and Politics*, pp. 164–167. The latter was one-time Zennoren chairman, Tsunejima Masaoki, who was originally elected to the Diet as an Independent and who later joined the Japan Farmers Party. He joined the Liberal Party in 1949 and unsuccessfully contested the 1949 election for a seat in Nagasaki (2) constituency. He won for the Liberals in 1952 and subsequently joined the LDP. Although Zennoren has been classed by some authors as a farmers' union, it belongs to a different organisational genre, given its historical and organisational associations with the agricultural cooperative movement. See chapter 3 on 'Farmers' Politics'.

214 Kyosanto Bukkuretto, *Gaiatsu no Naka no Nihon*, p. 42.

215 Kyosanto Bukkuretto, *Gaiatsu no Naka no Nihon*, pp. 42–43.

216 Kyosanto Bukkuretto, *Gaiatsu no Naka no Nihon*, p. 42.

217 Ishida and George, 'Nokyo', p. 204, quoting a *Mainichi Shinbun* interview with Miyawaki.

218 Muramatsu and Krauss, 'The Dominant Party', p. 286.

219 Muramatsu and Krauss, 'The Dominant Party', p. 294.

220 Muramatsu and Krauss, 'The Dominant Party', p. 289. This work is probably reliant on the research done for the Muramatsu, Ito and Tsujinaka volume on Japanese pressure groups, which established that amongst the various categories of pressure groups surveyed, agricultural groups scored only 56.5 per cent on the question whether support for the LDP was 'extraordinarily strong → fairly strong'. This compared with 61.4 per cent for economic groups, and 66.7 per cent each for administration-related, educational and specialist groups. See Table 4.2 in *Sengo Nihon no Atsuryoku Dantai*, p. 173. Other research for the same book revealed that only 22 per cent of agricultural groups perceived themselves to be very close to the LDP, compared to 48 per cent who perceived themselves to be fairly close, 13 per cent not very close, and 17 per cent not close at all (p. 180).

221 Muramatsu, Ito and Tsujinaka, *Sengo Nihon no Atsuryoku Dantai*, p. 182.

222 According to Muramatsu, Ito and Tsujinaka, because the JSP was quite strong, the LDP had to make flexible and responsive policies. Their study also revealed that although agricultural groups contacted other political parties, they still supported the LDP. *Sengo Nihon no Atsuryoku Dantai*, pp. 183–184, 229.

223 Muramatsu and Krauss, 'The Dominant Party', p. 291.

224 Sone and Kanazashi, *Nihon no Seiji*, pp. 115–116.

225 Kobayashi, Shinohara and Soma, *Senkyo*, p. 78.

226 Tachibana, *Nokyo*, pp. 314–315. As he points out, the power of Nokyo's farmers' political leagues are as different as heaven and earth, depending on the region (p. 314).

227 For example, the general observation was made by Calder that: 'Group norms and specific group instructions to members appear more important [in Japan] than elsewhere in determining voting and other political activity. Accordingly, Japanese political culture gives those in a position to generate group consensus . . . the ability to powerfully influence policy output. The strategic problem for Japanese conservative leadership thus becomes more effectively coopting the leadership of formally apolitical groups, such as neighbourhood associations

and chambers of commerce, rather than appealing directly to the general electorate as possible in less organized societies like the United States.' *Crisis and Compensation*, p. 184.

228 Sone and Kanazashi, *Nihon no Seiji*, p. 116.

229 *Tohyo Kodo*, p. 54.

230 Sakaguchi, *Kyodai Nokyo*, p. 111.

231 Amano Hiroyuki, ' "Hoshu no Jo" no Hikari to Kage' ['Light and Shadow in the "Castle of Conservatism" '], in Nosei Jyaanarisuto no Kai (ed.), *Tatoka Jidai no Nosei*, pp. 184–185.

232 Goto and Imamura, 'Japanese Agriculture', p. 19. See also chapter 4 on 'Organisational Politics'.

233 Fujitani, *Nokyo*, p. 16.

234 See also above.

235 Kobayashi, Shinohara and Soma, *Senkyo*, p. 78.

236 Arimitsu, *Seito to Beika Seisaku*, pp. 105–106.

237 Hirose Michisada, *Hojokin to Seikento* [*Subsidies and The Ruling Party*], Tokyo, *Asahi Shinbunsha*, 1981, p. 43.

238 Ono, 'Nokyo to Senkyo', p. 83.

239 Ono, 'Nokyo to Senkyo', p. 87.

240 This was just the national poll and it was reported in Zenkoku Nogyosha Nosei Undo Soshiki Kyogikai, *Nogyosha no Seiji Ishiki ni Kansuru Chosa Hokoku*, April 1995, p. 8. The results of this particular question, interestingly, were not reproduced in the *Nosei Undo Jyaanaru* journal publication produced by the organisation as its main politics-related information outlet.

241 These figures compare with the same question asked in relation to the influence of information coming from the secondary workplace of part-time farmers. In the view of 7.9 per cent, it was very important; 33.5 per cent thought it was quite important; whilst 58.6 per cent claimed that it was not important at all. Zenkoku Nogyosha Nosei Undo Soshiki Kyogikai, *Nogyosha no Seiji Ishiki*, p. 8.

242 'Toitsu Chiho Senkyo e no Kakuchi no Torikumi' ['Each Region's Grappling with the Local Elections'], *Nosei Undo Jyaanaru*, No. 24, March 1999, p. 29.

243 Ono Masakazu, 'Hoshu Okoku no Hokai' ['Collapse of a Conservative Kingdom'], in Nosei Jyaanarisuto no Kai (ed.), *Shu, San Senkyo to Nomin no Sentaku* [*Lower and Upper House Elections and Farmers' Choices*], Tokyo, Nihon Nogyo no Ugoki No. 91, Norin Tokei Kyokai, 1990, p. 134.

244 Tachibana, *Senkyo*, pp. 318–319.

245 Interview with Tomioka Yoshiyuki, Agricultural Editor, *Nihon Keizai Shinbun*, Tokyo, 4 July 1974. For a discussion of Nokyo's vote control in the new electoral system in the Lower House, see below.

246 The large number of candidates in 1950 was probably a reflection of the relative inexperience of the agricultural cooperative organisation in fielding candidates in national constituency UH elections at that time and the relatively large number of candidates representing various 'vocational' interests contesting seats in the early postwar elections to the Upper House. It was not yet clear how many NC candidates the national Nokyo electorate could successfully sustain.

247 *Nihon no Nokyo*, p. 426.

248 *Nihon no Nokyo*, p. 421.

249 Curtis for example, argued that: 'Like many interest groups, the agricultural cooperative union organisation functions most effectively in support of Upper House candidates in the national constituency elections who run with the backing of the national organization'. *Election Campaigning*, p. 193.

250 Tanaka, *Nihon no Nokyo*, p. 426.

251 See above.

252 See chapter 2 on 'Interest Group Politics' and chapter 3 on 'Farmers' Politics'.

253 Although he stood as Chairman of Zenkyoren, Okamura's local support base was in Hokkaido where he had previously been Chairman of the Hokkaido Association of Agriculture (Hokkaido Nogyokai) and where he was also Director of Snow Brand Milk, a company which began as a Hokkaido-based dairy cooperative. Okamura shared this same regional support base with a JSP NC Nokyo candidate, Mori Masao, who was Vice-Chairman of the Hokkaido Nokyo Central Union at the time. The result of their competition for local Hokkaido farmers' votes was defeat for them both.

254 With one or two exceptions, MAFF bureaucrats have not retired into mainstream Nokyo organisations (and then represented them in the Diet), except for Norinchukin, which as noted in chapter 2, is of a different organisational genre (i.e. a *tokushu hojin* and thus an institutional interest group). There have been a number of examples of former high-level MAFF bureaucrats taking up top executive positions in Norinchukin and then obtaining seats in the Diet. See George, *The Strategies of Influence*, pp. 263–264.

255 See Tables 7.9 and 7.10.

256 For some early examples, see George, *The Strategies of Influence*, p. 264. See also chapter 7 on 'Representative Politics'.

257 In 1959, for example, Okamura competed successfully for a NC seat against six other candidates who represented agricultural and forestry organisations of various kinds, four of whom were ex-MAF officials. Yet another five others including a Nokyo leader (see Table 6.6) and an ex-MAF official from the National Chamber of Agriculture were unsuccessful. Similar breadth of competition for the farm vote occurred in 1962. See chapter 7 on 'Representative Politics', and George, *The Strategies of Influence*, p. 264.

258 See Table 7.9.

259 George, *The Strategies of Influence*, p. 265.

260 When interviewed, an official of Zendoren commented, for example, that Nokyo collected people – it consisted of people/farmers – whereas in the land improvement districts, land had first priority and it provided a narrower, single focus. Personal interview, Tokyo, July 1995.

261 The power of narrower sectional interests and more specific and immediate organisational loyalties was demonstrated in the 1968 election when Mori Yasoichi, standing as the national Nokyo candidate and Zenchu leader, was beaten on the hustings by Kobayashi Kuniji, a former MAF Structural Improvement Bureau Construction Department Chief, Director of MAF Hokuriku Agricultural Policy Bureau and agriculture and forestry engineering technical official, who on retirement became Vice-Chairman of the National Federation of Land Improvement Industry Groups, Chairman of the Japan Agricultural Engineering General Research Institute, Chairman of the Farmland Agriculture Promotion Association and adviser to the Agricultural Land League. Mori scored his highest vote tally ever in 1968 with 720,000 votes. It was his fourth election. Kobayashi, on the other hand, was an unknown new candidate. He won 780,000 votes and sixth place, the highest score of any agriculture and forestry candidate. As the land development industry depended enormously on government subsidies to fund its operations, political representation in the Diet was regarded as vital to keep open channels of communication and pressure on the MAF and MOF. Kobayashi's votes were linked directly to interests involved in this industry, and his executive roles in organisations related to the land improvement industry proved to be an effective pipeline to rice-roots voters participating in this kind of enterprise. His supremacy over Mori was attributed to the well-organised supporting votes he received from agriculture and forestry engineering tech-

nicians' associations, plus the backing of the National Land Improvement Political League and the Agricultural Land League. According to Tanaka, Mori's chairmanship of Zenchu, in contrast, encompassed too broad a field and made votes unexpectedly difficult to collect. *Nihon no Nokyo*, p. 466. Kobayashi also did extremely well in his second election in 1974. He gained 867,548 votes which put him in 8th place. In the 1980 UH elections, he stood for the prefectural constituency of Tottori. See chapter 7 on 'Representative Politics' and Table 7.10.

262 See the examples given in George, *The Strategies of Influence*, pp. 267–268.

263 Interview, Tokyo, July 1995.

264 For example, it was Mori Yasoichi's political independence for 18 years that identified him so clearly as Nokyo's representative in the Diet. This was reinforced by his chairmanship of Zenchu from 1968 onwards. Mori's political independence reputedly enabled him to operate in the 'demilitarised zone' between government agricultural Diet member members and the Opposition parties.

265 Tanaka, *Nihon no Nokyo*, p. 461.

266 The absence of a candidate in the 1974 elections to replace Mori Yasoichi hinged on the personal decision of Miyawaki Asao, Zenchu Chairman, not to replace Mori as Nokyo's national representative in the Diet. Prime Minister Tanaka offered LDP endorsement to Miyawaki in the 1974 elections to carry on in Mori's footsteps but Miyawaki refused. His past record as Socialist candidate for Kagawa in the 1964 elections had been one of failure. The reason he gave for declining Tanaka's offer was the political neutrality of the Nokyo organisation which he claimed prevented him from identifying with any particular party, and the demands of his job as Zenchu Chairman.

267 For a discussion of the current subdivision of agricultural interests in the national constituency, see chapter 7 on 'Representative Politics'.

268 See chapter 2 on 'Interest Group Politics' and chapter 7 on 'Representative Politics'.

269 *Sankei Shinbun*, 5 June 1974.

270 Sakaguchi, *Kyodai Nokyo*, p. 111.

271 'Genchi Rupo: Kumamoto Nogyosha Seiji Renmei no Katsudo' ['Local Report: Activities of the Kumamoto Farmers' Political League'], *Nosei Undo Jyaanaru*, No. 14, August 1997, p. 28. In fact it retained the same title.

272 Tachibana's research, however, revealed that Horinouchi Hisao from Miyazaki (2), owed about 40,000 votes, or 70 per cent of his total support to the Nokyo organisation. *Nokyo*, p. 315.

273 These figures do not vary significantly from those obtained by the author in the earlier questionnaire of Nosei Kenkyukai members in 1976–77 and reported in George, *The Strategies of Influence*, pp. 252–253. A total of 88.5 per cent of respondents agreed that electoral support from Nokyo groups contributed to their successful election, whilst estimations of the extent of this contribution varied from 5 per cent to 60–70 per cent of their total supporting votes (see Table 4.5, p. 255), although a number of respondents had no idea. Percentages varied quite significantly according to party, with LDP members estimating their Nokyo vote at an average of 49 per cent, and JSP members at 25 per cent.

274 Ito Kenzo, quoted in *Australian Financial Review*, 27 February 1986.

275 Nagao, 'Nihon no Seiji Taisei', p. 33.

276 Nagao, 'Nihon no Seiji Taisei', p. 33.

277 Aono, *Nokyo*, p. 21.

278 Ishikawa, 'Nogyo Kyodo Kumiai', p. 252.

279 *Far Eastern Economic Review*, 17 November 1988.

280 Aono, *Nokyo*, p. 21.

281 Sakaguchi, *Kyodai Nokyo*, p. 109.
282 Sakaguchi, *Kyodai Nokyo*, p. 54.
283 Nosei Jyaanarisuto no Kai, *Tenki ni Tatsu Norin Kinyu*, p. 53.
284 Ono, 'Nokyo to Senkyo', p. 78.
285 Personal communication, Zenkoku Noseikyo Secretariat official, September 1997.
286 Iwai, 'Nogyosha no Seiji Ishiki', p. 10.
287 Yanagida Akitoshi, 'Nominhyo ni "Gyakuryu Gensho"' ['The "Comeback Phenomenon" by Farmers' Votes'], in Nosei Jyaanarisuto no Kai (ed.), *Tatoka Jidai no Nosei*, p. 155.
288 Yamamoto, for example, undertook a study of all LH elections from 1960–93 from the perspective of the LDP's performance in agricultural constituencies, identifying possible factors in agricultural and other policies that might have influenced farmers' votes. 'Sengo Nosonhyo', pp. 23–69.
289 'Nokyo to Senkyo', p. 84.
290 Okamoto Matsuzo, 'Nokyo no Nosei Katsudo' ['Nokyo's Agricultural Policy Activities'], in Ouchi and Kajii (eds), *Nokyo Yonjunen*, p. 268. See also the discussion in Tanaka, *Nihon no Nokyo*, pp. 173–186, 472–481. He recounts how Nokyo informed the LDP that it would confront it in the elections the day before the announcement of the producer rice price freeze in 1969. There was, however, strife in the headquarters prior to this announcement because most Nokyo organisations were determined to defect from the LDP in the elections, while Zenchu Chairman, Miyawaki was alone in stressing that it would be inappropriate for Nokyo, as a politically neutral organisation, to confront a particular political party. An anti-LDP movement in the election was subsequently led by the youth and women's divisions, as well as the rice price headquarters in the *kenchu* of some rice-producing prefectures such as Yamagata. Nevertheless, although the general election was expected to reflect Nokyo's response to the rice price freeze and the introduction of the *gentan*, the impact of these policies was not as significant as expected. This was mainly because the LDP tenaciously persuaded Nokyo executives to prevent a Nokyo rebellion against the LDP. See also above.
291 Ishida and George, 'Nokyo', p. 208.
292 Ono, 'Nokyo to Senkyo', p. 85.
293 'Nomin no Seiji Ishiki', pp. 21–22.
294 This is despite the fact that the LDP candidate ultimately won. See Mori Koji, 'Murateki Jokyo o Koenai Kokusei Senkyo' ['National Elections That Can Never Go Beyond Local Elections'], in Nosei Jyaanarisuto no Kai (ed.), *Tatoka Jidai no Nosei*, pp. 165–173.
295 Atsumi, "Tohoku Kessen", pp. 176–178.
296 Ishiwata, 'Nomin to Seiji', p. 11.
297 Ishiwata, 'Nomin to Seiji', p. 11.
298 See for example Yamamoto, 'Sengo Nosonhyo', pp. 23–70. See also chapter 4 on 'Patronage Politics' in my forthcoming volume, *Politicians and Bureaucrats*.
299 Examples of this are given in chapter 4 on 'Patronage Politics' in my forthcoming volume, *Politicians and Bureaucrats*.
300 See chapter 4 on 'Patronage Politics' in my forthcoming volume, *Politicians and Bureaucrats*.
301 Tsuchiya Shigeru, 'Jiminto Nosei de Nominhyo o Torimodoseru ka' ['Is It Possible to Regain Farmers' Votes with the LDP's Agricultural Policy?'], *Nogyo to Keizai*, Vol. 56, No. 1, January 1990, p. 51. These figures compare with those from the *Asahi Shinbun* surveys reported by Miyake, which revealed a similar order of decline from 56 per cent in the 1986 LH election to 41 per cent in the 1989 UH election. See Table 1 in '89-Nen Sangiin Senkyo', p. 36. See also below and chapter 5 on 'The Political Demography of Agriculture'.

302 Kyosanto Bukkuretto, *Gaiatsu no Naka no Nihon*, p. 54.
303 Takabatake Michitoshi, 'Naze Nomin wa Jiminto o Mikagitta Ka' ['Why Did Farmers Desert the LDP?'], *Ushio*, September 1987, p. 77.
304 This was effectively an unprecedented decision, because the earlier decision to lower the rice price in 1956 was a slight adjustment in the price owing to a change in the formula for calculating the rice price. *Asahi Nenkan*, 1988, p. 144.
305 *Asahi Shinbun*, 21 April 1989.
306 These issues are discussed more fully in chapter 8 on 'Gaiatsu Politics' in my forthcoming volume, *The Challenge to Vested Interests*.
307 *Asahi Shinbun*, 21 April 1989.
308 See Table 8.3 in my forthcoming volume, *The Challenge to Vested Interests*.
309 See Table 8.2 in my forthcoming volume, *The Challenge to Vested Interests*.
310 According to a Zenchu survey in March 1986, 59.7 per cent of 87,000 livestock farming households (out of which 60 per cent were beef producers) were suffering in their business, and 1.3 per cent of them were unable to recover. *Asahi Shinbun*, 1 June 1986.
311 *Asahi Shinbun*, 1 June 1986.
312 *Australian Financial Review*, 29 October 1990.
313 *Asahi Shinbun*, 20 February 1989.
314 *Asahi Shinbun*, 21 April 1989.
315 Takabatake, 'Naze Nomin wa Jiminto o Mikagitta Ka', p. 77.
316 *Asahi Shinbun*, 21 April 1989.
317 Tsuchiya, 'Jiminto Nosei', p. 51. In a general public opinion survey reported by Kobayashi, 79.3 per cent of those surveyed said that the consumption tax was the most important factor influencing their vote, whilst 13.4 per cent said it was agricultural policy issues (*nosei mondai*), 6.1 per cent the Recruit scandal and 1.2 per cent PM Uno's 'woman problem' (*josei mondai*). *Gendai Nihon no Senkyo*, p. 100.
318 *Asahi Shinbun*, 21 April 1989.
319 Kyosanto Bukkuretto, *Gaiatsu no Naka no Nihon*, p. 55.
320 *Sydney Morning Herald*, 7 July 1989.
321 *Asahi Shinbun*, 21 April 1989.
322 *Asahi Shinbun*, 21 April 1989.
323 *Asahi Shinbun*, 21 April 1989.
324 *Asahi Shinbun*, 21 April 1989.
325 *Asahi Shinbunn*, 22 April 1989.
326 The Yamagata Prefecture Nokyo Political League followed the advice of the Nokyo *seinenbu* that they should not support the LDP and recommend their own candidate. Chairman Nakajima of the Yamagata Prefecture *seinenbu* recounted to one analyst that the anger against the LDP had not been a recent phenomenon. It had begun in the 1960s when the government had instituted production control of rice followed by the rice price freeze, rising debts amongst farmers for agricultural machinery purchases and liberalisation of agricultural imports. Despite the government's pledge that it would not liberalise beef and oranges, it had done so. Agriculture had clearly not been protected by the ABL and that was why farmers had been cheated by the LDP's glib lies. The party's real intention (*honne*) reflected the Nakasone line which was to protect export industry. What was intolerable for farmers was uncertainty about the future of agriculture which also impacted on farmers' marriage chances and encouraged young people to move to the cities. However, it was not easy to push the anti-LDP line in Yamagata because the LDP candidate had put a lot of effort into obtaining subsidies for which farmers were grateful. The best option was to have a farmers' candidate,

but unfortunately this was not possible. The only alternative was to hand in a blank voting paper on election day, in spite of the fact that he was a member of the LDP. Takabatake, 'Naze Nomin wa Jiminto Mikagitta Ka?', p. 81. See also below.

327   *Asahi Shinbun*, 7 April 1989; *Mainichi Shinbun*, 14 June 1989.

328   The list included the following: in Aomori, the four Nokyo federations cooperated with a candidate supported by the Farmers' Executive Committee to Block the Construction of a Nuclear Fuel Facility (45,000 members) with anti-nuclear and anti-LDP slogans; in Iwate, the Shizukuishi Town Nokyo youth division (220 members), decided not to support the LDP in the national constituency; the Nishiwaga (46 members), Hiraizumi (1,242 members) and Murone (1,193 members), Nokyo's decided not to support the LDP in the national constituency, and the Higashiyama Nokyo youth division (25 members) decided not to support the LDP in either the Upper or Lower House elections; in Akita, the Noshiro City Nokyo (3,270 members) decided not to support the LDP; in Fukushima, the Ippa City Nokyo Youth League (17 members) decided not to support the LDP in either the national or prefectural constituency; in Ibaraki the prefectural Nokyo youth league (1,100 members) terminated its rec-ommendation for LDP candidates which it had observed hitherto and allowed a 'free vote'; in Tochigi the prefectural Nokyo youth league (6,819 members) decided on a 'free vote'; in Gumma the Meiji Nokyo livestock organisation council (50 members) decided not to support the LDP; in Nagano the Shinonoi Nokyo youth division (152 members) decided not to support the LDP and the Koshoku Nokyo youth division (45 members) decided not to support the LDP; in Okayama, agricultural cooperatives in Ukan and Mabi towns (1,706 and 2,083 members respectively) and Kojo Nokyo (1,151 members) decided not to support LDP candidates in national elections; in Ehime, Shuso Nokyo, the biggest agricultural cooperative in the prefecture with 10,000 members decided not to support LDP candidates in future national elections; in Fukuoka the prefectural *noseiren* (135,000 members) decided not to support the LDP in the national constituency; in Oita the Kokonoe Nokyo youth division (64 members) recommended the JSP incumbent and decided on policy cooperation, and Ono Nokyo (1,380 members) decided not to support the LDP in national elections for one year; in Saga, Nagasaki and Miyazaki, the prefectural Nokyo youth organisation councils (5,178, 3,000 and 4,352 members respectively) decided not to support the LDP in the national constituency; and in Kagoshima the prefectural Nokyo youth organisation council (2,436 members) decided not to support the LDP in the national constituency. *Mainichi Shinbun*, 14 June 1989.

329   Personal interview with Nosei Kenkyukai, Secretary, Tokyo, March 1990.

330   *Nihon Nogyo Shinbun*, 11 March 1989.

331   *Nokyo Nenkan*, 1990, p. 148.

332   *Nokyo Nenkan*, 1990, p. 148.

333   'Sokatsu Toron: Nomin no Seiji Ishiki wa Kawatta Ka' ['Summary Discussion: Has Farmers' Political Consciousness Changed?'], in Nosei Jyaanarisuto no Kai (ed.), *Shu, San Senkyo*, p. 97.

334   *Nihon Nogyo Shinbun*, 27 July 1989. See also Mizusaki Tokifumi, 'Ichininku ni okeru Jiminto no Kampai' ['The Complete Defeat of the LDP in Single-Member Constituencies'], *Rebuaiasan*, Vol. 10, Spring 1992, pp. 82–108.

335   *Japan Agrinfo Newsletter*, Vol. 7, No. 2, October 1989, p. 6.

336   All Rengo candidates were also recommended by the JSP, DSP and SDL. See Table 2 in Mizusaki, 'Ichininku', p. 88.

337   These Independents were jointly recommended by the JSP in Tottori and the JSP and SDL in Shimane. See Table 2 in Mizusaki, 'Ichininku', p. 88.

338 According to an agricultural journalist, antipathy to Nokyo bosses who were pressing for Nokyo's amalgamation was a stronger factor in this election than criticisms over the LDP's agricultural policy. 'Sokatsu Toron: Nomin no Seiji Ishiki', p. 97.

339 See Tables 3-1 and 3-2 in Mizusaki, 'Ichininku', p. 92.

340 For a list of the leadership positions Higaki held in MAFF *gaikaku dantai*, see chapter 7 on 'Representative Politics'.

341 According to one of these farmers: 'There is no resentment against Higaki personally in spite of the government's agricultural policy. But, liberalisation, the Recruit scandal and the consumption tax are piling up, and dissatisfaction with the LDP has spread.' *Asahi Shinbun*, 21 April 1989.

342 *Japan Agrinfo Newsletter*, Vol. 7, No. 2, October 1989, p. 2.

343 Tagawa Norio, 'Saninsen to Nokyo to Nomintachi' ['The Upper House Election and Nokyo and Farmers'], in Nosei Jyaanarisuto no Kai (ed.), *Shu, San Senkyo*, pp. 149–151.

344 Kajiwara Yosuke, 'Jiyuka ni Itten o Mukuita Mikan Noka' ['Mikan Farmers Who Revenged Liberalisation'], in Nosei Jyaanarisuto no Kai (ed.), *Shu, San Senkyo*, p. 139–140.

345 Kajiwara, 'Jiyuka ni Itten o Mukuita Mikan Noka', p. 141.

346 Kajiwara, 'Jiyuka ni Itten o Mukuita Mikan Noka', p. 145.

347 *Japan Agrinfo Newsletter*, Vol. 7, No. 2, October 1989, p. 3.

348 *Japan Agrinfo Newsletter*, Vol. 7, No. 2, October 1989, p. 3.

349 *Japan Agrinfo Newsletter*, Vol. 7, No. 2, October 1989, p. 3.

350 *Japan Agrinfo Newsletter*, Vol. 7, No. 2, October 1989, p. 3.

351 'Sokatsu Toron: 'Nomin no Seiji Ishiki', p. 97.

352 Kawasaki Soichiro, 'Saninsen to Nosonhyo no Doko' ['The Upper House Election and the Movement of Rural Votes'], in Nosei Jyaanarisuto no Kai (ed.), *Shu, San Senkyo*, p. 40.

353 'Sokatsu Toron: Nomin no Seiji Ishiki', p. 103.

354 Takabatake, 'Naze Nomin wa Jiminto o Mikagitta ka', p. 80.

355 See also above.

356 Kawasaki, 'Saninsen to Nosonhyo', p. 25.

357 Kawasaki, 'Saninsen to Nosonhyo', p. 25.

358 Kawasaki, 'Saninsen to Nosonhyo', p. 25.

359 *Financial Times*, 19 July 1989.

360 Quoted in *Asahi Shinbun*, 26 June 1986, p. 3.

361 Takabatake, 'Naze Nomin wa Jiminto o Mikagitta ka', p. 81.

362 Takabatake, 'Naze Nomin wa Jiminto o Mikagitta ka', p. 81.

363 See chapter 4 on 'Opposition Party Politics' in my forthcoming volume, *The Challenge to Vested Interests*.

364 Takabatake, 'Naze Nomin wa Jiminto o *Mikagitta ka*', p. 83.

365 Kyosanto Bukkuretto, *Gaiatsu no Naka no Nihon*, p. 34.

366 One report commented that part-time rice farmers opposed not only rice import liberalisation but also the new rice price (either frozen or reduced) and the government's policy of promoting the rationalisation of agricultural land owner-ship in the hands of full-time farmers and their development. 'Sokatsu Toron: Nomin no Seiji Ishiki', p. 97.

367 Takahata Masamichi, 'Henka ni Taio Dekinakatta Jiminto' ['The LDP That Could Not Respond to Changes'], in Nosei Jyaanarisuto no Kai (ed.), *Shu, San Senkyo*, p. 90.

368 JSP support amongst primary industry workers jumped from 6 per cent in the 1986 LH elections to 17 per cent in the 1989 UH election. These figures are from the *Asahi Shinbun* surveys mentioned above and in chapter 5 on 'The Political

Demography of Agriculture'. See Table 1 in Miyake, '89-Nen Sangiin Senkyo', p. 36.

369 Kyosanto Bukkuretto, *Gaiatsu no Naka no Nihon*, p. 55.

370 Kyosanto Bukkuretto, *Gaiatsu no Naka no Nihon*, p. 55.

371 See chapter 4 on 'Opposition Party Politics' in my forthcoming volume, *The Challenge to Vested Interests*.

372 Kyosanto Bukkuretto, *Gaiatsu no Naka no Nihon*, p. 34.

373 One commentator observed that the LDP's poor showing reflected the intention of farm voters to punish the LDP. The result was not caused by voters who supported the policies of the JSP. 'Sokatsu Toron: Nomin no Seiji Ishiki', p. 97.

374 See Tables 5.9, 5.10, 5.13 and 5.14.

375 *Asahi Shinbun*, 3 June 1990.

376 Kobayashi also reports that across his spectrum of constituency categories, the LDP's vote tally dipped by the most percentage points in rural districts (from 68.51 per cent of votes in 1986 to 60.58 per cent in 1990). Conversely it rose slightly in strongly urban electorates. *Gendai Nihon no Senkyo*, p. 128.

377 Kaiin Toron, 'Nosei Fushin o Hanei Shita Sosenkyo' ['A General Election That Reflected Distrust of Agricultural Policies'], in Nosei Jyaanarisuto no Kai (ed.), *Shu, San Senkyo*, p. 14.

378 Kaiin Toron, 'Nosei Fushin', p. 14. Kobayashi also reports anti-LDP and pro-JSP sentiments being expressed by farmers in surveys around the time of the 1990 election. Furthermore, he notes that the JSP increased its vote tally in rural and semi-rural districts in the 1990 elections compared with the 1986 elections (from 19.75 per cent to 25.43 per cent of the total vote and from 20.40 to 26.33 of the total vote respectively). See *Gendai Nihon no Senkyo*, pp. 121–122, 128.

379 Kawasaki, 'Saninsen to Nosonhyo', p. 27.

380 Support rates were obtained from the *Asahi Shinbun* data reported Miyake, Table 1 in '89-Nen Sangiin Senkyo', p. 36. See also chapter 4 on 'Opposition Party Politics' in my forthcoming volume, *The Challenge to Vested Interests*.

381 In this situation, Kobayashi reports that some farmers, especially in rice-producing regions expressed continuing dissatisfaction with the LDP, but also said that they could only appeal to a party with power (i.e. the LDP). *Gendai Nihon no Senkyo*, p. 122.

382 Kaiin Toron, 'Nosei Fushin, p. 14. Once again, as noted by Kobayashi, a comment made by producers with respect to agricultural issues was that 'we cannot trust the LDP's agricultural policies, but the Opposition parties don't have an agricultural policy'. See *Gendai Nihon no Senkyo*, p. 122.

383 See chapter 4 on 'Opposition Party Politics' in my forthcoming volume, *The Challenge to Vested Interests*.

384 *Gendai Nihon no Senkyo*, p. 123.

385 Sakai, ' "To yori Hito" ', p. 96.

386 Sakai, ' "To yori Hito" ', p. 100.

387 Kaiin Toron, 'Nosei Fushin o Hanei Shita Sosenkyo', p. 14.

388 *Far Eastern Economic Review*, 2 March 1992.

389 *Far Eastern Economic Review*, 2 March 1992.

390 *Japan Agrinfo Newsletter*, Vol. 9, No. 9, May 1992, p. 2.

391 *Japan Agrinfo Newsletter*, Vol. 9, No. 9, May 1992, p. 2.

392 *Far Eastern Economic Review*, 17 November 1988.

393 See chapter 2 on 'Party Politics' in my forthcoming volume, *Politicians and Bureaucrats*.

394 Seisaku Koso Fuooramu, 'GATTO Uruguai Raundo no Seiko ni Mukete'

['Towards the Success of the GATT Uruguay Round'], *Nogyo to Keizai*, Vol. 58, No. 3, March 1992, Appendix, p. 3.

395 A farmer from Kumamoto was quoted as saying: 'Nobody, especially the farmers, believes that their [the politicians'] promises will be kept [about protecting the rice market] . . . The international community is not going to allow Japan alone to shut out foreign rice completely.' *Nihon Keizai Shinbun*, 3 March 1990. Another farmer was quoted as saying: 'The politicians, they keep saying, "No imports! Not a single grain of American rice!" . . . But nobody believes that. We know the foreign rice is coming, and we know we don't compete on price. So my job is to make the best rice I can possibly grow, and find a market that will buy it.' *The Washington Post*, 1 November 1992.

396 As one newspaper commented: 'What large-scale rice producers of Japan want to hear is not extreme protectionism but realistic countermeasures to take when liberalization of the rice market eventually takes place.' *Asahi Evening News*, 16 February 1990.

397 Personal interview with Zenchu official, Tokyo, February 1990.

398 *Nikkei Weekly*, 27 November 1995.

399 Arimitsu, 'Seito to Beika Seisaku', p. 108.

400 See the discussion of changing rural society and farm voters in chapter 5 on 'The Political Demography of Agriculture'.

401 *Tohyo Kodo*, p. 54.

402 Yamaguchi, *Ima Nokyo o Do Suru Ka*, pp. 71–73.

403 Yamaguchi, *Ima Nokyo o Do Suru Ka*, p. 73.

404 Ono, 'Nokyo to Senkyo', p. 76. See also relevant comments on the eroding basis of Nokyo's membership in chapter 4 on 'Organisational Politics'.

405 *No to Shoku*, p. 81.

406 *Far Eastern Economic Review*, 11 November 1988, encapsulating the view of one of Zenchu's former executive directors, Matsumoto Tokuo.

407 *Japan Agrinfo Newsletter*, Vol. 15, No. 6, February 1998, p. 6.

408 *Japan Agrinfo Newsletter*, Vol. 13, No. 10, June 1996, p. 8.

409 See chapter 8 on 'Policy Campaigning'.

410 *The Internationalization of the Japanese Economy*, p. 127.

411 See chapter 4 on 'Organisational Politics'.

412 Fujitani, *Nokyo*, p. 180.

413 Iwai, 'Nogyosha no Seiji Ishiki', p. 9.

414 Fujitani, *Nokyo*, p. 12.

415 Saeki, *Nokyo Kaikaku*, p. 32.

416 Goro Takahashi, 'Growing Conflicts: Government Cash Helps Farm Groups Crop Reform', *Japan Update*, No. 40, January 1995, p. 9.

417 *Nokyo Daikakushin*, p. 2.

418 Fujitani, *Nokyo*, p. 2.

419 *Sogo Nokyo Tokeihyo*, annual, various issues.

420 Sakaguchi, *Kyodai Nokyo*, p. 122.

421 Sakaguchi, *Kyodai Nokyo*, p. 122.

422 Kaiin Toron, 'Nosei Fushin, p. 18.

423 Nosei Jyaanarisuto no Kai, *Hanjutsu Hatten to Keiei Kakushin*, p. 92.

424 Personal interview, Tokyo, July 1995. See also chapter 8 on 'Policy Campaigning'.

425 Fujitani, 'Keito Nokyo no Nosei Katsudo', p. 53.

426 An earlier version of this commentary can be found in Aurelia George Mulgan, 'Electoral Determinants of Agrarian Power: Measuring Rural Decline in Japan', *Political Studies*, Vol. 45, No. 5, December 1997, pp. 875–899.

427 See chapter 5 on 'The Political Demography of Agriculture'.

428 See Sugita, 'Seiji Kiban no Henka', p. 7.

429 But see also the cross-cutting factors working to reduce the clearer differentiation of electorates.

430 See also the qualifying analysis below about the need to build a broader cross-section of support in the new SMDs.

431 *The Australian*, 19 October 1996.

432 The Fukui model has been generally followed by *noseiren* in other prefectures. See, for example, a similar report of internal restructuring for election activities by the Kanagawa Prefecture Nosei Suishin Renmei (Agricultural Policy Promotion League) in 'Suishin Giin to Meiyu', pp. 20–21.

433 'Hatsu no Shosenkyokusei Senkyo', pp. 28–29.

434 *Nikkei Weekly*, 20 November 1995.

435 This observation was made by the author after calculating the percentage of the total vote obtained by successful candidates across a range of constituencies in the 1996 LH election.

436 See J. M. Ramseyer and Frances McCall Rosenbluth, *Japan's Political Marketplace*, Cambridge, MA, Harvard University Press, 1993, p. 10. See also Mathew McCubbins and Frances McCall Rosenbluth, 'Party Provision for Personal Politics: Dividing the Vote in Japan', in Peter Cowhey and Mathew McCubbins (eds), *Structure and Policy in Japan and the United States*, Cambridge University Press, 1995, pp. 35–55.

437 'Seiji Kiban no Henka', p. 8. Other implications of this development for the existence of the *zoku* and the relative policymaking powers of party politicians versus the bureaucrats are discussed in chapter 2 on 'Party Politics' in my forthcoming volume, *Politicians and Bureaucrats*.

438 Sugita, 'Seiji Kiban no Henka', p. 7.

439 See also below.

440 See also chapter 7 on 'Representative Politics'.

441 *Seikan Yoran* [*A Handbook of Politics and the Bureaucracy*], 1997 Special Edition, Tokyo, Seisaku Jihosha, 1997 (hereafter *Seikan Yoran*), p. 95.

442 See chapter 5 on 'The Political Demography of Agriculture'.

443 *Nikkei Weekly*, 16 October 1995.

444 See also below.

445 Sugita, 'Seiji Kiban no Henka', p. 9.

446 'Heisei 10-Nendo "Nosei Undo Soshiki Genchi Kenkyu Shukai" Hiraku' ['Opening the 1998-Year "Agricultural Policy Campaign Organisations in the Field Research Assembly" '], *Nosei Undo Jyaanaru*, No. 23, February, 1999, p. 2.

447 Sugita, 'Seiji Kiban no Henka', p. 9.

448 See chapter 5 on 'The Political Demography of Agriculture'.

449 'Nogyosha Nosei Undo no Kongo no Arikata', *Nosei Undo Jyaanaru*, No. 1, July 1995, p. 17. See also chapter 7 on 'Representative Politics'.

450 'Nogyosha Nosei Undo no Kongo no Arikata', p. 17. Such a league was established in October 1995 called the Japan Agricultural Policy-Nokyo Diet Members' League (Nihon Nosei-Nokyo Giin Renmei). See chapter 7 on 'Representative Politics'.

451 'Hatsu no Shosenkyokusei Senkyo', p. 29.

452 Sasaki Takeshi, 'Post-Election Prospects', *Japan Echo*, Vol. 24, No. 1, Spring 1997, p. 9.

453 Cowhey, 'Domestic Institutions', p. 325.

454 Wada argues from an electoral theory point of view why this is unlikely in the context of the new electoral system in the Lower House. *The Japanese Election System*, pp. 17–27.

455 This is the view of Sato Seizaburo, reported by Mikuriya Takashi, 'Evaluating the Election', *Japan Echo*, Vol. 24, No. 1, Spring 1997, p. 7. Since then, of course, the

parties have undergone further rounds of fission and fusion, but the observation remains apt just the same.
456 Sakaguchi, *Kyodai Nokyo*, p. 113.
457 This accords with an observation made by LDP LH Diet member Kato Koichi to the effect that: 'Under the new single-seat electoral system, policy differences among political parties will be less clear than before, making it difficult for any single party to easily win a majority'. *Nikkei Weekly*, 29 January 1996. Ishii Satoshi, an SDP Diet member made a similar point, warning that Diet politicians would generalise their opinions under the new system to avoid conflicting with voters. *Nikkei Weekly*, 22 April 1996.
458 Wada offers a convincingly argued thesis why this will not occur. See chapter 2 on 'A Game Theory Analysis of Duverger's Law', in his book, *The Japanese Election System*, pp. 17–27.
459 *Viz.* 'Only when the LDP manages to jettison farmers and other uncompetitive sectors from its coalition – which it is attempting to do through electoral reform – can the United States expect to see dramatic changes in Japan's trade policy.' McCall Rosenbluth, 'Comment', p. 422. The weight attached to the electoral basis of policies such as Japan's agricultural protection also arises from the rational choice explanation of Japanese politics as noted in chapter 1.
460 *Nikkei Weekly*, 20 November 1995.
461 In one poll, 65 per cent of respondents said candidates' personalities came first, as opposed to 28 per cent who said party affiliation was more important. *Nikkei Weekly*, 7 October 1996.
462 The NFP candidate won with 83,490 votes, the LDP candidate got 55,491 votes and the Democratic Party candidate got 41,565 votes. *Asahi Shinbun*, 21 October 1996.
463 *The Australian*, 21 October 1996.
464 *Nikkei Weekly*, 3 November 1997.
465 See above.
466 *Nikkei Weekly*, 19 February 1996. This is also in line with Kato Koichi's prediction above.
467 Fukumitsu Toshio, 'Minami no Chikusan Kichi ni Miru Nominhyo no Yukue' ['The Direction of Farmers' Votes in Southern Livestock-Producing Districts'], in Nosei Jyaanarisuto no Kai (ed.), *Senkyo, Beika, Nokyo*, pp. 145–146.
468 Fukumitsu, 'Minami no Chikusan Kichi', p. 146.
469 Zenkoku Nogyo Kyodo Kumiai Chuokai Noseibu, *Nosei Katsudo Taisei ni tsuite* [*Concerning the System of Agricultural Policy Activities*], October 1973, p. 4.
470 Sakaguchi, *Kyodai Nokyo*, p. 111.
471 Sakaguchi reported that even amongst people called *nosui giin* (agriculture and fishery Diet members), the phenomenon of 'distancing themselves from Nokyo' had arisen. *Kyodai Nokyo*, p. 55.
472 Sakaguchi, *Kyodai Nokyo*, p. 113.
473 See chapter 8 on 'Policy Campaigning'.
474 *Yomiuri Shinbun*, 24 October 1997.
475 *Yomiuri Shinbun*, 24 October 1997.
476 *Yomiuri Shinbun*, 24 October 1997.
477 *Yomiuri Shinbun*, 24 October 1997.
478 See chapter 8 on 'Policy Campaigning'.
479 *Nikkei Weekly*, 22 June 1998.
480 'Sokatsu – Nosei Soshiki Undo no Mezasu Mono' ['Summary – Aim of the Agricultural Policy Organisation Campaign'], *Nosei Undo Jyaanaru*, No. 14, August 1997, p. 17.

7 Representative politics

1 This is a position in outside organisations commonly held by politicians.
2 The validity of these criteria were confirmed by the results of a questionnaire distributed to members of APRA, the Diet members' organisation attached to Nokyo. Respondents were asked whether they considered themselves to be *Nokyo giin*. Replies accorded with the above definition in 87 per cent of cases. See George, *The Strategies of Influence*, pp. 243–246.
3 Enoki Akira, Takagi Sanae and Hirata Masami, 'Han Jiyuka Giin' ['Anti-Liberalisation Diet Members'], *Keizai Mondai*, No. 36, April 1971, p. 242.
4 Arimitsu, 'Seito to Beika Seisaku', p. 108.
5 Enoki, Takagi and Hirata, 'Han Jiyuka Giin', p. 242.
6 Arimitsu, 'Seito to Beika Seisaku', p. 108.
7 Arimitsu, 'Seito to Beika Seisaku', p. 109.
8 According to Tachibana's data on the number of self-proclaimed *norin giin* from each prefecture, districts like Aomori, Iwate, Ishikawa, Yamanashi, Ehime and Kumamoto had the highest numbers of self-styled *norin giin* as a proportion of the total number of Diet representatives from the prefecture (an average of 83 per cent), while prefectures like Tokyo, Kanagawa, Osaka, Kyoto and Hyogo had the lowest (an average of 13 per cent). See *Nokyo*, pp. 366–369.
9 Arimitsu, 'Seito to Beika Seisaku', p. 109.
10 Arimitsu, 'Seito to Beika Seisaku', p. 109.
11 See chapter 3 on 'Consumer Politics' in my forthcoming volume, *The Challenge to Vested Interests*.
12 An exception to this was the Diet members' League to Protect the Diet Resolution on Rice (Kome no Kokkai Ketsugi o Mamoru Giin Rengo) formed in October 1993 by Kamei Shizuka who was Chairman of the LDP's Organisation Committee and Takeuchi Takeshi from the SDP and member of the LH Agriculture, Forestry and Fisheries Committee. This group was formed to oppose rice liberalisation and to try and force the coalition government into respecting the Diet resolution in favour of food self-sufficiency and thus opposing rice market opening at the GATT Uruguay Round.
13 Tachibana, *Nokyo*, p. 338.
14 See chapter 2 on 'Party Politics' in my forthcoming volume, *Politicians and Bureaucrats*.
15 There were 226 members of this group in 1972 (including those who were defeated in the 1972 elections). Yoshihara, *Zenno o Kiru*, p. 231. See also chapter 2 on 'Party Politics' in my forthcoming volume, *Politicians and Bureaucrats*.
16 It was maintained, for example, that even former Prime Ministers and faction leaders Tanaka Kakuei and Fukuda Takeo were essentially *norin giin*. Arimitsu, 'Seito to Beika Seisaku', p. 107.
17 Arimitsu, 'Seito to Beika Seisaku', p. 107.
18 Arimitsu, 'Seito to Beika Seisaku', p. 105.
19 Kaiin Toron, 'Norin Kanryo Ikigai to Kikikan', p. 108.
20 *The Economist*, 20 February 1988.
21 *Australian Financial Review*, 27 February 1986.
22 *Australian Financial Review*, 27 February 1986.
23 Sone and Kanazashi, *Nihon no Seiji*, p. 116.
24 Arimitsu, 'Seito to Beika Seisaku', p. 109.
25 Sakaguchi, *Kyodai Nokyo*, p. 102.
26 See chapter 6 for Noseiken funding in the 1971 and 1972 general elections for example.

27 See chapter 2 on 'Party Politics' in my forthcoming volume, *Politicians and Bureaucrats*.

28 Because of low numbers in the Diet, the executives of Komeito, DSP and JCP policy committees are not always Diet members, but party officials.

29 The author relied on sources such as Diet Handbooks, mimeographed lists of agricultural committee members, private interviews, and a privately compiled, comprehensive listing of Japanese politicians with connections to agriculture since 1946.

30 This same exercise was not repeated for the Upper House because prefectural and constituency boundaries are coterminous. It is, therefore, more meaningful to differentiate the smaller geographic areas represented by LH constituencies in one of the five categories of constituencies.

31 These categories are those used in Table 5.10.

32 Consumer attitudes towards agricultural support and protection are discussed extensively in chapter 3 on 'Consumer Politics' in my forthcoming volume, *The Challenge to Vested Interests*, while the ideology of agricultural support and protection is examined in chapter 7 on 'Ideological Politics'. See also my remarks on a possible shift to a zero sum calculus in the wake of the 1998 UH election.

33 Other nominated categories such as semi-rural/semi-urban (6 per cent), semi-urban (12 per cent), urban-rural (1 per cent) and urban (3 per cent) constituencies. The balance were from the national constituency of the Upper House or did not indicate what type of constituency they represented.

34 The exact percentages in the nominated years mean less than the maintenance of the general level of agricultural representation over the 1986–96 period. This is because the percentages at the margins are influenced by the quality of infor-mation available to the author regarding agriculture-related politicians in any one election year. Furthermore, the numbers of agriculture-related Diet members is in one sense cumulative. It contains all those who have been on agriculture-related committees in the past as well as in the present and therefore tends to exaggerate the number of these politicians over time.

35 This reflects the loss of a number of LDP farm politicians in the 1989 UH elections. See chapter 6 on 'Electoral Politics'.

36 There were some exceptions. Yamahara Genjiro from Kochi, for example, has consistently shown a keen interest in agricultural issues and has remained Chairman of the JCP's Agricultural, Forestry and Fisheries Division over a long period of time. He has also been a member of the LH Agriculture, Forestry and Fisheries Committee.

37 See chapter 6 on 'Electoral Politics'.

38 See chapter 6 on 'Electoral Politics'.

39 See chapter 4 on 'Opposition Party Politics' in my forthcoming volume, *The Challenge to Vested Interests*.

40 See chapter 4 on 'Opposition Party Politics' in my forthcoming volume, *The Challenge to Vested Interests*.

41 See chapter 4 on 'Opposition Party Politics' in my forthcoming volume, *The Challenge to Vested Interests*.

42 The list included: Fukita Akira, former LDP *norin zoku*; Hoshino Yukio, former AFD member; Ide Shoichi, former Vice-Chairman of the AFD; Kaneko Tokunosuke, former member of CAPIC; Koga Takaaki, former Chairman of the Agriculture, Forestry and Fisheries Committee in the Yamaguchi prefectural assembly; Mashiko Teruhiko, former member of CAPIC; Mihara Asahiko, son of former agricultural politician Mihara Asao; Nakajima Mamoru, former member of CAPIC; Oishi Masamitsu, former member of the AFD and CAPIC; Sato Moriyoshi, former MAFF Minister; Tanaka Shusei, former Vice-Chairman of

the AFD and member of CAPIC; Yamaoka Kenji, former Chairman of the Shinshinto policy committee on agriculture; and Yanase Susumu, former member of CAPIC.

43 In the 1993 elections, for example, as Table 7.2 shows, the Nihon Shinto elected four new agricultural Diet members (two were former MAFF officials and one was a former executive of the Japan Agricultural Newspaper and Nokyo executive). This was out of a total of 35 new members. The Shinseito elected only three new agricultural Diet members (two of these were ex-LDP prefectural politicians), out of a total of 55 candidates elected.

44 See chapter 5 on 'The Political Demography of Agriculture'.

45 Inoguchi and Iwai, '*Zoku Giin*', p. 187.

46 The importance of agriculture in the Abe faction can be partly explained by the fact that Abe represented an agricultural constituency, was MAF Minister in the 1970s and was a *norin zoku*.

47 The predominance of agriculturally-connected Diet members in the Komoto faction is largely explained by historical factors. The Komoto faction descended from the Miki faction, and in Miki's early political career he was prominent in the Japan Cooperative Party, which had close links to the agricultural cooperative movement. See chapter 3 on 'Farmers' Politics'.

48 'Sokatsu Toron: Shusan Dojitsu Senkyogo no Nakasone Seiji' ['Summary Discussion: Politics Under Nakasone After the Double Lower and Upper House Elections'], in Nosei Jyaanarisuto no Kai (ed.), *Senkyo, Beika, Nokyo*, p. 168. See also chapter 8 on 'Policy Campaigning'.

49 Data on the factional affiliations of JSP members are not available to the author from published sources, and therefore the questionnaire survey was used to obtain this sort of information.

50 Table 8 shows that 40 per cent of agricultural groups had Diet politicians as 'members', whilst the proportion for welfare groups was 37 per cent, educational groups 13 per cent and economic groups 21 per cent. Muramatsu, 'Nihongata Atsuryoku Dantai', p. 80.

51 This is very close to other figures which have revealed the proportion of the total number of Diet members with leadership ties to outside groups. A study of the 1981–83 Diet established that 33 per cent of the Diet were current or former interest group officials. See George, 'The Comparative Study of Interest Groups in Japan', pp. 9–10.

52 *Seikan Yoran*, 1990, First Half Year Issue, pp. 475–478. It is interesting to note, however, that in the case of trade union executives, they are obliged to relinquish union office prior to entry to the Diet. This is not the case with agricultural group executives.

53 An observation made by Komiya Ryutaro is also relevant to this discussion. He argues that 'the number of Diet members tied to a particular organisation is not necessarily a reflection of that organisation's political power. Take Japanese trade unions for example. There are quite a few socialist and communist Diet members who are trade union leaders and who are supported by unions at election time. Their numbers are not declining in the Diet, but their influence is. See his 'Comments', in Aurelia George (ed.), *Japanese Agricultural Policy: A Review*, Research Paper No. 87, Canberra, Australia–Japan Research Centre, 1981, p. 52.

54 See chapter 6 on 'Electoral Politics' for a list of his positions in agricultural groups.

55 See, for example, Sone Yasunori, 'Interest Groups and the Process of Political Decision-making in Japan', in Yoshio Sugimoto and Ross E. Mouer (eds), *Constructs for Understanding Japan*, London, Kegan Paul International, 1989, pp. 259–295. The 1982 George study showed that 29 per cent of the Lower

House were interest group officials, and 41 per cent of the Upper House. See 'The Comparative Study of Interest Groups in Japan', pp. 9–10.

56 The figure of 54 may in fact be understating the situation somewhat, because data gathered for the 1990 figures was assisted by the questionnaire survey, which elicited much more information from Diet members regarding their organisational connections than was available from Diet handbooks and other published sources.

57 Other associated categories of representatives include the politicians with links to unions of workers in agricultural and forestry organisations and to food industry companies and unions. In this book, these Diet members are not strictly considered 'farmers' representatives' and therefore no detailed analysis of their representational characteristics is attempted, although from time to time they are mentioned in passing.

58 Tanaka, *Nihon no Nokyo*, p. 427. Research by the *Asahi Shinbun* in 1970 disclosed that one-third of the chairmen of *kenchu* were LDP members and members of either local assemblies or the Diet. If those who were not members of local assemblies or the Diet were included, LDP members accounted for half the total number of *kenchu* chairmen. Mitsukawa, *Nogyo Dantai Hattenshi*, p. 631.

59 *Japan Agrinfo Newsletter*, Vol. 14, No. 1, September 1996, p. 2.

60 As Ward points out: 'One does not usually distinguish at the village level among a community's political, economic, and social leaders. There is a high probability that they will be the same individuals.' See Robert Ward, 'Urban-Rural Differences and the Process of Political Modernization in Japan: A Case Study', *Economic Development and Cultural Change*, Vol. 9, Part 2, October 1960, p. 144.

61 Personal interview with Zenkoku Noseikyo Secretariat Chief, Tokyo, July 1995.

62 There was one exception to this, Higaki Tokutaro, formerly the MAFF. See chapter 6 on 'Electoral Politics' for Higaki's details.

63 Personal interview with Zenchu official, Tokyo, July 1995.

64 The Zenkoku Noseikyo Secretariat Chief, however, pointed out that while the number of former Nokyo executives in the Diet had been decreasing in recent times, the fact that the numbers in prefectural assemblies were still considerable was due to the prefectural branches supporting the election campaigns of ex-Nokyo candidates running for local election. Personal interview, Tokyo, July 1995.

65 Amongst the 1995 group, for example, Horigome was former Vice-Chairman of Nagano Prefecture Labour Council (the prefectural branch of Sohyo), and Kunii was an adviser to Rengo Tochigi (the Japanese Trade Union Confederation branch in Tochigi Prefecture). He received support from Rengo in the 1995 elections as well as being the Confederation's party (i.e. Minkairen) candidate for Tochigi. *Seikan Yoran*, 1995, Second Half Year Issue, pp. 152, 440. See also below.

66 According to earlier research done by the author, 77 per cent of all prefectural constituency UH Nokyo Diet members between 1950 and 1977 had held or were holding official positions in prefectural Nokyo organisations at the time of election, with the central unions best represented politically. The corresponding figure for national Nokyo organisational representation was 39.5 per cent (in some cases, Nokyo Diet members represented both levels of the organisation). Amongst national Nokyo organisations, the marketing, livestock and silk federations were the best represented. The same pattern was evident amongst LH *Nokyo giin* over the same period. See George, *The Strategies of Influence*, pp. 270–271.

67 See chapter 6 on 'Electoral Politics'.

68 One commentator argued that national Nokyo leaders were so powerful that they did not have to enter politics to get their opinions heard. It was well known, for

instance, that during Miyawaki Asao's tenure as Chairman of Zenchu in the 1970s, he had an open line to PM Tanaka. Clearly, Zenchu leaders carried enormous political weight in their own right. Personal interview with the Secretary of APRA, reported in George, *The Strategies of Influence*, p. 270.

69 Earlier research by the author showed that 52 per cent of *Nokyo giin* in the Upper House had held positions in local government, the vast majority in prefectural assemblies. The figure for LH *Nokyo giin* was 66.6 per cent, once again the vast majority in prefectural assemblies. George, *The Strategies of Influence*, pp. 271, 273.

70 Earlier research by the author showed that one-third of prefectural constituency UH Nokyo Diet members had held the position of party prefectural federation leader, whilst 35 per cent of LH Nokyo Diet members had held leading positions in party prefectural federations, in most cases the chairmanship. See George, *The Strategies of Influence*, pp. 272–273.

71 This information was obtained from the author's card system of Japanese farm politicians, 1949–97.

72 See also chapter 8 on 'Policy Campaigning'.

73 Mitsukawa, *Nogyo Dantai Hattenshi*, p. 632.

74 Kyosanto Bukkuretto, *Gaiatsu no Naka no Nihon*, p. 89.

75 *Asahi Shinbun*, 23 October, 1994.

76 Tanaka, *Nihon no Nokyo*, p. 437.

77 Nosei Jyaanarisuto no Kai, *Hanjutsu Hatten to Keiei Kakushin*, p. 87.

78 Nosei Jyaanarisuto no Kai, *Hanjutsu Hatten to Keiei Kakushin*, p. 91.

79 Nishimoto, 'Nokyo', pp. 321–322.

80 Hanaoka Taro, 'Zaibatsuka Sareta Nokyo' ['Nokyo has Become a *Zaibatsu*'], *Hoseki*, February 1974, p. 112.

81 These type-categories are an adaptation of the classification system proposed by Tanaka. See chapter 6 on 'Electoral Politics'.

82 Tanaka, *Nihon no Nokyo*, p. 437.

83 See George, *The Strategies of Influence*, pp. 213–215.

84 A survey of the backgrounds of APRA members by the author revealed that a majority but not all Nokyo Diet members in any one year were members of the organisation (around 70–75 per cent of LH Nokyo Diet members and around 85 per cent of UH Nokyo Diet members).

85 See chapter 3 on 'Farmers' Politics'.

86 Its early members included some who later became APRA members in the post-war Diet including Miyake Shoichi, JSP, Niigata (3), 1946–63 and 1967–80, adviser to Zennichino, former Chairman of the National Committee of Nichino, who had been active in the farmers' movement in the 1930s, and who was a former member of the Executive Committee of the Labour Farmer Party; Sugiyama Genjiro, Right Socialist member for Osaka (4), 1946–63, former Nichino *Kumiaicho* (Chairman), Nomin Sodomei adviser and Zennichino adviser; Morita Jujiro, LDP, Aomori (1), 1949–55 and 1960–72; Najima Isamu, 1946–49, Progressive Party member for Chiba (1), former chairman of a *nogyokai*; and Matsuura Shutaro, 1946–76, Japan Cooperative Party then LDP member for Hokkaido (2).

87 'Kokusei to Nosei', published material supplied to the author by the Secretary of APRA, source unknown, p. 189. According to Figure 3.1, the Japan Cooperative Party won only 14 seats in the 1946 elections, so the actual numbers of Japan Cooperative Party Diet members at that time is in dispute.

88 Leading members of the Nosei Kenkyukai thereafter were *Nokyo giin* such as Mori Yasoichi, first elected to the UH national constituency in 1950 as a member of the Green Breeze Society and later Independent/LDP member and Chairman

of Zenchu; Ide Ichitaro, first elected to the Diet in 1947 as a member of the Kokumin Kyodoto, later LDP member in the Lower House for Nagano (2) and a Director of Norinchukin and MAF Minister; Sakata Eiichi, first elected from Ishikawa (1) to the Lower House in 1949 as a member of the Democratic Liberal Party, former MAF bureaucrat and later MAF Minister; and Sakamoto Chikao, a Zenchu Director and LDP politician, first elected to the Lower House for Miyazaki (2) in 1969 and later a member of the Upper House for Miyazaki. All except Mori were members of the Miki faction, signifying that faction's strong link to cooperative interests.

89 Personal interview with the Secretary of APRA, Tokyo, November 1972.
90 'Kokusei to Nosei', p. 189.
91 In the author's questionnaire survey of APRA members, to the question: 'What do you think is the main function of the Nosei Kenkyukai?', the respondents were virtually united in the 'policy emphasis' of the organisation. Twenty respondents answered this question (the remaining 15 gave no answer). Their replies ranged as follows: 'To promote a comprehensive and constructive agriculture'; 'research and inquiry into agricultural policy'; 'agricultural promotion'; 'a pipeline to the agricultural policies of government and opposition parties'; 'members plan for policy promotion'; 'the study of agricultural policy'; 'to investigate new agricultural policies'; 'research on an agricultural policy framework'; 'to treat topics in agricultural policy in order to realise and resolve food problems etc. in such a way as to improve the farmers' livelihood'; 'general research on agricultural policy and liaison with Nokyo'; 'to establish a national agricultural policy; 'to promote an agricultural policy for the farmers'; 'in order to guarantee food for the nation, the APRA negotiates with the administration on matters relating to agricultural policy in general'; 'it performs political activities for the advancement agriculture'; 'to improve the farmers' livelihood and build prosperous rural villages'; 'promotion of agricultural policy activities'; 'proposals concerning agricultural policy, the improvement of agricultural finance and budget acquisitions'; 'it functions as a pipeline between the farmers and politics'; 'to advance the promotion of agriculture'; 'the APRA is inactive except during budget time when it holds formal meetings'. Two other APRA members answered in the negative, and two failed to answer the question.
92 'Kokusei to Nosei', p. 195.
93 Figures obtained from successive 'Kaiin Meibo' ['Membership Lists'], personally supplied to the author by the APRA Secretary.
94 For a more detailed breakdown of the party affiliations of APRA members, see George, *The Strategies of Influence*, p. 216.
95 'Heisei 10-Nendo "Nosei Undo Soshiki Genchi Kenkyu Shukai" Hiraku', p. 2.
96 'Heisei 10-Nendo "Nosei Undo Soshiki Genchi Kenkyu Shukai" Hiraku', p. 2.
97 'Heisei 10-Nendo "Nosei Undo Soshiki Genchi Kenkyu Shukai" Hiraku', p. 2.
98 The connection that was reported with the Agriculture, Forestry and Fisheries Finance Corporation in Appendix A was from a former staff member. This corporation does not employ politicians in leadership positions.
99 See Aurelia George Mulgan, 'The Politics of Deregulation and Japanese Agriculture', in T. J. Pempel, Tony Warren, Aurelia George Mulgan, Purnendra Jain, Keiko Tabusa, and Hayden Lesbirel, *The Politics of Economic Reform in Japan: Collected Papers*, Pacific Economic Papers, No. 270, August 1997, pp. 3.1–3.38.
100 Personal interview, Canberra, October 1995.
101 Personal interview, Canberra, October 1995.
102 See chapter 4 on 'Patronage Politics' in my forthcoming volume, *Politicians and Bureaucrats*.

103 Personal interview with agricultural economist, Professor Yuize Yasuhiko, Tokyo, July 1995.
104 Ranking is also influenced by factional decisions, but votes and funds are the two most important candidate-based criteria.
105 See chapter 4 on 'Patronage Politics' in my forthcoming volume, *Politicians and Bureaucrats*.
106 *Nikkei Weekly*, 7 July 1997.
107 Tanaka, *Nihon no Nokyo*, p. 466. See also chapter 6 on 'Electoral Politics'.
108 *89 Gendai Seiji Joho*, p. 413.
109 Personal interview with dairy federation executives, Tokyo, July 1995.
110 *Nikkei Weekly*, 7 July 1997. As the *Nikkei* reports, the scandals involving bureaucrats in recent years and the growing criticism of government ministries as well as of large public works outlays dissuaded some former bureaucrats from running for public office for the LDP, as well as the NFP's vote-getting power in the PR segment of the UH election.
111 See chapter 6 on 'Electoral Politics'.
112 See also chapter 6 on 'Electoral Politics'.
113 Nosei Jyaanarisuto no Kai, *Hanjutsu Hatten to Keiei Kakushin*, p. 89.
114 No further information is available on these organisations, which clearly had a brief and unnoteworthy history.
115 Nosei Jyaanarisuto no Kai, *Hanjutsu Hatten to Keiei Kakushin*, p. 89.
116 See chapter 4 on 'Patronage Politics' in my forthcoming volume, *Politicians and Bureaucrats*.
117 See chapter 6 on 'Electoral Politics'.
118 Personal interview with National Chamber of Agriculture personnel, July 1995.
119 *Chikusan Shinko Jigyodan Nenpo*, 1990, pp. 247–298. The author was unable to obtain data for both direct subsidies and cumulative totals for subsidised investments beyond 1990.
120 This was discussed at some length in Yokota Tetsuji, *Gyuniku Wa Naze Takai Ka* [*Why is Beef Expensive?*], Tokyo, Simul Press, 1977. There were also rumours circulating about the SSPSC recycling some of its profits into the pockets of politicians as financial donations. Even though the LIPC and the SSPSC came together to form ALIC in 1996, each organisation may have continued to hide their work from the other and thus maintain 'secret areas'. As long as these two organisations concealed their activities, it was still possible for politicians to get money from these bodies to which they were connected. There are always rumours about other public corporations as well. Personal interview with *Asahi Shinbun* journalist, Tokyo, July 1995.
121 An examination conducted on the organisational affiliations of livestock Diet members over the three decades from 1947 to 1977 revealed that a leadership position in prefectural livestock associations was extremely common. George, *The Strategies of Influence*, pp. 459–460.
122 The activities of this group are discussed in chapter 2 on 'Party Politics' in my forthcoming volume, *Politicians and Bureaucrats*. A list of *kome giin* (either current or former) is as follows (all are members of the LDP unless otherwise stated): Watanabe Kozo from Fukushima, former Chairman of Tajima Nokyo, but also a *norin zoku* and Chairman of Noshinkyo; Sakurauchi Yoshio from Shimane, former MAF Minister, *norin zoku* and chairman of the rice 'Vietcong'; Watanabe Michio from Tochigi, also one of the rice 'Vietcong' and former MAFF Minister, *norin zoku* and one-time holder of all prominent agricultural policy positions in the LDP; Kano Michihiko (ex-LDP, now NFP) from Yamagata, former MAFF Minister and active in promoting increases in the producer rice

price as Secretary-General of Noshinkyo; Fujio Masayuki from Tochigi and Tamura Hajime from Mie, both leaders of the rice Diet members in the 1960s; and JSP Diet member Hino Ichiro from Miyagi, Zennichino leader, prominent in the LH Agriculture, Forestry and Fisheries Committee and Vice-Chairman of the JSP Rice Struggle Central Headquarters. All these politicians were in the Diet in 1995, although Watanabe Michio later died.

123 Sone and Kanazashi, *Nihon no Seiji*, p. 167.

124 Examples are Eto Takami from Miyazaki (see Table 7.8 for his leadership connections to livestock organisations), Vice-Chairman of the Diet Members' League for the Promotion of Livestock Farming (Chikusan Shinko Giin Renmei) and holder of all top-level positions in the LDP on agricultural policy; Horinouchi Hisao also from Miyazaki (see Table 7.8 for his leadership positions in agricultural groups), Secretary-General of the Diet Members' League for the Promotion of Livestock Farming, holder of leadership positions in the LDP on agricultural policy and also former MAFF Minister; Okawara Taiichiro, former MAFF Vice-Minister, NC member in the Upper House, Adviser to the Central Livestock Association, holder of all major agricultural policy positions in the LDP and Vice-Chairman of the Diet Members' League for the Promotion of Livestock Farming; Kato Koichi from Yamagata, holder of all major LDP agricultural policy positions and Vice-Chairman of the Diet Members' League for the Promotion of Livestock Farming; Yamanaka Sadanori from Kagoshima (see Table 7.8 for connections to livestock-related organisations) and Adviser to the Diet Members' League for the Promotion of Livestock Farming; Ozato Sadatoshi, also from Kagoshima, Assistant Secretary-General of the Diet Members' League for the Promotion of Livestock Farming and holder of LDP agricultural office; Suzuki Seigo from Fukushima, chairman of a range of livestock-related organisations (see Table 7.8) and holder of leadership positions in the Diet and in the LDP on agricultural policy; Tani Yoichi from Hyogo, Assistant Secretary-General of the Diet Members' League for the Promotion of Livestock Farming, *norin zoku* and a member of LDP agricultural policy committees; Mizuno Kiyoshi from Chiba, holder of leadership positions in livestock-related organisations, a *norin zoku*, and Vice-Chairman of the Diet Members' League for the Promotion of Livestock Farming; and Nakao Eiichi from Yamanashi, holder of party and Diet leadership positions on agricultural policy, Vice-Chairman of the Diet Members' League for the Promotion of Livestock Farming, specialist on agricultural liberalisation problems and negotiator with the United States on agricultural trade problems. All these politicians were in the Diet in 1995. Others are listed in George, *The Strategies of Influence*, pp. 457–458.

125 Examples are Hachiro Yoshio, a dairy farming specialist from Hokkaido and JSP/Independent Nokyo Diet member (see Table 7.8); Kitamura Naoto from Hokkaido (LDP/NFP) Diet member elected with support from Hokkaido dairy farmers and a member of LDP agricultural policy committees; Mitsuzuka Hiroshi from Miyagi, member of the Dairy Farmers' Political Federation of Japan and member of LDP agricultural policy committees. These politicians were all in the Diet in 1995.

126 Examples are Mitsubayashi Yataro from Saitama (see Table 7.8 for leadership connections to horticultural groups) and holder of all major positions in the LDP on agricultural policy; and Otsuka Seijiro from Saga (see Table 7.8 for leadership connections to agricultural groups) and holder of party and Diet agricultural policy leadership positions. Both these politicians were in the Diet in 1995, although Otsuka Seijiro later died.

127 The distinction between the categories of 'beef' and 'dairy' politician is somewhat

spurious given the high regional coincidence of dairy and beef production and the fact that substantial quantities of domestic beef come from dairy herds.

128 Personal interview with federation executives, Tokyo, July 1995.

129 Personal interview with federation executives, Tokyo, July 1995.

130 Personal interview with federation executives, Tokyo, July 1995.

131 'Hatsu no Shosenkyokusei Senkyo', p. 30. See also 'Suishin Giin to Meiyu', pp. 20–23, which details meetings held between prefectural *noseiren* and their Diet representatives all over the country in the year following the LH election.

132 See below.

133 *Seikan Yoran*, 1997, Special Issue, p. 211.

134 See also chapter 8 on 'Policy Campaigning'.

135 Tetsuhisa Matsuzaki, 'Slowing Parties: Inertia Will Keep Bureaucrats and Ex-LDP Members at the Fore', *Japan Update*, June 1994, pp. 10–11.

136 Career information on Saito Juro available from the author's card index system of farm politicians.

137 See chapter 6 on 'Electoral Politics'.

138 Inoguchi and Iwai, '*Zoku Giin*', p. 103.

139 See also my earlier comments on this issue and in chapter 6 on 'Electoral Politics'.

140 These details were obtained from Diet handbooks and the author's own card index system of Japanese farm politicians 1949–97.

141 See also above.

142 This substantiates an argument made in the Inoguchi and Iwai study of LDP policy tribes, which pointed out that 'unlike the ministries or business circles which represent rather specific interest groups, an LDP Diet member can represent various interest groups, from agricultural workers to small-scale entrepreneurs, or both consumers and producers, depending on the issue. In short, interests represented by LDP Diet members are pluralistic and multilayered.' '*Zoku Giin*', p. 102.

143 It was not clear from the information available what career the remaining Diet members had prior to their gaining national political office.

144 This particular feature of Japanese interest group behaviour has been identified by a number of Western analysts including William E. Steslicke, *Doctors in Politics: The Political Life of the Japan Medical Association*, New York, Praeger, 1973, and Donald R. Thurston, *Teachers and Politics in Japan*, Princeton, Princeton University Press, 1973.

145 David Truman, *The Governmental Process*, 2nd edition, New York, Alfred A. Knopf, 1971, p. 264.

146 Agricultural groups scored the best average access to government administrative personnel (78.3 per cent of agricultural groups), Diet members (43.5 per cent) and 'friendly' Diet members (60.9 per cent). See Table 1.8 in *Sengo Nihon no Atsuryoku Dantai*, p. 36. A total of 81 per cent of so-called 'friendly' Diet members, for example, were from the LDP (p. 36).

147 A total of 73.9 per cent of agricultural groups had contacts with the LDP. The next highest were administration-related groups (73.3 per cent). *Sengo Nihon no Atsuryoku Dantai*, p. 173.

148 Muramatsu and Krauss, 'The Dominant Party', p. 297.

149 Muramatsu and Krauss, 'The Dominant Party', p. 296.

150 Muramatsu and Krauss, 'The Dominant Party', p. 293.

151 This topic is discussed explicitly in the British case, for example, in Allen Potter, *Organized Groups in British National Politics*, London, Faber, 1961, especially chapter 15, pp. 271–292.

152 As Izumi has pointed out, LDP Diet politicians have traditionally been 'mainly former bureaucrats, executives of larger corporations, and leaders of farming,

forestry, or fishing organizations. Socialist party members are largely former labor union leaders, including those from the teachers' union . . . Clean Government party Diet members are usually former executives of small and medium-size firms or officials of the party secretariat. Former labor union leaders and executives of small and medium-size firms form the bulk of Democratic Socialist party'. Shoichi Izumi, 'Diet Members', in Francis R. Valeo and Charles E. Morrison (eds), *The Japanese Diet and the U.S. Congress*, Boulder, CO., Westview Press, 1983, p. 71.

153 Two examples are George, 'The Comparative Study of Interest Groups' and Bradley Richardson and Scott Flanagan, 'Interest Articulation and Aggregation', in *Politics in Japan*, Boston, Little, Brown & Co., 1984, pp. 290–328.

154 See chapter 6 on 'Electoral Politics'.

155 See chapter 2 on 'Interest Group Politics'.

156 Matsuzaka, 'Koritsuka Suru Norin Kanryo', p. 13.

157 Matsuura Tatsuo, ' "Hokaku Ainori" Doko Made Tsuzuku' [' "The Collusion" between the Conservatives and Progressives: How Long Will It Last?'], in Nosei Jyaanarisuto no Kai (ed.), *Tatoka Jidai no Nosei*, p. 13.

158 See chapter 4 on 'Patronage Politics' in my forthcoming volume, *Politicians and Bureaucrats*.

159 'Kumagai Ichio Kokkai Ripooto' ['Kumagai Ichio's Diet Report'], *Nosei Undo Jyaanaru*, No. 22, December 1998, p. 25.

160 In the case of the LDP, agricultural policy groups and committees tested were the AFD, CAPIC and the party's Agriculture, Forestry and Fisheries Bureau. In the case of the JSP, it was the Agriculture, Forestry and Fisheries Division, the Agriculture, Forestry and Fisheries Office, the Policy Committee on Agriculture, Forestry and Fisheries Market Opening Problems, the Special Committee on Forestry Policy, the Livestock Division Office, the Agriculture and Food Policy Project Office and the Special Committee on Sweet Resources Policy. For the DSP it was the Special Committee on Agricultural Basic Problems Policy and the Special Committee on Urban Agricultural Policy, and for the Komeito, it was the Special Committee on Agricultural Problems.

161 Koichi Kishimoto, 'Diet Structure, Organization, and Procedures', in Valeo and Morrison (eds), *The Japanese Diet*, pp. 43–44.

162 Izumi, 'Diet Members', p. 63.

163 Izumi, 'Diet Members', p. 63.

164 Inoguchi and Iwai, 'Zoku Giin', p. 142.

165 Inoguchi and Iwai, 'Zoku Giin', p. 142.

166 Inoguchi and Iwai, 'Zoku Giin', p. 143.

167 See chapter 2 on 'Party Politics' in my forthcoming volume, *Politicians and Bureaucrats*.

168 See chapter 2 on 'Party Politics' in my forthcoming volume, *Politicians and Bureaucrats*.

169 Quoted in *Seikan Yoran*, Special Issue, 1997, p. 10.

170 One of his other main claims to fame came when he was MAFF Minister in the Uno Cabinet. He reportedly said that 'women were useless in politics'.

171 Tachibana, *Nokyo*, pp. 340–343.

172 Amongst this group were Watanabe Michio, Hata Tsutomu, Kato Koichi and Tamazawa Tokuichiro, all prominent *norin zoku*.

173 Arimitsu, 'Seito to Beika Seisaku', p. 109.

174 This was in fact done by Tachibana, *Nokyo*, pp. 340–343.

175 Tachibana, *Nokyo*, p. 339.

176 Tachibana, *Nokyo*, p. 339.

177 Ishida, 'Interest Groups Under A Semipermanent Government Party', pp. 1–10.

178 Kan Ori, 'The Diet in the Japanese Political System', in Valeo and Morrison (eds), *The Japanese Diet*, p. 15.
179 See chapter 6 on 'The Politics of Agricultural Policymaking' in my forthcoming volume, *Politicians and Bureaucrats*.
180 George, 'Japanese Interest Group Behaviour', p. 132.
181 George, 'Japanese Interest Group Behaviour', p. 106.
182 Hiroshi Fukunaga, 'If That's Democracy, I'll Take Chocolate', *Tokyo Business Today*, February 1996, p. 5.
183 For an elaboration of this theme in a number of different policy contexts, see Stockwin *et al.*, *Dynamic and Immobilist Politics in Japan*.
184 See chapter 2 on 'Party Politics' in my forthcoming volume, *Politicians and Bureaucrats*.
185 The organisational lineage of some of these groups was not clear from the data.
186 The organisational lineage of some of these groups was not clear from the data.

8 Policy campaigning

1   Goto and Imamura, 'Japanese Agriculture', p. 19.
2   Takeuchi and Otawara, *Asu no Nokyo*, p. 251.
3   Muramatsu, Ito and Tsujinaka's study of agricultural groups revealed that they utilised organisational size as a useful resource. *Sengo Nihon no Atsuryoku Dantai*, p. 234.
4   As Imamura and Inuzuka argue, because of the mutual dependence of Nokyo and the government, Nokyo is given much power to intervene in agricultural policymaking as a pressure group. *Seifu to Nomin*, p. 74. But as they also point out, for the same reason, its independence as a cooperative is largely limited. See chapter 2 on 'Interest Group Politics' for a discussion of this question.
5   Takeuchi and Otawara, *Asu no Nokyo*, p. 251.
6   Asuwa, *Nokyo no Genjo*, p. 252.
7   See chapter 2 on 'Interest Group Politics'.
8   Muramatsu, Ito and Tsujinaka's study of Japanese pressure groups revealed that agricultural groups scored very high (95 per cent) on exchanges of opinion with administrative authorities. *Sengo Nihon no Atsuryoku Dantai*, p. 204. Earlier work by Muramatsu indicated that agricultural groups mainly lobbied administrative organs relative to political parties (78.3 per cent as opposed to 17.4 per cent). He speculated that pressure groups come to depend more on the bureaucracy if their interests had already been well reflected in existing policies. This was simply because administrative institutions actually executed policies. On the other hand, politicians (i.e. political parties) took leadership in introducing new policies, and therefore, pressure groups that demanded completely new policies had to communicate with political parties or individual politicians. 'Nihongata Atsuryoku Dantai', p. 79. This author's research does not strongly support this contention. Very close ties are maintained with LDP politicians in order to influence LDP intervention in agricultural policymaking and the ruling party's 'political' amendment of agricultural policies. See below, chapter 2 on 'Party Politics' and chapter 6 on 'The Politics of Agricultural Policymaking' in my forthcoming volume, *Politicians and Bureaucrats*.
9   Muramatsu, Ito and Tsujinaka's analysis scored agricultural groups very high on an index of 'mass strategies' (they were below labour, citizens' and political groups), but much higher than professional, economic, welfare, educational and administrative groups. See Table 4-18 in *Sengo Nihon no Atsuryoku Dantai*, p. 206.
10   According to Muramatsu, Ito and Tsujinaka's survey, agricultural groups scored moderately high for contacts with the PM (30.4 per cent), slightly lower for the

MAFF Minister (26.1 per cent), very high for bureau directors (73.9 per cent) and extremely high for section chiefs (95.7 per cent). Table 4-20 in *Sengo Nihon no Atsuryoku Dantai*, p. 209.

11 Muramatsu, Ito and Tsujinaka's survey of Japanese pressure groups showed that 71.4 per cent of them, including agricultural groups, worked through 'people who support the position of one's group'. See Table 4-15 in *Sengo Nihon no Atsuryoku Dantai*, p. 198. Their survey also suggested that agricultural groups were very active in political negotiations to obtain benefits. This was part of the author's general thesis that agricultural groups changed from being sectoral groups to 'policy beneficiary groups' (*seisaku rieki dantaika*) (pp. 202–203).

12 Ono, *No to Shoku*, p. 84.

13 See chapter 7 on 'Representative Politics'.

14 Nagata and Saito, *Nokyo no Hanashi*, p. 21. See also below.

15 Tachibana, *Nokyo*, p. 334. The policy central headquarters system was set up in 1970.

16 In the 1970s and 1980s, there used to be four central headquarters for price problems: one for grains, one for livestock, one for dairy farming and one for fruit and vegetables, with offices set up in the Agriculture and Livestock Department of Zenchu. Tachibana, *Nokyo*, p. 334.

17 Since reaching a post-WWII peak in 1960 of 115 kg per person, annual rice consumption has been falling steadily. By fiscal 1988–89, it had fallen to 70.9 kg. In 1987, Japanese people for the first time consumed more milk and dairy products than rice. Each citizen consumed 75 kg of milk and dairy products in that year, twice the amount in 1965, compared with 71 kg of rice, about half the all-time record of 1939. In percentage terms, consumption of meat grew even faster – tripling from 1965 to reach 27 kg in 1987.

18 Zenchu organised a new rice consumption countermeasures strategy in 1990. With the backing of the MAFF, it turned to modern American rock'n'roll to bolster rice's fading fortunes. It launched a three-year 'I Love Rice' campaign at major railway stations nationwide, with young women performing aerobics to rock music played at disco-level decibels on stage. This was for the purpose of attracting commuters to displays of pamphlets, new rice-based products and samples of new rice dishes to disseminate both the cultural and nutritional value of rice. The campaign emphasised that rice consumption was an Asia-wide food habit, while bread was only used in Western food, that rice was nutritious and that few Japanese were obese because rice was the main course. Nokyo's offensives to halt the decline in rice consumption, however, have generally been remarkable for their lack of success. The Japanese continue to eat less of it every year. Farmers are cutting back on consumption even faster than city-dwellers.

19 See chapter 7 on 'Ideological Politics' in my forthcoming volume, *The Challenge to Vested Interests*.

20 See chapter 3 on 'Consumer Politics' in my forthcoming volume, *The Challenge to Vested Interests*.

21 Ishida and George, 'Nokyo', p. 205; Ito, 'Nokyo to Seiji Katsudo', p. 150.

22 Hiroshi Yamato, 'Political Parties and the Diet', in Valeo and Morrison (eds), *The Japanese Diet*, p. 31.

23 See chapter 2 on 'Party Politics' and chapter 6 on 'The Politics of Agricultural Policymaking' in my forthcoming volume, *Politicians and Bureaucrats*.

24 Sakurai, 'Nokyo no Nosei Katsudo', p. 63.

25 Muramatsu Michio, 'Center-Local Political Relations in Japan: A Lateral Competition Model', *Journal of Japanese Studies*, Vol. 12, Summer 1986, p. 318. The original reference for this was Tachibana, *Nokyo*, pp. 336–337.

26 Ishida, *Gendai Soshikiron*, pp. 2–3.

27 Zenkoku Nogyo Kyodo Kumiai, *Hayawakari JA no Subete*, p. 81.
28 Muramatsu and Krauss, 'The Dominant Party', p. 297.
29 Sakaguchi, *Kyodai Nokyo*, p. 97.
30 See chapter 4 on 'Organisational Politics'.
31 A list of the major resolutions emanating from these conventions over the period 1952–88 can be found in Zenkoku Nogyo Kyodo Kumiai Chuokai, *Hayawakari JA no Subete*, pp. 82–85.
32 *Japan Agrinfo Newsletter*, Vol. 12, No. 4, December 1994, p. 2.
33 *Japan Agrinfo Newsletter*, Vol. 12, No. 4, December 1994, p. 2.
34 Kaiin Toron, 'Norin Kanryo', p. 104.
35 The extent of the responsibility of the full-time executives of Zenchu for agricultural policy matters within the organisation is the fact that these officials are those who are sacrificed when Zenchu suffers spectacular policy failures such as the beef and orange liberalisation of 1988 and the minimum access agreement for rice in 1993. Those in charge (Matsumoto Tokuo and Ishikura Teruka respectively) were both fired from their executive positions following these liberalisation agreements by the government. Matsumoto was demoted and sent to the equivalent of Nokyo Siberia – Zenchu's cooperative college in Hachioji. In the 1960s, such policy 'failures' were more likely to result in the resignation of the Zenchu Chairman, as happened in 1969 over the introduction of the IDR system. Miyawaki Asao resigned over the introduction of the system, but was, however, immediately re-elected to the position. See also Tanaka, *Nihon no Nokyo*, pp. 175–182 191–194.
36 Internal interest group processes and the extent to which group leaders represent the policy preferences of members is subjected to more theoretical treatment in James L. Franke and Douglas Dobson, 'Interest Groups: The Problem of Representation', *Western Political Quarterly*, Vol. 38, No. 2, June 1985, pp. 224–237.
37 Saeki, *Nokyo Kaikaku*, p. 179.
38 'Nogyo Kyodo Kumiaiho', in *Nogyo Roppo*, 1976, p. 116. Election rights are for choosing executives and representatives; voting rights are for voting on issues such as the establishment of representatives' meetings (*sodaikai* – see below), and the dissolution and amalgamation of agricultural cooperatives. For a full explication of the voting and election rights of agricultural cooperative members, see Zenkoku Nogyo Kyodo Kumiai Chuokai, *Shinpan: Nogyo Kyodo Kumiaiho*, p. 139.
39 In fact the *noji kumiai hojin* often exercise stronger rights in management than individual farmers because of their purchasing and marketing power. Even though they may only exercise one voting right, they can, for instance, buy huge amounts of farm inputs and generate 10–20 per cent of a co-op's profits.
40 Takeuchi and Okawara argue that as far as management of the agricultural cooperatives are concerned, the job of the board of directors is to provide basic management direction only, with daily management of the cooperatives committed to the full-time directors. *Asu no Nokyo*, p. 235. On the other hand, the *sokai* or *sodaikai* is the supreme body for deciding the intention or purpose of the agricultural cooperative (*saiko ishi kettei kikan*). Takahashi, 'Kyodo Kumiainai Shijo Genri', p. 226.
41 Moore, *Japanese Agriculture*, p. 165.
42 Fujitani, *Nokyo*, p. 14.
43 General meetings may also be requested by members with the consent of more than one-fifth of the entire membership. They are usually called twice a year.
44 Fujitani, 'Nokyo at a Crossroads', p. 379. This has become rarer because of co-op mergers.

45 Other matters decided at the general meeting include the annual budget reports, all levies on members and other organisational matters. See Dore, *Land Reform in Japan*, p. 279.
46 Saeki, *Nokyo Kaikaku*, p. 182.
47 'Nogyo Kyodo Kumiaiho', in *Nogyo Roppo*, 1976, p. 118.
48 Fujitani, 'Nokyo at a Crossroads', p. 371.
49 Kajii, 'Nogyo Kosho', p. 128.
50 'Nokyo Kyodo Kumiaiho', in *Nogyo Roppo*, 1976, p. 118.
51 An amendment to Nokyo Law permitted members of prefectural and national organisations to be given more than two votes, depending on the number of members each organisation has. This means that large-scale *tankyo* can be given more than two votes, while small-scale *tankyo* have only one vote. Similarly, large-scale prefectural federations can be given more than two votes while small-scale federations only have one. Tanaka, *Nihon no Nokyo*, pp. 20–21.
52 Nokyo's internal organisational decisionmaking procedures are elaborated in George, *The Strategies of Influence*, pp. 82–105.
53 'Toitsu Chiho Senkyo e no Kakuchi no Torikumi', p. 29.
54 Central Union of Agricultural Cooperatives, 1972, p. 17.
55 Both *senmu riji* and *jomu riji* mean 'managing director' in Japanese. The figures are for October 1997. Until very recently, Zenchu had five *jomu riji*.
56 'Nokyo Kyodo Kumiaiho', in *Nogyo Roppo*, 1976, p. 128.
57 Nokyo Pamphlet, *JA Zenchu Soshiki Kozu*, 1998, p. 2.
58 This system is replicated across the other national federations. Personal communication, Kobayashi Shinichi, Nihon University, 20 May 1998.
59 *Nokyo Kaikaku*, p. 182.
60 In fact Zenchu explains that the leadership side of the cooperatives has been historically differentiated into the executive machinery, the management machinery and the machinery to decide the will of the organisation. These correspond to the board of directors, full-time executives and general meetings respectively. See Zenkoku Nogyo Kyodo Kumiai Chuokai, *Shinpan: Nogyo Kyodo Kumiaiho*, p. 194.
61 Takeuchi and Otawara, *Asu no Nokyo*, p. 235.
62 See chapter 2 on 'Interest Group Politics'.
63 *Nokyo no Genjo*, p. 66.
64 *Ima Nokyo o Do Suru Ka?*, pp. 73–74.
65 Zenkoku Nogyo Kyodo Kumiai Chuokai, *Hayawakari JA no Subete*, p. 80.
66 Yamaguchi, *Ima Nokyo o Do Suru Ka?*, p. 54.
67 Yamaguchi, *Ima Nokyo o Do Suru Ka?*, pp. 155–156.
68 This is the description of the process by the head of Zenchu's Agricultural Policy Department in the early 1970s. See Sakurai, 'Nokyo no Nosei Katsudo', pp. 62–63.
69 Zenkoku Nogyo Kyodo Kumiai Chuokai, *Hayawakari JA no Subete*, p. 81.
70 Yamaguchi, *Ima Nokyo o Do Suru Ka?*, pp. 155–156.
71 But see also below.
72 The role of MAFF bureaucrats in agricultural policymaking is examined in chapter 6 on 'The Politics of Agricultural Policymaking' in my forthcoming volume, *Politicians and Bureaucrats*.
73 Kyosanto Bukkuretto, *Gaiatsu no Naka no Nihon*, p. 30.
74 Ono, 'Nokyo to Senkyo', pp. 84–85.
75 Ono, 'Nokyo to Senkyo', p. 87.
76 Ono, 'Nokyo to Senkyo', p. 87.
77 Amongst the 15 Zenchu *riji* in 1997, eight were prefectural *kenchu* chairmen. The balance consisted of a representative from Zenkyoren's Board of Directors,

Chairman of the Board of Directors of Norinchukin, the Chairman of Ie no Hikari Kyokai, a representative of the Zenkoku Koseiren Board of Directors, a representative of the Zenno Board of Directors, a representative of the Nichienren Board of Directors and the Chairman of the National Nokyo Tourism Association. Nokyo Pamphlet, *Zenkoku Nogyo Kyodo Kumiai Chuokai Yakuin* [*National Agricultural Cooperative Union Central Union Executives*], 1998, p. 2.

78 Personal Interview with MAFF official, Tokyo, November 1994.

79 Domon Takeshi, 'Shoeki ni Hashita Nosei Kanryo no Hyaku Hi' ['One Hundred Days of Agricultural Policy Bureaucrats Pursuing Their Interests'], *Chuo Koron*, Vol. 109, No. 6, June 1994, p. 132. As noted earlier, Ishikura's resignation was in the end demanded by the Zenchu leadership as a sop to the regions.

80 See chapter 4 on 'Organisational Politics'.

81 See chapter 4 on 'Organisational Politics'.

82 See chapter 2 on 'Interest Group Politics'.

83 See chapter 2 on 'Interest Group Politics'.

84 Yamaji Susumu, 'Atsuryoku Dantai Toshite no Nokyo' ['Nokyo As A Pressure Group'], in Kondo Yasuo (ed.), *Nokyo Nijugonen: Sokatsu to Tenbo* [*Twenty-Five Years of Nokyo: Summary and Outlook*], Nihon Nogyo Nenpo, Vol. 22, Tokyo, Ochanomizu, 1973, p. 239.

85 Nagata and Saito, *Nokyo no Hanashi*, p. 76.

86 This covers a whole range of issues, for example. As far as its taxation demands in relation to fiscal 1992 tax policy are concerned, Zenchu requested extension of the agricultural cooperative merger support law, treating subsidies paid to farmers for the establishment of 'rice paddy agriculture' (i.e. rice acreage reduction) as temporary income, increasing the special tax deductions where farming land had been transferred to rationalise farmland ownership, and exceptional treatment for the agricultural income of those newly engaged in agriculture or who had expanded their scale of farming. These demands were presented to Diet members and the LDP, including the LDP's taxation system investigation committee. They were all more or less realised except for the increase in the amount of special tax deduction in cases where farmland was transferred for the purpose of rationalising farmland ownership. *Nokyo Nenkan*, 1993, pp. 81–84.

87 See chapter 4 on 'Organisational Politics'.

88 Kobayashi, Shinohara and Soma, *Senkyo*, p. 78.

89 Muramatsu, Ito and Tsujinaka, *Sengo Nihon no Atsuryoku Dantai*, p. 139.

90 *Yomiuri Shinbun*, 14 September 1994.

91 A detailed analysis of these campaigns can be found in George, *The Strategies of Influence*, pp. 371–489. See also below.

92 See also below.

93 A detailed analysis of these campaigns can be found in George, *The Strategies of Influence*, pp. 317–362.

94 Enoki, Takagi and Hirata, 'Han Jiyuka Giin', p. 245.

95 See chapter 2 on 'Party Politics' in my forthcoming volume, *Politicians and Bureaucrats*.

96 *Nokyo Nenkan*, 1978, p. 99. Its campaign to protect agriculture involved a series of activities including the holding of an 'Assembly to Present Demands on Livestock Commodity Prices to Political Parties' (Chikusanbutsu Kakaku Yokyu Seito Yosei Shukai) which was aimed selectively at the ruling party. The programme of *nosei katsudo* also extended to a campaign of demands by the permanent executives of the Zennofukyo to LIPAC.

97 *Nihon Nogyo Nenkan*, 1996, p. 370.

98 For examples of the latter, see chapter 6 on 'Electoral Politics'.

99 A comprehensive discussion of *seinenbu* political activities can be found in Zenkoku Nokyo Seinen Soshiki Kyogikai, 'Nokyo Seinenbu to Seiji Katsudo' ['The Nokyo Youth Division and Political Activities'], *Chijo*, August 1967, pp. 88–97.

100 Nosei Jyaanarisuto no Kai, *Nogyo Kihonho no Soten*, p. 153.

101 *Nokyo Nenkan*, 1978, p. 101.

102 Domon, 'Shoeki ni Hashita Nosei Kanryo', p. 132.

103 *Nihon Nogyo Nenkan*, 1996, p. 371.

104 *Nihon Nogyo Nenkan*, 1996, p. 371.

105 These used to appear in *Nokyo Nenkan*, but since the demise of this annual volume in 1994, the author is not aware of any other published source of this list.

106 *Nokyo Nenkan*, 1993, pp. 378–411.

107 *Nokyo Undo*, p. 262. Zenchu, for its part, claims that while its agricultural policy activities continued their focus on demand price campaigns, in fact in the 1980s when issues such as the rice *gentan*, crop diversion (*tensaku*) and rice paddy utilisation reorganisation policies were introduced, its agricultural policy activities extended into many fields such as tax, subsidy and structural policies and it promoted campaigns in these areas. Furthermore, when external pressures mounted to liberalise Japan's agricultural market, Nokyo's *nosei katsudo* took on struggles to prevent and oppose import liberalisation as an important mission. Zenkoku Nogyo Kyodo Kumiai Chuokai, *Hayawakari JA no Subete*, pp. 80–81. See also below.

108 Ishikawa, 'Nogyo Kyodo Kumiai', p. 252. See also chapter 3 on 'Bureaucratic Politics' in my forthcoming volume, *Politicians and Bureaucrats*.

109 See chapter 2 on 'Interest Group Politics' and chapter 4 on 'Patronage Politics' in my forthcoming volume, *Politicians and Bureaucrats*.

110 See chapter 7 on 'Representative Politics'.

111 Personal interview, Tokyo, July 1995.

112 The micro-politics of subsidies is discussed at length in chapter 4 on 'Patronage Politics' in my forthcoming volume, *Politicians and Bureaucrats*.

113 Ishikawa, 'Nogyo Kyodo Kumiai', p. 251. See also chapter 4 on 'Organisational Politics'.

114 See chapter 2 on 'Interest Group Politics'.

115 Tachibana, *Nokyo*, p. 335.

116 Tachibana, *Nokyo*, p. 335.

117 See chapter 2 on 'Interest Group Politics'.

118 Ono, *No to Shoku*, p. 65. As he describes it: 'Nokyo created its own campaign style in which agricultural cooperative representatives gathered in Tokyo. This crowd-gathering method involved holding meetings of more than 10,000 participants for demanding producer rice price increases, demonstration parades and sit-down demonstrations at the LDP headquarters.' Sakurai comments that in 1961, Nokyo organised demonstration marches, opened demand conventions in each prefecture and appealed to regional assemblies, thus invigorating its producer rice price campaigns. *Beika Seisaku*, pp. 125–126.

119 Sakurai comments that in 1962, Nokyo's producer rice price convention in Tokyo rallied 10,000 people. *Beika Seisaku*, p. 126.

120 See Table 2.1 in my forthcoming volume, *Politicians and Bureaucrats*. The factors involved in these fluctuations are discussed in George, *The Strategies of Influence*, pp. 297–370.

121 Sakaguchi, *Kyodai Nokyo*, p. 112.

122 Tachibana, *Nokyo*, p. 336.

123 These are spelled out respectively in 'Beihyoka Kettei', p. 221.

124 'Beihyoka Kettei', pp. 221–222.
125 In 1970, for example, Zenchu switched from a so-called 'annual income balance method' to a 'bulk line method'.
126 Tachibana, *Nokyo*, p. 336.
127 Nosei no Shoten I [Focus on Agricultural Policy I], 'Beihyoka Kettei ga Nokoshita Mono' ['Matters Left Over After the Rice and Wheat Price Decisions'], in Nosei Jyaanarisuto no Kai (ed.), *Tatoka Jidai no Nosei*, p. 223.
128 Moore, *Japanese Agriculture*, p. 156.
129 Moore, *Japanese Agriculture*, p. 163.
130 In 1970, for example, Nokyo put an advertisement in the popular weekly magazine *Shukan Asahi* for the first time, with a view to promoting public understanding of the situation with respect to domestic agriculture.
131 See chapter 2 on 'Party Politics' in my forthcoming volume, *Politicians and Bureaucrats*.
132 Sakaguchi, *Kyodai Nokyo*, p. 97.
133 See chapter 2 on 'Party Politics' in my forthcoming volume, *Politicians and Bureaucrats*.
134 Arimitsu, *Seito to Beika Seisaku*, p. 110.
135 Moore, *Japanese Agriculture*, p. 163.
136 Arimitsu, *Seito to Beika Seisaku*, p. 110. See also chapter 2 on 'Party Politics' in my forthcoming volume, *Politicians and Bureaucrats*.
137 Tachibana, *Nokyo*, p. 339.
138 Arimitsu, *Seito to Beika Seisaku*, p. 110.
139 The influence of elections on producer rice price outcomes is examined extensively in chapter 2 on 'Party Politics' in my forthcoming volume, *Politicians and Bureaucrats*.
140 See chapter 2 on 'Party Politics' in my forthcoming volume, *Politicians and Bureaucrats*.
141 These are all listed in *Nokyo Nenkan*, annual, relevant years.
142 Nosei no Shoten, pp. 118–119.
143 *Chikusan Shinko Shingikai Iin Meibo* [*Livestock Industry Promotion Advisory Council Membership Register*] and *Chikusan Shinko Shingikai Tokubetsu Iin Meibo* [*Livestock Industry Promotion Advisory Council Special Membership Register*], MAFF Home Page, http://www.maff.go.jp.
144 This is the national organisation of Seikyo, referred to earlier. Terminologically speaking, Seikyo is the equivalent of Nokyo. See chapter 3 on 'Consumer Politics' in my forthcoming volume, *The Challenge to Vested Interests*.
145 Personal interview with league executives, Tokyo, July 1995.
146 See chapter 2 on 'Party Politics' in my forthcoming volume, *Politicians and Bureaucrats*.
147 See chapter 2 on 'Party Politics' and chapter 3 on 'Bureaucratic Politics' in my forthcoming volume, *Politicians and Bureaucrats*.
148 See Table 2.3 in my forthcoming volume, *Politicians and Bureaucrats*.
149 Tachibana, *Nokyo*, p. 338.
150 *Nokyo Nenkan*, relevant years.
151 This policy is detailed in chapter 3 on 'Bureaucratic Politics' in my forthcoming volume, *Politicians and Bureaucrats*.
152 Since 1987, Zenchu has presented its budget request to the government and to the Diet in September – after the MAFF's presentation of its *gaisan yokyu* to the MOF – even though the process of formulating Nokyo's budget demands still begins in March or April. This suggests that the Nokyo budget campaign no longer feeds into the formulation of the MAFF's draft budget, but is reserved for a later stage of the budget formulation process.

153 The last time one of these was held was 1984.
154 *Nokyo*, p. 354. See also chapter 3 on 'Bureaucratic Politics' and chapter 4 on 'Patronage Politics' in my forthcoming volume, *Politicians and Bureaucrats*.
155 *Nokyo Nenkan*, 1993, p. 80.
156 Kibo Gennosuke, 'Remon Yunyu Jiyuka no Kyokun' ['A Lesson From the Liberalisation of Lemons'], *Nogyo Kyodo Kumiai*, Vol. 29, No 3, March 1983, pp. 76–81. This study shows that, as soon as lemons were liberalised, the wholesale price of lemons plunged sharply, and as a result, domestic lemon production slumped dramatically.
157 Okamoto, 'Nomin no Seiji Ishiki', p. 21.
158 See chapter 2 on 'Party Politics' in my forthcoming volume, *Politicians and Bureaucrats*.
159 *Nokyo Nenkan*, 1972, p. 361.
160 See Table 8.1 in Aurelia George Mulgan, *The Challenge to Vested Interests: Contesting Agricultural Power in Japan*, forthcoming.
161 See chapter 8 on '*Gaiatsu* Politics' in my forthcoming volume, *The Challenge to Vested Interests*.
162 Ito, *Nosanbutsu Yunyu Jiyuka*, p. 25.
163 See chapter 2 on 'Party Politics' in my forthcoming volume, *Politicians and Bureaucrats*, and chapter 5 on 'The Role of Business' and chapter 6 on 'The Media and Other Critics' in my forthcoming volume, *The Challenge to Vested Interests*.
164 Ito, *Nosanbutsu Yunyu Jiyuka*, p. 25.
165 Mishima Tokuzo, 'Nosanbutsu Jiyuka Rongi no Keifu' ['The Genealogy of Agricultural Product Liberalization Debates'], in Ouchi and Gomi (eds), *Keizai Masatsuka*, p. 207.
166 Ito, *Nosanbutsu Yunyu Jiyuka*, pp. 25–26.
167 Ito, *Nosanbutsu Yunyu Jiyuka*, p. 230.
168 Ito Kenzo, 'Nosanbutsu-Wakukakudai Soshi Undo No Keii to Tenbo' ['The Details and Outlook for the Campaign to Prevent Quota Expansion for Agricultural Products'], *Nogyo Kyodo Kumiai*, Vol. 29, No 3, March 1983, p. 46.
169 Ito, 'Nosanbutsu Wakukakudai Soshi Undo', p. 46.
170 Ito, 'Nosanbutsu Wakukakudai Soshi Undo', p. 46.
171 Ito, 'Nosanbutsu Yunyu Jiyuka', p. 47.
172 *Australian Financial Review*, 10 March 1988.
173 *Australian Financial Review*, 10 March 1988.
174 'Conclusion of Uruguay Round and Countermeasures for JA Group', *JA-Zenchu News*, No. 3, March 1994, p. 3.
175 'Conclusion of Uruguay Round', pp. 3–4.
176 *Japan Times*, 18 December 1992; *New York Times*, 17 December 1992.
177 Quoted in Fujitani, 'Keito Nokyo', p. 50.
178 *Reuter Textline*, Comline News Service – 25 June 1993.
179 'Conclusion of Uruguay Round', p. 4.
180 *Nokyo Nenkan*, 1993, p. 86.
181 Zenkoku Nogyo Kyodo Kumiai Chuokai, *Hayawakari JA no Subete*, p. 80.
182 Zenkoku Nogyo Kyodo Kumiai Chuokai, *Hayawakari JA no Subete*, p. 80.
183 Matsumoto Tokuo, 'Nokyo Nosei Undo no Tenkan: Sono Yoin to Hoko' ['Changes in Nokyo's Agricultural Policy Campaigns: Their Causes and Direction'], in Nosei Jyaanarisuto no Kai (ed.), *Senkyo, Beika, Nokyo*, p. 40.
184 See chapter 3 on 'Bureaucratic Politics' in my forthcoming volume, *Politicians and Bureaucrats*.
185 Matsumoto, 'Nokyo Nosei Undo', p. 40.

186 'Japan's Rice Policy', in *JEI Report*, No. 2A, 14 January 1983, quoted in Balaam, 'Self-Sufficiency in Japanese Agriculture', p. 99.
187 This was the Provisional Commission on Administrative Reform (Rinji Gyosei Chosakai, or Rincho) set up in the Prime Minister's Office in March 1981. See chapter 5 on 'Budget Politics' in my forthcoming volume, *Politicians and Bureaucrats*.
188 This was the Research Council for the Adjustment of the Economic Structure for International Harmony (Kokusai Kyocho no Tame no Keizai Kozo Chosei Kenkyukai, or Keikoken) chaired by Maekawa Haruo and established by PM Nakasone in 1985.
189 Kajii, 'Ima Naze Nokyo Ka', p. 4.
190 Inoguchi and Iwai, 'Zoku Giin', p. 246.
191 *Nihon Keizai Shinbun*, 31 July 1986.
192 *Asahi Shinbun*, 5 August 1986.
193 Higashi and Lauter, *The Internationalisation of the Japanese Economy*, p. 127.
194 *Sankei Shinbun*, 10 August 1986.
195 Inoguchi and Iwai, '*Zoku Giin*', p. 249.
196 *Sankei Shinbun*, 10 August 1986.
197 Kajii, 'Ima Naze Nokyo Ka', pp. 3–4.
198 Sakaguchi, *Kyodai Nokyo*, p. 100.
199 Sakaguchi, *Kyodai Nokyo*, p. 100.
200 *Mainichi Shinbun*, 9 August 1986. See also below.
201 *Mainichi Shinbun*, 9 August 1986.
202 Toyokura Yasuhiro, *Raisu Pawaa: Tsuba Kara Kona E* [*Rice Power: From Grain to Flour*], Tokyo, Niceday Books, 1989, p. 82.
203 Inoguchi and Iwai, '*Zoku Giin*', pp. 248–249.
204 As early as March 1987 the Managing Director of Zenchu publicly acknowledged that 'the producers' rice price should be lowered eventually.' Yamaguchi, 'Don't Push Japanese Farmers Too Far', p. 3.
205 *Nokyo Nenkan*, 1989, p. 493.
206 *Asahi Shinbun*, 26 June 1986, p. 3.
207 Imamura and Inuzuka, *Seifu to Nomin*, p. 67.
208 *Asahi Shinbun*, 26 June 1986, p. 3.
209 Otawara, 'Nokyo no Ichi to Yakuwari', p. 28. This conference was called a 'Festival of Life' and was held in the National Sports Stadium. It attracted around 4,000 participants, 1,500 of whom were consumer representatives. Okamoto, 'Nokyo no Nosei Katsudo', p. 266.
210 Ito Isao, 'Sengo Nokyo no Hensen to Nokyoron no Tenkai' ['The Transformation of Postwar Nokyo and the Development of Nokyo Theory'], in Ouchi Tsutomu and Kajii Isao (eds), *Nokyo Yonjunen*, p. 48.
211 Okamoto, 'Nokyo no Nosei Katsudo', pp. 265–266.
212 *Japan Times*, 12 June 1992.
213 *Asahi Shinbun*, 31 May 1990.
214 Personal interview with Zenchu official, Tokyo, July 1995.
215 *Wall Street Journal*, 18 December 1992.
216 This was a comment by the Chairman of Hokkaido Nokyo Chuokai and reported in Kyosanto Bukkuretto, *Gaiatsu no Naka no Nihon*, p. 35.
217 Ito, 'Nosanbutsu Yunyu Jiyuka', p. 230.
218 See chapter 3 on 'Consumer Politics' in my forthcoming volume, *Politicians and Bureaucrats*.
219 *Zenchu News*, No. 12, December 1982, p. 3.
220 Ito, *Nosanbutsu Yunyu Jiyuka*, p. 26.
221 *Japan Agrinfo Newsletter*, Vol. 1, No. 12, July 1984, pp. 7–8.

222 Elipidio R. Sta. Romana, *The Politics of Liberalization of the Japanese Agricultural Market*, Papers in Japanese Studies, No. 12, Department of Japanese Studies, National University of Singapore, July 1991, p. 29.
223 *Nokyo Nenkan*, 1975, p. 66.
224 David Vogel, 'Consumer Protection and Protectionism in Japan', *Journal of Japanese Studies*, Vol. 18, No. 1, 1992, p. 151.
225 One in the rather more objective category was Nosei Jyaanarisuto no Kai, *Towareru Yunyu Shokuhin no Anzensei [The Safety of Imported Food Questioned]*, Nihon no Ugoki, No. 83, Tokyo, Norin Tokei Kyokai, 1987.
226 *International Herald Tribune*, 29 March 1988.
227 Quoted in Vogel, 'Consumer Protection', p. 133.
228 Quoted in Vogel, 'Consumer Protection', p. 133.
229 Quoted in Vogel, 'Consumer Protection', p. 133.
230 Carol Luffy, quoted in Vogel, 'Consumer Protection', p. 134.
231 The Japanese title of this organisation is not supplied, so it is difficult to know which organisation he means exactly.
232 Vogel, 'Consumer Protection', p. 134.
233 Kyosanto Bukkuretto, *Gaiatsu no Naka no Nihon*, p. 61.
234 Kazuko Nishikawa, 'Why Japanese Consumer Groups Oppose Market Opening Measures', *Tokyo Business Today*, March 1990, p. 41.
235 Reuter Newswire, Far East, 7 October 1992.
236 *Zenchu News*, No. 12, December 1982, p. 3.
237 See chapter 3 on 'Consumer Politics' in my forthcoming volume, *The Challenge to Vested Interests*.
238 Ito, 'Nosanbutsu Yunyu Jiyuka', p. 226.
239 Ito, 'Nosanbutsu Yunyu Jiyuka', pp. 226–227.
240 *Australian Financial Review*, 14 January 1988.
241 *Zenchu News*, No. 13, 1 March 1983, p. 5.
242 'Conclusion of Uruguay Round', p. 5.
243 *Zenchu News*, No. 12, December 1982, p. 3.
244 'Conclusion of Uruguay Round', p. 4.
245 *Nosanbutsu Yunyu Jiyuka*, p. 1.
246 'Conclusion of Uruguay Round', p. 3.
247 See chapter 7 on 'Ideological Politics' in my forthcoming volume, *The Challenge to Vested Interests*.
248 For a comprehensive evaluation of this ideological justification, see chapter 7 on 'Ideological Politics' in my forthcoming volume, *The Challenge to Vested Interests*.
249 'Conclusion of Uruguay Round', p. 3.
250 *The Economist*, 20 February 1988.
251 See chapter 3 on 'Consumer Politics' in my forthcoming volume, *The Challenge to Vested Interests*.
252 'Conclusion of Uruguay Round', p. 5.
253 *Japan Agrinfo Newsletter*, Vol. 12, No. 4, December 1994, p. 5.
254 *Japan Agrinfo Newsletter*, Vol. 12, No. 4, December 1994, p. 6.
255 For an interesting discussion on the difficulties of measuring interest group influence, see Berry, *Lobbying*, pp. 272–275.
256 See chapter 3 on 'Bureaucratic Politics' in my forthcoming volume, *Politicians and Bureaucrats*.
257 See chapter 8 on 'Gaiatsu Politics' in my forthcoming volume, *The Challenge to Vested Interests*.
258 See chapter 3 on 'Bureaucratic Politics' in my forthcoming volume, *Politicians and Bureaucrats*.

259 Mitsukawa, *Nogyo Dantai Hattenshi*, p. 636.
260 See also below for the latest example of concessions made to Nokyo in relation to the new rice policy.
261 See Tables 8.1–8.4 in my forthcoming volume, *The Challenge to Vested Interests*.
262 See chapter 5 on 'Budget Politics' in my forthcoming volume, *Politicians and Bureaucrats*.
263 See chapter 2 on 'Party Politics' in my forthcoming volume, *Politicians and Bureaucrats*.
264 See Table 5.4 in *Sengo Nihon no Atsuryoku Dantai*, p. 229.
265 See Table 5.4 in *Sengo Nihon no Atsuryoku Dantai*, p. 229.
266 *Sengo Nihon no Atsuryoku Dantai*, p. 229.
267 Muramatsu, 'Nihongata Atsuryoku Dantai', p. 79.
268 Muramatsu, 'Nihongata Atsuryoku Dantai', p. 79. Muramatsu speculated that in the case of administrative, educational and professional organisations, they held rather 'exclusive' power in a particular policy field (i.e. there were a limited number of dominant pressure groups), and they were often closely connected to administrative institutions.
269 See chapter 3 on 'Bureaucratic Politics' in my forthcoming volume, *Politicians and Bureaucrats*.
270 *Yomiuri Shinbun*, 2 November 1994.
271 Hokkaido Koiki Nogyo Kyodo Kumiai and Kajiura, *Datsu Nokyo*, p. 78.
272 See chapter 3 on 'Consumer Politics' in my forthcoming volume, *The Challenge to Vested Interests*.
273 Takeuchi and Otawara, *Asu no Nokyo*, p. 261.
274 Hokkaido Koiki Nogyo Kyodo Kumiai and Kajiura, *Datsu Nokyo*, p. 79.
275 See chapter 4 on 'Organisational Politics'.
276 Takeuchi and Otawara, *Asu no Nokyo*, p. 253. The authors report research in Hokkaido which showed that 65.2 per cent of respondents thought that farmers should pursue agricultural policy activities through their own independent farmers' organisations (like the Hokkaido Farmers' League), rather than leaving it up to Nokyo to provide leadership on agricultural policy matters (18.4 per cent) (p. 253).
277 Sakaguchi, *Kyodai Nokyo*, p. 111.
278 Tachibana, *Nokyo*, pp. 345–346.
279 Hokkaido Koiki Nogyo Kyodo Kumiai and Kajiura, *Datsu Nokyo*, p. 79.
280 Sakaguchi, *Kyodai Nokyo*, p. 111.
281 Sakaguchi, *Kyodai Nokyo*, p. 111.
282 This survey was reported in Ono, 'Senkyo to Nokyo', p. 91.
283 Iwai, 'Nogyosha no Seiji Ishiki', p. 9. The average percentage for this item was the third highest behind farm guidance and marketing. In fact it could indicate several contradictory trends. Firstly, as the third highest, it could reflect quite high levels of dissatisfaction amongst farmers with the conduct of Nokyo's *nosei katsudo*, as the even higher figures for farm guidance and marketing are interpreted to reflect. On the other hand, because less than a quarter of those polled marked this item, it could indicate increasing apathy amongst farmers about Nokyo's *nosei katsudo*, or alternatively, satisfaction with these activities, with the low proportion suggesting that farmers did not think *nosei katsudo* needed strengthening. Iwai has interpreted the percentage to mean that only a low proportion of farmers wanted Nokyo to undertake more political lobbying and an increasing reluctance on their part to get behind such lobbying. 'Japan's Agricultural Politics', p. 193.
284 See chapter 8 on '*Gaiatsu* Politics' in my forthcoming volume, *The Challenge to Vested Interests*.

285 Fujitani, 'Keito Nokyo', p. 53.
286 Personal interview with Nokyo official, Tokyo, July 1995.
287 Fujitani, 'Keito Nokyo', p. 49.
288 'Conclusion of Uruguay Round', p. 5.
289 *Asahi Shinbun*, June 21, 1994.
290 'Conclusion of Uruguay Round', p. 5.
291 'Conclusion of Uruguay Round', p. 5.
292 Personal interview, Tokyo, July 1995.
293 Ishikura Teruka and Moroi Ken, 'Nogyo no Ninaite o Do Kakuho Suru Ka' ['How to Secure Successors in Japanese Agriculture'], *Ekonomisuto*, 15 June 1993, p. 20.
294 Quoted in *Japan Agrinfo Newsletter*, Vol. 12, No. 4, December 1994, p. 5.
295 *Japan Agrinfo Newsletter*, Vol. 12, No. 4, December 1994, p. 5.
296 Saeki, *Nokyo Kaikaku*, p. 27.
297 Domon, *Nokyo Ga Tosan Suru Hi*, pp. 77–80.
298 See also the discussion in chapter 4 on 'Organisational Politics'.
299 This limited price movements on a year-on-year basis to a 10 per cent drop or rise to protect the agricultural cooperatives and rice farmers.
300 Domon, *Nokyo Ga Tosan Suru Hi*, p. 75. It was later raised to 13 per cent. *Nikkei Weekly*, 6 January 1998.
301 See the figures in chapter 4 on 'Organisational Politics'.
302 Telegraphic Report, US Consulate Sapporo, 20 September 1994, p. 2.
303 *Yomiuri Shinbun*, 14 September 1994.
304 Domon, *Shinshokuryoho de*, p. 132.
305 Domon, *Shinshokuryoho de*, p. 133.
306 Domon, *Shinshokuryoho de*, p. 86.
307 See also chapter 4 on 'Organisational Politics'.
308 Domon Takeshi, 'Shinshokuryoho de Toku', p. 83.
309 Yamauchi, 'Analytical Institutional Economics', p. 25.
310 Fujitani, *Nokyo*, p. 9.
311 *Japan Agrinfo Newsletter*, Vol. 13, No. 10, June 1996, p. 3.
312 Fujitani, *Nokyo*, p. 202.
313 *Nihon no Nokyo*, pp. 213–214.
314 *No to Shoku*, pp. 70–71.
315 See chapter 5 on 'The Political Demography of Agriculture'.
316 Kajii, 'Ima Naze Nokyo Ka', p. 4. See also chapter 4 on 'Organisational Politics'.
317 Ono, *No to Shoku*, p. 72.
318 Ono, 'Nokyo to Jiminto', pp. 72–74.
319 Ono, 'Nokyo to Jiminto', p. 75.
320 Ono, 'Nokyo to Jiminto', pp. 75–76.
321 Ono, *No to Shoku*, p. 74.
322 Ono, *No to Shoku*, pp. 76–78.
323 Ono, *No to Shoku*, pp. 74–75.
324 *No to Shoku*, p. 82.
325 See below for more biographical details.
326 *Asahi Shinbun*, 22 June 1994.
327 *Asahi Shinbun*, 23 June 1994.
328 'Yori Kyoryoku na Nosei Undo o Mezashite' ['Aiming At An Even More Powerful Agricultural Policy Campaign'], *Nosei Undo Jyaanaru*, No. 17, January 1998, p. 31.
329 See also the comments below.
330 It was officially called the 'Uruguay Round Agricultural Agreement-Related Policy Outline'.
331 As it happened, about half the package (¥3 trillion) would ultimately end up in

the pockets of construction companies for land improvement projects. Personal interview with Zenchu official, Tokyo, July 1995.

332 See chapter 2 on 'Party Politics' in my forthcoming volume, *Politicians and Bureaucrats*, for an argument about the reduced political sensitivities of LDP farm politicians to constituency considerations after general elections.

333 'UR Taisaku to Nogyo Kankei Yosan Kakuho de Undo', *Nosei Undo Jyaanaru*, No. 13, May 1997, p. 3.

334 'Tokushu Taidan: 21 Seiki no Nogyo, Noson o Katsuryoku to Miryoku aru Mono ni' ['Special Interview: Changing 21st Century Agriculture and Farm Villages to be Full of Vitality and Appeal'], *Nosei Undo Jyaanaru*, No. 1, July 1995, p. 4.

335 As the Secretary-General of Zenkoku Noseikyo explained, 'the consensus reached through the new Agricultural Basic Law will determine the position on which Japan will stand at the WTO negotiations.' 'Sokatsu – Nosei Soshiki Undo no Mezasu Mono', p. 17.

336 'Tokushu Taidan', p. 5.

337 See chapter 2 on 'Interest Group Politics', and chapter 4 on 'Organisational Politics'.

338 *MAFF Update*, No. 245, 6 February 1998, http://www.maff.go.jp. The basic idea of the income compensation scheme is that the government and producers will make an outlay together to establish a fund, and when the rice price falls drastically, a part of the loss of those producers who followed production adjustment will be covered by the fund. If the rice price continues to fall, the government's burden also continues to increase. *Yomiuri Shinbun*, 24 October 1997.

339 *Nikkei Weekly*, 27 November 1997; *MAFF Update*, No. 245, 6 February 1998, http://www.maff.go.jp.

340 *Asahi Shinbun*, 28 November 1996.

341 This is the Independently Distributed Rice (IDR) Price Formation Centre which replaced the IDR Price Formation Organisation when the new Staple Food Law took effect in 1995.

342 *Nikkei Weekly*, 1 June 1998.

343 *Nikkei Weekly*, 22 December 1997.

344 Personal interview with Zenchu official, Tokyo, July 1995.

345 ' "Shokuryo-Nogyo-Noson Chiiki ni kansuru Arata na Kihonho" Seitei ni tsuite no Yosei' ['Requests Relating to the Enactment of the "New Basic Law Concerning Food, Agriculture and Rural Areas" Enactment'], *Nosei Undo Jyaanaru*, No. 17, January 1998, p. 18.

346 'Arata na Kihonho Rongi ni okeru JA-Guruupu no Iken to Shucho' ['The JA-Group's Opinions and Assertions in the Debate About a New Agricultural Basic Law'], *Nosei Undo Jyaanaru*, No. 16, November 1997, p. 13.

347 'Genchi Rupo: Hiroshima Nokyo Nosei Kyogikai no Katsudo' ['Local Report: Hiroshima Nokyo Agricultural Policy Council's Activities'], *Nosei Undo Jyaanaru*, No. 17, January 1998, p. 30.

348 One national representatives' assembly was held in October 1998, for example, which invited leading *norin giin* from the LDP so that the voice of the farmers and farm households could be reflected in the new law. Three prominent invitees were Tani Yoichi, a *norin zoku*, former member of APRA, a member of CAPIC and the Norin Bukai, and former Vice-Chairman of the Livestock Industry Promotion Diet Members' League; Matsuoka Toshikatsu, a Director of the LH Agriculture, Forestry and Fisheries Committee and former Chairman of the LDP's Norin Bukai; and Miyaji Kazuaki, another ex-MAFF agricultural policy heavyweight and member of CAPIC and the Norin Bukai. A similar gathering (of 400 participants) met one month later, with the same invited LDP guests.

349 At present, the law restricts company farming to agricultural production companies that are private limited companies, not jointstock companies. According to a nationwide survey conducted by the *Nihon Keizai Shinbun*, about 20 per cent of those who run agricultural production companies or agricultural cooperatives support the idea of allowing companies engaged in commercial agriculture to become jointstock companies. *Nikkei Weekly*, 28 September 1998.

350 *Japan Agrinfo Newsletter*, Vol. 16, No. 2, October 1998, p. 6.

351 *Nikkei Weekly*, 22 June 1998.

352 Outline of the Report Submitted to the Prime Minister by the Investigative Council on Basic Problems Concerning Food, Agriculture and Rural Areas, Part 2, *MAFF Update*, No. 283, 30 October 1998, http://www.maff.go.jp.

353 *Asia Pulse*, 18 September 1998; 23 September 1998.

354 Outline of the Report, http://www.maff.go.jp.

355 *Yomiuri Shinbun*, 11 December 1998.

356 The restrictions on jointstock company ownership of farmland will include prohibitions on companies' purchasing farmland for speculative purposes.

357 *Jiji Press Newswire*, 3 February 1999. Basic plans for food, agriculture and rural areas that will incorporate goals for self-sufficiency to be achieved in food will be drawn up by the new Food, Agriculture and Rural Areas Advisory Council which was established by the new law, and which replaces APAC.

358 In anticipation of this change, in December 1998 the MAFF announced the establishment of a new commodities market for bid trading in dairy products designed to promote pricing mechanisms that reflect demand and supply levels. The new market is scheduled to open for business in the fall of 1999. *Nikkei Weekly*, 16 November 1998. In early 1999 the MAFF announced a changeover in the deficiency payments scheme for raw milk for processing to a system of dairy farmers' farm management stabilisation measures in FU 2001.

359 *Jiji Press Newswire*, 1 March 1999.

360 *Nikkei Weekly*, 14 December 1998.

361 For a thorough evaluation of the new ABL and associated policies, see chapter 4 on 'Bureaucratic Politics' in my forthcoming volume, *Politicians and Bureaucrats*.

362 '21 Seki o Tenbo Shita "Nosei Kaikaku"', p. 3. See also chapter 7 on 'Ideological Politics' in my forthcoming volume, *The Challenge to Vested Interests*.

363 The full text of these public demands is given in 'Aratana Kihonho Seitei to Kanren Seisaku no Suishin ni Mukete' ['Towards the Promotion of the New Basic Law Enactment and Related Policy'], *Nosei Undo Jyaanaru*, No. 22, December 1998, pp. 6–9.

364 See, for example, 'Tokushu: WTO Kyotei to Jiki Nogyo Kosho' ['Special: The WTO Agreement and the Next Round of Agricultural Negotiations'], *Nosei Undo Jyaanaru*, No. 22, December 1998, pp. 12–16. This is appended with a list of the 'assertions' of Nokyo which lays out its counter-ideology to free trade ideology. See chapter 7 on 'Ideological Politics' in my forthcoming volume, *The Challenge to Vested Interests*.

365 Personal interview with Zenchu official, Tokyo, July 1995.

366 See chapter 2 on 'Party Politics' in my forthcoming volume, *Politicians and Bureaucrats*.

367 'Shashin Gurafu', *Nosei Undo Jyaanaru*, No. 22, December 1998, p. 3.

368 *Australian Financial Review*, 9 December 1998.

369 If Japan shifted to a tariff scheme before fiscal 2001, the WTO required it to raise the import ratio by only 0.4 percentage points each year, as opposed to 0.8 percentage points every year under the six-year minimum access agreement spanning 1995–2000. *Kyodo News*, 13 December 1998.

370 *Comline News Service*, 15 December 1998.

371 *Asia Intelligence Wire*, 18 December 1998.
372 The exact rate was ¥351.17. This is equivalent to a tariff rate of 1,100 per cent. *Asahi Shinbun*, 18 December 1998. In and after 2000, the tariff will be reduced to ¥341 per kilogram. *Kyodo News Service*, 18 December 1998.
373 Although tariffication meant that private importing firms could import rice freely, the ¥351.17 tariff was in fact set far too high for these firms to break even on rice imports. *Yomiuri Shinbun*, 21 December 1998.
374 *Nikkei*, 7 December 1998. At a press conference following the tripartite meeting, Harada said that there was 'no other choice for preserving Japan's rice farming under the WTO-based system'. *Kyodo News*, 17 December 1998.
375 This would expand the earlier scheme introduced in 1998 with respect to farmers who cut back rice acreage. See above.
376 *Asahi Shinbun*, 18 December 1998. It was subsequently announced in early 1999, however, that the MAFF had decided to continue its rice production adjustment policy in the coming fiscal years (unspecified), but envisaged letting producer organisations use their own initiative in setting annual goals for rice production adjustment and management. The contemplated reforms would be included in detailed policies for FY 2000 finalised in the fall of 1999. *Japan Agrinfo Newsletter*, Vol. 16, No. 7, March 1999, p. 2.
377 *Yomiuri Shinbun*, 30 September 1994.
378 *Yomiuri Shinbun*, 2 November 1994. This is in spite of the fact that Northern Nokyo leaders (i.e. from the rice belt) continued to push for such campaigns even after the passage of the new Staple Food Law. Personal interview with Zenchu official, Tokyo, July 1995.
379 *Nikkei Weekly*, 2 March 1998.
380 This was followed in November 1998 with a further reduction of 1.75 per cent in the producer price for the 1999 rice crop – to nearly the same level as in 1975.
381 Along with the RPAC, LIPAC is also scheduled for abolition. As in the case of the RPAC, liberalisation of domestic marketing systems has rendered the price advisory role of this council more or less redundant.
382 Personal interview, Tokyo, July 1995.
383 Personal interview with former Zenchu Managing Director, Tokyo, July 1995.
384 Kuwabara, 'Nogyo Kyodo Kumiai no Nosei Katsudo', p. 270.
385 See chapter 4 on 'Organisational Politics'.
386 Personal interview with MAFF official, July 1999.
387 Matsumoto, 'Nokyo Nosei Undo', p. 43.
388 Franke and Dobson, 'Interest Groups', p. 226.
389 *Nikkei Weekly*, 1 March 1999.
390 See chapter 3 on 'Bureaucratic Politics' in my forthcoming volume, *Politicians and Bureaucrats*.
391 Personal interview, Tokyo, July 1995.
392 This approach was recommended in 'Shokuryo, Nogyo, Noson Mondai wa Kakuto Kyotsu no Kokuminteki Kadai' ['Food, Agriculture and Rural Issues are Each Party's Common National Themes'], *Nosei Undo Jyaanaru*, No. 20, August 1998, p. 4.
393 See chapter 5 on 'The Political Demography of Agriculture'.
394 *Asahi Shinbun*, 21 June 1994.
395 Personal interview with Zenchu official, Tokyo, July 1995.
396 This pledge was prominently featured in *Nosei Undo Jyaanaru*, No. 21, October 1998, p. 21.
397 '21 Seki no Nihon Nogyo o Hiraku "Kokumin Kyosei Undo"' ['"A Campaign of Symbiosis with the People" to Cultivate Japanese Agriculture in the 21st Century', *Nosei Undo Jyaanaru*, No. 22, December 1998, p. 4.

398 Fujitani, *Nokyo*, p. 134.
399 *Nokyo*, p. 346.
400 Matsumoto, 'Nokyo Nosei Undo', p. 43.

9 Conclusion

1 Nishida Yoshiaki, 'From a Train Window: Why is Japanese Farmland so Different From That in Europe?', *Social Science Japan*, April 1995, p. 11.
2 Mitsukawa, *Nogyo Dantai Hattenshi*, p. 621.
3 Culpepper, 'Organisational Competition', p. 295.
4 Lowi's proposition as summarised by Andrew S. McFarland, 'Interest Groups and Theories of Power in America', *British Journal of Political Science*, Vol. 17, Part 2, April 1987, p. 132.
5 In particular, Standard & Poor's pointed to the declining value of real estate assets, the exposure of agricultural cooperative financial institutions to non-banks and the increasing vulnerability of farm borrowers which raised the risks of further credit losses. *PR Newswire*, 4 September 1998.
6 *PR Newswire*, 4 September 1998.
7 The commodities involved include dairy products, raw milk for processing, wheat, barley, soybeans and sugar. The trading centres for dairy products opened in 1999, the new measures for raw milk processing will take effect in FY 2001, and the new schemes for the remaining products will be implemented in FY 2003.
8 Ishikura and Moroi, 'Nogyo no Ninaite', p. 18.
9 Minoru Morita, 'Advice for a Party Stuck in Quicksand', *Tokyo Business Today*, January 1994, p. 10.
10 See, for example, Pempel, *Regime Shift*, p. 211.
11 *Asia Pulse*, 23 September 1998.
12 *Nikkei Weekly*, 21 September 1998.

Bibliography

Aguri, Fuooramu, 'Nokyo Shinjikeeto' ['The Noyko Syndicate'], in 'Tokushu: Nihon no Kome' ['Special Report: Japanese Rice'], *Chuo Koron*, Vol. 102, No. 2, February 1987
—'Tokushu: Nihon no Kome' ['Special Report: Japanese Rice'], *Chuo Koron*, Vol. 102, No. 2, February 1987
Amano, Hiroyuki, ' "Hoshu no Jo" no Hikari to Kage' ['Light and Shadow in the "Conservative Kingdom" '], in Nosei Jyaanarisuto no Kai (ed.), *Tatoka Jidai no Nosei* [*Agricultural Policy in the Era of Party Proliferation*], Nihon Nogyo no Ugoki No. 44, Tokyo, Norin Tokei Kyokai, 1977
Anderson, Kym and Yujiro Hayami *et al.*, *The Political Economy of Agricultural Protection: East Asia in International Perspective*, Sydney, Allen & Unwin, 1986
Aoki, Masahiko, 'The Japanese Bureaucracy in Economic Administration: A Rational Regulator or Pluralist Agent?', in J. Shoven (ed.), *Government Policy Towards Industry in the United States and Japan*, Cambridge, Cambridge University Press, 1988
Aono, Bunsaku, *Nokyo, Soshiki to Hito to Senryaku* [*Nokyo: Organisation, People and Strategies*], Tokyo, Daiyamondosha, 1976
Arai, Yoshio, 'Kyodo Kumiai Genten Rongi no Yukue' ['Where the Debate Stands on the Fundamentals of Cooperative Unionism'], *Norin Keizai*, 28 June 1973
'Arata na Kihonho Rongi ni okeru JA-Guruupu no Iken to Shucho' ['The JA-Group's Opinions and Assertions in the Debate About a New Basic Law'], *Nosei Undo Jyaanaru*, No. 16, November 1997
'Arata na Kihonho Seitei to Kanren Seisaku no Suishin ni Mukete' ['Towards the Promotion of the New Basic Law Enactment and Related Policy'], *Nosei Undo Jyaanaru*, No. 22, December 1998
Arimitsu, Reimin, 'Seito to Beika Seisaku' ['Political Parties and Rice Price Policy'], in Nosei Jyaanarisuto no Kai (ed.), *Beisaku no Shintenkai* [*New Developments in Rice Cultivation*], Nihon Nogyo No Ugoki No. 5, Tokyo, Kyodo Kumiai Kyokai, April 1966
Asahi, Shinbunsha (ed.), *Asahi Nenkan* [*Asahi Yearbook*], Tokyo, Asahi Shinbunsha, annual
Asano, Naonobu, 'Jigyo, Soshiki Kaikaku no Hoko to Kadai' ['Directions and Issues of the Reform in Business and Organisation'], *Nogyo to Keizai*, Special Issue, Vol. 61, No. 2, 1995
Asuwa, Shinzaburo, *Nokyo no Genjo to Kadai* [*Nokyo's Present Condition and Themes*], Tokyo, Toyo Keizai Shinbunsha, 1979

Atsumi, Shigeyuki, ' "Tohoku Kessen" de Nani ga Kawatta Ka' ['What Has Changed in the "Tohoku Showdown"?'], in Nosei Jyaanarisuto no Kai (ed.), *Tatoka Jidai no Nosei* [*Agricultural Policy in the Era of Party Proliferation*], Nihon Nogyo no Ugoki No. 44, Tokyo, Norin Tokei Kyokai, 1977

Australian Bureau of Agricultural and Resource Economics (ABARE), *Japanese Agricultural Policies: A Time of Change*, Policy Monograph No. 3, Canberra, Australian Government Publishing Service, 1988

—*Proposed Strategies for Reducing Agricultural Protection in the GATT Uruguay Round: A Synthesis and Assessment*, Discussion Paper, 90.6, Canberra, Australian Government Publishing Service, 1990

Balaam, David N., 'Self-Sufficiency in Japanese Agriculture: Telescoping and Reconciling the Food Security-Efficiency Dilemma', in William P. Browne and Don F. Hadwiger (eds), *World Food Policies: Toward Agricultural Interdependence*, Boulder, CO., Lynne Rienner Publishers, 1986

Berger, S. D., *Organizing Interest in Western Europe: Pluralism, Corporatism and the Transformation of Politics*, New York, Cambridge University Press, 1981

Berry, Jeffrey M., *Lobbying for the People: The Political Behavior of Public Interest Groups*, Princeton, N.J., Princeton University Press, 1977

Boonekamp, Loek, *Agriculture in Japan: Current Issues and Possible Implications of the Uruguay Round Agreement*, Tokyo, National Research Institute of Agricultural Economics, Ministry of Agriculture, Forestry and Fisheries, March 1995

Bureau of Agricultural Economics (BAE), *Japanese Agricultural Policies: An Overview*, Occasional Paper, 98, Canberra, Australian Government Publishing Service, 1987

Calder, Kent, *Crisis and Compensation: Public Policy and Political Stability in Japan, 1949–1986*, Princeton, Princeton University Press, 1988

Cargill, Thomas F., *Asia's Financial Crisis and Japan*, Briefing Paper, Japan–U.S. Friendship Commission in Cooperation with Japan Information Access Project, 15 December 1997

Central Union of Agricultural Cooperatives, *Central Union of Agricultural Cooperatives*, 1972

Chikusan Shinko Jigyodan, *Chikusan Shinko Jigyodan Nenpo* [*Livestock Industry Promotion Corporation Annual Report*], Tokyo, Chikusan Shinko Jigyodan, annual

'Cooperative Trade and Unicoop Japan', *Japan Agricultural Coop News*, Vol. 13, No. 2, July 1972

Cowhey, Peter F., 'Domestic Institutions and The Credibility of International Commitments: Japan and the United States', *International Organization*, Vol. 47, No. 2, Spring 1993

Coyle, William T., *U.S.–Japan Agricultural Trade Issues in Perspective*, Economic Research Service, United States Department of Agriculture, 1983

Culpepper, Pepper D., 'Organisational Competition and the Neo-Corporatist Fallacy in French Agriculture', *West European Politics*, Vol. 16, No. 3, July 1993

Curtis, Gerald, *Election Campaigning Japanese Style*, New York, Columbia University Press, 1971

—*The Japanese Way of Politics*, New York, Columbia University Press, 1988

'Dai 41-Kai Shugiin Giin Sosenkyo: Zenkoku Noseikyo Suisen Tosen Giin Ichiran' ['The 41st House of Representatives Election: List of Successful Diet Members Recommended by the National Agricultural Policy Council], *Nosei Undo Jyaanaru*, No. 10, November 1996, pp. 19–22

Dai-41 Shugiingiin Sosenkyo Ichiran Heisei 8-nen 10-gorbu 20 Shikko [*The 41st House of Representatives Election Held on 20 October 1996*], Shugiin Jimukyoku, 18 March 1997.

'Daremo Iwanai Nokyo no Judai Sekinin' ['No one Says Anything About Nokyo's Huge Responsibilities'], *Aera*, No. 8, 26 February 1996

Domon, Takeshi, *Yoi Nokyo: Jiyukago ni Ikinokoru Senryaku* [*The Good Nokyo: A 'Post-Liberalisation' Survival Strategy*], Tokyo, Nihon Keizai Shinbunsha, 1988

—*Nokyo ga Tosan Suru Hi* [*The Day that Nokyo Goes Bankrupt*], Tokyo, Toyo Keizai Shinposha, 1992

—'MAFF Fiddles While Taxpayers Burn: Rice Market Opening Close at Hand', *Tokyo Business Today*, January 1994

—'Shoeki ni Hashita Nosei Kanryo no Hyaku Hi' ['One Hundred Days of Agricultural Policy Bureaucrats Pursuing Their Interests], *Chuo Koron*, Vol. 109, No. 6, June 1994

—'Kome Gyosei: Kengyo Noka o Mamori, Shokuryocho o Mamotta' ['The Administration of Rice: Protection for Part-Time Farmers and the Food Agency?'], *Ekonomisuto*, 22 November 1994

—*Shinshokuryoho de Nihon no Okome wa ko Kawaru* [*The New Food Law Changes Japanese Rice in This Way*], Tokyo, Toyo Keizai Shinposha, 1995

—'Shinshokuryoho de Toku o Suru no wa Ittai Dare' ['Who Will Profit from the New Food Law?'], *Ekonomisuto*, 7 November 1995, pp. 80–83

—'The Inside Story of the Troubled Farm Co-ops', *Japan Echo*, Vol. 23, No. 2, Summer 1996, pp. 21–27

—'Jusen Kokkai ni Katte Kinyu Senso ni Yabureru' ['Nokyo Won the *Jusen* Diet But Was Defeated in the Financial War'], *Kinyu Bijinesu*, July 1996

Donnelly, Michael, 'Setting the Price of Rice: A Study in Political Decisionmaking', in T. J. Pempel (ed.), *Policymaking in Contemporary Japan*, Ithaca and London, Cornell University Press, 1977

Dore, Ronald P., *Land Reform in Japan*, London, Oxford University Press, 1966

—*Land Reform in Japan*, 2nd edition, London, The Athlone Press, 1984

—'The Socialist Party and the Farmers', in Allan D. Cole, George O. Totten, and Cecil H. Uyehara (eds), *Socialist Parties in Postwar Japan*, New Haven and London, Yale University Press, 1966

Dunleavy, Patrick and O'Leary, Brendan, *Theories of the State: The Politics of Liberal Democracy*, Houndmills, Macmillan, 1987

East Asia Analytical Unit, Department of Foreign Affairs and Trade, 'Agriculture and Food', Draft Chapter 11, in *Japan at the Crossroads: Strategies for the 21st Century*, n.d.

Enoki, Akira, Takagi Sanae and Hirata Masami, 'Han Jiyuka Giin' ['Anti-Liberalisation Diet Members'], *Keizai Mondai*, No. 36, April 1971

Flanagan, Scott, 'The Japanese Party System in Transition', *Comparative Politics*, Vol. 3, No. 2, January 1971

Food Agency, *An Outline of the Staple Food Law: The Law for Stabilization of Supply-Demand and Price of Staple Food*, January 1995

—*An Outline of New Food Systems: Based on the Law for Stabilization of Supply-Demand and Price of Staple Food*, March 1996

Foreign Agricultural Service, United States Department of Agriculture, *Agricultural Trade Policy*, June 1972

Foreign Press Center, Japan, *The Diet, Elections, and Political Parties*, 'About Japan' Series, No. 13, January 1985

Franke, James L. and Dobson, Douglas, 'Interest Groups: The Problem of Representation', *Western Political Quarterly*, Vol. 38, No. 2, June 1985

Fujitani, Chikuji, 'Nichibei Nosanbutsu Boeki' ['Japan–US Agricultural Trade'], in Ouchi Tsutomu and Gomi Kenkichi (eds), *Keizai Masatsuka no Nihon Nogyo [Japanese Agriculture Under Economic Friction]*, Nihon Nogyo Nenpo 34, Tokyo, Ochanomizu Shobo, 1986

—'Eino Shido' ['Agricultural Management Guidance'], in Ouchi Tsutomu and Kajii Isao (eds), *Nokyo Yonjunen – Kitai to Genjitsu [Forty Years of Nokyo: Expectation and Reality]*, Nihon Nogyo Nenpo, Vol. 36, Tokyo, Ochanomizu Shobo, 1989

—'Nokyo at a Crossroads', *Japan Quarterly*, Vol. 39, No. 3, July–September 1992

—*Nokyo Daikakushin [Revolution in the Nokyo]*, Tokyo, Ie no Hikari Kyokai, 1994

—'Keito Nokyo no Nosei Katsudo wa Naze Shippai Shita Ka' ['Why Did The Agricultural Policy Activities of Nokyo Fail?'], *Nogyo to Keizai*, Vol. 60, No. 4, April 1994

—'JA Zenkoku Taikai no Yakuwari to Kitai Sareta Mono' ['The Role and Expectations of the JA National Convention'], *Nogyo to Keizai*, Vol. 61, No. 2, Special Issue, 1995

Fukuda, Jun, Shigeki Kakinuma and Hiroshi Fukunaga, 'When in Doubt, Cut it Out: Trimming Uselsss Organs of the Bureaucracy', *Tokyo Business Today*, June 1994

Fukui, Haruhiro, 'The Japanese Farmer and Politics', in Isaiah Frank (ed.), *The Japanese Economy in International Perspective*, Baltimore and London, The Johns Hopkins University Press, 1975

—'Studies in Policymaking: A Review of the Literature', in T. J. Pempel (ed.), *Policymaking in Contemporary Japan*, Ithaca and London, Cornell University Press, 1977

—'Cooperative Democratic Party', in Haruhiro Fukui (ed.), *Political Parties of Asia and the Pacific*, Westport, Connecticut, Greenwood Press, 1985

—'Democratic Liberal Party', in Haruhiro Fukui (ed.), *Political Parties of Asia and the Pacific*, Westport, Connecticut, Greenwood Press, 1985

—'Japan Cooperative Party-1', in Haruhiro Fukui (ed.), *Political Parties of Asia and the Pacific*, Westport, Connecticut, Greenwood Press, 1985

—'Japan Farmers Party-1', in Haruhiro Fukui (ed.), *Political Parties of Asia and the Pacific*, Westport, Connecticut, Greenwood Press, 1985

—'Japan Farmers Party-2', in Haruhiro Fukui (ed.), *Political Parties of Asia and the Pacific*, Westport, Connecticut, Greenwood Press, 1985

—'Japan Socialist Party-2', in Haruhiro Fukui (ed.), *Political Parties of Asia and the Pacific*, Westport, Connecticut, Greenwood Press, 1985

—'National Cooperative Party', in Haruhiro Fukui (ed.), *Political Parties of Asia and the Pacific*, Westport, Connecticut, Greenwood Press, 1985

—'National Democratic Party', in Haruhiro Fukui (ed.), *Political Parties of Asia and the Pacific*, Westport, Connecticut, Greenwood Press, 1985

—'National Party', in Haruhiro Fukui (ed.), *Political Parties of Asia and the Pacific*, Westport, Connecticut, Greenwood Press, 1985

—'Ryokufukai-1', in Haruhiro Fukui (ed.), *Political Parties of Asia and the Pacific*, Westport, Connecticut, Greenwood Press, 1985

—'Shinseikai-1', in Haruhiro Fukui (ed.), *Political Parties of Asia and the Pacific*, Westport, Connecticut, Greenwood Press, 1985

—'Social Reformist Party', in Haruhiro Fukui (ed.), *Political Parties of Asia and the Pacific*, Westport, Connecticut, Greenwood Press, 1985

Fukui, Jun, 'Japan Agriculture on the Ropes', *Tokyo Business Today*, December 1994

Fukumitsu, Toshio, 'Minami no Chikusan Kichi ni Miru Nominhyo no Yukue' ['The Direction of Farmers' Votes in Southern Livestock-Producing Districts'], in Nosei Jyaanarisuto no Kai (ed.), *Senkyo, Beika, Nokyo* [*Elections, the Rice Price and Nokyo*], Nihon Nogyo no Ugoki No. 79, Tokyo, Norin Tokei Kyokai, October 1986

Fukunaga, Hiroshi, 'If That's Democracy, I'll Take Chocolate', *Tokyo Business Today*, February 1996

Fukutake, Tadashi, *Nihon no Noson* [*Japan's Agricultural Villages*], Tokyo, Tokyo University Press, 1971

—*Japanese Rural Society*, Ithaca and London, Cornell University Press, 1972

'Genchi Rupo: Hiroshima Nokyo Nosei Kyogikai no Katsudo' ['Local Report: Hiroshima Nokyo Agricultural Policy Council's Activities'], *Nosei Undo Jyaanaru*, No. 17, January 1998

'Genchi Rupo: Kumamoto Nogyosha Seiji Renmei no Katsudo' ['Local Report: Activities of the Kumamoto Farmers' Political League'], *Nosei Undo Jyaanaru*, No. 14, August 1997

George, Aurelia, 'The Japanese Beef Import Controversy', *New Zealand International Review*, Vol. 3, No. 2, March/April 1978

—*The Strategies of Influence: Japan's Agricultural Cooperatives (Nokyo) as a Pressure Group*, unpublished doctoral thesis, Australian National University, 1980

—'Politics of Agricultural Protectionism in Northeast Asia: The Japanese Experience', in Kym Anderson and Aurelia George (eds), *Australian Agricultural and Newly Industrialising Asia: Issues for Research*, Canberra, Australia–Japan Research Centre, 1980

—*Japan's Beef Import Policies 1978–84: The Growth of Bilateralism*, Pacific Economic Papers, No. 113, July 1984

—*The Comparative Study of Interest Groups in Japan: An Institutional Framework*, Pacific Economic Papers, No. 95, Canberra, Australia–Japan Research Centre, December 1982, revised and reprinted as 'Japanese Interest Group Behaviour: An Institutional Approach', in J. A. A. Stockwin *et al.*, *Dynamic and Immobilist Politics in Japan*, London, Macmillan, 1988

—'The Politics of Interest Representation in the Japanese Diet: The Case of Agriculture', *Pacific Affairs*, Vol. 64, No. 4, Winter 1991–1992

George, Gilbert C., *Japan's Post-War Agricultural Cooperative Movement*, M.Econ. Thesis, Hitotsubashi University, Tokyo, 1976

George Mulgan, Aurelia, 'The Politics of Deregulation and Japanese Agriculture', in T. J. Pempel *et al.*, *The Politics of Economic Reform in Japan: Collected Papers*, Pacific Economic Papers, No. 270, August 1977

—'Electoral Determinants of Agrarian Power: Measuring Rural Decline in Japan', *Political Studies*, Vol. 45, No. 5, December 1997

Gikai Seido Nanajunenshi: Shugiin, Sangiin [*A 70 Year History of the Diet System: House of Representatives, House of Councillors*], Tokyo, Okurasho Insatsu Kyoku, 1961

Goto, Junko and Imamura, Naraomi, 'Japanese Agriculture: Characteristics, Institutions, and Policies', in Luther Tweeten, Cynthia L. Dishon, Wen S. Chern, Naraomi Imamura and Masaru Morishima (eds), *Japanese & American Agriculture: Tradition and Progress in Conflict*, Boulder, CO., Westview Press, 1993

Haigo Shiryo Kyokyu Antei Kiko, *Haigo Shiryo Kyokyu Antei Kiko no Gaiyo* [*Outline of the Compound Feed Supply Stabilisation Organisation*], 1997

Hanaoka, Taro, 'Zaibatsuka Sareta Nokyo' ['Nokyo has Become a *Zaibatsu*'], *Hoseki*, February 1974

Hasegawa, Hiroshi, 'A Petition to Open the Rice Market', *Japan Quarterly*, Vol. 34, No. 1, January–March 1987

'Hatsu no Shosenkyokusei Senkyo ni Mitsu no "Chiku Honbu" Sosetsu de Taio' ['Coping with the First Small-Constituency System Election with the Establishment of the "Three District Headquarters"'], *Nosei Undo Jyaanaru*, No. 22, December 1998

Havens, T. R. H., *Farm and Nation in Modern Japan*, Princeton, Princeton University Press, 1974

Hayami, Yujiro, *Japanese Agriculture Under Siege*, London, Macmillan and St Martin's Press, 1998

—'Kaikaku no Keiki Nogasu Kome Kanzeika Kaihi' ['Japan May Lose the Opportunity of Reform if it Avoids Rice Tariffication'], *Nogyo to Keizai*, Vol. 60, No. 6, June 1994

Hayami, Yujiro and Yamada Saburo *et al.*, *The Agricultural Development of Japan: A Century's Perspective*, Tokyo, University of Tokyo Press, 1991

Hayashi, Nobuaki, 'Shijo Kaiho – Endaka no Nihon Nogyo' ['Market Opening and Japan's Agriculture under High Yen Conditions'], in Ouchi Tsutomu and Gomi Kenkichi (eds), *Keizai Masatsuka no Nihon Nogyo* [*Japanese Agriculture Under Economic Friction*], Nihon Nogyo Nenpo 34, Tokyo, Ochanomizu Shobo, 1986

—*Nogyo wa Nihon no Onimotsu Ka* [*Is Agriculture a Burden to Japan?*], Tokyo, Ie no Hikari Kyokai, 1987

'Heisei 10-Nendo "Nosei Undo Soshiki Genchi Kenkyu Shukai" Hiraku' ['Opening the 1998-Year "Agricultural Policy Campaign Organisations in the Field Research Assembly"'], *Nosei Undo Jyaanaru*, No. 23, February 1999

Higashi, Chikara and Lauter, Peter G., *The Internationalization of the Japanese Economy*, Boston, Kluwer Academic Publishers, 1987

Hirose, Michisada, *Hojokin to Seikento* [*Subsidies and The Ruling Party*], Tokyo, Asahi Shinbunsha, 1981

—'Dojitsu Senkyo ni Miru Nominhyo no Ugoki' ['The Movement of Farmers' Votes Seen in the Double Elections'], in Nosei Jyaanarisuto no Kai (ed.), *Senkyo, Beika, Nokyo* [*Elections, the Rice Price and Nokyo*], Nihon Nogyo no Ugoki No. 79, Tokyo, Norin Tokei Kyokai, October 1986

Hokkaido Koiki Nogyo Kyodo Kumiai and Kajiura Yoshimasa, *Datsu Nokyo: Nihon Nogyo Saisei e no Michi* [*Getting Out of Nokyo: The Road to the Revival of Japanese Agriculture*], Tokyo, Daiyamondosha, 1995

Honma, Masayoshi, *Nihon no Nogyo to Zaisei Kozo* [*Japan's Agriculture and Financial Structure*], Tokyo, Seisaku Koso Fuooramu, January 1987

Honma, Masayoshi and Hayami, Yujiro, 'The Determinants of Agricultural Protection Levels: An Economic Analysis', in Kym Anderson and Yujiro Hayami *et al.*, *The Political Economy of Agricultural Protection: East Asia in International Perspective*, Sydney, Allen & Unwin, 1986

Horiguchi, Kenji, 'Issues for a Country Dependent on Imported Foodstuff to Consider: Implications of Recent Structural Changes in Farm Products Trade', unpublished manuscript, n.d.

Houck, James P., 'Agricultural Trade: Protectionism, Policy, and the Tokyo/Geneva Negotiating Round', *American Journal of Agricultural Economics*, Vol. 61, No. 5, December 1979

Kiyomi, Ikeyama, 'Sengo Seiji no Sokessan ni Jishin Tsuyomeru Nakasone Shuso' ['Prime Minister Nakasone's Strengthening Confidence in Settling the Postwar Political Accounts'], in Nosei Jyaanarisuto no Kai (ed.), *Senkyo, Beika, Nokyo* [*Elections, the Rice Price and Nokyo*], Nihon Nogyo no Ugoki No. 79, Tokyo, Norin Tokei Kyokai, October 1986

Imamura, Naraomi and Akiharu, Inuzuka, *Seifu to Nomin* [*Government and the Farmers*], Shokuryo Nogyo Mondai Zenshu No. 10, Tokyo, Nosan Gyoson Bunka Kyokai, 1991

Imamura, Naraomi, Tsuboi, Nobuhiro and Odagiri, Tokumi, 'Japanese Farm Structure: Trends and Projections', in Luther Tweeten, Cynthia L. Dishon, Wen S. Chern, Naraomi Imamura and Masaru Morishima (eds), *Japanese & American Agriculture: Tradition and Progress in Conflict*, Boulder, Co., Westview Press, 1993

Inoguchi, Takashi and Tomoaki, Iwai, '*Zoku Giin' no Kenkyu* [*Research on 'Tribe Diet Members'*], Tokyo, Nihon Keizai Shinbunsha, 1987

Inoue, Akira, *The Widening Gap between U.S. and Japanese Agricultural Policies and Its Implications for Agricultural Production*, USJP Occasional Paper 95-04, Program on U.S.–Japan Relations, Harvard University, 1995

The Institute for the Development of Agricultural Cooperation in Asia, *Agricultural Cooperative Movement in Japan*, n.d.

Ishida, Takeshi, *Interest Groups in Japan*, unpublished monograph, n.d.

—*Gendai Soshikiron* [*Discourse on Contemporary Organisation*], Tokyo, Iwanami Shoten, 1961

—'The Development of Interest Groups and the Pattern of Political Modernization in Japan', in Robert E. Ward (ed.), *Political Development in Modern Japan*, Princeton, Princeton University Press, 1968

—'Interest Groups Under A Semipermanent Government Party: The Case of Japan', *Annals of the American Academy of Political and Social Science*, Vol. 413, May 1974

—'Organizations and Symbols in Contemporary Politics: A Political Scientist's View of Postwar Japan', *Annals of the Institute of Social Science*, No. 20, 1979

Ishida, Takeshi and George, Aurelia D., 'Nokyo: The Farmers' Representative', in Peter Drysdale and Hironobu Kitaoji (eds), *Japan and Australia: Two Societies and their Interaction*, Canberra, ANU Press, 1980

Ishikawa, Hideo, 'Nogyo Kyodo Kumiai no Mitsu no Kao' ['The Three Faces of the Agricultural Cooperative Unions'], in Usui Yoshimi (ed.), *Kanryo, Seito, Atsuryoku Dantai* [*Bureaucracy, Political Parties, Pressure Groups*], Gendai Kyoyo Zenshu, Vol. 21, Tokyo, Chikuma Shobo, 1960

Ishikura, Teruka and Ken, Moroi, 'Nogyo no Ninaite o Do Kakuho Suru Ka' ['How to Secure Successors in Japanese Agriculture'], *Ekonomisuto*, 15 June 1993

Ishimi, Takashi, *Nokyo: Sangyo no Showa Shakaishi* [*Nokyo: The Social History of Industries in the Showa Period*], Tokyo, Nihon Keizai Kyoronsha, 1986

Ishiwata, Sadao, 'Nomin to Seiji' ['Farmers and Politics'], in Ishiwata Sadao (ed.), *Nomin to Senkyo: Nomin no Seiji Ishiki to Hyo no Yukue* [*Farmers and Elections: The Political Consciousness of Farmers and Trends in the Farm Vote*], Tokyo, Ochanomizu Shobo, 1984

Ishizuka, Masahiko, 'Black Hole in Japanese Economy', *Japan Economic Journal*, 13 September 1986

Ito, Isao, 'Sengo Nokyo no Hensen to Nokyoron no Tenkai' ['The Transformation of Postwar Nokyo and the Development of Nokyo Theory'], in Ouchi Tsutomu and Kajii Isao (eds), *Nokyo Yonjunen – Kitai to Genjitsu* [*Forty Years of Nokyo: Expectation and Reality*], Nihon Nogyo Nenpo, Vol. 36, Tokyo, Ochanomizu Shenbo, 1989

Ito, Kenzo, *Nozanbutsu Yunyu Jiyuka Mondai to Nihon Nogyo* [*The Problem of Liberalising Imports of Agricultural Products and Japan's Agriculture*], Tokyo, Tsukuba Shobo, 1984

Ito, Momoko, 'Soshiki Nidankaika mo Saisei no Kimete de wa nai' ['The Shift to the Two-Step Organisation is Not a Decisive Measure of Revival'], *Kinyu Bijinesu*, July 1996

Ito, Toshio, 'Nokyo to Seiji Katsudo' ['Nokyo and Political Activities'], in Kondo Yasuo (ed.), *Nokyo Nijugonen: Sokatsu to Tenbo* [*Twenty Five Years of Nokyo: Summary and Outlook*], Nihon Nogyo Nenpo, Vol. 22, Tokyo, Ochanomizu Shobo, 1973

Iwahashi, Y., 'Why Do Farmers Have Such Great Power', *Tokyo Business Today*, May 1986

Iwai, Tomoaki, 'Nogyosha no Seiji Ishiki ni kansuru Chosa Hokoku' ['Survey Report on Farmers' Political Consciousness], *Nosei Undo Jyaanaru*, Vol. 1, July 1995

—'Japan's Agricultural Politics At A Turning Point', in Purnendra Jain and Takashi Inoguchi (eds), *Japanese Politics Today: Beyond Karaoke Democracy?*, South Melbourne, Macmillan, 1997

Iwamoto, Isao, *Hachiju Nendai Nihon Seiji to Sekai* [*Japanese Politics and the World in the 1980s*], Kyoto, Koyo Shobo, 1988

Izumi, Shoichi, 'Diet Members', in Francis R. Valeo and Charles E. Morrison (eds), *The Japanese Diet and the U.S. Congress*, Boulder, CO, Westview Press, 1983

Japan Company Handbook, Tokyo, Toyo Keizai Inc., 1993

Japan Productivity Center for Socio-Economic Development, *International Comparison of Labour Productivity*, Tokyo, September 1995

'Japan: The Top 300', *Tokyo Business Today*, June 1988

JA Zenno Beikoku Jigyo Honbu, *Beikoku ni kansuru Shuyo Tokei* [*Main Statistics Relating to Rice*], 1996, Tokyo, Zenkoku Nogyo Kyodo Kumiai Rengokai Beikoku Jigyo Honbu, 1997

JA Zenno Sogo Kikakubu Kikaku Chosaka (ed.), *JA Guruupu Keizai Jigyo Kiso Tokei* [*JA Group Basic Economic Business Statistics*], Tokyo, Zenno Sogo Kikakubu Kikaku Chosaka, annual

Johnson, Chalmers, *Japan's Public Policy Companies*, Washington, DC, American Enterprise Institute for Public Policy Research, 1978

Kabashima, Ikuo, *Kokusaika to Nihon no Seiji* [*Internationalisation and Japanese Politics*], Tokyo, Zenkoku Noseikyo, 1997

Kabashima, Ikuo and Ishio, Yoshito, 'The Instability of Party Identification Among Eligible Japanese Voters', *Party Politics*, Vol. 4, No. 2, April 1998

Kada, Ryohei and Goto, Junko, 'Present Issues of Sustainable Land Use Systems and Rural Communities in Japan', in Luther Tweeten, Cynthia L. Dishon, Wen S. Chern, Naraomi Imamura and Masaru Morishima (eds), *Japanese & American Agriculture: Tradition and Progress in Conflict*, Boulder, CO, Westview Press, 1993

Kaiin Toron [Members' Discussion], 'Norin Kanryo Ikigai to Kikikan' ['The Agriculture and Forestry Bureaucracy's Meaning of Life and Sense of Crisis'], in Nosei Jyaanarisuto no Kai (ed.), *Norin Kanryo o Kaibo Suru* [*Dissecting the Agriculture and Forestry Bureaucracy*], Nihon Nogyo no Ugoki No. 11, Tokyo, Nihon Norin Keikaku Kyokai, January 1968

—'Nosei Fushin o Hanei Shita Sosenkyo' ['A General Election Which Reflected Distrust of Agricultural Policies'], in Nosei Jyaanarisuto no Kai (ed.), *Shu, San Senkyo to Nomin no Sentaku* [*Lower and Upper House Elections and Farmers' Choices*], Nihon Nogyo no Ugoki No. 91, Tokyo, Norin Tokei Kyokai, 1990

Kaiin Toron Kai [Members' Debate], 'Goto-Zaikai no Nogyokan o Ryori Suru' ['Examination of the Views on Agriculture Among Five Parties and Zaikai'], in Nosei Jyaanarisuto no Kai (ed.), *Yukizumaru Nokiho* [*The Agricultural Basic Law At A Standstill*], Nihon Nogyo no Ugoki No. 6, August 1966

Kajii, Isao, 'Ima Naze Nokyo Ka' ['Why Nokyo Now?'], in Ouchi Tsutomu and Kajii Isao (eds), *Nokyo Yonjunen – Kitai to Genjitsu* [*Forty Years of Nokyo: Expectation and Reality*], Nihon Nogyo Nenpo, Vol. 36, Tokyo, Ochanomizu Shobo, 1989, pp. 3–14

—'Nogyo Kosho no Zasetsu to Nihon Nogyo no Saihensei' ['The Failure of the GATT Agricultural Trade Negotiations and the Reorganisation of Japanese Agriculture'], in Ouchi Tsutomu and Saeki Naomi (eds), *GATTO Nogyo Kosho to Nihon Nogyo* [*The GATT Agricultural Negotiations and Japanese Agriculture*], Nihon Nogyo Nenpo 37, Tokyo, Norin Tokei Kyokai, 1991, pp. 112–182

Kameya, Sho, 'Nokyo Chuokai no Genjo Bunseki' ['Analysis of the Current State of the Nokyo Central Unions'], in Nogyo Kaihatsu Senta (ed.), *Nokyo Undo no Genjo Bunseki* [*Analysis of the Current State of Nokyo's Activities*], Gendai Nogyo Kyodo Kumiai Soshikiron 2, Tokyo, Ie no Hikari Kyokai, 1974, pp. 395–412

Kamiya, Mitsugi and Korenaga, Tohiko (eds), *Nogyo Hogo to Nosan Butsu Boeki Mondai* [*Agricultural Protection and Agricultural Trade Issues*], Research Monograph No. 105, Tokyo, Nogyo Sogo Kenkyujo, 1985

Kano, Yoshikazu, 'Hojokin Sakugen, Noka "Senbetsu" De Shijoka Isogu' ['Reducing Subsidies and "Selecting" Farm Households for the Introduction of the Market Mechanism'], *Ekonomisuto*, 22 November 1994

'Kanzeika to Shokkan Seido Wa Ryoritsu Shinai' ['Tariffication and the Food Control System are Incompatible'], *Shukan Toyo Keizai*, 20 November 1993

Kasuga, Masashi, 'The Transformation in the *Chiku Suisen* (District Recommendation) System in Postwar Japan', Paper presented to the Seventh Japanese Studies Association of Australia Conference, 11–13 July 1991

Kawagoe, Toshihiko, 'The Origins of Protectionism in Japanese Agriculture', Seminar, Department of Economic History, Australian National University, September 1996

Kawasaki, Isonobu, *Shokuryocho-dono: Watashi Wa Yamigomeya Desu* [*Mr Food Agency: I Am Running A Black Market Rice Shop*], Tokyo, Gendai Shorin, 1992

Kawasaki, Soichiro, 'Saninsen to Nosonhyo no Doko' ['The Upper House Election and the Movement of Rural Votes'], in Nosei Jyaanarisuto no Kai (ed.), *Shu, San Senkyo to Nomin no Sentaku* [*Lower and Upper House Elections and Farmers' Choices*], Tokyo, Nihon Nogyo no Ugoki No. 91, Norin Tokei Kyokai, 1990

Keeler, John T. S., 'Agricultural Power in the European Community: Explaining the Fate of CAP and GATT Negotiations', *Comparative Politics*, Vol. 28, No. 2, January 1996

Kibo, Gennosuke, 'Remon Yunyu Jiyuka no Kyokun' ['A Lesson From the Liberalisation of Lemons'], *Nogyo Kyodo Kumiai*, Vol. 29, No. 3, March 1983

Kile, O. M., *The Farm Bureau Movement*, New York, Macmillan, 1921

—*The Farm Bureau Through Three Decades*, Baltimore, Waverly Press, 1948

Kishimoto, Koichi, 'Diet Structure, Organization, and Procedures', in Francis R. Valeo and Charles E. Morrison (eds), *The Japanese Diet and the U.S. Congress*, Boulder, CO, Westview Press, 1983

Kobayashi, Yoshiaki, *Gendai Nihon no Senkyo [Contemporary Japanese Elections]*, Tokyo, Tokyo Daigaku Shuppankai, 1991

Kobayashi, Naoki, Shinohara Hajime and Soma Masao, *Senkyo [Elections]*, Tokyo, Iwanami Shoten, 1960

Kobayashi, S., Morison, J. B. and Riethmuller, P., 'A Review of Recent Developments in Japanese Agriculture and Agricultural Policy', *Review of Marketing and Agricultural Economics*, Vol. 59, No. 3, December 1991

Kohno, Masaru, 'Rational Foundations for the Organization of the Liberal Democratic Party in Japan', *World Politics*, Vol. 44, No. 3, April 1992

Komiya, Ryutaro, 'Comments', in Aurelia George (ed.), *Japanese Agricultural Policy: A Review*, Research Paper No. 87, Canberra, Australia–Japan Research Centre, 1981

'Kore Kara no Seikyoku o Do Miru Ka' ['How Does the Political Situation Look After This?'], *Nosei Undo Jyaanaru*, No. 2, September 1995

Korenaga, Tohiko, 'Senshinkoku Nosei no Tenkai to Nosan Boeki Mondai' ['The Development of Agricultural Policy in Advanced Countries and Agricultural Trade Problems'], in Kamiya Mitsugi and Korenaga Tohiko (eds), *Nogyo Hogo to Nosan Butsu Boeki Mondai [Protectionist Policies and Agricultural Trade]*, Research Monograph No. 105, Tokyo, Nogyo Sogo Kenkyujo, 1985

Kudo, Taishi, 'Nokyo Hatan de Hisoka ni Tsukawareta "Koteki Shikin" ' [' "Public Funds" Secretly Used for Nokyo Failures'], *Kinyu Bujinesu*, July 1996

'Kumagai Ichio Kokkai Ripooto' ['Kumagai Ichio's Diet Report'], *Nosei Undo Jyaanaru*, No. 22, December 1998

Kurata, Jun, *Nogyo Kyodo Kumiairon [A Discourse on Nokyo]*, Tokyo, Zenkoku Nogyo Kyodo Kumiai Chuokai, 1985

Kurihara, Rumi, 'Nogyo Ninaite Mondai' ['The Agricultural Bearers' Issue'], in Ouchi Tsutomu and Gomi Kenkichi (eds), *Nogyo Ninaitezo no Hikari to Kage [The Lights and Shadows of Pictures of Agricultural Bearers]*, Nihon Nogyo Nenpo 38, Tokyo, Norin Tokei Kyokai, 1992

Kuwabara, Masanobu, 'Nogyo Kyodo Kumiai no Nosei Katsudo' ['The Agricultural Policy Activities of Nokyo'], in Nogyo Kaihatsu Senta (ed.), *Nokyo Undo no Genjo Bunseki [Analysis of the Current State of Nokyo's Activities]*, Gendai Nogyo Kyodo Kumiai Soshikiron 2, Tokyo, Ie no Hikari Kyokai, 1974

Kyodo Kumiai Tsushinsha, *Nogyo Kyodo Kumiai Rengokai Yakushokuin Meibo [Executive and Staff Members' Register of the Agricultural Cooperative Union Federations]*, Tokyo, Kyodo Kumiai Tsushinsha, annual

Kyosanto, Bukkuretto, *Gaiatsu no Naka no Nihon no Shokuryo, Nogyo [Japan's Food and Agriculture Under Foreign Pressure]*, Tokyo, Nihon Kyosanto Chuo Iinkai, 1988

Kyoto Daigaku Bungakubu Kokushi Kenkyu Shitsu (eds), *Nihon Kindaishi Jiten [A Dictionary of Modern Japanese History]*, Tokyo, Toyo Keizai Shinposha, 1964

Lehmbruch, Gerhard, 'Liberal Corporatism and Party Government', *Comparative Political Studies*, Vol. 10, No. 1, April 1977

Livestock Industry Promotion Corporation, *LIPC*, 1975

Livestock Industry Promotion Corporation: Corporate Profile, 1996

Longworth, John, *Beef in Japan*, St Lucia, University of Queensland Press, 1983

McCall Rosenbluth, Frances, 'Comment', to Ito Takatoshi, 'U.S. Political Pressure and Economic Liberalization in East Asia', in Jeffrey Frankel and Miles Kahler (eds), *Regionalism and Rivalry: Japan and the United States in Pacific Asia*, Chicago, University of Chicago Press, 1993

McCalla, Alex F. and Josling, Timothy E., *Agricultural Policies and World Markets*, New York, Macmillan, 1985

McCormack, Gavan, 'Afterbubble: Fizz and Concrete in Japan's Political Economy', *JPRI Working Paper* No. 21, June 1996

McCubbins, Mathew and McCall Rosenbluth, Frances, 'Party Provision for Personal Politics: Dividing the Vote in Japan', in Peter Cowhey and Mathew McCubbins (eds), *Structure and Policy in Japan and the United States*, Cambridge, Cambridge University Press, 1995

Mamiya, Atsushi, 'Kongo wa Nogarerarenai! Nonbanku Shori no Arashi' ['This Time It is Impossible to Escape! The Storm of Non-Bank Credit Disposal'], *Kinyu Bijinesu*, July 1996, pp. 6–8

Masuda, Yoshiaki, 'Nokyo no Keiei Bunseki' ['An Analysis of Nokyo's Management'], in Ouchi Tsutomu and Kajii Isao (eds), *Nokyo Yonjunen – Kitai to Genjitsu* [*Forty Years of Nokyo: Expectation and Reality*], Nihon Nogyo Nenpo, Vol. 36, Tokyo, Ochanomizu Shobo, 1989, pp. 51–70

Matsumoto, Tokuo, 'Nokyo Nosei Undo no Tenkan: Sono Yoin to Hoko' ['Changes in Nokyo's Agricultural Policy Campaigns: Their Causes and Direction'], in Nosei Jyaanarisuto no Kai (ed.), *Senkyo, Beika, Nokyo* [*Elections, The Rice Price and Nokyo*], Nihon Nogyo no Ugoki No. 79, Norin Tokei Kyokai, 1986

Matsushima, Masahiro, 'Kome Zenmen Jiyuka wa Mondai' ['Total Liberalisation of Rice is a Problem'], *Asahi Shinbun*, 17 March 1990

Matsuura, Tatsuo, ' "Hokaku Ainori" Doko Made Tsuzuku' [' "The Collusion" between Conservatives and Progressives: How Long Will It Last?'], in Nosei Jyaanarisuto no Kai (ed.), *Tatoka Jidai no Nosei* [*Agricultural Policy in the Era of Party Proliferation*], Nihon Nogyo no Ugoki No. 44, Tokyo, Norin Tokei Kyokai, 1977

Matsuzaka, Shojiro, 'Koritsuka Suru Norin Kanryo' ['The Increasingly Isolated Agriculture and Forestry Bureaucracy'], in Nosei Jyaanarisuto no Kai (ed.), *Norin Kanryo o Kaibo Suru* [*Dissecting the Agriculture and Forestry Bureaucracy*], Nihon Nogyo no Ugoki No. 11, Tokyo, Nihon Norin Keikaku Kyokai, January 1968

Matsuzaki, Tetsuhisa, 'Slowing Parties: Inertia Will Keep Bureaucrats and Ex-LDP Members at the Fore', *Japan Update*, June 1994

Midoro, Tomiyuki, *Rodosha Nomin Undoron* [*A Treatise on Workers' and Farmers' Movements*], Tokyo, Tsukuba Shobo, 1994

Mikuriya, Takashi, 'Evaluating the Election', *Japan Echo*, Vol. 24, No. 1, Spring 1997

Minami, Tetsuo, 'Jiminto no Nogyo Seisaku' ['The LDP's Agricultural Policy'], in Nosei Jyaanarisuto no Kai (ed.), *Tatoka Jidai no Nosei* [*Agricultural Policy in the Era of Party Pfoliferation*], Nihon Nogyo no Ugoki No. 44, Tokyo, Norin Tokei Kyokai, 1977

Ministry of Agriculture, Forestry and Fisheries, *The Long-Term Prospects for Demand and Production of Agricultural Products*, Japan's Agricultural Review, Vol. 25, March 1996

Mishima, Tokuzo, 'Nosanbutsu Jiyuka Rongi no Keifu' ['The Genealogy of Agricultural Product Liberalization Debates'], in Ouchi Tsutomu and Gomi Kenkichi (eds),

Keizai Masatsuka no Nihon Nogyo [*Japanese Agriculture Under Economic Friction*], Nihon Nogyo Nenpo 34, Tokyo, Ochanomizu Shobo, 1986

Mitsukawa, Motochika, *Nogyo Dantai Hattenshi* [*A History of the Development of Agricultural Groups*], Tokyo, Meibun Shobo, 1972

Miyagawa, Takayoshi (ed.), *Seiji Handobukku* [*A Handbook of Politics*], Tokyo, Seiji Koho Senta, annual

Miyake, Ichiro, *Tohyo Kodo* [*Voting Behaviour*], Tokyo, Tokyo Daigaku Shuppankai, 1989

—'89-Nen Sangiin Senkyo to "Seito Saihensei" '['The 1989 Upper House Election and "Party Realignment" '], *Rebuaiasan*, Vol. 10, Spring 1992

Moore, Richard, *Japanese Agriculture: Patterns of Rural Development*, Boulder, CO, Westview Press, 1990

Mori, Koji, 'Murateki Jokyo o Koenai Kokusei Senkyo' ['National Elections That Can Never Go Beyond Local Elections'], in Nosei Jyaanarisuto no Kai (ed.), *Tatoka Jidai no Nosei* [*Agricultural Policy in the Era of Party Proliferation*], Nihon Nogyo no Ugoki No. 44, Tokyo, Norin Tokei Kyokai, 1977

Morita, Minoru, 'Advice for a Party Stuck in Quicksand', *Tokyo Business Today*, January 1994

Muramatsu, Michio, 'Nihongata Atsuryoku Dantai no Kenkyu' ['Research on Japanese Pressure Groups'], *Shukan Toyo Keizai*, 2–9 May 1981

—'Center–Local Political Relations in Japan: A Lateral Competition Model', *Journal of Japanese Studies*, Vol. 12, Summer 1986

Muramatsu, Michio and Ellis Krauss, 'The Conservative Policy Line and the Development of Patterned Pluralism', in Kozo Yamamura and Yasukichi Yasuba (eds), *The Political Economy of Japan*, Vol. 1, Stanford, Stanford University Press, 1987

—'The Dominant Party and Social Coalitions in Japan', in T. J. Pempel (ed.), *Uncommon Democracies: One Party Dominant Regimes*, Ithaca, Cornell University Press, 1990

Muramatsu, Michio, Ito Mitsutoshi and Tsujinaka Yutaka, *Sengo Nihon no Atsuryoku Dantai* [*Pressure Groups in Postwar Japan*], Tokyo, Toyo Keizai Shinposha, 1986

—*Nihon no Seiji* [*Politics in Japan*], Tokyo, Yuhikaku, 1992

Nagao, Satoru, 'Nihon no Seiji Taisei to Kome no Jiyuka Mondai' ['Japanese Political Institutions and the Rice Liberalisation Issue'], *Outlook*, No. 10, Fall 1990

Nagase, Meitoku, 'Nosei Kyogikai no Kaiso to Nosei Domei no Kessei' ['The Reorganisation of the Agricultural Policy Council and the Formation of the Agricultural Policy League'], *Nogyo Kyodo Kumiai*, Vol. 19, No. 2, February 1973

Nagata, Shozo and Saito Misao, *Nokyo no Hanashi* [*Story of Nokyo*], Tokyo, Tokyo Keizai Shinposha, 1982

Nakajima, Chihiro, 'A Peaceful End to Urban Farming', *Economic Eye*, March 1987

Nakamura, Yoshijiro, 'Nominhyo no Pawaa' ['The Power of the Farm Vote'], in Ishiwata Sadao (ed.), *Nomin to Senkyo: Nomin no Seiji Ishiki to Hyo no Yukue* [*Farmers and Elections: The Political Consciousness of Farmers and Trends in the Farm Vote*], Tokyo, Ochanomizu Shobo, 1984

—'Kaifuku Shita Jiminto Shiji: Noringyogyosha no Seiji Ishiki' ['Recovery of the LDP's Popularity: The Political Consciousness of Farmers, Foresters and Fisherfolk'], in Nosei Jyaanarisuto no Kai (ed.), *Tatoka Jidai no Nosei* [*Agricultural Policy in the Era of Party Proliferation*], Nihon Nogyo no Ugoki No. 44, Tokyo, Norin Tokei Kyokai, 1977

Nakayasu, Sadako, 'Japan's Agricultural Structure: Characteristics and Changes', in The Committee For the Japanese Agricultural Session, XXI IAAE Conference (ed.), *Agriculture and Agricultural Policy in Japan*, Tokyo, University of Tokyo Press, 1991

The National Chamber of Agriculture, *The National Chamber of Agriculture: Its Organization and Activities*, March 1982

'Nenpyo: Nokyo 25-nen' ['A Chronology: The 25 Years of Nokyo'], in Kondo Yasuo (ed.), *Nokyo Nijugonen: Sokatsu to Tenbo* [*Twenty Five Years of Nokyo: Summary and Outlook*], Nihon Nogyo Nenpo Vol. 22, Tokyo, Ochanomizu Shobo, 1973

Nihon Keizai Shinbunsha (ed.), *Kaisha Nenkan 1996* [*Annual Corporation Reports, Trust Business 1996*], Tokyo, Nihon Keizai Shinbunsha

'Nihon Nogyo Ikinokori e no Michi – Ogura Takekazu-kun ni Kiku' ['The Road to Survival for Japanese Agriculture – Listening to Takekazu Ogura'], in Ouchi Tsutomu and Saeki Naomi (eds), *GATTO Nogyo Kosho to Nihon Nogyo* [*The GATT Agricultural Negotiations and Japanese Agriculture*], Nihon Nogyo Nenpo 37, Tokyo, Norin Tokei Kyokai, 1991

Nihon Nogyo Nenkan Kankokai (ed.), *Nihon Nogyo Nenkan* [*Japan Agricultural Yearbook*], Tokyo, Ie no Hikari Kyokai, annual

Nishida, Yoshiaki, *The Rise and Decline of the Farmers' Movement and Transformation of the Rural Community in Postwar Japan*, Occasional Papers in Labor Problems and Social Policy, No. 19, Institute of Social Science, University of Tokyo, September 1994

—'From a Train Window: Why is Japanese Farmland so Different From That in Europe?', *Social Science Japan*, April 1995

Nishihira Shigeki, 'An Anatomy of the 1976 Election', *Japan Echo*, Vol. IV, No. 2, 1977

—'Shosenkyoku Bunrui Kijun no Teian' ['Proposals for a Classification Standard for the Single-Member Electorate System'], *Chuo Chosaho*, No. 449, March 1995

Nishimoto, Koichi, 'Nokyo: Pressure from the Co-ops', *The Japan Interpreter*, trans. by V. Dixon Morris, Vol. 7. Nos. 3–4, Summer–Autumn 1972

Nishikawa, Kazuko, 'Why Japanese Consumer Groups Oppose Market Opening Measures', *Tokyo Business Today*, March 1990

'Nogyosha Nosei Undo no Kongo no Arikata' ['What Farmers' Agricultural Policy Campaigns Should Be in the Future'], *Nosei Undo Jyaanaru*, No. 1, July 1995

Nokyo, Kanren Kigyo Meikan, 1995 [*The Directory of Agricultural Cooperatives and Related Corporations, 1995*], Tokyo, Nokyo Kyokai, 1995

Nokyo Pamphlet, *JA Guruupu no Jigyoryo* [*The Quantity of Business of the JA Group*], 1998

—*JA Zenchu Soshiki Kozu* [*JA Zenchu Organisational Composition*], 1998

—*Kumiaisu to Kumiaiinsu oyobi Shokuinsu* [*Numbers of Cooperatives, Cooperative Members and Staff Members*], 1998

—*Zenkoku Nogyo Kyodo Kumiai Chuokai Yakuin* [*National Agricultural Cooperative Union Central Union Executives*], 1998

Nomin Kumiai Goju Shunen Kinensai Jikko Iinkai (ed.), *Nomin Kumiai Gojunenshi* [*A Fifty-Year History of the Farmers' Unions*], Tokyo, Ochanomizu Shobo, 1972

Nomin Mondai Kenkyukai (ed.), *Sengo Nihon no Nomin Undo to Kyosanshugi Katsudo* [*Farmers' Movements and Communist Activities in Postwar Japan*], Tokyo, Nikkan Rodo Tsushinsha, 1962

Norinchukin Research Institute, *Funding and Investment of Agri. Coops Credit Institutions of Three Levels*, as of 31 March 1997

Norinsuisansho, *Nogyo Hakusho* [*Agricultural White Paper*], Tokyo, Norin Tokei Kyokai, annual

Norinsuisansho, Daijin Kanbo Chosaka (ed.), *Nokyo Hakusho Fuzoku Tokeihyo* [*A Statistical Compendium to the Agricultural White Paper*], Tokyo, Norin Tokei Kyokai, annual

Norinsuisansho, Keizai Kyoku Nogyo Kyodo Kumiaika, *Sogo Nokyo Tokeihyo* [*Statistics on Agricultural Cooperatives*], Tokyo, Norin Tokei Kyokai, annual

Norinsuisansho Meibo [*Ministry of Agriculture, Forestry and Fisheries Officials' Register*], Tokyo, Norin Shuppansha, annual

Norinsuisansho, Tokei Johobu, *Poketto Norinsuisan Tokei* [*Pocket Agriculture, Forestry and Fisheries Statistics*], Tokyo, Norin Tokei Kyokai, annual

—*Norinsuisansho Tokeihyo* [*Statistical Yearbook of the Ministry of Agriculture, Forestry and Fisheries*], Tokyo, Norin Tokei Kyokai, annual

Norinsuisansho (ed.), *Nogyo Roppo* [*A Compendium of Agricultural Laws*], Tokyo, Gakyuo Shobo, 1976, 1993, 1998

Nosei Jyaanarisuto no Kai, *Tenki ni Tatsu Norin Kinyu* [*Agricultural and Forestry Finance at a Turning Point*], Kikan Nosei no Ugoki, 3, Tokyo, Kyodo Kumiai Kyokai, 25 June 1958

—*Teimei Suru Nosei Undo* [*Lukewarm Agricultural Policy Campaigns*], Kikan Nosei no Ugoki, 5, Tokyo, Kyodo Kumiai Kyokai, 20 December 1958

—*Hanjutsu Hatten to Keiei Kakushin: Atarashii Nominzo o Motomete* [*The Development of Marketing Techniques and Management Reform: Searching for a New Farmers' Image*], Kikan Nosei no Ugoki, 7, Tokyo, Kyodo Kumiai Kyokai, 30 June 1959

—*Nogyo Kihonho no Soten* [*Points at Issue in the Agricultural Basic Law*], Kikan Nosei no Ugoki, 14, Tokyo, Nokyo Kyokai, 15 May 1961

—*Chiho Gyosei to Noson* [*Regional Administration and Agricultural Villages*], Kikan Nosei no Ugoki, 19, Tokyo, Nokyo Kyokai, 10 October 1962

Nosei Kenkyukai, 'Nosei Kenkyukai Kaisoku' ['The Constitution of the Agricultural Policy Research Association'], *Kaiin Meibo* [*Membership List*], 1972

'Noseikyo no Ugoki' ['Activities of Agricultural Policy Councils'], *Nosei Undo Jyaanaru*, No. 1, Inaugural Issue, 1995

Nosei no Shoten I [Focus on Agricultural Policy I], 'Kotoshi no Beika Undo no Tokucho' ['Special Features of This Year's Rice Price Campaign'], in Nosei Jyaanarisuto no Kai (ed.), *Nihon Nogyo ni Mirai Wa Aru Ka* [*Does Japanese Agriculture Have a Future?*], Nihon Nogyo no Ugoki No. 23, August 1971

Nosei no Shoten V [Focus on Agricultural Policy V], 'Saninsen ni Miru Nominhyo no doko' ['Movement of Farmers' Votes in the Upper House Election'], Nosei Jyaanarisuto no Kai (ed.), *Nihon Nogyo ni Mirai Wa Aru Ka* [*Does Japanese Agriculture Have a Future?*], Nihon Nogyo no Ugoki No. 23, August 1971

Nosei no Shoten II [Focus on Agricultural Policy II], 'Sanjiko no Koso o Megutte' ['Concerning the Third Structural Plan'], in Nosei Jyaanarisuto no Kai (ed.), *Tatoka Jidai no Nosei* [*Agricultural Policy in the Era of Party Proliferation*], Nihon Nogyo no Ugoki No. 44, Tokyo, Norin Tokei Kyokai, 1977

'Noseiren Suisen no Sangiingiin Ichiran' ['List of Upper House Diet Members Recommended by the Noseiren'] *Nosei Undo Jyaanaru*, No. 2, September 1995

Noson, Soshiki Kenkyukai (ed.), *Mura to Nokyo: Sogo Toron* [*Villages and Nokyo: General Debate*], Tokyo, Nihon Keizai Hyoronsha, 1979

OECD, *Agricultural Policies, Markets and Trade in OECD Countries*, Paris, OECD, 1996

Ogura, Takekazu B., *Can Japanese Agriculture Survive?*, Tokyo, Agricultural Policy Research Centre, 3rd edition, 1982

Okamoto, Matsuzo, 'Nomin no Seiji Ishiki no Henka' ['Changes in the Farmers' Political Consciousness'], *Gijutsu to Fukyu*, Vol. 8, No. 10, September 1971

—'Nomin Dantai no Genjo to Undo no Tokucho' ['The Current State of Affairs Amongst Farmers' Groups and the Special Features of their Campaigns'], *Nogyo Kyodo Kumiai*, Vol. 19, No. 2, 1973

—'Nokyo no Nosei Katsudo' ['Nokyo's Agricultural Policy Activities'], in Ouchi Tsutomu and Kajii Isao (eds), *Nokyo Yonjunen – Kitai to Genjitsu [Forty Years of Nokyo: Expectation and Reality]*, Nihon Nogyo Nenpo, Vol. 36, Tokyo, Ochanomizu Shobo, 1989

Okazaki, Isamu, 'Seiken Seito no Jikkoryoku ni Kitai o Kaketa ga' ['Placing Hopes on the Ruling Party's Ability to Take Action'], in Nosei Jyaanarisuto no Kai (ed.), *Senkyo, Beika, Nokyo [Elections, the Rice Price and Nokyo]*, Nihon Nogyo no Ugoki No. 79, Tokyo, Norin Tokei Kyokai, October 1986

Okino, Yasuharu, *Showa 30 Nendai ni Okeru Toshika, Kogyoka to Tohyo Kodo Henka [Urbanisation, Industrialisation and Changes in Electoral Behaviour, 1995–65]*, Tokyo, Minshushugi Kenkyukai, 1966

Okurasho, Insatsu Kyoku (ed.), *Shokuinroku [List of Staff Members]*, 1987, Tokyo, Okurasho Insatu Kyoku, 1986

Okuyama, Taro, 'Hojokin 4-cho En Nosei wa Kuni o Horobosu' ['The ¥4 Trillion Agricultural Policy That is Damaging the Country'], *Shukan Daiyamondo*, 8 February 1986

Olson, Mancur, *The Logic of Collective Action: Public Goods and the Theory of Groups*, Cambridge, MA, Harvard University Press, 1965

Ono, Kazuoki, 'Nokyo to Senkyo' ['Nokyo and Elections'], in Ishiwata Sadao (ed.), *Nomin to Senkyo: Nomin no Seiji Ishiki to Hyo no Yukue [Farmers and Elections: The Political Consciousness of Farmers and Trends in the Farm Vote]*, Tokyo, Ochanomizu Shobo, 1984

—*No to Shoku no Seiji Keizaigaku [The Political Economy of Agriculture and Food]*, Tokyo, Ryokufu Shuppan, 1994

Ono, Masakazu, 'Hoshu Okoku no Hokai' ['Collapse of a Conservative Kingdom'], in Nosei Jyaanarisuto no Kai (ed.), *Shu, San Senkyo to Nomin no Sentaku [Lower and Upper House Elections and Farmers' Choices]*, Tokyo, Nihon Nogyo no Ugoki No. 91, Norin Tokei Kyokai, 1990

Onodera, Yoshiyuki, *Janbo Nokyo no Sugao [The Unpainted Face of Jumbo Nokyo]*, Tokyo Jutaku Shinposha, 1970

Ori, Kan, 'The Diet in the Japanese Political System', in Francis R. Valeo and Charles E. Morrison (eds), *The Japanese Diet and the U.S. Congress*, Boulder, CO, Westview Press, 1983

Orio, Yoshiharu, *Dame na Nokyo, Genki na Nokyo no Kenkyu [Research into Good and Bad Noyko]*, Tokyo, Yell Books, 1992

Ornstein, Norman J. and Elder, Shirley, *Interest Groups, Lobbying and Policymaking*, Washington, D.C., Congressional Quarterly Press, 1978

Otake, Hideo, 'Forces for Political Reform: The Liberal Democratic Party's Young Reformers and Ozawo Ichiro', *Journal of Japanese Studies*, Vol. 22, No. 2, 1996

Otani, Tetsumaru, *Nokyo no Ryutsu Senryaku [Nokyo's Distribution Strategies]*, Tokyo, Nihon Keizai Shinbunsha, 1973

Otawara, Takaaki, 'Nokyo no Ichi to Yakuwari' ['Nokyo's Position and Role'], in Ouchi Tsutomu and Kajii Isao (eds), *Nokyo Yonjunen – Kitai to Genjitsu* [*Forty Years of Nokyo: Expectation and Reality*], Nihon Nogyo Nenpo, Vol. 36, Tokyo, Ochanomizu Shobo, 1989

Ozawa, Kenji, 'A New Phase for Rice in Japan: Production, Marketing, and Policy Issues', in Luther Tweeten, Cynthia L. Dishon, Wen S. Chern, Naraomi Imamura and Masaru Morishima (eds), *Japanese & American Agriculture: Tradition and Progress in Conflict*, Boulder, CO, Westview Press, 1993

Pempel, T. J., *Regime Shift: Comparative Dynamics of the Japanese Political Economy*, Ithaca and London, Cornell University Press, 1998

Pincus, J. J., 'Pressure Groups and the Pattern of Tariffs', *Journal of Political Economy*, Vol. 83, No. 4, 1975

Potter, Allen, *Organized Groups in British National Politics*, London, Faber, 1961

Quigley, Harold S. and Turner, John E., *The New Japan*, Minneapolis, University of Minnesota Press, 1956

Ramseyer, J. Mark and McCall Rosenbluth, Frances, *Japan's Political Marketplace*, Cambridge, MA, Harvard University Press, 1993

Reading, Brian, *Japan: The Coming Collapse*, London: Weidenfeld and Nicolson, 1992

Reed, Steven, 'The Nomination Process for Japan's Next General Election: Waiting for the Heiritsu-sei', *Asian Survey*, Vol. 35, No. 12, December 1995

Reforming World Agricultural Trade: A Policy Statement by Twenty-nine Professionals from Seventeen Countries, Washington, D.C., Institute for International Economics, Canada, The Institute for Research on Public Policy, May 1988

Richardson, Bradley and Flanagan, Scott, *Politics in Japan*, Boston, Little, Brown & Co., 1984

Robinson, Pearl T., 'Niger: Anatomy of a Neotraditional Corporatist State', *Comparative Politics*, Vol. 24, No. 1, October 1991

Runge, Carlisle Ford, 'The Assault on Agricultural Protectionism', *Foreign Affairs*, Vol. 67, No. 1, Fall 1988

Saeki, Naomi, 'Nogyo Kosho no Tenkai to Kiketsu' ['The Development and Results of the Agricultural Trade Negotiations'], in Ouchi Tsutomu and Saeki Naomi (eds), *GATTO Nogyo Kosho to Nihon Nogyo* [*The GATT Agricultural Negotiations and Japanese Agriculture*], Nihon Nogyo Nenpo 37, Tokyo, Norin Tokei Kyokai, 1991

—*GATTO to Nihon Nogyo* [*GATT and Japanese Agriculture*], Tokyo, Tokyo Daigaku Shuppankai, 3rd edition, 1992

—*Nokyo Kaikaku* [*Reform of Nokyo*], Tokyo, Ie no Hikari Kyokai, 1993

Sakaguchi, Takashi, *Kyodai Nokyo no Sugosa* [*The Power of Massive Nokyo*], Tokyo, Ginko Jihyosha, 1987

Sakai, Yoshiaki, ' "To yori Hito" o Jissho Shita Nominhyo' ['Farmers' Votes Demonstrated "The Man Rather Than The Party" '], in Nosei Jyaanarisuto no Kai (ed.), *Senkyo, Beika, Nokyo* [*Elections, the Rice Price and Nokyo*], Nihon Nogyo no Ugoki No. 79, Tokyo, Norin Tokei Kyokai, October 1986

Sakizaki, Chihiro, *Yomigaere Nokyo* [*Come Back to Life Nokyo*], Tokyo, Zenkoku Myodo Shuppan, 1991

Sakurai, Makoto, 'Nokyo no Nosei Katsudo' ['Nokyo's Agricultural Policy Activities'], *Nogyo Kyodo Kumiai*, February 1972

—*Beika Seisaku to Beika Undo* [*Rice Policy and the Rice Price Campaign*], Tokyo, Zenkoku Nogyo Kyodo Kumiai Chuokai, 1977

Salisbury, Robert H., 'Interest Representation – The Dominance of Institutions', *American Political Science Review*, Vol. 78, No. 1, 1984

Sasaki, Takeshi, 'Post-Election Prospects', *Japan Echo*, Vol. 24, No. 1, Spring 1997

Sato, Seizaburo, 'LDP Redivivus: The Failure of Electoral Reform', *Japan Echo*, Vol. 24, No. 1, Spring 1997

Saxon, E. A., *Farm Production in Japan: Determinants, Performance and Prospects*, Bureau of Agricultural Economics, Occasional Paper No. 35, Canberra, Australian Government Publishing Service, 1976

—*Recent Developments in Food Consumption and Farm Production in Japan*, Bureau of Agricultural Economics, Occasional Paper No. 43, Canberra, Australian Government Publishing Service, 1978

Scalapino, Robert A. and Masumi, Junnosuke, *Parties and Politics in Contemporary Japan*, Berkeley and Los Angeles, University of California Press, 1962

Schmitter, Philippe, 'Still the Century of Corporatism?', in Philippe C. Schmitter and Gerhard Lehmbruch (eds), *Trends Toward Corporatist Intermediation*, London and Beverly Hills, Sage Publications, 1979

Seikan Yoran [*A Handbook of Politics and the Bureaucracy*], Tokyo, Seisaku Jihosha, biannual

Seisaku Koso Fuooramu, 'GATTO Uruguai Raundo no Seiko ni Mukete' ['Towards the Success of the GATT Uruguay Round'], *Nogyo to Keizai*, Vol. 58, No. 3, March 1992, Appendix

Seligmann, Albert L., 'Japan's New Electoral System: Has Anything Changed?', *Asian Survey*, Vol. 37, No. 5, May 1997

'Shashin Gurafu' ['Photographs'], *Nosei Undo Jyaanaru*, No. 22, December 1998

Shinohara, Hajime, 'Postwar Parties and Politics in Japan', *The Developing Economies*, Vol. 4, No. 4, December 1968

'Shinpojiumu "Kokusaika Jidai ni Okeru Nogyo", Noson Mondai' ['Symposium on "Agriculture and Farming Villages in an Era of Internationalisation"'], *Nogyo to Keizai*, Vol. 55, No. 5, 1989

Shiraishi, Masahiko, 'Gyunyu' ['Milk'], in Ouchi Tsutomu and Kajii Isao (eds), *Nokyo Yonjunen – Kitai to Genjitsu* [*Forty Years of Nokyo: Expectation and Reality*], Nihon Nogyo Nenpo, Vol. 36, Tokyo, Ochanomizu Shobo, 1989

—'Kyodo Katsudo Senryaku no Tenkan ni yoru Chiiki Shakai Zukuri no Shintenkan' ['The New Development of the Formation of the Regional Society By Revising the Strategy of Cooperative Activity'], *Nogyo Kyodo Kumiai*, Vol. 61, No. 2, 1995

'Shokkan Seido o Nokoshita Kanzeika wa Kiken: Chikazuku Kome Shijo no Kaiho' ['It is Dangerous to Introduce Tariffication Without Abolishing the Food Control System: The Liberalisation of the Rice Market is Approaching'], *Shukan Toyo Keizai*, 20 November 1993

'Sokatsu – Nosei Soshiki Undo no Mezasu Mono' ['Summary – Aim of the Agricultural Policy Organisation Campaign'], *Nosei Undo Jyaanaru*, No. 14, August 1997

Shokuryocho, *Beika ni kansuru Shiryo* [*Materials Relating to the Rice Price*], June 1995

' "Shokuryo-Nogyo-Noson Chiiki ni kansuru Arata na Kihonho" Seitei ni tsuite no Yosei' ['Requests Relating to the Enactment of the "New Basic Law Concerning Food, Agriculture and Rural Areas Enactment"'], *Nosei Undo Hyaanaru*, No. 17, January 1998

Smiley, Ross, *Japanese Electoral Distribution and Its Political Consequences 1947–1990*, MA Thesis, University of Sydney, March 1990

'Sokatsu Toron: Nomin no Seiji Ishiki wa Kawatta ka' ['Summary Discussion: Has Farmers' Political Consciousness Changed?'], in Nosei Jyaanarisuto no Kai (ed.), *Shu, San Senkyo to Nomin no Sentaku* [*Lower and Upper House Elections and Farmers' Choices*], Tokyo, Nihon Nogyo no Ugoki No. 91, Norin Tokei Kyokai, 1990

'Sokatsu Toron: Shusan Dojitsu Senkyogo no Nakasone Seiji' ['Summary Discussion: Politics Under Nakasone After the Double Lower and Upper House Elections'], in Nosei Jyaanarisuto no Kai (ed.), *Senkyo, Beika, Nokyo* [*Elections, the Rice Price and Nokyo*], Nihon Nogyo no Ugoki No. 79, Tokyo, Norin Tokei Kyokai, October 1986

Soma, Masao, *Nihon no Senkyo Seiji* [*Election Politics in Japan*], Tokyo, Aoki Shoten, 1963

—*Kokumin no Sentaku: 1972-nen Sosenkyo no Bunseki* [*The People's Choice: An Analysis of the 1972 General Election*], Tokyo Sanichi Shobo, 1974

Somucho, Gyosei Kanri Kyoku, *Shingikai Soran* [*A Compendium of Advisory Councils*], Tokyo, Somucho, Gyosei Kanri Kyoku, annual

Somucho, Tokei Kyoku, *Nihon Tokei Nenkan* [*Japan Statistical Yearbook*], Tokyo, Somucho, Tokei Kyoku, annual

Sone, Yasunori, 'Interest Groups and the Process of Political Decision-making in Japan', in Yoshio Sugimoto and Ross E. Mouer (eds), *Constructs for Understanding Japan*, London, Kegan Paul International, 1989

Sone, Yasunori and Kanazashi, Masao, *Nihon no Seiji* [*Japanese Politics*], Tokyo, Nihon Keizai Shinbunsha, 1989

Sta. Romana, Elipidio R., *The Politics of Liberalization of the Japanese Agricultural Market*, Papers in Japanese Studies, No. 12, Department of Japanese Studies, National University of Singapore, July 1991

Steslicke, William E., *Doctors in Politics: The Political Life of the Japan Medical Association*, New York, Praeger, 1973

Stockwin, J. A. A., *Japan: Divided Politics in a Growth Economy*, London, Weidenfeld and Nicolson, 1975

—'Cooperative Party', in Haruhiro Fukui (ed.), *Political Parties of Asia and the Pacific*, Westport, Connecticut, Greenwood Press, 1985

—'Farmers Cooperative Party', in Haruhiro Fukui (ed.), *Political Parties of Asia and the Pacific*, Westport, Connecticut, Greenwood Press, 1985

Suda, Toshihiko, 'Nihon Nogyo Saisei no Joken o Kangaeru' ['Considering Conditions for the Revival of Japanese Agriculture'], *Keizai Zeminaru*, Tokyo, Nihon Hyoronsha, December 1993

Sugita, Yuji, 'Seiji Kiban no Henka to Nosei no Hoko o Do Miru Ka' ['How Should We View Changes in the Basis of Politics and Directions in Agricultural Policy?'], *Nogyo to Keizai*, Vol. 63, No. 4, March 1997

'Suishin Giin to Meiyu no Paipu o Futoku' ['Thickening the Pipe Between Recommended Diet Members and Supporters'], *Nosei Undo Jyaanaru*, No. 15, September 1997

Suzuki, Saichiro, 'Kobai Jigyo' ['Purchasing Business'], in Ouchi Tsutomu and Kajii Isao (eds), *Nokyo Yonjunen – Kitai to Genjitsu* [*Forty Years of Nokyo: Expectation and Reality*], Nihon Nogyo Nenpo, Vol. 36, Tokyo, Ochanomizu Shobo, 1989

Tabusa, Keiko, 'The 1996 General Election in Japan', *Australian Quarterly*, Vol. 69, No. 1, 1997

Tachibana, *Nokyo: Kyodai na Chosen* [*Nokyo: The Enormous Challenge*], Tokyo, Asahi Shinbunsha, 1980

Tagawa, Norio, 'Saninsen to Nokyo to Nomintachi' ['The Upper House Election and Nokyo and Farmers'], in Nosei Jyaanarisuto no Kai (ed.), *Shu, San Senkyo to Nomin no Sentaku* [*Lower and Upper House Elections and Farmers' Choices*], Tokyo, Nihon Nogyo no Ugoki No. 91, Norin Tokei Kyokai, 1990

Taguchi, Fukuji, 'Pressure Groups in Japanese Politics', *The Developing Economies*, Vol. 6, No. 4, December 1968

—'Sosenkyo to Nominhyo no Yukue' ['General Elections and Trends in Farmers' Votes'], *Nogyo Kyodo Kumiai*, February 1973

Takabatake, Michitoshi, 'Naze Nomin wa Jiminto o Mikagitta ka' ['Why Did the Farmers Desert the LDP?'], *Ushio*, September 1989

Takahashi, Goro, ' "Kyodo Kumiainai Shijo Genri" to Nokyo no Soshiki Saihen' [' "Market Principles in Cooperative Unions" and the Reformation of the Nokyo Organisation'], in Ouchi Tsutomu and Kajii Isao (eds), *Nokyo Yonjunen – Kitai to Genjitsu* [*Forty Years of Nokyo: Expectation and Reality*], Nihon Nogyo Nenpo, Vol. 36, Tokyo, Ochanomizu Shobo, 1989

—'Growing Conflicts: Government Cash Helps Farm Groups Crop Reform', *Japan Update*, No. 40, January 1995

Takahata, Masamichi, 'Henka ni Taio Dekinakatta Jiminto' ['The LDP That Could Not Respond to Changes'], in Nosei Jyaanarisuto no Kai (ed.), *Shu, San Senkyo to Nomin no Sentaku* [*Lower and Upper House Elections and Farmers' Choices*], Tokyo, Nihon Nogyo no Ugoki No. 91, Norin Tokei Kyokai, 1990

Takeuchi, Tetsuo, 'Keito Sandankaisei no Saihen' ['Reorganisation of the Federated Three-Stage System'], in Ouchi Tsutomu and Kajii Isao (eds), *Nokyo Yonjunen – Kitai to Genjitsu* [*Forty Years of Nokyo: Expectation and Reality*], Nihon Nogyo Nenpo, Vol. 36, Tokyo, Ochanomizu Shobo, 1989

Takeuchi, Tetsuo and Takaaki, Otawara, *Asu no Nokyo: Rinen to Jigyo o Tsunagu Mono* [*Tomorrow's Nokyo: The Connection Between Principle and Enterprise*], Tokyo, Nosangyoson Bunka Kyokai, 1994.

Tanaka, Toyotoshi, *Nihon no Nokyo* [*Japan's Nokyo*], Tokyo, Nokyo Kyokai, 1971

Tanimoto, Takashi, 'Nomin Undo to Senkyo Toso' ['The Farmers' Movement and Election Struggles'], in Ishiwata Sadao (ed.), *Nomin to Senkyo: Nomin no Seiji Ishiki to Hyo no Yukue* [*Farmers and Elections: The Political Consciousness of Farmers and Trends in the Farm Vote*], Tokyo, Ochanomizu Shobo, 1984

'The TBT 300: 1994 Corporate Ranking', *Tokyo Business Today*, September 1994

Thurston, Donald R., *Teachers and Politics in Japan*, Princeton, Princeton University Press, 1973

'Toitsu Chiho Senkyo e no Kakuchi no Torikumi' ['Each Region's Grappling with the Local Elections'], *Nosei Undo Jyaanaru*, No. 24, March 1999

'Tokushu Taidan: 21 Seiki no Nogyo, Noson on Katsuryoku to Miryoku aru mono ni' ['Special Interview: Changing 21st Century Agriculture and Farm Villages to be Full of Vitality and Appeal'], *Nosei Undo Jyaanaru*, Vol. 1, July 1995

'Tokushu: WTO Kyotei to Jiki Nogyo Kosho' ['Special: The WTO Agreement and the Next Round of Agricultural Negotiations'], *Nosei Undo Hyaanaru*, No. 22, December 1998

'Toron' ['Discussion'], in Saito Makoto, 'Shimeikan no Henshitsu wa Tozen' ['It is Natural that the Nature of the Mission Has Changed'], in Nosei Jyaanarisuto no Kai (ed.), *Norin Kanryo o Kaibo Suru* [*Dissecting the Agriculture and Forestry Bureaucracy*], Nihon Nogyo no Ugoki No. 11, Tokyo, Nihon Norin Keikaku Kyokai, January 1968

Toyokura, Yasuhiro, *Raisu Pawaa: Tsuba Kara Kona E* [*Rice Power: From Grain to Flour*], Tokyo, Niceday Books, 1989

Tsuboi, Nobuhiro, 'Keito Shinyo Jigyo' ['Federated Trust Business'], in Ouchi Tsutomu and Kajii Isao (eds), *Nokyo Yonjunen – Kitai to Genjitsu* [*Forty Years of Nokyo: Expectation and Reality*], Nihon Nogyo Nenpo, Vol. 36, Tokyo, Ochanomizu Shobo, 1989

Tsuboi, Nobuhiro, 'Appendix: Limitations and Potential of Family Farmers in Japan: Can Japanese Family Farms Survive?', in Luther Tweeten, Cynthia L. Dishon, Wen S. Chern, Naraomi Imamura and Masaru Morishima (eds), *Japanese & American Agriculture: Tradition and Progress in Conflict*, Boulder, Westview Press, 1993

Tsuchiya, Shigeru, 'Jiminto Nosei de Nominhyo o Torimodoseru Ka' ['Is It Possible to Regain Farmers' Votes with the LDP's Agricultural Policy?'], *Nogyo to Keizai*, Vol. 56, No. 1, January 1990

Tweeten, Luther, 'Overview', in Luther Tweeten, Cynthia L. Dishon, Wen S. Chern, Naraomi Imamura and Masaru Morishima (eds), *Japanese & American Agriculture: Tradition and Progress in Conflict*, Boulder, CO, Westview Press, 1993

van Wolferen, *The Enigma of Japanese Power: People and Politics in a Stateless Nation*, London, Macmillan, 1989

Vogel, David, 'Consumer Protection and Protectionism in Japan', *Journal of Japanese Studies*, Vol. 18, No. 1, 1992

Wakabayashi, Hideyasu, 'Mikan-Kaju' ['*Mikan*-Fruit Juice'], in Ouchi Tsutomu and Kajii Isao (eds), *Nokyo Yonjunen – Kitai to Genjitsu* [*Forty Years of Nokyo: Expectation and Reality*], Nihon Nogyo Nenpo, Vol. 36, Tokyo, Ochanomizu Shobo, 1989

Ward, Robert, 'Urban–Rural Differences and the Process of Political Modernization in Japan: A Case Study', *Economic Development and Cultural Change*, Vol. 9, Part 2, October 1960

Wilson, Graham K., *Interest Groups*, Oxford, Basil Blackwell, 1990

Yamaguchi, Hiroshi, 'Nyuku Funso to Rakuno no Tachiba' ['The Milk Price Dispute and Dairy Farmers' Standpoint'], *Ekonomisuto*, March 1967

Yamaguchi, Ichimon, *Ima Nokyo o Do Suru Ka* [*What Should be Done About Nokyo?*], Tokyo, Ie no Hikari Kyokai, 1987

Yamaguchi, Iwao, 'Don't Push Our Farmers Too Far', *Japan Echo*, Vol. 14, No. 1, Spring 1987

Yamaguchi, Taro, 'Nihon Shakaito no Nogyo Seisaku' ['The Japan Socialist Party's Agricultural Policy'], in Nosei Jyaanarisuto no Kai (ed.), *Tatoka Jidai no Nosei* [*Agricultural Policy in the Era of Party Proliferation*], Nihon Nogyo no Ugoki No. 44, Tokyo, Norin Tokei Kyokai, 1977

Yamaji, Susumu, 'Atsuryoku Dantai Toshite no Nokyo' ['Nokyo As A Pressure Group'], in Kondo Yasuo (ed.), *Nokyo Nijugonen: Sokatsu to Tenbo* [*Twenty Five Years of Nokyo: Summary and Outlook*], Nihon Nogyo Nenpo, Vol. 22, Tokyo, Ochanomizu Shobo, 1973

Yamaji, Susumu and Ito, Shoichi, 'The Political Economy of Rice in Japan', in Luther Tweeten, Cynthia L. Dishon Wen S. Chern, Naraomi Imamura and Masaru Morishima (eds), *Japanese & American Agriculture: Tradition and Progress in Conflict*, Boulder, Co., Westview Press, 1993

Yamamiya, Junko, 'Japan's Declining Food Self-sufficiency Rate', *Mitsui Research Institute Business Report*, March 1991

Yamamoto, Eiji, 'Sengo Nosonhyo no Rekishiteki Bunseki' ['An Historical Analysis of the Farm Vote in the Postwar Period'], in Ishiwata Sadao (ed.), *Nomin to Senkyo:*

Nomin no Seiji Ishiki to Hyo no Yukue [*Farmers and Elections: The Political Consciousness of Farmers and Trends in the Farm Vote*], Tokyo, Ochanomizu Shobo, 1984

Yamamoto, Osamu, 'Sogo Nokyo to Senmon Nokyo' ['Multi-Purpose Agricultural Cooperatives and Special-Purpose Cooperatives'], in Ouchi Tsutomu and Kajii Isao (eds), *Nokyo Yonjunen – Kitai to Genjitsu* [*Forty Years of Nokyo: Expectation and Reality*], Nihon Nogyo Nenpo, Vol. 36, Tokyo, Ochanomizu Shobo, 1989

Yamashita, Juntaro, 'Nezuyoi Hoshu–Kyoto Isshiki' ['Strongly-Rooted Conservatism–Local Party Consciousness'], in Nosei Jyaanarisuto no Kai (ed.), *Tatoka Jidai no Nosei* [*Agricultural Policy in the Era of Party Proliferation*], Nihon Nogyo no Ugoki No. 44, Tokyo, Norin Tokei Kyokai, 1977

Yamato, Hiroshi, 'Political Parties and the Diet', in Francis R. Valeo and Charles E. Morrison (eds), *The Japanese Diet and the U.S. Congress*, Boulder, CO, Westview Press, 1983

Yamauchi, Hiroshi, 'Analytical Institutional Economics of Japanese Agricultural Policy', Seminar, Research Institute for Asian Development, University of Hawaii, May 1993

Yanagida, Akitoshi, 'Nominhyo ni "Gyakuryu Gensho"' ['The "Comeback Phenomenon" by Farmers' Votes'], in Nosei Jyaanarisuto no Kai (ed.), *Tatoka Jidai no Nosei* [*Agricultural Policy in the Era of Party Proliferation*], Nihon Nogyo no Ugoki No. 44, Tokyo, Norin Tokei Kyokai, 1977

Yokota, Tetsuji, *Gyuniku Wa Naze Takai Ka* [*Why is Beef Expensive?*], Tokyo, Simul Press, 1977

'Yori Kyoryoku na Nosei Undo o Mezashite' ['Aiming At An Even More Powerful Agricultural Policy Campaign'], *Nosei Undo Jyaanaru*, No. 17, January 1998

Yoshihara, Shizuo, *Zenno o Kiru* [*I Criticise Zenno*], Tokyo, Nisshin Hodo, 1975

Zadankai, 'Seiji no Gekido to Nogyo, Noson no Shinro' ['Dramatic Movements in Politics and the Direction of Agricultural and Farming Villages'], *Zenei*, June 1989

Zaisei Chosakai (ed.), *Hojokin Soran* [*A Compendium of Subsidies*], Tokyo, Nihon Densan Kikaku Kabushiki Kaisha, annual

Zenkoku Nogyo Kozo Kaizen Kyokai, *Zenkoku Nogyo Kozo Kaizen Kyokai no Goannai* [*A Guide to the National Agricultural Structural Improvement Association*], 1997

Zenkoku Nogyo Kyodo Kumiai Chuokai, *Nogyo Kyodo Kumiai Nenkan* [*The Yearbook of Agricultural Cooperatives*], Tokyo, Zenkoku Nogyo Kyodo Kumiai Chuokai, annual

—*Shinpan: Nogyo Kyodo Kumiaiho* [*New Publication: Agricultural Cooperative Union Law*], Tokyo, Ie no Hikari Kyokai, 1995

—*Hayawakari JA no Subete* [*An Easy Guide to All of JA*], Tokyo, Ie no Hikari Kyokai, 1994

Zenkoku Nogyo Kyodo Kumiai Chuokai Noseibu, *Nosei Katsudo Taisei ni tsuite* [*Concerning the System of Agricultural Policy Activities*], October 1973

Zenkoku Nogyosha Nosei Undo Soshiki Kyogikai, *Nogyosha no Seiji Ishiki ni kansuru Chosa Hokoku* [*Research Report Relating to the Farmers' Political Consciousness*], April 1995

'Zenkoku Nokyo no Toppu Jinji ni Irei no Zohan' ['An Unusual Anti-Establishment Move in National Nokyo's Top Personnel'], *Aera*, 27 July 1993

Zenkoku Nokyo Seinen Soshiki Kyogikai, 'Nokyo Seinenbu to Seiji Katsudo' ['The Nokyo Youth Division and Political Activities'], *Chijo*, August 1967

Zenkoku Noseikyo, *Sanin Senkyo Taisaku Shiryo* [*House of Councillors' Election Policy Materials*], June 1995

Zenno Sogo Kikakubu Kikaku Chosaka (ed.), *Keito Keizai Jigyo Kiso Tokei* [*Federated Economic Business Basic Statistics*], Tokyo, Zenno Sogo Kikakubu Kikaku Chosaka, annual

'Zento Tanan na Yato Shuketsu' ['The Road Ahead is Full of Difficulties for the Opposition Parties' Concentration'], *Nosei Undo Jyaanaru*, No. 17, January 1998

Zenkoku Tochi Kairyo Jigyo Dantai Rengokai [*National Federation of Land Improvement Associations*], Pamphlet, 1998

'21-Seki o Tenbo Shita "Nosei Kaikaku" ' [' "Agricultural Policy Reform" With a View to the 21st Century'], *Nosei Undo Jyaanaru*, No. 23, February 1999

'21-Seki no Nihon Nogyo o Hiraku "Kokumin Kyosei Undo" ' [' "A Campaign of Symbiosis with the People" to Cultivate Japanese Agriculture in the 21st Century'], *Nosei Undo Jyaanaru*, No. 22, December 1998

89 Gendai Seiji Joho: Shusanhyoin Giin Paanaru Deeta Banku [*1989 Current Politics Report: Lower and Upper House Diet Members' Panel Data Bank*], Seikai Jihosha, 1991

Index

Agricultural Policy Countermeasures
Council (Nosei Taisaku Kyogikai),
191
Agricultural Policy Promotion Council
(Nosei Suishin Kyogikai), 85, 130,
415
Agricultural Policy Promotion League
(Nosei Suishin Renmei), 188,
416
Agricultural Policy Reform League
(Nosei Kakushin Renmei), 187
Agricultural Policy Reform League
(Nosei Sasshin Renmei), 187, 189,
389–90
Agricultural Policy Research
Association (Nogyo Seisaku
Kenkyukai – Noseiken), 391–92,
419–20
Agricultural Policy Research
Association (APRA) (Nosei
Kenkyukai), 388, 389, 393–94,
410–11, 419, 488, 504, 505–8,
536–37, 541, 543, 549, 566
Agricultural Problems Research
Association (Nogyo Mondai
Kenkyukai), 390–91
Agricultural Promotion Regional
Consolidation Law, 74
Agricultural Public Works Association,
520
Agricultural Public Works Techniques
League, 521
Agricultural Reconstruction Policy
Research Association (Nogyo
Saiken Seisaku Kenkyukai), 495
agricultural representation. *See* Diet
agricultural societies (*nogyokai*), 40–41,
43, 47, 48, 65–66, 67, 70, 84, 135,
153, 167, 171–78, 186, 196, 212
agriculture,
efficiency, 23–26
land, 2
producer prices, 6–7
role in economy, 3
See also farm vote; Ministry of
Agriculture, Forestry and Fisheries;
livestock; Nokyo; *nosei katsudo*
(agricultural policy activities); rice;
Uruguay Round etc.
Agriculture and Fisheries' Industries
Cooperative Union Savings
Insurance Organisation
(Nosuisangyo Kyodo Kumiai
Chokin Hoken Kiko), 116

Agriculture and Forestry Broadcasting
Corporation, 512
Agriculture and Forestry Division
(AFD) (Norin Bukai). *See* Liberal
Democratic Party
Agriculture and Forestry Promotion
Diet Members' League (Norin
Shinko Giin Domei), 166
Agriculture, Forestry and Fisheries
Finance Corporation (Noringyogyo
Kinyu Koko), 114, 115, 123, 132,
139, 142, 521, 595
Agriculture, Forestry and Fisheries
Finance Corporation Law, 114
Agriculture, Forestry and Fishery
Groups Staff Members' Mutual
Aid Association (Noringyogyo
Dantai Shokuin Kyosai Kumiai),
115, 139, 217
Agriculture, Forestry and Fishery
Groups Staff Members' Mutual
Aid Law (*Noringyogyo Dantai
Shokuin Kyosai Kumiaiho*) (1958),
115
Agriculture, Forestry and Fisheries
Statistics Observation Advisory
Council, 35
Agriculture and Livestock Industries
Corporation (ALIC)
(Nochikusangyo Shinko Jigyodan),
111–14, 123, 131, 132, 133, 136,
148, 218
See also Livestock Industry
Promotion Corporation (LIPC)
Agriculture and Livestock Industries
Corporation Law (*Nochikusangyo
Shinko Jigyodanho*) (1996),
111
Agriculture and Nokyo Problems
Research Institute (Nogyo, Nokyo
Mondai Kenkyujo), 219
Agriculture Reconstruction Council
(Nogyo Fukko Kaigi), 48–49
Agriculture Reconstruction Policy
Research Association, 543
Aichi Kazuo, 373
Aino Kochiro, 531
Akagi Munenori, 603
ALIC. *See* Agriculture and Livestock
Industries Corporation
All-Japan Compound Feed Price
Stabilisation Fund (Zennihon
Haigo Shiryo Kakaku Antei Kikin),
131

Sudo Ryutaro, 514, 520, 521
sugar, 113–14, 326
Sugar Price Stabilisation Corporation
  (Toka Antei Jigyodan), 113–14
Suishigen Kaihatsu Kodan. *See*
  Fisheries' Resources Development
  Corporation
Sun Party (Taiyoto), 374, 467
Sunaga Ko, 168
Suzuki Seigo, 546
Sweet Resources Advisory Council
  (Kanmi Shigen Shingikai), 35

tabako giin. See Diet
Tabako Kosaku Kumiaiho. See Tobacco
  Cultivation Association Law
Tahara Takeo, 388
taisaku chuo honbu (policy central
  headquarters). *See* Nokyo
Taiseiyoku Sankai. *See* Imperial Rule
  Assistance Association
Taiyoto. See Sun Party
Takeshita Noboru, 264
Tamaki Kazuo, 262, 264, 627
Tamazawa Tokuichiro, 530
Tanaka Shoichi, 523
Tanaka Tsunetoshi, 499
tankyo (unit cooperative). *See* Nokyo
Tax Party, 488
tea, 94, 326
Teikoku Nokai. *See* Imperial
  Agricultural Association
tobacco, 94, 521
Tobacco Cultivation Association Law
  (*Tabako Kosaku Kumiaiho*),
  94
Tochi Kairyo Kensetu Kyokai. *See* Land
  Improvement Construction
  Association
Tochi Kairyoho. See Land Improvement
  Law
tochi kairyoku. See land improvement
  district
Toka Antei Jigyodan. *See* Sugar Price
  Stabilisation Corporation
tokushu hojin. See public corporations
Toyoda Hakaru, 271, 504, 623
Tsuji Kazuhiko, 531
Twenty-First Century Village
  Construction School, 512

UFO Party, 367
UH (Upper House). *See* Diet
United Kingdom, 646

United States, 4, 28, 97, 102, 144, 263,
  440, 584, 596, 602–5, 612, 614, 616,
  618, 637, 646, 650
Upper House (UH). *See* Diet
UR. *See* Uruguay Round
Urata Masaru, 376, 446, 447
Uruguay Round (UR), 3, 4, 89, 112, 157,
  327, 442, 454, 458, 504, 569, 584,
  603, 605, 618, 622–23, 629–30, 637,
  638
  See also General Agreement on Tariffs
    and Trade; World Trade
    Organisation

Vegetable Supply Stabilisation Fund
  (Yasai Kyokyu Antei Kikin), 116
Vegetable Production Shipment
  Stabilisation Law (1966), 138
vegetables, 7, 19
  electoral importance, 326–27
  and Nokyo, 58
  number of producers, 20
  producer subsidy equivalent (PSE), 25
  regions, grown in, 21–22, 23
Voice of the People (Kokumin no Koe),
  374
vote mobilisation. *See* electoral activities

Watanabe Michio, 406, 453, 492, 546,
  605, 606
wheat, 7, 19, 59, 148, 327
  number of producers, 20
  producer price, 597
  producer subsidy equivalent (PSE),
  25
  public interest corporation, 126
  regions, grown in, 21
World Trade Organisation (WTO), 5,
  473, 630, 636–38, 643, 649–50
  See also General Agreement on Tariffs
    and Trade; Uruguay Round
WTO. *See* World Trade Organisation

Yamaguchi Iwao, 394
Yamanaka Sadanori, 451, 493, 503–4,
  545
Yasai Kyokyu Antei Kikin. *See*
  Vegetable Supply Stabilisation
  Fund

Zenchikuren (Zenkoku Chikusan Nogyo
  Kyodo Kumiai Rengokai). *See*
  National Livestock Nokyo
  Federation